KV-105-915

BRILLIANT WOMEN

WRITTEN BY GEORGIA AMSON-BRADSHAW
ILLUSTRATED BY RITA PETRUCCIOLI

WAYLAND
www.waylandbooks.co.uk

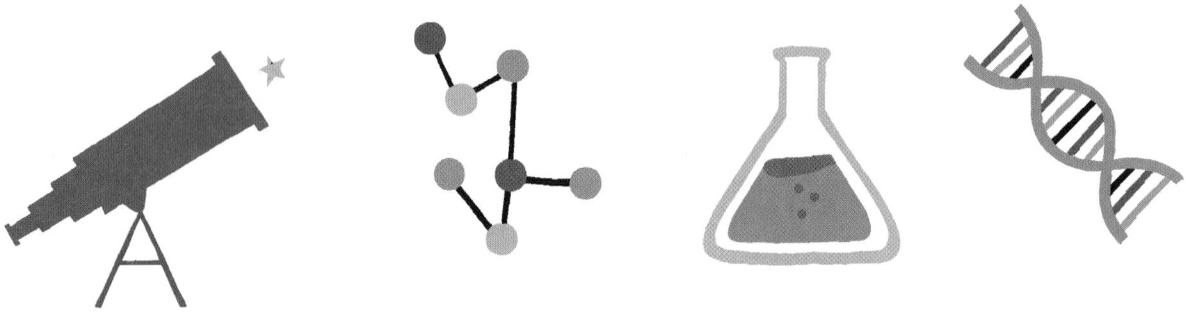

PIONEERS OF SCIENCE AND TECHNOLOGY

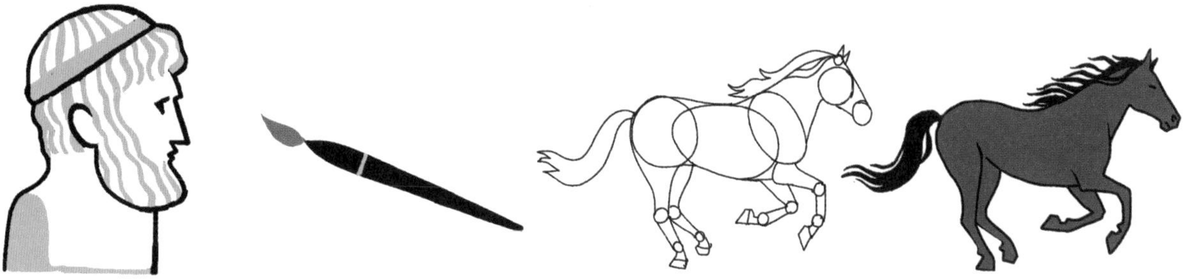

AMAZING ARTISTS AND DESIGNERS

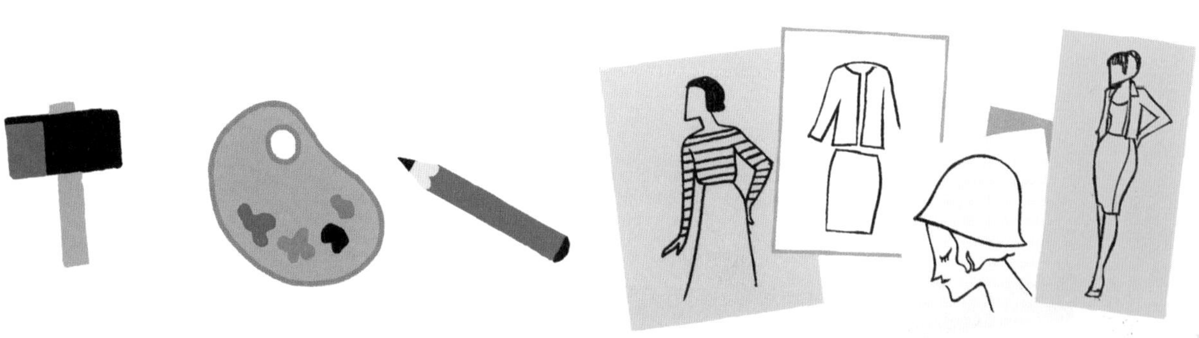

INCREDIBLE SPORTING CHAMPIONS

HEROIC LEADERS AND ACTIVISTS

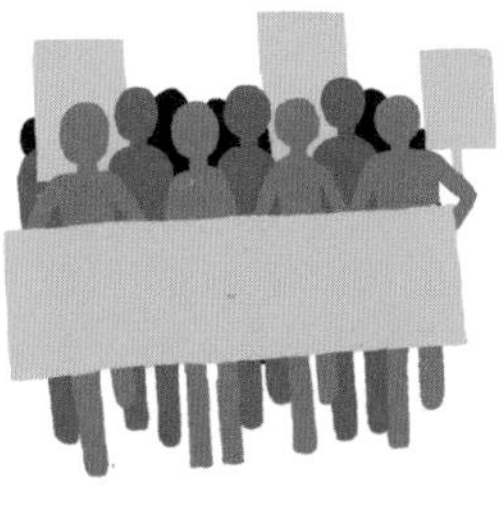

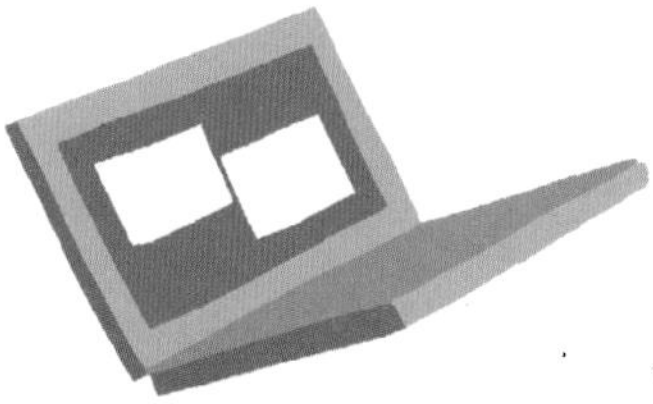

PIONEERS OF SCIENCE AND TECHNOLOGY

HERE'S A QUICK RIDDLE FOR YOU TO TRY OUT ON YOUR FRIENDS.

A boy and his dad go to watch a football game. As they are driving home, their car is involved in an accident. The boy is rushed to hospital in an ambulance, where a surgeon is ready and waiting to treat him. But when he arrives, the surgeon says, 'Oh no! This boy is my son!' How can this be?

If you are feeling a bit flummoxed by this riddle, you're not alone. Most people can't think of the right answer. If you guessed correctly that the surgeon is the boy's mother, give yourself a big pat on the back!

Even in today's modern world, not everyone automatically imagines women working in science and technology professions, such as being a surgeon, an engineer, a physicist or a mathematician. But, as the brilliantly brainy women in this book show, women have been working – and excelling – in science and technology for a very long time.

Some of the names you might already know. Double Nobel Prize-winning scientist, Marie Curie, and mathematician, Ada Lovelace, are famous figures from history. But you'll also get to meet some of the brilliant women who are pushing boundaries and solving problems today – from leprosy specialist Indira Nath to technology entrepreneur Juliana Rotich.

CAROLINE HERSCHEL

Starting out as her brother's assistant, Caroline later became the first woman to earn a salary for the scientific study of the night sky.

ASTRONOMER

Caroline Herschel was a scientific expert on celestial bodies, such as stars, moons, comets and nebulae.

LIVED:	16 March 1750 – 9 January 1848
BORN IN:	Hanover (Germany)
WORKED IN:	Hanover (Germany) and Bath (UK)

Caroline was born in Germany, the eighth child in her family. Being a child wasn't a lot of fun for Caroline, as her mum didn't want her to study and instead made her do most of the housework. When Caroline was ten years old she caught the deadly disease typhus. She survived, but because of the illness she never grew taller than 1 m 33 cm (4 ft 3 in). Because of this, her family assumed she would never marry, and thought it was better she learned to be a house servant than get an education.

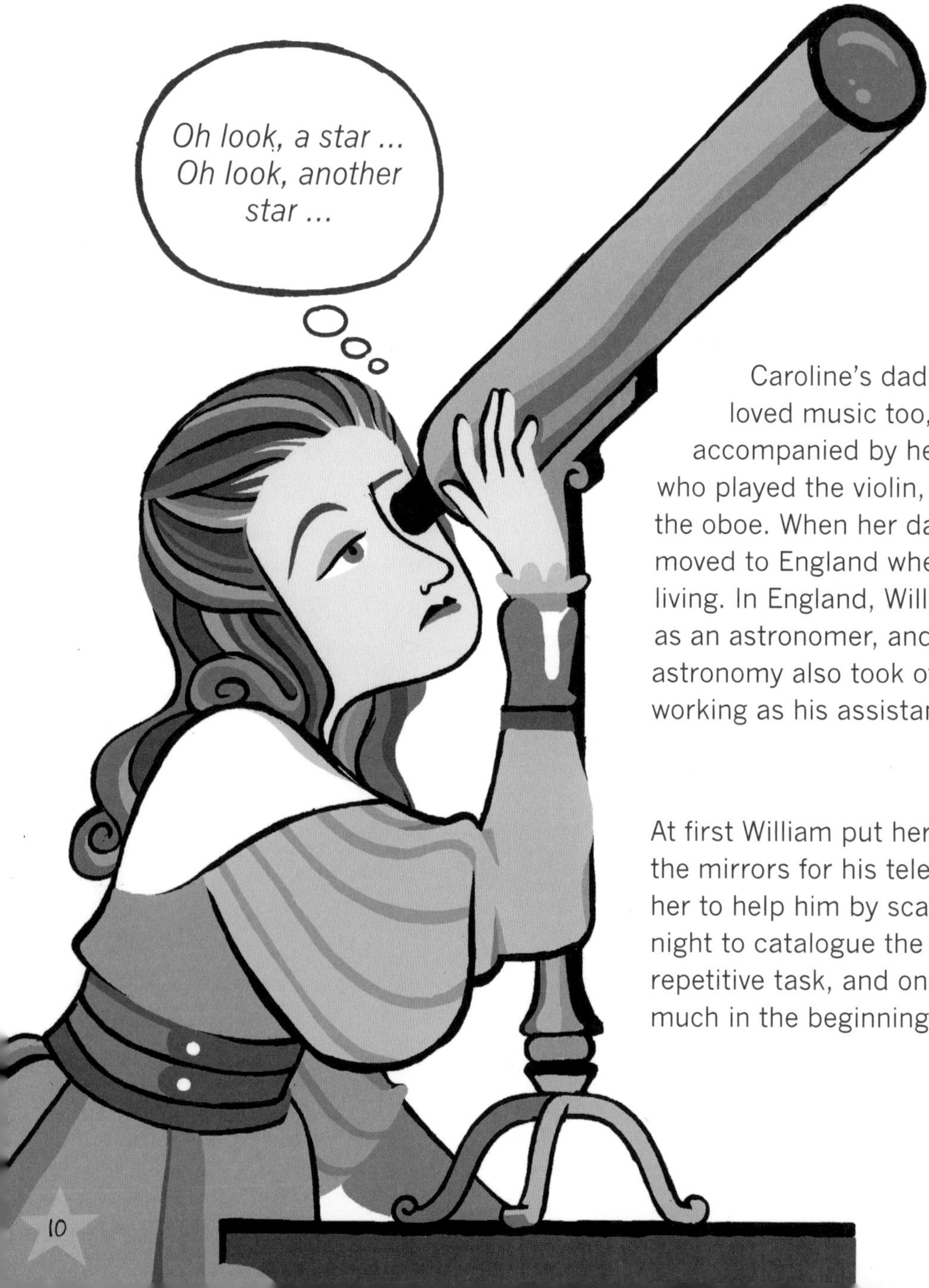

Oh look, a star ... Oh look, another star ...

Caroline's dad was a musician. She loved music too, and learned to sing accompanied by her brother, William, who played the violin, harpsichord and the oboe. When her dad died, Caroline moved to England where William was living. In England, William began working as an astronomer, and Caroline's career in astronomy also took off when she started working as his assistant.

At first William put her to work polishing the mirrors for his telescopes. Later he got her to help him by scanning the skies every night to catalogue the stars. It was a slow, repetitive task, and one she didn't enjoy much in the beginning.

After a while Caroline began to really enjoy astronomy, and during her stargazing she discovered several comets and nebulae. William became the official astronomer for King George III, and as William's assistant the King started to pay Caroline a salary of £50 per year for her work. That is the equivalent of £5,700 in today's money, a considerable sum in those days. This made her the first woman to be paid for astronomy at a time when most men were not paid for their scientific work.

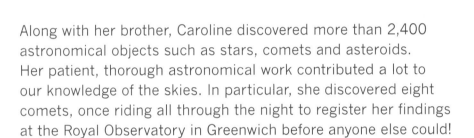

Along with her brother, Caroline discovered more than 2,400 astronomical objects such as stars, comets and asteroids. Her patient, thorough astronomical work contributed a lot to our knowledge of the skies. In particular, she discovered eight comets, once riding all through the night to register her findings at the Royal Observatory in Greenwich before anyone else could!

In 1828, she was awarded the Gold Medal of the Royal Astronomical Society, something a woman was not awarded again until 1996 – 168 years later! Along with Mary Somerville, who was another prominent woman scientist of the era (see page 42), Caroline was elected as an honorary member of the Royal Astronomical Society. The two of them were the first women members.

STARGAZE LIKE CAROLINE

The best way to see stars is to get away from any street lights, floodlights and house lights. What better excuse to get your family and friends together and go on a countryside camping trip to look at the night sky? Wrap up warm, bring marshmallows for toasting and, once it gets dark, see what constellations you can spot.

There are apps that can be downloaded for smartphones that will help you identify constellations and individual stars in the sky. If you have a telescope, see if you can spot the patterns of craters on the Moon that have been formed by asteroids hitting its surface. One of the Moon's craters is called C. Herschel, after Caroline herself.

Even if you can't travel very far, it's still worth stargazing from your garden or local park. For regular stargazing practice, search online for astronomy clubs in your local area.

MARY ANNING

Born in poverty, Mary began fossil-hunting to earn money. Her discoveries changed our thinking about how life developed on Earth.

PALAEONTOLOGIST

Mary Anning collected and studied fossils of ancient creatures, advancing our understanding of prehistoric life.

LIVED:	21 May 1799 – 9 March 1847
BORN IN:	Lyme Regis (UK)
WORKED IN:	Lyme Regis (UK)

Mary Anning's family was very poor. She and her brother Joseph were the only two of ten siblings who survived childhood, though as a baby Mary had a lucky escape when she was being looked after by a neighbour. Three women and baby Mary were underneath a tree when it was struck by lightning! The three women were instantly killed, and only baby Mary miraculously survived. As she grew up, people in her village said the lightning strike was the cause of her intelligence and curiosity.

To help her family earn money, Mary collected fossils along the Dorset coast, which they sold to collectors and geologists. She searched bravely and tirelessly, especially in winter when storms exposed more fossils. The unstable cliffs were dangerous and she was once nearly killed in a landslide.

The geologists wrote about the fossils, but Mary herself was not included in the exclusive, scientific community – despite the importance of her findings. In 1811, Mary discovered the skeleton of the prehistoric sea creature, the ichthyosaur. The finding caused a sensation, as it began to make scientists question the history of the Earth, at a time when most people believed that God had created the planet 6,000 years ago. But despite the buzz about the skeleton, the scientific papers written about it never mentioned Mary's name.

As well as the ichthyosaur, Mary also discovered plesiosaurs and pterosaurs. She even solved a scientific puzzle that none of the other experts could crack: she worked out that stones, called coprolites, found in the intestine area of the skeletons, were fossilised dinosaur poo!

What on Earth could it be?
How shall I tell him he's holding a poo?

Mary found so many different fossils that, in 1830, geologist and artist Henry de la Beche painted a picture of prehistoric Dorset called *Duria Antiquior* based on her finds. It became the first illustration of prehistory to be widely circulated, and was used for educational purposes.

Mary's poor background and the fact she was a woman meant that she received very little recognition for her work during her lifetime. After her death her friend and president of the Geological Society, Henry de la Beche, published a eulogy for her. The famous writer Charles Dickens also wrote an article about Mary, and she may have inspired the famous tongue-twister, 'She sells seashells on the seashore.' In recent times, due to her expertise in finding fossils, she has come to be recognised as one of the most important British women in science.

DISCOVER PREHISTORY LIKE MARY

The painting *Duria Antiquior* shows an 'action shot' of the fossilised animals that had been discovered by Mary along the Dorset coast. Henry de la Beche sold prints of his painting to raise money for Mary. In the image an ichthyosaur is biting the neck of a plesiosaur, and the plesiosaur is even shown making the droppings that will become coprolite.

The split-level view reveals the scene both above and below the surface of the water. Research what dinosaurs and prehistoric creatures lived in your area, and create your own 'action shot' in the style of the *Duria Antiquior*.

ADA LOVELACE

Creative and brilliant, Ada Lovelace developed the first 'computer program' nearly a hundred years before the first computers were actually built.

COMPUTER PROGRAMMER AND MATHEMATICIAN

Ada Lovelace was an expert at maths, and she theorised how a machine could be used to calculate more than just numbers.

LIVED: 10 December 1815 – 27 November 1852

BORN IN: London (UK)

WORKED IN: London (UK)

Augusta Ada Byron was the daughter of the famous poet Lord Byron, and the English aristocrat Lady Anne Isabella Byron. It was her dad who chose the name, Ada, that she was known by, but when baby Ada was only one month old her parents separated. Her mum did not trust Lord Byron because of his reckless behaviour, always spending all his money and breaking his promises!

Anne Isabella thought that Lord Byron's rash behaviour and poetic imagination was a kind of 'madness' and she was worried Ada would take after her dad. When Ada told her mum of her idea to build a steam-powered flying horse, Lady Byron became even more concerned! She wanted Ada to be sensible, so she insisted Ada be taught maths and science from a young age. This was a very unusual education for girls at the time, but Ada was very clever and excelled at her studies.

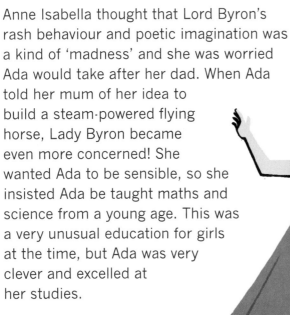

When she was 17, she met the mechanical engineer and mathematician Charles Babbage at a party. Charles Babbage had no time for people he thought were foolish or stupid, and he often became very cross when other people made mistakes. But even though Ada was a young woman, her mathematical talent was so great they became good friends.

Charles Babbage came up with the idea of a mechanical computer that could complete mathematical calculations, which he called his Analytical Engine. Instructions could be fed into the machine using hole-punched cards. The Analytical Engine really captured Ada's imagination. She worked with Charles, translating some writings about the machine, to which she added many pages of her own notes about how the machine could be used.

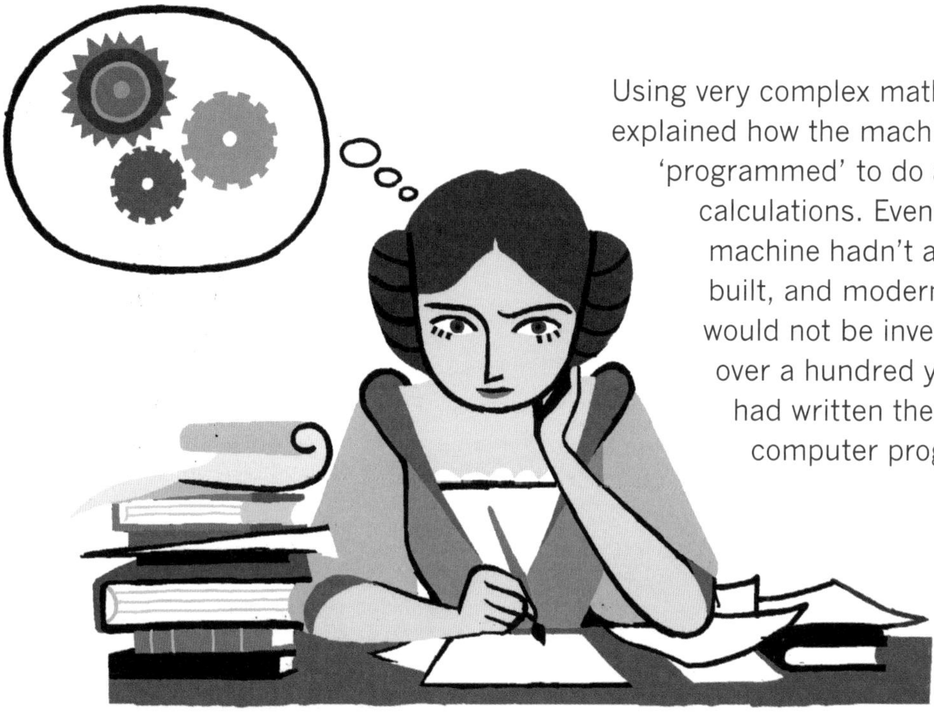

Using very complex maths, Ada explained how the machine could be 'programmed' to do all sorts of calculations. Even though the machine hadn't actually been built, and modern computers would not be invented for over a hundred years, Ada had written the first ever computer program!

Thanks to her powerful imagination and intelligence, Ada was also able to think about possible future tasks that computers would be able to complete beyond simply calculating numbers. She suggested they could do things such as compose music, or be useful to science – which has come true.

Ada knew that her visionary qualities were unique. She said, 'I believe myself to possess a most singular combination of qualities exactly fitted to make me pre-eminently a discoverer of the hidden realities of nature.'

PROGRAM COMPUTERS LIKE ADA

Nowadays computers are in every area of our lives and do all sorts of things, just like Ada predicted. In fact, you can write a program to make music with your computer, just as she imagined! Visit the website scratch.mit.edu. To program a musical track, click on the 'create' tab at the top of the page. Next, click on the link on the right-hand side of the page for the step-by-step tutorial called 'Make Music'. This will take you through steps to program your own musical melody and animation.

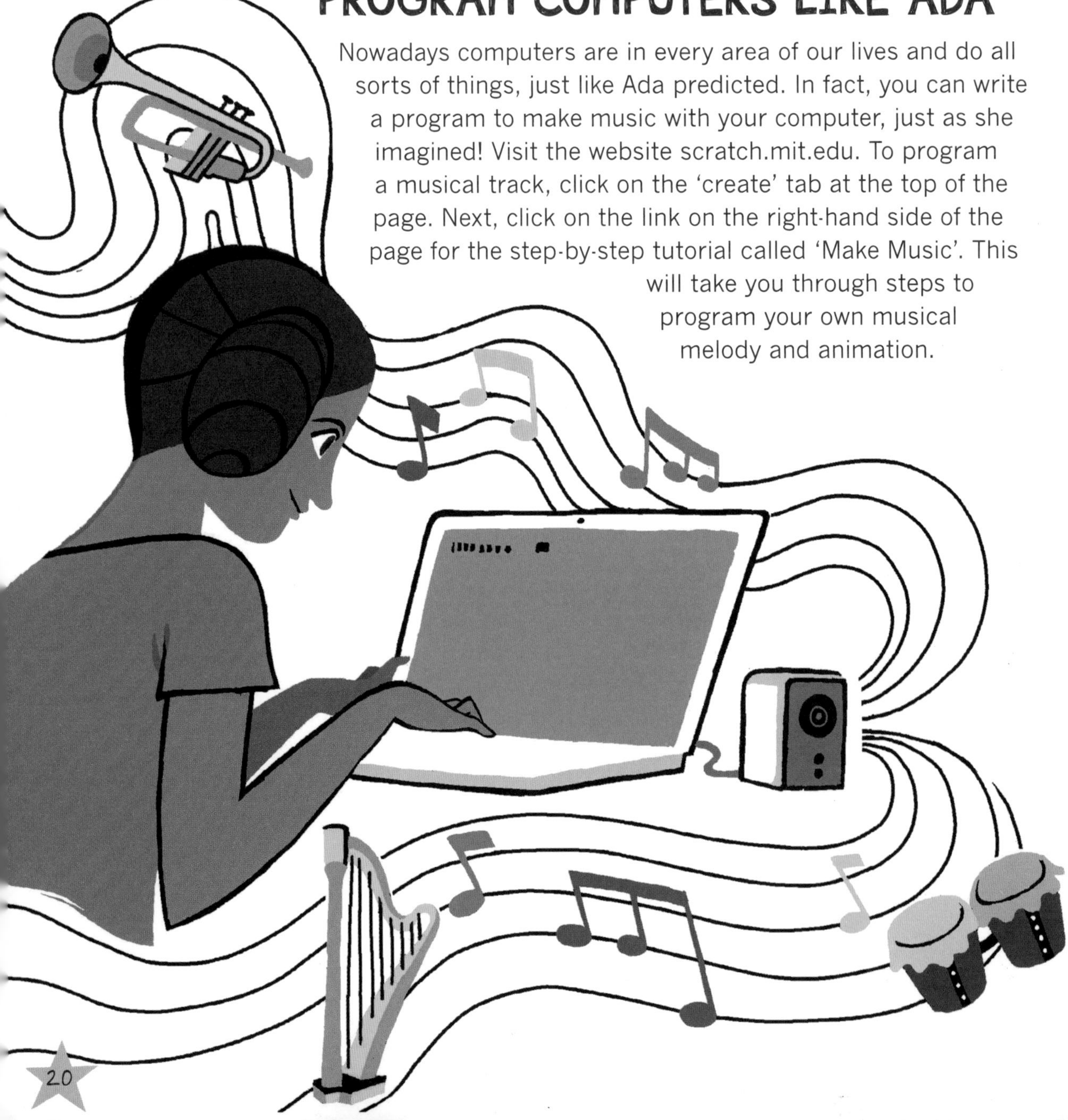

MARIE CURIE

This double Nobel Prize-winning woman made history several times over, discovering radioactivity and new chemical elements.

PHYSICIST AND CHEMIST

Marie Curie's study of radioactivity advanced our scientific understanding in physics (the study of matter and energy) and chemistry (the study of substances).

LIVED: 7 November 1867 – 4 July 1934

BORN IN: Warsaw (Poland)

WORKED IN: Paris (France)

When she was a young girl, Marie's dad taught her and her brothers and sisters at home. He was a maths and physics teacher, and he brought home laboratory equipment from the school he taught at. Marie loved science and wanted to go on and study at university, but in Poland at that time it was forbidden for women to enter higher education.

She attended an illegal underground school called the 'Flying University' that taught women students in secret. The classes would regularly change locations around the city, so as to avoid the teachers and students being arrested! However, Marie knew that to get a proper education she would have to go to an official university. She saved up for several years until she had enough money to go to the famous university, the Sorbonne, in Paris, France.

Marie completed two degrees in Paris, one in physics and one in maths. She also met and fell in love with a young professor named Pierre Curie. They worked together studying the mysterious 'X-rays' that some materials give off. Marie described these materials as 'radioactive'. She was the first person to use this word, and through her experiments she discovered two new elements. They were called radium and polonium (after her homeland, Poland).

In 1906, Pierre was killed in an accident. Marie was devastated, but was determined to honour his memory. She continued her work and took over his role as professor at the Sorbonne, becoming the first woman to teach there. Experiments with radium showed Marie that it could be used to kill cancerous cells.

At the beginning of the 20th century this new material radium really fired people's imaginations and was believed to have all sorts of wonderful, magical healing properties. It was put in lots of products, from chocolate to children's toys! People did not know at that time how dangerous radioactive materials were.

Marie won two Nobel Prizes for her work, in 1903 and 1911. She was the first woman to be awarded the prestigious award, and she was also the first (and so far, only) woman to win twice. She is now one of the most famous scientists in history.

EXPERIMENT LIKE MARIE

X-rays are far too dangerous to experiment with at home, however you can do an experiment to see the effect of a different type of radiation. X-rays are a type of light – but one that we can't see with our eyes. Ultra violet, or UV light, is another type of light that we can't see with our eyes, but we can see its effects. Along with visible light, they are both given off by the Sun.

To see the effects of UV rays, place a piece of coloured sugar paper in a sunny spot with a cardboard cut out shape in the centre. Leave it for a few days, then remove the cardboard shape. You should see a dark outline where the paper has been protected from the UV rays.

LISE MEITNER

Facing discrimination for being a woman, then in danger for being Jewish, Lise Meitner tirelessly battled many obstacles to pursue her passion for physics.

NUCLEAR PHYSICIST

Lise Meitner studied atoms, the tiny building blocks of all stuff, and the energy that can be released when they are split even smaller.

LIVED:	7 November 1878 27 October 1968
BORN IN:	Vienna (Austria)
WORKED IN:	Berlin (Germany) and Stockholm (Sweden)

Lise's family lived in Vienna, Austria. They were a well-off Jewish family, and Lise was one of eight children. She was a very curious child, full of questions. A natural scientist, by the age of eight she was studying things about the world around her, such as how light splits into colours on oil slicks. She kept a notebook of her scientific observations under her pillow.

In Austria at that time, women were not allowed to continue school after the age of 14, but her parents were supportive of her scientific enthusiasm and paid for her to have a private education. This meant Lise was able to study at the University of Vienna, and later the University of Berlin. When the First World War broke out in 1914, Lise helped wounded soldiers by taking X-rays of their injuries.

In Berlin, Lise met a chemist called Otto Hahn, and together they worked on particles and radioactivity. She enjoyed her work very much, but when the National Socialists (Nazis) rose to power in the 1930s the situation became very dangerous for Lise, who had Jewish heritage.

The Nazis passed a law banning scientists from leaving the country, and it became clear that Lise would have to escape Germany secretly. Her colleagues helped with her escape preparations, and Otto Hahn gave her his mother's diamond ring in case she needed it to bribe Nazi guards.

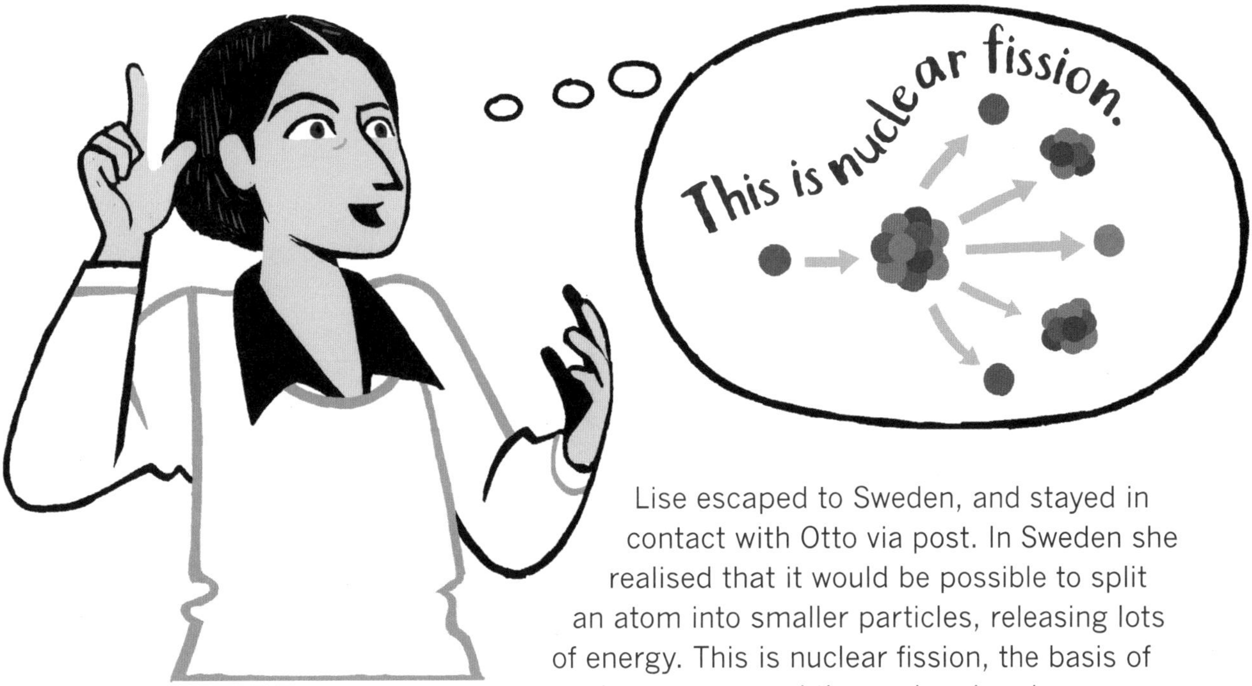

Lise escaped to Sweden, and stayed in contact with Otto via post. In Sweden she realised that it would be possible to split an atom into smaller particles, releasing lots of energy. This is nuclear fission, the basis of nuclear power, and the nuclear bomb.

Lise was very disapproving of the use of nuclear technology in weapons-making, and she refused a job offer from the USA to work on nuclear weapons, saying, 'I will have nothing to do with a bomb!' She faced great danger and was disadvantaged throughout much of her life due to prejudice she faced as both a woman and a Jew, but she never gave up. She said, 'Life need not be easy, provided only that it is not empty.'

EXPLORE LIKE LISE

It's not very safe or practical to try and recreate nuclear experiments in your bedroom! But that doesn't mean you can't explore like Lise. Being a proper scientist starts with observing the world around you, just like Lise did with her notebook when she was little.

Get a notebook and go outside. Look at the world around you and try to really notice small details and patterns in the way things are. Look at how things move, for example, watch how spilled water runs and collects on a pavement. Look at plants through a magnifying lens. Touch different materials to see how warm or cold they feel. Record your observations in your notebook, and try to figure out ideas as to why things are the way they are. This is how scientists come up with 'hypotheses', or theories.

BARBARA McCLINTOCK

Barbara McClintock made many ground-breaking discoveries about genetics by studying corn plants.

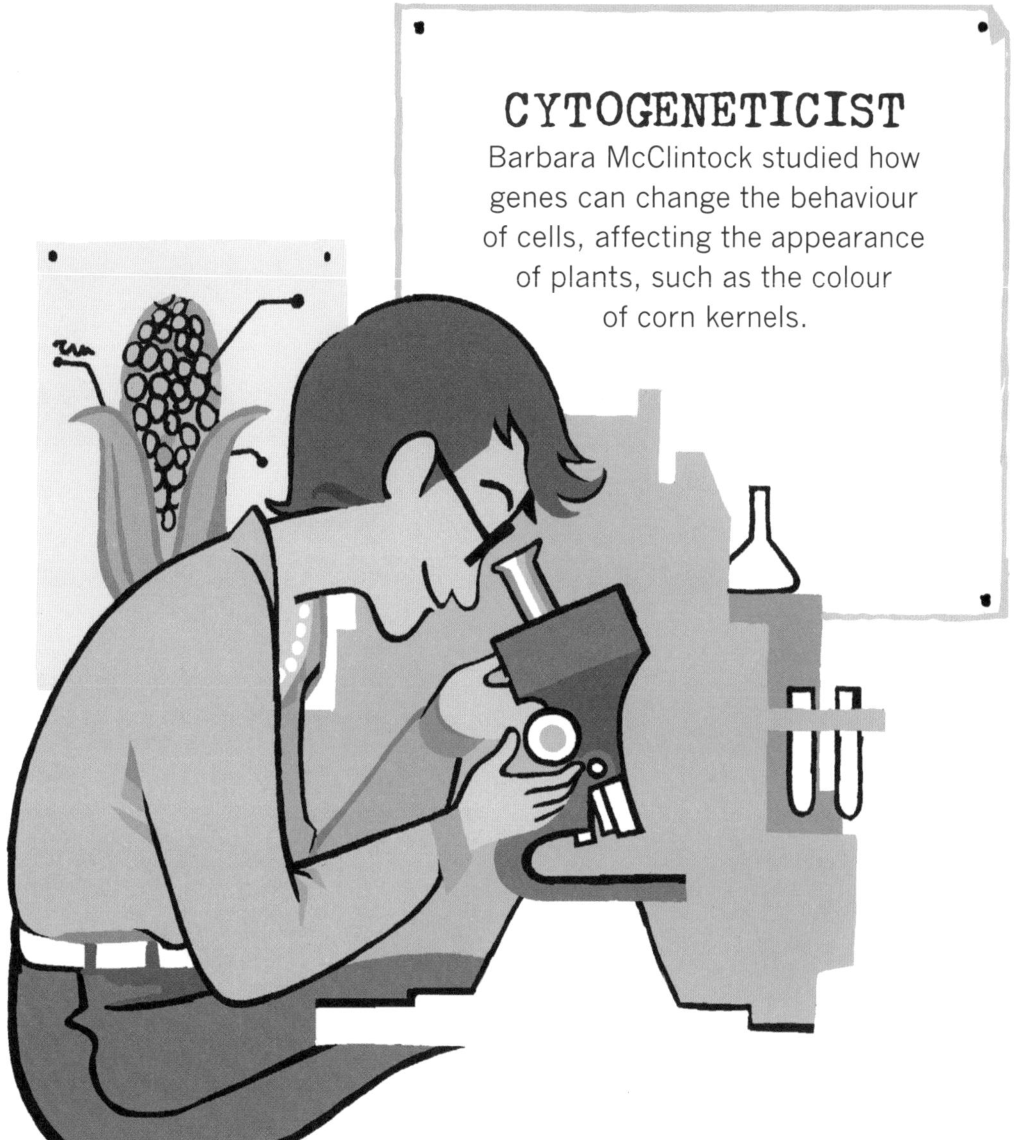

CYTOGENETICIST

Barbara McClintock studied how genes can change the behaviour of cells, affecting the appearance of plants, such as the colour of corn kernels.

LIVED:	16 June 1902 – 2 September 1992
BORN IN:	Hartford, Connecticut (USA)
WORKED IN:	Ithaca and Long Island, New York (USA)

When she was born, Barbara was given the name Eleanor McClintock, but as a young girl her parents noticed a strong independent streak in her. They decided to rename Eleanor Barbara, because they thought it was better suited to her strong personality. At school Barbara discovered a love for science, and told her parents she wanted to go to university to study. Her mum worried that no man would want a scientist for a wife! But Barbara didn't care one bit about that. She was determined to pursue her passion. Her dad, who was a doctor, supported her and in 1919 she went to Cornell University to study biology.

At Cornell Barbara began to work on the subject that would occupy most of her career, studying the genetics of corn plants (which are also called maize). She was fascinated by how some purple kinds of corn had kernels of different colours: some that were purple, some that were white, and some that were speckled.

Barbara's work centred around the study of chromosomes, which are tiny structures that all living things have inside their cells. These structures contain genes, which are like microscopic instructions in our bodies that control things, such as how we look (for example, whether we have blue or brown eyes). Barbara wanted to figure out how these genes affected the appearance of the corn.

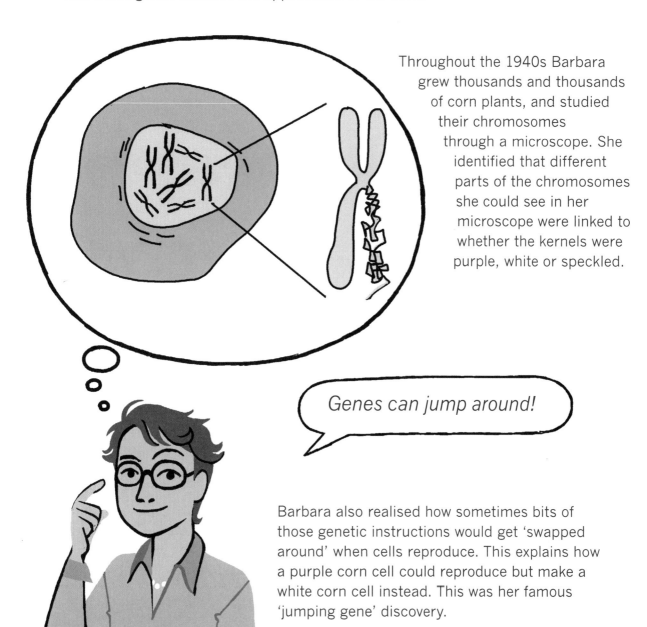

Throughout the 1940s Barbara grew thousands and thousands of corn plants, and studied their chromosomes through a microscope. She identified that different parts of the chromosomes she could see in her microscope were linked to whether the kernels were purple, white or speckled.

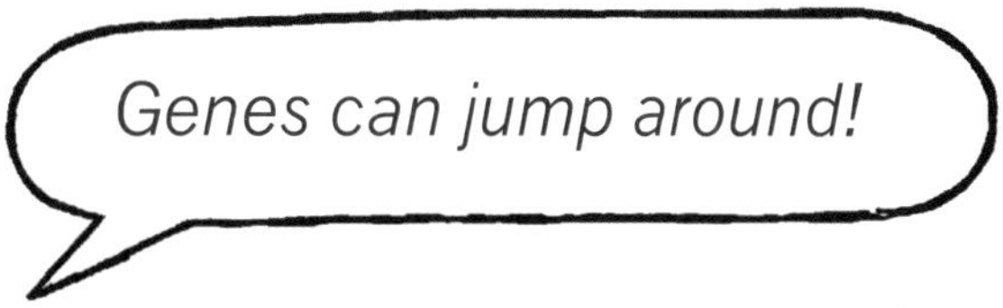

Barbara also realised how sometimes bits of those genetic instructions would get 'swapped around' when cells reproduce. This explains how a purple corn cell could reproduce but make a white corn cell instead. This was her famous 'jumping gene' discovery.

Barbara liked to work alone and her research was way ahead of its time, so was largely ignored by fellow scientists. It was only in the 1960s and 1970s that people began to understand the importance of her findings, and she was finally recognised with the Nobel Prize in Physiology or Medicine in 1983, for her contribution to the understanding of genetics.

Often, the Nobel Prize is awarded to teams of people, however Barbara's prize was awarded to her alone, the first Nobel Prize of this type to go to an individual woman.

OBSERVE LIKE BARBARA

You are probably familiar with the yellow sweetcorn that we eat, but why not try growing some of the purple corn that led to Barbara making her amazing discoveries? You can observe the different colours in the kernels up close, and compare the cobs of different plants to see how the patterns change. To find seeds for purple corn (also called 'Indian corn') search online, and follow the planting instructions on the seed packet.

KATHERINE JOHNSON

An incredibly talented mathematician, Katherine Johnson was one of the 'human computers' that helped put US astronauts into space.

ANALYTIC GEOMETRY

Katherine Johnson was an all-round talented mathematician, but her knowledge of analytic geometry (a type of maths that uses co-ordinates) was essential to her work at NASA.

BORN: 26 August 1918

BORN IN: White Sulphur Springs, West Virginia (USA)

WORKED IN: Hampton, Virginia (USA)

As a little girl, Katherine loved numbers. She counted everything – from the steps she took to reach the church, to the knives and forks when she did the washing up. Her mathematical talent was so obvious from such an early age that she started high school four years early at just ten years old, and went to university aged just 14!

In many states in the USA at that time, there were laws enforcing 'segregation', which meant black students were not allowed to go to the same schools and universities as white students. Getting a good education wasn't straightforward for Katherine, as the county her family lived in did not have any universities for black students. This meant she had to attend a university over 200 km away.

In 1952, she heard that NACA (the organisation that later became NASA) was hiring mathematicians. In those days, complex mathematical calculations were carried out mainly by humans, not machines. People who did the calculations were called 'computers' so Katherine became one of the 'computers in skirts' at NACA, the all-women team of mathematicians who did the number-crunching for the research team.

In keeping with the state laws, the workplace at NACA was segregated. This meant white women and black women worked separately, even having to use separate toilets and drinking fountains. When NACA became NASA in 1958 the workplace was desegregated, but there were still barriers against her as a woman. For a long time Katherine was not allowed to put her name as the author of research reports, and instead had to use the name of a male colleague.

Putting a man in space for the first time meant figuring out incredibly complex mathematics, and Katherine did a lot of the calculations for the USA's first ever human spaceflight, in 1961. She was so good at her work that, the following year, astronaut John Glenn specifically requested that Katherine check the calculations for his flight orbiting Earth, rather than rely on the calculations from the machines. John Glenn's flight was a success, and it marked a turning point in the Space Race between the USA and Russia as to who could put a man on the Moon first.

Katherine was employed at NASA for over 30 years, and during that time she worked extremely hard to overcome the barriers that were put in front of her as a black woman. As well as pushing to have her own name on research reports, she fought to attend high-level meetings, where previously women had not been welcome. In 2015, President Obama honoured Katherine with the Presidential Medal of Freedom, the highest honour a civilian can receive in the USA.

SOLVE PROBLEMS LIKE KATHERINE

Reckon you've got what it takes to solve maths problems about space? Flex your maths muscles on the NASA 'Space Math' website: spacemath.gsfc.nasa.gov/grade35.html. Try the maths problems to test your skills on the sorts of topics that Katherine herself worked on! Figure out how the orbit of the International Space Station changes, or use geometry – the same type of maths that Katherine excelled at – to calculate when planets will line up.

JANE GOODALL

A fearless explorer with big dreams, Jane Goodall made amazing scientific discoveries about chimpanzees by studying them in the wild.

PRIMATOLOGIST

Jane Goodall is an expert on primates, the group of animals that includes monkeys, chimpanzees, gorillas and humans.

BORN: 3 April 1934

BORN IN: London (UK)

WORKED IN: Gombe (Tanzania) and Cambridge (UK)

Jane Goodall was always fascinated by animals. Visiting a farm when she was just four years old, she hid in a hen house for hours to discover how chickens laid eggs. She didn't realise her poor mum was rushing around outside looking for her, absolutely worried sick!

When she was ten years old Jane read the book *Tarzan of the Apes*. It was about a man raised by apes, and his wife – who was also called Jane! That's when she knew that her dream was to move to Africa, live in the wild and write books about the animals there.

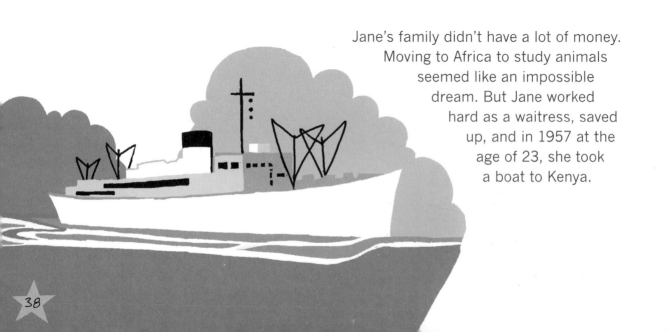

Jane's family didn't have a lot of money. Moving to Africa to study animals seemed like an impossible dream. But Jane worked hard as a waitress, saved up, and in 1957 at the age of 23, she took a boat to Kenya.

She soon got an opportunity to start studying the chimpanzees that lived in the jungle in Tanzania. At first the chimpanzees were frightened and ran away from her. Slowly, they got used to her presence, and allowed her to watch them close up.

Don't look now, she's back!

While observing the chimpanzees, Jane discovered something amazing. The chimpanzees were making simple tools for catching termites, by stripping the leaves off twigs, and poking them into termite mounds. Until that time, it was believed that humans were the only creatures to make and use tools. When she told her mentor Louis Leakey, he said, 'Now we must redefine man, redefine tools, or accept chimpanzees as humans.' This was a major scientific discovery!

We must respect animals like we respect other people.

Louis Leakey told Jane she needed to get a degree to get funding for her scientific work. She went to Cambridge University to study ethology – the study of animal behaviour – and became only the eighth person to be allowed to gain a PhD without having a degree.

In the beginning Jane got a rather frosty welcome at Cambridge. Many of the academics there accused her of being unscientific in her work, as she had given the chimpanzees names instead of numbers, and she had committed what in their eyes was a terrible sin – believing that the chimpanzees were feeling emotions, seeming happy, or sad. The idea that chimpanzees can feel emotions is much less controversial now, but at the time, as a young, self-educated woman, Jane had to fight hard to have her research taken seriously.

Jane worked with chimpanzees in Africa for many more years, and made several other important discoveries. In 1977 she founded the Jane Goodall Institute, a global wildlife and environment conservation organisation. She also founded Roots & Shoots, which helps young people get involved in environmental and wildlife conservation in their own local area.

CAMPAIGN LIKE JANE

Do you love animals and want to help protect the environment? Start a nature club with your friends. Study the plants and animals around where you live, and come up with ways to improve your local area for the resident insects and animals.

MORE SCIENCE AND TECHNOLOGY GENIUSES

The list of brilliant women in science and technology doesn't stop there! Here are even more ground-breaking women scientists that you should know about, from the present day right back to the ancient Greek period.

HYPATIA

LIVED: c. CE 355 – 415

BORN IN: Alexandria (Egypt)

WORKED IN: Egypt

Ancient Greek mathematician, philosopher and astronomer Hypatia was one of the earliest recorded female mathematicians. She was taught by her father, Theon, who was a well-respected scholar.

Hypatia was educated in Athens in mainland Greece, but as an adult lived in the city of Alexandria in ancient Egypt, which was part of the Eastern Roman Empire and had a famous library. She eventually surpassed her father's knowledge, and became the head of the Neoplatonist School in Alexandria, teaching the works of Plato and Aristotle to students who came from miles around. Hypatia was killed by rioting Christians, due to the religious unrest in the city.

MARY SOMERVILLE

LIVED: 26 December 1780 – 29 November 1872

BORN IN: Jedburgh (Scotland)

WORKED IN: Scotland and England

As a child Mary was not given much education. Following her family's wishes, she married her cousin, a Russian navy captain who also did not approve of her studying. After he died just three years later, Mary was free to dedicate herself to her love of maths and astronomy. Her second husband, who she married in 1812, was proud and supportive of his wife's self-taught knowledge. They moved to London, and Mary became friends with scientists such as Charles Babbage and Caroline Herschel.

Mary wrote many books on different scientific topics, including a book called *Physical Geography* which was used as a textbook until the early 20th century. She became a well-respected figure, being accepted into the Royal Astronomical Society alongside Caroline Hershel, the first women to be members of the respected scientific society.

RACHEL CARSON

LIVED: 27 May 1907 – 14 April 1964

BORN IN: Springdale, Pennsylvania (USA)

WORKED IN: USA

Rachel grew up on a large farm, where she learned about nature and animals. The ocean was a particular topic of interest for her, and she ended up studying biology, and later specialising in marine biology when she went to university. After graduating she got a job writing environmental literature for the US Bureau of Fisheries. Rachel wrote several books about the ocean and the environment. Her most famous book, *Silent Spring*, is about the harmful effects of pesticides on the natural world. She became very involved in nature conservation, and she testified before a government committee about the dangers of pesticides.

DOROTHY HODGKIN

LIVED: 12 May 1910 – 29 July 1994

BORN IN: Cairo (Egypt)

WORKED IN: UK

Dorothy's father was an archaeologist, so she was born in Cairo, in Egypt, and spent much of her childhood travelling around different places in the Middle East. She did well at school, and then went to university to study chemistry. After graduating, she worked at Cambridge and then at Oxford Universities. Her work was on protein crystallography which is a technique that uses X-rays to look at the atoms of proteins. Dorothy found crystallography absolutely fascinating, and through her dedication to the work she identified the structure of penicillin, insulin and the vitamin B12.

CHIEN-SHIUNG WU

LIVED: 31 May 1912 – 16 February 1997

BORN IN: Liuhe, Taicang (China)

WORKED IN: USA

Chien-Shiung Wu was born near Shanghai in China. Her parents were strongly in favour of her having a good education, and they encouraged Wu to study hard. She studied physics at university in China, but at her academic advisor's suggestion she left China in 1936 to continue her studies in the USA.

She became an expert in nuclear physics, and was recruited to the Manhattan Project – a team that developed nuclear weapons. After the Second World War she became a professor again, and made further breakthroughs in nuclear physics, for which she was awarded a Nobel Prize as well as being given the nickname 'the Queen of Nuclear Research'.

ROSALIND FRANKLIN

LIVED: 25 July 1920 – 16 April 1958

BORN IN: London (UK)

WORKED IN: UK

Rosalind Franklin was born into a well-off Jewish family in London. Her parents helped settle Jewish refugees from Europe who had escaped the Nazis, and her mother was involved in the struggle for votes for women. Rosalind was a very talented student, and went on to study chemistry at Cambridge University. She became an expert on X-ray images of substances, and in 1950 she started working on making X-ray images of DNA. This work led to the discovery of the structure of DNA. Rosalind died aged only 39 from ovarian cancer, but her colleagues on the same project were awarded a Nobel Prize in 1962 for their work.

INDIRA NATH

BORN: 14 January 1938

BORN IN: Andhra Pradesh (India)

WORKS IN: India

Indira knew when she was ten years old that she would become a doctor. When she was old enough to go to university, Indira travelled to the UK to study for her medical degree, but she was committed to returning to India after graduating so she could use her skills and knowledge to the benefit of her home country.

India has the highest rates of leprosy in the world, and she was determined to make a breakthrough in the treatment and prevention of the disease. Indira identified a problem with sufferers' immune systems, which was a big step forward in developing treatments and vaccines. Thanks in large part to her research, the number of people in India suffering from leprosy has dropped from 4.5 million people, to fewer than 1 million today, and better treatments mean that the worst disfigurements from leprosy are now rare.

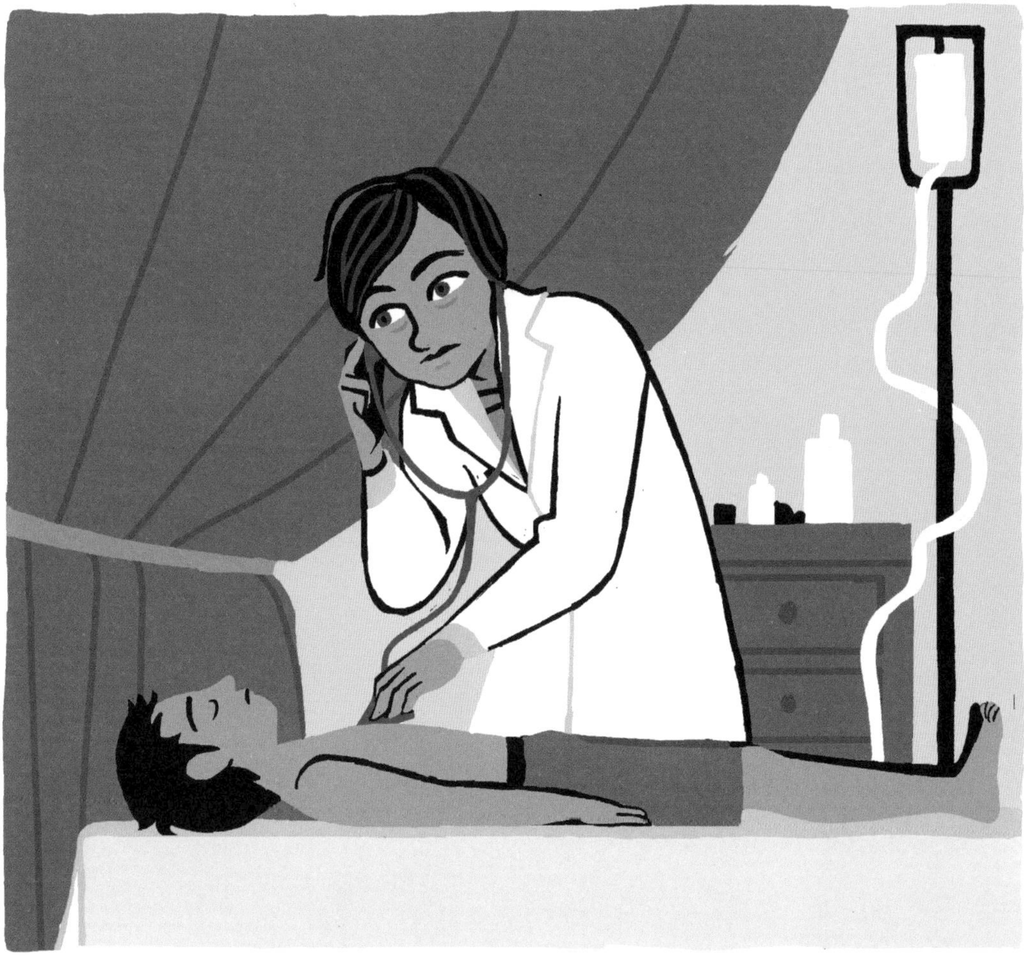

WANDA DÍAZ-MERCED

BORN: 7 February 1974

BORN IN: Gurabo (Puerto Rico)

WORKS IN: Puerto Rico, South Africa and UK

As young girls growing up in Puerto Rico, Wanda and her sister used to dream of visiting distant galaxies in a space shuttle. Her family were poor, but Wanda's hard work led to her winning places on several science summer programmes. She went on to study physics at university, but tragedy struck when she lost her sight through illness.

Wanda thought she wouldn't be able to continue with astrophysics, but rather than letting her disability prevent her from continuing in the field she loved, Wanda came up with a solution. Instead of relying on visual graphs of data, she translated the data into sound. She has since made scientific breakthroughs, finding patterns that would not have been noticed using visual methods alone.

JULIANA ROTICH

BORN: 1977

BORN IN: Kenya

WORKS IN: Kenya

Always passionate about technology, Juliana was the chair of her school computer club. She studied computer science at university and worked in the computer industry after she graduated. Then, in Kenya in 2008, violence broke out after the elections. During the confusion, Juliana realised how difficult it was to get accurate, up-to-date information about what was happening. She created Ushahidi, a website and communication platform that could be used by anyone to report and map incidents. The same technology is now used in many countries in various situations, for example after natural disasters like earthquakes, or during conflicts, as well as for on-going issues such as pollution. She also developed the BRCK, a self-powered portable WiFi router to ensure good Internet access in places without an Internet connection.

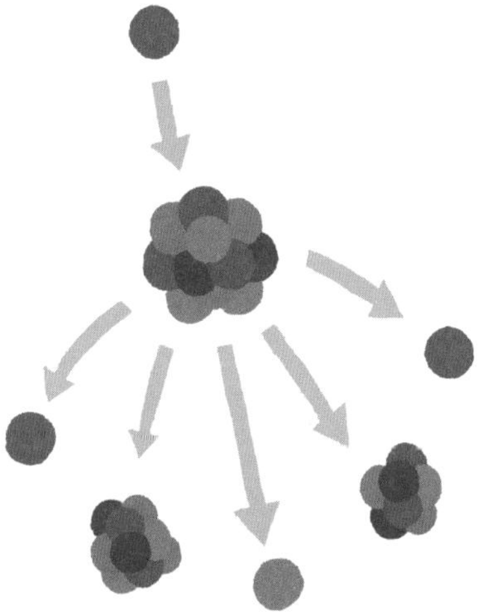

COUNTLESS OTHERS ...

There are so many more incredible women making amazing discoveries and important contributions to science, technology and maths that there isn't space for on these pages. At this very moment, all around the world, some of the most cutting-edge science in the fields of robotics, materials science, medicine, environmental science and anything else you can think of is being done by women. Who knows what astonishing scientific breakthroughs women will make next?

GET INVOLVED IN SCIENCE AND TECHNOLOGY!

There are hundreds of fun ways to pursue your passion for science and technology. Here are just a few suggestions to get you started.

GET INVOLVED IN CITIZEN SCIENCE!

Citizen science is a practical way to help out with actual, cutting-edge scientific research. Scientists often need tons of data to test and prove their theories, and sometimes this data can be very time-consuming or expensive to collect. Enter citizen science. In citizen science projects, normal people can go out and make observations, or take part in quizzes and activities online, which all go towards a scientist's REAL research project.

Citizen science projects range from things such as the RSPB's Big Garden Birdwatch, which asks people to record what bird species they spot in their gardens on specific days of the year, to online projects about all sorts of subjects. Search online for 'citizen science' to see what you can find.

FIND A SCIENCE CLUB, OR START ONE YOURSELF

You can use the Internet or ask at a local library to see if there are any science clubs in your area. If there aren't, don't be put off – just start one yourself! Find some friends who are also interested in science, and ask a teacher or parent to help you organise space and resources. What sort of activities would you like to do in your club? If you want to do hands-on experiments you can find ideas for science projects and fun activities online, or in your local library. You might want to try new activities each week, or you might want to work on one big project – and even enter it into a competition.

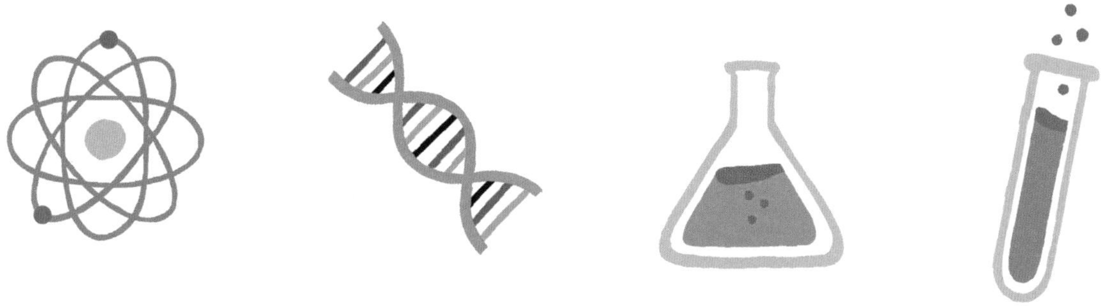

ENTER A YOUNG PERSON'S SCIENCE COMPETITION

There are lots of national science competitions you can enter, either in teams or individually. If you need to put a team together or you need access to equipment, it's worth talking to your school to see if they can help.

GO TO A SCIENCE FESTIVAL

Science festivals can be an awesome way to witness some super cool fizzing and whizzing science. Events range from explanatory talks and expert-led demonstrations, to fun hands-on workshops where you get to test out the scientific principles for yourself! Look online to find out if any festivals are coming to a town near you.

LEARN TO CODE

If computers and digital technology are what really get you excited, look out for code clubs in your local area that can teach you how to write computer programmes. Some volunteer-led organisations also run digital technology summer camps, where you can explore robotics, game development and other cool skills.

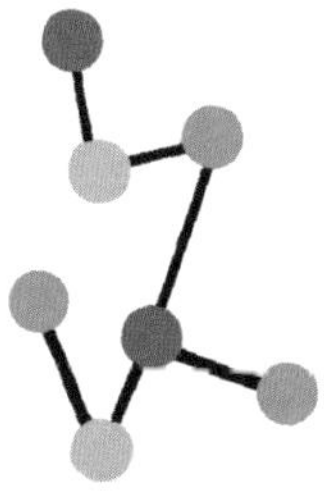

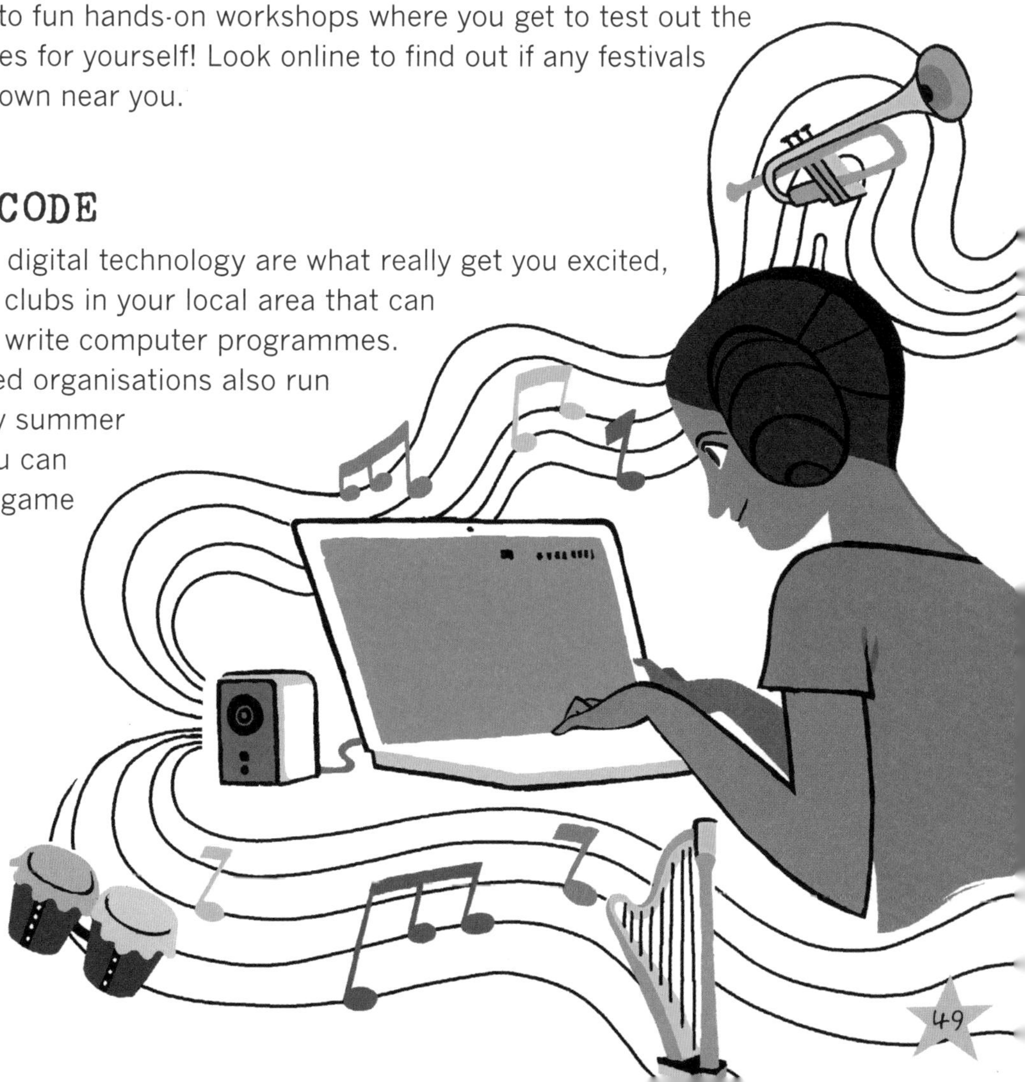

AMAZING ARTISTS AND DESIGNERS

What's the most famous painting you can think of? Probably the *Mona Lisa*, right? Many of the most famous paintings in the world are of beautiful women. Pictures like Leonardo da Vinci's portrait of Mona Lisa or Sandro Botticelli's *The Birth of Venus*, are instantly recognisable works of art, famous the world over.

But although galleries and art museums might be full of pictures of women, when it comes to pictures made by women, it's a different story. Only between three and five per cent of the artworks on display in the most famous galleries across Europe and the USA are by women artists.

Despite not always being given prominence in museum and gallery collections, women have been making incredible art for hundreds of years. The styles of art might be very different, ranging from Artemisia Gentileschi's baroque painting to Louise Bourgeois' huge, twisted metal sculptures and Lee Miller's surrealist photography, but they are united by their talent and dedication to their art.

Some of the women in this book were well-known in their lifetime, some of them were not. Some are still working to break the boundaries of art as we know it today, but all of them are amazingly gifted and talented women, who created important art, design, fashion and architecture.

If you are a budding artist or designer, you'll find ideas in this book for how to follow in the footsteps of these incredible women. Perhaps in a few years' time your work will be on display around the world.

So read on, and be inspired by these brilliant women's stories.

ARTEMISIA GENTILESCHI

An incredibly talented painter, Artemisia Gentileschi created scenes full of passion and drama.

BAROQUE

Artemisia was an artist in the baroque style, which typically shows scenes from the Bible painted in an atmospheric, dramatic and detailed way.

LIVED: 8 July 1593 – c. 1656

BORN IN: Rome (Italy)

WORKED IN: Italy and England

Artemisia was born in Rome, Italy in 1593, the eldest child of the painter Orazio Gentileschi. Although there were many famous painters and sculptors in Italy around at that time, women were not normally allowed to train as artists. But Orazio saw that Artemesia was much more talented than her brothers, and realised it was worth teaching her. Despite becoming a very accomplished painter, unlike other artists of the time she was never taught to read or write!

In her dad's studio Artemesia learnt to draw, to mix pigments and how to paint in the chiaroscuro style. Chiaroscuro is a technique that was popularised by the famous artist Caravaggio, who was a friend of Orazio Gentileschi. It uses areas of strong light and shade to create very dramatic scenes. Artemisia excelled in this style.

When she was only 17, Artemesia painted a scene from the Bible, *Susanna and the Elders*. It shows two old men spying on Susanna as she bathes. Unlike other versions of the scene from the same era, Artemisia's version of the story shows Susanna's emotion and suffering. Her eyes are full of tears, and her body is twisted in embarrassment.

Artemisia moved to Florence in 1614, and became very successful. She was commissioned to produce artworks for the rich and powerful Medici family, as well as King Charles I of Great Britain. She became the first woman to be allowed to join the Accademia della Arti del Disegno (the Academy of the Arts and Design) and became friends with other influential people, including the scientist Galileo Galilei.

Throughout her career she painted many images of strong and defiant women. One of her most famous paintings is called *Judith Slaying Holofernes*, which is a gory picture of the beautiful widow Judith, killing Holofernes, an army general who was about to destroy her city. During her lifetime Artemisia's work was very well known and admired. A portrait of her painted by another artist at the time describes her as 'the famous Roman painter'.

After her death Artemisia was mostly forgotten by art critics, and many of her paintings were assumed to be done by male artists. In the 20th century, art historians began to reassess her importance as an artistic figure. Through painstakingly examining artworks from the period, historians have been able to identify from tiny details, such as types of brushstroke, which paintings were in fact created by Artemisia. She is now considered one of the most talented painters of her generation.

PAINT LIKE ARTEMISIA

Create your own chiaroscuro artwork. Set up a still-life scene that you would like to draw or paint, perhaps a selection of fruit, or an ornament or figurine. Draw the curtains or dim the light, so the room is dark, and place a torch so that it shines light on your still-life scene from an angle. Sketch the object or objects, trying to capture how the light falls on one side, while the other side is in shade.

ROSA BONHEUR

An animal-lover with a strong independent streak, Rosa Bonheur painted horses, bulls and other animals in a naturalistic style.

ANIMALIER

Rosa Bonheur was known as an animalier, an artist skilled in the realistic portrayal of animals.

LIVED: 16 March 1822 – 25 May 1899

BORN IN: Bordeaux (France)

WORKED IN: France, Scotland and England

Rosa always loved animals. What Rosa did NOT love was school. Even as a very young child she would sit happily sketching animals for hours on end, but when her mum tried to teach her to read and write, Rosa would stubbornly refuse. Eventually her mum came up with the idea of getting Rosa to draw an animal for each letter of the alphabet, and she learned her letters that way!

Rosa was the eldest child in a family of artists. Her family belonged to a Christian sect called the Saint-Simonians who, unusually for the time, believed in the equal education of women. But formal education did not suit Rosa. She was a very naughty pupil, and was expelled from many different schools due to her disruptive behaviour. After being expelled from another school when she was 12, her father decided to teach Rosa to be a painter.

Rosa began by copying pictures of animals from books, before moving on to making studies of live animals. She would travel to the outskirts of Paris to paint the horses, sheep, cows and goats there. Her most famous painting is *The Horse Fair*, a huge artwork that measures 2.5 m tall and 5 m wide. It shows the horse market in Paris, and is now on display in the Metropolitan Museum in New York, USA.

When Rosa's work was displayed in Britain it caught the attention of the art critics and collectors there, and she met Queen Victoria who admired her paintings. Her rise in popularity abroad was not matched at home, as French art critics began to consider her style 'too English'. They started referring to her with the English title 'Miss' rather than 'Mademoiselle'.

In spite of the criticism from her fellow countrymen, Rosa became very famous in Britain and the USA. During the 1860s American girls could own Rosa Bonheur dolls, and engravings of her painting *The Horse Fair* were given away with American newspapers as a free gift.

Rosa did things differently throughout her whole life. She had a fifty-year relationship with her partner, artist Nathalie Micas, at a time when gay relationships were considered scandalous. She was also well known for wearing men's clothing, for which she had a special permit from the police in Paris! She refused to conform to the behaviour expected from women at the time, and although it wasn't always easy, she was a happy and successful artist.

DRAW ANIMALS LIKE ROSA

The real challenge when drawing animals (and people!) is getting the proportions right. An easy way to start is to draw the very simple shapes and lines that make up an animal's body first, before fleshing out the details. Try copying the circles and lines from the horse outline below, then add colour and detail to create a fully-realistic drawing of a horse in motion.

EDMONIA LEWIS

A trailblazing and gifted sculptor, Edmonia Lewis was the first woman of African-American and Native American heritage to become internationally famous for her skill in fine arts.

NEOCLASSICAL SCULPTURE

Edmonia created marble sculptures in the neoclassical style, that drew inspiration from ancient Roman and ancient Greek art.

LIVED: 4 July 1844 – 17 September 1907

BORN IN: Greenbush, New York (USA)

WORKED IN: Boston, Massachusetts (USA) and Rome (Italy)

There is nothing so beautiful as the free forest.

Edmonia Lewis' parents died before she was nine years old, so she went to live with her aunts. They were Native American craftswomen, and Edmonia started using her Native American name, Wildfire. Many years later she described her childhood as 'wild', as she would spend her time wandering through nature, fishing and swimming. It was a happy time for her, and she enjoyed the freedom of running through the forest.

In 1859, aged 15, Edmonia was sent by her brother Samuel to Oberlin College in Ohio to study art. Oberlin was one of the first colleges to allow women and African Americans to study. In 1864 she moved to Boston, looking for further training in sculpture. There she was turned down by three established sculptors before she was finally taken on by Edward A. Brackett, who made marble busts.

Edmonia held the first solo exhibition of her work in 1864, showing her sculptures of abolitionists (people who campaigned against slavery) and civil war heroes. From selling her work she made enough money to move to Rome, Italy, where she worked for most of her career.

In Rome she began creating more sculptures in the neoclassical style, for example showing people dressed in Roman robes, rather than contemporary clothing. Many of her sculptures also had African-American and Native American themes and figures, such as her sculpture *The Arrow Maker* which shows a Native American man teaching his daughter how to make an arrow.

Unlike other marble sculptors, Edmonia did the carving and chiselling of her pieces herself. Other artists would often create wax or clay models, then pay tradespeople to produce the finished marble piece, but Edmonia preferred to do all the work herself to ensure accuracy and originality.

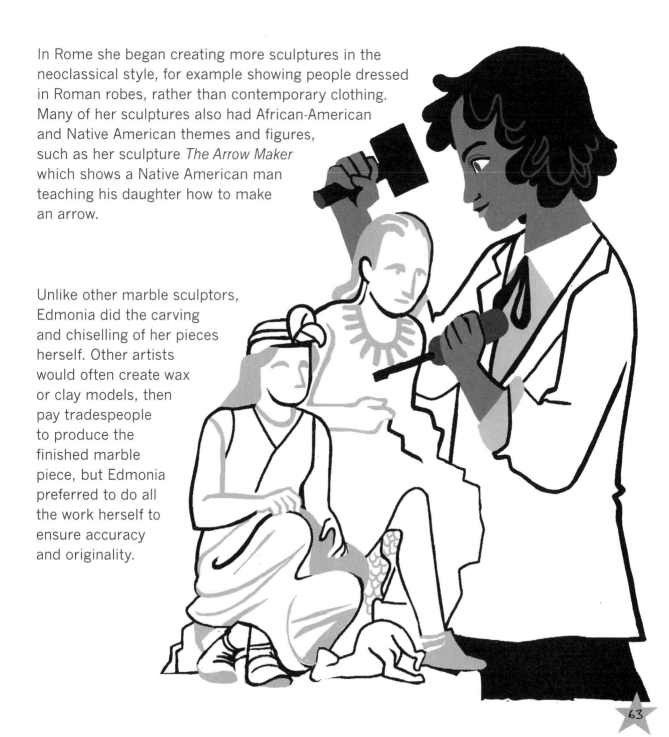

Edmonia was very commercially successful, and received two commissions for US$50,000 each, an incredible sum worth nearly £700,000 in today's money. However, despite her financial success, audience reactions to her work could sometimes be frustrating.

The white people who viewed her work would often assume that her sculptures of women were self-portraits, which Edmonia wished to avoid. She did this by deliberately giving her female figures distinctively European-looking features, but the assumptions people made about her art and the way her pieces were interpreted differently to white male artists was sometimes annoying for Edmonia.

SCULPT LIKE EDMONIA

Artists who create marble sculptures like Edmonia don't start carving the stone straight away. Instead, they make a version of their artwork in clay first, then copy it in marble. Why not try this first stage yourself? Get some modelling clay and create a portrait of someone you admire using the neoclassical style. Give them Roman robes and classical hairstyles. You could even show them slaying a mythical beast!

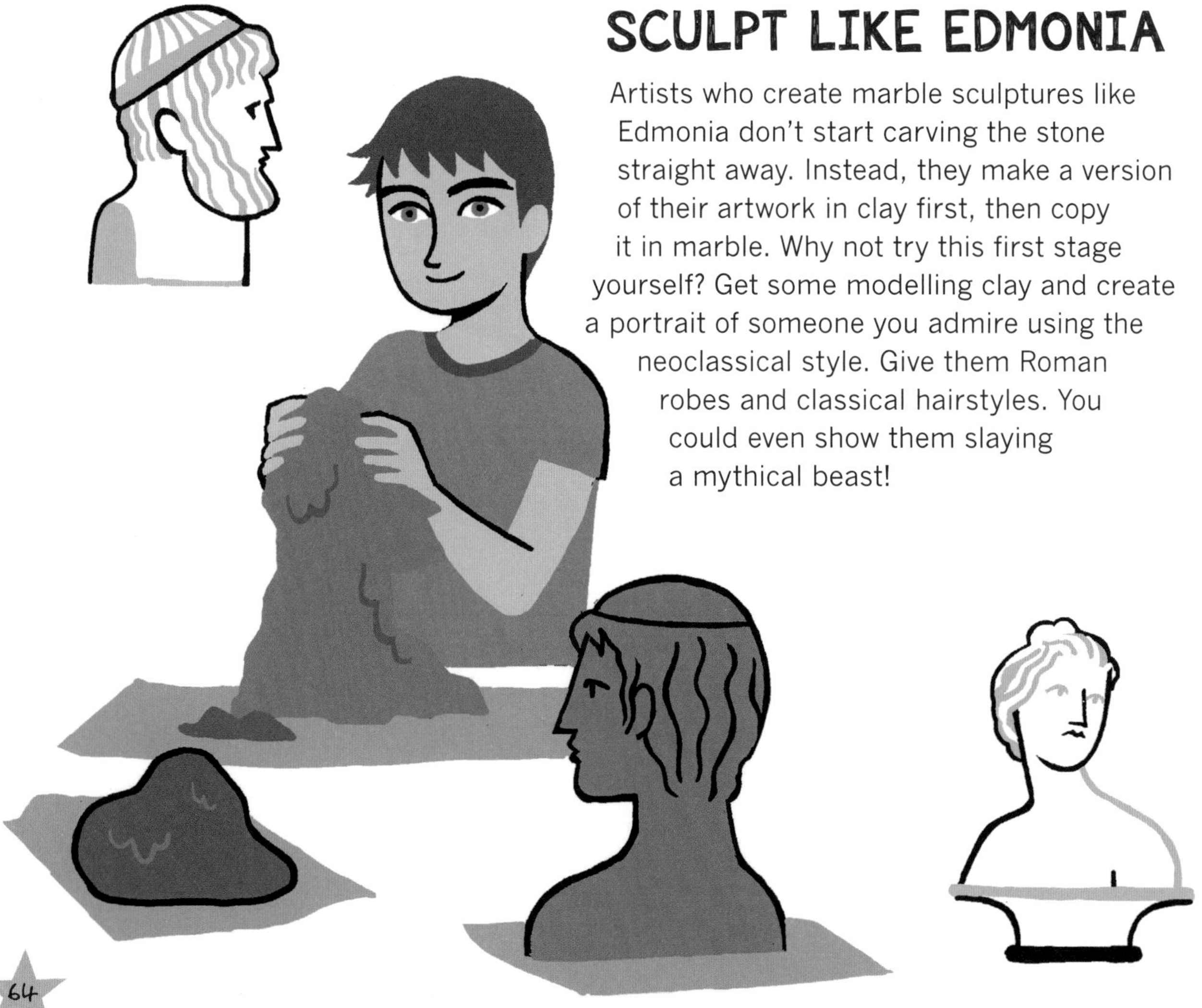

COCO CHANEL

Coco Chanel was a fashion designer and trendsetter who revolutionised clothing for women in the 20th century.

FASHION DESIGN

Coco Chanel created totally new looks and styles of clothing which changed the way people dressed around the world.

LIVED:	19 August 1883 – 10 January 1971
BORN IN:	Saumur (France)
WORKED IN:	Deauville, Biarritz and Paris (France)

In August 1883 Gabrielle Chanel was born to a poor laundry woman and a pedlar. Her mum died when she was only 12 years old, and her dad sent Gabrielle and her sisters to an orphanage. It was a very strict, hard place to live, but it was there that she learned to sew. Her talent with a needle would end up changing her fortunes.

Gabrielle had to leave the orphanage when she turned 18, so she began working as a seamstress during the daytime, and as a singer during the evenings. She would often sing the popular songs 'Ko Ko Ri Ko', and 'Qui qu'a vu Coco', and so the soldiers who came to watch gave her the nickname 'Coco'. Unfortunately, Coco was not a very good singer, and so her career as a performer did not last very long!

She began designing hats instead, and opened a shop in Paris. Her hats did not have huge fancy feathers and bows as was the style at that time, but were simple and chic. When a famous actress wore one of her hats in a play, Coco's business really took off.

As well as hats, Coco started to design clothes, but her clothes for women were like nothing people had seen before. She used lightweight fabrics such as cotton jersey that were previously only used for men's underwear. She created simple, easy-to-wear clothes for active women, without fussy frills and restrictive corsets.

Coco's enjoyment of sailing led her to add striped sailor-style tops to her collection, as well as trousers for women. She started another trend when she cut her hair short in a boyish style. She had a totally modern approach to fashion, and at the time her whole look was revolutionary.

In 1926, Coco designed her iconic 'little black dress'. It was hailed by the fashion magazine *Vogue* for its elegant simplicity. They called it 'the frock that all of the world will wear'. And they weren't far wrong! The 'little black dress' became a classic piece of design which is still referenced by fashion designers today.

At the end of her life, Coco lived in the fashionable Hotel Ritz in Paris, France. She died in 1971, aged 87. Even in her last moments, Coco was determined to set the trend. Her last words to her maid were, 'You see, this is how you die.'

The frock all the world will wear

DESIGN LIKE COCO

Many of the innovations Coco Chanel introduced are still extremely popular today, such as sailor-style striped shirts, bobbed hair cuts and simple black dresses for elegant occasions. Her designs were loved because they were stylish, but comfortable and modern. Try and design a fashion collection of your own in the style of Coco Chanel. Draw a set of clothes using simple, elegant shapes and comfortable fabrics.

FRIDA KAHLO

Frida's colourful and emotionally complex art explored the tragedies that she suffered in her life, as well as her identity as a Mexican woman.

SURREALISM

Frida's very personal artwork does not neatly fit into any categories, but she often used surreal, dream-like images to express her feelings.

LIVED: 6 July 1907 – 13 July 1954

BORN IN: Coyoacán (Mexico)

WORKED IN: Cuernavaca and Mexico City (Mexico) and Detroit (USA)

On a summer's day, in a village just outside Mexico City, Frida Kahlo was born. Her mum was Mexican, and her dad was an immigrant from Germany. When she was six years old Frida caught polio, a disease which forced her to stay in bed for nine months. The polio caused one of her legs to be thinner than the other and gave her a limp forever afterwards.

During her illness Frida became very close to her dad. He taught her about art, nature and philosophy and encouraged her to take up sports such as boxing and roller-skating to regain her strength, even though at this time these sports were considered only for boys.

Frida was very clever, and aged 18 she was training to be a doctor when tragedy struck again. A bus she was travelling on crashed into a tram, and she was almost killed. She spent many months in hospital with terrible injuries, and was in pain for the rest of her life. She began to paint while she was recovering, as it was something she could do while lying down.

After two years, Frida was no longer confined to her bed, and she began spending time with her old school friends who were involved in politics. She joined the Mexican Communist Party and met the artist Diego Rivera. She was much younger than he was, but they fell in love and got married.

She began to use Mexican folk art styles in her painting, and wore traditional Mexican clothing. Many of Frida's paintings show self-portraits in which she would emphasise her eyebrows and facial hair to show that she rejected Western ideas about what is 'beautiful', and to express her Mexican heritage. Her paintings often showed strange, dream-like scenes which symbolised her feelings, such as one painting that shows her as a deer being hunted with arrows.

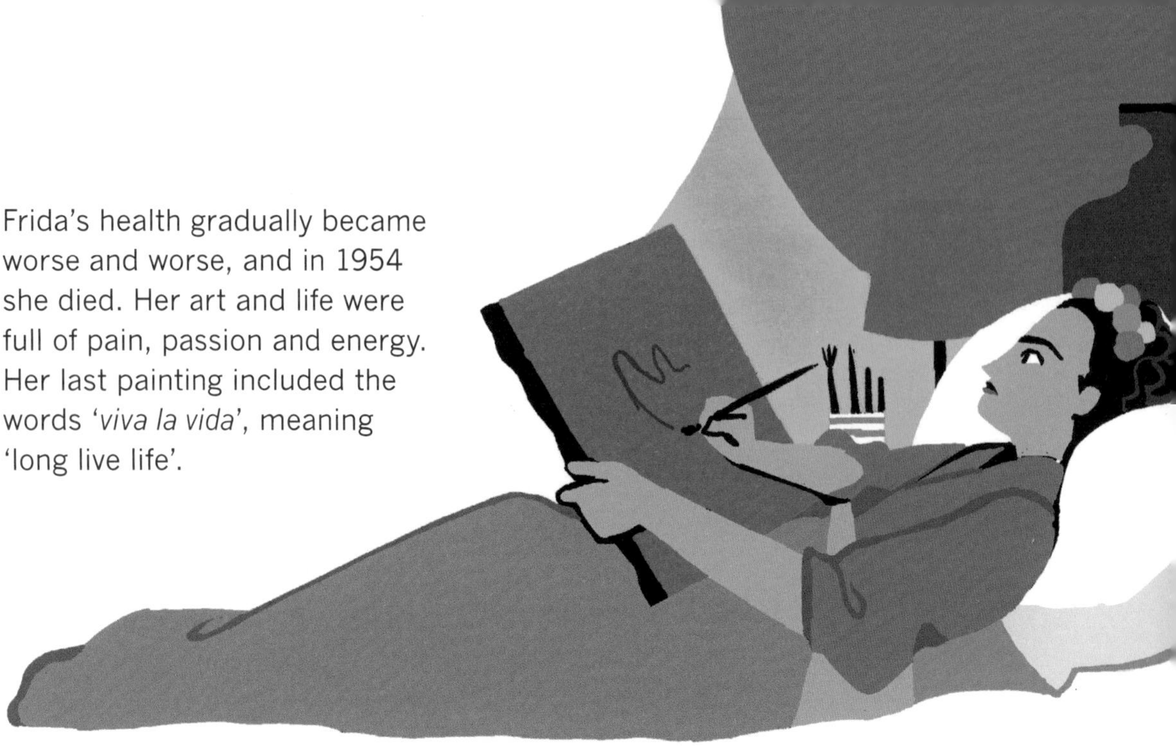

Frida's health gradually became worse and worse, and in 1954 she died. Her art and life were full of pain, passion and energy. Her last painting included the words '*viva la vida*', meaning 'long live life'.

EXPRESS YOURSELF LIKE FRIDA

Frida used surreal images in her paintings to tell the viewer about her emotions and thoughts. She also exaggerated parts of her appearance to make statements about her identity.

Try creating a self-portrait in the same style. Consider what parts of your clothing and appearance would tell the viewer something about who you are and where you are from. Add details or other elements to your picture, such as animals or objects that can represent your personality or feelings. For example, if you think you are usually a brave person, you could add a lion to your picture, or if you have been feeling like the odd-one-out, you could show yourself alongside a black sheep.

YAYOI KUSAMA

Describing herself as 'obsessive', and voluntarily living in a mental health hospital for decades, Yayoi's incredible, colourful art has consistently challenged the expectations of the art world.

AVANT-GARDE

Yayoi Kusama has had a very varied career, spanning different media and movements. Her art can be described as 'avant-garde', as for much of her career she has been pushing at the boundary of what can be called art.

BORN: 22 March 1929

BORN IN: Matsumoto (Japan)

WORKED IN: Tokyo (Japan) and New York City (USA)

Yayoi was born into a traditional Japanese family in an area surrounded by high mountains. As a little girl she longed to explore what lay beyond. She once wrote a letter to the president of France that said: 'Dear Sir, I would like to see your country, France. Please help me.' She got a reply from the French Embassy in Japan advising her to study French!

Yayoi loved to make art, but her parents were not supportive of her interest. Her mum would tear her drawings away from her, but Yayoi would not give up and when she ran out of art supplies, she would look around the house for alternative things to make her pictures with.

Aged ten, Yayoi began to have hallucinations, which were bright flashes of light with dense patterns of dots. These hallucinations went on to greatly influence her work. A psychiatrist suggested she continue with her art and so, against her mum's wishes, she went to art school in Japan.

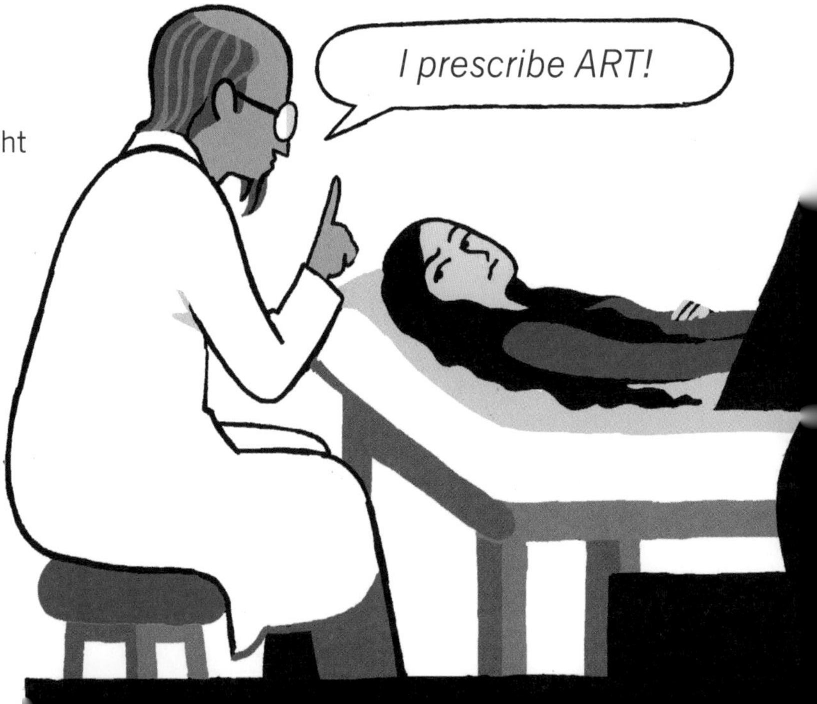

Yayoi became very interested in European and American avant-garde art, and in 1957, fed up with Japan which she felt was too conservative, she moved to the USA. She began creating huge artworks covered in polka dots, from massive 9-m-long canvas paintings of repeated dots, to clothing mannequins that she also covered in dots. She was fascinated by the idea of infinity, and used polka dots to create 'infinity rooms'.

Polka dots are a way to infinity.

At first Yayoi struggled to make money and often went hungry, but she quickly became an important figure in the New York avant-garde art scene. She created an astonishing range of strange artworks, including installations such as mirror-lined rooms filled with neon balls, huge open air sculptures of pumpkins and performance art in public spaces.

Yayoi worked incredibly hard, however she continued to struggle with her mental health. In 1973 she moved back to Japan, and in 1977 she checked herself into a hospital for the mentally ill, where she has been living by choice ever since.

Her creativity and uniqueness have made Yayoi a hugely successful artist. In 2014 she was the most popular artist in the world according to the visitor numbers of her galleries, and a recent retrospective tour of her work attracted over two million visitors. A five-storey museum dedicated to Yayoi was opened in Tokyo in 2017.

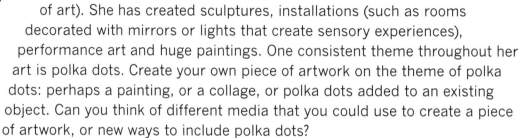

CREATE LIKE YAYOI

Yayoi works in many different media (which means the material and method that an artist uses to create a piece of art). She has created sculptures, installations (such as rooms decorated with mirrors or lights that create sensory experiences), performance art and huge paintings. One consistent theme throughout her art is polka dots. Create your own piece of artwork on the theme of polka dots: perhaps a painting, or a collage, or polka dots added to an existing object. Can you think of different media that you could use to create a piece of artwork, or new ways to include polka dots?

VIVIENNE WESTWOOD

Creating radical and rebellious clothing designs inspired by music and politics, Vivienne Westwood is a very successful fashion designer and business woman.

PUNK FASHION

Vivienne Westwood was largely responsible for creating the 'punk' fashion style of ripped fabrics, safety pins, tartan fabrics and chains.

BORN: 8 April 1941

BORN IN: Tintwistle, Derbyshire (UK)

WORKS IN: London (UK)

From a very young age Vivienne had strong feelings about injustice. In her aunt's shop aged five, she saw an image of Christ on the cross. When she asked her cousin about it, she could not believe what she was told and that people could be so cruel. Vivienne became dedicated to opposing injustice at that point.

Vivienne was born into a working-class family in the north of England, but they moved to London when she was a teen. She briefly studied silversmithing at college, but dropped out, believing a working-class girl could not succeed in art. However, she continued to make and sell her own jewellery while working as a teacher.

Vivienne began to get very involved in fashion when she started a relationship with Malcolm McLaren, an art student who she met through her brother. Malcolm and Vivienne opened a shop in 1971 selling Vivienne's clothing designs. Malcolm was the manager of the punk band, the Sex Pistols, and Vivienne's clothes dressed the band and helped them create their signature look.

Punk was all about a rebellious, counter-culture attitude. Punk artists and musicians believed that mainstream culture was restrictive and materialistic. It was a political and cultural movement, and the clothing style reflected its provocative themes. Vivienne created outfits that featured ripped fabrics, accessorised with bicycle chains and dog-collars, safety pins and aggressive slogans. These were the looks that started the iconic punk style of the 1970s and 80s.

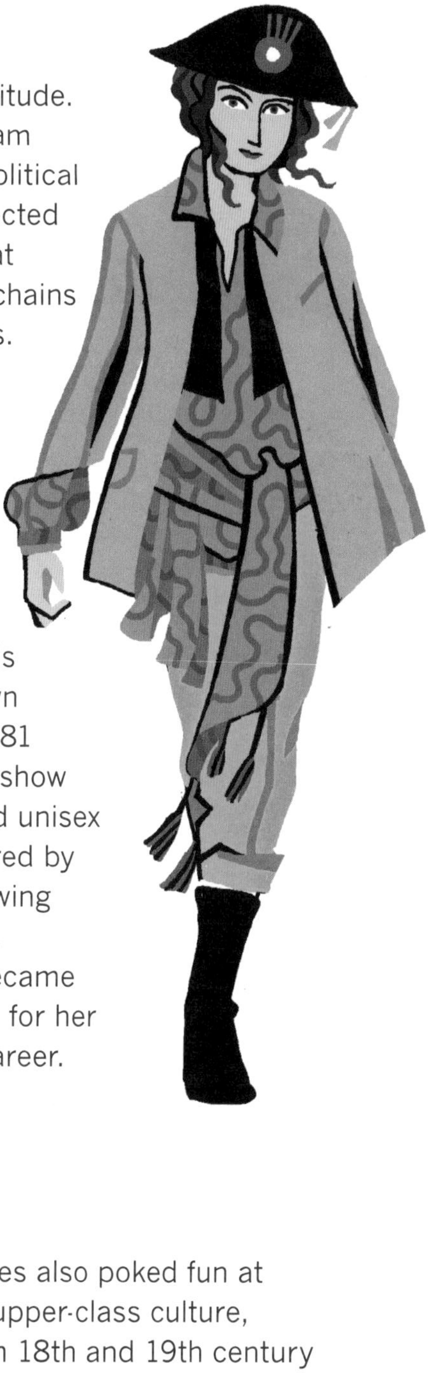

The fame of the Sex Pistols made Vivenne a well-known name in fashion, and in 1981 she held her first catwalk show called 'Pirate'. It featured unisex clothing designs inspired by pirates with big billowing sleeves and trousers. Historical costumes became an important inspiration for her design style across her career.

Her later fashion lines also poked fun at establishment and upper-class culture, using elements from 18th and 19th century aristocratic clothing, such as Victorian crinoline skirts. She always wanted her fashion to be fun and outrageous, and she had no time for pompous attitudes! Vivienne's use of historic references in her styles were hugely influential to fashion at the time.

NO TO AUSTERITY
CLIMATE REVOLUTION
FRACKING DESTROYS THE ENVIRONMENT

Throughout Vivienne's career she has often been very outspoken about political issues, campaigning on climate change and on behalf of civil rights groups. In 2015 her catwalk show featured models holding placards with slogans protesting against fracking and austerity. These designs continued to be influential on fashion, in the same way as her punk styles of the 1970s.

She is a hugely successful fashion designer, with many stores selling her collections around the world, as well as being made a Dame of the British Empire by the Queen. Despite her role as an international businesswoman, Vivienne still believes it is better not to be materialistic, advising people to, 'Buy less. Choose well. Make it last.'

MAKE A STATEMENT LIKE VIVIENNE

Vivienne's clothing designs have always had an element of social or political commentary, since her beginning as a fashion designer in the 1970s punk movement. Think about an issue you really care about – it could be the environment, or perhaps women's equality. Create a fashion collection that makes a statement about your chosen issue. Think about things such as what materials you would use for the clothes – does your choice of fabric say something relating to your message or cause?

ZAHA HADID

A forward-thinking and ambitious architect, Zaha Hadid created unconventional, artistic building designs.

ARCHITECT

Zaha Hadid designed buildings. Like art, architecture has different styles. Some people called Zaha's style 'deconstructivist' because of her use of unusual shapes and angles.

LIVED: 31 October 1950 – 31 March 2016

BORN IN: Baghdad (Iraq)

WORKED IN: London (UK)

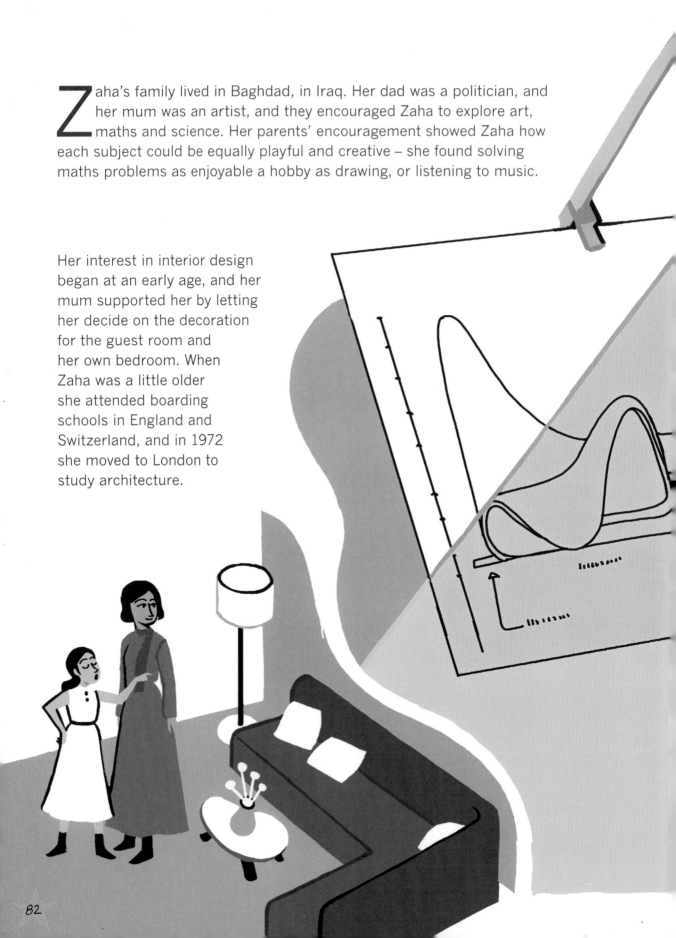

Zaha's family lived in Baghdad, in Iraq. Her dad was a politician, and her mum was an artist, and they encouraged Zaha to explore art, maths and science. Her parents' encouragement showed Zaha how each subject could be equally playful and creative – she found solving maths problems as enjoyable a hobby as drawing, or listening to music.

Her interest in interior design began at an early age, and her mum supported her by letting her decide on the decoration for the guest room and her own bedroom. When Zaha was a little older she attended boarding schools in England and Switzerland, and in 1972 she moved to London to study architecture.

Architecture was the perfect combination of her twin loves maths and art, and even as a student Zaha immediately rejected conventional architecture styles. Her designs were much more radical, and she insisted on avoiding 90 degree angles in all of her work, instead using unusual diagonals and curves. Her tutor nicknamed her 'the inventor of 89 degrees' because of her refusal to use boring right-angled shapes! She later went on to design the famously curved Heydar Aliyer Centre in Azerbaijan.

After graduating, Zaha taught architecture herself at a number of universities including Harvard in the US, and Cambridge in the UK. Then in 1980 she opened her own architectural firm. In the early years not many of her building designs went on to be constructed, and instead she built up a portfolio of design ideas.

One of Zaha's first designs to actually be constructed was for a small fire station in Germany, although it ended up being used as an exhibition space instead. A very sculptural design with lots of sharp, diagonal angles, it was the start of her career as an internationally successful architect.

In the 1990s and 2000s Zaha gained larger and more prestigious commissions, including the Guangzhou Opera House in China, and the London Aquatics Centre for the 2012 London Olympics, among many others. Her buildings continued to use flowing shapes and avoid straight lines and 90 degree angles. She became nicknamed the 'queen of the curve'.

Zaha won many prizes and awards for her architecture, including the prestigious Stirling Prize for excellence in architecture in both 2010 and 2011. In 2012 she was made a Dame Commander of the British Empire.

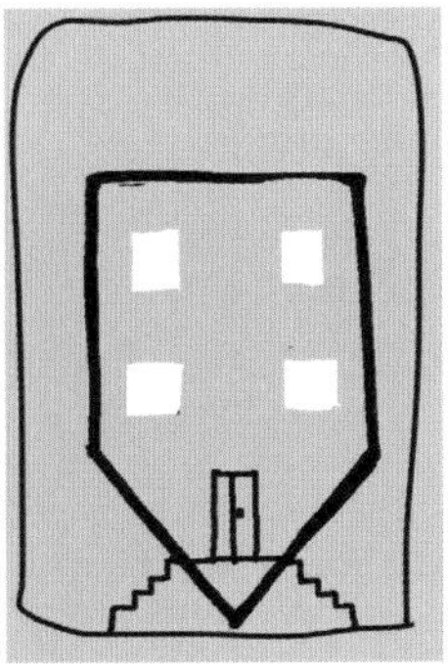

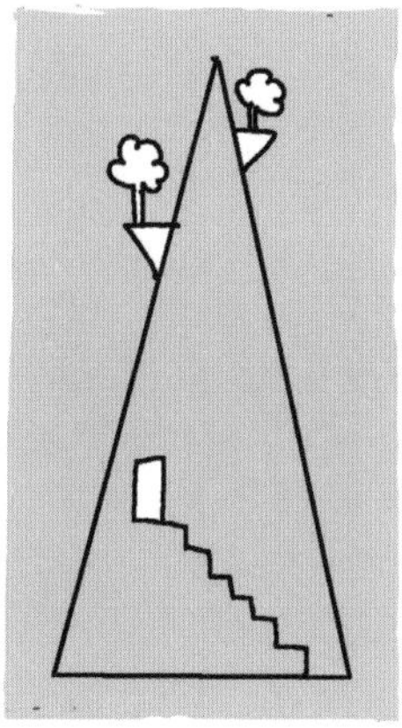

SKETCH IDEAS LIKE ZAHA

Imagine you could design and build your dream home. What would it look like? When architects like Zaha first start designing a building, they begin by sketching ideas. These first sketches can be as crazy and imaginative as they like, before the later stages of forming a building that can realistically be built! Create a series of sketches for the most over-the-top amazing dream home you can think of. What strange shapes will you use? What bizarre features will your house have? Let your imagination run wild.

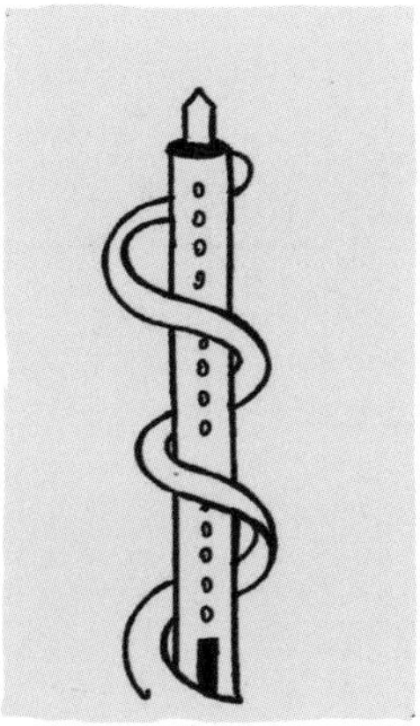

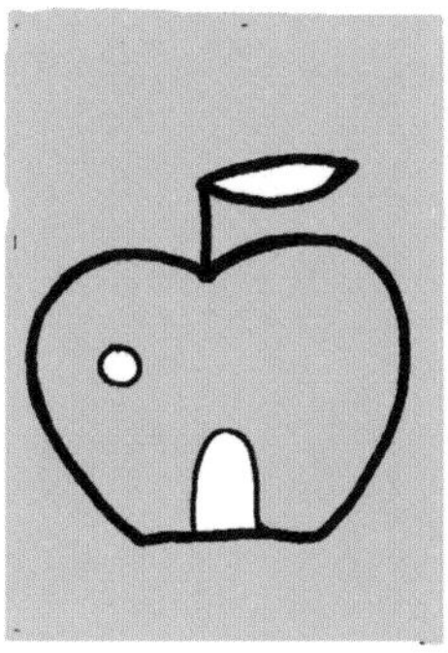

MORE ART AND DESIGN VISIONARIES

The list of visionary women in art and design doesn't stop there! Here are even more pioneering women artists that you should know about, from Renaissance artists of the 17th century to today's rising stars.

JUDITH LEYSTER

LIVED: 28 July 1609 – 10 February 1660

BORN IN: Haarlem (Netherlands)

WORKED IN: Netherlands

Judith was the eighth child of a brewer and cloth-maker in Haarlem in the Netherlands. It is thought she began painting after her father became bankrupt, and she needed to earn money to support her family. She joined an artists' guild in 1633, which was extremely unusual for women at that time.

She painted a self-portrait in 1633 looking very relaxed and smiling, another break in tradition, as women's self-portraits were much more formal in that era and usually showed serious facial expressions. Her work was well-respected, and she took on several young apprentices.

After Judith died in 1660 she became largely forgotten until 1893, when her signature was found on a painting. Recently, art historians have been restoring her reputation as a pioneering female artist.

HARRIET POWERS

LIVED: 29 October 1837 – 1 January 1910

BORN IN: Clarke County, Georgia (USA)

WORKED IN: USA

Talented quilt designer Harriet Powers was born into slavery in Georgia, USA. She learned to sew, probably taught by her mother. She used traditional appliqué techniques, where shapes are cut out of coloured fabric and stitched onto a background, to create quilts showing scenes from stories. Her quilts told Bible stories, local legends and recorded astronomical events.

During her lifetime a newspaper article described Harriet as illiterate, assuming she learned her Bible stories from other people. However, Harriet could read and write, and may well have used her quilts as a teaching tool herself. Only two of her quilts survive, and they are now on display in museums as beautiful and historically important examples of African-American folk art.

GEORGIA O'KEEFFE

LIVED: 15 November 1887 – 6 March 1986

BORN IN: Sun Prairie, Wisconsin (USA)

WORKED IN: USA

By the age of ten Georgia had already decided she would be an artist and her family arranged for tuition from a local watercolour artist for her and her sister. At art college she was top of her class, and she was very skilled at realistic painting. However, the realist style did not excite her, and she began experimenting with abstract styles.

Georgia painted simplified images of natural things, such as flowers and rocks, as well as abstract and colourful pieces representing her feelings about music. Wherever she travelled, she created artworks that expressed a strong sense of the place and landscape. She became attached to the desert landscape of New Mexico, and she lived and worked there for many years.

BARBARA HEPWORTH

LIVED: 10 January 1903 – 20 May 1975

BORN IN: Wakefield (UK)

WORKED IN: UK

When Barbara was a girl, she would look at the shapes of the hills and fields as her family drove through the English countryside. This fascination with the landscape stayed with her throughout her life. She studied art at college, then became a sculptor, creating abstract works of art from wood and stone. She wanted to create art that was calming and beautiful and preferred the method of working directly in the chosen material, rather than the more traditional process of making models from which someone else would produce the work.

Barbara moved from London to the seaside town of St Ives in Cornwall in 1939 and lived there for the rest of her life. Her love of the landscape continued to inspire her, and some of the large sculptures that she created were designed so that they could be used as a 'frame' for the landscape around and behind them. Audiences could look through the centre of her pieces to see the world in a different way. She was a very important figure in Modernism, an art movement that used simple, abstract shapes.

LEE MILLER

LIVED: 23 April 1907 – 21 July 1977

BORN IN: Poughkeepsie, New York (USA)

WORKED IN: USA, France and UK

American fashion model, photographer, war correspondent and artist Lee Miller lived an extraordinarily varied life. Aged 19, she was about to step in front of a car in New York, but the publisher of *Vogue* magazine spotted the danger and pulled her to safety. This was how she was 'discovered' as a model, and she appeared on the cover of *Vogue* in 1927.

In 1929 she travelled to Paris to study with the surrealist photographer Man Ray. She became friends with famous artists including Pablo Picasso, and created many photographic artworks. She moved to London, and after the outbreak of the Second World War in 1939, she became a photojournalist for *Vogue* magazine. One of her stories documented the Blitz, the German campaign of air raids on London and other UK cities from September 1940 to May 1941.

After the war Lee travelled to mainland Europe and photographed images of Nazi concentration camps for *LIFE* magazine. Due to the horrific things she saw, she suffered from a period of mental ill-health, and gave up most of her photographic work, becoming a gourmet cook.

EMILY KAME KNGWARREYE

LIVED: 1910 – 3 September 1996

BORN IN: Utopia (Australia)

WORKED IN: Australia

Emily was nearly 80 years old before she began to paint. She was an Indigenous Australian woman from the Anmatyerre community, and the area where she was born was settled by white cattle farmers when she was around ten years old. She spent much of her life working on cattle farms, until the land where she was born was returned to Indigenous Australian people in 1976. In 1977 she learned batik-making, a method for printing designs onto silk fabric. The patterns she used were inspired by traditional body markings, as well as being symbolic of important plants that grow in the Australian desert. She moved from batik to painting with acrylic paints on canvas in the 1980s, and created many incredible, colourful artworks that became internationally popular and sold for hundreds of thousands of dollars.

LOUISE BOURGEOIS

LIVED: 25 December 1911 – 31 May 2010

BORN IN: Paris (France)

WORKED IN: USA

Louise was named after her father, Louis, who had wanted a son. Family life was difficult when Louise was a child, as her father had an explosive temper and was unfaithful to her mother. As a teenager she cared for her frail mother, who died when Louise was 21.

Louise met her husband Robert in 1938, and emigrated from France to the USA where she studied art. She used her art to express her difficult feelings from her childhood. She created many different kinds of art including huge metal sculptures of spiders, strange installations and drawings of body parts.

BASTARDILLA

BORN: ?

BORN IN: Colombia

WORKS IN: Colombia

No one knows exactly who Bastardilla is. Like the British graffiti artist Banksy, she keeps her identity a carefully guarded secret. What is known is that she is a very talented and unique street artist from Colombia, whose artworks cover powerful topics such as violence against women, police violence and poverty. She has gathered an international following, and has created large pieces not only in her home country of Colombia but in cities around the world, including in Mexico and Italy. Although her art features serious and often dark topics, her murals are brightly coloured, and she even uses glitter to make the artworks sparkle at night.

KARA WALKER

BORN: 26 November 1969

BORN IN: Stockton, California (USA)

WORKS IN: USA

Art has been a passion for Kara since she can remember. One of Kara's earliest memories is sitting on her father's lap, aged two-and-a-half, watching him draw, and thinking 'I want to do that too'. Born in California where she lived until she was 13, she then moved to Georgia, where she found that racism in society was much more out in the open. Her experiences in Georgia inform her art, which explores race and the history of slavery in the southern states of the USA.

Her most well-known artworks include large cut-paper silhouettes showing exaggerated caricatures of figures from the era of slavery. At the age of 27 she became the second youngest recipient of the John D. and Catherine T. MacArthur Foundation's 'genius' grant, which is a prize for extraordinary individuals working in any field.

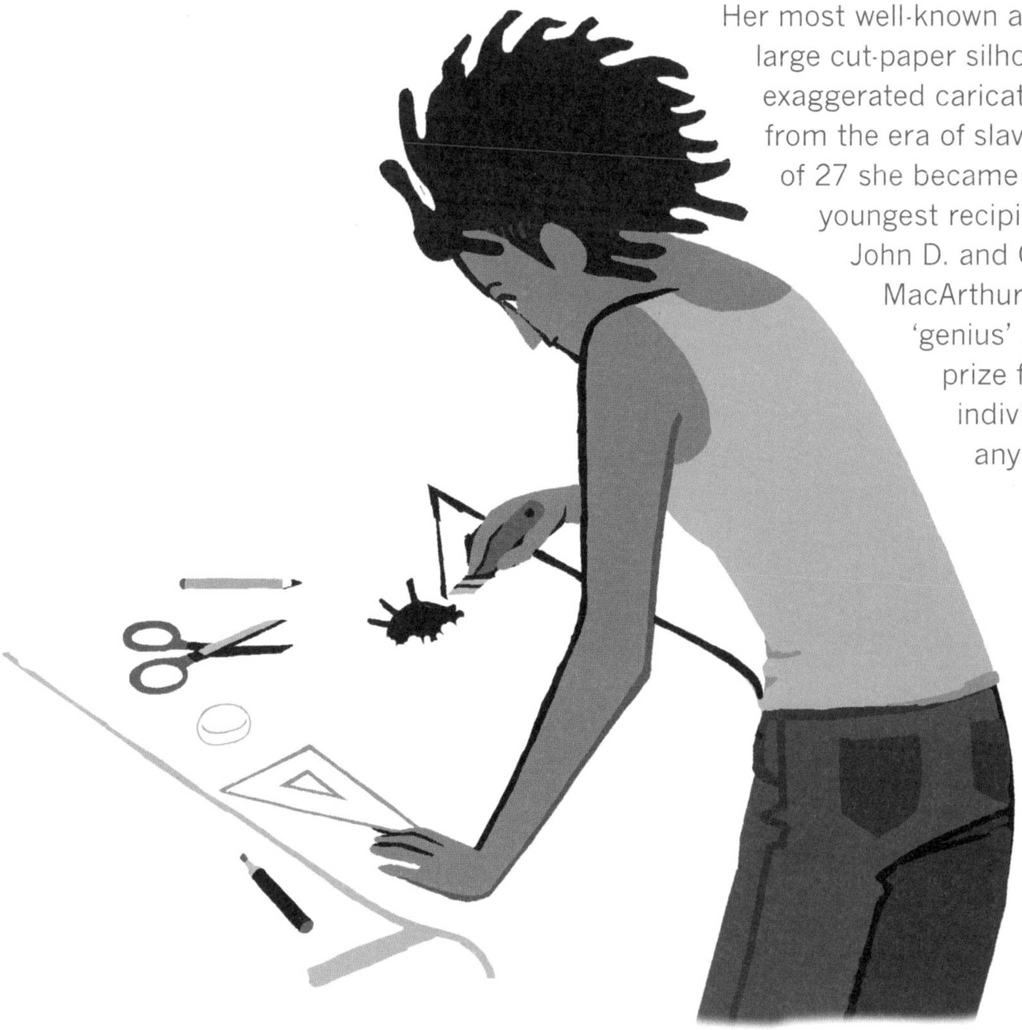

COUNTLESS OTHERS ...

The women included in this book are just a very few of the amazingly talented, visionary artists and designers who have made art, and continue to make art around the world right now.

GET INVOLVED IN ART AND DESIGN!

It doesn't take much to get started on the path to being an artist. Just pick up a pencil and paper, a piece of clay, some fabric or a camera and have a go. That's it! Kara Walker said, 'There's no diploma in the world that declares you an artist ... You can declare yourself an artist and then figure out how to be one.' But if you need a bit of inspiration, here are some other ideas for how to learn more and get involved in different types of art.

GO TO GALLERIES AND MUSEUMS

It sounds obvious, but one of the best ways to get started creating your own art is to look at the work of other artists. Visiting galleries and museums can give you great ideas for different topics and styles to try out yourself. Lots of people teach themselves to make great art by copying some of their favourite pieces by famous artists; this is why you'll often see people in galleries sketching.

Museums and galleries often run special events and workshops for kids, too. Look online to find a gallery near you, and find out what interactive events and activities they are putting on.

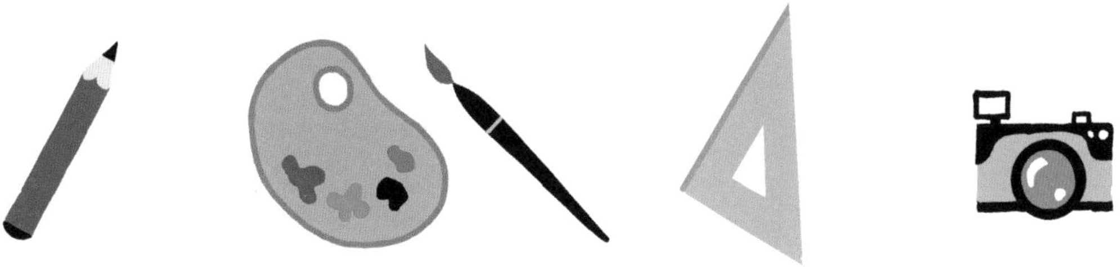

FIND AN ART CLUB, OR START ONE YOURSELF

Look for an after-school art club you can join, and if there isn't one, start one yourself! You can try out different art styles and techniques each week. Books from the library can give you project ideas, or look for tutorials on YouTube to learn drawing techniques. At the end of term, you could put on an exhibition of your artworks for your family and friends to enjoy.

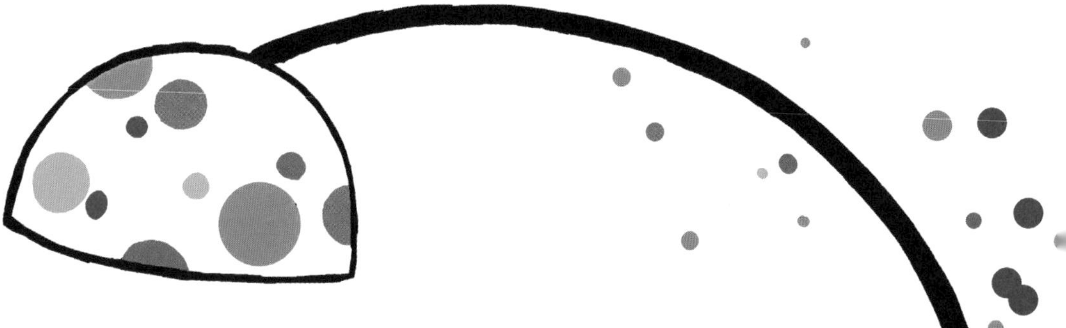

ENTER A YOUNG PERSON'S ART COMPETITION

Perhaps you're the kind of person whose competitive spirit will help get your creative juices flowing. If so, there are tons of art competitions for children and young people on various different subjects. Search online to find a competition on a subject or style that particularly interests you.

INCREDIBLE SPORTING CHAMPIONS

Imagine a footballer running as fast as they can down the field – sweating, muddy, muscles working at full strength, skilfully manoeuvring the ball. Eyes fixed on the goal, grimacing with effort, focused on taking down the opponent and winning – nothing else. At the last moment, she pivots, shoots – and scores!

Did that last sentence change the picture you had built up in your mind?

For many people that 'she' feels unexpected. Even today, the idea of a tough, competitive sporting champion is still largely presented to us as a man rather than a woman and that can stick unhelpfully in our minds.

Women's sport is more popular today than it has ever been, in terms of taking part and watching others play. It is finally starting to get at least some of the respect and the funding that it deserves, but it's a slow process. Women in sport still make far less money than men and get fewer opportunities to reach their full potential with top-class professional training, resources and big competitions that get lots of media coverage.

Throughout history, women and girls have been given all sorts of ridiculous reasons why they shouldn't enjoy sports just like men do. They're too fragile, it's bad for their health, they're not good enough to bother trying, they're not strong enough, it's just not 'ladylike' (whatever that is supposed to mean these days) ...

In this book you will meet just a few of the incredibly talented, dedicated and brave women who have refused to let people decide for them what they are capable of achieving. They have often not received the respect and the fame they deserve – in many cases, they've been laughed at, called names and struggled to even be allowed to take part in the sports to which they've dedicated their lives.

Read about athletes from many different sports, including tennis, running, swimming, boxing, cycling, gymnastics – even sword fighting and skateboarding! The sporting champions and pioneers in this book show that women can excel at any kind of sport, so let their stories inspire you.

MARIE MARVINGT

Marie Marvingt never accepted any limits put on her as a woman, from disguising herself as a man to serve in the army to cycling the Tour de France route despite being excluded from the men-only race.

ALL-ROUNDER

Marie Marvingt swam, canoed, cycled, climbed, skied, skated and flew her way into history with a huge range of impressive sporting 'firsts' for women.

LIVED: 20 February 1875 – 14 December 1963

BORN IN: Aurillac (France)

COMPETED FOR: France and herself

Marie was required to take care of the house for her father and brother, after her mum died when she was just 14 years old. But her head was always full of dreams of adventure, and she read lots of books about explorers. Ignoring her dull, household duties, at the age of 15 she canoed over 400 km from Nancy, France to Koblenz, Germany.

She loved the challenge of long-distance events, and in 1905 she became the first woman to swim the length of the River Seine in Paris. The press called her 'the red amphibian' because of her red swimming costume and impressive ability in the water.

Marie dominated the French winter sports seasons (which include events such as skiing, ice skating and bobsleigh) from 1908 to 1910, winning first place on 20 occasions. She was a keen cyclist, but was refused entry to the 1908 Tour de France because she was a woman. Not put off that easily, she cycled the course after the race had finished. In doing so, she completed a ride that only 36 out of the 114 men in the race had managed to finish that year – and her times would have beaten some of the men in the official race. Even today, the Tour de France is a men-only event.

During the First World War (1914–1918), Marie disguised herself as a man and attempted to fight on the frontline. She was discovered and ended up serving as a nurse and pilot, becoming the first woman to fly combat missions. After the war she was awarded the Croix de guerre (War Cross) for her achievements, and she campaigned for the introduction of air ambulances.

She was the first woman to climb many of the mountains in the French Alps, and the first woman to cross the English Channel in a hot-air balloon. Due to her risk-taking exploits, Marie was given the nickname 'The Fiancée of Danger', which she loved and used for the title of her autobiography. As well as the sports she won medals for, she had a wide range of sporting hobbies, such as martial arts, boxing and even trapeze!

The French Academy of Sport awarded Marie a Medaille d'Or (gold medal) for her accomplishments in all sports. It is the only multi-sport medal that the Academy has ever awarded. Finally, at the age of 86, two years before her death, Marie cycled between Nancy and Paris – a distance of over 320 km.

EMBRACE ADVENTURE LIKE MARIE

Marie Marvingt had an exciting life full of challenges and adventures, from her teenage years right up until the end of her life. Imagine that someone is writing a newspaper article about you, 20 years from now. What amazing adventures have you already had? Where have you been? What have you done? And what are you planning to do next? It's your life, so think big!

BABE DIDRIKSON ZAHARIAS

Babe Didrikson Zaharias took on any new challenge with confidence and flair. When she was once asked if there was anything she did not play, she shot back: 'Yeah, dolls.'

ALL-ROUNDER

With her almost unbelievable range of achievements in golf, basketball, baseball and athletics, Babe has been described as the most talented athlete, male or female, ever seen in the USA.

LIVED: 26 June 1911 – 27 September 1956

BORN IN: Port Arthur, Texas (USA)

COMPETED FOR: Her employer, the USA and herself

Babe's real name was Mildred Didrikson, but she got her nickname in a childhood baseball game where she was so impressive that people started calling her 'Babe Ruth' after the male baseball legend. At high school she was the star of the basketball, tennis, golf, baseball, swimming and volleyball teams.

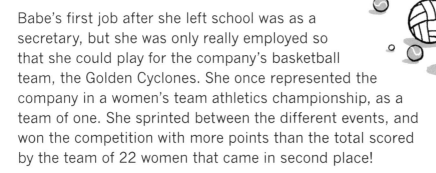

Babe's first job after she left school was as a secretary, but she was only really employed so that she could play for the company's basketball team, the Golden Cyclones. She once represented the company in a women's team athletics championship, as a team of one. She sprinted between the different events, and won the competition with more points than the total scored by the team of 22 women that came in second place!

Babe competed at the 1932 Olympic Games in the only three events that women were allowed to enter at the time. She won gold for the 80-m hurdles and for javelin, breaking two world records in the process. She won silver for high jump, missing out on a clean sweep of gold medals, after one of her jumps was ruled illegal because her head had cleared the bar before her body – this rule no longer exists.

After the Olympics, Babe was a celebrity, but there were no real opportunities for professional female athletes. So she toured the USA performing a variety show as 'The World's Greatest Woman Athlete'. This earned her a lot of money – around US$1,200 a week in a time when the average woman earned a few cents an hour. Although she was paid well, she was often mocked and criticised in newspapers, with some writers saying that it wasn't 'nice' for a woman to play sport, that she only did it because she was too ugly to find a husband, and that she must be a man in disguise.

In 1935, Babe decided to focus on golf, and it was in this sport that she most excelled. She practised by hitting as many as 1,000 golf balls a day, and kept going until her hands were so raw with blisters that she had to bandage them! Babe dominated women's golf through the 1930s and 1940s, with a total of 82 tournament wins. By 1950 she had won every possible women's golf championship in the USA. She made history by qualifying and doing extremely well in a number of men's golf competitions, too. Babe was diagnosed with cancer in 1953. She won five further golf tournaments before dying at the age of just 45.

COMPETE LIKE BABE

Babe Didrikson Zaharias had a huge amount of confidence in herself and her sporting abilities, and she tried to enter every competition she could – even when, as a woman, she wasn't welcomed! Entering sports competitions is good practice, and can be really good fun. Find out what competitions you can enter at school, or through sports clubs in your local area.

CATHY FREEMAN

Cathy made history when she became the first Australian indigenous woman to win an international medal in any sport.

RUNNER

Cathy's talent is sprinting. She competed in several sprint events, including the 100 m, 200 m, 100-m relay, and her best event, the 400 m.

BORN: 16 February 1973

BORN IN: Mackay, Queensland (Australia)

COMPETED FOR: Australia

Cathy was born to Norman and Cecelia Freeman in 1973. Her dad and her grandad had both been gifted sportsmen, but due to the laws governing what indigenous Australian people were and were not allowed to do, her grandad had been prevented from developing his rugby league career abroad.

During much of the 20th century, indigenous Australians did not have the same rights as non indigenous people. They were forced to live in certain places, and families were often forcibly split up with children taken away from their parents.

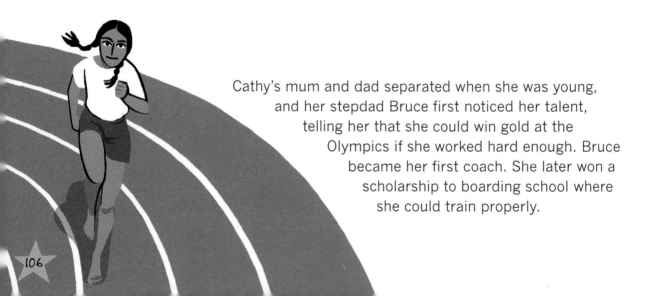

Cathy's mum and dad separated when she was young, and her stepdad Bruce first noticed her talent, telling her that she could win gold at the Olympics if she worked hard enough. Bruce became her first coach. She later won a scholarship to boarding school where she could train properly.

In 1990 Cathy was picked to join Australia's 4 × 100-m relay team for the 1990 Commonwealth Games. Her team won the gold medal, making Cathy the first-ever Aboriginal Commonwealth Games gold medallist at just 16 years old.

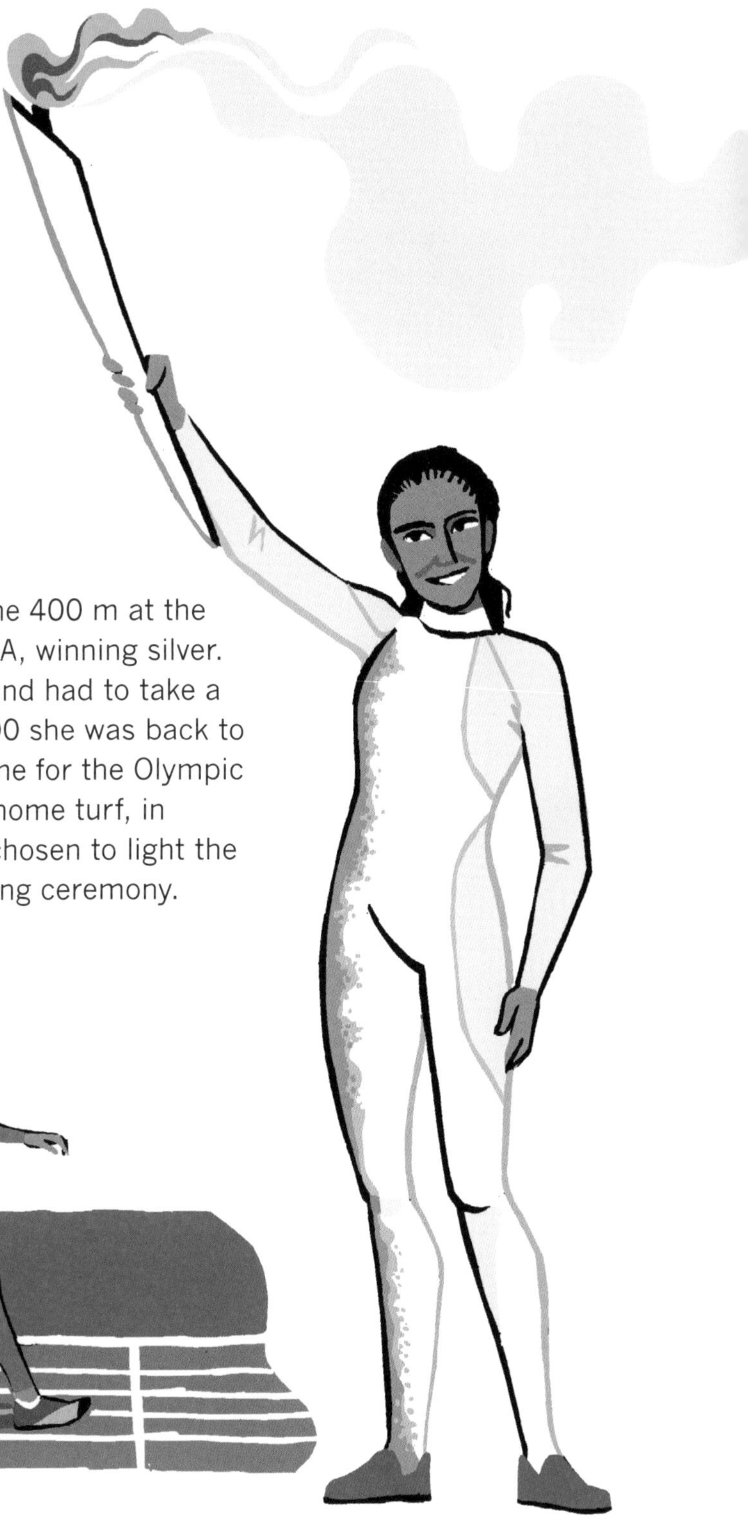

In 1996, Cathy competed in the 400 m at the Olympic Games in Atlanta, USA, winning silver. In 1997 she injured her foot, and had to take a year off to recover, but by 2000 she was back to full fitness. This was just in time for the Olympic Games that were held on her home turf, in Sydney, Australia. Cathy was chosen to light the Olympic cauldron at the opening ceremony.

She was determined to win gold this time, on behalf of her fellow Australians, and in particular, the Aboriginal people. When she won the 400 m race with a time of 49.11 seconds, she fell to her knees with relief, before doing a victory lap with both the Australian and Aboriginal flags.

Since retiring from competitive sport in 2003, Cathy has set up an organisation that works to improve education for children in several remote Australian indigenous communities. Although Australian indigenous people have the same rights according to the law as non indigenous people have now, there is still inequality in educational achievement which the Cathy Freeman Foundation aims to help address.

RUN LIKE CATHY

Cathy ran barefoot for much of her childhood. Barefoot running requires a slightly different running style. In barefoot running, when your foot hits the ground, it's important to land on the ball of your foot rather than your heel to protect your joints. Try running slowly and paying attention to what part of your foot hits the ground first. Is it your heel or another part of your foot? Do you land on the outside or the inside of your foot? Try simple exercises like jumping up and down on the spot, and balancing on each leg in turn, to increase the level of control you have over the muscles in your feet and legs.

SARAH STOREY

Sarah is the most successful British Paralympian of all time, with a total of 14 gold medals. She also holds an amazing 72 world records.

SWIMMER AND CYCLIST

An outstanding athlete, Sarah began in the pool, collecting many medals and records in swimming before switching to cycling to continue her winning streak.

BORN:	26 October 1977
BORN IN:	Manchester (UK)
COMPETES FOR:	England and Great Britain

Despite being born without a working left hand, Sarah was a very active child who loved all sports. Watching the Olympics aged seven, she knew she wanted to be an athlete, and by the time she was ten she'd chosen swimming as her main sport. Her parents were supportive and she began to train seriously, and at just 14 years old she competed for Great Britain in the Paralympic Games in Barcelona. She won an amazing two golds, three silvers and a bronze medal in the pool.

Ha! Your hair is wet!
Brilliant observation, genius.

Sarah may have been an internationally successful athlete, but school was a different matter. She was bullied by other girls, who would tease her for showing up with wet hair after training, and would move the chairs and tables at lunchtime so Sarah had nowhere to sit. Sarah stopped eating lunch to avoid the bullies, which made her lose a lot of weight. Eventually her mum intervened, and Sarah began to regain her weight and her confidence.

She represented Great Britain as a swimmer at three more Paralympic Games, winning a further three gold medals, five silvers and two bronze, until persistent ear infections forced her to switch sports. In 2005, Sarah became a cyclist instead. At her first international cycling event, the Para-cycling European Championships, she won triple gold. Then, in the Beijing Paralympics in 2008, she won gold in the individual pursuit with a time that also put her in the top eight of the Olympic finals, as well as winning the road time trial.

Just eight days after winning Paralympic gold, Sarah competed in the British Cycling National Track Championships against able-bodied cyclists, where she won the individual pursuit. She went on to become the first para-cyclist to compete for England at the Commonwealth Games against able-bodied cyclists.

At the London 2012 Paralympics, Sarah won gold in all four of her events, and also set a world record in the pursuit. She continued her winning streak at the Rio Paralympic Games in 2016, winning three gold medals. This secured her position as Great Britain's most decorated female Paralympian of all time.

LEARN SPORTS LIKE SARAH

When Sarah was forced to switch to cycling from swimming, she started off by watching professional cyclists on TV and in live races to observe their techniques. Try doing the same with your favourite sport. For example, if you like cycling, look at the riding position of professional cyclists during races. How do they have their bikes set up? If you like running, watch whether the athletes are taking long or short strides, and what they do with their arms.

SERENA WILLIAMS

Serena has made history time and time again, playing both alongside her sister Venus and alone. She has been world number one for 318 weeks in her career – more than six years.

TENNIS WORLD-CHAMPION

Serena Williams has the third fastest serve ever recorded in women's tennis, but her consistent strength, speed and accuracy make her the most successful player of her time.

BORN: 26 September 1981

BORN IN: Saginaw, Michigan (USA)

COMPETES FOR: USA

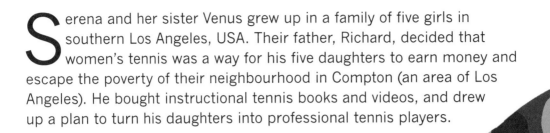

Serena and her sister Venus grew up in a family of five girls in southern Los Angeles, USA. Their father, Richard, decided that women's tennis was a way for his five daughters to earn money and escape the poverty of their neighbourhood in Compton (an area of Los Angeles). He bought instructional tennis books and videos, and drew up a plan to turn his daughters into professional tennis players.

Serena began playing tennis at the age of just four, and was coached intensively by her father on the poor-quality public courts in their local area. The courts were uneven and full of potholes, and there were threats of violence from gang members who hung around by the courts.

OK, Serena, try that again with more backspin.

When Serena was nine, the family moved to Florida so she and Venus could attend a prestigious tennis academy. Her father stopped the girls from entering junior tournaments for several years so they could focus on school and be protected from the intense competition and racism that he saw at these matches.

Serena began winning major championships in 1999, when she was still a teenager, and by the end of the year she was ranked the 4th best women's tennis player in the world. She moved up the ranks and became World Number One in women's tennis in 2002. She once held this position for 186 consecutive weeks – that's over three-and-a-half years!

Serena has won all the most important world tennis competitions, known as the four 'Grand Slams'. In 2002–03 and 2014–15 she won all four of the Grand Slams in the same year.

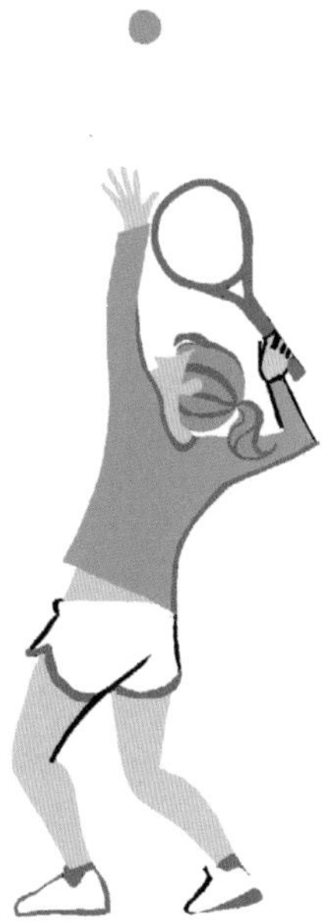

As well as competing individually, Serena and Venus often play together in tennis doubles, and have never been beaten when playing together in a Grand Slam doubles final. They also share an Olympic record of each having won four Olympic gold medals, one in women's singles and three in women's doubles.

In 2017 Serena beat Venus in the Australian Open Final, winning her 23rd Grand Slam title. She later revealed that she had been around eight weeks pregnant at the time of her victory.

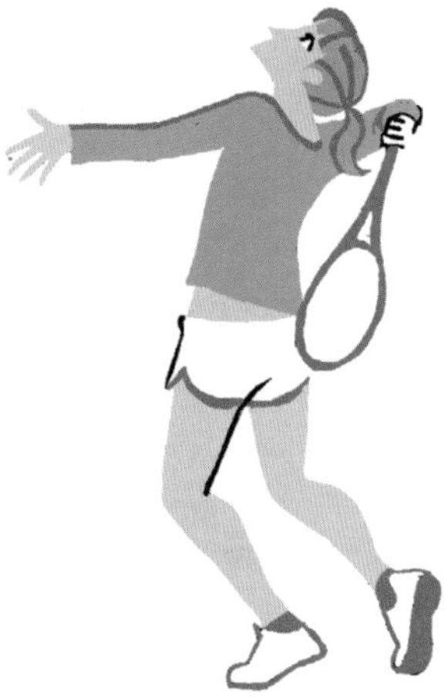

PRACTISE LIKE SERENA

Serena Williams is an incredibly talented player, but that means nothing without lots and lots of hard work. Ever since she was a young girl, Serena has practised the same movements over and over again, getting better and better each time. Whatever sport you like to do, think about the main movements you make and act them out in slow motion. Concentrate on what your body is doing at each stage of the movement. If you are serving a tennis ball, think about how you are throwing the ball up in the air to hit it – how fast, how high, how far from your body. Find the version of the movement that works best for you, and do it again and again.

MARTA

Marta has been described as an artist on the field, using her imagination as well as her skills to get past her opponents and find the perfect path to a goal.

FOOTBALL SUPERSTAR

Considered the most skilful women's football player in the world, Marta Vieira da Silva has reached the superstar heights of being known by her first name alone.

BORN: 19 February 1986

BORN IN: Dois Riachos, Alagoas (Brazil)

COMPETES FOR: Various clubs including Vasco de Gama, Umeå IK, and Brazil national team

Marta's father left her family when she was a baby, and by the time she was 11 she was selling fruit and clothes on a market stall to help her mum feed the family. During her time off, Marta played football with the boys out on the street. Some of the boys told Marta that she couldn't play football because she was a girl, or made fun of her for being 'like a boy'. But although they teased her, they put up with her because she was such a good player that they wanted her on their team!

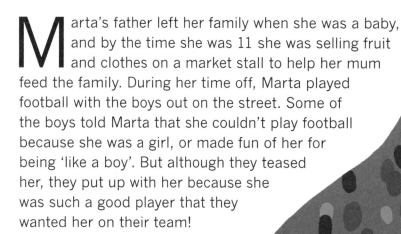

At 14, Marta was discovered by a well-known female football coach and left home to play for Vasco de Gama football club in Rio de Janeiro. She travelled for three days by bus to reach the city from her family home in the north-east. With professional coaching, she excelled and became part of the Brazilian teams that competed at the 2002 Under-19 World Championship and 2003 FIFA Women's Cup.

When she was 18, Marta joined Umeå IK football club in Sweden and the team went on to win the UEFA Europa League that year. She became the youngest woman to ever win the FIFA World Player of the Year Award when she was 20, and has since won this award a further four times, as well as a huge range of other awards and honours.

Marta is considered part of the Brazilian tradition of skilful players such as Pelé, Ronaldinho and Rivaldo. She has been the star of the Brazil national team, making 101 appearances for them and scoring a total of 105 goals. Only one football player in the world, Germany's Miroslav Klose, has scored more goals than her in World Cup matches – 16 to her 15. Pelé scored 12 World Cup goals over his career.

Even for one of the best players in the world, it can be difficult to make a steady living in women's football. Many of the teams that Marta has joined have had money problems and gone bankrupt. Although she is the highest-paid female football player in the world, she still makes a fraction compared to the highest-paid male footballers.

PLAY LIKE MARTA

Marta likes to trick her opponents into thinking she is going to run one way with the ball, and then speeds off past them in the opposite direction. Try it for yourself by turning your body in one direction as you approach your opponent, faking like you're about to kick the ball past them. Then suddenly lift your leg over the ball and turn the other way – using your other foot to kick the ball away ahead of you. Check out UEFA's Star Skills videos at *uefa.com/women/video* and learn tips, tricks and techniques from Marta and other world-class players.

TATYANA McFADDEN

Tatyana McFadden has incredible upper-body strength, using her powerful arms to propel herself forwards in her wheelchair to reach great speed in races.

WHEELCHAIR RACER

Tatyana has become a champion racer over huge and short distances, not believing in putting limits on what she can achieve.

BORN: 21 April 1989

BORN IN: Russia, moved to USA aged 6, now an American citizen

COMPETES FOR: USA

Tatyana was born paralysed from the waist down. Her birth mum couldn't look after her, so Tatyana went to live in an orphanage. The orphanage couldn't afford a wheelchair, so she had to crawl around using her hands. When Tatyana was six years old, Deborah McFadden visited the orphanage in Russia. She felt an instant connection with Tatyana, and she and her partner Bridget O'Shaughnessy adopted the little girl.

When she came to the USA, doctors said Tatyana was so ill that she did not have long to live. But she got better, and took part in a variety of sports to strengthen her muscles, such as swimming, gymnastics and athletics.

You can't race!
I'll race you to court!

In high school, she was not allowed to compete with athletes who did not have disabilities, and so had to race around an empty track on her own. Tatyana and her mum Deborah went to court, and Tatyana won the right to race at the same time as her fellow athletes.

Tatyana was just a schoolgirl when she made her Paralympic debut at the age of 15, in Athens, Greece. She won a silver medal in the women's 100 m race and a bronze medal in the women's 200 m. At the 2008 Beijing Paralympic Games she added another three silvers and one bronze to her name.

In 2009 Tatyana entered the Chicago Marathon. As she specialised in shorter distance sprints, she thought it would be fun but didn't imagine she would do that well. She unexpectedly won, and finished so quickly that her mum wasn't yet ready with the camera to film her victory!

In 2013 Tatyana became the first person, able-bodied or disabled, to win all four Grand Slam marathons (London, Boston, Chicago and New York) in one year. At the World Championships in the same year, Tatyana won gold in every distance from 100 m to 5,000 m.

At the 2014 Winter Paralympic Games in Sochi, Russia, Tatyana won silver in cross-country skiing in front of her adoptive and birth mothers. This was a very meaningful moment for Tatyana. She said afterwards it made her feel 'fulfilled'. In 2016, Tatyana won the Chicago, Boston and London marathons once more, and took home four gold and two silver medals at the 2016 Rio Paralympics. She describes herself as 'the fastest woman on three wheels'!

CHALLENGE YOURSELF LIKE TATYANA

Athletes like Tatyana are always trying to beat their own 'personal best', and do better than they did before. They keep records of how well they do in each training session, and see if their performance is improving. Using a stopwatch, try recording and challenging your own personal best every few days over a few weeks (in running, or swimming, or another individual sport of your choice). It is important to make sure you are always testing yourself across the exact same time and distance to see if you are getting better.

ELLIE SIMMONDS

Ellie shot to fame during the 2008 Beijing Paralympics, where she won two gold medals for Great Britain despite being the youngest team member at just 13 years and nine months old.

CHAMPION SWIMMER

Ellie has won dozens of championship medals and broken several world records – including being the youngest person ever to receive an MBE from the Queen, at the age of 14.

BORN: 11 November 1994

BORN IN: Walsall, West Midlands (UK)

COMPETES FOR: Great Britain

Ellie was born with a condition called achondroplasia dwarfism. Among other symptoms, achondroplasia restricts how tall people grow. Ellie began swimming when she was five, and she immediately loved being able to move fast in the water. From a young age she put a huge amount of hard work into swimming, getting up at 5.30 a.m. during the week to train for two hours before school and then going back to the pool for another 90-minute session in the afternoon.

When she was 10, her talent was spotted at a disability event, and she was entered onto the British Swimming talent programme. Her family knew this was a serious achievement, and was very supportive of her ambition. When Ellie was 11, she and her mother moved to Swansea, Wales, so that Ellie could train during the week at the city's world-class swimming pool. Her father, brother and three sisters continued living in the West Midlands and she saw them at weekends.

In 2008, at the age of 13, Ellie competed in her first Paralympics in Beijing. As well as winning two gold medals, she also set two world records in the 100 m and 400 m freestyle. She rounded off 2008 by winning the BBC Young Sports Personality of the Year Award.

After doing well in international para-swimming over the next few years, Ellie repeated her impressive Paralympics performance in the London 2012 Paralympics. She took home two gold medals and set two new world records, as well as a silver and a bronze medal for good measure. In 2013, she was awarded the even higher honour of an OBE.

The 2016 Rio Paralympics saw her win another gold in the 200-m individual medley, moving the world record to under three minutes for the first time in history. She also took another bronze for Team GB in the 400 m freestyle. By this time, Ellie had won 13 World titles and 10 European titles and broken various world record times along the way. She, and everyone else, felt that she deserved a break.

Ellie took a gap year and travelled to nine countries around the world. She camped in Australia's outback, learned to surf and snorkel (overcoming her fear of the sea in order to do so!), revisited the site of her first Paralympic triumph in Beijing, competed in the World Dwarf Games in football in Canada and even swam with whale sharks. She wanted to travel anonymously but was upgraded to first class on her very first flight when the air steward recognised her!

TRAIN LIKE ELLIE

When Ellie Simmonds started out, she trained with able-bodied swimmers. These children obviously had an advantage compared to her, with longer bodies that made covering distances in the pool easier. But she had the determination to get to the front of the pack no matter what. If you're good at something or you like doing it, don't give up if you're not the absolute best or if someone seems to have advantages that you don't. Use the competition as motivation to do better and better each time, and feel good about the improvements you make.

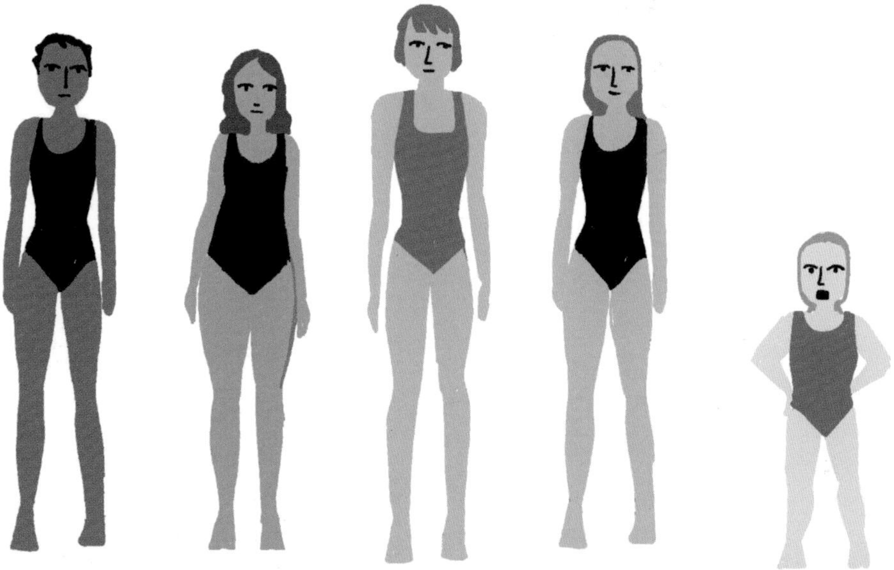

MORE SPORTING HEROINES

The list of fast, strong, determined and talented women in sport goes on and on. Here are some more brilliant women who have excelled through history, as well as some athletes who will no doubt be beating records into the future.

YUENÜ

LIVED: 5th century BCE

BORN IN: Yue (China)

SPORTS: Sword fighting and archery

Yuenü, which means literally 'The Lady of Yue', was a swordswoman and archer of legendary skill and wisdom. From a young age she hunted with her father and in this way learned how to use a sword and a bow. Yuenü developed her skills alone in the forest and based her techniques around the possibility of defeating multiple attackers.

King Gouijan of Yue province called upon Yuenü to train his army for his planned war against another Chinese province. She explained that she thought of the sword as a door that can be divided into yin and yang. She believed in being outwardly calm, rather than putting energy into raging and showing off to an opponent. Instead everything should be focused on internal strength, expressed in powerful, smooth movements and precise, practised footwork. These ideas were at the heart of Chinese martial arts for generations, and Yuenü is considered the first person in history to put forward these ideas.

LIS HARTEL

LIVED: 14 March 1921 – 12 February 2009

BORN IN: Copenhagen (Denmark)

SPORT: Dressage

Lis Hartel became the Danish dressage champion in 1943 and again in 1944. Then, in September of 1944 she contracted polio and was initially almost entirely paralysed. However, she didn't give up her favourite sport. She never regained the feeling below her knees, and at first fell off her horse many times even at a walking pace. But by 1947 she had improved so dramatically that she entered the Scandinavian Riding Championships and won second place. No one on the international scene knew about her paralysis. In the 1952 Helsinki Olympics, women were allowed to compete in dressage with the men for the first time. Lis could not mount or dismount without help, but still won silver. This incredible achievement also made her the first woman to ever win an Olympic medal in direct competition with men. Lis won another Olympic silver medal in dressage in 1956, and was the Danish dressage champion in 1952, 1953, 1954, 1956 and 1959. After retiring, she dedicated her life to supporting riding for people with disabilities and opened the first ever therapeutic riding centre.

BILLIE JEAN KING

BORN: 22 November 1943

BORN IN: Long Beach, California (USA)

SPORT: Tennis

Billie Jean King took up tennis aged 11, learning to play at free local courts. Just four years later, she competed in her first Grand Slam. At the age of 17, in her first time at Wimbledon, she unexpectedly won the women's doubles title. Billie Jean went on to take her first Wimbledon singles title at 22, and to win the singles title six more times. In 1973, Billie Jean beat Bobby Riggs in an infamous $100,000 challenge match watched by a crowd of 30,000 and a TV audience of 50 million. Riggs, a former world number one in tennis, believed – wrongly – that he could beat the top female player in the world. Billie Jean has long fought for equality in sport, and founded the Women's Tennis Association and the Women's Sports Foundation. She came out as a lesbian in 1981, losing around $2 million in sponsorship deals. In 1987 she fell in love with her doubles partner, Ilana Kloss, and they are still together.

PATTI McGEE

BORN: 23 August 1945

BORN IN: Santa Monica, California (USA)

SPORT: Skateboarding

Patti McGee was the first female professional skateboarder and the first women's National Skateboarding Champion. She started skateboarding as a distraction when she was unable to surf. Her signature trick was the handstand, a move that made her the national champion, and a photograph of her doing the trick was used on the front cover of *Life* magazine. She was the first woman to be inducted into the Skateboarding Hall of Fame and the first woman to be on the cover of *Skateboarder* magazine. She set the world record at the time for 'fastest girl on a skateboard', reaching 75 kph. After becoming National Skateboarding Champion in 1965, she toured the USA for a year and was one of the first people to demonstrate skateboarding on national TV shows. Now in her seventies she still skates at local parks.

NICOLA ADAMS

BORN: 26 October 1982

BORN IN: Leeds (UK)

SPORT: Boxing

Nicola loved watching videos of boxing legend Muhammad Ali as a child. She got into boxing by accident when she was 12 years old. Her mum, who raised Nicola and her brother as a single parent, couldn't find a babysitter to watch them while she went to the gym. She enrolled Nicola in a children's boxing class, and Nicola was hooked. Nicola was the only female boxer at her gym and struggled to find opponents. It wasn't until 1997 that a women's boxing match in the UK was authorised by the Amateur Boxing Association. Nicola told her mum she would grow up to become an Olympic boxing champion, but that wasn't technically possible at the time – women were not allowed to compete in boxing at the Olympics until 2012. Nicola made history as the first female Olympic Boxing Champion, winning gold at the 2012 London Olympics, in the flyweight (lightest) category. She defended her title at the 2016 Olympics in Rio, Brazil, winning another gold medal.

KAORI ICHO

BORN: 13 June 1984

BORN IN: Hachinohe, Aomori (Japan)

SPORT: Freestyle wrestling

Kaori started wrestling around the age of four, encouraged by her older sister's passion for the sport. Kaori's training was very intense, as the culture of wrestling in Japan is incredibly tough. Kaori won her first World Championship in 2002. Then for 13 years, between 2003 and 2016, she was undefeated over a total of 189 contests! She won nine World Championships and three Olympic gold medals during that time. After the shock of finally losing a match in January 2016, she bounced back to win a fourth Olympic gold medal in Rio only a few months later. Despite her success, Kaori is driven by trying to wrestle a perfect match rather than by breaking records and winning medals. This attitude has led to her being described as a samurai – a noble warrior – although she modestly says that she doesn't understand this label.

TIRUNESH DIBABA

BORN: 1 June 1985

BORN IN: Bekoji (Ethiopia)

SPORT: Long-distance runner

Tirunesh grew up with her family on their farm in Ethiopia. As a girl, she would run with buckets of water that she fetched from the river for her mum. She thinks this early training helped her be successful. She began running for sport when she moved to the capital city, Addis Ababa, at the age of 14. When she was 18 years old, Tirunesh became the youngest woman to win an individual gold medal in the 5,000 m at the 2003 World Championships. In 2005 she became the first woman to win both the 5,000 m and 10,000 m races in the World Championships. In 2007 she became the only woman to ever win back-to-back 10,000 m titles, when she managed to defend her title despite falling during the race.

Because of her young age, she gained the nickname 'the Baby-Faced Destroyer'. Tirunesh has six Olympic medals, and has also won a total of ten gold medals from the World Championships, World Cross Country Championships and African Championships. Her 5,000 m record still stands as the world's fastest.

IBTIHAJ MUHAMMAD

BORN: 4 December 1985

BORN IN: Maplewood, New Jersey (USA)

SPORT: Fencing

Ibtihaj is the first American woman to ever wear a hijab (a headscarf that usually covers the head and chest) at the Olympics. She began fencing at the age of 13, choosing the sport partly because she was frustrated by having to alter the uniforms she wore for other sports to cover her arms and legs, in line with her religious beliefs about dressing modestly. The fencing uniform is designed to cover most of the body, to protect it against the jabbing end of the foil (sword). At the 2016 Rio Olympics Ibtihaj won bronze in the team fencing competition, and became one of the first two Muslim-American woman to ever win an Olympic medal. Dalilah Muhammad was the other, winning a gold medal in the 400 m hurdles at the same Olympic Games, but she received far less attention in the press because she didn't wear a hijab. Ibtihaj runs a clothing line for Muslim women who want to dress modestly but fashionably, and she works to promote sports and education for girls in the USA and other countries.

SIMONE BILES

BORN: 14 March 1997

BORN IN: Columbus, Ohio (USA)

SPORT: Gymnastics

Simone was adopted by her grandparents, as drug and alcohol addiction problems meant her mum and dad were unable to care for her and her siblings. Aged six, Simone was on a field trip with her day care group to a gymnastics centre. Little Simone watched the gymnasts, and then tried to copy their moves. The instructors at the gym were amazed by her natural talent. She began training, and by the age of ten she was competing nationally. At the age of 16, she won the all-round title at the World Championships. She went on to win the world title three times in a row. Then, at the 2016 Rio Olympics, she won four gold medals, making her the the most decorated (highest medal-earning) American gymnast of all time.

COUNTLESS OTHERS ...

The women included in this book are just a very few of the amazingly talented, determined and downright revolutionary women in sport today and throughout the past. Some have made history and paved the way for women in sport; some continue to compete, win and inspire all around the world today. All are true sporting champions. Will you be the next one to join their ranks?

GET INVOLVED IN SPORT!

There are loads of different ways to get started with a new sport, or to take things further with a sport that you already play and love. Here are a few suggestions.

FIND A SPORTS CLUB, OR START ONE YOURSELF

You'd be amazed at all the different types of sports that you might be able to try out in your area. Have a look at what is on offer – your school or local leisure centre should have some classes and clubs where you can learn something new or practise your skills, but you may also find local groups that run all sorts of different outdoor sports from kayaking to archery. If there isn't a club, start one yourself!

JUNIOR PARKRUNS

If running or wheelchair racing is your thing, then look into junior parkruns. Junior parkruns are free weekly 2-km runs that are open to all children and young people between the ages of 4 and 14. If you want to improve your fitness level, speed or stamina for other sports, this is also a great way to do it.

GO TO WATCH LIVE SPORT

It can be really inspiring to see professionals competing in a sport that you love, or just think you might be interested in doing yourself. Most women's sport is cheaper to go and watch than men's sport, and organisers really want to encourage young people to come along so you might find that you can watch it for free in many cases!

DISCOVER A NEW SPORT ONLINE

If you want to find out more about sports you haven't tried before, and learn how you could have a go yourself, try searching online. You can watch clips of sports on YouTube.com to inspire you, and find video tutorials for particular techniques.

HEROIC LEADERS AND ACTIVISTS

Do you have a favourite superhero? A character who fights evil, battles the bad guys and stands up for the weak against the strong? From Hercules to Wonder Woman, stories of brave heroes who risk life and limb to defeat the forces of darkness have been told and enjoyed for thousands of years.

But although tales of warriors and strong men and women fighting monsters and criminals are thrilling, the real-life challenges faced by real-life heroines are much harder. The incredible, fearless women in this book have fought battles for many years of their lives, and they haven't always been celebrated for it.

Social activists who challenge injustice have to fight their own societies. They need to have the wisdom, strength and heart to see that the situation they are living in is unfair, even when many of the people around them are telling them they are wrong.

Meet the early feminists who first stood up for women's rights around the world, including Mary Wollstonecraft and Qiu Jin. Read about the astonishing Helen Keller, who despite being deaf and blind, became a political activist and writer. Discover the women who have used their art to promote social justice, such as writer Maya Angelou.

These inspiring activists for peace, human rights and the environment have all, in their own ways, made their mark on history.

If you feel deeply about a particular cause, or if you can see a way in which the world could be changed for the better, you'll find ideas in this book for how to make a difference. There are suggestions for how to raise awareness for your favourite cause, raise money for charity and contact your elected politicians to make your voice heard!

Anyone can make a difference. Even you. Especially you. So get ready to be inspired by these brilliant, real-life superheroes!

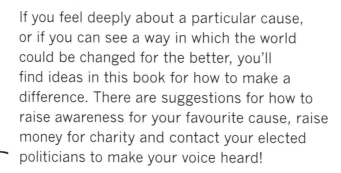

MARY WOLLSTONECRAFT

A trailblazing writer and thinker, Mary Wollstonecraft argued for women's rights and education at a time when women were treated as men's property.

FEMINIST PHILOSOPHER

Mary Wollstonecraft wrote about big ideas such as morality, what an ideal society should be like, and equality between men and women.

LIVED: 27 April 1759 – 10 September 1797

BORN IN: London (UK)

WORKED IN: London (UK)

As a girl, Mary was treated unfairly from the day she was born. Her parents gave her brother Edward much more attention. During the time that Mary was born, boy children were celebrated, whereas girl children were considered a financial burden. Daughters were not able to carry on the family name once they married, and everything they owned became the property of their new husband. Women were also expected to obey their husbands entirely, and while men could divorce their wives for having an affair, women could not get a divorce from their husband for the same reason.

Mary left home when she was 19, and worked as a teacher and then a governess. She was very frustrated by the lack of job opportunities for women, and in 1787 she decided to take a radical step – trying to earn her living by becoming an author. This was not at all normal for women at the time, and Mary told her sister she would be 'the first of a new genus'.

She worked for a publisher in London, translating political and philosophical pamphlets. It was during this time that she met political activists and philosophers such as Thomas Paine. Thomas Paine wrote a book called *Rights of Man*, which set out the rights that a citizen should have in their country. During the 18th century, countries such as France and the USA were experiencing a lot of political change, and the ideas in *Rights of Man* were very influential.

I do not wish women to have power over men; but over themselves.

Mary wrote her most famous pamphlet, *A Vindication of the Rights of Woman*, in 1792. In it, she argued that women should not be considered 'ornaments' or the property of men, but that they should be treated as human beings with the same basic rights. She argued that, as women were responsible for teaching and raising children, it was for the good of everyone that women be educated properly. At the time, many people assumed that women could not think rationally like men.

When Mary published her pamphlet, it was initially well-received, but later people dismissed her work because of 'scandalous' things she had done (which included having a daughter with a man she wasn't married to). Nowadays, her work is considered incredibly important, as she was one of the earliest feminist writers.

WRITE A PAMPHLET LIKE MARY

During the 18th century, many political thinkers and philosophers wrote pamphlets that set out their opinions on how society ought to be. Write your own political pamphlet! Think about what you believe to be unfair or wrong about the world at the moment. Perhaps you think children shouldn't be forced by their parents to go to school? Or do you think people shouldn't eat animals? Decide what would be different in your perfect world, and write your arguments down on a piece of paper. Give it to your friends and family to read.

HARRIET TUBMAN

Born a slave, the tireless and brave Harriet Tubman escaped from her masters and then risked her life over and over again to help other slaves reach freedom.

ABOLITIONIST

Harriet was part of the abolition movement, which was the campaign to end slavery in the USA and Europe. Campaigners and activists spoke out against slavery, and helped slaves escape.

LIVED: c. 1820 – 10 March 1913

BORN IN: Dorchester County, Maryland (USA)

WORKED IN: Pennsylvania and Maryland (USA)

Harriet Tubman was born in Maryland, USA. Her mum was called Harriet, too, and her dad was called Benjamin. They were both slaves, and this meant Harriet was a slave too. Her master treated her very cruelly, and when she was only five years old she was given the job of looking after a baby. When she couldn't stop the baby from crying, she was whipped.

Harriet's master died when she was 27 years old. She decided it would be better to try and run away, rather than be sold again. She knew that if she could get to the neighbouring state of Pennsylvania, where slavery was illegal, she would be free. Harriet headed north using the Underground Railroad. This wasn't an actual railway, but a network of slaves, freed slaves, and white abolitionists who would help runaway slaves escape by hiding them in their houses, or transporting them to a new safe house.

Harriet travelled at night to avoid detection. When she crossed over into Pennsylvania, she had to check her hands to see if she was the same person! She later said, 'there was such a glory over everything ... I felt like I was in heaven.' She lived in Pennsylvania and worked odd jobs to earn money, but she was not content with just her own freedom. She wanted to help others to be free.

Over the next 11 years, Harriet returned to Maryland again and again, to guide first her family, and then other slaves, to freedom. She made about 13 expeditions, and guided around 70 slaves to freedom, as well as providing directions to another 50 or 60. During her rescue missions she would travel at night, or disguise herself as a slave on an errand by carrying a chicken.

When the American Civil War (1861–1865) began between the Unionists (made up of northern US states where slavery was illegal) and the Confederates (made up of southern US states where slavery was legal), Harriet worked as a nurse and a spy for the Union forces. Despite her service during and after the war, she did not receive a salary from the US government and spent her whole life living in poverty.

CAMPAIGN AGAINST SLAVERY LIKE HARRIET

Did you know there are more people enslaved around the world today than there were when Harriet was alive? Although slavery is illegal worldwide, in many places the law is not enforced. As a result, up to 30 million people, many of whom are women and children, are slaves right now. Many famous abolitionists during Harriet's day were preachers, who stood up and made speeches against slavery. Why don't you research, write and perform your own speech about modern-day slavery to your family and friends? You can find out about which organisations are working to combat it, and tell your friends and family how they can help.

EGLANTYNE JEBB

Although she came from a well-off background, Eglantyne was outraged by the suffering of the poor, particularly children.

HUMANITARIAN

Eglantyne felt her calling in life was to save human lives and reduce human suffering.

LIVED: 25 August 1876 – 17 December 1928

BORN IN: Ellesmere (UK)

WORKED IN: UK and Switzerland

Eglantyne had a happy childhood. She was born into a well-off family in England with a big house. She loved horse riding, and spent her summers climbing trees, swimming and boating on the lake. In the winter she would go ice skating. She was very imaginative, and loved reading, writing and telling stories. She would tell stories to her younger brothers and sisters about heroes and monsters, magicians and witches.

Although Eglantyne's family wealth meant she didn't have to work, she was determined to do something useful. After graduating from university she started working as a primary school teacher. While she was training to be a teacher in East London she saw many children in poverty, who were ill and weak due to lack of food. Later, while doing charity work in Cambridge, she realised that poverty in England was a serious and widespread problem.

During and after the First World War (1914–1918), Great Britain, France and Russia blockaded Germany and its allies. This meant they stopped food and other goods being imported into the countries, in order to weaken them and bring about the end of the war. However, food shortages in Germany after the First World War meant many children were starving.

Eglantyne was appalled that British actions were causing children to die. She gave out leaflets in Trafalgar Square in London showing two starving German children, with the caption 'Our blockade has caused this!'. She was arrested and tried for her protest, but the prosecutor was so impressed with her actions that he paid her fine himself!

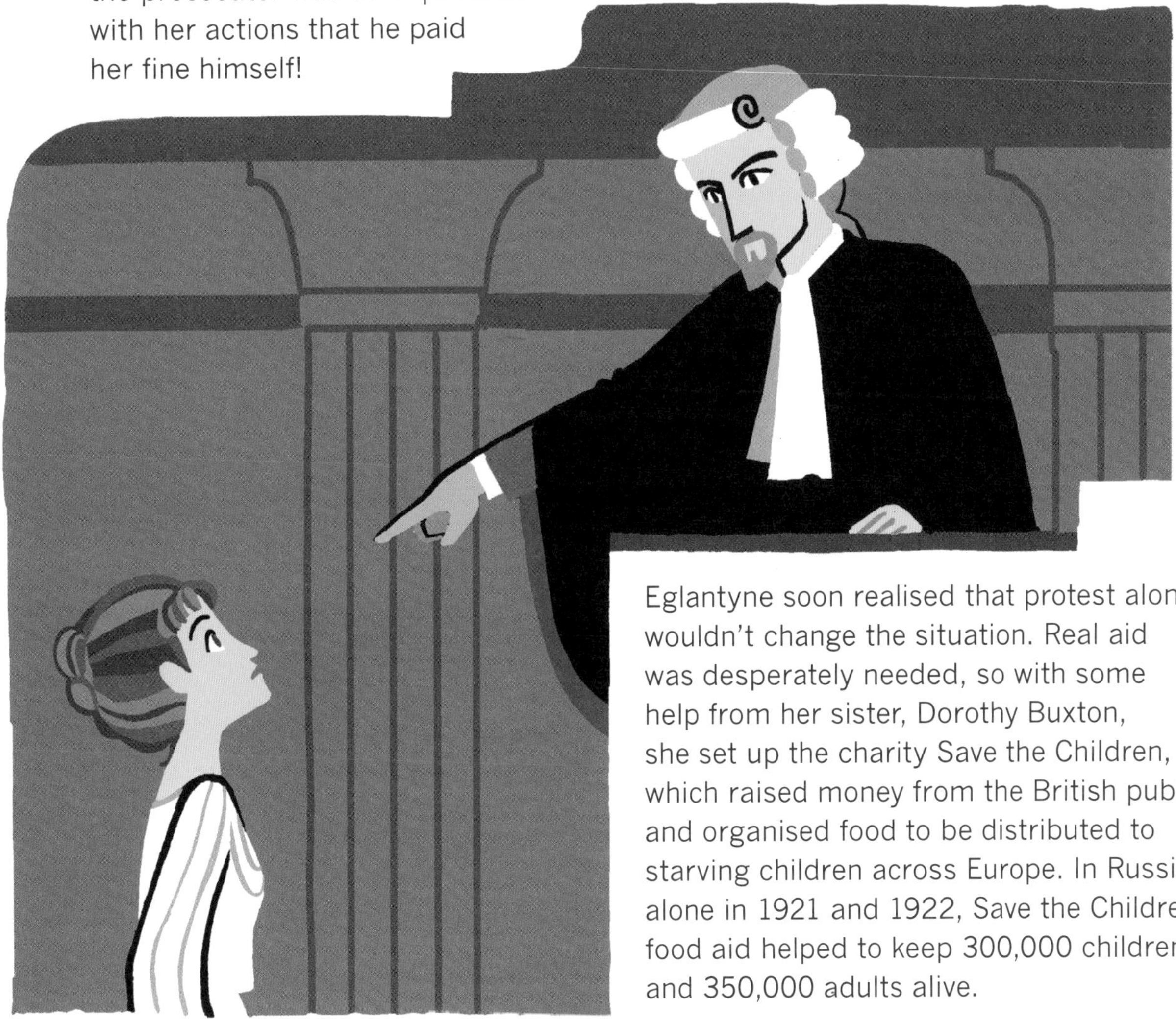
You're fined ...
but I'm paying!

Eglantyne soon realised that protest alone wouldn't change the situation. Real aid was desperately needed, so with some help from her sister, Dorothy Buxton, she set up the charity Save the Children, which raised money from the British public and organised food to be distributed to starving children across Europe. In Russia alone in 1921 and 1922, Save the Children food aid helped to keep 300,000 children and 350,000 adults alive.

But Eglantyne also realised that no matter how generous, charity was not enough either. To make a lasting change, children's rights needed to be defended by the law. She drafted a document, the 'Declaration of the Rights of the Child', which was adopted by the international organisation, the League of Nations, in 1924. This document also became the basis of current international law on children's rights, which is outlined in the United Nations Convention on the Rights of the Child.

RAISE FUNDS FOR SAVE THE CHILDREN LIKE EGLANTYNE

Save the Children is still a large and successful international organisation that fights for children's rights and provides relief to children suffering from disasters around the world. Save the Children have lots of ideas for ways you can help raise money to support the work that they do on their website, from hosting den-building parties to sponsored walks or bike rides. Take a look and see which ideas appeal to you, and organise a fundraising event of your own. There are lots of other charities that help children. See if you can find one in your local area that needs support.

HELEN KELLER

Despite losing her sight and hearing as a baby, Helen Keller's incredible intelligence and determination enabled her to become a world-famous author and political activist.

ADVOCATE FOR THE BLIND

An advocate argues for the rights of a particular person or group. Helen Keller travelled and advocated for improvements in the conditions of blind peoples' lives.

LIVED: 27 June 1880 – 1 June 1968

BORN IN: Tuscumbia, Alabama (USA)

WORKED IN: USA and worldwide

A healthy, happy baby named Helen was born into a well-off family in Alabama in the summer of 1880. But, when she was only 19 months old, Helen lost her sight and hearing after a mysterious illness. As she got older, being unable to communicate properly made Helen a bad-tempered, naughty child.

Helen's parents arranged for her to have a teacher, Anne Sullivan, who came to live with them. Anne arrived in 1897 and began teaching Helen using finger spelling. She would teach Helen words by spelling them out on the palm of Helen's hand. For example, Anne spelled D-O-L-L, then passed Helen her doll. Helen didn't understand at first, and became very frustrated. Then, about one month after Anne began using finger spelling, Anne traced the letters W, A, T, E, R on Helen's hand, while holding her hand to water. Helen suddenly understood! She was so excited that she learned the hand spelling for 30 different objects in one day.

With Anne to help her, Helen went to school in 1888. She was a very bright student, and she learned several methods of communication, including lip-reading by touch (where she would place her fingers against the mouth of the speaking person), braille (a system of written letters that use raised dots on paper that can be felt by the fingertips), typing, and even speech!

Helen learned to speak by feeling the vibrations and lip-movements of her teachers, and copying them. Although her speech was not perfect, it was an incredible achievement. She went to university, studying at Radcliffe College. She was accompanied by Anne who translated her texts and lectures for her. Helen was the first deaf-blind person ever to graduate from university. It was while she was a student that Helen wrote her first book, *The Story of My Life*.

After graduating Helen became a writer, political activist and advocate. She gave many speeches as well as writing books and essays on various topics, including religion, disabled people's rights and politics. She was appointed to a role within the American Foundation of Overseas Blind, and she travelled to over 40 different countries arguing in favour of education, treatment and rights for the blind.

COMMUNICATE LIKE HELEN

Sighted and hearing people can help blind and deaf people by learning ways to communicate with them. Using the braille alphabet below, have a go at writing a letter using braille. Get a piece of paper, a piece of cardboard and a biro. Put the paper on top of the cardboard, and press the biro down to make raised bumps on the reverse side of the paper. But wait! The braille is read on the reverse side of the paper. This means you need to write it as though it is a mirror image of what you want to end up with, so start on the right-hand side of your paper and move left, and flip the dot patterns of the letters too. Keep practising until you figure it out!

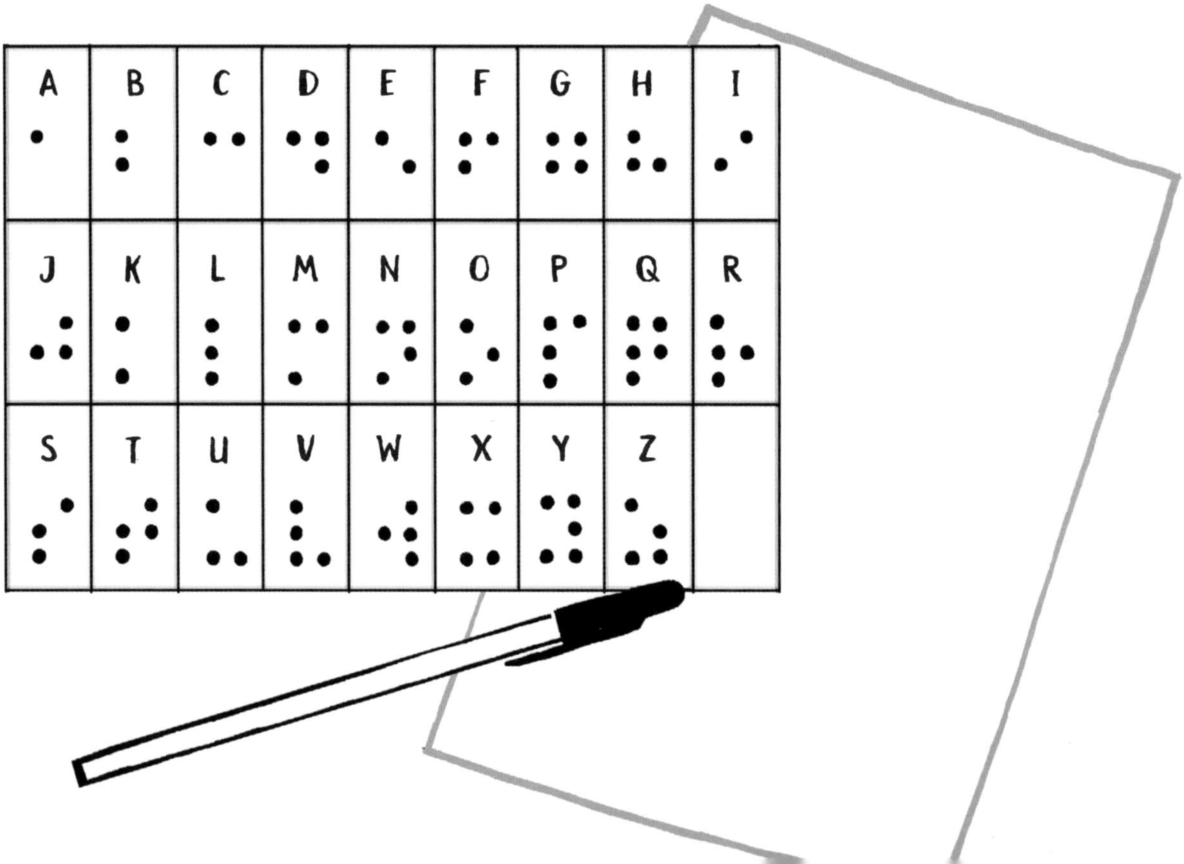

FAITH BANDLER

Faith's own experiences of injustice, as well the suffering of her father, propelled her to fight for equality in a deeply unfair society.

INDIGENOUS RIGHTS CAMPAIGNER

Faith organised petitions and meetings to get Australian law changed to recognise equal rights for indigenous people.

LIVED: 27 September 1918 – 13 February 2015

BORN IN: Tumbulgum, New South Wales (Australia)

WORKED IN: Australia

Faith was one of eight children. Her mum, Ida, had Scottish and Indian heritage. Her dad, Wacvie Mussingkon (who later changed his name to Peter Mussing) was an indigenous South Sea Islander. For much of his life, Wacvie had worked as a slave labourer on Australian sugar plantations, after being 'blackbirded' from the small South Sea nation of Vanuatu when he was 13 years old. 'Blackbirding' was the term for capturing and kidnapping indigenous people, taking them away on boats and forcing them to work as cheap or unpaid labourers. This was a common method of finding workers for the sugar industry in Australia in the 19th century.

After 20 years on the plantations, Wacvie escaped, but his life story inspired Faith in her activism. Faith was a very good student at school, but the Great Depression in the 1930s stopped her studies. She worked various jobs, including on farms, where she was paid less than the white workers, as were the Aboriginal Australians and other indigenous people from the region.

Indigenous people were treated very badly by the Australian government, and weren't even considered worthy of counting when the government did a census. Indigenous people were forced to live in designated areas, and the children of indigenous families were often forcibly removed from their parents.

After working as a seamstress and on fruit farms, Faith became a full-time activist in 1956, campaigning for indigenous people's rights. She led a campaign to change the Constitution of Australia to remove the discrimination against indigenous people, organising several huge petitions and hundreds of large public meetings. Eventually, in 1967 her campaign was successful. A key referendum was held that changed the law in Australia so that indigenous people were included in the census as well, making it possible for the government to create laws that would help the indigenous population.

After her great success with the campaign that led to the 1967 referendum, Faith started to focus her energy on the plight of her own people, the descendants of South Sea Islanders who were still not eligible for certain benefits in education, health and housing. In 1976 she made an emotional journey to the South Sea island of Ambrym in Vanuatu, where her father was kidnapped so many years before.

CREATE POLITICAL CHANGE LIKE FAITH

Although children can't vote in referendums or elections, there are no age limits on learning about politics and campaigning during referendums or at election time! Why not look online to read up on the policies of the different political parties, and decide which ones sound the best to you. You might particularly want to look at what policies they have about children and young people. How would the ideas they put forward affect you? You can also write to your local politician to ask for their support on a campaign that you feel strongly about.

SOPHIE SCHOLL

Sophie's powerful sense of right and wrong led the young student to stand up against the Nazi regime in Germany, and ultimately to give her life for her beliefs.

PACIFIST

Being a pacifist means believing in non-violence. Sophie rejected the brutality of the Nazis, and encouraged others to resist them using peaceful means.

LIVED: 9 May 1921 – 22 February 1943

BORN IN: Forchtenberg (Germany)

WORKED IN: Munich (Germany)

Sophie was one of six children. Her dad, Robert, was the mayor of the small town of Forchtenberg where the family lived. Sophie's strong sense of justice was apparent from an early age. At school, the best pupils had to sit on the front row. On her younger sister Elizabeth's birthday, Elizabeth was moved by the teacher from the front row to the second row. Sophie was so angry at the unfairness of her sister being moved off the front row on her birthday, that she escorted her sister back to the front row and told the teacher 'It's Elizabeth's birthday, so I'm moving her back!'

Sophie was eleven when the Nazis, led by Adolf Hitler, came to power in 1933. At first she joined the League of German Maidens, which was the girls' wing of the Nazi youth movement, but as she learned more about Nazi ideology, she realised how wrong the ideas of the Nazi Party were.

The Nazis believed that white people were superior, that disabled people were a burden, and that any political opposition was treason. Activities like making jokes about the Nazis or forming a youth group that wasn't part of the Hitler Youth was made illegal. Jewish people were seen as 'subhuman', and a danger to society. In 1939 Nazi-led Germany invaded Poland, which started the Second World War (1939–1945).

After finishing school, Sophie began to work as a nursery teacher, and then started studying at the University of Munich in 1942 where her brother Hans was also a student. At university, Sophie and Hans and a group of friends who called themselves the 'White Rose' began to create pamphlets that called on people to resist the Nazis. The pamphlets argued that the Nazi regime was criminal and oppressive, and they condemned the mass-murder of Jewish people that the Nazi government was conducting. They urged people to take up non-violent resistance, through protest and political non-cooperation.

After dropping some leaflets, Sophie and Hans were spotted and reported to the secret police. A draft of a leaflet written by another member, Christoph Probst, was found in Hans' apartment. The three of them were put on trial and sentenced to death. They were executed by guillotine on 22 February, 1943. The incredible bravery of Sophie and all of the members of the White Rose group has since inspired millions of people. In Germany, they have become a symbol of resistance against tyranny, and many monuments have been erected in their honour.

PROTEST LIKE SOPHIE

Non-violent resistance has been an important technique for social activists for a long time, and continues to be used to make political change today. Key methods include going on demonstrations or protest marches. Join a demonstration for an issue that you care about – or if you can't find one, why not organise one yourself? Gather a group of friends and make signs that explain what you are demonstrating about. Ask an adult to accompany you and stand with your signs in a safe public place. A good idea is to make leaflets with information on, so passers-by can learn about the issue you are protesting. You could wear fancy dress to make your demonstration more eye-catching!

WANGARI MAATHAI

Wangari understood how caring for the environment and caring for people were part of the same cause.

ENVIRONMENTALIST

Wangari wanted to protect the natural environment, and improve the lives of rural women, so she started the Green Belt Movement to get people planting trees.

LIVED: 1 April 1940 – 25 September 2011

BORN IN: Ihithe Village, Nyeri District (Kenya)

WORKED IN: Nairobi (Kenya)

As a little girl Wangari felt a strong connection to nature. Near her house was a fig tree and a stream, and Wangari's mum would send her to collect firewood and water. In the stream, frogs would lay their eggs, and Wangari thought they looked like beautiful beads.

Most girls in rural Kenya like Wangari did not go to school, as education was not considered important for them, however Wangari was very clever and her parents were persuaded to let her study. At high school she was the best student in her class. In 1960, she won a scholarship to Mount St Scholastica College in Kansas, USA, to study biology, chemistry and German. She returned to Kenya to get her PhD – the first East African woman to receive one.

Wangari saw that people in Kenya were facing many problems. In rural areas, there was no firewood, and no water. Without firewood, people could not cook healthy food. Many people were suffering from malnutrition and also didn't have any work.

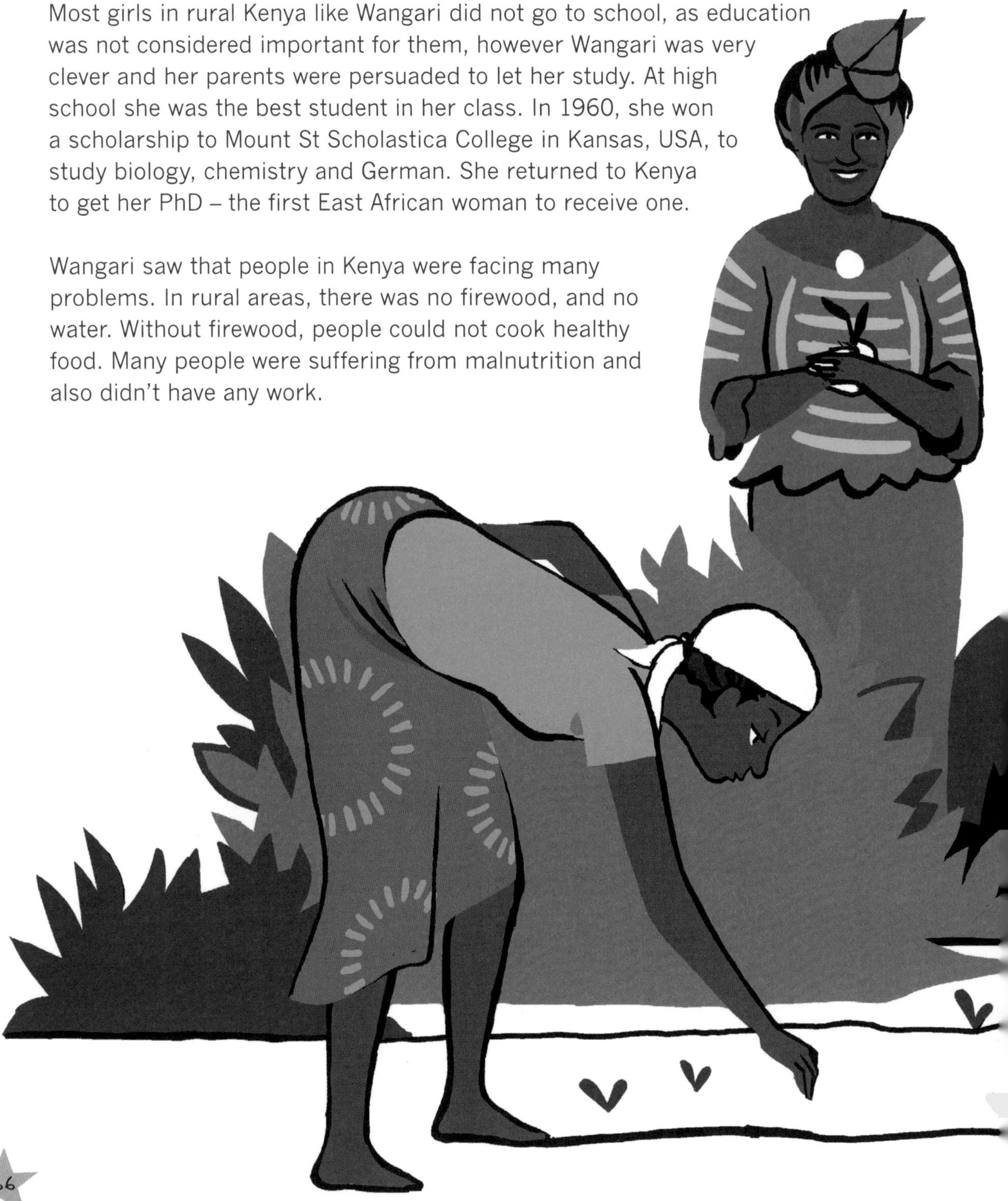

Wangari realised that many of the problems were due to deforestation. Trees had been cut down to make space for money-earning crops, such as tea. But this meant there was no firewood. The trees had previously helped the land store water and soil, but without the trees, water quickly ran off, taking the soil with it.

She had the idea to help women plant native trees to renew the health of the land, and provide firewood. This was the start of the Green Belt Movement. In the 1980s the government of Kenya was very repressive. Through the Green Belt Movement Wangari also carried out pro-democracy activism, by registering women to vote and pushing for political reform.

The government attempted to shut down the Green Belt Movement, and Wangari's pro-democracy activities. In 1992, Wangari was arrested and released on bail. But during another clash with the government – this time about pro-democracy campaigners who were being held in prison – Wangari was badly beaten and ended up in a coma.

Despite the government attempting to shut it down, the Green Belt Movement became extremely successful, and since it began in 1977 over 51 million trees have been planted in Kenya, and over 30,000 women have been trained in forestry and other environmental skills. In 2002 Wangari ran for Parliament, and was elected to a position in the Ministry for Environment and Natural Resources. In 2004, she won the Nobel Peace Prize for her environmental and pro-democracy work.

HELP THE ENVIRONMENT LIKE WANGARI

There are lots of ways we can help make our environment healthier and happier. Planting wild flowers can provide a home for animals and insects, as well as helping to protect the soil. Have you got any bare patches of ground at home or at school that could be planted with wild flowers? Ask your teacher if you can make a project of planting flowers or even a tree – you will be helping nature thrive, and making your environment a nicer place to be.

MALALA YOUSAFZAI

The youngest ever winner of a Nobel Peace Prize, Malala was just a schoolgirl herself when she was shot for standing up for the rights of girls to have an education.

EDUCATION CAMPAIGNER

Malala set up the Malala Fund, which is an organisation working to ensure every girl in the world receives a minimum of 12 years of education.

BORN: 12 July 1997

BORN IN: Mingora (Pakistan)

WORKS IN: Pakistan, the UK and worldwide

Malala was born in an area of Pakistan called the Swat Valley, in a town called Mingora. Her dad was a social activist who campaigned for human rights, and for the right of every child to go to school. He founded many schools in the Swat Valley. Malala understood from a very young age that the situation in the area where her family lived was not fair. The area was controlled by the Taliban, who are a political group that follow a very extreme and repressive version of Islam.

The Taliban use violence to enforce their rules, such as forbidding girls to be educated, banning music, films and television, and even banning women from leaving the house without a male relative. This is very different to the way most Muslims around the world, such as Malala and her family, practice their religion. The Taliban blew up nearly 400 schools, and many of the students in the schools set up by Malala's dad stopped attending due to the danger.

Aged 11, Malala began writing a blog on the BBC website, arguing for her right to continue attending school. She also spoke on a TV talk show, asking 'How dare the Taliban take away my right to a basic education?' When the blog was translated into English, many people around the world read it, and she became very well known. Malala gave more television interviews, and the famous activist and religious leader Desmond Tutu nominated her for the International Children's Peace Prize.

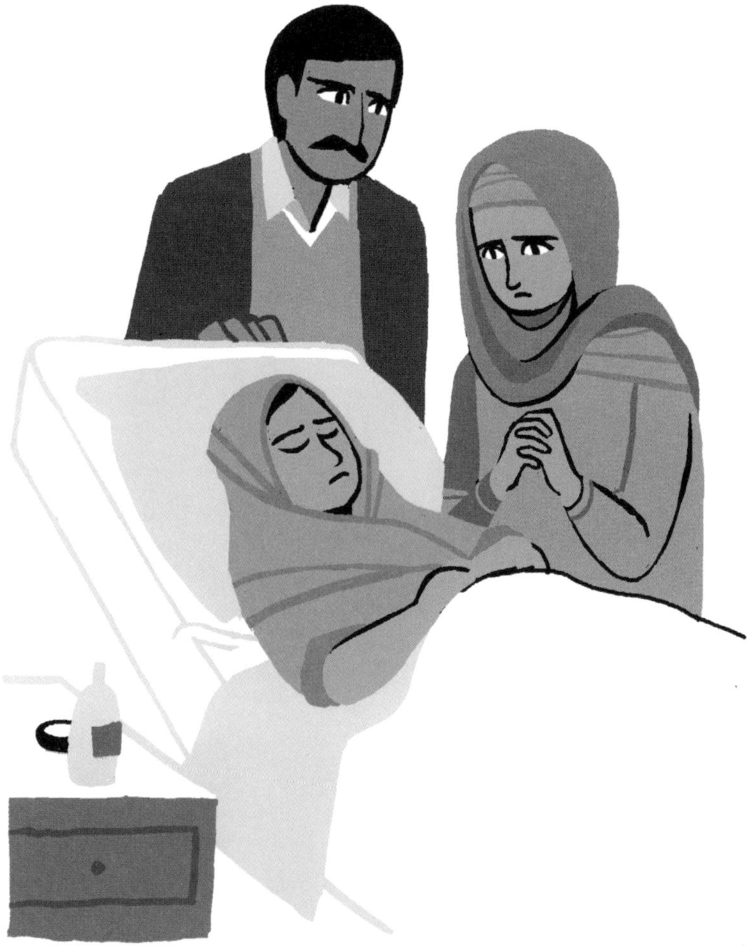

Then, when Malala was 15, a Taliban gunman boarded the bus that was taking her home from school and shot her in the head, in an attempt to kill her. Malala was very ill, but the bullet did not reach her brain. She was flown to hospital a few hours away, and then transferred to a hospital in England. She slowly recovered, and began going to school in Birmingham, England, where her family now also live.

A year later she gave a speech at the United Nations about her experiences and the right of all girls to get an education. In 2014, when she was only 17, she became the youngest ever recipient of the Nobel Peace Prize for her activism. She continues to mix campaigning for girls' rights to education with her own studies. She has called on world leaders to invest in 'books, not bullets'.

HELP EVERY CHILD LEARN LIKE MALALA

You might think that you aren't yet old enough to be a teacher. Wrong! No matter what your age is, you can help another young person learn. Get your friends involved too. Start a buddy scheme and pair up your friends with younger students in your school. You can then all meet up with your younger buddies for short reading sessions. Get the younger students to read aloud to their older buddy. The older students can help their younger buddies with any difficult words, and help them learn to read aloud.

MORE SOCIAL ACTIVISM HEROES

There are a great many other inspiring women who are social activists and leaders. Here are even more courageous and tireless campaigners for justice, from the past right up to the present day.

KATE SHEPPARD

LIVED: 10 March 1847 – 13 July 1934

BORN IN: Liverpool (UK)

WORKED IN: New Zealand

Kate grew up and went to school in Scotland, and from an early age she had a reputation for being very clever. She moved to New Zealand with her mum and siblings in 1868, where she began to get involved in various causes. She believed that women should be able to participate in all aspects of society, including politics, at a time when women did not have the vote anywhere in the world. Kate was a strong believer in equality of all kinds, saying, 'all that separates, whether of race, class, creed, or sex, is inhuman, and must be overcome.'

She wrote many pamphlets, and held meetings in favour of women's suffrage (the right to vote). During the late 1880s and 1890s Kate organised several petitions on women's suffrage which were presented to Parliament. Finally, in 1893, she presented the largest petition yet and that year a bill was passed granting women in New Zealand the vote – the first country in the world to do so. She continued to campaign for women's rights for several years until she was prevented by ill health. She is now considered a very important figure in New Zealand's history, and the history of women's suffrage worldwide. Kate's portrait is printed on the New Zealand ten dollar note.

QIU JIN

LIVED: 8 November 1875 – 15 July 1907

BORN IN: Shaoxing (China)

WORKED IN: China

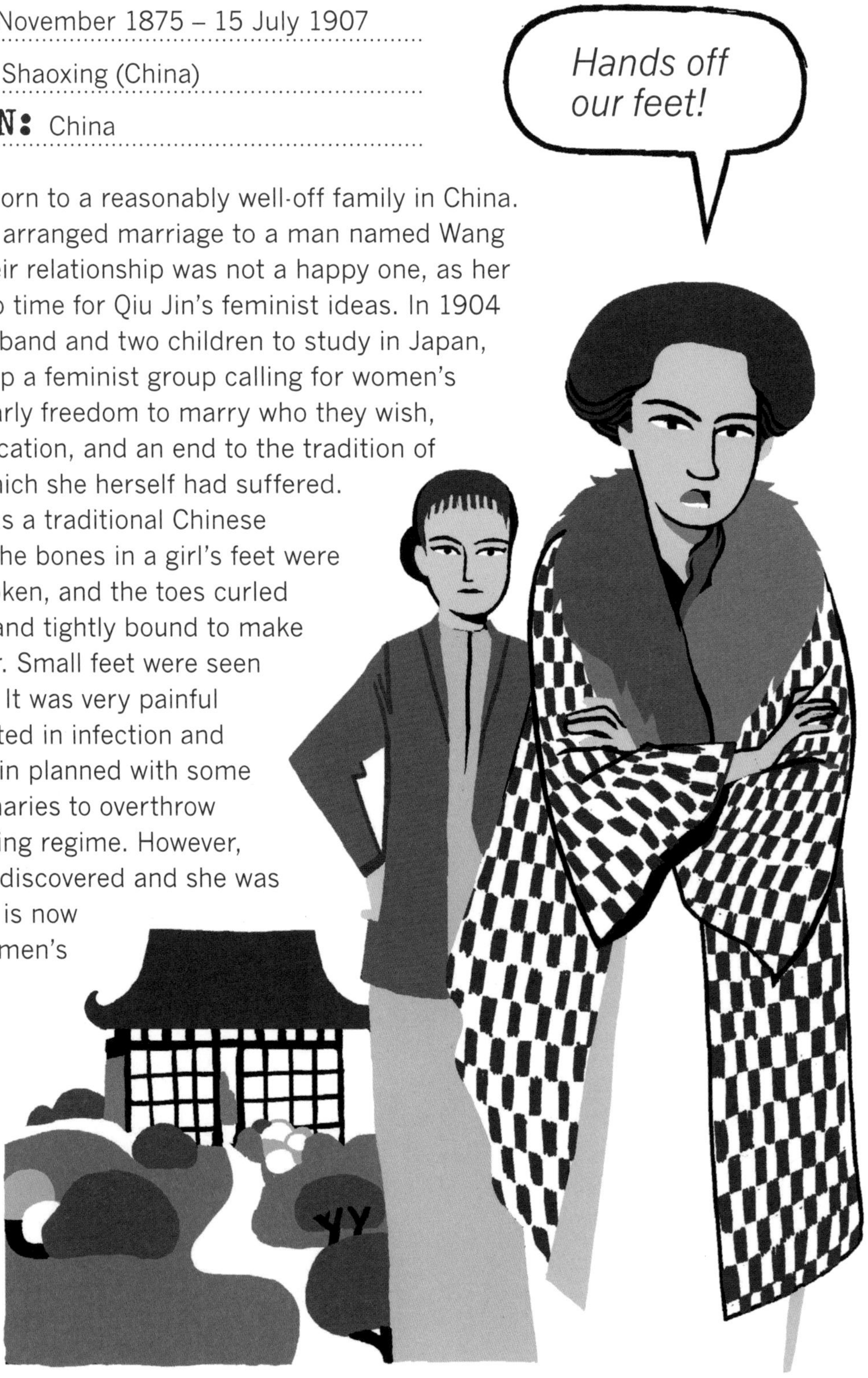

Qiu Jin was born to a reasonably well-off family in China. She had an arranged marriage to a man named Wang Tingjun, but their relationship was not a happy one, as her husband had no time for Qiu Jin's feminist ideas. In 1904 she left her husband and two children to study in Japan, where she set up a feminist group calling for women's rights, particularly freedom to marry who they wish, freedom of education, and an end to the tradition of foot-binding, which she herself had suffered. Foot-binding was a traditional Chinese custom where the bones in a girl's feet were deliberately broken, and the toes curled under the feet and tightly bound to make the foot smaller. Small feet were seen to be beautiful. It was very painful and often resulted in infection and disability. Qiu Jin planned with some other revolutionaries to overthrow the Chinese ruling regime. However, her plans were discovered and she was beheaded. She is now a symbol of women's independence in China.

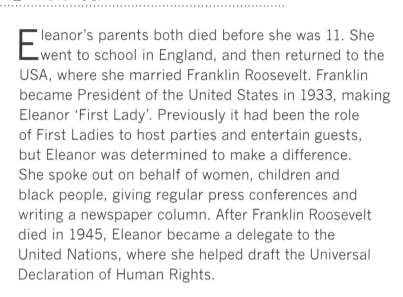

ELEANOR ROOSEVELT

LIVED: 11 October 1884 – 7 November 1962

BORN IN: New York City, New York (USA)

WORKED IN: USA

Eleanor's parents both died before she was 11. She went to school in England, and then returned to the USA, where she married Franklin Roosevelt. Franklin became President of the United States in 1933, making Eleanor 'First Lady'. Previously it had been the role of First Ladies to host parties and entertain guests, but Eleanor was determined to make a difference. She spoke out on behalf of women, children and black people, giving regular press conferences and writing a newspaper column. After Franklin Roosevelt died in 1945, Eleanor became a delegate to the United Nations, where she helped draft the Universal Declaration of Human Rights.

ROSA PARKS

LIVED: 4 February 1913 – 24 October 2005

BORN IN: Tuskegee, Alabama (USA)

WORKED IN: USA

In Alabama where Rosa lived, there was a set of laws called 'segregation' that kept black people and white people separate. Black people had to go to different schools to white people, and on buses, they had separate seating areas. If all the seats were full, black passengers had to give up their seats for white passengers. On 1 December 1955, Rosa was arrested when she refused to give up her seat to a white passenger. In response to her arrest, black people in the city of Montgomery boycotted (refused to use) the buses for over a year. The bus companies lost a lot of money, and eventually the law concerning the buses was changed. However, it wasn't until 1964 that segregation of public spaces was abolished across the USA.

MAYA ANGELOU

LIVED: 4 April 1928 – 28 May 2014

BORN IN: St Louis, Missouri (USA)

WORKED IN: USA

Maya's real name was 'Marguerite', but when she was little her brother would call her 'My-a sister', and the nickname 'Maya' stuck. It wasn't an easy childhood, as the society in southern USA where she lived was very racist. When she was eight, she was abused by her mum's boyfriend. She told her mum about it, and when her mum's boyfriend was later found murdered, Maya believed her voice had killed him. She didn't speak for five years after that. When she grew up, she had many jobs, working as a waitress, a singer, an actor and a dancer. She joined the civil rights movement, campaigning alongside well-known activists such as Malcolm X and Martin Luther King. But her true passion was always for writing. In 1969 she wrote the story of her life, *I Know Why the Caged Bird Sings*. It became a bestseller, and helped many people to understand what life was like for a black woman growing up in a racist society.

ELLEN JOHNSON SIRLEAF

BORN: 29 October 1938

BORN IN: Monrovia (Liberia)

WORKS IN: Liberia

Ellen is from Liberia, a country with a troubled history. Liberia was settled as a colony for freed black and mixed-heritage slaves from the USA in the early 19th century. However, the area of land already had people living there, and a very oppressive class-system was put in place, with immigrants holding power over the indigenous African people. Ellen had a mixture of immigrant and indigenous heritage, and she did very well in school. As an adult she began working in government.

In 1980, the President and many ministers were shot during a military coup. The leader of the coup, Samuel Doe, declared himself president, and later he put Ellen in prison for criticising him. In 1989 Samuel Doe was overthrown by another man, Charles Taylor, and Liberia was plunged into a violent civil war, which killed over a quarter of a million people.

After 13 years of fighting, Charles Taylor agreed to leave Liberia, and in 2005 Ellen was elected the president, the first woman president of any African country. She made education free and compulsory for all children. In 2011, alongside Nigerian peace activist Leymah Gbowee, Ellen won the Nobel Peace Prize, for their work in bringing in a period of peace and stability in Liberia.

I swear to clean up the mess you men have made.

EUFROSINA CRUZ

BORN: 1 January 1979

BORN IN: Santa Maria Quiegolani, Oaxaca (Mexico)

WORKS IN: Mexico

Eufrosina comes from an indigenous community in Mexico, where traditional laws and ways of life mean that most women have to get up very early to gather fuel, grind corn to make tortillas and look after the children. Girls have little education, and their husbands are often chosen for them by their fathers. Aged 11, Eufrosina decided she wanted a better life than this. She saved up money by selling chewing gum, and went away to study. When she returned, she was determined to make women's lives better in her community, so she became a candidate in the election for mayor. She won many votes, but the men who ran the community were furious, and cancelled the election result, saying she could not be mayor because she was a woman. Eufrosina wrote to the Human Rights Commission, and got the local laws changed so that women could participate fully in elections. She also started an organisation, QUIEGO, to achieve justice for indigenous women.

MANAL AL-SHARIF

BORN: 25 April 1979

BORN IN: Mecca (Saudi Arabia)

WORKS IN: Saudi Arabia

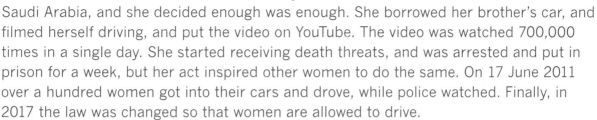

In Saudi Arabia the laws governing what women are allowed to do are very restrictive. Women have not been allowed to drive cars, or travel without a male relative's permission. After spending some time in the USA where she could drive freely, Manal returned to Saudi Arabia, and she decided enough was enough. She borrowed her brother's car, and filmed herself driving, and put the video on YouTube. The video was watched 700,000 times in a single day. She started receiving death threats, and was arrested and put in prison for a week, but her act inspired other women to do the same. On 17 June 2011 over a hundred women got into their cars and drove, while police watched. Finally, in 2017 the law was changed so that women are allowed to drive.

AMELIA TELFORD

BORN: 1994

BORN IN: Tweed Heads (Australia)

WORKS IN: Australia

Bundjalung country, where Amelia Telford is from, is a part of Australia with a beautiful and diverse landscape. There are beaches, rainforest and mountains, and it is an area where many indigenous Australian people live. Amelia loved the natural landscape of her home, but gradually realised how climate change was impacting both the environment, and the indigenous people who lived in the area. So she started working with the Australian Youth Climate Coalition to raise money to create the Seed Indigenous Youth Climate Network, an organisation dedicated to helping young indigenous people take action against climate change.

GET INVOLVED IN SOCIAL ACTIVISM!

There are lots of different ways to be an activist. Activists stand up for what they believe in. Activists let other people know about the unfair things that are happening around the world. Activists use their own special talents and gifts to get their words heard. Activists raise money for organisations that are challenging injustice. Activists see what needs to be done, and they don't give up. Here are some ideas for how you can get involved in social activism.

MAKE AN ONLINE VIDEO

Unless people know about an issue, they can't do anything about it! So raising awareness is a very important part of social activism. There are many different ways of spreading your message, but one great way is through online videos. These can be shared over and over again. Lots of charities and organisations use videos to get their messages across, so try watching some of them online for inspiration. While you watch, think about what makes their videos especially powerful or moving, and then try creating your own. Make sure you check with your parents before putting videos of yourself online.

START A PETITION

It can be difficult to convince the people in charge that things need to change. That's when you need to prove that you are not alone. You need to show that there are a lot of people on your side who also want things to be done differently. This is what a petition is for! A petition is a list of names of people who agree with you about what needs to be done, and the more people you can get to sign it, the louder your collective voice is. You can start petitions online or, if your issue is something close to home – perhaps you want to petition your school to compost the canteen food waste, or put up some nesting boxes for birds – you can simply collect names and signatures on sheets of paper and hand-deliver them to the person in charge.

RAISE MONEY FOR CHARITY

Effective action on big issues can take a lot of time and money, which is why non-governmental organisations (NGOs) and charities are needed to work in a long-term, and organised way. Raising money for an organisation of your choice can be a fun way to help support the causes you care about. There are tons of ways to raise money: you could do a sponsored walk or bike ride. You could collect up your old toys and clothes and hold a jumble sale. You could organise a party, or get your friends together to put on a musical performance and charge people for tickets. Be creative!

LEARN TO WIN AN ARGUMENT

Making change happen often requires a lot of people to be convinced of something that they disagree with, or maybe aren't sure about. Learning how to make a convincing argument for your point of view is a really useful skill, not only in social activism but in other areas of life too! One way to get better at arguing your case is through debating. Search for debate clubs in your local area, or read up about the rules of formal debating online. In debate clubs you often have to argue the case for something you don't actually agree with, which is a great way to sharpen your skills, as well as helping you understand other people's points of view.

GLOSSARY

PIONEERS OF SCIENCE AND TECHNOLOGY

Aristocrat Someone whose family has a high social rank, especially someone who has a title, such as Duke or Baroness.

Asteroid A chunk of rock travelling through space.

Astronomy The study of the Sun, Moon, planets, stars and other objects in space.

Astrophysics The study of the physical and chemical structure of the stars, planets, and other objects in space.

Atom One of the tiny building blocks that make up all stuff.

Cells Small building blocks that make up living things.

Chromosome Structures in a living thing's cells that contain genes.

Comet A chunk of dust and ice that travels through space.

Constellation A pattern of stars in the night sky.

Coprolite Fossilised dinosaur poo.

DNA The acid in the cells of living things that carries genetic information.

Element A substance that is made up of only one type of atom.

Eulogy A speech or piece of writing praising a person who has died.

Fossil The shape of a plant or animal that has been preserved in rock for a very long time.

Gene A microscopic 'instruction' in a living thing's cells that determine what it will look like or how it will behave.

Geologist A scientist who studies rocks and fossils.

Geometry A branch of maths that looks at shapes and angles.

Hypothesis A scientific theory about why or how something happens.

Jew A person who believes in and practises the religion of Judaism. Jewish people were discriminated against by the Nazis in Europe in the 1920s and 1930s.

Leprosy An infectious disease that affects the skin and nerves.

Matter The scientific term for all stuff.

Nazi A member of the right-wing political party, led by Adolf Hitler, which was in power in Germany from 1933 to 1945.

Nebula (plural: nebulae) A cloud of dust and gas in space where new stars are formed.

Nuclear fission A scientific process where atoms, the tiny building blocks of all matter, are split into even tinier pieces releasing huge amounts of energy.

Orbit A curved path followed by a planet or an object as it moves around another object.

Pesticide A chemical that is used to kill insects that eat farmer's crops.

PhD The abbreviation for doctor of philosophy, the highest college or university degree.

Radioactive A word that describes a substance that gives off certain types of rays that can't be seen with the naked eye.

Refugee A person who has been forced to leave their country, because there is a war or because of their political or religious beliefs.

AMAZING ARTISTS AND DESIGNERS

Abolitionist A person who campaigned to have slavery made illegal.

Abstract A style of art that does not try to show things realistically, but focusses on colour, shape and ideas.

Austerity Policies put in place by the government to reduce spending, which involve cutting public services or lowering payments for people who can't work.

Avant-garde An art movement that uses new, experimental methods and ideas.

Bust A model of a person's head and neck.

Caricature A cartoon-like image that exaggerates someone's features.

Chiaroscuro A style of painting (and photography) that uses strong areas of light and shade.

Deconstructivist A style of architecture that has very unconventional shapes, and can give the appearance of the building being broken up or fragmented.

Establishment The people and organisations that hold the most power within a country.

Fracking A process through which fossil fuels (coal, oil, gas) are extracted from the ground.

Illiterate Unable to read and write.

Indigenous people The first peoples to settle a land.

Materialistic Overly concerned with money and expensive objects, rather than more important issues.

Modernism A broad art movement in Western society at the end of the 19th and early 20th centuries that often used simple abstract shapes.

Native American People from one of the many groups who were living in North and South America before Europeans arrived.

Naturalistic A style of painting that aims to show things close to how they look in real life, as opposed to abstract styles.

Nazi A member of the right-wing political party, led by Adolf Hitler, which was in power in Germany from 1933 to 1945.

Neoclassical An art style that uses designs from ancient Greek and Roman art.

Pedlar Someone who travels from place to place in order to sell things.

Pigment A coloured powder that is mixed with liquid to make paint.

Psychiatrist A doctor who studies and treats mental illnesses.

Retrospective An exhibition showing an artist's body of work from over a long period of time.

Seamstress A woman whose job is sewing and making clothes.

Slavery The system by which people are owned by other people as slaves.

Still life A painting or drawing of inanimate objects, such as fruit or flowers.

Surrealism An art movement that shows strange, dream-like scenes, inspired by the unconscious mind.

INCREDIBLE SPORTING CHAMPIONS

Aboriginal A word used to describe indigenous people from mainland Australia and Tasmania.

Australian Open A major tennis tournament held every year in Melbourne, Australia.

Commonwealth Games An international sporting event held every four years, featuring athletes from the Commonwealth of Nations, which is a group of countries that used to be part of the British Empire.

Croix de guerre A military medal awarded in France for acts of heroism involving combat with the enemy.

FIFA The international governing organisation for football, which organises big tournaments including the World Cup.

Grand Slam A set of major matches or tournaments in a particular sport in any given year.

Hijab A head covering worn in public by some Muslim women.

Indigenous (people) The people who first lived in a particular region, rather than people who arrived later in history from another place.

MBE/OBE British honours that are awarded to a person by the King or Queen for a particular achievement. An OBE is a higher honour than an MBE.

Olympic Games The world's foremost sporting event featuring over 200 nations, held every four years. They began in the late 19th century but were inspired by the ancient Olympic Games which was a sporting event held in Olympia, in ancient Greece.

Paralympic Games International sporting event for athletes with a range of disabilities, held every four years, immediately after the Olympic Games.

Polio An infectious disease that can cause paralysis.

Professional A person who does a sport as a paid job rather than as a hobby.

Stamina The physical or mental strength needed to do something difficult for long periods of time.

UEFA Europa League An annual football competition for European football clubs held since 1971.

Variety show An entertainment made up of multiple different acts, such as acrobatics, music, comedy and juggling.

Yin and yang An idea from Chinese philosophy that says the world contains two forces which are always opposite one another but also connected at the same time.

HEROIC LEADERS AND ACTIVISTS

Abolitionist movement A campaign in Europe and the USA in the 18th and 19th centuries to make slavery illegal.

Aboriginal people Indigenous people from mainland Australia.

Advocate Someone who argues on behalf of another person or group of people.

American Civil War A war fought in the USA from 1861 to 1865 between southern and northern states over issues such as the right to own slaves.

Census An official survey of the population of a country to find out how many people live there and to collect other information about them.

Democracy A system of government in which all the people of a country can vote to elect their representatives.

Feminism A belief that women should have the same rights as men.

Genus A category of something.

Governess A woman who was employed to look after and teach children in a private house.

Great Depression An economic event that occurred across many countries in the 1930s where businesses went bankrupt and many people were unemployed.

Ideology A set of political beliefs and ideas.

Indigenous people Descendants of people who have always lived in a particular area, as opposed to later immigrants and their descendants.

Islam The religion of Muslims.

League of Nations An organisation set up after the First World War to try and promote world peace through international negotiation.

Malnutrition Poor health caused by not having enough food or a healthy diet.

Morality The belief that some behaviour is right and acceptable and that other behaviour is wrong.

Nazi A member of the right-wing political party, led by Adolf Hitler, which was in power in Germany from 1933 to 1945.

Oppression Cruel or unjust treatment.

Pacifism The belief that violence is never justified.

Pamphlet A short book or leaflet containing arguments about a particular subject.

Philosophy The study of the nature and meaning of human life and of the universe.

Preacher A person who gives religious speeches.

Referendum A vote to decide a specific political question.

Seamstress A woman who makes a living from sewing.

Segregation A historical set of laws in the USA ruling that black and white people had to use different services and facilities such as schools or drinking fountains.

Suffrage The right to vote.

Treason The crime of betraying your country.

United Nations An international organisation formed in 1945 to try and improve human rights around the world and maintain peace.

FURTHER INFORMATION

PIONEERS OF SCIENCE AND TECHNOLOGY

WEBSITES

For a large selection of citizen science projects visit this platform for people-powered research. **www.zooniverse.org**

The Big Bang Competition is an annual science competition for young people. **www.thebigbangfair.co.uk**

Check out a list of science festivals in the UK at the British Science Association website. **www.britishscienceassociation.org/uk-science-festivals-network-members**

BOOKS

Women in Science: 50 Fearless Pioneers Who Changed the World by Rachel Ignotofsky (Wren & Rook, 2017)

Good Night Stories for Rebel Girls by Elena Favilli and Francesca Cavallo (Particular Books, 2017)

Fantastically Great Women Who Changed the World by Kate Pankhurst (Bloomsbury, 2016)

Scientists Who Made History series (Wayland, 2014)

Girls Think of Everything by Catherine Thimmesh (Houghton Mifflin, 2002)

AMAZING ARTISTS AND DESIGNERS

WEBSITES

Check out the Tate galleries' kids' website for lots of ideas for fun and crafty activities that could be done at home or in an art club setting. **kids.tate.org.uk/create**

Art charity National Open Art runs a competition for young people in the UK and Ireland aged up to 14 years. **www.nationalopenart.org/children.php**

Find out about American artist Aminah Brenda Lynn Robinson and create your own art. **aminahsworld.org**

BOOKS

The Story of Paintings by Mick Manning and Brita Granström (Franklin Watts, 2017)

13 Women Artists Children Should Know by Bettina Schümann (Prestel, 2017)

INCREDIBLE SPORTING CHAMPIONS

WEBSITES

Find out more about sports you haven't tried before on this BBC website.
bbc.co.uk/sport/get-inspired

Check out the Park Run website for details of junior park runs and wheelchair races around the country and see if there is an event near you.
parkrun.org.uk/events/juniorevents

Read inspiring stories and get some great ideas about different ways you can get active as part of the This Girl Can campaign. **www.thisgirlcan.co.uk**

BOOKS

Women in Sport by Rachel Ignotofsky (Wren and Rook, 2018)

Olympic Expert by Paul Mason (Wayland, 2016)

HEROIC LEADERS AND ACTIVISTS

WEBSITES

The BBC Children in Need, Save the Children and Unicef websites have lots of ideas for how to raise money for important causes.
bbcchildreninneed.co.uk/fundraisinghub
www.savethechildren.org.uk/how-you-can-help/events-and-fundraising
www.unicef.org.uk/fundraise/fundraise-in-your-community/at-school

Change.org is a website that allows you to set up and share a petition online.
www.change.org

Contact your local MP or politician to let them know about a problem affecting people in your local area or to ask for their support on a particular campaign that you feel strongly about.
www.parliament.uk/get-involved/contact-your-mp

BOOKS

Rebel Voices: The Rise of Votes for Women by Louise Kay Stewart and Eve Lloyd Knight (Wren and Rook, 2018)

This Book Will Help You Change the World by Sue Turton and Alice Skinner (Wren and Rook, 2017)

Suffragettes and the Fight for the Vote by Sarah Ridley (Franklin Watts, 2017)

I am Malala (young readers edition) by Malala Yousafzai and Patricia McCormick (Orion Children's Books, 2014)

INDEX

INDEX CONTINUED

First published in Great Britain in 2019 by Wayland
Copyright © Hodder and Stoughton, 2019

The material in this book has previously been published in the following titles: Brilliant Women: Amazing Artists and Designers; Brilliant Women: Heroic Leaders and Activists; Brilliant Women: Incredible Sporting Champions; Brilliant Women: Pioneers of Science and Technology.

All rights reserved.

Editor: Sarah Silver
Designer: Lisa Peacock

Wayland, an imprint of Hachette Children's Group
Part of Hodder & Stoughton
Carmelite House
50 Victoria Embankment
London EC4Y 0DZ

ISBN: 978 1 5263 1211 2

10 9 8 7 6 5 4 3 2 1

Printed and bound in China

MIX
Paper from responsible sources
FSC® C104740

An Hachette UK Company
www.hachette.co.uk
www.hachettechildrens.co.uk

ROCK MECHANICS: CAVERNS AND PRESSURE SHAFTS

FELSMECHANIK: KAVERNEN UND DRUCKSCHÄCHTE

MÉCANIQUE DES ROCHES: LES CAVERNES ET LES PUITS SOUS PRESSION

3

KV-638-575

ISRM SYMPOSIUM / AACHEN / 1982.05.26-28

ROCK MECHANICS: CAVERNS AND PRESSURE SHAFTS

FELSMECHANIK: KAVERNEN UND DRUCKSCHÄCHTE

MÉCANIQUE DES ROCHES: LES CAVERNES ET LES PUITS SOUS PRESSION

Editor / Redakteur / Rédacteur

W. WITTKE

Institut für Grundbau, Bodenmechanik, Felsmechanik und Verkehrswasserbau, Aachen

VOLUME 3

Conference Events / List of Participants /
Papers which could not be printed in volumes 1 and 2
Tagungsablauf / Teilnehmerverzeichnis /
Fachbeiträge, die in den Bänden 1 und 2 nicht berücksichtigt werden konnten
Déroulement du symposium / Liste de participants /
Communications n'ayant pu être publiées dans les tomes 1 et 2

Published for / Herausgegeben für / Publié pour
Deutsche Gesellschaft für Erd- und Grundbau e.V., Essen

A.A.BALKEMA / ROTTERDAM / BOSTON / 1984

05925990

The texts of the various papers in this volume were set individually by typists under the supervision of each of the authors concerned

For the complete set of three volumes, ISBN 90 6191 232 6
For Volume 1, ISBN 90 6191 233 4
For Volume 2, ISBN 90 6191 234 2
For Volume 3, ISBN 90 6191 235 0

© 1984 A.A.Balkema, P.O.Box 1675, Rotterdam, Netherlands

Distributed in USA & Canada by: A.A.Balkema Publishers, P.O.Box 230, Accord, MA 02018
Published for the Deutsche Gesellschaft für Erd- und Grundbau e.V., 4300 Essen 1, Kronprinzenstrasse 35a

Printed in the Netherlands

D
624.1513
Roc

ISRM SYMPOSIUM / AACHEN / 1982.05.26-28

ROCK MECHANICS RELATED TO CAVERNS AND PRESSURE SHAFTS
FELSMECHANIK IN VERBINDUNG MIT KAVERNEN UND DRUCKSCHÄCHTEN
MÉCANIQUE DES ROCHES EN LIAISON AVEC LES CAVERNES ET LES PUITS SOUS PRESSION

CHAIRMAN / VORSITZENDER / PRÉSIDENT

Prof. Dr.-Ing. W. Wittke	President of the International Society for Rock Mechanics Präsident der Internationalen Gesellschaft für Felsmechanik Président de la Société Internationale de Mécanique des Roches

ADVISORY COMMITTEE / BEIRAT / COMITÉ DE PATRONAGE

Direktor H. Heiderhoff	Vorstandsmitglied des Rheinisch-Westfälischen Elektrizitätswerkes AG, Essen
Dr.-Ing. W. Krabbe	Vorstandsmitglied der Philipp Holzmann AG, Frankfurt
Direktor L. Meyer	Geschäftsführer, Lahmeyer International GmbH, Frankfurt
Prof. Dr.-Ing. K. Roske	Kreditanstalt für Wiederaufbau, Frankfurt

SCIENTIFIC COMMITTEE / WISSENSCHAFTLICHER BEIRAT / COMITÉ SCIENTIFIQUE

Prof. Dr.-Ing. H. Blind	Lehrstuhl für Wasserbau und Wassermengenwirtschaft, TU München
Prof. Dr. K.H. Heitfeld	Lehrstuhl für Ingenieurgeologie und Hydrogeologie, RWTH Aachen
Prof. Dr.-Ing. H.J. Kayser	Lehrstuhl für Strassenwesen, Erd- und Tunnelbau, RWTH Aachen
Prof. Dr.-Ing. G. Rouvé	Lehrstuhl für Wasserbau und Wasserwirtschaft, RWTH Aachen

ORGANIZING COMMITTEE / ORGANISATIONSKOMITTEE / COMITÉ D'ORGANISATION

Dipl.-Ing. S. Babendererde	Leiter der Zentralen Tiefbauabteilung der Hochtief AG, Essen
Prof. Dr.-Ing. K.H. Idel	Geschäftsführer der Deutschen Gesellschaft für Erd- und Grundbau e.V., Essen
Prof. Dr. M. Langer	Bundesanstalt für Geowissenschaften und Rohstoffe, Hannover
Dr. R. Wolters †	Generalsekretär der Internationalen Vereinigung für Ingenieurgeologie, Krefeld

Assistance at the organization: / Mitwirkung bei der Organisation: / Organisé avec le concours de:

Mitarbeiter des Instituts für Grundbau, Bodenmechanik, Felsmechanik und Verkehrswasserbau, RWTH Aachen

CONTENTS / INHALT / TABLE DES MATIÈRES

CONFERENCE EVENTS / TAGUNGSABLAUF / DEROULEMENT DU SYMPOSIUM

PAPERS / FACHBEITRÄGE / CONTRIBUTIONS

1 PART / TEIL / PARTIE

Rock mechanical investigation programs for large caverns in rock masses
Felsmechanische Untersuchungsprogramme für grosse Felskavernen
Programmes de recherches en mécanique des roches dans le cas de cavernes rocheuses de grandes dimensions

4 PART / TEIL / PARTIE

Limitation of the applicability of tunnel boring machines as seen from the rock mechanical point of view
Einsatzgrenzen von Tunnelvortriebsmaschinen aus felsmechanischer Sicht
Limites d'emploi de foreuses pour le creusement de tunnels, du point de vue de la mécanique des roches

CONFERENCE EVENTS

TAGUNGSABLAUF

DEROULEMENT DU SYMPOSIUM

PROGRAM / PROGRAMM / PROGRAMME

WEDNESDAY / MITTWOCH / MERCREDI, 26.05.1982

	EUROPA SAAL
8.15 h	Opening session and honours Eröffnung und Ehrungen Séance d'ouverture et hommage
9.30 h	Rock mechanical investigation programs for large caverns in rock masses Felsmechanische Untersuchungsprogramme für grosse Felskavernen Programmes de recherches en mécanique des roches dans le cas de cavernes rocheuses de grandes dimensions Chairman / Leitung / Direction: Prof. K.H. HEITFELD *Lehrstuhl für Ingenieurgeologie und Hydrogeologie, RWTH Aachen, Bundesrepublik Deutschland*
10.45 h	Underground caverns with large span Untertägige Hohlräume mit grosser Spannweite Cavités souterraines de grandes portées Chairman / Leitung / Direction: Prof. L. MÜLLER-SALZBURG *Ing. Büro für Tunnel- und Felsbau GmbH Müller-Hereth, Freilassing, Bundesrepublik Deutschland*
14.15 h	Underground caverns with large span Untertägige Hohlräume mit grosser Spannweite Cavités souterraines de grandes portées Chairman / Leitung / Direction: Dr. E. BROCH *The Norwegian Institute of Technology, Trondheim, Norway*
	BRÜSSEL SAAL
14.15 h	Rock mechanical investigation programs for large caverns in rock masses Felsmechanische Untersuchungsprogramme für grosse Felskavernen Programmes de recherches en mécanique des roches dans le cas de cavernes rocheuses de grandes dimensions Chairman / Leitung / Direction: Prof. S. URIEL ROMERO *Laboratorio del Transporte y Mecánica del Suelo, Madrid, Spain*

THURSDAY / DONNERSTAG / JEUDI, 27.05.1982

	EUROPA SAAL
8.15 h	Underground caverns with large span Untertägige Hohlräume mit grosser Spannweite Cavités souterraines de grandes portées Chairman / Leitung / Direction: Dr. M. YOSHIDA *Kansai Electric Power Co., Osaka, Japan*

10.15 h — Load sharing capacity of the rock mass for pressure tunnels and shafts
Mittragende Wirkung des Gebirges bei Druckstollen und Druckschächten
Effet de la portance du terrain dans le cas des galeries forcées et des puits sous pression
Chairman / Leitung / Direction:
Prof. H. BLIND
Lehrstuhl für Wasserbau und Wassermengenwirtschaft, TU München, Bundesrepublik Deutschland

14.00 h — Underground caverns with large span
Untertägige Hohlräume mit grosser Spannweite
Cavités souterraines de grandes portées
Chairman / Leitung / Direction:
A. ZAGARS
Harza Engineering Comp., Chicago, USA

BRÜSSEL SAAL

14.00 h — Load sharing capacity of the rock mass for pressure tunnels and shafts
Mittragende Wirkung des Gebirges bei Druckstollen und Druckschächten
Effet de la portance du terrain dans le cas des galeries forcées et des puits sous pression
Chairman / Leitung / Direction:
Prof. H.R. HARDY, Jr.
Pennsylvania State University, University Park, USA

FRIDAY / FREITAG / VENDREDI, 28.05.1982

EUROPA SAAL

8.00 h — Rock mechanical problems in association with underground storage
Felsmechanische Probleme im Zusammenhang mit der untertägigen Speicherung
Problèmes de mécanique des roches en relation avec le stockage souterrain
Chairman / Leitung / Direction:
Prof. H.J. KAYSER
Lehrstuhl für Strassenwesen, Erd- und Tunnelbau, RWTH Aachen, Bundesrepublik Deutschland

9.40 h — Limitation of the applicability of tunnel boring machines as seen from the rock mechanical point of view
Einsatzgrenzen von Tunnelvortriebsmaschinen aus felsmechanischer Sicht
Limites d'emploi de foreuses pour le creusement de tunnels, du point de vue de la mécanique des roches
Chairman / Leitung / Direction:
Prof. G. GIRNAU
Präsident der International Tunnelling Association (ITA), Köln, Bundesrepublik Deutschland

11.00 h — Panel discussion
Podiumdiskussion
Colloque
Chairman / Leitung / Direction:
Dr. W. KRABBE
Philipp Holzmann AG, Frankfurt, Bundesrepublik Deutschland

14.00 h — Rock mechanical problems in association with underground storage
Felsmechanische Probleme im Zusammenhang mit der untertägigen Speicherung
Problèmes de mécanique des roches en relation avec le stockage souterrain
Chairman / Leitung / Direction:
Dr. B. GILG
Elektrowatt Ingenieurunternehmung AG, Zürich, Schweiz

BRÜSSEL SAAL

14.00 h — Limitation of the applicability of tunnel boring machines as seen from the rock mechanical point of view
Einsatzgrenzen von Tunnelvortriebsmaschinen aus felsmechanischer Sicht
Limites d'emploi de foreuses pour le creusement de tunnels, du point de vue de la mécanique des roches
Chairman / Leitung / Direction:
Prof. A. EBER
Institut für Bauingenieurwesen IV, TU München, Bundesrepublik Deutschland

EUROPA SAAL

16.30 h — Closing session / Schlussitzung / Séance de clôture

OPENING SESSION AND HONOURS
ERÖFFNUNG UND EHRUNGEN
SÉANCE D'OUVERTURE ET HOMMAGE

DR. ING. W. KRABBE
Stellvertretender Vorsitzender der Deutschen Gesellschaft für Erd- und Grundbau e. V. (DGEG)
Deputy Chairman of the German Geotechnical Society (DGEG)
Président représentant la Société Allemande des Travaux de Terrassements et de Fondations (DGEG)

Meine sehr geehrten Damen, meine Herren!

Im Namen der Deutschen Gesellschaft für Erd- und Grundbau heiße ich Sie zum Internationalen Symposium "Felsmechanik in Verbindung mit Kavernen und Druckschächten" in Aachen herzlich willkommen.

Unsere Gesellschaft hatte immer eine Vielzahl profilierter Persönlichkeiten auf den Gebieten der Geologie, der Fels- und Bodenmechanik sowie des Grundbaus als Mitglieder. Deshalb widmet sie sich auch den entsprechenden Fachthemen und bemüht sich, den Gedankenaustausch unter den Fachkollegen im Rahmen von Tagungen zu beleben. Neben der Baugrundtagung, die den Mitgliedern aller bei uns vertretenen Sektionen etwas bieten soll, dienen die Fachtagungen der einzelnen Sektionen der Vertiefung in den jeweiligen speziellen Bereichen. Wir freuen uns, daß mit dem heute beginnenden Symposium die Reihe dieser anspruchsvollen Fachtagungen fortgesetzt wird.

Unser besonderer Dank gilt Herrn Prof. Dr. Wittke, der schon seit mehr als zehn Jahren als Leiter der Fachsektion Felsmechanik dem Vorstand der Deutschen Gesellschaft für Erd- und Grundbau angehört und zur Zeit ebenfalls Präsident der Internationalen Gesellschaft für Felsmechanik ist. Wir danken ihm, daß es ihm gelungen ist, die Schirmherrschaft der Internationalen Gesellschaft für Felsmechanik für dieses Symposium zu gewinnen und ein vielseitiges und ansprechendes Programm vorzubereiten. Sicherlich ist es auch seiner persönlichen Arbeit und seinem Erfolg auf nationalem und internationalem Gebiet zuzuschreiben, daß soviel profilierte Fachleute als Referenten oder auch als Zuhörer hierher nach Aachen gekommen sind. Es haben sich etwa 500 Teilnehmer aus 40 verschiedenen Ländern angemeldet, um sich aus 130 Beiträgen aus 25 Ländern informieren zu lassen. Sie werden Verständnis dafür haben, daß ich nicht alle Damen und Herren einzeln begrüßen kann, es seien mir aber einige wenige Ausnahmen gestattet. So begrüße ich sehr herzlich den Bürgermeister der Stadt Aachen, Herrn Gläßer, der anschließend einige Begrüßungsworte an uns richten wird. Ebenso begrüße ich den Prorektor der Rheinisch-Westfälischen Technischen Hochschule in Aachen, Herrn Prof. Dr. Eversheim, der die Grüße der hiesigen Hochschule überbringt. Weiterhin ist es mir eine Freude, den Herrn Präsidenten, fünf Vizepräsidenten und den Generalsekretär, also die gesamte Führungsspitze der Internationalen Gesellschaft für Felsmechanik, hier willkommen zu heißen. Und zusätzlich eine größere Anzahl von Präsidenten befreundeter Fachverbände. Ich möchte Herrn Prof. Wittke, aber auch seinen Mitarbeitern, den herzlichen Dank der Deutschen Gesellschaft für Erd- und Grundbau für die Vorarbeiten zu diesem Symposium aussprechen. Herr Wittke, Sie haben bereits ein zweites Mal diese Mühe auf sich genommen, denn schon 1972 luden Sie zu einem Internationalen Symposium nach Stuttgart ein, das damals das Thema trug "Durchströmung von klüftigem Fels".

Die Internationale Gesellschaft für Felsmechanik besteht 20 Jahre, nachzulesen hier vorne auf dem Podium, ein willkommener Anlaß jetzt und hier die herzlichen Glückwünsche auszusprechen und auch für die Zukunft eine weitere erfolgreiche Tätigkeit zu wünschen.

Ich muß sicherlich im Kreis von Fachkollegen nicht begründen, daß eine Beschäftigung mit den Themen der Felsmechanik im Hinblick auf Planung und Bau sinnvoll und notwendig ist. Gerade die weltweite Verknappung und Verteuerung der Energie führt zu vielen neuen Objekten bei der Nutzung der Wasserkraft oder zur Lagerung von Öl, Gas und Abfällen. In all diesen Fällen spielen felsmechanische Arbeiten eine ausschlaggebende Rolle. Die zunehmende Mechanisierung bei der Herstellung dieser Bauwerke bringt in gleicher Weise viele Fragen an den Felsmechaniker hervor. Das Programm dieses Symposiums trägt diesen vielfältigen Problemen Rechnung und bietet sicherlich eine Fülle von neuen Anregungen.

Warum Aachen als Tagungsort eine gute Wahl war, dazu wird Herr Bürgermeister Gläßer sicher anschließend noch etwas sagen. Daß ein Tagungsort in Deutschland angebracht scheint, ist durch die vielseitige Tätigkeit deutscher Ingenieure und Firmen an Planung und Bau entsprechender Objekte im In- und Ausland begründet. Dabei glauben wir Deutschen sicher nicht, alles allein und besser als andere zu können. Unser Respekt gilt selbstverständlich unseren ausländischen Fachkollegen sowie der internationalen Unternehmerkonkurrenz. Beide betrachten wir als unsere Partner bei der Lösung der vielseitigen Ingenieurprobleme.

Meine Begrüßung beende ich mit den besten Wünschen für das Gelingen dieses Symposiums, das hiermit eröffnet ist. Ich danke Ihnen.

Musikalische Eröffnung des Symposiums durch das Kurorchester Aachen.

Musical opening to the symposium by Aachen's Spa Orchestra.

Ouverture musicale du symposium par l'orchestre de cure d'Aix-la-Chapelle.

DIPL. ING. C. GLÄSSER
Bürgermeister der Stadt Aachen
Mayor of the City of Aachen
Maire de la ville d'Aix-la-Chapelle

Herr Vorsitzender, meine sehr verehrten Damen und Herren!

Mit der Internationalen Gesellschaft für Felsmechanik begrüßen wir heute in Aachen eine wissenschaftliche Vereinigung, die mit mehr als 5000 Mitgliedern aus über 40 Ländern inzwischen Weltruf genießt. Wir in Aachen sind sehr froh darüber, daß in diesem Jahr in der alten Kaiserstadt ein Internationales Symposium stattfindet. Dem Veranstalter gratuliere ich zu dem ausgewählten Vortragsprogramm, das mit den aufgegriffenen Themen das Interesse so vieler Fachleute aus zahlreichen Ländern getroffen hat. Dieses Symposium steht unter dem Thema "Felsmechanik in Verbindung mit Kavernen und Druckschächten". Indirekt sind mit diesem Thema brennende Fragen unserer Zeit angesprochen, nämlich beispielhaft die Probleme der Energieversorgung und -gewinnung oder die Endlagerung und Entsorgung von Abfallstoffen. Die Felsmechaniker leisten die wissenschaftliche Voraussetzung für die Nutzung von Naturräumen, die in ihren felsmechanischen Belastungsgrenzen und Möglichkeiten genauestens erforscht werden müssen. Sie sind für einige Tage in diesem Eurogress in der Kongreßhalle der Stadt Aachen. Nicht nur diese Halle soll für Sie ein würdiger Rahmen sein, sondern ich bin überzeugt, daß auch die Stadt für Sie in diesen Tagen ein angenehmer Tagungsort sein wird. Wenn auch die Geschichte dieser Stadt, nämlich als Stadt Karls des Großen oder als Krönungsstadt von 30 deutschen Königen, den Namen Aachens geprägt hat, so gibt es doch auch eine Reihe von gegenwärtigen, markanten Faktoren, die diese Stadt attraktiv machen. Mehr als 30 000 Studenten, die die Technische Hochschule Aachen besuchen, zu der Rat und Verwaltung dieser Stadt ein außerordentlich gutes Verhältnis haben, prägen das Bild dieser Stadt mit. Eine breite Palette industrieller und gewerblicher Unternehmen, darunter auch einige internationale Konzerne wie der französische Glaskonzern St. Gobain oder Philipps sind Garanten für Arbeitsplätze der Menschen in dieser Stadt. Aachener Tuche gehen in alle Welt und mehr als 50 % der Kakaoeinfuhr nach Deutschland werden von Aachener Süßwarenkonzernen verarbeitet. Aachener Printen genießen einen guten Ruf und Nadeln aus Aachen werden in vielfältiger Form in viele Länder exportiert. Diese Tagung, dieses Symposium ist eine internationale Veranstaltung und vielleicht sei zum Schluß noch ein Gedanke angesprochen, nämlich der, daß auch diese Stadt eine internationale Stadt ist. Die Stadt Aachen ist gelegen an den Grenzen zu den beiden Nachbarländern Belgien und Niederlande. Zwei Drittel der Stadtgrenze sind auch gleichzeitig Bundesgrenze zu diesen beiden Nachbarländern hin. Das ist verbunden mit einigen Problemen, mit wirtschaftlichen Problemen. Die Entwicklung dieser Stadt ist durch diese Grenze, auch wenn es Grenzen geworden sind, die heute leichter passierbar sind, eng begrenzt. Aber diese Grenzlage ist auch eine Chance dieser Stadt, die diese Stadt im Laufe ihrer Geschichte vielfältig wahrgenommen hat, nämlich die Pflege zu den Menschen jenseits der Grenze, zu un-

seren befreundeten Nachbarländern hin. Ich glaube, nicht nur die Karlspreisverleihung vor 8 Tagen in dieser Stadt, sondern gerade das internationale Geschehen in dieser Stadt könnte auch Sie beeindrucken und ich hoffe, daß auch Sie in diesen Tagen von dieser Internationalität und von dem Willen nach Einheit in Europa in dieser Stadt einige Impulse bemerken werden.
Ich wünsche dem Veranstalter einen guten Verlauf dieser Tagung. Allen, die als Dozenten oder als Hörer an dieser Veranstaltung teilnehmen, wünsche ich, daß sie mit Erfolgen und mit neuem Gedankengut wieder in ihre Heimat, an ihre Arbeitsstelle zurückkehren. Ich hoffe, daß Ihnen der Aufenthalt in dieser Stadt angenehm sein wird. Vielleicht wird das gute Wetter, das wir heute morgen hier begrüßen können, das seinige dazu tun.
Ich danke Ihnen für Ihre Aufmerksamkeit.

Der "Eurogress" in Aachen - Kommunikationsort für über 450 Fachleute aus 40 verschiedenen Ländern.

"Eurogress" in Aachen - location for exchange between more than 450 specialists from 40 countries.

"L'Eurogress" à Aix-la-Chapelle, lieu de communication pour plus de 450 spécialistes de 40 pays différents.

PROF. DR. ING. W. EVERSHEIM
Prorektor der RWTH Aachen
Pro-rector of the Aachen Technical University
Prorektor de l'université RWTH d'Aix-la-Chapelle

Herr Vorsitzender, Herr Präsident, meine sehr verehrten Damen und Herren!

In Vertretung seiner Magnifizenz, des Rektors der Rheinisch-Westfälischen Technischen Hochschule Aachen, eröffne ich hiermit als dritter Redner dieses Kolloquium über Felsmechanik in Verbindung mit Kavernen und Druckschächten. Ich tue dies mit gemischten Gefühlen, einerseits mit dem Gefühl des Bedauerns, daß ich seine Magnifizenz wegen anderweitiger politischer Geschäfte entschuldigen muß. Sie wissen, daß wir um die Neustrukturierung in dieser Hochschule ringen. Ich tue es auf der anderen Seite mit dem Ausdruck der Freude, daß durch diese Entschuldigung nun ich als Ingenieur Gelegenheit habe, ein derartiges Kolloquium zu eröffnen.

Wenn man das Tagungsprogramm durchsieht, mit namhaften Rednern aus sehr vielen Ländern, dann kommt zum Ausdruck, daß mit einer Veranstaltung wie der heutigen wiederum ein Akzent gesetzt wird in den Fragen der Ingenieurwissenschaften. Wenn auch die Felsmechanik noch eine relativ junge Disziplin ist, wie ich bei dem Studium der Akten als Maschinenbauer lernen konnte, so ist sie jedoch ein typisches Betätigungsfeld für die Ingenieurwissenschaften, da sie mehrere Disziplinen umfaßt und gewisse Analogien, z.B. zu der Forschung in der Medizin, zuläßt. Wir haben auf der einen Seite die Naturgebilde, die Randbedingungen, die uns die Natur vorgibt, und auf der anderen Seite versuchen wir eben diese Beschaffenheiten zu nutzen, um sie für Wasserkraftanlagen, für Ablagerungen, für Tunnelbauten usw. dienstbar zu machen. Wir müssen uns in der Wissenschaft durch Diagnose, durch Untersuchung, durch Versuche immer mehr Wissen über das, was uns der Boden vorgibt, verschaffen. Wir müssen untersuchen, ob es Gesetzmäßigkeiten gibt, damit wir, wenn wir die Gesetzmäßigkeiten gefunden haben, eine Therapie entwickeln können, wie wir baulich derartige Randbedingungen nutzen können. Also ein typisches Gebiet für interdisziplinäre Zusammenarbeit, was wir insbesondere an dieser Rheinisch-Westfälischen Technischen Hochschule begrüßen und fördern, damit wir nicht in den Fachdisziplinen alleine stecken bleiben.

Mit derartigen Veranstaltungen ist aber neben dem Austausch der wissenschaftlichen Erkenntnisse und Erfahrungen auch verbunden die Weitergabe des Wissens, der Erkenntnisse an andere Fachkollegen und insbesondere natürlich an unseren Ingenieurnachwuchs. Und mit einer solchen Veranstaltung ist drittens verbunden ein nicht unerheblicher Aufwand an Vorbereitung, wie Sie sicherlich alle teilweise ersehen oder zumindest erahnen können. Ich weiß selber - wir veranstalten derartige Kolloquien in Abständen von 3 Jahren - Herr Kollege Wittke, daß in den letzten Tagen und Nächten vor einer solchen Veranstaltung in den Instituten wahre Wunder geschehen, damit Dinge fertig werden oder noch gerichtet werden, die man sich einige Tage vorher nicht hat erträumen lassen. Insofern beglückwünsche ich Sie auch zu Ihren Mitarbeiterinnen und Mitarbeitern, daß

Sie derartiges hier auf die Beine gestellt haben, und ich darf diese Glückwünsche verbinden mit der Hoffnung, daß wir auch an dieser Stelle ein Scherflein dazu beitragen, unseren Nachwuchs so zu prägen, daß er nicht nur in Anspruchsdenken verfällt, sondern sich darauf besinnt, daß jeder von uns einen entsprechenden Beitrag in unserer Volkswirtschaft zu leisten hat.

In diesem Sinne, daß es Ihnen gelingen möge, einerseits Ihre Erkenntnisse hier auszutauschen und weiter auszubauen, daß es Ihnen gelingen möge, junge Menschen zum Wohle unserer Volkswirtschaft zu motivieren und insbesondere aber auch natürlich zur Mehrung des Rufes unserer Rheinisch-Westfälischen Technischen Hochschule Aachen beizutragen, wünsche ich Ihnen und den Veranstaltern vollen Erfolg für die nächsten drei Tage.

Ehrung der ehemaligen Präsidenten der Internationalen Gesellschaft für Felsmechanik (ISRM) durch den amtierenden Präsidenten Prof. W. Wittke
Honouring of the former Presidents of the International Society for Rock Mechanics (ISRM) by the President in office, Prof. W. Wittke
Hommage aux anciens présidents de la Société Internationale de Mécanique des Roches (ISRM) par le président en fonction Prof. W. Wittke

Meine sehr geehrten Damen und Herren!

Vor 20 Jahren, das war im Jahre 1962, wurde unsere Gesellschaft gegründet. Sie hat sich zur Aufgabe gesetzt, die internationale Zusammenarbeit auf dem damals und wohl auch heute noch vergleichsweise jungen Wissensgebiet der Felsmechanik sowie die Lehre auf diesem Gebiet und auch die interdisziplinäre Zusammenarbeit mit den benachbarten Wissenschaften zu fördern.

Der Anlaß für die Gründung unserer Gesellschaft war - und ich habe dies zum Teil auch selbst während meiner damaligen Tätigkeit als Doktorand an der Universität Karlsruhe erfahren - die Notwendigkeit, große Aufgaben auf dem Gebiet des Baus von Wasserkraftanlagen und Verkehrswegen zu bewältigen. Denn bei der Felsmechanik handelt es sich um eine Ingenieurwissenschaft, deren Entwicklung - wie es für eine Ingenieurwissenschaft typisch ist - erst durch die Aufgaben, die sich aus der Praxis ergeben, angeregt wurde.

Sie können sich vorstellen, daß sich die Gründung unserer Gesellschaft nicht abrupt und plötzlich vollzogen hat, sondern daß einige Jahre der Vorbereitung sowie der Einsatz einzelner herausragender Persönlichkeiten auf unserem Fachgebiet hierfür erforderlich waren. Ich möchte an dieser Stelle daran erinnern, daß die Entwicklung der Felsmechanik in Salzburg ihren Ausgang genommen hat. Dies wurde uns erst wieder im letzten Jahr bewußt, als das Salzburger Kolloquium sein 30jähriges Jubiläum begehen konnte.

Aus diesem Grund sind wir sehr glücklich, daß wir am heutigen Morgen den Gründer und Förderer unserer Disziplin, Herrn Professor Leopold Müller, den ersten Präsidenten unserer Gesellschaft, begrüßen dürfen. Ich glaube das 20jährige Jubiläum unserer Gesellschaft ist ein würdiger Anlaß, ihm für seine Bemühungen und seinen Einsatz für unsere Gesellschaft zu danken. Diesem Einsatz haben wir es u.a. auch zu verdanken, daß neben Englisch und Französisch auch die deutsche Sprache zu einer offiziellen Sprache unserer Gesellschaft wurde und sie es bis heute geblieben ist.

Viele von Ihnen werden sich an den ersten Felsmechanik-Kongreß im Jahre 1966 in Lissabon als ein glanzvolles Ereignis, sowohl in wissenschaftlicher als auch gesellschaftlicher Hinsicht, erinnern. Dieser Kongreß war für mich der Anlaß, meine bis dahin vorrangige Neigung für das Gebiet der Bodenmechanik zu ändern und mich mehr der Felsmechanik zuzuwenden, ja sie sogar zu meiner Lebensaufgabe zu machen.

Auf diesem Kongreß in Lissabon wurde als Nachfolger von Leopold Müller unser sehr verehrter portugiesischer Kollege Manuel Rocha zum Präsidenten der Gesellschaft gewählt. Sein Elan und sein Organisationstalent bildeten die Voraussetzungen für eine weite Verbreitung der Felsmechanik. Dies wird besonders dadurch deutlich, daß während seiner 4jährigen Amtszeit die Zahl der Mitglieder von einigen Hundert auf ca. 5000 anstieg und sich die Zahl der Mitgliedsländer auf damals 38 erhöhte.

Ehrung der ehemaligen Präsidenten der ISRM durch den amtierenden Präsidenten Prof. W. Wittke.
Honouring of the former Presidents of the International Society for Rock Mechanics (ISRM) by the President in office, Prof. W. Wittke.
Hommage aux anciens présidents de l'ISRM par le président en fonction Prof. W. Wittke.

a) Prof. L. Müller, b) Mrs. M.T. Rocha (representing her late husband Prof. M. Rocha), c) Dr. L. Obert, d) Prof. P. Habib.

An dieser Stelle sollte auch erwähnt werden, daß Professor Manuel Rocha uns durch das Laboratório Nacional de Engenharia Civil in Lissabon die Möglichkeit geschaffen hat, auf ein permanentes Sekretariat zurückzugreifen. Den beiden Generalsekretären Dr. Ricardo de Oliveira und Dr. Arnaldo Silvério, die ebenfalls beide heute morgen unter uns sind, möchte ich sehr herzlich für ihren langjährigen großen Einsatz danken. Was wäre eine Gesellschaft ohne ihren Generalsekretär? Auf einen Präsidenten könnte man notfalls noch verzichten, auf einen Generalsekretär jedoch nicht!

Im Jahre 1970 wurde der zweite Felsmechanik-Kongreß in Belgrad - ein nicht minder glanzvolles Ereignis - von Professor Kujundzić, der heute wegen einer Krankheit leider nicht unter uns sein kann, und seinen jugoslawischen Kollegen organisiert und durchgeführt. Hier ging die Präsidentschaft in die Hände unserer amerikanischen Freunde über. Zum Präsidenten wurde Dr. Leonard Obert aus den USA, den ich hier heute morgen auch recht herzlich willkommen heißen möchte, gewählt. Ihm fiel die Aufgabe zu, unsere Gesellschaft auf die amerikanischen Kontinente Nord und Süd auszudehnen und in eine Phase der Konsolidierung zu überführen. Seine Präsidentschaft endete im Jahre 1974 mit dem Kongreß in Denver, der wunderschönen Stadt in den Rocky Mountains, an den wir uns noch alle gern erinnern.

In Denver nahm unser französischer Kollege Pierre Habib, den ich heute morgen ebenfalls herzlich begrüßen möchte, die Geschicke unserer Gesellschaft in die Hand. Aus seiner Tätigkeit ist besonders hervorzuheben, daß es ihm gelang, auch unsere Freunde und Kollegen aus der UdSSR und der Volksrepublik China als Mitglieder zu gewinnen. Der vorläufig letzte Kongreß wurde im Jahre 1979 in Montreux, am herrlichen Genfer See, von unseren Schweizer Kollegen mit ihren umfassenden Erfahrungen auf dem Gebiet des Talsperren- und Tunnelbaus in den Alpen durchgeführt.

In diesem Jahr, zum 20jährigen Jubiläum unserer Gesellschaft, wollen wir nun unsere ehemaligen Präsidenten für ihre vielen Verdienste mit einer Plakette ehren und würdigen und ihnen für ihren langjährigen Einsatz und ihr Engagement für die Gesellschaft danken. Diese Plakette möge Sie, meine sehr verehrten Kollegen, jederzeit an Ihre enge auch weiterhin bestehende Verbindung zu unserer Gesellschaft erinnern.

EHRUNG DER EHEMALIGEN PRÄSIDENTEN

Sehr geehrter Herr Kollege Müller. Ich möchte Ihnen im Namen unserer Gesellschaft für Ihre viele Mühe und Ihren großen Einsatz recht herzlich danken. Ferner möchte ich die Bitte an Sie richten, Ihr Engagement für die Sache der Felsmechanik auch in Zukunft fortzusetzen und uns weiterhin zur Verfügung zu stehen. Vielen herzlichen Dank.

Sehr verehrte gnädige Frau Rocha. Wir sind alle sehr traurig, daß unser lieber Kollege Manuel Rocha im vergangenen Jahr, von einer schweren Krankheit getroffen, von uns gegangen ist. Wir verdanken ihm viel und ich darf Ihnen versprechen, daß wir ihn stets in Erinnerung behalten werden. Darf ich Sie, meine sehr geehrten Damen und Herren, bitten, sich von den Plätzen zu erheben und unseres Kollegen Rocha zu gedenken.

\- Gedenkminute -

Sehr verehrte Frau Rocha. Meine Kollegen von der Gesellschaft und ich freuen uns sehr, daß Sie unserer Einladung nach Aachen gefolgt sind und die Plakette an Ihres Mannes Stelle entgegennehmen. Vielen herzlichen Dank.

Sehr geehrter Herr Dr. Leonard Obert. Ich freue mich sehr, daß Sie zu diesem Symposium zu uns nach Aachen gekommen sind. Ich möchte meine Kollegen daran erinnern, daß Sie unser erster Präsident waren, der auf dem Gebiet des Bergbaus tätig ist. Dies bringt den interdisziplinären Charakter unserer Gesellschaft in besonderer Weise zum Ausdruck. Auch Ihnen recht herzlichen Dank für die Dienste, die Sie der Gesellschaft erwiesen haben.

Sehr geehrter Herr Kollege Pierre Habib. Da Sie ein Nachbar von uns sind, waren Sie schon oft in Aachen, aber ich freue mich diesmal ganz besonders, Ihnen für Ihre Verdienste für unsere Gesellschaft diese Plakette hier in Aachen überreichen zu dürfen. Vielen herzlichen Dank.

Abschließend möchte ich noch in einigen Sätzen auf die Zukunft unserer Gesellschaft eingehen. Ich glaube, daß die Aufgaben der Gegenwart und insbesondere die Aufgaben, vor denen wir in den nächsten Jahren stehen werden, nämlich der weiteren Erschließung der Wasserkraft, insbesondere in Asien und Südamerika, große Anstrengungen von uns fordern werden. Ebenso bin ich der Meinung, daß wir in den kommenden Jahren unsere verstärkte Aufmerksamkeit auf den Bergbau richten müssen. Dies hat bereits seinen Ausdruck in der Wahl unseres nächsten Kongreßortes Melbourne, in Australien, gefunden. Es werden dort Fragen der Felsmechanik im Zusammenhang mit bergbaulichen Aufgaben im Vordergrund stehen. Weitere Aufgaben der Felsmechanik für die Zukunft stellen die Erschließung der Rohstoffe und der Wasserkraft als Energiequelle, die Felsbauwerke größerer Dimensionen erfordern werden, sowie der Ausbau der Verkehrswege dar. Ich möchte in diesem Zusammenhang den Bau der Neubaustrecken für die Deutsche Bundesbahn mit ihren zahlreichen Tunnels, sowie die Pläne für die Untertunnelung des Ärmelkanals und der Straße von Gibraltar hervorheben.

Da nun das Symposium vor uns liegt, möchte ich meine besondere Freude darüber zum Ausdruck bringen, daß so viele Kollegen hierher in meine zweite Heimat gekommen sind. Dies ist für mich eine große Ehre und wir werden mit Unterstützung der Stadt Aachen, der Technischen Hochschule, sowie unserer Gesellschaft alles unternehmen, um Ihnen diesen Aufenthalt sowohl fachlich interessant als auch menschlich angenehm zu gestalten. Da auch, wie es scheint, das Wetter mitspielt, werden Sie in den Pausen und an den Abenden die schöne Umgebung des Kongreßzentrums genießen können. Ich darf Sie recht herzlich willkommen heißen.

MRS. M. T. ROCHA
Wife of the late ISRM-President Prof. M. Rocha
Gattin des verstorbenen ISRM-Präsidenten Prof. M. Rocha
La veuve du ancien président de la ISRM Prof. M. Rocha

Dear Friends,

Should my husband be here amongst so many distinguished colleagues and should he have been presented the 20th Anniversary Plaque I am now holding in my hands, I believe he would wish to express his warm appreciation of the success of the ISRM in carrying out the tasks he usually listed of an international association, namely:

1. to formulate in a systematic way the problems considered of greatest importance at the time,

2. to encourage and coordinate research,

3. to organize frequent meetings with well defined purposes,

4. to diffuse knowledge by the varied means at present available, and

5. to concern itself with promotion of the effective use of knowledge, aiming at the progress and welfare of humanity.

I think he would also seize the opportunity to stress how international collaboration between scientists must be envisaged not only as a means of speeding up the progress of knowledge, but also - he considered this just as important - as a contribution towards a better understanding between men. In fact, he strongly believed, above all, that the experience gained through personal contacts plays a fundamental part in the destruction of those diverse barriers separating people, which, as he saw it, are due to prejudice and reciprocal ignorance of the problems and conditions peculiar to each human group, rather than to conflict of real interests. He regarded the prodigious means which science is putting at the service of humanity as an indispensable basis for banishing bias from knowledge and understanding, thus allowing us a glimpse of that unity of the human race preached at all times by saints and philosophers. This is why, I guess, he would then exhort you to go on taking advantage of every possible area of understanding and convergence of interests, so that men may carry forward the art of reciprocal respect and understanding. Science, with its own mental attitude, that is, the scientific spirit, is contributing in a decisive manner to the creation of common mental attitudes and common points of view in Mankind. And this, he would add, is one of the fundamental conditions for men to build up their future together. Thus, we see science serving values which he considered even higher than the development of knowledge itself.

Finally, to conclude these words - a mere collage of sentences my husband voiced in his speeches - I am sure he would thank all of you most warmly for your treasured contribution to a common good cause.

Thank you.

Conferring of the ISRM Manuel Rocha Medal
Verleihung der Manuel Rocha-Medaille der ISRM
Remise de la plaquette Manuel Rocha de l'ISRM

DR. A. SILVERIO
Secretary General of the ISRM
Generalsekretär der ISRM
Le sécretaire général de l'ISRM

At the ISRM Board and Council Meetings 1981 the decision was made to create an award — a bronze medal and a cash prize — to be conferred annually by the International Society, in memory of Manuel Rocha. The award, to be presented at the technical meeting concurrent with the annual ISRM Council Meeting, is for an outstanding doctoral thesis in rock mechanics, accepted during two calendar years preceding conferment of the medal. Thus, the award will contribute to encourage rock mechanics research amongst the young, in line with Prof. Rocha's ideals.

The Manuel Rocha Medal, which will now be presented for the first time, is the work of a prominent Portuguese sculptor, Helder Batista, who teaches at the National School of Art, Lisbon, and is the winner of a number of competitions for medals of all sorts. The artist's concept was that Manuel Rocha excelled in the civil engineering uses of rock mechanics aiming at solutions far beyond traditional construction. This he conveyed in his plastic discourse by opposing natural, rough "rock mass" sections of the medal space to "man-made", smooth sections of the surface.

The medal reverse is the true realm of the rock mass, as shown by the supremacy of the corresponding area. Except at rare testing patches of simplified geometry, man-made shapes here look tentative and rather complex; they bear testimony to the rock engineer's struggle to adapt his structures — sometimes unusual — to the imperfectly known condition — often unfa

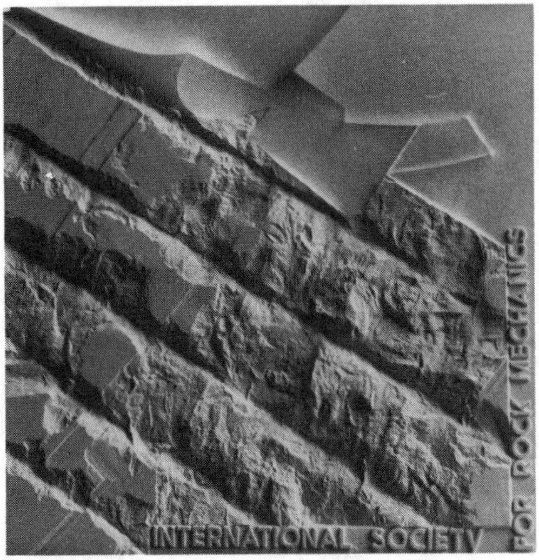

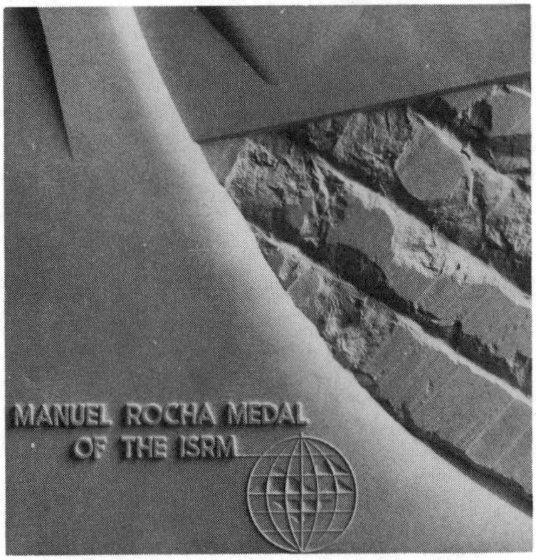

The Manuel Rocha Medal designed by the Portuguese artist Helder Batista.
Die von dem portugiesischen Künstler Helder Batista entworfene Manuel Rocha-Medaille.
La plaquette Manuel Rocha, créee par l'artiste portugais Helder Batista.

vourable — of their host rock masses. Obviously, the INTERNATIONAL SOCIETY FOR ROCK MECHANICS has a specific vocation for playing a major role at this research stage.

The medal anverse is the domain of Man, the Builder, with a predominance of structural elements as compared to rock outcrops. Once, through the agency of researchers like MANUEL ROCHA, sufficient understanding is gained of the rock mass behaviour, order creeps in to substitute for chaos; man-made shapes become simple, and flow over the medal surface with the elegance that is the watermark of accomplishment in structural design.

Ehrung des Manuel Rocha-Preisträgers durch den Präsidenten der ISRM Prof. W. Wittke
Honouring of the Manuel Rocha Prize-Winner by the President of the ISRM Prof. W. Wittke
Hommage du porteur de la plaquette Manuel Rocha par le président de l'ISRM Prof. W. Wittke

Der Vorstand und der Rat der ISRM hat beschlossen, mit der Manuel Rocha-Medaille alljährlich, anläßlich eines ISRM Symposiums oder Kongresses, einen jungen Wissenschaftler für eine hervorragende Arbeit auf dem Gebiet der Felsmechanik, eine Doktorarbeit, auszuzeichnen. Um diese Auszeichnung attraktiver zu gestalten und weil sich unsere Gesellschaft in einer guten finanziellen Situation befindet, haben wir uns entschlossen, mit der Verleihung der Rocha-Medaille auch einen Geldpreis in Höhe von 1000 US $ an den Preisträger zu vergeben. Da jedoch nur ein Kandidat diesen Preis erhalten kann, ist es sehr schwierig - ja eigentlich unmöglich - unter den verschiedenen aus aller Welt eingereichten Arbeiten die beste Doktorarbeit auszuwählen. Ich bin jedoch davon überzeugt, daß wir uns in diesem Jahr für eine der besten Arbeiten entschieden haben und freue mich, daß die Deutsche Gesellschaft für Erd- und Grundbau es ermöglicht hat, den Preisträger zu diesem Symposium einzuladen. Es ist mir eine große Ehre und zugleich eine Freude, die erste Manuel Rocha-Medaille an einen jungen Wissenschaftler zu verleihen, dessen Arbeit über lange Zeit von Professor Manuel Rocha persönlich betreut und gefördert wurde.

Ich möchte nun Herrn Dr. Antonio Pinto da Cunha zu mir bitten und die Manuel Rocha-Medaille für seine Doktorarbeit "Aplicação de models matemáticos ao estudo de túnlis maciços rochosos (auf Englisch: Mathematical modelling of rock tunnels)" entgegenzunehmen. Dr. da Cunha ist Mitarbeiter am Laboratório Nacional de Engenharia Civil in Lissabon und früherer Mitarbeiter von Manuel Rocha.

Dr. da Cunha, ich möchte Ihnen zum Gewinn des Preises gratulieren und Ihnen für Ihre zukünftige Arbeit alles Gute wünschen.

Verleihung der Manuel Rocha-Medaille an Dr. A.P. da Cunha durch Prof. W. Wittke.

Conferring of the Manuel Rocha Medal on Dr. A.P. da Cunha by Prof. W. Wittke.

Remise de la plaquette Manuel Rocha au Dr. A.P. da Cunha par le Prof. W. Wittke.

SOCIAL EVENTS
RAHMENPROGRAMM
PROGRAMME DES MANIFESTATIONS PARALLÈLES AU SYMPOSIUM

Mittwoch
Wednesday, 26.05.1982, 19.00 h
Mercredi

Reception given by the Lord Mayor of the City of Aachen in the "Krönungssaal", Coronation Hall, at the historic City Hall.

Empfang durch den Oberbürgermeister der Stadt Aachen im Krönungssaal des historischen Rathauses zu Aachen.

Accueil des participants par Monsieur le Maire de la ville d'Aix-la-Chapelle dans la Salle du Couronnement de l'hôtel de ville historique.

Lord Mayor K. Malangré welcomes symposium participants in the "Krönungssaal" at the historic City Hall.

Oberbürgermeister K. Malangré heißt die Teilnehmer des Symposiums im Krönungssaal des historischen Rathauses willkommen.

Monsieur le Maire K. Malangré souhaite la bienveune aux participants du symposium.

Members of the Board of the ISRM amongst the many present at the reception.

Mitglieder des ISRM-Vorstandes unter der zahlreichen Zuhörerschaft.

Membres du bureau de l'ISRM parmi les nombreux auditeurs.

Donnerstag
Thursday, 27.05.82, 20.00 h
Jeudi

ORGELKONZERT/ORGAN RECITAL/CONCERT D' ORGUE
IM HOHEN DOM ZU AACHEN

mit/with/avec

DOMORGANIST/CATHEDRAL ORGANIST/L' ORGANISTE DE LA CATHEDRALE
HERBERT VOSS

PROGRAMM/PROGRAM/PROGRAMME

Altitalienische und spanische Orgelmusik
Ancient Italian and Spanish Organ Music
Ancienne musique d'orgue italienne et espagnole

TOCCATA SESTA	H. Frescobaldi 1583 - 1643
PASTORALE	D. Zipoli 1688 - 1726
BATALLA IMPERIAL	J. Cabanilles 1644 - 1712

Altniederländische und französische Orgelmusik
Ancient Dutch and French Organ Music
Ancienne musique d'orgue hollandaise et francaise

ECHOFANTASIE IN A	J.P. Sweelinck 1562 - 1621
VIER VERSETTEN IM 1. TON	A.v.d. Kerckhoven 1627 - 1702
OFFERTOIRE SUR LES GRANDS JEUX	F. Couperin 1668 - 1733

Dom mit Elisengarten.
Aachen Cathedral.
La cathédrale d'Aix-la-Chapelle.

Der Barbarossaleuchter im Dom.
The chandelier of King Barbarossa in the Aachen Cathedral.
Le lustre du roi Barbarossa dans la cathédrale d'Aix-la-Chapelle.

Englische und deutsche Orgelmusik der Barockzeit
English and German Music from the Baroque Period
Musique anglaise et allemande tu temps baroque

CORNET-VOLUNTARY	J. Stanley 1713 - 1786
TRUMPET TUNE (eigentlich von J. Clarke 1659 - 1707)	H. Purcell ca. 1659 - 1695
KONZERT G-DUR (nach Herzog-Johann Ernst v. Sachsen-Weimar - BWV 592) Sätze: Vivace, Largo, Allegro	J.S. Bach 1685 - 1750

Orgelwerke deutscher und französischer Romantiker
Organ Music by German and French Romantic Composers
Musique d'orgue des romantiques allemands et françaises

MELUDIA	M. Reger 1873 - 1916
PIECE HEROIQUE	C. Franck 1822 - 1890
FREIE IMPROVISATION ÜBER "URBS AQUENSIS"	H. Voß 1922

Freitag
Friday, 28.05.1982, 20.00 h
Vendredi

Closing Banquet with Folklore and Musical Program
Festbankett mit folkloristischem Unterhaltungsprogramm
Banquet et programme de distraction folklorique

P R O F. O. M O R E T T O

ISRM-Vice-President for South America opens the banquet

Vize-Präsident der ISRM für Südamerika eröffnet das Festbankett

Le vice président de l'ISRM pour l'Amérique du Sud ouvre le banquet

Dear colleagues, ladies and gentlemen:

I habe been asked to open this banquet but, before conducting you to the buffet table, let me say a few words about the event that culminates tonight in what we expect will be a very nice evening.

The last three days we have been living in Aachen an event which I do not hesitate to qualify as outstanding.

It has been outstanding from the technical point of view, in the sense that we all have had an opportunity to update our knowledge about two important and highly complicated aspects of the civil engineering works necessary to develop hydraulic energy and to store underground, as do rock caverns and pressure shafts.

The contributions submitted to the Symposium and the presentations and discussions sustained during the technical sessions have brought forward all the important features that distinguish these types of works, which have been thoroughly analysed.

The development of the hydraulic energy is an event of the XX century made possible thanks to major technical advances in the civil, mechanical and electrical engineering sciences. Rock mechanics, together with soil mechanics, prestressed concrete and welding steel construction constitutes one of the major contributions made by the civil engineering science in the last fifty years. It is not by mere coincidence that rock mechanics developed in the second half of this century when the use of hydraulic energy acquired its great momentum. We engineers never say no to a challenge and rock mechanics became one. It was needed urgently to meet with adequate safety and minimum cost the requirements of hydraulic developments.

Hydropower will come to be known as a distinct development of the XX century because the available resources will be used up all over the world shortly after the end of this century. History will show that it came just in time to fill the gap between the times of abundant fossil fuels, particularly oil, and the times when new forms of energy will come into regular use. That is why those of us who devote their professional life to the development, design and construction of dams and hydraulic power stations can get the inner satisfaction that we are providing a particularly important service to the welfare of humanity, a sensation that gives a feeling of self gratification for the tasks we are fulfilling.

Development, design and construction of hydroelectric schemes is a multidisciplinary enterprise of which rock mechanics has become one of its very important branches. Within rock mechanics, caverns and pressure shaft constitute special challenges. They were met with professional efficiency and adequate imagination in the papers submitted to the Symposium and in the discussions presented during the sessions. That is why I feel that the Aachen Symposium will prove to have been a major contribution to our knowledges, "a milestone in the subject". For many years to come reference will be made to its proceedings and what is more important engineers engaged all over the world in the design and construction of caverns and pressure shafts will study them in search for ideas for the solution of their problems.

However, the Aachen Symposium has had another aspect, possibly more important and surely more touching than the technical one, that makes it still more outstanding. The warmth and kindness with which we have been received and taken care of by their organizers has turned our stay in this historic city particularly pleasant, both for ourselves the participants and for our accompanying wives and relatives.

Everybody in the Organizing Committee has been readily willing to do everything in his power to make us feel comfortable and help in whatever problem we had to solve. Even the sun decided to take its share of hospitality and came out shining during most of our stay in Aachen.

This many-sided hospitality, which included the civil and eclesiastic officers of the town through a reception by the Lord Mayor in the City Hall and an organ concert in the Dom, has deeply touched our gratitude. I believe I will interpret everybody present if in the name of all I say: thanks; we will cherish for a long time our stay in Aachen and everytime we open the Proceedings of the Symposium, which will be often, memories will come of nice days spent in the company of lovely people in the beautiful and friendly town of Aachen.

May I ask you all to follow me and my wife to the tables.

Chef awaiting the guests at the banquet buffet.

Der Küchenchef erwartet die Gäste zum festlichen Büffet.

Le chef de cuisine attend les invités au buffet

ISRM President Prof. W. Wittke hosting the conference

ISRM-Präsident Prof. W. Wittke als Conferencier

Le président de l'ISRM Prof. W. Wittke comme conférencier

Lively participation in the entertaining close to the symposium at Eurogress

Rege Teilnahme beim unterhaltsamen Abschluß des Symposiums im "Eurogress"

Une grande participation à la clôture divertissante

EXHIBITION OF ROCK MECHANICS TEST EQUIPMENT AND LITERATURE
AUSSTELLUNG FELSMECHANISCHER VERSUCHSGERÄTE UND LITERATUR
EXPOSITION D'APPAREILS D'ESSAI ET DE LIVRES DE MÉCANIQUE DES ROCHES

Register of exhibitors
Ausstellerverzeichnis
Répertoire des exposants

Bilfinger + Berger Aktiengesellschaft
Carl Reiß-Platz 1-5, Tel. 0621/4590
6800 Mannheim 1

Ingenieurbüro Dipl.-Ing. Egey
Im Herrenfeld 18, Tel. 07854/489
7640 Kehl 16

Solexperts AG
Dufourstr. 147, Tel. 01/47 42 00
CH-8008 Zürich

Stump Bohr GmbH
Im Lenzenfleck 1-3, Tel. 089/96191
8045 Ismaning

Mayer'sche Buchhandlung
Ursulinerstr. 17-19, Tel. 0241/48142
5100 Aachen

A.A. Balkema Publishers
P.O. Box 1675
NL-3000 BR Rotterdam

The Laboratorio Nacional de Engenharia Civil, Lisbon (Portugal) organized an exhibition commemorating the Life's work of Prof. M. Rocha.

Tagungsbegleitend organisierte das Laboratorio Nacional de Engenharia Civil, Lissabon (Portugal) im Foyer des "Eurogress" eine Ausstellung zur Würdigung des Lebenswerkes von Prof. M. Rocha.

En parallèle à la conférence le Laboratorio Nacional de Engenharia Civil, Lissabon (Portugal) a organisé au foyer de l'Eurogress, une exposition en commémoration à l'œuvre du Prof. M. Rocha.

CLOSING SESSION
SCHLUSSITZUNG
SÉANCE DE CLÔTURE

DR. A. SILVERIO
Secretary General of the ISRM
Generalsekretär der ISRM
Le sécretaire général de l'ISRM

LADIES AND GENTLEMEN

Now that we are coming close to the end of this memorable Congress (I knew it would happen: I knew it was no use trying to avoid this mistake, when the Aachen meeting proved to be such a major event in the life of our Society!) – to the end of this Symposium, I mean, I am delighted to be granted the opportunity to formally congratulate the Organizing Committee for their meticulous preparation of the meeting.

Because (i) surface, as a resource, is almost depleted in a number of regions, and (ii) surface vulnerability is not only universally acknowledged but also the object of increasing abuse, switching to the underground is a must at this development stage of mankind. I am sure most of you will accompany me in hoping that some day, even if in a rather distant future, we will join – mind and body – the underground community. No doubt, this Symposium on Rock Mechanics Related to Caverns and Pressure Shafts was a valuable contribution towards exploring a section of the surbsurface vast potential.

If you look at the themes – Investigation programs for large caverns in rock masses, Underground caverns with large span, Load sharing capacity of the rock mass for pressure tunnels and shafts, Rock mechanics problems in association with underground storage, and Limitation of the applicability of tunnel boring machines as seen from the rock mechanics point of view – you will recognize the key points in the Symposium topic, still calling for the concerted efforts of rock mechanics engineers and scientists. This means that, before rock mechanics can adequately assist construction of caverns and pressure shafts, most of the professional men and women now relaxing in this closing session atmosphere will have to pay a heavy tribute to such important themes; this also means that wives now enjoying their husbands' company will still have to bear sitting alone for many hours – eventually in front of their absent-minded husbands.

Just as the selection of themes was perfect, so was the Symposium Bulletin. To be quite frank, the weather forecast was an apparent flaw: "windy, rainy weather should be expected". However, after a couple of calm, sunny days everybody very much enjoyed, a mildly adverse climate was summoned in to clear the conscience of the Bulletin editor.

The Symposium Proceedings were distributed in time and the printers are to be commended for producing two very nice volumes. Because their third companion is still missing, the distributed volumes are just about right to cushion your head while you lie in one of the wonderful Aachen parks. But osmosis, mind you, is acknowledged as a very ineffective book to brain information transfer process. Nothing short of a careful reading of the papers will allow you to take full benefit from them.

The Technical Sessions were run smoothly by their tables and just a slight number of "traffic offenses" were committed by speakers who did not stop at the red light.

The Exhibition successfully avoided the pitfall of unmanageable size, though it covered the technical literature, testing and monitoring, construction, and design consultancy.

The Social Events, of which the climax is certainly going to be the banquet and Carnival soon to come, literally led us to the presence of Charlemagne, still very much alive in Aachen; and offered us un anthology of organ music at the precious Cathedral – such an exquisite environment as to raise the question of whether a nearby cathedral was built at Cologne to illustrate the difference between bigger and better.

And the Sightseeing and Short Trip offered were exciting enough to deserve the interest of a large number of accompanying persons and even, so I have heard, of a limited number of accompanying persons' accompanying persons — a tactical euphemism for regular Symposium participants.

All that was mentioned may already be looked at as a list of relevant services to the International Society for Rock Mechanics. But the Symposium was especially meaningful to the ISRM in that the Opening Session kindly hosted two ceremonies of great impact on our whole community.

On one hand, three Past-Presidents of the Society were good enough to accept our invitation to come to Aachen and be presented the 20th Anniversary Plaque "for the significant contributions Presidents have made to the establishment of ISRM as a major organization in the field of geotechnique" — a distinction which the Board unanimously wanted Professor Walter Wittke to share with his predecessors —; and a similar plaque, in memory of Past-President Rocha, was presented to Mrs Rocha, who succeeded in bringing her husband's image back to us, by cleverly making a collage of some the profound concepts his speeches were always packed full with.

On the other hand, a young researcher received the first Manuel Rocha Medal of the ISRM "for an outstanding thesis in rock mechanics".

Because, together, we have managed to keep it alive throughout two decades, our mature Society can be proud of its past, confident in its present, and hopeful of its future.

As Secretary-General of the International Society for Rock Mechanics I will now conclude by adding to my initial congratulations my "aufrichtiger Dank" to the Organizing Committee for the care they invested in preparing the meeting and, in what specifically concerns the ISRM, for the facilities they made available with efficiency and extreme courtesy.

PROF. DR. K.-H. IDEL
Geschäftsführer der DGEG
Managing Director of the DGEG
Le directeur commercial du DGEG

Im Namen der Deutschen Gesellschaft für Erd- und Grundbau e.V. als Veranstalter dieses Internationalen Symposiums möchte ich allen, die am wissenschaftlichen und organisatorischen Erfolg mitgearbeitet haben, recht herzlich danken, insbesondere der Internationalen Gesellschaft für Felsmechanik mit ihrem Präsidenten, Herrn Prof. Wittke und dem Generalsekretär, Herrn Dr. Silvério, die es verstanden haben, eine beachtliche Anzahl hervorragender Experten aus der ganzen Welt für diese Veranstaltung in unserem Lande zu interessieren.

Mehr als 130 Referenten und über 450 Teilnehmer aus 40 Ländern haben teilgenommen. Sie opferten ihre Zeit für die Vorbereitung eigener Beiträge für die Teilnahme und für die teilweise sehr weiten Reisen z.B. aus Australien, Argentinien, China und Japan. Ihr fachliches und wirtschaftliches Interesse war mit der Erwartung verknüpft, daß auf den behandelten Spezialgebieten der Felskavernen und großen Druckstollen weltweit der neueste Stand der Technik präsentiert und diskutiert wird.

Die Hauptlast der wissenschaftlichen Betreuung bei der Themenwahl, der Auswahl der Referate und der Vorbereitung für den Druck der zwei Tagungsbände und einem Diskussionsband, der nach der Tagung den Teilnehmern zur Verfügung stehen wird, lag bei Herrn Prof. Wittke, der sich mit vielen seiner Mitarbeiter einige Wochen zusätzlich zu seiner Arbeit im Institut engagiert hat.

Den Dolmetschern, die sich mit Hilfe der vorab eingereichten Referate in die schwierige Materie eingearbeitet hatten, möchten wir für ihre hervorragende Übersetzung besonders danken. Sie haben das gegenseitige Verstehen der Fachleute erheblich erleichtert.

Wir sind als Veranstalter auch froh, daß das Rahmenprogramm und die Besichtigungsreisen ohne Störungen - wie Herr Silvério erwähnt hat, verlaufen sind.

Danken möchten wir auch der Ausstellungsleitung Mückl + Fleischer, die die reichhaltige Ausstellung der Literatur, der Bauindustrie und Gerätehersteller betreut hat.

Wir sind ein wenig stolz darauf, daß wir durch das EUROGRESS in Aachen der internationalen Fachwelt den angemessenen Rahmen bieten konnten für gute Fachgespräche, sowie für die Vertiefung von Wirtschaftsverbindungen und Freundschaften, die uns nicht nur fachlich, sondern auch menschlich bereichern.

Ich schließe die Veranstaltung und wünsche Ihnen noch schöne Stunden in unserem Land und eine glückliche Heimreise.

LIST OF PARTICIPANTS

TEILNEHMERVERZEICHNIS

LISTE DE PARTICIPANTS

ARGENTINA

MORETTO, O. Prof., Vice-President of ISRM for South America
MORETTO, Mrs., E.
Bolognesi-Moretto, Ing. Consultores,
Luis S. Pena 250-6°.
1110 Buenos Aires

AUSTRALIA

BAMFORD, B., Prof. Dr., Vice-President of ISRM for Australasia
Senior Lecturer in Rock Mechanics
Mining Department, University of Melbourne
Parkville, Vic. 3052

ENDERSBEE, L.A., Prof., Dean
Faculty of Engineering, Monash University
Clayton, Vic. 3168

HAGAN, T.N., Dr., Principal Blasting Consultant
Golder Associates Pty. Ltd.
466 Malvern Rd., Prahran, Vic. 3181

AUSTRIA

AUREDNIK, H., Dipl.-Ing.
Dynamit Nobel Wien GmbH
Opernring 3-5, 1010 Wien

BONAPACE, B., Dipl.-Ing., Abteilungsleiter
Tiroler Wasserkraftwerke AG, Abt. WK 1,
Landhausplatz 2, 6020 Innsbruck

BÜHL, H., Direktor
Bühl & Faubel Ges. mbH
Zangerlestr. 49, 1237 Wien

FLÖGL, W., Dipl.-Ing. Dr. Techn.
Ingenieurkonsulent BR h.c. Dr. Techn. Helmut Flögl
Stockhofstraße 32, 4020 Linz

FUCHSBERGER, M., Univ. Prof.
TU Graz
Rechbauerstr. 12, 8010 Graz

GEHRING, K., Dipl.-Ing. Dr. Mont.
Voest-Alpine AG
8790 Zeltweg

GOBIET, W., Dr.
Pensionsweg 14, 8043 Graz

GÖBL, P., Dipl.-Ing.
GÖBL, Mrs.
Universale Bau
Reimgasse 10, 1010 Wien

GOLSER, J., Dipl.-Ing. für Bauwesen
Geoconsult Dipl.-Ing. E. Hack/Dipl.-Ing. J. Golser
Paracelsusstr. 2, 5020 Salzburg

HEIGERTH, G., Dr. Dipl.-Ing., Leitender Projektant
Tauernkraftwerke AG
Rainerstr. 29, 5020 Salzburg

HÖRSCHELMANN, G., Baumeister, Ing.
Tiefbaugesellschaft m.b.H.
Obersdorferstr. 14, 8600 Bruck/Mur

HOLZINGER, K., Obering., Bauleiter
Österr. Draukraftwerke AG
Kohldorferstr. 98, 9020 Klagenfurt

INNERHOFER, G., Dipl.-Ing., Prok.
Vorarlberger Illwerke AG
Batloggstr. 1062, 6780 Schruns

JÄGER, K. L., Dipl.-Ing.
Firma Ing. Karl Jäger, Unternehmung für Hoch- und Tiefbau
Batloggstr. 1080, 6780 Schruns

KÖNIG, F., Rat, Dipl.-Ing.
Bundesministerium für Land- und Forstwirtschaft
Stubenring 1, 1010 Wien

LACKNER, K., Dipl.-Ing. Dr. Techn.
TU Graz, Inst. f. Bodenmechanik, Felsmechanik und Grundbau
Rechbauerstr. 12, 8010 Graz

LAUFFER, H., Dipl.-Ing. Dr. Techn.
LAUFFER, Mrs. D., Dipl.-Ing.
Allgemeine Baugesellschaft A. PORR AG
Rennweg 12, 1031 Wien

MAYR, G.
Interfels GmbH
Schwarzstr. 27, 5020 Salzburg

MÜLLER, L., Univ.-Prof., Baurat h.c., Dipl.-Ing., Dr.Techn.
Dr.Mont.h.c.
Ingenieurkonsultant für Bauwesen
Paracelsusstr. 2, 5020 Salzburg

MÜLLER, P.-J., Dr. Geol.
Geoconsult Dipl.-Ing. E. Hack/Dipl.-Ing. J. Golser
Sterneckstr. 65, 5020 Salzburg

PÖCHHACKER, H., Dipl.-Ing., Direktor
PÖCHHACKER, Mrs. E.
Allgemeine Baugesellschaft A. PORR AG
Rennweg 12, 1031 Wien

RIEDLER, H., Dipl.-Ing., Oberingenieur
Österreichisch-Amerikanische Magnesit AG
9545 Radenthein

RUDAN, P., Dr., Ingenieurgeologe
Österreichische Elektrizitätswirtschaft AG
Am Hof 67, 1010 Wien

SAUER, G., Dr. Dipl.-Ing.
Ziviling. f. Wi.-Bauwesen
St. Jakob/Thurn 125, 5412 Puch/Hallein

SCHÖNAUER,J., Dipl.-Ing.
VOEST-ALPINE AG, Abt. Stahlbau TLS 23
Muldenstr. 5, 4010 Linz

SCHRAMM, J. M., Dr., Univ.-Dozent, Geologe
Institut für Geowisschenschaften, Universität Salzburg
Akademiestr. 26, 5020 Salzburg

SEEBER, G., o. Prof., Dipl.-Ing., Dr. Techn.
Institut für konstruktiven Wasserbau und Tunnelbau,
Universität Innsbruck, Technikerstr. 13, 6020 Innsbruck

STARJAKOB, F., Dipl.-Ing.
Ingenieurgemeinschaft Lässer-Feizlmayr
Framsweg 16, 6020 Innsbruck

VAVROVSKY, G. M., Dipl.-Ing.
Dipl.-Ing. Dr. Ing. h. c. Franz Pacher, Ingenieurconsiltant
für Bauwesen,
Franz-Josef-Str. 3, 5020 Salzburg

WISSER, E.K.R., Dipl.-Ing., Dr.Techn., Zivilingenieur
Vorarlberger Illwerke AG
Bochstr. 3, 6900 Bregenz

BELGIUM

BONNECHERE, F., Prof.
Université de Liège, Institut du Génie Civil
Quai Banning 6, 4000 Liège

BUTTIENS, E., Directeur R & D
BUTTIENS, Mrs., St.
N.V. Foraky S.A.
Barricadenplein, 13, 1000 Brüssel

DUVIEUSART, J.-C., Directeur de Travaux
C° Francois d'Entreprises CFE S.A.
Square Frère-Orban n° 10, 1040 Bruxelles

MARCHAL, J.-P., Ingenieur Techn.
Institut Geotechnique de l'Etat
Quai de Raome 33, 4000 Liège

MONJOIE, A., Professeur ordinaire
Université de Liège, Laboratoires de Géologie de l'Ingénieur et d'Hydrogéologie
7, place du XX Août, Liège

PETITJEAN, M., Ing. des Mines
Administration des Mines
4452 Juprelle, Chaussée de Tongres 106

WELTER, P., Ingenieur Civil
Institut Geotechnique de l'Etat
Square de Meeûs 28, 1040 Brüssel

BRAZIL

DE MELLO, V.F.B., Prof. Dr., President ISSMFE
DE MELLO, Mrs. M.L.
Rua Frederico Chopin 190, CEP 01454
Sao Paulo, S.P.

BULGARIA

PARASCHKEWOV, R., Prof. Dr.
Hochschule für Bergbau und Geologie
1156 Sofia

BUNDESREPUBLIK DEUTSCHLAND

ABRAHAM, K.-H., Dipl.-Ing., Obering.
Siemens AG, Energietechnik, E119
Postfach 32 40, 8520 Erlangen

ADAMS, F.-J., Oberbauleiter
Hochtief AG, Tiefbauabt.
Rellinghauser Str. 53-57, 4300 Essen 1

AGH-ACKERMANN, E., Dipl.-Ing.
Ortlindestr. 2, 8000 München 81

ALBERS, G., Dipl.-Ing.
Inst. f. Elektr. Anlagen u. Energiewirtschaft
RWTH Aachen, Schinkelstr. 6, 5100 Aachen

ALEX, H.E., Dipl.-Ing.
Gesellschaft für Reaktorsicherheit
Glockengasse 2, 5000 Köln

BABENDERERDE, S., Dipl.-Ing., Direktor
Hochtief AG, Tiefbauabt.
Rellinghauser Str. 53-57, 4300 Essen 1

BALTZER, W., Dipl.-Ing., wiss.Ass.
Lehrstuhl und Institut für Straßenwesen,
Erd- und Tunnelbau, RWTH Aachen
Mies-van-der-Rohe-Str. 1, 5100 Aachen

BECKMANN, U., Dipl.-Ing., Wiss. Assistent
Lehrstuhl für Grundbau und Bodenmechanik
TU Braunschweig
Gausstr. 2, 3300 Braunschweig

BECKMANN, W., Prof.
Westfalia Lünen, 4670 Lünen

BIENSTOCK, Dipl.-Ing., Bundesbahndirektor
Deutsche Bundesbahn, Projektgruppe M/S
der Bahnbauzentrale
Bahnhofstraße 5, 7500 Karlsruhe

BLIND, H., o. Prof. Dr.-Ing.
Lehrstuhl für Wasserbau und Wassermengenwirtschaft
TU München, Arcisstr. 21, 8000 München

BOGENRIEDER, W., Dipl.-Ing.
Rhein.-Westf. Elektrizitätswerke AG,
Abt. Wasserkraft, Kruppstr, 5, 4300 Essen

BOKEMEYER, R., Dipl.-Ing.
Hochtief AG, Tiefbauabt., Bockenheimer Landstr. 24
6000 Frankfurt

BRAACH, O., Wiss. Angestellter
Universität Bochum, Lehrstuhl Prof. Maidl, KIB V, IA 5/28
Universitätsstr. 150, 4630 Bochum

BRAUN, B., Dipl.-Ing.
Deilmann-Haniel GmbH
Haustenbecke 1, 4600 Dortmund-Kurl (13)

BREDER, R., Dipl.-Ing.
Institut für Grundbau, Bodenmechanik, Felsmechanik
und Verkehrswasserbau, RWTH Aachen,
Mies-van-der-Rohe-Str. 1, 5100 Aachen

BREM, G., Dipl.-Ing.
Hochtief AG, Tiefbauabt., Bockenheimer Landstr. 24
6000 Frankfurt

BÜCHNER, K.-H., Dr. Dipl.-Geol.
Niedersächsisches Landesamt für Bodenforschung
3000 Hannover 51

BUHL, G., Dipl.-Ing., Niederlassungsleiter
Bilfinger + Berger Bauaktiengesellschaft,
NL Hannover, Adenauerallee 18, 3000 Hannover 1

COSTINESCU, A., Dipl.-Ing.
Pipeline Engeneering GmbH
Moltkestr. 76, 4300 Essen 1

DACHROTH, W., Prof. Dr.
Geologisches Institut, Universität Heidelberg
Im Neuenheimer Feld 234, 6900 Heidelberg

DANNEMANN, H., Dipl.-Ing.
Erdbaulaboratorium Ahlenberg
Am Ossenbrink 40, 5804 Herdecke

DIETZ, W., Dipl.-Ing., Leiter der Tunnelbauabteilung
Hauptverwaltung Ed. Züblin AG
Jägerstr. 22, 7000 Stuttgart 1

DIMEL, E., Dr.-Ing., Direktor
Bilfinger + Berger Bau AG
Karl-Peters-Str. 1, 6200 Wiesbaden

DISTELMEIER, H., Dipl.-Ing., Leiter der
Abt. für Tunnel- und Stollenbau,
Bilfinger + Berger Bau AG
Carl-Reiss-Platz 1-5, 6800 Mannheim 1

DREYER, W., Prof. Dr.
Institut für Bergbau, TU Clausthal
Erzstr. 20, 3392 Clausthal-Zellerfeld

DUDDECK, H., o. Prof. Dr.-Ing.
Institut für Statik, TU Braunschweig
Beethovenstr. 51, 3300 Braunschweig

DÜLLMANN, H., Dr.-Ing.
Geotechnisches Büro Dr.-Ing. H. Düllmann
Habsburger Allee 25, 5100 Aachen

EBER, A., Prof. Reg. Bmstr.
TU München, Institut für Bauingenieurwesen IV
Tunnelbau und Baubetriebslehre
Arcisstr. 21, 8000 München

EDELING, H., Dipl.-Ing., Geschäftsführer
Maidl + Edeling, Ingenieurgesellschaft
für Bautechnik mbH
Kortumstr. 69, 4630 Bochum 1

EFFENBERGER, K., Dipl.-Geol.
Ingenieur-Geologisches Institut
Dipl.-Ing. S. Niedermeyer, 8821 Westheim

EGEY, Z., Dipl.-Ing., Beratender Ing.
EGEY, Mrs. B.
Ingenieurbüro Egey
Im Herrenfeld 18, 764 Kehl 16

EHRHARDT, T., Dipl.-Ing.
Baugrundinstitut Dr. J. Trischler, Dipl.-Ing. Th. Ehrhardt, Dipl.-Ing. U. Otto
Bergstr. 104-106, 6102 Pfungstadt

EISTERT, M., Dipl.-Ing., Geschäftsführer
Wirth GmbH, 5140 Erkelenz

ENGELHARDT, K., Dr., Direktor
Bilfinger + Berger Bauaktiengesellschaft
Carl-Reiss-Platz 1-5, 6800 Mannheim 1

ERBAN, P.-J., Dipl.-Ing.
Institut für Grundbau, Bodenmechanik, Felsmechanik und Verkehrswasserbau
RWTH Aachen, Mies-van-der-Rohe-Str. 1, 5100 Aachen

EVERLING, Dr.-Ing.
Bergbau Forschung GmbH
Postfach 13 01 40, 4300 Essen 13

FALTIN, J., Dipl.-Ing.
Strabag Bau AG, HA Technik und Projektbearbeitung
Siegburgerstr. 241, 5000 Köln 41

FISCHER, C., Dipl.-Ing., Vertriebsing.
Interfels, Deilmannstr. 1, 4444 Bad Bentheim

FISCHER, H., Dipl.-Ing.
Saarberg-Interplan GmbH
Stengelstr. 1, 6600 Saarbrücken

FLUNKER, H. J., Dipl.-Ing.
Hochtief AG, Tiefbauabt.
Rellinghauser Str. 53-57, 4300 Essen 1

FROHN, C., Dipl.-Ing.
Institut für Tieflagerung
Berliner Str. 2, 3392 Clausthal-Zellerfeld

GARBE, H. J., Dipl.-Ing.
Ingenieursozietät BGS, Zweigbüro Hannover
Andreaestr. 7, 3000 Hannover 1

GARTUNG, E., Dr.-Ing.
Landesgewerbeanstalt Bayern, Grundbauinstitut
Gewerbemuseumsplatz 2, 8500 Nürnberg 1

GEISSLER, H., Dr. Dipl.-Geol.
3167 Burgdorf, Gördelerstr. 39

GELL, K., Dipl.-Ing. Dipl.-Wirtsch. Ing.
Institut für Grundbau, Bodenmechanik, Felsmechanik und Verkehrswasserbau
RWTH Aachen, Mies-van-der-Rohe-Str. 1, 5100 Aachen

GIERER, H., Dr.
Schönestr. 31
7000 Stuttgart 50

GIERKE, H., Leiter Unternehmensbereich West
Eisenhütte Prinz Rudolph, Zweigniederlassung der Salzgitter Maschinen und Anlagen AG
Brokweg 75, 4408 Dülmen

GIRNAU, G., Prof. Dr.-Ing., President of ITA
STUVA, Mathias-Brüggen-Str. 41, 5000 Köln 30

GÖGGLER, W., Berging.(grad.)
Bundesanstalt für Geowissenschaften und Rohstoffe
Stilleweg 2, 3000 Hannover 51

GLORIA, K., Dipl.-Berging.
Pipeline Engineering GmbH
Moltkestr. 76, 4300 Essen 1

GÖTTE, K.-H., Ing.(grad.)
Lahmeyer International GmbH, Bauüberwachung S-Bahn
Stuttgart, Los 13
Leonberger Str., 7000 Stuttgart 1

GRAEFE, V., Dr.
Institut für Tieflagerung
Berliner Str. 2, 3392 Clausthal-Zellerfeld

GRÄFER, H., Dipl.-Bauing.
Rhein.-Westf. Elektrizitätswerke AG - HV, Bauabt.
Kruppstr. 5, 4300 Essen

GROSS, G., Baudirektor
Stadt Nürnberg, Tiefbauamt, U-Bahnbau
Karl-Bröger-Str. 9, 8500 Nürnberg 40

GRÜTER, R., Bundesbahndirektor
GRÜTER, Mrs. H.
Bundesbahndirektion Stuttgart, Neubauabteilung
Heilbronner Str. 7, 7000 Stuttgart 1

GRUNER, H., Oberbauleiter
Hochtief AG, Tiefbauabteilung
Rellinghauser Str. 53 - 57, 4300 Essen 1

HAGER, M., Prof. Dr.-Ing., Ministerialrat
HAGER, Mrs.
Merler Alle 99
5300 Bonn 1

HAIN, H., Prof. Dr.-Ing.
Universität Hannover
Callinstraße 32, 3000 Hannover

HARTH, W., Dipl.-Ing.
Dyckerhoff & Widmann AG
Gereonstr. 38, 5000 Köln 1

HARTMANN, E., Dr.-Ing.
Ed. Züblin AG, Tiefbauabteilung
Jägerstr. 22, 7000 Stuttgart 1

HARTMANN, J., Bergdirektor
Bergamt Bayreuth
Parsifalstr. 25, 8580 Bayreuth

HARTUNG, L., Bau-Ing.
Fa. Hermann Kirchner GmbH
Hermann Kirchner-Str. 6, 6430 Bad Hersfeld

HAUPT, G., Techn. Angest.
Stadt Frankfurt, Technische Aufsicht für den Stadt-
bahnbau
Zeil 53, 6000 Frankfurt/Main 1

HEBENER, H.-L., Dipl.-Ing., Wiss. Angestellter
Institut für Grundbau und Baubetrieb, TU Berlin
Kloedensstr. 1, 1000 Berlin 61

HEIDERHOFF, H., Direktor, Vorstandsmitglied
Rheinisch-Westfälische Elektrizitätswerke AG
Kruppstr. 5, 4300 Essen 1

HEILBRUNNER, J., Dipl.-Ing.
Alfred Kunz GmbH & Co.
Bavariaring 26, 8000 München 2

HEIM, W.A., Bergwerksdirektor, Mitglied des Vorstands
Kali und Salz AG
Friedrich-Ebert-Str. 160, 3500 Kassel

HEITFELD, K.-H., Prof. Dr.
HEITFELD, Mrs., Dr. H.
Lehrstuhl für Ingenieurgeologie und Hydrogeologie,
RWTH Aachen, Lochnerstr. 4 - 20, 5100 Aachen

HERBST, T., Dr.
Dyckerhoff & Widmann AG
Erdinger Landstr. 1, 8000 München 81

HEYNE, E., Prof.
Höfchensweg 53, 5100 Aachen

HÖNISCH, K., Dipl.-Ing.
Lahmyer Internat. GmbH
Lyonerstr. 22, 6000 Frankfurt/M. 71

HÖWING, K.-D., Dipl.-Geol.
Ruhr-Univ. Bochum, Inst. für Geologie, AG Felsmechanik
Universitätsstr. 150, 4630 Bochum 1

HOLLAUS, E., Dr. Geol.
Hans Broicher GmbH & Co.
Postfach 1445, 8500 Nürnberg 1

HOLFELDER, E., Dipl.-Ing.
8119 Kleinweil

HOLLINGER, J., Dr. Dipl.-Geol.
Adolf-Kolping-Str. 91, 6730 Neustadt/Wstr.

HORN, K., Dr.-Ing.
Bilfinger + Berger Bau-AG
Schnabelstr. 9, 4300 Essen

HORNEMANN, B., Dipl.-Ing.
Thyssen Schachtbau GmbH
Ruhrstr. 1, 4330 Mülheim-Ruhr

HURTZ, G., Obering., Prokurist
Wirth GmbH
5140 Erkelenz

IDEL, K.-H., Prof. Dr.-Ing., Geschäftsführer der DGEG
IDEL, Mrs.
Kronprinzenstr. 35a, 4300 Essen 1

JANCSECZ, S., Dipl.-Ing., Geotechniker
Wayss & Freytag AG, Abt. TA 3
Postfach 112042, 6000 Frankfurt/M. 11

JENEWEIN, G., Dipl.-Ing.
Bilfinger + Berger Bau-AG
Carl-Reiss-Platz 1 - 5, 6800 Mannheim

JESSBERGER, H.-L., Prof. Dr.-Ing.
Ruhr-Univ. Bochum, Lehrstuhl für Grundbau u. Bodenmechanik
Universitätsstr. 150, 4630 Bochum

JONASSON, G.
Technisches Büro G. Jonasson
Vosshösener Str. 90, 5802 Wetter 1

JÜTTE, H., Verkaufsing.
Gewerkschaft Eisenhütte Westfalia
Postfach, 4670 Lünen

KARLSSON, J.-A., Dipl.-Ing.
Polensky & Zöllner
Wächtersbacher Str. 89, 6000 Frankfurt/M. 61

KAST, K., Dipl.-Ing., Obering.
Dyckerhoff & Widmann AG
Postfach 810280, 8000 München 81

KAYSER, H.-J., Prof. Dr.-Ing.
Lehrstuhl für Straßenwesen, Erd- und Tunnelbau
RWTH Aachen, Mies-van-der-Rohe-Str. 1, 5100 Aachen

KIEHL, J., Dipl.-Phys.
Institut für Grundbau, Bodenmechanik, Felsmechanik und
Verkehrswasserbau, RWTH Aachen
Mies-van-der-Rohe-Str. 1, 5100 Aachen

KIRSCHNER, R., Dipl.-Ing.
Institut für Grundbau, Bodenmechanik, Felsmechanik und
Verkehrswasserbau, RWTH Aachen
Mies-van-der-Rohe-Str. 1, 5100 Aachen

KLEIN, J., Dr.-Ing.
Bergbau Forschung GmbH
Postfach 130140, 4300 Essen 13

KLEINSCHMIDT, E., Dipl.-Ing.
Großer Ring 53
4270 Dorsten 11

KOPPELBERG, W., Dipl.-Geol.
BUTENUTH, Mrs.
Lehrstuhl für Ingenieurgeologie und Hydrogeologie
RWTH Aachen, Lochnerstr. 4 - 20, 5100 Aachen

KÖNIG, H.W., Dr.-Ing.E.h.
Moorenstr. 33, 4300 Essen 1

KRABBE, W., Dr.-Ing., Vorstandsmitglied
Philipp Holzmann AG
Taunusanlage 1, 6000 Frankfurt/M. 1

KRAJEWSKI, W., Dipl.-Ing.
Institut für Grundbau, Bodenmechanik, Felsmechanik und Verkehrswasserbau, RWTH Aachen
Mies-van-der-Rohe-Str. 1, 5100 Aachen

KRAUSS, E., Dr.-Ing.
Philipp Holzmann AG
Taunusanlage 1, 6000 Frankfurt

KRAUSE, T., Dipl.-Ing., Wiss. Mitarbeiter
Gausstr. 2, 3300 Braunschweig

KREBS, E., Dipl.-Ing.
Eastman Instruments GmbH
Marktplatz 7, 3014 Laatzen 1

KRIMMER, H.-D., Dipl.-Ing., Oberbauleiter
Huta-Hegerfeld AG
Rosenheimer Str. 145, 8000 München 80

KUHNHENN, K., Dr.-Ing.
Ing. Büro Bung
Gartenstr. 4, 7500 Karlsruhe 1

KUNERT, N., Dr.rer.nat., Ingenieurgeologe
Geotechnisches Büro Dr. Kunert
Imbergstr. 5, 5960 Olpe

KUTTER, H.K., Prof.
AG Felsmechanik, Institut für Geologie
Ruhr-Universität Bochum, 4630 Bochum

LANGER, M., Prof. Dr., Direktor
Bundesanstalt für Geowissenschaften und Rohstoffe
Stilleweg 2, 3000 Hannover 51

LAUMANS, Q., Dr.-Ing.
Grundbauingenieure Steinfeld und Partner
Alte Königstr. 3, 2000 Hamburg 50

LEUSSINK, H., Prof. Dr.-Ing., Bundesminister a.D.
Strähler Weg 45, 7500 Karlsruhe 41

LEVEN, W., Dipl.-Ing., wiss.Ass.
Lehrstuhl und Institut für Straßenwesen, Erd- und Tunnelbau, RWTH Aachen
Mies-van-der-Rohe-Str. 1, 5100 Aachen

LIEDTKE, L., Dr.-Ing.
Bundesanstalt für Geowissenschaften und Rohstoffe
Stilleweg 2, 3000 Hannover 51

LIELUPS, L., Dipl.-Ing.
Ingenieurbüro Bung
Englerstr. 6, 6900 Heidelberg

LIERMANN, G., Dipl.-Ing., Leiter TB
Philipp Holzmann AG
Siegburger Str. 149-151, 5000 Köln 21

LUTHER, J.F., Dipl.-Ing.
Lahmeyer International GmbH
Lyoner Str. 22, 6000 Frankfurt/M.

LUX, K.-H., Dr.-Ing., Akad.Rat
Lehrgebiet für Unterirdisches Bauen, Universität Hannover
Callinstr. 32, 3000 Hannover

MAIDL, B., o. Prof. Dr.-Ing.
Ruhr-Universität Bochum
Universitätsstr. 150, 4630 Bochum

MARTIN, L., Dipl.-Ing.
Leonhard Moll GmbH & Co.
Konrad-Celtis-Str. 77, 8000 München 70

MASSON, C., Ass. d. Bergf., Prokurist
E. Heitkamp GmbH
Langekampstr. 36, 4690 Herne 2

MAURER, G., Dipl.-Ing.
Leonhard Moll GmbH & Co.
Konrad-Celtis-Str. 77, 8000 München 70

MAYER, H.W., Dipl.-Ing., stv. Geschäftsführer
Lahmeyer International GmbH
Lyoner Str. 22, 6000 Frankfurt/M. 71

MEISTER, D., Dr.-Ing.
Bundesanstalt für Geowissenschaften und Rohstoffe
Stilleweg 2, 3000 Hannover 51

MEYER, L., Direktor, Geschäftsführer
Lahmeyer International GmbH
Guiollettstr. 48, 6000 Frankfurt/M. 1

MÖKER, H., Bauing.
Bruchholzwiesen 15, 3006 Burgwedel 1

MÖRSCHNER, J., Dipl.-Ing.
Deutsche Bundesbahn
Baseler Str. 27, 6000 Frankfurt

MÜLLER, G., Dr.rer.nat., Geschäftsführer
Interfels GmbH
Deilmannstr. 1, 4444 Bad Bentheim

MÜLLER, G., Dipl.-Ing., Prokurist
Wirth GmbH, 5140 Erkelenz

NENDZA, H., Prof. Dr.-Ing.
Erdbaulaboratorium Essen
Susannastr. 31, 4300 Essen

NEUMAIER, W., Dipl.-Ing.
Lahmeyer International GmbH, BauÜ S-Bahn Stuttgart, Los 13
Leonberger Str., 7000 Stuttgart 1

NEUMANN, K., Obering.
Ed. Züblin AG, Tunnelabt., HV Stuttgart
7000 Stuttgart

VON NEUMANN-COSEL, E., Dipl.-Ing.
Wix + Liesenhoff GmbH
Unterste Wilms-Str. 11-13, 4600 Dortmund 1

NUSSMANN, W., Betriebsdirektor
Deilmann - Haniel GmbH
Postfach 130220, 4600 Dortmund 13

OBENAUER, P.W., Dipl.-Ing.
Ingenieurbüro Bung
Englerstr. 6, 6900 Heidelberg

PAHL, A., Dr., Geologiedirektor
Bundesanstalt für Geowissenschaften und Rohstoffe
Stilleweg 2, 3000 Hannover 51

PAPENFUSS, H., Dipl.-Ing., stv. Geschäftsführer
Lahmeyer International GmbH
Lyoner Str. 22, 6000 Frankfurt/M. 71

PAUL, A., Dipl.-Ing.
FMPA Baden-Württemberg, Abt. Baugrund, Ref. Felshohlraumbau
Pfaffenwaldring 4, 7000 Stuttgart 80

PETERS, M., Dipl.-Ing.
Huta-Hegerfeld AG
Hahnstr. 40, 6000 Frankfurt 71

PFEIFER, H., Obering.
Schluchseewerk AG
Rempartstr. 12 - 16, 7800 Freiburg/Br.

PIERAU, B., Dr.-Ing., Geschäftsführer
PIERAU, Mrs. B.
Prof. Dr.-Ing. W. Wittke, Beratende Ingenieure für
Grundbau und Felsbau GmbH
Alexianergraben 23, 5100 Aachen

PLISCHKE, B., Dipl.-Phys.
Institut für Grundbau, Bodenmechanik, Felsmechanik und
Verkehrswasserbau, RWTH Aachen
Mies-van-der-Rohe-Str. 1, 5100 Aachen

POHLE, G., o. Prof. Dipl.-Ing.
Institut für Baumaschinen und Baubetrieb, RWTH Aachen
Mies-van-der-Rohe-Str. 1, 5100 Aachen

PRECHTL, A., Dr., Geschäftsführer
PRECHTL, Mrs.
Schloßbrauerei Neunkirchen GmbH
Büchelstr. 7, 6680 Neunkirchen/Saar

PRINZ, H., Prof. Dr.
Hessisches Landesamt für Bodenforschung
Leberberg 9, 6200 Wiesbaden

QUAST, P., Dipl.-Ing.
Kavernen Bau- und Betriebs-GmbH
Rathenaustr. 13/14, 3000 Hannover 1

RAHN, W., Dr.rer.nat.
Ingenieur-Geologisches Institut Dipl.-Ing. S. Niedermayer
8821 Westheim

RAISCH, D., Dipl.-Ing.
Ed. Züblin AG, Tunnelbauabt., HV Stuttgart
7000 Stuttgart

RAMISCH, H., Dipl.-Ing.
Tiefbau-Berufsgenossenschaft
Am Knie 6, 8000 München 60

RAPP, R., Dr.-Ing.
Bayerische Wasserkraftwerke AG
Dom-Pedro-Str. 19, 8000 München 19

RAPPERT, D., Dipl.-Ing., Leiter Tiefbauabteilung
Philipp Holzmann AG
Siegburger Str. 149 - 151, 5000 Köln 21

RECHTERN, J., Dipl.-Ing.
Institut für Grundbau, Bodenmechanik, Felsmechanik und Verkehrswasserbau, RWTH Aachen
Mies-van-der-Rohe-Str. 1, 5100 Aachen

REINECKE, E., Bau-Ingenieur
Hermann Kirchner GmbH
Hermann Kirchner-Str. 6, 6430 Bad Hersfeld

REXHÄUSER, H., Prof. Dr., Vizepräsident
Bundesanstalt für Geowissenschaften und Rohstoffe
Stilleweg 2, 3000 Hannover 51

RICHTER, T., Dr.-Ing., Bauing.
GUD Grundbau u. Dynamik Consult GmbH
Mecklenburgische Str. 56, 1000 Berlin 33

RISSLER, P., Dr.-Ing., Abteilungsleiter
Ruhrtalsperrenverein, Entwurfsabt.
Kronprinzenstr. 37, 4300 Essen 1

ROBERTZ, F.L., Dr.h.c., Geschäftsführender Inhaber
Unternehmensgruppe Transportbeton Mülheim
Elbestr. 47, 4330 Mülheim/Ruhr

RODATZ, W., Dr.-Ing.
Ingenieurgemeinschaft Meerestechnik + Seebau GmbH
Millerntorplatz 1, 2000 Hamburg 4

ROKAHR, R.B., Dr.-Ing., Akad.Rat
Lehrgebiet für Unterirdisches Bauen, Univ. Hannover
Callinstr. 32, 3000 Hannover

ROSKE, K., Prof. Dr.-Ing.
Kreditanstalt für Wiederaufbau
Palmengartenstr. 5, 6000 Frankfurt/M.

ROTTENFUSSER, F., Dipl.-Ing., Direktor
Dyckerhoff & Widmann AG
Postfach 810280, 8000 München 81

SANIO, H.P., Dipl.-Ing.
Ruhr-Univ. Bochum, Institut für Geologie, AG Felsmechanik
Universitätsstr. 150, 4630 Bochum 1

SCHARDIN-LIEDTKE, Dipl.-Ing.
Institut für Bautechnik
Reichpietschufer 72-76, 1000 Berlin 30

SCHETELIG, K., Prof. Dr.
Institut für Geologie und Paläontologie, TU Darmstadt
Petersenstr. 13, 6100 Darmstadt

SCHIFFER, W., Dipl.-Ing., Leiter der Abteilung Tiefbau
Philipp Holzmann AG, Hauptniederlassung Hannover
Bothfelder Str. 35, 3000 Hannover 1

SCHMIDT, M.W., Dipl.-Geol.
Institut für Tieflagerung, Wiss. Abteilung
Berliner Str. 2, 3392 Clausthal-Zellerfeld

SCHNEIDER, H.J., Dr.-Ing., Dipl.-Geol.
Kavernen Bau- und Betriebs-GmbH
Rathenaustr. 13/14, 3000 Hannover 1

SCHRÖDER, A., Dipl.-Ing.
WETZEL, Mrs. G.
Ing.-Büro Schlegel - Dr.-Ing. Spiekermann GmbH & Co.
Duissernstr. 65, 4100 Duisburg 1

SCHUERMANN, F., Dr.-Ing., Wissensch. Mitarbeiter
SCHUERMANN, Mrs. S.
Steinkohlenbergbauverein
Franz-Fischer-Weg 61, 4300 Essen 1

SCHÜTZ, H., Prof. Dipl.-Ing.
Universität GH Wuppertal
Hohlenscheidterstr. 50, 5600 Wuppertal 12

SCHÜTZ, W., Dipl.-Ing.
Ing. Büro Philipp + Schütz, Beratende Ingenieure
Wagmüllerstr. 16, 8000 München 22

SCHULTER, A., Bauleiter
ARGE Hasenbergtunnel
Leonbergerstr., 7000 Stuttgart 1

SEIBERT, H., Vorstandsmitglied
Sieg Rhein. Germania Brauerei AG
Rheinstr. 90 - 100, 5303 Bornheim 2, Hersel

SEMPRICH, S., Dr.-Ing.
SEMPRICH, Mrs. A.
Bilfinger + Berger Bau AG, Abt. für Tunnel- und Stollenbau
Carl-Reiß-Platz 1 - 5, 6800 Mannheim 1

SIOR, G., Dr.-Ing., Beratender Ingenieur VBI
Grundbau-Institut Dr.-Ing. Sior
Eleonore-Sterling-Str. 3, 6000 Frankfurt 50

SOMMER, H., Prof. Dr.-Ing.
Universität - Gesamthochschule Kassel, FB 14
Wilhelmshöher Allee 71, 3500 Kassel

STOCK, G., Oberingenieur
Thyssen Schmiedetechnik/Bergbautechnik
Ehinger Str. 80, 4100 Duisburg 28

STAUPENDAHL, G., Dipl.-Ing., Wiss. Mitarbeiter
Gesellschaft für Strahlen- und Umweltforschung mbH, München
Institut für Tieflagerung, Wiss. Abteilung
Berliner Str. 2, 3392 Clausthal-Zellerfeld

THAUFELDER, G., Prokurist, Obering.
Lahmeyer International GmbH
Lyoner Str. 22, 6000 Frankfurt/M. 71

THOTE, P., Dipl.-Ing.
Bilfinger + Berger Bau AG
Karl-Peters-Str. 1, 6200 Wiesbaden

TROMBIK, J., Dipl.-Ing.
Stadtwerke München, Gas- und Wasserwerke, Badebetriebe,
Gruppe Wasser
Unterer Anger 3, 8000 München 2

UHLENBECKER, F.-W., Dr., Obermarkscheider
Kali & Salz AG
6433 Philippsthal

UNGER, E., Oberingenieur
Gewerkschaft Eisenhütte Westfalia
Postfach, 4670 Lünen

VOERCKEL, M., Dipl.-Ing.
Wirth GmbH
5140 Erkelenz

WAGNER, A., Dipl.-Ing.
'Universale-Bau' Ges. mbH
Johann-Clanze-Str. 51, 8000 München 70

WALLNER, M., Dr.-Ing.
Bundesanstalt für Geowissenschaften und Rohstoffe
Stilleweg 2, 3000 Hannover 51

WALTHER, C., Dr., Markscheider
DBE
Woltorfer Str. 74, 3150 Peine

WEBER, P., Dr., Obergeologierat
Geologisches Landesamt Nordrhein-Westfalen
De-Greiffstr. 195, 4150 Krefeld

WEBER, W., Dr.-Ing.
Wirth GmbH
5140 Erkelnz

WEMPE, H., Dipl.-Geologe
Projektleitung Energieforschung in der KFA Jülich
Postfach 1913, 5170 Jülich

WETJEN, D., Dipl.-Ing.
Lehrgebiet für Baumechanik, Universität Hannover
Callinstr. 32, 3000 Hannover

WETZEL, G., Dipl.-Ing.
Ingenieurbüro Schlegel - Dr.-Ing. Spiekermann
Duissenstr. 65, 4100 Duisburg

WILMS, J., Dipl.-Ing.
Hochtief AG, ZN Tiefbau Ruhr
Huyssenallee 22 - 30, 4300 Essen 1

WIND, H., Dipl.-Ing.
Philipp Holzmann AG
Taunusanlage 1, 6000 Frankfurt

WITTKE, W., Prof. Dr.-Ing., President of ISRM
WITTKE, Mrs. L.
Institut für Grundbau, Bodenmechanik, Felsmechanik und Verkehrswasserbau, RWTH Aachen
Mies-van-der-Rohe-Str. 1, 5100 Aachen

WOHNLICH, M., Dr.phil.nat., Engineer Geologist
Interfels GmbH
Deilmannstr. 1, 4444 Bad Bentheim

WOLFF, M., Dipl.-Ing. Leitender Bergdirektor
Bergamt Aachen, Deilmann - Haniel GmbH
Postfach 130220, 4600 Dortmund 13

WOLTERS, Mrs. I.
Heyes Kirchweg 12
4150 Krefeld-Fischeln

WÖSSNER, W., Dr.-Ing.
WÖSSNER, Mrs.
Valentinianstr. 54b, 6802 Ladenburg

WÜRSTLE, H., Dipl.-Ing., Oberingenieur
Dyckerhoff & Widmann AG
Postfach 810280, 8000 München 81

ZHANG, J.
Hochtief AG, Tiefbauabteilung
Rellinghauser Str. 53 - 57, 4300 Essen 1

ZIMMERMANN, J., Dr., Referatsleiter
Lahmeyer International GmbH
Postfach 710230, 6000 Frankfurt/M. 71

CANADA

BRECKON, J., Engineer
Crippen Consultants
224 West Esplanade, North Vancouver, B.C., V7M 1A4

KAISER, P.K., Dr., Associate Prof.
University of Alberta, Dept. of Civil Engg. 303
Edmonton TGG 2G7

LADANYI, B., Prof. Dr.-Ing.
LADANYI, Mrs. N.
Départment de génie civil, Ecole Polytechnique de Montréal
C.P.6079, Succ. A, Montreal, Que. H3C 3A7

LAJTAI, E.Z., Prof., Rock Mechanics
University of Manitoba, Dept. Geological Engineering
Manitoba

TAYLOR, E.
Geotechnical Engineering Dept., Ontario Hydro
700 University Ave., Toronto, Ontario M5G 1X6

WILKINS, B.T.S., Dr., Materials Scientist
Atomicenergy of Canada Limited, Whiteshell Nuclear Research
Establishment, Pinawa, Manitoba ROE ILO

CHILE

TRONCOSO, J.H., Prof. Dr.
Catholic University of Chile, Seccion Ing. Geotecnica,
V. Mackenha 4860, Santiago

CHINA

GE, X., Prof.
z.Z. Lehrstuhl für Felsmechanik, Inst. für Boden- und
Felsmechanik, Universität Karlsruhe
Kaiserstr. 12, 7500 Karlsruhe

GU, X., Dozent
z.Z. Institut für Grundbau, Bodenmechanik, Felsmechanik
und Verkehrswasserbau, RWTH Aachen
Mies-van-der-Rohe-Str. 1, 5100 Aachen
Universität Tianjin, Fakultät für Bauwesen
Tianjin

COLOMBIA

FORERO, M.M., Dipl.-Ing.
z.Z. Institut für Grundbau, Bodenmechanik, Felsmechanik und
Verkehrswasserbau, RWTH Aachen, Mies-van-der-Rohe-Str. 1,
5100 Aachen
Empresa de Energia Eléctrica de Bogotá, Calle 13 Kra 37,
Bogotá D.E.

DDR

HEINZE, F., Dr.-Ing.
VEB UGS Mittenwalde
1606 Mittenwalde/Mark, Berliner Chaussee

VOIGT, K., Dipl.-Ing.
Oberste Bergbehörde beim Ministerrat der Deutschen Demokratischen Republik, 7030 Leipzig, Friederikenstr. 60

DENMARK

ABRAHAMSEN, C., Engineer
Højgaard & Schultz A/S
Jaegersborg Allé 4, 2920 Charlottenlund

JACOBSEN, J., Engineer
Landsbyggifelagid, Faerøerne, c/o Højgaard & Schultz A/S
Jaegersborg Allé 4, 2920 Charlottenlund

PEDERSEN, E., Engineer
Højgaard & Schultz A/S
Jaegersborg Allé 4, 2920 Charlottenlund

FINLAND

GARDEMEISTER, R., Ph.D., Eng.geologist
GARDEMEISTER, Mrs. U.
Imatra Power Company Ltd.
P.O.Box 138, 00101 Helsinki 10

JOHANSSON, S., Chief Geologist
Neste Oy
Keilaniemi, 02150 Espoo 15

KOPPINEN, J., M.Sc.(Civ.Eng.), Section Manager
Finn-Stroi Oy
Melkonkatu 18, 00210 Helsinki 21

LAINE, T., Dipl.-Ing.
Ins. Tsto Saanio & Laine
Mannerheimintie 31 A 3, 00250 Helsinki 25

LEHTINIEMI, R., Civ.Eng. M.Sc.
Geotek Oy
Valimotie 23 D, 00380 Helsinki 38

PÖLLÄ, J., Office Head
PÖLLÄ, Mrs. H.
Geotechnical Department of City of Helsinki
Yrjönkatu 21 b A, 00100 Helsinki 10

SÄRKKÄ, P., Dozent
Technische Universität Helsinki, Abteilung für Bergbau u. Metallurgie, 02150 Espoo 15

FRANCE

ARNOULD, M., Professeur
Ecole Nationale Superieure des Mines
60 Boulevard Saint-Michel, 75272 Paris Cedex 06

BAUD, J.-P., Ingenieur Geologne
Techniques Louis Menard
B.P. 117, 91163 Longjummeau Cedex

BEREST, P., Ingenieur des Mines
Laboratoire de Mecanique des Solides, Ecole Polytechnique
91128 Palaiseau Cedex

BONTE, G., Ingénieur Divisionnaire
Department Etudes Fond - MDPA SA
11, av. d'Altkirch - BP 1270, 68055 Mulhouse Cedex

COLIN, P., Ingénieur Mécanique des Roches
GEOSTOCK
Tour Aurore - CB17, 92080 Paris Defense

DAVID, H., Ingénieur R
RATP
21 Boulevard Bourdon, 75004 Paris

EUVERTE
Service Etudes de Prix
3, avenue Morane Saulnier, 78140 Velizy

FOURMAINTRAUX, D., Docteur-Geotechnicien
Laboratoire Central des Ponts et Chaussées
58 Boulevard Lefebvre, 75732 Paris Cedex 15

FOURNIER, P., Ingénieur
Regie Autonome des Transports Parisiens (RATP)
21 Boulevard Bourdon, 75004 Paris

FRANCO, J., Ingénieur
Coyne & Bellier
5, Rue d'Héliopolis, 75017 Paris

GODARD, J.-P., Ingénieur Chef de Division
Régie Autonome des Transports Parisiens (RATP)
21 Boulevard Bourdon, 75004 Paris

HABIB, P., Prof., Directeur
Laboratoire de Mécanique des Solides, Ecole Polytechnique
91128 Palaiseau Cedex

LANTIER, F., Ingénieur Géophysicien
Compagnie de Prospection Geophysique Francaise - Bureau de Lyon, Lotis, Les Charpennes - Bat. A, 38290 Villefontaine

MARIN, G., Attaché au directeur de la Region d'Equipement ALPES - Lyon, Electricité de France
3, Rue Ronde, 73000 Chambery

MAURY, V., Ing.Docteur
Elf-Aquitaine
Avenue des Lilas, 64000 Pau

OTT, B., Ingénieur au Service Etudes Générales
Sites de la Région d'Equipement ALPES - Lyon,
Electricité de France, 3, Rue Ronde, 73000 Chambéry

PIRAUD, J., Dipl.-Ing.
B.R.G.M.
BP 6009, 45060 Orleans

GREECE

GARAGUNIS, C., Prof. Dr.
z.Z. Inst. Ingenieurgeol. u. Hydrogeol. RWTH Aachen,
Lochnerstr. 4 - 20, 5100 Aachen
Techn. Universität Athen, Patission Str. 42, Athen

KOLONIAS, E., Dipl.Bauing.
KOLONIA, Mrs. A.
Public Power Corporation, P. Fotioy 13, Marousi, Athen

MICHELIS, P., Dr.
Faneromenisstr. 26, Cholargos, Athen

PANTOPOULOS, T., Dipl.-Ing.
PANTOPOULOS, Mrs.
A.E.G.E.K. S.A., Elias Straße 12, Veria

GUATEMALA

MORALES, R., Dr.
Gerente Institutto
Nacional de Electrification
Guatemala City

HONGKONG

MALONE, A.W., Dr. Civ.Eng.
Hongkong Government, GCO 6/7 Empire Centre
Salisbury Road, Kowlon

HUNGARY

KERTÉSZ, P., Prof.
Technical University Budapest
BME Ásványtan, 1521 Budapest

GRESCHIK, G., Dr.
Hungarian Institut for Building Science
Budapest

ICELAND

PALMASON, P.R., M.S.Civ.Eng.
GUDMUNDSDOTTIR, Mrs. A.
VST Consulting Engineers
Ármúni 4, 105 Reykjavic

INDIA

JANAKIRAM, K.S., Dr., Senior Scientific Officer
VIJAYALKSHMI, Mrs. S.
Technology Utilization Division, Dep. of Science and Techn.
Technology Bhavan, New Mehrauli Road, New Delhi 110 016

MURALIDHARAN, K., Scientist
z.Z. Ruhr-Universität Bochum, Lehrstuhl Prof. Maidl
Structural Engineering Research Centre, Madras

IRELAND

DUFFY, W.P., Sectional Engineering Manager
Civil Works Department, Electricity Supply Board
18/21 St. Stephen's Green, Stephen Court, Dublin 2

O'FLAHERTY, R.M., Divisional Engineering Manager
Civil Works Department, Electricity Supply Board
18/21 St. Stephen's Green, Stephen Court, Dublin 2

ISRAEL

GOLDBERGER, M., Engineering Geologist
GOLDBERGER, Mrs.
Tahal Consulting Engineers Ltd.
P.O.B. 11170, Tel-Aviv 61111

HARASH, A., Dr., Eng.Geologist
Tahal Consulting Engineers Ltd.
54 Ibn Gevirol Str., Tel-Aviv

KORB, M., Engineer
Tahal Consulting Engineers Ltd.
54 Ibn Gevirol Str., Tel-Aviv

SEBEL, J., Mining Engineer
Petroleum Services LTT
Tuoot H'Arez 3, Tel Aviv

ITALY

BONALDI, P., Dr.Eng., Chief Engineer
ISMES - Experimental Institute for Models & Structures
Viale Giulio Cesare, 29, 24100 Bergamo

BORSETTO, M., Dr.Eng., Engineer
ISMES - Experimental Institute for Models & Structures
Viale Giulio Cesare, 29, 24100 Bergamo

DOLCETTA CAPUZZO, M., President AGI - President ISMES
ISMES, Viale Giulio Cesare, 29, 24100 Bergamo

FRUGUGLIETTI, A., Dottore Ingegnere
Cogefar S/A
Via Rombon 11, Milano

GARBUBLIO, E., Ingegnere Idraulico
MARRONE, Mrs., P.
MORETTI, Mrs., B.
SELM S.p.A. Servizi Elettrici Montedison
Via Taramelli 26, 20124 Milano

LEMBO-FAZIO, A., Ingegnere
University of Rome, Ist. Arte Mineraria
Via Eudosiana 18, 00184 Roma

LUMARDI, P., Engineer
c/o Rocksoil S.r.l.
Piazza S. Marco 1, 20121 Milano

PALMIERI, A., Civil Engineer
Studio Ing. G. Pietrangeli
Via A. Poliziano 8, Rome

RIBACCHI, R., Professor of Rock Mechanics
University of Rome, Istituto Arte Mineraria
Via Eudossiana 18, 00184 Roma

ROSSI, P.P., Dr.-Ing.
ISMES
Viale Giulio Cesare 29, 24100 Bergamo

JAPAN

FUJITA, K., Dr.
Hazama-Gumi Ltd.
2-5-8, Kta-Anoyama, Minato-Ku
Tokyo 107

HIRANO, I., Research Engineer
Taisei Corporation
1-25-1, Nishi Shinjuku, Shinjuku-ku, Tokyo

HORI, M., Assistant Manager, Civil Eng. Design Dept.
Electric Power Development Ltd.
1-8-17 Yaesu, Chuo-ku, Tokyo

IGAKI, T., Manager Hydro-power Planning Sect.
The Kansai Electric Power Co., Inc.
33-22 Nakanoshima 3 - Chome Kita-Ku, Osaka 530

IIHOSHI, S., Chief of Section
Taisei Corporation
344-1 Nase, Totsuka-ku, Yokohama-shi

ISHIZUKA, Y., Research Engineer
Shimizu Construction Co.
3-4-17 Echujima, Koto-ku, Tokyo

KATO, N., Chief of Section
Chuo Fukken Consultants Co.
3-5-26 Higashi Mikuni, Yodogawa-ku, Osaka

KAWAMOTO, T., Professor
Nogoya University
Furocho, Chidane-ku, Nagoyashi

KOBAYASHI, Y., Chief Geologist
Geotechnical Laboratory, Technical Research Institute
Okumura Corporation & Engineering
3-5-8 Hamaguchi Nishi, Suminoe-ku, Osaka

KODAMA, T., Chief of Section
Nuclear Power Civ. Eng. Design Dept., Tokyo Electric Power
Services Ltd., 4-6 Nishi Shinbashi, I-chome, Mitato-ku, Tokyo

KUTSUZAWA, S., Chief Engineer
Engineering Dept., Chuo Kaihatsu Corp.
2-11-13 Nishi Waseda, Shinjuku-ku, Tokyo

MIYAKE, F., Deputy General Manager
Shimizu Construction Co.
2-16-1 Kyobashi, Chuo-ku, Tokyo

MORIYAMA, K., R & D Div. Senior Engineer
Civil Engineering Dept., Sato Kogyo Ltd.
4-8 Nihonbashi Honcho, Chuo-ku, Tokyo

SAKURAI, S., Professor
Dept. of Civil Eng., Kobe University
Rokko, Nada-ku, Kobe 657

SATO, Y., Assistant Manager
Tokyo Construction Co.
1-16-14 Shibuya, Shibuya ku, Tokyo

SOTOMURA, K.
Taisei Corporation, 25-1, Nishi-Shintuku,
I-Chome Shintuku, Tokyo

TADASHI, K., Dipl.-Ing., Architekt
c/c Shimizu Construction Co., Ltd.
Berliner Allee 25, 4000 Düsseldorf

YAMADA, I., Senior Research Engineer
Kajima Corporation
2-19-1 Hidakyu, Chofu-shi, Tokyo

YOICHI, H., Engineer
Hazama Gumi
1233 Yono, Yono-shi, Saitama

YOSHIDA, M., Dr.Eng., Vice-President of ISRM for Asia
Executive Vice-President & Director, The Kansai Electric
Power Co., Inc., 3-22 Nakanoshima 3-Chome, Kita-ku, Osaka

YOSHITADA, I., Assistant General Manager
Nuclear Power Department, Electric Power Development Co.,Ltd.
8-2, Marunouchi I-chome, Chiyoda-ku, Tokyo 100

LUXEMBURG

ARTCIS, F., Ingénieur - Chef de Service
MecanARBED Dommeldange S.à.r.l.
B.P. 34, 1050 Dommeldange

PELLIN, J., Ingénieur en chef
Societe Electrique de l'Our S.A.
Boite postale 37, 2010 Luxembourg

MEXICO

BELLO, A., Civil Engineer
Geosistemas S.A., Grupo ICA
A. Ortega 1306, 03100 Mexico D.F.

RUIZ-VÁZGUEZ, M., Ingenieur Geologue
RUIZ-VÁZGUEZ, Mrs.
Univers. National Autonom. de México
Av. San Francisco No. 551, Magdalena Contreras
México, 20, D.F. (10500)

MOROCCO

CHAOUI, A., Vice-President of ISRM for Africa
B.P. 325, Rabat-Chella

NETHERLANDS

BRAAT, K.B., B.Sc., Civil Engineer
Royal Volker Stevin
P.O.Box 2695, 3000 CR Rotterdam

BUCK, J., Bauingenieur
Grabowsky en Poort B.V.
Oude Malsbergerweg 18, 6369 GR Simpelveld

LORENZEN, H., Dipl.-Ing.
Billiton International Metals B.V.
19 Louis Couperusplein, 2514 HP Den Haag

LUGER, H.J., Dipl.-Ing.
Delft Soil Mechanics Laboratory
P.O.Box 69, 2600 AB Delft

UITTENBOGAARD, R.E., Ir.
Delft Hydraulics Laboratory
P.O.Box 177, 2600 MH Delft

NORWAY

AARVOLL, M., Civil Engineer
Ingeniør Chr. F. Gruner A.S.
Kjørbuveien 14, 1300 Sandvika

AAS, G., Senior Chief Engineer
Ing. F. Selmer A/S
Postbox 6035 Etterstad, Oslo 6

ANDERSEN, U.H., Civil Engineer
Ing. Chr. F. Gruner A.S.
Kjørbuveien 14, 1300 Sandvika

BERGH-CHRISTENSEN, J., Dr.-Ing.
BERGH-CHRISTENSEN, Mrs.
A/S Geoteam
W. Thranesgt. 98, Oslo 1

BROCH, E., Dr.-Ing.
The Norwegian Institute of Technology, Dep. of Geology
University of Trondheim, 7034 Trondheim-NTH

BUEN, B., Dr.-Ing., Engineering Geologist
Ing. A.B. Berdal A/S, Partner of Norconsult A/S
Kjörbuveien 14, 1300 Sandvika

HELTZEN, A., Bergingenieur
N.T.N.F.
Bjarne Skausvei 14, 1347 Hosle

JOHANSEN, P.M., Civil Engineer
Norwegian Geotechnical Institute
P.O.Box 40, Taasen, Oslo 8

KJØLBERG, R.S., Siv.Ing.
KJØLBERG, Mrs.
A/S Geoteam
W. Thranesgt. 98, Oslo 1

KNUDSMOEN, M., Chartered Civ. Eng.
Siv.ing. Elliot Strømme A/S
Kjørbuvn. 16, 1300 Sandvika

MYRSET, Q., Senior Engineer
Norwegian Water Resources and Electricity Board
Middelthuns Gate 29, Oslo 3

MYRVANG, A.M., Dr.-Ing.
Mining Dept., The Norwegian Inst. of Technology
7034 Trondheim-NTH

NILSEN, B., Dr.-Ing.
Noteby, Norske Teknisk Byggekontroll A/S
Postboks 3544, Ilevouur, 7000 Trondheim

PALMSTRØM, A., Engineering Geologist
Ing. A.B. Berdal A/S, Partner of Norconsult A/S
Kjørbuvegen 14, 1300 Sandvika

TVEITAN, I., Dipl.-Ing.
Ing. A.B. Berdal A/S, Partner of Norconsult A/S
Kjörbuveien 14, 1300 Sandvika

POLAND

GERGOWICZ, Z., Prof. Dr. habil. Ing.
Institut für Geotechnik, Technische Hochschule Wroclaw
Al. Olimpijska 17, 51-612 Wroclaw

PORTUGAL

AZEVEDO, M.
Equipamento Hidraulico, Electricidade de Portugal
Bolhao

BARROSO, M., Research Officer
BARROSO, Mrs. N.
LNEC, 101 Avenida do Brasil, 1799 Lisboa Codex

PINTO DA CUNHA, A.J.V., Civil Engineer, Research Officer
PINTO DA CUNHA, Mrs. D.
LNEC, 101 Avenida do Brasil, 1799 Lisboa Codex

EUSEBIO, Mrs., Maria de Lourdes, Executive-Secretary, ISRM
LNEC, 101 Avenida do Brasil, 1799 Lisboa Codex

GROSSMANN, N.F., Dipl.-Ing.Bergbau, Research Officer
LNEC, 101 Avenida do Brasil, 1799 Lisboa Codex

MACEDO, R.
Equipamento Hidraulico, Electricidade de Portugal
Bolhao

PERES-RODRIGUES, F., Principal Research Officer
LNEC, 101 Avenida do Brasil, 1799 Lisboa Codex

ROCHA, Mrs., M.T.
95, Avenida Estados Unidos, 3rd Floor, 1799 Lisboa 5

DA SILVEIRA, A., Head, Dams Dep.
DA SILVEIRA, Mrs. I.
LNEC, 101 Avenida do Brasil, 1799 Lisboa Codex

SILVÉRIO, A., Dr. Secretary-General of ISRM
SILVÉRIO, Mrs. I.
LNEC, 101 Avenida do Brasil, 1799 Lisboa Codex

SOUSA, L., Civil Engineer
LNEC, 101 Avenida do Brasil, 1799 Lisboa Codex

SOUTH AFRICA

CAHNBLEY, H., Dr.-Ing., Rock Mechanics Engineer
Johannesburg Consolidated Investment Company Limited
P.O.Box 590, Johannesburg 2000

GEORGE, D., Engineering Geologist
George, Orr and Assocites
P.O.Box 3419, Pretoria, 0001

STACEY, D., Dr.
Steffen, Robertson and Kirsten
P.O.Box 8856, Johannesburg

VREEDE, F.A.
CSIR Geomechanics
Pretoria

SOUTH EAST ASIA

HSIEH, C.S., Engineer
Sinotech Engineering Consultants Inc.
10th Floor, 280 Chung Hsiao East Road, Sec. 4
Taipei

TSAI, C.T.
Taiwan Power Company
39 East Hoping Road, Sec. 1
Taipei

SPAIN

BRIONES, F., Ingeniero de Caminos
Hidroelectrica Espanola, S.A.
Hermosilla 3, Madrid-1

DE CELIS, J.R., Engineer
Iberduero, S.A.
Gardoqui 8, Bilbao 8

FERRANDIZ, E., Ingeniero de Caminos
SENER
Avda. Zugazarte 56, Las Arenas (Vizcaya)

GAZTANAGA, J., Civil Engineer
Hidroelectrica Espanola S.A.
Hermosilla 3, Madrid-1

PRESMANES, A., Ingeniero de Caminos
SENER
Avda. Zugazarte 56, Las Arenas (Vizcaya)

SALAS, J.A.Jimenez, Professor
Laboratorio Carreteras y Geotecnia
Alfonso XII no. 3, Madrid

SURROCA, P.L., Ingeniero de Caminos
Hidroelectrica Espanola S.A.
Hermosilla 3, Madrid-1

URIEL ROMERO, S., Prof., Vice President of ISRM for Europe
Laboratorio de Carreteras y Geotecnia
Alfonso XII,2, Madrid-7

SWEDEN

AHLGREN, B., Geologist
Sweco
P.O.Box 5038, 102 41 Stockholm

AKESSON, B., Prof.
Chalmers Technical University
412 96 Göteborg

BERGLIND, B., Dipl.-Ing.
Geodynamik AB
Regeringsgaten 111, 111 39 Stockholm

BJURSTRÖM, St., Research Director
BeFo, Box 5501, 11485 Stockholm

CALMINDER, A., M. Sc.
WP-System AB
Box 45118, 104 30 Stockholm

HAHN, T., Dr.
Conswede, Tegeluddsvagen 31
Box 29028, 10052 Stockholm

HELFRICH, H. K., Prof. Dr. Phil.
Brunsvägen 5, 182 45 Enebyberg

HOLMBERG, R.
Swedish Detonic Research Foundation
Box 32058, 12611 Stockholm

LINDQVIST, Senior Research Eng.
University of Lulea
951 87 Lulea

MÄKI, K., Research Eng.
SveDeFo,
Box 32058, 12611 Stockholm

MARTNA, J., Dr.-Ing., Chief Engineering Geologist
Swedish State Power Board
16227 Vällingby, Stockholm

OLSSON, L., Civil Engineer
Royale Inst. of Technology, Dept. of Soil and Rock Mechanics
10044 Stockholm

RASMUSSEN, P. H., Tekn. Dr.
RASMUSSEN, Mrs., R.
Firma Tre R
Ornbergsv 23, 14600 Tullinge

SAGEFORS, I., Civ. Eng.
SAGEFORS, Mrs., L.
WP-System AB
Box 45118, 10044 Stockholm

STEPHANSSON, O., Prof.
University of Lulea,
95187 Lulea

THURNER, H., Dr. Ing. Dozent
Geodynamik AB
Regeringsgatan 111, 111 39 Stockholm

WIKING, T., Engineer
VBB AB
Box 5038, 10241 Stockholm

SWITZERLAND

AMSTAD, C., Dipl. Bauing. ETH
Institut für Straßen-, Eisenbahn- und Felsbau,
ETH Zürich
Hönggerberg, 8093 Zürich

BÜCHI, E., Geologist
Atlas Copco Jarva
Obere Hauptgasse 78, 3600 Thun

DAWANS, P., Ing. dipl. EPFL, Chef de service genie civil
Societe Anonyme, L'Energie de L'Quest-Suisse (EOS)
Place de la Gare 12, Case postale 1048, 1001 Lausanne

DEMONT, J.-B., Ingenieur en chef
Compagnie d'Etudes de Travaux Publics (CEPT) SA
Saint-Martin 9, 1003 Lausanne

DIETRICH, H.
c/o Losinger AG
Könizstr. 74, 3000 Bern

EGGER, P., Prof. Dr.-Ing., Chef de Section
Lab. mecanique des roches-EPFL, 1015 Lausanne

EPPINGER, G., Dipl. Bauing. (F.H.)
Elektrowatt Ingenieurunternehmung AG
Bellerivestr. 36, 8022 Zürich

FELLMANN, W., Dipl.-Ing. ETH
Elektrowatt Ingenieurunternehmung AG
Bellerivestr. 36. 8022 Zürich

FERENCZI, G., Dipl. Bauing.
Suiselektra Ing. Unt. AG
Malzgasse 32, 4010 Basel

GILG, B., Dr.-Ing.
Elektrowatt Ingenieurunternehmung AG
Bellerivestr. 36, 8022 Zürich

GRABER, F., Ing. HTL
Losinger AG, VSL Internat.
Könizstr. 74, 3001 Bern

HALDEMANN, K., Dipl.-Ing. ETH
HALDEMANN, Mrs.
AG Ingenieurbüro Maggia
6601 Locarno

HAMBACH, P., Dipl.-Ing. Geschäftsführer
HAMBACH, Mrs.
Murer AG, Niederlassung Genf,
13 Chemin des Fraisiers, 1212 Grand-Lancy

HEGLAND, R., Dipl.-Ing. ETH/SIA
Jenatsch + Hegland Dipl.-Ing. ETH/SIA
Bahnhofplatz 8, 7000 Chur

JENNI, J.-P., Dr., Abteilungschef
Motor-Columbus Ingenieurunternehmung AG
Parkstr. 27, 5401 Baden

KARNELO, E., Ing.
Atlas Copco Jarva
Obere Hauptstr. 78, 3600 Thun

KESSLER, E., Bauing.
Ing. Büro Heierli AG
Postf. 248, 8033 Zürich

LECHNER, E., Ingenieur
Robbins Comp. Zürich
Bellariastr. 82, 8038 Zürich

MATHIS, R., Verkaufsingenieur
CHARZYNSKI, Mr., P.
Alira AG
Bellikonerstr. 218, 8967 Widen

MEYER, D., Dipl.-Ing., wiss. Adjunkt
Bundesamt für Verkehr
Bundeshaus Nord, 3003 Bern

MIKSICEK, R., Dipl. Bauing.
Elektrowatt Ingenieurunternehmung AG
Bellerivestr. 36, 8022 Zürich

PANTUCEK, P., Dipl.-Ing.
c/o Stump Bohr AG, Ing. Abt.
Mühlebachstr. 20, 8032 Zürich

PFISTER, E., Dipl.-Ing. ETH / SIA, M.Sc.
Nagra,
Parkstr. 23, 5401 Baden

ROELLI, P. E.
Losinger AG, VSL Internat.
Könizstr. 74, 3000 Bern

RUPPANNER, H.-J., ETH/SIA, Prokurist
Prader AG, Waisenhausstr. 2, 8001 Zürich

SCHLEISS, A., Dipl. Bauing. ETH
Versuchsanstalt für Wasserbau 3, ETH Zürich
Hönggerberg, 8093 Zürich

SCHMID, R., Bauing. ETHZ
Motor-Columbus Ingenieurunternehmung AG
Abt. Untertag- und Wasserbau
Parkstr. 27, 5401 Baden

SPRIANO, S., Dipl. Bauing. ETH
Elektrowatt Ingenieurunternehmung AG
Bellerivestr. 36, 8022 Zürich

STEINER, W., Dr., Dipl. Bauing. ETH
ELC Electroconsult eng.
Via Monte Ceneri 17, 6900 Lugano

VORACEK, J., Dipl.-Ing.
Societe Anonyme, l'Energie de L'Quest-Suisse (EOS)
Place de la Gare 12, Postale 1048, 1001 Lausanne

WANNER, H., Dr. Geologe
Geologisches Büro Dr. H. Wanner AG
Friedhofstr. 9, 9014 St. Gallen

WERNER, Ch., Dipl.-Ing. ETH
Ingenieurbüro A. Birchlek AG
Riedstr. 7, 6430 Schwyz

WINDLER, H., Dipl.-Ing. ETH, Prokurist
Prader AG, Waisenhausstr. 2, 8001 Zürich

ZURBUCHEN, W., Dipl.-Ing.
Giovanola Fréres S.A.
1870 Monthey

THAILAND

FREIMANIS, I., Senior Design Engineer
Snowy Mountains Engineering Corporation
8th Floor, Shell House, 140 Wireless Road
Bangkok

RATANAKUL, P.
RATANAKUL, Mrs.
Electricity Generating Authority of Thailand
Kanchanaburi

WATAKEEKUL, S.
WATAKEEKUL, Mrs.
Electricity Generating Authority of Thailand
Kanchanaburi

TURKEY

AYDIN, B., Lecturer, Mining Engineer
Mining Engineering Department, Middle East Technical
University (METU) Ankara-Turkey
Maden Mühendisligi Bölümü, Orta Dogu Teknik Üniv.
Ankara

UNITED KINGDOM

ALSOP, I., Chief Engineer
ALSOP, Mrs., J.
Diyam Consultants, c/o B.T.Seddon, Binnie & Partners
Artillery House, Artillery Row, London Swip 1RX

BROWN, E.T., Prof.
Imperial College of Science and Technology, Dept. of
Mineral Resources Engineering, Imperial College
London SW7 2BP

DAY, C.J., Civil Engineer
Dames Moore
123 Mortlake High Street, London SW14 8SN

DOUGLAS, T. H., Civil Engineer
James Williamson & Partners
231 St.Vincent Street, Glasgow G2 5QZ

FOWELL, Dr.
University of Newcastle upon Tyne
Newcastle upon Tyne, NE1 7RU

GOLDER, H.Q., Dr.
Golder Associates
5 Forlease Road, Maidenhaed, Berkshire SL6 1RP

GONANO, L.P., Dr.
Golder Associates
5 Forlease Road, Maidenhaed, Berkshire SL6 1RP

LEGGE, F., Chartered Engineer
W.L.P.U. Consultants
35 Station Road, Ashford, Kent

MACFARLANE, I. M., Technical Director, Civil Engineer
Cementation Specialist Holdings Ltd.
Denhem Way, Maple Cross, Rickmansworth, Herts WD3 2SW

MELLORS, T.W., Dr.
Golder Associates
5 Forlease Road, Maidenhaed, Berkshire S16 1RP

PASSARIS, E., Dr., University Lecturer
Unversity of Newcastle upon Tyne
Newcastle upon Tyne, NE1 7RU

ROWLAND, A., Civil Engineer
Binnie & Partners, Artillery House,
Artillery Row, London SW1P 1RX

SCOTT, R.A., Cosultant, Civil Engineer, Physicist
Cementation Specialist Holdings Ltd.
Denham Way, Maple Cross, Rickmanworth, Herts WD3 2SW

SEDDON, B.T., Civil Engineer
Binnie & Partners, Artillery House,
Artillery Row, London SW1P 1RX

SHARP, J.C., Dr.
Golder Associates
5 Forlease Road, Maidenhaed, Berkshire SL6 1RP

USA

ATCHISON, T. C., Prof., Vice-President of ISRM for
North America
University of Minnesota, Dept. of Civil and Mineral Eng.
221 Church Street SE, Minneapolis, Minnesota 55455

BANKS, D., Dr., Chief
Engineering Geology and Rock Mechanics
USAE Waterways Experiment Station
P.O. Box 631, Vicksburg, MS 39180

BARTON, N., Ph.D.
Terra Teck
420 Wakara Way, Salt Lake City

BREKKE, T., Prof.
University of California, College of Engineering
434, B Davis Hall, T2B, Berkeley, California 94720

COULSON, J.H., Principal Civil Engineer
Tennessee Valley Authority
400 West Summit Hill Drive
Knoxville, Tennessee

FAIRHURST, C.H., Prof.
Dept. of Civil and Mineral Engineering
University of Minnesota
Minneapolis, MN 55455

HAIMSON, B., Prof.
Univ. of Wisconsin
1509 University Av., Madison, Wisconsin 53706

HARDY, H. R., Prof. Dr.
HARDY, Mrs., M. M.
Pennsylvania State University
Room 117 MS Bldg., University Park, Pennsylvania 16802

LANG, T. A., Consulting Engineer
LANG, Mrs., A. H.
1 Doral Drive, Moraga, California 94556

OBERT, L., Dr.
OBERT, Mrs.
2680 South Ames Way, Denver, Colorado 30227

ROBBINS, R. J., President
ROBBINS, Mrs. B.
Robbins Company
Box C8027, Kent, Wa. 98031

ROEGIERS, J. C., Dr., Senior Associate Scientist
Dowell Inc., 5051, S. 129th. E. Avenue
Tulsa, Oklahoma 74139

THOMS, R. L., Dr.
Applied Geomechanics Inc.
P.O.Box 80619, Baton Rouge, LA 70890

WAGNER, JOHN E., Dr.
Arlington, Virginia 22201
3229 First Place, North

ZAGARS, A., Civil Engineer
Harza Engineering Company
150 S. Wacker Drive, Chicago, Illinois 60606

USSR

FILATOV, N.A., Prof. Dr., Chief of a Laboratory
The All-Union Research Institute of Mine Geomechanics and Surveying (VNIMI)
199026 Leningrad, Sredrij Avenue 82

MARKOV, G., Prof. Dr.Sc.(Tech)
Mining Institute Kola Branch, Academy of Sciences of the USSR
Fersman St. 24, 184200 Apatity Murmansk

SHIBAKOVA, V., Dr.Sc.
Geological Institute of AS of USSR
Moscow 117 234

YUFIN, S., Associate Professor of Engineering
Moscow Institute of Civil Engineering
Shlyuzovaya Embankment 8, Moscow, 113113

YUGOSLAVIA

CALGOVIĆ, M., Prof. Dipl.-Ing.
Universität Zagreb
Rokova ul. 9, 41000 Zagreb

DRAGAĆEVAE, D., Dipl.-Ing.
IBT Aeroinzenjering Beograd
Proleterskih Brigada 76, Beograd

FINGERHUT, L., Bergbau Dipl.-Ing.
FINGERHUT, Mrs. N.
Geotehnika - Zagreb
41000 Zagreb, Kupska 2

GOTIĆ, I., Dipl.-Ing.
GOTIĆ, Mrs. K.
RGN Fakultet Zagreb, Oour Varazdin
Hinkovicéva 7, 42000 Varazdin

IVANOVIC, K., Ingenieur
Institut J-Cerni
Beograd

KORICA, M., Dipl.-Ing.
Energoprojekt Beograd
Lenjinon Bulevar 12, Beograd

KORPAR, St., Dipl.-Ing.
KORPAR, Mrs. L.
RGN Fakultet Zagreb, Oour Varazdin
Hinkovicéva 7, 42000 Varazdin

MIJAJLOVIĆ, R., Civil Engineer
Centroprojekt
11 Belgrad, Zahnmska 26

NIKOLIĆ, Z.
Design Office, Hydraulic Engineering Department
The Energoprojekt Company
Belgrade

OCONOHID, M., Dipl.-Ing.
Institut la Putene Beograd
Kuuodrasko 257, Beograd

PERŠIČ, S., Civil Engineer
Energoprojekt
11070 Belgrad, Yugoslavija Bulevar Lenjina 12

PETKOVŚEK, B., Engineering Geologist
Geoloski Zauod Ljubljana
Parmova 37, 61000 Ljubljana

PODOBNIK, I., Dipl.-Ing. Mont.
Geoloski Zauod Ljubljana
61000 Ljubljana-Dimiceva 16

PROKOPOVIĆ, S., Dipl.Berg.Ing.
Institut Geoexpert
41000 Zagreb

PROTIC, M., Bauingenieur
Centroprojekt
11 Belgrad, Ivaija Milutinovica, SRP No. 102

SELJAMOVIĆ, M., Dipl.-Ing., Geologe
Centroprojekt
11 Belgrad, Zahnmska 26

* 1 *

ROCK MECHANICAL INVESTIGATION PROGRAMS FOR LARGE CAVERNS IN ROCK MASSES

Felsmechanische Untersuchungsprogramme für grosse Felskavernen

Programmes de recherches en mécanique des roches dans le cas de cavernes rocheuses de grandes dimensions

UNTERSUCHUNGEN ZUM FRAC-VERHALTEN VON SALZGEBIRGE

Investigations concerning the fracturing of rock salt

Recherches concernant les conditions de rupture d'un terrain de sel

C.FROHN, V.GRAEFE, M.W.SCHMIDT & A.URFF

Gesellschaft für Strahlen- und Umweltforschung mbH, Braunschweig, Bundesrepublik Deutschland

SUMMARY:

Underground boreholes in rock salt must be safely sealed from potential fluids of petrostatic pressure. Fracture of the surrounding rock must be prevented. However, measurements in the Asse-salt mine indicate that the pressure, at which cracking occurs, is decreasing in the vicinity of galleries. This influence is very strong, so that no increase of frac-pressure with depth could be found within a radius of 20 m. Finite element calculations can give an idea of the dependence of the frac-pressure from the gradually changing state of stress about an open borehole.

ZUSAMMENFASSUNG:

Für untertägige Bohrungen im Salzgebirge werden sichere Bohrlochabschlüsse verlangt gegen Fluide, die unter petrostatischem Druck zusitzen können. Ein Brechen des umgebenden Gesteins muß vermieden werden. Messungen, die im Rahmen eines Versuchsprogramms im Salzbergwerk Asse ausgeführt werden, zeigen aber , daß der Brechdruck des Salzgesteins in der Nähe der Strecken stark abnimmt. Der Einfluß des Streckenhohlraums ist so groß, daß im Umkreis der Strecken von über 20 m keine Zunahme des Brechdrucks mit der Teufe festgestellt werden kann. Finite-Element-Rechnungen geben Hinweise auf den Zusammenhang zwischen Brechdruck und dem sich langsam ändernden Spannungszustand um ein offenes Bohrloch.

RESUME:

On demande pour les sondages souterrains, qui sont faits dans le terrain de sel, que les fermetures des trous de sonde peuvent resiter à la pression pétrostatique des fluids. On doit éviter, que la roche englobante brise. Le programme de recherche est fait dans la mine de sel. Mais les mesures montrent, que la cassure des bancs compétents de l´évaporite diminue dans le voisinage des galeries. L´influence du vide de la voie ou de la galerie est si grande, que la cassure de bancs compétents, qu´on mesure dans un rayon des galeries de plus que vingt mètres, n´accroît pas avec la profondeur. Il existe une relation entre la cassure de bancs compétents et l´état de contrainte, qui existe autour du trou de sonde ouvert et qui se change lentement. La méthode, FINITE-ELEMENT, montre cette relation.

1 EINLEITUNG

Im Hinblick auf eine geforderte sichere säkulare Lagerung von radioaktiven Abfällen ist der Gesellschaft für Strahlen- und Umweltforschung (GSF) das ehemalige Steinsalzbergwerk Asse zur Durchführung von einschlägigen Forschungs- und Entwicklungsarbeiten übertragen worden.

Zu den Problemen, die sich hier bei den Standsicherheitsuntersuchungen ergeben, gehört die Frage, wie sich das aus der Praxis des Salzbergbaus bekannte gute mechanische Tragverhalten des Salzgebirges langfristig erhalten läßt, wenn einzelne Hohlräume im Salinar unter hydraulischen Innendruck gesetzt werden. Diese Frage wird hier für untertägig ansetzende Bohrungen untersucht, wo unerwartete Flüssigkeits- oder Gasaustritte erfolgen können, für die die Bergbehörde sichere Bohrlochabschlüsse fordert. Die Bohrlochverschlüsse müssen so ausgeführt sein, daß sie den Druck der zusitzenden Fluide aufnehmen können, ohne daß es in der Umgebung der Verschlüsse zu einem

Aufreißen des Gebirges kommt und die Fluide unkontrolliert austreten. Es ist also zu untersuchen, bei welchem Innendruck einer Bohrung das Gebirge bricht (fract).

Bei der Behandlung dieser Fragestellung soll in Analogie zu allgemeinen Prinzipien einer Standsicherheitsanalyse vorgegangen werden.
Demnach
- ist zu untersuchen, welche Erfahrungen aus der Praxis über das geomechanische Verhalten vergleichbarer untertägiger Hohlräume vorliegen,
- ist eine Modellvorstellung für das Problem zu entwickeln, mit deren Hilfe das Spannungs-, Verformungs- und Bruchverhalten numerisch abgeschätzt werden kann,
- sind in-situ-Untersuchungen vorzunehmen, so daß ein Vergleich zwischen dem vorausberechneten und dem tatsächlichen Gebirgsverhalten möglich ist.

Eine derartige Analyse ist entsprechend dem jeweiligen Kenntnisstand gegebenenfalls fortzuschreiben.

2 ERFRAHRUNGEN DER PRAXIS

Als ein wesentliches Bauelement des Bohrlochverschlusses werden in der Praxis "Standrohre" verwendet. Dies sind koaxial in die Bohrungen einzementierte, einige Meter lange Rohre, die am Stoß durch eine Kopfplatte fest verschlossen sind. Sie halten den radial wirkenden Innendruck von der Bohrlochwand fern und wandeln den axial auf die Kopfplatte gerichteten Druck in axial gerichtete Schubspannungen auf der Bohrlochwand um. Diese allein verbleibende Beanspruchung der Bohrlochwandung kann beliebig klein gemacht werden, wenn das Standrohr hinreichend lang gewählt wird.
Eine solche zuverlässige Möglichkeit, die Beanspruchung des Gebirges im Bereich des Stoßes herabzusetzen, hat sich als notwendig erwiesen, da der Druck angebohrter Fluideinschlüsse so hoch sein kann, daß das Gebirge ohne diese Maßnahme in der Umgebung des Verschlusses brechen würde.

Experimentell ermittelte Bohrloch-Innendrücke, die zum Bruch des Gesteins führten ("Brechdrücke", "Fracdrücke"), streuen stark. Bedingt ist dies durch die Einwirkung folgender Parameter:
- Inhomogenität und Anisotropie des Gebirges
- äußeres Spannungsfeld um die Bohrung
- elastische und plastische Eigenschaften des Gesteins
- Existenz von Mikrorissen und Art ihrer Ausbildung
- Porenwasserdruck.

Möglich erscheint auch eine Zunahme des Brechdrucks mit der Teufe. Wenn man annimmt, daß der Spannungszustand im Gebirge wesentlich durch die Gewichtskraft des überlagerten Gesteins bestimmt wird, müßte ein solcher petrostatischer Druck vor dem Aufreißen des Gesteins erst überwunden werden. Diese Abhängigkeit des Brechdruckes von der Teufe konnte aber bisher nicht nachgewiesen werden, eventuell deshalb, weil die Meßpunkte in Stoßnähe lagen, wo das Spannungsfeld stark verändert ist.

Zur Überprüfung der Sicherheit werden die Standrohre vor Inbetriebnahme unter den örtlichen petrostatischen Druck gesetzt. Das ist erforderlich, da auch Fluideinschlüsse unter diesem Druck stehen können.

Man hat daher die Situation, daß die Standrohre proportional zur Teufe gegen immer größeren Innendruck ausgelegt werden müssen, ohne daß jedoch bisher beim umgebenden Gestein eine ebenfalls mit der Teufe zunehmende Brechfestigkeit festgestellt werden kann. Um zu einer vernünftigen Dimensionierung zu kommen, scheinen weitere Untersuchungen zum Brechverhalten des Gesteins geboten.

3 NUMERISCHE UNTERSUCHUNG DER SPANNUNGSVERHÄLTNISSE AM BOHRLOCH

Ziel der numerischen Untersuchungen war, eine qualitative Vorstellung von den Spannungsumlagerungen zu erhalten, die beim Aufbringen des Brechdruckes (Fracdruckes) in der Umgebung des Bohrlochs ablaufen.

In die Rechnungen einzubeziehen ist der Zeitraum zwischen der Fertigstellung der Bohrung und dem Beginn des Druckversuchs, da schon während dieser Zeit - verursacht durch die Kriecheigenschaft des Salzgesteins - erhebliche Spannungsumlagerungen in der Bohrlochumgebung erfolgen und damit der Spannungszustand zu Beginn des Versuches stark von der Standzeit des offenen Bohrlochs abhängt.

Es wird angenommen, daß die auftretenden Verformungs- und Belastungszustände im Gestein rotationssymmetrisch bezüglich der Bohrlochachse sind und ein ebener Dehnungszustand vorliegt. Für die Berechnung kann daher aus dem Gestein eine Scheibe senkrecht zur Bohrlochachse herausgegriffen werden; deren Material soll isotrop sein.

Der ursprüngliche Spannungszustand im umgebenden Gebirge wird durch ein Feld kugelsymmetrischer Spannungstensoren beschrieben. Die Komponenten sollen sich wie bei einer ruhenden Flüssigkeit aus der Gewichtskraft des überlagerten Materials berechnen. Hiernach wurde für eine

Teufe von 775 m auf die Hauptspannungen $\sigma_r = \sigma_\phi = \sigma_z = 17{,}8$ MPa geschlossen (petrostatischer Spannungszustand).

Der Scheibenradius ist mit 1,60 m so groß gewählt, daß sich am äußeren Scheibenrand keine Belastungsänderungen bemerkbar machen, die vom Bohrlochinnenrand herrühren.

Als Randbedingung hat man daher am äußeren Scheibenrand den Druck $p_a = 17{,}8$ MPa. Senkrecht zu den Scheibenoberflächen sollen Verschiebungen nicht zugelassen sein. Am Innenrand des Bohrlochs herrscht der Atmosphärendruck $p_i = 0{,}1$ MPa für den Zeitraum von 300 Stunden (offene Standzeit), dann wird innerhalb von 5 Minuten der Innendruck linear bis auf $p_i = 20$ MPa erhöht, was der Durchführung des Brech- (Frac-) Versuchs entspricht.

Für den elastischen Anteil des Stoffgesetzes wird das Hocksche Gesetz benutzt mit dem Elastizitätsmodul $E = 2{,}84 \cdot 10^{10}$ Pa und der Querkontraktionszahl $\nu = 0{,}28$ /1/.

Als Stoffgesetz für das Primäre Kriechen, das bei den hier betrachteten Zeiträumen auftritt, kann die Gleichung

$$\dot{\varepsilon} = a\,\sigma^n \exp(-Q/RT) \quad \text{mit}$$

$a = 2{,}083 \cdot 10^{-36}\ \text{Pa}^{-5}\text{s}^{-1}$
$n = 5$
$Q = 54{,}21\ \text{MJ}\cdot\text{kmol}^{-1}$
$R = 8{,}314\ \text{kJ}\cdot\text{kmol}^{-1}\cdot\text{K}^{-1}$
$T = 313$ K
$\dot{\varepsilon}$ = Dehnungsgeschwindigkeit
σ = Effektivspannung

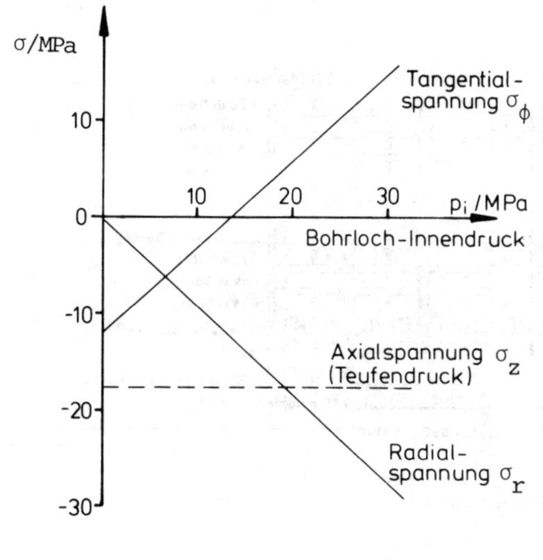

Abb. 1 Änderung der drei Hauptspannungen am Bohrlochrand beim Aufbringen des Bohrloch-Innendrucks

verwendet werden. Sie ergibt sich aus der Gleichung für Sekundäres Kriechen /2/ durch Vergrößerung des Koeffizienten a um den Faktor 40 /1/. Die Primäre Kriechgeschwindigkeit $\dot{\varepsilon}$ ist also bezüglich der Zeit linearisiert.

Die Lösung des so gestellten Problems erfolgt numerisch mit der Finite-Element-Methode. Benutzt wurden Acht-Knoten-Elemente mit quadratischem Verschiebungsansatz. Die Scheibe wurde in fünfzehn rotationssymmetrische Elemente eingeteilt, wobei die Einteilung zum Bohrlochrand hin feiner wird.

Als Ergebnis der Rechnung gibt die Abb. 1 die zeitliche Entwicklung der Spannungskomponenten in der Umgebung des offenen Bohrlochs. Da das Salzgestein wegen seiner Kriecheigenschaft in das offene Bohrloch ausweichen kann, vermindert sich allmählich der Betrag der Radialspannung. Der Betrag der Tangentialspannung hat anfangs am Bohrlochrand ein Maximum, das aber unter Abflachung ins Gebirge hinein abwandert.

Für die Phase der raschen Druckerhöhung im Bohrloch ist in Abb. 2 der Zusammenhang zwischen Bohrlochinnendruck und den drei Hauptspannungen am Bohrlochrand dargestellt. Mit dem Aufreißen (Fracen) des Gesteins ist bei steigendem Innendruck dann zu rechnen, wenn der zum Wertetripel (σ_r, σ_ϕ, σ_z) gehörige Punkt im Hauptspannungsraum die Bruchfläche erreicht. Gerade im hier betrachteten Bereich ist aber die Lage der Bruchfläche nur ungenügend bekannt. Der Brechdruck (Fracdruck) kann nur ungefähr zu 12 MPa abgeschätzt werden.

4 IN-SITU-UNTERSUCHUNGEN

Bei den in-situ-Untersuchungen im ehemaligen Salzbergwerk Asse II (Abb. 3) wurde das Verfahren des Hydraulic Fracturing /3/, das zunächst in der Erdölindustrie von obertägigen Bohrungen aus eingesetzt wurde, in zwei unterschiedlichen Varianten angewandt.

Beim Verfahren von F. RUMMEL /4/ wird eine Bohrlochsonde benutzt, bei der ein Bohrlochabschnitt von etwa einem Meter Länge durch zwei Packer abgedichtet werden kann. Dieser Abschnitt ist mit Öl gefüllt, das über eine Pumpe unter Druck gesetzt wird.

Beim selbst entwickelten Verfahren wird das Bohrloch durch ein Standrohr verschlossen, das um einige Meter kürzer als die Bohrung ist. Als Druckflüssigkeit wird Lauge verwendet, die im hinteren Teil der Bohrung auf das Salzgestein wirkt.

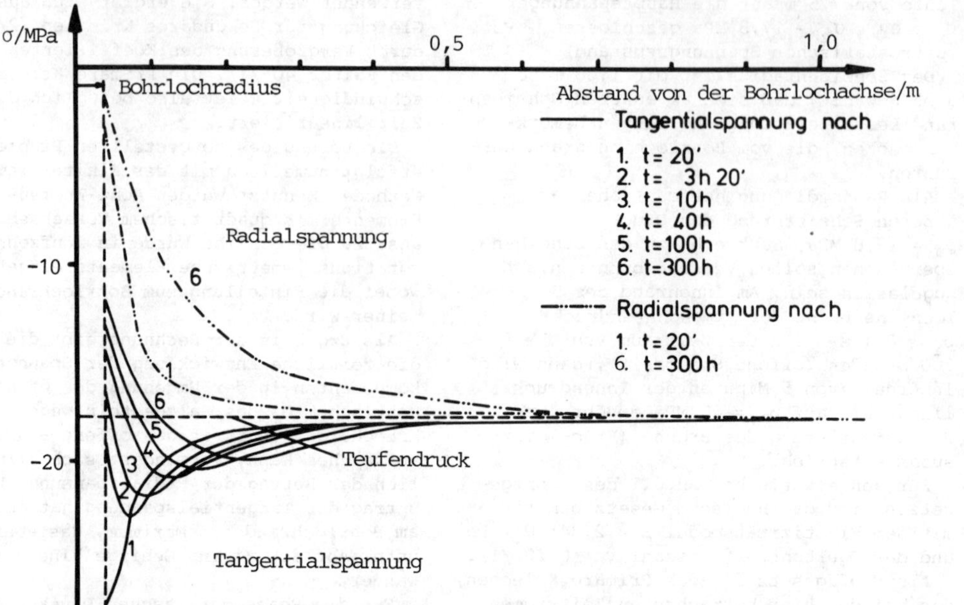

Abb. 2 Zeitliche Entwicklung der Hauptspannungen um ein offenes Bohrloch im Salzgestein. Berechnungen für die ersten 300 Stunden.

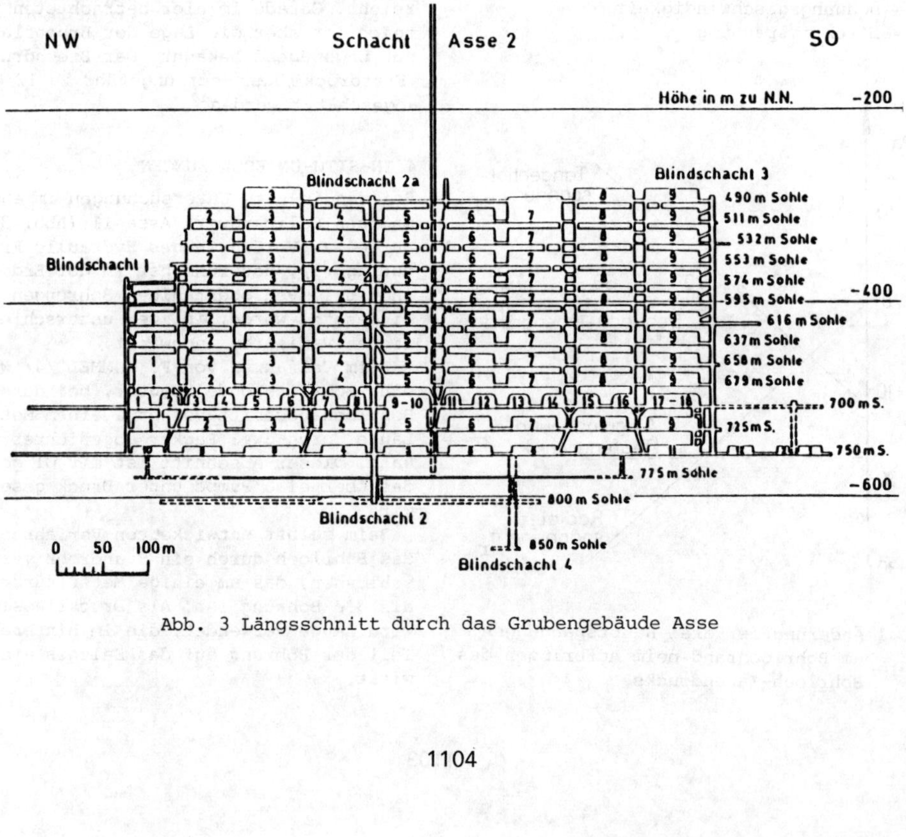

Abb. 3 Längsschnitt durch das Grubengebäude Asse

Bei beiden Verfahren wird der Druck der Bohrlochflüssigkeit zunächst bis zum Aufreißen des Gebirges erhöht (Brechdruck, Fracdruck p_C). Injiziert man keine weitere Flüssigkeit, fällt der Bohrlochinnendruck dann auf einen konstanten Wert, bei dem der entstandene Riß offengehalten wird, sich aber nicht weiter ausbreitet (Shut-in-Druck p_{si}, entspricht der senkrecht zur Rißfläche wirkenden Spannungskomponente). Bei weitere Flüssigkeitszufuhr steigt der Druck wieder soweit an, daß sich die Rißfläche weiter ausbreitet (Refracdruck p_R).

Der Refracdruck ist dabei kleiner zu erwarten als der Fracdruck, da der Riß beim Refrac im Kerbgrund eines Spaltes entsteht, beim Frac aber von einem zylinderförmigen Hohlraum ausgeht.

In Abb. 4 sind diese Druckwerte, die nach dem Rummelschen Verfahren in einer Reihe von 56 mm-Bohrungen im Bereich der 775 m-Sohle gemessen wurden, als Funktion des Abstandes von der Strecke aufgetragen. Zunächst ist die Erwartung bestätigt, daß der Fracdruck größer ist als der Shut-in-Druck, dieser wieder größer als der Refracdruck. Dann ist erkennbar, daß die Drücke in Streckennähe kleiner werden. Das wird auf Spannungsumlagerungen nach Auffahren der Strecke zurückgeführt. Es dürften sich ähnliche Spannungsverteilungen eingestellt haben, wie sie in Abschnitt 3 für die Umlagerung eines offenen Bohrlochs berechnet wurden.

Die schraffierten Flächen machen nach F. RUMMEL /5/ auf einen Druckverlauf aufmerksam, der proportional zur Radialspannung um die Strecke ist (vgl. den Radialspannungsverlauf um das Bohrloch in Abb. 1). Starke Streuungen der Meßwerte fallen auf. Besonders hohe Druckwerte bei 17 m Streckenabstand sind vielleicht auf festeres Gestein zurückzuführen.

Abdruckversuche in den Bohrlöchern zeigten Bruchflächen parallel zur Bohrlochachse an. Trifft man zusätzlich die Annahme, daß eine Hauptspannungsrichtung parallel zur Bohrlochachse liegt, dann läßt sich nach der Theorie des Hydraulic Fracturing für ein elastisch reagierendes Gestein

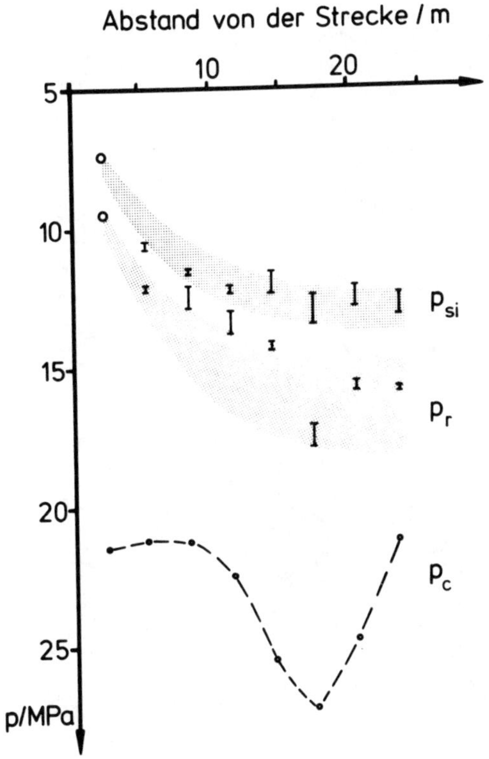

Abb. 4 Fracdruck p_c, Shut-in-Druck p_{si} und Refracdruck p_r in Abhängigkeit von Abstand zur Strecke

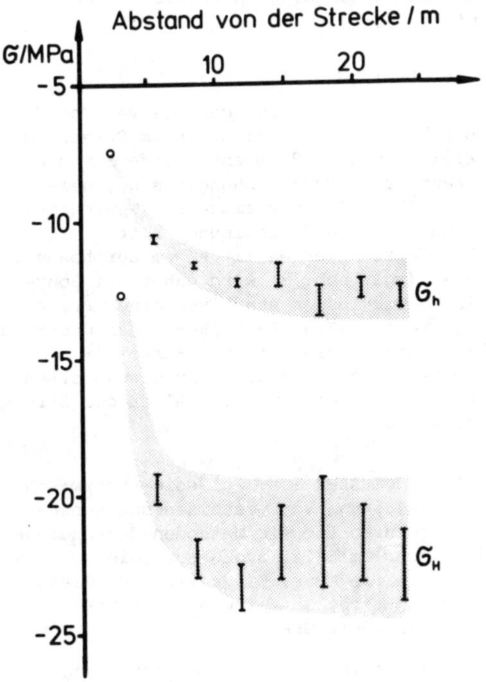

Abb. 5 Extremale Spannungen in Ebenen senkrecht zu den Bohrlochachsen in Abhängigkeit vom Abstand zur Strecke

die Größe der beiden anderen Hauptspannungen berechnen. Sie liegen in der Ebene senkrecht zur Bohrlochachse, die eine dabei senkrecht zur Rißfläche, die andere in der Rißfläche.
Diese Spannungen wurden formal aus den Meßergebnissen berechnet, obwohl natürlich nicht bekannt ist, ob eine Hauptspannungsrichtung mit der Bohrlochachse zusammenfällt und auch die Kriecheigenschaft des Salzgesteins außer Betracht bleibt. Man hat dann nur näherungsweise eine größte und eine kleinste Spannung in einer Ebene senkrecht zur Bohrlochachse. Diese Spannungen σ_h und σ_H sind in Abb. 5 über dem Abstand von der Strecke aufgetragen. Sie unterscheiden sich um den Faktor 2, ein kugelsymmetrischer Spannungszustand liegt daher im Meßbereich sicher nicht vor. Der Verlauf der Spannungen erscheint wieder proportional zur Radialspannung um die Strecke.

Die Messungen mit der Rummelschen Sonde zeigen den starken Einfluß, den der Streckenhohlraum auf den Brechdruck des Gebirges hat. Brechversuche mit dem Standrohr-Verfahren auf der 490 m-Sohle und der 775 m-Sohle bestätigten diese Abhängigkeit vom Streckenabstand. Unterschiede im Brechdruck, die auf den großen Teufenunterschied zurückzuführen gewesen wären, konnten nicht festgestellt werden.

5 ERGEBNISSE

Die Versuche zeigen, daß die verschiedenen Brechdrücke im Salzgestein im Streckenumkreis von über 20 m entscheidend vom Abstand zur Strecke abhängig sind, demgegenüber ein zu vermutender Teufeneinfluß nicht in Erscheinung tritt.
Bei Salzbergwerken mit hohem Durchbauungsgrad (vgl. Abb. 3) wird daher bei Bohrlochverschlüssen stets von einer Brechfestigkeit (Frac-Festigkeit) des Gebirges auszugehen sein, die vom Streckenabstand und - wie Berechnungen am offenen Bohrloch nahelegen - vom Alter der Strecke abhängt.

/1/ K. GESSLER aus: Zulässige thermische Belastung von Gesteinen und Konsequenzen für die Methoden der Endlagerung im Salz, Synthesestudie. G. Frommeyer, K. Gessler, H. Gies, W. Lutze, G. Malow u. P. Winske. Mai 1981. GSF.

/2/ M. LANGER et al.: Das Verformungs- und Bruchverhalten von Steinsalz. Zusammenfassende Darstellung einiger Forschungsergebnisse der BGR zur Salzmechanik, Hannover 1980; Salzmechanik II.

/3/ F. RUMMEL; R. JUNG: Hydraulic-fracturing stresses measurements near the Hohenzollerngraben-Structure. SW-Germany, Pageophys., Vol. 113, 1975.

/4/ B. HAINSON, F. RUMMEL: Hydrofracturing Stress Measurements in the IRDP Drillhole. Journ. of Geophys. Research, Special Issue, 1981

/5/ F. RUMMEL: Hydraulic-Fracturing-Spannungsmessungen in der Schachtanlage Asse. Unveröffentlichter, interner Bericht 1981.

ÉTUDE GÉOLOGIQUE, GÉOPHYSIQUE ET GÉOTECHNIQUE DE L'USINE SOUTERRAINE DU VERNEY

A geological, geophysical and geotechnical study of the Le Verney underground power station

Geologische, geophysikalische und geotechnische Studie für das unterirdische Wasserkraftwerk in Verney

A.MARTINET & G.AKERMANN
Electricité de France, Paris, France
J.LAKSHMANAN & F.LANTIER
Compagnie de Prospection Géophysique Française, Rueil Malmaison, France

SUMMARY :

The Le Verney underground power station is sited in marly schists of the Liassic period. An extensive drilling campaign has positioned it precisely. The geomechanical study of the rock has provided the information necessary for calculation of stability using the method of finite elements. The volume of future excavation has been determined by an original geophysical method described in this article.

ZUSAMMENFASSUNG :

Die unterirdische Anlage von Verney wird im Mergelschiefer des Lias gebaut. Eine umfangreiche Aufschliessungskampagne hat eine sehr genaue Positionierung ermöglicht. Diegeomechanische Untersuchung des Gesteins hat die erforderlichen Daten geliefert, um die Stabilität mit Hilfe der Finite Elementemethode zu berechnen. Das Aushubvolumen wurde mit einer in diesem Artikel beschriebenen originellen géophysikalischen Methode erkundet.

RESUME :

L'usine souterraine du Verney est implantée dans les schistes marneux du Lias. Une importante campagne de sondages a permis de la positionner avec précision. L'étude géomécanique du rocher a fourni les renseignements nécessaires à un calcul de stabilité par la méthode des élements finis. Le volume de la future excavation a été reconnu par une méthode géophysique originale décrite dans cet article.

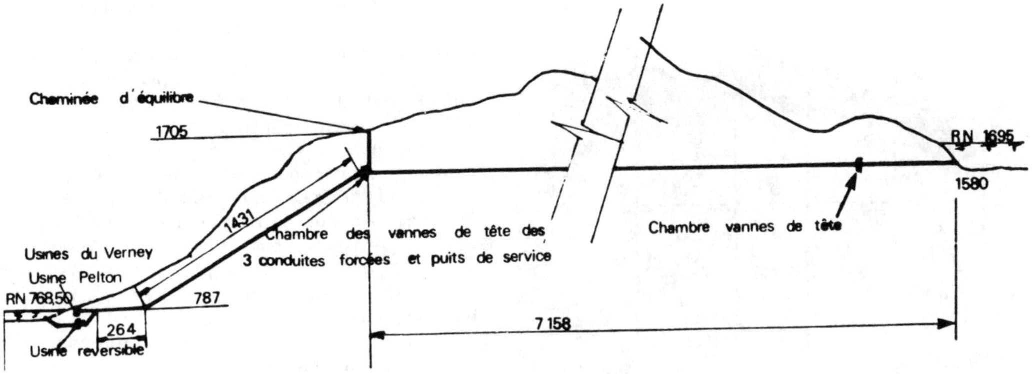

Fig. 1. Profil en long

L'Aménagement de Grand'Maison intéresse le cours de l'Eau d'Olle qui, prenant sa source à proximité du Col de la Croix de Fer, s'écoule entre les deux massifs cristallins de Belledonne et des Grandes Rousses pour rejoindre la Romanche à 7 km à l'aval de Bourg-d'Oisans et 30 km en amont de son confluent avec le Drac.
Les apports naturels de l'Eau d'Olle sont accumulés dans la cuvette formée par le barrage du Verney. Les eaux stockées sont turbinées en heures pleines par les usines du Verney : une usine extérieure comprenant 4 groupes Pelton (total 600 MW) et une usine souterraine comprenant 8 groupes réversibles (total 1 200 MW).
A l'installation gravitaire classique, se superpose donc une puissante station de transfert d'énergie par pompage permettant des échanges journaliers, hebdomadaires et saisonniers entre les bassins amont et aval.

1. RECONNAISSANCES GEOLOGIQUES

L'usine souterraine du Verney est implantée dans les schistes marneux du Lias. Son axe est parallèle à la vallée de l'Eau d'Olle. La position de l'usine a été déterminée à la suite d'une reconnaissance très complète par plus de 50 sondages qui ont permis de mettre en évidence une zone de rocher de bonne qualité et de dresser une carte du toit du rocher.
La couverture rocheuse est de 45 m à l'emplacement de l'usine. Le rocher est recouvert par une moraine sableuse épaisse de 20 à 30 m.
Le rocher est formé de schistes marneux à schistosité subverticale. L'axe de l'usine fait un angle de 65° avec la schistosité pour améliorer la tenue des longpans. Pour mieux connaître les caractéristiques du rocher on a réalisé un puits et deux galeries de 160 m situées l'une en voûte, l'autre au niveau le plus bas de l'usine. Le rocher présente des fissures subhorizontales inégalement réparties dans la masse.

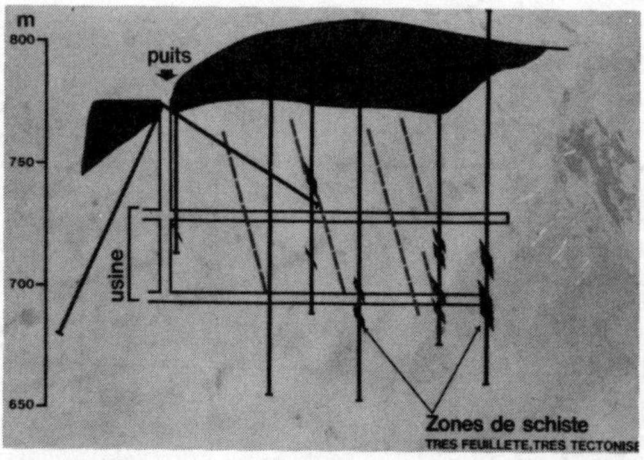

Fig. 2. Coup verticale longitudinale de l'usine

Sur les 30 derniers mètres des galeries, le rocher est plus tectonisé et il est injecté selon la schistosité de filons de calcite et quartz de 1 à 3 m d'épaisseur (figure 2).
Les galeries ont permis d'effectuer diverses reconnaissances in-situ et en laboratoire.
En laboratoire nous avons mesuré les résistances à la compression et à la traction, ainsi que les modules.
Le matériaux est fortement anisotrope comme le montre la figure 3 (coefficient d'anisotropie = 2,3).
La résistance à la traction brésilienne est égale à 7,5 ou 3,5 MPa selon l'orientation de la schistosité.
Les modules sont très élevés et varient de 58 000 à 104 000 MPa. Ils ne tiennent pas compte de la fracturation du massif.
Nous avons donc fait des mesures de modules in-situ à la plaque de charge et au vérin, parallèlement et perpendiculairement à la schistosité (charge maximum 8 MPa).
Les valeurs trouvées correspondent au module du rocher décomprimé, parallèlement à la schistosité 5 500 MPa, perpendiculairement à la schistosité 3 200 MPa.
Nous avons également réalisées des mesures de contraintes au vérin plat dans les deux galeries pour connaître l'état de contrainte initiale. Nous avons étudié 7 sections et les valeurs étaient assez dispersées. Leur interprétation donnent les contraintes initiales suivantes :

galerie supérieure : P = 3,9 à 4,3 MPa
k = 1,7
Galerie inférieure : P = 2,9 à 3,2 MPa
k = 2,2.

(où P est la contrainte verticale et Q = kP la contrainte horizontale).
Les valeurs trouvées pour la galerie inférieure correspondent sensiblement au poids du terrain qui est de 2,7 MPa. Par contre, le résultat aberrant de la galerie supérieure est vraisemblablement dû au fait que les axes principaux des contraintes in-situ ne sont pas vertical et horizontaux.
Toutes ces reconnaissances sont ponctuelles. Nous avons voulu contrôler l'homogénéité du rocher et nous avons réalisé pour cela une importante étude de géophysique.

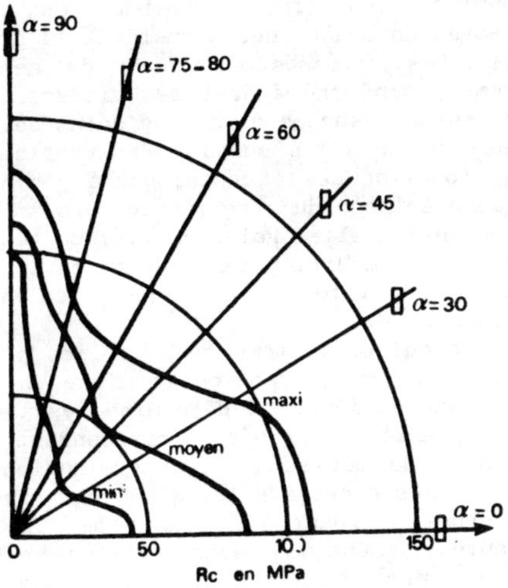

Fig. 3. Anisotropie

2. PRINCIPES GENERAUX DES METHODES GEOPHYSIQUES UTILISEES

2.1. Les dispositifs microsismiques

Ces mesures, tout-à-fait classiques, consistent à déterminer la répartition des vitesses des ondes de compression à travers les terrains, suivant les lois de la réfraction.
Le but essentiel de ces mesures était de déterminer l'épaisseur de la zone altérée ou décomprimée autour de la galerie.

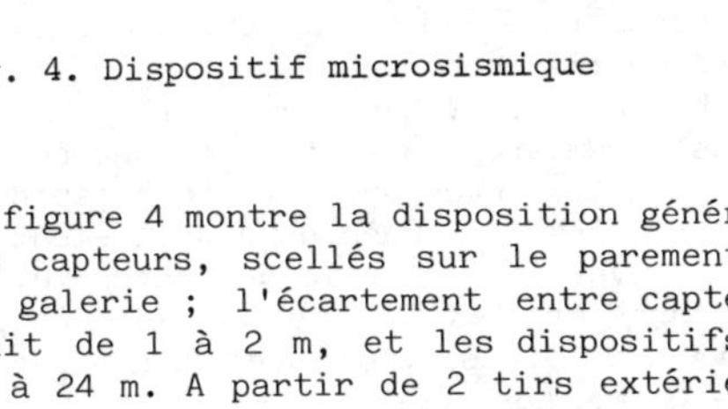

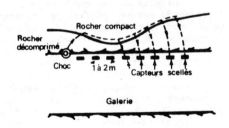

Fig. 4. Dispositif microsismique

La figure 4 montre la disposition générale des capteurs, scellés sur le parement de la galerie ; l'écartement entre capteurs était de 1 à 2 m, et les dispositifs de 12 à 24 m. A partir de 2 tirs extérieurs on a pu aussi déterminer, pour le rocher non affecté par la décompression, les vitesses des ondes de cisaillement.

2.2. Les carottages sismiques

Des forages au wagon-drill d'un diamètre de 50 mm ont été exécutés à l'horizontale, de façon régulière sur le parement de chaque galerie. Leur profondeur était comprise entre 3 et 5 m.
Le carottage sismique consiste à mesurer la vitesse de propagation des ondes de compression, et, quand celà est possible, des ondes de cisaillement, à partir de l'onde incidente provoquée à la surface du parement par un choc ou un faible tir.

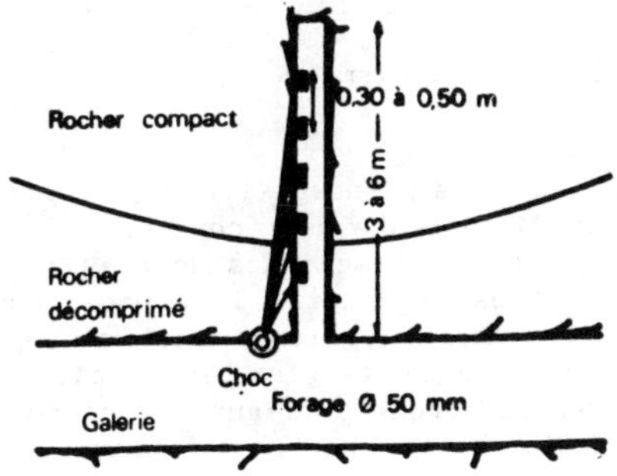

Fig. 5. Carottage sismique

La figure 5 représente une coupe horizontale passant par la galerie et un forage. On dispose à l'intérieur du forage d'une série de capteurs solidaires de la paroi, espacés de 30 à 50 cm.
Comme sur les mesures précédentes, le but principal des carottages était de déterminer l'épaisseur du rocher fissuré, altéré ou décomprimé au voisinage direct de la galerie, et de déterminer si possible, les modules dynamiques du rocher.

2.3. Méthode du panneau sismique

Cette méthode consiste à étudier la répartition des vitesses des ondes de compression et de cisaillement par transparence entre 2 forages situés dans un même plan, ou, comme sur le site du Verney, entre 2 galeries parallèles (figure 6).
Ce procédé, issu des techniques pétrolières (tirs de forages à forages) est surtout original par le traitement informatique des données de terrain.
On a disposé sur le parement de la galerie inférieure, une série de 24 capteurs répartis sur 100 m environ.
On a réalisé successivement 5 à 6 tirs à l'aide de petites charges dans la galerie supérieure, à l'intérieur de courts forages (1 m environ).
Le temps d'arrivée des ondes sismiques de

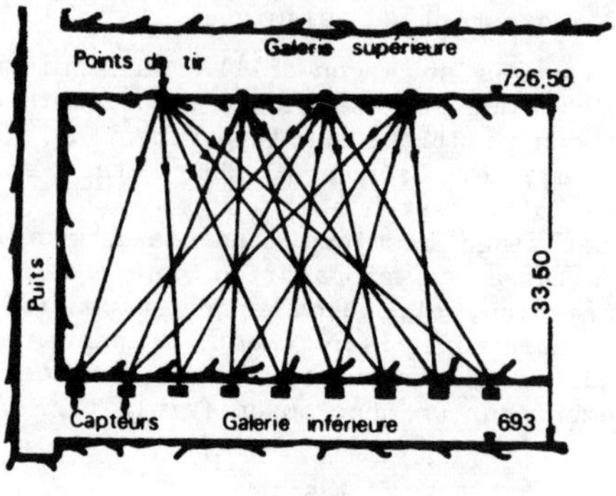

Fig. 6. Panneau sismique

chaque tir est enregistré simultanément sur les 24 capteurs de réception.

Principe du traitement des données :

Ce calcul est itératif. Il suppose que le panneau entre les galeries est décomposé en carrés ou rectangles élémentaires de vitesses différentes (figure 7) et dont le nombre est lié au nombre de rayons sismiques à traiter et à la dimension du panneau. Dans le cas présent, le panneau était décomposé en 42 rectangles de 17 m par 6 m. Le choix des dimensions des rectangles (ou carrés) qui constituent ces plages homogènes dépend du problème posé. Une dimension trop grande ferait perdre de la finesse de résolution à la méthode, alors qu'une maille trop serrée donnerait une précision illusoire.

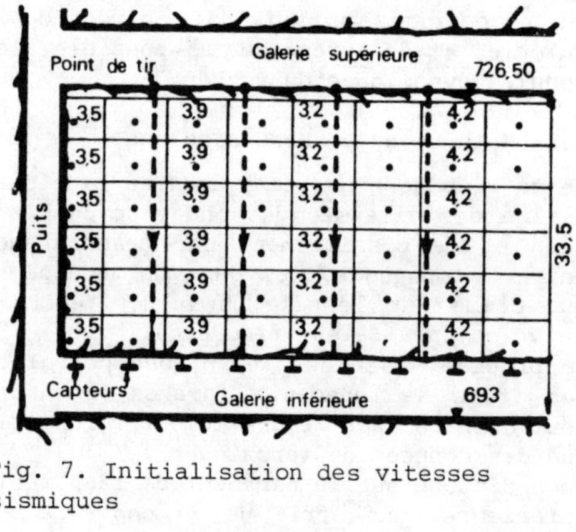

Fig. 7. Initialisation des vitesses sismiques

Le processus de calcul est le suivant :

- on se donne à priori un schéma de vitesses sismiques au départ. Le schéma est bâti sur les valeurs attribuées aux vitesses en chacun des sommets de la grille. Les vitesses sismiques de départ (km/s) sont en général les vitesses apparentes mesurées de chaque point de tir au capteur situé sur la même verticale. En fonction de la connaissance géologique préalable du site (forages, sismique conventionnelle, galeries,...) ce schéma peut être modifié, dans certaines zones, avec des vitesses sismiques les plus plausibles.
- Le calcul ordinateur applique les principes de la réfraction sismique en milieu hétérogène, et détermine les temps de première arrivée correspondant au schéma de départ ; la détermination de ces temps nécessite le calcul des rayons courbes joignant les points de tir aux capteurs. Chaque rayon sismique s'obtient par intégration de son équation intrinsèque :

$$d\alpha = \frac{dv}{v} \text{ tgi où}$$

$d\alpha$ est la variation, entre deux points du rayon infiniment voisins de l'angle α que fait la tangente au rayon avec l'axe des x.

dv est la variation de la vitesse v (x,z) entre ces deux mêmes points.

i est l'angle d'incidence, c'est-à-dire l'angle que fait le rayon avec le vecteur Grad V.

- A partir des désaccords constatés entre les temps mesurés et les temps précédemment calculés, on retouche le schéma de départ en agissant sur les valeurs de la vitesse aux sommets du réseau. Ces retouches s'effectuent grâce à un processus de moindres carrés pondérés.
- A l'aide du schéma modifié, on recommence le calcul, et ainsi de suite, jusqu'à ce que la différence entre les temps calculés et les temps mesurés soit jugée suffisamment petite ou stationnaire.
- Le programme présente alors une répartition bi-dimensionnelle des vitesses correspondant à ces temps modifés, avec le désaccord résiduel moyen t, et le désaccord résiduel maximal t max. entre temps mesurés et temps calculés, exprimés en millisecondes.

Ce traitement a pu être fait pour les temps premières arrivées (ondes de compression) et pour les temps correspondant aux arrivées des ondes de cisaillement.

Dans la version actuelle du programme, les capteurs et les points de tir peuvent avoir une disposition quelconque dans un même plan horizontal, vertical, ou même incliné.

3. APPAREILLAGE

La chaîne de mesures utilisée pour les dispositifs microsismiques et les panneaux sismiques sont similaires à celle de la sismique surface, avec cependant, utilisation pour le laboratoire, d'un appareil à multi-mémoire avec amplificateur d'entrée et de sortie, et possibilité de sommation et de filtration du signal.
Par contre, l'appareillage utilisé pour les carottages sismiques nécessite une très grande précision sur les temps (10 microsecondes). On a utilisé un enregistreur magnétique à six pistes, et parfois des capteurs tridirectionnels.

4. RESULTATS OBTENUS SUR L'USINE DU VERNEY

4.1. Dispositifs microsismiques

La figure 8 représente les résultats synthétiques de la galerie supérieure. Sur le schéma du bas, qui représente une coupe horizontale passant par la galerie, on n'a représenté l'épaisseur de terrain décomprimé qui ne dépasse guère 1 m au début de la galerie et avoisine 2,5 à 3 m sur les 30 derniers mètres.
La galerie inférieure présente en moyenne une épaisseur de rocher décomprimé un peu plus grande (2 m environ) que la galerie supérieure. On remarque donc que le matériau rocheux semble fragile et sensible aux tirs dans certaines zones (décompression égale au diamètre de la galerie). Les vitesses sismiques, pour la zone décomprimée sont les suivantes :
1700 VL 3400 m/s - 900 VT 1650 m/s.
Pour la zone saine, les vitesses sont les suivantes :
4000 VL 5900 m/s - 1900 VT 2650 m/s.

4.2. Carottages sismiques

Les carottages sont représentés sous forme de dromochroniques. S'ils n'est pas possible de déterminer la vitesse de l'onde de cisaillement dans le rocher décomprimé lorsque celui-ci est peu épais, on peut par contre la déterminer lorsque celui-ci devient plus épais (partie droite de la galerie).
On note que les vitesses sismiques mesurées sont en moyenne plus élevées lorsqu'elles ont été déterminées par carottage, que lorsqu'elles ont été déterminées par dispositif.
Ceci est lié à la disposition des capteurs et au fait que la détermination de la vitesse d'un même horizon est réalisée dans 2 plans perpendiculaires l'un par rapport à l'autre.
Modules dynamiques :
Le graphique central de la figure 8 représente les modules dynamiques d'élasticité sous forme d'histogramme, et le coefficient dynamique de Poisson, déterminé par les 2 méthodes précédentes.
En moyenne, pour la galerie supérieure :
Ed = 15 600 MPa pour la zone décomprimée, et Ed = 34 400 MPa pour la zone saine.
Coefficient de Poisson 0,33 (localement 0,15) pour les 2 zones.

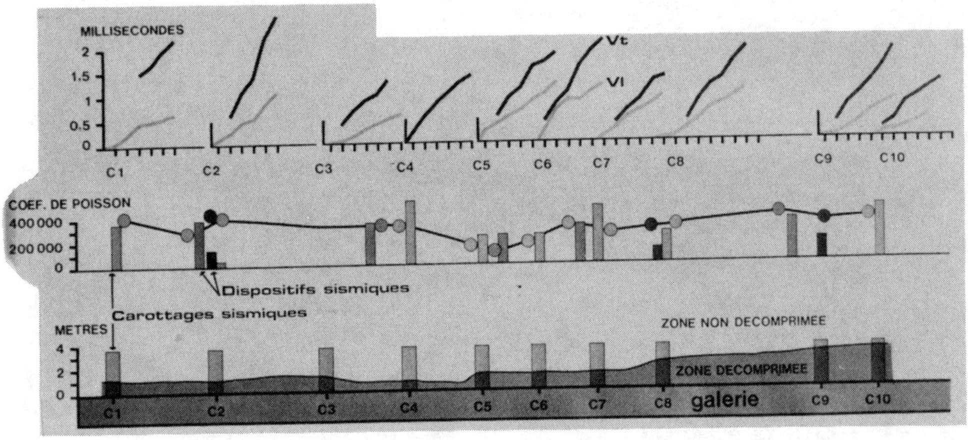

Fig. 8. Mesures microsismiques

Pour la galerie inférieure :
Ed = 10 200 MPa pour la zone décomprimée, et Ed = 34 200 MPa pour la zone saine. Coefficient de Poisson : 0,37

4.3. Panneaux sismiques

Vitesses mesurées :
Toutes les vitesses déterminées par la méthode du panneau correspondent à la partie de rocher non affecté par la décompression.
Les vitesses de l'onde de compression s'échelonnent de 3 500 m/s à plus de 5 000 m/s. Les faibles vitesses étant surtout localisées au voisinage du puits d'accès - galerie supérieure, et à l'extrémité droite de la galerie inférieure.
La figure 10 montre la répartition des vitesses transversales de 1 850 m/s à 2 500 m/s avec 2 zones à faible vitesse dans la partie supérieure gauche du panneau, et dans sa partie inférieure droite. Module dynamique d'élasticité (figure 11) :
Ils vont de 25 000 MPa à plus de 50 000 MPa ; l'axe à fort module part du début de la galerie inférieure et va tangenter la fin de la galerie supérieure.
Coefficient de Poisson (figure 12) :
On retrouve les constatations faites avec les autre mesures réalisées antérieurement : coefficients plus élevés (0,35 - 0,40) au voisinage de la galerie inférieure, et moins forts vers la galerie supérieure (0,25 - 0,35).

4.4. Corrélations entre modules dynamiques obtenus et modules statiques

Sur les échantillons, on a vu que le module d'élasticité est très élevé,

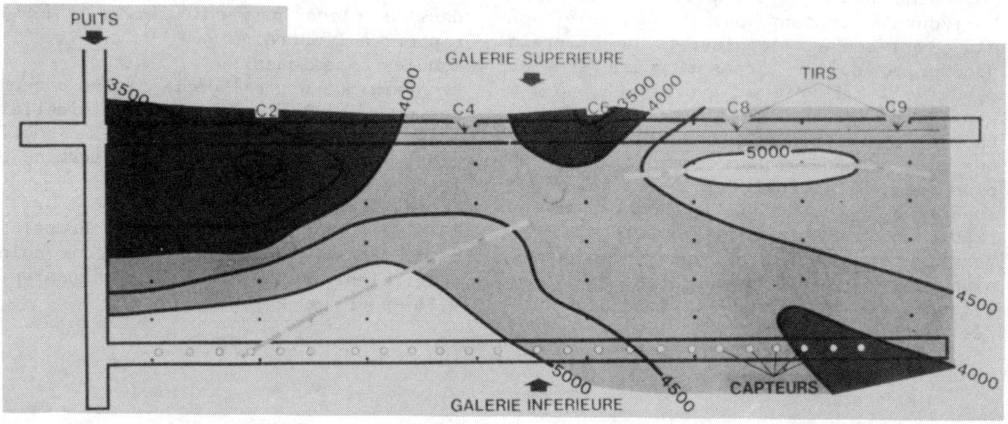

Fig. 9. Carte des vitesses longitudinales

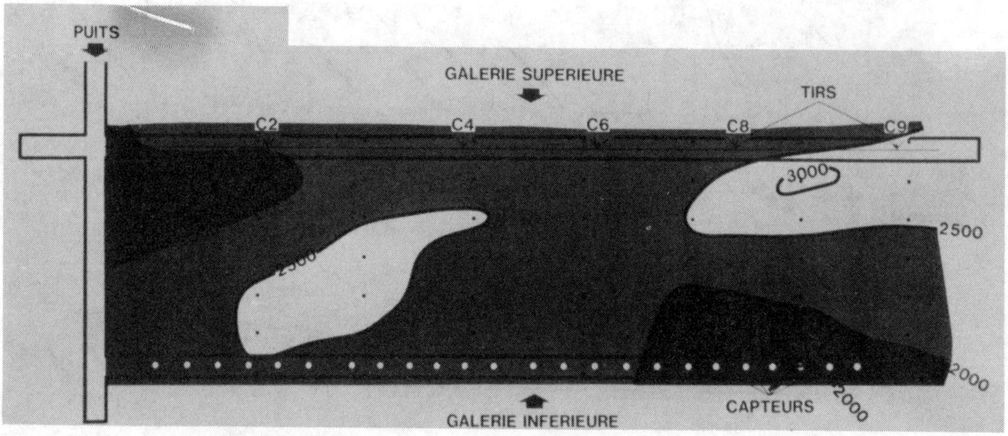

Fig. 10. Carte des vitesses transversales

58 000 MPa à 105 000 MPa suivant que les déformations aient été mesurées suivant le plan perpendiculaire à la schistosité ou dans le plan de celle-ci.
Il existe donc une très forte anisotropie (2,3) mise en évidence par les essais de résistance à la compression.
Les valeurs de modules mesurées correspondent à ceux de la matrice rocheuse et ne sont pas corrélables, semble-t-il avec les essais in-situ, car ils ne tiennent pas compte, ou peu compte de la fracturation du massif rocheux.
Les essais au vérin et à la plaque de charge circulaire, qui sollicitent le matériau sur une faible profondeur permettent d'établir une corrélation entre les modules d'élasticité réversible En et le module d'élasticité dynamique Ed' déterminé pour la zone décomprimée.
Le rapport entre module d'élasticité et module dynamique est, pour ce site, de 0,35.

Pour le rocher sain, nous ne disposons pas d'essais de chargement comme les essais au dilatomètre - médératec par exemple, qui auraient pu permettre une corrélation statistique semblable avec les modules dynamiques correspondants.
On a donc adopté, pour ce site, en admettant le rapport de 0,35 constant pour ce rocher, un module réversible moyen du rocher sain égal à 12 000 MPa, compte tenu des modules dynamiques mesurés entre 2 galeries.

4.5. Corrélation avec la géologie

Sans qu'on puisse absolument établir des corrélations avec des résultats géologiques ponctuels fragmentaires (sondages carottés essentiellement), et qui pourraient être complétés dès la terminaison de l'excavation, en cours, il est intéressant de noter que les faibles modules dynamiques situés au voisinage de l'extré-

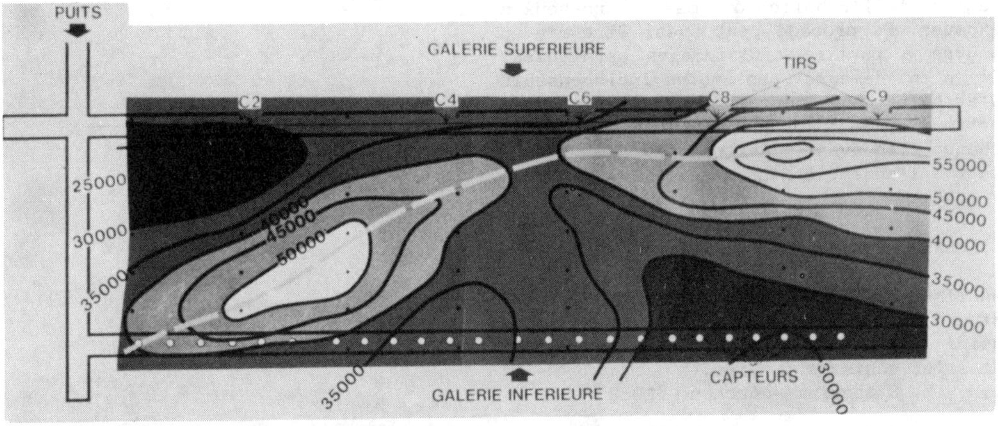

Fig. 11. Carte des modules d'élasticité dynamique

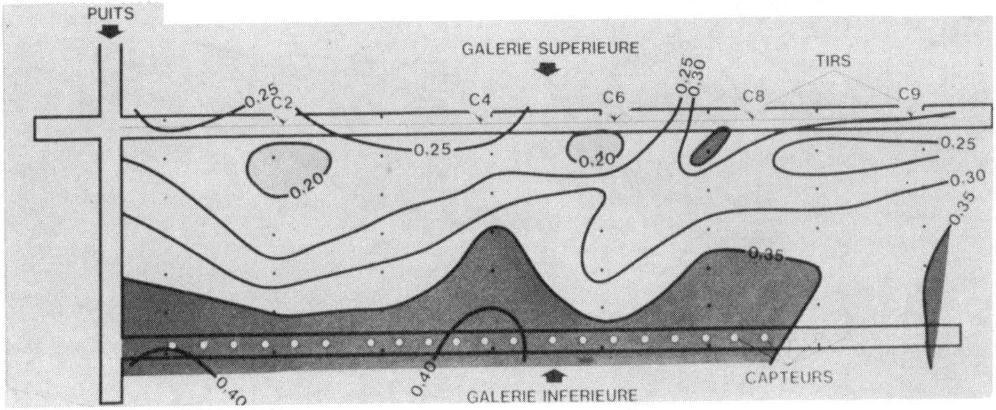

Fig. 12. Carte des coefficients de poisson dynamiques

mité de la galerie inférieure correspon - dent à des zones fissurées, à remplissage secondaire de calcite et de quartz.

5. CONCLUSION

En conclusion, retenons parmi l'éventail des moyens de reconnaissance in-situ un procédé original, le panneau sismique, permettant une auscultation bidimensionnelle d'un massif rocheux. Ce procédé met en évidence des structures qui peuvent ne pas apparaître en sismique de surface (couches lentes sous des couches rapides, par exemple).

Ces mesures, globales peu onéreuses (le coût global d'une telle opération ne dépasse pas le prix de 1 ou 2 essais au vérin et à la plaque de charge, et des sujetions nécessaires à leur exécution), permettent une approche plus réaliste des paramètres mécaniques mesurés sur échantillons, car ils tiennent compte et intègrent la fissuration à l'échelle du massif rocheux à excaver. Ce procédé peut aussi être mis en oeuvre à partir de 2 forages parallèles.

Il n'en demeure pas moins indispensable d'établir des corrélations statistiques entre modules statiques et dynamiques pour chaque site avant d'extrapoler les résultats à l'ensemble d'un massif.

6. REFERENCE

MARTINET Alain
Etude et Contrôle de la stabilité d'une usine hydro-électrique souterraine excavée dans les schistes du Lias.
I.S.R.M. Symposium - Aachen - 1982.

ZUSAMMENFASSENDE DARSTELLUNG VON VERSUCHSERGEBNISSEN ZUM SPANNUNGS- UND TEMPERATURABHÄNGIGEN FESTIGKEITS- UND VERFORMUNGSVERHALTEN VON SALZGESTEINEN

Condensed presentation of experimental results about the stress and temperature dependent strength and strain behaviour of salt rocks

Résultats résumés d'expériences de résistance et de déformation de roches évaporitiques en fonction de l'état de contrainte et de la température

G.STAUPENDAHL & K.GESSLER

Gesellschaft für Strahlen- und Umweltforschung mbH, Braunschweig, Bundesrepublik Deutschland

M.WALLNER

Bundesanstalt für Geowissenschaften und Rohstoffe, Hannover, Bundesrepublik Deutschland

SUMMARY:
From creep experiments with Younger Halite Na 3ß a material model is derived for the steady state creep. This multi-mechanism model represents the dependence of stress and temperature. The results of uniaxial und multiaxial stress und strain controlled laboratory experiments show that the failure behaviour of this rock salt not only depends on the stress but also on the strain rate and the temperature. The failure law derived, which includes the creep behaviour too, has to be quantified by further experiments.

ZUSAMMENFASSUNG:
Aus Kriechexperimenten an Leine-Steinsalz Na 3ß wird für stationäres Kriechen als wesentlichem Anteil der Langzeitverformung ein Stoffmodell abgeleitet,das als additives Mehrmechanismenmodell die Temperatur- und Spannungsabhängigkeit des Kriechens beschreibt.Die Ergebnisse ein- und mehrachsiger spannungs- und dehnungsgeregelter Versuche zeigen, daß das Festigkeits- bzw. Bruchverhalten dieses Steinsalzes nicht nur von der Spannung,sondern auch von der Dehnungsgeschwindigkeit und der Temperatur bestimmt werden. Das daraus entwickelte Bruchkriterium, das zudem noch das Kriechverhalten erfaßt, muß noch durch weitere Versuche quantitativ abgesichert werden.

RESUME:
Des expériences de fluage faites avec le sel gemme "plus jeune" Na 3ß ont permis de décrire le fluage stationnaire, à long terme la part essentielle de la déformation, par un modèle plurimécanique qui dépend additivement de la température et de l'état de contrainte. Les résultats d'expériences uni-et multiaxiales, à compressions préréglées, montrent que la résistance et le comportement à la rupture de ce sel gemme sont déterminés, non seulement par l'état de contrainte, mais aussi par la vitesse de déformation compressive et par la température. Un critère de rupture, qui de plus rend compte du comportement du fluage, a ainsi été développé. Mais d' autres expériences sont nécessaires pour le déterminer numériquement.

1. Einleitung

Im Rahmen von Forschungs- und Entwicklungsarbeiten zur Endlagerung von radioaktiven Abfällen in Salzformationen werden seit einigen Jahren von der Gesellschaft für Strahlen- und Umweltforschung mbH München (GSF), gemeinsam mit der Bundesanstalt für Geowissenschaften und Rohstoffe (BGR), Hannover, experimentelle Untersuchungen zum thermomechanischen Verhalten von Salzgesteinen der Schachtanlage Asse der GSF, Remlingen/ Wolfenbüttel, durchgeführt.

Aufgabe dieser Laborexperimente ist es, ein möglichst umfassendes Bild über das spannungs- und temperaturabhängige rheologische Verhalten von Salzgesteinen zu ermitteln. Dabei werden folgende Teilziele verfolgt:

1. Die Erforschung physikalischer Grundlagen der Verformbarkeit und Festigkeit einschließlich Kriech- und Bruchmechanismen von Salzgesteinen.
2. Bereitstellung von geotechnischen Kennwerten von Salzgesteinen und physikalisch begründeten Stoffgleichungen.
3. Anwendung und Weiterentwicklung standardisierter experimenteller Untersuchungstechniken zur Ermittlung der maßgeblichen mechanischen Parameter.

Die Untersuchungen werden im Rahmen eines mit der Kommission der Europäischen Gemeinschaften abgeschlossenen Forschungsvertrages durchgeführt und von dieser finanziell gefördert, wofür an dieser Stelle besonders gedankt sei.

2. EXPERIMENTELLER UNTERSUCHUNGSRAHMEN

Die experimentellen Arbeiten, über deren bisherigen Ergebnisse an dieser Stelle zusammenfassend berichtet wird, erstrecken sich dabei auf

1. ein- und mehrachsige Experimente zum Kriechverhalten von Salzgesteinen unter zeitlichen konstanten, jedoch unterschiedlichen Differenzspannungen und Temperaturen sowie
2. spannungs- und verzerrungsgeregelte ein- und mehrachsige Experimente zum Verformungs- und Bruchverhalten von Salzgesteinen.

Die Kriechexperimente an zylindrischen Proben wurden überwiegend als einachsige Versuche unter konstanten Mantelspannungen bis zu 18 MPa und konstanten Temperaturen im Bereich von 300 bis 573 K durchgeführt. Zusätzliche Experimente wurden als Temperaturwechselversuche bei konstanter Spannung und als Spannungswechselversuche bei konstanter, jedoch erhöhter Temperatur vorgenommen.

Die einachsigen Kriechversuche konnten inzwischen durch triaxiale Kriechexperimente bei Raumtemperatur ergänzt werden. Sie bestätigen, daß eine hydrostatische Be- und Entlastung bei gleichbleibender Differenzspannung keinen nennenswerten Einfluß auf die Kriechrate nimmt.

Die ein- und mehrachsigen spannungs- und verzerrungsgeregelten Experimente wurden bei Mantelspannungen bis zu 20 MPa mit Raten für die Zunahme der Differenzspannung im Bereich von $2\cdot10^{-3}$ bis zu 10MPa/min bzw. mit axialen Verzerrungsraten im Bereich von $6{,}7\cdot10^{-8}$ bis $6{,}7\cdot10^{-2}$ s^{-1} durchgeführt. Sie wurden im wesentlichen bei Raumtemperatur an zylindrischen Proben als Kompressionsversuche durchgeführt, jedoch in Experimenten an würfelförmigen Proben unter erhöhten Temperaturen bis zu 533 K auch als Extensionsversuche.

Die Standardabmessungen zylindrischer Prüfkörper sind 100 mm Durchmesser und 250 mm Höhe, die der Würfel im allgemeinen 11,5cm Kantenlänge.

Die hier vorgetragenen Untersuchungsergebnisse beziehen sich ausschließlich auf Liniensalz Na 3ß der Leine-Serie (Zechstein 3). Es handelt sich hierbei um ein überwiegend mittelkristallines sehr reines Steinsalz, welches sich in seinem Mineralgehalt durch hohe Halit-Anteile von meist 97 - 99% und geringe accessorische Beimengungen von Anhydrit, untergeordnet von Polyhalit und bisweilen von Kieserit auszeichnet. Wegen seiner Reinheit und weitgehenden Homogenität erwies sich dieses Steinsalz für grundlegende Experimente, auch als Referenzmaterial für vergleichende Untersuchungen an anderen Salzgesteinen am besten geeignet.

An dieser Stelle soll nicht näher auf die eingesetzten Prüfstände und -einrichtungen eingegangen werden. Teilweise wurden sie von M. Langer (1979) und M.Wallner et al. (1979) näher beschrieben.

Die einzelnen Prüfmaschinen werden hinsichtlich Arbeitsweise, technischer Ausstattung und angewandter Meßtechnik laufend verbessert. Für spezielle Experimente wird in zunehmenden Maße ein prozessgeregelter Versuchsablauf eingeführt.

3. ERGEBNISSE DER KRIECHVERSUCHE

Die phänomenologischen Beobachtungen aus den verschiedenen Kriechexperimenten lassen sich wie folgt zusammenfassen:

- Nur deviatorische Beanspruchungen nehmen Einfluß auf die Kriechverformungen.
- Unter konstanter thermo-mechanischer Beanspruchung stellt sich eine stationäre Kriechrate konstanter Geschwindigkeit ein.
- Die stationäre Kriechrate ist dabei überproportional vom herrschenden Temperatur- und Spannungszustand abhängig.
- Entlastungen von einem höheren Spannungsniveau führen zu geringeren Kriechraten als Belastungen auf den gleichen Spannungsdeviator von einem niedrigeren Spannungsniveau aus.
- Jede Spannungs- und Temperaturänderung ist mit anteiligen, reversiblen elastischen Verzerrungen verbunden.

Die Summe der aus den bisherigen Experimenten abgeleiteten Erkenntnisse gestattete schließlich die Formulierung eines Stoffmodells für das Langzeit-Verformungsverhalten von Asse-Liniensalz.

Dieses Stoffgesetz schließt gleichzeitig mikrophysikalisch begründete Modellvorstellungen über die Verformungsmechanismen im Kristallgitter ein. In seiner gegenwärtigen Fassung repräsentiert das Stoffgesetz unter Einschluß eines anteiligen elastischen Verhaltens das stationäre Kriechen als wesentlichsten Mechanismus einer Langzeit-Kriechdeformation unter konstanter Beanspruchung. Die Tabelle in der Abb. 1 faßt die mathematische Formulierung dieses kontitutiven Modells nach M.Wallner (1981b) zusammen. Dabei wird, beruhend auf einem von D.E.Munson und P.R.Dawson (1979) auf der Grundlage theoretischer und experimenteller Befunde entwickelten stofflichen Ansatz, das stationäre Kriechverhalten, gekennzeichnet durch die effektive Kriechrate $\dot{\varepsilon}^{cr}_{eff}$, gemäß Gleichung (6) von der Summe dreier unterschiedlicher Kriechmechanismen bestimmt, nämlich

1. einem Kriechen aufgrund von Versetzungsklettern bei niedrigen Spannungen und höheren Temperaturen,
2. einem Kriechen aufgrund eines "Übergangs"-Versetzungsmechanismusses bei norma-

$$\underline{\varepsilon}_{ges} = \underline{\varepsilon}^{el} + \underline{\varepsilon}^{cr} \,|\, \underline{\varepsilon}^{f} \quad (1)$$

$$\underline{\varepsilon}^{el}_{ij} = -\frac{\nu}{E}\,\underline{\sigma}_{kk}\,\delta_{ij} + \frac{1+\nu}{E}\,\underline{\sigma}_{ij} + \alpha_t\,\Delta\vartheta\,\delta_{ij} \quad (2)$$

$$\dot{\underline{\varepsilon}}^{cr}_{ij} = \frac{3}{2}\,\frac{\varepsilon^{cr}_{eff}}{\sigma^{cr}_{eff}}\,\underline{s}_{ij} \quad (3)$$

$$\dot{\varepsilon}^{cr}_{eff} = \sqrt{\frac{2}{3}\,\dot{\underline{\varepsilon}}_{ij}\,\dot{\underline{\varepsilon}}_{ij}} \quad (4)$$

$$\sigma_{eff} = \sqrt{\frac{3}{2}\,\underline{s}_{ij}\,\underline{s}_{ij}} \quad (5)$$

$$\dot{\varepsilon}^{cr}_{eff} = \sum_{i=1}^{3} \dot{\varepsilon}^{cr}_{eff}\,i\,(S, \sigma_{eff}, \vartheta) \quad (6)$$

$$\dot{\varepsilon}^{cr}_{eff}1 = A_1\, e^{\frac{-Q_1}{R\vartheta}} \left(\frac{\sigma_{eff}}{G}\right)^{n_1} \quad (7)$$

$$\dot{\varepsilon}^{cr}_{eff}2 = A_2\, e^{\frac{-Q_2}{R\vartheta}} \left(\frac{\sigma_{eff}}{G}\right)^{n_2} \quad (8)$$

$$\dot{\varepsilon}^{cr}_{eff}3 = 2\left(B_1 e^{\frac{-Q_1}{R\vartheta}} + B_2 e^{\frac{-Q_2}{R\vartheta}}\right) \sinh\left(D < \frac{\sigma_{eff} - \sigma^{o}_{eff}}{G} >\right) \quad (9)$$

$$\dot{\underline{\varepsilon}}^{f}_{ij} = \dot{\lambda}\,\frac{\delta f}{\delta \sigma_{ij}} \quad (10)$$

$$f = II_s - fkt\,(I_\sigma, II_{\dot{e}}, \vartheta, m, S) = 0 \quad (11)$$

$$f = \tau_o - C_1 \sigma_o^{\beta} \cdot e^{-C_2 \sigma_o\,(\vartheta - \vartheta_o)^2} \left(1 + C_3 \ln \frac{II_{\dot{e}}}{II^{o}_{\dot{e}}}\right) \quad (12)$$

Abb. 1 Stoffgesetzformulierungen für Salzgestein

I. ELASTISCHE PARAMETER GEMÄß GLEICHUNG (2)				
E	= 25000 ± 5000	[MPa]	-	Elastizitätsmodul
ν	= 0,25 ± 0,05	[-]	-	Querdehnungszahl
G	= 9600	[MPa]	-	Schubmodul
α_t	= $0{,}45 \cdot 10^{-4}$	[K^{-1}]	-	lin. therm. Ausdehnungskoeffizient
II. PARAMETER FÜR SEKUNDÄRES KRIECHEN GEMÄß GLEICHUNG (7) UND (8)				
Q_1	= 27	[kcal · mol^{-1}]	-	Aktivierungsenergie
Q_2	= 12,9	[kcal · mol^{-1}]	-	Aktivierungsenergie
n_1	= 5,5	[-]	-	Spannungsexponent
n_2	= 5,0	[-]	-	Spannungsexponent
A_1	= $1{,}2 \cdot 10^{22}$	[s^{-1}]	-	Strukturfaktor
A_2	= $1{,}7 \cdot 10^{14}$	[s^{-1}]	-	Strukturfaktor
R	= 1,987	[cal · mol^{-1} · K^{-1}]	-	allgem. Gaskonstante
III. PARAMETER FÜR SEKUNDÄRES KRIECHEN GEMÄß GLEICHUNG (9)				
Q_1	= 27	[kcal · mol^{-1}]	-	Aktivierungsenergie
Q_2	= 12,9	[kcal · mol^{-1}]	-	Aktivierungsenergie
B_1	= $1{,}5 \cdot 10^{7}$	[s^{-1}]	-	Strukturfaktor
B_2	= $3{,}6 \cdot 10^{-2}$	[s^{-1}]	-	Strukturfaktor
D	= $3{,}5 \cdot 10^{3}$		-	Aktivierungsvolumen
σ^{o}_{eff}	= 20	[MPa]	-	Bereichs-Grenzspannung für Versetzungsgleiten

Abb. 2 Materialkennwerte von Asse-Steinsalz Na 3 für das Stoffgesetz

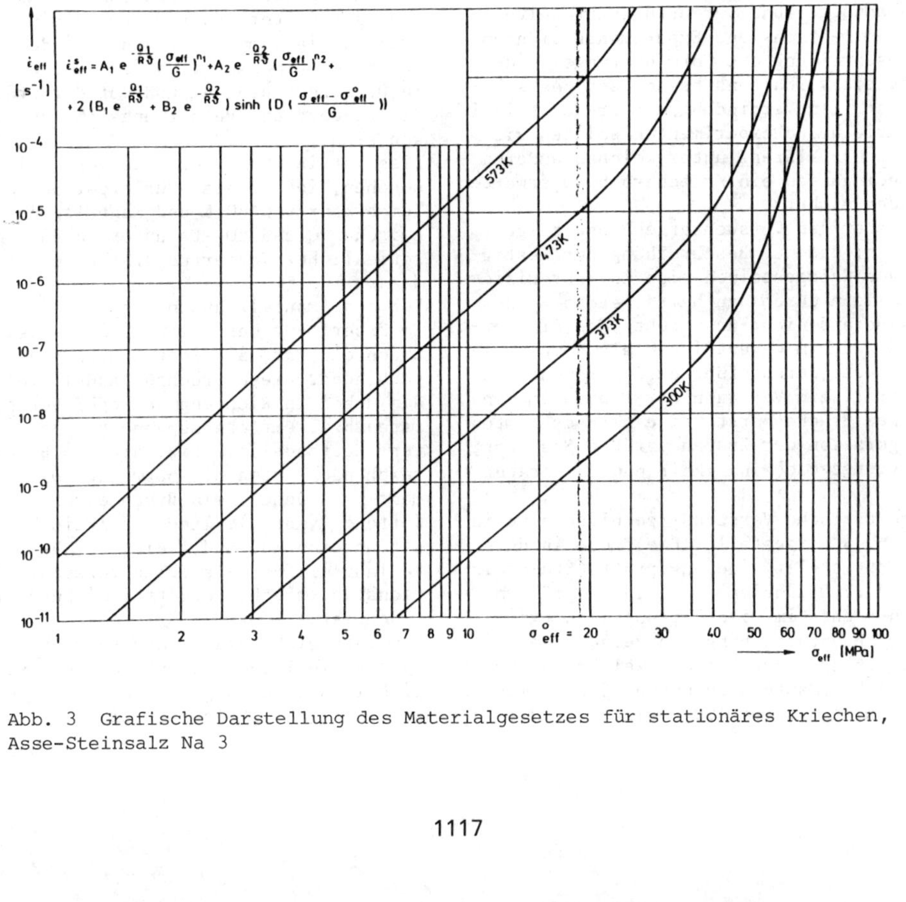

Abb. 3 Grafische Darstellung des Materialgesetzes für stationäres Kriechen, Asse-Steinsalz Na 3

len Lagerstättentemperaturen und -spannungen sowie

3. einem Kriechen aufgrund des Versetzungsgleitens bei höheren Spannungen.

Die entsprechenden skalaren Beziehungen für die aus diesen drei Mechanismen resultierenden effektiven stationären Kriechraten ε^{cr}_{eff} als Funktion der effektiven Spannung σ^{o}_{eff} sind in den Gleichungen (7) bis (9) dieser Abb. dargestellt.

Für die beiden erstgenannten Mechanismen ergibt sich eine Spannungsabhängigkeit nach einem Potenzgesetz mit unterschiedlichen Strukturfaktoren A, Aktivierungsenergien Q und Spannungsexponenten n. Beim dritten Mechanismus ergibt sich eine Spannungsabhängigkeit nach einem hyperbolischen trigonometrischen Ansatz.

Die Abb.2 faßt die nach diesem Ansatz für das Stoffgesetz ermittelten Materialparameter zusammen, welche aus den bisherigen Experimenten an Jüngerem Steinsalz der Grube Asse ermittelt wurden.

Abb.3 stellt schließlich die effektive sekundäre Kriechrate ε^{cr}_{eff} in Abhängigkeit von der Effektivspannung σ^{o}_{eff} unter Verwendung dieser Stoffkennwerte für vier Temperaturstufen zwischen 300 und 573 K dar.

4. ERGEBNISSE DER EXPERIMENTE ZUM FESTIGKEITS- UND VERFORMUNGSVERHALTEN

Die spannungs- und verzerrungsgeregelten ein- und mehrachsigen Experimente dienten der Beschreibung des Formänderungs- und Festigkeitsverhaltens bei dieser Beanspruchungsart. In Verbindung mit ersten triaxialen Kriechbruchexperimenten sollten sie aber auch abklären, unter welchen äußeren Randbedingungen ein Kriechbruch zu erwarten ist oder nicht.

Die bisherigen Versuchsergebnisse zeigen deutlich, daß zur Beschreibung der Festigkeit von Salzgesteinen eine Charakterisierung allein durch den herrschenden Spannungszustand nicht ausreicht. Wie die verschiedenen, im wesentlichen als Kompressionsversuche durchgeführten Experimente zeigen, tritt ein Versagen der Proben im Sinne eines Bruches erst bei einer bestimmten Konfiguration der Zustandsgrößen Spannung, Verzerrungsgeschwindigkeit und Temperatur ein.

Einige typische Versuchsergebnisse sind in der Abb. 4 dargestellt. Die Probe in der Bildmitte stellt eine ungeprüfte Steinsalzprobe dar. Die beiden triaxial geprüften Proben rechts im Bild zeigen einen typischen Schubbruch. Hingegen zeigen die beiden Prüfkörper zur Linken, welche bei zwar identischen Mantelspannungen, jedoch mit einer um den Faktor 100 geringeren axialen

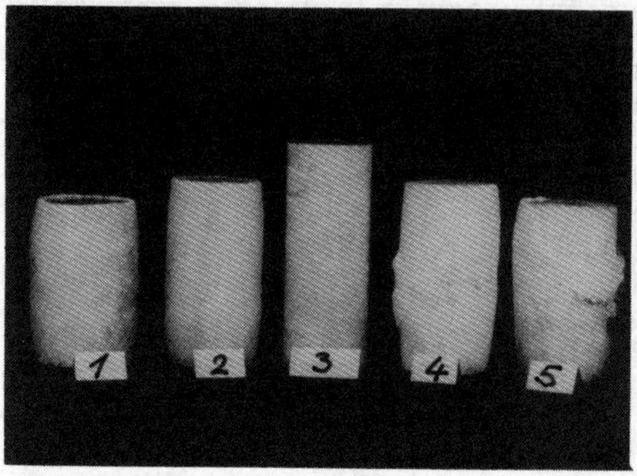

Abb.4 Triaxial geprüfte Steinsalzprüfkörper, Asse-Liniensalz Na 3ß
1: p_i = 50 bar; s = 0,01 mm/min
2: p_i = 25 bar; s = 0,01 mm/min
3: ungeprüfter Kern
4: p_i = 25 bar; s = 1 mm/min
5: p_i = 50 bar; s = 1 mm/min

Verformungsrate getestet wurden, trotz grosser Verzerrungen keine Brucherscheinungen.

Analog zur Darstellung der Ergebnisse für das stationäre Kriechen kann man nun die Ergebnisse solcher verzerrungs- und spannungsgeregelter Experimente in einem gleichartigen Diagramm eintragen, auf dessen Abszisse die im Experiment erreichte maximale Differenzspannung und auf der Ordinate die zugeordnete Verzerrungsrate aufgetragen sind.

Dies ist in Abb.5 für eine Testserie geschehen, in der die Prüfkörper bei einer Temperatur von 305K und Mantelspannungen zwischen 0 und 20 MPa unter Vorgabe unterschiedlicher Verzerrungsraten geprüft wurden.

Für jede Mantelspannung lassen sich nun die im Experiment bestimmten Punkte, bei denen Bruch eintrat, zu einer Bruchzustandslinie verbinden. Diese Bruchzustandslinien münden dabei in Richtung geringer Verzerrungsraten bzw. Differenzspannungen in eine untere Zustandslinie ein, die den Bruchbereich nach unten hin begrenzt. Die Experimente, in denen kein Bruch erreicht wurde (offene Symbole), liegen praktisch auf dieser unteren Zustandslinie, welche in ihrem Verlauf mit der aus Kriechversuchen für stationäres Kriechen ermittelten Kurve identisch ist.

Ein Vergleich gezielt angesetzter, jedoch unterschiedlicher Testprozeduren ist schließlich in Abb. 6 vorgenommen. In diese Abbildung sind schematisch die Versuchsspu-

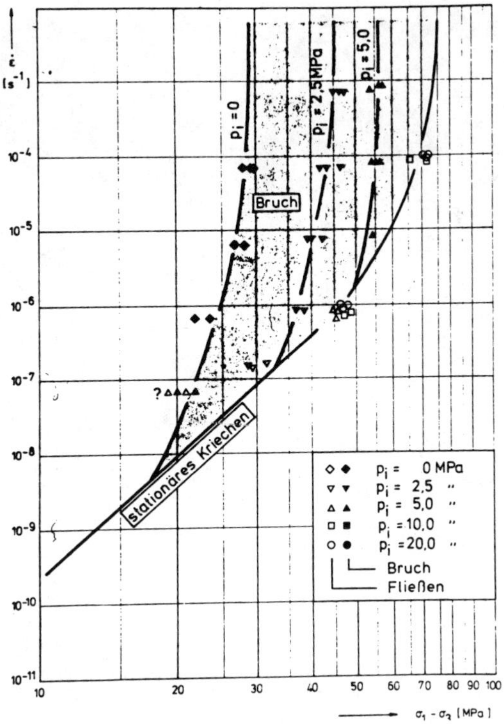

Abb. 5 $\dot{\varepsilon}/(\sigma_1 - \sigma_2)$-Diagramm weggeregelter Triaxialversuche, Leine-Steinsalz Na 3ß

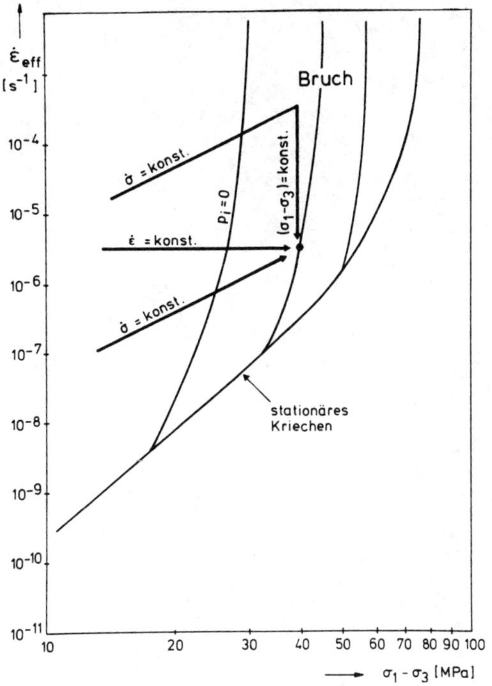

Abb. 6 Schematische Darstellung des Kriechbruchmodells mit Versuchsspuren unterschiedlicher Versuchsarten

ren dreier unterschiedlicher Experimente eingetragen, nämlich
1. die Versuchsspur eines Kompressionsversuches mit konstanter Spannungsrate,
2. die Versuchsspur eines Kompressionsversuches mit konstanter Verzerrungsrate,
3. die Versuchsspur eines Kompressionsversuches mit höherer Spannungsrate als im ersten Fall, jedoch anschließender Retardation nach Erreichen einer bestimmten Differenzspannung.

Im Ergebnis führen diese unterschiedlichen Experimente unter vergleichbaren Versuchsbedingungen zu dem gleichen Bruchpunkt auf der Bruchzustandslinie, die für den entsprechenden Manteldruck gültig ist.
Obwohl inzwischen von M.Wallner (1981 a) ein erster vorläufiger Ansatz für das Eintreten eines Kriechbruches formuliert werden konnte, reichen die bisher durchgeführten Experimente zur exakten quantitativen Beschreibung des Kriechbruches allerdings noch nicht aus. Hierzu sind noch weitere Untersuchungen notwendig, die insbesondere die Bruchmechanismen im Mikrogefüge klären sollen.

5. LITERATUR

Langer, M. 1979; Rheologisches Verhalten von Gesteinen und Fels-Generalbericht, Proc.4. Int.Congr.Rock Mech., Montreux 1979, Vol. 3, P. 63 - 96

Munson, D.E. u. P.R.Dawson 1979; Constitutive model for the low temperature creep of salt (with application to WIPP), Sand-79-1853, Sandia National Laboratories, Albuquerque, NM

Wallner, M., C.Cainenberg u. H. Gonther 1979; Ermittlung zeit- u. temperaturabhängiger mechanischer Kennwerte von Salzgesteinen, Proc.4. Int.Congr. Rock Mech., Montreux 1979, Vol. 1, P. 313 - 318

Wallner, M. 1981 a; Criterial examination of conditions for ductile fracture in rock salt, Proc. OECD/NEA Workshop on Near Field Phenomena in Geologic Repositories for Radioactive Waste, Seattle, August 31 - September 3, 1981, P. 243 - 253

Wallner, M. 1981 b; Analysis of thermo-mechanical problems related to the storage of heat producing radioactive waste in rock salt, Vortrag, 1. Conf. on the Mechanical Behavior of Salt, The Pennsylvania State Univ., Nov. 9 - 11.

INTERPRETATION OF VIRGIN STRESS MEASUREMENTS WITH REGARD TO LARGE CAVERNS

Interpretation von Messungen der Primärspannung beim Bau von grossräumigen Kavernen

L'interprétation des mesures de contraintes naturelles au regard de l'exécution des cavernes à grandes dimensions

F.A.VREEDE

National Mechanical Engineering Research Institute, Pretoria, South Africa

SUMMARY

The stability of large caverns depends to a great extent on the stresses in the rock mass. A survey must therefore be conducted to obtain the virgin stress field. Among stress measuring equipment in general use the CSIR triaxial strain cell holds a prominent place. Procedures have been developed to check the reliability of the results using this instrument.

To provide a practical basis for cavern design the test data must be analysed in order to separate the local residual stresses from the basic stress field which is caused by tectonic and gravitational forces. It is proposed to describe this field in cartesian coordinates by six linear functions for which 24 parameters are needed. A computer program for regression analysis can be used to calculate these parameters.

When measuring virgin stresses from an exploration tunnel it is common practice to restrict the tests to points outside the region of stress disturbance caused by the tunnel. This limitation can be removed if the disturbance is expressed in terms of the parameters of the basic stress field. The formulae for disturbed stresses have recently been derived for the case of a cylindrical hole in a classical material subjected to a linear stress field and are presented in the paper.

ZUSAMMENFASSUNG

Die Standfestigkeit grossräumiger Kavernen hängt massgeblich von den im Gebirge herrschenden Spannungen ab. Das Primärspannungsfeld muss daher vorab ermittelt werden. Unter den üblicherweise verwendeten Spannungsmessgeräten nimmt die CSIR Triaxial-Dehnungsmesszelle einen vorderen Platz ein. Zur Überprüfung der Zuverlässigkeit der mit ihr gemessenen Daten sind bestimmte Verfahrensweisen entwickelt worden.

Um eine ausreichende Grundlage für den Entwurf einer Kaverne zu erhalten, müssen die Messdaten analysiert werden im Hinblick auf die Trennung örtlich vorhandener Restspannungen vom Grundspannungsfeld, das durch tektonische Kräfte und Gravitationskräfte bestimunt wird. Es wird vorgeschlagen, dieses Feld in kartesischen Koordinaten mittels sechs linearer Funktionen zu beschreiben, wofür 24 Parameter benötigt werden. Diese Parameter werden mittels eines Computerprogramms für Regressionsanalyse berechnet.

Bei der Messung der Primärspannungen von einem Erkundungstollen aus ist es allgemein üblich, die Messungen ausserhalb des Bereichs zu nehmen, der vom Stollenausbruch beeinflusst ist. Diese Einschränkung kann entfallen, wenn die Beeinflussung über die Parameter des Grundspannungsfeldes zum Ausdruck gebracht wird. Die Formeln zur Beschreibung von "Störspannungen" sind vor kurzem abgeleitet worden für den Fall eines zylindrischen Hohlraums in einem klassischen Material, auf das ein lineares Spannungsfeld einwirkt; sie werden in vorliegendem Beitrag vorgestellt.

RESUME

La stabilité des cavernes à grandes dimensions dépend largement des contraintes naturelles qui règnent dans le massif rocheux. Ce champ de contraintes naturelles doit être établi avant que les travaux ne commencent. Parmi les appareils de mesure de contraintes naturelles, la cellule CSIR triaxiale à jauges de déformation représente un instrument de premier ordre. Dans le but de vérifier l'exactitude des résultats ainsi obtenus, certaines méthodes de contrôle ont été développées.

Afin d'obtenir une base de départ pour l'étude d'un projet de caverne, les résultats de mesure doivent être analysés en vue de séparer les contraintes locales résiduelles de celles qui sont causées par les forces tectoniques et de gravitation. On propose de décrire ce champ en coordonnées cartésiennes au moyen de six fonctions linéaires qui nécessitent vingt-quatre paramètres. Un programme d'ordinateur, conçu pour l'analyse de régression peut être utilisé afin de calculer ces paramètres. En mesurant les contraintes naturelles à partir d'une galerie de reconnaissance il est recommandé de conduire un programme de mesure hors de la région influencée par le creusement de cette galerie. Cette restriction peut être négligée si elle est exprimée en termes de paramètres du champ de contraintes naturelles. Les formules décrivant ces "contraintes perturbées" ont été trouvées récemment pour le cas d'une cavité cylindrique d'un matériel classique qui était soumis à un champ de contraintes linéaires.

1 INTRODUCTION

The virgin stress in rock masses is a deciding factor for the design of caverns. It is not possible to predict the magnitude of the stress components since the stress distribution is inherently statically indeterminate. Comprehensive measurements are therefore the only way of obtaining practical knowledge of the virgin stress field in a rock mass.

Measurement results generally show great variation, even over short distances (Hiltscher et al 1979, Saxena et al 1979). This can be attributed to local residual stresses, which are normally of little interest, but which give rise to considerable complications when interpreting the results of a test programme in terms of the basic stress field caused by tectonic and gravitational forces. Two problems therefore have to be solved in measuring virgin stress, namely obtaining reliable data and interpreting the data in a practical way. Both problems will be discussed mainly in relation to the CSIR triaxial strain cell.

2 THE RELIABILITY OF TEST RESULTS

The triaxial strain cell for measuring virgin stress which was designed at the Council for Scientific and Industrial Research of South Africa (Leeman and Hayes 1966) is well known. It measures the strains at three points of the wall of an EX borehole with strain gauge rosettes by relieving the stresses through overcoring. In the latest version the rosettes of the strain cell have four instead of three strain gauges in a regular star pattern. The directions in which the strains ε_1 to ε_4 are measured differ by 45 degrees, so that the strain function $r = \varepsilon_1 - \varepsilon_2 + \varepsilon_3 - \varepsilon_4$ must equal 0. In practice r is subject to stochastic variation through unavoidable measurement errors. When its values conform to a normal distribution the tests can be accepted and the three local strain components can be calculated, but when an excessively high value of r is found the instrument's behaviour has been faulty during the test and the result is therefore unreliable.

The strains are known functions of the six virgin tensor components if the deformation conditions are isotropic and linear-elastic and the stress field gradients have no effect over the width of the borehole (Hiltscher 1976). All six virgin tensor components can be calculated from the test results when these assumptions are true. Possible deviations from the assumptions can be investigated (Vreede 1981a) and the various cases are briefly discussed in the following paragraphs.

- The rock is anisotropic

For an anisotropic material the number of elastic constants may be as high as 5 or 9 or 13 or even 21. The calculations are however based on "the" elastic modulus and Poisson's ratio. This has the consequence that stresses in the direction of a low modulus are overestimated and stresses in the direction of a high modulus are underestimated. Rahn (1981) proposes a correction method for a simple case of anisotropy, but for more complicated cases no practical method exists.

- The deformation is non-linear

When the borehole axis is taken as z axis, the three plane stress components $\sigma_{\theta a}$, σ_{za} and τ_a at any point of the borehole wall r=a are known functions of the six virgin tensor components and the position angle θ. The state of stress at the borehole can be expressed by the two principal stresses

$$p = \frac{1}{2}(\sigma_{\theta a}+\sigma_{za}) \pm \{\frac{1}{4}(\sigma_{\theta a}-\sigma_{za})^2 + (\tau_a)^2\}^{\frac{1}{2}}$$

This equation defines a curve in the p_1p_2 plane with θ as curve parameter (Vreede 1981a). Figure 1 shows examples for three given virgin stress tensors (σ_i, τ_{ij}). When the curve anywhere exceeds the biaxial strength of the rock the deformation is decidedly non-linear and the results are unreliable.

- A strong stress gradient is present

The three local strain components mentioned before are measured at three points of the borehole wall, a total of nine values. When the virgin stress field is homogeneous these values must satisfy three homogeneity equations, but even then deviations occur because of measurement errors. The expected deviations can be calculated from the observed distribution of the strain function r. If excessively high deviations are found the homogeneity condition must have been violated by a strong local stress gradient, such as may occur in areas of large residual stress. The test results are then misleading since the basic stress field is often completely swamped.

3 THE INTERPRETATION OF A STRESS SURVEY

3.1 The tectonic/gravitational stress field

Measurements of virgin stress can only be conducted at isolated points which must be at least a metre apart to avoid interference. A complete picture of a virgin stress field would require some ten tests in each of the three dimensions, that is one thousand tests in all. No such test programme has as yet been undertaken and the actual nature of virgin stress fields is unknown. There is however clear evidence that stress values can vary quite considerably over short distances. Such variations are caused by local, self-compensating, residual stresses (Voight 1966). The residual stresses cannot be separated by theoretical principles from the basic tectonic/gravitational field which influences the rock-mechanical behaviour of a cavern, so the following definition is proposed as a practical solution:

VIRGIN STRESS	σ_x	σ_y	σ_z	τ_{xy}	τ_{yz}	τ_{zx}	UNIT	V
CURVE 1	9,8	4,6	11,2	-1,2	2,5	-0,5	MPa	0,2
CURVE 2	4,0	14,2	6,2	1,6	0,4	1,2	MPa	0,2
CURVE 3	3,2	2,2	5,6	-0,1	4,0	2,5	MPa	0,2

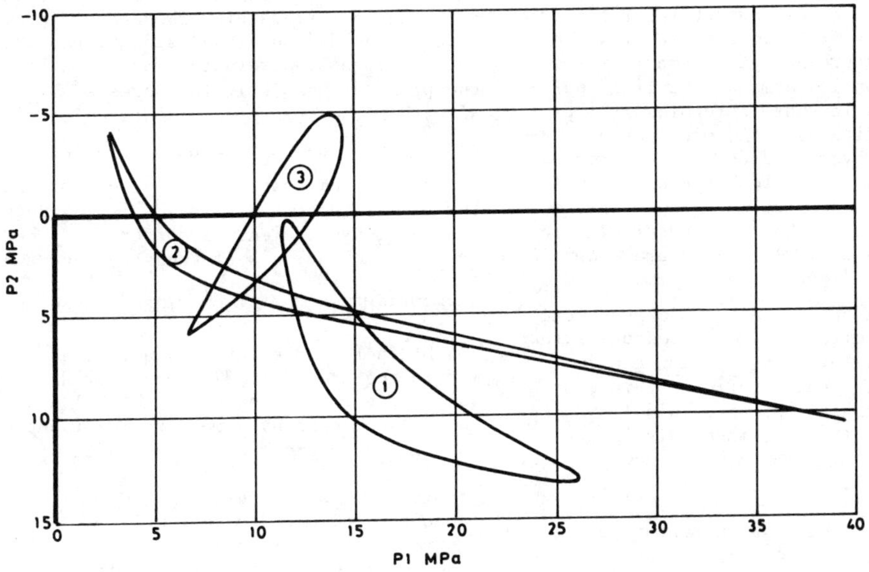

FIG. 1 : PRINCIPAL STRESSES AROUND A BOREHOLE.

The tectonic/gravitational field at a site is given by linear equations in cartesian coordinates which satisfy the law of gravity and give the best fit to the test data. These equations have the form:

$$\bar{p}_i = a_i x + b_i y + c_i z + d_i \quad (i=1 \text{ to } 6)$$

where $\bar{p}_i$ are the six tensor components of the field in the directions of the coordinate axes.

This definition introduces 24 parameters a_i, b_i, c_i and d_i (i=1 to 6) which must satisfy the three equations of equilibrium which contain the gravitational constant g. It has the same form after any linear transformation. It defines a homogeneous field when all parameters except d_i vanish, but then the conditions of equilibrium have to be ignored.

3.2 The problem of stress disturbance through the construction of an adit

To gather sufficient data for a reliable determination of the parameters it is necessary to perform a large number of tests. Usually an exploration tunnel (adit) is opened for a detailed investigation of geological and rock-mechanical conditions. Measurements of virgin stress can be performed conveniently from this adit as well.

It is standard practice to measure in long boreholes to avoid the area of stress disturbance which extends at least two adit diameters away from the adit wall. If, however, the disturbance of the basic stress field is known in terms of the field parameters, tests in short boreholes will provide information as well, with obvious advantages on layout and cost. The formulae for the disturbed field has been found for the case that the adit is cylindrical and the rock behaves like a classical elastic material (Vreede 1981b). They are shown in Table 1; the effect of the parameters d_i has been left out since this is identical to the known effect of a homogeneous stress field. A circular cross section can be achieved using tunnel boring machines or smooth blasting techniques. This leaves the rock in the adit wall reasonably intact which is a great advantage for geotechnical investigation.

3.3 The problem of bias in test results

A full scale stress survey is only worthwhile at a site which has shown its suitability for construction of a cavern. It will consist of both tests in boreholes drilled from the surface which were part of the primary exploration and tests conducted from an adit. Experience has shown that there may be correlation between stress and location (inhomogeneity) and between stress and direction (anisotropy), therefore the test stations should be evenly spread in space and orientation to avoid bias.

Bias may still creep into the data because tests in poor rock tend to fail while tests in hard rock will succeed. This bias leads to an over-estimate of the virgin stress, so it is desirable to reduce the data obtained in uncommonly stiff rock to values which could have been expected if the rock had been of average quality. It is proposed that this be done while leaving the strain energy unchanged:

$$p_m^2/(2E) = p_o^2/(2E_o)$$

where p_m = measured stress
E = local elastic modulus
p_o = reduced stress
E_o = average elastic modulus at site

This yields the reduction formula:

$$p_o = p_m (E_o/E)^{\frac{1}{2}}$$

3.4 The influence of faults

In sound rock the basic field can be expressed by one set of 24 parameters for the whole site. If the site is traversed by a fault it is to be expected that due to the accompanying stress disturbance, different sets are needed on either side of the fault. When through a coordinate transformation, the plane of the fault is expressed by x'=o then the stress components $\bar{\sigma}_x'$, $\bar{\tau}_{xy}'$ and $\bar{\tau}_{xz}'$ must be continuous at the fault, so their parameters b', c' and d' must be the same in both sets. The decision whether one set is sufficient or not can only be based on an analysis of the stress data.

4 REQUIREMENTS FOR A COMPUTER PROGRAM

To obtain reliable data for all 24 parameters requires some 30 tests providing 180 values and it is clear that the calculation can only be done by computer. The input must contain the geometrical survey data of:

- adit (when applicable)
- position of mouth of borehole
- direction of borehole
- depth of test station in borehole
- orientation of strain cell

TABLE 1: DISTURBED LINEAR STRESS FIELD AROUND A CYLINDRICAL HOLE

$$
\begin{aligned}
P_{rr} = \; & \{-\rho g_x(-\kappa^4-2\kappa^2+3) + (a_3-b_2-3c_4)(-\kappa^4+1)\}\ \tfrac{1}{4}r\cos\theta \\
+ \; & \{-\rho g_y(-\kappa^4-2\kappa^2+3) + (b_1-a_2-3c_5)(-\kappa^4+1)\}\ \tfrac{1}{4}r\sin\theta \\
+ \; & \{(a_1-a_3-2b_2)\cos 3\theta + (b_1-b_3+2a_2)\sin 3\theta\}\ \tfrac{1}{4}r(4\kappa^6-5\kappa^4+1) \\
+ \; & \tfrac{1}{2}(c_1+c_3)(-\kappa^2+1)\ z + \{\tfrac{1}{2}(c_1-c_3)\cos 2\theta + c_2\sin 2\theta\}\ (3\kappa^4-4\kappa^2+1)\ z
\end{aligned}
$$

$$
\begin{aligned}
P_{r\theta} = \; & -\{\rho g_y(\kappa^4-2\kappa^2+1) + (b_1-a_2)(-\kappa^4+1) + c_5(3\kappa^4-4\kappa^2+1)\}\ \tfrac{1}{4}r\cos\theta \\
+ \; & \{\rho g_x(\kappa^4-2\kappa^2+1) + (a_3-b_2)(-\kappa^4+1) + c_4(3\kappa^4-4\kappa^2+1)\}\ \tfrac{1}{4}r\sin\theta \\
+ \; & \{(b_1-b_3+2a_2)\cos 3\theta - (a_1-a_3-2b_2)\sin 3\theta\}\ \tfrac{1}{4}r(-4\kappa^6+3\kappa^4+1) \\
+ \; & \{c_2\cos 2\theta - \tfrac{1}{2}(c_1-c_3)\sin 2\theta\}\ (-3\kappa^4+2\kappa^2+1)\ z
\end{aligned}
$$

$$
\begin{aligned}
P_{\theta\theta} = \; & \{-\rho g_x(\kappa^4-2\kappa^2+1) + (a_3-b_2)(\kappa^4+3) - c_4(3\kappa^4+1)\}\ \tfrac{1}{4}r\cos\theta \\
+ \; & \{-\rho g_y(\kappa^4-2\kappa^2+1) + (b_1-a_2)(\kappa^4+3) - c_5(3\kappa^4+1)\}\ \tfrac{1}{4}r\sin\theta \\
- \; & \{(a_1-a_3-2b_2)\cos 3\theta + (b_1-b_3+2a_2)\sin 3\theta\}\ \tfrac{1}{4}r(4\kappa^6-\kappa^4+1) \\
+ \; & \tfrac{1}{2}(c_1+c_3)(\kappa^2+1)\ z - \{\tfrac{1}{2}(c_1-c_3)\cos 2\theta + c_2\sin 2\theta\}\ (3\kappa^4+1)\ z
\end{aligned}
$$

$$
\begin{aligned}
P_{rz} = \; & \{(1-\nu)(c_1-c_3)(-\kappa^4+\kappa^2) + \tfrac{1}{2}(a_4-b_5)(-\kappa^4+1)\}\ r\cos 2\theta \\
+ \; & \{(1-\nu)(2c_2)(-\kappa^4+\kappa^2) + \tfrac{1}{2}(a_5+b_4)(-\kappa^4+1)\}\ r\sin 2\theta \\
+ \; & \{-\tfrac{1}{2}(\rho g_z+c_6)\ r + (c_4\cos\theta + c_5\sin\theta)\ z\}\ (-\kappa^2+1)
\end{aligned}
$$

$$
\begin{aligned}
P_{\theta z} = \; & \{(2c_2)(\kappa^4-\nu\kappa^4-\nu\kappa^2) + \tfrac{1}{2}(a_5+b_4)(\kappa^4+1)\}\ r\cos 2\theta \\
- \; & \{(c_1-c_3)(\kappa^4-\nu\kappa^4-\nu\kappa^2) + \tfrac{1}{2}(a_4-b_5)(\kappa^4+1)\}\ r\sin 2\theta \\
+ \; & \tfrac{1}{2}(a_5-b_4)\ r + (c_5\cos\theta - c_4\sin\theta)(\kappa^2+1)\ z
\end{aligned}
$$

$$
\begin{aligned}
P_{zz} = \; & \{\nu\rho g_x(\kappa^2) + 2(1+\nu)c_4(\kappa^2) + a_6\}\ r\cos\theta \\
+ \; & \{\nu\rho g_y(\kappa^2) + 2(1+\nu)c_5(\kappa^2) + b_6\}\ r\sin\theta \\
- \; & \{(a_1-a_3-2b_2)\cos 3\theta + (b_1-b_3+2a_2)\sin 3\theta\}\ \nu r(\kappa^4) \\
- \; & \{(c_1-c_3)\cos 2\theta + (2c_2)\sin 2\theta\}\ 2\nu(\kappa^2)\ z + c_6\ z
\end{aligned}
$$

where: κ = R/r $\qquad$ ρ = density of rock
R = radius of hole $\qquad$ g_i = gravity component

and the stress data obtained with the strain cell:

- value of six tensor components
- standard deviation of each value.

All measured tensor components must be expressed as linear functions of the 24 parameters defined on a fixed coordinate system through repeated directional transformations. Three parameters are finally eliminated through the equilibrium equations and the result can be written in matrix notation as:

$$\underset{(n\times 1)}{\underline{m}} = \underset{(n\times 21)}{H}\ \underset{(21\times 1)}{\underline{p}} + \underset{(n\times 1)}{\underline{e}}$$

where $\underline{m}$ = measured stress vector
$\underline{p}$ = reduced parameter vector
H = factor which links any stress component with any parameter
$\underline{e}$ = vector of deviation terms, assumed to be independently and normally distributed.

The least square estimate is then calculated in the usual way:

$$\underline{\hat{p}} = (H^{1}H)^{-1}\ H^{1}\ \underline{m}$$

The measured stress data can be weighted through their standard deviations since the CSIR strain cell supplies this information (Vreede 1981a). The residuals

$$\underline{\hat{e}} = \underline{m} - H\ \underline{\hat{p}}$$

should be used in plotting routines to obtain information about certain statistical questions, such as

- have the residuals the same variance?
- are there outliers in the data?
- does the linear field fit the data?
- are the data from the same population?
- are some parameters superfluous?

The least square estimate and the plotting routines are included in an existing regression package (Galpin 1981). With its aid stress survey data are analysed and useful information on tectonic/gravitational fields at cavern sites can be obtained.

5 CONCLUSION

With the CSIR triaxial strain cell a reliable virgin stress survey can be conducted, but an intuitive appraisal of the results is inadequate when a large cavern is to be designed. A numerical interpretation is possible through the concept of the basic linear tectonic/gravitational field. Tests performed in short boreholes drilled from cylindrical adits are relevant since the relations between the disturbed stress around the adit and the linear field parameters have been derived.

A computer package based on statistical theory is available to determine a reliable estimate of the parameters. With this estimate stress boundary conditions can be calculated for applying the finite element or boundary element technique to predict stresses for any stage of the cavern excavation.

6 REFERENCES

Galpin, Jacqueline S., 1981, Regression package REGPAC (version 3), Special report SWISK 25, Nat. Research Inst. Math. Sci., CSIR Pretoria.

Hiltscher, R., 1976, Bemerkungen zur Technik der Gebirgsspannungsmessungen, Rock Mechanics, Vol.8, No.3, pp.199-206.

Hiltscher, R., Martna, J. and Strindell, L., 1979, The measurement of triaxial rock stresses in deep boreholes, Proc. 4. Congr. Int. Soc. Rock Mechanics, Montreux, Vol.2, pp.227-234.

Leeman, E.R. and Hayes, D.J., 1966, A technique for determining the complete state of stress in rock using a single borehole, Proc. 1. Congr. Int. Soc. Rock Mechanics, Lisboa, Vol.2, pp.17-24.

Rahn, W., 1981, Zum Einflusz der Gebirgsanisotropie und des bruchbedingten nichtlinearen Materialverhaltens auf die Ergebnisse von Spannungsmessungen im Bohrloch, Bochumer geol. u. geotechn. Arb. Heft 5, Inst. f. Geologie, Ruhr-Universität-Bochum.

Saxena, P.C., Mokhashi, S.L. and Rame Gowda, B.M., 1979, Rock stress measurements at Nagjhari tunnels, Kalinadi hydro-electric project India, Proc. 4. Congr. Int. Soc. Rock Mechanics, Montreux, Vol.2, pp.589-594.

Voight, B., 1966, Interpretation of in situ stress measurements, Proc. 1. Congr. Int. Soc. Rock Mechanics, Lisboa, Vol.2, pp. 45-50.

Vreede, F.A., 1981a, Critical study of the method of calculating virgin rock stresses from measurement results of the CSIR triaxial strain cell, Report ME 1679 Nat. Mech. Eng. Research Inst., CSIR Pretoria.

Vreede, F.A., 1981b, Elasto-mathematical investigation of holes in sound rock with a linear virgin stress field, Report ME 1733 Nat. Mech. Eng. Research Inst., CSIR Pretoria.

2

UNDERGROUND CAVERNS WITH LARGE SPAN
Untertägige Hohlräume mit grosser Spannweite
Cavités souterraines de grandes portées

GEOMECHANICAL STUDIES OF THE CARAGUATATUBA PUMPED STORAGE CAVERNS

Geomechanische Untersuchungen für die Kavernen des Caraguatatuba Pumpspeichers

Recherches de la méchanique des roches pour les cavernes de la centrale de pompage Caraguatatuba

W.M.DE CAMARGO & SOHRAB SHAYANI
Hidroservice, Sao Paulo, Brazil

SUMMARY:

Caraguatatuba 2,000 MW pumped storage powerplant to be constructed in the next years near the city of São Paulo (Brazil), required a complete FEM rock mechanics analysis, the aims, methodology, and results of which are the subject of this paper. The correlation among the structural analysis and the geologic survey resolved many conceptual, constructive and operational aspects of the design.

ZUSAMMENFASSUNG:

Das Caraguatatuba 2000 MW Pumpspeicherkraftwerk, das in den nächsten Jahren in der Nähe von São Paulo (Brasilien) gebaut werden soll, erforderte eine vollständige FEM-Berechnung, deren Ziele, Vorgehensweise und Ergebnisse Gegenstand dieses Beitrags sind. Die Abhängigkeit zwischen statischer Berechnung und geologischen Untersuchungen machte eine große Anzahl von Entwurfskriterien hinsichtlich Planung, Konstruktion und Ausführung notwendig.

RÉSUMÉ:

Caraguatatuba, une centrale électrique de pompage de 2000 MW, qui devra être construite durant les prochaines années aux environs de São Paulo (Brésil) exige un calcul complet par la méthode des éléments finis, dont les buts, la marche à suivre et les résultats font l'objet de cet exposé. La dépendance entre le calcul statique et les investigations géologiques rend, en ce qui concerne la planification, le dimensionnement et l'exécution, un grand nombre de critères de conception nécessaire.

1 INTRODUCTION

The High Paraíba do Sul river course at medium levels between 1,000 and 700 m over the sea, contained by Serra do Mar and Serra da Mantiqueira, in Southeast Brazil Atlantic shore, at distances ranging from 15 to 60 km from the Atlantic Ocean, enabled the formation of one of the highest industrial concentrations in the country along its valley, connecting the two major South American cities: Rio de Janeiro and São Paulo (see Figure 1).

In order to meet the electric power production requirements of this region, a number of works were implemented which enabled the partial diversion of watercourses and its water resources to locations technically more convenient for hydroelectric use.

It is very well known that the industrial activities are characterized by the continuous power consumption unbalance (the so-called demand peak) and, therefore, the installed power generating plants were the ones more economically suitable to this situation: high-head hydroelectric power plants located close to the power centers and easily supermotorizable to consume the available reasonably small flows.

The development of the region in the last decades was based on this scheme.

However, studies performed have shown that large peak power demands of approximately 10,000 MW, not covered by the installations presently included in the planning for power supply to the Rio-São Paulo area, shall occur in the year 2000.

Therefore, new hydroelectric possibilities shall be found, however taking into account the compatibilization of increasing power requirements with other essential factors: the maximum conservation of the water resources for ecological preservation and, consequently, for preservation of the living conditions in the region.

Among these possibilities, one is feasible even in a short-term basis, i.e. the use of the plateau water for power generation taking advantage of the high hydraulic head attained by the mountains and the sea. In addition to this, after total or partially stored in suitable reservoirs on the coastal area, these waters, when pumped back to the plateau, make possible the total reconstitution of the valley's water resources, they are the so-called Pumped Storage Plants, one of the latest innovations in the hydroelectric field.

Installed in underground cavern and equipped with high-power compact generator sets, the Caraguatatuba powerplant will produce at least 1,000 MW in its first phase. When pumped, it can reach 2,000 MW of installed power. It will be embedded in the rock mass of the Serra do Mar foot, near the place called Caraguatatuba with accesses to the roads which cross the area.

The water flow required for its initial operation with discharges to the ocean is estimated as 30 cubic meters per second. This will make possible peak power generation during the 1985-1995 decade without imparing the other activities of the Upper Paraíba Valley. In the initial stage, these water will be discharged through a short tailrace up to Santo Antônio River and from there on to the Atlantic Ocean. The pumped storage operation anticipates the water storage in a lower reservoir built in the coastal plains, most likely in the Juqueriquerê river headwaters where different dam alternatives were preliminary designed for this purpose.

2 BASIC CONCEPTS

To complete the rock engineering studies relative to the construction feasibility of the Caraguatatuba Pumped Storage underground works, the definition of the stress and strain fields that affect the rock mass after the execution of the different excavation stages were computerized. In the light of the results obtained, an attempt was made to determine the necessity and the dimensioning of the temporary supports, as well as the stability of the top and walls of the caverns.

In a study of this nature, it is imperative to correctly represent the basic factors which affect the mechanical behavior of the rock.

The simulation of the following was of particular importance:

- in situ stress conditions of the rock;
- physical non-linearity of the stress/strain ratios;
- excavation stages;
- existing faults.

In this case, the in situ stresses were estimated using the $\sigma h/\sigma v = 2$ ratio, inasmuch as the results from the corresponding tests were not yet available.

In another study, the structure of the blocks that is formed with the system of existing fractures shall be considered, simulating them by means of joints, in which the aperture and closure limits of the joint and the respective resistance variation, as well as the limits of resistance to compression and shearing shall be controlled. These calculations shall also be linear, repetitious.

In studies that shall follow, the effects of the anchorings and eventual supports that are specified shall also be dealt with.

3 PHYSICAL CHARACTERISTICS OF THE PROJECT

For the execution of the Caraguatatuba Pumped Storage, the following works shall be constructed (see Figure 2).

a.- Principal Works:

- Upper headrace.
- Upper water intake.
- Low pressured tunnels - 7.65 m Ø - circular section.
- Upstream penstocks.
- High pressure tunnels - 5.50 m Ø - circular section.
- Cable and ventilation tunnel - 3.50 m x 6.00 m.
- Cavern for valves and SF6 substation.
- Powerhouse.
- Downstream penstock.

- Acess tunnel - 8.00 m x 9.00 m.
- Tailrace tunnel - 10.20 m Ø - horseshoe section.
- Lower headrace.
- Lower water intake.
- Dam of the lower reservoir.
- Bottom outlet of the spillway.

b.- Auxiliary Works:

- Cofferdam of the upper water intake.
- Adit I - 8.00 m x 9.00 m for access to the low pressure tunnels.
- Adit II - 8.00 m x 9.00 m for access to the powerhouse.
- Temporary access tunnel, 8.00 m x 9.00 m.
- Adit III - 8.00 m x 9.00 m for access to the valve cavern.
- Adit IV - 8.00 m x 9.00 m for access to the exit of the tailrace tunnel.

During the first phase of the implementation of the work, corresponding to a generating installation of 1,000 MW, the underground excavations corresponding to the caverns, water mains, draft tubes, one of the low pressure tunnels, one of the upstream penstocks, one of the high pressure tunnels, the downstream penstock, the tailrace channel, the upstream and downstream water intakes, the downstream dam, the spillway and the tailrace tunnel.

For the final phase of the implementation of the project (2,000 MW), there shall remain the underground excavations of the other diffusers, of the second high pressure tunnel, of the second upstream penstock and of the second low pressure tunnel.

The project of the underground caverns, in their different stages of construction are examined in this study.

The configuration of the caverns, whose length prevails over the other dimensions, made possible the formulation of this study as bidimensional.

4 GEOLOGICAL STUDIES

Various geological surveys were carried out in the area of the Caraguatatuba Hydro Plant, both on the occasion of the studies for the Underground Power Plant and the Pumped Storage Scheme. The regional geology studies and the local geological and geotechnical conditions determined the alignment of 9 km long tunnels and an underground cavern measuring 140 m long, 110 m wide and 60 m high, located at 450 m above the surface of the land and at 40 m bellow sea level.

The geological research work was developed

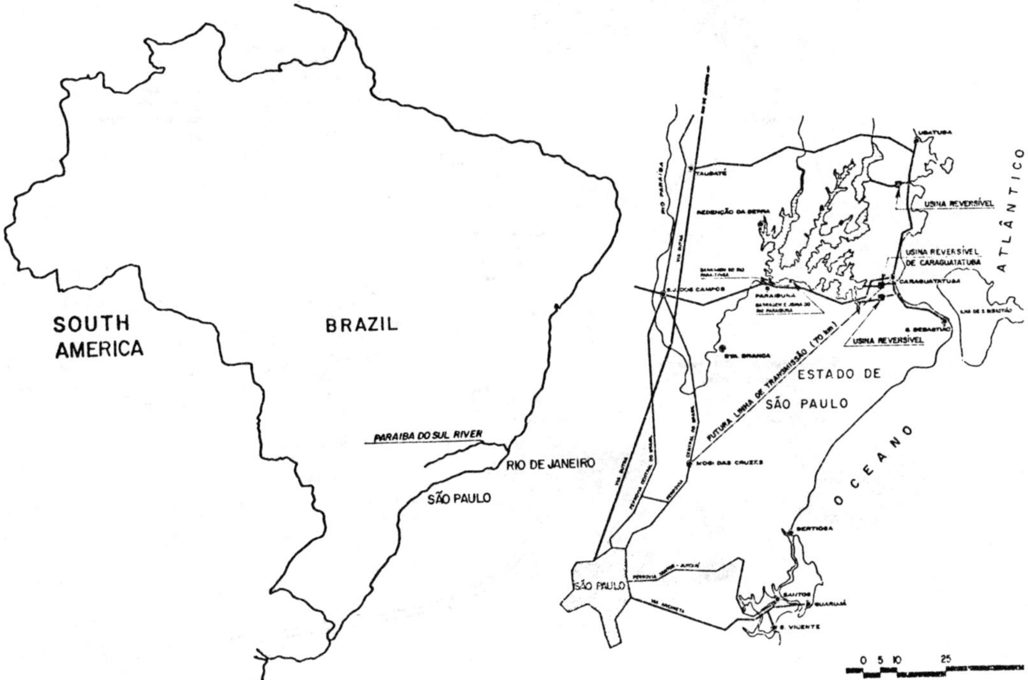

FIGURE 1

CARAGUATATUBA PUMPED STORAGE POWERPLANT - GENERAL LOCALIZATION in the plateau area and the slopes of the "Serra do Mar", near the city of Caraguatatuba, State of São Paulo. Bearing in mind the hydraulic conditions, the most feasible alignment was defined after the geological configuration of the area of interest of the project was known.

With this purpose in mind, a sequence of studies was developed, comprising the following:

. Photogeological studies for the purpose of preliminarily delimiting the main geological and structural units, including the indication of accesses for the execution of the research owing to the characteristics of the even topography and local thick vegetation.

. Geophysical Studies with a view to the initial delimiting of the rock summit and assisting the execution of a rational program of mechanical borings.

. Geological Mapping, for the purpose of verifying the photogeological studies and the delimitation of the different geological lithologies and structures of the areas of interest of the project.

. Deep boring: a total of 16,000 meters of boring by percussion and rotation were effected, along the tunnels and the underground caverns area.

These borings were schedules to be executed both vertically and inclined, for the purpose of crossing the different geological anomalies present in the area, supplying sufficient information for the preparation of the excavation projects and the lining in a safe and economical way.

. In the area of the underground caverns, according to HIDROSERVICE programming, two rotation borings were executed that reached the foreseen distance for the base of the excavations, reaching depths over 400 m. These borings have been the deepest so far in Brazil, in the field of Civil Engineering.

. All the geological and geotechnical services were specified, programmed, supervised, inspected and analyzed by specialized HIDROSERVICE teams.

. As can be observed in the annexed illustrations, the main existing rock in the area of the caverns of the Powerhouse

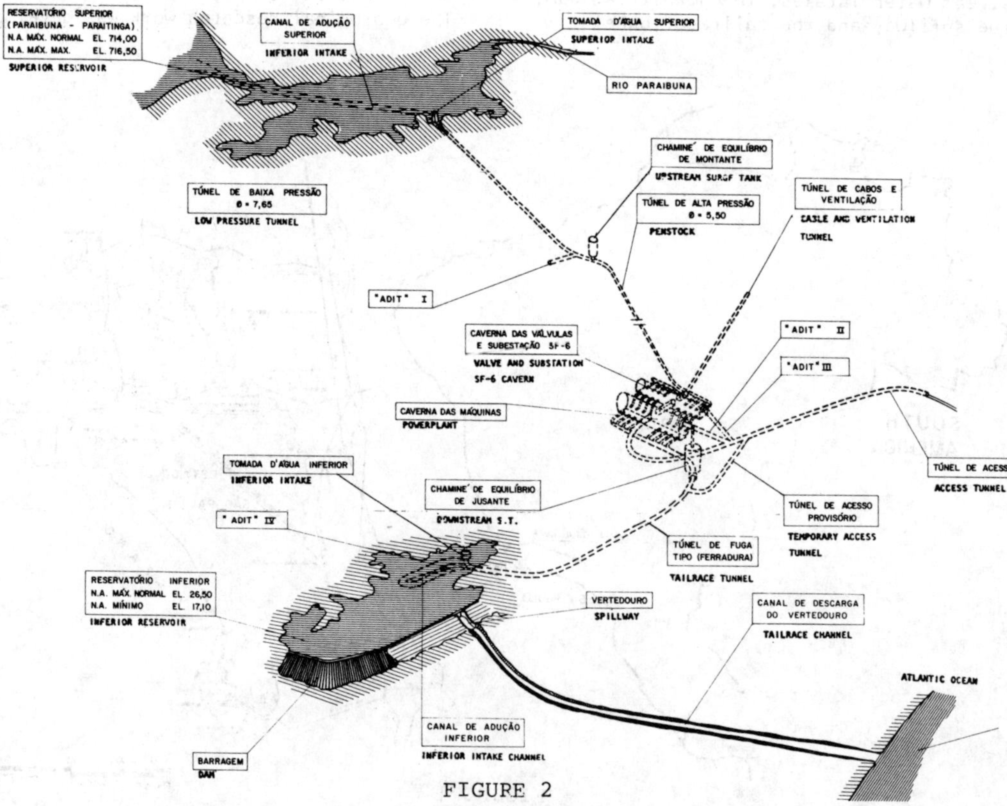

FIGURE 2

CARAGUATATUBA PUMPED STORAGE HYDRO-SCHEME: GENERAL LAYOUT

and the substation is a slightly fractured sound phacoidal gneiss.

. Occasionally in the region, diabase dikes with variable thicknesses occur. There is evidence of strips of sheared material in contact with the gneiss in this rock, despite its soundness.

. One of the dikes detected by the borings and which cuts the area of the powerhouse cavern has approximately 80 m wide and shows in its contact with the gneiss a strip of sheared and decomposed rock of about one meter.

Caraguatatuba Pumped Storage. Powerhouse and Substation Cavern. Geological and Geomechanical Parameters. Adopted for FEM Calculation

Type of Material	γ t/m^3	E 10^3 kg/cm^2	ν	φ	t/m^2	kg/cm^2
Sound Phacoidal Gneiss	2,65	350	0,22	45°	150	5
Sound Fractured Diabase	2,90	200	0,25	70°	100	5
Altered Diabase Contact Gneiss	2,0	10	0,30	36°	5	0
Fractured Rock by Blastings	2,6	20	0,30	25°	10	0

5 CONCEPT OF THE CALCULATION WITH THE FEM - FINITE ELEMENT METHOD

According to the above description, the objective of the calculation with the FEM, is to verify the effect of the excavation of the cavern in the redistribution of the stress in the rock mass, as well as the interaction with the temporary and final linings, if these exist.

The possibility of respecting the mutual influence of the structure and of the surrounding rock constitutes one of the great advantages of the FEM, applied to the project of underground structures.

The quality of the results obtained depends, among other factors, upon a correct simulation of:

. the different construction phases;

. the representation of the in-situ stress conditions in the still intact rock; and

. the correct representation of the characteristics of the materials (stress/strain ratios, strength criteria, etc.).

The program applied was developed by HIDROSERVICE, and is in conditions of taking into consideration all of these aspects.

The consideration of the different phases of construction is taken automatically into account by means of the activation and/or deactivation of elements. The resulting conditions of stress in the rock mass, calculated for a certain phase, is considered as an in-situ stress condition for the next phase. The lack of equilibrium due to the supression of a rock section is simulated by a system of forces in knots equivalent to the stresses that act upon the surroundings of the excavated region on that occasion.

The physical non-linearity that characterizes the behavior of the rock is considered through successive repetitions. For the yield curves, the Mohr criterion was used, despite the computer program used allows any type of pre-established criteria.

6 RESULTS

The following tables show the results obtained in the calculations.

The calculation was performed simulating the construction of the caverns in three basic stages, as can be observed in Figure 4, which is an acceptable simplification of actual excavation plan, partially shown at Figure 3. The characteristics of the three different materials that were considered are also shown in said figure.

The structure was represented by a discretization consisting of 992 knots and 1,023 elements.

In Figures 5 to 7 the strains of the surroundings of the excavated areas can be found, while Figures 8 to 10 show the configuration of the stress condition which affect the rock mass after each excavation phase. Lastly, in Figures 11 to 13 are shown the yielded areas after each stage of excavation.

7 ACKNOWLEDGEMENTS

The authors are indebted with Companhia Energética de São Paulo - CESP for the authorization for publication of the data contained in this paper which is a summary of the involved studies under development by HIDROSERVICE for Caraguatatuba Pumped Storage Powerplant. A special remark must be done for the relevant and specialized works of computer programming and calculation, and civil engineering studies, performed by HIDROSERVICE's technical structural engineering staff, managed by Eng. René Zalszupin, and executed by Eng. Antonio Bugan and Eng. Israel Burmann.

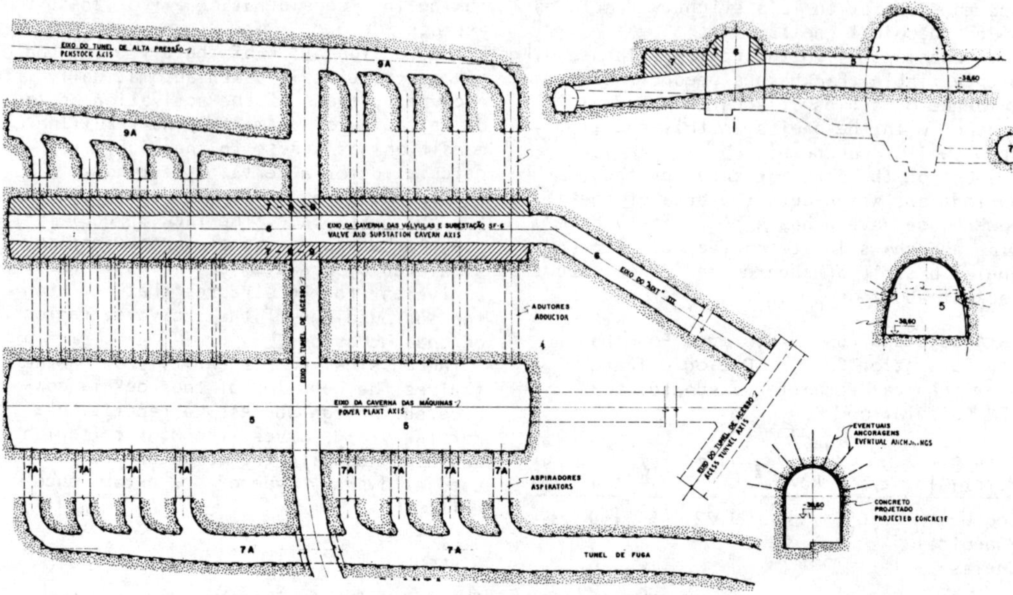

FIGURE 3

CARAGUATATUBA PUMPED STORAGE HYDRO-SCHEME: POWER HOUSE EXCAVATION PLAN

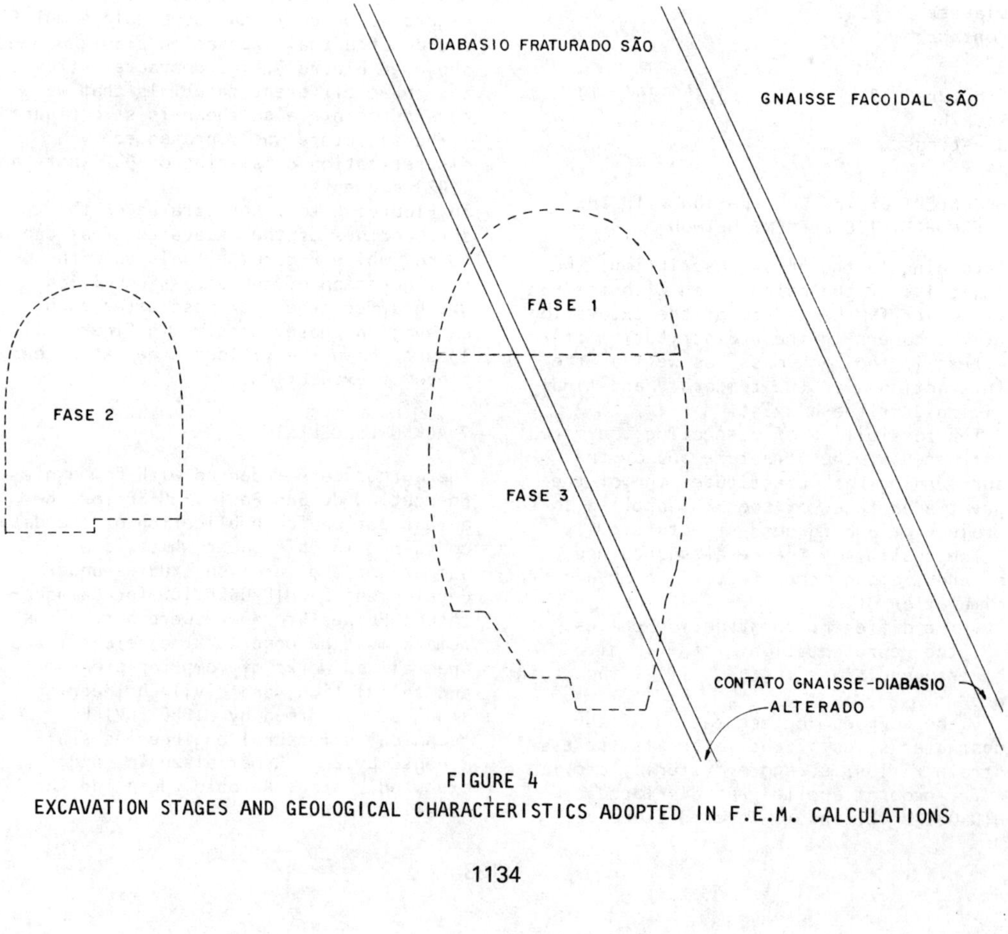

FIGURE 4

EXCAVATION STAGES AND GEOLOGICAL CHARACTERISTICS ADOPTED IN F.E.M. CALCULATIONS

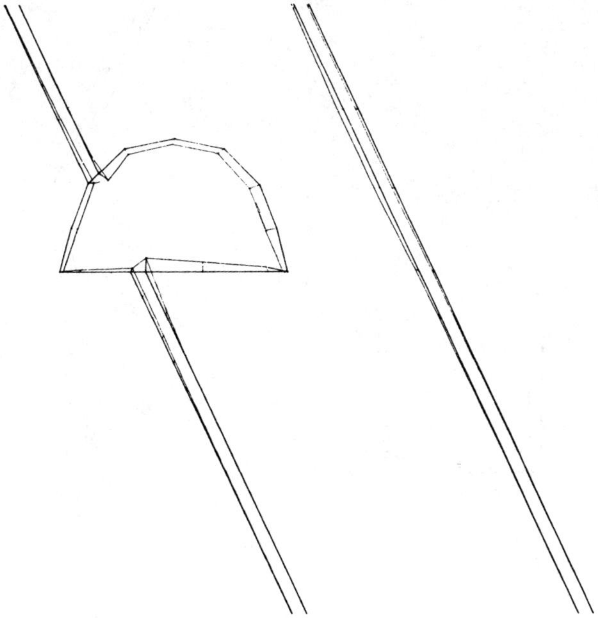

FIGURE 5
CONTOUR POINT DEFORMATION: STAGE 1

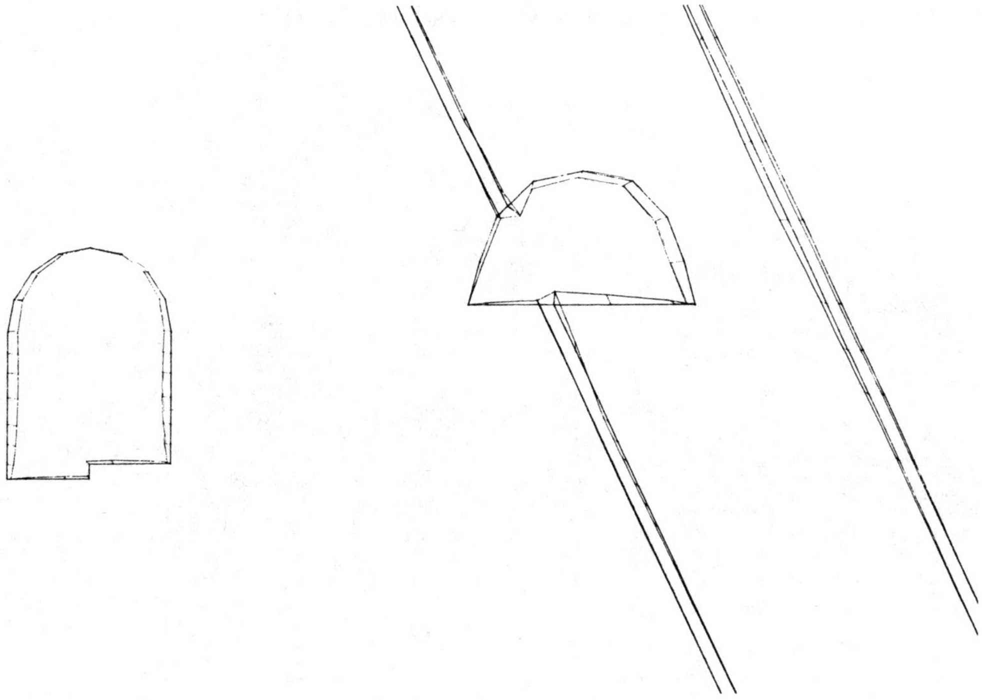

FIGURE 6
CONTOUR POINT DEFORMATION. STAGE 2

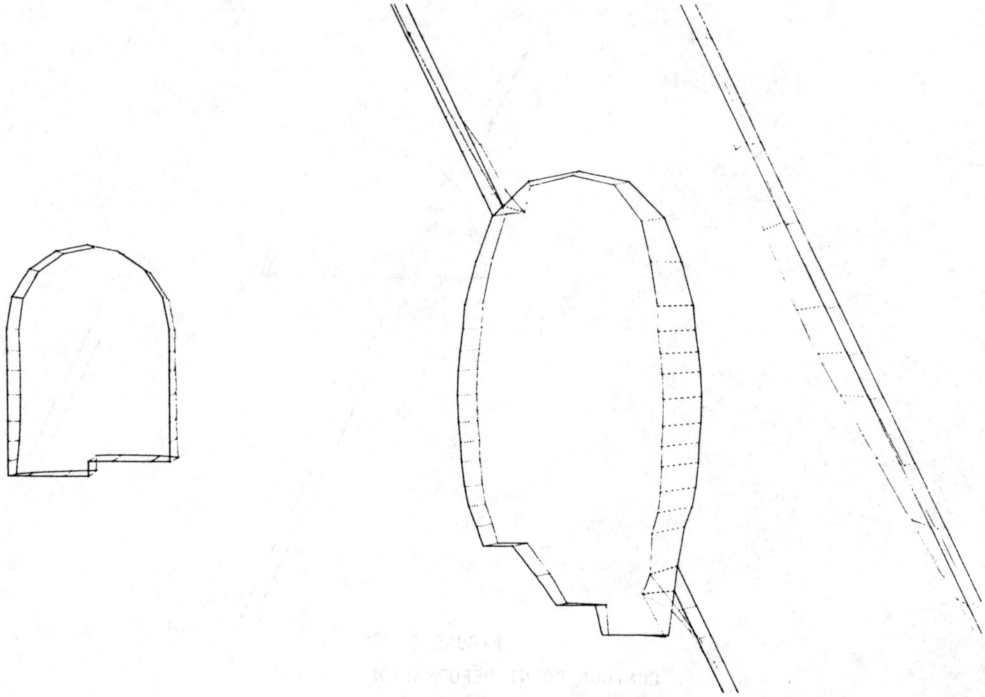

FIGURE 7

COUNTOR POINT DEFORMATION: STAGE 3

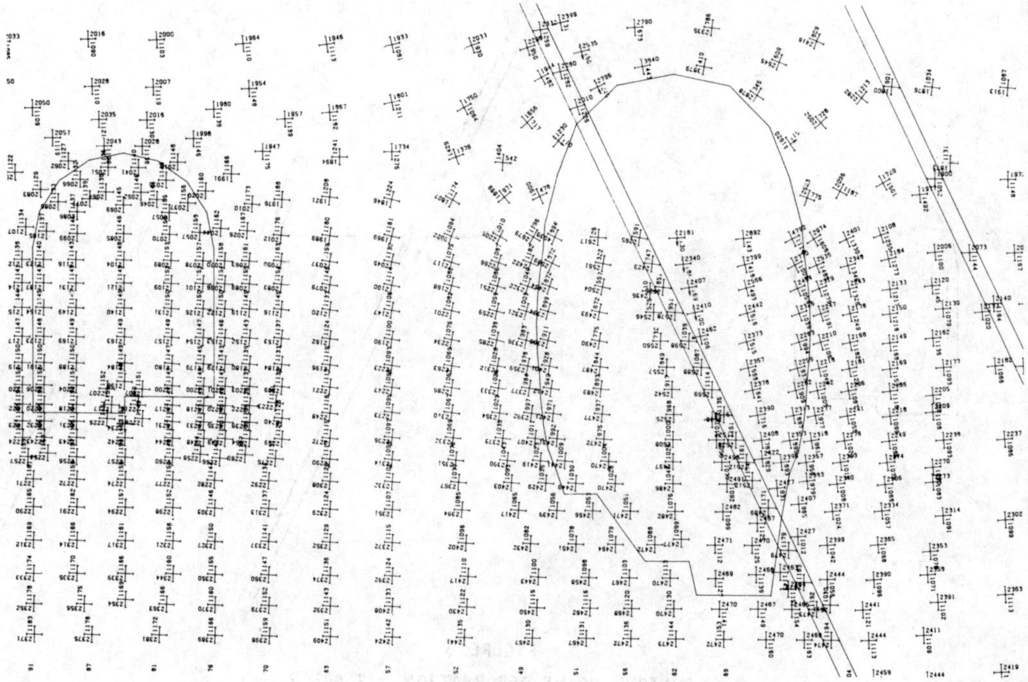

FIGURE 8

PRINCIPAL STRESS: STAGE 1

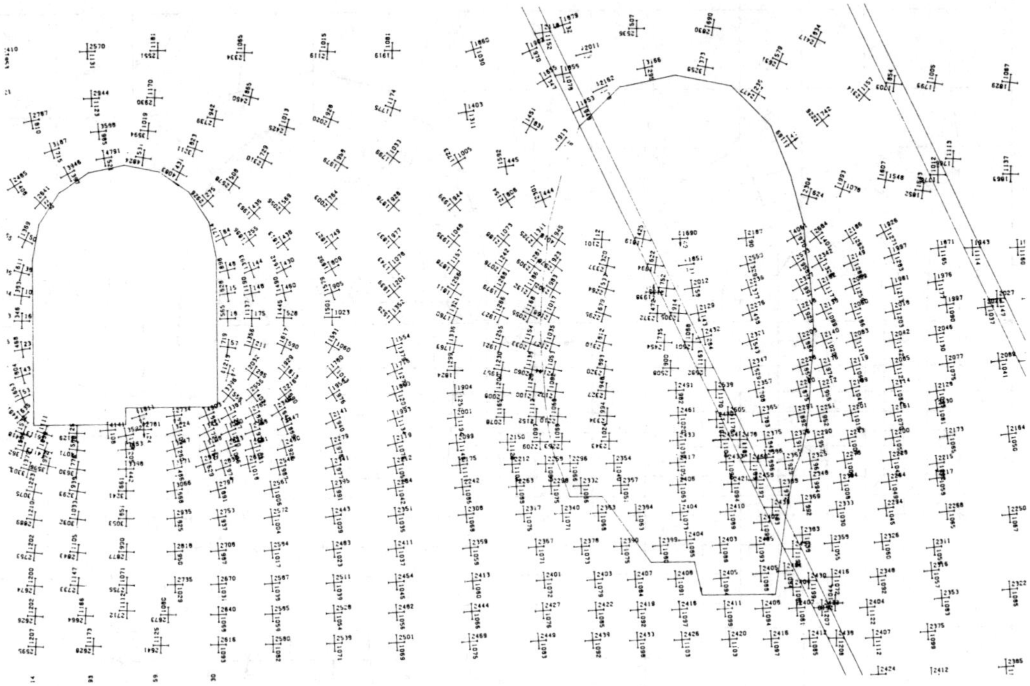

FIGURE 9

PRINCIPAL STRESS: STAGE 2

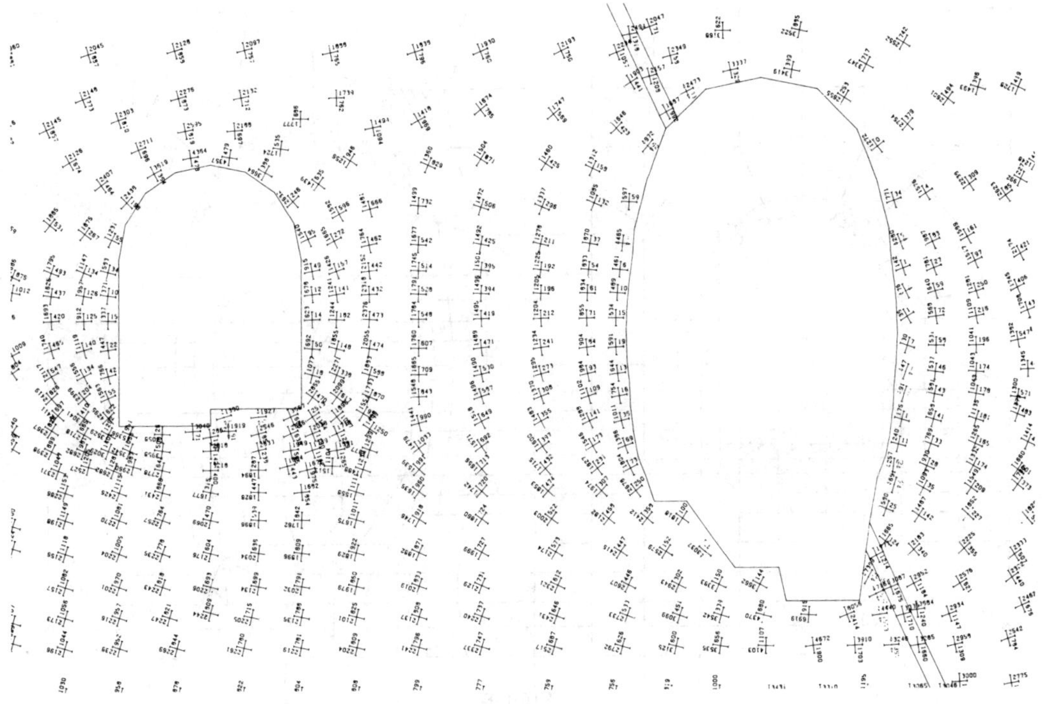

FIGURE 10

PRINCIPAL STRESS: STAGE 3

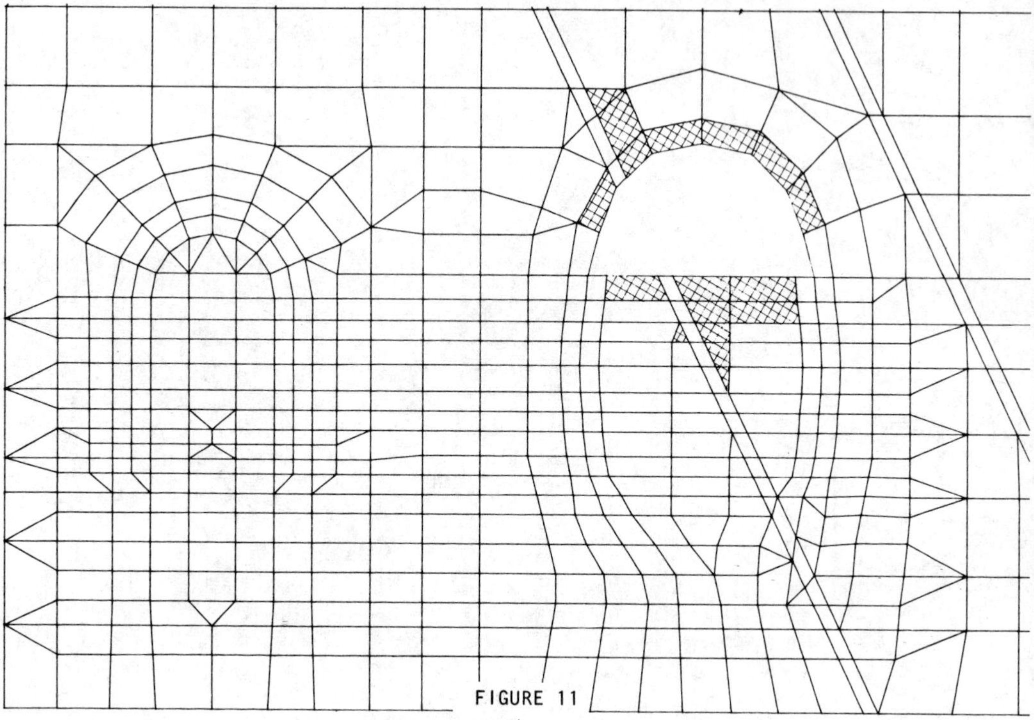

FIGURE 11

YIELD ZONES AFTER FIRST STAGE EXCAVATION

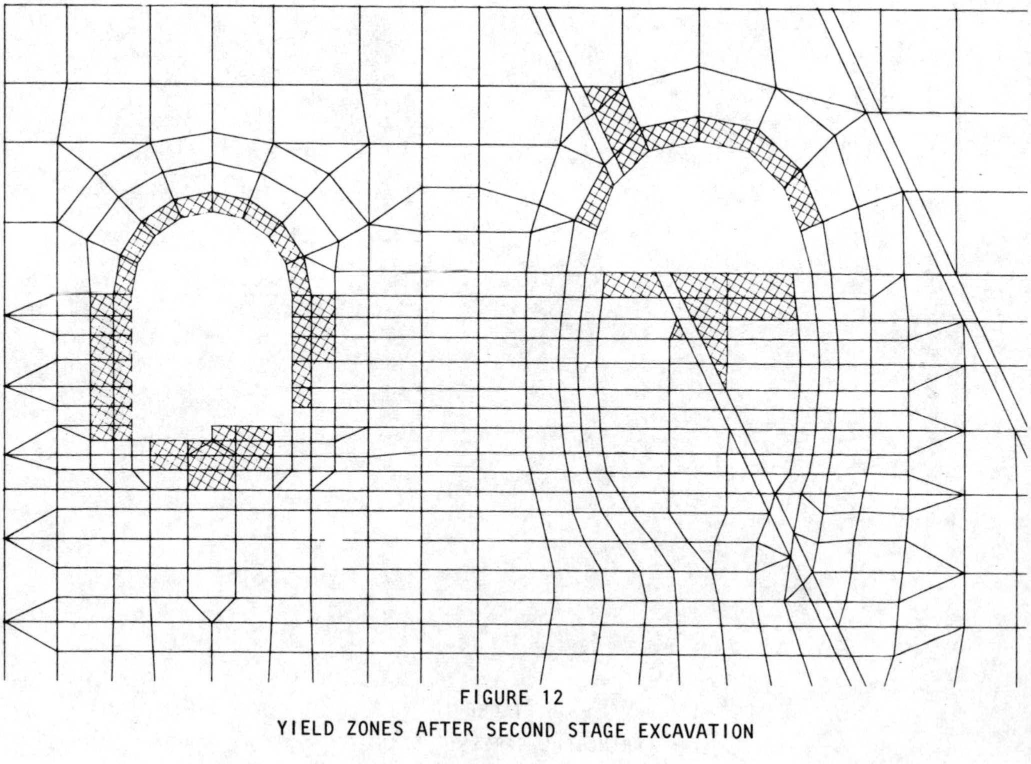

FIGURE 12

YIELD ZONES AFTER SECOND STAGE EXCAVATION

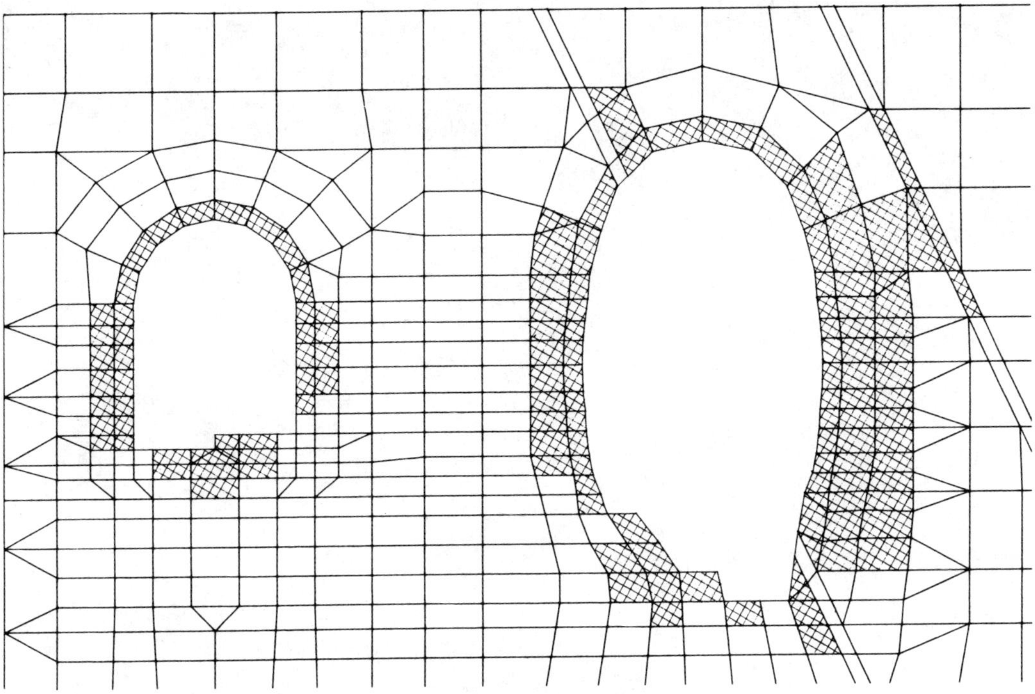

FIGURE 13
YIELD ZONES AFTER FINAL EXCAVATION

ENEL'S RECENT EXPERIENCES IN THE CONSTRUCTION OF LARGE UNDERGROUND POWERHOUSES, SHAFT AND PRESSURE TUNNELS

Neueste Erfahrungen von ENEL beim Bau von grossen unterirdischen Kraftwerken, Druckschächten und Druckstollen

Expériences nouvelles d'ENEL lors de la construction de grandes installations hydrauliques souterraines, de puits forcées et de galeries forcées

MORANDO DOLCETTA
ISMES, Bergamo, Italy

SUMMARY. In Italy, during the last decade, several hydroelectric plants - particularly pumped storage plants - have been constructed by ENEL. Improvements made in the performance of in situ tests, in the use of numerical tools, in the design of monitoring systems and in construction technologies are reported.

ZUSAMMENFASSUNG. Während der letzten Jahrzehnten sind in Italien mehrere Wasserkraftwerke - besonders Pumpspeicherwerke - vom ENEL gebaut worden. Es wird hier über den Entwicklungen in der Ausfuhrung von in-situ Versuchen, in der Benutzung numerischer Rechenmethoden, im Entwurf von Überwachungsystemen und in den Bautechnologien berichtet.

RESUME. In Italie, pendant la dernière décennie, beaucoup d'installations hydrauliques, en particulier installations de pompage, ont été construites par ENEL.On reporte ici les améliorations faites dans l'exécution d'essais en 'situ', l'emploi de methodes numériques, le projet de systèmes de contrôle et les technologies de construction.

1.0 EVOLUTION OF DESIGN CRITERIA

In the sixties ENEL first tackled the design of pumped-storage power plants which reached the installed power of 1000 MW with 125 MW per unit. It became evident that the most suitable solution was to install huge underground groups (see Dolcetta 1971 a, 1971 b, 1972).

On the one hand, this minimizes the inertia of the hydraulic system by shortening the length of pressure tunnels, and at the other it solves, in a satisfactory manner, all the problems related to the preservation of environment, and to the availability of areas.

Besides, a clear financial advantage with respect to the out-door solution was achieved in most cases.

However the required size of caverns turned out to be considerably bigger than that of previous Italian achievements.

In fact the new powerhouses required an excavation volume of 250.000 m^3, while in general those built previously didn't reach 100.000 m^3 each. Moreover the openings were of a remarkable height (about 60 m) since they had to house ternary units (alternator-turbine-right pump) and because of pumps cavitation problems (Fig.1). Later the introduction of new single or multi-stages reversible machines allowed to reduce the height of the main cavern to less than 40 m, and required some increment of its width. The construction of the pumped-storage stations made clear that the underground location might be the right solution also for other kinds of plants.

Therefore this choice was made even in the casé of plants for power production only, when the characteristics of the environment were difficult because of lack of building area and poor stability conditions of the site. Studies about possible underground installations of nuclear powerplants were also started.

In view of such an amount of work from the outset a program was sketched out to improve the knowledge about the real behaviour of the rock mass. More advanced design criteria were established as soon as new information was available particularly from construction experience. The Geotechnical Service of ENEL Central Construction Direction has followed all the design and construction activities carried out by Peripheral Operational Centers, thus assuring the organization of the information in a comprehensive theoretical frame, and its prompt diffusion. During the last twenty years ENEL's activities in the afore mentioned field stimulated a process which progressively updated and improved the rock mass behaviour models to be used in design. Their complexity, however, was made, each time, compatible with the available knowledge about the characteristic geotechnical parameters, and with the stage of their experimental determination.

In the above mentioned process the monitoring of the excavation play a very important role. Besides its usefulness in the construction phase it represents the base for further evolution of the design itself, either with regard to the individuation, and better determination of characteristic geotechnical parameters, or with regard to adaptation of interpretative models. However it is important to stress (Martinetti, 1977) the difficulty of selecting reliable instruments and planning measurements in order to assure regular surveys, even for critical situations as those of underground excavation stope. This implies the necessity of a certain redundancy in the monitoring system.

In fact in the case of a first group of new underground powerhouses the loss of essential information about real behaviour of the excavation was avoided in spite of the ill-functioning of some instruments of the main monitoring system. It was indeed possible to rely on supplementary information provided by other equipment and measurement systems which were less sophisticated and less expensive, but much more positive and reliable.

FIG.1 - S.Fiorano pumped storage power station View of the pump zone from the turbine level.

The wealth of information, gathered during the construction of the most important powerhouses listed in table 1, hasn't been completely analyzed yet. Nevertheless advances in the knowledge of the rock mass behaviour and in the computer simulation capabilities suggest the possibility that a new back-analysis programme, worked out also on the base of a first attempt (Martinetti, 1977), could give additional important explanations and ideas.

The completion of such a program will obviously require a long period of time; however the successful schematization employed during the design of the recent Timpagrande, Entracque, and Edolo powerhouses, makes a rational, safe and economical design and construction of openings already possible (such as Solarino and Piedilago which are expected to be complete in three years' time).

The pumped storage plants also involved the need of building power tunnels penstocks and surge shafts of unusual size.

TABLE 1 - ENEL's main underground plants: short description.

PLANT	STATION	ESCAVATION PERIOD	MACHINE HALL HEIGTH	MACHINE HALL WIDHT	MACHINE HALL LENGHT	ROCK
LAGO DELIO	RONCOVALGRANDE	1967-70	60.5	20.4	191.5	FINE GRAINED GREY GNEISS
LAGO D'ARNO S.FIORANO	S.FIORANO	1969-72	64.7	19.3	95.5	QUARTZITIC-FELDSPAR PHILLITES
PELOS	PELOS	1972-75	29.1	13.2	26.1	THINLY-BEDDED LIMESTONE WITH MARLY INTERLAYERS
TALORO	TALORO	1972-77	37.5	18.1	81.1	FINELY GRAINED GRANITE GRANITIC MILONITE
ARVO-AMPOLLINO	TIMPAGRANDE	1976-79	29.1	17.4	89.1	MEDIUM GRAINED GRANITE
ALBI MIGISANO	ALBI	1977-80	26.0	15.0	37.0	GNEISS KINZIGITES
GESSO	ENTRACQUE	1975-78	41.5	16.8	195.2	ANATEXITES PALEOMILONITES
EDOLO	EDOLO	1978-81	41.5	16.0	174.6	PHYLLITIC MICA SCHISTS
PIEDILAGO	PIEDILAGO	DESIGN	41.	17.	190.	GNEISS MICA SCHISTS
SOLARINO	SOLARINO	DESIGN	40.	20.	155.	CALCARENITE

The know-how gained from the main caverns was also ingeniously and largely used in the design and construction of tunnels and shafts. Obviously, taking into account the different size and stress condition of these openings, it was also necessary to give prominence to different aspects with regard to either the preliminary investigation, or the building procedures, or eventually the final lining. However, it must be pointed out that the increasing understanding of the real rock mass behaviour brought about a re-examination of the design criteria of the lining for shafts and pressure tunnels.Such a process, still to be completed, has already led to important practical results.

2.0 DESIGN CRITERIA AND INTERPRETATION OF THE BEHAVIOUR OF LARGE UNDERGROUND OPENINGS

2.1 Introduction

The design process relating to an underground powerhouse, currently adopted at ENEL, can be summarized in the following phases, which are put into practice, after a preliminary feasibility study.

- Preliminary determination of a rock mass model on the basis of a geologic-structural survey, and of simple analyses and laboratory tests.

- In situ investigation and laboratory tests for direct measurement of some relevant geotechnical parameters.

- Monitoring of minor excavations (e.g. properly equipped tunnels and chambers), and backanalysis of the observation aiming either at verifying a set of evaluated parameters or at obtaining an estimate of those which can't be directly measured.

- Working out of an adequate mathematical model for the excavation design and for possible support systems. Determination of the excavation sequence. Design and realization of the monitoring system. Behaviour prediction.

- Comparison between forecasted and measured behaviour, starting from the first excavation stage; possible updating of the model and design modification.

2.2 Rock mass models

The mechanical behaviour of a rock mass depends both on the rock matrix and on its discontinuities. Generally it's possible to represent a rock mass as a 'continuum'. The parameters defining such a continuum have to be established taking into account the presence of the discontinuity sets.

However, in some cases, it's also necessary to enquire about wedge stability (Hock, Bray, 1974; Martinetti, Ribacchi, 1977) by adopting a 'discontinuum' model. This happens when some discontinuity sets have particular geometric characteristics (persistence, spacing, and orientation) and namely when their extension is comparable with the size of the opening, Fig.2.

The characterization of joints is made according to procedures that are well-established in practice, having as conceptual reference the model described in a recent paper by Barton, and Choubey (1977).

The stabilization design involves the usual limit equilibrium method, and the forecast of dangerous wedges; the most important wedges will have to be located as soon as the excavation enable the inspection.

Once the local stability is ensured, the designer will examine the rock mass behaviour with regard to overall stability, immediate and rheologic deformation, and interaction with support structures. Such a behaviour, as previously said, is investigated from the stand-point of continuum mechanics, assuming that suitable constitutive laws account for the complex fabric of the rock mass. The geomechanical model generally assumed for design (Fig.3) is of the elasto-visco-plastic kind with fragile softening. Peak and residual strength are described by a simple Mohr- Coloumb criterion and tensile cutoff. The elastic strains are governed by a linear law while a non-associate flow rule controls the unrecoverable strains development. It is assumed that the relevant viscous phenomena are related to the plastic behaviour only.

This simple model can be specified on the basis of 8 parameters which are assumed constant within the frame of a specific problem:

- E elastic moduli
- ν Poisson's ratio
- Ψ dilatancy angle
- c_p peak cohesion
- φ_p peak friction angle
- c_r residual cohesion
- φ_r residual friction angle
- η viscosity coefficient

The evaluation of these parameters is basic for the design. Obviously, the other essential point is the evaluation of forces acting on the structure.

As, generally, the openings are at a considerable depth, the preminent forces derive from the relief of initial stresses. Besides, the selfweight of the rock must be taken into account in the equilibrium equations.

The simplification of the model is self-evident; e.g. it is unlikely that a fractured rock mass exhibits a neat peak

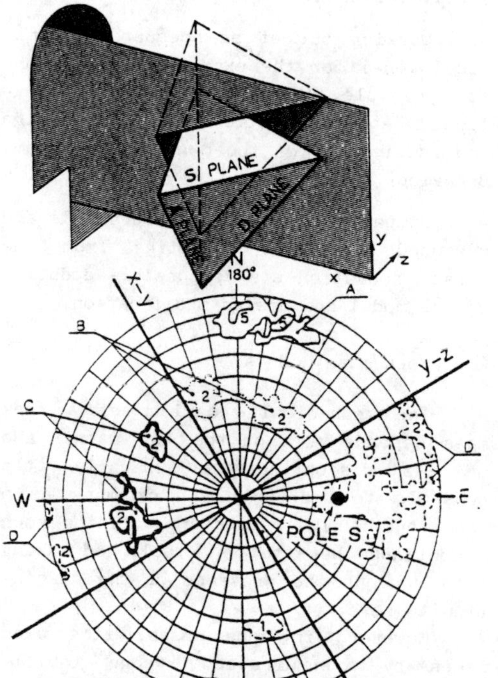

FIG.2 - Edolo machine hall. Geometry of the most severe design wedge expected on the base of the orientation of the main joint sets.

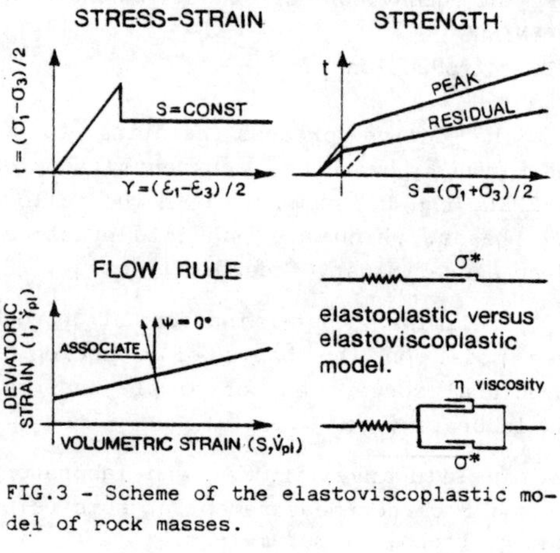

FIG.3 - Scheme of the elastoviscoplastic model of rock masses.

or a sudden softening, or that dilatancy could not be modified at large deformation. In addition two further points must be stressed. The residual strength of the rock mass is of primary importance in the design. The residual behaviour generates for most rocks, a plateau in the stress-strain curve both in triaxial tests and in joints shear tests. On the other hand the residual cohesion, at the rock mass scale, can be deteriorated at large deformations expecially at low confinements loads, when it is of vital importance for stability. Moreover a lowering of strength with time, and much more developed delayed deformations, must be expected, as mentioned before, at low stresses.

Such critical conditions should be avoided by an appropriate design.As a consequence, the above-mentioned simple model can have good chances of being accurate enough to reproduce working conditions. Another point to stress is that, being undrestood that the model retains the main features of the rock mass behaviour, its response largely depends on the selected values of the parameters. Therefore the model keeps its validity within a definite stress and strain range for which the parameter values have been selected.

The present know-how shows that such a model may be adequately adapted to various kind of rocks masses, provided that the parameter values are evaluated according to the same procedures and identification criteria.

Actually the setting up of the model and that of the methodologies and criteria for parameter identification are two, continuously interacting, phases of the same conceptual process. In fact each parameter must be considered as the expression of an important feature of the global behaviour, as it is detected by the specific test used to determine it.

Therefore the determination of a parameter by means of a 'generally speaking' better method must be considered with caution.

2.3 Supportive calculation methods for design

The wedge stability calculation methods have been briefly mentioned previously.

In the following the calculation methods used in the context of continuum mechanics will be described.

Most metodologies have been developed in connection with the use of computers, and probably they will be able to improve thanks to the evolution of such devices. A recent review of this subject has been published (Borsetto and Peano, 1981). The impact of numerical methods on design has become more and more significant in the last few years: note that this is also due to a better understanding of why and when such methematical tools are to be used.

Different approaches such as purely elastic, fully plastic, elastoplastic analyses are used to a different extent throughout the design stage. As a general rule elastic computations are used in very early stages, even when all design parameters have not been definitively selected. This approach was adopted since the construction of the Lago Delio plant in the late sixties, in connection to a finite element model (Fanelli, Riccioni, 1970). A recent example of usefull elastic computation is the three-dimensional analysis carried out for a separated-shafts excavation of the pumps zone of the Solarino machine hall, to be compared with the full section alternative (Fig.4). In most cases this computation gives only rough information, as for example the potential yield zone. This can be defined on the basis of the peak strength and of the stress level reached. Reasonable estimates of the actual failure zone, taking into account softening phenomena, may then be infered by means of judgement based on experience.

In many cases, however, both the stress and the strain fields are likely to be strongly modified by yieding. Such a phenomenon is easily taken into account if the void may be assumed to be circular in shape, and in situ stresses are not too anisotropic.

In fact, analytical tools, widely used for tunnels, are available for such situations (Amberg, Lombardi, 1974; Ribacchi, Riccioni, 1977).

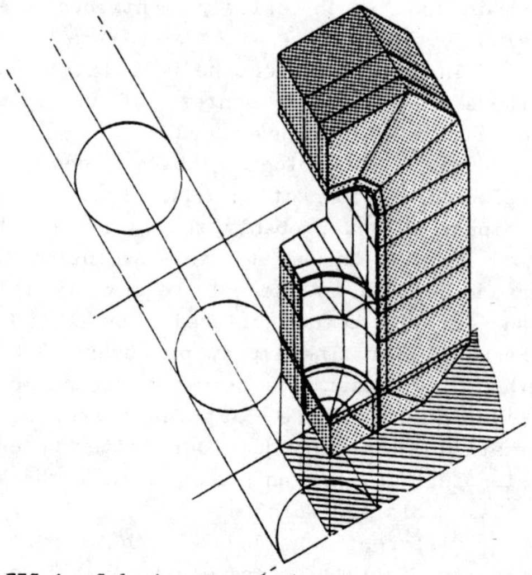

FIG.4 - Solarino pumped-storage power station. Partial view of the 3-D F.E. mesh used for the analysis of a ripetitive modulus of the excavation by FIESTA programme.

This approach is quite often followed for the interpretation of trial excavations (see paragraph 2.3) but it has been also used for the design of Timpagrande power station (Borsetto et al, 1982).

Actually the approach doesn't allow to point out a static problem which is peculiar to vertical walls and important when the height of the cavern is remarkable as for pumped-storage plants.

The wall equilibrium is, in fact, governed by the available residual strength and without arching effect the self weight action may produce very low minor principal stresses or even traction. A simplified method of analysis has been developed (Borsetto, Ribacchi 1978) to individuate the potentially dangerous zone. It is also useful to calculate a suitable stabilization pressure and the tendons length necessary to find adequate anchoring on the compression zone which develops from the crown and the bottom of the cavern.

The method was firstly adopted during the design of Albi power station (ISMES, 1978) and then employed for the dimensioning of the sistematic wall bolting of the Edolo plant. In this case the calculated pressure resulted in accordance with the one required to stabilize wedges of medium size and of appreciable expected frequency; more important, infrequent, wedges were stabilized individually after site inspection.

The whole calculations referred so far permit to obtain a reasonable view of the structure and to conceive at least a preliminary design. At this stage, however, the site investigations are in general completed and it is possible to decide if deeper analysis are needed. In this case more sophisticated methods, namely FEM, are used, which allow a more thorough simulation of the material behaviour and, at the same time, they take into account openings shape and the actual in situ stress field.

The computer program used for the analysis of the Taloro and Entracque plants provides for a non-dilatant variant of the initial stress method. This method does not fully comply with the presented rock mass model, and besides there are some limitations in anchor load analyses (Manfredini et al, 1976). In recent years, starting from the Albi plant design, the viscoplastic algorithm (Zienkiewicz et al, 1975) has been preferred, because it allows an all-though handling of the rock mass model, it has good numerical performaces, and finally because its results are more easily interpreted by the designers.

At any rate the mathematical model, which is more complex from a mechanical point of view and more sophisticated from a numerical one (e.g. eight excavation stages, and more than 3000 degrees of freedom), is usually developed in order to provide the design forecast of the excavation behaviour to be compared, step by step, with the measured performances.

3. DETERMINATION OF DESIGN PARAMETERS

3.1 Original state of stress

With some original contributions ENEL, in cooperation with the Institute of Mining of the University of Rome, has developed the doorstopper in situ measurements technique, that had at first been suggested and set up by CSIR (Leeman, 1969). Particular attention has been paid to its application to fractured rock masses and to the statistical interpretation of measurements (Martinetti, Ribacchi, 1974).

In a few words the strains caused by the stress release due to 'overcoring' are measured on the flattened bottom of a borehole. An estimated value of the in situ stresses, and its confidence limits, are obtained by means of an appropriate redundancy of measurements in differently oriented boreholes.

The stress concentration factors, that link the original state of stress to the state of stress at the flattened bottom, are well-known (Hocking, 1976) in the isotropic case only. In case of anisotropic rocks, analogous coefficients must be determined borehole by borehole.- This has been done by means of a 3-D FEM model for the Piedilago site (ISMES, 1981). In our opinion the method gives very satisfactory results. Their validity is also supported by the fact that in no case, in which 'a posteriori' analyses of the excavation behaviour were done by us, it was possible to attribute to an erroneous evaluation of the principal original stresses and in particular of their directions, possible deviation between the mathematical model forecasts and the survey measurements.

At last it must be recalled that the size of the underground stations is not negligible if compared with the thickness of the overburden. In the layer influenced by the excavation, therefore, the original state of stress is, in general, rapidly variable with depth. This is duly taken into account in the design computations which are described in paragraph 2.1.

To estimate this stress field a finite element model of the slope which houses the station is set up.

The excavation of the walley is simulated from two initial conditions, the first one corresponding to a purely gravitational equilibrium and the second one to a uniform horizontal compression of value f.The two derived stress fields (fig.5) are superposed and the free parameter f is evaluated in order to fit the experimental values at the measurement point.

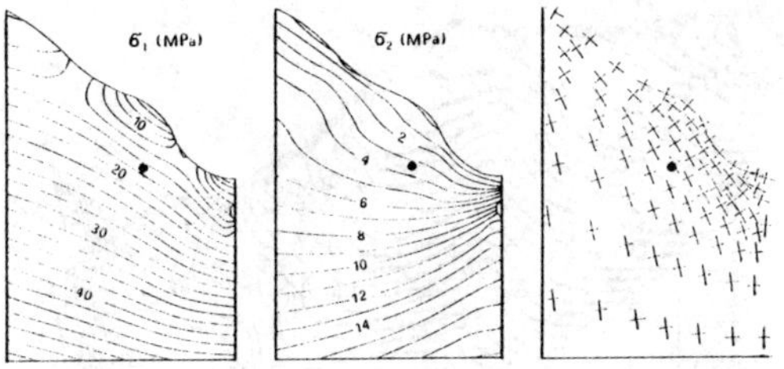

FIG.5 - State of stress at the Piedilago site evaluated by means of a finite element elastic analysis. The state of stress before the excavation of the valley is assumed to be purely gravitational.

Usually a two-dimensional idealization is sufficient. In other cases a 3-D model is more satisfying, see fig.6: the additional freedom for the choice of the horizontal extragravitational stress is counterbalanced by the additional experimental stress components to be fitted with.

3.2 Rock mass mechanical properties

As previously referred, the rock mass characterization leads to the definition of suitable values of the parameters listed in paragraph 2.2.

The procedure presently used by ENEL is as follows:

- Poisson's coefficient is 'a priori' assumed in a range of 0.2-0.3, as it is not thought to be influent.

- The peak c_p and residual c_r friction angle are estimated on the basis of a global interpretation of laboratory tests on samples (generally, triaxial tests on stiff machine) and on joints (direct shear tests).

- The elasticity modulus E is evaluated from in situ plate bearing tests.

- The value of c_r residual cohesion is estimated by means of flat jack tests performed in trial excavations.

- Two of the three remaining parameters (c_p, ψ) are evaluated on the basis of the deformations of trial excavations; in practice the state of stress (measured as in paragraph 3.1), and the values of E, ν, and of φ_p, c_r, φ_r

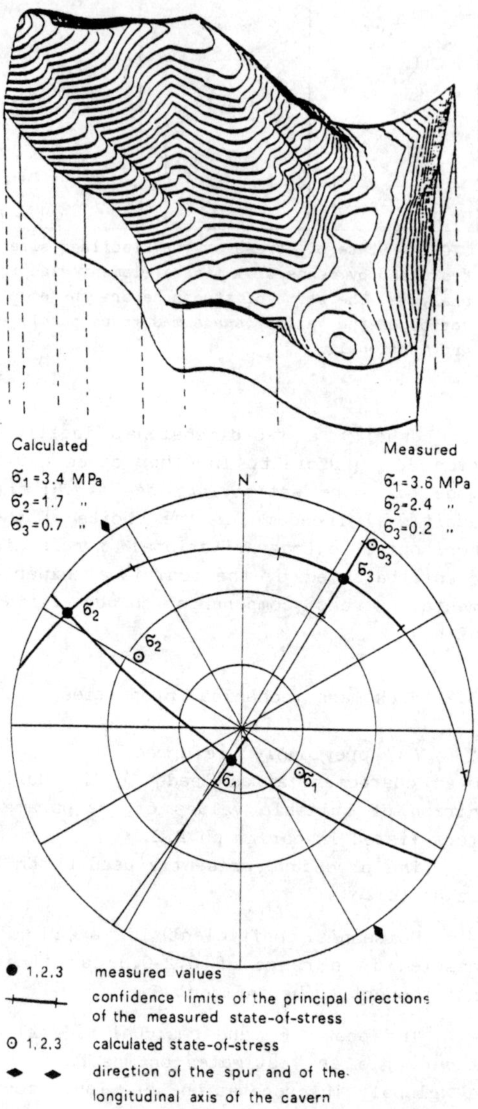

FIG.6 - Timpagrande site.
a) F.E. mesh of the valley, topographical contour lines are plotted on the surface.
b) Comparison between measured and calculated principal stresses after best fitting.

(determined as the previous points) are assumed to be known.

By means of a trial and error procedure a suitable couple of values (c_p, ψ) is determined, which, put into the elastoviscoplastic model, gives a satisfactory fitting of measured deformations.It is assumed that the measurement is made

TABLE 2 - Solarino Site. Mean elasticity modulus (MPa 10^{-3}) evaluated on different zones under the plate of fig.7.

DEPTH (m)	.07÷.25	.07÷3.5	.25÷3.5	.50÷3.5
P=4.5 MPa	59	129	224	243
P=6.5 MPa	59	126	212	225

when the gross rheological movements are exausted.

The evaluated parameters set is used in design although there are reasons to introduce some reduction factor, in order to take into account that the rock mass behaviour at scale of the final excavation may be less favourable than at the scale of the trial excavations. It is evident that previous procedure must rely upon some 'standardization', as far as possible, of the in situ tests which are more significant in the choice of the design characteristics.

With regards to the plate bearing tests, for example, tecnology and data interpretation procedures have been selected with satisfactory results (Manfredini et al, 1974).The state of the art of the experimental set up has been recently published (Oberti et al., 1979). The interpretation of the test is given, as an example, by the data of table 2 from which is possible to recognize in addition to the good test performance, the importance of readings at depth (Fig.7) in order to avoid the effect of the more deformable surface layer. It is worthwhile noting that the surface readings would furnish an elasticity modulus of 13.000 MPa instead it is estimated to be at least 23.000 MPa. It is thought that hydraulic chamber test, (with deep readings too, Rossi 1980), is conceptually very satisfactory but it cannot be used routinely.

The flat jack test is performed under an unusual perspective. That is not for deformability or in situ stresses determination (Jager and Kook, 1969). Its usage for the evaluation of residual strength is an original contribution to the solution of a uneasily solvable problem of rock mechanics.A theoretical introduction to the subject and a suitable interpretation model are given in (Borset-

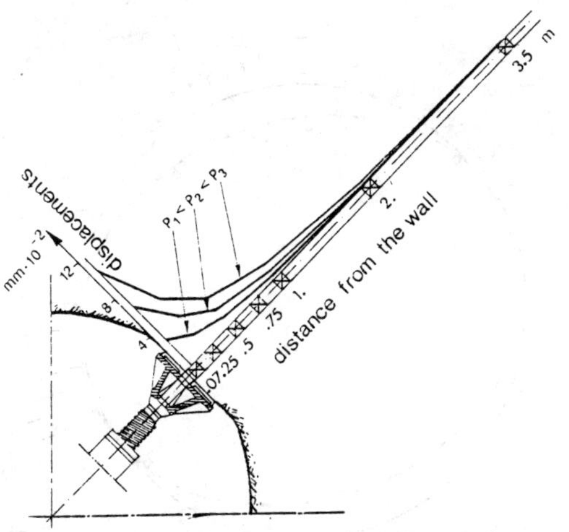

FIG.7 - Plate bearing test scheme. Mechanical estensometer anchors are shown.

to, 1980). The background of the test is the following: if the yield zone around the excavation undergoes sufficient deformations, the stresses in this layer will be in a state of limit equilibrium and will depend on the excavation geometry and on residual strength only. The test can be divided into three logical stages:

a) excavation of the tunnel: the residual strength is fully mobilized at the wall, and a related stress field is generated.

b) Cutting of the slot: displacements generated by the stress relief are monitored at various points (Fig.8). A mathematical model is used in order to identify the unknown stress field and, in the end, if an estimate of the deformability is available and residual friction was identified in other ways, the unknown parameter C_r is evaluated.

c) Re-charge: the flat jack is inserted and a known modification of the stress field is generated. Monitored displacements are used to calibrate the deformability of the afore-mentioned model.

A reliable geomechanical investigation requires that the rock mass interested by the trial excavation be as closed as possible to the site where the main cavern will be excavated. The execution of the afore-mentioned tests requires carefully excavated tunnels and drifts. As a logical consequence taking into account these needs and the low increment of the involved costs, portions of tunnel, nearly circular in shape, are instrumented in order to register the partial (convergence measurement) or the total deformation of the walls. The measured displacements provide a basis for the identification of the parameters, namely c_p and Ψ, which can not be estimated in a more direct way.

In the case of the Timpagrande plant (Borsetto et al, 1982) a trial enlargement of the adit tunnel has been attempted for this purpose, but unsatisfactory results have been obtained, mainly due to the disturbance induced by the installation of estensometers. The method could be refined, but usually the full face excavation method is preferred.

Additional information on strength parameters may, in principle, be obtained by fitting, again with the elastoviscoplastic model and some mathematical tool, the extension of the yield zone. This latter may be estimated, as has been done for the Albi adit tunnel (Silvestri, 1977), by means of seismic refraction on short bases and sonic logging. Since the reliability limit of the approach is low, it is conveniently used only for a qualitative undependent check of the parameter set which has been evaluated according to the general procedure.

In the previous discussion it has been assumed that a yield zone has developed. However, this could not happen in case of slightly fractured rocks or, in

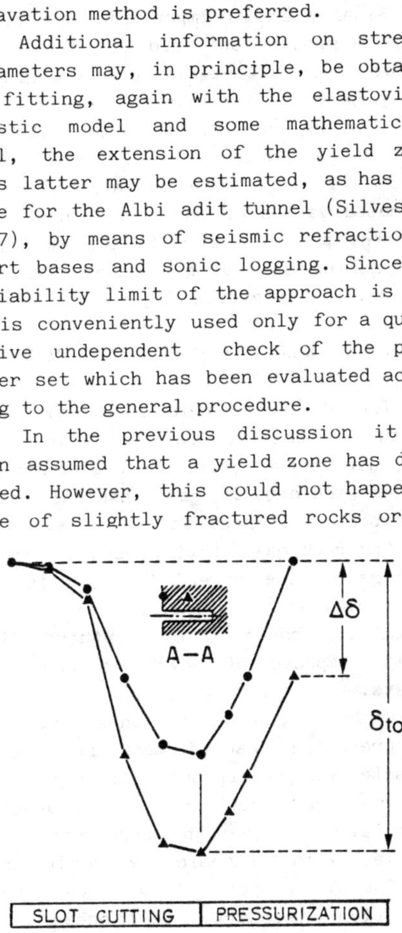

FIG.8 - Flat jack test. The diagram refers to a square slot cut from a test tunnel in a low cohesion rock mass.

general, when the in situ stresses are low in comparison to the peak strength. In such a case the cohesion parameters cannot be estimated directly by this methodology.

The elastic behaviour of the trial excavation is apparent from the conventional procedure results, if a convenient number of measures are taken. A lower bound of the peak cohesion may be infered and could be used, if no scale effects are likely to occur, for the design of the main chamber. A similar case occurred in a trial excavation of the Solarino Plant (Fig.9): the in situ strength of the calcarenite mass compares very well with the sample strength in the laboratory.

Finally it is important to remember that the process outlined in this section is not fully deterministic and engineering judgement is requested in each new plant. In any case the designer is involved in the evaluation of the design consequences of reasonable variations of the estimated values of the parameters. This, in turn, provides a basis for the decision making involving further rock mechanical investigations.

4. AN EXAMPLE. EDOLO POWER STATION

The Edolo pumped-storage power plant is the latest complete experience of ENEL, and serves well to illustrate the state-of-the-art of geomechanical design described in the previous sections.

The rock mass which houses the three openings of the power plant consists of "Edolo schists", a formation of the crystalline basement of southern Alps, mainly composed of phyllites and micaschists.

The study of general tectonics and photo interpretation results made it possible to site the underground openings at a location that combined the hydraulic-financial optimization requirements of the plant with the geological conditions.

The 700 m-approx long access tunnel excavation was started well ahead of the contract for the main works, so as to attain an advanced geomechanical characterization of the rock mass. The principal in situ tests carried out are indicated in Fig. 10.

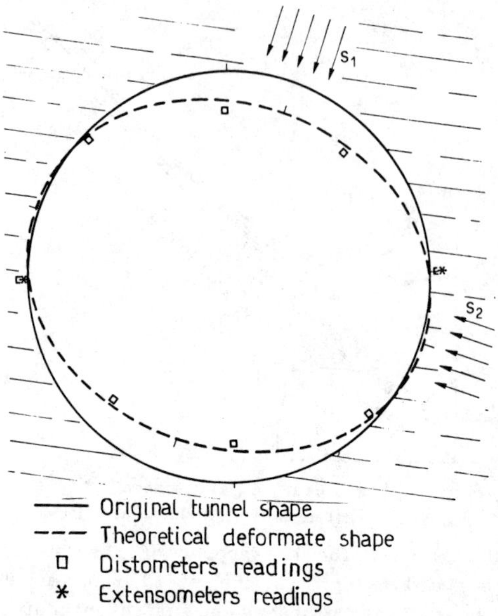

FIG.9 - Solarino trial excavation results. Comparison between measured displacements and the ones computed by a plane strain homogeneous elastic model on the basis of measured in situ stresses and elasticity modulus.

Following the general directions so far set forth, the design values of the two basic lithotype properties affecting the works were determined. These values are indicated in the Table 3.

The monitoring system was planned to provide the designer with the elements that would bear out the validity of the design or with well-grounded information for any possible modification.

A characteristic element of this system is an instrumented section with a high information content, shown in Fig.11, as well as a series of measuring stations intended to cover the widest excavation surface. Displacements recorded during excavation were rather high, reaching about 100 mm of convergence at the machine hall in the southern section and

TABLE 3 - Edolo Site. Values of design parameters (MPa, degrees)

Litho type	E	ν	c_p	φ_p	c_r	φ_r	ψ
1	40000	0.2	3.0	43°	1.5	38°	0°
2	25000	0.2	1.5	43°	1.1	38°	0°

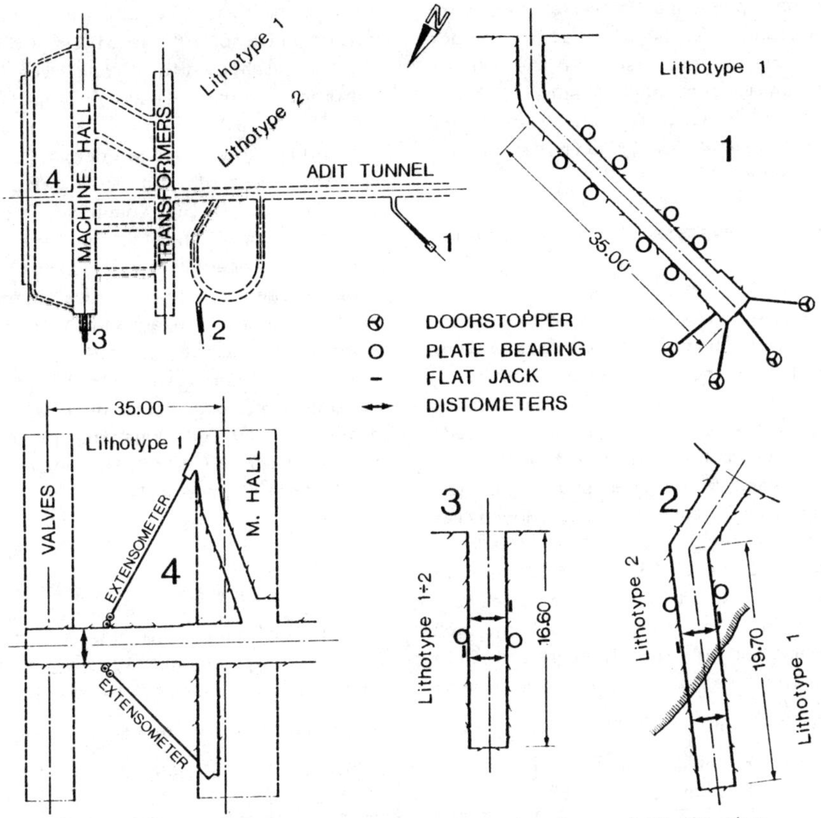

FIG.10 - Edolo site. Layout of the in situ tests. Zones where the mica shists are more intensively laminated are defined as lithotype 2.

230 mm in the northern section.

However, the substantial agreement between measurements and design forecast, based on the results of the mathematical model, at all excavation stages made it possible to carry on with confidence the excavation of benches according to the original design.

5. PRESSURE TUNNELS AND SHAFTS. SPECIFIC POINTS

In the past decade, the construction of hydroelectric power plants in Italy involved the excavation of some 50 km of pressure tunnels and of about 8 km of vertical or steeply inclined shafts forming surge shafts or emplacements for penstocks.

The problems of construction, of the stability of the openings and water-tightness in relation to occasionally

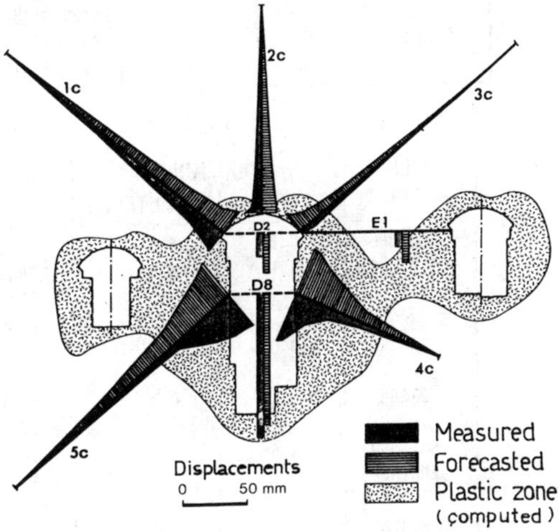

FIG.11 - Edolo plant. Comparison between measured and forecasted displacements in the main control section.

high internal pressures were solved both by conventional methods and, in many cases, by procedures based on the use of up-to-date equipment, and of special techniques and materials. The main works are listed in Table 4 and 5 with some descriptive notes.

5.1 Excavation systems. Tunnel boring machines

It is worth mentioning that T.B.M. were used for about 50% of excavations carried out for horizontal or sub-horizontal tunnels. In all cases, fullfacers of various sizes and types were involved. These were used both in relatively soft rocks (the sandstones and shales of the Suviana-Brasimone tunnel, with monoaxial compressive strength of saturated specimens between 30 and 130 MPa) and in medium-hard to hard rocks (compressive strength of between 150 and 350 MPa, such as the granites of the Taloro and Sila tunnels). The positive results achieved, notwithstanding the actual average utilization limits of machines (50 - 60% of the available time) and the high investment costs, lead to the conclusion that the T.B.M. can be relied on covering virtually all future needs, except for special cases of extremely hard rock.

In particular, machines with a double telescopic shield, coupled with a device for immediate prelining by precast ring segments, like those used for the Orichella and Timpagrande tunnels in Calabria, represent in general a favourable solution. This is particularly true when medium-hard rocks alternate with rocks of modest or quite thrusting properties, as the typical case of the Appenines zones of Central-Southern Italy.

5.2 Lining

Power tunnel linings as indicated in Table 4 are generally subjected to high operating pressures (10 to 12 bar), the

TABLE 4 - Surge shaft of ENEL's main underground plants: short description.

PLANT	SURGE SHAFT		ROCK	EXCAVATION METHODS	LINING
	HEIGHT	DIAMETER			
S.FIORANO	110	8.2	SANDSTONE	TRAD	REINFORCED CONCRETE
TALORO	U 96 L 77	14.8 14.8	GRANITE	TRAD	PRESTRESSED CONCRETE CONCRETE
GESSO	U 125 L 60	6.1 14. 10.	ANATEXITES PALEOMILONITES	TRAD	PARTIALLY PRESTRESSED CONCRETE
SUVIANA BRASIMONE	68	26.4	SANDSTONE WITH MARLY INTERLAYERS	TRAD	PRESTRESSED CONCRETE
EDOLO	U 105 L 48	18. 18.	PHILLITIC MICA SCHIST	TRAD + RAISE BORER	PRESTRESSED CONCRETE GUNITE-PVC-CONCRETE

U upper shaft

L lower shaft

TABLE 5 - Power tunnel of ENEL's main underground plants: short description.

PLANT	POWER TUNNEL		ROCK	EXCAVATION METHODS	LINING
	LENGHT(KM)	DIAMETER(M)			
LAGO DELIO	5.9	6.2	GNEISS	TRAD	REINFORCED CONCRETE
S.FIORANO	4.1	3.6	SANDSTONE TONALITIES LIMESTONE	TRAD	CONCRETE(MOST PART), REINFORCED CONC.(20%) STEEL (10%)
TALORO	3.9	5.5	GRANITE	T.B.M.	CONCRETE(MOST PART), PRESTRESSED CONCRETE
GESSO	7.4	6.1	ANATEXITES PALEOMILONITES	TRAD	CONCRETE(MOST PART), REINFORCED CONCRETE
SUVIANA BRASIMONE	4.5	5.4	SANDSTONE WITH MARLY INTERLAYERS	T.B.M.	REINFORCED CONCRETE INJECTION PRESTRESSING
EDOLO	8.1	6.4	GRANODIORITES MICA SCHISTES	TRAD	CONCRETE(MOST PART) WITH REINFORCED P.V.C.(20%)
PRESENZANO	2X2.2	5.6	LIMESTONE	T.B.M.	-

tunnel diameter being relatively high (5-7 m).

The pressure-diameter product in a sub-horizontal tunnel may reach 90 bar.m, and in some surge shafts 170 bar.m. Therefore, the designers had to face problems, especially when weak rock masses are encountered.

The power tunnel (diam. 6.40 m) of the Suviana-Brasimone pumped-storage power plant was excavated by means of T.B.M. in the Tusco-Emilian Appennines. A lining was carried out inside a prefabricated prelining made some twenty meters away from the excavation face. This lining is a typical example of a design that took into account not only the rock mass properties, but also the excavation and immediate support systems.

The tunnel crossed a formation of thinly bedded marl and sandstone, with an elasticity modulus lower than 5000 MPa. To provide immediate support to the rock after the T.B.M. head passed a prelining ring was placed. This ring consisted of precast segments and was slightly prestressed by interposing hydraulic jacks and fixing wedges.

The inner surface of the segments presented some grooves, which were covered with a steel plating, before the final lining was poured (Fig.12). The resulting annular and longitudinal channels were then pressure grouted in order to prestress the inner lining. Measurements carried out during 8 years by means of vibrating- wire straingauges indicated that the prestressing is still working. These measurements clearly show that the elastic modulus of the concrete increases with time, and that the deformations remain elastic.

At the same Suviana-Brasimone pumped-storage plant there was a marked design and construction problem for the surge shaft. This shaft, of the concentric cylindrical pipe differential type, is 68 m high. Diameters of external and internal pipes are 26.40 m and 12.40 m, respectively.

The remarkable size of the structure and the extent of pressure involved, along with the impossibility of relying on the support of the sorrounding rock (given the high local cracking of marls and the vicinity of the slope surface) have led to the use of prestressed reinforced concrete structures (ungrouted cables). Here too, periodical measurements carried out by electroacustic straingauges have shown the satisfactory behaviour of the structure.

Alternatives similar to those described for the Suviana power plant were used for S.Fiorano and Chiotas shafts; in the latter case, the results were proved satisfactory also on the basis of measurements made in the rock mass.

For Edolo pressure tunnel, a simple concrete lining was used, relying on the rock strength. Where the concrete fissuring could give rise to untolerable leaks a deformable, steel reinforced, waterproof polivinilchloride coating was placed between the preliminar and the final concrete linings (Moro, Vallino, 1982).

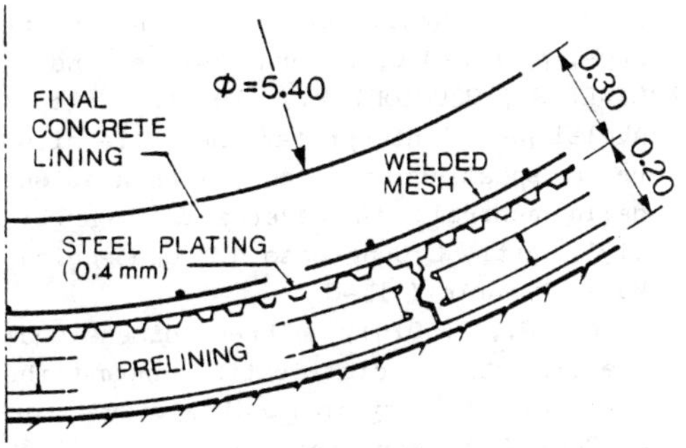

FIG.12 - Suviana-Brasimone power tunnel. Detail of the lining.

REFERENCES

AMBERG W.A., LOMBARDI G., (1974): 'Une méthod de calcul élastoplastique de l'état de tension et de deformation autur d'uné cavité soutteraine'. Proc. 3rd IRSM Congr., 2B, Denver.

BARTON N.S., CHOUBEY V., (1977): 'The shear strength of rock joints in theory and practice'. Rock Mech., 10.

BORSETTO M. (1980), 'Una metodologia per l'identificazione delle caratteristiche di resistenza degli ammassi rocciosi'. Atti XIV Nat. Geoth. Cong., Florence.

BORSETTO M., PEANO A., (1981) 'Numerical simulation of the escavation of large underground openings: an assessement of some past, present and future techniques', European Simulation Meeting, Capri.

BORSETTO M., GIUSEPPETTI G., MARTINETTI S., RIBACCHI R., SILVESTRI T., (1982), Rock Mech., in press.

BORSETTO M., RIBACCHI R., (1978), 'Metodi di calcolo per la valutazione dell'efficacia di tiranti di grandi scavi in sotterraneo', Giornata di studio sulla bullonatura, Torino.

DOLCETTA M. (1971a), 'Problems with large underground stations in Italy' Atti ASCE National WeterResources Engineering Meeting, Phoenix, USA, pp.243-286.

DOLCETTA M., (1971b), 'Pumped-storage stations in Italy. Present and future trends', Atti Int. Cong. on pumped- storage development and its environmental effects, Milwaukee, I Sect., USA.

DOLCETTA M., (1972), 'Rock loads on the support structures of two large underground hydroelectric power stations' Proc. Int. Symp. on Underground Openings, pp.405-446, Lucern, Switzerland.

FANELLI M., RICCIONI R., (1970), 'Calcoli svolti per l'interpretazione delle misure di spostamento durante l'escavazione della centrale in caverna di Lago Delio'. Atti X Congresso di Geotecnica, Bari, Memorie T 11-6.

HOCKING G., (1976), 'Three dimensional elastic stress distribution around the flat end of a cylindrical cavity' Int. J. Rock Mech. Min. Sci., 13.

HOEK E., BRAY J.W., (1974), 'Rock Shape Engineering' The Inst. of Mining and Methodology, London.

JAEGER C., COOK N.C.W., (1969), 'Foundamentals of Rock Mechanics', Methuen & Co. Ltd., London.

ISMES (1981), ISMES (1978), Technical reports to Enel, unpubliced.

MANFREDINI G., MARTINETTI S., RIBACCHI R., RICCIONI R., (1976), 'Design criteria for anchor cables and bolting in underground openings', Proc., IInd Int. Conf. Num. Meth. in Geomechanics, Blackburg.

MANFREDINI G., MARTINETTI S., ROSSI P., SAMPAOLO A. (1974), 'Observations on the procedures and interpretation of Plate Bearing Test'. Proc. III Cong. IRSM, Denver.

MARTINETTI S., (1977), 'Experience in field measurements for underground power-stations in Italy'. Proc. Int. Symposium: 'Field Measurements in Rock Mechanics'., Zurich, Switzerland.

MARTINETTI S., RIBACCHI R., (1974), 'Results of state of stress measurements in different types of rock masses'. 3rd Congr. Int. Soc. Rock Mech., Vol.2A, pp.458-463, Denver.

MARTINETTI S., RIBACCHI R., (1980), 'In situ stress measurements in Italy'. Rock Mechanics, Suppl.9, pp.31-47.

MARTINETTI S., RIBACCHI R., (1977), 'Stabilità di scarpate di roccia'. Rassegna Tecnica Problemi Energia Elettrica, n.133-134-135.

MORO T., VALLINO G., (1982), 'Criteri di progettazione della galleria di derivazione in pressione dell'impianto di Edolo', Gallerie e grandi opere sotterranee, VI, 14.

OBERTI G., CARABELLI E., GOFFI L., ROSSI P.P., (1979), 'Study of an orthotropic rock mass: experimental techniques, comparative analysis of results, IV ISRM Congr., Montreux.

RIBACCHI R., (1977), 'Rock stress measurements in anisotropic rock masses'. Proc. Int. Symp. 'Field Measurements in Rock Mechanics', 1, pp.183-196, Zurich.

RIBACCHI R., RICCIONI R., (1977), 'Stato di sforzo e di deformazione intorno ad una galleria circolare'. Gallerie e grandi opere sotterranee, II, 4.

ROSSI P.P., (1976), 'In situ verzusche zur bestimmung des verformugsmodulus von fels'. 2nd Rock Mech. Cong. Aachen.

SILVESTRI T., (1977), 'Criteri di progettazione della centrale in caverna di Albi (Sila); Internal Report ENEL-CPCIE Naples, unpublished.

ZIENKIEWICZ O.C., CORMEAU I.C., (1974), 'Viscoplasticity Plasticity and creep in Elastic Solids', Int. J. Num. Meth. in Engineering.8.

CONTROLLING BLAST-INDUCED CRACKING AROUND LARGE CAVERNS

Die Kontrolle der durch Sprengen hervorgerufenen Brüche in der Umgebung von grösseren unterirdischen Hohlräumen

Contrôle des fractures causées par des explosions aux environs des parois de grandes cavernes

T.N.HAGAN
Golder Associates Pty. Ltd., Melbourne, Australia

SUMMARY:
Overbreak is least in strong rocks, and especially in those which contain few discontinuities. Controlling overbreak and ground vibrations demands that blastholes have the optimum orientation and inclination.
Overbreak can be largely but not totally controlled by applying the smoothwall blasting technique (i.e., by using low explosion energy concentrations in perimeter blastholes and by firing these charges last, as simultaneously as possible, and with a burden: spacing ratio of 1.25 - 1.40).
If a primary blast is poorly designed and/or carried out, there is a high probability that overbreak will occur even with the application of smoothwall blasting. This is especially the case where fewer larger-diameter blastholes are used in an effort to reduce both the cost and period of excavation. However, in strong rocks, larger-diameter blastholes and acceptable overbreak can be surprisingly compatible, provided that progressive relief of burden is achieved by carefully selecting the energy factor, initiation sequence and delay timing for each charge. Where large-diameter blastholes are used in horizontal benching and especially in downhole benching, it may well be preferable to presplit the walls of the cavern.

ZUSAMMENFASSUNG:
Das Überprofil ist in solidem Gestein am kleinsten, insbesondere in Gestein, welches wenige natürliche Unregelmäßigkeiten aufweist. Die Kontrolle des Überprofils und der Erdschwingungen erfordert die bestmögliche Ortung und Neigung der Sprenglöcher.
Das Überprofil kann weitgehend, jedoch nicht völlig, durch Anwendung der Glattmauer-Sprengmethode unter Kontrolle gebracht werden, d.h. durch Anwendung niedriger Sprengenergiedichte in Kranzsprenglöchern, und durch Zündung dieser Sprengladungen zuletzt und so gleichzeitig wie möglich mit einem Vorgabe : Abstandsverhältnis von 1,25 - 1,40.
Falls eine Hauptsprengung mangelhaft entworfen oder ausgeführt worden ist, ist es höchstwahrscheinlich, daß ein Überprofil auftreten wird, sogar bei Anwendung der Glattmauer-Sprengmethode. Dies ist insbesondere der Fall, wenn weniger Sprenglöcher von größerem Durchmesser angewandt werden, um die Kosten und auch die Ausschachtungszeit zu verringern. Jedoch können in solidem Gestein Sprenglöcher größeren Durchmessers zu gleicher Zeit mit hinnehmbarem Überprofil existieren, solange die schrittweise Entlastung der Vorgabe durch die sorgfältige Auswahl des Energiefaktors, der Zündreihenfolge und der Verzögerungszeit jeder Sprengladung zuwegegebracht wird. Wenn Sprenglöcher größeren Durchmessers im horizontalen Stufenbau, und insbesondere in nach unten gerichtetem Abbau angewandt werden, mag die Vorspaltung der Wandung dos unterirdischen Raumes vorteilhafter sein.

RESUME:
L'exces de fissurage au dela de l'excavation est moindre dans la roche dure, particulierement dans celle qui contient peu de failles. Le controle du fissurage et des vibrations du sol necessite que les trous de mine aient une orientation et une inclinaison optimales.
L'exces de fissurage peut être controlé en grande partie, mais non completement, par la technique de "fracture lisse" (c'est à dire en plaçant une faible concentration d'energie explosive dans chaque trou de mine sur la péripherie et en amorçant ces charges en dernier et, autant que possible, simultanement; avec un rapport distance a la face libre/ecartement des trous de 1,25 a 1,40).
Si un tir primaire est mal preparé et/ou mal executé, il est probable que des fissures excessives se produiront au dela de l'excavation malgré l'application des charges péripheriques decrites ci-dessus. C'est en particulier le cas quand le nombre de trous de mine a été reduit et leur diametre aggrandit afin de reduire le cout et la durée du forage.
Cependant en roche dure, les charges de grand diametre peuvent être compatibles avec un degré de fissuration acceptable pourvu que l'abattage progressif de la roche soit obtenu par le choix soigneux du facteur d'énergie, de la séquence d'amorçage et du retard d'armorcage de chaque charge. Quand des trous de mine à grand diametre sont employés pour l'abattage horizontal ou plus particulierement pour l'abattage vertical il est souvent préferable de "pré-tailler" la parois de la caverne par un tir a deux temps.

1. INTRODUCTION

The last two decades have witnessed the excavation of many large caverns for both hydro-electric power projects and the storage of crude oil. There are strong indications that, in the remaining years of this century, far greater numbers of such underground openings will be required for these and additional purposes.

In the stronger rocks, at least, caverns will be excavated by drilling and blasting for many years to come. As is to be expected, there are appreciable incentives to fire larger blasts, since these effectively lessen the cyclicity of the operation and, hence, reduce both the period and cost of excavation. However, unless carefully designed and executed, larger blasts can create strains which produce more cracking beyond the design perimeter of a cavern. Minimum overbreak is desirable because
1. it promotes safety by reducing the probability of rockfalls,
2. it reduces the rock quantities to be removed and the cost of support or lining, and/or
3. it restricts leakages both into and out of completed unlined caverns.
On the other hand, achieving minimum excavation costs demands that conventional blasting techniques be used as close as possible to the final rock surfaces. That the factors which influence blast-induced overbreak be fully understood and then controlled to the optimum levels is, therefore, of considerable importance.

2. OVERBREAK MECHANISMS

There are at least four identifiable mechanisms by which blast-induced overbreak can occur, viz.
1. radial fracturing,
2. internal spalling,
3. gas extension of natural discontinuities and strain wave-induced cracks, and
4. release-of-load fracturing.
The above mechanisms are listed approximately in their chronological order of occurrence but not necessarily in their order of decreasing importance.

The intensity and extent of overbreak resulting from mechanisms 1 and 2 (see above) are influenced most by
1. the characteristics of the rock, and
2. the nature and weight of charges nearest to the design cavern profile.
The presence of an extensive and reasonably close free face in front of these charges does not substantially reduce overbreak by these mechanisms, the amount of fracturing beyond the blast boundary being very similar to that in the burden rock. The natures of overbreak created by mechanisms 1 and 2 are shown in Fig. 1.

The amount of overbreak resulting from mechanisms 3 and 4 (see above) is affected not only by the properties of the rock and explosive charges; it is influenced to a greater degree by the energy factor, initiation sequence and delay timing of the entire blast.

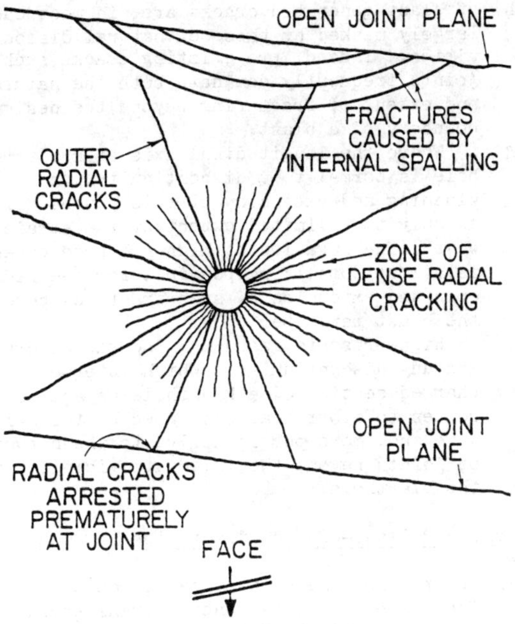

Fig. 1 Fracturing by relative radial motion and internal spalling

2.1 Radial fracturing

When a strain wave front passes, a cylindrical shell of rock immediately around the charge is subjected to intense radial compression, and tangential tensile strains then develop. If these tensile strains exceed the dynamic breaking strain of the rock, a zone of dense radial fracturing is created immediately around the blasthole (see Fig. 1). This intense fracturing terminates quite abruptly at that radial distance at which the wave's tensile strain attenuates to a value which is incapable of generating new cracks. The width of this zone decreases with
1. decreases in the blasthole diameter (d) and peak blasthole pressure (P_b), and
2. increases in the rock's dynamic tensile breaking strain and rate of absorption of strain wave energy.

Beyond this zone of dense radial fracturing, some evenly-distributed radial cracks propagate into the surrounding rock mass as long as wave-induced tension is applied normal to the crack tips (see Fig. 1). Crack lengths in both the inner and outer radial fracture zones usually increase linearly with both d and P_b.

An approximately linear relationship exists between crack extension and length of pre-existing cracks; longer cracks are preferentially extended. Where a natural discontinuity intersects the blasthole over much or all of the length of the charge, it opens under the action of the strain wave and limits the development of radial fractures in other directions.

A discontinuity which is parallel to but some distance behind a blasthole interrupts and arrests the propagation of radial cracks (see Fig. 1). Presplit planes also have this important property. In rocks in which discontinuities are widely spaced and persistent, the probability of blastholes being remote from a discontinuity is relatively high, and the full development of radial fracturing is promoted. Where discontinuities are more closely spaced and of more limited persistence, on the other hand, they are more capable of localizing radial fracturing as a result of
1. preferential extension of the discontinuities, and
2. termination of radial fractures.

Backward-facing radial cracks from a given blasthole tend to create interlocking sectors of rock beyond the blast perimeter. Where radial cracks from adjacent blastholes overlap and intersect other cracks or discontinuities, the newly-formed rock surface may suffer local wedge or block failures. For this reason, perimeter blastholes should be drilled on the widest practicable spacing and charged with the lowest suitable explosive concentration.

2.2 Internal spalling

Where a radial compressive strain wave strikes an effective free face (usually a pronounced rock/air interface), a reflected tensile wave is created. Since the dynamic strength of rock in tension is a small fraction of that in compression, tensile waves are a principal breaker of rock. If a reflected tensile wave is sufficiently strong, spalling occurs progressively from the effective free face back towards the blasthole.

Insofar as they affect reflection of the compressive wave, wide air-filled joints beyond peripheral blastholes can be regarded as effective free faces. Internal spalling produces more intense overbreak between the blasthole and such discontinuities but, because of reflection of the outward-propagating strain wave (and termination of radial cracks - see Section 2.1), overbreak beyond the joint is reduced (see Fig. 1). This breakage mechanism is expected to become appreciable only within about 15d of the blasthole. At water-filled and fine air-filled discontinuities, the reflected fraction of the strain wave energy is usually insufficient to cause internal spalling, much of the energy being refracted (see Fig. 1).

Internal spalling together with radial fracturing encourages intense overbreak between a perimeter blasthole and that discontinuity nearest to the blasthole. Overbreak beyond that discontinuity is not caused to any significant degree by these two mechanisms. Where discontinuities are closely spaced, therefore, the extent of fracturing which results from these two mechanisms is small. As a result of the dominant effects of mechanisms 3 and 4 (see Sections 2.3 and 2.4), however, highly-fissured rocks usually exhibit greater overall degrees of overbreak.

2.3 Gas extension of fractures

Immediately after the formation of radial cracks, explosion gases start to penetrate both strain wave-induced fractures and natural discontinuities. Where the charged section of a blasthole does not intersect a discontinuity, the high-pressure gases first jet into, wedge open and, hence, extend the radial cracks. In the absence of discontinuities running along the side of the charge, this mechanism can increase the lengths of strain wave-generated radial cracks by a factor of about five.

Because stress concentration at the crack tip increases with crack length, the longest crack (whether this be a discontinuity or a strain wave-generated crack) is the least stable and requires the lowest gaseous pressure for its further propagation. Therefore, longer fractures always extend first and propagate at a higher velocity than shorter adjacent fractures. The further they get ahead, the greater is the velocity difference until the shorter ones stop altogether. Where an open discontinuity intersects the blasthole alongside the charge, therefore, high gas flows cause this fissure to be preferentially expanded by a wedging action.

In highly-jointed strata, the extensions of blast-generated cracks are, in most case largely masked by those of natural disconti uities. Indeed, pre-existing cracks such a joints frequently dominate both the nature and extent of fracturing beyond the design boundary of a blast.

Where the longitudinal axis of a blasthole is normal to a discontinuity, the widening and extension of this can be assis ed only to a limited extent by the strain wave. The invasion of high-pressure gases is almost totally responsible for the wedgi open and extension of such fractures beyond the blast perimeter.

High-pressure gases use the radial crack and any discontinuities which intersect the charged section of a blasthole as access routes to other cracks created by the strai wave and, more particularly, to the network of joints beyond the immediate vicinity of the blasthole.

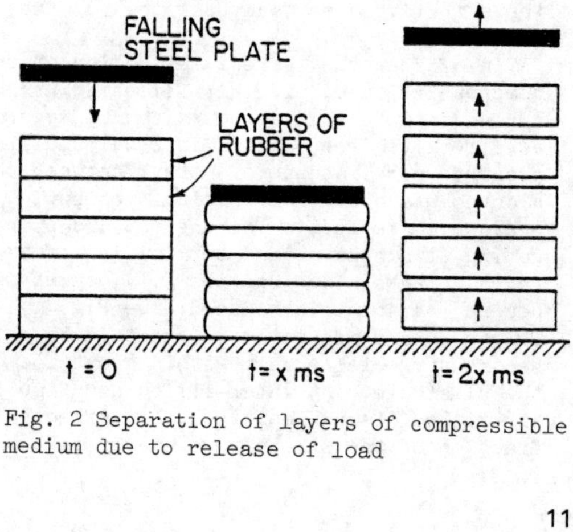

Fig. 2 Separation of layers of compressible medium due to release of load

2.4 Release-of-load fracturing

Before the strain wave reaches an effective free face, the total energy transferred to the strata by the initial compression of th rock can be as much as 60 - 70% of the blas energy. After the compressive strain wave has passed, a state of quasi-static equilibrium exists, the pressure in the blasthole being balanced by the strain at the blasthole wall. When the pressure in the blasthole subsequently falls (as gases push the burden rock forwards and escape via the collar of the blasthole), this strain energy is very rapidly relieved, rather like a compressed coil spring being suddenly released.

In rock bodies which exhibit discontinuities parallel to perimeter blastholes, the behaviour of the rock beyond the blast may be likened to that of a multi-layered mass of dense rubber which is impacted by a free-falling heavy steel plate (see Fig. 2). After contacting the upper surface of the rubber, the plate progressively compresses the layers until its momentum is exhausted. The highly compressed layers then expand, thereby accelerating the plate in the opposi direction; in propelling the plate upwards into the air, the layers of rubber separate from each other. Such separations are synonymous with release-of-load fractures.

When large multi-row blasts are fired wit excessive burdens and/or delays which do not allow sufficient progressive relief, many of the charges act in unison to create release-of-load fractures which are parallel to and beyond the blast boundary. As is indicated by the analogy to a multi-layered mass of rubber, the rock mass will fail preferential at pre-existing fractures such as joints.

3. EFFECTS OF BLAST PARAMETERS ON OVERBREAK

3.1 Effects of rock properties

Rock properties have a great influence upon the overbreak created by a blast. The most important rock properties are
1. the in-situ dynamic tensile breaking strain and, more particularly,
2. the spacing, orientation, persistence and nature of structural features such as joints.
Overbreak occurs when the blast-induced strain exceeds the dynamic tensile breaking strain of the rock mass. In the ideal case of a completely unfissured rock mass (a situation never fully realised in practice), all overbreak fractures would be of this type. As the amount of jointing increases, such new fractures account for a decreasing percentage of the total overbreak produced. A correspondingly greater proportion of the total overbreak is caused by explosion gases which stream into, wedge open and, hence, extend natural discontinuities in the rock. Close joint spacings have a detrimental effect upon overbreak control, irrespective of the blasting technique employed. As one would expect, less overbreak is obtained with tight and/or in-filled joints than with open joints.

3.2 Effects of drilling

The jumbo(s) used for drilling all except downhole benches (see Fig. 3) should have booms featuring

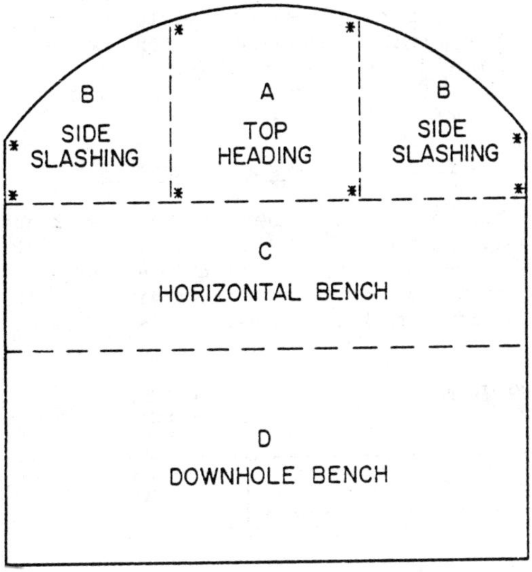

Fig. 3 Typical sequence of operations when creating a large cavern

1. parallel holding to minimise blasthole deviations, and
2. 180° feed roll-over to allow drilling perimeter blastholes with the smallest possible *look-out* angle.
As blasthole deviation decreases, so does the percentage of blastholes which suffer an excessive toe burden; such overburdening is a major cause of overbreak. As one would expect, any decrease in the *look-out* angle is responsible for
1. an increase in the overall (i.e., inter-round) smoothness of the cavern's surface, and
2. a reduced probability of overburdening the toes of perimeter charges (with a consequential lower risk of damage).

3.3 Effects of type and quantity of explosive

In general, the explosives selected for all blastholes other than perimeter blastholes should be such that they reliably break and displace their quotas of the burden rock with reasonable ease. If the energy concentration of the charge is too low for the selected burden distance, each charge will produce more overbreak.

Where groundwater can enter blastholes, explosives with adequate water resistance must be employed. If an ANFO charge were to be desensitised by water and, as a result, fail to undergo high-order detonation, one or more later-firing dependent charges would be overburdened and, therefore, would cause more overbreak.

Where large (say $\geqslant$ 51mm) diameter blastholes are used, it may be necessary to reduce the energy concentration in both the perimeter blastholes and those blastholes adjacent to the perimeter. The probability that this additional precaution will be required increases with
1. increases in the energy concentration for normal blastholes, and
2. decreases in rock strength.
Such measures are particularly necessary where the principal explosive for the round consists of pneumatically-charged ANFO or a pumped watergel explosive.

In rocks which exhibit only moderate strength, the optimum explosive for the penultimate arc or row of blastholes will depend largely upon the amount of groundwater present. In dry conditions, the damaging effects of ANFO charges can be reduced somewhat by introducing an upline of $10g.m^{-1}$ detonating cord. In the majority of cases, however, this change is not sufficient to prevent such charges breaking beyond the design cavern profile. It is usually preferable to use a low-density mixture of ANFO and expanded polystyrene beads, the density and polystyrene content (volume basis) of the charge being within the 0.20 - 0.50 $g.cm^{-3}$ and 80 - 50% ranges respectively. In wet blastholes, untamped continuous column charges of a moderately decoupled gelignite or watergel explosive should be selected; for 51mm blastholes, a cartridge diameter of 25mm or 29mm may well prove to be suitable.

3.3.1 Explosives for perimeter blastholes

In order to achieve the required smoothwall effect, it is usually necessary to charge those perimeter blastholes on the arch and walls of the cavern with an explosive which exhibits a relatively low energy yield per metre of charge length. Blow-loaded or loose-poured ANFO charges are invariably too powerful and, therefore, create excessive overbreak. In all but the strongest rocks, 20 ANFO/80 polystyrene mixtures are also too powerful.

Where conditions are too wet for ANFO/polystyrene, it may be possible to use a small-diameter column of butted (but untamped) cartridges of a low-density explosive. In 51mm blastholes in a consistently strong rock, for example, a 22mm diameter column of explosive is sufficiently decoupled to provide a moderately good smoothwall effect.

When smoothwall blasting is to be carried out in caverns which pass through strata which exhibit varying strength and wetness, however, it is prudent to select perimeter charges which exhibit

1. an energy yield per metre length which can be varied between wide limits, and
2. a high degree of water resistance (so as to cope with the wettest possible conditions).

These two requirements are best met by using equispaced cartridges of a 25 x 200mm gelignite within a slotted cartridge holder (see Figure 4). The energy concentration is reduced simply by lengthening the air gap between consecutive cartridges. Because one cannot rely upon the detonation wave to consistently propagate from one cartridge to the next over long air gaps, it is necessary to *trace* each charge with an upline of 10$g.m^{-1}$ or, preferably, 5$g.m^{-1}$ detonating cord. Needless to say, the operator's degree of control over energy yield per unit length is better with a slotted cartridge holder than with any other water-resistant explosive system.

3.3.2 Concentration and distribution of energy in perimeter blastholes

The optimum energy concentration in perimeter blastholes depends very largely upon the strength of (and especially the number and distribution of structural discontinuities in) the rock. Overcharging leads to overbreak. Wherever perimeter blastholes are undercharged, an annulus (not necessarily continuous) of partially fragmented rock remains within the design perimeter; removal of this annulus then necessitates the introduction of a trimming operation, this being both expensive and time-consuming.

The optimum charge concentration for perimeter blastholes cannot yet be selected on a purely scientific basis. Selection is based very largely upon previous experience in rocks with similar properties. As the blasthole diameter increases from 32mm to 51mm (the common current range), the optimum charge concentration usually increases from about 0.1$kg.m^{-1}$ to about 0.25$kg.m^{-1}$.

As one would expect, the optimum charge distribution is represented by a continuous column of explosive having a uniform diameter. Unfortunately, such charges exhibit an effective energy concentration which can be modified only slightly by changing the blasthole diameter (rarely a practicable solution). For this reason, it is far preferable to gain a high degree of control over energy concentration by using slotted cartridge holders (despite the slight disadvantage of non-uniform charge distribution with this method - see Figure 4).

3.4 Effects of blasthole diameter

Although it is an important factor in the study of overbreak control, blasthole diameter, per se, does not have an influence of the magnitude ascribed to it. For strong massive rocks, at least, it is suggested

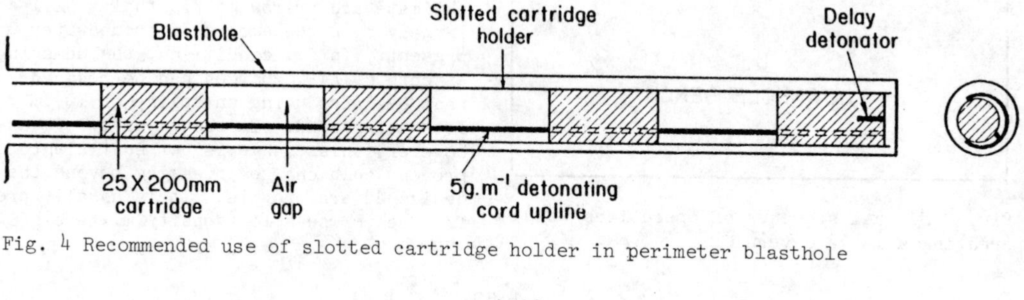

Fig. 4 Recommended use of slotted cartridge holder in perimeter blasthole

that overbreak can be controlled even with large (say 51 - 89mm) diameter blastholes, provided that other influential parameters (viz., blasthole pattern, energy concentration, initiation sequence and delay timing) are given sufficient attention.

As is widely appreciated, there is an economic incentive to drill blastholes with the largest practicable diameter (Hagan, 1981). However, the selection of blasthole diameter (d) needs to be tempered by the fact that overbreak increases with d unless steps are taken to counter this effect.

In many cases, and especially where large-diameter tunnels are driven in strong massive rocks, the replacement of 45mm by 55 - 64mm blastholes need not increase the amount of overbreak. Although not necessarily reduced in absolute terms, drilling deviation would be effectively less with an increase in d, since a given amount of deviation represents a smaller percentage error in (the larger) toe burdens and toe spacings. For this reason, charges will exhibit a greater overall capability of providing progressive relief of burden without creating the excessive overbreak which is associated with overburdened blastholes.

Any anxiety about the effects of larger-diameter blastholes on overbreak and the stabilities of the arch and walls of a cavern can be largely overcome by paying particular attention to selecting the optimum energy concentration per metre for

1. perimeter charges (see Sections 3.3.1 and 3.3.2) and
2. those charges adjacent to perimeter charges (see Section 3.3).

It would also be necessary, of course, to ensure that the selected blasthole pattern, initiation sequence and delay timing promote progressive relief of burden throughout the entire round.

Because horizontal bench blasts have extensive free faces to which they can shoot, their charges create ground vibration levels which are lower than those produced (by charges of the same diameter) in burn cut rounds. Also, larger-diameter blastholes can be drilled deeper before the amount of deviation exceeds that percentage of the toe burden or spacing beyond which overbreak starts to increase appreciably. For these reasons, there is an incentive to use relatively large-diameter blastholes, provided that particular attention is paid to other parameters which exert a considerable influence over the amount of overbreak. In wide deep benches in a strong massive rock, blasthole diameters of 51 - 70mm would be expected to exhibit high cost-effectiveness. If the use of larger-diameter blastholes gives considerable cost savings, but increases overbreak significantly, a highly compatible system may well be developed by presplitting the walls of the bench (see Section 4).

In high wide downhole benches, it may well be practicable to drill 76 - 89mm diameter blastholes. If, prima facie, the cost-effectiveness of such blastholes is precluded by excessive overbreak in a given rock, operators should consider

1. presplitting the walls of the bench,
2. drilling smaller-diameter perimeter blastholes and/or
3. using two individually-delayed deck charges in each large-diameter blasthole (see Section 3.8.5).

3.5 Effect of blasthole inclination

Despite considerable recent advances in both the design and operation of drilling equipment, it is not possible to drill perimeter blastholes which are exactly parallel to the axis of a cavern. Although *look-out* angles are currently as small as about 2°, this divergence tends to limit the operator's control over the profile, especially when pulling long rounds or when blasting high downhole benches.

In shallow downhole benches in which blasts are fired to a free face, adequate progressive rock movement along the invert can often be achieved with vertical blastholes. As the height of a free face increases, vertical front-row blastholes become progressively overburdened at invert level (because the face is never vertical). Therefore, the replacement of vertical by inclined blastholes maintains toe burdens at their design value, thereby preventing the increases in overbreak associated with overburdened charges. In benches higher than about 4m, blastholes are usually angled at 10 - 15° to the vertical.

In the common situation in which downhole bench blasts are fired into a buffer of broken rock, and especially in 4 - 10m high benches in a strong massive rock, angled blastholes are much more effective. Because the buffer largely restricts lateral movement of the newly-broken rock, blastholes should be inclined so that their charges provide sufficient upward displacement to avoid the increases in overbreak caused by effective overconfinement. As one would expect, the upward heaving action with angled blastholes is appreciably greater than that with vertical blastholes. The optimum blasthole inclination increases with both bench height and rock strength. For buffer blasts in a 10m high bench in a strong massive rock, a blasthole inclination as high as 25° may be beneficial.

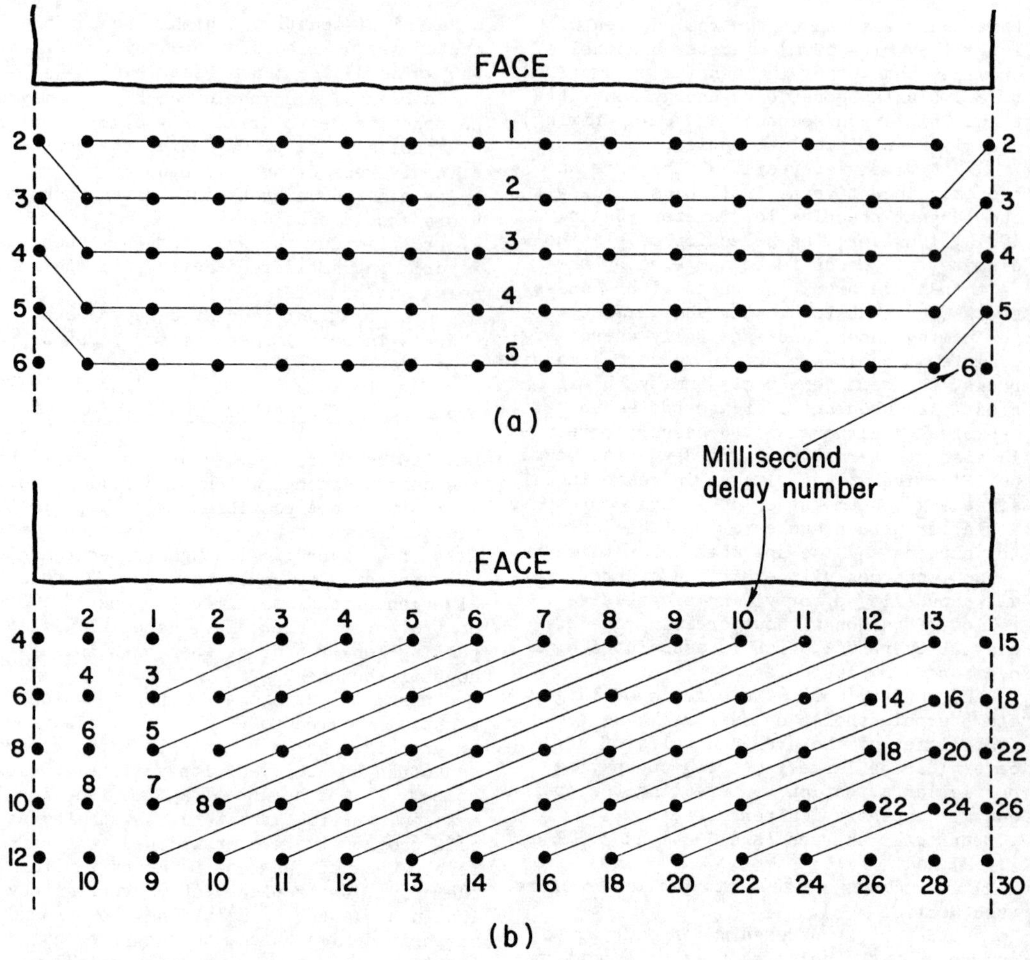

Fig. 5 Horizontal bench blast that produces (a) considerable and (b) little overbreak

3.6 Effects of blasthole pattern

When driving a top heading and, to a lesser extent, in side slashing (see Figure 3), constant burden distances and blasthole spacings cannot be applied. For this reason, it is necessary to ensure that each individual charge has
1. an effective burden that is not excessive and
2. an extensive free face to which it can shoot.
Because burdens and spacings are non-uniform, there is a greater probability that errors will contribute to overbreak.

In general, the overbreak produced by a burn cut round is greater than that created by a round based on the wedge cut. Overbreak from burn cut rounds can be reduced substantially, however, by providing the greatest practicable number of large-diameter relief (i.e., empty) holes to which the burn cut charges can shoot. These relief holes shoul be 150 - 300mm longer than the adjacent blastholes.

When (as is usual) smooth blasting is carried out in top heading and side slashing operations (see Fig. 3), the optimum spacing of perimeter blastholes increases from about 0.5m for 32mm blastholes to about 0.8m for 51mm blastholes. It is important to ensure that the burden distance for perimeter blast holes is 1.25 - 1.40 times their spacing.

Where the walls of a cavern are vertical, horizontal benches should be drilled out wit slightly rectangular patterns (see Figure 5) Where the walls converge appreciably towards the invert, it is necessary to vary the blas hole spacing and/or number of blastholes in each row; needless to say, the resulting irregular pattern demands that greater attention be given to the marking and collaring of blastholes. Downhole benches should be drilled on rectangular patterns. If, in either horizontal or downhole benching, it is decided to reduce the energy concentration in penultimate blastholes by a factor of (say) two, the product of burden and blasthole spacing should also be halved; charges for such blastholes could consist of 50ANFO/50 polystyrene or a highly-decoupled untamped column of watergel or, preferably, gelignite.

Should the walls of horizontal or vertical bench blasts be presplit, it is important to ensure

1. that the distance between the perimeter blastholes and presplit plane is $\nless$ 0.35 times the spacing (for perimeter blastholes), and
2. that the presplit plane extends at least two burden distances beyond the longitudinal extremity of the blast.

3.7 Effects of energy factor

One of the most common misconceptions in blast design is that overbreak increases with energy factor (i.e., explosion energy yield per m^3 of excavated rock). Provided that the initiation sequence and delay timing are selected carefully, high energy factors will provide good progressive relief of burden and, hence, surprisingly small amounts of overbreak. It is the overburdened blastholes of undercharged blasts that have the greatest ability to cause damage beyond the design profile of a cavern.

3.8 Effects of initiation sequence and delay timing

These are most important blast parameters, but ones that often receive less attention than they deserve. Even from one round to the next, the operator's degree of control over sequence and timing is relatively high (cf. that over parameters such as blasthole diameter, explosive type, etc.) but is never absolute. In large blasts, the range of delay detonators may be somewhat smaller than that actually desired; but the recent introduction of sequential timers (i.e., multi-channel delay exploders) has effectively increased the ranges of such detonators.

In any round in which overbreak must be minimised, it is most important that blastholes detonate in that sequence and with those inter-hole delay intervals which maximise the successive development of free faces which are

1. sufficiently near and
2. as extensive as possible.

When allocating delay numbers in the blast design phase, the operator should construct lines of breakage as shown in Fig. 6. By doing this, any instances of poor sequencing are exposed, and alternative superior delay allocations can then be made.

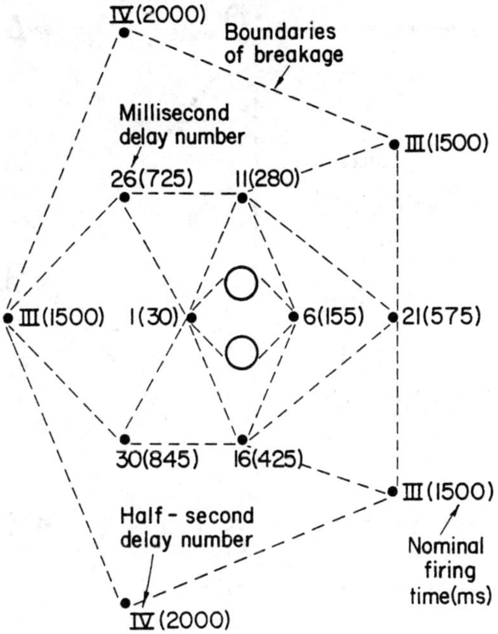

Fig. 6 Recommended use of millisecond delays in burn cut

3.8.1 Sequence and timing in burn cuts

In burn cuts, the earliest-firing charge should be that which is closest to the relief hole(s). The sequence of detonation for all other charges in the cut should be consistent with the order of increasing burdens on these blastholes (see Fig. 6).

Rock fragmented by the first one or few charges in the cut is ejected laterally into the void(s) provided by the relief hole(s) before being swept outwards along the heading's axis. In rounds with pulls of $\geqslant$ 3m, the time taken for these rock fragments to be completely ejected is considerable (typically $\geqslant$ 100 ms). It follows, then, that the delay between consecutive detonations should exceed 100 ms if the probability of choking is to be minimised. Where charges are fired on consecutive numbers of a series of millisecond delay detonators, progressive relief of burden is rarely achieved and, as a consequence, there is a relatively high risk of choking and a frozen cut (Hagan, 1979). Whenever millisecond detonators are used in burn cuts, therefore, every effort

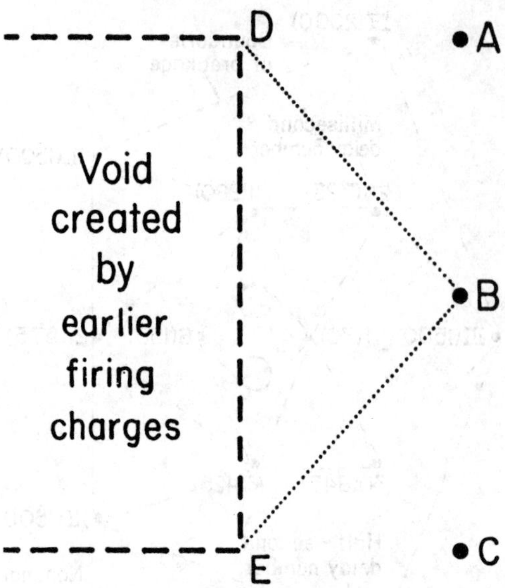

Fig. 7 Blasting alongside a burn cut

should be made to fire consecutive charges on every fourth or, preferably, fifth delay number. Overbreak decreases as the inter-charge delay increases in the approximate range 0 - 100 ms. The allocation of delay detonators shown in Fig. 6 discourages freezing by promoting progressive relief of burden.

The required number of delay periods increases with the cross-sectional area of a heading. In headings with medium or large cross sections, it is not possible to achieve inter-hole delays of ⩾ 100 ms when using only millisecond detonators. It is mainly for this reason that the use of spaced millisecond detonators in the cut and half-second delays outside the cut is recommended. Being aware of the considerable *scatter* (i.e., delay time variability) of half-second delay detonators, some operators tend to rely on this scatter by initiating the first two or more charges in the cut with the same delay number (say No. 1). Because the time between consecutive detonations is then a matter of chance rather than positively planned and controlled, the use of spaced millisecond delays is to be preferred.

The uninitiated might fondly imagine that events in the cut are so remote from the perimeter of the blast that their effects on overbreak are insignificant. But such is not the case. If progressive relief of burden is not achieved in the cut, all later-firing charges will be effectively overconfined as a result of the choked conditions in front of them. Each charge will then create more overbreak. It is important to realise that minimal blast damage requires that each and every charge fragments and displaces its burden rock forwards with reasonable ease. If, at a certain point within the blast, this progressive relief of burden ceases to be achieved, it is unlikely to be restored by the efforts of later-firing charges.

3.8.2 Sequence and timing outside the cut

In those parts of the face which are remote from the cut, it is sometimes possible to drill blastholes on a regular square or rectangular grid. Where such patterns are employed, one frequently observes poor sequencing which results from
1. a desire to simplify the blast design and, hence, to facilitate the allocation of delay detonators at the face, and
2. inadequate consideration of the effects of *scatter*.

In the common situation depicted in Fig. 7, for example, charges A, B and C are often initiated by detonators having the same delay number. Because of *scatter*, each charge will have an equal probability of firing before the other two. It is clear that the free face (DE) for charge B is about twice as extensive as that for either A or C. It follows, then, that less overbreak results when steps are taken to ensure
1. that charge B always fires first, and
2. that face DBE is fully developed before A and C shoot to it.

The firing of B before A and C enables identical blasting results to be achieved with lighter charges. When A or C fires first, this charge will *see* a free face of inadequate lateral extent; because such charges experience difficulty in breaking out of their tight corner positions, a relatively large percentage of their energy is manifested as overbreak.

Blasts should be such that the entire time span of the available range of detonators is used to full advantage. If the number of available delays exceeds that actually required, alternate delay numbers should be used for those adjacent charges where *scatter* and *crowding* are to be avoided most.

3.8.3 Sequence and timing for perimeter blastholes

Where smoothwall blasting is carried out, best results are achieved by firing perimeter charges simultaneously. In practice, this ideal situation is never fully realised. *Scatter* prevents the precision needed for true simultaneity. In the few cases in which only millisecond delay detonators are used,

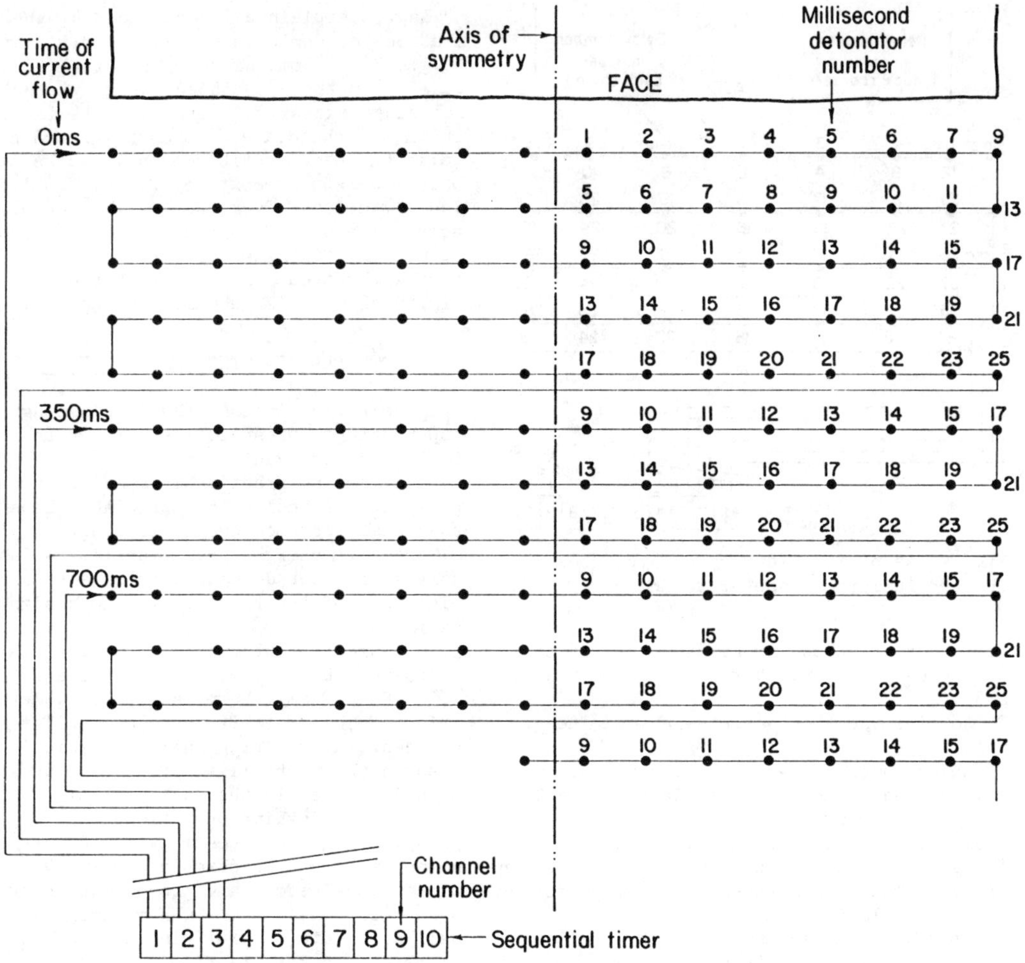

Fig. 8 Use of sequential timer to fire larger blasts in downhole benching

all perimeter blastholes should be fired on the highest delay number. The inter-charge delay then usually lies in the 0 - 90 ms range. More commonly, perimeter charges are fired on one or more of the higher numbers of the half-second delay series. In this latter case, inter-charge delays frequently lie in the 0 - 800 ms range.

Although neither of these cases resembles truly simultaneous initiation, very satisfactory results can be achieved, provided that the energy concentration, spacing and burden for perimeter blastholes have suitable values. Only slightly better results have been obtained in the few cases in which a detonating cord trunkline has been used to minimise the delay between the detonations of perimeter charges (to approximately $\leqslant$ 0.15 ms). This observation suggests that the reduction in performance caused by non-simultaneous detonations is small in comparison to that resulting from overcharging and/or unsuitable blasthole geometry. Nevertheless, perimeter charges should be initiated with the minimum practicable spread of the highest delay numbers. Charges which are in tight locations (e.g., those shown by asterisks in Fig. 3) should be initiated after all other blastholes in their vicinity.

3.8.4 <u>Sequence and timing in horizontal benching</u>

Where there is a sufficient number of millisecond delay detonators, initiation should commence close to, but not at, the end of the top row (see Fig. 5b). Delays should be allocated so as

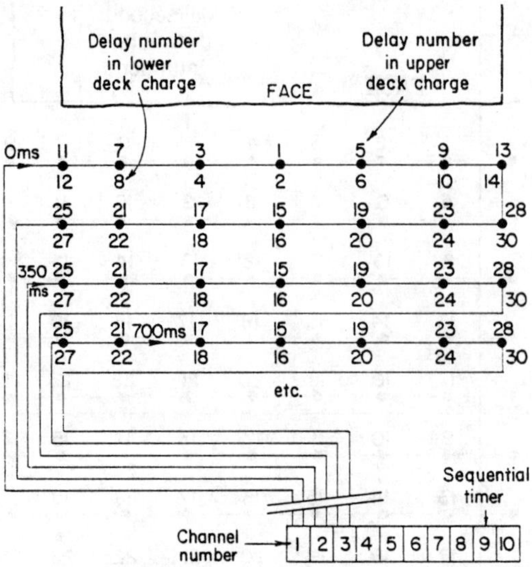

Fig. 9 Use of individually-delayed deck charges in large-diameter downholes

1. to maximise both progressive relief of burden and the total duration of the blast, and
2. to minimise the charge weight per delay number.

If delay numbers 0 - 30 (inclusive) of a millisecond detonator series are available to fire the round shown in Fig. 5, for example, the sequence and timing shown in (b) are considerably better than those shown in (a). The design shown in (b) is superior for the following reasons.

1. It takes full advantage of the available range of delay detonators.
2. Progressive relief of burden is improved by the use of some alternate delay numbers.
3. The maximum number of charges detonating simultaneously is reduced from 16 to 7.
4. Perimeter blastholes cause less overbreak, as a result of the double delay between themselves and adjacent charges.

3.8.5 Sequence and timing in downhole benching

Whilst maintaining overbreak within reasonable limits, operators should make every effort to maximise the mean size of blast (so as to reduce the cyclicity of blasting). When a large number of effective delays are allocated with skill and care, these two aims are surprisingly compatible.

Where it is desirable to fire blasts with more rows than that permitted by the entire range of millisecond delay detonators, the use of sequential timers should be considered. Fig. 8 shows how such equipment can be used to fire adjacent sections of a large blast.

As was explained in Section 3.4, there is a strong economic incentive to drill large (e.g., 76 - 89mm) diameter blastholes, provided that the associated energy yields do not cause excessive overbreak. It is suggested that large diameter blastholes and sound walls can be compatible even in rocks of only moderate strength by firing two individually-delayed deck charges in each blasthole. The use of a sequential timer would permit the firing of large blasts of this type without causing overbreak problems. Fig. 9 shows this recommended concept.

4. SMOOTHWALL BLASTING VERSUS PRESPLITTING

When compared with smoothwall blasting in top headings, presplitting suffers the following disadvantages.

1. The maximum practicable spacing for presplit blastholes is appreciably less than that for smoothwall blasting.
2. Presplit charges create an inter-blasthole split, but do not contribute to displacement of the rock within the design perimeter.
3. Because the outermost production blastholes must be very close to (typically 0.2 - 0.5m from) the presplit line, detonation of the presplit charges can dislocate adjacent later-firing charges. This increases the probability of finding unexploded charges in the muckpile.

In side slashing operations (see Fig. 3) presplitting could possibly cause lateral movement of a considerable percentage of the blast block before all production charges have been initiated. Such movement could well dislocate later-firing charges and, therefore, cause cut-offs and misfires.

For the above reasons, smoothwall blasting is preferred to presplitting in both top heading and side slashing operations.

But the situation in horizontal and downhole benching is somewhat different. The important advantage of presplitting is that it can arrest the propagation of cracks created by the nearest production blastholes. (Where smoothwall blasting is carried out, there is no peripheral fracture plane to arrest the extension of these cracks.) Where there is a desire to use larger-diameter blastholes (as is the case in benching operations), this feature of presplitting

1. assumes far greater significance, and
2. tends to outweigh the disadvantages of this technique.

Where larger-diameter blastholes are employed within presplit walls, therefore, drilling costs, blasting costs and the cycle period may well be reduced substantially.

5. ACKNOWLEDGEMENT

The author extends his thanks to Golder Associates Pty. Ltd. for permission to publish this paper.

6. REFERENCES

Hagan, T.N. 1979. Understanding the burn cut - a key to greater advance rates. Proc. 2nd Int. Tunnelling Symp., March 12-16, London.

Hagan, T.N. 1981. Larger diameter blastholes - a proposed means of increasing advance rates. Proc. 4th Australian Tunnelling Conf., March, Melbourne.

BESTIMMUNG DES EINFLUSSES RHEOLOGISCHER EIGENSCHAFTEN DES GESTEINSMASSIVS AUF DIE LASTVERTEILUNG DES AUSBAUS UNTERTÄGIGER ABBAURÄUME MIT GROSSEM QUERSCHNITT

The effect of rheologic properties of rock mass on the distribution of loads in linings of tunnels with big cross-sections

Détermination de l'influence des propriétées rhéologiques du massif rocheux sur la distribution des sollicitations du soutènement des tunnels des grandes sections

J.KACZMAREK
Technische Hochschule Wrocław, Polen

SUMMARY:
Load distribution in tunnel lining, executed by means of German tunnelling method, were determined. Six typical stages of tunnelling and lining were distinguished in this method. Calculations were performed for an idealized model of rock mass using the finite elements method. The assumed model of rock mass is characterized by the occurrence of elastic and viscose properties. The concrete lining is modelled by the material described by Hooke's law. The results of calculations are presented in the form of diagrams illustrating load changes occurring in the course of realizing successive stages of the construction.

ZUSAMMENFASSUNG:
Die Lastverteilung des nach dem deutschen Verfahren ausgeführten Grubenausbaus mit einem Rundquerschnitt wurde bestimmt. Es wurden 6 für dieses Verfahren typische Bauabschnitte des Grubenvortriebs und der Ausführung des Ausbaus dardestellt. Die Berechnungen wurden für ein idealisiertes Modell des Gesteinsmassivs unter Anwendung der Methode der finiten Elemente durchgeführt. Das angenommene Gebirgsmodell ist durch Auftreten der Elastizitäts- und Viscositätserscheinungen gekennzeichnet. Der durch das Hookesche Gesetz beschriebene Material modeliert den Gussbetonausbau. Die Ergebnisse der Berechnungen wurden in Form von Diagrammen vorgestellt, die den während der Ausführung von einzelnen Bauabschnitten auftretenden Lastwechsel darstellen.

RESUME:
Nous avons déterminé la distribution des sollicitations du soutènement du tunnel d'une section circulaire, creusé à l'aide de la méthode allemande. Typiquement pour cette méthode on a distingué six étapes dans le creusement du tunnel et dans la pose du soutènement. Les calculs ont été effectués pour un modèle idéalisé du milieu rocheux en utilisant la méthode des éléments finis. Le modèle appliqué du massif est caractérisé par la donnée des paramètres d'élasticité et de viscosité. Un soutènement en béton coulé est modelisé par un matériau satisfaisant à la loi de Hooke. Les résultats des calculs sont présentés sous forme de diagrammes qui montrent les changements dans les sollicitations ayant lieu lors de la réalisation des étapes particuliers de l'exécution des travaux.

1. EINLEITUNG

Aus den ökonomisch-technischen Gründen wird bei Ausführung von untertägigen Objekten mit grossem Querschnitt sehr häufig das "Kernbau"-Verfahren, die sog. deutsche Tunnel-Bauweise, angewendet. Abhängig von den bestimmten Gebirgsverhältnissen kann das Verfahren in verschieden Abarten auftreten, wobei man in jedem Fall typischen Vortriebs- und Ausbauphasen, die in einer streng bestimmten Reihenfolge auftreten, unterscheidet (Müller, 1978).

Die für das "Kernbau" Verfahren charakteristische Bauweise der untertägigen Konstruktion wurde schematisch am Beispiel eines Grubenbaus mit Kreisquerschnitt (Abb. 1.) dargestellt. Die

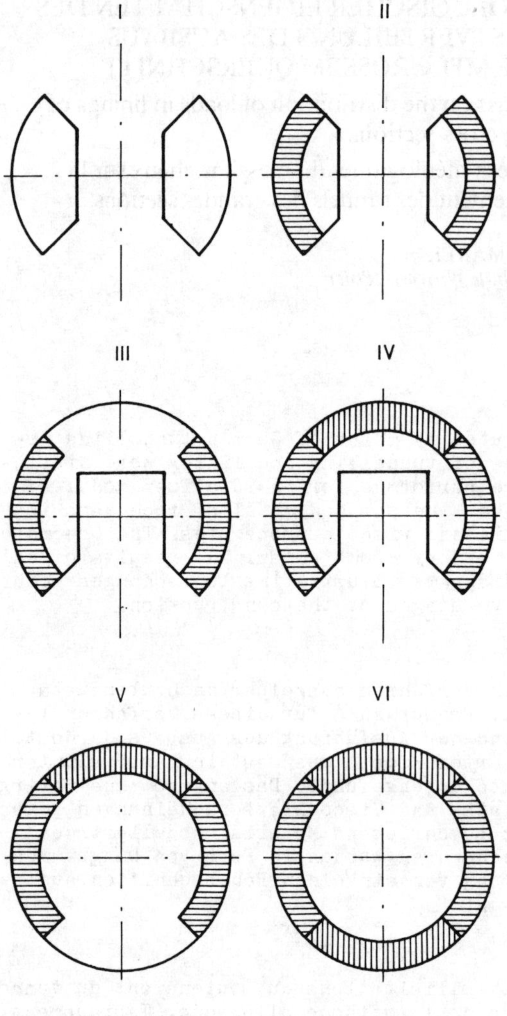

Abb. 1. Die für die deutsche Tunnel-Bauweise typische Reihenfolge der Ausführung von Grube und Ausbau.

Reihenfolge der einzelnen Bauabschnitte ist wie folgt :
- Aufschluss der Seitenstösse (I),
- Ausbau von Stössen (II),
- Aufschluss des Hangenden (III),
- Ausbau des Hangenden (IV),
- Entfernung des Stützkerns (V),
- Ausbau des Liegenden (VI).

Solcher Arbeitsgang hat zur Folge, dass die früher errichteten Ausbaufragmente der veränderlichen Belastungen ausgesetzt werden, die mit den durch die nächste Erweiterung des Grubenquerschnitts verursachten Änderungen des Spannungs- und Deformationszustandes des Gebirges übereinstimmen. Es wurde versucht die Grösse, verteilung und Änderung dieser Belastungen zu bestimmen, indem die auf der Abb. 1. dargestellte Geometrie des Systems und die Ausführungsweise des Objekts als Grundbedingungen angenommen wurden. Die Aufgabe wurde für ein idealisiertes Modell des Gesteinsmassivs gelöst, das durch Auftreten von Elastizitäts- und Viskositätseigenschaften gekennzeichnet ist. Die Berechnungen wurden mit Hilfe der Methode der finiten Elemente durchgeführt.

2. MATHEMATISCHES MODELL DES GESTEINSMASSIVS

Für Berechnungen wurde ein Modell des isotropen Körpers angenommen, dessen Verhalten durch folgende Gleichungen beschrieben ist (Kisiel, 1980):

$$\sigma_o = 2\,H\,\gamma_o$$

$$\tau_{ik} = 2\,G_1\,\psi\,\vartheta_{ik}$$

$$\psi = \frac{1 + 2\,T\,s}{1 + T\,s}\,, \qquad T = \frac{\eta}{G}\,,$$

wo: σ_o - Axiator des Spannungszustandes, γ_o - Axiator des Formänderungszustandes, τ_{ik} - Deviator des Spannungszustandes, ϑ_{ik} - Deviator des Formänderungszustandes, s - Mikusinski's Operator, G, G_1 - Kirchoffsche Moduln (Abb. 2.), H - Helmholtzsches Modul, η - Zähigkeitskoeffizient.

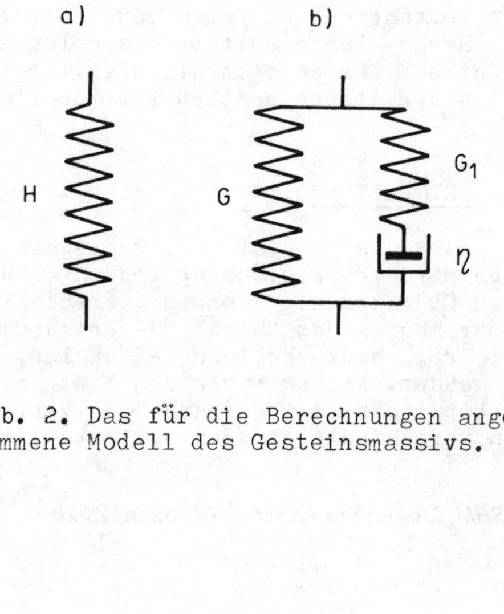

Abb. 2. Das für die Berechnungen angenommene Modell des Gesteinsmassivs.

Die Berechnungen wurden für folgenden Werte durchgeführt: G = 2200 MPa, G_1 = 9000 MPa, H = 15400 MPa, η = = 10000 MPa[t]. Bei der Dimension des Zähigkeitskoeffizienten η wurde die Zeiteinheit nicht eindeutig bestimmt und daher ein Symbol [t] verwendet, das in diesem Fall eine beliebige konventionelle Zeiteinheit bezeichnet. Die Werte des Elastizitätsmoduls E und der Poissonschen Zahl ν sind für das angenommene Modell variabel und hängen u.a. von Zeit ab. Bei dem in der Zeit (von t = 0 bis t = ∞) bestimmten Spannungswert betragen diese Werte entsprechend:
für t = 0 E_0 = 24640 MPa, ν_0 = 0,1
für t = ∞ E_∞ = 6160 MPa, ν_∞ = 0,4.
Manche Schiefersorten sind durch ähnliche, wie die übernommenen Werte E_0 ν_0 gekennzeichnet.

3. GEOMETRISCHES MODELL DES AUSBAU--GEBIRGE-SYSTEMS

Als geometrisches Modell der Aufgabe wurde eine homogene, gewichtslose Quadratscheibe mit einer Einheitsdicke und den Seiten A = H = 56 m angenommen. Die Scheibe unterliegt der Formänderungen im ebenen Formänderungszustand bei gemischten Spannungs-Verschiebungs-Randbedingungen (Abb. 3.). Auf die oberen und unteren Scheibenkante wirkt auf ihren ganzen Längen die gleichmässig verteilte, zeitkonstante Vertikallast, die 18 MPa beträgt. Das entspricht ungefähr dem Druck, der im Gebirge in der Tiefe von 800 m auftritt. Wenn es sich um die horizontale Spannung handelt, wurde angenommen, dass nach Abschluss der Gebirgsbildung eine unendlich lange Zeit abgelaufen ist. Unter Verwendung von elastischen Konstanten des Gebirges E_∞ und ν_∞ wurde der Spannungswert p_x = 12 MPa und die Werte der anfänglichen Formänderungen des Gebirges bestimmt. Hinsichtlich der vertikalen Scheibenkanten wurden Verschiebungs-Randbedingungen so angenommen, dass horizontale Verschiebung (u =0) und in den Punkten auf der X--Achse zusätzlich vertikale Verschiebungen (v = 0) begrenzt wurden.

Das in der Scheibe gemachte Öffnung mit einem Durchmesser von D = 18 m bildete das Modell des Grubenbaus. Modelliert wurde ebenfalls der 2 m dicke Gussbetonausbau. Es wurde die volle Übereinstimmung der vertikalen und horizontalen Verschiebungen an der Kontaktstelle des Ausbaus mit dem Gebirge vorausgesetzt. Für den Beton wurden folgende elastische Parameter angenommen:

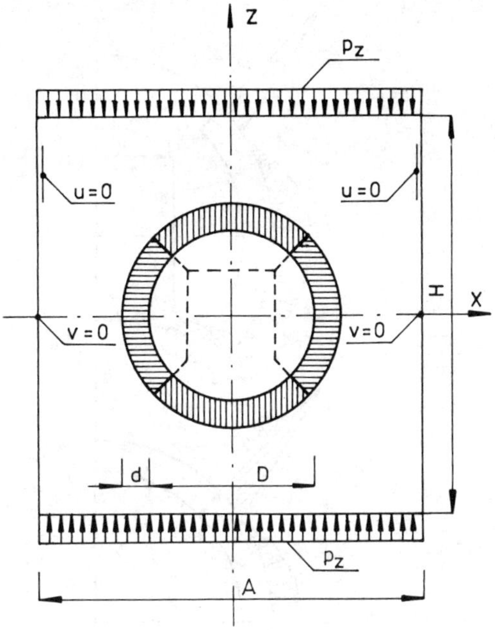

Abb. 3. Geometrisches Modell des Problems.

Eb = 24640 MPa, ν_b = 0,1.

4. BERECHNUNGSVERFAHREN

Die Berechnungen wurden in zwei Etappen, für zwei verschiedene Zeitintervalle durchgeführt. In der ersten Etappe wurde die Ausführungsweise des Grubenbaus und Ausbaus, unter Voraussetzung, dass der ganze Prozess in einem Moment verläuft, modelliert. In der zweiten Etappe wurde die durch die rheologischen Eigenschaften des modellierten Gesteinsmassivs hervorgerufene Lastzunahme des Ausbaus bestimmt. Die zweite Etappe entspricht also der Betriebsphase des ausgefürten Objekts.

Die einzelnen Phasen des Grubenvortriebs wurden durch Änderung der elastischen Parametern an der Stelle des vorgesehenen Hohlraums modelliert. Für die "hohlen" Elemente wurden folgende elastische Konstante angenommen: E = 1 MPa, ν = 0,25. Am Rand des neu aufgeschlossenen Teile des Grubenquerschnitts wurde eine Last angebracht, die den Randspannungen gleich, doch entgegengerichtet ist. Damit wurden die Randwerte der Spannungen auf Null reduziert. Die Modellierung der Ausbauele-

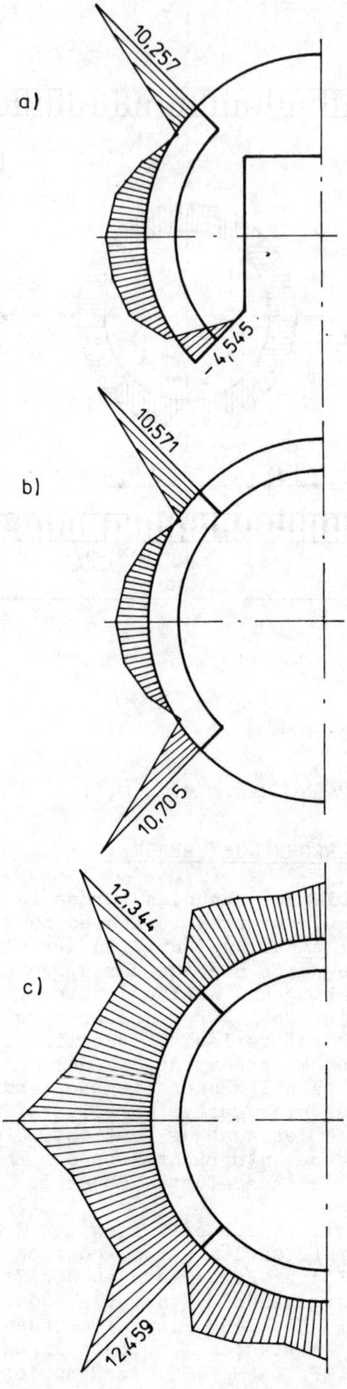

Abb. 4. Verteilung der zur Oberfläche des Ausbaus senkrechten Belastungen σ_N in einzelnen Bauabschnitten.

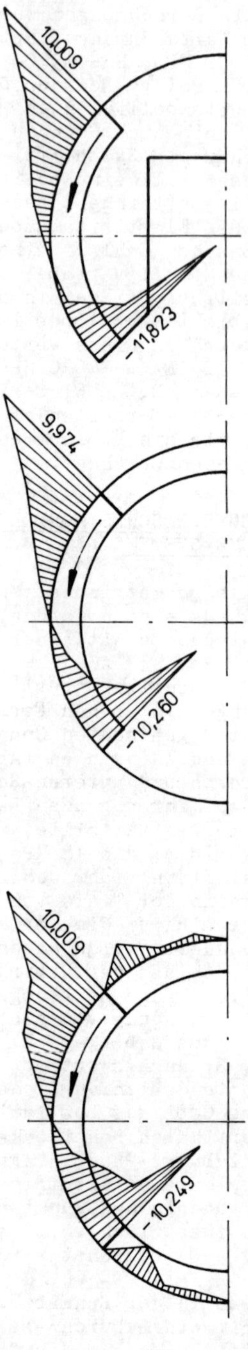

Abb. 5. Verteilung der zur Oberfläche des Ausbaus tangentialen Belastungen σ_S in einzelnen Bauabschnitten.

mente began nach dem erwähnten Randausgleich des Hohlraumes und daher erst die Beseitigung des nächsten an der Reihe Gebirgsteils beeinflusste die Änderung der Belastungen, die auf die schon bestehenden Ausbaufragmente wirken. Die Neuverteilung der Spannungen in dieser Modellierungsphase erfolgte bei elastischen Konstanten des Gesteinmassivs, die E_o und ν_o gleich sind.

Wie schon früher gesagt wurde, wurde der Einfluss der rheologischen Eigenschaften auf die Lastgrösse des Ausbaus in der zweiten Etappe untersucht, wobei für das Zeitintervall Δ_t bei der Berechnungen den Wert 5 angenommen wurde. Aus den mehreren bekannten Methoden der Berücksichtigung der rheologischen Eigenschaften in der Methode der finiten Elemente, zur Berechnungen wurde die numerische Integration von Funktionen der Spannungen und Formänderungen in der Zeit ausgewählt(Zienkiewicz, 1972, Winnicki, 1980).

5. ERGEBNISSE DER NUMERISCHEN BERECHNUNGEN

Die Lastverteilung des Ausbaus in den einzelnen Ausführungsphasen des Objekts und nach dem Zeitintervall $\Delta_t = 5$ wird auf den Abbildungen 4 und 5 dargestellt.

Erste Belastungen des Ausbaus treten nach der Ausführung des Etappes III, d.h. nach dem Aufschluss des Hangenden, auf. Diese Belastungen weisen grosse Asymetrie gegenüber Horizontalachse auf, wobei der grösste Gradient im oberen und unteren Teil des ausgefürten Ausbaufragmentes beobachtet wird. Was die zum Ausbau senkrechten Belastungen σ_N anbelangt, ist das Auftreten von negativen Werten beobachtet worden, was auf eine Tendenz auf Ablösen dieses Ausbaufragmentes vom Stoss hinweisen könnte. Das Entfernen des Stützkerns ruft keine wesentliche Belastungen des hangenden Ausbauteile hervor; im Stossausbau bilden sich die Belastungen symetrisch gegenüber der X-Achse, wobei die grössten Änderungen, hinsichtlich der vorhergehenden Phase, im unteren Abschnitt des Stossausbaus sichtbar sind.

Die grösste Lastzunahme des Ausbaus ist nach vollständiger Ausführung des Objekts beobachtet worden, als die rheologischen Eigenschaften des modellierten Gebirges aufgetreten sind. Eine Veränderung haben vor allem die zum

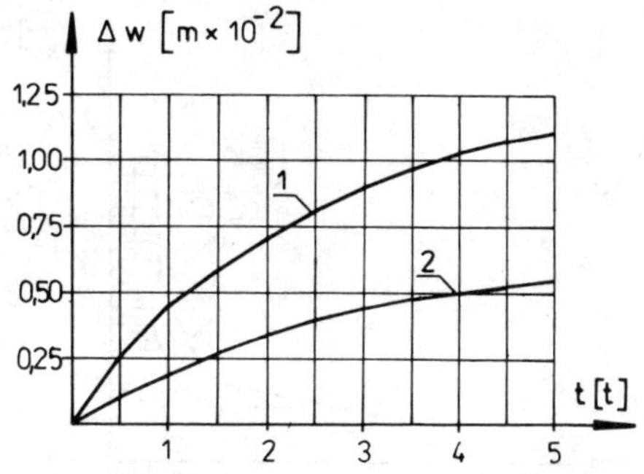

Abb. 6. Zunahme der Radialverschiebungen des Ausbaus Δw in der Zeit $\Delta_t=5$.

Ausbau senkrechten Spannungen σ_N erlitten. Die maximalen Werte dieser Belastungen treten im Stossteil des Ausbaus auf.

Die Abbildung 6 stellt die Zunahme der Radialverschiebungen Δw in der Zeit $\Delta_t = 5$. Die Kurve 1 bezieht sich auf die Mitte des hangenden Teils, die Kurve 2 dagegen auf die Mitte des Stossteils. Aus dem Bild ist ersichtlich, dass die Zunahme der Radialverschiebung des Ausbaus in der Mitte des Hangenden doppelt so gross als in der Mitte des Stosses ist.

Im Berechnungsverfahren wurde der Spannungszustand des Gebirges analysiert. Zur Analyse wurde die Bruchbedingung der Hypothese der Invarianten in der folgenden Form verwendet (Jakubowicz, Orłoś, 1972) :

$$\sigma_r = \frac{1+\kappa}{2}(\sigma_x+\sigma_y+\sigma_z) + \frac{1}{2}\sqrt{(1+\kappa)^2(\sigma_x+\sigma_y+\sigma_z)^2 - 2\kappa\left[(\sigma_x-\sigma_y)^2 + (\sigma_y-\sigma_z)^2 + (\sigma_z-\sigma_x)^2 + 6(\tau_{xy}^2 + \tau_{yz}^2 + \tau_{zx}^2)\right]}$$

wo: $\kappa = R_r : R_c$, R_r - Zugfestigkeit, R_c - Druckfestigkeit. Es wurde angenommen, dass $\kappa = 0,07$.

An der Abb. 7. wurden Diagramme der Anstrengung des Gesteinmassivs in den Symetrieachsen des Grubenbaus dargestellt. Die Kurve 1 bezieht sich auf die Anstrengung des Gesteinsmassivs unmittelbar nach der Ausführung des Grubenbaus; die Kurve 2 auf den Zustand, welcher nach dem Zeitverlauf $\Delta_t = 5$ entstanden ist. Aus der Abbbildung ergibt sich, dass in der unmit-

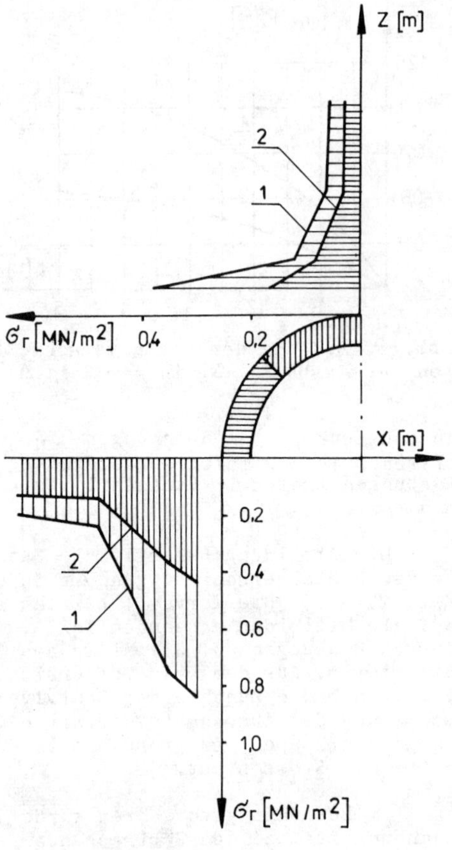

Abb. 7. Anstrengung des Gesteinsmassivs in den Symetrieachsen des Grubenbaus.

telbar an den Grubenbau grenzenden Zone die Anstrengung des Gesteinsmassivs ungefähr doppelt so gross in der Mitte des Stosses als in der Mitte des Hangenden ist. Nach dem Ablauf des untersuchten Zeitintervals hat sich die Anstrengung im ganzen Bereich rundum den Grubenbau verringert.

6. SCHLUSSFOLGERUNGEN

Aus vorgestellten Erwägungen geht hervor, dass die benutzte Berechnungsmethode kann in der Ingenieurpraxis verwendet werden. Ferner, obwohl die durchgeführten nummerischen Berechnungen nur für das angenommene Modell wichtig sind, ermöglichen sie eine Reihe von für die Bergbaupraxis belangreichen Schlüssen zu ziehen. Man kann beispielweise annehmen, dass trotz der für die deutsche Bauweise typischen Asymetrie des Arbeitsganges, in den Verhältnissen, die diesen des Modells ähneln, fast vollständige Symetrie der Belastungen des Ausbaus auftritt, welche durch mehrere Bauabschnitte umfassende Ausführung des Objekts hervorgerufen wird. Diese Belastungen charakterisieren sich jedoch durch grosse Veränderlichkeit längs des Ausbauumfangs, wobei sie ihre maximale Werte oft im Stossteil, in der Nähe von technologischen Verbindungen, sowie im mittleren Teil erreichen. Die grösste Zunahme der auf die fertige Ausbaufragmente wirkenden Belastungen wird durch des Aufschluss des hangenden Teils hervorgerufen. Die Ergebnisse der zweiten Berechnungsphase (die das Verhalten der abgebauten Grube betreffen) haben ausgewiesen, dass die rheologischen Eigenschaften des Gesteinsmassivs einen bedeutenden Einfluss auf die Belastungsgrösse des Ausbaus ausüben könnten. Gleichzeitig kann man anhand der Analyse der Anstrengungsänderung des Gesteinsmassivs rundum des Grubenbaus in der Zeitfunktion der Meinung sein, dass während des Betriebs des Objekts keine Ausdehnung der entspannten Bereiche im Gebirge auftritt.

LITERATUR

Jakubowicz, A., Orłoś, Z., 1972, Wytrzymałość materiałów, WNT, Warszawa.

Kisiel, I., 1980, Reologiczne równania stanu ośrodkow quasiliniowych, Wyd. PAN, Wrocław-Warszawa.

Müller, L., 1978, Der Felsbau/ Tunnelbau, Enke Vlg., Stuttgart.

Winnicki, L.A., 1980, Zastosowanie metody elementow skończonych w geotechnice, Praca zbiorowa, Wyd. PAN, Wrocław-Warszawa, 105-143.

Zienkiewicz, O.C., 1972, Metoda elementow skończonych, Arkady, Warszawa.

ÉTUDE ET CONTRÔLE DE LA STABILITÉ DE L'USINE HYDRO-ÉLECTRIQUE SOUTERRAINE DU VERNEY

Study of and checks on the stability of the underground hydroelectric power station at Le Verney

Stabilitätsstudie und Kontrolle des unterirdischen Wasserkraftswerks in Verney

ALAIN MARTINET

Electricité de France, Paris, France

SUMMARY :

The study of the stability of the Le Verney power station has been carried out using the method of finite elements.
An extensive system for auscultation by means of extensometric cables, invar wires and extensometers built into the concrete of the station vault provides a method of checking on the structure during the excavation phase, which is at present in course.

ZUSAMMENFASSUNG :

Die Stabilitätsstudie der Verney-Anlage wurde mit Hilfe der Finite Elementemethode durchgeführt.
Ein umfangreiches Prüfsystem mit Dehnungsmessakabeln, "Invar"-drähten und Dehnungsmessern im Gewölbebeton ermöglicht die Kontrolle des Bauwerks bei den gegenwärtigen Aushubarbeiten.

RESUME :

L'étude de la stabilité de l'usine du Verney a été réalisée par la méthode des éléments finis.
Un important dispositif d'auscultation par câbles extensométriques, fils invar, et extensomètres dans le béton de la voûte, permet de contrôler l'ouvrage lors de l'excavation, actuellement en cours.

L'aménagement de GRAND'MAISON intéresse le cours de l'Eau d'Olle qui, prenant sa source à proximité du Col de la Croix de Fer, s'écoule entre les deux massifs cristallins de Belledonne et des Grandes Rousses pour rejoindre la Romanche à 7 km à l'aval de Bourg-d'Oisans et 30 km en amont de son confluent avec le Drac.
Les apports naturels de l'Eau d'Olle sont accumulés dans la cuvette formée par le barrage de GRAND'MAISON. Le complément de remplissage annuel est assuré par un pompage des hautes eaux de printemps dans le bassin inférieur créé par le barrage du Verney. Les eaux stockées sont turbinées en heures pleines par les usines de l'Eau d'Olle : une usine extérieure souterraine comprenant 4 groupes Pelton (total 600 MW) et une usine extérieure souterraine comprenant 8 groupes réversibles (total 1 200 MW).
A l'installation gravitaire classique, se superpose donc une puissante station de transfert d'énergie par pompage permettant des échanges journaliers, hebdomadaires et saisonniers entre les bassins amont et aval.

1. CALCUL AUX ELEMENTS FINIS

Pour étudier la stabilité de l'usine souterraine du Verney, ELECTRICITE DE FRANCE a réalisé un calcul bidimensionnel par la méthode des éléments finis.
Les reconnaissances effectuées sur le site ont permis de définir les caractéristiques du rocher à prendre en compte pour le calcul :

- . p = 2 750 kg/m3
- . E = 10 000 MPa
- .   = 0,3

ainsi que les contraintes initiales insitu, orthotropes à axe vertical :

- pression verticale : P = 3 MPa à la cote 728,

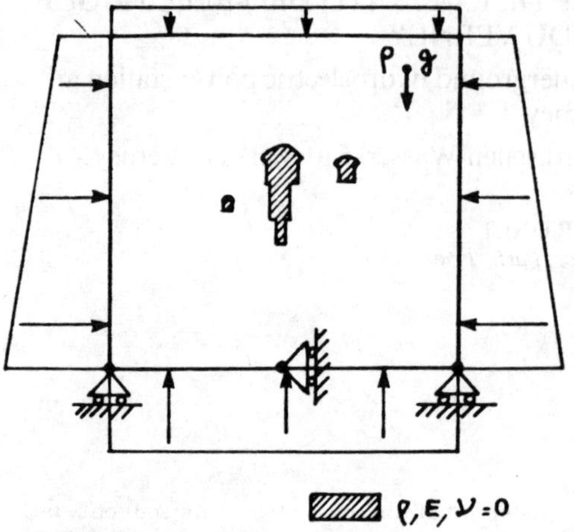

Fig 1 Modèle numérique

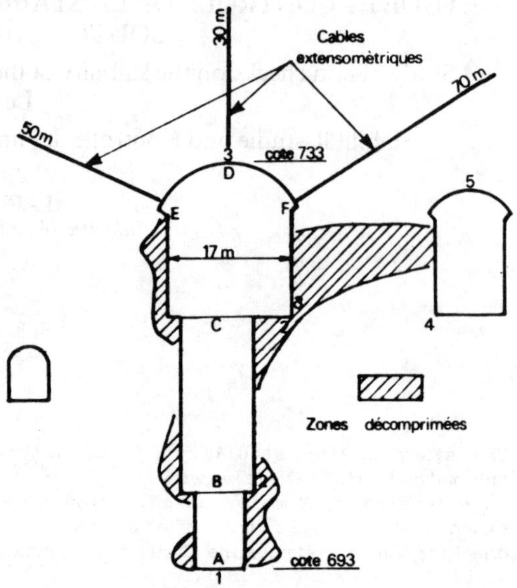

Fig 2 Resultats du calcul

- coefficient de poussée horizontale : k = 1,7.

Les conditions aux limites adoptées pour simuler ces contraintes initiales sont indiquées sur la figure 1, à savoir pressions normales sur les quatre côtés du modèle égales au contraintes initiales exercées dans la même direction, et déplacements nuls en trois points du modèle pour le stabiliser.

Les résultats du calcul mené en élasticité linéaire, en déformation plane, avec un modèle pesant sont les suivants (figure 2) :

- le rocher est décomprimé dans les zones grises, mais la traction n'y dépasse pas 1 MPa ;
- les compressions les plus fortes apparaissent en 1 : 23 MPa, en 3 : 16 MPa, en 4 : 11 MPa et en 5 : 12 MPa. Elles ne dépassent donc pas la valeur la plus faible de la résistance à la compression simple, mesurée en laboratoire, qui est de 25 MPa ;
- les déformations calculées sont : en A, déplacement vertical faible et convergence de 12 mm. La convergence augmente en remontant vers la voûte : 43 mm en B et 50 mm en C. Aux retombées de voûte elle est de 26 mm. La déformation verticale de la voûte, vers le bas, est dissymétrique : 2 mm en E, 2,5 mm en D et 0,5 mm en F.

2. AUSCULTATION

Pour contrôler les résultats du calcul et surveiller la stabilité de l'ouvrage nous avons mis en place un important système d'auscultation : 2 sections de mesures comportant chacune 3 câbles extensométriques LOSINGER, et une mesure de convergence au fil invar DISTOMATIC ont été instrumentés avant le début de l'excavation. De plus, au fur et à mesure de l'ouverture de la cavité, on dispose d'autres mesures de convergences réparties en 8 points tout au long de l'usine.

Actuellement, les convergences au niveau + 8,7 m atteignent 14 à 27 mm (au lieu de 30 calculé).

Les longrines du niveau zéro ont accusé un déplacement vertical vers le haut de 10 à 25 mm, dû à la décompression de la "marche d'escalier", et une convergence de 13 à 32 mm, au lieu de 50 calculé.

Mais il reste encore quelques mètres de stross à abattre et les déplacements ne sont pas stabilisés.

- Les mesures extensométriques indiquent des déplacements pouvant atteindre 13 mm (comparable à la convergence calculée de 26 mm), qui ont peu évolué lors de l'abattage sous le niveau zéro.
- Des mesures de contraintes dans la voûte en béton montre qu'elle est partout en compression et que celle-ci ne dépasse pas 5 MPa.

3. CONCLUSION

L'importante campagne de reconnaissance du site a permis de connaître avec précision les paramètres nécessaires à un calcul par la méthode des éléments finis. L'auscultation mise en place a permis d'en contrôler les hypothèses qui s'avèrent satisfaisantes.

4. REFERENCE

A. MARTINET, G. AKERMANN,
J. LAKSHMANAN, F. LANTIER
ELECTRICITE DE FRANCE - PARIS
Compagnie de Prospection Géophysique Française, RUEIL MALMAISON - FRANCE

Etude géophysique et géotechnique de l'usine souterraine du Verney

ISRM Symposium, Aachen 1982.

STANDSICHERHEIT UND BAU VON KAVERNEN IN ABHÄNGIGKEIT VON DEN BAUGEOLOGISCHEN BEDINGUNGEN

Stability and construction of caverns related to the engineering geological conditions

Stabilité et construction de cavités souterraines en fonction des conditions de la géologie de l'ingénieur

LEOPOLD MÜLLER-SALZBURG
Ingenieurkonsulant für Bauwesen, Salzburg, Österreich
PETER EGGER
Ecole Polytechnique Fédérale de Lausanne, Schweiz

SUMMARY

Whereas tunnelling experience shows difficulties to increase with the diameter, underground caverns with large span often caused astonishingly little trouble. This can be explained only to a small extent by the fact that caverns are generally built in favourable rock conditions which can be predicted with a good accuracy already in the design stage. But the observed successes were essentially made possible by modern geological and rock mechanical investigation methods, by a careful interpretation of the geological conditions and by adapting to them the design of the cavern, particularly the cross section, temporary and final rock support.

This progress is still going ahead : in the future, still more attention should be paid to the detailed interpretation of the geological data which will not only allow to avoid trouble but also to optimize the design, e.g. with respect to the layout and the orientation of the cavern, by the consideration of favourable geological elements, of the initial stresses and the joint pattern of the rock mass.

KURZFASSUNG

Während es im Tunnelbau als allgemeine Erfahrung gilt, dass die baulichen Schwierigkeiten mit dem Hohlraumdurchmesser wachsen, haben Kavernen sehr grosser Spannweite oft erstaunlich geringe Schwierigkeiten geboten. Dies ist nur zu einem geringen Teil darauf zurückzuführen, dass Kavernen meist in günstigen Gebirgsverhältnissen angelegt werden, welche mit grosser Genauigkeit der Vorhersage schon vor dem Bau erhoben werden können; sondern zu einem wesentlichen Teil wurden die verzeichneten Erfolge durch fortschrittliche Methoden der geologischen und felsmechanischen Bauvorbereitung, durch eine sorgfältige Interpretation der geologischen Bedingungen und eine Anpassung der Konstruktion, insbesondere auch der Querschnittsform und der vorläufigen wie der definitiven Abstützung des Gebirges an die geologischen Bedingungen ermöglicht.

Dieser Fortschritt ist noch im Gange. Noch wesentlich mehr Aufmerksamkeit als bisher sollte der Dateninterpretation gewidmet werden, wobei es gilt, nicht nur Schwierigkeiten zu vermeiden, sondern auch Vorteile, insbesondere der Lage und der Achsrichtung wahrzunehmen und sich dabei den vorhandenen Spannungen sowie dem Flächengefüge anzupassen.

RESUME

Tandis que l'expérience faite dans la construction des tunnels montre une augmentation des difficultés avec le diamètre, la réalisation de cavités souterraines de grandes dimensions a souvent posé peu de problèmes. Ceci ne peut être expliqué que très partiellement par le fait que les cavernes sont généralement construites dans des conditions géologiques favorables, bien prévisibles déjà à l'état de l'étude. Mais les succès observés ont été rendus possibles essentiellement par l'utilisation des méthodes modernes de la géologie et de la mécanique des roches, par l'interprétation soignée des données et par l'adaptation du projet, p. ex. section transversale, support provisoire et permanent, aux conditions géologiques.

Ce progrès n'est pas arrêté : à l'avenir une attention encore accrue devrait être portée sur l'interprétation détaillée des données géologiques qui permettra non seulement d'éviter des déboires, mais aussi d'optimiser le projet, p. ex. disposition et orientation de la cavité, en tirant profit d'éléments géologiques favorables et en considérant les contraintes initiales et la structure du massif.

Beim Bau der ersten Krafthauskavernen in den Vierzigerjahren hatte man Neuland betreten, ohne sich auf gesicherte theoretische Grundlagen stützen zu können. Noch gab es keine Geomechanik, welche eine bautechnische Interpretation geologischer Daten ermöglicht hätte. So wagte man zunächst Großräume nur unter günstigen geologischen Verhältnissen anzulegen, baute aber dennoch äußerst starke Gewölbe ein, - "zur Sicherheit" - d.h. aus innerer Unsicherheit. Erst im Laufe der Zeit tastete man sich an weniger günstige geologische Verhältnisse heran, riskierte auch größere Spannweiten. Der Anwendungsbereich des Untertage-Großraumbaues wuchs weiter zusehends, als das Bedürfnis nach Großraumlagern für Treibstoffe, Chemikalien, Wasser usw. die Verlegung größerer Speicher in den Untergrund nahelegten.

Gefördert wurde diese Entwicklung durch zunehmende praktische Erfahrung, aber auch durch vermehrte theoretische Kenntnisse. Doch auch jüngste Beispiele zeigen immer wieder, wie wenig sich bislang die Erkenntnis durchgesetzt hat, daß vornehmlich die geologischen Verhältnisse über das Ob und Wie des Untertage-Großraumbaues entscheiden bzw. entscheiden sollten.

GROSSHOHLRAUMBAU EINE SPEZIFISCH GEOMECHANISCHE AUFGABE

Ziel, aber auch Problem eines jeden Hohlraumbaues ist die Anpassung an die geologischen Verhältnisse, welche unabdingbare Gegebenheiten sind. Diese Probleme beziehen sich weniger auf das, worin viele Fachleute der Felsmechanik den Schwerpunkt sehen, nämlich auf die theoretisch-rechnerische Erfassung der statischen Verhältnisse aufgrund von geologischen Daten, welche als gegeben betrachtet werden; sie beziehen sich viel mehr auf die Repräsentativität und Variabilität der Parameter und auf die geologische Situation im ganzen bzw. deren Auswirkungen auf das Felsbauwerk, also auf Fragenkomplexe, welche z.B. der Salzburger Kreis vorzugsweise als Geomechanik im weiteren Sinne bezeichnet.

Immer noch stellt, trotz neuer Versuche auf diesem Felde, der Durchtrennungsgrad des Trennflächengefüges, seine Begriffgebung und seine Quantifizierung eines der ungelösten Hauptprobleme; von seiner richtigen Einschätzung hängt aber die zutreffende Bewertung der Gebirgsfestigkeit und deren Anisotropie ab. Mit Absicht sagen wir: Einschätzung, da eine rechnerische Erfassung aufgrund der Gesteins- und Gefügeangaben immer noch nicht gelungen ist und wohl auch nicht leicht in befriedigender Weise gelingen wird. Die einzig realistische Ermittlung der Gebirgsfestigkeit ist wohl die aufgrund von Großversuchen in situ. Doch stoßen Großversuche, so sehr sie zur Selbstverständlichkeit geworden sind, wenn es sich um die Bestimmung von E- und V-Modul handelt - auch seismische Feldversuche zur E-Modul-Bestimmung sind Großversuche in situ - häufig auf eine (rational nicht recht zu verstehende, aber starke) Aversion, sobald sie der Ermittlung der Gebirgsfestigkeit dienen sollen. Deshalb bleibt wohl nur die Möglichkeit, einen Abminderungsfaktor von der Gesteins- zur Gebirgsfestigkeit in der Weise zu gewinnen, wie dies von Hoek et al. (1980) und von John (1969) vorgeschlagen wurde; oder aber auf dem von Müller, Mühlhaus,

Reik und Sharma (1977a und 1977b, s.a. Reik, 1977) eingeschlagenen Kompromißweg einer Bestimmung mit Hilfe von natursimulierenden Modellversuchen.

Verläßliche Angaben über die Gebirgsfestigkeit wären für die Beurteilung der Standsicherheit einer Kaverne von fast noch größerer Bedeutung als die Kenntnis des Verformungsverhaltens des Gebirges, obwohl z.B. die Verformungsarbeit bis zum Höchstwert der Lastaufnahme - und auch jenseits davon - wertvolle Aussagen über die Zähigkeit oder Sprödigkeit des Gebirges, über seine Neigung zu Fließdeformationen, und damit über die Beurteilung seiner Standfestigkeit aufgrund gemessener Deformationsgrößen ermöglicht.

Nicht wenige Fachleute halten es für einen Ausweg aus dem Dilemma der angesprochenen Problematik, aus einer Anzahl von Einflußgrößen einen die Standfestigkeit (oder auch den Grad der erforderlichen Abstützung) des Gebirges charakterisierenden Index zu errechnen; mehrere Arten solcher Indexbildung sind in Gebrauch.

Allen diesen Versuchen einer "Index"-Klassifizierung des Gebirges ist das Bestreben gemeinsam, die unendliche Vielfalt der Natur in eine einzige Ziffer zu pressen.

Wir halten derartige Versuche - zumindest mit ihrem allgemeingültigen Anspruch - von vornherein für aussichtslos,

- weil nicht alle maßgebenden Einflußgrößen quantifizierbar sind;

- weil die wirklich quantifizierbaren unter ihnen nicht in linearen Funktionen dargestellt werden können und deshalb weder additiv noch multiplikativ überlagert werden dürfen;

- weil diese Einflußgrößen zumeist selbst variabel sind, ihre funktionale Abhängigkeit von anderen Größen jedoch nicht leicht erfaßt und in Rechnung gestellt werden kann;

- weil die Wechselbeziehungen und die gegenseitigen Beeinflussungen der durch Teilfaktoren ausgedrückten Einflußgrößen nicht erfaßt werden können. (Z.B. kann ein und dieselbe Kluftkombination bei Vorhandensein gewisser Primärspannungen sehr maßgebend, bei anderen Primärspannungen oder einer anderen Orientierung derselben völlig belanglos sein, ohne daß der Zusammenhang zwischen diesen Einflüssen als mathematisch faßbare Gesetzmäßigkeit angegeben werden könnte;

- vor allem aber deshalb, weil vielen Einflußgrößen nicht nur Quantität sondern auch Qualität zugesprochen werden muß, durch eine Quantifizierung jedoch nur Quantitäten, nicht Qualitäten erfaßt werden können.

Da ist es doch viel bescheidener und naturentsprechender, die Gebirgsfestigkeit durch Angabe des Zerklüftungsgrades und der Substanzfestigkeit oder -entfestigung zu charakterisieren und für den konkreten Einzelfall nach Erfahrung geschätzte Grenzbereiche, z.B. etwas gemäß Abb. 1, anzugeben.

Angesichts dieser vielen offenen Probleme ist es beruhigend, daß es immer noch, wenngleich verkümmert, eine menschliche Fähigkeit zu einer mehr intuitiven als rationalen, mehr die Gesamtsituation ganzheitlich erfassenden als das Detail bewertenden Einschätzung des Gebirgsverhaltens gibt. Beispiele zeigen dies. So mußten (und konnten) wir bei der Projektierung der Kaverne Waldeck II die Entscheidung darüber, ob (erstmals) ein Untertagehohlraum von so großen Abmessungen (Spannweite 33,5m) in dem Gesteinsverband des Rheinischen Schiefergebirges erstens überhaupt und zweitens ohne Firstgewölbe - lediglich durch eine Verbundkonstruktion aus Ankern, Fels und Spritzbeton gesichert - riskiert werden könne, bereits vor aller Berechnung treffen; und zwar vor dem Studium spannungsoptischer Versuche, lediglich aufgrund des augenscheinlichen Verhaltens im Zugangsstollen und einem kleinen Probehohlraum.

DIE ABHÄNGIGKEIT VON DEN GEOLOGISCHEN VORAUSSETZUNGEN

Mehr als jeder andere Felsbau hängt die Ausführung von Kavernenbauten, hängen Schwierigkeiten einerseits

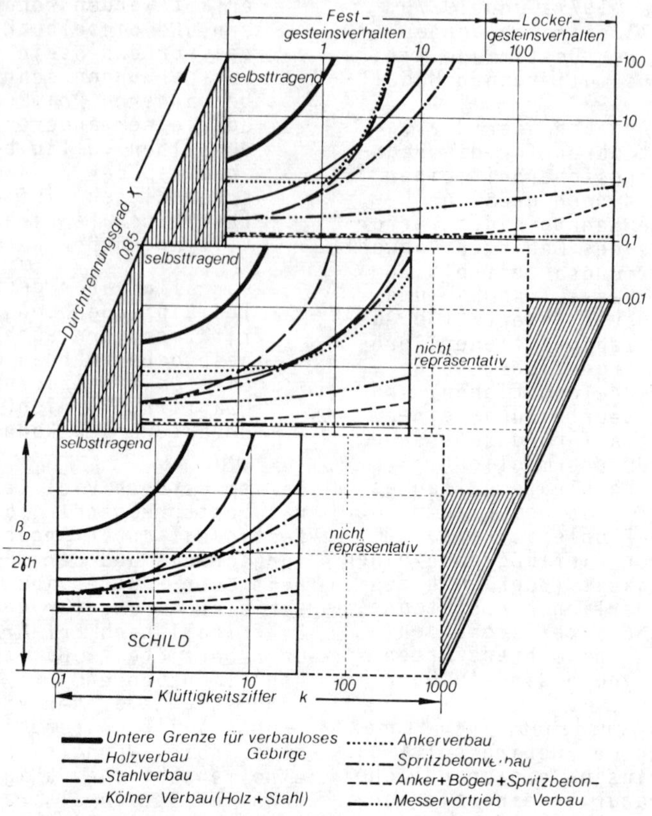

Abb. 1: Durchschnittliche Anwendungsbereiche für verschiedene Verbauarten in Abhängigkeit von Gesteinsfestigkeit, Klüftigkeit und Durchtrennungsgrad

und Ausführungsvorteile anderseits von der Gunst und Ungunst der geologischen Verhältnisse ab. Je mehr es schon bei der Projektierung, insbesondere bei der Situierung und Orientierung eines Großhohlraumes gelingt, ungünstige Einflüsse zu vermeiden und vorteilhafte Gegebenheiten, die die Natur bietet, zu nutzen, desto wirtschaftlicher und sicherer, auch rascher, kann das Bauwerk hergestellt werden. Je nachdem, ob das Projekt unmittelbar aus den geologischen Gegebenheiten heraus gestaltet wird oder ob der Projektant einen favorisierten Bauwerkstyp in die Natur hineinzwingen zu dürfen glaubt, können die Baukosten innerhalb viel weiterer Grenzen variieren, als es den meisten bewußt ist.

Gute Ingenieure haben sich immer darin ausgezeichnet, ein "Gefühl" für die geologische Situation zu entwickeln. Schwierigkeiten sind nicht dazu da, um überwunden zu werden, sondern gerade im Vermeiden von Schwierigkeiten zeigt sich die Kunst des Ingenieurs. Viel zu selten aber wird von der Möglichkeit Gebrauch gemacht, das Untertagebauwerk in den geologisch günstigsten Bereich zu schieben und ihm die felsmechanisch günstigste Form und Achsrichtung zu geben. Wie wichtig eine weiträumige Untersuchung der geologischen Verhältnisse ist, zeigt das Beispiel der Kaverne Belviso (Abb. 2 Kuhnhenn und Spaun, 1976), bei der sich die Kranbahn in 30 Jahren um mehr als

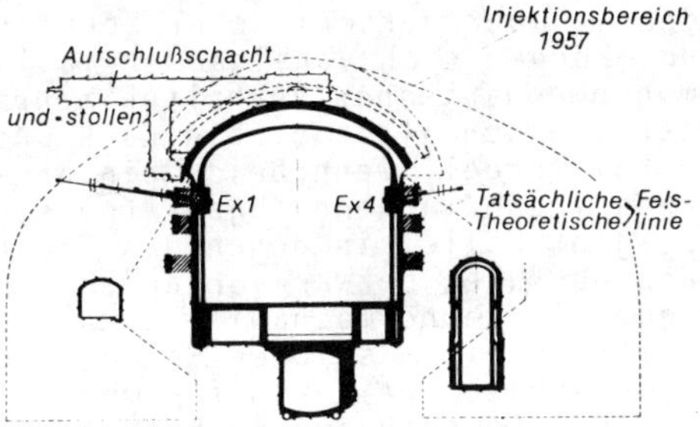

Abb. 2: Maschinenkaverne des Kraftwerkes Belviso. Querschnitt durch die Kaverne mit Darstellung der Verhältnisse in den Seitenwandbereichen (aus Kuhnhenn und Spaun, 1976)

6 Zentimeter verengte und die Maschinenfundamente derart verkippten, daß schwere Achslagerschäden auftraten. Die nachträgliche Untersuchung deckte auf, daß die Kaverne im Bereich eines aktiven Talzuschubes liegt, dem mit vertretbaren Mitteln auf die Dauer nicht begegnet werden kann.

Das Beispiel der ersten Kariba-Kaverne (Abb. 3), bei welcher sich die Projektierung auf nur vier - noch dazu vertikal abgestoßene - Kernbohrungen stützte, wobei Störungen, die die Kavernenwände durchzogen und äußerst ungünstige Kluftstellungen der Vorerkundung entgingen, sei als Warnung hingestellt.

Bohrungen sind nur Nadelstiche; sie sind vonnöten, um sich ein allgemeines Bild von den geologischen Verhältnissen zu verschaffen; doch zur Erkundung des felsbaulichen Gebirgsverhaltens geben einige hundert Meter Erkundungsstollen ein deutlicheres Bild als viele tausend Meter von Bohrungen. Man sollte sich aber nicht scheuen, das Netz der Aufschlußstollen nach mehreren Richtungen zumindest einen Kavernendurchmesser weiter ins Unbekannte vorzutreiben.

Planung ist ein schöpferischer Vorgang, bei welchem wissenschaftliche Kenntnisse allein nicht genügen, sondern welcher jene Kräfte und Fähigkeiten herausfordert, welche aller Baukunst erst Qualität und Niveau geben. Ein jedes Bauwerk ist anders, weil die Natur an jedem Orte immer wieder anders ist. Die Pläne einer Kaverne nach denen einer anderen zu kopieren, verrät deshalb geistige Armut.

GESTEINSVERHÄLTNISSE

Als Beispiel für Gesteinsverhältnisse, welche an sich so günstig sind, daß eine so ausführliche geologische Erkundung, wie im Vorigen angesprochen, nicht unbedingt nötig erscheint, können die Kaverne Braz (Vorarlberg, Abb. 4) im quarzitischen Glaukonit, die Kaverne Sylvenstein (Bayern) in fast homogenem Dolomit, schließlich auch die Kavernen Franz (Steiermark) im Dolomit und Grimsel (Schweiz) im Granodiorit genannt werden.

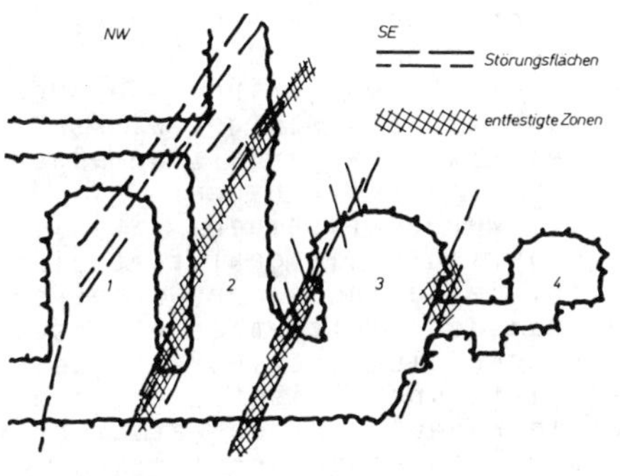

Abb. 3: Kariba-Kraftwerk (Rhodesien); Querschnitt durch die unterirdischen Anlagen. 1 Schieberkammer, 2 Druckschächte, 3 Maschinenhalle, 4 Transformatorenhalle (Müller, 1960c)

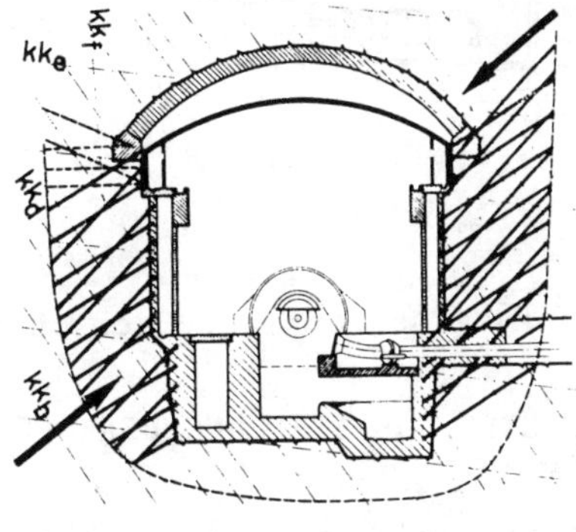

Abb. 4: Erste ankergesicherte Kaverne Braz, Österreich (1949)

Weniger günstig und daher größerer Vorerkundungen und vorsichtigerer Projektierung bedürftig sind Schichtgesteine (auch metamorphisierte), wie sie z.B. in der Kalkschiefer-Serie (Dogger) von Veytaux (Rescher, 1968) zu einer intensiven engständigen Ankerung Anlaß gegeben haben (Abb. 5). In Morrow Point (Utah, USA) hat eine Großkluft zu einem drohenden, aber schließlich durch Felsanker abgefangenen Abgleiten geführt. In Waldeck II wurde eine von Ort zu Ort wechselnde, von der Radialen abweichende Richtung der Vorspannanker erforderlich. Als Beispiel für Schwierigkeiten durch ungünstige Gefügestellungen wurde bereits die erste Kariba-Kaverne genannt, bei welcher während des Aushubes durch Teilkörperverschiebungen entlang zweier sich spitzwinkelig schneidender Kluftscharen unerwünschte zunehmende Ulmkonvergenzen von ca. 50 mm pro Woche auftraten, denen nur durch eine sofortige Intensivst-Ankerung mit vorgespannten Litzenankern Einhalt geboten werden konnte.

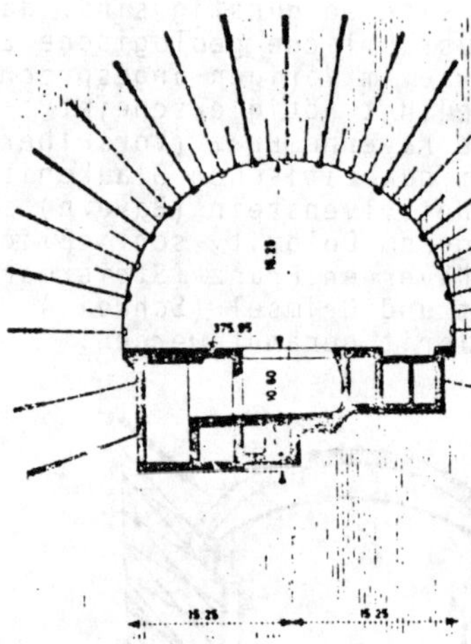

Abb. 5: Kaverne Veytaux: Querschnitt

DIE DOMINIERENDE STELLUNG DER GEFÜGEBEDINGUNG

Die Unterschiede im mechanischen Verhalten verschiedener Gebirgsarten sind in weit höherem Grade Auswirkung der Trennflächengefüge als der Gesteinsart und -substanz. Zwei massige Kalke gleicher stratigraphischer Einordnung, aber verschiedener Zerklüftung, können sich voneinander in ihrem geomechanischen Verhalten mehr unterscheiden als z.B. ein Kalk und ein Kalkmergel, wenn beide ein ähnliches Trennflächengefüge aufweisen.

Es gibt Fälle, in denen das Trennflächengefüge, obzwar vorhanden, so gut wie keine mechanische Rolle spielt. In einem solchen Falle wird die Übertragbarkeit von felsmechanischen Untersuchungsergebnissen im Labor, im Stollen oder Kleinhohlraum auf die Bedingungen des Großhohlraumes kaum Probleme aufwerfen. Hingegen kann diese Übertragbarkeit äußerst problematisch werden, wo das Trennflächengefüge oder gewisse Komponenten desselben (z.B. Großklüfte, Bankungsklüfte, Schichtklüfte, Schieferungsklüfte oder sogar Schieferungsflächen) mechanisch wirksam sind. Ob das der Fall ist, hängt keineswegs nur von der Scherfestigkeit entlang der Trennflächen und von ihrer Häufigkeit ab, sondern in hohem Maße von den Richtungsbeziehungen zwischen der Kavernenachse und den Anisotropierichtungen sowohl des Flächengefüges als auch des herrschenden Primärspannungszustandes.

Descoeudres und Egger (1977) haben anläßlich des Baues der Kaverne Grimsel-Oberaar Überlegungen zu dem Maßstabeffekt angestellt, welcher durch das Verhältnis zwischen dem mittleren Kluftabstand und den Dimensionen des Felshohlraumes bewirkt wird (Abb. 6). Bei der Kaverne Waldeck II haben (s.z.B.Abraham et al., 1974 sowie Baudendistel et al., 1970) Störungen und Großklüfte eine mechanisch wesentliche Rolle gespielt, während sich die Schichtfugen trotz ihres geringen Reibungskoeffizienten als weniger wirksam, die Kleinklüfte sogar als unmaßgeblich herausgestellt haben.

Je "verworrenklüftiger" (Stini), je weniger intensiv geklüftet ein Gestein, je geringer der Durchtrennungsgrad des Kluftnetzes einerseits, je geringer die Gesteinsfestigkeit anderseits, und je isotroper, d.h. je weniger deviatorisch betont drittens der Primärspannungszustand im Gebirge ist, desto monolithischer wird sich der Gesteinverband verhalten und desto eher wird dieses Verhalten kontinuumsmechanisch untersucht werden können. Und Umgekehrt.

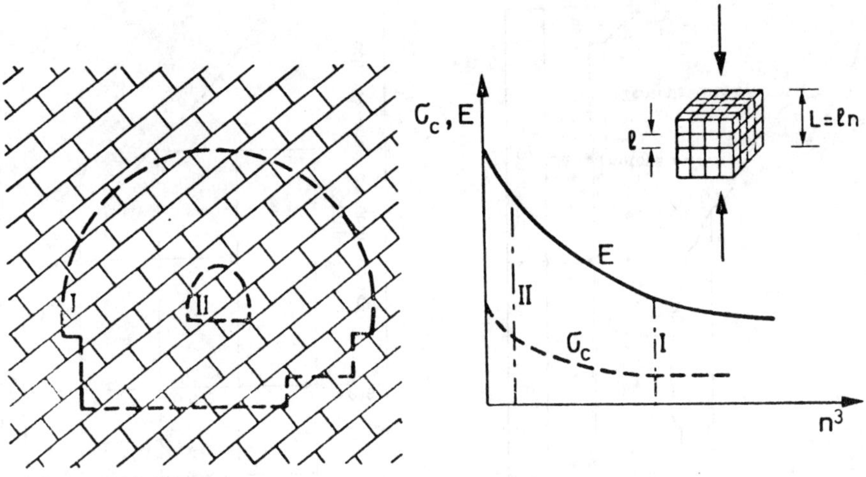

Abb. 6: Einfluß der Kluftdichte von Verformbarkeit und Festigkeit. Sowohl Verformbarkeit als auch Festigkeit werden durch die Zahl der auftretenden Klüfte beeinflußt, wobei mit wachsender Kluftdichte die Verschiebungen rasch anwachsen.

Daß gefügebedingte Schwierigkeiten weitgehend ausgeschaltet werden können, wenn man die Stellungen der Kavernenwände mit den anisotropiebedingten Richtungen großer und kleinster Teilkörperbeweglichkeit des Kluftkörperverbandes (Sander, 1948) in Einklang bringt, wurde bereits bei den Voruntersuchungen für die Kaverne Huben erkannt. Damals hat Müller (1951) ein Verfahren zur quantitativen Einschätzung der Teilkörperbeweglichkeit in Hohlraumbegrenzungen gegeben, welches z.B. durch Kombination mit dem Gleitkörper-Ermittlungsverfahren von John (1969) noch verbessert werden konnte. Auf jeden Fall ist eine gefügerelevante Orientierung der Kavernenachse geboten, sobald ein mechanisch wirksames Trennflächengefüge vorhanden ist, und eine gefühlsmäßige Berücksichtigung dieser Zusammenhänge kann heute nicht mehr als befriedigend angesehen werden.

DER EINFLUSS DER PRIMÄRSPANNUNGEN IM GEBIRGE

Im Gebirge vorhandene, vom Einfluß der Schwerkraft abweichende Spannungen, seien sie durch aktuelle Tektonik oder post-tektonisch oder aber auch, wie das in söhligen Sedimenten sogenannter ruhiger, ungestörter Lagerung vorkommt, durch Massenabtragungen und Spannungsumlagerungen bedingt, werden erst seit verhältnismäßig kurzer Zeit ernst genommen und konstruktiv berücksichtigt. Diese Berücksichtigung geschieht nicht nur in der Berechnung, was bei Verwendung der Finite-Element-Methode ohne weiteres möglich ist, sondern man versucht, soweit dies mit der Gefügesituation in Einklang zu bringen ist, auch schon die Kavernenachse so auszurichten, daß sie tunlichst quer zu den größten Horizontalspannungen im Gebirge liegt.

Einer der ersten Untertagegroßräume, bei welchem der Einfluß größter Primärspannungen erkannt wurde, dürfte die Kaverne Poatina in Tasmanien gewesen sein, bei welcher nach einem Vorschlag von Endersbee (1963) diese Spannungen durch Schlitze seitlich der Firste, welche mit Quetschhölzern verbolzt wurden, zu einem gesteuerten Abklingen gebracht wurden. Wenn die größten Firstsetzungen der Kaverne Waldeck (mit einer einzigen Ausnahme) nicht mehrals 18,5 mm betrugen, während nach sorgfältigen Berechnungen ca. 70 mm erwartet werden mußten, so ist dies ohne Zweifel darauf zurückzuführen, daß die quer zur Kavernenachse gerichteten Spannungskomponenten größer waren, als in der Berechnung angenommen. Wird die Form des Hohlraumes folgerichtig gewählt,

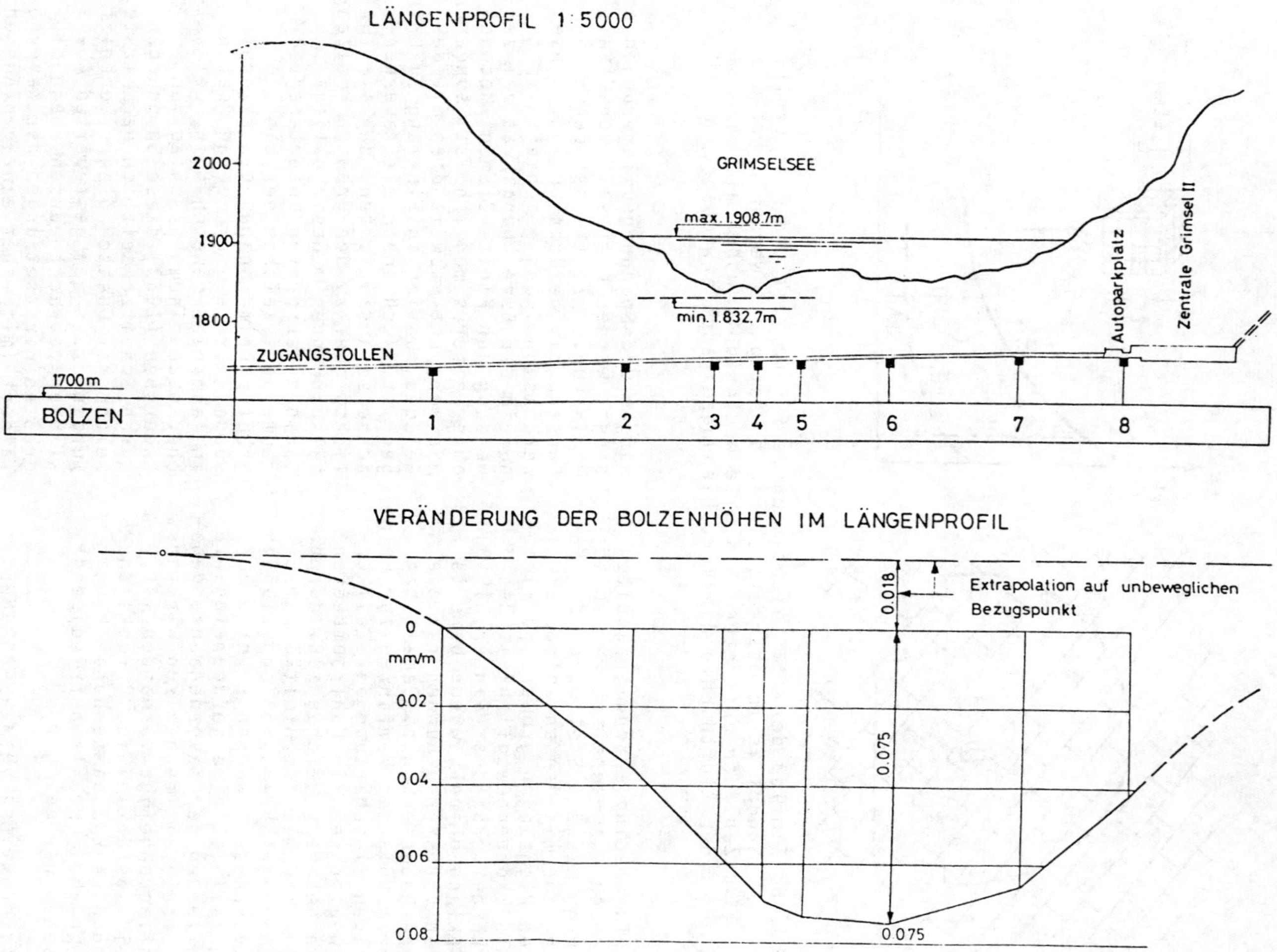

Abb. 7: Zugangsstollen zur Kaverne Grimsel (Schweiz): Setzungen in Abhängigkeit von den Stauspiegelschwankungen

wirken sich große Horizontalspannungen günstig aus, weil sie das Firstgewölbe des Gebirgstragringes nach oben drücken und damit stützen.

Das Beispiel Waldeck - siehe auch das von Egger (1971) mitgeteilte Beispiel des Kraftwerksschachts Vianden - hat gezeigt, wie wesentlich eine rechtzeitige Kenntnis von der Größe und Richtung der Primärspannungen ist. Zu diesem Behufe müssen nach heutigem Stand der Technik gründliche Spannungsmessungen in situ als unentbehrlich angesehen werden. Besonders bewährt hat sich die von der Interfels geschaffene Spannungsmeßeinrichtung in Bohrlöchern von 920 mm Durchmesser, weil diese Abmessung wenigstens einigermaßen groß genug ist, um den Einfluß des Kleinflächengefüges in der Messung zu berücksichtigen, was bei Spannungsmessungen in Bohrlöchern üblichen Durchmessers nicht der Fall ist.

In manchen Fällen besteht die Möglichkeit, die Primärspannungen indirekt und unter Ausschaltung des Maßstabeffektes kostengünstig folgendermaßen zu ermitteln: einerseits werden die durch den Ausbruch verursachten Verformungen z.B. an einem Nebenbauwerk der Kaverne (Wasserschloß o.ä.) mittels Extensometer gemessen, die bereits vor Beginn der Ausbrucharbeiten von einem Stollen auseingebaut wurden; andererseits wird ein FE-Modell des betrachteten Gebirgskörpers mit verschiedenen Primärspannungen durchgerechnet und die Verschiebungen der Extensometer-Meßpunkte in Abhängigkeit vom Seitendruckbeiwert aufgetragen. Der Vergleich zwischen den Ergebnissen der Feldmessung und der Parameteranalyse liefert auch bei komplexeren Gebirgsverhältnissen einen wahrscheinlichen Wert der horizontalen Primärspannungen, sofern nur das Rechenmodell einigermaßen naturgetreu ist.

Die bedeutende Wirkung höherer Primärspannungen auf das Deformationsgeschehen in der Hohlraumumgebung wird verständlich, wenn man sich eine Anschauung darüber bildet, wie "weich" alle geologischen Körper, auch solche von sehr großer Steifigkeit, im Grunde gebettet sind, weil diese Bettung eine große Mächtigkeit aufweist. Wenn man von Fachleuten der Satelliten-Geodäsie erfährt, daß der winterliche Schneefall die Alpen um ca. 10 cm einsinken und nach der Schneeschmelze wieder um diesen Betrag anheben läßt, so stimmt das bestens überein mit den jüngst an der Grimsel in einem Stollen unter dem Stausee gemessenen Senkungen und Hebungen des Gebirges bei vollem und leerem Becken, welche nach Descoeudres und Egger (1977) eine Bewegungsamplitude von über 4 mm (ca. 0,1 mm je Meter Wasserspiegelschwankung) erkennen lassen (Abb. 7). Hat man diese Tatsachen erst einmal auch zu einer Anschauung werden lassen, dann ist man auch nicht mehr überrascht, wenn manche Finite-Element-Berechnungen Gesteinsverschiebungen voraussagen, die oft mehrere Durchmesser weit in dieUmgebung des Hohlraums reichen. Alle diese Zusammenhänge macht man sich viel leichter klar, wenn man sich übt, in Deformationen zu denken, während man als Techniker ja im allgemeinen dazu erzogen ist, in Spannungen zu denken. Egger (1973) hat eine Ableitung gegeben, aufgrund deren geschlossen werden kann, wie groß die Ankerlänge bei Kavernensicherungen gewählt werden muß, um dem jeweiligen Deformationsbild Rechnung zu tragen.

FELSBAULICHE BESONDERHEITEN DES KAVERNENBAUES

Nach heutiger Auffassung muß das den Hohlraum unmittelbar umgebende Gebirge nicht nur als ein wesentlicher, sondern als der wesentlichste Teil der Konstruktion betrachtet werden. Dann werden gewisse bauliche Grundsätze immer wichtiger, denen beim traditionellen Kavernenbau älteren Stils eine nicht annähernd gleich große Bedeutung zukam. Die möglichst weitgehende Erhaltung der Eigenschaften des ungestörten Gebirges (nach dem Motto "Vorbeugen ist besser als Heilen") muß in konsequenter Weise sowohl bei der Projektierung als auch bei der Ausführung im Auge behalten werden.

Wegen der meist bedeutenden Abmessungen von Kavernenbauten spielt die Formgebung, d.h. das tunlichste Vermeiden von Spannungskonzentrationen und Zugbereichen - wie sie bei klassischen Querschnitten mit hohen vertikalen Wänden und Auflagernischen für das Deckengewölbe auftreten und oft zu metertiefen Auflockerungszonen im Gebirge führen - eine wesentlich größere Rolle als beispielsweise im Stollenbau. Selbst bei Teilausbrüchen strebt man heute, seit dem hervorragenden Ergebnis der Erstausführung in Waldeck (Abb. 8) an, durch Formgebung derselben, insbesondere durch Ausrundungen und Vermeidung scharfer Profilecken Spannungskonzentrationen zu vermeiden (s. Müller, 1978, S. 607).

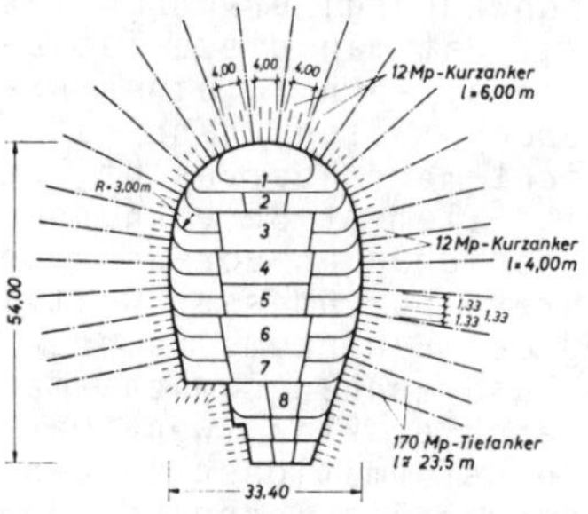

Abb. 8: Kaverne Waldeck II: Querschnitt mit Ausbruch- und Felsankerschema. 12 Mp-Kurzanker; 170 Mp-Tiefanker

Als hervorragendes Hilfsmittel zur Sichtbarmachung solcher Spannungsspitzen und Zugbereiche im Gebirge hat sich die Spannungsoptik bewährt, die überdies besonders einfach und anschaulich den Einfluß der horizontalen Primärspannungen auf das Spannungsfeld im Hohlraumbereich zu erkennen gestattet. Ebenso können Trennflächen im spannungsoptischen Modell gut simuliert werden (Abb.9), so daß diese Versuchstechnik auch im Zeitalter des Computers durchaus noch eine Daseinsberechtigung hat.

Abb. 9: Spannungsoptisches Modell für Kalottenausbruch in geklüftetem Gebirge

Aus dem gleichen Grunde wird die Zahl der Spannungsumlagerungen im Gebirge durch Vermeidung überflüssig vieler Teilausbruchphasen geflissentlich vermieden.

Daß bei der Bauausführung das Gebirge im Bereich der Ausbruchlaibung durch unsachgemäßes Sprengen stark in Mitleidenschaft gezogen werden kann, soll nur deshalb erwähnt werden, weil sich offenbar die Erkenntnis, daß der Zeitgewinn beim Sprengen meist durch stark erhöhten Sicherungsbedarf mehr als wettgemacht wird, noch nicht allgemein durchgesetzt hat.

Eine besondere Schwierigkeit der Bauausführung stellt die - ebenfalls zur Schonung des Gebirges notwendige - rechtzeitige Aufbringung der Querstützung durch vorgespannte Anker dar, weil die Vorspannkraft erst nach Abbinden des Injektionsgutes aufgebracht werden kann. Eine geradezu ideal zu nennende Konstruktion wurde bei der Krafthauskaverne Yamuna II in Uttar Pradesh, Indien, erdacht: dort wurden die Bohrlöcher für die meisten Ulmanker von achsparallel verlaufenden Seitenstollen aus bereits vor dem Ausbruch der Kaverne vorgebohrt, sodaß die Spannkabel jeweils sofort eingesetzt und ohne Injektionsvorgang gespannt werden konnten, sobald eine weitere Aushubsohle erreicht war.

In weniger schwierigen Fällen hat sich eine zweistufige Vorgangsweise für die Ankerung bewährt: Zunächst wird - dem Abschlag dicht folgend - eine systematische vollvermörtelte Kurzankerung eingebracht und dann in einigem Abstand eine vorgespannte Tiefenverankerung nachgezogen (Abb. 8). Diese Vorgangsweise entspricht sowohl den Baustellenbedingungen (Platzbedarf) als auch den Erkenntnissen aus neueren Forschungsarbeiten: Scherversuche entlang von Trennflächen zeigten eine Erhöhung der möglichen Scherbewegung bis zum Erreichen des Spitzenwiderstandes von wenigen Millimetern für unverankerte, auf mehrere Zentimeter für verankerte Proben, sowie im letzteren Fall einen bedeutend langsameren Abfall der Scherfestigkeit bei grösseren Verschiebungen. Ähnlich wurde auch für homogenes, also nicht durch diskrete Trennflächen zerlegtes Gebirge eine Erhöhung der Verformbarkeit bis zum Erreichen des Bruchs sowie ein sanfteres Abfallen der Festigkeit bei weitergehender Verformung infolge einer voll gebetteten Ankerung (Vernagelung) beobachtet (Egger, 1979a, S. 599).

Da wohl die am Umfang eines Felshohlraums auftretenden Verformungen (ϵ) prinzipiell vom Ausbruchsradius unabhängig sind, die Verschiebungen jedoch - die bevorzugt entlang von Trennflächen stattfinden - proportional mit der Größe wachsen und bei Kavernen üblicher Abmessungen leicht Zentimeterbeträge erreichen (Abb. 6), ist der in den Versuchen beobachtete Effekt der Ankerung von besonderer Bedeutung für die Erhaltung des ursprünglichen Gebirgsverbandes im hohlraumnahen Bereich.

Die Aufgabe der tiefgreifenden Stabilisierung des Gebirges, insbesondere die Sicherung von größeren, etwa durch Störungen begrenzten Felskeilen, wird hingegen vorteilhaft mit entsprechend langen vorgespannten Freispielankern gelöst: durch die Vorspannung bleibt die ursprüngliche Verzahnung bestmöglich erhalten; treten dennoch Verschiebungen auf, so wirkt das Spannglied wie eine elastische Feder, deren Wirksamkeit auch bei größeren Verformungen erhalten bleibt. Ankerkraft- und Verschiebungsmessungen mittels Extenso- oder Deflektometer (Abb.10) erlauben, dem Gebirge gleichsam den Puls zu fühlen und die Sicherungsmaßnahmen optimal den jeweiligen Gegebenheiten anzupassen. Im Kavernenbau bedeutet das nicht nur eine kontinuierliche Kontrolle der Standsicherheit des Bauwerks, sondern gewöhnlich auch eine nennenswerte Einsparung an Stützmitteln.

ZUSAMMENSPIEL VON INGENIEURGEOLOGIE UND GEOMECHANIK

Die heutige Praxis bei Projektierung und Bau von Kavernen wird von vielen Praktikern in der Weise charakterisiert, daß zwar den geologischen Untersuchungen viel mehr Raum eingeräumt wird als in früheren Zeiten, daß aber die gegenseitige Abstimmung zwischen der Arbeit der Geologen und der der Ingenieure weit weniger gut funktioniert, als dies vor wenigen Jahrzehnten der Fall war. Weltweit bedauern Ingenieurgeologen, daß die Ingenieure viel weniger als früher bereit seien, die geologischen Gegebenheiten zu beachten und echte Konsequenzen daraus zu ziehen. Ebenso weltweit aber klagen Ingenieure darüber, daß ihnen die geologische Situation in einer viel zu akademischen Weise und in einer Darstellungsform präsentiert werde, welche nicht in ihrer Sprache geschrieben und nicht in ihrer Zeichensprache dargestellt sei.

Heutigen Tages ist es um die Vorerhebung der geologischen, auch der Gefügedaten meist bestens bestellt. Nicht das gleiche kann gesagt werden von der ingenieurgeologischen Präsentation dieser Daten, welche bereits eine Auswahl aus den Beobachtungen darstellen muß und in

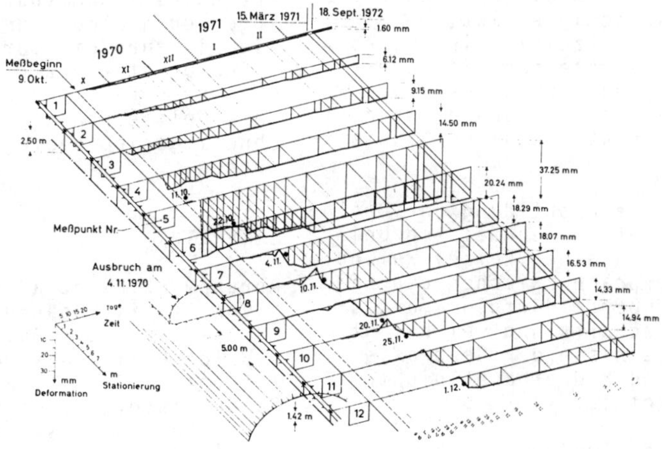

Abb. 10: Deformationsverlauf der IDI-Meßkette in der Kaverne Waldeck II

einer Form geschehen sollte, welche dem Ingenieur verständlich, ja für diesen sogar möglichst anregend sein sollte. Der schwierigste aber ist der dritte Schritt geotechnischer Vorbereitung: die felsmechanisch-felsbauliche Interpretation der geologischen Daten und deren Umsetzung (oder Übersetzung) in ein geomechanisches Modell. Eben diese Transformation, zu welcher viel Intuition, ebenso viel Ingenieurerfahrung wie geologische Kenntnisse gehören, bietet dann die Grundlage für Konstruktion und Berechnung des Bauwerkes. Dabei sollte die interdisziplinäre Zusammenarbeit keineswegs in einem Abschließenden Bericht einer geotechnischen Arbeitsgruppe enden, welcher dann einer Gruppe von Projektanten übergebenwird, sondern sie sollte fortgesetzt werden bis zum Ende der Projektierung, ja bis über das Ende der Bauherstellung hinaus.

Drei Ursachen können für die neuerlich wieder auftretenden Unvollkommenheiten geotechnischer Zusammenarbeit genannt werden:

- Aufseiten der Ingenieure fehlt fast an allen heutigen Universitäten der von Stini und seiner ganzen Generation für unerläßlich gehaltene gründliche Einführungsunterricht in die Möglichkeiten und Methoden der Ingenieurgeologie, welcher allein imstande ist, eine Verständnisgrundlage abzugeben für das so notwendige Gespräch zwischen den in völlig anderen Gedankenzusammenhängen denkenden Technikern und Geologen, und welcher allein geeignet ist, beim Ingenieur rechtzeitig ein ausreichendes Interesse für die Untergrundbedingungen zu wecken, von denen er ja mehr abhängig ist als von vielen statischen und Baustofffragen.

- Aber auch die Ausbildung der Geologen geschieht an den meisten Universitäten in einer Weise, welche für das Gespräch zwischen den Fakultäten äußerst dürftige Voraussetzungen schafft und welche auf die Erfordernisse der Geopraxis nur wenig oder überhaupt nicht ausgerichtet ist.

  Wenn Geologen meinen, sich die erforderlichen Kenntnisse durch eine Ergänzungsausbildung in Bodenmechanik oder Felsmechanik aneignen zu können, ist das ein Irrtum. Ingenieurgeologie ist nicht gleich Geologie plus Bodenmechanik oder Felsmechanik, ist auch mehr als Angewandte Geologie, sondern ist eine eigene Disziplin, welche die geologischen Sachbestände unter einem gänzlich anderen Gesichtswinkel betrachtet, als es der Fachgeologe tut.

  Sie arbeitet mit gänzlich anderen Forschungs- und Untersuchungsmethoden; sie kennt und beantwortet alle den Ingenieur bedrängenden Fragen, die der Fachgeologe in der Regel nicht beantworten kann und welche der Ingenieur mangels Einfühlung in die Gesteinswelt oft gar nicht stellt.

- Bodenmechanik und Felsmechanik haben quantitative Methoden der Berechnung und Beurteilung entwikkelt, welche in weit höherem Maße das Interesse der Ingenieure finden als die niemals ganz zu quantifizierenden, oft nur qualitativ anzugebenden geologischen Fakten. Die Freude am Quantifizieren schlägt in ein Mißbehagen an allem nicht so recht Quantifizierbarem und in dessen Mißachtung um.

Wir stehen nicht an zu erklären, daß die Anwendungen der Felsmechanik in der Felsbaupraxis geradezu gefahrbringend sein können, wenn sie nicht auf eine enge Vertrautheit mit der geologischen Materie und auf eine intensive Zusammenarbeit zwischen Ingenieurgeologen und Geoingenieur, wie sie zur Zeit vorbildlich in China praktiziert wird, gegründet ist. Eher kann Ingenieurgeologie ohne Felsmechanik als Felsmechanik ohne Ingenieurgeologie praktiziert werden.

LITERATUR

Abraham, K.H. et al.1974, Vergleich von Statik, Spannungsoptik und Messungen beim Bau der Kaverne Waldeck II, Rock Mechanics, Suppl.3, S. 143, Springer-Verlag

Baudendistel, M. et al. 1970, Einfluß von Diskontinuitäten auf die Spannungen und Deformationen in der Umgebung einer Tunnelröhre, Rock Mechanics, Vol. II, S. 17

Descoeudres, F. u. Egger, P. 1977, Monitoring System for Large Underground Openings - Experiences from the Grimsel-Oberaar Scheme, Internat. Sympos. on "Field Measurements in Rock Mechanics", Zürich

Egger, P. et al 1971, Die Ankerung für den Kraftwerksschacht Vianden, Sympos. SIMR, Nancy 1971, III-4

Egger, P. 1973, Einfluß des Post-Failure-Verhaltens von Fels auf den Tunnelbau, Veröff. Inst.f. Bodenmech. u. Felsmech., Univ. Karlsruhe, H. 57

Egger, P., 1979, I più recenti aspetti degli ancoraggi in galleria, (Diskuss.), Boll.Ass.Min.Subalp., XVI, no.3, S. 599

Endersbee, L.A. u. Hofto, E.O.,1963, Civil Engineering Design and Studies in Rock Mechanics for Poatina Underground Power Station, Tasmania, Engg.Conf., The Institution of Engineers, Australia

Föppl, L., 1957, Störungen des Spannungszustandes in der Umgebung eines Druckstollens durch Spalten, Geol.u.Bauw., Jg.23, H.1, S.4

Hoek, E. and E.T. Brown 1980, Empirical strength criterion for rock masses, ASCE, Vol. 106, GT9, S. 1013

John, K.W. 1969, Ein Ingenieurverfahren zur rechnerischen Abschätzung von Festigkeit und Verformbarkeit regelmäßig geklüfteten Felsens, Rock Mechanics, Vol. I, S. 183, Springer-Verlag

Kuhnhenn, K. u. Spaun, G. 1976, Schäden an einer Kaverne und Druckrohrleitung durch Felsgleitungen, Rock Mechanics, Suppl.5, S. 245, Springer-Verlag

Müller, L., 1951, Über das Maß der Auflockerung von Gesteinen, Geol.u.Bauw., Jg.18, S. 96

Müller, L. et al. 1977, Stability of Foundations in Complex Rock Formations, Int. Sympos. on the Geotechnics of Structurally Complex Formations, Sept. 1977 Capri

Müller, L., 1978, Der Felsbau - Bd. 3 "Tunnelbau", S. 607, Enke-Verlag, Stuttgart

Reik, G., 1977, Methoden zur Ermittlung der Felsmasseneigenschaften geklüfteter Sedimentgesteine, Jahresbericht 1976, SFB 77 "Felsmechanik" Karlsruhe

Rescher, O.J. 1968, Erfahrungen beim Ausbau der Kavernenzentrale Veytaux mit Spritzbeton und Felsankern, Felsmech.u.Ing.Geol., Suppl. 4, S. 216, Springer-Verlag

Sander, B. 1948, Einführung in die Gefügekunde, 1. Teil, Springer, Wien

Stini, J. 1955, Die Begriffsbildung in der Gebirgsdrucklehre, Geol.u.Bauw., Jg. 21, S. 169, Springer-Verlag

Vardar, M. 1977, Zeiteinfluß auf das Bruchverhalten des Gebirges in der Umgebung von Tunneln, Veröff. Inst.f. Bodenmech. u. Felsmech.,Univ. Karlsruhe, H. 72

Anschrift der Verfasser:

Leopold Müller, Univ.Prof., Baurat h.c., Dipl.-Ing. Dr.techn., Dr.mont. h.c., Ingenieurkonsulent für Bauwesen, Paracelsusstr. 2, A-5020 Salzburg, Österreich

Peter Egger, Dozent, Dr.-Ing., Laboratoire de Géotechnique, Département de Genie Civil, EPFL-ECUBLENS, CH-1015 Lausanne, Schweiz

NUCLEAR POWER PRODUCTION IN AN UNDERGROUND CHAIN

Kernenergieproduktion in einer unterirdischen Anlage

Production d'énergie nucléaire dans une installation souterraine

OVE STEPHANSON
University of Luleå, Luleå, Sweden

STEN G.A.BERGMAN
Stocksund, Sweden

BENGT Å.ÅKESSON
Chalmers University of Technology, Gothenburg, Sweden

BENGT STILLBORG
Swedish Mining Research Foundation, Kiruna, Sweden

K.IVAR SAGEFORS
WP-System AB, Stockholm, Sweden

SUMMARY

Environmental disturbances and risks of surface nuclear energy production can be considerably reduced by locating all the components of the system underground. Reactors and turbines and also intermediate and final storage for spent fuel are then linked together by tunnels. Surface transports of radioactive fuel and waste are thus eliminated. Safety in handling, transportation and storage is improved.

The halls for the reactors and turbines will need caverns with large spans and a rock cover of 40-70 m. Such caverns can also be built in medium-rated rock masses using the Rib-in-Roc method. The risk of polluting the surface environment with radioactivity after a core meltdown and vessel collapse can be considerably reduced by using safety tunnels filled with crushed rock. The contaminated gas can then expand into these tunnels instead of reaching the atmosphere.

ZUSAMMENFASSUNG

Umweltzerstörung und Risiken von Kernenenergieproduktion an der Erdoberfläche können erheblich reduziert werden, wenn alle Teile des Systems underirdisch lokalisiert werden. Reaktoren, Turbinen und auch Zwischen- und Endlager für verbrauchten Brennstoff sind durch Tunnels miteinander verbunden. Dadurch werden Oberflächentransporte von radioaktivem Brennstoff und Abfall vermieden. Die Sicherheit von Hantierung, Transport und Lagerung wird verbessert.

Für die Reaktor- und Turbinenhallen werden Kavernen mit grosser Spannweite und einer Gesteinsdecke von 40-70 m benötigt. Solche Kavernen können auch in Bergmassen von mittlerer Qualität unter Ausnutzung der Rib-in-Roc Methode gebaut werden. Das bei einer Herdschmelze und Kollaps der Reaktoreinschliessung bestehende Risiko der Oberflächenumweltverschmutzung mit Radioaktivität kann durch Einbau von mit gebrochenen Gesteinmassen gefüllten Sicherheitstunneln erheblich reduziert werden. Die giftigen Gase können dann in diese Tunnels expandieren, anstatt in die Erdathmosphäre zu entweichen.

RESUME

Les nuisances et risques de l'environnement de la production d'énergie nucléaire à la surface peuvent être considérablement réduits en plaçant sous terre tous les composants du système. Les réacteurs et turbines ainsi que le stockage intermédiaire et final de combustible utilisé sont ensuite reliés par des tunnels. Les transports de surface de combustible radioactif et de déchets sont ainsi éliminés. La sécurité dans la manutention, transport et stockage est améliorée.

Les salles pour les réacteurs et turbines nécessiteront des cavernes à grandes ouvertures et une couverture de roche de 40-70 m. De telles cavernes peuvent aussi être construites dans des masses de roche de qualité moyenne, en utilisant la méthode Rib-in-Roc. Le risqu de pollution en surface par radioactivité après une fusion du coeur et un effondrement de l´enceinte peut être réduit considérablement par la mise en oeuvre de tunnels de sécurité remplis de roche broyée. Le gaz pollué se dilate ensuite dans ces tunnels sans atteindre l´atmosphère.

1 MAIN ADVANTAGES

Nuclear power production in an underground chain has many advantages. Some are as follows:

- better land use, improved aesthetics and simplified decommissioning
- possibilities for siting near new urban areas
- safe handling, transportation and storage of radioactive fuel and waste
- controlled and limited outlet of radioactive gases and particles after a core meltdown and reactor tank failure
- good protection against sabotage, earthquakes and acts of war

2 BACKGROUND

In many countries, for example the U.S. and Sweden, the first era of nuclear power is nearly over. In the U.S. no new nuclear reactors have been ordered since 1978 (Weinberg, 1982) and previous orders for 60 new reactors have been cancelled.

In connection with the safety of nuclear power, a widespread feeling of distrust has been aroused in the public sector, reaching a peak after the accident at Three Mile Island. This in turn has led to a situation where many countries have temporarily halted further development of their nuclear power technology. In Sweden, the future of nuclear power became the subject for a referendum. It was decided that Sweden would build twelve reactors at four sites over a period of about 30 years. Of course, this decision could only be based upon the nuclear technology which was then available for public presentation.

It can be argued that nuclear energy has many advantages over conventional energy sources like oil and gas. However, it is likely that public acceptance can only be achieved by major improvements in the environmental safety of nuclear energy. One method of improving the environmental safety would be to locate the nuclear power production plant in an underground chain. It is often stated that public concern about safety of nuclear plants is emotional rather than rational. However, it should be noted that, since the 1960´s the Supreme Military Command in Sweden has recommended that nuclear power plants be placed in rock caverns.

3 COMPONENTS OF AN UNDERGROUND CHAIN

The basic idea behind nuclear power production in an underground chain is to locate the individual components in rock caverns and connect them with transport tunnels, Fig 1. The plant is reached by access tunnels from the surface. These tunnels can be protected against weapon effects.

3.1 Nuclear power plant

Recent feasibility studies in a number of countries have proposed conceptual designs for full scale nuclear power plants sited in rock caverns, see Bach (1977) and Oberth and Lindbo (1981). These investigations, conducted in Europe and North America, have demonstrated a number of potential benefits of underground siting. Small scale underground nuclear facilities have been built in Norway and Sweden and were commissioned in 1959 and 1963, respectively. The change from underground construction to surface siting of the Swedish power plants now in operation was chosen mainly for economic reasons.

A modern design for an underground nuclear power plant consists of a network of multiple caverns with interconnecting tunnels. Oberth and Lindbo (1981) state that the cavern span required for a 1300 MWe boiling water reactor (BWR) is 45 m. The largest hitherto man-made reinforced rock cavern has a span of about 35 m. Investigations made and cited by Oberth and Lindbo show that spans of 45 m or more are possible in very competent hard rock using known support methods. In less competent rock, however, such big spans will require a major technological step and special reinforcing methods will then be necessary. One such method is the Rib-in-Roc method presented by Stephansson and Stillborg at his symposium (see also inset in Fig 1).

Caverns for turbines, generators, auxiliary equipment, transformers and control station are assumed to be mined with conventional techniques.

3.2 Containment System

The rock cavern for a rock-sited nuclear plant has a concrete-steel lining that is gas-tight and also serves to strengthen the rock walls. Extreme and highly improbable accidents could possibly result in a core meltdown. When the gas pressure reaches a critical value of about 100 kPa, a valve automatically opens to an expansion tunnel filled with rock fragments and supplied with a condensation pool, Neretnieks (1980). This safety tunnel, shown at the upper left corner in Fig 1, is designed to contain all radioactive gases and particles released from the core meltdown.

At present the construction of a similar containment system is under way at one of the existing Swedish surface nuclear reactor plants.

3.3 Intermediate storage

Sweden has taken the first step towards the underground siting of nuclear energy production. An intermediate storage for spent nuclear fuel from all the Swedish nuclear power stations is now under construction, Gustafsson et al (1980). The mining of a cavern with span 22 m, height 28 m and length 55 m is now completed. The cavern will store 3000 metric tons of spent fuel in water basins.

The proposed caverns, shown in Fig 1, for intermediate storage, can be mined and reinforced using conventional techniques. Transport tunnels connect the storage with the power plant and the final repositories as indicated.

3.4 Final repository

After a limited time of storage in water at the power plant the spent fuel is transferred either to a reprocessing plant or directly to an intermediate storage facility. The concept presented here concerns the latter alternative with spent fuel. The intermediate storage time can vary between 10 and 40 years in various projects.

Final deposition could follow the WP-Cave method as described by Åkesson et al (1982) and used for example as indicated in Fig 1. The figure shows a farm of WP-Cave repositories, each one storing about 350 tons of spent fuel after 10 years of intermediate storage. The fuel is mounted in porous concrete balls placed in a heat stack centrally located in a large, almost spherical cavern. The remaining space in the cavern is filled with "dummy" concrete balls. The heat produced by the fuel is circulated and transferred to the surrounding rock by natural convection. About 40 m outside the central 40 m span cavern a clay barrier is constructed which completely surrounds the storage cavern. This engineered barrier is about 5 m thick and consists of a mixture of 20 % bentonite clay and 80 % quartz sand. The barrier has a high swelling capacity and a very low hydraulic conductivity. The barrier is built by use of modified cut-and-fill mining technique. The WP-Cave is estimated to be completely dry for more than 1000 years after closure of the repository.

One of the main advantages of the WP-Cave concept is that the repositories can be constructed in rock masses of mediocre quality. Thus no rock quality above that needed for the other components in the production line is required. The design can also be adapted for fairly easy retrieval of the spent fuel during the first hundreds of years. The limited volume of an individual WP-Cave means that the concept is easily adaptable to any number and size of reactors included in a particular plant, and that it is possible to have a continuous construction program in progress for big plants.

The more "conventional" repository layouts intended for igneous rock masses might also be used. One example is the Swedish KBS-concept, Nilsson (1980). These lay-outs use a horizontal system of parallel storage tunnels at a depth of 500-1000 m with appurtenant transport and service tunnels and shafts. The pattern of the storage tunnels will be adapted to the geologic conditions as encountered at the site. The waste canisters are stored in vertical boreholes drilled at intervals in the storage tunnel floors. The drillholes are lined with about 0.3 m thick blocks of highly compacted bentonite. The blocks will swell upon up-take of water and then form a buffer with very low conductivity against the ground water in the rock mass.

At present it seems to be a general consensus of opinion in Sweden that the KBS concept will require rock masses with high quality as regards strength, lack of joints and low hydraulic conductivity. If this opinion prevails, it will make this type of repository concept less adaptable to the idea of an underground chain presented here (Fig 1), since it would impose restrictions on the choice of sites for the reactor plants.

4 DISCUSSION

Statutory guidelines for siting and public opinion do not permit near-urban siting of surface nuclear power plants. A close study

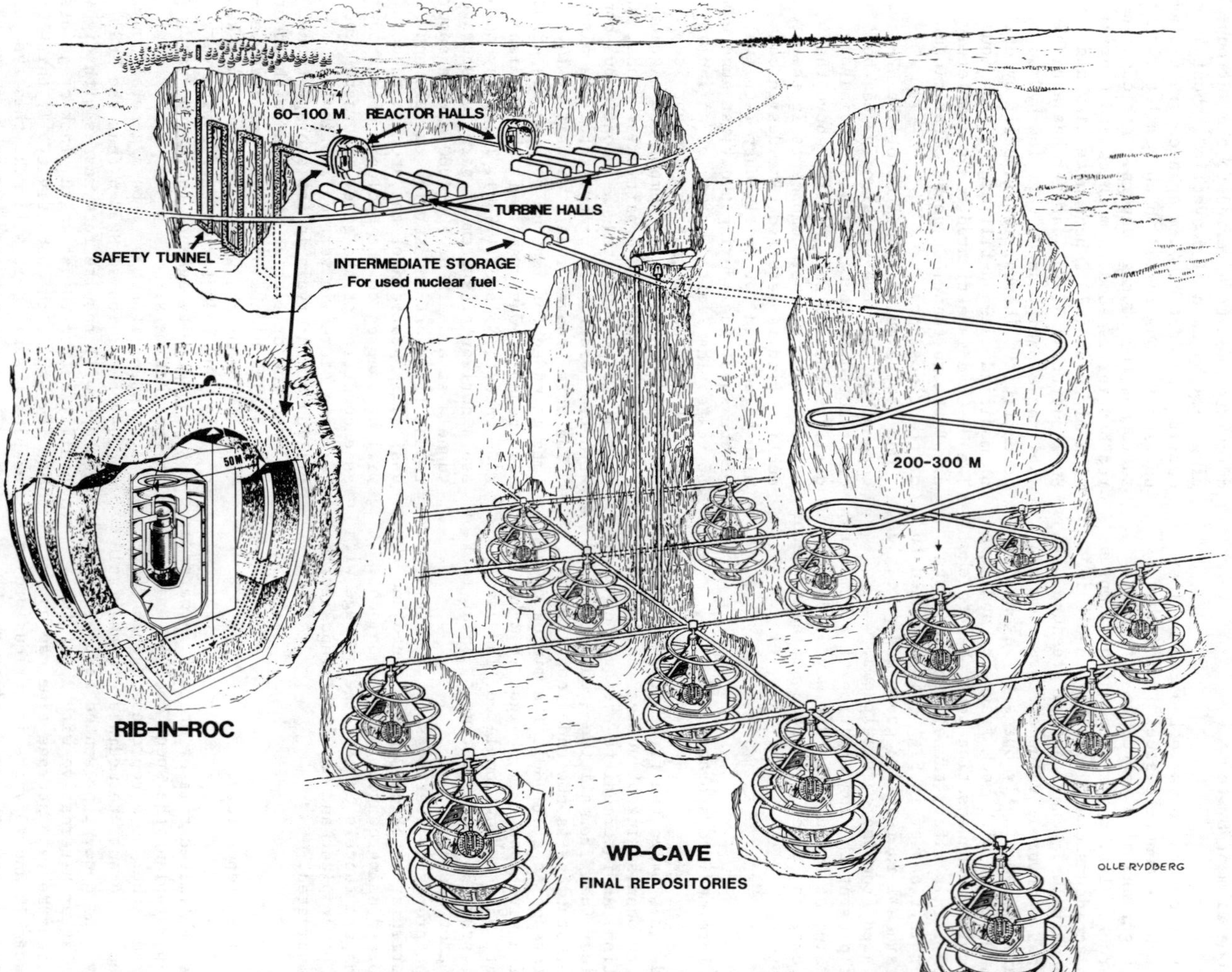

Fig 1 Nuclear power production in an underground chain. Reactor halls, turbine halls, intermediate storage and final repositories are connected with tunnels.

of the advantages and risks of underground siting of the total nuclear production line may result in permission to construct near-urban sited underground nuclear plants and storage facilities. A near-urban siting would make the use of waste heat attractive and thus make the site more economic.

Recent feasibility studies in a number of countries have revealed a number of benefits of underground siting of nuclear power plants, e.g. improved containment of radionuclides, increased plant protection and security and reduction in seismic loading on nuclear equipment and structures. These benefits can be realized only in combination with higher plant construction costs as listed by Obert and Lindbo (1981). There are also certain operational penalties such as risks for submersion and fire as well as construction delays of the order of 7 to 30 months depending upon the design used.

If we pay due regard to the growing educated public opinion, which means that the risks of surface nuclear reactors are acceptable neither in peace-time nor in war, and if we note the growing public distrust in the old infallibility dogma of technical experts, we should rate the benefits of underground siting much higher than the operational and economic penalties. It is conceivable that the latter might be reduced or indeed eleminated by new ideas and intellegent work. We might even be humble enough to acknowledge the possibility that there are rational motives behind the views expressed by the public.

A number of countries, including Sweden, face the problem of adding containment systems to the nuclear plants in operation today. An underground location of the total nuclear power chain would facilitate the design and construction of containment systems.

A central intermediate storage for spent fuel is now under construction in Sweden, and the final central repository is at present planned to be located at about 500 m depth in granitic rocks. Hence, two components of the nuclear power chain are already in the process of being located underground. One further step towards a complete production of nuclear energy underground will lead to safer handling, tranportation and storage of radioactive fuel and waste. It will improve the use of land and cause less environmental disturbances, reduce the consequences of possible accidents and facilitate the decommissioning of nuclear power stations and the demolishing and removal of nuclear structures.

5 REFERENCES

Åkesson, B., Bergman, S.G.A. and Sagefors, I. 1982, WP-Cave for dry underground storage of high-level nuclear waste. International Symposium on Rock Mechanics related to Caverns and Pressure Shafts, Aachen, May 26-28, 1982, vol. 2, pp. 861-872.

Bach, P. 1977, A summary of studies on underground nuclear power plant siting. Underground space. vol. 2, no.1. pp. 47-51.

Gustafsson, H., Hedman, T. and Larsson, H. 1980, An underground storage for spent nuclear fuel in Sweden. Proceedings of the International Symposium Rockstore 80, Stockholm, June 23-27, 1980, pp. 881-888.

Neretnieks, I. 1980, Safety Tunnels for Core Melting in Nuclear Power Plants. Underground Space, vol. 5, pp. 179-180.

Nilsson, L.B. 1980, Condensed version of the Swedish KBS concept regarding final storage of high level radioactive waste and spent fuel. Proceedings of the International Symposium, Rockstore 80, Stockholm, June 23-27, 1980, pp. 955-961.

Oberth, R.C. and Lindbo, T. 1981. Underground Nuclear Power Plants: State-of-the-Art. Underground Space, vol. 5, pp. 375-383.

Stephansson, O. and Stillborg, B. 1982, Rib-in-Roc prereinforcement system for large caverns. International Symposium on Rock Mechanics related to Caverns and Pressure Shafts, Aachen, May 26-28, 1982, vol. 1, pp. 451-458.

Weinberg, A.M. 1982, Reinventing nuclear power. Science 82, May, p. 3.

FELSMECHANISCHE PROBLEME BEI DER PLANUNG VON KAVERNEN FÜR WASSERKRAFTANLAGEN

Rock mechanics problems arising during the planning of caverns for hydroelectric power plants

Problèmes de mécanique des roches en rapport avec la planification des cavernes pour des centrales hydroélectriques

WALTER WITTKE
Rheinisch-Westfälische Technische Hochschule Aachen, Bundesrepublik Deutschland

SUMMARY
Both an appropriate description of the rock mass stress-strain behaviour and a reliable estimation of the in-situ stresses represent important prerequisites for the economic design of large underground openings in rock. The influence of the in-situ state of stress on the secondary stresses and deformations induced in the rock mass during excavation of a cavern are investigated on the basis of analysis results obtained using the finite element method. These investigations enable recommendations for an economic design of the support. Finally, some problems for the design of underground openings with very large span are discussed.

ZUSAMMENFASSUNG
Eine wesentliche Voraussetzung für den wirtschaftlichen Entwurf großer Felshohlräume ist eine zutreffende Beschreibung des Spannungsdehnungsverhaltens des Gebirges sowie die richtige Einschätzung des Primärspannungszustandes. Auf der Grundlage von Berechnungsergebnissen nach der Methode der Finiten Elemente wird der Einfluß des Primärspannungszustandes auf die Spannungen und Verformungen im Fels beim Ausbruch einer Kaverne untersucht. Daraus ergeben sich Hinweise für eine wirtschaftliche Dimensionierung und Bemessung der Sicherungsmittel. Abschließend wird auf die Probleme, die sich daraus für den Entwurf von Hohlräumen mit sehr großen Abmessungen ergeben, eingegangen.

RESUME
Une condition importante pour le projet économique des cavités rocheuses est une description précise de la relation entre les contraintes et les déformations de la roche ainsi qu'une estimation exacte de l'état de contrainte naturel. Les effets de l'état de contrainte naturel sur les contraintes et les déformations dans la roche lors de l'extraction d'une caverne sont examinés sur base de résultats calculés suivant la méthode des éléments finis. Il en résulte des remarques concernant le calcul économique et le dimensionnement du revêtement et du boulonnage du rocher. Pour conclure les problèmes concernant le projet de cavités à très grand métrage sont commentés.

1 EINLEITUNG

In diesem Beitrag soll über einige felsmechanische Probleme berichtet werden, die im Zusammenhang mit dem Entwurf und der Ausführung von Kavernen für Wasserkraftanlagen häufig auftreten. Nach den Erfahrungen des Autors, der in den letzten Jahren an mehreren Projekten dieser Art als Berater beteiligt war, liegt der Schlüssel zur Lösung dieser Probleme in der richtigen Einschätzung des Spannungsdehnungsverhaltens des Gebirges sowie der Primärspannungen.

Deshalb wird zunächst kurz eine Modellvorstellung für das Spannungsdehnungsverhalten von Fels erläutert, die in den vergangenen Jahren vom Autor und seinen Mitarbeitern entwickelt wurde [9, 14]. Dabei wird insbesondere auf die Schwierigkeit eingegangen, die erforderlichen felsmechanischen Kennwerte zu ermitteln. Es wird gezeigt, daß einige weit verbreitete und sehr oft angewendete felsmechanische Versuche bei bestimmten Gebirgsverhältnissen hierfür nicht oder nur begrenzt geeignet sind. Anschließend wird auf den Einfluß der Primärspannungen auf die Spannungsumlagerung und die Verformungen beim Ausbruch einer Kaverne eingegangen. Daraus ergeben sich einige Hinweise auf Probleme, die sich für die Standsicherheit von Kavernen ergeben können. Diese Probleme, wie auch die Vorgehensweise bei der Bemessung und Überprüfung von Sicherungsmaßnahmen, werden an einigen Beispielen erläutert.

Abschließend werden einige Schlußfolgerungen, die sich daraus für den Entwurf von Kavernen mit großen Abmessungen ergeben, gezogen.

2. SPANNUNGSDEHNUNGSVERHALTEN VON FELS

Die Trennflächen im Fels, die in Form von Kleinklüften, Großklüften sowie von weit durchgehenden Störungen auftreten können, haben bekanntlich einen maßgeblichen Einfluß auf das Spannungsdehnungsverhalten. An einer Vielzahl von Felsarten läßt sich zeigen, daß, durch die Entstehung bedingt, eine oder mehrere Scharen annähernd ebener und zueinander paralleler Trennflächen vorhanden sind, die das Gestein entweder teilweise oder vollständig durchtrennen. Es hat sich bewährt, einen solchen Fels durch ein Gefügemodell zu beschreiben, das sowohl ein Modell für das Korngefüge des ungeklüfteten Gesteins als auch für das Trennflächengefüge beinhaltet [14]. In den Bildern 1 bis 4 sind vier Beispiele für die Zuordnung unterschiedlicher Felsarten zu entsprechenden Gefügemodellen dargestellt.

Der in Bild 1a dargestellte Granit läßt sich durch die Kombination eines richtungslosen Korngefüges für das ungeklüftete Gestein und eines allgemeinen räumlichen Trennflächengefüges beschreiben (Bild 1b). Bei dem in Bild 2a dargestellten Schiefer handelt es sich um einen Fels mit flächigem Korngefüge und einem allgemeinen räumlichen Trennflächengefüge, wobei die Schieferung sowohl die flächenhafte Textur des Gesteins bestimmt, als auch als Trennflächenschar S ausgebildet ist (Bild 2b). Auch ein Sandstein mit

a Granit

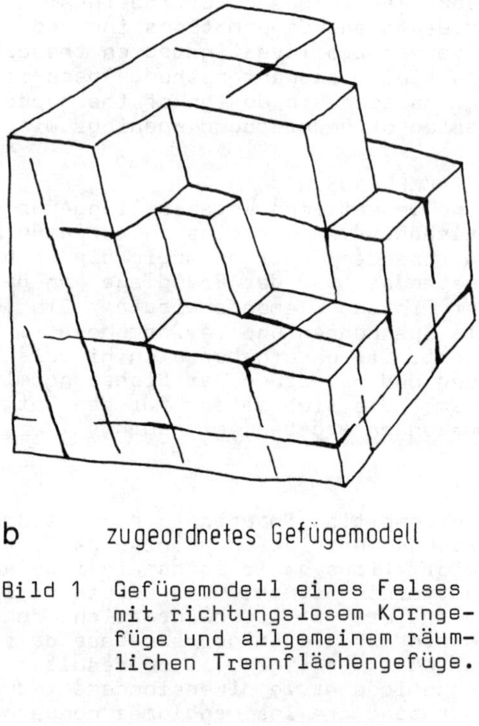

b zugeordnetes Gefügemodell

Bild 1 Gefügemodell eines Felses mit richtungslosem Korngefüge und allgemeinem räumlichen Trennflächengefüge.

a Schiefer

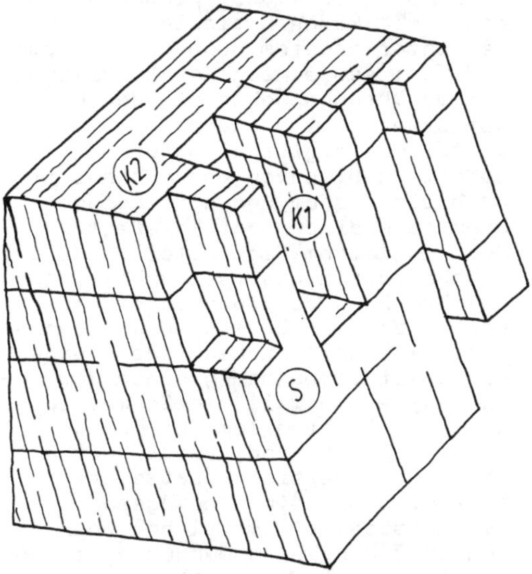

b zugeordnetes Gefügemodell

Bild 2 Gefügemodell eines Felses mit flächigem Korngefüge und allgemeinem räumlichen Trennflächengefüge.

a Sandstein

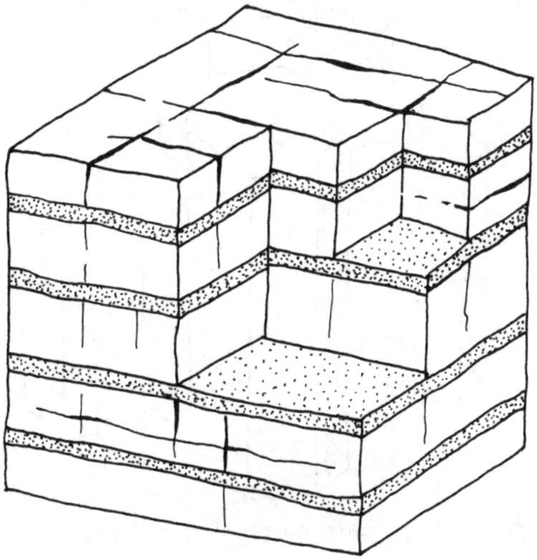

b zugeordnetes Gefügemodell

Bild 3 Gefügemodell für einen Fels mit gefüllten Schichtfugen.

gefüllten Schichtfugen aus feinkörnigen Böden kann einem geometrischen Gefügemodell zugeordnet werden (Bild 3). Der in Bild 4a dargestellte Basalt ist ein Beispiel für einen Fels mit richtungslosem Korngefüge und "linearem" Trennflächengefüge (Bild 4b).

Wenn man diese Gefügemodelle in mechanische Modelle umsetzen will, dann stellt sich zunächst die Frage, ob es dabei notwendig ist, jede Trennfläche mit ihren mechanischen Eigenschaften einzeln nachzubilden, um das Spannungsdehnungsverhalten des Felses zutreffend zu beschreiben. Abgesehen davon, daß es nicht mög-

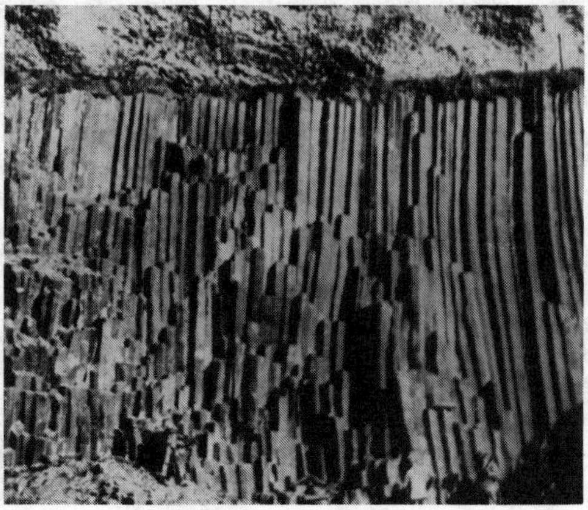

a Basalt

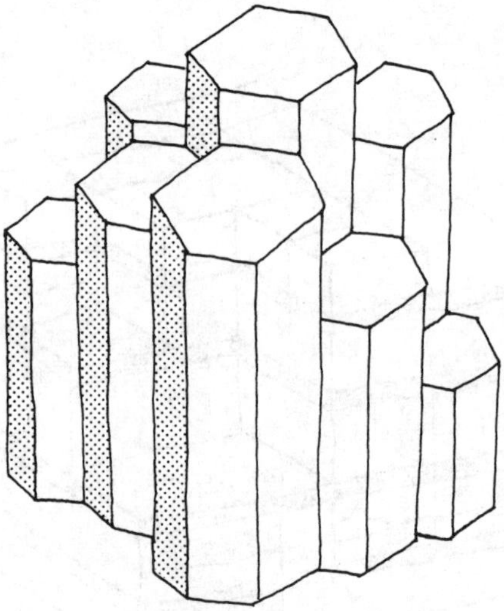

b zugeordnetes Gefügemodell

Bild 4 Gefügemodell eines Felses mit richtungslosem Korngefüge und "linearem" Trennflächengefüge.

lich sein wird, alle Trennflächen in ihrer Lage und ihrer Ausbildung in der Natur zu erkunden und somit geometrisch zu erfassen, wird vom Autor die Auffassung vertreten, daß man in vielen Fällen auch gar nicht danach streben sollte, weil der Fels unter bestimmten Bedingungen durch ein sogenanntes "homogenes Modell" beschrieben werden kann, das im folgenden näher erläutert werden soll [14].

Der Grundgedanke für dieses homogene Modell ist im Grunde nicht neu und soll zunächst an einer analogen Vorgehensweise aus der Bodenmechanik erklärt werden. Bekanntlich ist auch ein Boden - wie ein Fels - ein inhomogenes System, das aus den drei Phasen Feststoff, Luft und Wasser besteht. Ein Ausschnitt aus einem mit grobkörnigem Boden gefüllten Volumen zeigt das Bild 5. Das dargestellte Korngerüst, für das der Einfachheit halber angenommen wird, daß die Poren nur mit Luft gefüllt sind, sei durch die Normalspannung $\overline{\sigma}$ belastet. Führt man einen horizontalen Schnitt A-A' durch den Boden, so ergibt sich eine inhomogene Spannungsverteilung. Überall dort, wo ein Bodenkorn geschnitten wird, ist eine Spannung wirksam und im Bereich der Poren ist die Spannung gleich Null. Die Größe der Spannungen in den Einzelkörnern richtet sich dabei unter anderem nach deren Größe und Form sowie nach der Ausbildung der Berührungspunkte mit den Nachbarkörnern. Eine andere Spannungsverteilung ergibt sich für den Schnitt B-B' durch das Korngerüst. Auch die Verformungen in beiden Schnitten sind nicht konstant, sondern ungleichmäßig verteilt (Bild 5a)

Theoretisch wäre es denkbar, zur Beschreibung des Spannungsdehnungsverhaltens des Bodens, das Korngerüst im Detail nachzubilden. Wegen des damit verbundenen hohen Rechenaufwandes und weil die Geometrie der Körner und vor allem des Korngerüstes nicht bekannt sind, verzichtet man aber auf derartige Ansätze. Vielmehr wird mit einem homogenen Ersatzmaterial mit mittleren Spannungen $\overline{\sigma}$ und Verformungen $\overline{\delta}$ gerechnet (Bild 5b). Eine solche rechnerische Betrachtungsweise ist allerdings nur zulässig, wenn die Abmessungen l des betrachteten Bereichs groß sind im Vergleich zu den mittleren Abmessungen der Bodenkörner $\overline{d}$ (Bild 6).

Analog ist der Grundgedanke hinsichtlich der Formulierung eines homogenen Modells für einen klüftigen Fels, zu dessen Veranschaulichung Bild 7 dienen soll. Hier ist ein Fels mit einer Schar teilweise durchtrennter und abschnittweise offener Trennflächen dargestellt. Bei einer Belastung normal zu den Trennflächen ergeben sich auch hier inhomogene Spannungsverteilungen und Verformungen, die sich außerdem

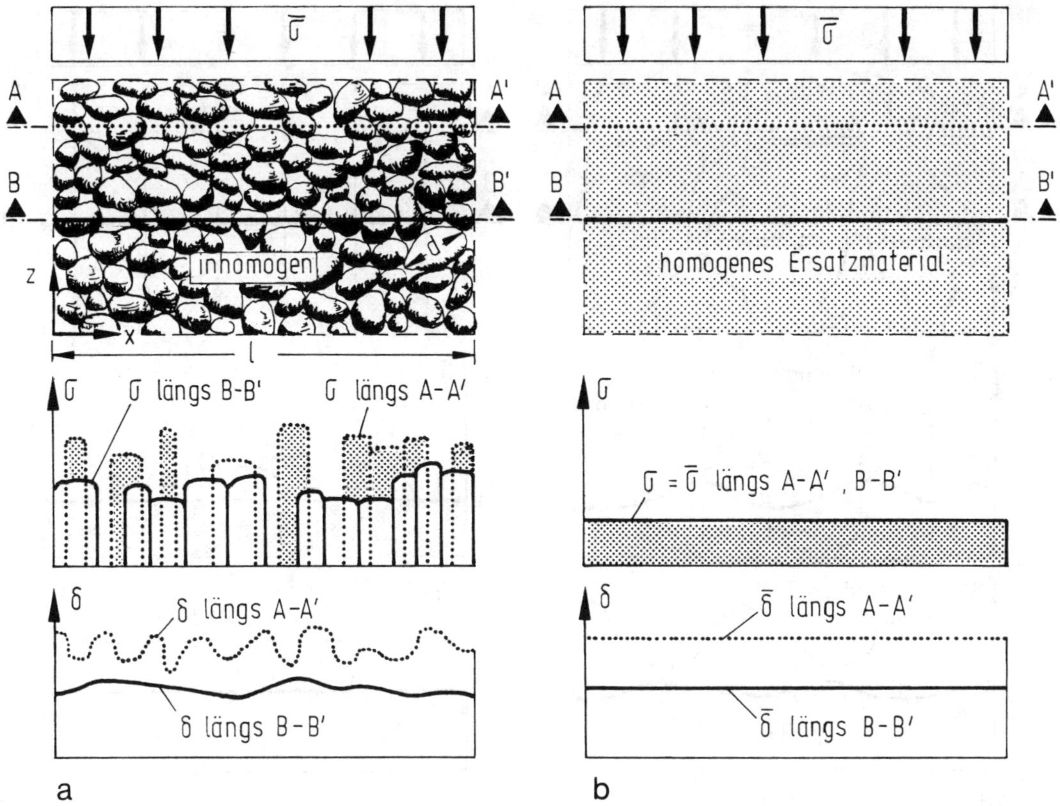

Bild 5 Homogenes Modell für das Spannungsdehnungsverhalten eines Bodens.

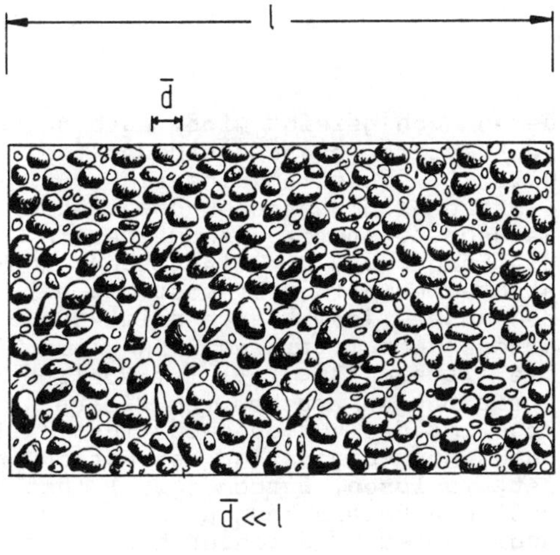

Bild 6 Ausschnitt, für den die Anwendung des homogenen Modells auf das Spannungsdehnungsverhalten eines Bodens zulässig ist.

je nach Lage des jeweiligen Schnitts (A-A', B-B', Bild 7a) deutlich voneinander unterscheiden. Mit dem homogenen Modell kann auch hier mit einem Ersatzmaterial mit mittleren Spannungen $\overline{\sigma}$ und Verformungen $\overline{\delta}$ gerechnet werden (Bild 7b). Auch bei einem klüftigen Fels ist jedoch die Anwendung des homogenen Modells nur zulässig, wenn die Abmessungen des betrachteten Bereichs groß sind im Vergleich zur Größe der durch die Trennflächen begrenzten Körper bzw. zur Erstreckung der Trennflächenabschnitte und zum Abstand der Trennflächen (Bild 8).

Wenn man also ein homogenes Modell anwenden darf, dann stellt sich als nächstes die Frage, wie man die Verformbarkeit des Gebirges beschreibt. Solange die Spannungen in bestimmten Grenzen bleiben, nämlich unterhalb der Festigkeit, ist dies in vielen Fällen durch eine linear elastische Spannungsdehnungsbeziehung möglich. Diese Annahme läßt sich, wie weiter

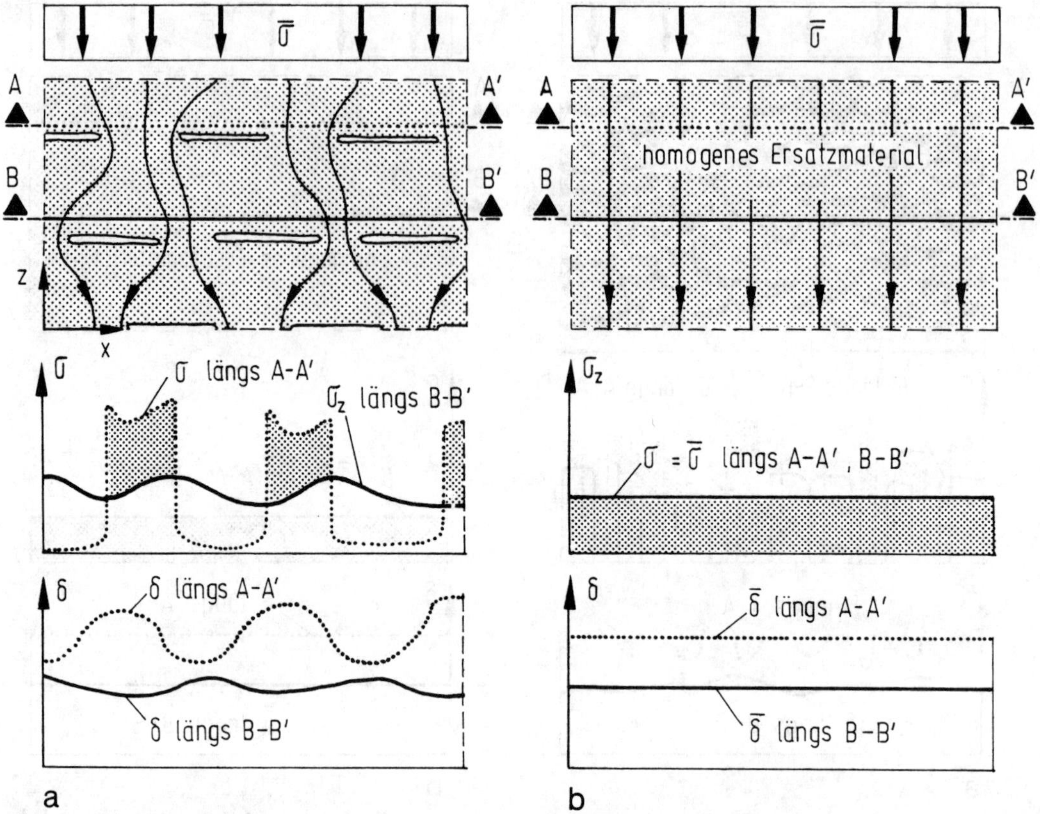

Bild 7 Homogenes Modell für das Spannungsdehnungsverhalten eines klüftigen Felses.

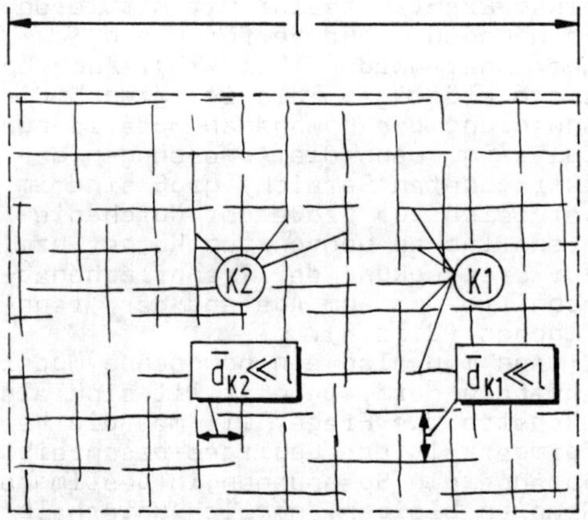

Bild 8 Klüftiger Fels mit zwei Trennflächenscharen.

unten noch gezeigt wird, auch durch Versuchsergebnisse begründen (vgl. Bild 12). Wenn man eine linear elastische Spannungsdehnungsbeziehung verwendet, stellt sich weiterhin die Frage, wie die elastischen Konstanten gewählt oder bestimmt werden müssen, damit sich beim Aufbringen der mittleren Spannungen $\overline{\sigma}$ die Mittelwerte $\overline{\delta}$ der tatsächlichen Verformungen ergeben. Um dieses Problem, das zum gegenwärtigen Zeitpunkt noch Gegenstand der Forschung ist, zu lösen, werden sowohl theoretische Untersuchungen als auch Modellversuche durchzuführen sein, die durch Feldversuche und -messungen zu ergänzen sind. Es handelt sich hierbei um eine der Hauptaufgaben der Felsmechanik überhaupt.

Im folgenden soll erläutert werden, wie die Festigkeit des Gebirges im Sinne des homogenen Modells beschrieben werden kann. Die Festigkeit des ungeklüfteten Gesteins läßt sich in den Fällen, in denen das Korngefüge keine ausgezeichneten Richtungen aufweist, in guter Näherung durch eine Mohr-Coulomb'sche Bruchbedingung beschreiben (Bild 9a). Flächen mit abgeminderter Festigkeit, wie sie Trennflächen oder auch Flächen latenter Spaltbarkeit im Gestein (Schieferung oder Schichtung) darstellen, können durch ein bilineares Bruchkriterium beschrieben werden, wie dies schon von Patton [5] vorgeschlagen wurde (Bild 9b). Streng genommen wird sich bei rauhen Trennflächen eine nichtlineare Bruchbedingung ergeben [1, 3, 8], die sich aber in vielen Fällen durch zwei Geraden annähern läßt [14].

Die Überlagerung beider Bruchkriterien führt bei einem klüftigen Fels zu einer stark anisotropen Festigkeit, wie dies in Bild 10 am Beispiel eines Felses mit zwei aufeinander senkrecht stehenden Trennflächenscharen dargestellt ist. Dieses Verhalten wurde vielfach durch Modellversuche und auch durch Laborversuche an Gesteinsproben bestätigt [2, 6].

Um das in Bild 10 dargestellte

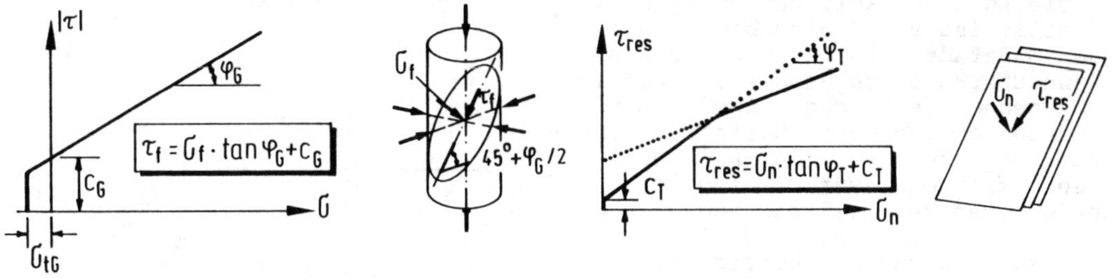

a Gestein (isotrop)

b Trennflächen mit abgeminderter Festigkeit

Bild 9 Bruchkriterien für Gestein und Trennflächen.

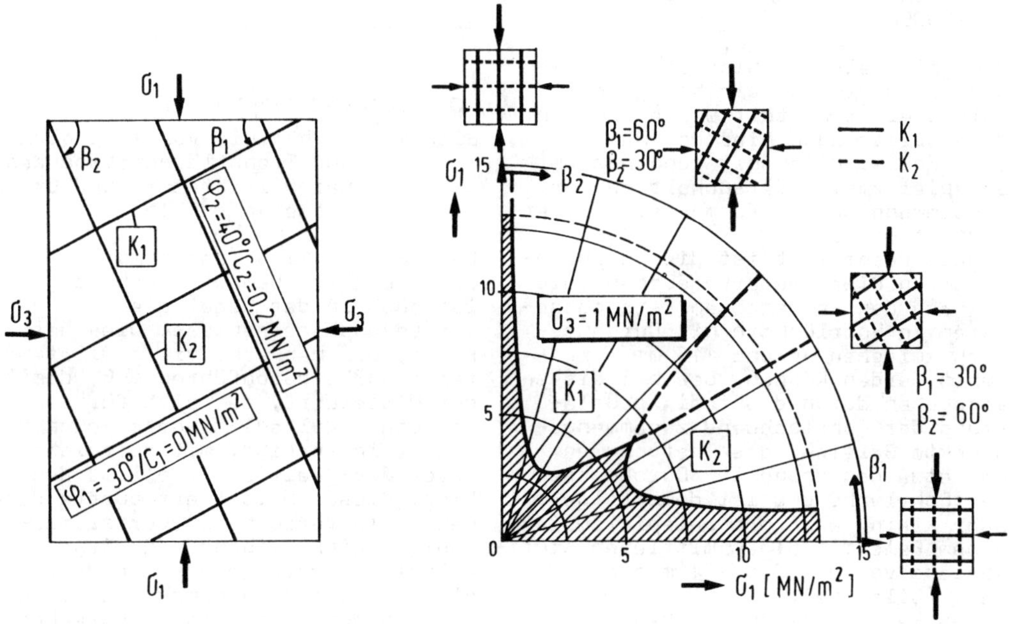

Bild 10 Anisotrope Festigkeit von klüftigem Fels mit zwei Trennflächenscharen.

Festigkeitsverhalten, das streng genommen nur dort zutreffend ist, wo beide Trennflächen K_1 und K_2 mit den mittleren Scherparametern $\varphi_1 = 30^o$, $c_1 = 0$, $\varphi_2 = 40^o$, $c_2 = 0{,}2$ MN/m^2 vorhanden sind, auf das homogene Modell zu übertragen, geht man davon aus, daß diese Festigkeitsanisotropie in jedem Punkt des Gebirges vorhanden ist. Auch hinsichtlich der Festigkeit ist die Anwendung eines homogenen Modells nur dann zulässig, wenn die Abmessungen des betrachteten Bereichs l groß sind im Vergleich zu den mittleren Erstreckungen und Abständen der Trennflächen (vgl. Bild 8).

Die Anwendbarkeit des homogenen Modells ist somit also eine Frage des Maßstabs. Eine Grenze für die Anwendbarkeit des homogenen Modells anzugeben, ist jedoch schwierig und dürfte von der betrachteten Aufgabenstellung abhängig sein. Als Faustregel kann man aber wahrscheinlich davon ausgehen, daß das homogene Modell angewendet werden darf, wenn die Abmessungen des betrachteten Bereichs, z.B. eines Kavernendurchmessers im Vergleich zum Kluftabstand, etwa im Verhältnis 10 : 1 stehen.

3. FELSMECHANISCHE UNTERSUCHUNGSMETHODEN

Wenn mit felsmechanischen Versuchen die Kennwerte für ein homogenes Felsmodell ermittelt werden sollen, dann spielt auch hier der Maßstab eine Rolle. Dies soll zunächst am Beispiel zweier Versuchsarten zur Bestimmung des Verformungsmoduls erläutert werden.

Weit verbreitet ist die Durchführung von Dilatometerversuchen, die je nach den verwendeten Versuchsgeräten in Bohrlöchern mit Durchmessern zwischen 46 und 116 mm ausgeführt werden können. Der bei diesen Versuchen durch die radiale Belastung der Bohrlochwand zusammengedrückte Bereich, das Testvolumen, hat etwa den doppelten Durchmesser des Bohrlochs und ist demzufolge sehr klein, wenn man beispielsweise einen Fels mit einem mittleren Kluftabstand von $\overline{d} = 0{,}5 - 1$ m zugrunde legt (Bild 11a).

Man kann in einem solchen Fall nicht erwarten, daß man durch einen Dilatometerversuch eine gute Beschreibung der Verformbarkeit des

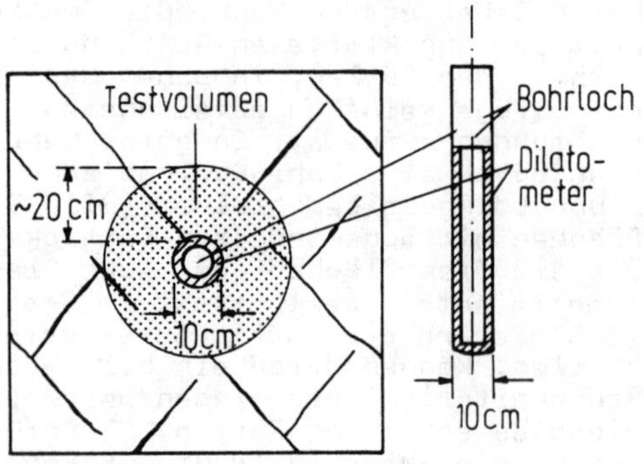

a Dilatometerversuch

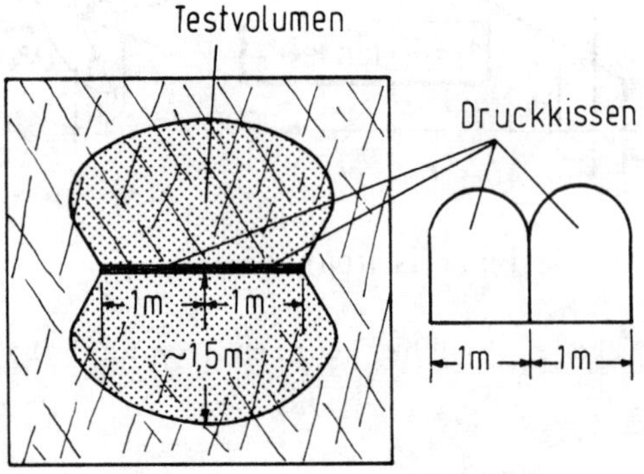

b Druckkissenversuch [7]

Bild 11 Verhältnis von Testvolumen und Trennflächenabständen bei Dilatometer- und Druckkissenversuchen.

Gebirges im Sinne des homogenen Modells erhält. Dementsprechend groß ist auch in der Regel die Streuung der Versuchsergebnisse. Dies hat zur Folge, daß man sehr viele Dilatometerversuche durchführen muß, damit der Mittelwert, der sich für den Verformungsmodul aus einer solchen Versuchsreihe ergibt, mit ausreichender Zuverlässigkeit ermittelt werden kann. Dieser Mittelwert dürfte dann, wenn alle Versuche in verhältnismäßig gleichbleibenden Gebirgsverhältnissen durchgeführt werden, in etwa dem Verformungsmodul im Sinne des homogenen Modells entsprechen [14].

Bei einem Druckkissenversuch, bei dem ein oder mehrere in den Fels gesägte Schlitze aufgeweitet werden [7], ist das Testvolumen erheblich größer und man kann auch bei größeren Kluftabständen brauchbare Ergebnisse für den Verformungsmodul erhalten (Bild 11b). In Bild 12 sind einige aus Druckkissenversuchen in verschiedenen Felsarten erhaltene Spannungsverformungslinien dargestellt, die zugleich zeigen sollen, daß die Annahme einer linearen Spannungsdehnungsbeziehung für den Fels gerechtfertigt ist, solange die Festigkeit des Gebirges nicht erreicht wird, d.h. keine größeren irreversiblen Verformungsanteile auftreten.

Bild 12a zeigt das Ergebnis für einen Granit, der einen Fels mit einer sehr geringen Verformbarkeit und hohen Festigkeit darstellt. Es ergibt sich ein für die Be- und Entlastung nahezu gleiches, linear elastisches Verhalten. Aus den für einen Schiefer erhaltenen Versuchsergebnissen ist erkennbar, daß die Verformbarkeit parallel zur Schieferung deutlich geringer als senkrecht dazu ist (Bild 12b). Auch für diesen Schiefer kann man sicherlich näherungsweise von einem linearen, wenn auch anisotropen Spannungsdehnungsverhalten ausgehen, das für Be- und Entlastung in etwa gleich ist. Die in Bild 12c und d dargestellten Spannungsverformungslinien zeigen eine deutliche Hysterese zwischen Be- und Entlastung. Die irreversiblen Verformungsanteile sind beim Sandstein (Bild 12c) im wesentlichen zeitabhängige Verformungen, die bei Dauerbelastungsversuchen bei den Laststufen 4 bzw. 6 MN/m^2 eingetreten sind. Wie sich auch bei anderen Felsarten herausgestellt hat, sind diese im Vergleich zu den Gesamtverformungen für Laststufen, die deutlich unterhalb der Festigkeit liegen, jedoch gering und konvergieren in der Regel nach wenigen Stunden. Bei dem verhältnismäßig stark verformbaren Tonstein (Bild 12d) bestehen die irreversiblen Verformungsanteile wahrscheinlich aus örtlich begrenzten plastischen Verformungen entlang von Trennflächen mit gegenüber dem Gestein

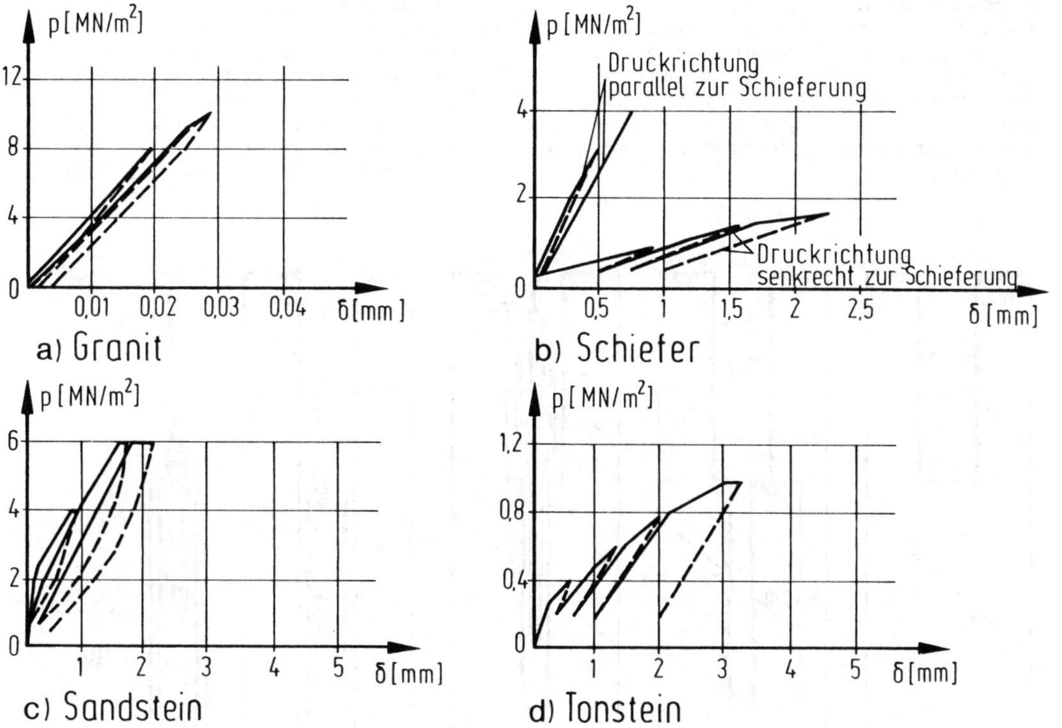

Bild 12 Aus Druckkissenversuchen in verschiedenen Felsarten erhaltene Spannungsverformungslinien.

abgeminderter Festigkeit. Daraus ergibt sich für die Erstbelastung eine immerhin noch bereichsweise lineare Spannungsverformungslinie mit einer allerdings geringeren Steigung als bei der Ent- und Wiederbelastung.

Allgemein läßt sich aus diesen Ergebnissen ableiten, daß die Abweichungen von einem linear elastischen Spannungsdehnungsverhalten umso größer sind, je geringer die Festigkeit und je größer die Verformbarkeit des Felses ist.

Auch bei den Primärspannungsmessungen spielt der Maßstab eine Rolle. Mit einer Triaxialzelle, die in ein Pilotloch mit einem Durchmesser von 38 mm eingesetzt wird, werden die Dehnungen gemessen, die infolge der Entspannung durch den Überbohrvorgang an der Bohrlochwand entstehen [4]. Da der Uberbohrdurchmesser mit 86 mm nicht viel größer ist als der Durchmesser des Pilotlochs, ist die Wanddicke des entspannten hohlzylindrischen Felskörpers sehr gering. Auch die Länge des Hohlzylinders liegt mit 45 cm allenfalls nur in der Größenordnung der Trennflächenabstände d (Bild 13). Infolge dieses kleinen Testvolumens vermitteln die Ergebnisse von Messungen, die z.B. im Einflußbereich einer trennflächenbedingten Inhomogenität des Spannungsfeldes durchgeführt werden, oft ein falsches Bild von dem großräumig vorhandenen Spannungszustand.

Dies soll am Beispiel eines mit einer vertikalen Spannung σ_0 homogen belasteten Felses erläutert werden. Besitzt dieser Fels geöffnete horizontale Trennflächen, die keine Normalspannungen über die Trennflächenufer übertragen können, dann kommt es im Bereich einer solchen Trennfläche zu der in Bild 14 skizzierten inhomogenen Spannungsverteilung. Würde man etwa in dem in Bild 14 mit A gekennzeichneten entlasteten Bereich unterhalb der Trennfläche eine Primärspannungsmessung mit einer Triaxialzelle durchführen, dann würde man eine sehr kleine vertikale Spannungskomponente ($\sigma_A = 0{,}25\sigma_0$) messen. Würde man dagegen in dem in Bild 14 mit B gekennzeichneten Bereich einer Spannungskonzentration seitlich neben der Trennfläche eine Messung durchführen, dann würde man eine sehr viel größere vertikale Spannungskomponente ($\sigma_B = 1{,}5\sigma_0$) messen. Entsprechende Unterschiede würden sich auch für andere Spannungskomponenten bei der Messung des räumlichen Spannungszustandes ergeben. Das bedeutet, daß trennflächenbedingte Inhomogenitäten des Spannungsfeldes sowohl die Größe als auch die Richtung der mit Triaxialzellen an verschiedenen Versuchsorten gemessenen Hauptspannungen beeinflussen. Nur in weitgehend ungeklüfteten Gebirgsverhältnissen führen derartige Versuche zu befriedigenden Ergebnissen.

Aufgrund der hier exemplarisch

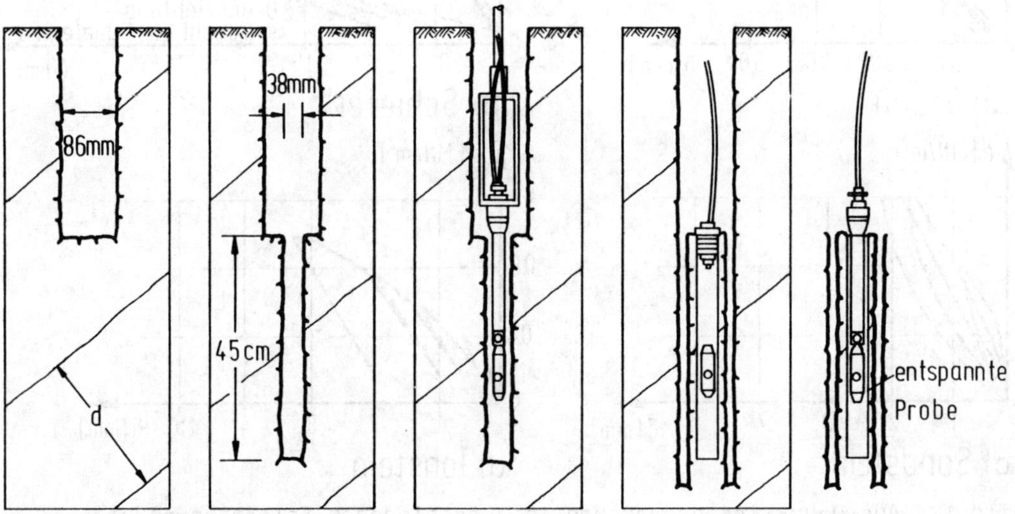

Bild 13 Primärspannungsmessungen mit einer Triaxialzelle [4].

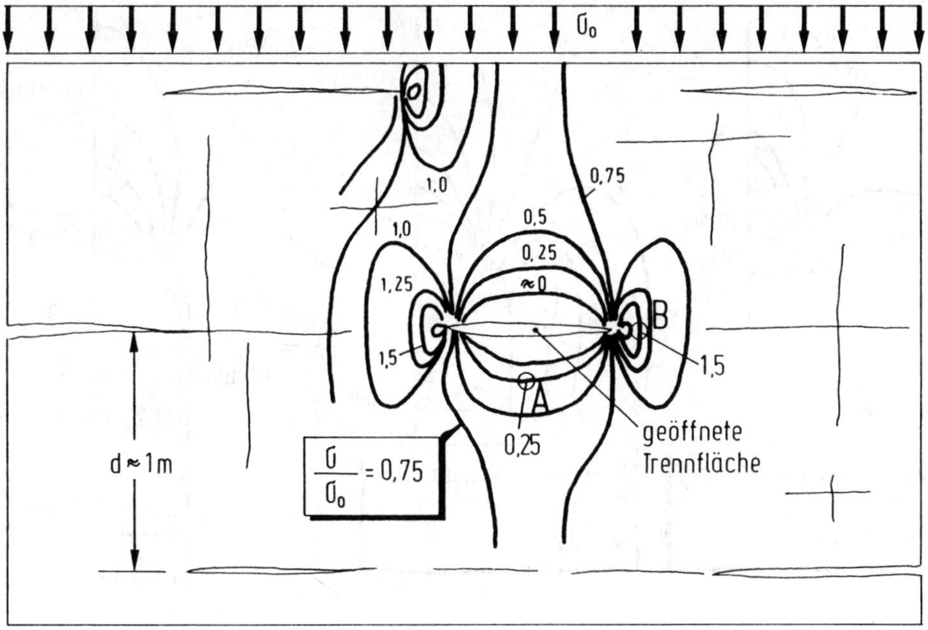

Bild 14 Spannungsverteilung um eine Trennfläche in einem homogen belasteten Fels.

aufgeführten Schwächen felsmechanischer Versuche in klüftigem Fels sollten felsmechanische Versuche, wenn es irgend geht, durch Messungen am Bauwerk ergänzt werden. Durch die Interpretation derartiger Messungen mit Hilfe numerischer Berechnungen gelangt man in vielen Fällen zu einem besseren Verständnis des großmaßstäblichen Spannungsdehnungsverhaltens und der Primärspannungen [11, 12, 14].

4. FELSMECHANISCHE GESICHTSPUNKTE BEIM ENTWURF VON KAVERNEN

In diesem Abschnitt soll zunächst am Beispiel einer 40 m hohen und 25 m breiten Kaverne der Einfluß der Primärspannungen des Gebirges auf die Spannungen und Verformungen im Bereich der Hohlraumwand in verschiedenen Ausbruchstadien verdeutlicht werden. Dazu werden die Ergebnisse einiger zweidimensionaler Berechnungen nach der Methode der Finiten Elemente (FEM) mit einem am Institut für Grundbau, Bodenmechanik, Felsmechanik und Verkehrswasserbau der RWTH Aachen entwickelten Rechenprogramm, das in [9, 14] ausführlich beschrieben ist, dargestellt und erläutert. Für den Fels wurde bei den Berechnungen von einer linear elastischen Spannungsdehnungsbeziehung mit einem Verformungsmodul von $E = 5000\ MN/m^2$ und einer Poissonzahl von $\nu = 0,2$ ausgegangen.

Zunächst soll der Fall betrachtet werden, daß das Gebirge durch das Gewicht der Überlagerung (h = 200 m) überwiegend vertikal belastet wird (σ_{z0}, Bild 15). Durch den Ausbruch der Kalotte bildet sich oberhalb der Firste der Kaverne ein entlasteter Bereich ($\Delta\sigma_z < 0$) und seitlich der Ulme ein belasteter Bereich ($\Delta\sigma_z > 0$) aus (Bild 15, links). Mit fortschreitendem Ausbruch der Kaverne breitet sich der belastete Bereich neben den Seitenwänden der Kaverne weiter aus, während der entlastete Bereich oberhalb der Firste sich nur noch geringfügig verändert (Bild 15, Mitte und rechts). Dementsprechend stellt sich bereits mit dem Kalottenausbruch ein großer Teil der Firstsetzungen, nämlich etwa 2/3 der Endsetzungen, ein. Die Horizontalverformungen der seitlichen Kavernenwände sind in allen Ausbauphasen sehr gering.

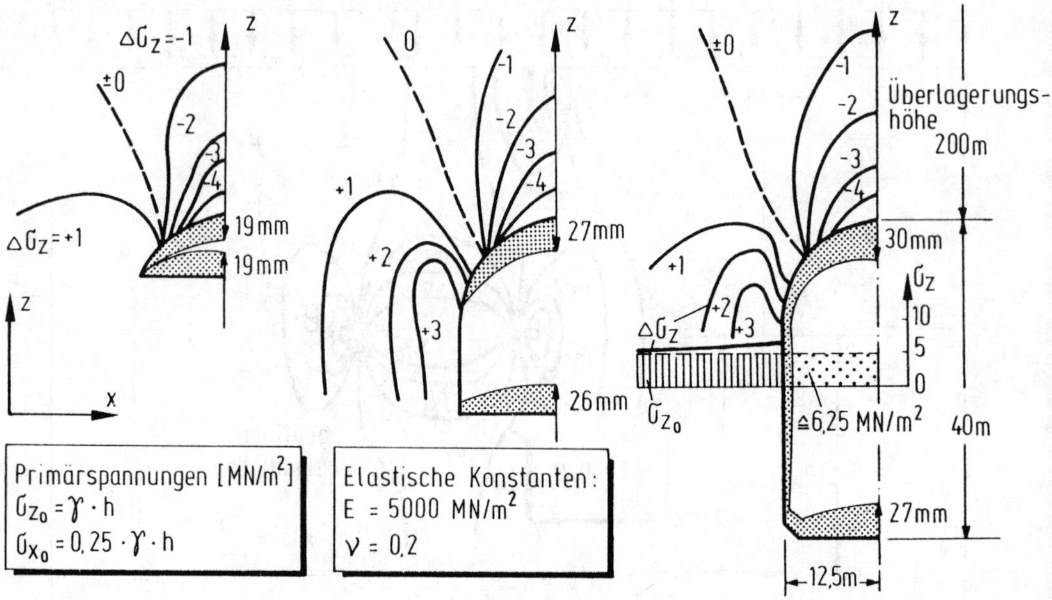

Bild 15 Spannungen und Verformungen beim Ausbruch einer Kaverne in einem überwiegend vertikal belasteten Gebirge.

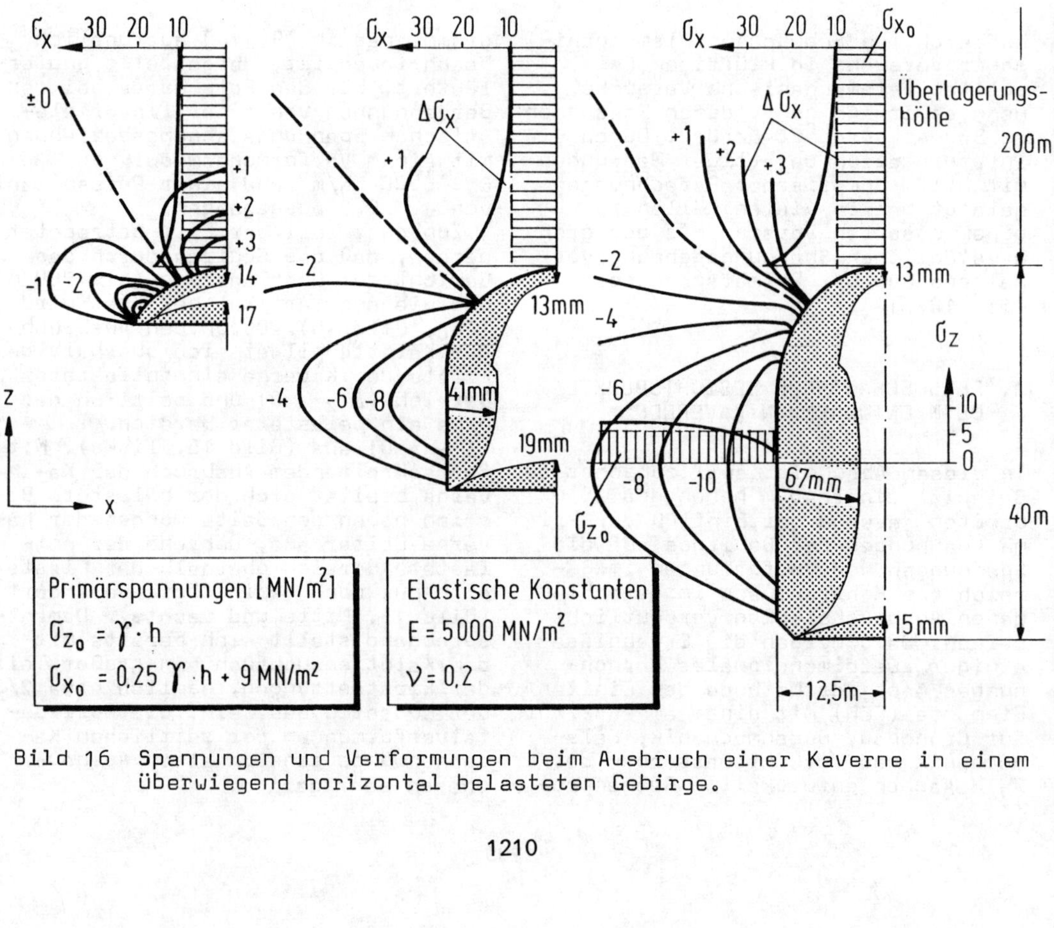

Bild 16 Spannungen und Verformungen beim Ausbruch einer Kaverne in einem überwiegend horizontal belasteten Gebirge.

In Bild 16 sind die Verhältnisse beim Ausbruch des gleichen Kavernenquerschnitts in einem überwiegend horizontal belasteten Gebirge dargestellt. Dabei wurde die horizontale Primärspannungskomponente σ_{x0} gegenüber dem in Bild 15 dargestellten Fall um 9 MN/m^2 erhöht, während die vertikale Komponente σ_{z0} unverändert blieb. In diesem Fall kommt es schon beim Kalottenausbruch oberhalb der Firste zu einer Konzentration der horizontalen Druckspannungen, während der Bereich neben der Ulme entlastet wird (Bild 16, links). Mit fortschreitendem Ausbruch nimmt die Horizontalspannung oberhalb der Firste weiter zu und neben der seitlichen Kavernenwand kommt es zu einer weit in das Gebirge reichenden, horizontalen Entlastung. Diese Entlastung führt zu großen Horizontalverschiebungen der seitlichen Kavernenwand, die ebenfalls mit fortschreitendem Ausbruch zunehmen, während die Firstsetzungen konstant bleiben (Bild 16, Mitte und rechts). In diesem Ergebnis kommt die für eine horizontale Beanspruchung ungünstige Formgebung des Hohlraums zum Ausdruck.

Die in den Bildern 15 und 16 dargestellten Ergebnisse elastischer Berechnungen zeigen bereits, daß der Fels schon bei mittleren Überlagerungshöhen die Haupttragwirkung übernehmen muß. Die beim Ausbruch auftretenden Spannungsänderungen können durch Sicherungsmittel nicht in vollem Umfang aufgenommen werden, wenn man die Kaverne wirtschaftlich bemessen will. Besonders deutlich wird dies für den Fall großer horizontaler Spannungen (Bild 16). Beim Vollausbruch kommt es neben der seitlichen Kavernenwand zu einer horizontalen Entlastung um $\Delta\sigma_x = 10\ MN/m^2$. Die daraus resultierenden Druckkräfte können von einer Sicherung nur zu einem kleinen Teil aufgenommen werden. Eine Spritzbetonsicherung müßte in diesem Bereich besonders nachgiebig ausgebildet werden, damit sie die Gebirgsverformungen zu einem großen Teil mitmachen und sich damit der Beanspruchung weitgehend entziehen kann. Auch bei der Dimensionierung einer Vorspannankerung müßte berücksichtigt werden, daß die Anker die ausbruchbedingten Verformungen zu einem Teil mitmachen müssen und somit eine Längung erfahren. Je nach Größe der auftretenden Verformungen müßte deshalb bei der Vorspannung eine entsprechende Spannkraftzunahme berücksichtigt werden. Auf diese Weise tragen Sicherungsmittel wie Spritzbeton und Felsanker dazu bei, die Tragwirkung des Gebirges zu verbessern, ohne dabei jedoch die Hauptttragfunktion zu übernehmen.

Die Tragwirkung des Gebirges muß durch Sicherungsmittel immer dort unterstützt werden, wo es infolge der Umlagerung der Primärspannungen während des Ausbruchs der Kaverne zu Überschreitungen der Zug- oder Scherfestigkeit im Fels kommt.

Ein Beispiel hierfür ist in Bild 17 dargestellt. Beim Ausbruch einer Kaverne in einem überwiegend vertikal belasteten Gebirge kommt es, wie bereits in Bild 15 dargestellt, oberhalb der Firste zu einer Entlastung, die im Fall eines elastischen Spannungsdehnungsverhaltens des Gebirges zu Zugspannungen sowohl in vertikaler als auch in horizontaler Richtung führen kann. Sind im Gebirge, wie in Bild 17 dargestellt, horizontale und vertikale Trennflächen ausgebildet, dann können diese Trennflächen keine Zugspannungen übertragen, und es bilden sich Felskeile aus, die herunterfallen können.

Bei einer überschläglichen Bemessung einer Sicherung kann man in einem solchen Fall häufig von der vereinfachenden Vorstellung ausgehen, daß das Gewicht des entlasteten Bereichs über eine Betonschale oder

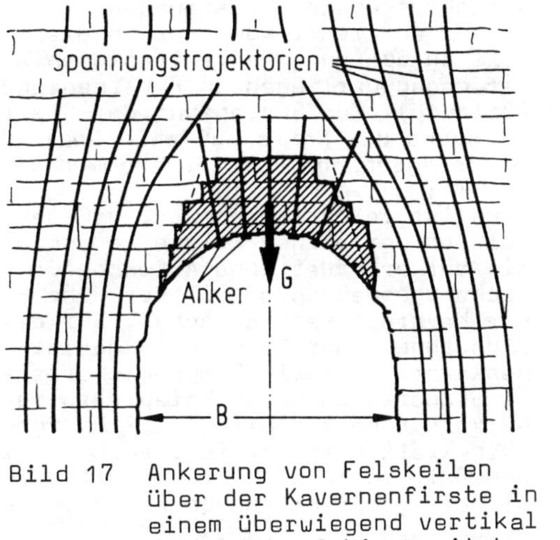

Bild 17 Ankerung von Felskeilen über der Kavernenfirste in einem überwiegend vertikal belasteten Gebirge mit horizontalen und vertikalen Trennflächen.

aber, wie in Bild 17 dargestellt, mittels einer Ankerung aufgenommen werden muß. Das bedeutet für den in Bild 17 skizzierten Fall, daß das Gewicht des durch die horizontalen und vertikalen Trennflächen begrenzten, in Bild 17 gestrichelt eingezeichneten, Gebirgskörpers durch eine Ankerung aufgehängt werden muß. Die Größe des zu verankernden Bereichs läßt sich allerdings durch eine elastische Berechnung nur überschläglich ermitteln. Mit dem o.g. Berechnungsverfahren lassen sich jedoch auch Berechnungen durchführen, in denen ein elastisch-viskoplastisches Spannungsdehnungsverhalten des Felses berücksichtigt werden kann. Derartige Berechnungen haben gezeigt, daß die Bereiche, in denen es zu Festigkeitsüberschreitungen kommt, zumindest teilweise entlastet werden, und es bildet sich - falls die Standsicherheit der Kaverne überhaupt gegeben ist - im Gebirge ein Gewölbe aus, das die plastischen Zonen sozusagen einschließt und dessen Spannweite größer ist als die der Kaverne [14]. Mit derartigen Berechnungen läßt sich die Wirksamkeit einer angenommenen Sicherungsmaßnahme, z.B. die Ankerung eines Felskeils bestimmter Größe, überprüfen.

In Bild 18 ist ein Beispiel für die Gefährdung der Standsicherheit einer Kaverne durch einen Gebirgskeil, der von einer Störung und der Hohlraumwand begrenzt wird, dargestellt. Da sich der Keil durch eine Gleitbewegung der Lastaufnahme weitgehend entzieht, kommt es in diesem Fall zu Spannungskonzentrationen an der gegenüberliegenden Kavernenwand (Bild 18). Zur Begrenzung der Gleitbewegung des Keils muß sein Gewicht durch Vorspannanker aufgenommen werden [10].

Es ist leicht erkennbar, daß das Volumen derartiger Felskeile und damit der erforderliche Aufwand für Sicherungsmaßnahmen mit der Höhe H der Kaverne stark anwächst. Für die Sicherung einer 32 m hohen Maschinenkaverne für ein Pumpspeicherwerk im Schwarzwald waren beispielsweise 82 Vorspannanker mit je 1,7 MN Vorspannkraft erforderlich. Auch in diesem Fall wurde die Wirksamkeit der Sicherung mit Hilfe von FEM-Berechnungen überprüft [10].

Ganz entsprechend ist die Vorgehensweise beim Auftreten räumlicher Keile. Auch in diesem Fall kann die Sicherung auf dem oben beschriebenen Weg bemessen und mit Hilfe von FEM-Berechnungen überprüft werden.

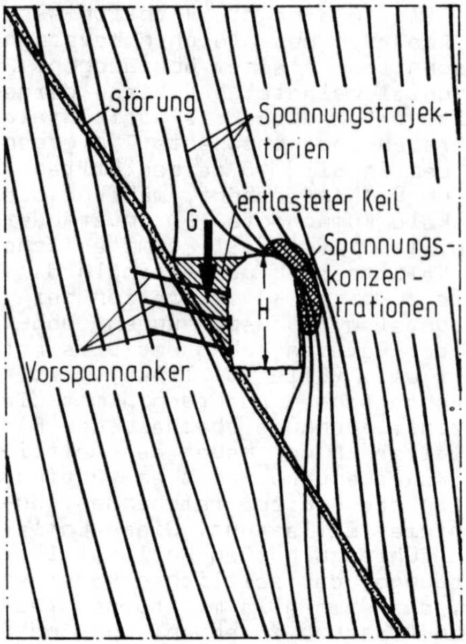

Bild 18 Ankerung eines von einer Störung und der Kavernenwand begrenzten Felskeils, der sich durch eine begrenzte Gleitbewegung der Lastaufnahme entzogen hat [10].

Ein weiteres Problem für die Standsicherheit von Kavernen, das insbesondere bei Hohlräumen mit hohen Wänden und wandparallelen Klüften auftritt, bildet die Knickstabilität. Die bei Kavernen in einem Gebirge mit überwiegend vertikaler Belastung neben den seitlichen Wänden der Kaverne auftretenden Spannungskonzentrationen (vgl. Bild 15) nehmen noch zu, wenn im Fels wandparallele vertikale Trennflächen ausgebildet sind. Weil die Trennflächenufer nur geringe Schubspannungen übertragen können, beschränkt sich in diesem Fall die Umlenkung der Vertikalspannungen auf einen sehr schmalen Bereich neben dem Hohlraum. Die Spannung, bei der es zum Ausknicken der durch die vertikalen Trennflächen begrenzten Felsscheiben kommen kann, kann in einem solchen Fall unter der Annahme einer gelenkigen Lagerung an den Enden der Felsscheibe durch die aus der Baustatik bekannte Formel

$$\sigma_K = \frac{\pi^2 E t^2}{12 h^2} \qquad (1)$$

abgeschätzt werden. Hierin ist E der Verformungsmodul des Gebirges, t die Dicke und h die Höhe der knickgefährdeten Felsscheiben (Bild 19). Beim Auftreten von erhöhten Horizontalspannungen in einem Fels mit horizontalen Trennflächen können derartige Stabilitätsprobleme entsprechend an der Firste und Sohle der Kaverne auftreten.

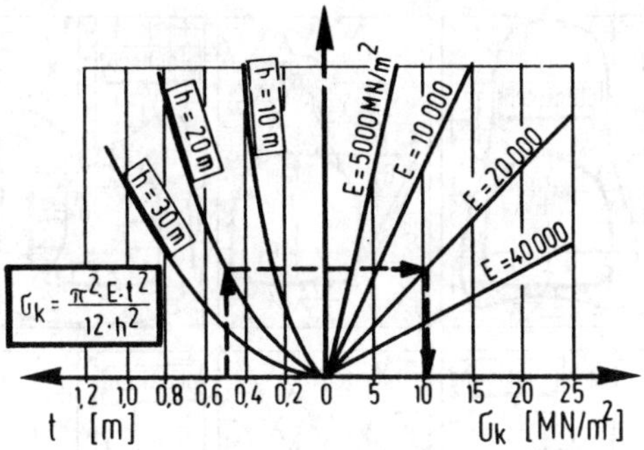

Bild 20 Nomogramm zur Ermittlung der Knickspannung σ_K. Beispiel für t = 0,5 m, h = 20 m und E = 20000 MN/m^2 [14].

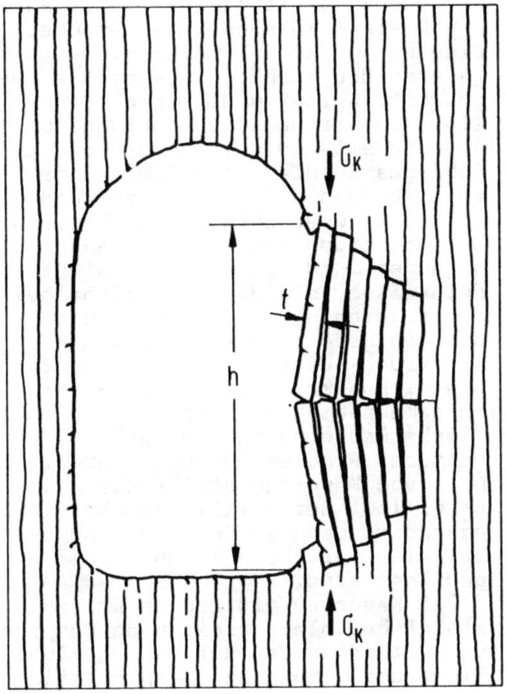

Bild 19 Ausknicken von Felsscheiben an der Kavernenwand bei großen Vertikalspannungen und vertikalen Trennflächen.

Da die rechnerische Untersuchung dieser Stabilitätsprobleme in der Felsmechanik zur Zeit noch Gegenstand der Forschung ist, erscheint es zum gegenwärtigen Zeitpunkt sinnvoll, aus der bei einer Standsicherheitsberechnung erhaltenen Spannungsverteilung mit Hilfe der Beziehung (1) eine überschlägliche Abschätzung der Knickstabilität vorzunehmen. Diese Abschätzung kann für die bei Felskavernen üblichen Größenordnunger für E, t und h mit Hilfe des in Bild 20 dargestellten Nomogramms vorgenommen werden [14].

5. ALLGEMEINE HINWEISE FÜR DEN ENTWURF VON KAVERNEN MIT GROSSEN ABMESSUNGEN

Aus dem vorangegangenen Abschnitt ergeben sich einige allgemeine Hinweise für den Entwurf von Hohlräumen mit großen Abmessungen, die im folgenden kurz zusammengefaßt werden sollen. Der wichtigste Aspekt besteht darin, Hohlräume mit sehr großen Abmessungen möglichst nur in einem Gebirge auszuführen, das sich unter den vorliegenden Beanspruchungen weitgehend elastisch verhält. Je größer die Abmessungen des Hohlraums werden, umso größer wird auch die Erstreckung plastischer Zonen sein, die infolge von Festigkeitsüberschreitungen auf Trennflächen entstehen können (Bild 21a). Bei der Überbeanspruchung auf Trennflächen oder Störungen können sich oberhalb der Firste oder seitlich der Ulme Gebirgsbereiche oder Felskeile mit Abmessungen ausbilden, deren Sicherung einen unverhältnismäßig großen Aufwand erfordert, weil deren Gewicht G mit den Abmessungen der Kaverne zunimmt (Bild 21b). Ebenso ist der Bau von Hohlräumen mit großen Höhen dann sehr schwierig, wenn im Gebirge größere Horizontalspannungen wirksam sind, weil es in solchen Fällen insbesondere an der Firste

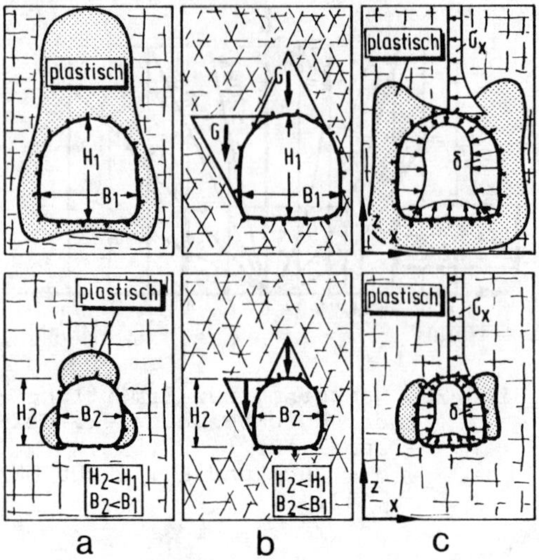

Bild 21 Probleme bei Hohlräumen mit großen Abmessungen.
a) Erstreckung plastischer Zonen,
b) Abmessungen von Felskeilen,
c) große Horizontalspannungen.

zu großen Spannungskonzentrationen und an der Ulme zu großen Horizontalverformungen kommen kann, die mit der Höhe der Kaverne zunehmen (Bild 21c) [13].

6. ZUSAMMENFASSUNG UND SCHLUSSFOLGERUNGEN

Eine wesentliche Voraussetzung für den wirtschaftlichen Entwurf großer Felshohlräume ist eine zutreffende Einschätzung des Spannungsdehnungsverhaltens des Gebirges und der Primärspannungen. Da die Abmessungen einer Kaverne i.a. groß im Vergleich zu den Erstreckungen und Abständen der den Fels durchtrennenden Klüfte sind, kann bei der Berechnung der Standsicherheit von Kavernen das Spannungsdehnungsverhalten von Fels oft durch ein homogenes Modell beschrieben werden, bei dem der Fels im Hinblick auf seine Verformbarkeit und Festigkeit vereinfacht als homogenes Kontinuum aufgefaßt wird. Die Bestimmung geeigneter Kennwerte für ein solches Modell ist jedoch schwierig und mit felsmechanischen Versuchen allein oft nicht möglich, weil die untersuchten Felsvolumina zu klein und damit für den Fels im Sinne des homogenen Modells nicht repräsentativ sind. Daher gelingt häufig erst durch die Interpretation von Verformungsmessungen, an Probeausbrüchen oder am Bauwerk selbst, eine zuverlässige Einschätzung der Verformbarkeit und der Primärspannungen des Gebirges.

Die Spannungen und Verformungen beim Ausbruch einer Kaverne werden entscheidend durch den Primärspannungszustand beeinflußt. Bei einer überwiegend vertikalen Belastung des Gebirges wird der Bereich oberhalb der Firste entlastet und neben der seitlichen Kavernenwand treten Spannungskonzentrationen auf. Beim Ausbruch einer Kaverne in einem überwiegend horizontal belastetem Gebirge sind die Verhältnisse gerade umgekehrt. Für eine wirtschaftliche Dimensionierung der Sicherung muß in beiden Fällen die Tragfähigkeit des Gebirges in die Standsicherheitsuntersuchungen mit einbezogen werden. Bei einer überschläglichen Bemessung der Sicherung kann häufig davon ausgegangen werden, daß das Gewicht von Felskeilen, die die Standsicherheit der Kaverne durch Herabfallen oder Gleiten gefährden können, von der Sicherung aufgenommen werden muß. Die Wirksamkeit derartiger Sicherungsmaßnahmen läßt sich durch numerische Berechnungen überprüfen. Ein weiteres Problem für die Standsicherheit von Kavernen stellt die Knickstabilität der seitlichen Wände dar, besonders wenn im Gebirge wandparallele, vertikale Trennflächen ausgebildet sind.

Bei Kavernen mit großen Abmessungen steigt bei gleichbleibenden Gebirgsverhältnissen der Aufwand etwaiger Sicherungsmaßnahmen überproportional an.

7. LITERATUR

[1] Barton, N.R. Review of a new shear-strength-criterium for rock joints. Eng. Geology 7 (1973): 287-332.

[2] John, K.W. 1969, Festigkeit und Verformbarkeit von druckfesten, regelmäßig gefügten Diskontinuen. Veröffentl. des Institutes für Boden- und Felsmechanik, Univ. Karlsruhe, Heft 37.

[3] Ladanyi, B., Archambault, G. 1969, Simulation of shear

behaviour of a jointed rock mass. Proc. 11th U.S. Symp. Rock. Mech.: 105-125.

[4] Leeman, E.R., Hayes, D.J. 1966, A technique for determining the complete state of stress in rock using a single borehole. Proc. 1st ISRM Congress, Lisbon, Vol. II: 17-24.

[5] Patton, F.D. 1966, Multiple modes of shear failure in rock. Proc. 1st ISRM Congress, Lisbon, Vol. I: 509-513.

[6] Reik, G., Hesselmann, F.J. Verfahren zur Ermittlung der Gebirgsfestigkeit von Sedimentgesteinen. Rock Mech. Suppl. 11 (1981): 59-71.

[7] Rocha, M., da Silva, J.N. 1970, A new method for the determination of deformability in rock masses. Proc. 2nd ISRM Congress, Belgrade, Vol. I: 423-437.

[8] Schneider, H.J. 1975, Reibungs- und Verformungsverhalten von Trennflächen im Fels. Veröffentl. des Institutes für Boden- und Felsmechanik, Univ. Karlsruhe, Heft 65.

[9] Semprich, S. 1980, Berechnung der Spannungen und Verformungen im Bereich der Ortsbrust von Tunnelbauwerken im Fels. Veröffentl. des Institutes für Grundbau, Bodenmechanik, Felsmechanik und Verkehrswasserbau der RWTH Aachen, Heft 8.

[10] Wittke, W., Pfisterer, E., Rißler, P. 1974, Felsmechanische Untersuchungen für die Maschinenkaverne Wehr. Berichte der 1. Nationalen Tagung über Felshohlraumbau, Essen: 123-148.

[11] Wittke, W. 1976, Neues Entwurfskonzept für untertägige Hohlräume in klüftigem Fels. Veröffentl. des Institutes für Grundbau, Bodenmechanik, Felsmechanik und Verkehrswasserbau der RWTH Aachen, Heft 1: 48-116.

[12] Wittke, W., Plischke, B., Hosang, K.-H. 1979, Interpretation der Ergebnisse eines felsmechanischen Versuchsprogramms für ein untertägiges Krafthaus mit Hilfe numerischer Berechnungen. Proc. 4th ISRM Congress, Montreux, Vol. III: 209-218.

[13] Wittke, W. 1981, Felsmechanische Aspekte in bezug auf Planung und Bau von großen Hohlräumen in Fels. Int. Symp. über "Unterirdische Bauweise von Kernkraftwerken", Hannover: 217-232.

[14] Wittke, W. 1984, Felsmechanik - Grundlagen für wirtschaftliches Bauen im Fels. Berlin, Heidelberg, New York, Tokyo, Springer.

STABILITY PREDICTION AND EVALUATION FOR THE SYSTEM OF LARGE-SPAN CAVERNS OF UNDERGROUND POWERPLANTS

Prognostizierung und Gewährleistung der Stabilität von Hohlräumen unterirdischer Wasserkraftwerke mit grosser Spannweite

Prévision et évaluation de la stabilité des cavités des centrales hydroélectriques souterraines d'une grande portée

S.A.YUFIN, V.I.TITKOV, I.R.SHVACHKO, A.A.ANTIPOV
Moscow Institute of Civil Engineering, Moscow, USSR

SUMMARY

The well understood tendency of placing the systems of underground structures of powerplants in the rock masses with favorable geologic conditions rarely can be realized in practice. Generalization of in-situ and model data obtained for already completed projects (in our case the powerhouse of Inguri powerplant) is the best basis for choice of a numerical method and model to be used during the design stage of a new structure.

ZUSAMMENFASSUNG

Das Bestreben komplexe unterirdische Bauwerke von Wasserkraftwerken in Bereichen von Bergmassiven unter günstigen ingenieur-geologischen Bedingungen zu errichten, kann in der Praxis nur selten realisiert werden. Die Verallgemeinerung von in-situ Werten und Ergebnissen aus Untersuchungen an Modellen, die durchgeführt wurden für bereits bestehende und im Bau befindliche unterirdische Maschinenräume von Wasserkraftwerken machte es möglich, rechnerische Prinzipien zur Begründung von Vortriebsschemen und Konstruktionen zur Verankerung des Systems großer, dicht beieinander angeordneter Hohlräume der zu projektierenden Kavernen zu verwenden.

RESUME

La tendance à construire des complexes souterrains de centrales hydroélectriques dans des massifs rocheux dans des conditions géologiques favorables peut être concrétisée rarement dans la pratique. La généralisation des données in-situ et des résultats des études des modèles provenant des projets qui ont été déjà éxécutés (dans notre cas, les salles des machines souterraines de la centrale hydroélectrique Inguri) est la meilleure base de choix d'une méthode numérique et d'un modèle devant être utilisés durant la phase de dimensionnement d'une nouvelle structure.

1 INTRODUCTION

Design of the support systems for the large-span underground openings is an intricate problem without a sole solution. Systems of caverns for underground hydraulic powerplants usually include openings for powerhouse, transformer hall, valve chambers and sometime underground surge shafts or reservoirs. In some cases this caverns are at sufficient distances from one another and for layout at shallow depths the transformer hall is placed usually on the ground level, so each cavern may be regarded separately from other openings, but quite often the analysis has to be made for the whole system of underground structures. The difficulties arise from the existence of access adits, ventilation and cable shafts, draft tubes, etc.

From the analyst's point of view this is a typically three-dimensional problem which only in rare cases can be solved as a two-dimensional one. Sole reliable source of information on the stress-state of the structure and surrounding rock mass is in situ measurement. Regretfully this kind of data is available only during and after the construction process takes place and is not at hand during the design stage. One can use only the data from the analogous structures already in operation or apply to mathematical or physical models. Further parallel analysis of data obtained from models and in situ during and after construction provides the basis for drastic improvements of models in use and higher level of design for new projects.

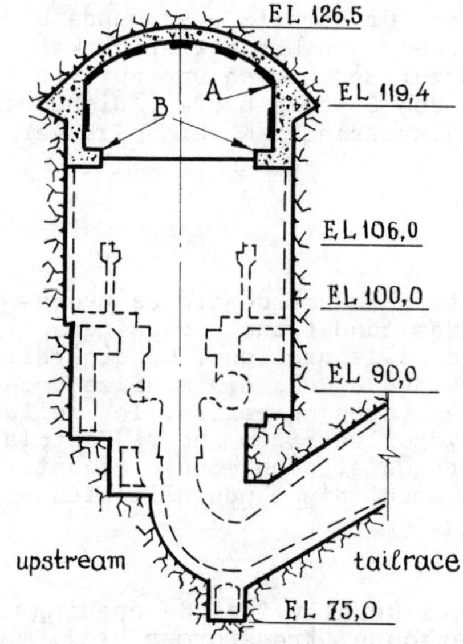

Fig. 1 Cavern of the Inguri powerhouse

2 EXAMPLE OF A COMPREHENSIVE ANALYSIS OF AN UNDERGROUND POWERHOUSE

At the Moscow Institute of Civil Engineering (MICE) investigations for the Inguri underground powerhouse were initiated by Eristov et al in 1969 (1972,1974). The cavern (Fig.1) is 126 m long, 21.8 m wide and 52.3 m high. The support consists of a reinforced-concrete arch with suspended crane beam-walls. The arch axis is a circular arc with radius of 14.05 m with a central angle of 120°. The arch thickness at the crown and that of the crane wall is 1.3 m and the arch thickness at the abutments is 2.23 m. The height of the opening supported by the concrete arch and the crane beam-walls is 13.33m.

The cavern is located in thick-layered medium-jointed limestones. The dip of the rock strata is 30-40° and the rock shows considerable anisotropy. Preliminary geological investigations gave the values for the Young's modulus in the direction along the strata E = 8000 - 10000 MN/m^2 and in perpendicular direction E = 6000 - 8000 MN/m^2.

For model analysis materials prepared of plaster and grounded limestone mixtures were used. The MICE has gained quite a reputation for physical static and dynamic modelling of different kinds of hydraulic structures (dams and foundations, tunnels, etc.) and model materials were selected from an abundance of mixture recipes. Wide-ranging test program was carried out for the determining both the physical-mechanical characteristics of the model materials and that of interlayer joints.

Several two-dimensional models were analyzed for cases of isotropic and anisotropic jointed rock mass. For isotropic homogenous conditions the model was made by direct pouring of the model material mixture into the 1.8x1.8x0.2 m rigid steel framework and subsequent drying. Anisotropic jointed and layered rock mass was modelled either by pouring different model materials in order to make thin layers with different properties or by assembling the model from prefabricated bricks made of dryed model material. In some mo-

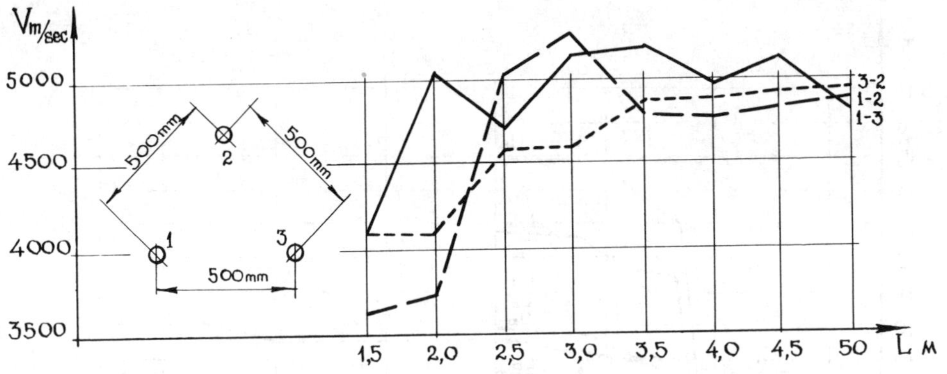

Fig. 2 Set up of boreholes for ultrasonic measurements and wave velocities along the borehole length at site "2", upstream wall, EL 100.0

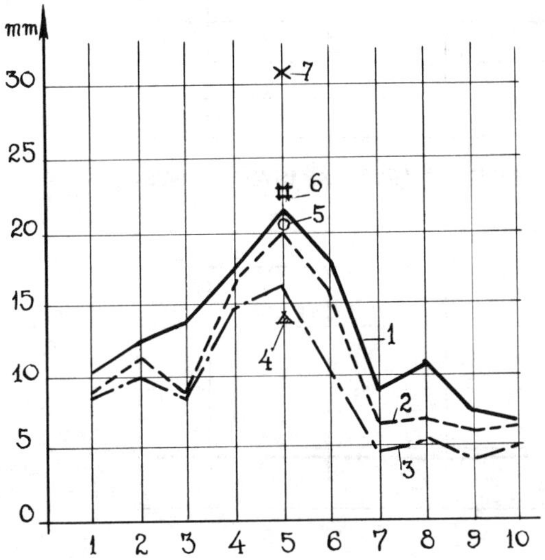

Fig. 3 Horizontal closure of the Inguri powerhouse cavern at the crane beams level (point B, Fig.1) 1,2,3 - measured in situ at 10 equally spaced along the axis of the cavern sites with excavation at EL 90.0, 100.0, and 106.0 respectively; 4,5 - FEM analysis; 6 - layered model; 7 - model with sleak interlayer joints

dels granular paraffin was used to reduce interblock or interlayer friction.

Biaxial state of stress was applied to the model by means of special mechanical device which provides stability of pressure during long period of time. The model of concrete arch was made independently of the main models and installed at the appropriate stage of excavation process. The step-by-step excavation technique has been modelled either by drilling adjoining holes on the contour of the opening or by sawing. The models (there were six models with different material parameters for the rock mass) were equipped with precision mechanical deformometers and strain-gaige rosettes to measure stresses and displacements around the opening and in the model of the arch. Once the attempt was made to model rock bolting in the walls of the opening, somehow this experiment failed due to unappropriate modelling of bolts, their models were too rigid and the support provided was unrealistically high. For some later investigations nylon and PVC models for anchors w ere used with success.

In situ investigations were made in the cavern of Inguri powerhouse during period of 1971-1976, some measurements are being taken up to present time. Some part of the measuring devices was taken out of operation by blasting, so the results regarded in this publication concern

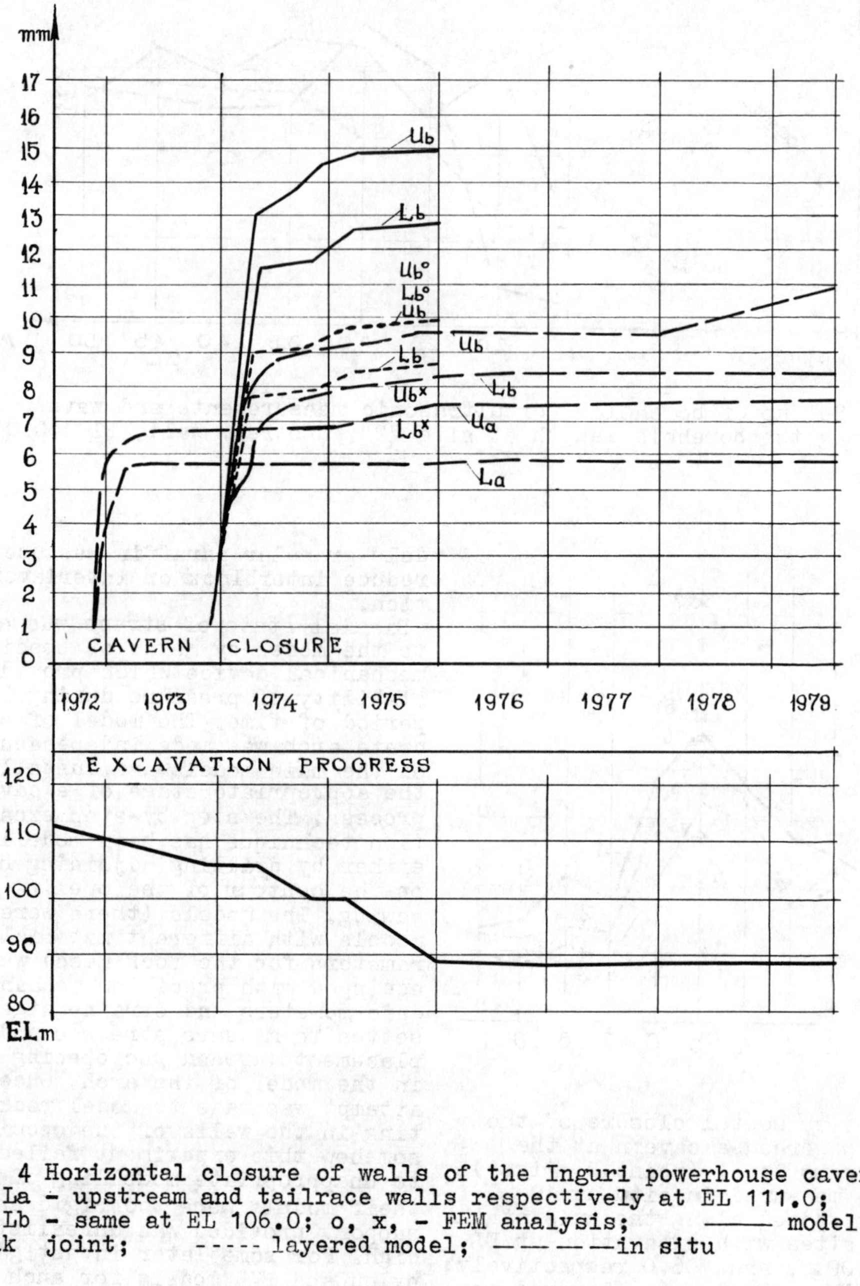

Fig. 4 Horizontal closure of walls of the Inguri powerhouse cavern Ua, La - upstream and tailrace walls respectively at EL 111.0; Ub, Lb - same at EL 106.0; o, x, - FEM analysis; ——— model with sleak joint; ---- layered model; — — — —in situ

ning contour deformations and stresses in the concrete arch correspond to the period of time starting in november 1972.

The investigations included:

- evaluation of rock mass characteristics and of the degree of loosening of the rock in the zone close to the contour of the opening;
- evaluation of stresses in rock and in concrete arch;
- measurements of the crane wall-beams and powerhouse wall displacements.

Rock mass characteristics in the zone close to the contour of the opening were obtained by the ultrasonic method. Every measuring site consisted of three 5 m deep boreholes placed at the nodes of a triangle with 0.5 m side length. Borehole deviation from the designed orientation was measured with special anglemeasuring device and appropriate corrections of the results were made. The velocities of the ultrasonic waves were measured between every pair of boreholes in the triangle in order to evaluate the contribution of the anisotropy to the changes of the obtained data. Measurements were taken every 0.5 m along the borehole axis. Typical ultrasonic wave velocities distribution in rock in one of the sites on the wall of the cavern is shown on Fig.2. The even values of velocities at the end of boreholes point that the loosened zone around the cavern has the depth close to the length of the borehole, i.e. 5 m. The average depth of the loosened zone was evaluated as 1.5 m.

Stress-release and compensation techniques were used for the rock mass state of stress and deformation parameters measuring. Average Young's moduli were E = 18000 MN/m^2, E = 12000 MN/m^2 (Yufin and Chincharauli, 1978).

Along with in situ tests FEM analysis was performed (Yufin, 1974). Calculations were made for the transverse-isotropic elastic medium regarding sequential excavation and support installement. As an input data in situ-measured parameters were used. The comparison of the results of in situ, model and FEM analysis is performed on Fig. 3 and Fig. 4. The "o" points on Fig. 4 relate to the ubiquitous joint method analysis made in 1979 to verify this approach with in situ data on loosened zone parameters.

Rock mass shows practically linear deformability without apparent creep deformations and due to low stress level (approx. 0.5 MPa), no plastic zones were found. The model with low interlayer friction gives high values of contour displacements but for the second modell and for the FEM analysis resulting values are very close to real. Small rise in displacements at the upstream side wall in 1978-1979 can be related to the effect of the power equipment under operation.

3 PROGRAM BASE FOR THE NUMERICAL ANALYSIS OF UNDERGROUND STRUCTURES

Relatively unsophisticated programs for linear-elastic analysis do not satisfy the demands of the present period of time. Design and construction of large underground structures in complicated engineering - geological conditions call for the development of a comprehensive basis for their mathematical modelling. Such a program or rather a set of programs has to be able to perform two- and three-dimensional static and dynamic analysis of structures using complex models of materials and regarding some additional factors such as typical for geomechanics problems sequential process of excavation and/or construction, etc. This ideas are incorporated in the comprehensive "STATAS" code, developed by the first two authors of this publication and used for solving different hydraulic construction and geomechanics problems. The code is based on the finite element method.

Element library of the "STATAS" code include CST, LST and isoparametric quadrilaterals up to the third order. Degraded elements are used to connect higher-order elements to the lower-order ones. For joint modelling special family of first-second and third-order isoparametric slip elements were developed. For rock bolts one-dimensional elements of appropriate order are being used along the sides of solid elements. The crossing of the bolt with joint is represented by link element (De Ngo,1975). Slip and link elements use relative displacement approach (Ghaboussi,Wilson and Isenberg,1973, Wilson,1977). Curved thin isoparametric "sheet" elements surve the purpose of modelling steel linings in pressure tunnel analysis. "Infinite" elements are to be used at the mesh boundaries (Bettes, 1977, Brebbia and Walker, 1980).

The input to the program is organised in such a way, that slip and link elements can appear at the side of any given element in the mesh, i.e. no predetermined pattern of joints is used during the mesh preparation and coding, so different joint patterns can be regarded with the same mesh. A preprocessor code is being developed for statistical data preparation on joint properties and distribution. Two main models are adopted for joint properties - elasto-plastic and dilatant, first as proposed by Kratichvil (1976) and the second according to Heuze and Barbour (1978).

Three-dimensional variant of the "STATAS" code use isoparametric eight to twenty-node brick elements.

Some nonlinear material models are incorporated into the program but their use needs tedious and costly laboratory and in situ analysis of rock properties as a source of input data.

Much attention has been paid to the sequentional excavation modelling in the FEM analysis (Chandrasekaran and King, 1974, Desai and Abel, 1972, Desai, 1977, Desai and Christian, 1977, Wittke, 1977). Somehow equilibrium and stress problems were successfully solved at the earliest stages of the work described herein (Yufin,1974).

The "STATAS" code regards sequential modifications of the analyzed area (excavation/construction, etc.) as a non-linear process in which altered are either system stiffness matrix or the right hand part of the main equation or both. If the exact solution of the system of equations is desired (understanding that round-off and truncation operations would cause some deviations in results) and say the Gauss elimination procedure is used, the stiffness matrix triangulization consumes most of the computer time of the particular run. Time needed can be evaluated as:

$$t = (a_1 n + a_2)(a_3 p^2 + a_4 p + a_5) + a_6$$

where n- number of degrees of freedom in the system; p-the bandwidth of the stiffness matrix, a_i - parameters, depending on the characteristics of the computer in use (speed, available core, algorithm realisation, programming language and qualities of a compiler) and on the mastership of the programmer.

For the given program and computer configuration parameters a_i become constants.

The process is regarded as a multi iterational one and we consider that every i-th iteration needs alteration of some rows of the stiffness matrix used in the (i-1)th iteration, i.e. the problem is to minimize the time for alterations in the existing triangular matrix. It is obvious, that Gauss elimination process is symmetric regarding the direction of the elimination of unknowns (the time needed to obtain upper or lower triangilar matrixes is equivalent). The most economical way is to modify the stiffness matrix in such a way as shown on Fig.5. The time gain related to the time needed for complete triangulization of stiffness matrix obtained due to this modification is proportional to n/m (n - number of the system's degrees of freedom, m - width of a modifiable area of the matrix).

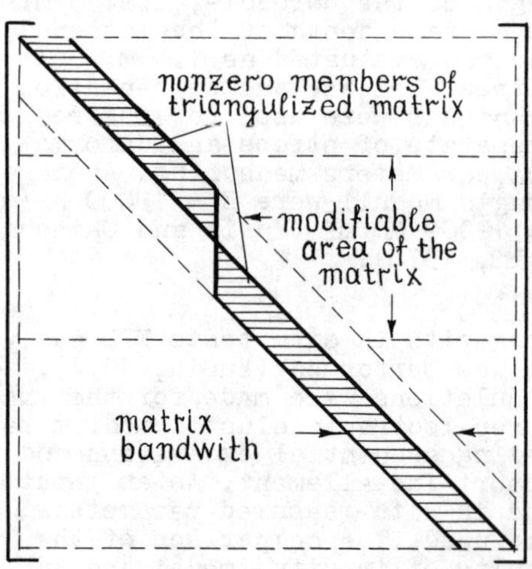

Fig.5 Scheme of matrix modification

Some complications arise when the right hand part of the matrix equation is also to be modified for consequent iteration. Formally, during each iteration we have to solve the matrix equation of the form AD = F, where A is the stiffness matrix of the system, D - vector of unknowns, F - force vector. Any mentioned matrix modification can be regarded as a multiplication of both parts of equation by some matrix B : BAD=BF. If A'=BA, than A'D=BF (A' is a triangular matrix of one of the two kinds mentioned earlier). Under these conditions our additional problem is to preserve non-zero elements of the modification matrix B. The time needed for obtaining new matrix equation A'D=F is given as:

$$t=2(na_1+a_2)(a_3p^2+a_4p+a_5)+a_6+a_7pn$$

where multiplier 2 accounts for modification of matrix B along with matrix A and the last member accounts for matrix multiplication B'F.

Same algorithm can be used in analysis with nonlinear material properties and proves to be effective and economical, especially in multistage analysis.

The imput data is analyzed by the preprocessor programs and if there are no errors the computational process is performed in order to obtain needed results under the supervision of the program controlled by parameters specifying the sequence and the special features of the analysis. It needs to be mentioned that in every particular case only some of the computational system's abilities are in use.

Performance of the program at every stage of it's development is controlled during the analysis of the hypothetical cavern (Heuze and Yufin 1978, Heuze and Barbour, 1978, Yufin, 1978). The central part of the FEM mesh used in this analysis is presented on Fig.6 and the problem set up - on Fig.7. The cavern is 13.5m high and 30.0m wide. Joint pattern can be easily redefined but in series of analysis described herein is as shown on the picture. Fig.8 represents cavern closure as a result of linear elastic analysis (1), non-linear analysis - rheology viscoelastic material, no joints (4), jointed rock with (3) and without (2) rock bolting. Line (6) represents horizontal closure of the cavern at the end of the bolt "N" for analysis case (3). Line (5) shows vertical displacements at the lock end of bolt "G" for the same case.

For ubiquitous joint method (de Rouvray and Goodman, 1972, Goodman, 1977) we use failure criteria proposed by Kasparyan (1977) as an extended Coulomb formulation for known direction of a joint plane:

$$\frac{\sigma_2-\sigma_1}{2}\cos 2\alpha(tg 2\alpha - tg\varphi) < C + \frac{\sigma_1+\sigma_2}{2} tg\varphi$$

$$\frac{\sigma_3-\sigma_1}{2}\cos 2\alpha(tg 2\alpha - tg\varphi) < C + \frac{\sigma_3+\sigma_1}{2} tg\varphi$$

$$\frac{\sigma_2-\sigma_3}{2}\cos 2\alpha(tg 2\alpha - tg\varphi) < C + \frac{\sigma_2+\sigma_3}{2} tg\varphi$$

here α is the angle between direction of a joint and minimum principal stresses σ_1, φ and C are the angle of internal friction and cohesion respectively.

Unhomogenuity of the real rock mass and usual uncertainty of the designer concerning material parameters and distribution of the discontinuities calls for use of stohastic models at the design stage for complex rock structures.

4 FURTHER DEVELOPMENTS

As an example of the extended numerical analysis of the system of underground structures the set of caverns of Rogun powerplant can serve. Fig.9 shows two alternative configurations of the powerhouse and of the adjoining transformer hall caverns. The rock mass is represented by brown jointed sandstones with intrusions of argillites and aleurolites. Most of the joints have clayish material as a filling. The most significant joints are shown on Fig.9. The goal of the analysis is the evaluation of the most rational sequence of excavation and anchoring, and the stability prediction for both configurations of caverns and types of support. The results will serve as a basis for final project and due to the limited space herein will be presented separately from this publication.

5 CONCLUSIONS

Physical and mathematical modelling of underground structures is the

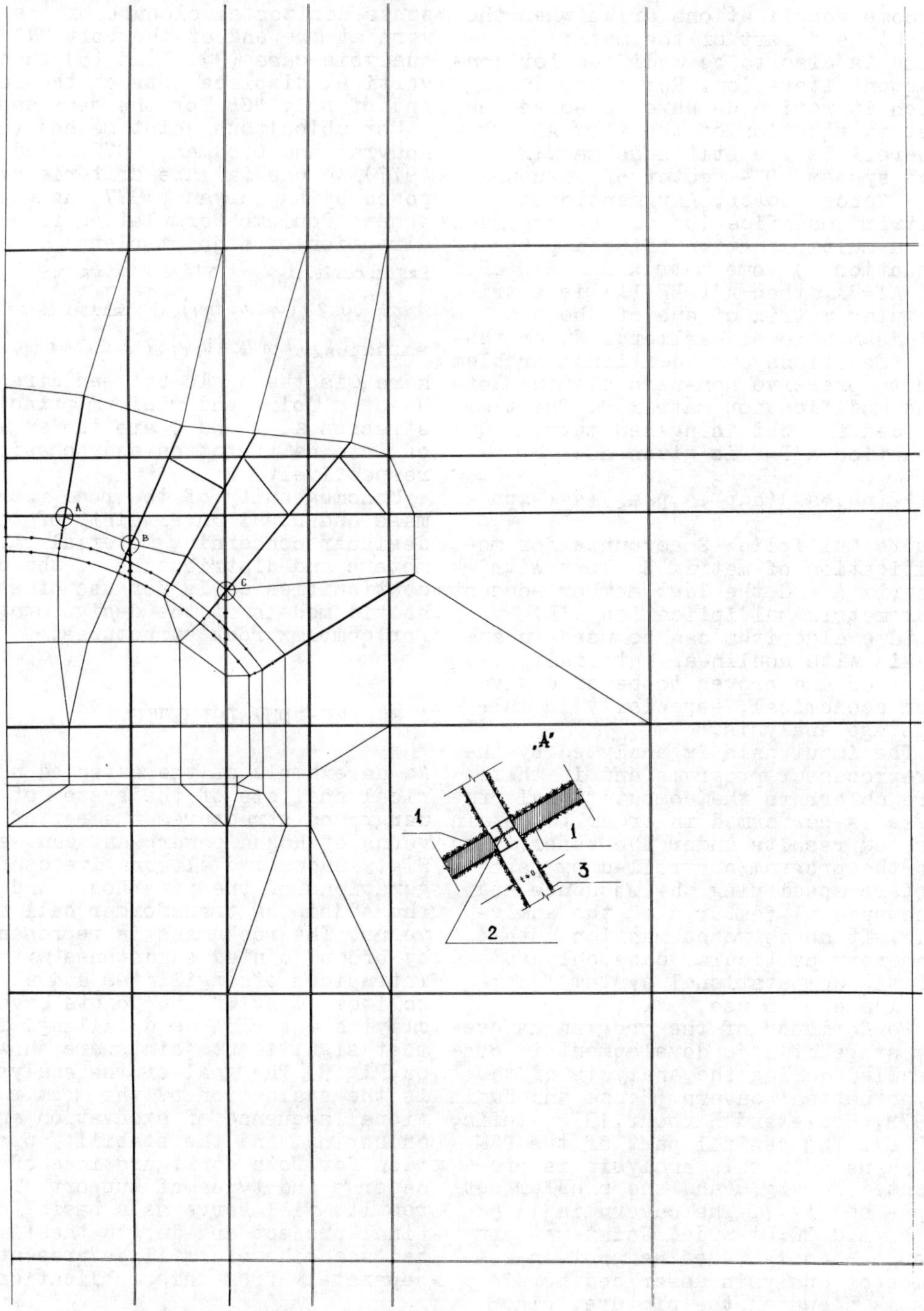

Fig. 6 Central part of the finite element mesh for test cavern "A" - explication of rock bolt/joint crossing;
1 - rock bolt; 2 - link element; 3 - joint

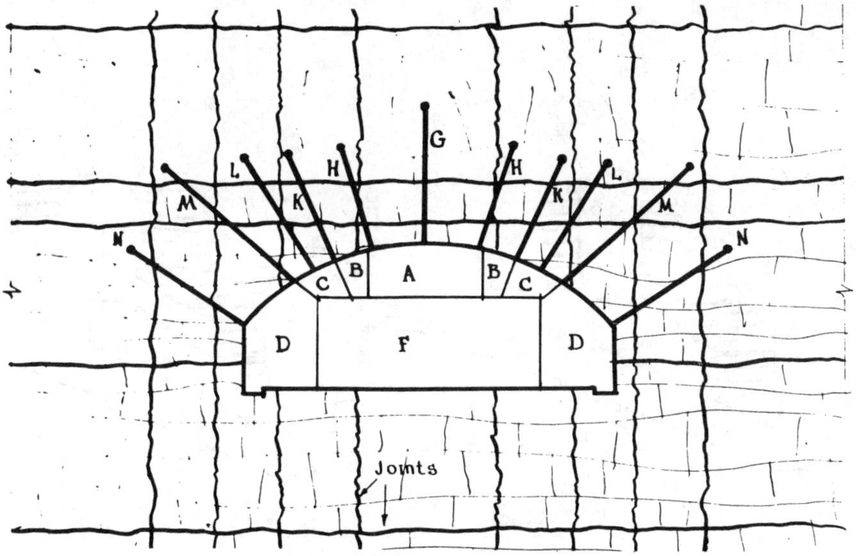

Fig. 7 Test cavern in jointed rock
A,B,C,D,F - excavation stages; G,H,K,L,M,N - optional rock bolts

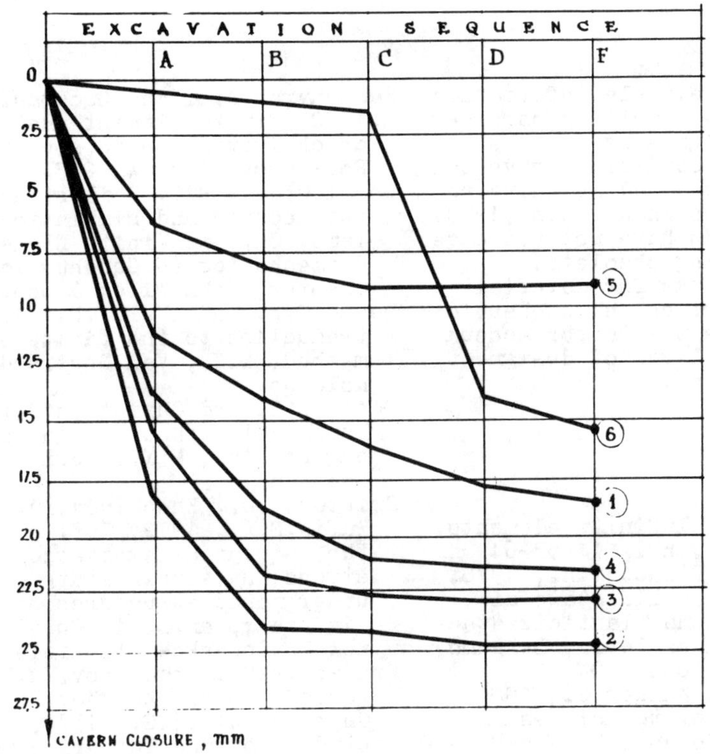

Fig. 8 Closure of the test cavern. FEM analysis
1,2,3,4 - vertical at the head of rock bolt "G", 5 - vertical at the lock of rock bolt "G"; 6 - horizontal at the head of rock bolt "N"

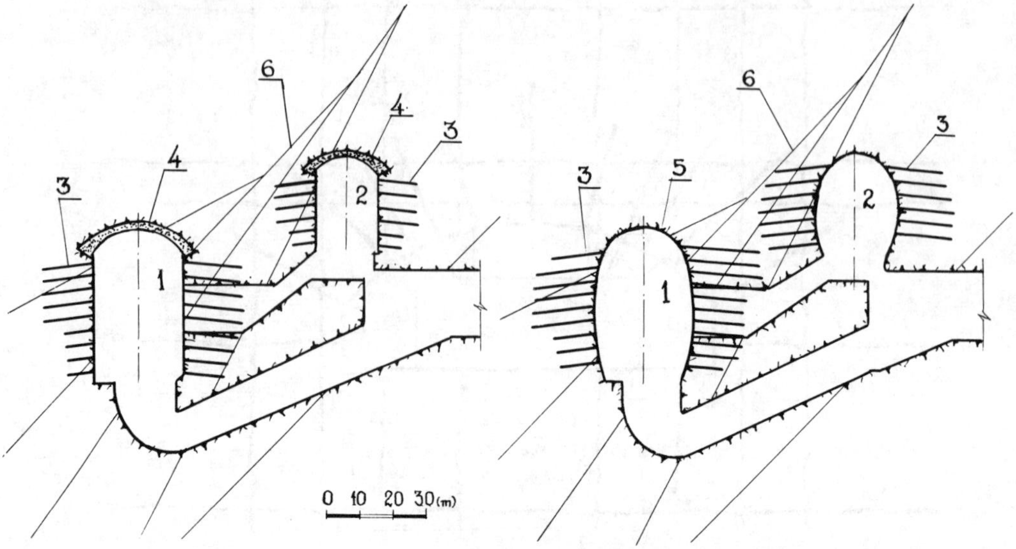

Fig. 9 Setup of the problem for further analysis

main source of reliable information on the predicted stability parameters at the design stage.

Under complex conditions physical models can be used and as quite recent publications show (Rossi,1979), numerical methods have not yet made physical modelling obsolete.

Information banks for material and joint properties and stohastic modelling can be the factor accounting for higher level of design of structures in rock.

6 REFERENCES

Bettes,P., 1977, Infinite elements, Int.J.Num.Meth.Eng. 11: 53-64

Borsetto,M. and Ribacchi,R., 1978, Determinazione dello stato di sforzo nella zona plasticizzata intorno ad una galleria, Bergamo, ISMES Publications, 104

Brebbia,C.A. and Walker,S., 1980, Boundary element techniques in engineering, London, Newnes-Butterworths

Chandrasekaran,V.S. and King,J.W., 1974, Simulation of excavation using finite elements, ASCE, J.S.M.& F.D., 100, GT9

de Rouvray,A.L. and Goodman,R.E., 1972, Finite element analysis of crack initiation in a block model, Rock mechanics, 4, 203

Desai,C.S., 1977, Soil-structure interaction and simulation problems, Ch.7 in Finite Elements in Geomechanics (G.Gudehus ed.), Chichester, John Wiley & Sons

Desai,C.S. and Abel,J.F., 1972, Introduction to the finite element method, N.Y., Van Nostrand Reinhold Co.

Desai,C.S. and Christian,J.T.,1977, Numerical methods in geotechnical engineering, N.Y., McGraw-Hill Book Co.

Eristov,V.S., Khechinov,Yu.E. and Yufin,S.A., 1972, Influence of the sequential excavation on the stress and strain-state of the underground structures of hydraulic powerplants, in Russian, Gidrotekhnicheskoe stroitelstvo*,7

Eristov,V.S., Khechinov,Yu.E., Andgouladze,G.P., Zhokhov,E.I. and Chincharauli,T.G., 1974, Field studies of the Ingouri powerhouse, Gidrotekhnicheskoe Stroitel'stvo*, 6 (See also Proc. 3rd ISRM Congress, Denver, Colorado)

Ghaboussi,J.,Wilson,E.L. and Isenberg,J., 1973, Finite element for

rock joints and interfaces, ASCE, J.S.M.& F.D., SM10
Goodman,R.E., 1977, Analysis in jointed rocks, Ch.11 in Finite Elements in Geomechanics (G.Gudehus ed.), Chichester, John Wiley & Sons
Heuze,F.E. and Barbour,T.G., 1978, Stability analysis for rock structures, Proc. 19th Symposium on Rock Mechanics, Stateline, Nevada
Heuze,F.E. and Yufin,S.A., 1978, Finite element modelling of sequential excavation and rock reinforcement, Proc. 107th AIME Annual Meeting, Denver, Colorado
Kasparyan,E.V., 1977, Stress state of rock and rock pressure development around openings, Ch. 11 in Fundamentals of Rock Mechanics, (Turchaninov I.A., Iofis M.A. and Kasparyan E.V. authors, in Russian), Leningrad, Nedra Publishers
Kratochvil,J., 1976, Solution of contact problems by finite element method, Stav.Cas., 24, c.5, Bratislava, VEDA
Manfredini,G., Martinetti,S., Ribacchi,R., Riccioni,R., 1977, Design criteria for anchor cables and bolting in underground openings, Bergamo, ISMES Publications, 91
Rossi,P.P., 1979, Bidimensional geomechanical models of large underground openings, Bergamo, ISMES Publications, 126
Wilson,E.L., 1977, Finite elements for foundations, joints and fluids, Ch. 10 in Finite Elements in Geomechanics (G.Gudehus ed.), Chichester, John Wiley & Sons
Wittke,W., 1977, New design concept for underground openings in rock, Ch. 13 in Finite Elements in Geomechanics (G.Gudehus ed.), Chichester, John Wiley & Sons
Yufin,S.A., 1974, Analysis of the stresses and displacements in the arch of an underground powerhouse and in the surrounding rock mass by considering the excavation stages, Gidrotekhnicheskoe Stroitel'stvo*, 9
Yufin,S.A., 1978, Analysis of underground structures in jointed rock considering excavation technology influence, Brno, Czechoslovakia, Proc. Brno Technical Univ., B80
Yufin,S.A. and Chincharauli,T.G., 1978, Stress analysis of the rock mass during the excavation of Inguri underground powerhouse, Gidrotekhnicheskoe Stroitel'stvo,2
Zienkiewicz,O.C. The Finite Element Method, 3rd edition, N.Y., McGraw-Hill Book Co.

* The journal "Gidrotekhnicheskoe Stroitel'stvo" (Hydrotechnical Construction) is translated into English for the American Society of Civil Engineers and published by Consultants Bureau, a division of Plenum Publishing Corporation

* 3 *

LOAD SHARING CAPACITY OF THE ROCK MASS FOR PRESSURE TUNNELS AND SHAFTS

Mittragende Wirkung des Gebirges bei Druckstollen und Druckschächten

Effet de la portance du terrain dans le cas des galeries forcées et des puits sous pression

ÉTUDE DU COMPORTEMENT D'UNE CONDUITE FORCÉE SOUTERRAINE BLOQUÉE AU ROCHER PAR LA RÉALISATION D'UN ESSAI EN CAVERNE

Study of the behaviour of an underground forced conduit lodged in the rock, using a cave test

Untersuchung des Verhaltens einer unterirdischen, gegen den Felsen blockierten Druckrohrleitung mit Hilfe eines Versuchs in einem Stollen

T.DOUCERAIN & A.MARTINET
Electricité de France, Paris, France

SUMMARY

The Super-Bissorte hydroelectric project has led to a review of the méthods employed for dimensioning the reinforcement of forced conduits lodged in the rock.

In order to arrive at better understanding of the actual behaviour of the steel-concrete-rock complex, a full-size test was carried out on a section 20 m long of a reconnaissance tunnel in the Super Bissorte power station.

The principal résults were as follows :

- The very high pressures (25 MPa) caused distorsions of the steel that were much greater than the limit of elasticity. However no breakage was experienced.
- Confirmation was obtained of play between the steel and the concrete of up to 80.10^{-5} (relative to the radius of the conduit).
- The participation of the rock depends largely on the geotechnical charactéristics of the decompressed zone in the neighbourhood of the excavation. Under the test conditions it varied form 50 to 60 %.

The results obtained have permitted calibration of a mathemetical model, which will thus be usable for dimensioning other forced conduits.

ZUSAMMENFASSUNG

Die in Super-Bissorte geplante Wasserkraftanlage erforderte ein Uberdenken der Dimensionierungsmethoden für die Austeifung von gegen den Felsen Blockierten Druchrohrleitungen.

Um jedoch besser das Verhalten des Verbunds Stahl/Beton/Gestein bestimmen zu können, wurde ein Versuch in Masstab 1 ausgeführt, und zwar in einem 20 m langen Abschnitt eines Aufschluss-stollen des Wasserkraftwerks Super-Bissorte.

Es ergaben sich folgende Hauptergebnisse :

- Die sehr hohen Drücke (25 MPa) haben den Stahl weit über die elastische Grenze hinaus verformt, ohne jedoch zu einem Bruch zu führen.
- Bestätigung des Vorhandenseins eines Spiels zwischen Blech un Beton bis zu 80×10^{-5} (relativ auf den Leitungsradius bezogen).
- Die Beteiligung des Gesteins hängt zum grossen Teil von den goetechnischen Daten des druckenlasteten Bereichs in Nähe der Ausschachtung ab. Sie bewegt sich je nach Versuchsbedingungen zwischen 50 und 60 %.

Die Messergebnisse haben die Abstimmung eines mathematischen Modells ermöglicht, das jetzt auch für die Dimensionierung anderer Durckrohrleitungen herangezogen werden kann.

RESUME

Le projet hydroélectrique de Super-Bissorte a conduit à revoir les méthodes de dimensionnement du blindage des conduites forcées bloquées au rocher.

Pour mieux cerner le comportement réel du complexe acier-béton-rocher, un essai en vraie grandeur a été réalisé sur un tronçon de 20 m de long, dans une galerie de reconnaissance de l'usine de Super-Bissorte.

Les principaux résultats sont les suivants :

- les pressions très élevées (25 MPa) imposées ont provoqué des déformations de l'acier très supérieures à la limite élastique. Cependant, aucune rupture n'a été constatée.
- L'existence d'un jeu entre tôle et béton pouvant atteindre 80.10^{-5} (relativement au rayon de la conduite) est confirmée.

- La participation du rocher dépend pour une grande part des caractéristiques géotechniques de la zone décomprimée située au voisinage de l'excavation. Elle varie dans les conditions de l'essai de 50 à 60 %.

Les résultats des mesures ont permis le calage d'un modèle mathématique qu'il sera donc possible d'utiliser pour le dimensionnement d'autres conduites forcées.

INTRODUCTION

L'étude du dimensionnement des conduites forcées du projet de SUPER-BISSORTE situé en Savoie dans la Vallée de l'Arc (voir Fig. 1) a montré la nécessité, pour les aménagements de haute chute en cours de réalisation ou d'étude, de revoir certaines hypothèses de calcul du blindage des conduites forcées.

Jusqu'à présent, les calculs concernant les conduites forcées bloquées au rocher étaient conduits en ne tenant compte que de la tôle ; l'influence du rocher n'intervenait qu'au niveau du choix du coefficient de sécurité fixé à 1,2 ou 1,3 alors qu'il est de 2 dans le cas d'une conduite libre. Avec l'augmentation des valeurs des hauteurs de chute et des puissances transitées ce type de calcul conduit à dépasser les limites constructives de l'acier ; il faut donc élaborer une méthode de calcul cernant de plus près la réalité et prenant en compte le complexe tôle + béton de blocage + rocher dans son ensemble. A cet effet, un modèle mathématique (qui utilise la méthode par éléments finis) a été mis au point par E.S.I. (Engineering System International). Pour caler ce modèle et vérifier sa validité, un essai en vrai grandeur a été réalisé sur un tronçon de conduite bloquée au rocher, implantée sur le site de SUPER-BISSORTE. Ce tronçon, long d'une vingtaine de mètres, a été équipé d'un dispositif d'auscultation de l'ensemble tôle-béton-rocher.

1. IMPLANTATION DE LA CAVERNE D'ESSAIS

1.1. Le choix de l'emplacement (voir Fig. 2)

Le tronçon de galerie destiné à l'essai, a été implanté sur l'un des rameaux de la galerie de reconnaissance de l'Aménagement de SUPER-BISSORTE.

Les galeries de reconnaissance de l'usine souterraine BISSORTE II, avaient permis de déceler la présence d'une importante zone faillée F1 (voir Fig. 2) conduisant à décaler légèrement vers le Sud l'emplacement de l'usine. Ceci eut pour effet de laisser, dans une roche malgré tout relativement saine, deux rameaux de galerie disponibles, dont les dimensions permettaient d'implanter une chambre d'essais. Afin de pouvoir étudier de plus près l'influence d'une zone faillée sur le comportement du complexe tôle + béton + rocher, on choisit le rameau central dont le déro-

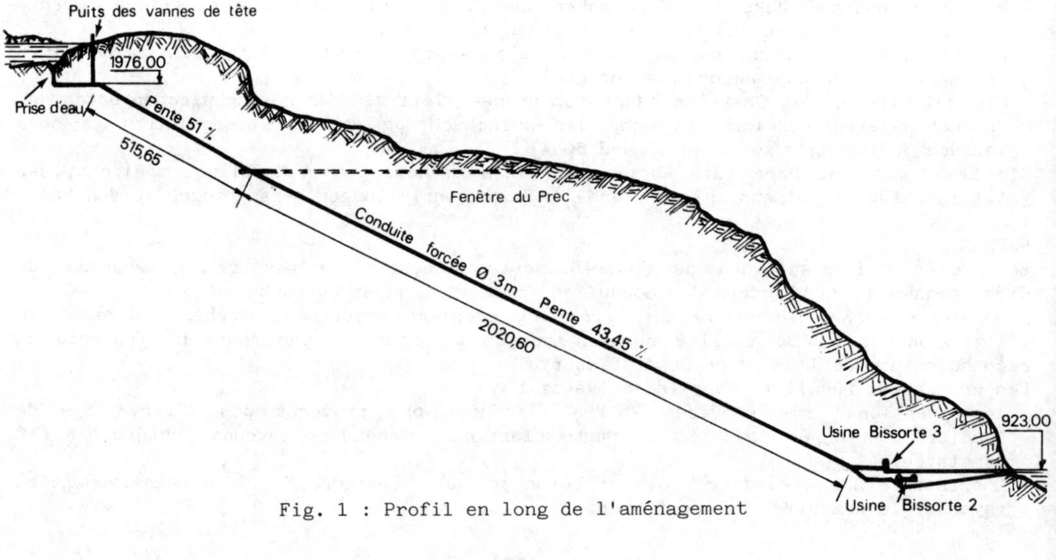

Fig. 1 : Profil en long de l'aménagement

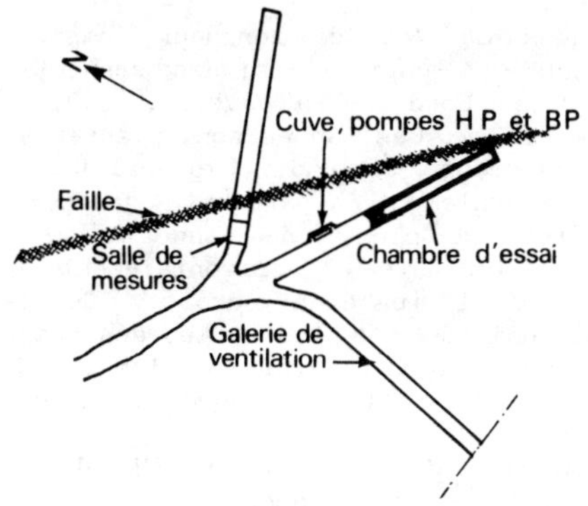

Fig. 2 : Schéma d'implantation

chement fut au préalable prolongé de cinq mètres.
L'emplacement de cette caverne d'essais s'est avéré idéal dans la mesure où 200 m seulement la séparent de la sortie de galerie de reconnaissance facilitant les allers et venues et l'approvisionnement en matériel et où la proximité de l'usine en construction a permis, lors de la mise en oeuvre des essais, de bénéficier du support logistique que représente un chantier en activité.

1.2. Relevé géologique

Le rocher de SUPER-BISSORTE appartient à ce qu'on appelle le Houiller externe de la zone briançonnaise.
Il est essentiellement constitué :
. de grès,
. de psammites,
. de schistes gris,
. de schistes charbonneux.
En ce qui concerne la caverne d'essais, elle est entièrement située dans les niveaux gréseux. Les bancs de grès, dont le pendage est inférieur à 20°, sont affectés par une schistosité de pendage identique. Il en résulte une certaine fissilité de la roche, plus ou moins marquée suivant la densité des minéraux phylliteux matérialisant la schistosité ou la stratification.

1.3. Description de la chambre

Il s'agit d'une galerie de 3,20 m de diamètre longue de 30 m. La virole a une longueur de 20 m et un diamètre intérieur de 2 m. Son blocage est assuré par un anneau de béton de 0,60 m d'épaisseur.

2. CARACTERISTIQUES DE L'INSTALLATION

2.1. Le rocher

Les caractéristiques sont les suivantes :

- densité = 2,75
- teneur en eau = 0,18 %
- porosité = 0,5 %
- rupture au cisaillement : C = 25 MPa
  Φ = 48°

Les mesures de résistance ont en outre montré l'anisotropie de ce matériau :

	stratification //	⊥ stratification
Rc (MPa)	108,5	175,7
RT (brésilien) (MPa)	3,75	12,0

Les valeurs du module réversible obtenus par essai au vérin plaque de charge sont les suivantes :

	Module de déformation réversible (moyen) en MPa
Radiers	3 000
Parements gauches	5 300
Parements droits	14 000
Calottes	9 000

Les faibles modules obtenus en radier et en parement gauche ne sont pas surprenants :
- d'une part, la zone du radier et du parement gauche se trouve affectée par la présence d'une faille,
- d'autre part, le rocher est particulièrement fracturé par le tir en radier section n° 1.

2.2. Le béton

Les essais sur des éprouvettes provenant du béton de blocage de la galerie d'essais ont fourni les résultats suivants :
- module d'élasticité (sous 15 MPa) : 30 950 MPa,
- résistance mécanique à la compression : 33,5 MPa, à la traction : 3,23 MPa,
- coefficient de dilatation linéaire : $5{,}7.10^{-6}$
- densité : 2,4

2.3. La tôle

Les tôles utilisées pour les viroles de la conduite d'essai sont en acier

ST 5 2-3 d'épaisseur 12 mm. Les caractéristiques mécaniques sont les suivantes :

	Minimum	Maximum
Lim élastique (MPa)	409	480
Résistance en traction (MPa)	550	564
Allongement à la rupture	25,6 %	26,7 %
Module	$2 \times 10^{+5}$ MPa	

3. DISPOSITIF D'AUSCULTATION

3.1. Choix des sections de mesure

Deux sections perpendiculaires à l'axe de la galerie ont été auscultées :
- la section S1, située à environ 12 m du fond de la caverne,
- la section S2 à 20 m du fond.

Les deux sections de mesure ne présentent pas les mêmes caractéristiques de déformabilité. Le radier et la calotte sont en section 1 beaucoup plus décomprimés qu'en section 2 : les modules de déformation y sont 2 à 3 fois plus faible. De plus la section 1 est plus proche de la faille que la section 2.
Le dispositif d'auscultation adopté permet donc de quantifier l'influence de zones de rocher plus déformables.

3.2. Mesures mises en oeuvre

3.2.1. Dans le rocher (voir sur Fig. 3 l'exemple de S1)

Les extensomètres à points multiples de type mini distofor version tubé mesurent des déplacements.
Chaque appareil est en fait une canne extensométrique ancré au fond d'un forage sur laquelle sont répartis des capteurs inductifs.
Chaque section est équipée de quatre cannes de 4 m de longueur comportant chacune 4 capteurs situés respectivement au bord de la caverne, à 0,50 m, 1 m et 2 m. Ces cannes sont placées verticalement (en radier et calotte) et horizontalement (parement gauche et droit). De plus, une canne de 40 m a été implantée horizontalement en section 1 (parement droit). Celle-ci est munie de 8 capteurs disposés respectivement à 0 ; 0,50 m ; 1 m ; 2 m ; 5 m ; 16 m ; 30 m du bord de la paroi rocheuse.
L'ancrage de cette canne (HD 40) est placé à 39 m du parement.

3.2.2. Au contact bétonrocher (voir Fig. 4)

Afin de mesurer la pression de contact entre le béton et le rocher, des cellules hydrauliques GLOTZL (de type F 10/20 QM 200) ont été disposées le long de la paroi, à raison de trois appareils par section de mesure. Elles ont toutes été orientées tangentiellement au contour et mesurent les pressions radiales.

3.2.3. Dans le béton (voir Fig. 4)

a) Afin de mesurer la pression totale dans le béton, chaque section a été équipée de six cellules "GLOTZL", type B 10/20 QS 300 dont la pression maximale d'utilisation est de 30 MPa.

b) Pour la mesure des déformations radiales dans le béton, (compression ou traction), on a choisi d'utiliser l'extensomètre à corde vibrante, type TELEMAC C 110. A raison de six par section de mesure, ces appareils ont été noyés dans le béton. Rappelons brièvement le principe général de l'extensomètrie à corde vibrante :
- on utilise une fine corde à piano,

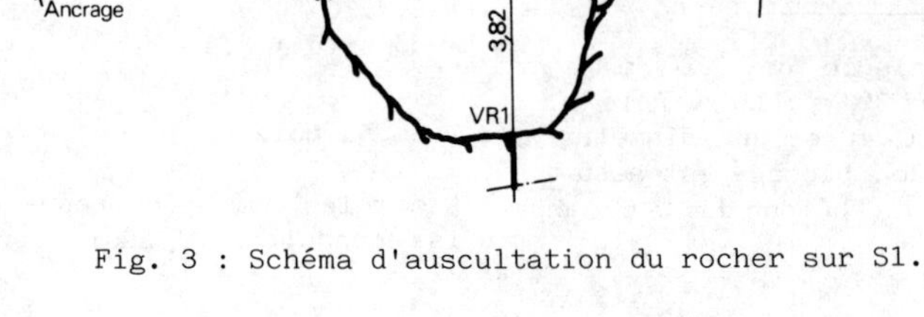

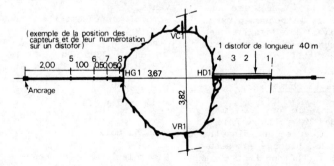

Fig. 3 : Schéma d'auscultation du rocher sur S1.

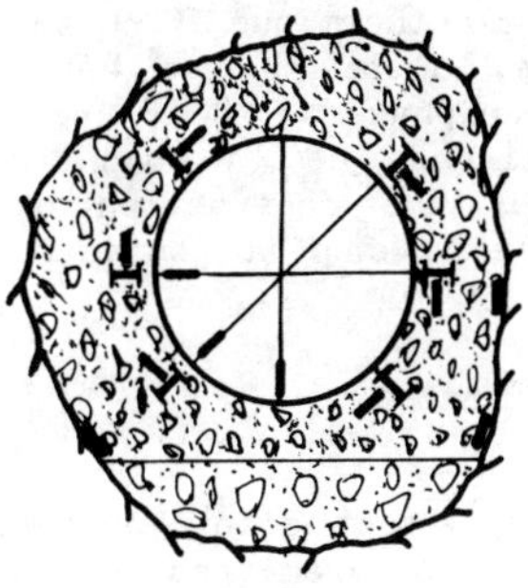

Fig. 4 : Schéma d'auscultation de l'acier et du béton en S1.

tendue entre deux points de la structure à étudier,

- une fois mise en vibration, cette corde est écartée au moyen d'électro-aimants,
- les signaux (fréquences) furent, dans notre cas, transmis par câble électrique et collectés sur l'armoire de mesures.

3.2.4. Dans l'acier (Fig. 4)

a) Extensomètres (mesures inductives)
Dans chaque section, on a mis en place trois extensomètres à fil "invar", de type "Espion de Rocher" afin de mesurer les déplacements diamètraux de la virole en acier.
Le principe de l'appareil consiste à utiliser un fil d'invar modérément tendu (8 daN), monté en série avec un ressort et un dispositif extensométrique.
L'invar utilisé a un coefficient de dilatation inférieur à 10^{-8}, ce qui permet d'obtenir des précisions de mesures de l'ordre du 1/100e de mm, sur une base de 3 m, avec une résolution de 1 micromètre.

b) Jauges de contraintes
Afin de mesurer les déformations tangentielles de la virole en acier, la D.T.G. a mis en place 32 rosettes, disposées par paires (chaque paire comportant une jauge transversale et une jauge longitudinale), à raison de 8 paires par section de mesure.
Ces jauges ont été collées sur l'acier puis reliées électriquement à un pont de Wheatstone placé dans la salle de mesures.

4. DEROULEMENT DES ESSAIS

La pression de fonctionnement de cette conduite serait, avec les méthodes de dimensionnement habituelles de 5 MPa.
Le but de l'essai était de monter en charge jusqu'à cinq fois cette pression soit 25 MPa, en cinq cycle (à 5 MPa, 10 MPa, 15 MPa, 20 MPa, 25 MPa), comportant chacun :

- une phase de mise en charge progressive (par increment de 1 MPa),
- une phase de déchargement progressif,
- une seconde phase de mise en charge progressive, plus rapide que la première,
- une seconde phase de déchargement,
- une série de matraquage (six par cycle en principe),
- un palier de fluage.

Les essais ont débuté le 15 octobre 1981 et se sont terminés le 3 février 1982.
La durée du palier de fluage a été variable d'un cycle à un autre. En particulier il a été décidé de prolonger le palier de fluage à 20 MPa pendant 1 mois de façon à atteindre la stabilisation du système et mieux cerner les paramètres viscoélastiques.

5. RESULTATS

5.1. Mesures in situ

L'exploitation des mesures réalisés in situ n'est pas complètement achevé. Un certain nombre de résultats relatifs à l'acier et au béton sont néanmoins disponibles.

5.1.1. Commentaire sur les déplacements de l'acier obtenus

Les déplacements atteignent lors du cycle à 25 MPa des valeurs variant de 0,35 à 1,3 %. Ces valeurs dépassent largement la limite élastique de l'acier (0,2 %). Néanmoins aucune déchirure de la virole n'a été constaté.

5.1.2. Part de pression prise par l'acier

Les courbes de pression intérieure - déplacement mettent en évidence un phénomène d'écrouissage de l'acier : lors de la deuxième montée en charge progressive et lors des matraquages, le comportement de l'acier apparaît approximativement comme linéaire et réversible.
On peut donc, dans les domaines de déplacements correspondant à ces phases, calculer à l'aide des lois de l'élasticité, la pression intérieure équivalente P' qui donnerait la même variation de déplacement si la conduite était seule (voir tableau ci-dessous).

Part de pression prise par l'acier (en MPa)					
	5 MPa	10MPa	15MPa	20MPa	25MPa
S1 1	2,1	3,2	4,9	6,7	8,6
S1 2	3,9	6,8	7,8	9,4	10,8
S1 3	3,9	6,2	7,5	9,1	10,5
Moy S1	3,3	5,4	6,7	8,4	10,0
S2 4	3,0	5,3	6,4	8,1	9,2
S2 5	2,5	4,3	5,6	6,9	8,4
S2 6	1,4	2,7	3,9	5,3	6,9
Moy S2	2,3	4,1	5,3	6,8	8,2

Ce tableau appelle les commentaires suivants :

- les efforts transmis à la tôle sont en section 1 nettement supérieurs à ceux transmis en section 2. Cette différence provient essentiellement des distancemètres 2 et 3, dont les réactions traduisent, comme on l'a vu, la mauvaise qualité du rocher en radier ainsi que la proximité plus grande de la faille ;
- les valeurs de P' supérieures à la résistance à la traction (P' = 6 MPa), ne sont que des valeurs fictives, puisque les hypothèses de base du calcul ne sont plus vérifiées. Dans ce cas l'acier a atteint "la phase de striction" dans laquelle le calcul des contraintes est beaucoup plus complexe.
- la part prise par le rocher diffère évidemment de S1 à S2, mais on constate qu'elle augmente au fur et à mesure de l'avancement de l'essai : de 34 à 60 % pour S1, de 55 à 66 % pour S2.

Cette variation montre l'amélioration de la rigidité de l'ensemble tôle - béton - rocher. La très forte augmentation de participation du rocher constatée sur S1 montre qu'elle résulte vraisemblablement du serrage des fissures dans les zones les plus décomprimées au voisinage de la galerie.

5.1.3. Présence d'un jeu entre tôle et béton

Les cellules de pression du béton ne réagissent qu'après un seuil de pression, variable selon les cellules et compris entre 1 et 2 MPa.
Ce retard traduit l'existence d'un jeu radial entre tôle et béton, variant d'après les distancemètres de 300 à 800 microns. En valeur relative, le rapport jeu radial/rayon vaut 30 à 80 x 10^{-5}.
Cette fourchette encadre la valeur couramment admise à E.D.F. : 45 x 10^{-5}.
Ce jeu serait dû aux variations du rayon de la tôle, consécutives aux variations de température ambiante. En effet, la prise exhothermique du béton dilate la virole, alors que le béton n'est pas encore en phase solide.
Le premier remplissage de la conduite crée, par contre, une contraction du rayon de la virole et donc un jeu entre tôle et béton.

5.2. Modèle mathématique

5.2.1. Phase de calage

Le but de ce modèle est d'interpréter l'influence des divers paramètres intervenant dans la structure et d'ajuster leur valeur de façon à caler le modèle sur les mesures réalisées.
Dans cette optique, il est apparu nécessaire de tenir compte de deux éléments, mis en évidence par les reconnaissances et mesures :

- le jeu entre tôle et béton,
- la zone de décompression présente autour de l'excavation.

De plus, il a fallu pour réaliser le modèle tenir compte d'une forte altération du béton conduisant à diviser son module par 3 (soit 10.000 MPa au lieu de 30.000 MPa).

5.2.2. Application à la conduite réelle

Il s'agit donc d'une deuxième phase de calcul où l'on reprend les principaux enseignements du calage et des mesures in situ pour estimer les efforts subis par la conduite forcée (réelle) du projet hydroélectrique de Super-Bissorte.
Ces efforts sont donnés sous la forme coefficient de sécurité : rapport limite élastique/contrainte de traction.
Ce calcul a été effectué avec les paramètres suivants :

a) Acier : son épaisseur (43 mm) a été dimensionné de telle façon que le coefficient de sécurité de la conduite libre soit de 1, pour une pression de fonctionnement (141 bars) et un diamètre de 3 m.

Les autres caractéristiques de l'acier sont :
norme AFNOR A 36201 nuance 460
limite élastique 440 MPa
limite de rupture 570 à 710 MPa
allongement à la rupture 17 %.

b) Béton : on tient compte d'une dégradation du béton se traduisant par :
   . l'absence de résistance en traction dès qu'apparaissent les fissures radiales,
   . la diminution du module de déformation.

Dans ces conditions les caractéristiques sont les suivantes :

Sain		Fracturé
30.500 MPa	E	10.000 MPa
3,0 MPa	RT	0 MPa

c) Rocher : on admet qu'il existe au voisinage immédiat de l'excavation une zone décomprimée de quelques mètres. Les caractéristiques du rocher sain et décomprimé sont les suivantes :

Sain		Décomprimé
30.500 MPa	E	10.500 MPa
0,15	ν	0,15 MPa
29 MPa	c	3 MPa
50°	Φ	0°

d) Résultat

Le calcul a permis d'étudier l'influence sur le coefficient de sécurité de deux paramètres :

- la valeur de jeu entre tôle et béton,
- l'épaisseur de la zone décomprimé.

Influence du jeu

Elle a été observée pour une épaisseur de la zone décomprimée égale à R/2, et pour des valeurs de jeu relatif valant 0, 20 x 10^{-5}, 40 x 10^{-5}, 100 x 10^{-5}, 200 x 10^{-5}. Les variations du coefficient de sécurité FS apparaissent dans le tableau suivant :

Jeu J/R	0	20x10^{-5}	45x10^{-5}	100x10^{-5}	200x10^{-5}
FS	2,5	2	1,80	1,2	1,0

Influence de l'épaisseur de la zone décomprimé

Pour un jeu relatif de 45 x 10^{-5} x R, les variations du coefficient de sécurité FS en fonction de l'épaisseur de la zone décomprimée sont les suivantes :

Epaisseur	0	R/2	R	2R
FS	1,9	1,8	1,75	1,7

Commentaire :

Ces résultats font donc apparaître une forte sensibilité du coefficient de sécurité (FS) au jeu radial entre tôle et béton.

Avec un jeu radial de 45 x 10^{-5} (conduite dimensionnée avec FS = 1 à l'air libre), FS atteint une valeur minimum de 1,7 lorsque le blocage de la roche est pris en compte.

6. CONCLUSION

Il se dégage de l'essai in situ et des calculs mathématiques deux enseignements essentiels. Il importe en premier lieu en effet de minimiser l'importance des zones de décompression. Le recours à des méthodes de creusement mécanisé est donc, partout où les caractéristiques géomécaniques le permettent, à recommander.

Il importe de plus, comme l'ont montré les calculs, de réduire l'importance du jeu initial acier-béton, au moyen par exemple d'injections.

DRUCKSTOLLEN UND DRUCKSCHÄCHTE IN SCHWACHEM MITTELS ANKER VERSTÄRKTEM GEBIRGE

Pressure galleries and pressure shafts in the weak rock mass reinforced by bolting

Conduites forcées et puits en charge dans les massifs tendres, renforcés par les boulons

Z.B.GERGOWICZ
Technische Hochschule Wrocław, Polen

SUMMARY:
One of the basic factors, on which the emphasis is put at designing of a lining of pressure galleries and pressure shafts, is to ensure a good collaboration between a steel shell and a rock mass surrounding the pit. The results of the analysis of generally applied methods of calculation as well as those of practice point out that this kind of collaboration can only by obtained either by the special technological operations or by the applying of adequate construction. The concept of such type of special construction, suitable for the weak rock mass, is presented in the paper. Applying of a provisional lining in form of rockbolting is an additional as well as a basic element. At adequate technology (an equalising coat of gunit) the lining permits to use the shrinkage-compensating concretes as an envelopment of the steel shell. Thanks to such type of construction there is a possibility of obtaining a good mutual contact among the particular member of a lining thus the chance of a due collaboration between a steel shell and a rock mass becomes greater.

ZUSAMMENFASSUNG:
Einer der wichtigsten Faktoren, dem bei Projektierung von Auskleidung der Druckstollen und Druckschächte grosses Gewicht beigelegt wird, ist das gute Zusammenwirken der Stahlpanzerung mit dem den Grubebau umgebenden Gebirge zu sichern. Aus der Analyse der allgemein angewandten Berechnungsmethoden und der Erfahrung geht hervor, dass solches Zusammenwirken entweder durch spezielle Konstruktion oder durch entsprechende technologische Massnahmen erzielt werden kann. Ein Entwurf solch einer Konstruktion vom speziellen Typ, die für Anwendung in schwachem Gebirge geeignet ist, vorgestellt wurde. Das grundlegende und zugleich zusätzliche Element ist hier die Anwendung der vorläufigen Auskleidung in Form eines Ankerausbaus. Bei entsprechender Technologie 5Torkret-Ausgleichschicht9 ermöglicht dieser Ausbau als Betonauskleidung der Stahlpanzerung Expansiv-Gegenschwindungsbeton zu verwenden. Durch solche Konstruktion kann ein guter gegenseitiger Kontakt zwischen den einzelnen Bauelementen erreicht werden und demzufolge die Möglichkeit des richtigen Zusammenwirkens der Stahlpanzerung mit dem Gebirge vergrössert sich.

RESUME:
Un des facteurs principaux lequel joue un rôle important dans les calculs des conduites forcées et des puits en charge est une bonne collaboration du blindage en acier avec les roches entourantes. De l'analyse des méthodes des calculs utilisées couramment ainsi que de la pratique il en résulte que ce genre de collaboration peut être obtenu ou bien par des traitements technologiques spéciaux ou bien par l'utilisation d'une construction appropriée. Dans ce travail nous présentons une telle construction du type spécial, construction qui peut être utilisée dans les cas des roches tendres. Ce soutènement permet, en adoptant la technologie appropriée (couche de régalage en torcret), a une utilisation des bétons expansifs, dites contre-retraits comme un enrobage en béton du blindage en acier. Grâce à ce type de construction on arrive à avoir un bon contact entre

les éléments respectifs du soutènement. Cela nous permet d'augmenter les chances d'une collaboration effective du blindage en acier avec le massif.

In der früheren Bearbeitung (Gergowicz, 1978) wurden die Druckstollen mit Betonauskleidung, die in schwachem mit Anker verstärktem Gebirge lokaliesiert werden, behandelt. Aus den Schlussfolgerungen ergibt sich, dass die Anker, die im Prinzip die Aufgabe des vorläufigen Ausbaus erfüllen, die Arbeit der endgultigen Stollenauskleidung günstig beeinflussen. Dieser günstige Einfluss ist die Folge der deutlichen Verbesserung der Bedingungen, in denen die Stollenauskleidung mit dem Gebirge zusammenwirkt. Durch das Zusammenwirken werden die durch den Innenwasserdruck hervorgerufenen Spannungen in der Auskleidung bedeutend reduziert, was im Falle der Beton- bzw. Stahlbetonauskleidung eine wichtige Rolle spielt. Es muss hier betont werden, dass die hier angeführten Probleme sich auf die Stollen mit Wasserdruck, der nicht grösser als 2,0 bis 2,5 MPa (20 bis 25 kG/cm^2) ist, beziehen.

Bei Stollen mit höherem Druck und vor allem bei Druckschächten wird in der Regel eine von innen mit Stahlpanzerung verstärkte Auskleidung verwendet. Man kann also eine Frage stellen, ob auch in diesem Fall die Verstärkung des Gebirges mit dem Anker insofern einen positiven Einfluss auf das ganze Konstruktionssystem ausübt, dass man ihn bei Projektierung berücksichtigen kann. Die Tatsache nämlich, dass dieser Einfluss überhaupt ausgeübt wird, und dass er positiv ist, ist zweifellos.

Die Antwort auf die oben gestellte Frage kann anhand der genauen Analyse der Arbeit aller Elemente des Systems: Stahlpanzerung, Betonauskleidung und Gebirge gegeben werden. Es ist daher notwendig, die in jedem der oben genannten Elemente auftretenden Erscheinungen und Änderungen genau zu bestimmen, indem gleichzeitig die konkreten, wirklichen Bedingungen unter welchem diese Erscheinungen auftreten, berücksichtigt werden.

Das Problem ist nicht neu und war schon Gegenstand zahlreicher, mehr oder weniger ausführlicheren Untersuchungen. Sehr ausführlich und eingehend hat sich Kastner (1971) mit diesem Problem befasst. Bei der Untersuchung des Zusammenwirkens der Stahlpanzerung mit dem Gebirge hat er alle diese Faktoren, die einen wesentlichen Einfluss auf den Verlauf dieser Erscheinung haben können, sehr genau bestimmt. Er hat sich also nicht nur auf die Bemessung von Verformungen und gleichzeitigen Verschiebungen der Stahlpanzerung, Betonauskleidung und des Gebirges beschränkt; sondern auch solche zusätzliche Einflussfaktoren, wie Betonschwindung, Temperatur, plastische Verformungen im Beton und im Gebirge berücksichtigt.

Leider, wenn man alle die Arbeit des ganzen Systems betreffenden Realien berücksichtigt, kommt man zur Überzeugung, dass die Kastners Erwägungen, obwohl sehr wertvoll, einen rein theoretischen Charakter haben. Schon bei der Bemessung der Verformungsgrössen der freiliegenden Panzerung, die dem Innenwasserdruck ausgesetzt wurde, entstehen die ersten Zweifel. Die von Kastner in seinem Buch angeführte Tabelle (Tab 1), die sich auf die ausgeführten Objekte bezieht, wurde mit den werten der Radialverschiebung der Panterung ergänzt. Wie man sieht, liegen diese Verschiebungen in den Grenzen von 1 bis 2 mm. Aus den Formeln, die Kastner zur Bestimmung anderer Faktoren ausnützt, erhält man nach Umrechnung die Ergebnisse einer Grössenreihe von zehntel Millimetern. Man kann also die allgemeine Bilanz von gegenseitigen Verschiebungen der Einzelnen Elemente des Systems feststellen und auf diesem Grund die Grösse und den Charakter des Zusammenwirkens der Auskleidung mit dem Gebirge bestimmen.

Die obigen Erwähgungen sind nur dann begründet, wenn die äusserst präzise Ausführung des Objekts gewährleistet ist. Es geht ja darum, dass die Betonauskleidung ideal, mit einer Genauigkeit von 0,1 mm, sowohl an die Panzerung als an das Gebirge anliegt. Die Gesamtbreite der Undichtheit darf nicht 1 mm überschreiten, sonst werden die durchgeführten Berechnungen irreal. Aus der bei Ausführung von mehreren Objekten gewonnenen Erfahrungen geht hervor, dass solch ein Ausführungspräzision praktisch unmöglich ist. Alle nach der Fertigung der Auskleidung getroffenen speziellen Massnahmen ebenfals nicht immer sichern eine ausreichende Füllung aller möglichen Klüfte und Hohlräume.

Es muss festgestellt werden, dass Kastner sich der negativen Auswirkungen von Ausführungstechnologie bewusst

Tabelle 1. Ausführungsdaten der Druckstollenpanzerungen (nach Kastner)

Kraftwerk	Bemessungsdruck ($kpcm^{-2}$)	Innendurchmesser (cm)	Blechdicke (mm)	Blechwerkstoff und Mindeststreckgrenze ($kpcm^{-2}$)	Ringspannung der freiliegenden Panzerung ($kpcm^{-2}$)	Radialverschiebung der Panzerung (mm)
Cavergno (Maggia-Kraftwerke AG Locarno)	57,5	220	30	COLTUF 28 2600	2180	1,14
Zervreila (Kraftwerke Zervreila AG, Vals)	73,7	210	24	UNION 36 3000	3370	1,68
Verbano (Maggia-Kraftwerke AG	31,0	285	18	ALDUR 41 2600	2600	1,76
Lienne (Walliser-Alpen)	93,7	160	23	COLTUF 32 3300	3400	1,30
Peccia (Maggia-Kraftwerke AG)	47,1	180	15	COLTUF 28 2600	3020	1,29
Fionnay (Grande Dixence S.A.)	93,5	280	33	ALDUR 50 3400	4090	2,73

war. Er hat also in seine Formeln, die die Reduktiongrösse des ausschliesslich durch Panzerung übertragenen Druckes bestimmen, zwei Grössen, bezeichneten Δ_1 und Δ_2 eingeführt. Die erste Grosse bezieht sich auf den Spalt zwischen der Panzerung und der Betonauskleidung, die zweite dagegen auf den Spalt zwischen der Betonauskleidung und dem Gebirge. Im Gegensatz zu den mit entsprechender Präzision bestimmten Einflüssen von Faktoren, die früher besprochen wurden, sollen nach Kastner die zwei letzt genannten Grössen schätzungsweise bestimmt werden. In seinen Erwägungen nimmt er für sie die Grössenordnung von zehntel Millimetern an. Wenn solche Stellung inbezug auf den Kontakt der Panzerung mit der Betonauskleidung akzeptabel sein könnte, so erweckt die Sache des Kontakts der Betonauskleidung mit dem Gebirge grosse Zweifel. Das Problem tritt besonders deutlich im Falle des schwachen Gebirges auf - von dem hier eben die Rede ist - das noch zusätzlich durch Sprengarbeiten gelockert werden kann. Ausserdem scheint hier eine genaue Bestimmung der Gebirgsverschiebung unter Anwendung der Grössenordnung von zehntel Millimetern überhaupt problematisch zu sein.

Alle oben angeführten Bemerkungen setzten sich zum Ziel nicht die von Kastner vorgestellte Berechnungsmethode einer Kritik zu unterziehen, sondern eine Bestätigung der grundsätzlichen Schlussfolgerung hinsichtlich der Möglichkeit des richtigen Zusammenwirkens der Auskleidung mit dem Gebirge zu erzielen. Aus der Analyse der eingehenden Kastners Erwägungen geht es indirekt hervor, dass das erforderte Zusammenwirken der beiden erwähnten Elemente entweder durch entsprechende technologische Massnahmen oder durch vorgenommene Änderungen in den tradizionellen Konstruktionsschemen gewährleistet werden kann.

Zur Gruppe der technologischen Massnahmen gehören alle diese Arbeiten, die erst dann ausgeführt werden, wenn die endgültige Auskleidung fertig ist. Es geht hier um allerlei Injektionen, die zur Füllung von zwischen den einzelnen Elementen der Auskleidung auftretenden Hohräumen und Klüften dienen. Die Praxis weist darauf hin, dass es kaum solche Objekte gibt, an denen die Massnahmen dieser Art nicht getroffen werden. Es ist auch bekannt, wie problematisch in manchen Fällen die auf diese Weise erzielten Ergebnisse waren. Dies bedeutet aber nicht, dass diese Handlungsweise schlecht ist, im Gegenteil, man muss weiter in diese Richtung gehen. Es scheint nur, dass man alle Bemühungen auf einer mehr radikalen und für Steuerung und Kontrolle leichteren Ausführungsmethoden konzentrieren muss.

Projekte der eventuellen Konstruktionsänderungen bieten sich im gewissem Sinne automatisch, nachdem wir die Wirkungsweisen der Injektionen erörtert haben, wovon die Rede früher war. Die Injektion beruht darauf, dass verschiedenartige Materialien unterm Druck ausser die Panzerung eingeführt werden. Die Anwendung vom Druck bei Pressung verursacht nicht nur die Beseitigung von Klüften und Hohlräumen sondern ruft auch einen Spannungszustand hervor, der mit einer eigenartigen Vorspannung der Konstruktion vergleichen werden kann. Es erhebt sich die Frage, ob es nicht möglich wäre, solche Materialien einzusetzen, die sowohl das dichte Anliegen der einzelnen Elemente aneinander gewährleisten als auch einen, genau bestimmten Spannungszustand in der Betonauskleidung hervorrufen können.

Als Antwort auf solche Fragestellung bietet sich sofort der Entwurf der Anwendung des Bettungsbeton aus Expansivbeton. Der Bettungsbeton dieser Art konnte durch das Vergrössern ihres Volumens während des Abbindens und der Verhärtung nicht nur alle Klüfte und Hohlräume beseitigen, sondern auch einen Druck auf den Stahlmantel und das Gebirge ausüben.

Der Sinn dieser Lösung ist jedoch unter Anwendung des traditionellen Konstruktionsschemas, bei dem der Bettungsbeton einen unmittelbaren Kontakt mit dem Gebirge hat, mehr als zweifelhaft. Das zerklüftete und zusätzlich infolge der Sprengarbeiten gelockerte Gebirge, das durch unregelmässige Abrisslinie gekennzeichnet ist, bildet für die Bettung aus Expansivbeton keine entsprechende Kontaktfläche. Man soll nämlich nicht vergessen, dass die obenerwähnte Volumenvergrösserung von 1 bis 4 % beträgt (Kesler, Pfeifer, 1970), also in Millimetern gemessen wird. Der Bettungsbeton soll daher an das Gebirge mit einer regelmässigen und nicht gelockerten Oberfläche anliegen.

Die Erfüllung dieser schwierigen und den Verlauf der Arbeiten komplizierenden Bedingung kann im hohem Grade die Anwendung von Ankerung als Vor-Auskleidung erleichtern. Das Hervorrufen von zusätzlichen Spannungen im Gebirge sowie Herstellung eines verstärkten Ringes rundum den Grubenbau sollte wesentlich zur Beseitigung der Risse und des Auflockerungszustandes beitragen. Dann wird die Anwendung einer Betonausgleichschicht, die nach einem Torkretierungsverfahren gefertigt wird, möglich und zugleich zweckmässig. Bei der Annahme solcher Technologie von Vorarbeiten gewinnt die Sache der Ausnutzung des Expansivbetons einen anderen Sinn als früher.

Der Expansivbeton, gemäss seinem Namen, vergrössert sein Volumen während des Quellungsprozesses wobei dieser Prozess durch die Wirkung gewissener zusätzlichen Zementbestandteile hervorgerufen ist, die hauptsächlich auf Kalziumaluminaten, Kalziumsulfaten und Kalziumoxiden basieren. Die Quellgrösse kann durch entsprechende Rezeptur der Mischung gesteuert werden, wobei sie in den Grenzen von 0,1 bis 3÷ 4 % liegt. Wenn die freie Quellung begrenzt ist, so treten im Beton Druckspannungen von 0,1 bis 0,7 MPa (von 1 bis 7 kG/cm^2) abhängig von der angewandten Rezeptur, auf.

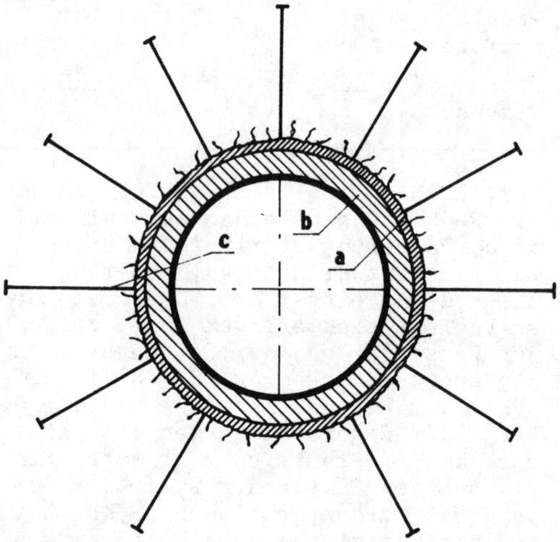

Abb. 1. Querschnitt des Druckschachtes in schwachem mittels Anker verstärktem Gebirge: a) Torkret-Ausgleichschicht, b) Bettungsbeton, c) Anker.

In Hinblick auf die Tatsache, dass der zum Betonieren vorbereitete Grubenbau eine regelmäsige Form aufweist, kann man etwas kleinere Dicke des Bettungsbetons (20 - 30 cm) annehmen. Bei Anwendung des Expansivbetons sog. Gegenschwindungsbetons und einer entsprechenden Rezeptur soll nicht die Volumenvergrösserung während des Abbindens 1 bis 2 %, also 2 bis 6 mm überschreiten. Gleichzeitig sollen die auf das Gebirge und den Stahlmantel übertragenen Druckspannungen in den Grenzen von 0,1 MPa liegen. In Hinblick auf die Betonentspannung (Relaxation) verschwinden allmählich die Druckspannungen nach der Abbindezeit. Die auf vorgeschlagene Bauweise ausgeführte Auskleidung wird, wie es auf der Abb. 1 in einfachster Form dargestellt wurde, aussehen.

Der Arbeitsgang ist zweifellos mehr kompliziert als im Falle der typischen Auskleidung von Druckschächten. Man darf aber nicht vergessen, dass es sich hier um das schwache Gebirge handelt, bei dem die vorläufige Auskleidung, deren Rolle die Anker übernehmen, unentbehrlich ist. Durch die Anwendung der Torkret-Ausgleichschicht werden die späteren Injektionen eliminiert und die Ausführung dieser Schicht kann in vollem Masse, u.a. dank der Ankerauskleidung, mechanisiert werden. Unter Beachtung der Tatsache, dass die Kosten des Expansivbetons sich wenig von den des Normalbetons unterscheiden, kann man feststellen, dass der vorgeschlagene Entwurf aus dem ökonomischen Gesichtspunkt keine ernste Vorbehalte erwecken sollte. Ausserdem ist die Einführung von mehr komplizierten Technologien und von einem speziellen Betontyp, um die beschwerlichen Injektionen, die die gewünschte Zuverlässigkeit nicht gewährleisten, zu vermeiden, nicht neu. Es genügt hier eine Betonauskleidung zu erwähnen, die nach dem Prepakt-Verfahren gefertigt ist.

Im Falle der richtigen und genauen Ausführung aller Arbeiten kann man annehmen, dass der Kontakt zwischen der Stahlpanzerung und dem Gebirge vollauf gesichert wird. Dann können die von Kastner vorgeschlagenen Formeln, die sich auf die Reduzierung des auf die Stahlpanzerung wirkenden Innenwasserdruckes beziehen, vereinfacht werden. Nach Einsetzen der konkreten Werte erhält man Ergebnisse, die um 40 % günstiger sind, im Verhältnis zu diesen, die nach Kastners Formeln erhalten werden. Man kann feststellen, indem dieser Überschuss als eine Art Sicherheitsreserve anerkannt wird, dass die Anwendung der vorgeschlagenen Konstruktion und Arbeitstechnologie den Anforderungen, die sich aus dem Kastners Berechnungsverfahren ergeben, entsprechen. Es werden jedoch die am Anfang erwähnten Zweifel und Verschweigungen, die sich auf die Bestimmungsweise des Zusammenwirkens der Auskleidung mit dem Gebirge beziehen, vermieden.

LITERATUR

Gergowicz, Z.B., Springer-Verlag 1978, Bemessung von Druckstollenauskleidungen unter Berücksichtigung des Einflusses der Gebirgsverankerung, Rock Mech., Suppl.7., 129-138.

Kastner, H., 1971, Statik des Tunnel- und Stollenbaues, Berlin-Heidelberg-New York, Springer-Verlag.

Kesler, C.E., Pfeifer, D.W. 1970, Expansive Cement Concretes-Present State of Knowledge, ACI J., 583-- 610.

NEUESTE ERKENNTNISSE ÜBER DIE MITWIRKUNG DES GEBIRGES BEI DRUCKSTOLLEN IN VULKANISCHEN ABLAGERUNGEN

Recent knowledge about the cooperation between rock and pressure tunnel lining in volcanic deposits

Connaissances récentes de la coopération entre le rocher et le revêtement des galeries sous pression dans des sédiments volcaniques

B.GILG

Beratender Ingenieur, Zürich, Schweiz

SUMMARY:

It is to-day more and more a necessity to transverse volcanic deposits with pressure tunnels of various size. Such constructions are requiring certain principle considerations for the design as well as for the performance of the excavation and the tunnel lining which are not new in the domain of underground works but cannot be neglected without creation of major difficulties. Of big importance are therefore f.i. a good correlation of the investigation work, the correct performance of the excavation following the prescripted profiles, a perfect dewatering system, the reliability of grouting work and the adequate choice of the quality and the content of cement. Deviations of the to-day generally well known standards will very often lead to time consuming repaire work and therefore to losses of energy.

ZUSAMMENFASSUNG :

Die Durchfahrung vulkanischer Ablagerungen mit Druckstollen verschiedener Durchmesser ist heute mehr und mehr eine Notwendigkeit. Dabei müssen für die Projektierung, vor allem aber beim Ausbruch und beim Bau der Tunnelverkleidung gewisse Grundsätze befolgt werden, welche zwar im Untertagebau schon seit längerer Zeit bekannt sind, deren Vernachlässigung jedoch hier besonders rasch zu Schwierigkeiten führen kann. Eine wichtige Rolle spielen vor allem die Korrelation der verschiedenen Voruntersuchungen, die sorgfältige profilgerechte Ausführung des Ausbruches, die saubere Wasser-Ableitung die Zuverlässigkeit der Injektionen sowie die adäquate Wahl der Zementqualität und insbesondere der Zementdosierung. Abweichungen von der heute zwar anerkannten aber nicht immer eingehaltenen Norm führen zu zeitraubenden Nachbehandlungen der Stollenverkleidung und damit zu Energieverlust.

RESUME:

La traverse des sédiments volcaniques moyennant des galeries sous pression de différents diamètres s'avère aujourd'hui de plus en plus nécessaire. Les travaux y relatifs demandent, en général, la considération stricte de certains principes concernant aussi bien le projet que l'exécution des excavations et de la construction du revêtement, qui sont d'ailleurs, bien connus depuis plusieurs années et dont la négligence amène dans ce genre de travail à des difficultés variées. La corrélation soigneuse des diverses prospections, l'exécution propre de l'excavation selon le profil prescrit, le drainage des eaux, la sûreté des injections ainsi que le choix adéquat de la qualité et du dosage de ciment jouent entre autre un rôle important. Toute abérration des normes, telles que reconnues normalement aujourd'hui dans les travaux souterrains peut engendrer des réparations du revêtement qui nécessitent beaucoup de temps et causent ainsi des pertes d'énergie.

1. EINLEITUNG

Weite Bereiche der Erdkruste bestehen in ihren äusseren Zonen aus vulkanischen Ablagerungen jüngeren und jüngsten Datums. Dieselben besitzen sehr unterschiedliche Entstehungsformen und weisen demnach auch verschiedenartige Qualitäten auf, was sich besonders deutlicn zeigt, wenn sie als Baugrund verwendet werden müssen. Sie reichen vom kompakten Basalt mit hoher Festigkeit und hohem Verformungsmodul bis zu den vulkanischen Tuffen und sogar bis zur Flugasche, wobei für die letzte Formationen der Begriff Gestein kaum noch verwendet werden kann.

Die Ausführung von Untertagebauten in Zonen vulkanischer Ablagerungen hat deshalb zu neuen Erkenntnissen geführt, deren Verbreitung nützlich scheint, da die Errichtung von Stollen, Schächten und Kavernen heute in fast allen Felsarten mehr und mehr zunimmt, sei es für Strassenbau, Bahnbau, Wasserkraftanlagen oder auch für nukleare Kraftwerke.

In den folgenden Kapiteln soll das Problem möglichst allgemein behandelt werden, wobei wir versuchen,an Hand eines praktischen Beispieles die spezifischen Fragen heraus zu kristallisieren und ihre Beantwortung in genereller Weise zu formulieren.

Vorerst ist zu betonen, dass es sich beim Testfall keineswegs um ein spektakuläres Bauwerk handelt. Dennoch zeigt er sehr deutlich, dass gerade bei geologisch ungewöhnlichen Randbedingungen dem bautechnischen Vorgang umso grössere Aufmerksamkeit geschenkt werden muss, wenn man verhindern will, dass relativ geringe Versäumnisse grosse Wirkungen nach sich ziehen. Im übrigen sind die gemachten Erfahrungen von so allgemeiner Natur, dass sie auch auf grössere Bauten übertragen und bei deren Dimensionierung berücksichtigt werden können.

Wir wählen als Beispiel für unsere Ueberlegungen einen Druckstollen von rd. 3 m Durchmesser welcher einem Mitteldruckkraftwerk als Triebwasserleitung dient. An und für sich ist dies ein harmloses Bauwerk, welches in der Literatur normalerweise kaum mehr Erwähnung finden dürfte. Man würde höchstens noch mögliche moderne Ausbruchsmethoden und eventuell die Durchquerung besonders schwieriger Fels- oder Lockergesteinpartien mit hohem Wasser- und Gebirgsdruck diskutieren. Aber auch im Falle scheinbar normaler Verhältnisse kann das Zusammentreffen von ausserordentlichen Umständen Schwierigkeiten bereiten, welche nur infolge des Kumulierungseffektes all dieser Ereignisse die kritische Schwelle überschreiten und dann allerdings ganz deutlich vor Augen führen, wie sehr auch die kleinen Einzelheiten des Felsbaues ins Gewicht zu fallen vermögen und wie der vielgerühmte Fortschritt bisweilen in der Praxis noch nicht seine Früchte zeitigt.

2. Beschreibung des Testbauwerkes

Der zu erstellende Druckstollen besitzt zwischen der Wasserfassung und dem Wasserschloss eine Länge von ca. 12 km, folgt dabei grösstenteils dem Haupttale und muss auf seinem Wege mehrere Seitentäler unterfahren oder queren. Die Ausbauwassermenge beträgt rd. 22 m3/s, sodass sein innerer Durchmesser auf 2.65 m beschränkt werden konnte, ohne dass selbst beim Vollbetrieb grössere Geschwindigkeiten als 4m/s auftreten. Wenn auch diese Geschwindigkeit für einen Dauerbetrieb etwas ungewöhnlich wäre, so kann sie hier doch toleriert werden, da der Normalbetrieb nicht der vollen Leistung entspricht und somit für die seltenen Fälle der Vollast ein grösserer Verlust in Kauf genommen werden darf.

Die bewusste Wahl eines relativ kleinen Durchmessers lässt ahnen, dass die Wirtschaftlichkeit der Anlage an der Grenze liegt, ein Zustand welcher sich nun freilich dank der steigenden Oelpreise zunehmend verbessert. Immerhin wurde bei der Optimierung des Stollendurchmessers eben nicht nur auf den Vollbetrieb abgestellt, sondern es wurden alle mutmasslichen Betriebszustände mit dem Gewicht ihrer prozentualen Dauer in die Optimierungsberechnung eingeführt, was dann zur Wahl der oben erwähnten Werte führte.

3. Geologie

Der Stollen durchläuft eine grosse Varietät von vulkanischen Formationen nämlich:

Vulkanische Tuffe Vulkanische Tuffbrekzien Vulkanische Konglomerate	8400 m
Vulkanische Asche	300 m
Ignimbrit	500 m
Basalt	1400 m
Andesit	900 m
Porphyrit	400 m

Um die Gesteinseigenschaften zu erkennen, wurden folgende Vorarbeiten durchgeführt:

Oberflächengeologie
1400 m Bohrungen
13000 m seismische Profile
Sondierstollen
Wasserstands-Messungen

Dabei liessen sich folgende Feststellungen machen :

- Die seismischen Geschwindigkeiten nehmen von der Oberfläche gegen die Tiefe systematisch zu und betragen im Bereiche des künftigen Stollentrassees 2000 m/s bis 3400 m/s. Lediglich bei der Umfahrung der Seitentäler muss man über eine Länge von einigen hundert Metern mit viel niedrigeren Werten rechnen.

- Der Stollen befindet sich über einen Grossteil seiner Länge in konsolidierten Konglomeraten und Tuffbrekzien, deren seismische Geschwindigkeit im Mittel rd. 2500 m/s beträgt.
- Ueber kurze Strecken verläuft der Stollen im Basalt and Andesit, teilweise sogar im Quarzporphyr, welche durchgehend seismische Geschwindigkeiten von mehr als 3000 m/s aufweisen.
- Der Grundwasserspiegel liegt in weiten Bereichen höchstens 20 m unter dem normalen Betriebs-Spiegel, sodass den aus dem Projekt resultierenden Innendrücken von 4 bis 8 atü meist ein Aussendruck von mindestens 2 bis 6 atü entgegenwirkt. Grössere Ueberschüsse an Innendruck sind nur bei der Umfahrung der Seitentäler möglich.
- Der ausgebrochene Fels ist teilweise sehr verwitterungsanfällig, was einen sofortigen Schutz der Stollenwände mit Spritzbeton erfordert. Dies gilt vor allem für die Tuffe.
- Einige kurze Verwerfungszonen werden einen stärkeren Einbau erfordern, im allgemeinen aber ist der Fels standfest.
- Der Fels ist im Bereich der Tuffe relativ dicht.

4. Das Projekt

Wie bereits erwähnt, bewegten sich zur Zeit der Projektierung die Anlagekosten an der Grenze der Wirtschaftlichkeit. Dies erforderte äusserste Sparsamkeit in allen Bereichen. Natürlich war es von Anbeginn klar, dass gewisse Teile des Stollens gepanzert werden mussten, so z.B. die Unterfahrung der zwei wichtigsten Seitentäler sowie die 600 m lange weniger als 100 m unter der Fels-Oberfläche liegende Schluss-Strecke vor dem Wasserschloss.

Ferner war anzunehmen, dass einige der durchfahrenen Verwerfungszonen mit bewehrtem Spritzbeton zu schützen waren. Ihre Ausdehnung sollte 300-400 m betragen. Für den Hauptteil des Stollens wurde ein unbewehrter Betonring von 25 cm vorgesehen sodass der Ausbruchdurchmesser 3.15 m betragen musste ; auch dies eine relativ bescheidene Dimension.

Eine generelle Berechnung der im Beton zu erwartenden Ringzugspannungen konnte auf folgende Annahmen abgestellt werden:

Raum-Gewicht der Felsmasse	= 2.0 t/m3
Querdehnung	= 0.25
seismische Geschwindigkeit v=	2500 m/s
und daraus	
Dynamischer Elastizitäts-modul E_{dyn}	= 106'000kg/cm2

Da diese Annahmen eher auf der ungünstigen Seite liegen, ist der E_{dyn} sicher nicht kleiner als der berechnete Wert.

Ein oft diskutiertes Problem ist bekanntlich die Berechnung des statischen Elastizitätsmoduls auf Grund des dynamischen Wertes. Natürlich weiss man, dass lediglich bei sehr hohen Moduln dieselben einander gleich sind, jedoch war man noch vor wenigen Jahren der Ansicht, dass das Verhältnis nur bei sehr verformbarem Fels unter 4 sinken würde. In unserem Fall wählte man die Zahl 3,5, was dann einen statischen Wert

$$E_{stat.} = 30'000 \text{ kg/cm2}$$

ergab.

Im weiteren steht bekanntlich fest, dass nach Beendigung der um den Stollen herum ausgeführten Konsolidationsinjektionen der Modul des Felsens zum mindesten um 50%, öfters aber noch stärker ansteigt. Somit war mit einem tatsächlich wirkenden Modul von ca. 55'000 kg/cm2 zu rechnen, was einer Erhöhung um 85% entspricht. Für den Felsbereich ausserhalb der injizierten Zone gilt E = 30'000 kg/cm2.

Die Druckverteilung auf Stollenwand und Fels wurde unter der Annahme intensiver Injektionen (E = 55'000 kg/cm2) und zur Kontrolle auch ohne Injektionen bestimmt (E = 30'000 kg/cm2). Der Betonmodul wurde üblicherweise mit E = 200'000 kg/cm2 angenommen. Für die Betonstärke erwiesen sich 25 cm als vernünftiger Wert, sodass folgende Ringzugspannungen resultieren:

Innendruck-Ueberschuss	Ringzugspannungen im Beton injizierter Fels	uninjizierter Fels
2 atü	5 kg/cm2	7 kg/cm2
4 atü	11 kg/cm2	13 kg/cm2
6 atü	16 kg/cm2	20 kg/cm2
8 atü	21 kg/cm2	26 kg/cm2

Diese Tabelle zeigt, dass die Zugspannungen das Mass des Zulässigen nicht einmal bei uninjiziertem Fels überschreiten, sodass die Betonverkleidung nicht mit einer Bewehrung zu versehen war.

Temperatur- und Schwindspannungen sind für die Ringbeanspruchung bei adäquatem Betoniervorgang nicht zu berücksichtigen, da sich der Beton beim Erkalten vom Fels ablösen kann. Nur in Längsrichtung treten dieselben auf, was bisweilen zu radialen Rissen führt. Diese sind im Stollenbau allgemein bekannt und bedeuten üblicherweise keine Schwächung des Bauwerkes.

5. Vorschriften für die Bauausführung

Wie schon in der Einleitung bemerkt wurde, sind auch Stollenbauten kleiner Abmessungen mit grosser Sorgfalt durchzuführen. Dies gilt insbesondere für die Durchfahrung von ungewöhnlichen Felsformationen. Im Fall eines Gesteins, dessen Verformbarkeit relativ gross ist und dessen Verwitterungsanfälligkeit sich als intensiv erwiesen hat, gelten folgende Massnahmen :

a) beim Ausbruch

- Verwendung einer minimalen Sprengstoffmenge, falls nicht ein mechanischer Aushub sich als beste Lösung erweist. 1 kg Sprengstoff pro m3 ist bereits relativ hoch !
- Sehr profilgerechter Ausbruch, möglichst wenig Ueberprofil
- Rascher Schutz der Stollenwände mit Spritzbeton
- Wirksame Wasserableitung zwecks Verhütung einer Aufweichung des Sohlenbereiches

b) bei der Betonierung

- Verwendung eines Zementes mit möglichst geringer Wärmeentwicklung
- Saubere Betonierung, namentlich im Gewölbe
- Gute Vibration des Betons
- Sauberes Abschalen der Arbeitsfugen
- Möglichst tiefe Herabsetzung des Zementgehaltes, was u.U. einen Betonverflüssiger nötig macht.

c) bei der Injektion

- Perfekte Füllinjektion, vorallem im stets heiklen Gewölbe-Schluss und bezüglich der Baudrainage
- Konsolidationsinjektion mindestens bis in die Tiefe eines Stollendurchmessers. Wahl der Bohrlochabstände entsprechend der Felsinjizierbarkeit. Vermeidung hoher Drücke, z.B. $>$ 15 atü.

Natürlich sind das alles recht gut bekannte Wahrheiten, aber erstaunlicherweise werden sie gerade bei kleinen Bauwerken in ihrer Wichtigkeit unterschätzt.

Sicher ist ein mechanischer Ausbruch mit einer Voll-Fräsmaschine ein Vorteil, da er verschiedene Inhomogenitäten verringert oder sogar verunmöglicht. Andererseits kann diese Methode nicht von vornherein für alle Stollenbauten vorgeschrieben werden, sodass wir sicher noch einige Zeit auch mit dem klassischen Vortrieb rechnen müssen.

Im vorliegenden Testfall waren nun mehrere Abweichungen von der Norm aufgetreten, welche man zwar immer wieder zu korrigieren versuchte, leider jedoch ohne die gewünschte Regelmässigkeit zu erzielen.

So wurde z.B. trotz der nicht grossen Härte des Gesteins ein relativ hoher Sprengstoff-Verbrauch von 3-4 kg pro m3 Ausbruch verzeichnet.

Diese etwas rauhe Ausbruchmethode führte zu grösseren Ueberprofilen, deren Tiefe bis zu 1 m betrug und welche in keiner Weise geologisch bedingt waren.

Der Fels wurde teilweise viel zu spät mit Spritzbeton geschützt, obschon selten ein Hinderungsgrund wie etwa Stahl-Einbau oder starker Wasseranfall diese Massnahme erschwert hätte.

Die Ableitung des Gebirgswassers geschah in unvollkommener Weise, weil die Pumpenleistungen zu gering waren und die Drainage-Gräben zu wenig Tiefe besassen. So wurden verschiedentlich längere Stollenstücke unter Wasser gesetzt, vor allem im fallenden Vortriebs-Ast. Dies wiederum hat natürlich die Qualität des verwitterungsanfälligen Felsens beeinträchtigt.

Infolge der Ueberprofile liess sich nicht vermeiden, dass der ausgeführte Betonring wegen der sehr variablen Dicke von 0,25m bis 1,25m von einem idealen Kreisring abwich und eine ungünstige Form aufwies. Das statische Verhalten eines solchen Querschnittes ist natürlich alles andere als ideal.

Ferner musste aus verschiedenen liefertechnischen Gründen ein Zement von ziemlich hoher Wärme-Entwicklung verwendet werden. Im weiteren wurde der Beton zur Erleichterung des Einbringens stark verflüssigt, wobei der relativ grosse Wassergehalt zwecks Erreichung einer genügend hohen Festigkeit einen erhöhten Zementgehalt erforderte. Waren auch die Festigkeiten durchaus im zulässigen Rahmen, so ergab sich doch beim Abbinden eine ausserordentliche Erwärmung, welche zu einer sehr ungleichmässigen Beanspruchung des Betons führte, da diese Wärme viel schneller an der Innenleibung abgeführt wurde, als dies im Fels möglich war.

Eine gewisse Schwierigkeit ergab sich vermutlich auch bei der Injektion. Der Beton war teilweise zu wenig intensiv vibriert worden, sodass im Scheitel ziemlich viel Injektionsgut einfloss. Ob dieses Injektionsgut wirklich in den bei Abkühlen zwischen Fels und Beton normalerweise entstehenden Hohlraum eingedrungen ist, muss in Frage gestellt werden, da die mittlere Temperatur des Betons nur langsam abnahm.

Auch die Konsolidationsinjektionen zeigten in den Tuffen mit 240 kg/m Stollen eine relativ geringe Zementabsorption. Dies war wohl in erster Linie eine Folge der Felsstruktur. In den harten Gesteinen (Basalt, Andesit) lag die Absorption zwischen 350 und 400 kg/Stollenmeter.

6. Die Probefüllung

Jeder Stollen sollte sehr sorgfältig geprüft werden, bevor er dem Betrieb übergeben wird. Nun ist oft für diese Prüfung die Zeit sehr knapp. Dies gilt vor allem für diejenigen Stollen, welche den Flaschenhals im Programm darstellen, sodass die Betriebsaufnahme sehnsüchtig auf die Freigabe des Tunnels wartet. Ganz besonders stellt sich dieses Problem bei einer Wasserkraftanlage, welche fix und fertig dasteht und gerne Kilowattstunden produzieren möchte.

Natürlich wird im Bauprogramm stets für die Stollenabnahme 2-3 Monate Zeit eingeräumt. Leider ist aber oft der Stollen am schwierigsten auszuführen und hat am meisten Rückstand auf das Bauprogramm. Sind endlich die Arbeiten fertig, so reduziert man das Prüfschema auf ein Minimum. Dieses besteht dann in einem Abschluss beim Wasserschloss und in einer Füllung der gesamten Tunnelröhre zwischen demselben und der Wasserfassung. Bleiben die Verluste klein, so ist jedermann zufrieden, treten aber grössere Verlust auf, so sind sie sehr schwer zu lokalisieren.

Eine wesentlich nutzbringendere Methode besteht daher in einem differenzierten Abpress-Versuch, wobei die gesamte Stollenstrecke - wenn möglich nach geologischen und nach bautechnischen Gesichtspunkten - in verschiedene Einzelstrecken aufgeteilt wird. Jeder Teilstollen wird dann mit provisorischen Pfropfen abgeschlossen und auf seine Dichtigkeit überprüft. Ein solches Vorgehen gibt sehr aufschlussreiche Werte, dauert aber bisweilen mehrere Monate und ist auch etwas kostspielig. Immerhin sollte es bei Stollen von mehr als 5 km Länge und mehr als 4 - 5 m Durchmesser stets angewandt werden.

Im Testfall musste die Prüfung aus Zeitmangel nach dem abgekürzten Verfahren durchgeführt werden. Sie ergab somit summarische Werte, welche nicht genau interpretiert werden konnten. Immerhin war es möglich, aus den bei der nachfolgenden Stolleninspektion gemachten Feststellungen wertvolle Schlüsse zu ziehen und gezielte Massnahmen zu beschliessen.

Schon bald nach Füllbeginn, d.h. also, als erst der tieferliegende Stollenabschnitt unter Wasser stand und einen noch sehr bescheidenen Innendruck von höchstens 1 atü aufwies, traten bereits Wasserverluste auf.

Während des weiteren Füllvorganges vermehrten sich dieselben in unerwarteter Weise und erreichten am Ende den Wert von 3.5 m3/s. Natürlich konnte der Stollen nicht dem Betrieb übergeben werden. Er wurde in wenigen Tagen geleert und eingehend inspiziert.
Die unmittelbare Ursache des Verlustes war leicht festzustellen, zeigten sich doch längs der gesamten Stollenstrecke eine grosse Zahl von Längs- und Querrissen, aus welchen teilweise grössere Wassermengen in den Stollen zurückflossen und deren Oeffnung zwischen einem Zehntelmillimeter und mehreren Millimetern schwankte. Eine systematische Aufnahme der Risse zeigte, dass diese sich nicht auf spezifische Felsbereiche konzentrierten sondern in allen Strecken, also auch im Basalt und Porphyrit, auftraten.

7. Ursachen der Rissbildung

Da der Stollen nur in einem einzigen Prüfvorgang getestet wurde, ist es nicht leicht, eine eindeutige Erklärung für die Ursachen der zahlreichen Risse zu geben; man ist auf Indizien angewiesen, welche sich in ihrer Aussagekraft unterscheiden.

7.1 Die Transversalrisse

Jeder Druckstollen weist eine geringere oder grössere Zahl von Transversalrissen auf ; dies sind Risse, welche praktisch kreisförmig in einer Ebene verlaufen, die zur Stollenaxe mehr oder weniger senkrecht steht. Sie sind eine Folge des Schwindens und der Abkühlung des Betons und ihre gegenseitigen Abstände hängen von der Qualität des Zementes, der Betonverarbeitung, dem umliegenden Fels und den ausgeführten Injektionen ab. Besitzt die Betonröhre einen innigen Kontakt mit dem Fels, zu welchem gut ausgeführte Injektionen wesentlich beitragen, so entstehen eine grössere Anzahl sehr feiner Risse, welche nur geringe Wasserverluste verursachen. In einem gut injizierten Gebirge werden sich diese kaum auswirken können, da keine Wasserwege vorhanden sind. Das gleiche gilt bei hohem Aussenwasserdruck. Haftet jedoch die Tunnelröhre schlecht am Fels, so besitzt sie in der Längsrichtung relativ grosse Beweglichkeit und reisst in grösseren Abständen, dann aber mit relativ grossen Rissen. Ein Wasseraustritt ist leicht möglich, und die Verluste hängen nur noch vom Aussendruck und den möglichen Wasserwegen im Gebirge ab, wobei die Qualität der Injektionen natürlich eine entscheidende Rolle spielt.

Im Testfall zeigte es sich eindeutig, dass in den Zonen höherer Felsqualität (Basalt, Andesit, Prophyrit) ein mittlerer Abstand von ca. 6 m zwischen den Transversalrissen auftrat, wogegen derselbe Abstand in den Tuffen auf 10-12 anwuchs.

7.2 Die Längsrisse

Das Entstehen der Längsrisse ist eine Folge der Kombination von Innendruck-Zugspannungen, Temperatur- und Schwindspannungen. Innendruck-Zugspannungen treten natürlich in jedem Druckstollen auf, solange der Aussendruck nicht gleich dem Innendruck ist oder diesen sogar übersteigt. Im Testfall betrugen diese Innendruckspannungen im maximum rd 20 kg/cm2 (mit Ausnahme der Panzerstrecken) und waren somit zulässig. Die aus Schwinden und Abkühlung resultierenden Ring-Zugspannungen sollten sich auf wenige kg/cm2 beschränken, da die Tunnelröhre sich eigentlich vom Fels abheben kann, wenn sie sich kontrahiert.

Beim Testfall scheint es sicher, dass die Superposition zu gross war, was nur durch übergrosse Temperatur- und Schwindspannungen zu erklären ist. Diese sind sehr wahrscheinlich auf folgende Ursachen zurückzuführen :

- Verwendung von Zement mit grosser Wärmeentwicklung
- Ueberdosierung des Zementes
- Konzentration von Wärmeentwicklung an Stellen mit Ueberprofil
- Unregelmässige Abkühlung des Betons von der Innenleibung bis zum Fels

Der letzte Punkt erweist sich als sehr wichtig, wenn man folgende Ueberlegung anstellt :

> Der beim Abbinden sehr stark erwärmte Beton hat sich relativ rasch erhärtet. In der daraufhin einsetzenden Abkühlungsphase hat sich zuerst die Innenleibung abgekühlt, während die mittlere Betontemperatur wegen der schlechten Abstrahlungs-Verhältnisse im Fels und wegen dessen niedriger Wärmeleitfähigkeit nur langsam abnahm.
>
> Bei einer nur unvollkommenen Ablösung vom Fels - falls diese überhaupt stattfand - haben sich an der Innenleibung Ringzugspannungen in der Grösse von $>$ 20 kg/cm2 entwickelt. Diese führten in Superposition mit den Schwindspannungen vermutlich bereits zu Anrissen im inneren Drittel des Betonringes.

Die voranstehenden Ueberlegungen zeigen also, dass die Längrisse ebenfalls <u>vor</u> der Druckprobe bereits vorgezeichnet waren und dass das Betonprofil den noch folgenden Innendruck <u>nicht</u> mit seiner ganzen Stärke aufnehmen konnte.

8. Die Reaktion des Gebirges

Im Falle eines Gebirges mit hohem E-Modul (z.B. 100'000 kg/cm2 ÷ 200'000 kg/cm2) und unter der Annahme, dass der eventuell freie Raum zwischen Betonring und Fels, welcher sich bei der Abkühlung bilden kann, gut mit Injektionsmaterial verfüllt ist, sollte bei einem kleinen Stollen und bei relativ geringen Innendruck-Ueberschüssen selbst ein reduziertes Betonprofil keine schädlichen Risse aufweisen.

Was nun im Testfall sich als ungünstig erwies, war die Kombination der unvorteilhaften Erscheinungen im Beton mit der mittleren Gebirgsqualität.

Nach der Leerung des Stollens wurden an einzelnen Stellen E-Modulmessungen in Bohrungen und auch an freigelegten Felsoberflächen hinter dem Betonring durchgeführt . Sie haben teilweise die ursprünglichen Messwerte bestätigt, teilweise haben sie sehr geringe Werte von 2000-5000 kg/cm2 ($E_{stat.}$) ergeben. Diese letzteren lassen sich wie folgt erklären :

An denjenigen Stellen in den Tuffen und Tuffbrekzien, an welchen der sofortige Schutz der freigelegten Stollenwand durch Spritzbeton unterblieb, hat - insbesondere im Zusammenhang mit der Einwirkung von Wasser oder feuchter Luft - ein Quellen, eventuell sogar eine Umstrukturierung des Gesteins stattgefunden, wodurch dessen E-Modul stellenweise stark herabgesetzt wurde. Gleichzeitig bewirkt dieser Vorgang eine Verminderung der Injizierbarkeit mit einer üblichen Zement-Mischung, sodass auch die normalerweise eintretende Zunahme des E-Moduls infolge Injektion nicht oder nicht genügend intensiv stattfand.

Es ist aber festzuhalten, dass diese Herabminderung des E-Moduls eher lokaler Natur war, dass sie deshalb wohl einige der Risse resp. Wasseraustritte erklärt, niemals aber allein für alle Längsrisse und Verluste verantwortlich gemacht werden kann.

Wie schon erwähnt, war es die Kombination aller in den vorangehenden Kapiteln beschriebenen Ereignisse, welche zu der starken Rissebildung führte, was sich auch im Resultat der Risse - Statistik augenfällig erweist :

Fels Bezeichnung	Qualität	Mittlere Anzahl der Längsrisse m Riss/ m. Stollen
Porphyrite	sehr gut	o.25
Basalt/Andesit	gut	1.35
Tuffe/ Tuffbrekzien	mittel	1.95
Ignimbrit	gering	3.00

Da die Porphyrite und die Ignimbrite nur über eine sehr kurze Strecke anstehen, sind die entsprechenden Werte wenig aussagekräftig, wenn sie auch recht gut ins allgemeine Bild passen. Wichtig aber ist der relativ geringe Unterschied zwischen der Rissehäufigkeit in den Basalten und Andesiten (20% der Totallänge) einerseits und den Tuffen und Tuffbrekzien (70% der Totallänge) andererseits. Sie verhalten sich wie 1:1.5, was eindeutig zeigt, dass die Felsqualität keinesfalls die Hauptursache darstellt.

9. Schlussfolgerungen

Die Mitwirkung des Gebirges bei vulkanischen Tuffen und Tuffbrekzien hängt natürlich weitgehend von seinem Verformungsmodul ab. Da dieser nicht sehr gross ist, muss die Qualität des Felsens während der Arbeiten besonders stark geschont werden .Dies bedingt :

- Vermeidung unnötigen Sprengstoff-Verbrauches
- Vermeidung von Ueberprofil
- Sofortiger Schutz nach Ausbruch durch Spritzbeton
- Gute Wasser-Ableitung

Da die Mitwirkung entsprechend der statischen E-Moduli von 20'000-30'000 kg/cm2 begrenzt ist, darf der Stollenbeton nicht bereits während der Abbinde-Phase durch grössere Zugspannungen beansprucht werden, was die Vermeidung von Zement-Ueberdosierungen und von Bindemitteln mit hoher Abbindewärme erfordert. Schlakkenzemente und Trass-Zusätze sind zu empfehlen. Im weiteren muss ein profilgerechter Betonring erstellt werden.

Die den E-Modul des Gebirges verbessernden Zementinjektionen sowie die Füllinjektionen im Zwischenraum zwischen Beton und Fels (insbesondere im Scheitel) sind sehr sorgfältig durchzuführen, damit ihre Wirksamkeit ein Maximum erreicht. Hohe Drücke sind nicht eine Abhilfe gegen geringe Zementaufnahme, dagegen wohl kleine Einpressgeschwindigkeiten und eventuell Vermehrung der Injektionsbohrungen längs des gesamten Umfanges.

Der Innendruckueberschuss sollte 6 atü nicht überschreiten. Ist dies unvermeidbar, so ist Armierung des Betons oder Panzerung zu empfehlen. Da diese Massnahmen teuer sind, ist ihre Anordnung aber von Fall zu Fall zu überprüfen.

10. Abschliessende Bemerkungen

Da die Umrechnung vom dynamischen auf den statistischen E-Modul oft von grosser Wichtigkeit ist, soll nachstehend eine empirische Formel gegeben werden, welche sich auf eine grosse Zahl von Erfahrungswerten bezieht :

$$E_{stat}\ (t/cm2) = 0.016\ E_{dyn}\ (t/cm2)^{1.6}$$

sie beweist die Abnahme des Verhältnisses

$E_{dyn} : E_{stat}$ mit abnehmendem E-Modul,

d.h.

E_{dyn}	985	310	159	100	70
E_{stat}	985	155	53	25	14
E_{dyn}/E_{stat}	1	2	3	4	5

Als weitere Bemerkung ist noch zu erwähnen, dass der Teststollen nach erfolgter Reparatur mittels Panzerung, armiertem Spritzbeton und Fugenabdichtung heute einwandfrei funktioniert. Die Verluste sind auf rd. 60 l/s abgesunken, was einem spezifischen Wert von

$$\frac{1\ l/s}{1000\ m2\ \text{Stollenwand}}$$

im ungepanzerten Teil entspricht.

ERFASSUNG DES GEBIRGSTRAGVERHALTENS UND ENTWURF DER AUSKLEIDUNG FÜR EINEN DRUCKSCHACHT MIT HOHEM INNENDRUCK

Determination of load bearing capacity of the rock mass and lining layout for a high stressed pressure shaft

Détermination du comportement statique du terrain massiv et projet du revêtement d'un puits blindé à haute pression intérieure

G.HEIGERTH
Tauernkraftwerke AG, Salzburg, Österreich

SUMMARY

The pressure shaft "Häusling" represents a section of operation conduit of the Ziller powerplant, a pump storage facility under construction, situated in Tyrol. Since the shaft is placed in solid gneiss formation of the Central alps, the rock mass offered a furthermost load capacity to bear the internal pressure (max. 93 bar).
However, the knowledge of rock behaviour has to be provided. Mechanical excavation, therefore was carried out as early, that shaft lining layout could be based on results of rock mechanic tests. For a continuous information of deformation behaviour, as far as possible, in-situ-load tests and laboratory test with drilling cores were executed, just as sound velocities were measured and rock penetration of the drilling-machine crippers too. The latter procedure, in any case, gives an idea of rock uniformity and possibly could be developed.
Results of rock-mechanical investigations allowed to design the lining only for sealing against seepage, up to a pressure rate of 78 bar. For that there were considered and explored in detail, including the construction: plastic-foils and steel sheets, each with pre-stressed concrete lining. Based on tender results a lining with sheet steel is built. First filling up the shaft will be in 1985.

ZUSAMMENFASSUNG

Der Druckschacht "Häusling" ist ein Abschnitt der Triebwasserführung des Zillerkraftwerkes, eines derzeit im Bau befindlichen Pumpspeicherwerkes in Tirol. Der Schacht liegt im massigen Gneis der Zentralalpen, so daß es nahe lag, für die Aufnahme des maximal 93 bar erreichenden Innendruckes weitestgehend den Fels heranzuziehen.
Voraussetzung dafür war jedoch die Kenntnis der Gebirgseigenschaften. Der Fräsvortrieb wurde daher so zeitgerecht durchgeführt, daß die Ergebnisse der felsmechanischen Versuche der Bemessung der Auskleidung zugrunde gelegt werden konnten. Um ein möglichst kontinuierliches Bild der Verformungseigenschaften des Felsens zu erhalten, wurden nicht nur Stempeldruckversuche und Laborversuche an Bohrkernen ausgeführt, sondern auch Schall-Laufzeiten und während des Vortriebes das Einpressen der Verspannplatten der Stollenfräse gemessen. Dieses Verfahren gibt jedenfalls ein Maß für die Gleichmäßigkeit des Felsens und scheint ausbaufähig.
Aufgrund der felsmechanischen Untersuchungen brauchte der Auskleidung bis zu einem Innendruck von 78 bar nur mehr eine Dichtfunktion zugewiesen werden. Dafür kamen Kunststoff-Folien oder dünnwandige Panzerbleche, jeweils mit einem vorgespannten Betoninnenring, in Frage, die einschließlich der Bauausführung näher untersucht wurden. Aufgrund des Ausschreibungsergebnisses wird eine "dünnwandige Panzerung" ausgeführt. Die erste Füllung des Schachtes ist für 1985 vorgesehen.

RESUME

Le puits blindé de "Häusling" est une partie de la conduite d'eau de l'aménagement Zillerkraftwerk, un aménagement a accumulation par poumpage, situé en Tyrol, qui se trouve a présent en construction. Le puits est situé dans le gneiss du massiv central des Alpes. Ce cette façon là on pouvait donner une partie assez grande de la pression intérieure (93 bar an maximum) au rocher.
Pour cela il était naturellement nécessaire de connaître la qualité du rocher. C'est pourquoi on a commencé à creuser le puit à un moment assez tôt, pour pouvoir faire des essais de la mécanique de roches et en profiter pour les calculs du revêtement du puits. Pour s'informer sur des qualités de la déformation du rocher, à action continue le long du puits, on a fait non seulement des essais de pression avec des étampes et dans les laboratoires avec les carottes de sondage; on a mésuré également le temps du son et le procède de la pression des étampes de la machine de traçage. Cette méthode donne en tout cas une représentation des divers qualités du rocher le long du puits et on peut bien l'exécuter dans l'avenir aussi.
Par suite des essais de la mécanique de roches on a constaté, qu'il suffit, de donner au revêtement la fonction d'étancheité dans la partie du puits blindé, qui est soumis a une pression intérieure au dessous de 78 bar. Pour l'étancheité on peut employer des lamelles de matière artificielle ou des feuilles de métal, avec un revêtement intérieur du beton précontrainte. Naturellement on a soumis les lamelles et les feuilles à une examination exacte. Par suite de l'adjudictation on a decidé à executer une feuille de métal mince.
La première replissage du puits blindé est prévue pour 1985.

1. EINLEITUNG

Druckstollen und -schächte von Wasserkraftwerken und anderen wasserwirtschaftlichen Anlagen werden zu-nehmend unter Ausnützung des Gebirgstragverhaltens entworfen und errichtet. Diese Entwicklung ermöglicht die Fortschritte in der Felsmechanik und die in-situ-Meß-

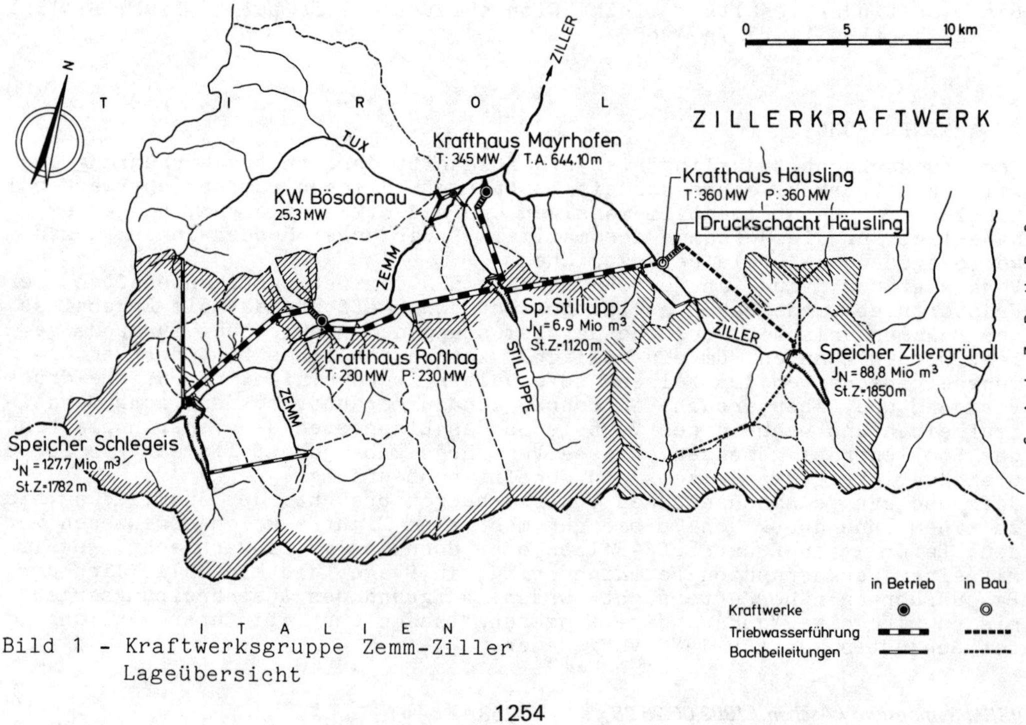

Bild 1 - Kraftwerksgruppe Zemm-Ziller
Lageübersicht

-verfahren zum Erfassen der Gebirgseigenschaften. Der wirtschaftlichen Auslegung der Auskleidung bei Beachtung der erforderlichen Sicherheit kommt auch die Entwicklung neuerer Materialien entgegen.
In Österreich sind die in den letzten 20 Jahren errichteten Triebwasserstollen, vor allem der Wasserkraftanlagen Kaunertal, Zemm, Malta und Sellrain-Silz, und im Montafon, Schritte in dieser Richtung. Im folgenden wird über einen Druckschacht des "Zillerkraftwerkes" berichtet, wobei neuere Entwicklungen näher beleuchtet werden sollen.

2. HAUPTDATEN UND AUFGABENSTELLUNG

2.1. Das "Zillerkraftwerk"

Die derzeit in Bau befindliche Anlage liegt in einem der Quelltäler des Zillertales in Tirol und ergänzt die in den Jahren 1966 bis 1971 errichtete Kraftwerksgruppe Zemm. Bild 1 zeigt eine Lageübersicht. Dieses Pumpspeicherwerk nützt die Abflüsse eines Abschnittes der vergletscherten Zentralalpen und bildet eine zweite Oberstufe zur bereits bestehenden Zweistufenanlage. Seine energiewirtschaftlichen Aufgaben sind mit der Erzeugung von Winterenergie und der Deckung von Lastspitzen gegeben. Das Kraftwerk ist seit 1979 in Bau; es ist geplant, den Betrieb in den Jahren 1986/87 aufzunehmen.
Der neue, in rd. 1800 m Seehöhe gelegene Jahresspeicher Zillergründl mit 88 hm3 Nutzinhalt wird von einer 190 m hohen Gewölbemauer mit 500 m Kronenlänge abgeschlossen und über zwei Beileitungssysteme gefüllt werden. Er wird über einen insgesamt 16,2 km langen Triebwasserweg mit 65 m3/s Ausbaudurchfluß mit einem bereits bestehenden Wochenspeicher in Verbindung stehen, wobei die Rohfallhöhe rund 700 m beträgt. Das Krafthaus "Häusling" wird mit zwei Maschinensätzen zu je 180 MW Turbinen- wie Pumpenleistung ausgerüstet. Nach Fertigstellung wird die Kraftwerksgruppe im Regeljahr 1072 GWh, vorwiegend im Winter, erzeugen; ein-

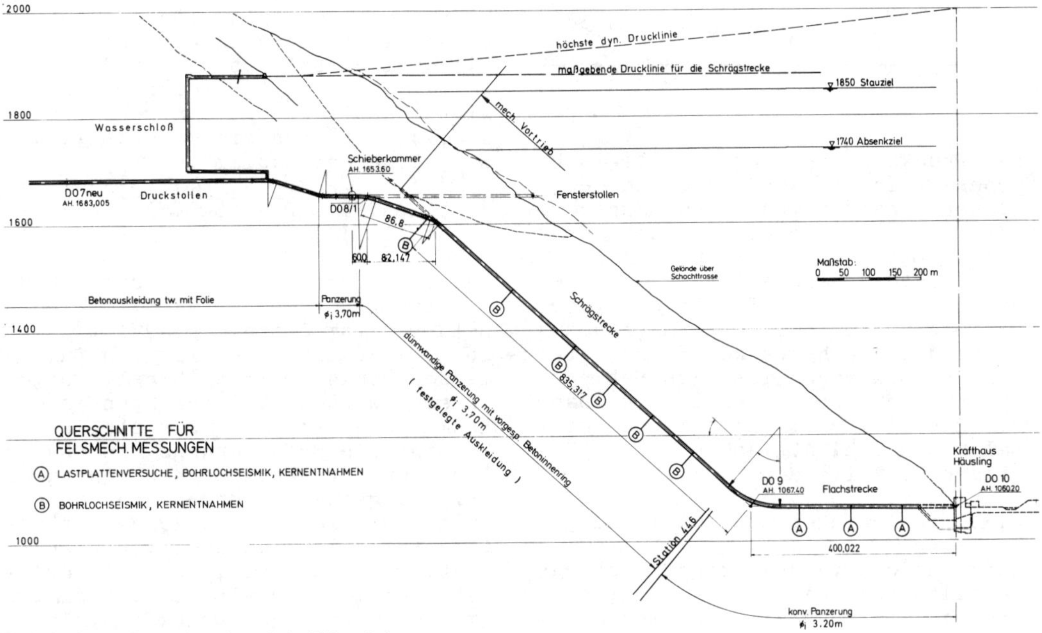

Bild 2 - Druckschacht Häusling
Längsschnitt

-schließlich Pumpwälzbetrieb kann die Erzeugung 1830 GWh an Spitzenenergie erreichen.

2.2. Druckschacht "Häusling"

Der hier näher beschriebene Druckschacht stellt den letzten Abschnitt des druckseitigen Triebwasserweges zwischen dem Wasserschloß und dem Krafthaus dar; den Längsschnitt zeigt Bild 2. Dieser Kraftabstieg wurde aus mehreren, nicht zuletzt wirtschaftlichen Gründen als Schacht in den im Mittel 32° steilen Hang gelegt; er setzt sich aus einer Schräg- und einer Flachstrecke zusammen.

Die Hauptabmessungen und maßgebenden Innendrücke sind:

Strecke		schräg	flach
Ø	m	3,70	3,20
Länge	m	900	360
Neigung	Neugrad	20,9/46,6	0,7
Maxim. Innendruck:			
stat.	m	7,45	7,86
dyn.	m	8,56	9,27

Der Druckschacht liegt, geologisch gesehen, in der Nordabdachung des "Tauernfensters", das den Hauptkamm der Ostalpen aufbaut. Er verläuft zum Großteil noch im Zentralgneis, sowie in der darüberliegenden Unteren Schieferhülle ("Schönachmulde"). Die Grenze der beiden Formationen quert die Flachstrecke. Es war standfestes vorwiegend massiges Gebirge zu erwarten, wobei der Schrägschacht die generell steil nach Norden einfallenden Schichtflächen unter günstigem Winkel quert.

2.3. Überlegungen zur Auskleidung

Aufgrund der zu erwartenden Gebirgsverhältnisse und der Erfahrungen von anderen Stollenbauten in diesem Gebiet war von vornherein vorgesehen, dem Gebirge eine volle Tragfunktion zuzuordnen, was beim relativ hohen Innendruck entsprechende Kosteneinsparungen bringt. Weil die maßgebende Drucklinie zum Großteil außerhalb des Geländes liegt, muß der Schacht allerdings dicht gegenüber Wasseraustritten sein. Da der vom Gebirge aufnehmbare Innendruck durch die Gebirgsüberlagerung begrenzt wird, wurde eine Trassenführung gewählt, die die insgesamt wirtschaftlichste Lösung erwarten ließ. Dabei war auch der als Außendruck wirksame Gebirgswasserspiegel zu berücksichtigen, der nach Angabe der Geologen mit etwa 2/3 der Überlagerungshöhe anzusetzen ist.
Voraussetzung war, den Stollen so früh vorzutreiben, daß Zeit für die erforderlichen felsmechanischen Messungen wie auch für die weiteren Untersuchungen zur Verfügung stand. Eine weitere Grundlage war der Fräsvortrieb, der außer Kostenvorteilen und Schonung des Gebirges, eine geometrisch eindeutige Stollenlaibung ergibt.
Es war geplant, in jenem Abschnitt, wo das Gebirge den vollen Innendruck übernehmen kann, der Auskleidung lediglich die erforderliche Dicht-Funktion zuzuordnen; dazu war eine vorgespannte Schalbetonauskleidung mit zusätzlicher Dichthaut vorgesehen. Für die anschließenden Strekken waren konventionelle hinterbetonierte Panzerungen geplant, die, wie üblich, bei Ausnützung der jeweils möglichen Gebirgsmitwirkung wirtschaftlich bemessen werden können, soweit dies die erforderliche Beulsicherheit zuläßt.

3. VORTRIEB UND FELSMECHANISCHE MESSUNGEN

Den o.a. Überlegungen entsprechend ist der Druckschacht Häusling im Zeitraum vom September 1979 bis April 1980 mit einem lichten Durchmesser von 4,20 m maschinell vorgetrieben worden. Bei Durchfahren des Krümmers am Übergang zur Steilstrekke sind die Schutterungs- und Nachlaufeinrichtungen auf den Schrägvortrieb umgestellt worden. Der ohne Zwischenfälle und mit Tagesleistungen bis 36 m ablaufende Vortrieb bestätigte im wesentlichen die erwarteten Gebirgsverhältnisse. Lediglich am oberen Ende des Druckschachtes ist eine stark aufgelockerte Zone aufgefahren worden, die den unteren

Rand einer tiefgreifenden, alten Sackungsmasse bildet.
Beim Vortrieb wurde versucht, die Verschiebungen beim Anpressen der Fräsen-Verspannplatten als Routinemessung zur zumindest qualitativen Erfassung der Gebirgsverformbarkeit heranzuziehen (Darüber hat der Autor beim 30. Geomechanik-Kolloquium in Salzburg in einem Diskussionsbeitrag bereits kurz berichtet). Da die bei jedem Hub erreichte Verspannkraft mit ca. 5000 kN in gleicher Größenordnung wie bei den üblichen Lastplatten-Geräten liegt, steht hiemit eine Reihe von Belastungsversuchen zur Verfügung. Beim Vortrieb wurde ca. alle 100 m, beim Rückzug der Maschine durchgehend bei etwa jedem fünften Schritt gemessen. Erfaßt wurde dabei die Summe der beidseitigen Verformung bei Laststufen zwischen einem Basiswert von 10 bis 15% und dem Endwert der Verspannkraft. Da die Verspannplatten mit je 6 kegelförmigen Dornen bestückt waren, ist das durch Kleinscherbrüche hervorgerufene Eindringen dieser Dorne gemessen worden. Diese Gesamtverschiebung stellt damit sicherlich kein eindeutiges Maß für die Verformbarkeit des Gebirges dar, erscheint als Beurteilungskriterium für die Gleichförmigkeit jedoch ebenso geeignet, wie die üblichen Routineverfahren, z.B. die Hammerschlagseismik. Bild 3 zeigt charakteristische Druck-Weg-Verläufe; die Endwerte erreichen maximal 23 mm.

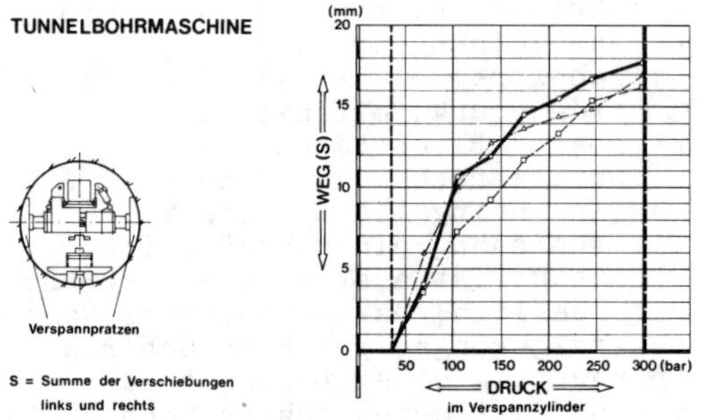

Bild 3 - Verspannplatten-Messungen

Konvergenzmessungen sofort hiner dem Fräskopf zeigten kaum meßbare Radius-Verkürzungen und damit nur sehr geringe Auflockerungen. Entspannungserscheinungen in Form schalenförmiger Ausbrüche traten nur in einem einzigen kurzen Abschnitt auf.
Zur quantitativen Erfassung des Verformungsverhaltens bzw. Eichung der Verspannplattenmessungen wurde folgendes felsmechanische Meßprogramm abgewickelt:

- Schall-Laufzeit mit Oberflächenseismik ... in der Flachstrecke
- Schall-Laufzeit mit Bohrlochseismik ... ca. alle 100 m
- Gesteinskennwerte an Bohrkernen (Labormessungen) ... ca. alle 100 m
- Deformationen mit 4000-kN-Lastplattengerät ... an 3 repräsentativen Querschnitten (spez. Flächendruck max. 8 N/mm2)

Die Lastplattenversuche zur quantitativen Erhebung der Verformbarkeit wurden nur in der Flachstrecke ausgeführt und gelten wegen fast isotroper Verhältnisse als repräsentativ für den gesamten Schacht.
Die Gegenüberstellung der Ergebnisse für die Flachstrecke zeigt Bild 4. Die Schallgeschwindigkeiten, um 4000 - 5000 m/s, bestätigen die Gleichförmigkeit des Gebirges und praktisch das Fehlen einer Auflockerung. Die Gesteinsfestigkeiten liegen für Druck im Bereich 30-80N/mm2, für Spalt-Zug bei 4-7N/mm2.
Die ermittelten Verformungsmoduli erlauben es, für die Verformung bereits vorbelasteten, mit Injektionen zusätzlich verfestigtem Gebirges mit Sicherheit einen durchgehenden Wert von 10000 N /mm2 anzusetzen.
Die geologische Detailaufnahme des Druckschachtes bestätigt, abgesehen vom obersten Ende der Steilstrecke, die Prognose. Im Bereich der Unteren Schieferhülle wurden Gneise mit vereinzelten Feldspatleisten, Granat, Pyrit, Schiefer- und Quarzbändern angetroffen. Die Zentralgneis-Formation zeigt Migmatite, Biotit, Bänder-, Augen- und Zwei-Glimmer-Granitgneise. Die steilstehende Schichtung ist im Zentralgneis zum Teil undeutlich ausgeprägt. Das Gebirge zeigt sich als durchwegs dicht, im unteren Abschnitt als sehr dicht; lediglich am Übergang zum lockeren Bereich am oberen Ende zeigen sich Klüfte mit Mylonit-Lagen.

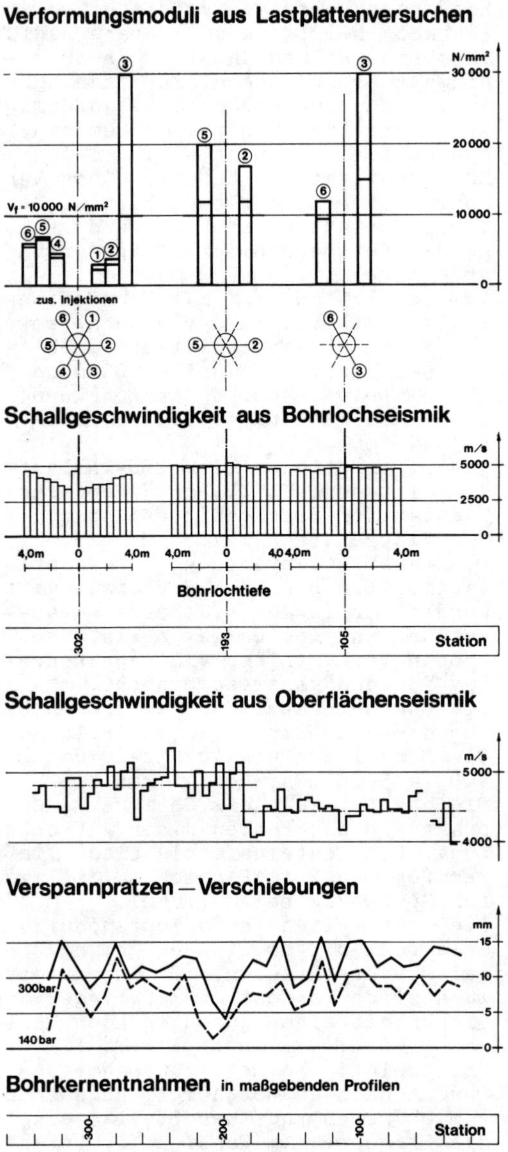

Bild 4 - Felsmechanische Messungen in der Flachstrecke

4. AUSLEGUNG DER AUSKLEIDUNG; VORGESPANNTE STAHLBETONSTRECKE

4.1. Statische Bemessung

Aufgrund obiger Ergebnisse wurde zunächst festgelegt, dem Gebirge jenen Innendruck zuzuordnen, der etwa dem lotr. Überlagerungsdruck entspricht. Als maßgebend wurde der ungünstigste Betriebslastfall mit längerdauernder Belastung angesetzt.

Höhere Werte, wie kurzzeitige Druckspitzen aus extremen instationären Vorgängen (Überlagerung extremer Wasserschloß-Schwingungen mit Druckstößen), wurden nur als Ausnahme-Lastfälle nachgewiesen; das zähe Gebirge eignet sich zur Aufnahme derartiger Druckschwankungen.

Für den üblichen statischen Nachweis war der Verformungsmodul mit V_{min} = = 10000 N/mm2 anzusetzen.

(Für konventionelle Panzerungen kommt ein Initialspalt zwischen Panzerblech und Beton hinzu). Für den Verformungsnachweis wurde, auch aus Sicherheitsgründen, angenommen, daß sich dieser Wert bei Überschreiten der kleinsten primären Gebirgsspannung auf die Hälfte reduziert. Dieser Nachweis ist maßgebend für die vorgespannte Betonauskleidung (siehe Regelprofil Bild 5).

Für die Vorspannung des Betons wird gefordert, daß nach Abzug von Temperatur- und Relaxationseinflüssen ein Wert verbleibt, der den Betonring bei maßgebenden Innendruck rissefrei hält, d.h., daß keine bzw. nur geringe Zugspannungen auftreten dürfen. Da beim Vorspannen selbst eine ausreichende Sicherheit gegen Erreichen der Druckfestigkeit verbleiben muß, soll der Beton bis zum Vorspannen möglichst lange aushärten können; dafür ist etwa ein Jahr vorgesehen.

Die Bemessung der Beton-Vorspannung für den Übergang Krümmer-Schrägstrekke zeigt das Diagramm in Bild 6.

Für die konventionelle Panzerung waren noch die Beulnachweise zu führen; der maßgebende Außendruck für die Betonauskleidung ist mit dem Vorspannvorgang gegeben.

Aus diesen Berechnungen, die wir mit Hilfe der Diagramme nach SEEBER ausgeführt haben, ergab sich das folgende Auskleidungssystem:

- Flachstrecke: Konventionelle Panzerung (mit nach innen abnehmbarer Blechstärke)
- Schrägstrecke: Vorgespannter Betoninnenring mit Dichthaut

Die Anordnung einer zusätzlichen Dichthaut ist aus Sicherheitsgründen erforderlich, da austretendes Wasser bei zu geringer primärer Gebirgsspannung zu einem Druckaufbau entlang von Gefügeflächen führen könnte. Da die Durchsickerungsfähigkeit zur Oberfläche hin zunimmt, käme es zwar zu keinem Druckaufbau in Oberflächennähe; dies wäre jedoch nicht mit Sicherheit auszuschließen.

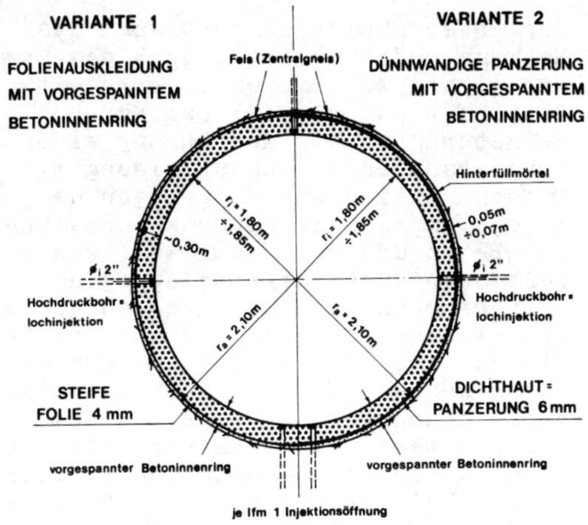

Bild 5 - Schrägstrecke, Regelquerschnitt-Varianten

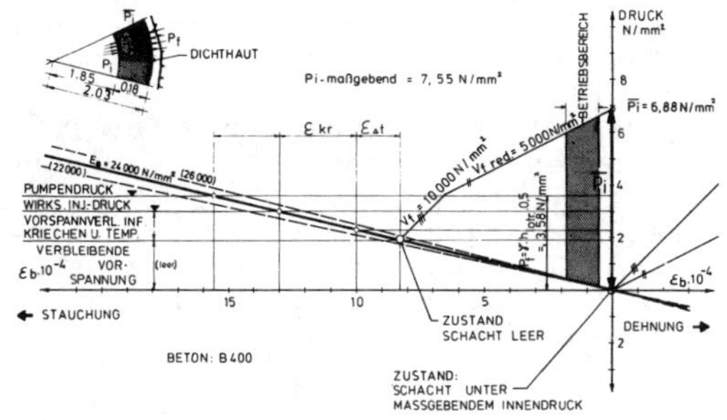

Bild 6 - Bemessung der Betonvorspannung

4.2. Untersuchungen zur Dichthaut

Wie das Regelprofil im Bild 5 zeigt, wurden für die zwischen Betoninnenring und Fels gelegene Dichthaut zwei Varianten untersucht, die als grundsätzlich gleichwertig anzusehen sind:

- Kunststoff-Folie
- Dünnwandiges Panzerblech

Die exakte Kreisform des gefrästen Schachtes läßt die Anwendung steifer Folien zu, die eine vergleichsweise hohe Robustheit und Alterungsbeständigkeit aufweisen.
Die Materialprüfstelle der Tauern-kraftwerke AG hat dazu eine Reihe von am Markt angebotenen, entsprechend adaptierten Folien im Labor erprobt. Außer den üblichen Kennwerten wurde vor allem die Fähigkeit der Überbrückung eines Spaltes unter Innendruckbelastung, bei schlaffer bzw. gezogener Folie überprüft. Hiezu wurden eigene Geräte entwickelt. Dem extremen Kriterium - Überbrückung eines 4-mm-Spaltes bei 60 bar Wasserdruck auf Dauer - konnten Foliensysteme zweier Hersteller standhalten, die bei der Entwicklung des Dichtsystems wesentlich mitarbeiteten. Aus mehreren Gründen war vorgesehen, zwischen Felsuntergrund und der 4 mm starken Dichtfolie ein Kunststoffvlies aufzubringen.
Vom Panzerblech wird hohe Dehnfähigkeit verlangt, womit ein nicht-vergüteter Stahl hoher Bruchdehnung in Frage kommt.

4.3. Einzelheiten zur Ausführung

Voraussetzung für die Ausführbarkeit war die Entwicklung bzw. Festlegung der konstruktiven Einzelheiten einschließlich optimaler Bauverfahren, wobei nur zum Teil auf Erfahrungen von ausgeführten Anlagen zurückgegriffen werden konnte.
Für die Variante Kunststoff-Folie war wegen der erschwerten Montagebedingungen im Schrägschacht besonderes Augenmerk auf das Einbringen der Folie, die Herstellung der Nähte und deren Dichtigkeitsprüfung, die Ableitung von zudringendem Wasser u.ä. zu legen.
Auch für die Montage der dünnen Panzerbleche sind gemeinsam mit Stahlbaufirmen mehrere Möglichkeiten studiert worden. Man legte schließlich fest, ebene Bleche mit 6 mm Mindeststärke an der Baustelle zu Rohrschüssen zu rollen, zu verschweißen und entsprechend ausgesteift in den Schacht einzubringen. Der verbleibende Spalt Rohr - Fels von 5 bis 7 cm muß mit Mörtel verfüllt werden.
Anschließend wird bei beiden Varianten der Innenring her- bzw. fertiggestellt.
Wesentlich für beide Varianten ist das Injiziersystem zum Verpressen einerseits des Spaltes Dichthaut - Gebirge, andererseits des Gebirges über entsprechende Bohrlöcher. Hiezu sind in die Dichthaut radiale Injizierstutzen eingesetzt. Die Variante Folie erfordert weiters in den Spalt

eingelegte "Sperren", die den Vorlauf des Injiziergutes weitgehend bremsen und damit einen abschnittsweise gestaffelten Druckaufbau ermöglichen.
Näher zu untersuchen war auch die Ausführung der Dichthaut-Anschlüsse an die konventionellen Panzerungen. Aufgrund v.a. der Ausschreibungsergebnisse hat die Tauernkraftwerke AG entschieden, die dünnwandige Panzerung auszuführen. Es kommt eine Montage-Form zur Ausführung, die ähnlich bereits im Kraftwerk Silz der TIWAG verwirklicht worden ist. In jeweils 4 m lange Rohrschüsse wird der Innenbetonring eingebracht und diese vorgefertigten Rohre eingefahren. Die Betonierung reduziert sich damit auf das Verfüllen ringförmiger Aussparungen im Bereich der Montageschweißnähte. Das Bild 7 zeigt den Längsschnitt der Auskleidung. Die Stahlgüte entspricht einem St 360, die Betongüte beträgt 40 N/mm2 nach 90 Tagen, der größte Injizierdruck rund 40 bar. Rohrfertigung und Montage werden in den Jahren 1983 und 1984, die Injektionsarbeiten im Jahr 1985 abgewickelt werden.

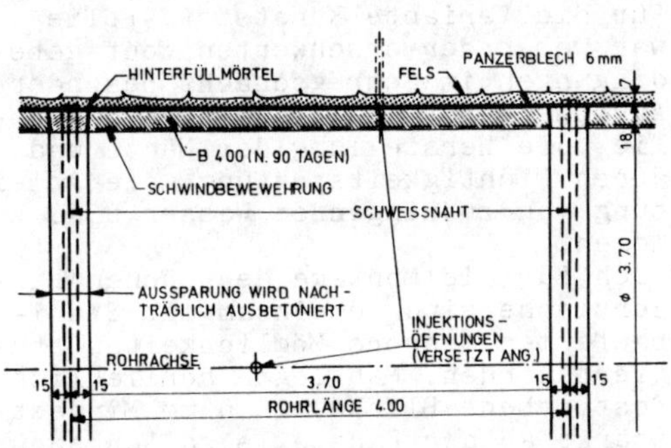

Bild 7 - Schrägstrecke, Längsschnitt (Ausführung)

6. SCHLUSSFOLGERUNGEN

Wie in der Praxis bei Druckstollen und -schächten schon mehrfach angewandt, ist auch bei hohen Innendrükken eine kostensparende und sichere Auskleidung ausführbar. Die Eignung ist durch geologische und geomechanische Untersuchungen nachzuweisen, für die genügend Zeit verfügbar sein muß.
Der Fräsvortrieb schont dabei das Gebirge und ermöglicht auch das unmittelbare Aufbringen einer steifen Dichthaut auf den Felsuntergrund. Maßgebend für die Ausführung einer vorgespannten Betonauskleidung mit Dichthaut sind das Aufbringen der Injektion, das Verformungsverhalten von Beton und Fels sowie die kostenbestimmenden Montagebedingungen. Weiters kann die durchlaufend gemessene Verschiebung der Verspannplatten zur Gebirgsbeurteilung herangezogen werden. Um hier auch quantitativ brauchbare Aussagen zu erhalten, wäre eine entsprechende Ausformung der Verspannplatten zu überlegen. Weiters sollten die Meßwerte selbsttätig erfaßt und ausgewertet werden.

LITERATUR

Gschaider, Ewy, Heigerth: Triebwasserführungen und Beileitungen der Zemmkraftwerke. Österr. Zeitschr. f. El.-Wirtschaft, 1972/10
Seeber: Neue Entwicklungen für Druckstollen und Druckschächte. Österr. Ing.-Zeitschrift, 1975/5
Seeber, Heigerth, Bärenthaler, Finger: Triebwasserweg der Hauptstufe Malta. Österr. Zeitschrift für El.-Wirtschaft, 1979/1,2

STABILITY OF VERTICAL LONG-LIFE SHAFTS IN TECTONICALLY INDUCED MASSIFS

Stabilität vertikaler Schächte mit langer Nutzungsdauer in tektonisch beanspruchtem Gebirge

Stabilité des puits verticaux dans les massifs contraints tectoniques pendant une longue durée de leur existence

G.A.MARKOV
Academy of Sciences of the USSR, Apatity, USSR

SUMMARY:
The laws are considered of the destruction process in time in vertical shafts which are sank in high-induced rock massifs. The initial design of a shaft of a circular section is changing into an ellipsoidal cavern. Besides the dimensions of a cross section of the cavern in the horizontal plane have 10 times exceeded the initial diameter of the shaft. Characteristic destruction of shafts in the cross section in the form of ellipse fully agrees with the calculated predictions if high horizonial stresses existing in a massif are taken into consideration.

The criteria and speeds are determined of the development of rock destruction in time at different relations including the overlimiting relations between strength and indices of the state of stress of rocks in the outline of shafts. A choice of a cross section of a shaft and of the disposal of adjacent workings is of great importance taking into consideration the direction of the greatest horizontal compression. In addition the intensity of destructions reduces here by the factor of 3-5 and in some cases of 10.

ZUSAMMENFASSUNG:
Man betrachtet die Gesetzmässigkeiten des Zeitzertrümmerungsprozesses von den in den hochgespannten Gebirgsmassiven abteuften Seigerschächten. Die Anfangskonstruktion des Schachtes mit runder Schachtscheibe verändert sich in ellipsenähnlicher Kaverne. In diesem Fall sind die Abmessungen des Querschnittes in der Horizontalebene zehnmal grösseren im Vergleich zum Anfangsdurchmesser des Schachtes. Die charakteristische Zerstöhrung der Schächte wird im Querschnitt nach der Ellipse mit den angerechneten Prognosen vollständig koordiniert, wenn man die im Massiv wirkenden grossen Horizontalspannungen berücksichtigt. Es werden die Kriterien und die Geschwindigkeiten der Gesteinszerstöhrungen während einiger Zeit bei den verschiedenen und nachäussersten Beziehungen zwischen der Festigkeit und der Kennziffer der Intensität der Gesteine auf der Kontur der Seigerschächte festgestellt. Eine grosse Bedeutung hat für Stabilitätsverwahrung die Auswahl der Schachtscheibe und der Lage von Nebenverhieben in Anbetracht der Richtung grösserer Horizontalpressung. In diesem Fall gelangt man bis zur Verminderung der Intensität der Zerstöhrungen um dreibis fünfmal und in einigen Fällen bis zehnmal.

RESUME:
On examine les régilarités du processus de la destruction dans le temps d'existence des puits verticaux creusés dans les massifs rocheux haut contraints. La construction primaire du puits de la section circulaire se régénère en caverne ellipsoïdale. Dans ce cas les dimensions de la section transversale d'une caverne du plan horizontal s'est augmentée de dix fois en comparaison avec le diamètre primaire du puits. La déstruction caractéristique de puits dans la section transversale sur une ellipse s'accorde complétement avec les pronostics calculés, si on prend en considération les grandes contraintes horizontales dans un massif. On a détérminé les critères et la vitesse du dévéloppement de ruptures des roches dans le temps avec différentes corrélations entre la résistance et les indices de l'intensité des roches sur le contour des puits. Une grande importance pour le maintien de la stabilité a le choix de la section du puits et de la disposition des ouvrages adjacents en considération de la direction de plus grande compression horizontale. Dans ce cas il y a la diminution de l'intensité de ruptures de 3-5 fois et dans certains cas jusqu'a 10 fois.

Modern investigations have proved the occurence of such a pnenomenon as the tectonic state of stress of rocks in most deposits which are composed of igneous rocks and in those which are represented by sedimentary rocks of metamorphic complex. The state of stress of rocks existing in tectonically induced massifs is written as follows:

$$\left.\begin{aligned} \sigma_1 &= \gamma H \\ \sigma_2 &= \frac{\nu}{1-\nu}\gamma H + \psi T \\ \sigma_3 &= \frac{\nu}{1-\nu}\gamma H + T \end{aligned}\right\} \qquad (1)$$

where $\sigma_1, \sigma_2, \sigma_3$ – the main stresses;
γH – the gravitation component of stresses determined by the depth (H) and volume weight (γ) of rocks;
ν – Poisson's ratio;
T – the tectonic component of stresses;
ψ – the anisotropy coefficient in the field of tectonic stresses.

The additional component (T) of stresses in tectonically induced massifs is a compressive one and can several times exceed the component which is conditioned by the weight of overburden rocks. In most cases the vector of the additional component has a horizontal direction. It follows that in tectonically induced massifs the main horizontal stresses σ_2 and σ_3 in absolute value exceed a vertical one $\sigma_1 = \gamma H$

Investigations have shown that in tectonically induced massifs rocks are highmonolithic, strong and elastic.

The properties of tectonically induced massifs mentioned above condition the peculiarities of rock pressure manifestation while constructing various underground structures. When driving a working one can observe cracking and flaking of rocks. In the most induced sections of an underground structure rock bursts and burstings may take place. These peculiarities of destruction of highly-stressed rocks are considered in publication (Markov et al. 1979). Different conditions of the development of destruction process were analized in our paper at the symposium on rock mechanics (Turchaninov et al. 1981).

Loss of stability of workings in tectonically induced massifs is conditioned by the process of brittle fracturing of rocks which takes place near the outline of a working and is accompanied by the forming of fractures and the caving of rock plates into the working. The surfaces of forming fractures are parallel to the outline of the surfaces of radial stress (σ_r) action. From the physical point of view this process is characterized by the imergence and development of destructions. This process may develop with the constant or increasing speed in the course of time up to the destruction similar to rock bursts or burstings. Under conditions of different relations between the stresses existing in the outline of a working and the strength of rocks the expected nature of destruction may be predicted on the base of the following relation:

$$\sigma_D \geqslant K_c \sigma_c \qquad (2)$$

where σ_D – the invariant characteristic of the existing stresses:
Kc – the empiric coefficient which characterizes the relation between the existing stresses and the strength of rocks in different processes of destruction.

Since in the outline of a working the radial stress $\tau = 0$, the invariant value of the stress σ_D is written as follows:

$$\sigma_D = \sigma_\theta + \sigma_L \qquad (3)$$

where σ_θ – the tangential stress in the outline of a working in a normal cross section of a working;
σ_L – the longitudinal stress in the section parallel to the axis of a working.

The process of destruction of highstressed, hard rocks has been studied experimentally when observing the stability of vertical shafts sank in one of the mines of the Kola peninsula (Markov et al. 1978). Shafts NN 1,2,3 (Fig.1) are sank into the depth of 600 m. The distance between them is 80 m. The design of all these three shafts is the same. The diametre of the main part of a shaft in its circular section is equal to 6 m. The lower part of the shaft is broadened and has 128 m^3 (8x16m) in its cross section area and 36 m in height. The shafts are connected with a tunnel. A system of passageways is driven around a shaft. They form four layers of workings situated one above another 18–20 m away from each ofher. The passageways are connected with the shaft. A raise working is sank parallel to a shaft and is of 5 m in its cross section area (2.5x2m). The distance between their centres is 23 m. The shafts are sank by a shorthole drilling-and-blasting method.

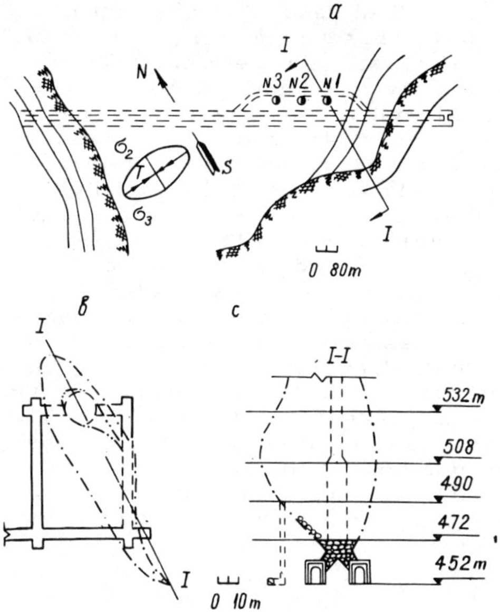

Fig.1: Disposal of vertical shaft and its destruction.
a – Plan of shafts disposal and the orientation of the ellipse of the greatest horizontal stresses;
b – The orientation of destruction ellipse in the horizontal section of a shaft;
c – Shaft destruction in a vertical section.

Geomechanical investigations have shown that the strength of rocks in which the shafts are sank is as follows: σ_c = 150–200 MPa where σ_r is the axil compression strength of rocks (in a piece) and σ_p = 10–15 MPa where σ_p is the axial tensile strength of rocks. The rocks are fine-grained, monolithic, tectonically fractured zones are absent, jointing is weak. Elastic modulus of rocks in the massif is $E = 5\cdot10^4 - 10\cdot10^4$ MPa. The initial stress field in the massif is characterized by the following relation: $\sigma_1 = \sigma_2 = \sigma_3 =$ 1:2:4 where $\sigma_1 = \gamma H$. The greatest horizontal stress σ_3 is directed latitudinally (Fig.1) and is equal to 70–80 MPa. When sinking the shafts one could observe an active rock bursting which was accompanied by plate scaling of rocks from the walls. The scale surfaces are parallel to the surface of shaft's walls regardless of the natural lamination and jointings of rocks. Rock burstings and scaling are characteristic of those zones of the shaft outline in which the concentration of existing stresses exceed the strength of rock. Zones of active destructions were situated in the northern and southern walls of the shaft. The following formula has been obtained to forecast general destruction process in the walls of vertical workings:

$$\gamma H\left(1+2\frac{\nu}{1-\nu}\right)+T\left[1-2\cos2\theta+\psi\left(1+2\cos2\theta\right)\right]>K_c\sigma_c \quad (4)$$

where θ – the radial angle composed by the direction of the T-vector and the radius-vector which determines the position of a point in the outline of a shaft.

After the auxiliary workings had been driven around and connected with the shaft the process of rock destruction activized sharply but not in all cases. The process of activization was observed when workings connected with or parallel to the shaft were disposed in plane perpendicular to the direction of the greatest stress σ_3, i.e. to the direction of stress T.

The calculations obtained allowed to determine the values of stresses in various elements of a structure. More than ten-year observations were then made over the characteristic points of the structure. These observations give a possibility to establish the regularities of the development of destructions, including such a factor as time (Fig.2).

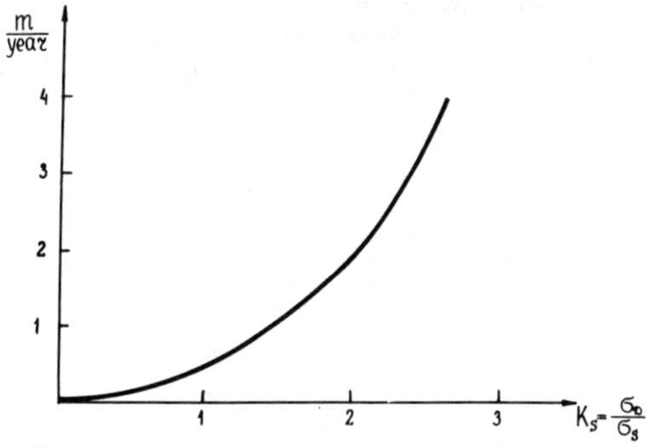

Fig.2: The dependence of speed (m/year) of shaft wall destruction on the exising stresses and rock strength relation ($K_c = \frac{\sigma_D}{\sigma_c}$)

The speed of rock destruction in the walls changes from 0.1–0.3 m per year (when $K_c = 0.5$) to 4–4 m per year (when $K_c = 2.5$) when the correlation of the main stresses $\sigma_1, \sigma_2, \sigma_3$ is the same in the region of the shafts disposal as that one mentioned above. The walls of the shaft preserve a stable state within the whole period of observation when $K_c < 0.3$.

During the period of obeservation the cross section of the shatts has changed its circular form into an elliptical one as a result of destructions in the norhern and southern walls and has streched in the me-meridional direction. The cross section dimensions of the shaft 4–10-fold (from 6–16 to 50–60 m). Thorough geological investisations have proved that it is impossible to explain the destruction of shafts as a result of fractures' affect or the exictence of zones of tectonically fractured rocks. The peculiarities of shaft destructions have been explained only by the determination of the initial state of stress of a massif and corresponding calculations of stress distribution around structures.

Practical results of these investigations are the recommendations for the rational disposal of adjacent workings parallel to or intersected with the shaft, for a choice of a rational form of a shaft cross section and corresponding spacial orientation of this form. These recommendations and their detailed substantiation are submitted in special paper (Markov 1977). Further practical experiments proved completely the correctness of the recomendations for taking into consideration the tectonic state of stress in vast and different conditions of various mines in reference not only to workings sank vertically but to these of any orientation and complex configuration intended for underground structures, including the systems of underground mining developments. The data obtained have shown that when choosing a design of a structure in terms of tectonic state of stress of rocks it is possible to influence the nature and intensity of rock pressure manifestation, to increase safety of updrivage works, to vary the duration of underground structure existence, and to secure free of damage exploitation of the structures during the appoined period of time.

References

1. Markov G.A. 1977, Tectonic stresses and rock pressure in mines (in Russian), Nauka, L., 212.
2. Markov G.A., Demidov Ju.V., Sazonov G.V., Sizov Ju.P. 1978, The influence of tectonic forces on the stability of deep ore chutes (in Russian), Gornyi zhurnal 7: 63–65.
3. Markov G.A., Kaspar'jan E.W. 1979, Erfassung der Struktureigenartigkeit und des Spannungzustandes des Felsgebirges bei der Ermittung der Standfestigkeit von bergmannischen Hohlraumen (in German), Rock Mechanics 11: 133–142.
4. Turchaninov I.A., Markov G.A., Lovchikov A.V. 1981, Conditions of changing of extra-hard rock into weak rock under the influence of tectonic stresses of massifs. International Symposium on Weak Rock, Tokyo, Japan 2: 194–198.

BEMESSUNG VON INJEKTIONSVORGESPANNTEN AUSKLEIDUNGEN IN DRUCKSTOLLEN

The design of concrete lined pressure tunnels prestressed by grouting

Le dimensionnement des revêtements, mises en précontrainte par injection, dans des galeries forcées

WALTER WITTKE & WOLFGANG KRAJEWSKI

Rheinisch-Westfälische Technische Hochschule Aachen, Bundesrepublik Deutschland

SUMMARY

The paper describes the application of a finite element program, developed for the computation of rock-statics problems, on the analysis of pressure tunnels. Concrete lined pressure tunnels prestressed by grouting are considered as well as non-prestressed tunnels. For a number of examples the influences of an anisotropic rock mass deformability as well as those of plastic zones induced in the rock mass during the prestressing and loading of the tunnel are investigated. The results indicate that the tensile stresses in the lining are underestimated in the cases considered if the above mentioned influences are ignored.

ZUSAMMENFASSUNG

Im vorliegenden Beitrag wird die Berechnung von Druckstollen mit einem für felsstatische Berechnungen entwickelten Finite-Element-Programm erläutert. Es werden sowohl nichtvorgespannte als auch durch Injektion vorgespannte Druckstollen betrachtet. Für einige ausgewählte Beispiele werden die Einflüsse einer anisotropen Verformbarkeit des Gebirges und von örtlichen Festigkeitsüberschreitungen im Gebirge auf die Beanspruchung der Druckstollenauskleidung untersucht. Die Berechnungsergebnisse zeigen, daß in den untersuchten Fällen bei einer Vernachlässigung dieser Einflüsse die Zugbeanspruchung der Auskleidung unterschätzt wird.

RESUME

Dans le texte suivant on trouvera des explications concernant le calcul des galeries forcées suivant un programme des éléments finis relatif au calcul statique des roches. Prises en considération sont des galeries forcées qui n'ont pas subi une précontrainte ainsi que celles qui ont subi une précontrainte par injection. Dans quelques exemples les influences de la déformation anisotrope de la roche et du dépassement local de la résistance de la roche sur les contraintes dans le revêtement des galeries forcées sont étudiées. Les resultats des calculs montrent que dans les cas étudiés, où ces influences sont négligées, la contrainte de traction du revêtement est sous-estimée.

1 EINLEITUNG

Beim Bau von Wasserkraftanlagen werden in zunehmendem Maße Triebwasserstollen mit hohen Innendrücken ausgeführt. Bei Durchmessern von 4 - 5 m betragen die Druckhöhen zum Teil mehr als 500 m. Dabei können die Innendrücke nur in seltenen Fällen unmittelbar auf das Gebirge übertragen und von diesem aufgenommen werden. In der Regel ist eine Stollenauskleidung erforderlich, die bei der Belastung durch den Innenwasserdruck in Wechselwirkung mit dem umliegenden Gebirge tritt und je nach den vorhandenen Steifigkeitsverhältnissen einen Teil der Belastung auf das Gebirge überträgt.

Neben dickwandigen Stahlpanzerungen, die aus wirtschaftlichen Gründen heute üblicherweise nur noch in Stollenabschnitten mit höchsten Beanspruchungen ausgeführt werden, kommen als Auskleidung in erster Linie Betonschalen in Frage. Um die erforderliche Dichtigkeit zu gewährleisten, erhalten die Betonschalen neuerdings häufiger eine außenliegende Dichtungsfolie. Darüber hinaus verwendet man in bestimmten Fällen auch eine dünne Stahlpanzerung.

Als sehr wirtschaftlich haben sich in vielen Fällen Betonauskleidungen erwiesen, bei denen durch eine Zementinjektion des Spaltes zwischen Auskleidung und Gebirge eine radiale Vorspannung der Betonauskleidung erzeugt wird. Diese Vorspannung bewirkt im Beton in tangentialer Richtung Druckspannungen, die größer sind als die aus dem Innenwasserdruck resultierenden Zugspannungen. Darüber hinaus führt die Zementinjektion auch häufig zu einer Vergütung des an den Stollen angrenzenden Gebirges.

Von Kieser [4] wurde in den 40er Jahren ein Injektionsverfahren für Druckstollen entwickelt, bei welchem die Stollenauskleidung aus einer außenliegenden Vorauskleidung und einem Kernring aus Betonformsteinen besteht (Fig. 1a). Der zwischen der Vorauskleidung und dem Kernring verbleibende 2 - 3 cm dicke Spalt wird mit Zementsuspension injiziert. Der radial auf den Kernring wirkende Injektionsdruck führt dabei zu einer Tangentialvorspannung dieser Schale, wobei die Vorspannung auch nach Erhärten des Injektionsgutes bestehen bleibt. Dieses Verfahren wurde von den Tiroler Wasserkraftwerken AG (TIWAG) weiterentwickelt, indem zwischen Gebirge und Betonauskleidung Injektionsschläuche angeordnet werden, durch die nach dem Erhärten des Betons die Vorspanninjektion erfolgt (Fig. 1b, [9]). In einigen Fällen wurde in einer Abwandlung dieses Verfahrens die Vorspannung auch durch eine Injektion nachträglich hergestellter, radial angeordneter Bohrlöcher bewirkt (Fig. 1c, [12]).

Dieser Beitrag befaßt sich mit der rechnerischen Erfassung des Spannungs- und Dehnungszustandes von injektionsvorgespannten Druckstollenauskleidungen durch Berechnungen nach der Methode der Finiten Elemente (FEM). Dabei wird anhand eini-

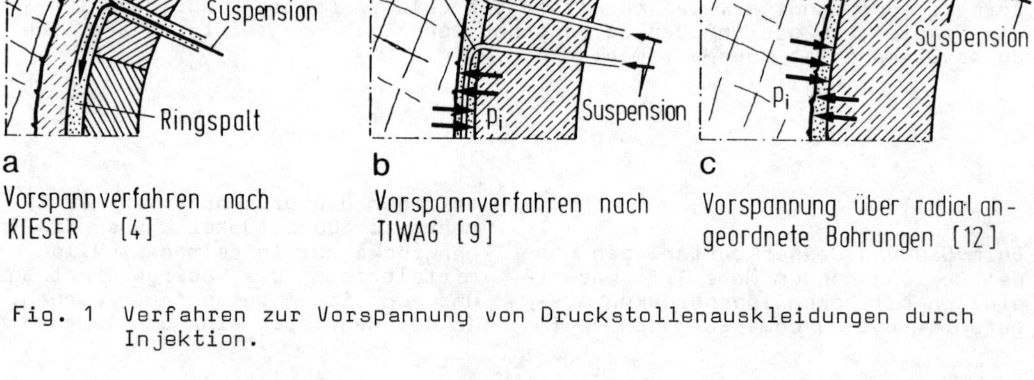

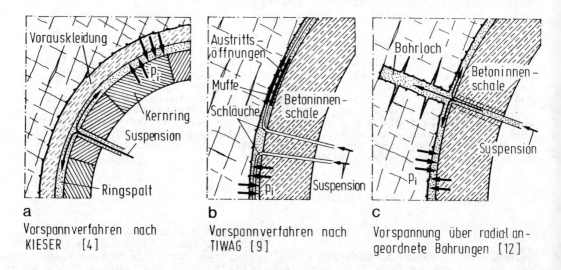

a
Vorspannverfahren nach KIESER [4]

b
Vorspannverfahren nach TIWAG [9]

c
Vorspannung über radial angeordnete Bohrungen [12]

Fig. 1 Verfahren zur Vorspannung von Druckstollenauskleidungen durch Injektion.

ger ausgewählter Beispielrechnungen der Einfluß einer anisotropen Verformbarkeit des Gebirges sowie der Einfluß von örtlichen Festigkeitsüberschreitungen im Gebirge auf den Spannungszustand in der Auskleidung untersucht.

2 BERECHNUNGSVERFAHREN

Im Hinblick auf eine wirklichkeitsnahe rechnerische Erfassung des Spannungszustandes in Druckstollenauskleidungen ist eine Berücksichtigung der Wechselwirkung zwischen Auskleidung und Gebirge von wesentlicher Bedeutung. Dementsprechend wurden schon frühzeitig kontinuumsmechanische Methoden zur Druckstollenberechnung entwickelt [2, 4]. Grundlage dieser Berechnungen ist i.a. die Annahme eines isotropen und elastischen Spannungs-Dehnungsverhaltens des Felses. Der nach Ausbruch des Stollenquerschnitts vor dem Einbau einer Sicherung im Gebirge vorhandene Spannungszustand, der sogenannte Sekundärspannungszustand, läßt sich hiernach aus einer geschlossenen Lösung für eine an den Rändern belastete, kreisrund gelochte Scheibe ermitteln. Die aus dem Innenwasserdruck und einem Injektionsdruck resultierenden Spannungen können nach der Theorie des dickwandigen Rohres berechnet werden. Die Betonauskleidung und das Gebirge werden hierbei jeweils als dickwandige Rohre angesehen, die zusammen einen Verbundkörper bilden. Für dieses statisch unbestimmte System des Verbundkörpers lassen sich die Spannungen infolge der radial wirkenden Wasser- bzw. Injektionsdrücke ermitteln. Diese Spannungen werden anschließend denen des Sekundärzustandes überlagert.

Neben der vorstehend genannten Möglichkeit werden gelegentlich auch großmaßstäbliche in-situ-Versuche zur Bemessung von Druckstollenauskleidungen ausgewertet. Hierzu wird das Gebirge von einem Stollen aus mit Hilfe einer Radialpresse oder einer Druckkammer belastet. Derartige Versuche lassen sich durch die Konstruktion einer Arbeitslinie, die den Zusammenhang zwischen der Belastung und der Verschiebung des Ausbruchrandes angibt, auswerten. Die Arbeitslinie kann, gemäß einem Vorschlag von Lauffer und Seeber, in eine Bemessungstafel eingearbeitet werden, in der auch das Spannungs-Dehnungsverhalten der Auskleidung berücksichtigt wird. Die Bemessung der Auskleidung erfolgt auf graphischem Wege [5]. Bei diesem Bemessungsverfahren kann neben dem Einfluß einer Injektionsvorspannung auch eine zusätzliche Beanspruchung der Auskleidung durch thermische Einflüsse berücksichtigt werden. Das Verfahren kann auch bei einer anisotropen Verformbarkeit des Felses angewendet werden, wie dies für Versuche, die mit der TIWAG-Radialpresse durchgeführt wurden, gezeigt wurde ([6], [3]).

Durch die Entwicklung von leistungsfähigen Großrechenanlagen in Verbindung mit umfangreichen Programmsystemen ist in den letzten Jahren mit der Methode der Finiten Elemente (FEM) ein weiteres Verfahren zur Berechnung der Spannungen und Verformungen im Gebirge und in der Auskleidung hinzugekommen. Ein Vorteil dieser Methode liegt darin, daß eine weitgehende Anpassung des Berechnungsmodells an die natürlichen Gegebenheiten möglich ist, wodurch z.B. auch Inhomogenitäten im Fels berücksichtigt werden können. Weiterhin erlaubt dieses Verfahren z.B. die Untersuchung des Einflusses einer anisotropen Verformbarkeit des Felses sowie des Einflusses von örtlichen Überschreitungen der Gebirgsfestigkeit auf die Spannungen in Fels und Auskleidung.

3 DIE BERECHNUNG VON DRUCKSTOLLEN MIT DEM FINITE-ELEMENT PROGRAMMSYSTEM FEST 03

3.1 Das Programmsystem FEST 03

In den vergangenen Jahren wurde am Institut für Grundbau, Bodenmechanik, Felsmechanik und Verkehrswasserbau der RWTH Aachen das Finite-Element Programmsystem FEST 03 für felsstatische Berechnungen entwikkelt. Das Programmsystem wurde an anderer Stelle [10, 13] bereits ausführlich beschrieben, so daß im folgenden nur eine zusammenfassende Darstellung der Leistungsfähigkeit des Programms gegeben werden soll.

Mit dem Programmsystem FEST 03 sind ebene und räumliche Berechnungen von Spannungen und Verformungen nach der Methode der Finiten Elemente möglich, wobei isoparametrische Raumelemente mit variabler Knotenzahl verwendet werden [14]. Das Spannungs-Dehnungsverhalten des Felses wird durch ein linear elastisch-viskoplastisches Stoffgesetz beschrieben. Solange die Verformbarkeit im elastischen Bereich isotrop ist, reichen zu ihrer Beschreibung der Elastizitätsmodul E und die Poissonzahl ν aus. Bei geschichtetem oder geschiefertem Fels ist die Verformbarkeit jedoch in der Regel senkrecht zu der Gefügeebene größer als parallel zu dieser Ebene, die in Fig. 2 als isotrope Ebene bezeichnet ist. Ein solches Verformungsverhalten wird im Programm FEST 03 im elastischen Bereich durch fünf voneinander unabhängige Elastizitätskonstanten E_1, E_2, G_2, ν_1 und ν_2 beschrieben (transversale Isotropie).

Die beiden Elastizitätsmoduln E_1 und E_2 beschreiben die Zusammendrückbarkeit parallel bzw. senkrecht zur isotropen Ebene (Schieferung, Schichtung) und der Schubmodul G_2 die Gleitung bei einer Scherbeanspruchung in der isotropen Ebene. Die beiden Poissonzahlen ν_1 bzw. ν_2 beschreiben die Querdehnung parallel bzw. senkrecht zur isotropen Ebene (Fig. 2).

Der Übergang vom linear elastischen zum viskoplastischen Spannungs-Dehnungsverhalten des Felses wird durch die Fließfläche F = 0 des Mohr-Coulomb'schen Bruchkriteriums gekennzeichnet. Für den Fall, daß die Festigkeit des Gebirges richtungsunabhängig, also isotrop, ist, kann die Fließfläche in Abhängigkeit von den Hauptspannungen dargestellt werden. In einem Raum, der durch die Richtungen der Hauptspannungen aufgespannt wird, bildet in diesem Fall die Fließfläche F = 0 die Oberfläche eines hexagonalen Pyramidenstumpfes, dessen Symmetrieachse mit der Achse $\sigma_1 = \sigma_2 = \sigma_3$ zusammenfällt (Fig. 3). Unter Berücksichtigung der Zugfestigkeit $\sigma_{t,G}$ des isotropen Gesteins wird der Pyramidenstumpf durch die Ebene $\sigma_1 = \sigma_{t,G}$ begrenzt (Fig. 3). Für Spannungszustände, die einem Punkt innerhalb der Fließfläche entsprechen (F<0), ergeben sich elastische Dehnungen, während bei Zuständen mit $F \geq 0$ irreversible Dehnungen auftreten.

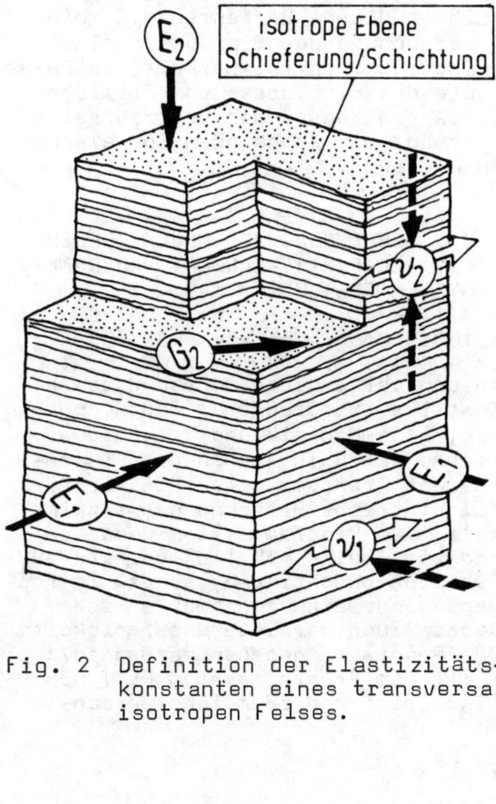

Fig. 2 Definition der Elastizitätskonstanten eines transversal isotropen Felses.

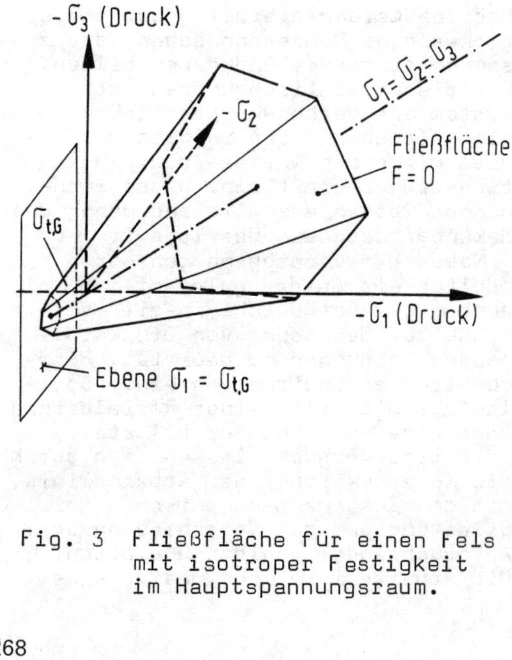

Fig. 3 Fließfläche für einen Fels mit isotroper Festigkeit im Hauptspannungsraum.

Mit dem Programmsystem FEST 03 kann darüber hinaus eine Anisotropie der Zug- und Scherfestigkeit, wie sie etwa in geklüftetem oder geschiefertem Fels auftritt, berücksichtigt werden. In diesen Fällen wird für die Ebenen mit verminderter Festigkeit der Spannungszustand in einem τ_{res} - σ_n - Koordinatensystem dargestellt (Fig. 4). Hierin bedeutet τ_{res} die resultierende Schubspannung in der betrachteten Ebene mit verminderter Festigkeit und σ_n die Normalspannung auf dieser Ebene. Unter Beibehaltung des Mohr-Coulomb'schen Bruchkriteriums ergeben sich dann für diese ausgezeichneten Ebenen Bruchgeraden ($F_T = 0$), die i.a. deutlich unter der für das Gestein maßgebenden Bruchgeraden ($F_G = 0$) liegen (Fig. 4).

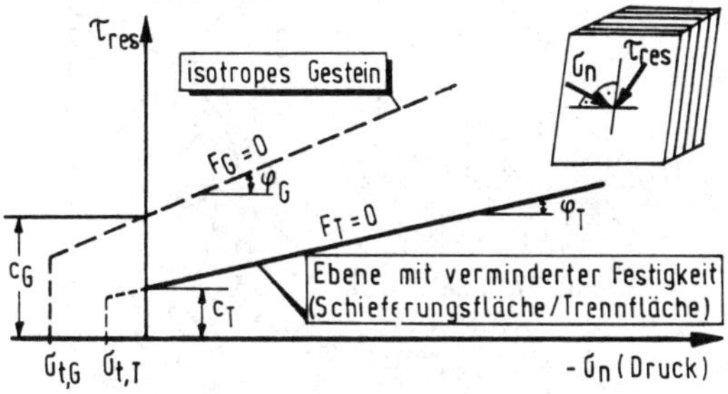

Fig. 4 Modifiziertes Mohr-Coulombsches Bruchkriterium für geklüfteten oder geschieferten Fels.

Treten Festigkeitsüberschreitungen im Gestein bzw. auf den Trenn- oder Schieferungsflächen auf, so werden die damit verbundenen irreversiblen Dehnungen nach der Theorie der Viskoplastizität berechnet. Dieser Vorgehensweise liegt die Vorstellung zugrunde, daß durch eine Belastung zunächst nur elastische Verformungen hervorgerufen werden, während irreversible plastische Verformungen aufgrund von Festigkeitsüberschreitungen erst im Laufe der Zeit eintreten. Dementsprechend sind zunächst auch Spannungszustände, für die $F > 0$ gilt, zulässig. Anschließend findet jedoch eine Spannungsumlagerung statt und es ergeben sich, falls für das Gesamtsystem ein Gleichgewichtszustand möglich ist, am Ende einer viskoplastischen Berechnung schließlich für alle Gebirgsbereiche Spannungszustände mit $F \leq 0$.

3.2 Simulation der Bau- und Betriebszustände von Druckstollen

In Anlehnung an den Bau- und Betriebsablauf erfolgt die Druckstollenberechnung in mehreren Schritten. Hierbei werden im einzelnen folgende Zustände untersucht:

1. Der Primärzustand, der im Gebirge vor dem Auffahren des Stollens vorhanden ist.
2. Der Sekundärzustand, wie er sich nach dem Auffahren des Stollens einstellt. Auch erforderliche Sicherungsmaßnahmen können in diesem Rechenschritt berücksichtigt werden.
3. Der Zustand nach fertiggestellter Auskleidung des Druckstollens.
4. Der Zustand mit aufgebrachter Injektionsvorspannung ohne Berücksichtigung eines Innenwasserdrucks. Dieser Zustand wird im folgenden als Bauzustand bezeichnet.
5. Der Betriebszustand mit Wirkung des Innenwasserdrucks.

In allen genannten Zuständen kann, falls erforderlich, ein Bergwasserspiegel berücksichtigt werden. Der Einfluß von Temperaturveränderungen und der des Schwindens und Kriechens des Auskleidungsbetons wurde nicht berücksichtigt. Eine entsprechende Erweiterung des Programms ist jedoch möglich.

Die rechnerische Simulation des Primärzustandes erfolgt im Programm FEST 03 dadurch, daß, vom unbelasteten, unverformten Elementnetz ausgehend, den Gebirgselementen die entsprechenden mechanischen Eigenschaften und die sich aus dem Eigengewicht ergebenden Spannungen zugeordnet werden. Gegebenenfalls können hier noch zusätzliche Spannungen, etwa aus tektonischen Einflüssen oder geologischer Vorbelastung, durch eine Vorverformung des Netzes rechnerisch berücksichtigt werden (Fig. 5a).

Der Sekundärzustand wird in einem zweiten Berechnungsschritt dadurch simuliert, daß den Elementen, die im Bereich des Ausbruchs liegen, eine sehr geringe Steifigkeit und eine Wichte von Null zugewiesen werden (Fig. 5b). Im gleichen Berechnungsschritt kann über den Ausbruch des Stollenquerschnitts hinaus auch der Einbau einer Sicherung,

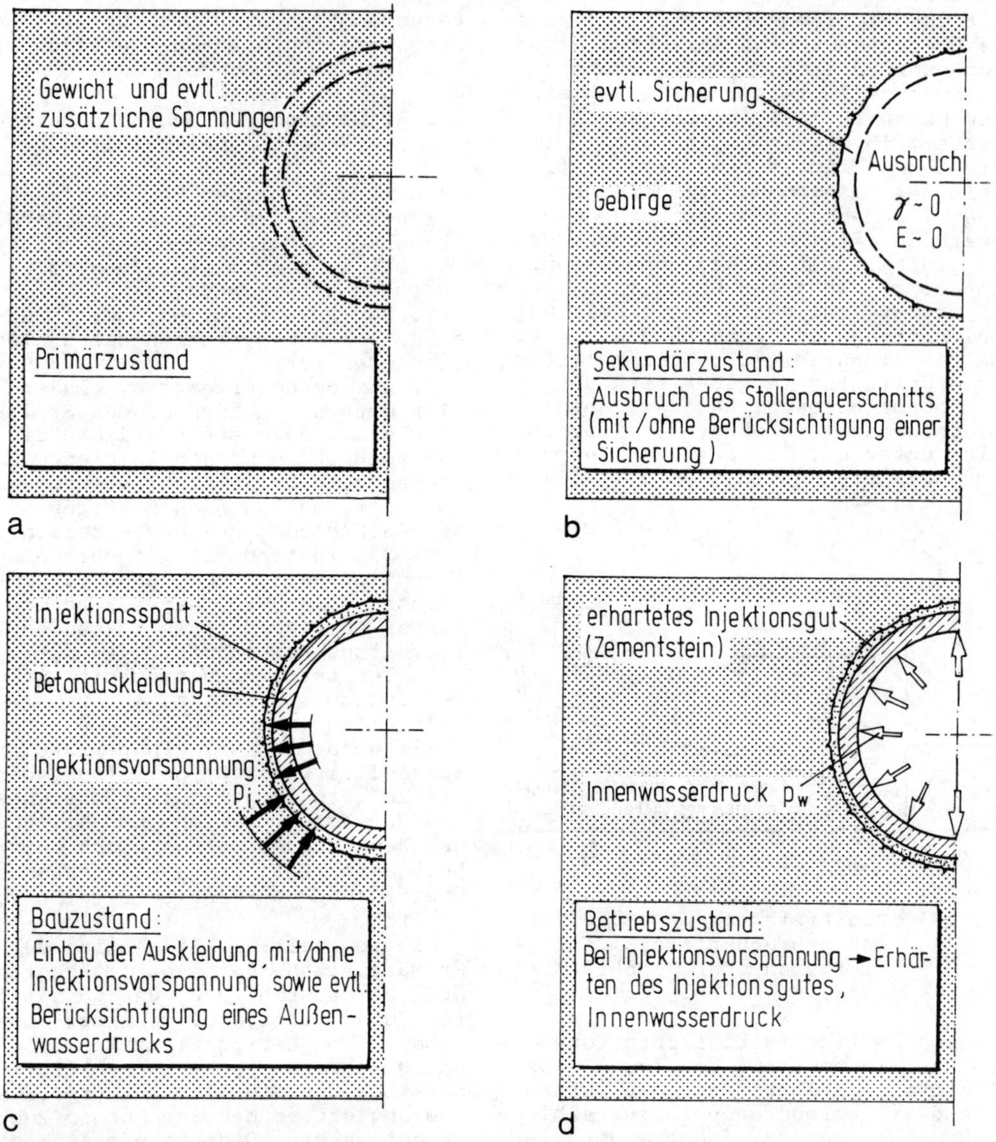

Fig. 5 Simulation der Bau- und Betriebszustände eines betonausgekleideten, vorgespannten Druckstollens in vier Rechenschritten.

beispielsweise einer Betonauskleidung simuliert werden, indem die Elemente, mit denen die Auskleidung nachgebildet werden soll, die Eigenschaften eines Betons erhalten. Ausgehend von einem unverformten Elementnetz werden hierbei die Auskleidungselemente in einem Zwischenschritt durch Eigenspannungszustände derart vorverformt, daß die Verformungen denen des Primärzustandes entsprechen. Durch diese rechentechnische Maßnahme wird ein spannungsloser Einbau der Auskleidung simuliert. Bei dieser Vorgehensweise wird jedoch nicht berücksichtigt, daß in der Natur bis zum Einbau der Auskleidung bereits ein Teil der vortriebsbedingten Gebirgsverformungen eingetreten ist. Dies führt in diesem Fall dazu, daß die Spannungen in der Auskleidung rechnerisch überschätzt werden.

In den durchgeführten Druckstollenberechnungen wurde deshalb ein anderer Weg zur Simulation des Einbaus der Auskleidung beschritten. Nachdem, wie vorstehend erläutert, die ausbruchbedingten Sekundärspannungen und -verformungen ermittelt worden sind, erhalten die Auskleidungselemente erst in einem darauffolgenden dritten Rechenschritt die Eigenschaften von Beton zugewiesen (Fig. 5c). Auch hierbei wird ein spannungsloser Einbau des Betons simuliert, indem die Auskleidungselemente entsprechend dem Sekundärzustand vorverformt werden. Dies bedeutet, daß davon ausgegangen wird, daß die vortriebsbedingten Verformungen des Gebirges bis zum Einbau der Auskleidung in voller Größe eingetreten sind. Diese Annahme ist in den meisten praktischen Fällen gerechtfertigt, da der Einbau der Auskleidung in einem vom Ausbruch und dem Einbau der Sicherung zeitlich getrennten Arbeitsgang erfolgt. Im Falle eines vorgespannten Druckstollens wird die Injektionsspannung p_i im gleichen Rechenschritt in Form von äquivalenten, radialen Knotenkräften simuliert. Hierbei wird der Injektionsspalt durch eine gesonderte Reihe dünner Elemente nachgebildet (Fig. 5c, 7), die in diesem Rechenschritt einen sehr kleinen Elastizitätsmodul erhalten, so daß sich der Spalt ohne Behinderung durch die Steifigkeit des Injektionsgutes aufweiten kann.

Im vierten Berechnungsschritt wird dann unter Berücksichtigung der vorangegangenen Aufweitung des Injektionsspaltes die Erhärtung des Injektionsgutes simuliert, indem den entsprechenden Elementen die Eigenschaften eines Zementsteins zugewiesen werden. Im gleichen Schritt wird auch der Innenwasserdruck p_w simuliert, indem auf die Auskleidung wirkende, äquivalente Knotenkräfte aufgebracht werden (Fig. 5d).

Die Schnittgrößen für die Bemessung der Auskleidung werden im Anschluß an diese Berechnungen aus den ermittelten Verformungen der Auskleidung nach einem von Pierau [8] entwickelten Verfahren an einem System von Schalenelementen berechnet. Diese getrennte Rechnung ist deshalb erforderlich, weil der Spannungsverlauf in den isoparametrischen Elementen für die Ermittlung der Biegemomente in der Auskleidung nicht hinreichend genau ist [8].

Druckstollen stellen in der Regel linienförmige Bauwerke dar, deren Länge um ein Vielfaches größer ist als ihr Durchmesser. Unter den Voraussetzungen, daß der rechnerisch untersuchte Stollenquerschnitt nicht im Bereich der räumlichen Spannungsabtragung an der temporären Ortsbrust liegt und daß sich die mechanischen Eigenschaften des Felses und die Primärspannungen entlang der Stollenachse nicht ändern, kann die Berechnung von Druckstollen an ebenen Elementscheiben erfolgen. Dies gilt sowohl für einen Fels mit isotroper Verformbarkeit, bei dem in Stollenlängsrichtung keine Verformungen auftreten, als auch für einen Fels mit anisotroper Verformbarkeit, bei dem unter diesen Voraussetzungen zwar Verformungen, jedoch keine Dehnungen in Stollenlängsrichtung auftreten können [13].

4 ANWENDUNGSBEISPIELE

4.1 Beschreibung der untersuchten Fälle

Die nachfolgend erläuterten Beispielrechnungen erfolgten für einen Druckstollen mit einem Innendurchmesser von D = 5,20 m und einer Dicke der Betonauskleidung von t = 40 cm. Die Höhe der Gebirgsüberlagerung oberhalb der Firste wurde mit $H_ü$ = 100 m und die Wichte des Felses mit γ = 25 kN/m^3 gewählt (s. hierzu auch Fig. 7). Ein Bergwasserspiegel wurde nicht berücksichtigt.

Es wurden vier verschiedene Fälle untersucht (Fig. 6). Im Fall a wurde elastisches, isotropes Spannungs-Dehnungsverhalten des Felses angenommen. Der E-Modul wurde verhältnismäßig hoch mit E = 40 000 MN/m^2 gewählt. Die Poissonzahl wurde zu ν = 0,25 angesetzt. Bei einem verhältnismäßig geringen Innenwasserdruck von p_w = 1,0 MN/m^2 (≙ 10 bar) wurde in diesem Fall auf eine Vorspannung der Auskleidung verzichtet (Fig. 6a). Für dieses erste Beispiel, das als Referenzfall für die weiteren Berechnungen dienen soll, ist wegen der verhältnismäßig einfachen Verhältnisse ein Vergleich der Berechnungsergebnisse mit denen herkömmlicher Berechnungsmethoden, z.B. von Kastner [2], möglich.

In einem zweiten Fall, dem Fall b, wurde, wiederum ausgehend von elastischem Spannungs-Dehnungsverhalten des Felses, der Einfluß einer anisotropen Verformbarkeit des Gebirges auf die

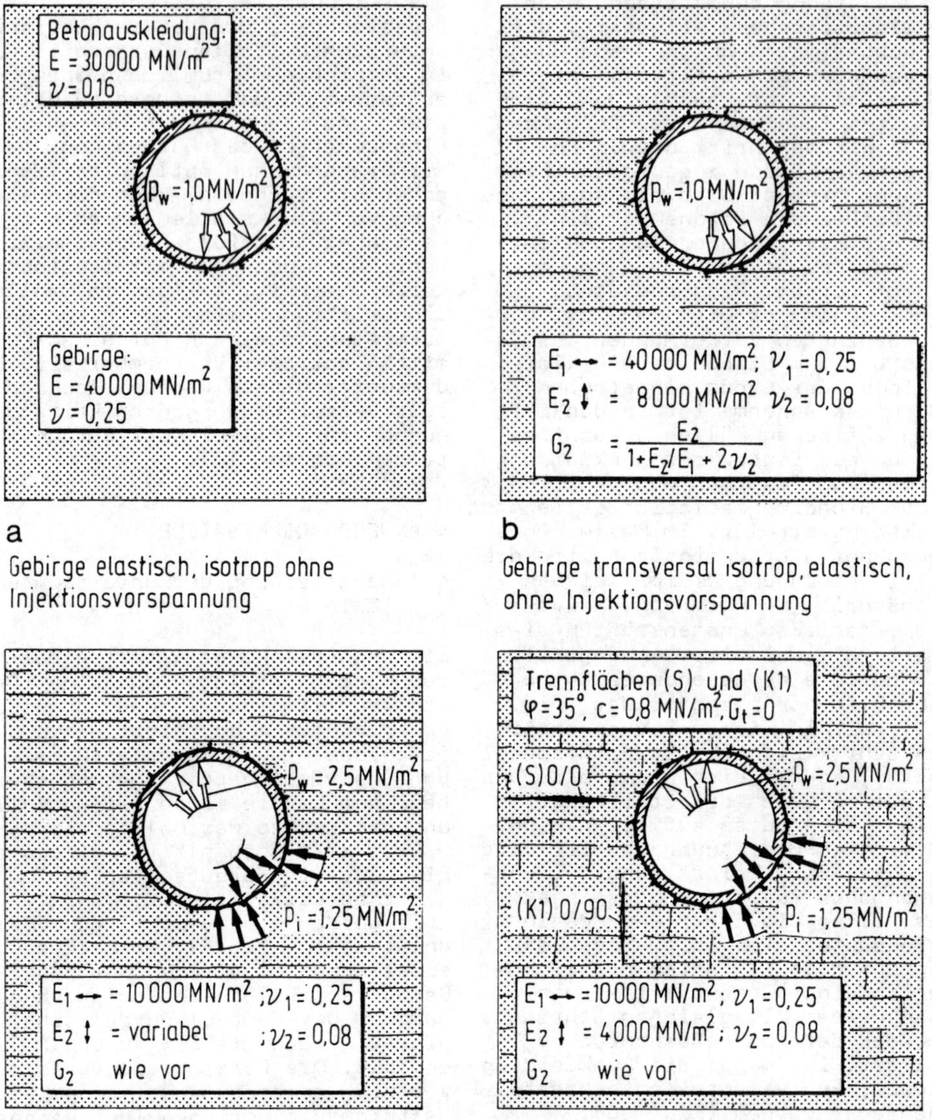

Fig. 6 Untersuchte Fälle.

Spannungen in der Auskleidung untersucht. Hierzu wurde angenommen, daß die Verformbarkeit des Gebirges in vertikaler Richtung größer ist als in horizontaler. Der E-Modul E_1, der das Verformungsverhalten des Gebirges in der horizontalen, isotropen Ebene beschreibt, blieb gegenüber dem E-Modul des Referenzfalls a unverändert, während E_2, der E-Modul in vertikaler Richtung, auf 1/5 des Wertes für E_1 abgemindert wurde (Fig. 6b). Der Schubmodul G_2 wurde in diesem und den nachfolgenden Fällen nach einer Beziehung von Barden [1] aus den Kennwerten E_1, E_2 und ν_2 wie folgt angesetzt:

$$G_2 = \frac{E_2}{1 + \frac{E_2}{E_1} + 2\nu_2}$$

Für die Poissonzahl ν_1 wurde der gleiche Wert wie für ν des Falls a zugrundegelegt, während ν_2 gegenüber ν auf 0,08 abgemindert wurde (Fig. 6b). Der Innenwasserdruck betrug wie im Fall a $p_w = 1,0$ MN/m^2.

Im Fall c (Fig. 6c) wurde für das Gebirge gegenüber Fall b eine größere Verformbarkeit zugrundegelegt. Unter der Annahme elastischen und transversal isotropen Spannungs-Dehnungsverhaltens wurde E_1 zu 10 000 MN/m^2 angesetzt. Um den Einfluß der Anisotropie und im besonderen des Verhältnisses E_1/E_2 zu untersuchen, wurde E_2 in einer Parameterstudie von 2 000 MN/m^2 bis zur Größe von E_1 variiert. Voruberlegungen führten zu dem Schluß, daß bei den angenommenen Gebirgsverhältnissen und einem Innenwasserdruck von $p_w = 2,5$ MN/m^2 eine Injektionsvorspannung der Auskleidung notwendig ist. Die erforderliche Größe der Vorspannung wurde mit $p_i = 1,25$ MN/m^2 abgeschätzt.

Schließlich wurde in einem vierten Fall, dem Fall d, in einer elastisch-viskoplastischen Berechnung der Einfluß von Festigkeitsüberschreitungen auf den Trennflächen auf die Spannungsverteilung in Gebirge und Auskleidung untersucht. Hierzu wurden, ausgehend von den Verhältnissen des Falls c mit $E_2 = 4000$ MN/m^2, zusätzlich zwei Trennflächenscharen S und K1 berücksichtigt (Fig. 6d). Die Festigkeit in der horizontalen Schichtung oder Schieferung (S) und der parallel zur Stollenachse streichenden und senkrecht einfallenden Kluftschar K1 wurde durch den Reibungswinkel $\varphi = 35^o$ und die Kohäsion $c = 0,8$ MN/m^2 beschrieben. Eine Zug-

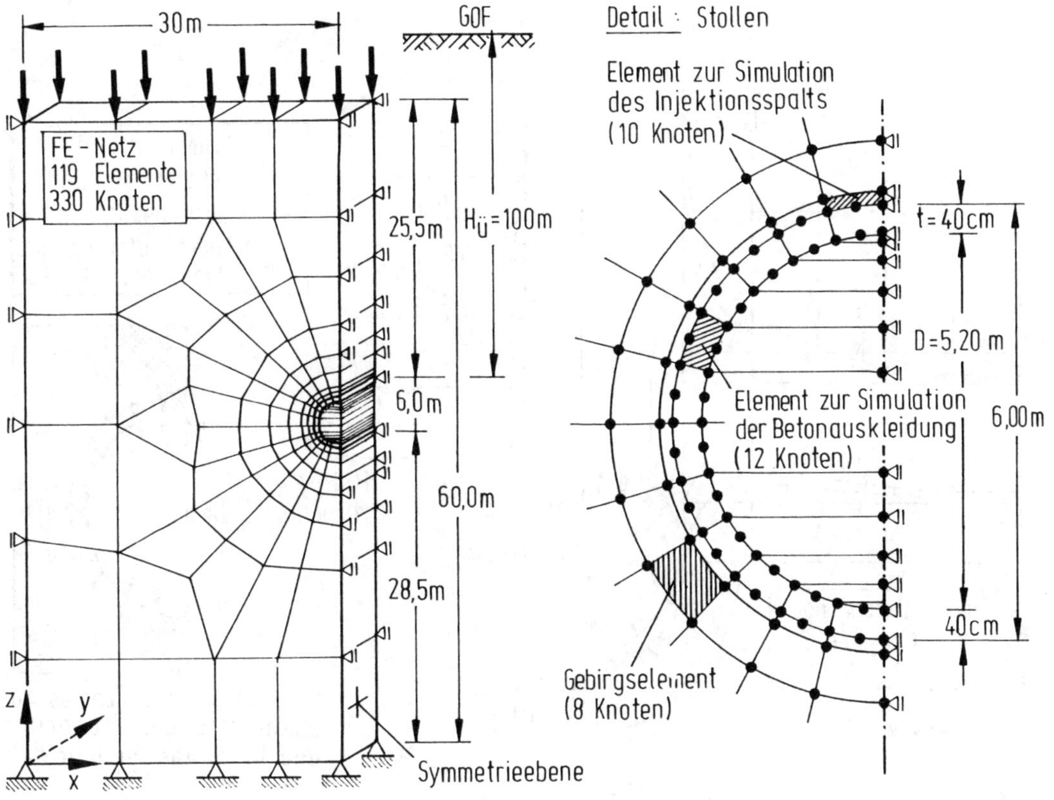

Fig. 7 Berechnungsausschnitt und Elementnetz.

festigkeit in den Trennflächen (Fig. 6d) wurde nicht berücksichtigt.

4.2 Berechnungsausschnitt und Elementnetz

Alle Berechnungen wurden mit dem in Fig. 7 dargestellten Elementnetz durchgeführt, in welchem berücksichtigt wurde, daß die Vertikalebene durch die Stollenachse aufgrund der getroffenen Berechnungsmaßnahmen eine Symmetrieebene bildet.

Als Randbedingungen wurden die Knotenpunkte der Grundfläche des Berechnungsausschnitts (z = 0) als unverschieblich, die der Seitenflächen als vertikal verschieblich und horizontal unverschieblich angenommen. Da die Oberfläche des Berechnungsausschnitts nicht mit der Geländeoberfläche identisch ist, wurde ein Teil des Überlagerungsgewichtes durch äquivalente, auf dem oberen Rand des Netzes (z = 60 m) angreifende Knotenkräfte simuliert. Das in Fig. 7 abgebildete Elementnetz umfaßt insgesamt 119 isoparametrische Elemente mit 330 Knotenpunkten. Der Fels wurde dabei mit 8-Knotenelementen, der Injektionsspalt mit 10-Knotenelementen und die Betonauskleidung mit 12-Knotenelementen nachgebildet.

4.3 Berechnungsergebnisse

Fall a

In Fig. 8 sind die aus den Berechnungen erhaltenen Radial- (σ_r) und Tangentialspannungen (σ_ϑ) des Gebirges für einen Horizontalschnitt durch die Ulme und die vertikale Symmetrieebene dargestellt. Die Darstellung der Spannungen im Vertikalschnitt beschränkt sich hierbei, wie auch in allen folgenden Fällen, auf den Firstbereich, da sich unter den gegebenen Verhältnissen die Spannungsverläufe im Sohl- und Firstbereich nur unwesentlich voneinander unterscheiden. Für den Betriebszustand sind in Fig. 8 außerdem die in der Betonauskleidung wirksamen Tangentialspannungen $\sigma_{\vartheta,b}$ aufgetragen.

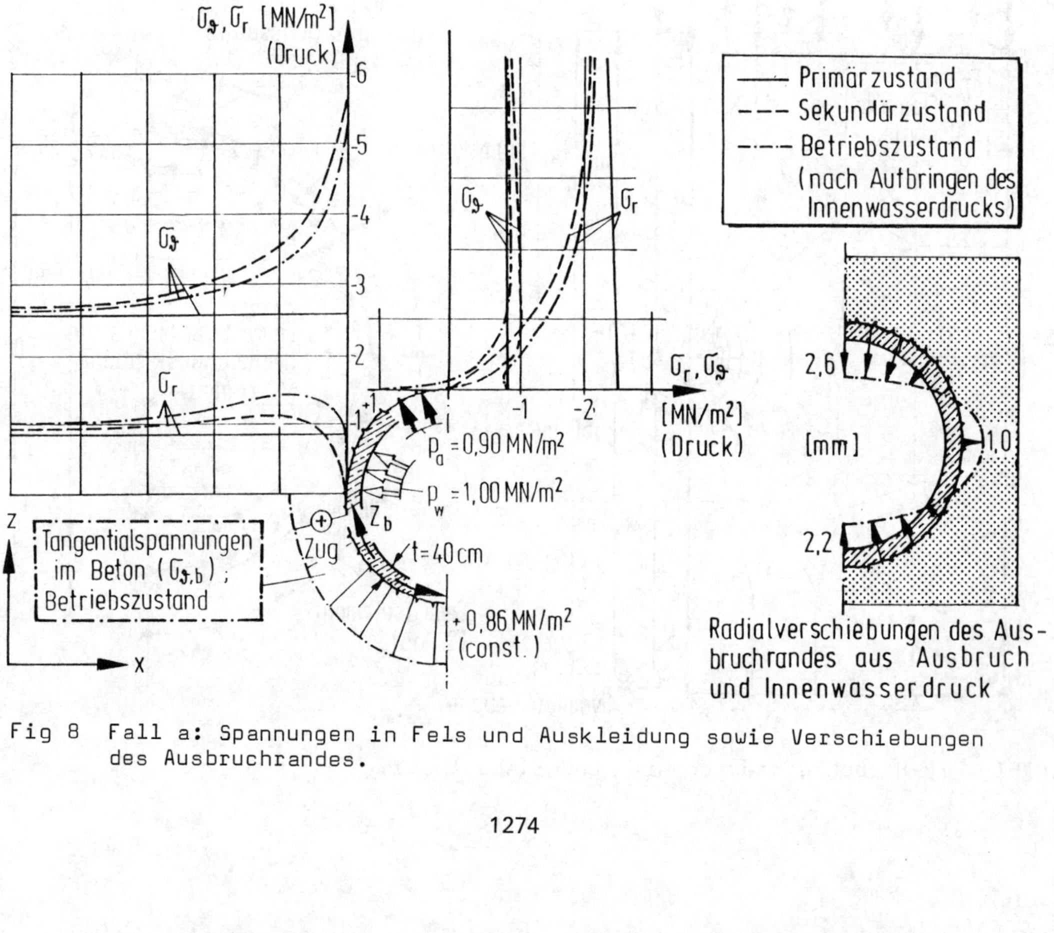

Fig 8 Fall a: Spannungen in Fels und Auskleidung sowie Verschiebungen des Ausbruchrandes.

Weiterhin sind in Fig. 8 auf der rechten Seite auch die Radialverschiebungen des Ausbruchrandes infolge des Ausbruchs und des Innenwasserdrucks dargestellt. Man erkennt, daß der Innenwasserdruck in der Betonauskleidung eine gleichmäßige Tangentialzugspannung $\sigma_{\vartheta,b}$ = 0,86 MN/m^2 bewirkt. Die hieraus resultierende Zugkraft $Z_b = \sigma_{\vartheta,b} \cdot t$ = 0,34 MN/m kann allerdings ohne weiteres von einer schlaffen Bewehrung aufgenommen werden. Die von der Betonauskleidung auf das Gebirge übertragene Radialspannung p_a beträgt 0,90 MN/m^2 und entspricht 90 % des Innenwasserdrucks. Der Traganteil des Gebirges ist also groß im Vergleich zu dem der Auskleidung. Dies läßt sich durch die geringe Verformbarkeit des Felses erklären, dessen E-Modul mit E = 40 000 MN/m^2 größer ist als der des Auskleidungsbetons, der mit E_b = 30 000 MN/m^2 angesetzt wurde. Infolge des Ausbruchs wird das Gebirge im Firstbereich sowohl in radialer als auch in tangentialer Richtung entlastet. Im Betriebszustand treten im Firstbereich tangentiale Zugspannungen bis zur Größe von 0,9 MN/m^2 auf, die durch die verhältnismäßig große Radialspannung zwischen Gebirge und Auskleidung bedingt sind. Die Ausdehnung des Zugkeils ist jedoch klein. An der Ulme treten im Sekundärzustand Spannungskonzentrationen auf, die dazu führen, daß auch im Betriebszustand keine Zugspannungen auftreten (Fig. 8).

Dieses Beispiel wurde auch mit dem Verfahren von Kastner [2] nachgerechnet. Dabei ergab sich eine gute Übereinstimmung mit den Ergebnissen der FE-Berechnung.

Fall b

Als Folge der anisotropen Verformbarkeit des Gebirges ergibt sich für diesen Fall im Betriebszustand eine ungleichmäßige und gegenüber dem Fall a wesentlich höhere Zugbeanspruchung der Auskleidung bei gleichem Innenwasserdruck (Fig. 8, 9). Die maximale Betonspannung stellt sich an der Ulme, d.h. an der Stelle mit der in radialer Richtung geringsten Verformbarkeit, ein und ist dort fast dreimal so groß wie im Fall a. Ein Vergleich der Radialverschiebungen des Ausbruchrandes im Betriebszustand für die Fälle a und b zeigt, daß im Fall b (Fig. 9), wegen der größeren Verformbarkeit des Felses in vertikaler Richtung, die First- und Sohlverschiebungen fast viermal so groß sind wie im Fall a (Fig. 8). An den Ulmen unterscheiden sich die radialen Verschiebungen in beiden Fällen dagegen praktisch nicht.

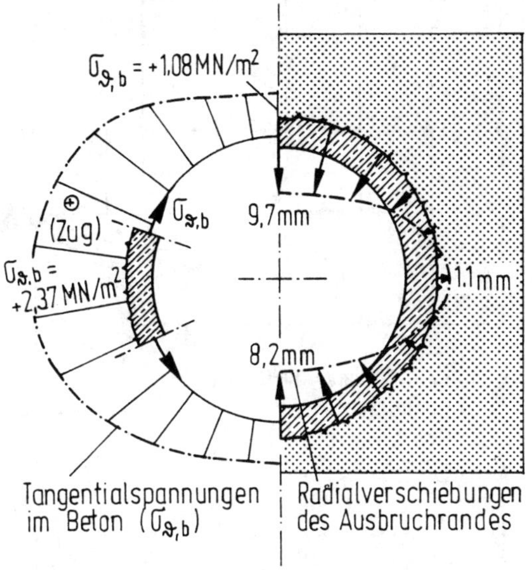

Fig. 9 Fall b: Tangentialspannungen in der Auskleidung und Radialverschiebungen des Ausbruchrandes für den Betriebszustand.

Fall c

In Fig. 10 sind für den Fall c mit E_2 = 4000 MN/m^2 (s. Fig. 6) in einem Vertikal- und einem Horizontalschnitt die Tangentialspannungen σ_ϑ im Gebirge dargestellt. Außerdem sind für den Bau- und den Betriebszustand die Tangentialspannungen in der Betonauskleidung angegeben. Die Injektionsvorspannung bewirkt in der Betonauskleidung eine gleichmäßige tangentiale Druckspannung $\sigma_{\vartheta,b}$ = − 9,2 MN/m^2. Durch den Innenwasserdruck wird diese Druckspannung im Betriebszustand teilweise abgebaut. An der Ulme liegt im Betriebszustand nur noch eine Betondruckspannung $\sigma_{\vartheta,b}$ von − 1,3 MN/m^2, an der Sohle von − 3,3 MN/m^2 vor. Es ergeben sich jedoch an keiner Stelle der Auskleidung, auch unter Berücksichtigung der in Fig. 10 nicht dargestellten Biegemomente, Randzugspannungen.

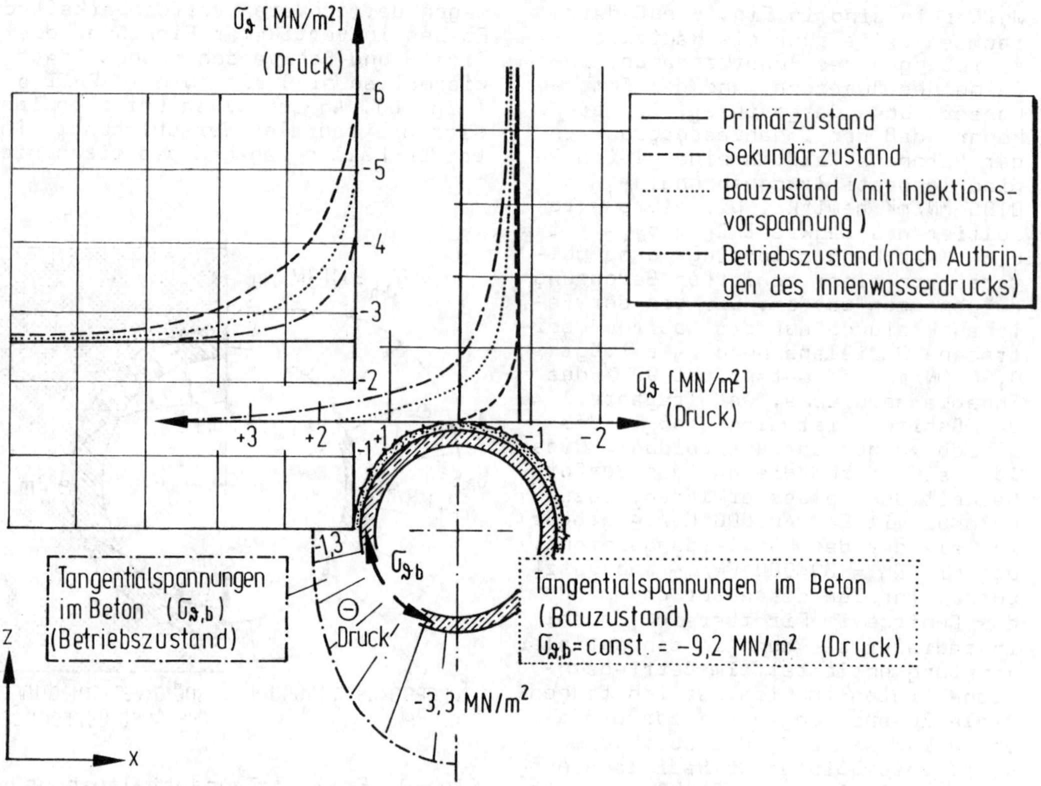

Fig. 10 Fall c: Tangentialspannungen in Gebirge und Auskleidung.

Demgegenüber führt die Injektionsvorspannung im Gebirge oberhalb der Firste zu tangentialen Zugspannungen, deren Maximalwert sich durch den Innenwasserdruck noch mehr als verdoppelt. In vergleichbarem Maße vergrößert sich auch die Erstreckung des Zugkeils. An den Ulmen treten in keinem der untersuchten Zustände Zugspannungen auf (Fig. 10).

In einer Parameterstudie wurde, von dem vorstehend erläuterten Fall ausgehend, zur Untersuchung des Einflusses der Anisotropie der Elastizitätsmodul E_2 variiert. Als ein Ergebnis dieser Untersuchung sind in Fig. 11 die Tangentialspannungen in der Betonauskleidung für den Betriebszustand in Abhängigkeit von E_2 dargestellt. Die Betrachtung beschränkt sich auf einen Schnitt in der Ulme und einen in der Firste. Man erkennt, daß eine Abnahme des E-Moduls E_2 zu einer Abnahme der Betondruckspannungen führt. Für Werte $E_2 < 2500$ MN/m^2 – dies entspricht einem Modulverhältnis $E_1/E_2 \geq 4$ – ergeben sich in der Ulme sogar Zugspannungen.

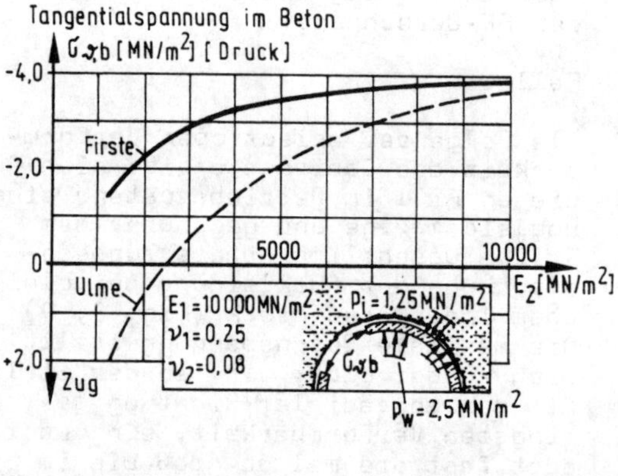

Fig. 11 Tangentialspannungen in der Betonauskleidung im Betriebszustand in Abhängigkeit vom Elastizitätsmodul E_2.

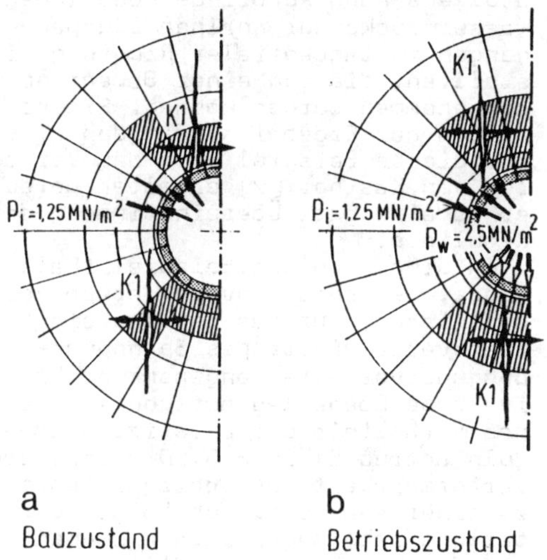

Fig. 12 Fall d: Zugbrüche auf K1 im Bereich von Firste und Sohle des Stollens.

Fall d

Für den Bau- und Betriebszustand ergaben sich im Fall c (Fig. 10) oberhalb der Firste und - in Fig. 10 nicht dargestellt - unterhalb der Sohle tangentiale Zugspannungen im Gebirge. Diese können in einem Gebirge mit parallel zur Stollenachse streichenden steil einfallenden Kluftscharen geringer Zugfestigkeit zu Zugbrüchen im First- und Sohlbereich führen. Erwartungsgemäß ergeben sich dann auch entsprechende Festigkeitsüberschreitungen für den Fall d, dem die gleichen Elastizitätskonstanten zugrundegelegt wurden wie dem vorhergehenden Fall (E_2 = 4000 MN/m²), bei dem aber zusätzlich zwei Trennflächenscharen mit abgeminderten Festigkeiten (S, K1, s. Fig. 6) berücksichtigt wurden. In Fig. 12 sind, getrennt für den Bau- und den Betriebszustand, die Bereiche dargestellt, für die die viskoplastische Berechnung Zugbrüche

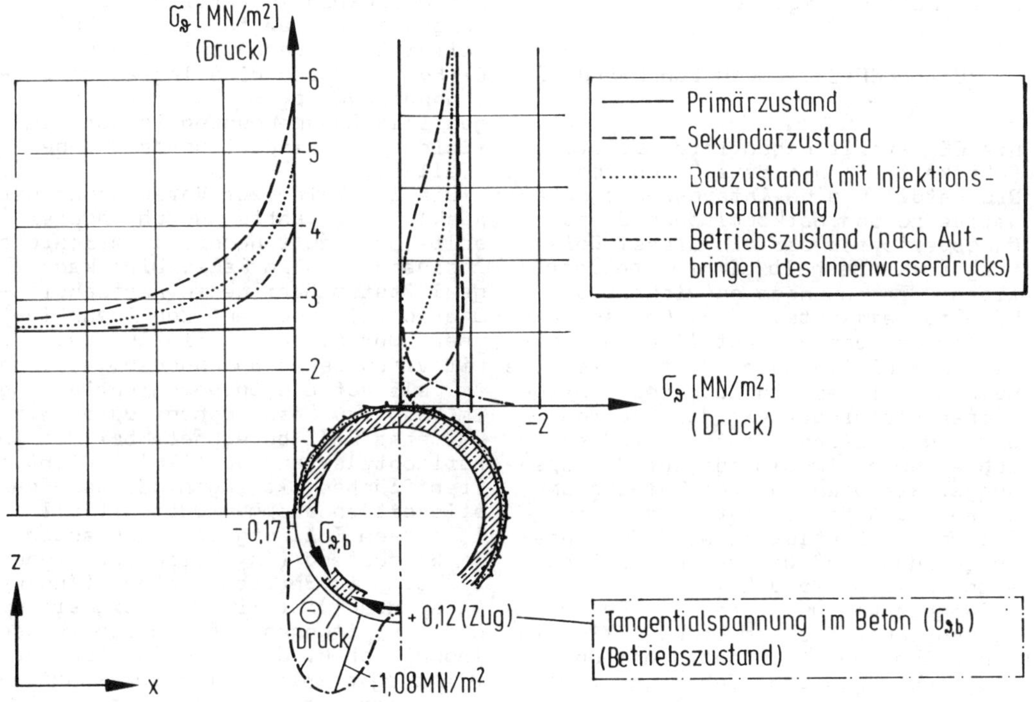

Fig. 13 Fall d: Tangentialspannungen in Gebirge und Auskleidung.

auf der parallel zur Stollenachse streichenden und senkrecht einfallenden Kluftschar K1 ergibt.

In Fig. 13 wurden die Gebirgs- und Betonspannungen in gleicher Weise wie für den Fall c (Fig. 10) dargestellt. Da im Sekundärzustand keine nennenswerten Zugspannungen an der Firste bzw. der Sohle auftreten, sind die entsprechenden Spannungsverläufe σ_ϑ in beiden Fällen annähernd gleich. Dies ist im Bau- und Betriebszustand jedoch nicht mehr der Fall. Infolge der hier auftretenden Zugbrüche (Fig. 12) treten Spannungsumlagerungen auf, die zu einem Abbau der Zugspannungen führen (Fig. 13).

Für die Tangentialspannungen in der Auskleidung ergibt sich daraus für den Betriebszustand eine deutliche Veränderung gegenüber dem Fall c (Fig. 10, 13). An der Sohle und entsprechend auch an der Firste treten Zugspannungen auf, während sich im entsprechenden elastischen Fall an diesen Stellen die größten Druckspannungen ergaben. In den übrigen Bereichen der Auskleidung sind noch Druckspannungen vorhanden, die jedoch geringer sind als im elastischen Fall c (Fig. 10, 13).

5. ZUSAMMENFASSUNG UND SCHLUSSFOLGERUNGEN

Die FEM stellt wegen ihrer Leistungsfähigkeit für die Berechnung von Druckstollen eine interessante Alternative zu den herkömmlichen Berechnungsverfahren dar. In diesem Beitrag wurde deshalb ein für felsstatische Berechnungen entwickeltes FEM-Programmsystem (FEST 03) auf die Berechnung von Druckstollen angewendet. Für einige ausgewählte Beispiele wurde dabei der Einfluß einer anisotropen Verformbarkeit des Gebirges und von örtlichen Festigkeitsüberschreitungen im Gebirge auf den Spannungszustand in der Auskleidung untersucht. Außerdem wurde in einigen Fällen der Einfluß einer Injektionsvorspannung auf Beton- und Gebirgsspannungen untersucht.

Ausgegangen wurde bei den Beispielrechnungen von einem Druckstollen in einem Gebirge mit elastischem und isotropem Spannungs-Dehnungsverhalten (Fall a). Der E-Modul des Gebirges wurde dabei so hoch gewählt, daß sich in der Betonauskleidung des Stollens nach Aufbringen des Innenwasserdrucks nur geringe Zugspannungen in tangentialer Richtung einstellten, die von einer Bewehrung aufgenommen werden können. Ein Vergleich der Ergebnisse mit denen, die für dieses Beispiel nach dem Verfahren von Kastner [2] erhalten werden, ergab eine gute Übereinstimmung der Resultate.

In einem zweiten Beispiel (Fall b) wurde, bei sonst unveränderten Verhältnissen, für das Gebirge ein transversal isotropes Spannungs-Dehnungsverhalten angenommen. Die isotrope Ebene lag horizontal und das Verhältnis der Elastizitätsmoduln betrug $E_1/E_2 = 5$. Die anisotrope Verformbarkeit des Gebirges führte zu einer sehr ungleichmäßigen Verteilung der Tangentialspannungen in der Betonauskleidung, die an den Ulmen nahezu das 3-fache des Wertes des Referenzfalls a erreichten.

In weiteren Berechnungen wurden die Elastizitätsmoduln E_1 und E_2 herabgesetzt und der Innenwasserdruck erhöht. Gleichzeitig wurde eine Injektionsvorspannung der Auskleidung berücksichtigt. In einer Parameterstudie, in der das Verhältnis der E-Moduln variiert wurde, zeigte sich, daß für das gewählte Beispiel für Verhältnisse von $E_1/E_2 < 4$ durch eine Injektionsvorspannung von $p_i = 1{,}25\ MN/m^2$ tangentiale Zugspannungen in der Auskleidung verhindert werden können (Fall c).

Die Injektion zur Vorspannung der Auskleidung führte jedoch andererseits auch zu tangential gerichteten Zugspannungen im Fels. Dies kann in geklüftetem Gebirge zu Festigkeitsüberschreitungen auf den Trennflächen führen. Um den Einfluß der hiermit verbundenen Spannungsumlagerungen im Fels auf die Spannungsverteilung im Beton zu untersuchen, wurde ein weiterer Fall berechnet, bei dem in horizontaler und vertikaler Richtung Trennflächen mit abgeminderter Festigkeit angenommen wurden (Fall d). In diesem Fall ergaben sich sowohl im Bauzustand (Injektionsvorspannung) als auch im Betriebszustand (Innenwasserdruck) örtliche Festigkeitsüberschreitungen auf den vertikalen Trennflächen, die dazu führten, daß die tangentialen Betondruckspannungen gegenüber den unter der Annahme elastischen Verhaltens erhaltenen Werten deutlich geringer waren.

An der Firste und Sohle des Stollens traten sogar Zugspannungen auf.

Aus den Ergebnissen der untersuchten Beispiele können folgende Schlußfolgerungen gezogen werden:

Eine Vernachlässigung der Anisotropie des elastischen Verhaltens des Gebirges kann zu einer Unterschätzung der Zugbeanspruchung einer Druckstollenauskleidung führen. Mit einer Injektionsvorspannung der Auskleidung können Zugspannungen in der Auskleidung zwar vermieden oder zumindest verringert werden, jedoch entstehen andererseits durch diese Maßnahme im Gebirge bereichsweise tangential gerichtete Zugspannungen. Für den Fall, daß das Gebirge diese Zugspannungen z.B. aufgrund von vorhandenen parallel zur Stollenachse streichenden Trennflächen mit geringer Zugfestigkeit nicht aufnehmen kann, treten im Fels Festigkeitsüberschreitungen auf, die zu Spannungsumlagerungen führen. Hierdurch kann es zu einer ungünstigen Beeinflussung der Spannungsverteilung im Beton kommen, indem die Druckspannungen abgebaut werden und örtlich sogar Zugspannungen auftreten können.

Eine Verallgemeinerung dieser Schlußfolgerungen ist über die Kennwerte und Randbedingungen der untersuchten Fälle hinaus nur begrenzt möglich. Die Beispiele zeigen jedoch eindrucksvoll, daß die Einflüsse, die sich aus der Anisotropie der Verformbarkeit des Gebirges sowie den Spannungsumlagerungen infolge örtlich auftretender Festigkeitsüberschreitungen auf die Spannungen im Fels und Druckstollenauskleidung ergeben, nicht vernachlässigt werden dürfen.

6. LITERATUR

[1] Barden, L., Stresses and displacements in a cross-anisotropic soil. Geotechnique Vol. XIII (1963): 198-210.

[2] Kastner, H. 1962, Statik des Tunnel- und Stollenbaus. Berlin, Göttingen, Heidelberg, Springer.

[3] Kawamoto, T. 1966, On the calculation of the orthotropic elastic properties from the states of deformation around a circular hole subjected to internal pressure in orthotropic elastic medium. Proc. 1st ISRM-Congress, Lisbon, Vol. I: 269-275.

[4] Kieser, A. 1960, Druckstollenbau. Wien, Springer.

[5] Lauffer, H., Seeber, G., Die Bemessung von Druckstollen und Druckstollenauskleidungen für Innendruck auf Grund von Felsdehnungsmessungen. Österreichische Ingenieur-Zeitschrift 5 (1962) Heft 2.

[6] Lauffer, H., Seeber, G. 1966, Die Messung der Felsnachgiebigkeit mit der TIWAG-Radialpresse und ihre Kontrolle durch Dehnungsmessungen an der Druckschachtpanzerung des Kaunertalkraftwerkes. Proc. 1st ISRM-Congress, Lisbon, Vol. II: 347-361.

[7] Lauffer, H., Vorspanninjektionen für Druckstollen. Der Bauingenieur (1968) Heft 7.

[8] Pierau, B. 1981, Tunnelbemessung unter Berücksichtigung der räumlichen Spannungs-Verformungszustände an der Ortsbrust. Veröffentlichungen des Institutes für Grundbau, Bodenmechanik, Felsmechanik und Verkehrswasserbau der RWTH Aachen, Heft 9.

[9] Seeber, G., Möglichkeiten und Grenzen im Druckstollenbau. Schweizer Ingenieur und Architekt (1981) Heft 29: 639-647.

[10] Semprich, S. 1980, Berechnung der Spannungen und Verformungen im Bereich der Ortsbrust von Tunnelbauwerken im Fels. Veröffentlichungen des Institutes für Grundbau, Bodenmechanik, Felsmechanik und Verkehrswasserbau der RWTH Aachen, Heft 8.

[11] Wittke, W., Carl, L., Semprich, S., Felsmessungen als Grundlage für den Entwurf einer Tunnelauskleidung. Straße Brücke Tunnel (1975) Heft 1.

[12] Wittke, W. Injektionsvorspannungen von Stollenauskleidungen. Heitkamp Mitteilungen 1 (1976).

[13] Wittke, W. 1984, Felsmechanik - Grundlagen für wirtschaftliches Bauen im Fels. Berlin, Heidelberg, New York, Tokyo, Springer.

[14] Zienkiewicz, O.C. 1977, The Finite Element Method, London Mc-Graw-Hill.

DER SPANNUNGSZUSTAND IN BETON- UND STAHLBETONAUSKLEIDUNGEN VON DRUCKSTOLLEN IN NICHTLINEAR DEFORMIERTEN GESTEINEN

Stress state of the concrete and reinforced concrete linings of pressure tunnels in rocks with non-linear deformability

État de contrainte dans les revêtements en béton plein et en béton armé des galeries en pression dans les roches à déformation non linéaire

S.A.YUFIN, O.K.POSTOLSKAYA & E.I.ZHOKHOV
Moscow Institute of Civil Engineering, Moscow, USSR

SUMMARY

Analysis for pressure tunnel lining considering its working together with adjoining rock mass can be devided into several different problems which are discussed in the paper. Physical geomechanical modelling, laboratory investigations on material properties and numerical analysis of pressure tunnel linings were performed. Finite element method is the basis of numerical analysis. Non-linear numerical models were used for rock and some types of concrete. The material is considered as a elastovisco-plastic hardening/softening medium. Operation experience of the completed tunnels will give the basis for a more wider use of as far experimental design criteria.

ZUSAMMENFASSUNG

Das Problem der Berechnung der Verkleidungen von Druckstollen unter den Bedingungen des Zusammenwirkens mit dem ihn umgebenden Gesteinsmassiv kann in verschiedene Fragenkomplexe eingeteilt werden. Die Autoren haben Forschungen an Modellen und im Labor bezüglich der Eigenschaften von Stoffen durchgeführt, wobei für Felsgesteine und einige Betonmarken mathematische Modelle auf der Grundlage der F.E.M. erstellt wurden. Das Material wird als festwerdender Körper mit zähplastischen Eigenschaften betrachtet. Insgesamt drücken die Ergebnisse den realen Zustand aus und ermöglichen damit praktische Schlußfolgerungen sowohl in technischer als auch ökonomischer Hinsicht.

RESUME

Le calcul du revêtement de galerie forcée considérant son action simultanée avec les massifs rocheux environnants peut être divisé en plusieurs problèmes différents, lesquels sont discutés dans cet exposé. Des recherches sur les modèles et au laboratoire relatives aux propriétés de la matière et la calcul numérique des revêtements des galeries forcées ont été éxécutés. La méthode des éléments finis est la base du calcul numérique. Des modèles numériques non linéaires ont été utilisés pour la roche et quelques types de béton. La matière a été considérée comme un milieu passant à l'état solide avec des propriétés viscoplastiques. Au total, les résultats expriment l'état réel, ce qui rend possible des conclusions pratiques non seulement du pont de vue technique mais aussi sous l'angle économique.

1 EINLEITUNG

Bei der Projektierung der Konstruktion der Auskleidung der Druckstollen ist natürlicherweise erwünscht, den grössten Teil der Belastung des Innendruckes des Wassers auf den Einfassungsmassiv des Berggesteines zu übertragen. Dieses Problem enthält eine Reihe verschiedener Fragen:
- die Bestimmung der Minimaltiefe der Lage des Druckstollens, bei der die Übertragung eines Teils der Belastung auf das Gestein möglich ist;
- die Beurteilung des Einflusses der realen Form des äusseren Umrisses der Auskleidung, bedingt durch den Aufbau des Massivs und resultierende Verausbrüche beim Stollenvortrieb auf die Beanspruchungen in der Auskleidung beim Zusammenwirken mit dem Gestein;
- die Auswahl der Konstruktion und des Stoffes der Auskleidung für die Schaffung des günstigeren Spannungzustandes, und nähmlich, die Benutzung der Polymer- und Fibrobetonen mit dem niedrigen Modul;
- die Berücksichtigung bei der Projektierung der Reihenfolge der Errichtung und der Inbetriebsetzung der Auskleidung, was besonders wichtig ist beim Vorhandensein der parallelen Wasserleitungsstrecken, die der Reihe nach in Betrieb gesetzt werden, auch die Verteilung der Arbeitsbedingungen der Konstruktion in der Zeit der Errichtung, des Betriebs, der Reparatur und Prophilaktik;
- der Einfluss der zusätzlichen Massnahmen für die Verbesserung der Eigenschaften des Einfassungsmassivs, und nähmlich der Zementierung, auf die Trägfahigkeiten des Gesteines.

Die genannten Fragen sind grundlegend, obwohl sie nicht vollkommen das Problem behandeln.

2 AUFGABENSTELLUNG

Die angenommenen Methoden der Bestimmung des Spannungszustandes der Befestigungskonstruktionen der Druck stollen kann man bedingungsweise in zwei Gruppen unterteilen:
- die rechnerische Methode, die die Beanspruchungen in der Auskleidung von den angegebenen Belastungskombination zeigen können;
- die Methoden, in denen das Zusammenwirken des Einfassungsmassivs und der Auskleidung berücksichtigt werden, dabei wird die Belastung auf die Konstrution im Verlauf der Berechnungen bestimmt.

Die erste Gruppe der Methoden gibt keinen realen Bild der Arbeitsweise der Konstruktion und wird nur wegen der Einfachkeit verwendet. Zur zweiten Gruppe gehört die Mathematik und Strukturmodelierung.

Die durchgeführten theoretischen und experimentalen Forschungen des Spannungszustandes der Auskleidungen der Druckstollen sind sehr umfangreich und die vorliegende Arbeit erhebt keinen Anspruch auf ihre ausführliche Analyse. Es werden hier nur die Forschungsergebnisse gegeben die gewissermassen Tendenz der vorliegender Arbeit festgestellt haben.

Als Ergebnis der Versuchsarbeit von Eristow (1967), war die effektive Berechnungsmethodik der Auskleidungen der Druckstollen im Anisotropgestein. Dabei wurde doch die Belastung der Auskleidung unter der Einwirkung des Bergmassivslastes und der anderen Belastungen nicht behandelt. Als Fortsetzung dieses Arbeit wurden von Tschurakow und Kalandarischwili (1970), die Ergebnisse der Modelluntersuchungen der Druckstollen mit Flachgründung veröffentlicht Diese Untersuchungen wurden auf den Flachmodellen aus Gips- und Kalkstoffen durchgeführt. Es wurde auch die Frage über die zulässige minimale Tiefgründung des Druckstollens behandelt, bei der die Übertragung eines Teils der Belastung vom Wasserdruck auf das Einfassungsmassiv möglich ist. Diese Frage soll doch, der Autorenmeinung nach, für jeden konkreten Fall einzeln gelost werden.

Auf den ähnlichen Modellen haben Andguladze und Yufin (1974) experimental gezeigt, dass die Verausbrüche beim Stollenvortrieb verschlechtern ihre statische Arbeit wegen der Veränderung der Aussenumrisse der Auskleidung, doch die Betonmenge dabei bedeutend grössen wird. Sowohl die Modellen, als auch die Berechnungen mit der F.E.-Methode zeigen die Konzentrationen der Spannungen, die die rechnerischen Spannungen 2.2 mal übertreffen. Aber die Annahme, dass in der Verkleidung keine Risse sind, wird nicht real.
Mit den sowjetischen Bauforschriften werden die Menge und die zulässige Rissaufdeckung in den Auskleidungen der hydrotechnischen Druckstollen

reglamentiert, und die entsprechende Berechnungen sollen mit Berücksichtigung der realen Umrissen der Auskleidungskonstruktion durchgefürt werden.

Es wurde vielmals der Einfluss der Reichenfolge beim Stollenvortrieb und bei der Errichtung der Auskleidung in einem oder zwei parallelen Tunnels auf den Spannungszustand der Konstruktion erforscht.

Ghaboussi und Ranken (1977) erforschen dieses Problem sehr ausführlich und sammelten Bibliographie. Sie Unterstrichen, dass diese Aufgabe dreidimensionalgelöst werden soll, aber sie haben die Bedingungen gezeigt, bei denen zweidimensionale Lösung gute Ergebnisse für die Praxis gibt. Sehr ausführlich wird der Einfluss der Grösse des Pfeiles und die Reihenfolge der Errichtung auf den Spannungszustand der Konstruktion beschrieben. Von Kovari (1977), wird eine Reihe mathematischer Modellen vorgeschlagen, die für die Berechnung der Tunnelkonstruktionen gebraucht werden. Patzold (1979) zeigt die Ergebnisse der Messungen in situ für die Auskleidung des schildvorgetriebener Tunnel.

Lux (1979) vergleicht die in der Auskleidung gemessenen Beanspruchungen für den Schildvortrieb mit den theoretischen Berechnungen mit Hilfe der F.E.-Methode, mit Berücksichtigung, in einigen Fällen, der physikalischen Nichtlinearität des Stoffes. Sehr ausfühliche Analyse der Berechnungsvoraussetzungen, begründet auf F.E.-Methode, gibt Wittke (1977). Dabei handelt es sich um die Notwendigkeit, bei der Projektierung der Konstruktionen die Vorspannung in Betracht zu ziehen, die bei der Zementierung mit dem hohen Druck entsteht.

3 DIE ERFORSCHUNG DES ZEMENTIERUNGSPROZESSES DER FELSGESTEINE MIT RISSEN, DIE DEN TUNNEL MIT BETONAUSKLEIDUNG EINFASSEN

Die Zementierung der Rissgesteine mit hohem Druck wird weitgehend vorwendet. Es wird gemeint, dass bei bestimmten Bedingungen der hohe Druck der Injektion zur Schaffung der Vorspannung nicht nur in der Tunnelauskleidung sondern auch im Tunneleinfassungsmassiv beitragen kann.

Der Prozess der Befestigung der Rissgesteine ist sehr kompliziert und hat zur Zeit kein mathematisches Adäquatmodell. Effekt der Vorspannung der Tunnelauskleidung wegen des Zementierungsdruckes wurde beim Bau vieler Tunnels verwendet, auch in der UdSSR beim Bau Inguri- und Tscharwakwasserkraftwerken.

Die Angaben zu diesem Problem wurden von Kujundzic u.a. (1970), von Pavlovic (1970) und von anderen Erforschern veröffentlicht. Aber diese Angaben sind nur uber den Vorspannungszustand der zusammengepressten Auskleidung und der Spannungszustand des Einfassungsmassivs wird dabei nicht betrachtet.

Für die quantitative Beurteilung des Spannungszustandes sowohl der Konstruktion der Betonauskleidung, als auch Felsgesteinmassivs bei der Zementierung beim hohen Druck wurden die Forschungen sowohl auf dem mathematischen als auch auf dem Strukturmodell durchgeführt.

Das Raummodell, bestimmt für solche Forschungen, stellt 20 mal verkleinertes Fragment der Tunnelstrecke dar. (Durchmesser - 10m, Länge - 16 m, die Betonauskleidungdicke - 0.6 m (ohne Bewehrung), der Einfassungsmassiv mit Rissen der mittleren Stärke) Für die Modellierung

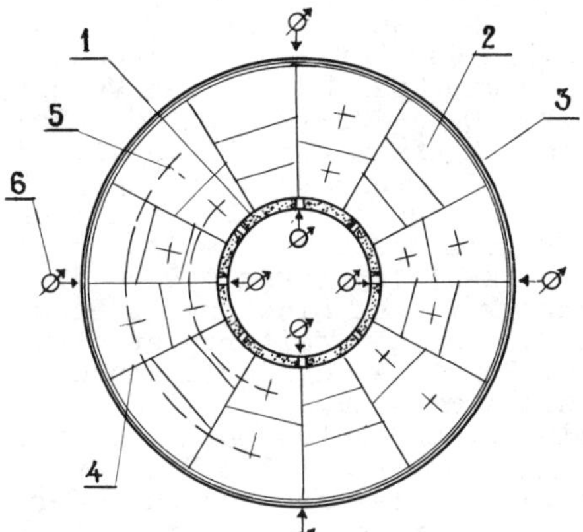

Bild 1 Schema des Modells
1 - Auskleidung; 2 - Gesteinmassivblocken; 3 - die metallische Zwinge;
4 - Risse zwischen den Blocken;
5 - die Stellen der Tensoresistoren;
6 - mechanische Deformometer

des die Auskleidung einfassenden Gesteinmassiv und für die Auskleidung selbst waren die zement-sandige Mörtel angewendet. Nach den Versuchsangaben hatten der Auskleidungstoff und der Felsgesteinmassiv folgende physikalisch-mechanische Kennziffer: für die Auskleidung - E=10130 **MPa**, ν=0.16, R_t =10.7 MPa, R_c =1.8 MPa; für den Felsmassiv - E=6000 MPa, ν=0.22, R_t =3.9 MPa, R_c=0.5 **MPa**.

Vorgenommen, dass der Stoff des Modelierungsgesteines und der Auskleidung dem Naturstoff ähnlich ist, und die bemessene Belastung (Injektionsdruck) der realen Beanspruchung auf das Bauwerk entspricht, sind zur Meinung gekommten, dass dieses Modell praktisch ein reales unterirdisches Bauwerk des Kleinen Ausmasses darstellt. Der Spannungszustand des Massivs wurde mit Hilfe der in den Gestein hingestellten Tensoresistoren bemessen, die vorher im Stabilometer geeicht wurden. Tensoresistoren waren in zwei mittleren Rangen des Modells auf zwei Bemessungskonturen untergebracht, die von der Auskleidung 0.2 und 0.6 ihres Durchmessers abstehen. Für die Injektion gebrauchte man Zementmörtel auf der Grundlage des Portlandzementes 400 mit dem 5% Gipszuschlag.

Der Injektionstoff unter dem Druck 1 MPa wurde ins Modell durch zwölf gleichmässig verteilte Bohrlöcher in die Modellauskleidung gepumpt. Das Einpressen dauerte ungefähr 4 Stunden bis zur Erstarrung des Mörtels. In der Zeit des Einpressens betrug die Spannung in den Massivblocken 0.6 - 0.9 MPa mit der Relaxation ungefähr von 40% in die ersten fünf Tagen. Die Spannungsstabilisation begann in 3 Monaten nach dem Beginn des Experiments. Zu dieser Zeit verringerte sich die Spannung in den Blocken des Massivs 1.5-2.0 mal. Im weiteren erfolgte keine Verringerung der Spannungen im Gesteinmassiv.

Ein vereinfachtes mathematisches Modell, gebaut mit F.E.M., wurde für die Vergleichenschätzung der Experimentergebnisse gebraucht. Es wurde Blockfelsmassiv mit regelmässiger Lage der Risse genommen. Die Gesteinmassivblocken hatte die Kriecheneigenschaften mit in-situ Angaben von Kubetsky. Die Druckverteilung in den Rissen zwischen den Blocken wurde nach den Experimentangaben angenommen. Die Messergebnisse haben die Annahme über die Entstehung des Vorspannungszustandes im Tunneleinfassungsgestein des Folge der Zementierung unter dem Druck und die bedeutende Steigerung der Tragfähigkeiten des Massivs bestätigt, was dünne Beton- und Stahlbetonauskleidungen für grosse Druckstollen zulässig macht.

4 PARALLELEN LINIEN DER DRUCKSTOLLEN MIT VORGEFERTIGTEN-MONOLITSTAHLBETONAUSKLEIDUNGEN

4.1 Angaben zum Bauwerk

Im Projekt des Selentschuk Wasserkraftwerkes im Nordkaukasus wird der Bau von zwei parallelen Strecken der Druckstollen vorgesehen. Der Innendurchmesser der Tunnels - 4.9 m die Länge - 2200 m. Die Tunneltrasse geht durch die dünn-schichtigen Tonaleurolithen. Die Schichtung ist sehr deutlich mit der praktisch waagerechen Fläche der Anlagerung zu sehen.

Im Zerstörungszustand sind die Gesteine durch folgende Kennwerte charakterisiert: $E_{\parallel}$=4400 MN/m^2, $E_{\perp}$= 2500 MN/m^2, $\nu_{\parallel}$=0.23, $\nu_{\perp}$=0.19, φ=36°, γ=2700 kg/m^3. Auf den Strecken, geschwächt durch Risse, $E_{\parallel}$=1540 MN/m^2 $E_{\perp}$=1070 MN/m^2, C=0.75 MN/m^2.

Die Gesteine haben die Kriecheneigenschaften mit dem rheologischen Parameter 0.77 und die Formbarkeit bei hohen Belastungen.

Der Tunnelvortrieb wird der Reihe nach von dem mechanisierten Schild verwirklicht, der vom Leningrader "Metrostroj" konstruirt wurde. Der Tunneldurchmesser in dem vortrieb hat 5.6 m; der Abstand zwischen den Achsen der parallelen Strecken - 20 m. Die Tiefe der Tunnellage ist etwa 50 m. Unmittelbar hinter dem Schild wird die vorgefertigte Stahlbetonblockauskleidung mit der Dicke von 0.15 m errichtet. Der Stoff dieser Blocken ist durch Modul E_{cb}=24500 MN/m^2 gekennzeichnet. Die vorgefertigten Auskleidungssektionen haben die Länge von 1 m und werden ins Gestein mit Hilfe der hydraulischen Bockwinde mit der Beanspruchung von 0.4 MN gedruckt. Zum Abschluss der Vortriebsarbeit wird der innere Stahlbetonring mit E_{cA}=22000 MN/m^2

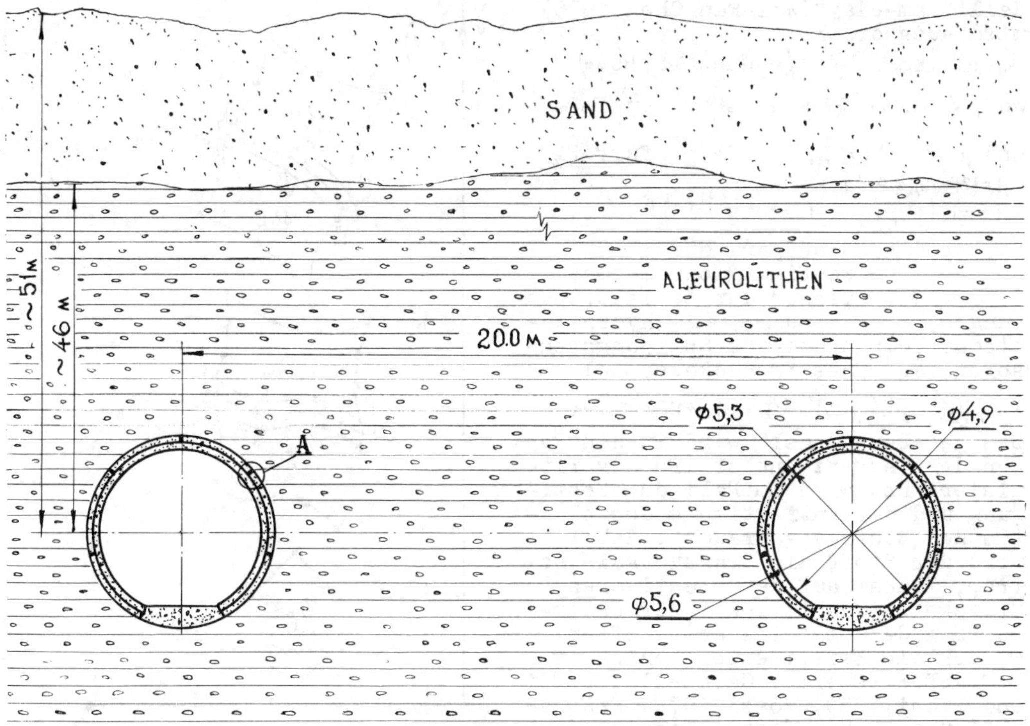

Bild 2 Schema der Lage der Druckstollen

errichtet. Der innere Tunnelwasserdruck während des Betriebs beträgt 0.74 MPa. Die Inbetriebsetzung der ersten Tunnelstrecke ist möglich bis zur vollenden der Vortriebsarbeiten der zweiten Strecke. Das Schema der Tunnellage ist auf dem Bild 2 gegeben.

4.2 Mathematisches Modell

Mathematisches Modell soll die Lösung der Kontaktaufgabe mit zeitverändlichen Grenzen des betreffenden Gebiets sichern. Die Grenzänderung ist durch Prozess des Vortriebs und der Errichtung der Auskleidungskonstruktion bedingt.

Wie viele Autoren festgestellt haben, ist die Modllierung der Kontakten zwischen den Schichten im Berggesteinmassiv nicht rationell und gibt keine verbesserten Ergebnisse, aber die Berücksichtigung der Kontaktbedingingen Auskleidung-Gestein, Monolitbeton - vorgefertigter Beton und die Fuge zwischen den Blocken ist für das vorliegende Problem vollkommen unbedingt.

Im Zusammenhang damit wird der Berggesteinmassiv hier als elastisch-zähplastisches Medium betrachtet, mit den Eigenschaften der Festigung und Entfestigung. Die Gesteinfestigung wird nur am Beginn des Vortriebs bis zur Inbetriebsetzung der vorgefertigten Auskleidung zulässig. Die Festigung wird im Prozess der Auskleidungdeformation bei der Zigabe des inneren Druckes in Tunnel zulässig. Die Aufgabe wird mit F.E.-Methode gelöst.

Die volle Deformation der Elementen wird durch Formel ausgerechnet:

$$\varepsilon_{ij} = \varepsilon^{(e)} + \varepsilon_{ij}^{(p)} + \varepsilon_{ij}^{(c)} + \varepsilon_{ij}^{(d)}\delta_{ij}$$

wo: $\varepsilon^{(e)}$ - zeitig-unabhängige elastische Komponente;
$\varepsilon_{ij}^{(p)}$ - plastische Komponente;
$\varepsilon_{ij}^{(d)}\delta_{ij}$ - räumliche Komponente;
$\varepsilon_{ij}^{(c)}$ - zähige Komponente;
δ_{ij} - das Kroneckersymbol

Das elastisch-plastische Inkrementverhältnis der Spannungen und Deformationen für ein modifiziertes Modell "Cam-clay"(Wai-Fan Chen,1975) wird ausgedrücht:

$$\dot{\sigma}_{ij}=\beta\varepsilon_{ij}-L\dot{\varepsilon}_{mm}\delta_{ij}-\frac{1}{\psi}\left(H\delta_{ij}+\frac{\beta}{M^2}S_{ij}\right)\left(\frac{\beta}{M^2}S_{k\ell}\dot{\varepsilon}_{k\ell}+H\dot{\varepsilon}_{mm}\right)$$

wo $\psi=(2P-P_o)H+\frac{2\beta j_2}{M^4}+P(2P-P_o)R$ fur $P\leq P_o/_2$

und $\psi=(2P-P_o)H+\frac{2\beta\vartheta_2}{M^4}$ fur $P>P_o/_2$

$$H=(2P-P_o)\left(\frac{1}{3}\beta-L\right)$$

$$R=-P_o\left(\frac{1+\ell\vartheta}{\lambda-\eta}\right) \qquad L=P\frac{(1+\ell\vartheta)}{\eta}+\frac{1}{3}\beta$$

η,λ,M - Stoffparameter;

P_o - Festigungsparameter;

$S_{ij}=\sigma_{ij}-P\delta_{ij}$ - Tensor der Deviatorspannungen, $P=(\sigma_x+\sigma_y+\sigma_z)$ - hydrostatische Komponente der Spannungstensoren, δ_{ij} - das Kroneckersymbol

$$J_2=\frac{1}{6}\left[(\sigma_x-\sigma_y)^2+(\sigma_y-\sigma_z)^2+(\sigma_z-\sigma_x)^2\right]+\tau_{xy}^2+\tau_{yz}^2+\tau_{zx}$$

Das gegebene Modell wird in den Rahmen der Tangenzionalsteife algoritmisiert und wird im Fall der Festigung und der Entfestigung des plastischen Stoffes gebraucht; dabei wird der Stoff als transversal-isotrop, linear auf der elastischen Strecke betrachtet. Bei der Untersuchung der Gesteineigenschaften wurden die Experimentergebnisse von I.S.M.E.S.(Oberti, Carabelli, Goffi und Rossi,1979, Rossi,1978, Manfredini u.a.,1974, Goffi, Rossi und Borsetto,1978) in Betracht gezogen. Da die Methodik der unmittelbaren Bemessung der einzelnen Parameter des Stoffes fehlte, wurden die Berechnungen für Experimentbedingungen durchgeführt.

In der vorliegenden Arbeit wird Beton für die Auskleidung als linear elastisches Isotropmedium angenommen. Aber die Experimentergebnisse weisen auf die Möglichkeit hin, den guten Spannungszustand der Auskleidung während der Betriebszeit dank der Anwendung der Polymerbeton mit niedrigen Modull zu bekommen. Dabei wird auch die Wasserundurchschlässigkeit der Konstruktion gesteigert. Das Modell solches Stoffes wird ausgearbeitet und wird zukünfig ausgenutzt.

Das Berechnungsmodell wird durch isoparametrische viereckige Elemente bis zur dritten Ordnung in der Grenzen der Auskleidung und der liegende Zone diskretiziert. Für die Modellierung der Kontakte zwischen den Auskleidungselementen und dem Gestein ist die Familie der isoparametrischen Kontaktelementen der ersten, zweiten und dritten Ordnung Formuliert (Bild 3).

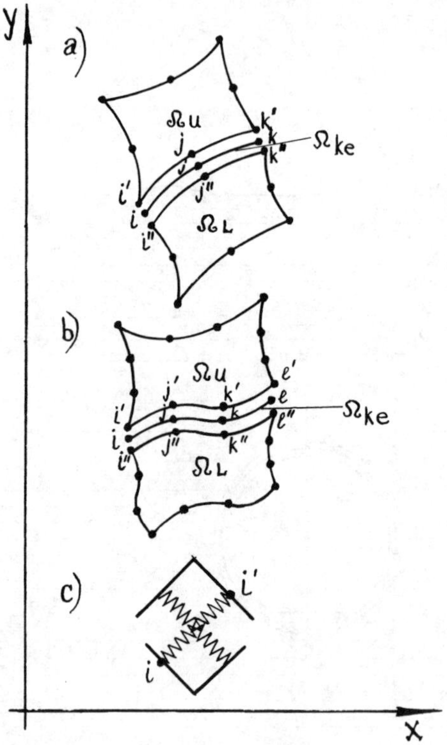

Bild 3 Kontaktelemente
a) - der zweiten Ordnung; b) - der dritten Ordnung; c) - "Link"-Element

Für Erhalten der Hauptabhängigkeiten für diese Elemente wurde der Relativverschiebungsprinzip realisiert, der für die Elemente dieses Types von Ghaboussi, Wilson und Isenberg (1973) formuliert wurde.

Die geschweissten Versatzteile der vorgefertigten Blocken werden von "Link"-Elemente modeliert, die den Elementen von De Ngo (1975) ähnlich sind und für die der Relativverschiebungsprinzip gebraucht wurde. Fragment der Berechnungsschema ist auf dem Bild 4 gegeben.

Der mechanisierte Schildvortrieb gibt verhältnismässig glatte Oberfläche des Vortriebsumrisses, dabei auch glatte Kontaktoberfläche zwischen dem Monolit- und Vorgefertigtem Beton. Ausserdem, wie eine der Varianten, wird eine nachgiebige Fuge zwischen dem Monolit- und Vorgefertigtem Beton mit dem bitumiosen Bestreichen analysiert. Dieser Umstand gab die Möglichkeit, für Kon-

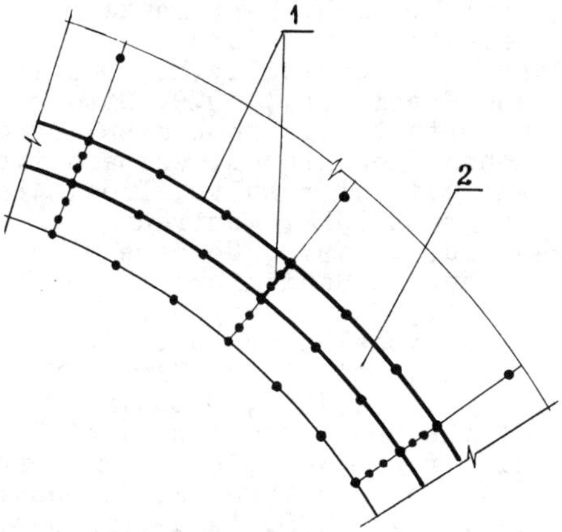

Bild 4 Fragment des Berechnungsschemas 1 - Kontaktelemente; 2 - zweidimensionale Elemente der dritten Ordnung

taktelemente die Verhältnisse des plastisch-elastischen Stoffes in Matrixform anzuwenden, die von Kratochvil (1976) eingeführt wurden. Das für vorliegende Arbeit genommene Berechnungsprogramm wird sehr ausführlich von Yufin und Berdzenischvili (1980), von Yufin u.a.(1982) betrachtet.

In Anfangsstadium der vorliegenden Arbeit gebrauchte man die Berechnungen für den einzelnen Tunnel mit dem mehrschichtigen Ring und dabei wurde auch die modifizierte Methode von Bodrow-Gorelik (Szechy,1966) angewendet. Die Bemessungsergebnisse bestätigen die Anwendbarkeit der gewählten Konstruktion und entsprechen den Standartergebnissen, die bei der Projektierung gebraucht werden, doch sie unterscheiden sich prizipiell von den mit F.E.M. Ergebnissen. Gewiss, hier kann man den komplizierten Spannungszustand des Massivs und der Konstruktion und ihr Zusammenwirken nicht berucksichtigen. Der Platzmangel in dieser Publikation lässt keine Illustrationen über die Forschungergebnisse geben.

5 SCHLUSSFOLGERUNGEN

Es ist hervorzuheben, dass die Parameter des Mediums auf den Spannungszustand der Auskleidung einen Einfluss üben, und dieser Einfluss ist bedeutend stärker in der Betriebszeit. Die gewählte Grösse des Pfeiles zwischen zwei Tunnels ist genug gross und der Einfluss des Vortriebs des mittleren Tunnels ist unbedeutend. Die parallele Vortriebsarbeit beim Vorhandensein des Druckes im Nachbartunnel ist nicht wünschenswert, oder es darf doch keinen Vortrieb ohne Auskleidung sein. Das Pressen der vorgefertigten Auskleidung ist sofort nach der Montage durchzuführen, dabei ist zu berücksichtigen die Ungleichkeit der Kraftferteilung in den Blocken wegen der Reibung zwischen dem Gestein und der Auskleidung. Das eingefuhrte mathematische Modell gibt die Möglichkeit, eine Vorstellung über das Zusammenwirken der Konstruktion und des Gesteines zu bekommen. Sie sichert auch die Angaben für die Projektierung von hoher Qualität und Inbetriebnahme der ökonomischen Konstruktion, die den grössten Teil der Beanspruchungen auf das Gestein überträgt. Leider, der notwendige Umfang und Nomenklatur der Experimentangaben für solche Berechnungen sind bedeutend grösser als gewöhnlicher Umfang der Forschungsarbeiten für die Mechanik der Felsgesteine und sind nicht immer zulässig.

DANKBARKEIT

Die Autoren sind Dr.-Ing. J.Kratochvil aus der technischen Hochschule der Stadt Brno, Tschechoslowakei, sehr dankbar für die Reihe wertvoller Bemerkungen und die Teilnahme an der Ausarbeitung der Familie der isoparametrischen Kontaktelementen.

LITERATUR

Andgouladze,G.P. und Yufin, S.A., 1974, Der Einfluss des faktischen Umrisses der Druckstollenauskleidungen auf ihre statische Arbeit, (im Russisch), Wasserbau*, 10

Borsetto,M., Ribacchi,R. and Rossi, P.P., 1981. Long-term cyclic plate loading tests in weak rocks, Int. Symp. Weak Rock, Tokyo, 1:137-142

Eristow,W.S.,1967, Fersuchforschungen der Druckstollenauskleidungen in der Anisotropgesteinen, Wasserbau*, 12

Ghaboussi,J. and Ranken, R.E., 1977, Interaction between two parallel tunnels, Int.J.Num.Anal.Meth. Geomech. 1: 75-103

Ghaboussi,J., Wilson,E.L. and Isenberg,J., 1973, Finite element for rock joints and interfaces, ASCE, J.S.M.& F.D., SM10: 833-848

Goffi,L., Rossi,P.P. and Borsetto, M., 1978, Proposte ed interpretazioni di tecniche sperimentali per la misura dei parametri di deformabilita di ammassi rocciosi ortotropi, Bergamo, ISMES Publications, 113

Iwlew,D.D., und Bykowtzew,G.I.,1971, Die Theorie des festwerdenden plastischen Korpers (im Russisch), Moskau, Wissenschaft

Kovari,K., 1977, The elasto-plastic analysis in the design practice of underground openings, Ch. 12 in Finite Elements in Geomechanics (G.GUDEHUS ed.), Chichester, John Wiley & Sons

Kratochvil,J., 1976, Solution of contact problems by finite element method, Staveb.Čas.,24,č.5, Bratislava, VEDA

Kubetsky,V.L. and Kozionov,V.A., 1981, Investigating rheological properties of fissured semirocks, Int.Symp.Weak Rock, Tokyo, 1

Kujundzic,B., Iovanovic,L. and Radoslavljevic,Z., 1970, Proc. 2nd Congress ISRM, 2, 4, Beograd

Lux,H.,1979, Zum Tragverhalten Schildvorgetriebener Tunnel-Messungen in-situ und theoretische Ansätze. Tunnelsymposium Math. und Phys. Modelle von unterirdischen Bauten, Spindleruv Mlyn, Tschechoslowakei

Manfredini,G., Martinetti,S., Rossi,P.P., Sampaolo,A., 1974, Observations on the procedures and on the interpolation of the plate bearing test, Proc. 3rd Congress ISRM, Denver, Colorado

Ngo,De, 1975, A network-topological approach to the finite element analysis of progressive crack growth in concrete members, Report UL SESM 75-6, Berkeley, University of California

Oberti,G., Carabelly,E., Goffi,L., and Rossi,P.P., 1979, Study of an orthotropic rock mass: experimental techniques, comparative analysis of results, Proc. 4th Congress ISRM, Montreux

Pätzold,J., 1979, Gemessene Beanspruchungen Schildforgetriebener Tunnel, Tunnelsymposium Math. und Phys. Modelle von unterirdischen Bauten, Spindleruv Mlyn, CSSR

Pavlovic,M., 1970, Grouting works at the headwater tunnel of hydroelectric power plant Rama, Proc. 2nd Congress ISRM, 2, 4, Beograd

Rossi,P.P., 1978, La determinazione delle caratteristiche di deformabilita degli ammassi rocciosi, Bergamo, ISMES Publications, 111

Széchy,K., 1966, The art of tunnelling, Budapest, Akademiai Kiado

Tschurakow,A.I. und Kalandarischvili,A.G., 1970, Modelluntersuchungen des Tunnelvortriebs im Anisotropgestein bei nicht tiefen Lagerung, Wasserbau*, 8

Tschurakow,A.I., Zhokhov,E.I., 1979, Model analysis of the pre-stress effect in rock mass around tunnel, Gidrotekhnicheskoe Stroitel'stvo*, 3

Wai-Fan Chen, 1975, Limit analysis and soil plasticity, Developments in Geotechnical Engineering, 7, N.Y., Elsevier scientific publishing Company

Wittke,W., 1977, New design concept for underground openings in rock, Ch. 13 in Finite Elements in Geomechanics (G.Gudehus ed.), Chichester, John Wiley & Sons

Yufin,S.A. and Berdzenishvili,T.L., 1980, A multipurpose computer code for the solution of some problems of geophysics, Bulletin of the Academy of Sciences of the Georgian SSR, Tbilisi, 97, 3

Yufin,S.A., Titkov,V.I., Shvachko, I.R. and Antipov,A.A., 1982, Stability prediction and evaluation for the system of large-span caverns, ISRM Symposium, Aachen

* 4 *

LIMITATION OF THE APPLICABILITY OF TUNNEL BORING MACHINES AS SEEN FROM THE ROCK MECHANICAL POINT OF VIEW

Einsatzgrenzen von Tunnelvortriebsmaschinen aus felsmechanischer Sicht

Limites d'emploi de foreuses pour le creusement de tunnels, du point de vue de la mécanique des roches

PODIUMSDISKUSSION ZUM THEMA 'DIE BEURTEILUNG DER EINSATZGRENZEN VON TUNNELVORTRIEBSMASCHINEN AUS FELSMECHANISCHER SICHT'

Panel discussion on 'The limitation of the applicability of tunnel boring machines as seen from the rock mechanical point of view'

Colloque sur le thème 'Limites d'emploi de foreuses pour le creusement de tunnels, du point de vue de la méchanique des roches'

EINLEITUNG

In zunehmendem Maße kommen im Tunnel- und Stollenbau, aber auch bei Rohrpressverfahren, Vortriebsmaschinen zum Einsatz. Im Vergleich zum konventionellen Vortrieb im Fels, bei welchem der Ausbruch mittels Sprengungen erfolgt, hat der Einsatz von Vortriebsmaschinen in der Regel den Vorteil, daß die über das geplante Profil hinausreichenden Mehrausbrüche gering sind und daß die mittragende Wirkung des Gebirges besser erhalten bleibt. Aber auch im Hinblick auf mögliche Kostenersparnisse stellt der maschinelle Vortrieb häufig eine günstige Alternative dar. Dies ist einerseits in der i.a. größeren Vortriebsgeschwindigkeit und damit möglicherweise verkürzten Bauzeit und andererseits in dem relativ geringen Personalaufwand begründet.

Diesen Vorteilen stehen aber auch verschiedene Probleme und Risiken gegenüber, die während des Symposiums in den Sitzungen zum Thema "Einsatzgrenzen von Tunnelvortriebsmaschinen aus felsmechanischer Sicht" erläutert wurden. In diesem Zusammenhang fand unter der Leitung von Herrn Dr. W. Krabbe, Philipp Holzmann AG, Frankfurt (Bundesrepublik Deutschland), zu diesem Thema eine Podiumsdiskussion statt. Eingeladen wurden zu dieser Veranstaltung Vertreter der Bauherrnschaft, der Bauunternehmungen, der Maschinenhersteller und der Forschung, wobei folgende Herren an der Diskussionsrunde teilnahmen:

S. Babendererde
Hochtief AG, Essen (Bundesrepublik Deutschland)

Prof. W. Beckmann
Westfalia Lünen, Lünen (Bundesrepublik Deutschland)

Prof. E.T. Brown
Imperial College of Science and Technology, Dept. of Mineral Resources Engg., London (England)

P. Hambach
Bauunternehmung Murer AG, Erstfeld (Schweiz)

G. Innerhofer
Vorarlberger Illwerke AG, Schruns (Österreich)

R.J. Robbins
The Robbins Company, Kent (USA)

Prof. W. Wittke
Institut für Grundbau, Bodenmechanik, Felsmechanik und Verkehrswasserbau, RWTH Aachen (Bundesrepublik Deutschland)

Im folgenden soll der Inhalt der im Rahmen dieser Podiumsdiskussion vorgetragenen Berichte und Diskussionsbeiträge kurz zusammengefaßt werden.

Das erste Diskussionsthema stellte die Voraussage der Lösbarkeit des Felses bzw. der Vortriebsleistung dar. Nach einigen einführenden grundsätzlichen Erläuterungen wurden anhand von Erfahrungsberichten die Möglichkeiten aber auch die Grenzen solcher Voraussagen aufgezeigt.

Teilnehmer an der Podiumsdiskussion
Participants in the panel discussion
participants au colloque
(v.l./from the left/de gauche): G. Innerhofer, Prof. W. Beckmann, R.J. Robb
Dr. W. Krabbe, Prof. W. Wittke, P. Hambach, S. Babendererde, Prof. E.T. Bro
(nicht im Bild/not pictured/ne pas sur l'image).

Probleme, die im Zusammenhang mit dem Einsatz von Tunnelvortriebsmaschinen

a) in druckhaftem Gebirge
b) bei der Durchörterung von Störungszonen und bei großem Bergwasseranfall

auftreten können, wurden wegen ihrer besonderen Bedeutung bzw. Komplexität anschließend gesondert behandelt. Insbesondere aus den Berichten dieses zweiten Abschnitts der Diskussion wurde deutlich, daß im Hinblick auf eine Verbesserung der Wirtschaftlichkeit des mechanischen Vortriebs gezielte Weiterentwicklungen nötig sind.

Hierzu wurde im dritten Diskussionsabschnitt auf einige richtungsweisende Entwicklungen in der Vortriebstechnik hingewiesen.

Schließlich wurde im vierten Abschnitt die Podiumsdiskussion durch einige Ausführungen zum Thema der Risikoverteilung beim Einsatz von Tunnelvortriebsmaschinen abgeschlossen.

GRENZEN DER VORAUSSAGE VON LÖSBARKEIT UND VORTRIEBSLEISTUNG

Bei der Beurteilung der Lösbarkeit eines Gebirges durch eine bestimmte Maschine muß, wie von Brown ausgeführt wurde, eine Reihe von Einflüssen und Wechselwirkungen berücksichtigt werden. So haben i.a. neben den Maschinenkennwerten verschiedene Gebirgseigenschaften, wie z.B. die Festigkeit des Gesteins, oder die Geometrie des Trennflächengefüges wesentlichen Einfluß auf die Lösbarkeit des Felses. Zwar liegen, wie z.B. von Beckmann berichtet wurde, bei den Maschinenherstellern und Anwendern Erfahrungswerte vor, doch lassen diese Werte im Einzelfall nur bedingt Rückschlüsse auf die zu erwartende Lösbarkeit zu. Dies gilt in verstärktem Maße für die Voraussage der Vortriebsleistung, wie von Robbins anschaulich anhand einiger Diagramme gezeigt wurde.

So wird aus diesen empirisch gewonnenen Zusammenhängen deutlich, daß die Abhängigkeit der Vortriebsleistung von einzelnen Kennwerten, wie z.B. der einaxialen Druckfestigkeit des Gesteins, i.a. sehr kompliziert ist und nicht isoliert von anderen Parametern betrachtet werden kann. Um trotz dieser Schwierigkeiten eine Voraussage zu ermöglichen, sind hierzu in der Vergangenheit verschiedene Laborversuche und Klassifizierungssysteme entwickelt worden. Besonders hervorgehoben wurde von Brown ein an der Universität von Newcastle upon Thyne entwickelter Schneidtest. Bei diesem Laborversuch wird aus der vom Schneidgerät geleisteten Arbeit auf die Lösbarkeit des Felses in der Natur geschlossen. In der Praxis hat sich jedoch noch keines der neu entwickelten Verfahren durchsetzen können und es wird eine Aufgabe der ISRM-Commission on Boreability, Cuttability and Drillability sein, entsprechende Empfehlungen zu erarbeiten.

Von Wittke wurde in einem Erfahrungsbericht anschaulich auf eine weitere Schwierigkeit bei der Abschätzung der Vortriebsleistung hingewiesen. In dem geschilderten Fall, einem ca. 2,8 km langen Freispiegelstollen, waren Sandsteinbänke, die mit der zum Einsatz gekommenen Teilschnittmaschine nicht gelöst werden konnten, nicht erkundet worden, obwohl der Abstand der Erkundungsbohrungen mit ca. 100 m verhältnismäßig gering war. Infolgedessen mußten die Bänke auf eine Länge von ca. 235 m händisch gelöst werden, was zu hohen zusätzlichen Kosten führte.

In der an diesen Erfahrungsbericht anschließenden Diskussion wurde von Babendererde die Meinung vertreten, daß auch in Fällen wie dem von Wittke beschriebenen, bei dem der überwiegende Teil des Stollenvortriebs für die Maschine keine Schwierigkeiten dargestellt hatte und nur kleine Teilstücke besondere Maßnahmen erforderten, der Maschineneinsatz noch eine wirtschaftliche Lösung darstellen kann.

GRENZEN FÜR DEN EINSATZ VON TUNNELVORTRIEBSMASCHINEN

Druckhaftes Gebirge

Bei einem Tunnelvortrieb in druckhaftem Gebirge treten in der Regel um den Hohlraum herum Festigkeitsüberschreitungen auf. Diese führen, wie von Wittke erläutert wurde, zu plastischen, zeitabhängigen Verformungen, die Dezimetergröße erreichen können. Wird in einem solchen Fall die Hohlraumwandung unmittelbar nach dem Ausbruch des Felses gesichert, sind für eine Stabilisierung des Tunnels sehr große Ausbauwiderstände erforderlich, die häufig weder vom Schild einer Vortriebsmaschine, noch von den Sicherungselementen (z.B. Ausbaubögen und bewehrter Spritzbeton) aufgebracht werden können. Bei solchen Verhältnissen ist die Wahl des richtigen Zeitpunktes für den Einbau der Sicherung von entscheidender Bedeutung für die Standsicherheit des Tunnels. Auch wenn inzwischen nachgiebige Schildsysteme, wie z.B. der flexible Messerschild, sowie auch sehr steife und kurze Schilde entwickelt wurden, sind auch beim heutigen Stand der Technik die Einsatzmöglichkeiten von Tunnelvortriebsmaschinen in druckhaftem Gebirge noch ziemlich begrenzt. Anschaulich wurde dieser Sachverhalt von Babendererde an einem Ausführungsbeispiel, einer Tunnelauffahrung in druckhaftem Tonschiefer, erläutert.

Störungszonen und Bergwasseranfall

Auch beim Durchfahren von Störungszonen größerer Erstreckung können beim Einsatz von Vortriebsmaschinen Probleme auftreten. Solche Zonen erlauben häufig nur einen verringerten Bohrandruck, da die Maschine nur eingeschränkt verspannbar ist. Die sich hierdurch ergebenden Schwierigkeiten treten insbesondere im Übergang von der Störungszone zu wieder festerem Gebirge auf, wenn die Verspannung noch in der Störungszone erfolgen muß, während sich der Bohrkopf bereits wieder in härterem Gestein befindet.

Hambach weist darauf hin, daß weitere Behinderungen auch auftreten können, wenn durch grobstückiges Lockergestein der Störungszone der Bohrkopf eingeklemmt wird. In solchen Fällen muß das eingeklemmte Lockergestein von Hand zerlegt und abtransportiert werden. In ungünstigen Fällen können durch das herabfallende Gestein im Bereich der Störungszone auch Beschädigungen der Maschine auftreten.

Wenn die angetroffenen Störungszonen Wasser führen, kann feinkörniges Bodenmaterial aus der Störungszone erodiert werden, was unter Umständen zu einem Verschlammen der Maschine führt. Hierdurch kann die Funktionsfähigkeit aufwendiger Tunnelvortriebsmaschinen, wie z.B. eines flexiblen Messerschilds, erheblich beeinträchtigt werden. Robbins empfiehlt für den Fall, daß mit Wasserzutritt zu rechnen ist, ähnlich wie bei einem Tunnelvortrieb in Lockergestein eine Schildmaschine einfacher Bauart einzusetzen, das einsickernde Bergwasser zu fassen und gegebenenfalls mit einer Schlammpumpe abzufördern.

TECHNISCHE WEITERENTWICKLUNGEN ZUR VERBESSERUNG DER WIRTSCHAFTLICHKEIT DES MECHANISCHEN VORTRIEBS

Da der Einsatz von Tunnelbohrmaschinen in druckhaftem Gebirge auch heute noch mit vielen Schwierigkeiten verbunden ist, ist eine Weiterentwicklung der Vortriebstechnik insbesondere für dieses Einsatzgebiet von großem Interesse. Babendererde wies in diesem Zusammenhang auf die Entwicklung des flexiblen Messerschilds und die Entwicklung von elastischen Ausbausystemen, z.B. mittels rückverankerter Tübbinge und verformbarer Fugenkonstruktionen hin. Darüber hinaus wurde angeregt, die Anwendungsmöglichkeiten für Teilschnittmaschinen auch im Tunnelvortrieb mit suspensionsgestützter Ortsbrust zu erweitern. Weiterverfolgt werden sollte nach Meinung der Diskussionsteilnehmer auch die bereits teilweise gelöste Aufgabe nicht kreisförmige Tunnelquerschnitte mit der Vollschnittechnik auffahren zu können.

RISIKOVERTEILUNG BEIM EINSATZ VON TUNNELVORTRIEBSMASCHINEN

Erkundungen, die der Tunnelausschreibung und der Baumaßnahme vorausgehen, erlauben in aller Regel noch keine zuverlässige Aussage über die beim Ausbruch des Tunnels angetroffenen Gebirgsverhältnisse. Selbst durch die vorgezogene Auffahrung eines Richt- oder Probestollens ist das Risiko, später beim Tunnelausbruch unerwartet ungünstige Gebirgsverhältnisse anzutreffen, nicht ausgeschlossen. Andererseits erfolgt die Entscheidung über den Einsatz und die Wahl einer bestimmten Vortriebsmaschine im wesentlichen auf der Grundlage der Erkundungsergebnisse. Deshalb wird auch in Zukunft der Einsatz von Tunnelvortriebsmaschinen mit Risiken verbunden sein. Die damit verbundene Frage der Risikoverteilung zwischen Bauherrn und Unternehmer, die Gegenstand des abschließenden Teils der Podiumsdiskussion war, behält daher wohl auch zukünftig ihre Aktualität.

Innerhofer führte zu diesem Thema aus, daß dem Unternehmer auf der Grundlage sorgfältiger Erkundungen vertraglich eine größtmögliche Freiheit hinsichtlich des Maschinen- und Personaleinsatzes gegeben werden sollte, wobei das damit verbundene Risiko eines Fehleinsatzes auch von ihm zu vertreten sei. Mehrkosten, die durch einen erhöhten Aufwand bei Antreffen von nicht vorhersehbaren geologischen und felsmechanischen Verhältnissen entstehen, sollten jedoch zu Lasten des Bauherrn gehen.

In diesem Zusammenhang berichtete Innerhofer von den guten Erfahrungen die seine Gesellschaft mit einem besonderen Vergütungssystem gemacht hat. Hierbei wird die Klassifizierung des Gebirges an dem tatsächlich erforderlichen Ausbau- und Sicherungsaufwand orientiert und nicht an der Standzeit des Gebirges oder ähnlicher konventioneller Kriterien. Erschwernisse, wie z.B. ein erhöhter Wasseranfall oder hoher Quarzgehalt des Gesteins, werden besonders vergütet. Diese Vorgehensweise, bei der der Vortriebspreis entscheidend vom Sicherungsaufwand beeinflußt wird, setzt jedoch in besonderem Maße ein Vertrauensverhältnis zwischen Bauherrn und Unternehmer sowie kontinuierliche Gesprächsbereitschaft voraus.

ERFAHRUNGEN BEIM DURCHÖRTERN GEOLOGISCHER STÖRUNGSZONEN MIT TUNNELBOHRMASCHINEN

Experiences with tunnel boring machines driving through geological fault zones

Enseignements acquis dans des creusements par tunneliers à travers des formations géologiques perturbées

J.HENNEKE & H.KÜBLER

Mannesmann Demag Bergwerktechnik, Duisburg, Bundesrepublik Deutschland

SYNOPSIS:

The technical potential of employing tunnelling machines in hard rock is determined by the extent and frequency of geological disturbances. For driving at great depths, in principle only tunnelling machines of open design are suitable rather than shield-driving types. Only those of open design can accommodate heavier rock convergences, allow for early completion of the walling and facilitate the effective employment of advance consolidation measures. There are 5 different levels of geological disturbance, and the required driving methods are similarly graded. These latter range from simple walling reinforcement, advance face zone injection and reinforcement, up to provisional manual drifting using special lining techniques. Driving through deformations by mechanical means is, as a rule, more efficient than conventional heading techniques without being more expensive. Future machine technology for driving at great depths will continue to follow the trend towards open designs with even greater accessibility in the face zone. For larger tunnel bore diameters, machines with their cutter heads inclined in the driving direction may be particularly suitable, as they improve the stability of the rock, particularly in geological deformations, by producing a sloped face.

ZUSAMMENFASSUNG:

Die technische Einsetzbarkeit von Tunnelbohrmaschinen in Hartgestein wird vom Ausmaß und Umfang geologischer Störungen bestimmt. Für Auffahrungen in großen Teufen eignen sich grundsätzlich nur Tunnelbohrmaschinen in, gegenüber Schildkonstruktionen, offener Bauweise. Denn allein sie ermöglichen die Hinnahme stärkerer Gebirgskonvergenzen, das frühzeitige Einbringen des endgültigen Streckenausbaus sowie die wirkungsvolle Anwendung vorauseilender Sanierungsmaßnahmen. Bei den geologischen Störungen lassen sich 5 Schweregrade unterscheiden mit entsprechender Abstufung der erforderlichen Vortriebsmaßnahmen. Letztere reichen von einfacher Ausbauverstärkung, über vorauseilende Vorfeld-Injektion und -Armierung, bis zu vorübergehendem Handvortrieb unter Verwendung von Sonderausbautechniken. Die maschinelle Störungsdurchörterung ist in der Regel leistungsfähiger als konventionelle Vortriebstechniken, ohne dabei kostspieliger zu sein. Die zukünftige Maschinentechnik für Auffahrungen in großen Teufen wird zu offenen Konstruktionen mit noch günstigerer Zugänglichkeit im Vorortbereich führen. Für größere Bohrdurchmesser mögen sich Maschinen mit in Auffahrrichtung geneigten Bohrköpfen besonders eignen, die über die Erzeugung einer geböschten Ortsbrust die Standfähigkeit des Gebirges insbesondere in geologischen Störungen weiter verbessern.

RÉSUMÉ:

La mise en oeuvre de tunneliers en roches dures est du point de vue technique conditionnée par le degré et l'importance des perturbations géologiques. Pour le creusement de galeries en grandes profondeurs, ne conviennent en principe que des machines du type sans bouclier. Ce sont les seules en effet à permettre la traversée de zones à forte convergence, la pose immédiate du soutènement définitif, ainsi que la mise efficace en application de mesures préliminaires de consolidation. Les perturbations géologiques peuvent être classées en cinq degrés de difficulté, impliquant chacun des mesures appropriées comprenant selon les cas le simple renforcement du soutènement,

l'injection préliminaire au front, le boulonnage immdédiat dans la partie excavée et enfin l'abattage manuel temporaire avec procédés spéciaux de soutènement.
Un creusement mécanisé à travers des formations perturbées est en général plus performant qu'un creusement conventionnel, sans pour cela être plus coûteux.
L'évolution de la technologie des machines de creusement en grandes profondeurs vavers des types ne comportant pas de bouclier et permettant une accessibilité encore meilleure à la zone du front. Pour grands diamètres de creusement, peuvent s'indiquer des machines à tête de foration inclinée dans le sens de l'avancement qui réalisent un front en talus augmentant encore la consistance des terrains, surtout dans les formations perturbées.

1 EINFÜHRUNG

Die technische Anwendbarkeit des maschinellen Vortriebs mit Tunnelbohrmaschinen wird im wesentlichen von 2 gesteins- und gebirgsabhängigen Faktoren bestimmt, der Bohrbarkeit des Gesteins und dem Gebirgsverhalten generell (Bild 1).

Unterstellt man, daß die Weiterentwicklung der Rollenbohrwerkzeuge inzwischen eine wirkungsvolle Hereingewinnung auch härtester und abrasivster Gesteine ermöglicht, d.h. bei beherrschbarem Werkzeugverschleiß und ausreichender Bohrgeschwindigkeit, so ist das erwartete Gebirgsverhalten letztlich maßgebend für die technische Entscheidung über einen Maschineneinsatz. Dazu gehören die Eigentragfähigkeit des Gebirges bis zum Einbringen des vorläufigen oder endgültigen Tunnelausbaus, falls erforderlich; ferner die Neigung des Gebirges zur Konvergenz sowie die Verspannbarkeit der Tunnelbohrmaschine, d.h. die Fähigkeit des Gebirges, der Vortriebsmaschine ein ausreichendes Widerlager zur Aufnahme der Reaktionskräfte

Gesteins- und gebirgsabhängige Faktoren für den maschinellen Vortrieb

Bohrbarkeit
Bohrwerkzeugverschleiß
Bohrgeschwindigkeit

Gebirgsverhalten
Eigentragfähigkeit
Konvergenz
Widerlagerfähigkeit

1 Geologisch-petrographische Parameter

aus Drehmomenten und Vorschubkräften zu bilden.

Das Gebirgsverhalten erreicht kritische Ausmaße in geologischen Störungszonen, insbesondere bei Auffahrungen in großen Teufen von 800 - 1300 m, z.B. im Steinkohlenbergbau der Bundesrepublik Deutschland, wovon im folgenden die Rede sein soll.

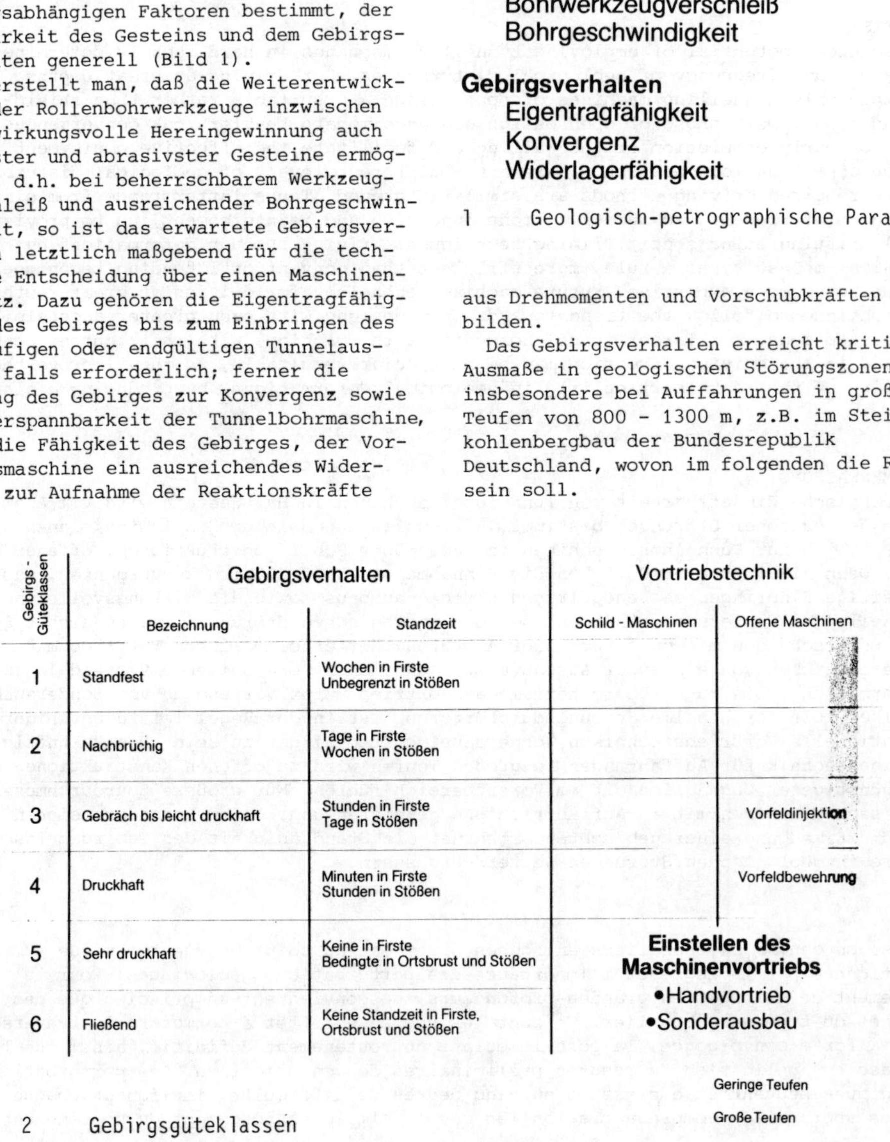
Gebirgs-Güteklassen
Gebirgsverhalten
Vortriebstechnik
Bezeichnung
Standzeit
Schild - Maschinen
Offene Maschinen
1
Standfest
Wochen in Firste
Unbegrenzt in Stößen
2
Nachbrüchig
Tage in Firste
Wochen in Stößen
3
Gebräch bis leicht druckhaft
Stunden in Firste
Tage in Stößen
Vorfeldinjektion
4
Druckhaft
Minuten in Firste
Stunden in Stößen
Vorfeldbewehrung
5
Sehr druckhaft
Keine in Firste
Bedingte in Ortsbrust und Stößen
Einstellen des Maschinenvortriebs
•Handvortrieb
•Sonderausbau
6
Fließend
Keine Standzeit in Firste, Ortsbrust und Stößen
Geringe Teufen
Große Teufen

2 Gebirgsgüteklassen

2 GEBIRGSKLASSIFIZIERUNG

In Anlehnung an die Lauffer'sche Gebirgsklassifizierung lassen sich über die Standzeit des Gebirges bekanntlich 6 Gebirgsgüteklassen von standfest bis fließend beschreiben (Bild 2) und davon Rückschlüsse auf den geeigneten Maschinentyp für Auffahrungen in geringen und großen Teufen ziehen. Eignen sich so z.B. Schildmaschinen bei oberflächennahen Auffahrungen selbst noch in druckhaftem Gebirge, sind sie in großen Teufen wegen der Konvergenzgefahr unbrauchbar.

Offene Maschinenkonstruktionen mit guter Zugänglichkeit in den Vorortbereich sind dagegen universell verwendbar; sie erfordern in der Regel zwar auch bei oberflächennahen Auffahrungen unter gebrächen bis druckhaften Gebirgsverhältnissen zusätzliche Ausbautechniken, wie Vorfeld-Konsolidierungen durch Injektionen und Armierungen bzw. Bewehrungen. Dagegen sind offene Maschinenkonstruktionen alleine geeignet für Auffahrungen in großen Teufen, so insbesondere auch bei der Durchörterung schwerer geologischer Störungen der Gebirgsgüteklassen V und VI, wo der Maschinenvortrieb zeitweise eingestellt werden muß und Handvortrieb unter Einsatz von Sonderausbautechniken zur Anwendung kommt. Dabei ist die Zugänglichkeit offener Tunnelbohrmaschinen in den Störungsbereich vor Ort entscheidend für die erfolgreiche Durchörterung derartiger Störzonen.

3 GEOLOGISCHE VERHÄLTNISSE IM UNTERTAGEBERGBAU

Charakteristisch für das Gebirgsverhalten in großen Teufen ist der quasi plastische Effekt der Konvergenz (Bild 3). Querschnittsverengungen von z.B. 1,2 m bei 6 - 6,5 m Ausgangs-Bohrdurchmesser, d.h. um ca. 20 % innerhalb des unmittelbaren Maschinenbereiches von 7 - 8 m Abstand von der Ortsbrust, bis zu 1,7 m oder fast 30 % in 100 m Entfernung von der Ortsbrust, sind nicht ungewöhnlich.

Die geologischen Störungen bei Auffahrungen im untertägigen Steinkohlenbergbau lassen sich in 5 Störungs- bzw. Schweregrade einteilen (Bild 4) entsprechend dem Ausbruchsverhalten des Gebirges. Die Tabelle gibt die erforderlichen Maßnahmen zur Störungsdurchörterung an, wie sie sich im Laufe der Jahre bei konsequenter Anwendung als erfolgreich erwiesen haben. Sie reichen von einer einfachen Verstärkung des Mattenverzuges und Auspfeilern des Ausbruchshohlraumes ohne Unterbrechung des Maschinenvortriebs bis zur manuellen Getriebezimmerung im Schutz von Hilfsbauen mit erweitertem Streckenquerschnitt vor dem Bohrkopf bei vorübergehender Einstellung des Maschinenvortriebes.

Streckenauffahrungen in gefaltetem Gebirge, wie der im(Bild 5)dargestellten "Bochumer Mulde" der Schachtanlage Victoria 1/2 bei Dortmund, mit ständigem

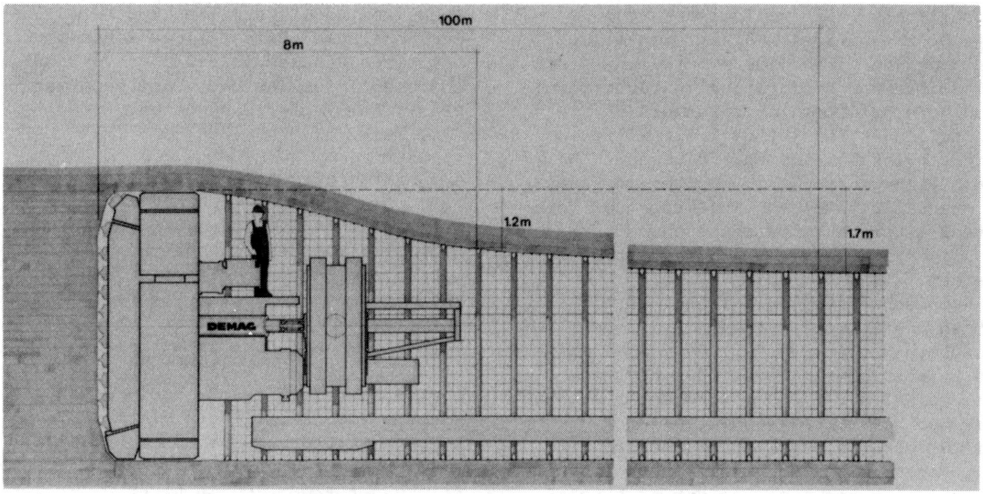

3 Konvergenzerscheinungen

Störungsgrad	Gebirgsverhalten	Maßnahmen
1	Örtliche Firstausbrüche bis 1 m Höhe	• Verstärkung des Mattenverzuges • Ausbruchverfüllung mit Holzpfeilern
2	Firstausbrüche 1-2 m hoch über 50 % der Streckenbreite in mehreren Metern Länge	• Flächenversiegelung mit Spritzmörtel • Ausbruchverfüllung mit Holzpfeilern
3	Firstausbrüche über 2 m Höhe, bedingte Gewölbebildung, Nachbruchtendenz	Unterbrechen des Maschinenvortriebs: • Fächerförmiges Vorbohren • Einbringen von Moniereisen als Schutzdach
4	Hereinbrechen von Ortsbrust und Firste mit Böschungsbildung (45°) über 3 m oberhalb der Streckenfirste	Einstellen des Maschinenvortriebs: • Hilfsbogenausbau im Überprofil • Ausbruchverfüllung mit Pumpbeton • Haufwerksverladung manuell
5	Hereinfließen von nasser, lettiger, rolliger Kluftausfüllung	Einstellen des Maschinenvortriebs: • Hilfsbogenausbau im Überprofil • Getriebezimmerung • Flächenversiegelung mit Spritzmörtel • Haufwerksverladung manuell

4 Störungsgrade

Wechsel von Gesteinsanteilen, Schichteinfallen und Spannungszuständen in der Ortsbrust sowie gelegentlichen Verwerfungen mit entsprechenden Zerrüttungszonen sind ganz typisch und normal. Auf kürzeren Strecken kann es dabei durchaus so turbulent zugehen wie in der "Donger-Störung" (Bild 6) der Schachtanlage Rheinland am Niederrhein, wo nach zuvor erläuterter Klassifikation der Störungsgrad 4 vorlag und der Vortrieb vorübergehend manuell fortgesetzt werden mußte.

4 TECHNIKEN DER STÖRUNGSDURCHHÖRTERUNG

Für mittelschwere geologische Störungen des Störungsgrades 2-3 hat sich in der Vergangenheit neben der Vorfeldbewehrung mit Hilfe von Moniereisen in fächerförmigen Vorbohrlöchern im Firstbereich die Vorfeldinjektion (Bild 7) mit Hilfe niedrigviskoser Kunstharze bewährt. Bei Vorbohrlängen von 15 m konnten in alternierendem Wechsel von Injektion und Vortrieb mittlere Vortriebsgeschwindigkeiten von immerhin noch 5 - 6 m/Tag erzielt werden.

Auch schwerste geologische Störungszonen des Störungsgrades 4 - 5 können bei vorübergehender Einstellung des Maschinenvortriebs manuell sicher durchörtert werden (Bild 8). Dabei wird unter Abfangen des Gebirges mittels Holzpfeiler zunächst die Strecke in erweitertem Querschnitt mit Bogen-Hilfsausbauen am Bohrkopf vorbei manuell vorgetrieben und der Ausbruchshohlraum in der Firste mit Asche- oder Pumpbeton verfüllt. Bei extrem rolligfließendem Störungsgestein kann sogar Getriebezimmerung erforderlich werden. Nach Vorfahren der Tunnelbohrmaschine und Einbringen des endgültigen Ringausbaus wird der Ringraum zwischen vorläufigem Bogen- und endgültigem Ringausbau ebenfalls verfüllt, um der Vortriebsmaschine ein sicheres Verspann-Widerlager zu bieten.

Die richtige Dimensionierung und Anordnung von Hilfs- und endgültigem Ausbau (Bild 9) sind wesentlich für die Leistung der Störungsdurchörterung. Sie erfordert eine rechtzeitige Planung und Bereitstellung der erforderlichen Materialien.

Das gilt insbesondere auch für die Techniken und Materialien zum Verfüllen der Hohlräume (Bild 10) des Mehrausbruchs sowie des Ringraumes zwischen vorläufigem und endgültigem Ausbau, bestehend aus Blas-, Pump- oder Sack-Beton.

4.1 Kosten der Störungsdurchörterung

Die Erfahrung hat gezeigt, daß geologische Störungen im Steinkohlenbergbau maschinell wirkungsvoller durchörtert werden können als mit konventionellen Mitteln im Sprengvortrieb (Bild 11). Selbst unter extremen Verhältnissen konnte immerhin noch eine Vortriebsleistung von 1,5 - 2,0 m/Tag erzielt werden, in der Regel jedoch 3 - 5 m/Tag. Zwar liegen die Vortriebskosten bei Störungsdurchörterungen um mehr als 50 % über denen normaler Maschinenvortriebe, trotzdem jedoch nicht höher als beim Sprengvortrieb unter vergleichbaren Bedingungen.

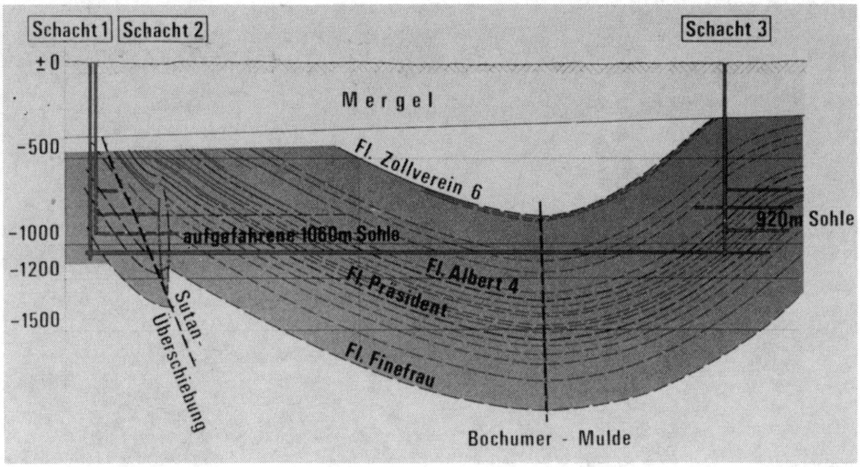

5 Geologisches Profil "Bochumer Mulde"

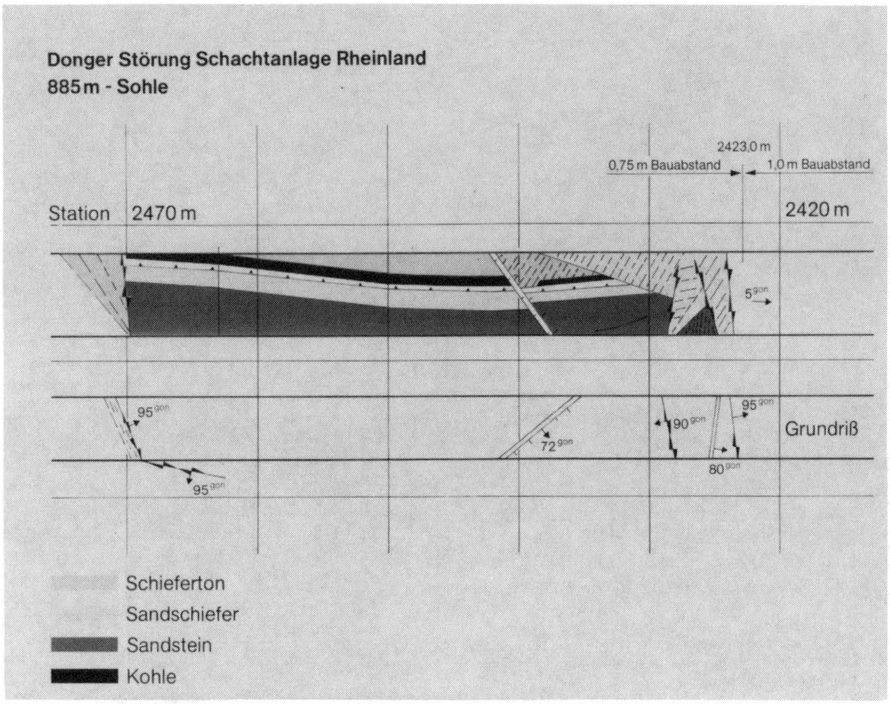

6 Geologisches Profil "Donger Störung"

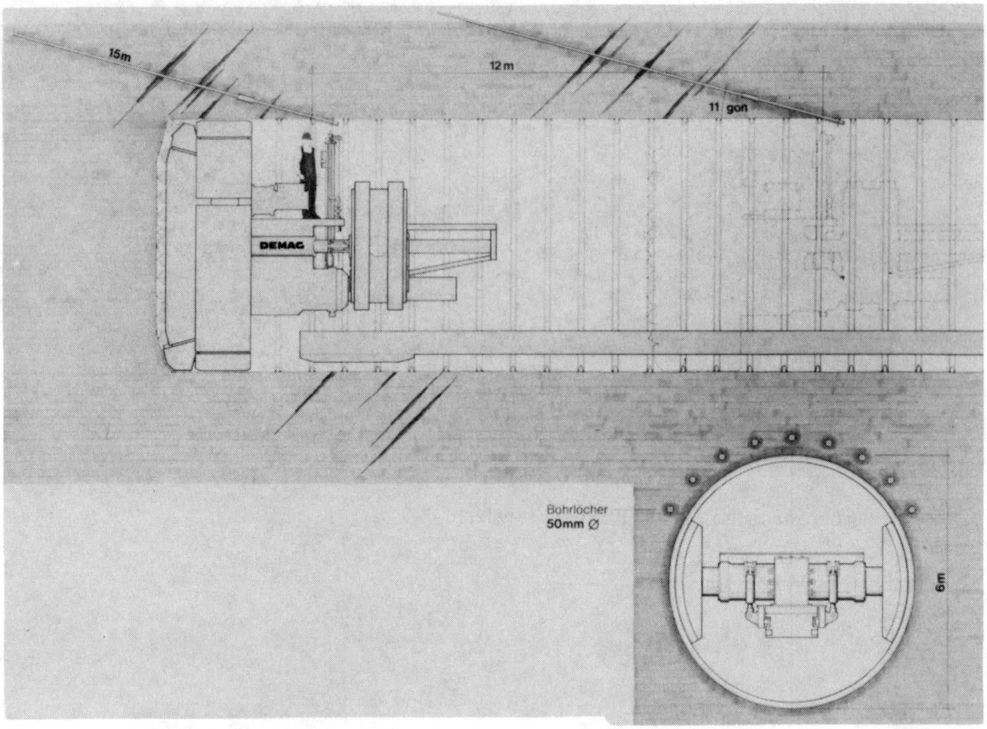

7 Vorfeldinjektion

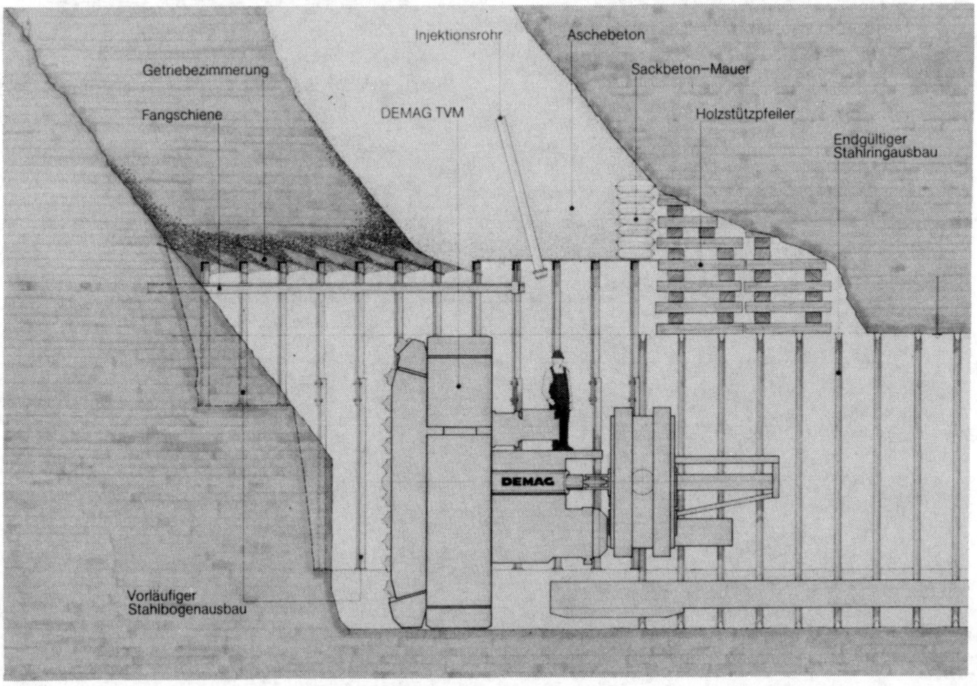

8 Kombinierte Sonderausbau-Techniken

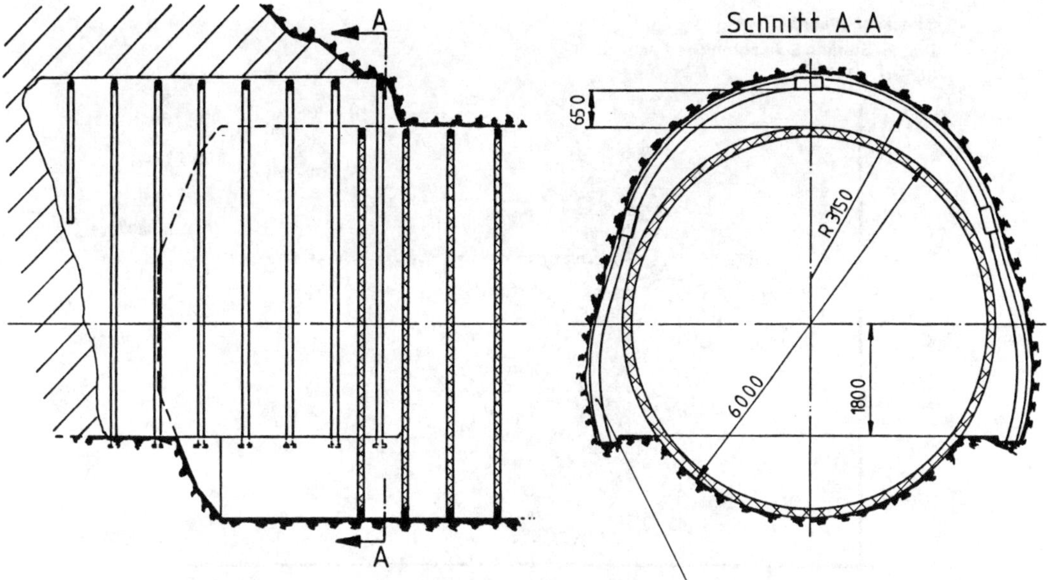

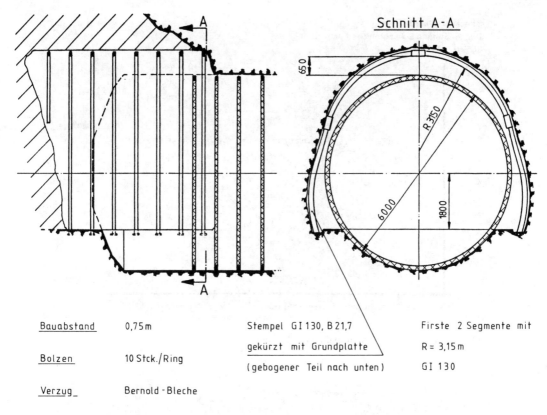

Bauabstand	0,75 m	Stempel GI 130, B 21,7	Firste 2 Segmente mit
Bolzen	10 Stck./Ring	gekürzt mit Grundplatte	R = 3,15 m
Verzug	Bernold-Bleche	(gebogener Teil nach unten)	GI 130

9 Sonderausbau (Längs- und Querschnitt)

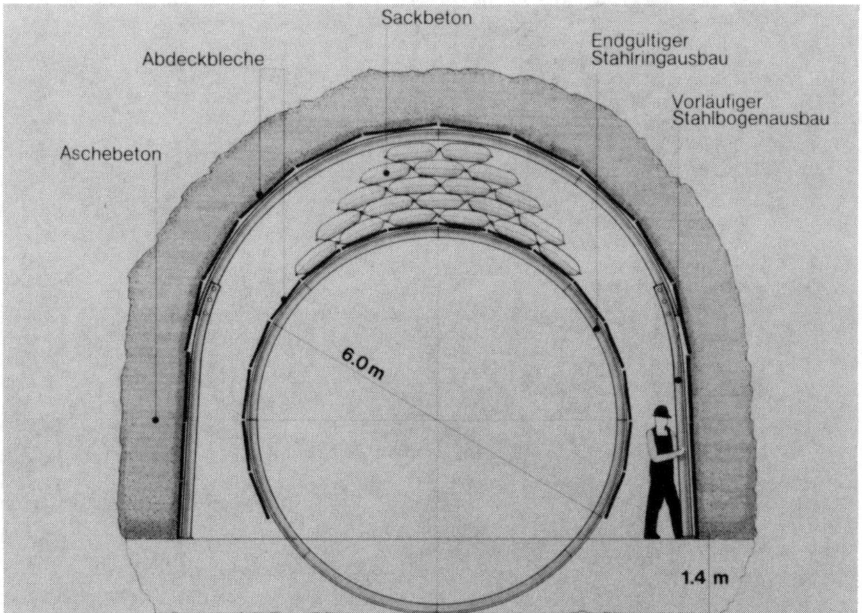

10 Sonderausbau (Querschnitt mit Verfüllmaterial)

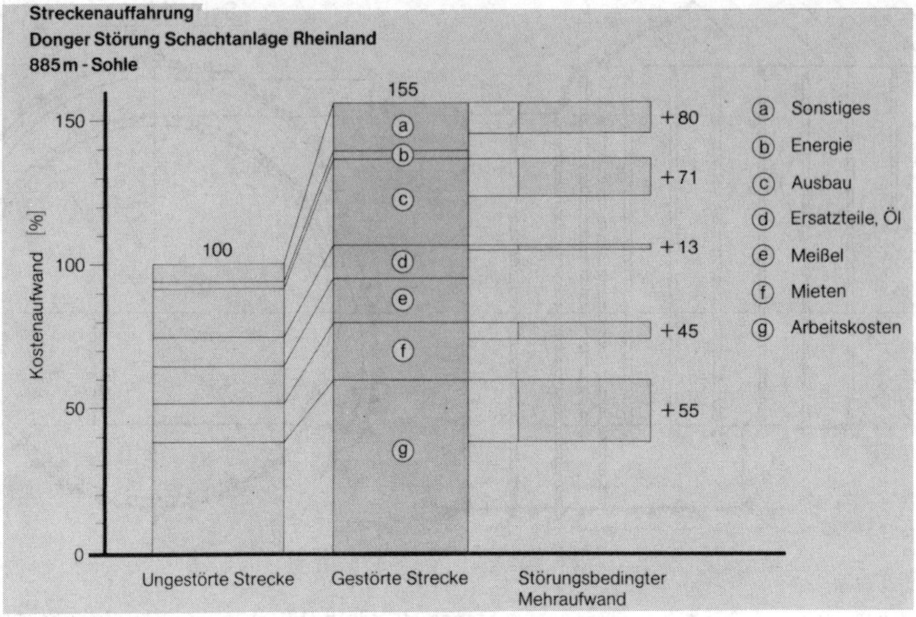

11 Kosten der Störungsdurchörterung

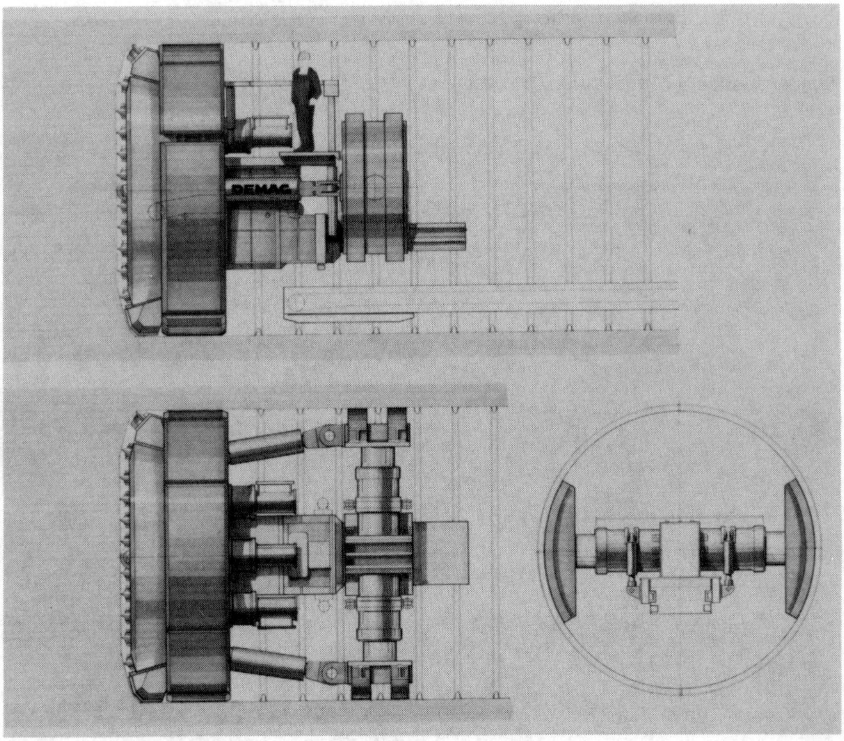

12 Leichte TVM

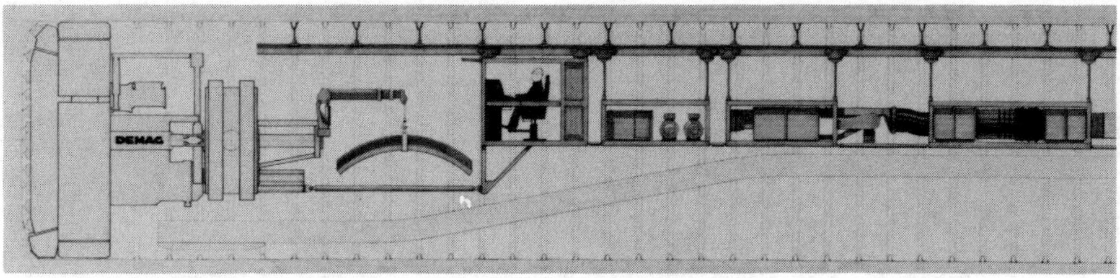

13 Leichte TVM mit Nachläufer

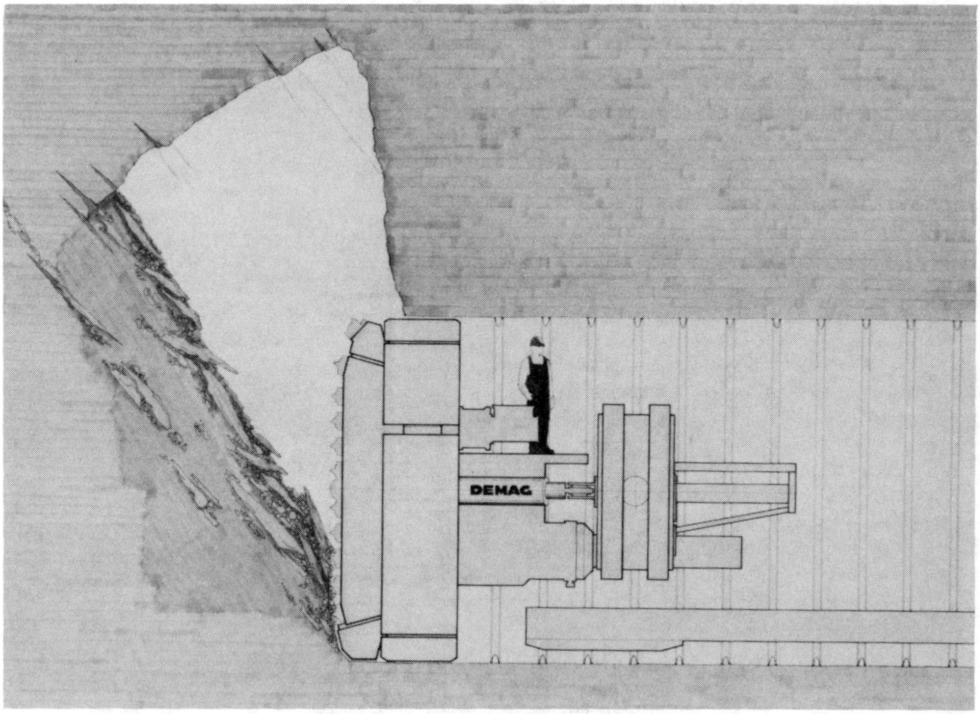

14 Ausbruchböschung

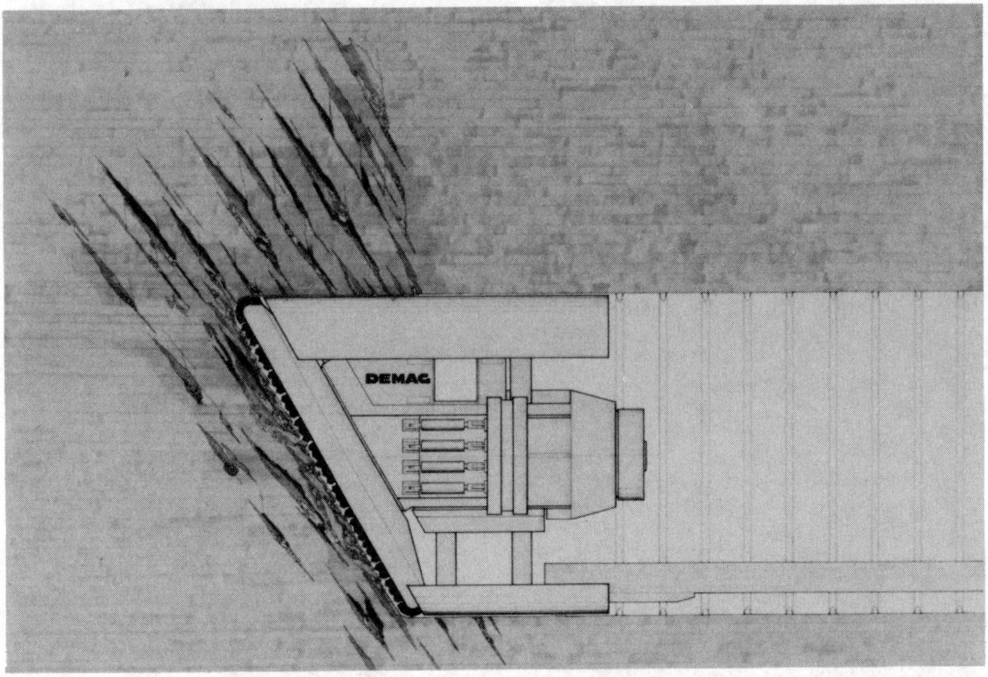

15 Ausbruchböschung mit TVM-Bohrkopf

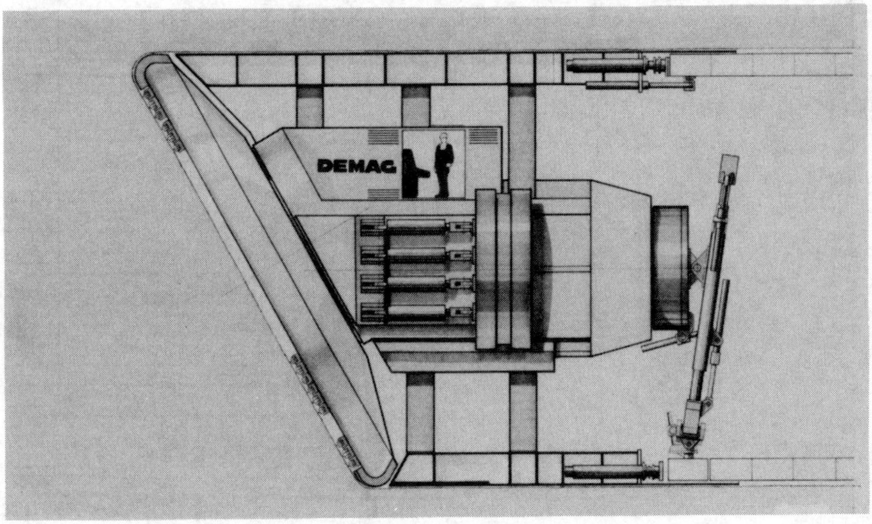

16 TVM mit geneigtem Bohrkopf

5 NEUE TUNNELBOHRTECHNIKEN

Auch in Zukunft wird man, im Hinblick auf unvermeidbare Störungsdurchörterungen, für die Tunnelauffahrung in großen Teufen, offene Maschinenkonstruktionen aus Erfahrung eindeutig bevorzugen (Bild 12). Dabei wird man versuchen, die Zugänglichkeit im unmittelbaren Vorortbereich weiter zu verbessern, um, gerade auch bei stark konvergierendem und nachbrüchigem Gebirge einen frühest möglichen Ausbau zu gewährleisten sowie Sanierungsmaßnahmen und manuelle Vortriebsarbeiten zu erleichtern.

Auch der nachgeschaltete Bereich (Bild 13) wird noch raumsparender ausgelegt werden, um die Bewegungsfreiheit für den Antransport von Hilfsgerät und -Material sowie den Abtransport von Störungsgestein zu erhöhen.

Überdenkt man die Vorgänge beim Hereinbrechen von Störungsgestein mit natürlicher Böschungsbildung (Bild 14) des Haufwerks, so drängt sich zwangsläufig der Gedanke auf, das Auslaufen von Ortsbrust und Firste durch eine entsprechende konstruktive Formgebung des Bohrkopfes zukünftiger Tunnelbohrmaschinen zu verhindern (Bild 15). Das kann beispielsweise durch eine Neigung des Bohrkopfes entsprechend dem Böschungswinkel des hereinbrechenden Störungsgesteins von 30 - 45° geschehen.

Eine derartig konzipierte Tunnelbohrmaschine (Bild 16) könnte ggf. eine Fortsetzung des maschinellen Vortriebs weiter in den Bereich geologischer Störungen hinein verlegen, wo im Augenblick noch zusätzliche Maßnahmen erforderlich sind.

Generell ist festzustellen, daß bisher kein Maschinenvortrieb im deutschen Steinkohlenbergbau an geologischen Schwierigkeiten gescheitert ist, und die gesammelten und systematisch ausgewerteten Erfahrungen einen Fächer an wirkungsvollen Maßnahmen bereithält, um allen denkbaren Problemen gerecht zu werden.

Die geologischen Probleme in den großen Teufen des Steinkohlenbergbaus gehören zu den wesentlichen Herausforderungen des Tunnelbaues. Ihre bisher erfolgreiche Bewältigung mag auch ausstrahlen auf andere Gebiete des Tunnelbaues und zu einer stärkeren Anwendung des maschinellen Vortriebs ermutigen.

GEOLOGISCH BEDINGTE GRENZEN FÜR DEN EINSATZ VON TUNNELVORTRIEBSMASCHINEN

Geological limitations for the application of tunnel boring machines

Conditions géologiques limitantes pour l'emploi des tunneliers

H.WANNER
Ingenieur-Geologe, St.Gallen, Schweiz

SUMMARY

The range of applications vor tunnel boring machines (TBM) has been expanded by improvements through the last years. Harder rocks are economically excavated due to higher forward thrust. Steel ring erectors directly behind the cutterhead help to overcome zones of fractured or loose rock. For safety reasons, in penstokes or other inclined shafts the mechanical excavation is the only possible even in very hard and abrasive rock. A better knowledge of the breaking mechanism of the rock under the load of the cutters allows a realistic estimation of machine performances for a given project.

ZUSAMMENFASSUNG

Durch Verbesserungen an Tunnelvortriebsmaschinen ist deren Einsatzbereich in den letzten Jahren stark erweitert worden. Höhere Vorschubkräfte erlauben den wirtschaftlichen Ausbruch immer härterer Gesteine. Durch Ausbauhilfen direkt hinter dem Bohrkopf können Störungszonen bewältigt werden. In Druckschächten und anderen Schrägschächten ist aus Sicherheitsgründen oft nur ein mechanischer Vortrieb möglich, selbst in sehr hartem und abrasivem Gestein. Vertiefte Kenntnisse über den Bruchvorgang im Gestein erlauben eine realistische Abschätzung der Maschinenleistung für ein bestimmtes Projekt.

RESUME

Pendant les derniers années les tunneliers ont été amélioré de sorte qu'ils sont aujourd'hui capable de travailler dans des roches dures aussi bien que dans des roches d'une faible stabilité. Dans les puits inclinée, l'excavation mécanisée est souvent la seule possible, même dans des roches très dures et abrasives. Des connaissances plus profondes sur la fracturation de la roche sous les outils permettent d'estimer d'une manière réalistique la vitesse d'avancement pour un certain project.

1. EINFUEHRUNG

Der Einsatzbereich für Tunnelvortriebsmaschinen ist in den letzten Jahren stark erweitert worden, und zwar in Richtung hätere Gesteine durch Erhöhung der Vorschubkraft, in Richtung Lockermaterial durch Entwicklung verschiedener Kombinationen mit Schildern und in Richtung nicht standfeste Felsgesteine durch systematische Einbaumöglichkeiten unmittelbar hinter dem Bohrkopf.

Für viele Gebirgsarten, bei denen früher ein mechanischer Vortrieb nicht in Frage kam, werden heute geeignete Maschinen oder Maschinenkombination angeboten. Es handelt sich dabei durchwegs um Geräte im Wert von mehreren Millionen DM. Bei Investitionen in solcher Höhe muss sorgfältig abgeklärt werden, wo die Grenzen der Einsetzbarkeit liegen. Es ist offensichtlich, dass diese von Gerät zu Gerät abweichen und daher jedesmal neu festzustellen sind.

Die folgenden Ausführungen beziehen sich hauptsächlich auf Vollschnittmaschinen.

2. BEDINGUNGEN FUER DEN EINSATZ VON VOLLSCHNITTMASCHINEN

Vollschnittmaschinen können nur dort eingesetzt werden, wo dies a) technisch möglich und b) wirtschaftlich ist, d.h. nicht teurer als der konventionelle Vortrieb.

Die technischen Möglichkeiten können abgeschätzt werden, wenn detaillierte Kenntnisse über das anzutreffende Gebirge vorliegen. Diese müssen in der Regel ausführlicher sein als für Sprengvortrieb, da der mechanische Vortrieb - wenn überhaupt - nur mit Mühe an veränderte Gebirgsverhältnisse angepasst werden kann.

Die Wirtschaftlichkeit eines Maschineneinsatzes hängt nicht nur vom Gestein und Gebirge, sondern auch von den Gegebenheiten des Bauwerks (Kreisprofil, Kurvenradien etc.) ab. Besonders beim Bau von Druckschächten sind seit mehr als einem Jahrzehnt fast ausschliesslich Vortriebsmaschinen eingesetzt worden, und zwar auch in sehr abrasivem Hartgestein. Eine maschinengerechte Projektierung der Stollen und Schächte kann hier wesentlich zur Hebung der Wirtschaftlichkeit beitragen. Sie ist Voraussetzung für einen optimalen Maschineneinsatz.

3. WIRTSCHAFTLICHE GRENZEN

Jeder Maschineneinsatz hat den Vergleich mit einem entsprechenden Sprengvortrieb zu bestehen.

In Druckschächten und anderen Schrägschächten stellt der Sprengvortrieb meist ein sehr hohes Sicherheitsrisiko dar. Nachbrüche, selbst von kleinen Gesteinsbrocken, gefährden die Mannschaft ausserordentlich, auch im gesamten rückwärtigen Bereich des Schachtes. Es finden sich heute kaum noch Mineure, die bereit sind, einen Schrägschacht nach konventioneller Methode im steigenden Vortrieb zu sprengen. In Schrägschächten werden daher heute meist Tunnelvortriebsmaschinen eingesetzt auch wenn sehr hartes und abrasives Gestein zu erwarten ist.

Die Meisselkosten können in solchen Fällen weit über 100 DM pro Kubikmeter Festgestein ansteigen, was kaum mehr als wirtschaftlich bezeichnet werden darf. Um einzelne extrem harte Zonen überhaupt auffahren zu können, sind gelegentlich Lockerungssprengungen vor dem Bohrkopf nötig. Solche Sprengungen sollen von der Ortsbrust eine Vielzahl von Trennflächen im Gestein erzeugen, ohne dass grössere Blöcke auf den Bohrkopf herunterfallen. Das so gelockerte Gebirge lässt sich dann mit wesentlich verbesserten Vortriebsleistungen ausbrechen.

Die Wirtschaftlichkeit eines Maschineneinsatzes darf nicht nur an den Ausbruchkosten abgeschätzt werden. Der mechanische Vortrieb kann die Gesamtkosten wesentlich beeinflussen. Durch den gebirgsschonenden Ausbruch werden die notwendigen provisorischen und dauernden Stützmassnahmen reduziert. Die glatte, regelmässige Ausbruchsoberfläche erlaubt es, minimale Betonstärken auszuführen, ohne dass Ueberprofil mit Beton verfüllt werden muss. Das ausgebrochene Material fällt so kleinstückig an, dass es in Schrägschächten auch bei geringer Neigung meist über eine Schwemmrinne abgeführt werden kann. Bei unverkleideten Druckstollen ergeben sich hydraulische Reibungsverluste, die wesentlich geringer sind als beim Durchfliessen eines gesprengten Stollens mit all seinen groben Unebenheiten. Alle erwähnten Faktoren führen zu Einsparungen, welche indirekt auf den mechanischen Ausbruch zurückzuführen sind, sich jedoch nicht unmittelbar in den Ausbruchskosten manifestieren.

4. GEOLOGISCH BEDINGTE GRENZEN

Die durch die geologischen Verhältnisse gegebenen Grenzen sind teils ultimativ (z.B. bei ungenügender Standfestigkeit des Gebirges oder wenn die Maschine nicht ausreichend verspannt werden kann), teils sind sie durch wirtschaftliche Gegebenheiten gesetzt (z.B. bei hohen Meisselkosten oder geringen Vortriebsleistungen). Die erwähnten Limitierungen werden nachstehend diskutiert.

4.1. Standfestigkeit des Gebirges

Viele, besonders ältere Vortriebsmaschinen sind für den Einsatz in standfestem Gebirge konstruiert worden. Die Möglichkeit, gebräches oder nachbrüchiges Gebirge wirksam zu stützen, besteht dabei erst in beträchtlichem Abstand von der Ortsbrust. Solche Maschinen können auch kleinere Störungszonen nur mit grösster Mühe durchfahren.

Neuere Maschinen wurden in Schilde eingebaut, was sich in Lockergesteinen recht gut brwährt hat. In Felsgesteinen ergeben sich daraus mehrere Probleme. In druckhaftem Gebirge kann der Schild völlig verklemmt werden. Die Steuerung einer Schildmaschine ist schwieriger. Vor dem Einsatz einer Schildmaschine sind daher sorgfältige Abklärungen nötig.

Maschinen der neuesten Generation bieten unmittelbar hinter dem Bohrkopf die Möglichkeit, nachbrüchiges Gebirge wirksam zu stützen, sei dies durch halbautomatisch versetzbare Stahlringe oder durch systematische Ankerung. Ausbau und Verspannvorrichtung der Maschine müssen aufeinander abgestimmt sein. Solche Maschinen sind effizient beim Einsatz in standfestem Gebirge, vermögen jedoch auch über längere Einbaustrecken gute Vortriebsleistungen zu erbringen.

4.2. Vortriebsleistungen

Die Vortriebsleistungen hängen sowohl vom Gestein und Gebirge als auch von den Maschinenparametern, insbesondere von der Vorschubkraft ab. In den letzten Jahren sind die Vortriebsleistungen laufend verbessert worden, wie in Fig. 1 dargestellt.

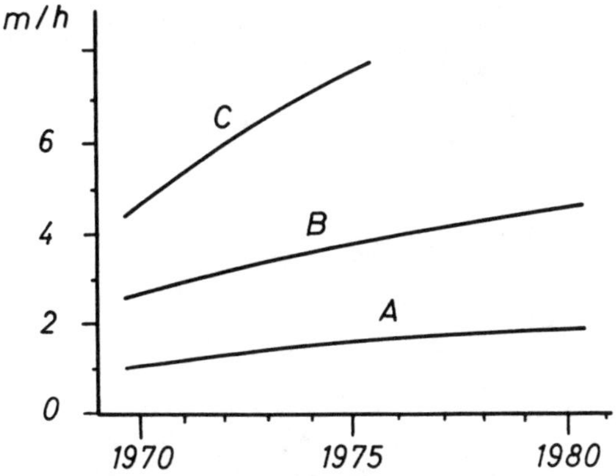

Fig. 1: Entwicklung der Netto-Vortriebsleistungen (nach Robbins 1980) für verschiedene Gesteins-Druckfestigkeiten.
A= 2'500 kp/cm^2, B=1000 kp/cm^2, C=500 kp/cm^2
Tunneldurchmesser = 3.7 m

Die Netto-Vortriebsleistung bildet zusammen mit dem Ausnützungsgrad der Maschine die wichtigste Einflussgrösse für die Gesamtkosten des Tunnelausbruchs. Der Ausnützungsgrad kann bei optimaler Baustellenorganisation, systemgerechtem Nachläufer etc. über 65% ansteigen, doch werden meist aus verschiedenen Gründen nicht wesentlich mehr als 50 - 55 % Ausnützung erreicht.

Die Gesteins-Druck- bzw. Zugfestigkeiten bestimmen im Wesentlichen die Netto-Vortriebsleistung. Aufgrund verschiedener Modellvorstellungen über den Bruchvorgang im Gestein unter der Last eines Rollenmeissels können Formeln hergeleitet werden zur Bestimmung der Meissel-Eindringtiefe und somit der Vortriebsgeschwindigkeit. Eine dieser Formeln ist nachstehend aufgeführt. Sie gilt für scharfkantige Diskenmeissel.

$$V = U \cdot \left(\sqrt[3]{X - \frac{B}{2}} - \sqrt[3]{X + \frac{B}{2}} \right)^2$$

wobei:

$$X = \sqrt{\frac{B^2}{4} + \frac{A^3}{27}}$$

$$A = \frac{\tau_t \cdot T}{N \cdot C}$$

$$B = \frac{P/N}{C\sqrt{D} \cdot \tan \alpha/2}$$

$$C = \frac{4}{3}\sigma_c - (4\tau_t \cdot \tan \alpha/2)$$

V = Netto-Vortriebsgeschwindigkeit
U = Bohrkopf-Drehgeschwindigkeit
D = Disken-Durchmesser
T = Tunneldurchmesser
P = Vorschubkraft
N = Anzahl Cutter
σ_c = einachsige Gesteinsdruckfestigkeit
τ_t = Scherfestigkeit des Gesteins
α = Keilwinkel der Disken

Die Formel berücksichtigt nicht die Gebirgseigenschaften wie z.B. den Zerlegungsgrad, die Häufigkeit und Orientierung der Klüfte etc. Sie erklärt jedoch deutlich den Einfluss der Vorschubkraft auf die Vortriebsleistung (Fig. 2). Die in Fig. 1 dargestellte Entwicklung ist demnach im Wesentlichen auf erhöhte Vorschubkräfte pro Rolle zurückzuführen.

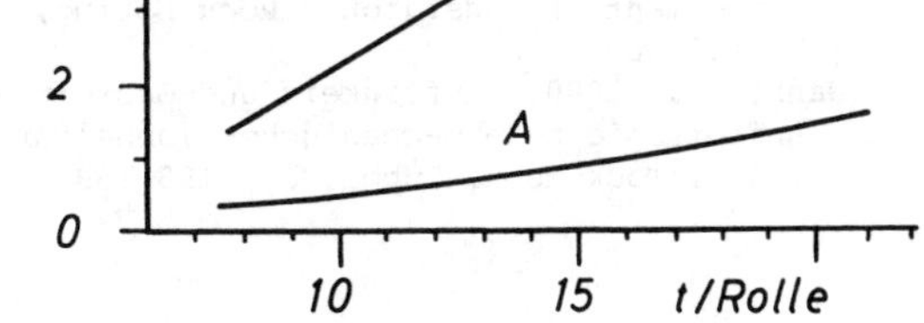

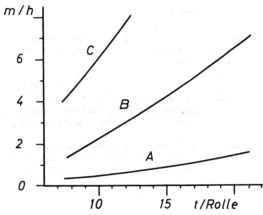

Fig. 2: Netto-Vortriebsleistungen bei steigender Vorschubkraft. Gesteinsdruckfestigkeiten und Tunneldurchmesser gleich wie in Fig. 1.

Die zu erwartende Vortriebsleistung kann recht zuverlässig abgeschätzt werden bei ausreichender Kenntnis der Gesteins- und Gebirgseigenschaften.

4.3. Werkzeugkosten

Obwohl in den letzten Jahren immer härtere und abrasivere Gesteine mechanisch abgebaut wurden, sind die Meisselkosten pro Kubikmeter Festgestein wesentlich gesunken und übersteigen Werte von 20-30 DM/m^3 nur selten. In nicht-abrasiven Gesteinen liegen sie meist bei oder unter 10 DM/m^3. Die Werkzeugkosten limitieren einen Maschineneinsatz nur in seltenen Fällen.

Die Abrasivität eines Gesteins kann auf verschiedene Art zuverlässig bestimmt werden, z.B. nach der Methode von Schimazek und Knatz aus Anteil und Grösse der abrasiven Mineralien und aus der Gesteins-Zugfestigkeit, oder durch Abrasionsversuche mit einem Stahlstift nach CERCHAR.

5. FOLGERUNGEN

Um die Grenzen der Einsetzbarkeit einer Tunnelvortriebsmaschine zuverlässig abschätzen zu können, sind detailliertere geologische Voruntersuchungen nötig als beim konventionellen Vortrieb. Dazu gehören Untersuchungen des Mineralgehalts der Gesteine, der Druck- und Zugfestigkeit, der Art, Orientierung und Häufigkeit der Trennflächen. Da die Vortriebsmaschinen sehr unterschiedlich ausgelegt sind, kann die Gesteins-Bohrbarkeit immer nur bezüglich einer bestimmten Maschine angegeben werden.

6. REFERENZEN

Henneke J. und Kübler H., 1981, Stand und Entwicklungen beim maschinellen Gesteins-Streckenvortrieb im deutschen Steinkohlenbergbau. Techn. Mittlg. 74; 225-235

Robbins R.J., 1980, Present Trends and future directions in tunnelling. S.Afr. Inst.Min.Met.Symp. on Economics and Management of Underground Rock Boring, Febr. 1980

Wanner H., 1980, Klüftigkeit und Gesteins-Anisotropie beim mechanischen Tunnelvortrieb. Rock Mech. Suppl. 10, 155-169

* 5 *

ROCK MECHANICAL PROBLEMS IN ASSOCIATION WITH UNDERGROUND STORAGE

Felsmechanische Probleme im Zusammenhang mit der untertägigen Speicherung

Problèmes de mécanique des roches en relation avec le stockage souterrain

EINFLUSS DER NUMERISCHEN UND STOFFLICHEN APPROXIMATIONEN AUF DAS ERGEBNISS VON KRIECHBERECHNUNGEN

Influence of numerical and material approximations on the results of creep calculations

Influence de l'approximation numérique et matériel sur le résultat des calculs de fluage

H.HEBENER
Technische Universität Berlin
T.RICHTER
Grundbau und Dynamik Consult GmbH, Berlin
K.-M.BORCHERT
Technische Universität Berlin

SUMMARY

In dimensioning deep underground excavations in rock-salt it is of particular importance to find a realistic way to take into account the time dependent deformation behavior of rock-salt. Developing and proving a useful material law requires a sufficient number of laboratory test results as well as in situ measurements. Furthermore an appropriate method of calculations or a computer program is needed to calculate even high complicated boundary value problems. In this work the influence of some numerical and material approximations on the results of creep calculations with the Finite Element Method is presented. As an example the rather simple boundary value problem of a deep borhole is noticable, whereas the chosen variations of the boundary conditions don't effect the results at all. It is evident that the calculated creep deformations vary with respect to the chosen material model. Therefore the effect of the variation of Poisson's-ratio in the range of instantaneous deformation and the effect of different 3-D generalisations for the steady-state creep on the overall time dependent behavior is examined.

ZUSAMMENFASSUNG

Für die Bemessung von Bauwerken im Salzgestein ist es von besonderer Wichtigkeit das zeitabhängige Verformungsverhalten des Salzes möglichst realistisch zu erfassen. Hierfür ist es einerseits erforderlich genügend zuverlässige Laborversuchsergebnisse und in situ Messungen zu besitzen, um ein brauchbares Stoffgesetz formulieren und testen zu können. Andererseits muß ein geeignetes Rechenverfahren bzw. Rechenprogramm verfügbar sein, um auch komplizierte Probleme zu lösen. Im Rahmen dieser Arbeit werden die Einflüsse dargestellt, die die numerischen und stofflichen Näherungen auf die Kriechberechnungen haben können. Hierbei wird das einfache Randwertproblem eines tiefen Bohrloches im homogenen Salzgebirge untersucht. Im Rahmen der numerischen Approximationen ergibt sich ein erheblicher Einfluß der Diskretisierung und des Elementtypes, während die Randbedingungen in den hier gewählten Variationen das Kriechverhalten kaum verändern. Da die errechneten Kriechverformungen naturgemäß stark von der Art des gewählten Stoffgesetzes abhängen, wird hier besonders der Einfluß verschiedener 3-D Verallgemeinerungen des sekundären Kriechens sowie der gewählten Querdehnungszahl des Sofortverformungsbereiches auf das Zeitverformungsverhalten des Bohrloches untersucht.

RESUME

Pour mesurer des constructions dans le minéral de sel il est très important de saisir la réaction de déformation du sel qui est dépendant du temps le mieux possible réalistement. Pour cela il est nécessaire d'une part d'avoir assez de résultats des essais de laboratoire et de mesurages du terrain à bâti pour formuler et tester une loi de matière utile. D'autre part une bonne méthode de calculer respectivement un programme de calculer doit être disponible pour solutionner aussi des problèmes compliqués. Dans le cadre de ce travail ils sont présentés ces influences que les approximations numériques et matériels avaient sur les calculs de fluage. Pour cela le simple problème d'une trou de mine dans un terrain de sel homogène est examiné. Dans le cadre de l'approximation numérique il se montre une influence considérable de la manière d'élément pendant que les conditions de bord dans la variation choisi ici modifient à peine l'attitude de fluage. Parce que les déformations de fluage calculées dependent naturellement trop de la manière du loi de matière choisi, l'influence de la nombre de Poisson choisi et encore plusieurs 3-D généralisations de fluage sécundaire sur l'attitude de déformation dépendent du temps de la trou de mine est examiné ici.

1. EINLEITUNG

Das aufgrund der technologischen und nicht zuletzt der politischen Entwicklung immer größer werdende Bedürfnis Primärenergieträger wie Erdöl und Erdgas oberflächennah zu speichern, hat den Bau von immer größeren und somit effektiveren Kavernen erforderlich gemacht. Dies bedingte dann die Notwendigkeit einer intensiven Erforschung der Mechanik des Salzgesteins.
Sehr wesentliche und teilweise gänzlich neuartige Impulse erhielt die Salzmechanikforschung durch die Suche nach einer Möglichkeit zur Endlagerung für den seit Jahren produzierten hochgiftigen radioaktiven Müll unserer Gesellschaft.
Damit wurde allerdings auch gleichzeitig ein sehr hoher Anspruch an die Ergebnisse und die Zuverlässigkeit der Forschung gestellt. Die Möglichkeit wie bei der Lösung anderer Ingenieurprobleme aus Erfahrungen zu lernen - auch aus negativen - mußte hier ausgeschaltet werden, da man in diesem Zusammenhang negative Erfahrungen eventuell nur einmal machen kann.
Die konkreten Aufgaben, die sich bei der Lösung von Ingenieurproblemen stellen, sind im allgemeinen die folgenden:

1. Berechnung der Struktur als Randwertproblem unter Verwendung eines geeigneten Rechenverfahrens.
2. Beschreibung des Materialverhaltens in möglichst realistischer Weise unter Berücksichtigung der Spannungs- und Verformungsbedingungen, denen das Material in situ ausgesetzt ist und Einfügen dieser Beziehung in das Rechenverfahren.
3. Bei dem Problem der Lagerung radioaktiven Mülls sind anders als z.B. bei Speicherkavernen noch die Einflüsse aus Temperatur und radioaktiver Bestrahlung in der Materialbeziehung zu berücksichtigen. Es ist außerdem zu beachten, daß der zu untersuchende Betriebszeitraum der Kaverne die labormäßigen Erfahrungen um ein vielfaches übersteigt und daher starke Extrapolationen des Erfahrungsbereiches notwendig sind.

Die bis vor wenigen Jahren noch ausschließlich verwendeten empirischen oder halbempirischen Rechenverfahren erweisen sich wegen der neuen "Dimension" dieser Probleme als völlig unzureichend. Besonders das Verfahren der finiten Elemente eröffnet dagegen die Möglichkeit, mechanisch fundiert bei selbst kompliziertestem Stoffverhalten und schwierigen Randwertproblemen realistische Rechenergebnisse zu erhalten. Aber auch im Rahmen dieses Rechenverfahrens, da es sich um ein numerisches Näherungsverfahren handelt, sind Vereinfachungen und Annahmen zu formulieren, die bei gewissen Randwertproblemen erheblich die Form des späteren Rechenergebnisses beeinflussen. Diese Näherungen liegen einmal im Bereich der Numerik und zum anderen in der Art der Formulierung des Materialverhaltens.

In der vorliegenden Arbeit sollen an Hand eines einfachen Beispieles beide Approximationen bezüglich ihrer Wirkung auf das Kriechverhalten von Salz untersucht werden.

Als Beispiel wird ein tiefes Bohrloch im ASSE-Steinsalz gewählt, für das aufgrund extensiver Laboruntersuchungen ausreichend abgesicherte Materialparameter gegeben sind und außerdem Ergebnisse von in situ Konvergenzmessungen vorliegen (vergleiche Wallner (1981)).

Eine nähere Untersuchung der materialspezifischen Einflüsse, wie sie bei der Lagerung von radioaktivem Abfall auftreten, soll hier nicht erfolgen, da nach Meinung der Verfasser schon bei den fundamentalen Fragen der Numerik und der Materialansätze Probleme bei der praktischen Berechnung auftreten, von denen im folgenden einige diskutiert werden sollen.

2. RECHENVERFAHREN

Die Methode der finiten Elemente (FEM) ist seit zwei Jahrzehnten ein Verfahren, mit welchem komplizierte Strukturen mit linearem, nichtlinearem und zeitabhängigem Materialverhalten unter statischer und dynamischer Belastung berechnet werden können.

Da diese Methode kein exaktes sondern ein Näherungsverfahren darstellt, sind die Ergebnisse, die mit ihr zu erzielen sind, abhängig von der Güte der gemachten Näherungen. Grundlegende Ableitungen sollen hier nicht erfolgen, sondern es werden nur einige für die weitere Betrachtung wesentliche Formeldarstellungen gegeben. Für ein detailliertes Studium sei auf das grundsätzliche Werk von Zienkiewicz (1971) verwiesen.

Die FEM analysiert das zu berechnende Problem in einem begrenzten Bereich, der über Randbedingungen mit der für die Betrachtung angenommenerweise nicht relevanten Umgebung verbunden ist. Die Absteckung dieses Bereiches ist neben der Formulierung der Art der Randbedingungen eine Näherung und erfordert vom Anwender Erfahrung und Einsicht in das Verformungsverhalten des Problems.

Der betrachtete Bereich wird in endliche Elemente eingeteilt, deren Dichte, Art und Form eine weitere Approximation darstellen. Die Elemente besitzen Randknoten, an denen sie miteinander verbunden sind, und für deren Freiheitsgrade die Bewegungsgleichungen aufgestellt werden. Bei einer dem Verschiebungsgrößenverfahren der Stabstatik entsprechenden Vorgehensweise sind alle Zustandsgrößen über die Verschiebungen darstellbar.

Im Element ergeben sich an jedem Punkt die Verschiebungen $\underline{u}$ aus

$$\underline{u} = \underline{N} \cdot \underline{v} \tag{1}$$

$\underline{v}$ ist der Knotenpunktverschiebungsvektor und $\underline{N}$ die Matrix der Ansatzfunktionen. Es läßt sich zeigen, daß je mehr Knoten ein Element besitzt, desto höherwertiger ist der Verschiebungsansatz und desto genauer lassen sich über das Element Verschiebungen, Verzerrungen und Spannungen berechnen. Die Güte des Ergebnisses ist also eine Funktion der geeigneten Elementwahl. Aus den Verzerrungen ergeben sich die Spannungen über ein Stoffgesetz der einfachsten Form:

$$\underline{\sigma} = \underline{C}\ (\underline{\varepsilon} - \underline{\varepsilon}_o) + \underline{\sigma}_o \tag{2}$$

$\underline{\varepsilon}_o$ = spannungsfreie Verzerrung
$\underline{\sigma}_o$ = Anfangsspannungszustand
$\underline{C}$ = Materialmatrix

Die spannungsfreien Verzerrungen beinhalten zum Beispiel plastische oder Kriechverzerrungen.
Die Güte des Stoffgesetzes, welches zumeist aus einfachen Laboruntersuchungen entwikkelt wird, mißt sich an seiner Fähigkeit bei beliebigen Problemen realistisches Verformungsverhalten darzustellen. Da jedoch bei jeder Ableitung eines Stoffgesetzes eine Reihe vereinfachender Annahmen zu treffen sind, können Rechenergebnisse komplizierter Strukturen unbewußte Fähigkeiten und Schwächen der Stoffgesetze aufdecken.

Nachfolgend unter 3. sollen zwei einfache und ein komplizierteres Stoffgesetz für weitere Berechnungen vorgestellt werden.

Bei der Lösung von Problemen mit nichtlinearem Materialverhalten ist eine iterative Lösung der Gleichungen nötig. Hierfür gibt es verschiedenste Iterationsstrategien, die abhängig vom Problem mehr oder weniger effektiv sind.

Bei Kriechproblemen ist es üblich in Richtung der Zeitachse eine inkrementelle Vorgehensweise zu wählen, d.h. den Verformungsprozeß in so kleine Zeitintervalle zu zerlegen, daß in jedem Zeitintervall mit konstanten Zustandsgrößen gerechnet werden kann. Die Wahl dieser Zeitschrittlänge ist daher für die Wirtschaftlichkeit aber besonders für die Konvergenz der Rechenergebnisse entscheidend. In der Literatur werden dabei für eine Zeitschrittsteuerung unterschiedlichste Formeln angegeben. Da all diese Kriterien schließlich empirisch sind, empfiehlt sich eine Überprüfung auch dieser Approximation durch Variation der Zeitschrittlängen.

3. STOFFMODELLE

3.1 Allgemeines

Es wird vereinfachend davon ausgegangen, daß das zeitliche Verformungsverhalten von Salz sich aus einem Sofortverformungs- und einem sekundären Kriechbereich zusammen - setzt. Es wird auf die Betrachtung von primärem Kriechen und von Kriechbrüchen verzichtet.

3.2 Stoffmodelle 1 und 2

Es werden hier zwei Modelle vorgestellt, bei denen jeweils die Sofortbelastung durch das Hooke'sche Gesetz dargestellt wird. Im Bereich sekundären Kriechens wird einmal ein rheologisches Modell in Form eines Newtonschen Dämpfers mit spannungsabhängiger Viskosität und zum anderen wird eine Exponentialfunktion analog Weertmann (1968) angesetzt. Die Materialkonstanten werden so gewählt, daß im einaxialen Kriechversuch, der als Referenzzustand gilt, identisches Verformungsverhalten auftritt. Es gilt

Modell 1 - NEWTON:

$$\dot{\varepsilon}_1^K = \frac{1}{\eta}\,\sigma_1 \tag{3}$$

$$\text{mit } \eta = \eta_o \cdot \left(\frac{\sigma_1}{G}\right)^{1-n} \tag{4}$$

Modell 2 - WEERTMANN:

$$\dot{\varepsilon}_1^K = B \cdot \exp\left(-\frac{Q}{RT}\right)\left(\frac{\sigma_1}{G}\right)^n = A\left(\frac{\sigma_1}{G}\right)^n \tag{5}$$

Für den mehraxialen Zustand wird für beide Modelle volumenkonstantes, d.h. rein deviatorisches, Kriechen angenommen. Modell 1 wird in Analogie zum Hooke'schen Gesetz, während Modell 2 über die der Plastizitätstheorie entlehnte Betrachtung der Koaxialität der Spannungen mit den Verzerrungszuwächsen entwickelt wird.

Modell 1 - NEWTON, nach Hooke gilt:

$$\varepsilon_1 = \frac{1}{E}\sigma_1 \text{ ergibt } \underline{\varepsilon} = \frac{1}{E}\,\underline{A}^{-1}\,\underline{\sigma} \tag{6}$$

Analog ist:

$$\dot{\varepsilon}_1^K = \frac{1}{\eta}\sigma_1 \text{ ergibt } \underline{\dot{\varepsilon}}^K = \frac{1}{\eta}\,\underline{\tilde{A}}^{-1}\,\underline{\sigma} \tag{7}$$

$$\text{mit } \underline{\tilde{A}} = \underline{A}_{(\nu=0.5)} \tag{8}$$

Modell 2 - WEERTMANN, es gilt $\underline{\dot{e}}^K = k\underline{s}$ (9)

"e" und "s" sind deviatorische Größen.

Weiterhin ist: $\varepsilon_1^K \rightarrow \bar{e}^K = \sqrt{\frac{2}{3}\, e_{ij}^K \cdot \cdot\, e_{ij}^K}$ (10)

$$\sigma_1 \rightarrow \bar{s} = \sqrt{\frac{3}{2}\, s_{ij} \cdot\cdot s_{ij}} \quad (11)$$

Es ergibt sich: $k = 1{,}5\ \dot{e}^K / \bar{s}^*$ (12)

$$\text{mit } \bar{s}^* = \sqrt{\frac{3}{2}(s_x^2 + s_y^2 + s_Z^2 + \tau_{xy}^2 + \tau_{xZ}^2 + \tau_{Zx}^2)} \quad (13)$$

Weitere Einzelheiten sind den Arbeiten von Borchert u.a. (1981) sowie Richter u.a. (1981a) zu entnehmen.

3.3 Endochrones Stoffmodell - Modell 3

Die Endochronentheorie verwendet eine mechanisch andere Vorgehensweise bei der Entwicklung eines Stoffgesetzes. Sie ist von Valanis (1971) für die Beschreibung des Verhaltens von Metallen entwickelt und von Bazánt/Bhat (1976) für Beton erweitert worden.

Die Theorie ist in der Lage unterschiedlichstes Materialverhalten darzustellen und somit wurde sie von Richter u.a.(1981b) auch zur Beschreibung des Kriechverhaltens von Salz verwandt. Die theoretischen Hintergründe und die speziellen Ableitungen sind in diesen Arbeiten ausführlich angegeben und es soll, da die Darstellung dieser Theorie recht aufwendig ist, hier auf eine Abteilung verzichtet werden. Die Leistungsfähigkeit aber auch die Beschränkungen dieses Types von Materialgesetzen sollen jedoch bezogen auf Salzgestein kurz dargestellt werden, um die später demonstrierten Rechenergebnisse verständlich zu machen.

Im Sofortverformungsbereich werden durch die Endochronentheorie von Beginn der Belastung an plastische Deformationen dargestellt. Hier ist keine Fließgrenze einzuführen, es ergibt sich vielmehr automatisch durch die vereinfachte Formulierung wie sie Valanis (1971) für Metalle verwandt hat, ein im Grenzwert der Fließbedingung von Prandle-Reuss identisches Verhalten. Bei Belastungsumkehr ergibt sich eine Versteifung des Materials, wodurch ein Hysteresisverhalten modellierbar ist, welches bei den meisten Materialien auftritt. Hierzu gibt Bild 1 einen anschaulichen Eindruck.

Für den Bereich sekundären Kriechens wurden die Stoffunktionen der Theorie so angesetzt, daß eine dem Modell 1-NEWTON äquivalente Darstellung gefunden wurde. Somit ist für den 1-D Referenzversuch das Verhalten im sekundären Kriechbereich identisch dem der unter 3.2 angegebenen Stoffmodelle.

3.4 Materialkonstanten

Die Materialkonstanten wurden in Abstimmung mit den bei Wallner (1981) angegebenen Werten berechnet. Der einaxiale Zylinderdruckversuch dient als Referenzversuch. Für die

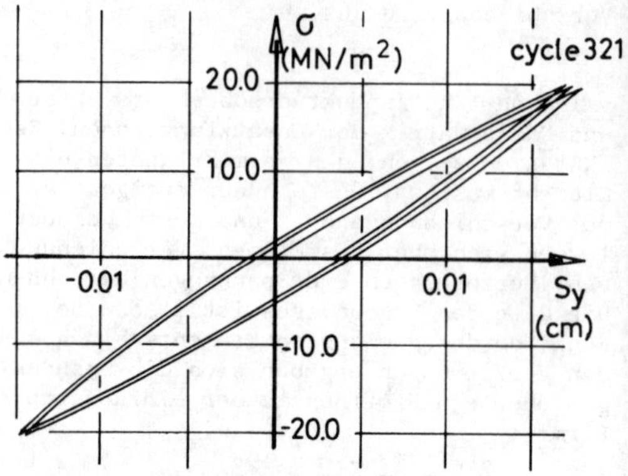

Bild 1: Zyklisches Verhalten eines Hohlzylinders unter Verwendung der Endochronentheorie

3 Stoffmodelle sind in den Berechnungen die folgenden Werte angesetzt worden.

Modell 1 - NEWTON:

$G = 9920$ MN/m²
$\nu = 0{,}25$
$n = 5$
$\eta_o = 0{,}907 \cdot 10^{-7}$ MN·d/m²

Modell 2 - WEERTMANN:

$G = 9920$ MN/m²
$\nu = 0{,}25$
$n = 5$
$A = 2{,}16 \cdot 10^{10}$ 1/d

Modell 3 - ENDOCHRONENTHEORIE:

$G = 9920$ MN/m²
$\nu = 0{,}25$
$a_1 = 0{,}025$
$n = 5$
$\eta_o = 0{,}907 \cdot 10^{-7}$ MN·d/m²

4. RECHENERGEBNISSE

Die vorliegenden Berechnungen wurden an einem Randwertproblem durchgeführt, für welches in situ Meßergebnisse aus Laborversuchen zur Beschreibung des Spannungs-Dehnungsverhaltens vorliegen.

Es handelt sich um ein tiefes Bohrloch im Asse-Steinsalz, für welches die entsprechende Elementierung sowie die Randbedingungen im Standardfall dem Bild 2 zu entnehmen sind.

Die Messungen und Rechnungen werden in einer Tiefe von 1042m unter der Annahme eines hydrostatischen Spannungszustandes vorgenommen. Als Wichte wird $\gamma = 0{,}0216$ MN/m³ angesetzt. Im Standardfall wird gemäß Bild 2 mit 4 Knoten-isoparametrischen Elementen gearbeitet. Da sich die Konvergenzmeßebene in

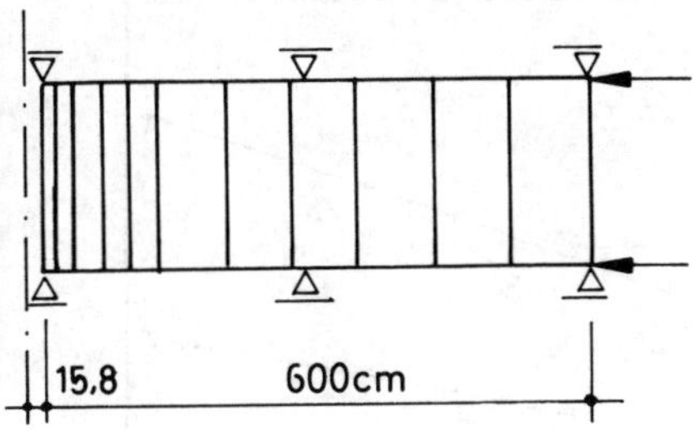

Bild 2: Elementierung des Problems tiefes Bohrloch

sehr großer Tiefe befindet, kann die Aufgabe in vertikaler Richtung als ebenes Verzerrungsproblem aufgefaßt werden (Bild 2). Eine andere mögliche Randbedingung erhält man durch Freischneiden in horizontaler Richtung am oberen Rand und unter Ansatz der dort freigeschnittenen vertikalen Spannungen (Δ im Bild 3).
Die unterschiedlichen Konvergenzraten beider Annahmen sind dem Bild 3 zu entnehmen.

Es ergeben sich recht ähnliche Systemantworten, sodaß der Einfluß der Gestaltung des oberen Randes nicht sehr wesentlich ist. Nach Ersetzen des horizontalen Gebirgsdrukkes durch feste Lager am rechten Rand des Bildes 2 ergibt sich (+ im Bild 3) keine Änderung des Konvergenzverhaltens. Das Elementnetz ist also genügend groß gewählt worden.
Von wesentlicher Bedeutung für die Güte der Ergebnisse ist die Art der Diskretisierung. In Bild 4 sind unterschiedliche Diskretisierungen verglichen. Die Standardlösung mit einem 4 Knotenelement ist mit einem Δ dargestellt. Bei einer Netzverfeinerung nahe des Bohrlochrandes (o in Bild 4) ergeben sich deutlich höhere Konvergenzraten und nicht so stark abfallende effektive Spannungen. Bei Verwendung eines höherwertigen 8-Knotenelementes (+ in Bild 4) ergeben sich bei nahezu gleichem Verlauf der effektiven Spannung im Vergleich zum feineren 4-Knotennetz deutlich größere Konvergenzen. Es zeigt sich also, daß der Einfluß der Diskretisierung sehr stark ist und daß das 4-Knotenelement keine optimalen Ergebnisse liefert. Betont sei an dieser Stelle, daß entgegen weit verbreiteter Meinung, daß ein 4-Knotenelement keine volumenkonstante Ver-

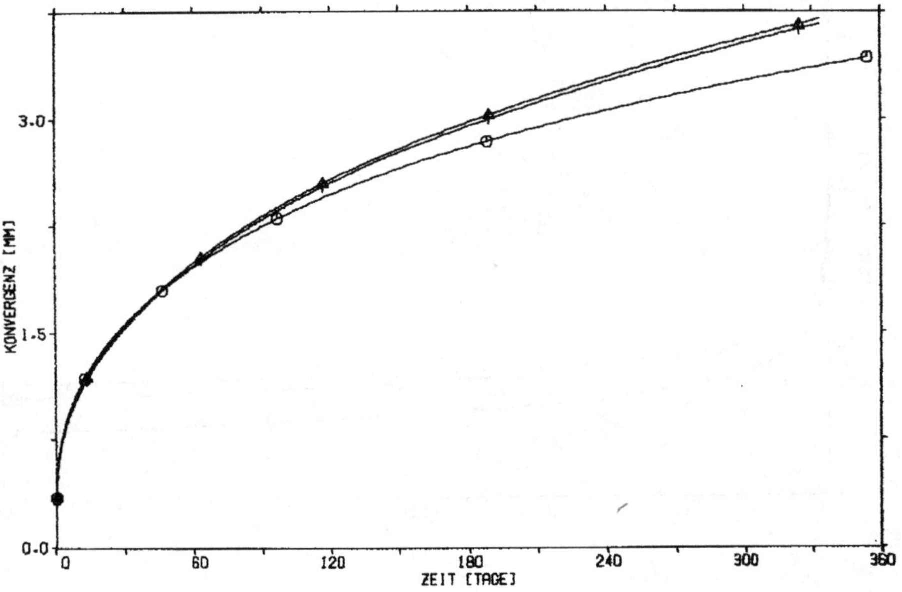

o Randbedingungen gemäß Bild 2
Δ oberer Rand freigeschnitten
+ oberer Rand freigeschnitten, rechter Rand festes Lager

Bild 3: Konvergenz bei unterschiedlichen Randbedingungen

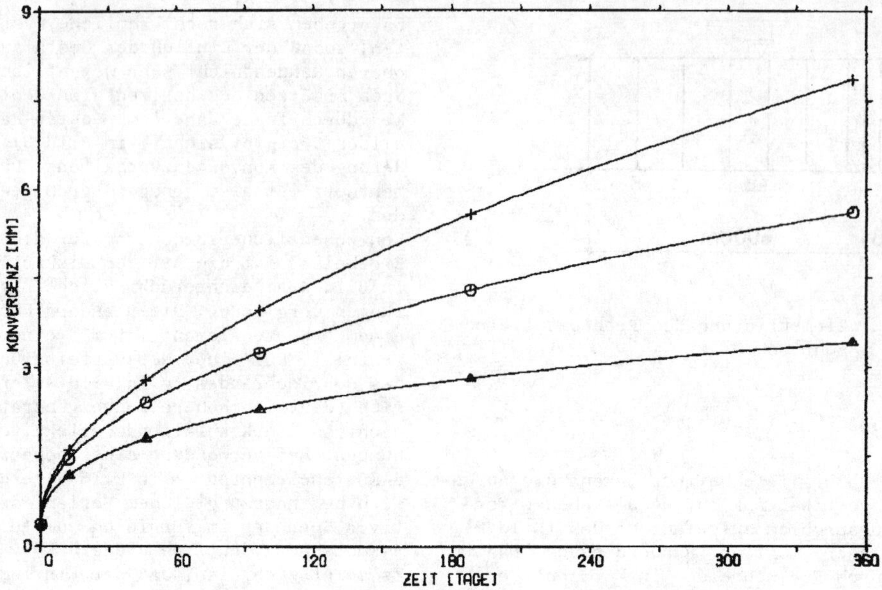

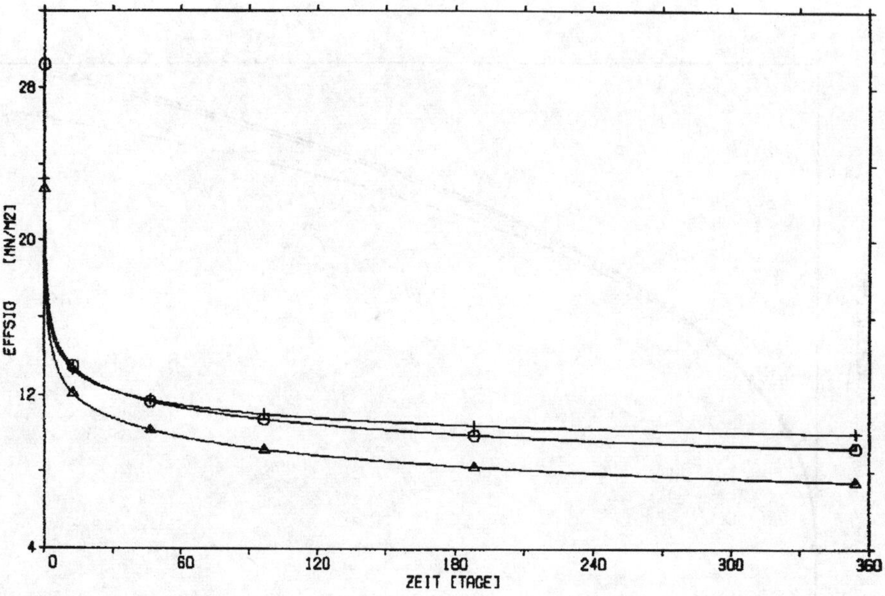

Δ	Konfiguration gemäß Bild 2	NEQ = 11
o	4-Knotenelement mit Netzverfeinerung	NEQ = 15
+	8-Knotenelement	NEQ = 23

Bild 4: Einfluß der Diskretisierung auf Konvergenz und effektive Spannung im ersten Element

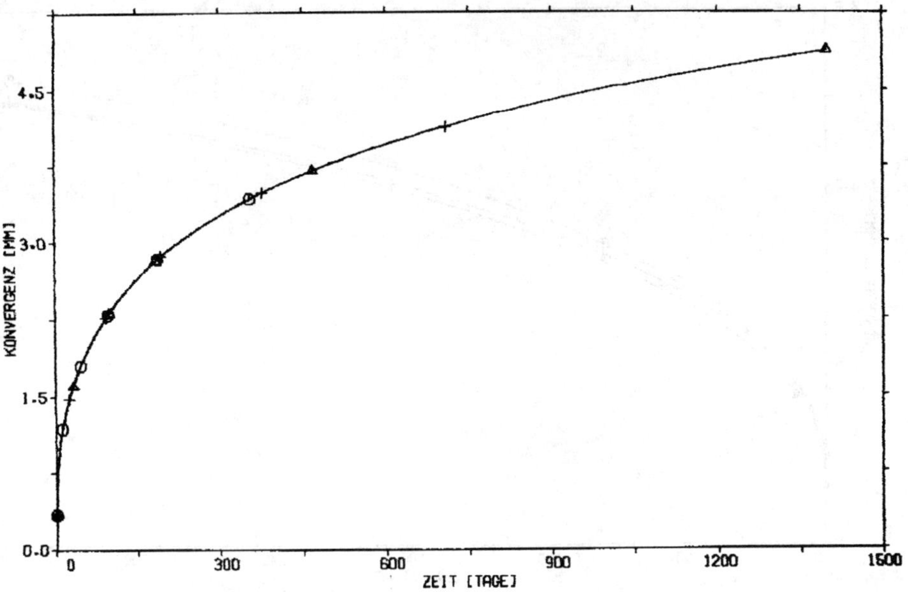

o $\Delta t_o = 0{,}05$ d $\Delta t_i = \Delta t_{i-1} \cdot 1{,}05$

Δ $\Delta t_o = 0{,}05$ d $\Delta t_i = \Delta t_{i-1} \cdot 1{,}10$

\+ $\Delta t_o = 0{,}10$ d $\Delta t_i = \Delta t_{i-1} \cdot 1{,}05$

Bild 5: Einfluß der Zeitschrittsteuerung auf die Konvergenz

formung darstellen kann, von den Autoren bei der Berechnung eines ebenen Biegebalkens ($\varepsilon_3 = 0$) nahezu ideal sekundäres Kriechen ohne jedwede numerische Verfestigung berechnet werden konnte.

Um die Empfindlichkeit des Ergebnisses gegen Veränderungen der Zeitschrittlänge zu untersuchen, sind im Bild 5 drei unterschiedliche Ansätze verglichen. Alle drei liefern identische Konvergenzen, womit die Stabilität der hier vorgestellten Ergebnisse demonstriert ist. Es darf dabei nicht außer acht gelassen werden, daß abhängig vom jeweiligen Problem unterschiedliches Stabilitätsverhalten auftritt, so daß bei empirischer Zeitschrittsteuerung Vorsicht geboten ist und auch dort Variationsrechnungen nötig sind.

Nach der Betrachtung einiger numerischer Approximation soll jetzt auf die stoffliche übergegangen werden.

In Bild 6 ist der Einfluß der unterschiedlichen Theorien auf das sekundäre Kriechen gezeigt. Die Endochronentheorie zeigt zwar erheblich größere Sofortverformungen, die aus dem nichtlinearen Ansatz für diesen Bereich zu erwarten waren, nach längerer Kriechzeit jedoch nähert sich ihr Ergebnis dem des rheologischen Newton Modelles an. Da das sekundäre Kriechen in der Endochronentheorie durch eben dieses Modell dargestellt wird, ist dies Ergebnis auf dem ersten Blick nicht verwunderlich. Bei diesem Randwertproblem wird jedoch das sekundäre mit dem Übergangskriechen, welches durch Spannungsumlagerungen hervorgerufen wird, überlagert, und dadurch wäre durch die andere Art des Sofortbereiches ein unterschiedliches Verhalten zu erwarten gewesen. Wie die effektiven Spannungen zeigen, sind diese bei allen Modellen sehr ähnlich, sodaß durch die gewählten Kriechgesetze, die nur von den Spannungen und nicht von den Verformungen abhängen, ein nahezu identisches Kriechverhalten hervorgerufen wird.

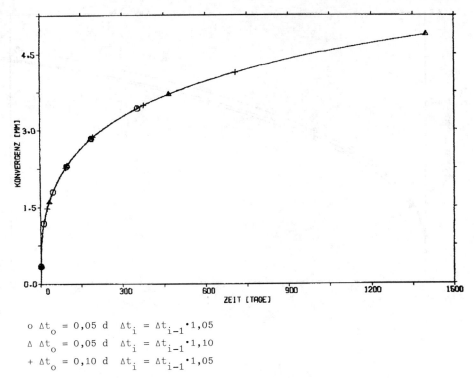

Im Gegensatz zum Kriechmodell hat eine Veränderung der Poisson-Zahl bei konstantem Schubmodul einen erheblichen Einfluß, sowohl auf die Konvergenz, als auch auf die effektiven Spannungen im bohrlochnahen Element (Bild 7).
Durch die unterschiedliche Kompressibilität fallen die effektiven Spannungen unterschiedlich schnell ab, für die höchste Poisson-Zahl ergibt sich die stärkste Redu-

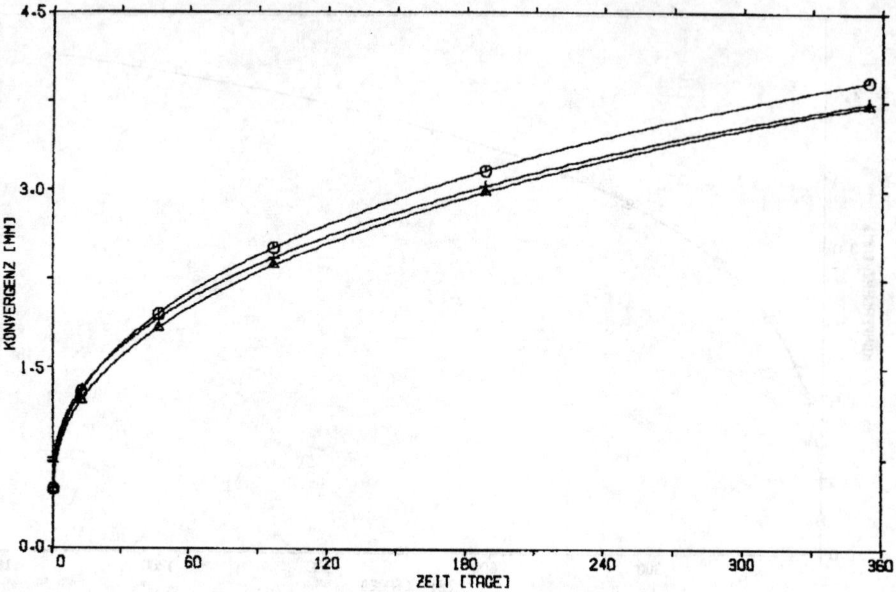

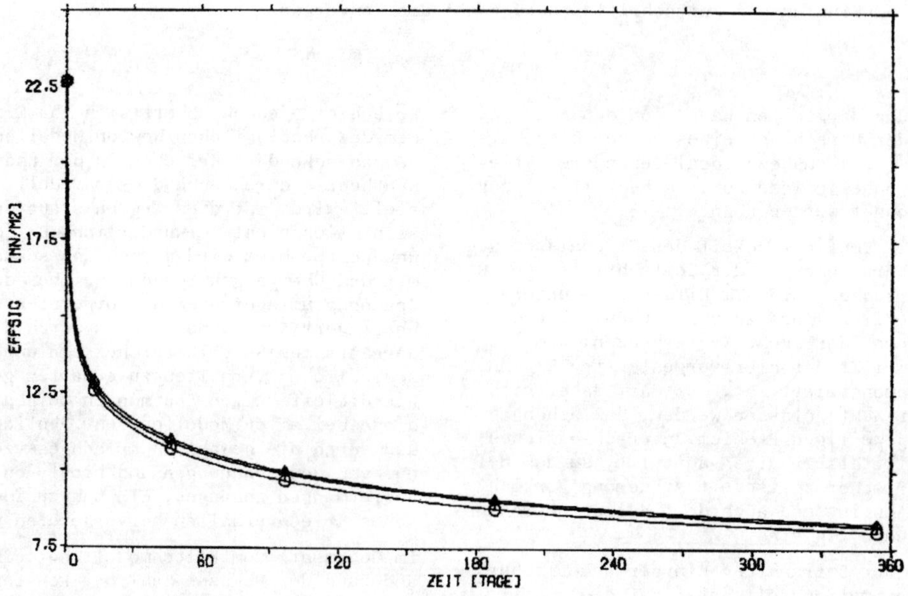

△ Modell 1 - Newton
o Modell 2 - Weertmann
+ Modell 3 - Endochronentheorie

Bild 6: Einfluß des Kriechmodelles auf Konvergenz und effektive Spannungen im ersten Element

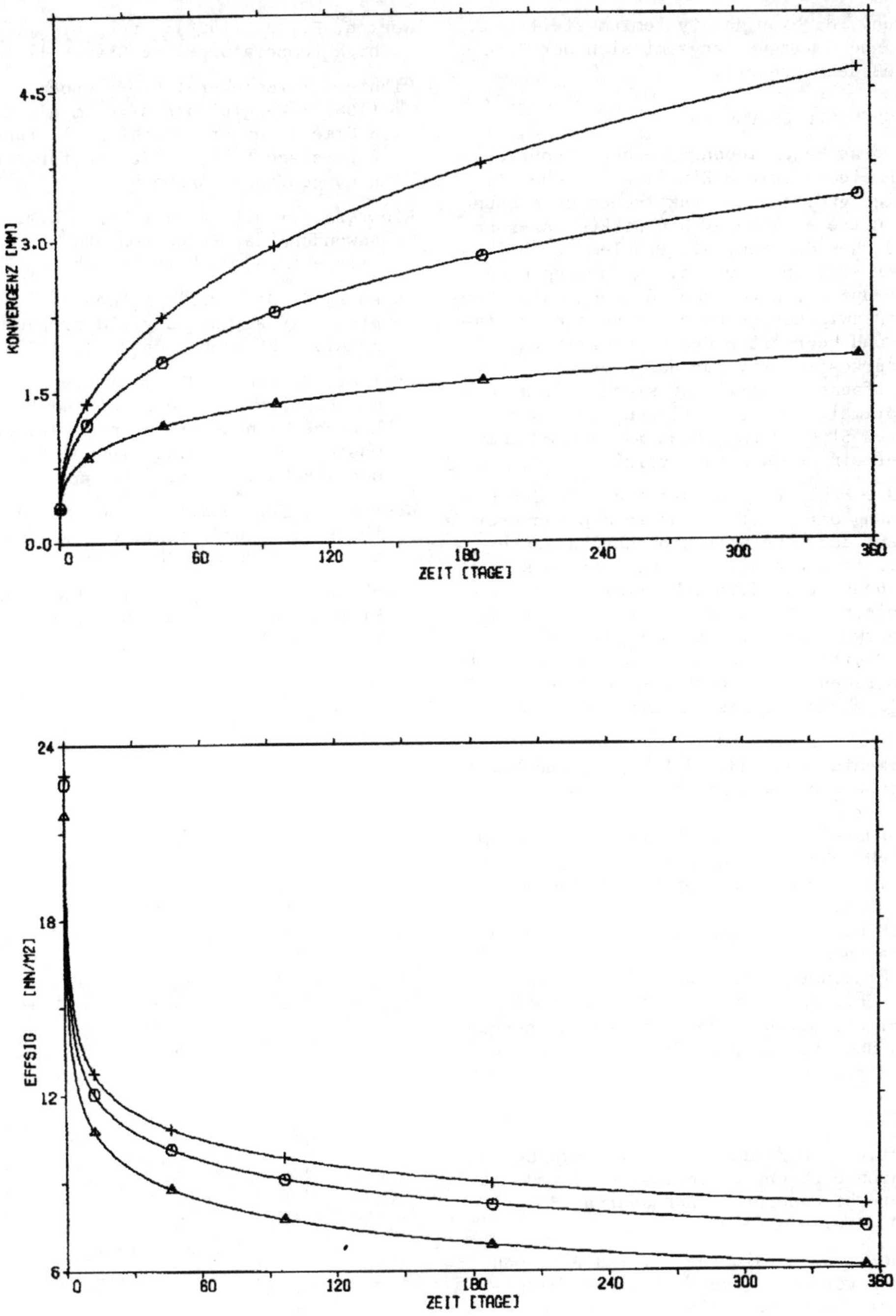

Δ $\nu = 0,40$
o $\nu = 0,25$
\+ $\nu = 0,10$

Bild 7: Einfluß der Poisson-Zahl auf Konvergenz und effektive Spannungen im ersten Element zierung, da hier das System am steifestem ist, und damit verlangsamt sich der Kriechprozeß sehr schnell.

5. SCHLUSSFOLGERUNGEN

Die voran beschriebenen Rechenergebnisse geben einen kleinen Einblick, welche Schwierigkeiten bei praktischen Berechnungen auftreten können. Die Diskretisierung ist sicher das zentrale Problem der Methode der Finiten Elemente, da der Ingenieur immer auf der Suche nach dem optimalen Kompromiß zwischen gewünschter Rechengenauigkeit und begrenzter Rechnerkapazität und Rechnerkosten ist. Für das hier vorgestellte einfache Beispiel ist sicher leicht eine optimale Lösung zu finden, bei komplizierten Strukturen jedoch muß dieses immer wieder ein neues Suchen sein.

Bei der Wahl des Stoffgesetzes und der Bestimmung der Stoffkonstanten muß beachtet werden, daß scheinbar grob abschätzbare Konstanten, wie dies oft von der Poisson-Zahl gedacht wird, bei bestimmten Problemen einen erheblichen Einfluß auf die Systemantwort haben. Eine Variation sämtlicher Stoffparameter ist also grundsätzlich anzustreben, wobei auch hier ein Kompromiß bezüglich Rechnerkosten gefunden werden muß.

Zusammenfassend läßt sich sagen, daß bei Kriechberechnungen vor allem zu beachten ist:

1. Ausreichend feine Diskretisierung im Bereich hoher Spannungsgradienten, die ursächlich für den Kriechprozeß verantwortlich sind.
2. Eine sehr sorgfältige Wahl der Randbedingungen.
3. Eine sorgfältige Wahl des Stoffgesetzes, wobei darauf zu achten ist, daß die natürliche Streuung der Laborversuchsergebnisse über Parameterstudien in die endgültige Berechnung einbezogen wird.

6. LITERATUR

Bazant, Z., P./Bhat, D., P. (1976): Endochronic theory of inelasticity and failure of concrete, ASCE Journal EM 4, 701-722.

Borchert, K.-M./Richter, T. (1979): Spannungsverformungsverhalten von Salzgestein unter mehraxialer Belastung, Kali und Steinsalz 10, 3-11.

Borchert, K.-M./Hebener, H./Richter, T. (1981): Creep calculations on salt by using an endochronic material law- compared to other creep formulations, First Conference of the Mechanical Behavior of Salt, Pennsylvania.

Norton, F., H. (1929): Creep of steel at high temperatures, Mc Graw-Hill.

Richter, T./Borchert, K.-M./Hebener, H. (1981): Vergleich einiger möglicher 3 dimensionaler Kriechformulierungen für Salzgestein, 3. Tagung für Ingenieurgeologie, Ansbach.

Richter, T./Wulf, A./Borchert, K.M.(1981): Anwendung der Endochronentheorie auf Salzgestein, Rock Mechanics 13,131-143.

Valanis, K.,D. (1971): A theory of viscoplasicity without a yield surface, Archives of Mechanics 23/4, 517 - 551.

Wallner, Manfred (1981): Analysis of Thermomechanical problems related to the storage of heat producing radioactive wastes in Salt rock, First Conf. of the Mech. Behav. of Salt, Pennsylvania.

Weertmann, J. (1968): Dislocation climb theory of steady state creep, Transactions, ASME 61, 668 - 694.

Zienkiewicz, O., C., (1971): The Finite Element Method in Engineering Science, Mc Grax-Hill.

A ROCK MECHANICS INVESTIGATION FOR THE STABILITY OF AN UNDERGROUND ORE STORAGE CHAMBER

Felsmechanische Untersuchung der Stabilität einer untertägigen Erzlagerkammer

Une investigation de la stabilité d'une caverne employée comme dépôt souterrain dans une mine

A.G.PAŞAMEHMETOĞLU, T.Y.IRFAN, A.BILGIN, A.ÖZGENOĞLU, C.KARPUZ

Middle East Technical University, Ankara, Turkey

SUMMARY:

In this paper, rock mechanics investigations carried out on the future behaviour and support requirements of a large cavern planned to be utilized as a chamber for ore storage which is under early stages of its construction are presented. This cavern which is to be excavated in weak granodiorite and scarn, will have the dimensions of 15 m width, 40 m height, and 60 m length when completed.

To reach the goal, rock mechanical parameters have been extensively studied. In this respect, major geological patterns and their strength characteristics have been established together with the physical and mechanical properties of the ore bearing rock (scarn) and the wall rock (marble and altered granodiorite). Moreover, the state of stress in the area was measured.

Large proportion of the data thus obtained was integrated into different rock mass classification systems. Back analysis has been carried out. Stability of ore storage cavern is studied and measures to be taken are suggested.

ZUSAMMENFASSUNG:

In der vorliegenden Arbeit werden die felsmechanische Untersuchungsergebnisse über das Zukunftsverhalten einer grossen Untertage-Aushöhlung vorgestellt und Abstützungserfordernisse für dieses Raum festgelegt, welches zum Lagern von Erz bestimmt ist und sich im Anfangsstadium der Herstellung befindet. Diese im minderfesten Granodiorit und Skarn auszuhöhlende Kaverne wird, wenn fertiggestellt, 40 m hoch, 15 m breit und 60 m lang sein.

Um das Ziel zu erreichen, wurden die felsmechanische Parameter ausführlich untersucht. In diesem Zusammenhang wurden die massgebenden geologischen Formen und deren Festigkeitseigenschaften sowie die mechanischen und physikalischen Eigenschaften des erzhältigen Gesteins (Skarn) und des Nebengesteins (Marmor und verwittertes Granodiorit) festgelegt. Ausserdem wurden die spannungszustände in dem Gebirge gemessen.

Ein grosser Teil der so erhaltenen Messdaten wurden in die verschicdene Klassifizierungssysteme der Gesteinsmassen hinein integriert und retrograden Analysen wurden duzchgeführt. Schliesslich wurde die standfestigkeit des Erzlagerkammersstudiert und die hierzu notwendigen Massnahmen vorgeschlagen.

RÉSUMÉ:

Dans cet ouvrage, les recherches pour le soutenemant et la tenue d'un large caverne à excaver comme le magasin pour le minerai produit dans la mine de scheelite à Uludağ(Bursa) sont faites. Ce caverne sera excavé dans une roche de faible grano-diorite et scarn, ayant des dimensions nettes de 15 metres de largeur, 40 metres de hauteur et 60 metres de longueur finalement.

A fin de pouvoir à accomplire cet oeuvre, les parametres mécaniques ont été étudieés soigneusement. Dans ce domain, les structures géologiques et les propriétés mecaniques de cettes roches ont été determinees. De plus, l'état de contraintes dans cette zône a été étudié.

Graces aux résultats ainsi obténus on est arrivé à un system de classification des masses rocheuse en question. Une analyse est faite et la stabilité de catte chambre est étudiée et les précautions à prendre ont été suggerées.

1 INTRODUCTION

Uludağ tungsten deposit is located in the province of Bursa, northwest Turkey. Ore bearing rock, scarn occurs between elevations of 2100 m and 2300 m above sea level. Lengthy and severe winter conditions prevail in the area. Near surface part of the deposit is exploited by open pit mining. Sublevel stoping method is applied to extract the ore underground (Figure 1). Stopes having dimensions of up to 15 m width, 30 m height and 100 m length are created as a result of this mining method.

Rock mechanical investigations under a project program covered the whole mine both underground and open pit. The work done to evaluate the future behaviour and support requirements of a large cavern, which is planned to serve as ore storage chamber for the output of open pit mine, will be given here. This cavern which is under early stages of its construction will have the dimensions of 15 m width, 40 m height and 60 m length when completed. The originality of this work is that the storage cavern will be opened up by the sublevel stoping method rather than conventional large excavation opening method.

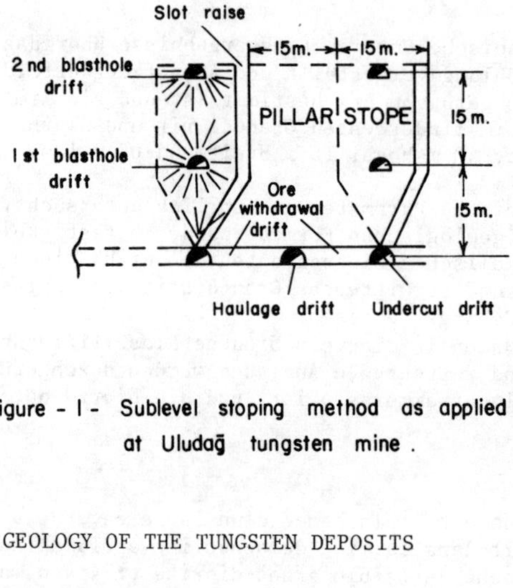

Figure - 1 - Sublevel stoping method as applied at Uludağ tungsten mine .

2 GEOLOGY OF THE TUNGSTEN DEPOSITS

2.1 Geological setting

Uludağ tungsten mine is situated between marbles of Palaeozoic-aged Metamorphic Series and the younger granodioritic batholith. The Metamorphic series of the Uludağ massif are composed of amphibolites, gneisses and marbles at the base overlain by mica-schists,phyllites and semi-marbles. These in turn are overlain by Permian - Carboniferous clastics and limestones (Erk 1942).

Tungsten bearing minerals are found in the scarn rocks which are formed as a result of contact metamorphism of marbles by the intrusion of a granodioritic batholith, and also at higher levels in the granodiorite close to the contact zone (Kaaden 1954). Marbles are very poor in tungsten ore and tungsten bearing scheelite mineral is present only in thin vein formations. Two types of scarn have been recognized (İnan 1979):

1. Endoscarn is formed as a thin band within the magmatic mass of the contact zone and represents the metasomatically altered granodiorite.
2. Exoscarn is formed within the marbles by contact metamorphism process.

Granodiorite in the mine area is a grey, medium-grained, biotite rich rock with plagioclase (40-45 %), alkalifeldspar (13-15 %), quartz, biotite and muscovite as the main constituents. Fine-grained aplitic dykes and granodioritic porphyrites cut marbles, amphibolites and gneisses and have been extensively altered within the scarn.

2.2 Structural properties

The location of scarn sheets is controlled by the structural elements in the mine area. Metamorphism has been controlled by the regional geologic structure and as a result scarn is formed as sheet, generally parallel to the bedding planes and sometimes cutting across the marble beds (Figure.2). Away from the granodiorite contact scarn zones thin away and disappear. Commercial scheelite mineralization is particularly developed in the brecciated, sheared contact zone and in the joints, fractures, shear zones within scarn and along scarn-marble contacts. Scarn-granodiorite contact zone is generally sheared, crushed and brecciated due to the forcible intrusion of the batholith and tectonism. Shear zones are also present within granodiorite, scarn and marbles. A number of these zones cross the proposed ore storage chamber presenting stability problems in the underground mine.

Thickness of individual scarn zones vary between 0 and 75 m and the total thickness of scarn reaches 250 m. Scarn sheets show a general dip of 15°-35° towards northeast. Relatively new, NE-SW striking faults which cut ore-bearing scarn and marbles are present in the area (Ketin 1947).

3 GEOTECHNICAL INVESTIGATIONS

Ore storage chamber is under early stages of its construction between 2150 m and 2190 m levels in the northwestern part of the present underground mine. Investigations carried out in various already opened galleries of the ore storage chamber and in nearby areas are summarized on an engineering geological plan (Figure 3) and on a geological section (Figure 4).

3.1 Physical and mechanical properties

The results of some physical and mechanical properties of the ore bearing rock (scarn) and the wall rocks (marble and altered granodiorite) as determined in the laboratory from core samples are given in Table 1.

3.2 Engineering geological properties

Extensive field studies have been carried out in various already opened galleries of the proposed cavern and in nearby galleries to establish the structural patterns. Discontinuities measured in the ore storage cavern area have been plotted on an equal area Schmidt net and the dominant discontinuity sets have been determined. The results of discontinuity analysis is shown in Table 2. The two most dominant discontinuity sets are joint sets 1a-b and 2a-b striking approximately N-S and E-W respectively. The most important discontinuities which will affect the stability of the ore storage chamber are the NNE-SSW striking shear and fault zones and the crushed, sheared contact zone.

Granodiorite in this area is moderately to highly altered to a rock-soil mixture by hydrothermal solutions and weathering (alteration has particularly affected plagioclase feldspars changing them into gritty-soft kaolinite minerals). Altered soil zones, which are mainly composed of quartz and kaolinized feldspars, are generally developed in N-S direction, thickness varying between a few mm and 750 mm. These soil zones enclose in between them less altered or relatively fresh granodiorite blocks. Granodiorite shows increased alteration in areas of intense quartz-pyrite veining and the effect of weathering increases towards the surface. Alteration grade scheme used for mapping the underground mine is shown in Table 3. This grading scheme is a modified form of the weathering grade scheme developed for granite (Dearman, Baynes and Irfan 1978) and the effects of hydrothermal alteration have been included in devising the system.

Rapid weatherability is one of the problems encountered in galleries opened in altered granodiorite. Shortly after the excavation of the galleries soil zones in contact with the atmosphere and water soften and failure occurs in the form of scaling and rock falls resulting in the enlargement of these galleries if left unsupported.

Towards the southeastern corner of the ore storage chamber at 2150 m level (Figure 3) sheared, brecciated endoscarn ("granitic scarn") is present at the contact between the granodiorite below and scarn above. This contact zone rises up towards the north and is met at 2165 m and 2180 m level. There are a number of shear zones cutting obliquely the present galleries and the ore storage cavern; the thickest one reaching 20 m and thinning upwards towards the surface in scarn and marbles (Figure 4). These zones are composed of sheared, kaolinized, epidotized weak rock and soil, and contain pegmatitic veins or pockets of quartz and pyrite in granodiorite.

3.3 Rock mass classification

The galleries, which are cut by shear zones, such as 2nd. and 3rd. haulage drifts and undercut drift are driven in Grade-III and

Table 1. Physical and mechanical properties

Rock type	Uniaxial compressive strength (MPa)	Modulus of elasticity ($1x10^4$ MPa)	Poisson's ratio	Cohesion (MPa)	Internal friction angle (degree)	Unit weight (kN/m^3)	Tensile strength (indirect) (MPa)
Marble	103	6.4	0.22	18.5	41	27.5	11
Granodiorite	64-83	2-5.25	0.14-0.19	21-34	53	25.5	7.8-8.6
Scarn	13-152	0.8-12	0.15-0.28	6-43	29-57	33.3	1.6-17

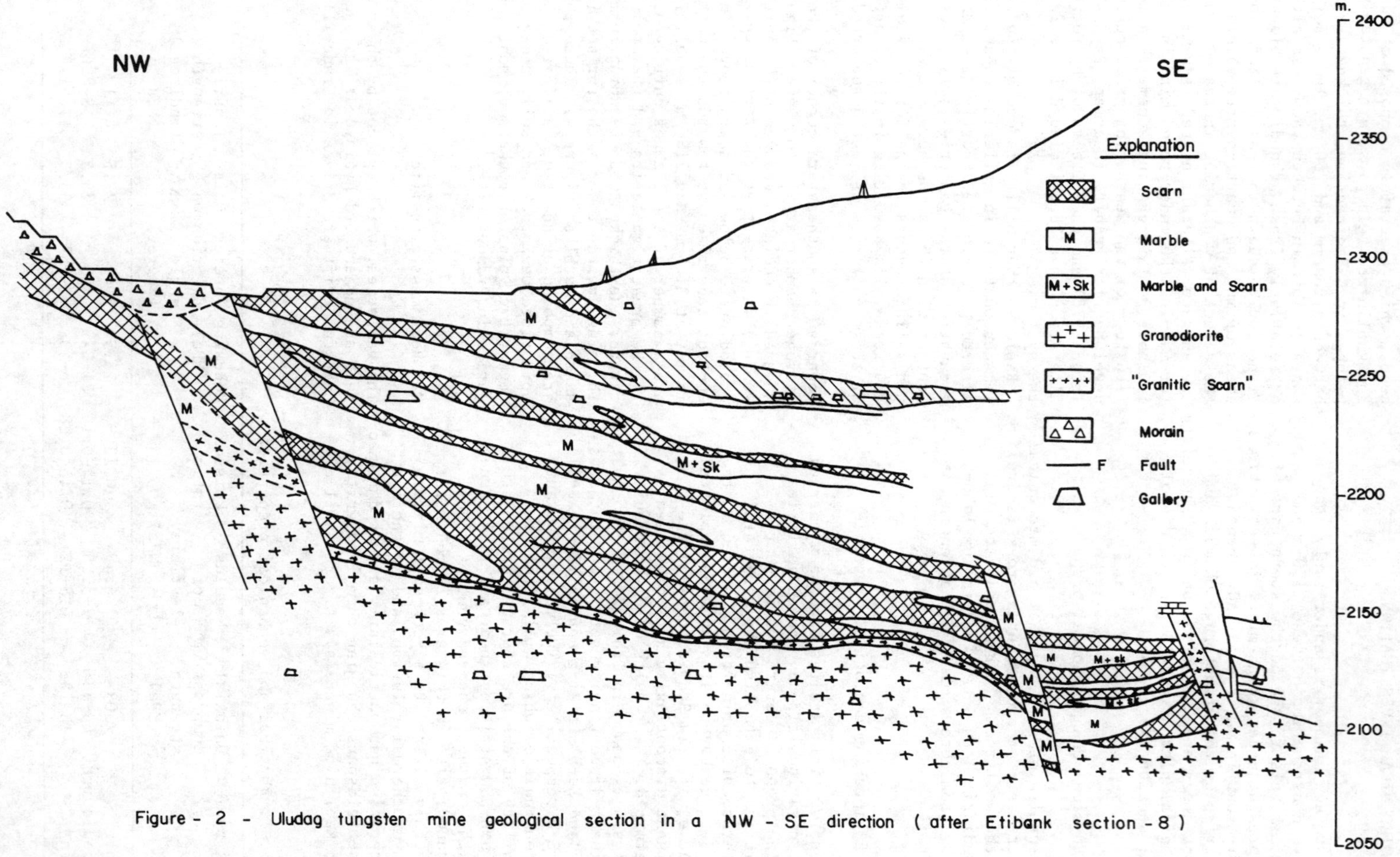

Figure - 2 - Uludag tungsten mine geological section in a NW - SE direction (after Etibank section - 8)

Table 2. Discontinuity sets and their general properties in ore storage chamber area (granodiorite and scarn)

Discontinuity No Type	Dip direction(°)	Dip amount(°)	Properties
1a Joint	263 ∓ 8	66(55-90)	Granodiorite is moderately to highly altered (Soil:
	and		20-50 %); intense quartz-pyrite veins and kaoliniza-
	092 ∓ 11	70(60-90)	tion on joint surfaces; occasional calcite veins
1b Joint	102 ∓ 5	88(80-90)	Joints in scarn contain chlorite, pyrite, calcite; altered clayey surfaces
2a Joint	187 ∓ 10	73(65-90)	Less frequent quartz-pyrite veins; thin (10-30 mm)
2b Joint	345 ∓ 6	70(65-75)	altered zones
3 Joint	066 ∓ 4	50(50-65)	Less dominant; some quartz-pyrite veins
Shear zones	NNE-SSW striking		In granodiorite : 3-20 m thick; intensely fractured, kaolinized, epidotized, pegmatitic weak rock and soil zones In scarn : A number of closely spaced fault zones with pyrite, calcite and/or clay fillings, highly altered surfaces

Table 3. A simplified alteration grading system used in geotechnical mapping of Uludağ tungsten mine

Term	Mass alteration grade	Description
Fresh granodiorite	GI	Fresh, no effects of weathering or alteration
Slightly altered granodiorite	GII	Slight discoloration on the joint surfaces
Moderately altered granodiorite	$GIII_i$	Occasional, altered (kaolinized) thin zones, soil : <10 %
	$GIII_{ii}$	Frequent altered (kaolinized) zones, soil : 10-50 %
Highly altered granodiorite	GIV	Altered (kaolinized), soil :> 50 %
Completely altered granodiorite	GV	Completely decomposed to soil

Grade-IV granodiorite. This rock is classified as poor-very poor rock according to Bieniawski (1979), poor-extremely poor rock according to Barton et al (1974)(Table 4). 4 m high, 4-5 m wide permanent galleries in the cavern area are generally supported by steel sets at 1-2 m intervals. Very dense timber support exits in the southern part of the 2nd haulage drift where a thick shear zone is present. Part of the blasthole drift which is driven in scarn at level 2170 m has no support (RMR=32, Q=1.5). At the contact zone and in granodiorite, steel supports are placed at 1.5-2 m intervals which becomes denser in the 6-8 m wide shear zone.

3.4 Measurement of in situ stress

Flat jack method which was the only method available is appealed to determine the state of stress in the area. Measurements are made with circular flat jacks at two locations. Horizontal and vertical field stresses are calculated from the tangential stresses measured at the bottom and at the sidewall of the gallery, the crosssection of which is assumed to be circular.

Calculations gave the vertical field stress as 4-4.5 MPa and the horizontal field stress as 2-2.3 MPa. The measured vertical stress was smaller than the vertical stress due to the weight of overburden. Limitations of the flat jack method is taken into consideration and the vertical stress due to overburden is used in Finite Element analysis. Nevertheless, as a result of these tests it has been understood that there

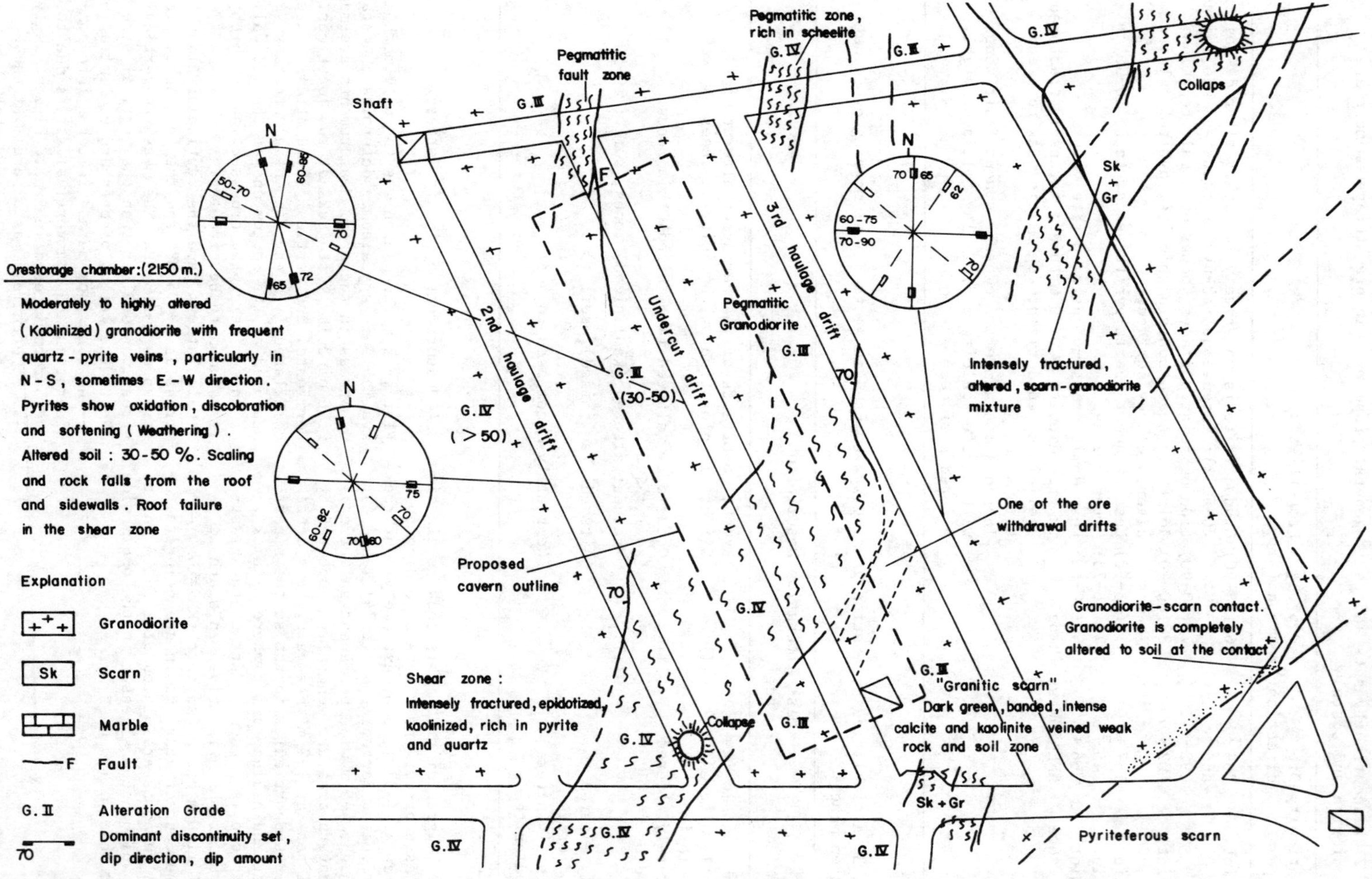

Orestorage chamber: (2150 m.)
Moderately to highly altered (Kaolinized) granodiorite with frequent quartz - pyrite veins, particularly in N - S, sometimes E - W direction.
Pyrites show oxidation, discoloration and softening (Weathering).
Altered soil : 30-50 %. Scaling and rock falls from the roof and sidewalls. Roof failure in the shear zone
Explanation
Granodiorite
Sk
Scarn
Marble
F
Fault
G. II
Alteration Grade
70
Dominant discontinuity set, dip direction, dip amount
(30-50) Altered soil amount
Shaft
G. III
Pegmatitic fault zone
F
Pegmatitic zone, rich in scheelite
G. IV
G. III
G. IV
Collaps
Sk
Gr
N
50-70
60-85
70
65
72
75
60-82
70
60
70
65
62
60 - 75
70-90
72
2nd haulage drift
Undercut drift
3rd haulage drift
G. III
(30-50)
G. IV
(> 50)
Pegmatitic Granodiorite
G. III
70
Intensely fractured, altered, scarn-granodiorite mixture
One of the ore withdrawal drifts
Proposed cavern outline
G. IV
Granodiorite-scarn contact. Granodiorite is completely altered to soil at the contact
Shear zone :
Intensely fractured, epidotized, kaolinized, rich in pyrite and quartz
G. IV
Collapse
G. III
G. III
"Granitic scarn"
Dark green, banded, intense calcite and kaolinite veined weak rock and soil zone
Sk + Gr
G. IV
G. IV
G. IV
Pyriteferous scarn

Figure - 3 - Engineering geological plan of ore storage chamber area (2150 m. level).

Table 4. Rock mass classification values, drift sizes and existing support

Location	Rock mass description	RMR	Q	Excavation year and support condition	Drift sizes(m)
Ore storage cavern blasthole drift 2170 m level	Scarn, pyrite rich, clay and calcite filled faults, slightly altered	32	1.5	1980, Unsupported	width:3.5 height:3.0
Ore storage cavern second and third haulage drifts 2150 m level	Moderately to highly altered granodiorite (GIII - GIV)	15	0.025	1980, closely spaced timber support, after trimming to 14 m^2 section steel sets placed, occasional spalling	width:4.0 height:5.0
Ore storage cavern undercut drift	Granodiorite, shear zone	8	0.04	1980, very closely spaced timber support (0-0.5 m), roof collapse and spalling	width:3.5 height:4.0

were no tectonic or residual stresses in the area.

4 FINITE ELEMENT ANALYSIS

Location and orientation of the ore storage cavern has already been chosen by the mine management at a place where adverse geologic conditions prevail. So, it became necessary to evaluate the stability of the cavern roof and walls, to determine the mode and extent of potential failures and to specify the extent of anchoring. Otherwise, without or with insufficient anchoring, several problems are to be expected ranging from dilution of ore to total collapse of the cavern. A FE analysis was performed with these ideas in mind.

Although the problem is three-dimensional in nature because of geological conditions, plane strain case is assumed in FE solution. Since the cavern has considerable cross-sectional area and the ring-holes are blasted in sequence from undercut drift to top blasthole drift (using delay firing), it can be accepted that cavern is excavated at once for each vertical slice; therefore, excavation sequence simulation is not necessary.

The applied FE program uses eight noded isoparametric quadrilateral elements. Totally 100 elements and 340 nodes were used for half section. Problem was solved for rectangular region assuming gravity loading with boundaries located at 60 to 80 m distance from the cavern outline. Except the upper boundary, normal displacement components were eliminated along the boundaries. Upper boundary nodes were free to move in both directions.

4.1 Results of the analysis

Major principal stress contours are shown in Figure 5. As it is seen from the figure the stresses are compressive and the largest major principal stresses are observed at the points where vertical and sloping sidewalls are met. Magnitude of the largest principal stress is 10 MN/m^2. Noting that the vertical in situ stress is roughly 5 MN/m^2, the excavation of the cavern produces a stress concentration of twice the original in situ stress. Recalling that the average quality scarn having a uniaxial compressive strength of 70 MN/m^2, the factor of safety against compression is (70/10) 7. However, as highly weathered or hydrothermally altered zones have a compressive strength of 12 MN/m^2, the safety factor reduces to (12/10) 1.2 at such zones.

Minor principal stress contours are shown in Figure 6. Tensile stress regions are observed at the roof (-0.5 MN/m^2), at the vertical sidewall (-0.2 MN/m^2) and at sloping sidewall near the floor. Highly weathered or altered zones having a tensile strength of 1.6 MN/m^2 yields a factor of safety of approximately (1.6/0.5) 3 against tensile failure. However, it must be emphasized that when the rock is sheared, jointed or altered as in the case of pegmatitic shear zones seen at various sections of the cavern, the tensile stresses may cause spalling and rock falls at such places.

5 ASSESSMENT OF DATA AND DISCUSSION

5.1 Stability of the cavern

With the geological and geotechnical information already given and under the light of FE analysis, the evaluation of stability

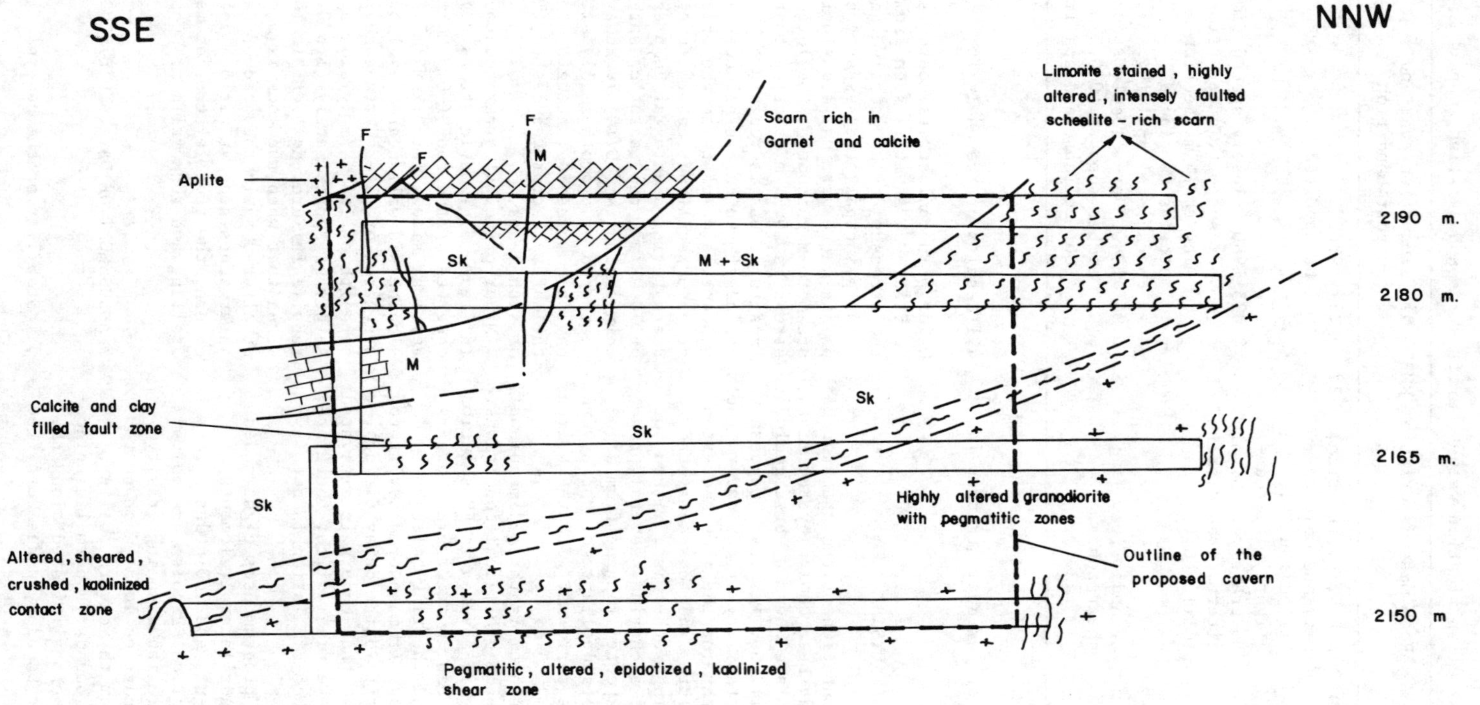

Figure - 4 - A simplified geological section of the ore storage chamber
Explanation : F = Fault, M = Marble, Sk = Scarn, M + Sk = Marble and Scarn

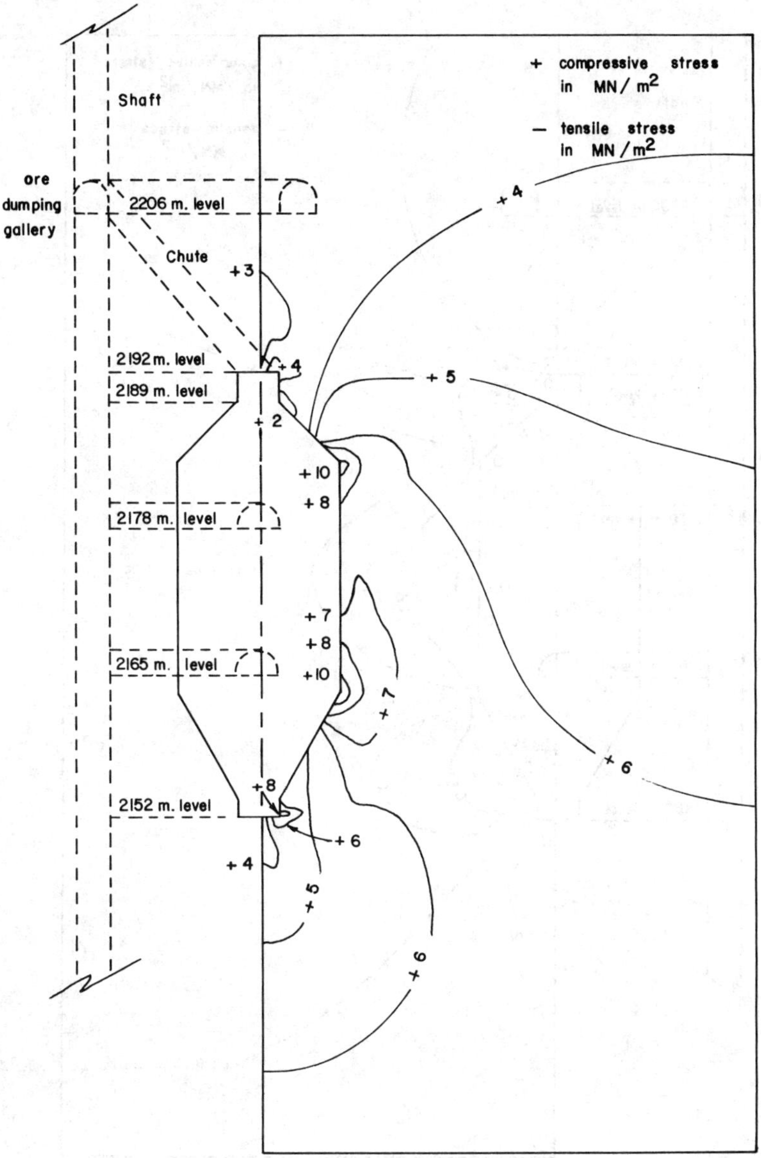

Figure - 5 - Major principal stress contours around ore storage cavern (cavern height 40 m., cavern width 15 m.)

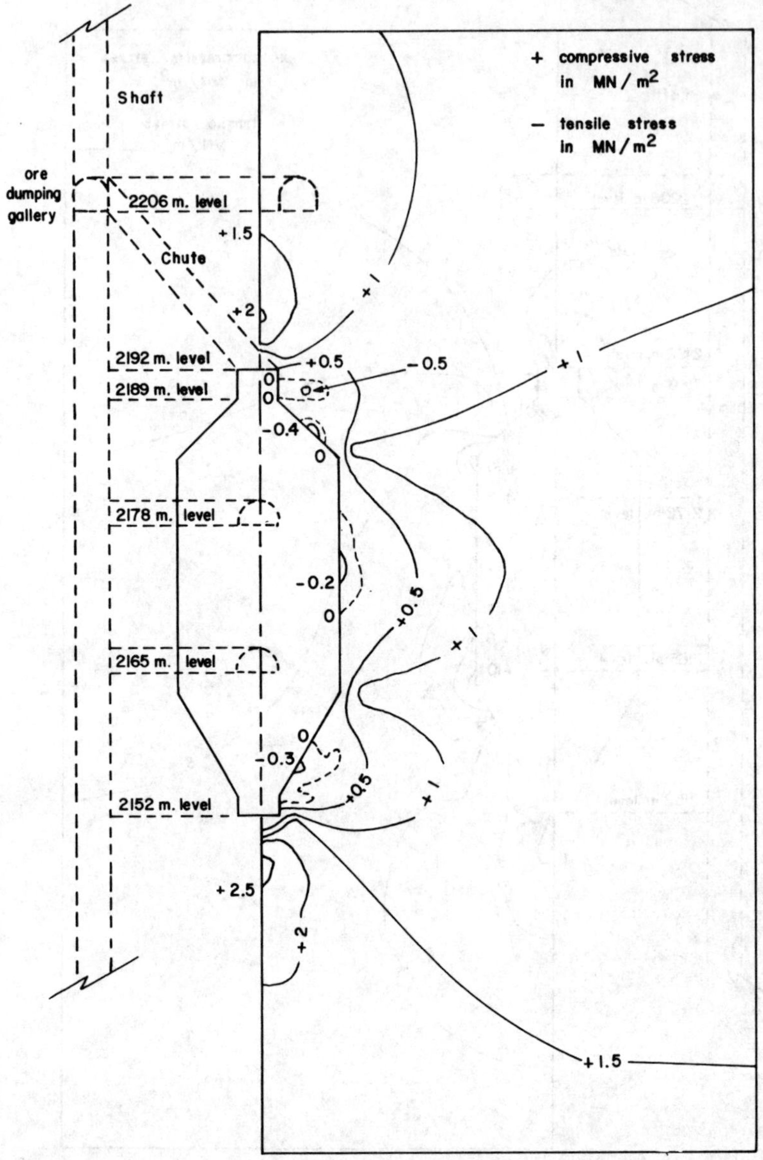

Figure – 6 – Minor principal stress contours around ore storage cavern (cavern height 40 m., cavern width 15 m.)

and the necessary preventive measures to be taken are as follows:

1. Cavern is located at the weaker part of the mine. However, its orientation is favorable with respect to orientation of discontinuities.

2. Cavern roof: Recalling that the factor of safety is low (F.S=3) against tensile failure and tensile region has a 4 m extent in the roof and the corresponding displacements amount to 15 cm, the shear zones, highly weathered scarn zones at various sections of the cavern roof may fail due to tensile stresses. For this reason, spalling and collapse of roof may take place and failure may continue depending upon the dimensions of the weak zone until natural stability occurs. Preventive measures could be the following:

a. 5-6 m long rock bolts cemented along full length should be applied in a regular ring pattern from 2189 m level before the excavation commences.

b. 10-15 m long cable bolting from 2206 m level towards 2189 m level before excavation starts.

3. Side wall: Tensile region penetrating 2 m into the sidewall and experiencing displacements up to 1 cm towards the cavern, when coincides with the weathered contact zone, may cause eventual failure. To eliminate failure possibilities at the sidewalls, it is proposed that the blasthole drifts should be opened, at both sides of the cavern instead of at the center, from where 4 m long rock bolts grouted along full length can be applied. This practice would also allow to apply shotcrete to sidewalls that prevents rapid weathering of granodiorite.

Drivage of blasthole drifts at the sides of the cavern also enables to apply cable bolting in ring pattern between the blasthole drift of a nearby cavern and that of one under consideration if a second cavern is to be excavated being symmetrical about the shaft (Figure 6). Such a practice will both strengthen the pillar between the caverns and decrease the extent of tensile regions at the sidewalls. However, it would be better to carry out a detailed analysis for the stability of pillar between the caverns if another cavern is to be opened up.

4. Inclined sidewalls at the bottom: The lower part of the cavern is to be excavated in highly weathered granodiorite where occurs a weathered, pegmatitic, kaolinized shear zone. Although FE analysis reveals safety factors of 2.5 and 5.0 against compression and tension respectively, highly weatherable character of granodiorite and presence of already weathered zone create potential failure dangers. Therefore, application of 4-5 m long nontensioned rock bolts grouted full length from both undercut drift and ore-withdrawal drifts is recommendable. Especially, the application of 2.5 cm thick shotcrete together with the bolts can decrease the rate of weathering and retain the stability of ore-withdrawal drifts. Rock bolts and shotcrete should be applied prior to excavation of the cavern.

5.2 Back analysis for ore-withdrawal drifts

The ore stored in the cavern will be drawn and loaded by Load-Haul-Dump cars from several ore-withdrawal drifts (Figure 1). Then, stability of these drifts which are planned to have 14 m^2 cross-sectional area becomes important. To estimate the support requirements for them, back analysis for the already existing galleries at various sections of the mine is carried out. That is, support system proposed by Bieniawski's (1979) and Barton et al's (1974) rock mass classification systems are compared with the applied supports (Table 5).

Under the light of this comparison it is found that Bieniawski's classification is rather conservative for this case. This is not surprising because Bieniawski's classification system is devised for tunnels of civil purposes. On the other hand, the support system proposed by Barton et al's Q-index is more consistent with the applied support sytem. Consistency is especially true for unsupported sections. Nevertheless, mine management tends to use the classical steel sets for supporting the ore-withdrawal drifts.

6 CONCLUSIONS

It is concluded that the ore storage chamber located at the weaker part of the mineralization can suffer from several types of instabilities. Together with the various types of supports assigned, a displacement monitoring program should be carried out. A detailed monitoring program making use of extensometers is given to the mine management. However, if it appears that the application of the stabilization measures is unjustified because of economical and practical reasons, this cavern should be regarded as a production stope.

Table 5. Support measures as proposed by different rock mass classification systems together with the existing supports in the mine for moderately weathered granodiorite

Rock type	According to Bieniawski's Geomechanics Classification	According to Barton et al's Tunnelling Quality Index	Applied Support in the mine
Moderately weathered granodiorite	RMR = 30 - 45 Systematic rock bolt 3-4 m long, spaced 1-1.5 m in crown and walls with wire mesh and shotcrete 100-150 mm in crown and 100 mm in sides and light to medium ribs spaced 1.5 m where required	Q = 0.3 - 0.5 (0.01-1.5) Tensioned rock bolts, spaced 1 m and 50 mm thick shotcrete reinforced with mesh	Steel sets spaced 1-1.5 m generally, 0.5-1 m occasionally, spalling with time if left unsupported

7 REFERENCES

Barton, N., R. Lien, J. Lunde 1974, Engineering classifications of rock masses for design of tunnel support, Rock Mechanics 6: 189-236.

Bieniawski, Z.T. 1979, The geomechanics classification in rock engineering applications, Proc. 4th. Cong. Int. Soc. Rock Mech., Montreux, 2:41-48.

Dearman, W.R., F.J. Baynes, T.Y. Irfan 1978, Engineering grading of weathered granite, Engng. Geol. 12:345-374.

Erk, S.A. 1942, Geologic study of Bursa-Gemlik district (in Turkish), M.T.A. Insitute 9.

İnan, K. 1979, Petrogenesis and geochemistry of Uludağ scarn belt (in Turkish), İstanbul, İ.T.Ü. Maden Fakültesi.

Kaaden, G. Vander 1954, Geologic report on Uludağ scheelite deposit (in Turkish), M.T.A. Institute 2202.

Ketin, I. 1947, About tectonics of Uludağ massif (in Turkish), İstanbul Geological Society Bulletin, Vol.1.

FLOW RATES OF AIR AND WATER FROM CAVERNS IN SOIL AND ROCK

Luft- und Wasserströmungsgeschwindigkeiten aus Kavernen in Erde und Fels

Vitesses d'écoulement de l'air et de l'eau à partir de cavernes dans un sol et dans un rocher

O.TOKHEIM
City of Oslo Geotechnical Division, Norway
N.JANBU
Norwegian Institute of Technology, Trondheim, Norway

SUMMARY:

Straightforward approximate formulas are presented for the estimation of flow rates of air (gas) and water (incompressible liquid) from a cavern in a permeable mass; the cavern acting as a source or a sink. The mass may be soil or fractured rock and the cavern may be a drill hole, a tunnel or a compressed air surge chamber among others. The idealized geometry of the cavern and the distance to a boundary equipotential, which may be the groundwater table, determines the value of a geometry factor appearing in the flow rate formulas. One formula applies to water flow in completely water saturated media and a slightly different formula to air flow in dry media. Special emphasize is given to the application of the formulas in questions regarding design of unlined compressed air surge chambers in jointed rock.

ZUSAMMENFASSUNG:

Vereinfachte, approximative Formeln sind für die Bestimmung der Stömungsgeschwingigkeit von Luft (Gas) und Wasser (unzusammendrückbarer Flüssigkeit) aus einer Kaverne in durchlässiger Materie präsentiert, wo die Kaverne als eine Quelle oder Senke fungiert. Die Materie könnte Erde oder klüftiger Fels sein, und die Kaverne könnte ein Bohrloch, ein Tunnel oder ein geschlossenes Wasserschloss das mit Druckluftpolster arbeitet sein, u.a. Der in den Strömungsformeln auftretende Geometriefaktor wird durch die ideale Geometrie der Kaverne und durch den Abstand von einem Randäquipotential (z.B. dem Grundwasserspiegel) bestimmt. Die eine Formel ist für die Wasserströmung in wassergesättigten Böden anwendbar, und eine ähnliche Formel für die Luftströmung in trockenen Böden. Besondere Betonung wird auf die Anwendung der Formeln in den Fragen der Konstruktion unausgekleideter geschlossener Wasserschlösser mit Druckluftpolstern in zerklüftetem Fels gelegt.

RÉSUMÉ:

Des formules approximatives et directes pour estimer les vitesses d'écoulement de l'air (gaz) et de l'eau (liquide incompressible) à partir d'une caverne dans une masse perméable sont présentées; la caverne agissant comme source ou comme drain. La masse peut être un sol ou un roc fracturé et la caverne peut être un trou de fourage, un tunnel ou une chambre d'equilibre à air comprimé entre autres. La géométrie idéalisée de la caverne et la distance à une équipotentielle limite, qui peut être la nappe d'eau souterraine, détermine la valeur d'un facteur de géométrie apparaissant dans les formules de vitesse d'écoulement. Une première formule s'applique à l'écoulement de l'eau dans un medium complètement saturé d'eau et une autre formule, légèrement différente, à l'écoulement de l'air dans un medium sec. Un accent spécial est mis sur l'utilisation des formules en question pour le calcul des chambres d'équilibre à air comprimé sans recouvrement intérieur dans un roc comprenant des joints.

1 INTRODUCTION

The planning of closed air surge chambers in Norway in the early seventies called for methods to predict air loss from caverns located in fractured rock. The work undertaken by the present authors (1973) was directed towards the development of appropriate formulas for estimating rock mass permeability from borehole tests (Lugeon tests) and measurements of water flow into tunnels and caverns. Furthermore to develop formulas for estimating water and air flow from a cavern knowing the effective permeability of the rock mass.

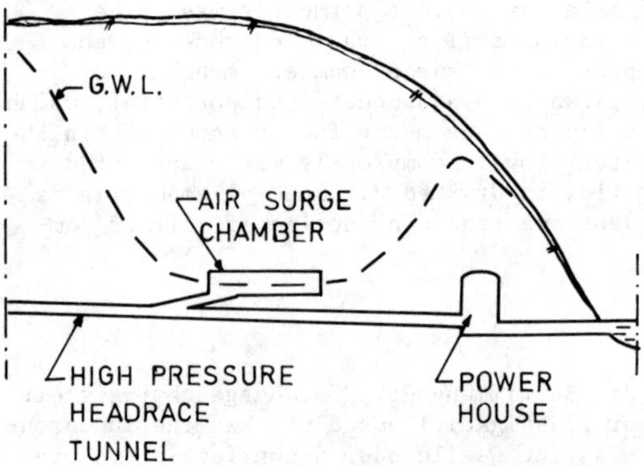

Fig.1. Closed air surge chamber in a fractured rock mass (not in scale).

Fig.1 shows the typical problem; an air surge chamber partially filled with compressed air. Under air pressure higher than, or even slightly below the original water pressure at the chamber location, compressed air will migrate into the rock joints intersecting the chamber. The air loss must be compensated for by compressors. One crucial question is the compressor capacity needed.

The analysis of flow problems in fractured rock is difficult for several reasons. The flow taking place in hard rock suitable for the location of air surge chambers is exclusively limited to fissures and joints. The spacing, distribution and openings of such are likely to be most irregular. Considering even a single joint parallel plate theory may not be correct as the flow may take place in channels.

In the theory to be presented the medium in which flow takes place is considered homogenous. Thus the theory itself is not developed particularly for flow problems in fissured rock. The flow equations to be presented applies to soils and other permeable media as well. In the present paper emphasize is, however, given to the application of the flow equations to inhomogenous rock.

The combined flow of air and water (two fluid system) is hard to analyse. Much easier is the analysis of water (liquid) flow in a completely water saturated porous medium and the analysis of air (gas) flow in a dry porous medium. When able to handle the latter problem at least an upper limit of the air flow in a mixed air-water flow problem is given. The theory to be presented is limited to single fluid flow, but some emphasis is given to the application of the results to the mixed flow problem of an air surge chamber.

During the filling of air into a surge chamber a transient period will take place under which air displaces water in some of the rock joints. The rate of air loss during the transient period is smaller than during the steady state reached after some time. Steady state conditions only will be considered in this paper.

Various analytical solutions to flow problems are available in the literature. Muskat (1937) presented solutions to fluid flow problems involving spherical and cylindrical flow, including also two-dimensional flow from a line source to a plane equipotential (isobar).

Zangar et.al.(1953) among aother problems analysed water flow from a short section of a test-hole below the groundwater table.

The analytical solutions available are as a general not readily applicable to the geometry of an air surge chamber without simplifications and approximations. One goal of this paper has been to rationalize the analytical solutions so as to present straight forward formulas applicable to a variety of flow problems as illustrated by the geometry in Fig.2.

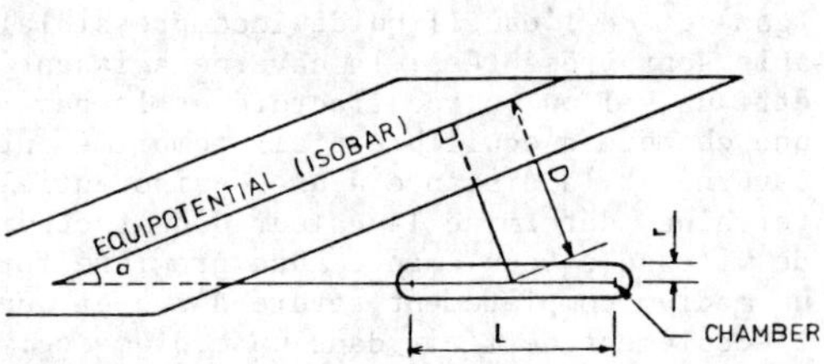

Fig.2. Geometry in an idealized flow problem.

The boundary of a cavern acting as a source or a sink shall be represented by a sylindrical surface with ballshaped ends. A plane equipotential or isobar is the other boundary; the plane normally being associated with the groundwater table. The center of the cavern is located at a distance D from the outer boundary while the axis of the cavern intersects the boundary at an arbitrary angle α.

2 FLOW EQUATIONS

2.1 Fluid flow theory.

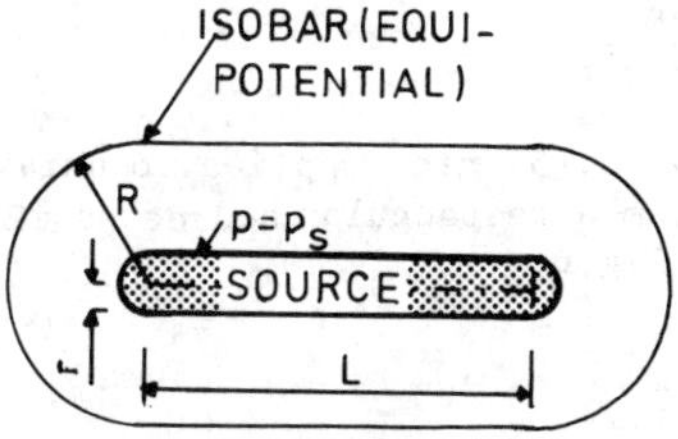

Fig.3. Section through source and equipotential (isobar) in an infinite porous medium

In the flow analysis below the more simple problem of fluid from a source in an infinite homogenous porous medium is considered first. The source is cylindrical with ball shaped ends as shown in Fig.3. The flow is governed by the generalized Darcy's law which, when ignoring gravity, may be written

$$v = -\frac{K}{\mu}\frac{dp}{dR} \qquad (1)$$

where v is the average velocity and $-dp/dR$ is the radial pressure gradient. Furthermore K[1] is the intrinsic permeability and μ is the dynamic viscosity.

The key to the simplified solution is to assume isobars and equipotentials having the same shape as the source. Comparison of the resulting flow rate equations with more acurate solutions developed for special cases indicate this being a fair approximation. If the length L of the cylinder is infinite (two-dimensional flow) or zero (strictly radial flow) no approximation is involved at all.

1) The intrinsic permeability K is related to the hydraulic conductivity (permeability coefficient) through $K=\mu k/\rho g$ in which ρg is the unit weight of the fluid.

The assumption above implies constant mean flow velocity v at distance R from the centre of the source. The volume flux Q follows as

$$Q = \frac{\rho}{\rho_0} vA \qquad (2)$$

where ρ and ρ_0 are the fluid density under the actual pressure p and the reference pressure p_0 respectively. "A" is the area of the equipotential surface; being readily expressed as a function of R and L.

Density and pressure are related to each other through the state equation

$$\rho/\rho_0 = (p/p_0)^m \qquad (3)$$

in which m is a thermal constant. Combining Eqs. (1) - (3) leads to the following pressure field:

$$\left(\frac{p}{p_0}\right)^{m+1} = \left(\frac{p_s}{p_0}\right)^{m+1} - \frac{(m+1)Q\mu}{2\pi\, KLp_0}\,\ell n\,\frac{(L+2r)R}{r(L+2R)} \qquad (4)$$

in which p_s is the pressure in the source ($R=r$). Given an equipotential with pressure $p=p_e$ at a distance $R=R_1$ from the source Eq.(4) may conveninetly be solved with respect to the flow rate Q. This solution shall be included in the more general solution to be presented shortly. As we are particularly interested in the case in which a plane equipotential or an isobar is a boundary, some further progress must be made.

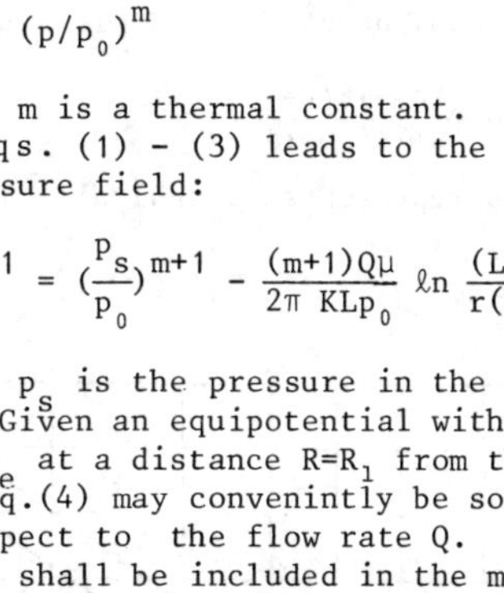

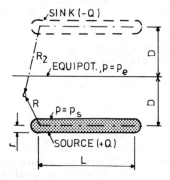

Fig.4. Section through source and imaginary sink.

Imagine a sink with capacity -Q located at a distance 2D from the source; D being the distance between the source and a plane equipotential as shown in Fig.4. The separate pressure distributions for a source and a sink are given in expressions similar to Eq.(4). In the joint case of a source and a sink the pressure at a given point is found by adding two pressure fields of the form given in Eq.(4); one field associated with the source and one with the sink. Given the pressure p_e at the plane equipotential the resulting pressure distribution may be solved with respect to the flow rate Q, yielding

$$Q = \frac{2\pi K L p_0}{(m+1)\mu G}\left[\left(\frac{p_s}{p_0}\right)^{m+1} - \left(\frac{p_e}{p_0}\right)^{m+1}\right] \quad (5)$$

In the equation above G is a geometry factor depending on r, L and D. In the general case involving a source or a sink and a plane equipotential G is given by:

$$G = \ln \frac{(2D-r)\,(L+2r)}{\left|L+2\,(2D-r)\right|\,r} \quad (6)$$

which is represented graphically in Fig.5.

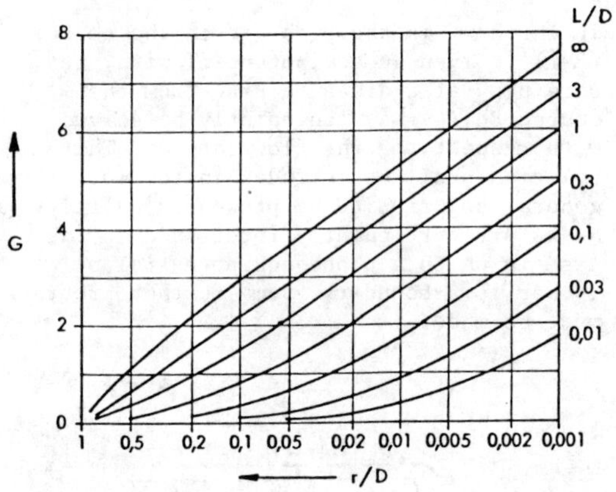

Fig.5. The geometry factor G for flow to a plane equipotential

Eq.(5) also applies to a spherical source, i.e. L = 0 Then

$$\frac{L}{G} = \frac{(2D - r)\,r}{D - r} \quad (7)$$

When developing the flow formula above the axis of the source has been parallel to the plane equipotential. Eq.(5) may, however, be applied with some care to provide approximate results also when this is not the case, i.e. $\alpha \neq 0$ as illustrated in Fig.2. It is required that the minimum distance between the source and the equipotential is not small as compared with the length L of the source.

In the extreme case when D becomes much greater than L and r the geometry factor G tends to becomes independent of D. Evidently the direction of source axis is of no concern in this case.

As already indicated Eq.(5) also applies to the case in which a boundary equipotential with pressure p_e has the same shape as the source (or sink) with pressure p_s, cfr. Fig.3. Then

$$G = \ln \frac{R\,(L+2r)}{(L+2R)\,r} \quad (8)$$

and for spherical flow (L=0)

$$\frac{L}{G} = \frac{2Rr}{R - r} \quad (9)$$

Finally Eq.(5) also applies to uniaxial flow from a rectangular source as illustrated in Fig.6.

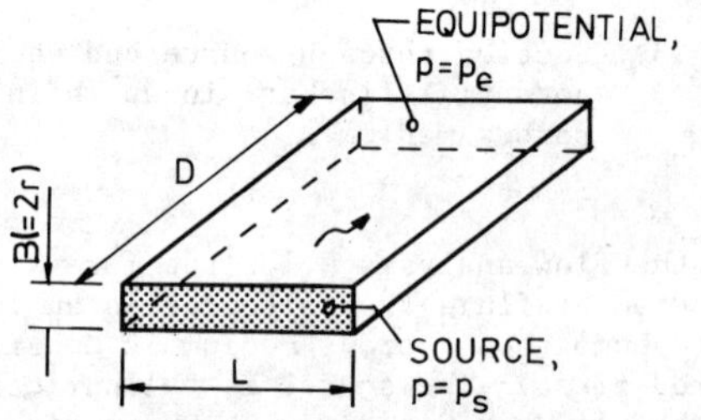

Fig.6. Linear flow from a rectangular source

The geometry factor for linear flow is simply

$$G = 2\pi\, D/B \quad (10)$$

2.2 Air (gas) flow

In the case of isothermal gas flow the thermal constant m = 1, reducing Eq.(5) to

$$Q_a = \frac{\pi K L p_0}{\mu_a G}\left[\left(\frac{p_s}{p_0}\right)^2 - \left(\frac{p_e}{p_0}\right)^2\right] \quad (11)$$

For the overview all symbols are repeated below, giving also preferenced dimensions;

Q_a = air (gas) flow rate through a dry porous medium in m^3/s under reference pressure p_0, normally 10^5 Pa (1 bar)
K = intrinsic permeability, m^2
L = length of source, m

μ_a = dynamic viscosity of air (gas); at 10^0C $\mu_a = 1.8 \cdot 10^{-5}$ kg/m • s

p_0 = reference pressure, normally 10^5 Pa

p_s = absolute pressure in source or sink, Pa

p_e = absolute pressure at a boundary isobar, normally athmospheric pressure ($\simeq 10^5$ Pa)

G = geometry factor as represented in Fig.5 and Eqs.(6)-(10)

2.3 Water (incompressible liquid) flow

Eq.(5) is valid for water flow when incerting m = 0. However, gravity has so far been ignored. This discrepancy may be overcome by substituting $p_s - p_e$ with p_r which is the pressure head in the source or sink. Eq.(5) thus yields

$$Q_W = \frac{2\pi K L p_r}{\mu_w G} \qquad (12)$$

The symbols are:

Q_w = water flow rate in m^3/s through a completely water saturated medium

K, L, G as in section 2.2

μ_w = dynamic viscosity of water; at 10^0C $\mu_w = 1.3 \cdot 10^{-3}$ kg/m • s

p_r = pressure head in source or sink, Pa

3 ROCK MASS PERMEABILITY ESTIMATES

The flow formulas, Eqs.(11) and (12) are developed for steady state flow in a homogenous permeable mass. The intrinsic permeability K is a constant for the particular medium in which flow takes place, regardless of whether the fluid is air or water.

It is recognized that rock is indeed no homogenous permeable mass. Considering hard rock no intergranular flow takes place, the flow being located in joints. In some cases the joint system may be fairly regular, but more often the distribution of water conducting joints is most irregular. As regards for the air surge chambers constructed so far in Norway, these are located where the rock conditions are favourable; the chambers being intersected only by one or two water conducting joints. It is also an experience of many geologists that water flow is by no means uniform over a joint, rather the flow is taking place in channels.

In conclusion hereof it is doubtful to consider hard rock as a homogenous permeable mass. However, an exhaustive exploration of the true system of water conducting joints and channels may become insurmountable. In many cases a rough estimate of the rock mass permeability will do. So is the case with a compressed air surge chamber where the key questions are compressor capacity, need for grouting or lining etc.

The applications of the flow equations presented above may be manyfold due to the variety of the geometry encountered.

Below we shall, however, be concerned with rock mass permeability estimates only, and the application of the results to the estimation of the air leakage rate from an unlined air surge chamber.

In consideration of the inhomogeneity of jointed rock one major concern is to take into account the jointing system. In this respect a key word is scale, i.e. the dimension of a subsurface opening as compared with the joint spacing. First we shall apply Eq.(12) to the determination of the equivalent rock mass permeability.

3.1 Borehole pumping tests (Lugeon tests)

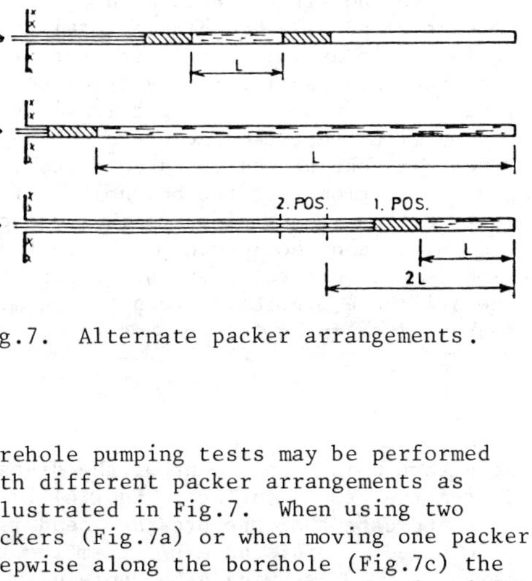

Fig.7. Alternate packer arrangements.

Borehole pumping tests may be performed with different packer arrangements as illustrated in Fig.7. When using two packers (Fig.7a) or when moving one packer stepwise along the borehole (Fig.7c) the distribution of the water conducting joints may be estimated as suggested by Snow (1968) One packer only in the outer end of the borehole (Fig. 7b) is a less time consuming set up, but the interpretation of the result is more severe.

It is important to get a rough view of the jointing system and the joint spacing. Depending on the scale of the joint system the flow will be considered two - or three - dimensional as will be explained below.

As the diameter of a borehole is typically a few centimetres only it is required that flow takes place in joints rather than in a few channels. Otherwis the chance of hitting a channel with a borehole is marginal and it must be expected that borehole pumping test by no means give a true picture of the water conducting joint system. If the requirement above is not satisfied, permeability estimates must be based on the recording of water flow into a cavern or a tunnel as shall be discussed in a section to follow.

Eq.(12) is in most cases accurate enough for the interpretation of borehole pumping tests; the solving with respect to the intrinsic permeability gives;

$$K = \frac{\mu_w Q_w G}{2\pi L p_r} \quad (13)$$

In borehole pumping tests it is customary to record the leakage in terms of the unit "Lugeon"; 1 Lugeon denoting 1 litre per minute and metre borehole at 10 kp/cm^2 ($\simeq 10^6$Pa) pressure head. As shall be seen below a rough proportionality exists between the Lugeon value and the intrinsic permeability.

Two approaches to the interpretation of borehole pumping tests shall be looked into. In the first approach the rock mass is considered as a homogenous pervious medium, thus assuming small fracture spacing and intersecting joints allowing flow to take place in three dimensions. Assume first that two packers are used in a test so that discharge takes place from a short section L of the borehole. If the test section is not close to the surface, i.e. D>>L, and the length of the test section is much greater than the radius of the drillhole,i.e. L>>r, then the geometry factor given in Eq.(6) reduces to

$$G = \ln \frac{L}{2r} \quad (14)$$

Note that G is independent of the distance D from the ground surface. Eq.(14) in fact indicate that the pressure head is eliminated at a distance L/2 from the borehole.[1] Assuming a borehole diameter in the order of 5 cm and test sections between 1 and 5 metres, Eqs.(13) and (14) indicate that 1 Lugeon corrsponds to K_b in the order of $1.0 \cdot 10^{-14} m^2$ to $1.6 \cdot 10^{-14} m^2$ at 10^0C water temperature.

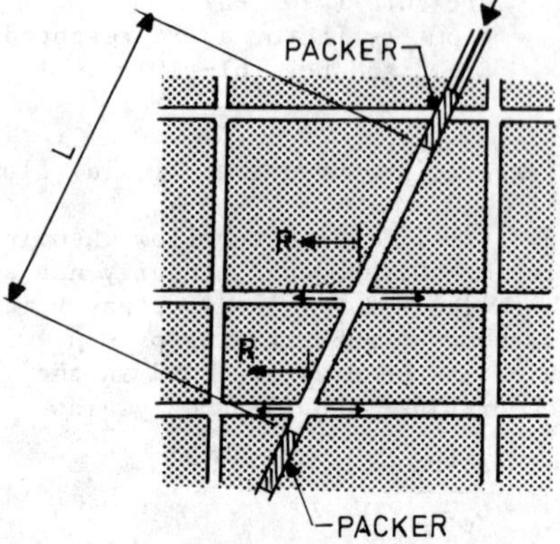

Fig.8. Drill hole with packers in fractured rock under idealized conditions.

In the approach above three-dimensional flow has been assumed. However, even in strongly fractured rock the joint spacing is likely to be great as compared with the diameter of the drill hole. Fig.8 illustrates two-dimensional flow likely to take place in random joints intersecting a borehole. The geometry factor, as given in Eq.(8), reduces to

$$G = \ln R/r \quad (15)$$

in which R is the radius from the borehole for which the pressure head is eliminated. If two or three intersecting joint sets exist, the water conducting joints intersecting the borehole will also intersect other joint sets at some distance from the borehole. As joint sets intersect the effective area subjected to flow increases substantially, thus causing the pressure head to drop rapidly. If the average joint spacing is in the order of say maximum 10 metres, the expected average distance between the borehole and the closest joint intersection is in the order of a few metres. Thus the pressure head is likely to be eliminated at a few metres distance from the borehole. The value of the geometry factor according to Eq.(15) is therefore likely to be slightly higher than, or in the same order as suggested by Eq.(14).

In the case of three-dimensional flow first considered a two-packer test arrangement was assumed.

1) One may have noticed that Eq.(14) differ somewhat from the corresponding geometry factor included in Glovers formula published by Zangar (1953), wherein G = $\ln$ L/r. As both formulas require L>>r the discrepancy is no great concern.

In the latter case two-dimensional flow has been assumed close to the borehole regardless of the distance between the packers. Thus the latter interpretation goes for all test arrangements illustrated in Fig. 7.

Keeping in mind the significant uncertainties involved in the determination of K from borehole pumping tests the following rough interpretation formula is suggested for all tests:

$$K_b \simeq Q_{wl} \cdot 1.5 \cdot 10^{-14} \; |m^2| \qquad (16)$$

where Q_{wl} is the flow rate in terms of Lugeon units. The sub b indicates K being determined from a borehole pumping test.

As pointed out already the flow in the proximity of a borehole is basicly two-dimensional due to the small diameter of the hole as compared with the joint spacing. On the other hand when analyzing problems involving flow around a tunnel or cavern for which the dimensions are larger- or in the same order as the average joint spacing, it is fair to consider the flow three-dimensional in as far as flow takes place in all joint systems simulanously. Due to scale effects it is fair to correct the intrinsic permeability K_b estimated from borehole pumping tests.

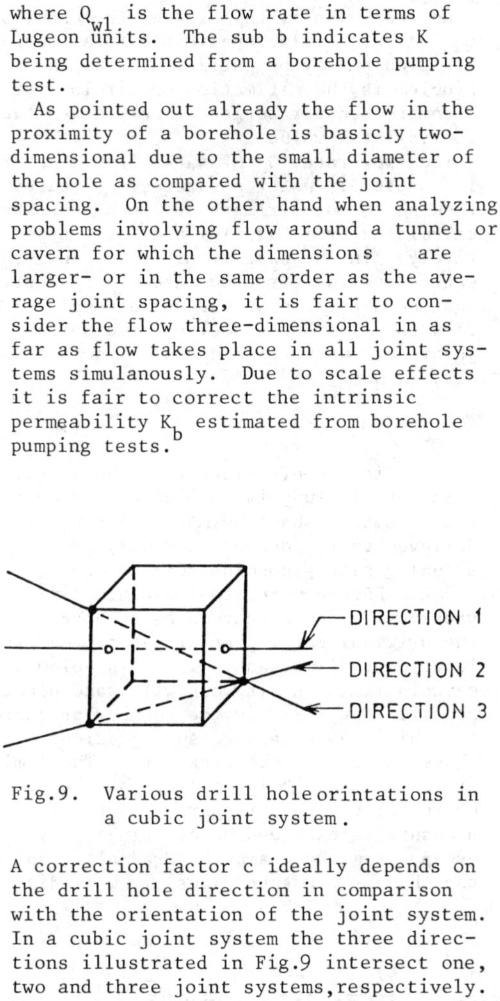

Fig.9. Various drill hole orintations in a cubic joint system.

A correction factor c ideally depends on the drill hole direction in comparison with the orientation of the joint system. In a cubic joint system the three directions illustrated in Fig.9 intersect one, two and three joint systems,respectively. When writing the correction due to scale

$$K = c \, K_b \qquad (17)$$

the correction factor c equals 2.0, 1.4 and 1.2 for directions 1, 2 and 3 respectively. When no detail analysis is made c = 1.5 is recommended.

As a joint system is likely to be irregular drill holes for pumping tests should if possible be made in 3 orthogonal directions. When averaging the results from borings in different directions most weight should be put on the borings in the direction exhibiting the highest permeability.

3.2 Water flow into a cavern or a tunnel

In the previous section some of the problems in borehole pumping tests were pointed out, such as a scale effect, as to whether several intersecting joint sets exists, the joint spacing, and to whether flow takes place in channels or joints of the parallel plate type. These problems are to some extent overcome when the permeability estimate is based on the recording of water flow into an excavated tunnel or a cavern. Thus if the problem is to estimate air loss from a compressed air surge chamber borehole pumping tests may be made at an early stage to select a suitable location for the chamber and to get a rough idea of the future air loss. However, the estimate of the compressor capacity needed for compensation of the air loss should be based on permeability estimates after the chamber is excavated. If the rock mass is permeabilitywise homogenous at a large scale, reliable results may also be obtained based on water flow into the nearby tunnel.

The interpretation formula in Eq.(13) is suitable for estimating the equivalent intrinsic permeability based on water flow into a cavern or tunnel. The actual K-value calculated depend on whether the flow is two-dimensional or three-dimensional; the former being the case when only one major set of parallel joints intersect the tunnel or the chamber. However, it is not so important to get a true picture of the joint system when the permeability estimate is based on waterflow into a cavern. Erros due to incorrect modelling are likely to cancel out when the same formulas subsequently are used for the estimation of air loss (reversed flow directions).

3.3 Special problems; only one or two major joints

So far we have assumed a basicly regular joint system justifying the notion of homogeneity at a large scale. More typical is perhaps the case in which one or two major water conducting joints intersect a cavern as illustrated in Fig.10. Then special consideration must be made.

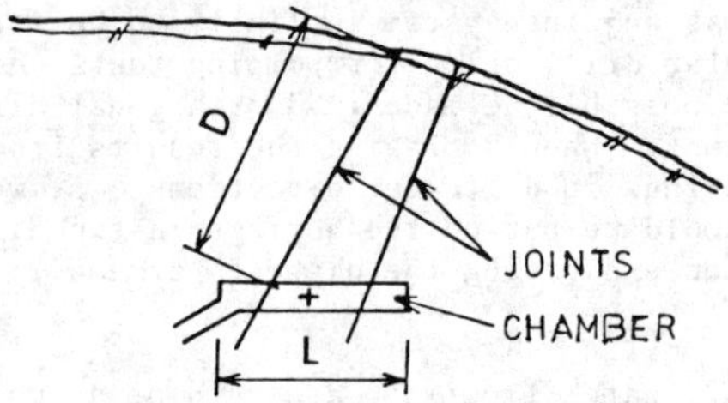

Fig.10. Two major joints intersecting a cavern.

In borehole pumping tests either significant flow or virtually no flow at all will be recorded depending on whether or not the drillhole intersects one of the water conducting joints. Evidently the average result of a number of borehole pumping tests may not give a true picture of the permeability when no homogeneity exists even at a large scale. Single joints must be treated individually.

Still borehole pumping test and recording of water discharge into a cavern may be used for permeability estimates. However, one may not determine a representative K-value for the rock mass at large. Rather a K-value applying to a specific tunnel section or cavern is estimated.

Regardless of whether permeability estimates are based on borehole pumping tests or water discharge into a cavern, the flow must be considered two-dimensional, i.e. $L/D = \infty$ must always be entered into the geometry factor formula.

When borehole pumping tests are made the drillholes must be set in order to detect all major joints intersecting the future chamber. The average discharge rate at a given pressure head must be recorded for each joint. When adding together the average flow rates for all joints intersecting the cavern, an equivalent rate over the cavern length is obtained. Accordingly a representative Lugeon value for the cavern may be calculated, or the intrinsic permeability may be calculated directly from Eq.(13).

When using borehole pumping tests for single joints no correction due to scale is necessary as two-dimensional flow is considered all the time.

4 AIR LOSS FROM A CHAMBER

In the previous chapter guidelines are given as to how the intrinsic permeability K of a rock mass may be calculated. As a rule the joint system must be fairly regular justifying the assumption of homogeneity at a large scale. However, it was also seen that even if this is not the case, an equivalent K-value applicable to a specific problem may be estimated. Now the problem is the estimation of air loss from a compressed air surge chamber, given the equivalent K-value.

The flow rates Q_w of water from a cavern in completely water saturated, fractured rock and Q_a of air in a dry rock mass are calculated from Eqs.(12) and (11) respectively. In the case of mixed air and water flow the air flow rate Q_{aw} evidently must be a portion of the corresponding flow rate Q_a in dry rock as some of the joints are water filled and may not conduct air. Hence

$$Q_{aw} = \psi Q_a \qquad (18)$$

where ψ is a coefficient less the unity.

No detail study is made on ψ. However, some comments shall be made. First, it is believed that ψ depends strongly on the actual geometry concidered, i.e. on D, r and L. Furthermore, the absolute air pressure P_s in the cavern as compared with the original water pressure at the cavern location is important. If P_s is below a certain limit no air loss will take place at all. The limit is the chamber pressure for which the water pressure gradient above the chamber becomes zero. The limit pressure is slightly smaller than the hydrostatic water pressure. As the limit pressure is exceeded an air finger may escape from the chamber. Gradually, as the chamber pressure rises air will dis-

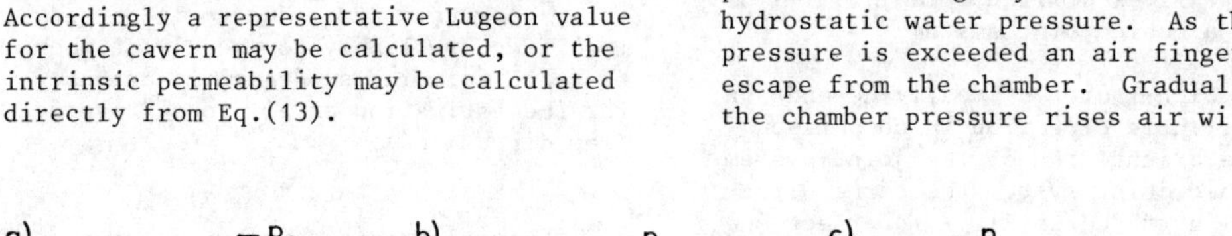

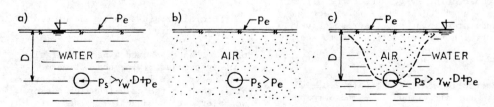

Fig.11. Water, air and mixed water-air flow from a cavern.

place water in the joints above the chamber.

The pressure in a chamber may be characterized in terms of the mean water gradient

$$i_m = \frac{p_r}{\gamma_w D} \tag{19}$$

in which p_r is the pressure head in the chamber and $\gamma_w D$ is the hydrostatic pressure at the chamber location.

As regards for compressed air surge chambers the value of i_m will often be in the order of 0.5, and never exceeding unity for flow to the ground surface. In the absence of detail analysis and to some extent supported by model tests by Barton (1972) it is believed that ψ is in the order of 0.2-0.5 for i_m in the order of 0.1-0.5.

The method described above has been used by Johansen and Vik (1982) for the prediction of air loss from compressed air surge chambers at three different sites in Norway. The intrinsic permeability K was estimated from Lugeon tests, water discharge into boreholes and water flow into the chamber. The predicted air loss is in reasonable agreement with the field observations. Best results are obtained from the measurement of water flow (including evaporation) into the chamber.

5 REFERENCES

Barton,N. 1972, A parallel plate model study of air leakage from underground openings situated beneath ground water level. Norwegian Geotechnical Institute, Oslo, internal report 54203-2, 66 p.

Johansen,P.M. and G.Vik 1982, Prediction of air leakages from air - cushion surge chambers. Paper to be published in International Symposium on Rock Mechanics related to Caverns and Pressure Shafts, Aachen, 5 p.

Muskat,M. 1937, The flow of homogenous fluids through porous media. McGraw-Hill, New York, reprinted 1946 by Edwards Inc., Ann Arbor, Michigan.

Snow,D.T. 1968, Rock fracture spacings, openings, and porosities. Proc.ASCE, 94 (SM1), pp.73-91.

Tokheim,O. and N.Janbu 1973, Overslag over luftlekkasjer fra lukkede fordelingsbasseng i fjell (in Norwegian). Publ. in: Lukket fordelingsbasseng med luftpute, samlerapport. Ed. by River and Harbour Research Laboratory, NTH, Trondheim, pp. 75-113.

Zangar,C.N. 1953, Theory and problems of water percolation. U.S. Dept. of Interior, Bur. of Reclam., Denver, Colorado, Eng. Monograph No.8, 76 p.

EXCAVATION DESIGN IN ROCK SALT - LABORATORY EXPERIMENTS, MATERIAL MODELING AND VALIDATIONS*

Entwurf eines Hohlraums in Salzgestein – Laborversuche, Modellgesetze und Berechnungen

Plan d'une excavation dans le sel-gemme – essais de laboratoire, modèles constitutifs et calculs

W.R.WAWERSIK, W.HERRMANN, S.T.MONTGOMERY & H.S.LAUSON
Sandia National Laboratories, Albuquerque, USA

SUMMARY:
A cycle of laboratory measurements, constitutive modeling and validation calculations is described as a basis for excavation design in rock salt. The results of triaxial creep tests were fitted by a creep model with exponentially decaying transients and power law thermally activated steady state creep which are functions only of deviatoric stress and temperature. The corresponding three-dimensional constitutive equation, including elastic terms, is then applied in finite element simulations of the known closure of an isolated mine drift.

ZUSAMMENFASSUNG:
Ein Zyklus von Labormessungen, konstitutiver Beschreibung und Rechnungen wird vorgestellt als Grundlage fuer den Entwurf untertaegiger Hoghlraeume in Salzgesteinen. Die Ergebnisse triaxialer Kriechversuche wurden im Ausgleichsverfahren zur Bestimmung eines Kriechgesetzes behandelt. Danach ist das Uerbergangskriechen als Exponentialfunktion und das stationaere Kriechen als Potenzfunktion mit thermischer Aktivierung gegeben. Ein entsprechendes dreidimensionales Stoffgesetz wird dann unter Einschluss elastischer Terme mit Hilfe des Verfahrens der finiten Elemente angewendet, um die Konvergenzen in einer isolierten Strecke untertage zu berechnen. Die errechneten Werte werden mit bekannten in situ Messungen verglichen und bestaetigt.

RESUME:
Cette communication décrit un cycle de mesures en laboratoire, des modèles constitutifs, ainsi que les calculs confirmant et servant de base au dimensionnement d'une excavation dans le sel-gemme. Les résultats d'essais triaxiaux de fluage furent ajustés à un modele mathématique comportant une phase transitoire declinant exponentiellement, ainsi qu'un fluage thermique permanent, suivant une puissance. Ces deux lois sont fonctions seulement de la contrainte deviatorique et de la temperature. L'équation tridimensionnelle constitutive correspondante, contenant aussi les termes elastiques, fut alors appliquée à des simulations par elements finis d'une galerie de mine isolée dont la convergence était connue.

1. INTRODUCTION

The design of a radioactive waste isolation facility and of oil storage caverns in the U.S. is supported by thermostructural design calculations using a variety of finite element codes. This paper describes three prerequisites for the successful application of such calculations.

1. Laboratory measurements of the thermomechanical properties of rock salt,
2. Constitutive modeling of rock salt creep, and
3. A comparison of design calculations with in situ measurements.

Descriptions of laboratory measurements and material modeling include a discussion of important implications and uncertainties of the proposed creep model which bear on its use for arbitrary stress and temperature histories. The uncertainties may also affect the extrapolation of the model to low stresses which are probably encountered around underground structures after long times.

*This work performed at Sandia National Laboratories supported by the U.S. Department of Energy under Contract Number DE-AC04-76DP00789.

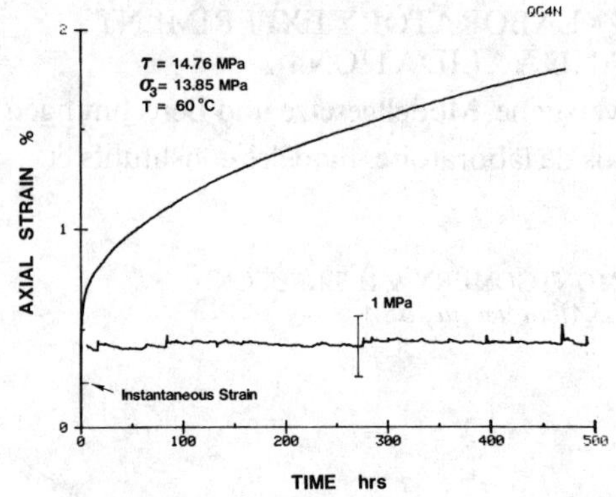

(a) Measurements in single stage test with superimposed history of principal stress difference to different scale.

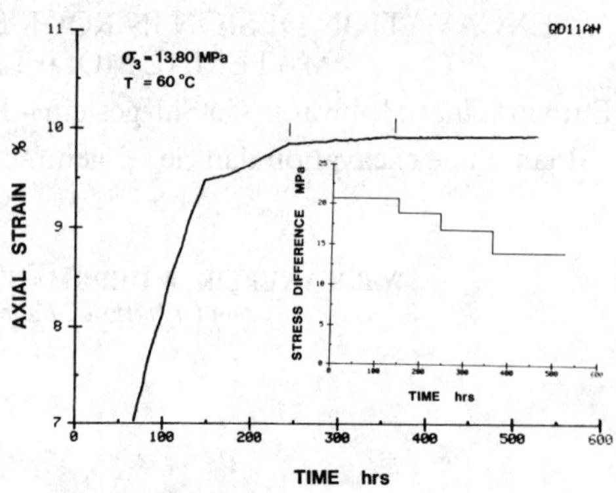

(c) Data from four stage stress decrement test. Inset shows stress history. Axial strains below 7% were omitted to retain unloading details.

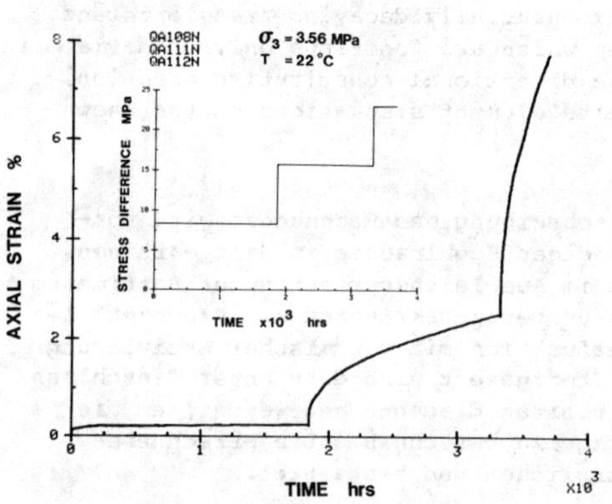

(b) Data from three stage stress increment experiment. Inset shows stress history.

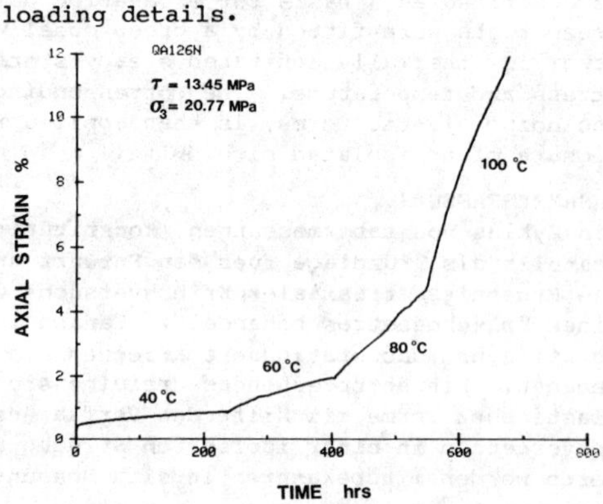

(d) Measurements in temperature change test.

Figure 1: Creep data for rock salt with average values of principal stress difference, confining pressure and temperature.

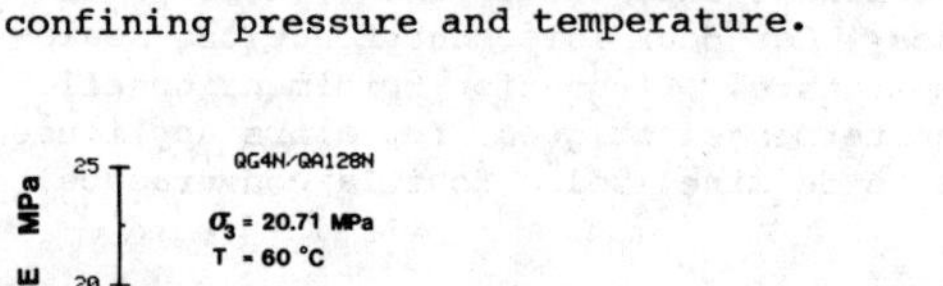

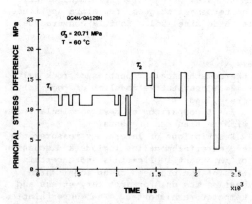

Figure 2: Special purpose creep experiments -- (a) Complex stress history of a "stress dip" test.

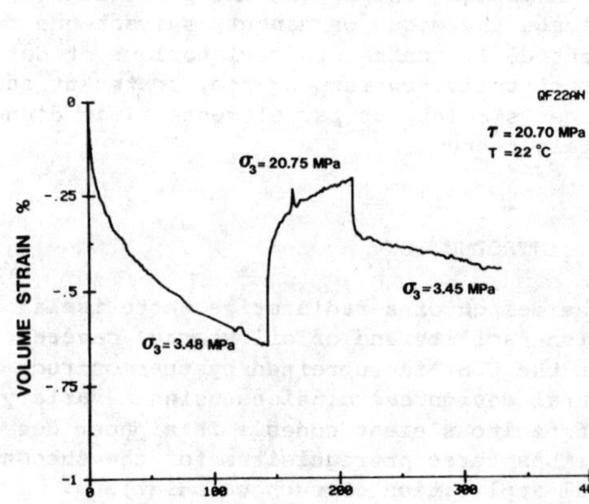

(b) Volumetric strain history at constant principal stress difference and varying confining pressure.

2. LABORATORY MEASUREMENTS

Thermomechanical properties of rock salt are measured in specially designed machines using specimens which measure up to 10.8 cm in diameter and 21 cm in length. Details of the apparatus and procedures are described elsewhere (Wawersik and Preece, 1982; Wawersik, 1979).

Short-term tests are conducted to determine the elastic properties of salt, failure envelopes and short-term inelastic properties. Short-term tests are carried out in hydrostatic compression ($\sigma_1 = \sigma_2 = \sigma_3$), triaxial compression ($\sigma_1 > \sigma_2 = \sigma_3$) and in triaxial extension ($\sigma_1 = \sigma_2 > \sigma_3$) at constant stress rate up to 6.5 MPa/s, at constant strain rate up to 10^{-2} 1/s and at constant stress. These tests include stress paths which are not ordinarily realized in axisymmetric experiments, for example, principal stress variations at constant mean stress and confining pressure variations at constant maximum compression σ_1 (Wawersik and Hannum, 1980). The maximum confining pressure and the maximum temperature are 70 MPa and 250°C.

Creep experiments are performed to ascertain the long-term response of salt. Creep experiments are conducted at approximately constant true stress by means of frequent adjustments of the applied loads. In past tests, stress variations of up to ± 10% were experienced in confining pressure and deviatoric stress, either because of fluctuations in confining pressure or because of rapid creep with attendant changes in sample dimensions. Recent improvements limit confining pressure variations to ± 1% (± .04 MPa) and deviatoric stress variations to ± 3% (± .2 MPa).

Experimental measurements include test time, principal stress difference $\tau = (\sigma_1 - \sigma_3)$, confining pressure σ_3, true (logarithmic) axial and radial strains e_1 and e_3. Strains are determined indirectly by monitoring changes in sample length and sample diameter. Maximum strains are limited to 35 percent. Finite element calculations have confirmed that the strains inferred up to these levels are good measures of the homogeneous strains under ideal conditions with no frictional restraints (Wawersik and Preece, 1982).

Creep tests fall into two categories.

1. Single stage tests where each sample is subjected to one constant stress and temperature.
2. Multistage experiments or "change tests" where principal stress difference, confining pressure or temperature are changed from time to time. These changes may occur upward or downward. Accordingly, for example, a distinction is made between stress increment tests and stress decrement tests.

Examples of creep experiments are shown in Fig. 1. Fig. 1a shows data for a typical single stage experiment. The superimposed record of principal stress difference τ versus time, drawn to a different scale, indicates the quality of stress control. Fig. 1b shows the result of a multistage test with increases in stress difference. Fig. 1c gives the strain histories for a series of stress decrements, while Fig. 1d depicts data at several temperatures between 40 and 100°C.

Additional tests aid the interpretations and the generalizations of the basic experimental data in Fig. 1. Thus, the complex stress history in Fig. 2a serves two purposes. First, the development of identical transients following equal stress drops is employed to determine when steady state creep is reached at the reference stress τ_1. Subsequently, observations of transients following stress drops of different magnitudes are used, for example, to infer the role of glide in the low temperature creep of rock salt, to measure recovery times and to test the uniqueness of steady state creep. Fig. 2b shows a history of volumetric strain as a function of confining pressure which is important in creep fracture and healing studies.

3. CREEP MODEL AND CONSTITUTIVE EQUATION

Creep and constitutive models were derived to describe the rate dependent behavior of bedded salt from the Salado formation, southeastern New Mexico, depths 645-655 m and 810-875 m. Both salts are medium to coarse grained and exhibit little or no preferred grain orientation. They contain up to eight percent of impurities, primarily polyhalite and anhydrite along grain boundaries (Powers et. al., 1978). Anhydrite impurities are typical for the deeper salt.

The creep model which is presented here is based on data from sixty-two single and multistage tests which were carried out during a continuing test and design program (Wawersik and Hannum, 1978; Hansen and Mellegard, 1977, 1979). Fifty-four of these tests were performed on the deeper salt. Only stress increment data were considered up to 21 MPa confining pressure, 41 MPa principal stress difference and 200°C. More than half of the results were obtained at ambient temperature. The duration of each test stage varied between 1.4×10^4 s ($\approx$ 4 hours) and 6.75×10^6 s (1875 hours). The average test duration was 2.4×10^6 s. The greatest and smallest observed creep rates during the last 25 to 50 hours of each test were on the order of 10^{-7} 1/s to 10^{-10} 1/s. More recently, a minimum strain rate of 2×10^{-11} 1/s was recorded which lies at the low end of the current experimental resolution.

Material modeling proceeded in several steps. First, all data were smoothed and fitted by a creep function of the form (Jefferson, 1974; Herrmann et al., 1980a).

$$e = e_0 + e_a(1 - e^{-\xi t}) + \dot{e}_s t \qquad (1)$$

where e and t denote strain and time. The quantitites $\dot{e}_s$, e_a and ξ are constants at constant stress and temperature. Data taken during the first hour were usually excluded from the fits. The constant e_0 ensures the best fit to all the creep data which were used from a given test. It does not correspond to the instantaneous elastic or plastic strains on loading.

The fits (1) represent each data set of up to 2000 data points by three constants together with their standard errors. The form of equation (1) is consistent with the common phenomena of transient and steady state creep in sodium chloride which are well established, at least at intermediate and high temperatures (Blum and Ilschner, 1967; Burke, 1968; Heard, 1972). The model predicts a maximum transient strain equal to e_a and steady state creep rate of $\dot{e}_s$. With few exceptions very good fits were obtained with overall standard errors well below 10^{-3}. Example fits to axial and radial strain data during a first stage experiment are shown in Fig. 3.

Fitting to individual experiments was followed by multiple regression analyses of data from all tests (Herrmann et al., 1980b). Differences in the creep behavior of salt from the two depths, 645-655 m and 810-875 m were statistically significant. The stress and temperature dependence of all fitting parameters far outweighed the influence of confining pressure. The assumed pressure invariance is consistent with the fact that observed values of dilatancy or compaction almost always were less than 10 percent of the shear strains $\gamma = e_1 - e_3$.

The final step in modeling consisted of correlating the fitting parameters e_a, ξ, and $\dot{e}_s$ with stress and temperature (Herrmann et al., 1980b,c). These cor-

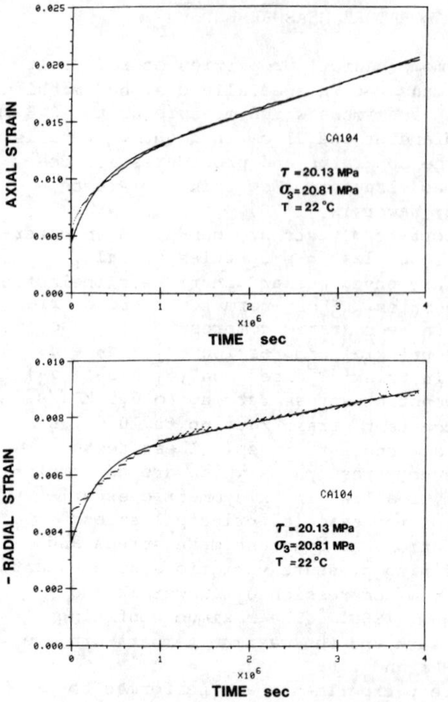

Figure 3: Typical fit of equation (1) to axial and radial creep measurements (Herrmann, Wawersik and Lauson, 1980a).

relations were performed in terms of the shear strain, γ. If good radial strain data were lacking it was assumed that $\gamma = 3/2\, e_1$. Excellent fits were obtained by means of the following expressions for steady state and transient creep.

$$\dot{\gamma}_s = A e^{-Q/RT} \left(\frac{\tau}{G}\right)^n \qquad (2)$$

$$\gamma_p = \gamma_a(1 - e^{-\xi t}) \qquad (3)$$

where

$$\gamma_a = \frac{B}{\xi} \dot{\gamma}_s \qquad (4)$$

$$\xi = C\dot{\gamma}^* \text{ for } \dot{\gamma}_s < \dot{\gamma}^* = \text{const.}$$
$$\xi = C\dot{\gamma}_s \text{ for } \dot{\gamma}_s > \dot{\gamma}^* \qquad (5)$$

The total creep shear strain is given by

$$\gamma - \gamma_0 = \gamma_p + \dot{\gamma}_s t \qquad (6)$$

where γ_0 corresponds to e_0.

Differentiating, the creep shear strain rate is given by

$$\dot{\gamma} = \dot{\gamma}_p + \dot{\gamma}_s \qquad (7)$$

where, from (3), the transient creep rate is described by the evolution equation

$$\dot{\gamma}_p = \xi(\gamma_a - \gamma_p) \quad (8)$$

T denotes absolute temperature. Constant B is based on a proportionality between the initial creep rates according to (1) and subsequent steady state creep rates (Herrmann et al., 1980c; Garafalo et al., 1963; Conway and Milliken, 1966; Evans and Wilshire, 1968; Webster et al., 1969; Threadgill and Wilshire, 1972; Amin et al., 1972; Amadieh and Mukherjee, 1975). The different dependence of relaxation frequency ξ on creep rate at low rates, eq. (5) may be due to a contribution of grain boundary sliding to the creep process. This was first suggested from observations on austenitic stainless steel (Garafalo et al., 1963; Webster et al., 1969;).

The numerical values of all constants and their standard errors were determined as

$A = (2.5 \pm 0.53) \times 10^{14}$ 1/s

for salt from 645-655 m,

$A = (6.7 \pm 1.42) \times 10^{14}$ 1/s

for salt from 810-875 m,

$Q = 50 \pm 2.7$ kJ/mole

$n = 4.9 \pm 0.27$

$G = 12.4$ GPa

$B = 6.69 \pm 1.19$

$C = 190.5 \pm 63$

$\dot{\gamma}^* = 8.1 \times 10^{-8}$ 1/s

The shear modulus G was determined in separate quasi-static measurements.

The correlation between γ_a and $\dot{\gamma}_s$ is indicated in Fig. 4. Fig. 5 shows a comparison between the model for steady state creep with the data for the deeper salt which were scaled to the nearest common nominal stress values using $n = 4.9$.

The creep equations (2) to (6) can be nondimensionalized by the steady state creep rate $\dot{\gamma}_s$ to obtain a master creep curve. This master curve is shown in Fig. 6 together with the nondimensionalized data for creep tests at $\tau = 31$ MPa and 24°C. The solid line represents the model with mean values for B and C $\dot{\gamma}^*$

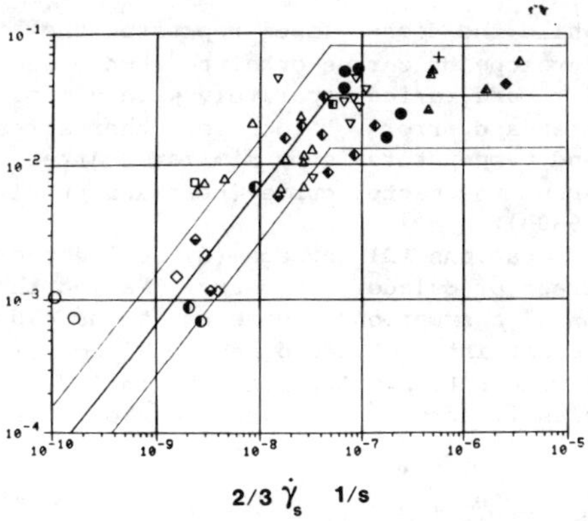

Figure 4: Correlation between asymptotic transient creep parameter γ_a and steady state creep rate $\dot{\gamma}_s$, equation (4) (Herrmann, Wawersik and Lauson, 1980c).

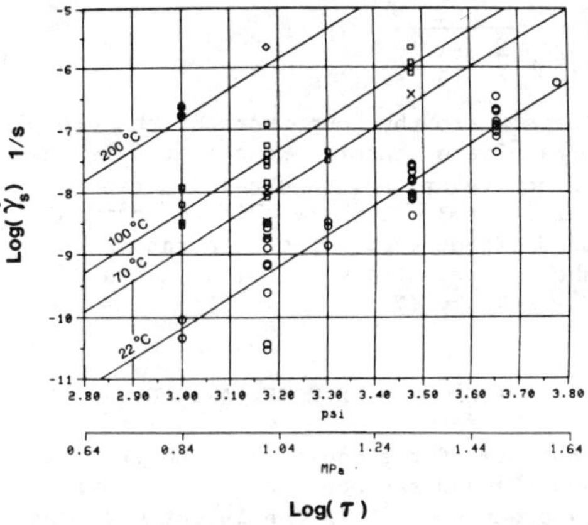

Figure 5: Comparison of steady state creep data with fit, equation (2) (Herrmann, Wawersik and Lauson, 1980b). Creep rates were scaled to nearest common principal stress difference.

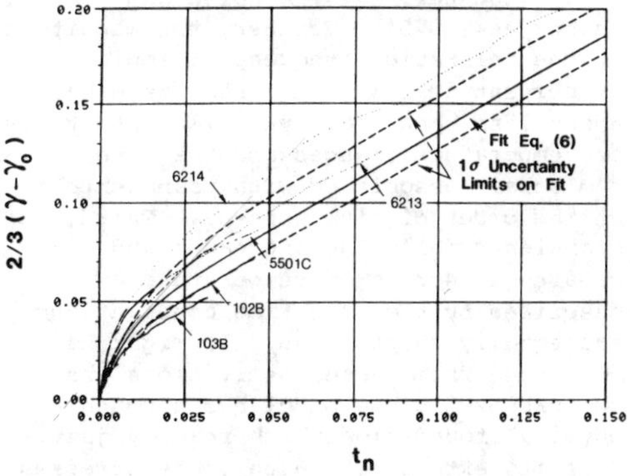

Figure 6: Comparison of nondimensionalized transient and steady state creep data with master curve (Herrmann, Wawersik and Lauson, 1980c).

while the dashed lines represent the envelope of curves obtained when B and C $\dot{\gamma}^*$ are varied separately within their standard errors. Plots for other stresses and temperatures show similar scatter about the master curve (Herrmann et al., 1980b).

Equations (2) through (6) define the creep of Salado salt tests. Making the usual assumptions, these equations can be recast into a three-dimensional constitutive equation. Accordingly, including an elastic term e^e_{ij} and using a flow rule,

$$\dot{e}_{ij} = \dot{e}^e_{ij} + \frac{\dot{\gamma}}{\bar{\sigma}} \sigma'_{ij} \tag{9}$$

where

$$\bar{\sigma} = \sqrt{\frac{3}{2} \sigma'_{ij} \sigma'_{ij}} \tag{10}$$

$$\dot{\gamma} = \sqrt{\frac{3}{2} \dot{e}^c_{ij} \dot{e}^c_{ij}} \tag{11}$$

The $\dot{e}^c_{ij}$ are the components of the creep strain rate tensor. Note that $\bar{\sigma}$ is the effective stress, as usually defined, while $\dot{\gamma} = 3\,\dot{\bar{e}}/2$ where $\dot{\bar{e}}$ is the commonly used effective creep strain rate. The shear creep strain rate $\dot{\gamma}$ is given directly by (7).

4. IMPLICATIONS OF MODEL AND UNCERTAINTIES

The form of the model (7) with (2), (3) and (8) and the magnitude of the stress exponent $n = 4.9$ is consistent with the assumption that creep of Salado salt is controlled by dislocation climb (Weertman, 1968) and that this process is rate controlling throughout steady state creep as well as transient creep (Webster et al., 1969; Ilschner, 1973; Amadieh and Mukherjee, 1975). Further, the magnitude of the relaxation frequency ξ implies that 99 percent of all transients are exhausted after less than 7.8 days following stress or temperature changes and that the maximum strain associated with transients is on the order of five percent. Third, transients following increases and decreases in stress or temperature are described by the same time constant and are equally short lived. It might be concluded from these observations that the proposed creep model has a sound physical foundation which readily justifies its extrapolation to other stresses and temperature and to long times (Weertman, 1968; Webster et al., 1969; Amin et al., 1970). It might also be assumed that transients are negligible for the time scales of any underground structure whose design life is going to be at least twenty years. Although these tenets are highly welcome, caution is suggested in accepting them without also evaluating known uncertainties and inconsistencies.

While steady state creep is described quite well by the power law for diffusion controlled dislocation climb, it is not yet possible to relate an effective activation energy $Q = 50$ kJ/mole to the diffusivity of any known atomic species within the sodium chloride lattice. This raises the possibility of other participating or rate controlling mechanisms, such as glide or cross-slip (Sherby and Burke, 1967; Nix and Ilschner, 1977).

There also are uncertainties concerning transients. It was mentioned that model (7) was formulated by means of creep measurements in stress increment tests. Although this model captures the qualitative features of unloading transients measured in more recent stress drop tests, it does poorly in quantitative comparisons. For example, using the material constants listed earlier and starting from steady state creep, the unloading history at strain rates below $\dot{\gamma}^* = 8.1 \times 10^{-8}$ 1/s consist of inverse transients with negative slope immediately following any stress decrement exceeding 4.1 percent of the starting stress. The strain rate then increases continuously through zero until, after 7.8 days it recovers fully to the steady state creep rate for the current stress and temperature. Several experimental observations run counter to that prediction. For example, Fig. 7 shows the creep record

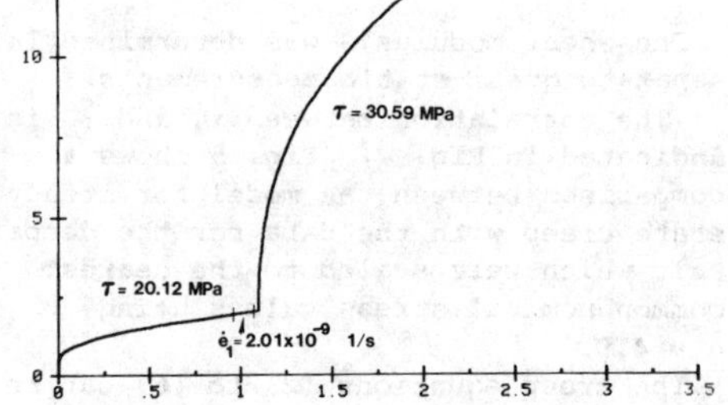

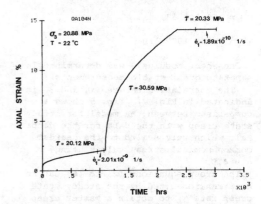

Figure 7: Creep data for rock salt subjected to stress difference of 20.33 MPa before and after creep at higher stress (Wawersik and Hannum, 1978).

of a Salado salt specimen subjected to τ = 20.3 MPa before and after an intermediate stage at τ = 30.6 MPa. The creep rate after the stress drop from 30.6 MPa appears to be positive and constant throughout but only about 1/10th as high as it was at the same stress before the stress was increased to 30.6 MPa. No recovery, i.e. no increase in creep rate with time from its low initial value is evident within the scatter of data over a period of 675 hours following the stress decrement.

Fig. 1c shows another example of a set of stress decrement tests on a domal salt whose properties are almost identical to those of Salado salt. In this second case, recovery is clearly evident after the first and second stress decrements. It also appears that the creep rates become constant relatively quickly, particularly after the first stress drop. Both of these observations are consistent with expectations using equations (2) - (6). However, surprisingly, the creep rates at the end of stage 2 and at the end of all subsequent stages of the experiment lay considerably below the creep rates which were determined at the same stresses in stress increment tests on two other samples. This comparison of results is shown in a plot of minimum observed creep rates versus stress in Fig. 8. If the data are fitted to a power law, then the stress increment data yield a stress exponent n = 5.06 while the stress decrement data yield n = 14.9. Similar observations have been reported previously for sodium chloride, aluminum, copper and α-brass (Pontikis and Poirier, 1975; Parker and Wilshire, 1976; Langdon et al., 1977).

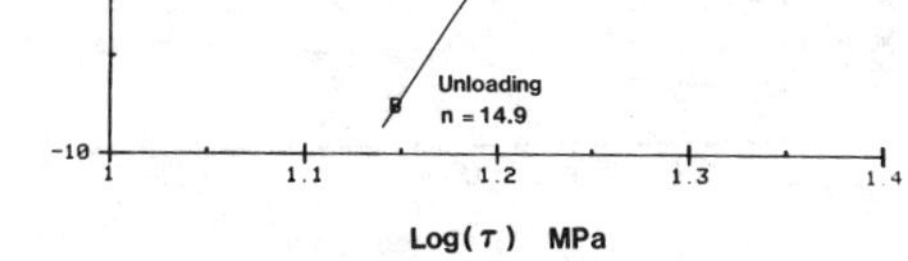

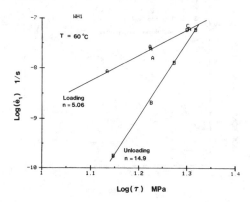

Figure 8: Comparison of minimum observed creep rates measured in stress increment (loading) and stress decrement (unloading) experiments at roughly equal test times.

If recovery was incomplete following the stress decrements of Fig. 1c, then the observed transients are not only underestimated by the model but could conceivably affect the design of an underground structure. Total creep might be overpredicted which is probably safe, but discrepancies in predicted and measured deformations might jeopardize field validation studies. On the other hand, if recovery was complete, new history dependent steady state creep rates were obtained contrary to previous assumptions. It is clear that the data of the tests shown in Fig. 7, 1c and 8 must be considered further.

One more uncertainty will be mentioned although it is not the only remaining one. It is well known that effective activation energies and power law stress exponents can be underestimated if creep rates are used which are not steady state creep rates (Woodford, 1969). Because of very low creep rates in the Salado salt experiments it was difficult to decide unambiguously when steady state creep had been reached. This decision was particularly difficult at ambient temperature. Because nearly half of the data were obtained at ambient temperature, it is possible, therefore, that the creep parameters Q and n obtained in fits are only lower bound estimates. Recent measurements (Wawersik, 1981; Hunsche, 1981) have yielded activation energies between 67 and 71 kJ/mole confirming this possibility.

5. COMPARISON OF PREDICTION AND MEASUREMENTS

Design calculations which utilize finite element methods with laboratory based constitutive equations are relatively new in predicting the long-term performance of underground structures in rock salt masses. This is particularly true where high temperatures are anticipated which have no precedence in mining experience. Therefore, confidence in design requires validation of the design procedures by comparing well documented, independent measurements with predictions. These evaluations must address a number of questions. Can laboratory measurements be extrapolated to the low stresses and long times pertinent to many in situ problems? How important is the inclusion of elastic properties in design calculations involving considerable creep? How important are transients due to changes in stress and temperature? How significant is the influence of stratigraphic features ranging from anhydrite, polyhalite and clay impurities to clay stringers, clay seams and anhydrite or shale layers? What is the effect of statistical variations in rock salt properties? What are the limitations and inaccuracies which are introduced by computational simplifications? Ultimately, all these considerations determine what design accuracies are achievable and whether errors are likely to be acceptable.

Several of the foregoing questions are dealt with in the following example of predicted and measured convergences in an isolated mine opening at the Esterhazy mine, IMC Corp., Canada (Mraz, 1978). The opening which was modeled is 6.0 m wide and 2.35 m high. It was driven in a shaft pillar in a horizontal evaporite bed. The rock composition over the height of the opening was 58.5% halite, 40.2% sylvite, .5% carnallite and .8% clay (Mraz, 1978). Clay stringers and up to 2% disseminated clay were reported to occur above the drift. The floor rocks were described to consist primarily of rock salt interbedded with anhydrite. The nearest hard rock layer was located approximately 30 m above the opening. Following excavation the drift was instru- with anchor bolts to monitor horizontal and vertical convergences.

To simulate the response of the evaporites around the Esterhazy drift, several assumptions were made. The rock mass properties were assumed to fit the model for Salado salt, depth 645-655 m. Based on published data it was deemed reasonable to equate the properties of sylvite to those of halite (Dreyer, 1972). The properties of the shallower Salado salt were believed to be more representative of the rock salt of mixed purity at Esterhazy. Also, the use of these properties made it possible to integrate the present predictions with those of an earlier study which did not include elastic terms in the material model (Munson and Dawson, 1980).

Closure calculations were done with the finite element code SANCHO (Morgan et al., 1981) which uses dynamic relaxation to solve plane strain, plane stress or axisymmetric problems involving large deformations and inelastic materials. Plane strain conditions were assumed using vertical symmetry planes at the drift center and 80 m from the drift center to define the vertical boundaries of the simulation. The horizontal boundaries of the model lay 42 m above and below the drift center. The top 12 m of the model consisted of a shale layer. The remaining material was halite. It was also assumed that the salt was under an initial lithostatic stress of 20.7 MPa, that the drift was excavated instantaneously and that the model temperature was 27°C and constant. Constant normal tractions were then maintained at 20.7 MPa across the top of the shale and across the bottom salt surface while the lateral boundary of the shale layer at 80 m was held fixed.

Two cases were considered:

A. The behavior of the salt mass was determined by its elastic and steady state creep properties.

B. The salt response was determined by its elastic and by both the steady state and transient creep properties (Montgomery, 1981).

Fig. 9 shows the calculated horizontal convergences between points at the surface and at 1.52 m and 6.1 m into the drift walls for case A. Regimes of almost constant convergence rates are predicted after approximately one year at the surface of the drift and after less than eight months at the other two stations. The rapid initial convergence rates are caused by high initial stresses due to the elastic rock properties. For example, the initial effective stresses at zero and 1 m into the drift wall are 42 MPa and 14 MPa. These stresses change to 23 MPa and 13 MPa after three days. At that time they are probably representative of the highest stresses in the immediate wall of the Esterhazy drift at the end of a finite excavation period.

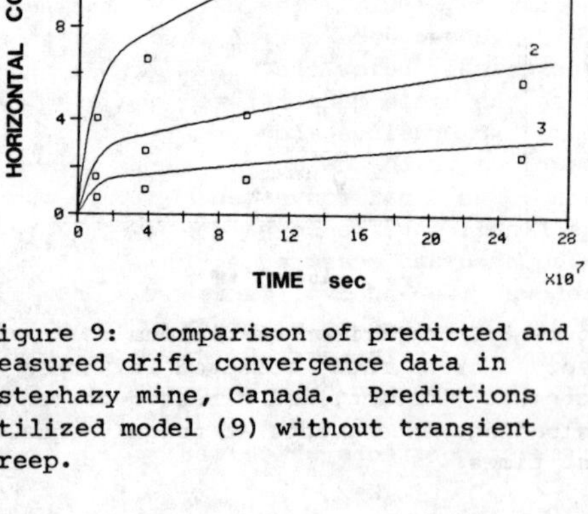

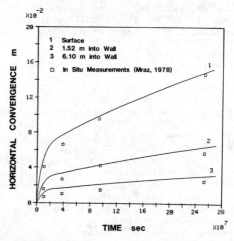

Figure 9: Comparison of predicted and measured drift convergence data in Esterhazy mine, Canada. Predictions utilized model (9) without transient creep.

Detailed stress histories are shown in Figs. 10a and 10b as functions of the horizontal distance from the drift wall. The stresses right below the surface of the drift wall are highest at early times (Fig. 10a) while the far-field stresses (Fig. 10b) are almost unaffected by the drift. As time goes on, the stress field perturbation due to the drift propagates outward causing the far-field stresses to rise. These stress increases are followed by stress drops to almost stationary values everywhere.

Fig. 11 gives a comparison of the predicted and horizontal convergence histories at the drift surface with and without the contributions of transient creep during the first 27 days after the simulated drift excavation (case B). Differences in results are limited to convergence rates at very early times. Essentially no difference remains thereafter. Therefore, the predictions of Figs. 9 and 10 which were made only by means of elastic and steady state creep terms appear to be representative for the behavior which corresponds to the complete constitutive model (9).

Further details of the Esterhazy drift simulation will be given elsewhere. However, several observations are important within the context of this paper. Overall, remarkably good agreement is attained between a simulation and completely independent in situ measurements. Although the closeness of the predicted and measured convergence histories may be fortuitous, it raises hope that the design procedures which are described here may be valid in rock salt masses.

The results in Figs. 9 and 10 are directly comparable to an earlier analysis (Munson and Dawson, 1980) which also describes the creep around the Esterhazy drift but did not consider the elastic salt properties. The comparison is possible because the creep models in both simulations were equivalent (Herrmann and Lauson, 1981). The earlier analysis yields convergence curves which first lie considerably below the field data, then cross the field data between one and 5 1/2 years and continue above the in situ measurements to the end of the simulation. The final convergence rates and the final convergence values which were calculated and measured differed by factors 1.75 and 1.4 (Munson and Dawson, 1980). Although this agreement is quite favorable, it is less satisfactory than that shown in Fig. 9. This fact is believed to demonstrate again the importance of elastic effects which set up a more

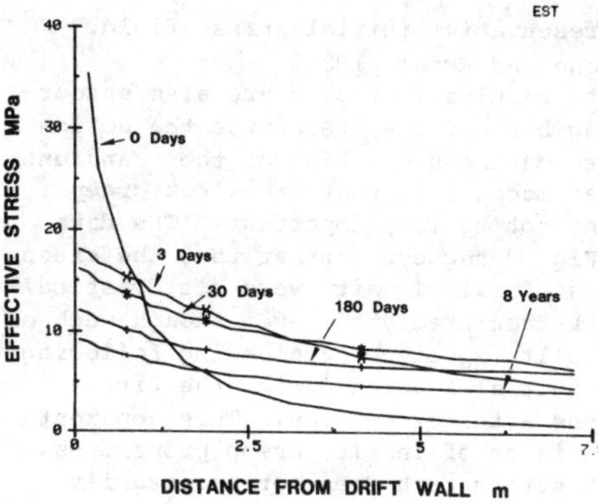

(a) Near-field stresses,

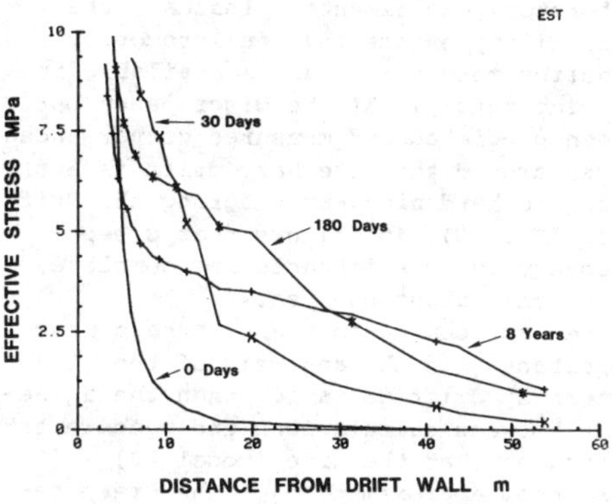

(b) Far-field stresses.

Figure 10: Predicted stress distribution along horizontal distance from drift wall, using model (9) without transient creep.

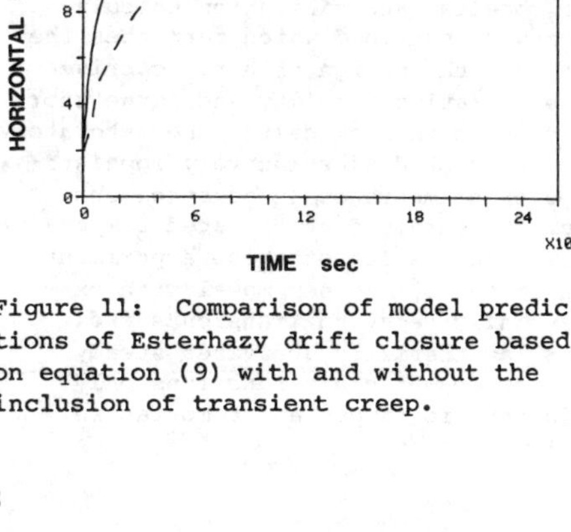

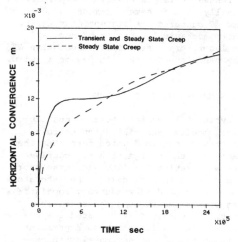

Figure 11: Comparison of model predictions of Esterhazy drift closure based on equation (9) with and without the inclusion of transient creep.

representative initial stress field. (Stone and Krieg, 1981)

The results in Fig. 9 are also encouraging because they reinforce the notion, based on the properties of the transient creep model (3), that transient creep might not be very important. The data in Fig. 9 suggest further that the creep rates of salt in situ were not drastically lower than predicted, even though much of the salt experienced unloading following the initial loading during the first months after excavation. This apparent invariance of in situ creep properties with stress path does not necessarily contradict the measurement of anomalously low creep rates upon stress drops in some laboratory experiments. Instead, the possibility exists that full recovery requires more time than is available in the laboratory. If the discrepancy between predicted and measured convergences rates around the Esterhazy drift is attributed to hardening early during the drift life (Fig. 9), it follows that creep recovery in this instance was complete after only about one year.

The last conclusions are perhaps most important. If the analysis of the Esterhazy drift is valid, then the agreement between calculations and measurements indicates that the creep model (2) - (6) is a good approximation of the creep behavior of rock salt regardless of the nature and number of rate controlling deformation mechanisms. The model also would appear to apply to low stresses which are only half as large as the lowest stresses in laboratory creep experiments. Finally, the agreement demonstrated in Fig. 9 supports the assumption that the thermomechanical behavior of rock salt in laboratory tests is representative of the behavior of rock salt masses in situ.

6. SUMMARY AND CONCLUSIONS

A cycle of laboratory tests, constitutive modeling and validation calculations was described which furnishes the basis for the design of a radioactive waste isolation facility and large storage caverns in rock salt. The laboratory tests consisted of relatively sophisticated experiments on large specimens under pressure and at elevated temperature. The results of these experiments were fitted by a creep model with exponentially decaying transients and power law thermally activated steady state creep which are functions only of deviatoric stress and temperature. The model was then cast into a three dimensional constitutive equation.

As a third step, the constitutive model was tested against published convergence measurements in an almost isolated mine drift. This was accomplished by means of a finite element code for large deformations using inelastic material properties. The agreement between calculated and measured convergence rates and absolute convergences is remarkably good and, therefore, supports the validity of the entire design procedure, in spite of several uncertainties concerning the mechanistic interpretation of the creep model, the generalization of available laboratory data to arbitrary stress histories and the extrapolation of the proposed constitutive model to long times and low stresses. The finite element simulation further demonstrates the importance of the elastic properties of salt in the prediction of the behavior of salt masses.

Considering the difficulties of gathering and interpreting laboratory creep data at low strain rates, the finite element computations which have been presented underline the need and the value of analyzing case histories to validate the procedures for excavation design in salt and to establish that the present agreement between predictions and in situ measurements is not fortuitous.

7. REFERENCES

Amadieh, A. and A. K. Mukherjee 1975, Transient and steady state creep curves in Ni-Fe alloy system, Scripta Met. 9: 1299-1304.

Amin, K. E., A. K. Mukherjee and J. E. Dorn 1970, A universal law for high-temperature diffusion controlled transient creep, J. Mech. Phys. Solids, 8: 413-426.

Blum, W. and B. Ilschner 1967, Ueber das Kriechverhalten von NaCl-Einkristallen, Phys. Stat. Sol. 20: 629-642

Burke, P. M. 1968, High temperature creep of polycrystalline sodium chloride, PhD Thesis, Stanford Univ.

Conway, J. B. and M. J. Mullikin 1966, Techniques for analyzing combined first- and second-stage creep data, Trans. Met. Soc. AIME 236: 1629.

Dreyer, W. 1972, The Science of Rock Mechanics, Part 1, Trans. Tech. Publications, Clauthal-Zellerfeld.

Evans, W. J. and B. Wilshire 1968, Transient and steady state creep behavior of nickel, zinc and iron, Trans. Metal Soc. AIME 242: 1303.

Garafalo, F., C. Richmond, W. F. Domis and F. von Gemmingen 1963, Strain-time, rate-stress and rate-temperature relations during large deformations in creep, ASME, Joint Int. Conf. on Creep, p. 1-31.

Hansen, F. D. and K. D. Mellegard 1977, Creep behavior of bedded salt from Southeastern New Mexico at elevated temperatures, RSI-0062, RE/SPEC, Inc., Rapid City, SD.

Hansen, F. D. and K. D. Mellegard 1979, Further creep behavior of bedded salt from Southeastern New Mexico at elevated temperatures, RSI-0104, RE/SPEC, Inc., Rapid City, SD.

Heard, H. C. 1972, Steady-state flow in polycrystalline halite at pressure of 2 kb, Geophys. Monogr. 16, Flow and Fracture of Rocks, AGU, p. 197-209.

Herrmann, W. and H. S. Lauson 1981, Review and comparison of transient creep laws used for natural rock salt, SAND81-0738, Sandia National Laboratories, Albuquerque, New Mexico.

Herrmann, W., W. R. Wawersik and H. S. Lauson 1980a, Creep curves and fitting parameters for Southeastern New Mexico bedded salt, SAND80-0087, Sandia National Laboratories, Albuquerque, New Mexico.

Herrmann, W., W. R. Wawersik and H. S. Lauson 1980b, A model for transient creep of Southeastern New Mexico salt, SAND80-2172, Sandia National Laboratories, Albuquerque, New Mexico.

Herrmann, W., W. R. Wawersik and H. S. Lauson 1980c, Analysis of steady state creep of Southeastern New Mexico bedded salt, SAND80-0558, Sandia National Laboratories, Albuquerque, New Mexico.

Hunsche, U. 1982, Results and interpretation of creep experiments on rock salt, Proc. First Conf. Mech. Beh. of Salt, Penn State Univ., Nov. 1981 (in press).

Ilschner, B. 1973, Hochtemperatur-Plastizitaet, Springer Verlag.

Jefferson, H. 1974, TJMARI-A FORTRAN subroutine for nonlinear least squares parameter estimation, SLL73-0305, Sandia National Laboratories, Albuquerque, New Mexico.

Langdon, T. G., R. B. Vastava and P. Yavari 1977, The influence of substructure on creep behavior following stress changes, Strength of Metals and Alloys, ICSMA5 1: 271-276.

Montgomery, S. T. 1981, Implementation of a transient creep model for natural rock salt as a material response subroutine for SANCHO, SAND81-1163, Sandia National Laboratories, Albuquerque, New Mexico.

Morgan, H. S., R. D. Krieg and R. V. Matalucci 1981, Comparative analysis of nine structural codes used in the second WIPP benchmark problem, SAND81-1389, Sandia National Laboratories, Albuquerque, New Mexico.

Mraz, D. 1978, Theoretical predictions confirmed by in situ rock behavior in deep potash mine, Proc. 19th U.S. Rock Mechanics Symposium, Y. S. Kim, ed., University of Nevada, Reno, Nevada.

Munson, D. E. and P. R. Dawson 1980, Numerical simulation of creep closure of deep potash mines with application to waste isolation, SAND80-0467, Sandia National Laboratories, Albuquerque, New Mexico.

Nix, W. O. and B. Ilschner 1977, Mechanisms controlling creep of single phase metals and alloys, Strength of Metals and Alloys, Pergamon Press, ICSMA5 3: 1503-1530.

Parker, J. D. and B. Wilshire 1976, On the subgrain size dependence of creep, Phil. Mag. 34 3: 485-489.

Pontikis, V. and J. P. Poirier 1975, Phenomenological and structural analysis of recovery-controlled creep, with special reference to the creep of single-crystal silver chloride, Phil. Mag., 32, 3, 577-592.

Powers, D. W., et al. 1978, Geological characterization report, waste isolation pilot plant (WIPP) site, Southeastern New Mexico, Vol. II, SAND78-7076, Sandia National Laboratories, Albuquerque, New Mexico.

Sherby, O. D. and P. M. Burke 1967, Mechanical behavior of crystalline solids at elevated temperature, Progr. Mat. Sci. 13: 325-389.

Stone, C. S. and R. D. Krieg 1981, personal communication, Sandia National Laboratories, Albuquerque, New Mexico.

Threadgill, P. L. and B. Wilshire 1972, Mechanisms of transient and steady-state creep in a γ'-hardened austenitic steel, Creep Strength in Steel and High-Temperature Alloys, The Metals Soc.: 8-14.

Wawersik, W. R. and D. W. Hannum 1978, Interim summary of Sandia creep experiments from the WIPP study area, Southeastern New Mexico, SAND79-0115, Sandia National Laboratories, Albuquerque, New Mexico.

Wawersik, W. R. 1979, Indirect deformation (strain) measurements and calibrations in Sandia triaxial apparatus for testing to 250°C, SAND79-0114, Sandia National Laboratories, Albuquerque, New Mexico.

Wawersik, W. R. and D. W. Hannum 1980, Mechanical behavior of New Mexico rock salt in triaxial compression up to 200°C, J. Geophys. Res. B2, 85: 891-900.
Wawersik, W. R. 1981, New comparisons of creep rates for rock salt as a function of temperature to 160°C ($\tau = 0.4\ \tau_m$), Trans. Am. Geophys. Union, 62, 45 (abstact).
Wawersik, W. R. and D. S. Preece 1982, Creep testing of salt - procedures, problems and suggestions, Proc. First Conf. Mech. Behavior of Salt, Penn. State Univ., November 1981 (in press).
Webster, G. A., A. P. O. Cox and J. E. Dorn 1969, A relationship between transient and steady-state creep at elevated temperature, Metal Sci. J. 3: 221-225.
Weertman, J. 1968, Dislocation climb theory of steady state creep, ASM Trans. Quart 61: 681-694.
Woodford, D. A. 1969, Measurement and interpretation of the stress dependence of creep at low stress, Mat. Sci. Engr. 4: 146-154.

KV-638-576

ROCK MECHANICS: CAVERNS AND PRESSURE SHAFTS
FELSMECHANIK: KAVERNEN UND DRUCKSCHÄCHTE
MÉCANIQUE DES ROCHES: LES CAVERNES ET LES PUITS SOUS PRESSION

2

ISRM SYMPOSIUM / AACHEN / 1982.05.26-28

ROCK MECHANICS: CAVERNS AND PRESSURE SHAFTS

FELSMECHANIK: KAVERNEN UND DRUCKSCHÄCHTE

MÉCANIQUE DES ROCHES: LES CAVERNES ET LES PUITS SOUS PRESSION

Editor / Redakteur / Rédacteur

W. WITTKE

Institut für Grundbau, Bodenmechanik, Felsmechanik und Verkehrswasserbau, Aachen

VOLUME 2

Pressure Tunnels / Tunneling Machines / Underground Storage
Druckstollen / Tunnelvortriebsmaschinen / Untertägige Speicherung
Galeries forcées / Foreuses de tunnels / Stockage souterrain

Published for / Herausgegeben für / Publié pour
Deutsche Gesellschaft für Erd- und Grundbau e.V., Essen

A.A.BALKEMA / ROTTERDAM / 1982

05846456

The texts of the various papers in this volume were set individually by typists under the supervision of each of the authors concerned

For the complete set of three volumes, ISBN 90 6191 232 6
For Volume 1, ISBN 90 6191 233 4
For Volume 2, ISBN 90 6191 234 2
For Volume 3, ISBN 90 6191 235 0

© 1982 A.A.Balkema, P.O.Box 1675, Rotterdam, Netherlands
Distributed in USA & Canada by: MBS, 99 Main Street, Salem, NH 03079, USA
Published for the Deutsche Gesellschaft für Erd- und Grundbau e.V., 4300 Essen 1, Kronprinzenstrasse 35a

Printed in the Netherlands

D
624.1513
Roc

CONTENTS / INHALT / TABLE DES MATIÈRES

3 PART / TEIL / PARTIE

Load sharing capacity of the rock mass for pressure tunnels and shafts
Mittragende Wirkung des Gebirges bei Druckstollen und Druckschächten
Effet de la portance du terrain dans le cas des galeries forcées et des puits sous pression

5 PART / TEIL / PARTIE

Rock mechanical problems in association with underground storage
Felsmechanische Probleme im Zusammenhang mit der untertägigen Speicherung
Problèmes de mécanique des roches en relation avec le stockage souterrain

* 3 *

LOAD SHARING CAPACITY OF THE ROCK MASS FOR PRESSURE TUNNELS AND SHAFTS

Mittragende Wirkung des Gebirges bei Druckstollen und Druckschächten

Effet de la portance du terrain dans le cas des galeries forcées et des puits sous pression

DESIGN OF UNLINED PRESSURE SHAFT AT MAURANGER POWER PLANT, NORWAY

Entwurf eines nicht ausgekleideten Druckschachtes bei der Wasserkraftanlage Mauranger, Norwegen

Dimensionnement d'un puits sans soutènement de la centrale hydroélectrique Mauranger, Norvège

J.BERGH-CHRISTENSEN
A/S GEOTEAM, Oslo, Norway

SUMMARY:
The Mauranger Hydro-Electric Power Plant in Western Norway utilizes a 455 metre static head unlined pressure shaft. The paper describes the investigations performed and the criteria applied for the design of the shaft.

ZUSAMMENFASSUNG:
Die Wasserkraftanlage Mauranger in West-Norwegen nützt das Wasser mit einer statischen Druckhöhe von 455 m durch eine unverbaute Druckschacht aus. Es wird über die ausgeführten Untersuchungen berichtet zusammen mit den angewandten Kriterien für den Entwurf der Schacht.

RESUME:
Le complexe hydro-électrique de Mauranger dans la Norvège de l'ouest comporte un puits sans revêtement sous pressión hydrostatique de 455 mètres. Le présent article deċrit les reconnaissances effectuées et les critères de désign pour le puits de pression.

INTRODUCTION

The Folgefonni Hydro-Electric Power Project, developed and owned by the State Power Board, utilizes run-off from the great Folgefonn glacier in Western Norway. The Project comprises the Jukla Pumped-Storage Station (Bergh-Christensen 1982) and the Mauranger Power Station, as shown in Fig. 1.

The general layout of the Mauranger Power Plant is indicated in Figs. 2 and 3. It includes a 20 m^2 unlined pressure shaft with a maximum static head of 455 metres.

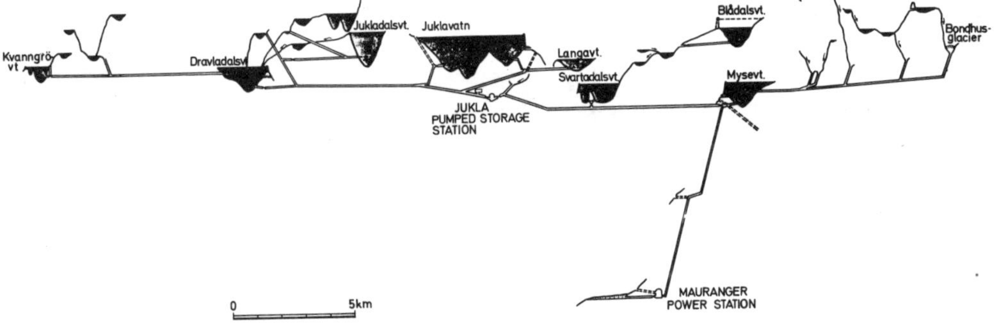

Fig. 1: The Folgefonni Hydro-Electric Power Project.

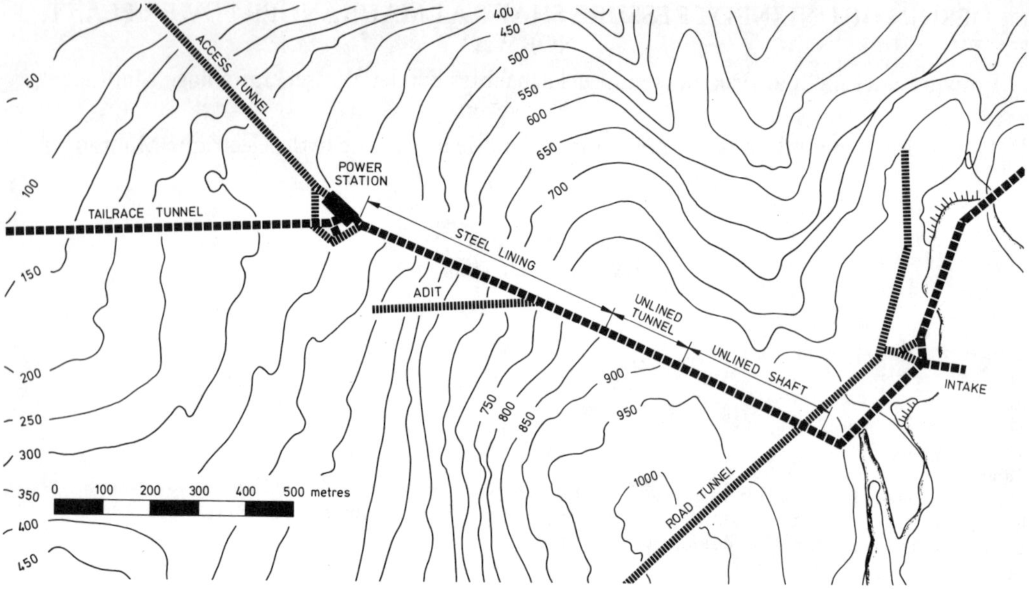

Fig. 2: Mauranger Power Plant, general layout.

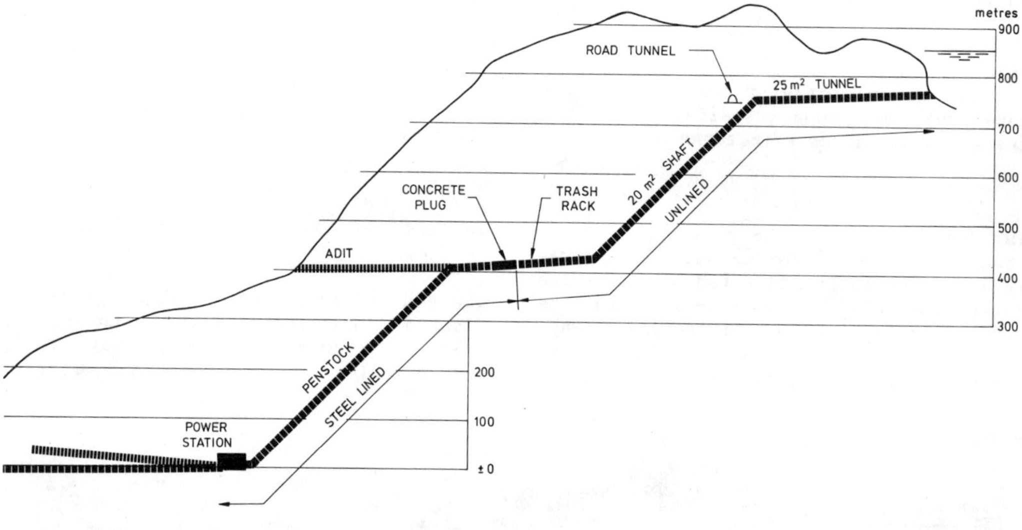

Fig. 3: Mauranger Power Plant, section.

The utilization of unlined tunnels and pressure shafts in hydro-electric power plants has long traditions in Norway. More than 50 unlined shafts or tunnels with heads higher than 150 metres have been put into operation (Broch and Selmer-Olsen 1982).

Detailed planning of the Mauranger project started in 1970. The failure of a 300 metre static-head unlined pressure shaft at Brokke Power Plant in 1968 (Selmer-Olsen 1970), and then the failure of a 200 metre static-head unlined pressure tunnel at Åskåra Power Plant in 1970 (Bergh-Christensen 1975), indicated the need for detailed geological investigations for this type of project, as well as the need for re-evaluation of the "rule of thumb" design criteria applied up to then for siting of unlined shafts and tunnels.

SITE INVESTIGATIONS

Acting as engineering geological consultant to the State Power Board, A/S GEOTEAM was responsible for all site investigations and rock mechanics design evaluations performed prior to and during the construction of the Mauranger pressure shaft.

As the first step in the field investigations, a geological survey of the site was performed, followed by detailed geological logging during excavation of tunnels and shafts. The rock is a Pre-Cambrian granitic gneiss. The head-race tunnel and the upper 70 metres of the pressure shaft are cut by a series of faults containing swelling clay gouge. The close proximity of a road tunnel called for extensive sealing and grouting works to be performed in these parts of the project in order to avoid excessive leakages. The main part of the unlined pressure shaft and pressure tunnel designed for a maximum 455 metre static head was, however, placed in moderately jointed rock.

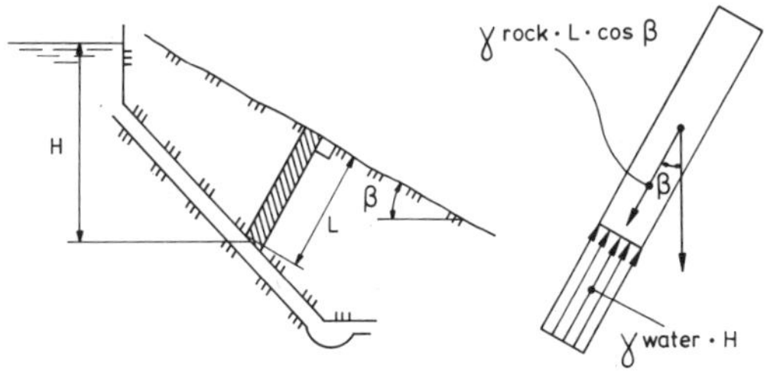

Fig. 4: Limit equilibrium condition.

For assessment of rock stress conditions, borehole in situ rock stress measurements were performed at two locations in the unlined high pressure tunnel. These measurements showed the rock stress to be highly anisotropic, with σ_3 -values of only 5 to 12 MPa(kp/cm^2); i.e. only a fraction of the intended water pressure.

"STATE OF THE ART" STUDY

In order to establish design criteria for the project a "state of the art" study was performed, including:

- Review of proposed design guidelines for unlined pressure shafts.
- Case studies of existing unlined high pressure tunnels and shafts, including known projects where total failure or severe leakages had occurred.
- Theoretical study of potential failure modes, including induced "hydraulic fracturing".

A review of the failures of unlined shafts/tunnels at the Brokke and Åskåra power plants revealed that the two incidents had certain features in common:

- Both are situated in steep valley slopes.
- Both are cut by steep, permeable joints and weakness zones striking nearly parallel to the slope.
- The "side cover" of the tunnel/shaft -measured as the shortest distance out to the valley slope - is moderate, and lower than the vertical rock cover.

At both sites, the failure mechanism was thought to be as follows:

leakage from the unlined shaft/tunnel allowed the build-up of high joint water pressures, which in turn caused a deformation of the "side-burden" rock and opening of joints to form a composite failure plane. This in turn caused washing out of gouge material and large scale water out-bursts in the valley slope.

Both incidents illustrated the importance of geological detail, and the importance of adequate rock cover for the safe construction of unlined shafts.

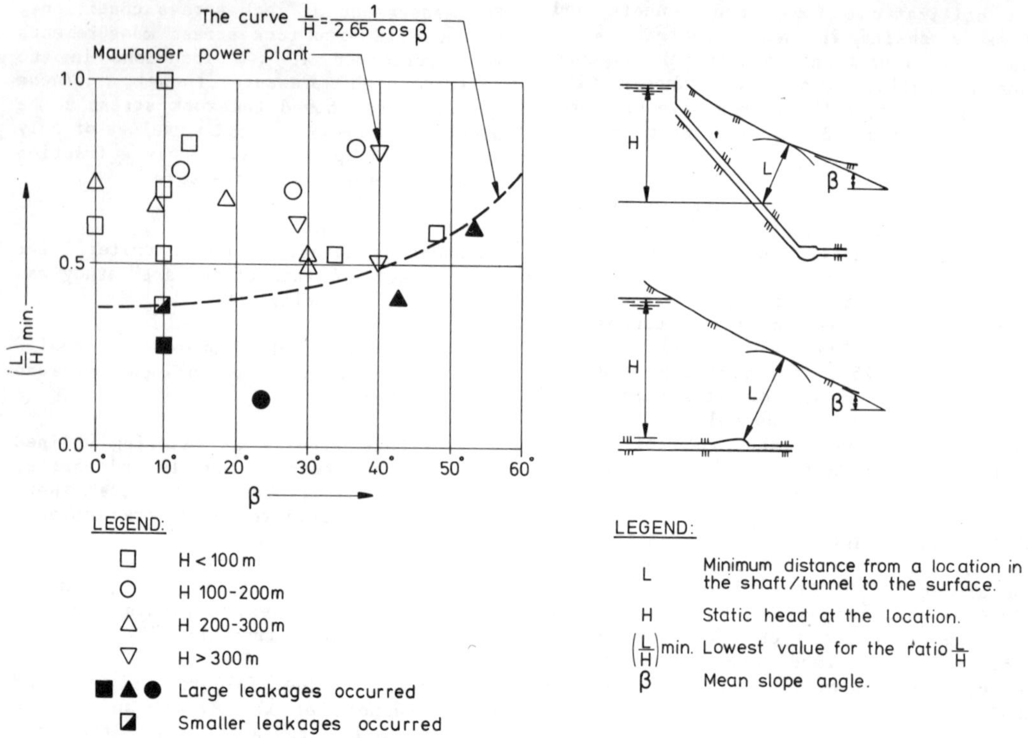

Fig. 5: Rock cover conditions at unlined shafts and tunnels.

ROCK COVER CONDTIONS

A review was performed of rock cover conditions at the major unlined shafts and tunnels completed in Norway at that time (Bergh-Christensen and Dannevig, 1971), resulting in a diagram, as shown in Fig. 5.

A simple equation defining the limit equilibrium between water pressure and rock weight for a potential displacement towards a free surface as defined in Fig. 4 indicates necessary rock cover

$$\frac{L}{H} \geq \frac{1}{2.65 \cos\beta}$$

When this limit curve is plotted onto Fig. 5, it is seen to give a fair agreement with the empirical data. It is also found to be in agreement with criteria defined by Kieser (1960) for shafts without steel lining.

As shown in Fig. 5 the rock cover at Mauranger should be adequate compared with the above criteria and the empirical data.

HYDRAULIC FRACTURING EVALUATIONS

However, the very low values found by the in situ rock stress measurements necessitated an analysis of the potential for failure by "hydraulic fracturing". Hydraulic fracturing is a term well known in petroleum engineering as a method of increasing well yield. It comprises creating and propagating fractures in the reservoir rock by injecting fluid under pressure through a well bore to overcome native stresses and cause material failure. The same failure mechanisms might under certain conditions apply when high water pressures are applied to the large diameter "well-bore" of a pressure shaft or tunnel.

The basic mechanisms of hydraulic fracturing have been discussed by Hubert and Willis (1957), Barenblatt (1962), Geertsma (1966), Howard and Fast (1970), and others. Some simple conclusions may be drawn from these papers:

a) The basic condition for the opening up of a permeable joint is that the fluid pressure in the joint exceeds the native in situ normal stress on the joint plane.

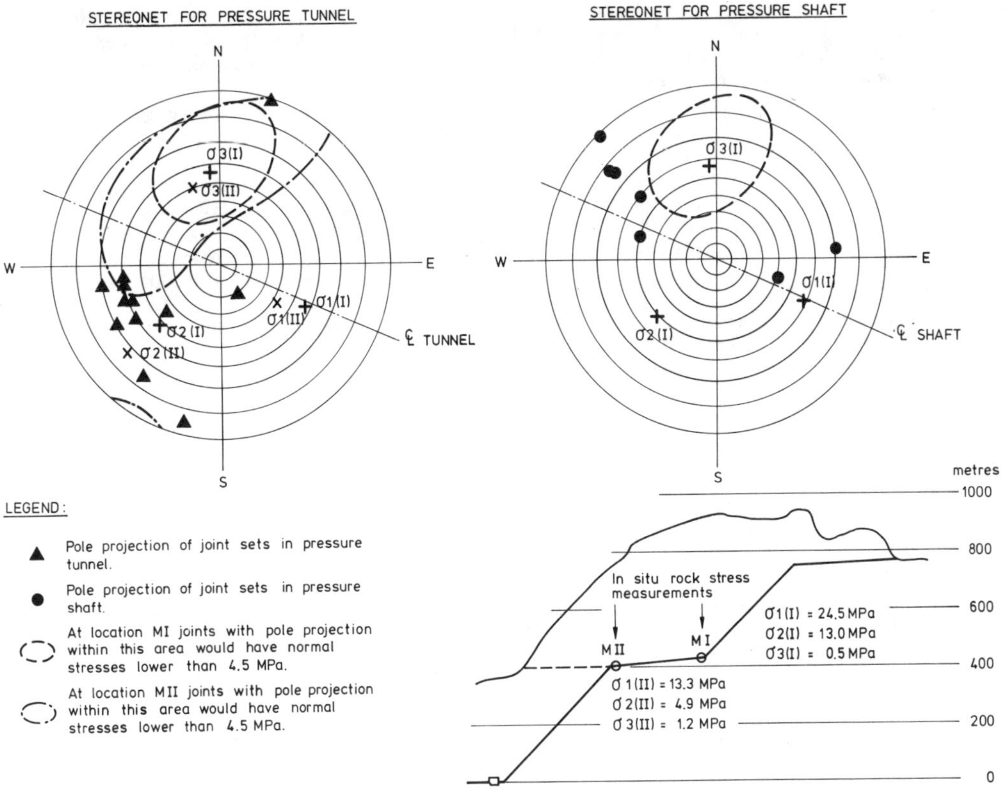

Fig. 6: Comparison of in situ joint data with critical normal stress orientations.

b) When condition a) is fulfilled, the propagation of a fracture may <u>theoretically</u> continue as long as injection of fluid is continued and the fracure acts as a closed system (without drainage or pressure loss).

c) Field data from hydraulic fracturing of oilwells show that the "breakdown pressure" needed for initiation of fractures from a well is higher than the inferred effective overburden pressure, and also higher than the pressure needed for propagation of the fractures once initiated.

Applying these conditions on the Mauranger shaft, it was assumed that a potential composite failure due to hydraulic fracturing would have to develop along pre-existing joints (tensile strengh of the rock being higher than the intended water pressure). The basic question might then be put as:

Is the pressure tunnel or shaft intersected by any joint-sets with an orientation such that the native normal stress on the joints is less than the intended water pressure?

A detailed logging of joint-sets was performed in the pressure tunnel and shaft. Based on the in situ rock stress measurements, the orientation of planes with a theoretical normal stress lower than 45 MPa was calculated, and compared with the joint orientation data, as visualized in Fig. 6. Based on this analysis it was concluded that none of the native joint sets had an orientation that would facilitate a hydraulic fracturing type large scale failure.

Based on the above evaluations it was concluded that the conditions at Mauranger, as revealed by the site investigations, would allow the pressure shaft and pressure tunnel to remain unlined.

However, some modifications in the design were recommended and a detailed programme for systematic grouting of a number of potential leakage sections were specified.

CONCLUDING REMARKS

The tunnel and shaft was completed in 1973. During the first water filling of the system, joint water pressures and leakages were closely monitored. The total leakages from the pressure tunnel and shaft - with an exposed rock area of the order of 13,000 m^2, dropped from an initial value of 0.5 litres/second to 0.1 litres/second when the surrounding rock had been fully saturated.

The unlined pressure shaft and pressure tunnel at Mauranger has been in continuous operation since 1974 without any problems with leakage or stability.

Current pre-investigation methods for unlined pressure shafts and pressure tunnels include both detailed geological site investigations, in situ rock stress measurements and the use of finite-element models for computer analysis of assumed stress conditions, as described by for instance Broch and Selmer-Olsen (1982) and Bergh-Christensen and Kjølberg (1982).

The present paper summarizes some of the investigations that constitute part of the basis for current Norwegian design methods. In particular, the concept of "hydraulic fracturing" related to pressure shafts and pressure tunnels is discussed.

REFERENCES

Barenblatt, G.J., 1962: The mathematical theory of equilibrium cracks in brittle fracture. Advances in Applied Mechanics, 7, pp. 55-129.

Bergh-Christensen, J., 1975: Brudd i uforet trykktunnel ved Åskåra kraftverk (Failure of unlined pressure tunnel at Åskåra Power Plant). Proc. Bergmekanikkdagen 1974. Tapir, Trondheim.

Bergh-Christensen, J. 1982: Unlined compressed air surge chamber for 24 atmospheres pressure at Jukla Power Plant. Proc. Int. Symp. on Rock Mech. related to Caverns and Pressure Shafts, Aachen 1982.

Bergh-Christensen, J. and Dannevig, N.T., 1971: Ingeniørgeologiske vurderinger vedrørende uforet trykksjakt ved Mauranger Kraftverk, Folgefonnanleggene. A/S GEOTEAM Report number 2398.03.

Bergh-Christensen, J. and Kjølberg, R.S., 1982: Investigations for a 1,000 metre head unlined pressure shaft at the Nyset-Steggje Project, Norway. Proc. Int. Symp. on Rock Mech. related to Caverns and Pressure Shafts, Aachen 1982.

Broch, E. and Selmer-Olsen, R., 1982: The development of unlined shafts and tunnels in Norway. Proc. Int. Symp. on Roch Mech. related to Caverns and Pressure Shafts, Aachen 1982.

Geertsma, J., 1966: Problems of rock mechanics in petroleum production engineering. Proc. 1st. Congr. I.S.R.M. Vol I -3.59. Lisboa 1966.

Howard, G.C. and Fast, C.R., 1970: Hydraulic fracturing. AIME Soc. of Petr. Eng. New York, Dallas.

Hubbert, M.K. and Willis, D.G., 1957: Mechanics of hydraulic fracturing. Trans AIME 210, P. 153.

Kieser, A., 1960: Druckstollenbau. Wien, Springer Verlag.

Selmer-Olsen, R., 1970: Experience with unlined pressure shafts in Norway. Proc. Int. Symp. on Large Permanent Underground Openings, Oslo 1969.

INVESTIGATIONS FOR A 1000 METRE HEAD UNLINED PRESSURE SHAFT AT THE NYSET/STEGGJE PROJECT, NORWAY

Untersuchungen für einen nicht ausgekleideten Druckschacht mit 1000 Meter statischer Druckhöhe der Nyset/Steggje Wasserkraftanlage, Norwegen

Reconnaissances en vue d'un puits sous pression sans soutènement d'une hauteur de refoulement de 1000 m du projet Nyset/Steggje, Norvège

J.BERGH-CHRISTENSEN & R.S.KJØLBERG
A/S GEOTEAM, Oslo, Norway

SUMMARY:
The paper describes pre-investigations for a 1000-metre head unlined pressure shaft at the Nyset-Steggje Hydro-Power Project in Western Norway.

The field investigations performed have included a thorough engineering geological mapping of rock types, joint patterns and zones of weakness. Rock samples have been collected for laboratory investigations of rock mechanics properties.

The rocks in the shaft area consist of gneiss and granite, only slightly jointed and with few zones of weakness. The drillability and wear investigations indicate medium to good drillability and medium to low wear.

To locate the shaft, a finite element analysis of the rock stresses have been performed. The main condition imposed is that the minimum in situ compressive stresses must be higher than the water pressure at any point along the shaft. Because of complicated topography a simplified topographic model has been established. The planned shaft has a location oblique in relation to the valley side. The calculations are therefore performed by means of 3 two-dimensional models representing vertical sections cutting the shaft at critical points.

In situ stresses will be measured. If these differ appreciably from the calculated stresses, a re-evaluation of the shaft will have to be undertaken.

ZUSAMMENFASSUNG
Die Voruntersuchungen für eine unverbaute Druckschacht von 1000 meter statischer Druckhöhe bei der Wasserkraftanlage Nyset-Steggje in West-Norwegen werden beschrieben.

Gebirgsarten, Kluftscharen und zerstörte Zonen wurden im Felde ingenieurgeologisch kartiert. Ausgewählte Felsproben wurden auf felsmechanischen Eigenschaften im Laboratorium untersucht.

Die Gebirgsarten im Gebiet der Druckschact bestehen aus Gneiss und Granit, wenig zerklüftet und fast ohne zerstörte Zonen. Spezielle Laboruntersuchungen indikieren dass mittlere Bohrbarkeit und mittlerer bis geringer Verschleiss der Bohrwerkzeuge zu erwarten sind.

Eine endliche Element Analyse der Felsspannungen wurde ausgeführt um eine sichere Lage der Druckschacht zu finden. Eine grundlegende Bedingung ist dass die kleinste in situ auftretende Druckspannung in irgend einem Punkt entlang der Schacht kleiner sein muss als der dort Auftretende Wasserdruck. Die topographischen Verhältnisse sind recht kompliziert weshalb ein vereinfachter topographischer Model verwendet wurde. Die geplante Schacht hat zur Talseite eine schräge Orientierung. Die Berechnungen wurden mit Hilfe von drei zweidimensionalen Modellen durchgeführt. Diese Modelle repräsentieren Vertikalschnitte durch die Schacht in kritischen Punkten.

Die Spannungen in situ werden gemessen werden. Falls die so gemessenen Spannungen erheblich von den errechneten Spannungen abweichen werden, müssen neue Uberlegungen bezüglich der Schacht unternommen werden.

RESUME:
L'article decrit les reconnaissances préliminaires menées pour le projet hydroénergétique de Nyset-Steggje, dans la Norvège de l'ouest. Le projet comporte un puits non-revêtu destiné à des pressions de 1000 mètres d'eau.

Les reconnaissances effectuées en chantier ont inclus une cartographie detailleé des conditions geólogiques, formation rocheuse, plans de fissuration et zones de faiblesse. Des eĉhantillons de roches ont été prélevés pour fins d'essais des propriétés mécaniques en laboratoire.

Dans les environs du puits, la formation rocheuse consiste de gneiss et de granite, avec peu de fissures et peu de zones de faiblesse. Les études de la forabilité et de l'index d'usure de la tête de forage indiquent une forabilité moyenne à bonne, et une usure moyenne à faible.

A fin de déterminer la position optimum du puits, une analyse par éléments finis des contraintes dans le rocher a été faite. La critere principal imposé requiert que la contrainte minimale in situ soit superieure à la pression maximale de l'eau sur les parois due puits. Les conditions topographiques complexes au site ont nécessité le recours à un modèle topographique simplifié. Le puits proposé est localisé sur une oblique relativement à la pente de la valleé. Les calculs ont été faits au moyen de trois modèles bi-dimensionnels que representent des sections verticales intersectant le puits à divers points critiques.

Les contraintes in situ seront mesureés. Si celles-ci diffèrent de facon importante des contraintes pfedites au moyen de calculs, une réévaluation du puits sera entreprise.

INTRODUCTION

Årdal og Sunndal Verk, one of the main producers of aluminium in Norway, is planning a new power project at Årdal in Western Norway.

The main part of the project area is rugged mountain terrain, about 1,000 - 1,200 metres above sea level.

Figure 1 shows how the Nyset River and Steggje River are regulated. Water from the lake Berdalsvatnet in the northern part of the area will be taken through a 12 kilometre long tunnel to the reservoir. The Steggje River and a tributary river are also taken into the tunnel on the way to the reservoir. In the reservoir area a 43 metre high earth fill dam with a bitumate membrane will be constructed. The maximum water level here will be 980.3 metres above sea level.

From the reservoir the water is led through a headrace tunnel to the top of the pressure shaft at an altitude of 800 metres. The pressure shaft itself will have an inclination of 45°, with its lower end (at sea level) just inside the power plant. The shaft is planned to be unlined. From the power station a 2.5 kilometre long tailrace tunnel will lead to an outlet in the fjord.

The terrain in the shaft area consists of a high altitude plane at elevation 1,100-1,200 metres, with steep irregular rocky slopes down towards the fjord and the valley along the Nyset River, as shown on the map in Figure 2.

Originally a steel penstock was planned from the headrace tunnel located at ground level and down the steep slope to the power plant, also located at ground level. The investigations along the pipe alignment showed, however, that there was a high risk of rock falls and slides and therefore the possibility of damage to the pipe was great. Because of this an alternative site was chosen with the shaft and power plant underground.

GEOLOGICAL SETTING

The sequence of rocks found in this part of Norway is:

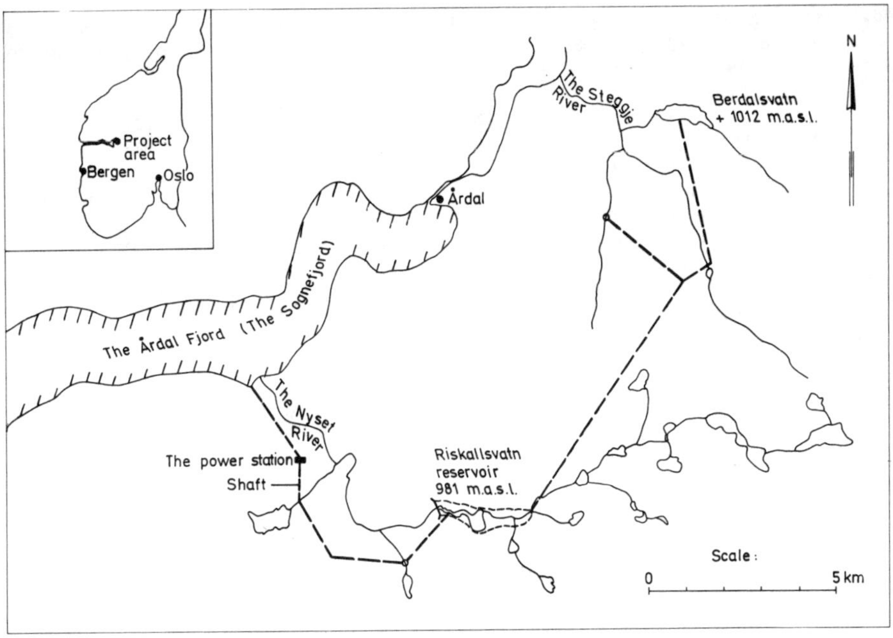

Fig. 1. The Nyset-Steggje Hydropower Project.

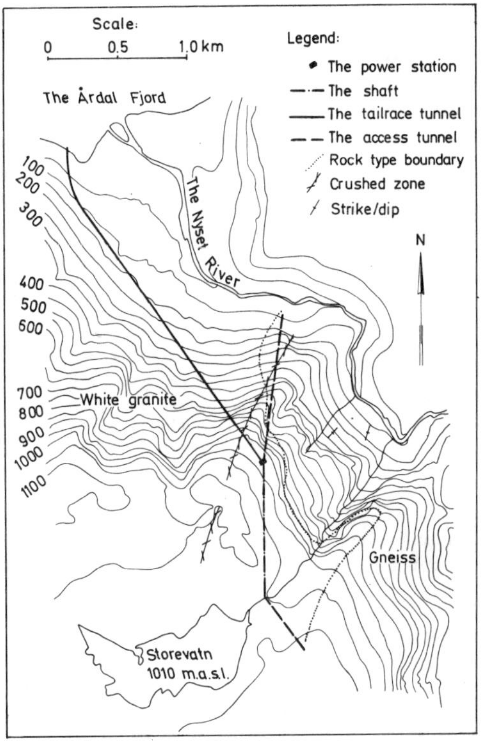

Fig. 2. Map of the power station area.

Top: The Jotun Nappe.
Mylonite.
Camro-Ordovician sediments.
Bottom: Pre-Cambrian basement.

The tunnels in this area, as well as the pressure shaft and power station, will be situated mainly in the upper formation, the Jotun Nappe. Only on a very short section will the tunnel between Berdalsvatn Lake and the reservoir penetrate the thrust plane and pass into the Mylonite zone.

The Jotun Nappe has a very complex structure with a varying mineralogic composition and degree of metamorphism. The rocks are mainly gneisses and granites but diorites and gabbros are also encountered.

The tectonic structure of the area is dominated by the over-thrust of the Jotun Nappe. The thrust plane itself is located within the Mylonite zone but differential shear zones can be found above the thrust plane.

INVESTIGATION PROGRAMME
As mentioned, the pressure shaft is planned

to be unlined. With a static head of 980 metres, this will be the unlined shaft with the highest water pressure in Norway, and probably also in the world.

Due to difficult topographic conditions it is impossible to establish any access to the shaft in the steep valley slope, so the shaft will have to be driven in one continuous section from the bottom to the top.

In this situation the following investigation programme was established:

a) Geological mapping and sampling.
b) Laboratory testing of rock samples.
c) Evaluation of the feasibility of full-face boring of the shaft.
d) Rock mechanics calculations as a basis for siting of the shaft.

GEOLOGY OF THE SHAFT AREA

The rocks in the area belong, as mentioned, to the Jotun Nappe. At the bottom, along the Nyset River and above elevation 75 metres, the rock is gneiss. The gneiss is overlain by a white granite which is intruded as a sandwich layer in the rock sequence. The boundary between these two rocks is very irregular, but can be followed up the valley side and also on the mountain plateau on the northwestern side of Storevatn. West of the boundary, only white granite is found. The boundary zone itself has originally been crushed, but due to injection of granite material into these masses, it is now massive and sound. The zone consists of a very irregular mixture of the two rock types, and the total thickness is about 200-250 metres. The rock distribution as mapped can also be seen on Figure 2.

The underlying gneiss has a foliation with north-northwesterly strike and a 70-90° dip towards west. The white granite has developed a very pronounced exfoliation jointing parallel to the surface, especially in the steep slopes. The plates have a thickness of 0.1-1.0 metre. Otherwise the rock in the area is very moderately jointed. A vertical joint set with north-south strike is also found, but the joint spacing is rather large. A fracture zone cuts the area, as shown on Figure 2. It is of great importance that the shaft does not intersect this zone. The zone has an easterly dip of 80°.

DRILLABILITY PREDICTIONS

Typical samples of the rocks have been collected and laboratory tested for drillability evaluations. The methods used have been presented earlier by O.T. Blindheim et.al (1979).

The indexes used are the DRI (Drillability Rate Index) and the BWI (Bit Wear Index). Besides these, the degree of jointing of the rock mass is also taken into account.

Table I shows the measured values of the DRI and BWI indexes and in Figures 3 and 4 the values of DRI and BWI are plotted. The diagram in Figure 3 shows the expected net penetration rate for a 3.5 metre TBM (Tunnel Boring Machine) as a function of the DRI and the average joint spacing in the rock mass. Figure 4 shows the expected cutter costs for a 3.5 metre TBM (with single disc cutters) as a function of the BWI-index and of the joint spacing. As mentioned the rocks are very moderately jointed, hence the curve designating distance between joints and partings longer than 20 cm is used.

Table I

Drilling Rate Index DRI Bit Wear Index BWI	Sample I Granitic gneiss	Sample II Gneiss	Sample III White granite
DRI	64 high	54 medium	69 high
BWI	20 low	21 low	25 low

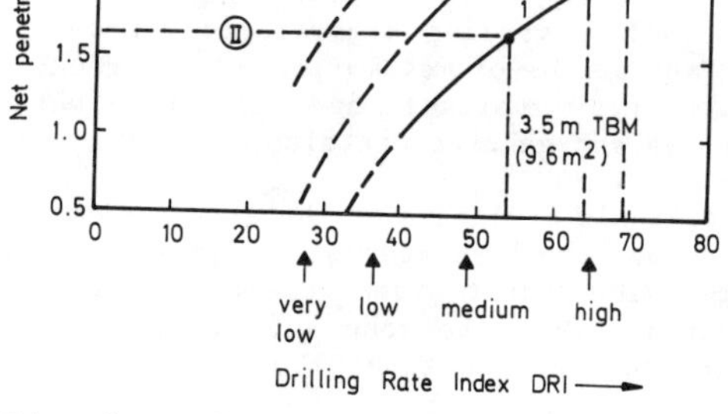

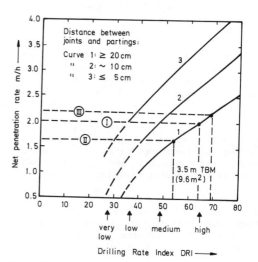

Fig. 3. Drilling Rate Index (DRI) versus penetration rate (sample I, II and III values indicated)

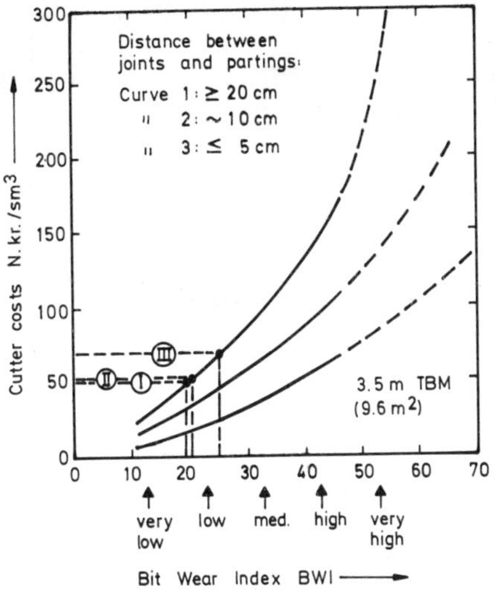

Fig. 4. Bit Wear Index (BWI) versus cutter costs (sample I, II and III values indicated)

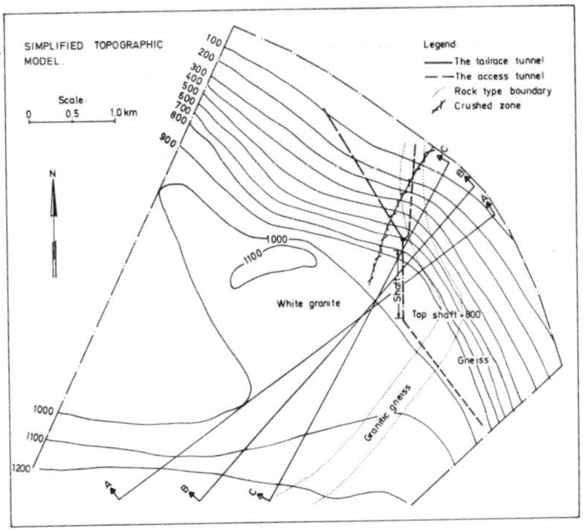

Fig. 5. Simplified topographic model.

The diagrams show that in our case the net penetration rate is expected to be of the order of 1.7-2.1 metres per hour, and the cutter costs are expected to be 50-80 Norwegian kroner (8-13 USD) per cubic metre of solid rock. This may be characterized as medium to good drillability and medium to low wear. The investigations thus indicate that the use of TBM will be feasible.

ROCK MECHANICS CALCULATIONS

The method used for evaluation of the shaft siting is based on a calculation of total stresses by finite element plain strain analysis. This method of calculation was developed at the Geological Institute, Technical University of Norway, and is described by Selmer-Olsen (1974) and Broch and Selmer-Olsen (1982). The main condition imposed is that the minimum in situ total stress should be higher than the water pressure at every point along the shaft, in order to avoid the risk of failure by hydraulic fracturing.

The computer programme used is developed by SINTEF (The Foundation of Scientific and Industrial Research at the Norwegian Institute of Technology) for solving plain, linear elastic problems.

In this case the terrain is very irregular, and in order to make a plain element analysis possible it was necessary to establish a simplified topographic model in which all the protruding "noses" were cut away. The simplified topographic model is shown in Figure 5. Based on a very simple calculation a preliminary location for the shaft was chosen. This location is also shown on the terrain model.

The computer programme used gives, for this type of finite element analaysis, the stress distribution along a vertical plane normal to the contour lines of the terrain model. Pressure shafts are usually located in the direction normal to the contour lines, and the programme then gives a complete picture of the stresses along the shaft. But in this particular case, the shaft has to be located obliquely in relation to the valley side, and consequently the standard programme does not give the complete stress distribution along the shaft in a single run.

A three-dimensional model was found to be unrealistic and it was therefore decided to perform the calculations with the use of 3 two-dimensional models representing profiles cutting the lower end of the shaft and at 225 metres and 425 metres above the bottom. Earlier calculations show that these points are critical.

When evaluating hydraulic fracturing the total stresses are of interest for comparison with the water pressure, and therefore transformation of the stresses to the shaft direction is unnecessary. The

Table II

Sample	Bulk density	Poissons ratio	Young's mod. E
(I) (Granitic gneiss)	2.78		
∥ Foliation		0.05	$0.026 \cdot 10^6$ MPa
⊥ Foliation		0.14	$0.035 \cdot 10^6$ MPa
(II) Gneiss	2.93		
∥ Foliation		0.11	$0.025 \cdot 10^6$ MPa
⊥ Foliation		0.14	$0.025 \cdot 10^6$ MPa
(III) White granite*	2.62	0.07	$0.027 \cdot 10^6$ MPa

* The granite is homogeneous without foliation.

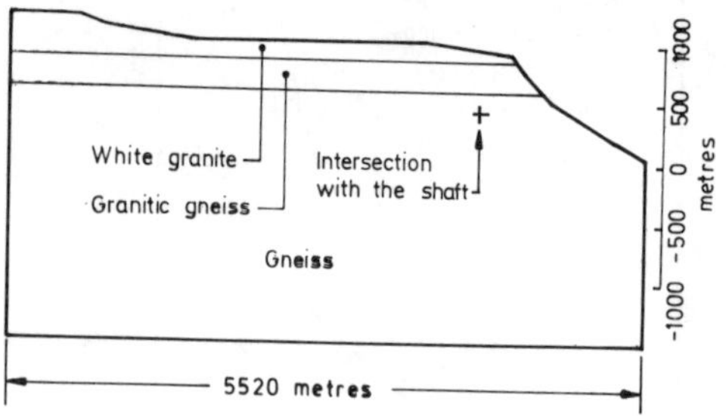

Fig. 6. Geometry of finite element model.

rock material is supposed to be linearly elastic and orthotropic (with different values in the X-and Y-direction). The bulk density, Poissons ratio and E-modulus for the different rock types are given in Table II.

The locations of the three sections A-A, B-B and C-C, designating the three two-dimensional models are shown in Figure 5. The geometry of one of the models is shown in Figure 6. All analyses have been done with models of the same dimensions, i.e. the same number of elements and a length of 5,250 metres. The models (shown on Figure 7) are designed with a horizontal roller bearing at the bottom and a vertical bearing on the right hand side. A horizontal pressure equal to 50% of the overburden pressure is applied at the left hand side of the model.

Each model is divided into 4 substructures. The shaft is located in substructure 1 and the results of this substructure are of the greatest interest.

RESULTS

The calculation results are shown in Figures 8 and 9.

Figure 8 shows the distribution of the total stresses in substructure 1, section A-A. The direction and magnitude of maximum and minimum total stresses are shown as crosses. Notice that the maximum total stress is mainly parallel to the valley side. In the shaft area the ratio between the minimum and maximum total stress is from 1:1.7 to 1:2.1.

Figure 9 shows the calculated minimum total stress at the intersection points between

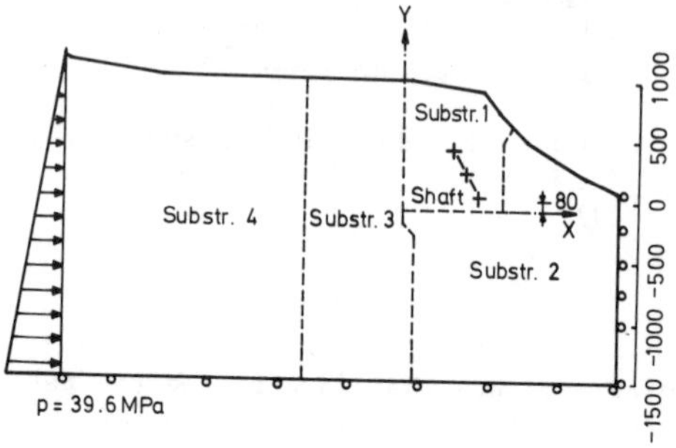

Fig. 7. The model divided in substructures.

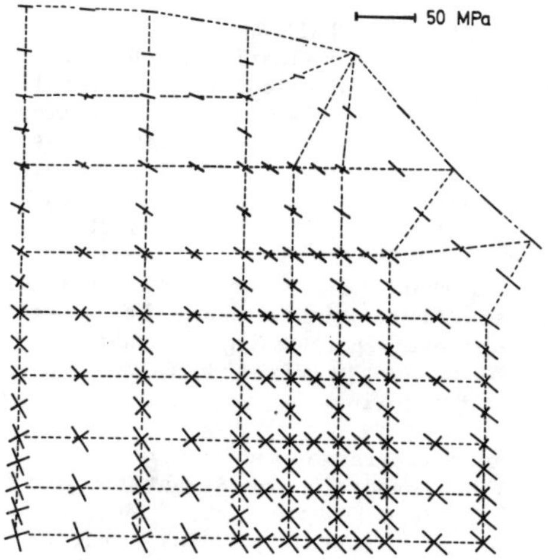

Fig. 8. Stress distribution in substructure 1.

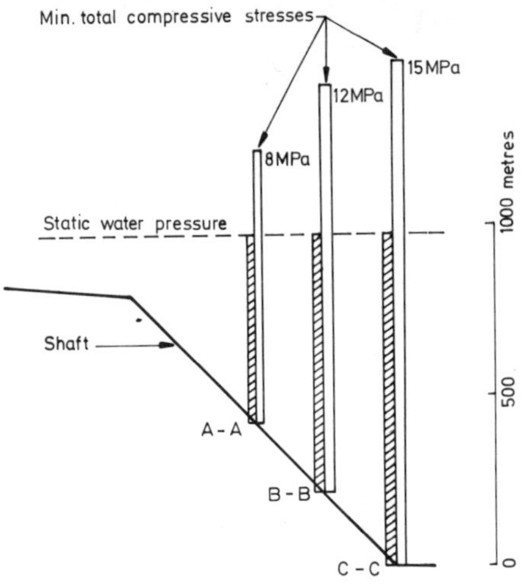

Fig. 9. Minimum total stress versus water pressure.

the shaft and three sections A-A, B-B and C-C. The corresponding water pressure is also shown. The following values for the ratio between minimum total stress and water pressure are found.

Section A-A : 2.1
Section B-B : 1.7
Section C-C : 1.5

According both to earlier experience and the above calculations, it was concluded that the preliminary location of the shaft should be sufficiently safe, and this location was chosen for final design of the power station.

FURTHER INVESTIGATIONS

It is of basic importance for the final decision on shaft design that the calculated stresses are fairly correct, i.e. similar to the stress conditions found in situ. When the tunnelling works start, the access tunnel to the power plant and a pilot adit towards the bottom of the shaft will have highest priority. As soon as access to the bottom of the shaft is possible, in situ rock stress measurements will be performed. Hydraulic fracturing tests are also planned to be performed in situ. If the rock stress measurements indicate more adverse stress conditions than calculated, and hence lining of the shaft is found necessary, the time schedule will allow for this.

If full steel lining should be found necessary a very expensive ropeway has to be built up to the top of the slope. However, another alternative would be to line only the lower part of the shaft. By driving a tunnel with a rise of 1:10 from the access area up to an elevation of about 250 metres in the shaft, the lower part of the shaft only can be lined.

These alternative solutions are less desirable economically than the unlined shaft, so good agreement between in situ measurements and the calculations performed are hoped for.

REFERENCES

BLINDHEIM, O.T., DAHL JOHANSEN, E. and JOHANNESSEN, O. (1979).
Criteria for the selection of fullface tunnel boring or conventional tunnelling. Proc. 4th Congr. Int. Soc. Rock Mech. Montreux 1979.

BROCH, E and SELMER-OLSEN, R (1982).
The development of unlined pressure shafts and tunnels in Norway. Int. Symp. on Rock Mech. related to Caverns and Pressure Shafts, Aachen 1982.

SELMER-OLSEN, R (1974).
Underground openings filled with high-pressure water or air. Bull. Int. Ass. of Engineering Geology No. 9 pp. 91-95.

THE DEVELOPMENT OF UNLINED PRESSURE SHAFTS AND TUNNELS IN NORWAY

Die Entwicklung von nicht ausgekleideten Druckschächten und Tunnels in Norwegen

Le développement des puits sous pression sans soutènement et des tunnels en Norvège

E.BROCH
University of Trondheim, Norway

SUMMARY:
Sixty years ago four unlined pressure shafts with water heads up to 150 m were constructed in Norway. Three of them are still in operation. During the last twenty years underground powerhouses and unlined pressure shafts have become the conventional design for hydropower plants. Norway has today 150 underground powerhouses and 64 unlined pressure shafts and tunnels with water heads varying between 150 and 780 m. This paper describes the development of the general lay-out for hydropower plants. Older rules of thumb as well as new computer based design charts for unlined pressure shafts are presented.
Also unlined, closed surge chambers with compressed air cushions are briefly described. Such chambers with internal air pressure of up to 75 atmospheres on unlined rock is now in operation. Geological conditions which may have a serious influence on the behaviour of unlined pressure shafts, are discussed. Finally, an example of the layout of tunnels and shafts around an underground powerhouse is presented.

ZUSAMMENFASSUNG:
Vor 60 Jahren wurden in Norwegen vier Druckschächte mit Fallhöhen bis zu 150 m ohne jegliche Auskleidung gebaut. Drei werden heute noch benutzt. Während der letzten 20 Jahren wurden unterirdische Kraftwerksstationen und nicht-ausgekleidete Druckschächte zu einer allgemeine üblichen Konstruktionsmethode für Wasserkraftanlagen entwickelt. Norwegen besitzt heute ungefähr 150 unterirdische Kraftwerke sowie 64 nicht-ausgekleidete Druckschächte und Tunneln mit Fallhöhen die zwischen 150 und 780 m variieren. Diese Ausarbeitung beschreibt die Entwicklung der genereller Gestaltung von Wasserkraftanlagen. Alte "Dummen-Regeln" werden ebenso dargestellt wie rechnergestützte Methoden für nicht-ausgekleidete Druckschächte.
Ebenso werden nicht-ausgekleidete, geschlossene Wasserschlösser, die mit Druckluftpolster arbeiten, kurz beschrieben. Solche Druckkammern, mit einem inneren überdruck bis zu 75 Atmosphären auf dem blossen Fels, arbeiten jetzt bereits. Die geologischen Bedingungen, die einen erheblichen Einfluss auf das Verhalten der nicht-ausgekleidete Druckschäfte ausüben können, werden diskutiert. Zum Schluss wird ein Beispiel für die Anlage von Tunneln und Schächten in der Umgebung eines unterirdische Kraftwerksanlage dargestellt.

RESUMÉ:
Il y a 60 ans que quatre puits en charge non-revêtus avec des hauteurs d'eau allant jusqu'à 150 m etaient construits en Norvège. Trois d'entre eux sont encore en service. Durant ces 20 dernières années, les centrales souterraines et les puits en charge non revêtus sont devenus la pratique courante pour les aménagements hydro-électriques.
La Norwège possède aujourd'hui 150 centrales souterraines et 64 puits et galeries non revêtus avec des charges d'eau variant entre 150 m et 780 m. La communication décrit le développement des dispositions generales des aménagements. De vieilles méthodes empiriques de dimensionnement sont présentées, de meme que des nouveaux abaques établis a l'aide d'ordinateur.

D'autre part, des chambres d'équilibre non revêtues, fermées et avec coussins d'air comprimé sont brièvement décrites. De telles chambres avec une pression d'air allant jusqu'à 75 atm sur de la roche non revêtue sont actuellement en service. Les conditions géologiques, qui peuvent avoir une influence décisive sur le comportement des puits non revêtus, sont discutées. Enfin un exemple de la disposition des puits et galeries autour d'une centrale souterraine est présenté.

INTRODUCTION

The topographical conditions in Norway are especially favourable for the development of hydro electric energy. More than 99% of a total annual production of 90 TWh of electric energy is thus generated from hydropower. Figure 1 shows the installed production capacity in Norwegian hydro electric power stations. It is interesting to notice that since 1950 the underground powerhouses are dominating. In fact, of the world's 300 - 350 underground powerhouses almost one half, i.e. 150 are situated in Norway. Another proof of the Norwegian electricity industry being an "underground industry" is that it has approximately 2.500 km of tunnels.

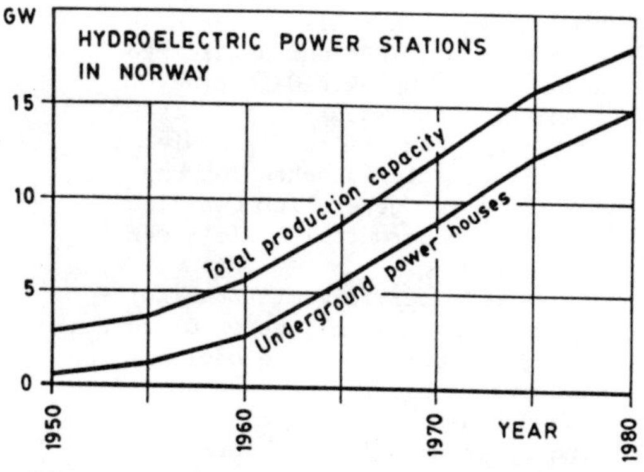

Fig. 1. The development of hydro electric power production in Norway, after Myrset (1980).

Through the design, construction and operation of all these tunnels and underground powerhouses valuable experiences have been gained. Also special techniques and design concepts have during the years been developed. One such Norwegian speciality is the unlined high pressure tunnels and shafts, which this paper will describe.

Before starting the description it should, however, be mentioned that the rocks in Norway are of Precambrian and Paleozoic age. Although they consist of a wide variety of rock types, highly metamorphic rocks are dominating. From an engineering point of view they may in general be classified as typical hard rocks.

Most of our hydropower tunnels have only 2 - 4 per cent of concrete or shotcrete lining. Only in a few cases has it been necessary to increase this percentage to 30 - 60. The low percentage of lining is not only due to favourable tunnelling conditions. It is also the consequence of a supporting philosophy which accepts minor down-falls of rock during the operation period of water tunnels. As long as rock falls in certain parts of the tunnel don't develop considerably and thus increase the head loss, a reasonable number of small blocks spread along the tunnel will not harm the tunnel or disturb the operation of the hydropower station. If necessary, they may be removed during later inspection and maintenance.

THE EARLY UNLINED PRESSURE SHAFTS

During and shortly after the Great World War there was a shortage of steel leading to uncertain deliveries and very high prices. As a result of this four Norwegian hydropower stations with unlined pressure shafts were put into operation, see Table 1.

Already in 1922 three of the pressure shafts were described in detail in a publication from the Norwegian Geological Survey by J.H.L. Vogt (1922) called "Pressure Tunnels and Geology". Herlandsfoss, Svelgen and Toklev is later investigated and described by Broch and Christensen (1962) and Herlandsfoss by Selmer-Olsen (1970).

Name	Year	Water head (m)	Diam. (m)	Rock	Remarks
Herlandsfoss	1919	136	3,20	Mica-schist	Partly failed
Skar	1920	129		Gneiss-granite	Completely failed
Svelgen	1921	152	2,40	Sand-stone	Minor leakages
Toklev	1921	72	2,50	Monzonite	No leakages

Table 1. The first unlined pressure shafts in Norway.

The pressure shaft at Herlandsfoss is shown in Figure 2. According to the original design the penstock and the concrete plug was placed only 50 m from the turbine leaving 150 m of the high pressure tunnel unlined. During the first filling of the tunnel and the shaft increasing leakages through the mica-schist layer was observed. The tunnel was then emptied and a 60 m long reinforced concrete lining was placed inside the penstock. After two months of operation rapidly increasing leakages were again observed. Inspection in the emptied tunnel unveiled open cracks in the concrete on both sides of the tunnel near the springline. After this failure the penstock was extended through the whole tunnel to the foot of the shaft as the figure shows. No leakages from the shaft have been observed since that, and the power station has now operated without unplanned stops for 60 years.

The pressure shaft at Skar was, to make a long and miserable story short, a complete failure and was substituted by an ordinary penstock except for the upper part of the tunnel. The reason for the unacceptable leakages was first of all the low overburden of rock, only 22 m where the water head was 116 m.

At Svelgen leakages of 3 - 5 l/sec were observed as two small polluted streams during the first filling of the pressure shaft. A short part of the shaft was then lined with concrete and grouted with cement. Since then the shaft has operated perfectly.

The Toklev pressure shaft has functioned without any reported problems since it was put into operation.

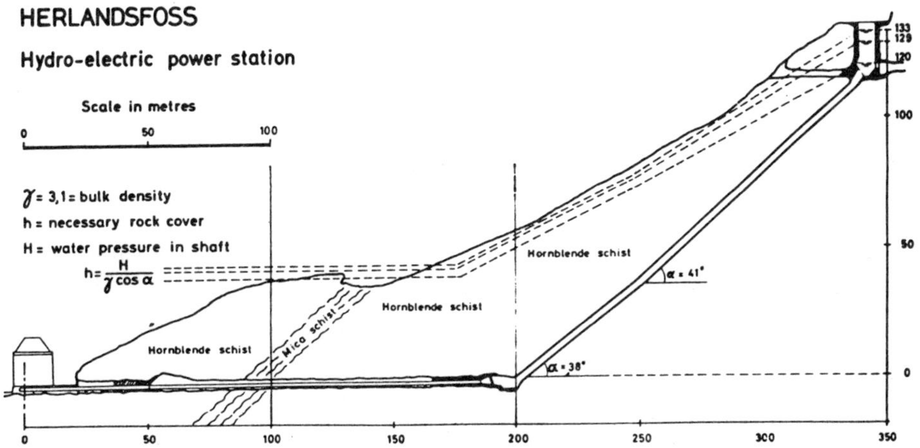

Fig. 2. The Herlandsfoss hydro electric power station, in operation since 1919, from Selmer-Olsen (1970).

DEVELOPMENT OF THE GENERAL LAY-OUT FOR HYDROPOWER PLANTS

Although three out of four pressure shafts constructed around 1920 were operating perfectly after some "birth problems" had been solved, it should take almost 40 years before the world record of 152 m water head on unlined rock at Svelgen should be beaten. Until 1958 another nine unlined pressure shafts were constructed, but all with water heads below 100 m. Before 1950 the above-ground powerhouse with penstock(s) was the conventional lay-out for hydropower plants as shown in Figure 3.

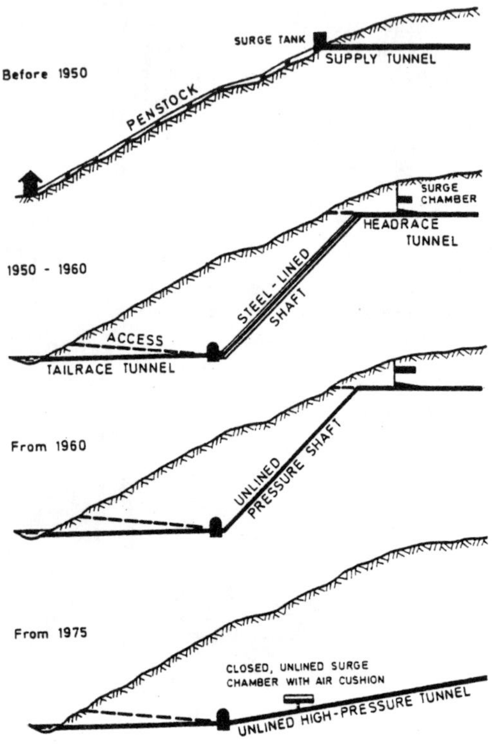

Fig. 3. The development of the general lay-out of hydro electric plants in Norway.

When the hydropower industry "went underground" in the early 50's, they brought the steel pipes with them. Thus, for a decade or so, most pressure shafts were steel-lined. During the period 1950-65 a total of 36 steel-lined shafts with heads varying between 50 and 967 m and with an average of 310 m were constructed.

The new record shaft of 286 m at Tafjord K3 which successfully was put into operation in 1958, gave the industry new confidence in the unlined shafts. As Figure 4 is demonstrating, new unlined shafts were constructed in the early 60's. Since 1965 the unlined pressure shafts have been the conventional solution for heads up to 500 - 600 m. Last year the Tafjord Kraftselskap set their third world record by putting into operation an unlined pressure shaft with a water head of 780 m. However, as another paper at this symposium is describing, plans are already completed for a new unlined pressure shaft with water head of 1000 m, Bergh-Christensen & Kjølberg (1982). By the end of this year altogether 64 unlined pressure shafts with water heads varying between 150 and 780 m and with an average of 314 m will be in operation in Norway. Figure 4 is clearly demonstrating how the increasing water heads are reflecting an increasing confidence in the unlined pressure shafts during the last 20 years.

This confidence in the tightness of the unlined rock mass was additionally increased in 1973 when the first closed, unlined surge chamber with an air cushion successfully entered into service at the Driva hydro electric powerplant. This new innovation in surge chamber design is described in detail by L. Rathe (1975). The bottom sketch in figure 3 is showing how the new design influences the general lay-out of a hydropower plant. The steeply inclined pressure shaft normally at 45°, is replaced by a slightly inclined tunnel, 1:10 to 1:15. Instead of the conventional open surge chamber near the top of the pressure shaft, a closed chamber is excavated somewhere along the high pressure tunnel, preferably not too far from the powerhouse.

After the tunnel system is filled with water, compressed air is pumped into the surge chamber. At Driva where the water head at the chamber is 425 m, the total volume of the chamber is 6.000 m^3. 3.000 of this is filled with compressed air. This compressed air acts like a "cushion" to reduce the waterhammer effect on the hydraulic machinery and the waterways, and also ensures the stability of the hydraulic system. Table 2 gives some basic information about the air cushion surge chambers in service.

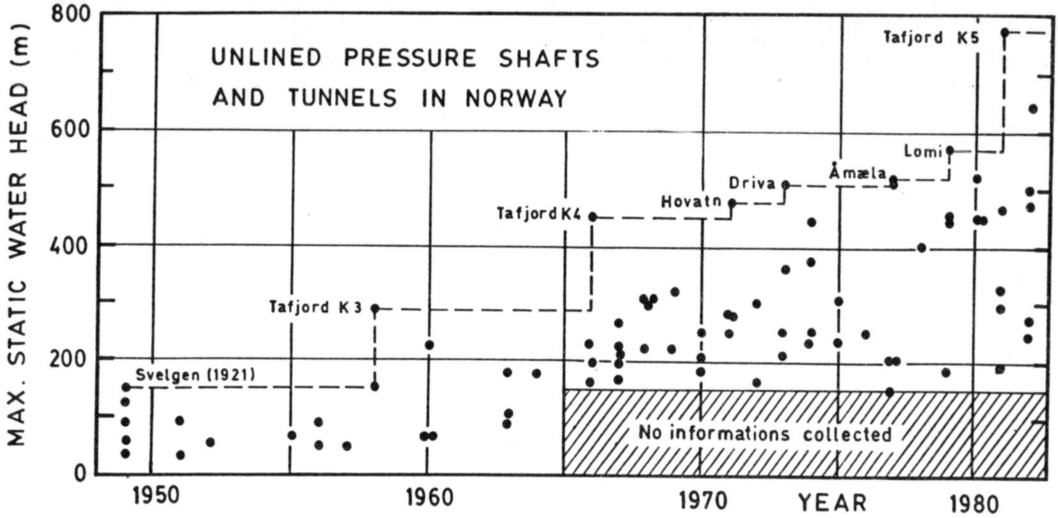

Fig. 4. The development of unlined pressure shafts and tunnels in Norway.

Name	Year	Air pressure in bar	Volume of chamber (m^3)
Driva	1973	42,5	6.000
Jukla	1974	24	6.200
Oksla	1980	46	17.300
Sima	1980	50	7.100
Kvilldal	1981	43	100.000
Nye Osa	1981	18	12.000
Tafjord K5	1981	75	2.000
Brattset	1982	26,5	3.000

Table 2. List of closed, unlined surge chambers with air cushions.

THE FIRST DESIGN CRITERIA

In summarizing the experiences from the early unlined pressure shafts Vogt (1922) states that the first and foremost requirement for a pressure shaft is that leakages are avoided. He is disagreeing with those who at that time claimed that an unlined pressure tunnel is safe when the weight of the rock overburden is greater than the water pressure. He even says that to get this dogma out of the world, is one of his main reasons for writing the report. According to Vogt the main risk for unlined pressure tunnels and shafts is bad rock masses like weathered zones, joints etc. Hence the best way of avoiding leakages is to place the tunnel as deep into the rock mass as possible.

In the years before 1968 the "rule of thumb" used in the planning of unlined pressure shafts in Norway was connected with the general lay-out for hydropower plants which was used at that time, see figure 3. For constructional reasons the inclination of the unlined shafts varied between 31° and 47° with 45° as the most common angle. The rule was expressed as: (see Figure 5)

$h > c \cdot h$ (for every point of the shaft)

where h = vertical depth of the point studied (in m).

H = static water head (in m) at the point studied.

c = a constant, which was 0,6 for valley sides with inclinations up to 35° and increased to 1,0 for valley sides of 60°.

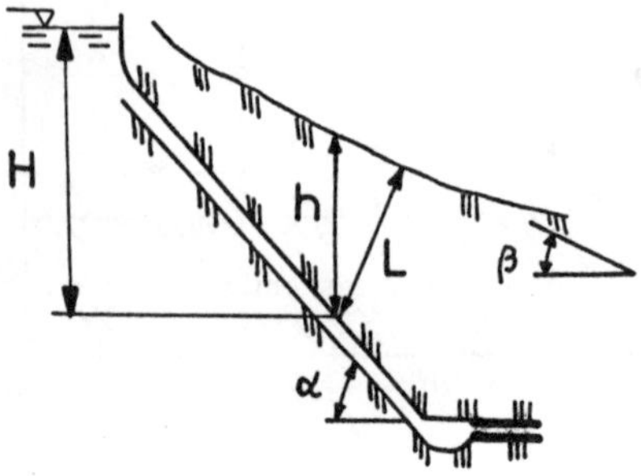

Fig. 5. Definitions for the rule of thumb.

High valley sides steeper than 60° are rather uncommon in Norway. This simple rule was, of course, to be used with care under special geological conditions.

In 1968 the unlined pressure shaft at Byrte with a maximum static water head of 300 m failed. The shaft had the uncommon inclination of 60°. A revised rule of thumb which should also cover shafts steeper than the commonly used 45° was presented by Selmer-Olsen (1970). It was expressed in a more general way as: (see figure 5)

$$h > \frac{\gamma_w \cdot H}{\gamma_r \cdot \cos\alpha}$$

where γ_w = density of water.

γ_r = density of the rock mass.

α = the inclination of the shaft.

(h and H as earlier explained).

The failure of the Byrte shaft was also for the first time analyzed by the use of a finite element model, Brekke et al. (1970).

In the autumn of 1970 another failure occurred at Åskora where an unlined tunnel in sandstone with a water head of approximately 200 m was hydraulicly splitted. The split followed sandfilled, steeply dipping joints with a strike parallel to the very steep valley side (55°) and normal to the tunnel. The failure is described in detail by Bergh-Christensen (1975).

After this failure a new rule of thumb was introduced by Bergh-Christensen and Dannevig (1971) where the inclination of the valley side was taken directly into account:

$$L > \frac{H}{\gamma_r \cdot \cos\beta}$$

where L = shortest distance between the surface and the point studied (in m).

β = average inclination of the valley side.

H and γ_r as earlier, see also figure 5.

Based on this a diagram showing existing unlined pressure shafts with or without leakages was presented. This was further supplied with information by the Norwegian Geotechnical Institute (1972) and is shown here in a slightly revised version as Figure 6. It is worth noticing that the unlined pressure shafts where leakages are observed, are, with the exception of Bjerka, plotting below the curves defined by the rule of thumb. At Bjerka unfavourable geological conditions with steeply dipping, permeable joints with strike parallel to the valley side gave leakages at a distance of up to 1 km from the pressure tunnel.

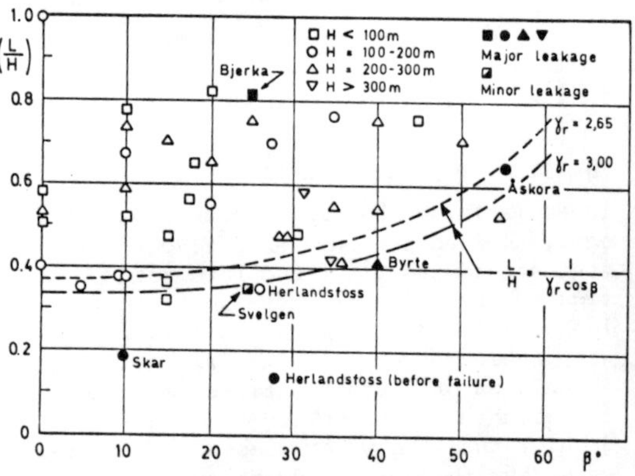

Fig. 6. Unlined pressure shafts in valley sides with various inclinations, β. See text for further explanation.

DESIGN CHARTS BASED ON FINITE ELEMENT MODELS

Parallel with the revisions of the rule of thumb the search for a better and more general design criterium was intensivated at the Department of Geology, University of Trondheim. This should not only be valid for unlined pressure shafts and tunnels, but also for unlined surge chambers with compressed air cushions. The first hydropower plant with this new solution, Driva, was already under construction.

The new design tool was taken into use in 1971-72 and is described in detail by Selmer-Olsen in 1974. It is based on the use of computerized finite element models (FEM), and the concept that nowhere along an unlined pressure shaft or tunnel shall the internal water pressure exceed the minor principal stress in the surrounding rock mass.

Very briefly, the FEM-models are based on plain strain analysis. Horizontal stresses (tectonic plus gravitational) increasing linearly with depth are applied. Bending forces in the model are avoided by making the valley small in relation to the whole model. If required, clay gouges (crushed zones containing clay) may be introduced.

In addition to real cases a number of idealized, but still typical valley sides have been analyzed. One example of an idealized model is shown in Figure 7. In this case the inclination of the valley side $\beta = 40^{o}$, the bulk density of the rock mass $\gamma_r = 2,75$, Poisson's ratio $\nu = 0,2$ and the $\frac{\sigma_{hor.}}{\sigma_{vert.}}$ ratio at a distance of 5 d from the valley is 0,5. d is the depth of the valley and H the maximum static head. (As Young's modulus E is kept constant, it will not influence the results). To make the model dimensionless, the static water pressure is expressed as the ratio H/d where the water head is expressed as a height in the same units as the valley depth, e.g. in meter. The curved lines run through points where the internal water pressure in a shaft equals the minor principal stresses in the surrounding rock mass ($\sigma_3 = H$).

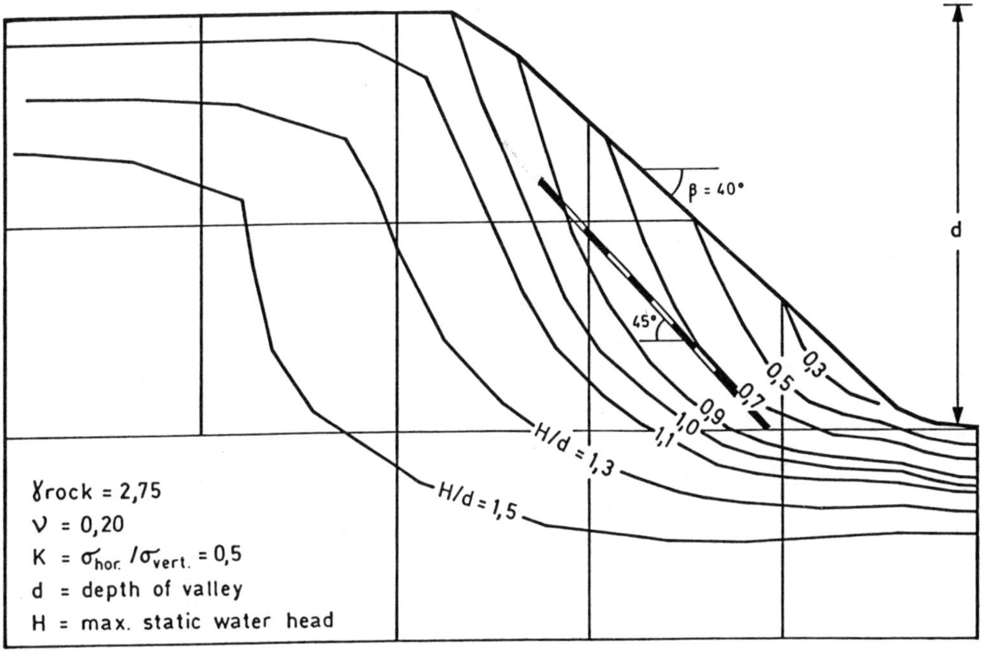

Fig. 7. Design chart for unlined pressure shafts based on a finite element model. The curves run through points where the internal water pressure in the shaft equals the minor principal stress in the surrounding rock mass, $H = \sigma_3$. See text for further explanation.

The use of the design charts is illustrated by an example. Let the bottom of the valley, where the power station is located, be situated 100 m.a.s.l. and the top of the valley side 600 m.a.s.l. This makes d = 500 m. The maximum water level in the intake reservoir is 390 m.a.s.l. This makes H = 290 m and the H/d-ratio = 0,58. At all points inside or below the 0,58 line, the minor principal stress in the rock mass exceeds the water pressure in an unlined shaft, and hence no hydraulic splitting should occur. If a factor of safety of 1,2 is introduced, the critical line will be the $1{,}2 \cdot 0{,}58 = 0{,}7$-line. As a demonstration, a 45° inclined shaft is placed in this position in figure 7.

Design charts for a number of valley side inclinations, β, are available. To fit the actual valley side to one of these is normally possible. In this fitting process it is necessary to simplify and idealize the valley side by smoothening the actual profile and ignoring protuding parts. It is also possible to make interpolations between two standard design charts. It is important that the profiles are made at a right angle to the conture lines of the map. In cases where the pressure shaft is placed in a part of the valley side which is protuding in the horizontal section, a series of profiles through the protuding part should be studied.

Through a number of analyses all factors influencing the results have been carefully evaluated within natural limits. If, for example, a measured bulk density, γ_r, varies from the "standard" 2,75, this can be compensated by a correction of the overburden by the ratio $2{,}75/\gamma_r$. Also in cases with an upper layer of topsoil or weathered rock masses, this can be compensated for by reducing the thickness of the overburden in accordance with the bulk density of these masses.

Measurements as well as observations indicate that the $\sigma_{hor.}/\sigma_{vert.}$-ratio in topographically undisturbed areas in Norway normally varies between 0,5 and 1,3 and very seldom exceeds 1,5. As a conservative solution a ratio of 0,5 is used in the standard charts. An increase in Poisson's ratio, ν, will give σ_3 = H-lines that go deeper in the valley side. For the standard charts $\nu = 0{,}2$ is used.

The chape and width of the valley have a major influence on the stress distribution near and under the bottom of the valley. The analyses have, however, shown that the σ_3 = H-lines on levels above the bottom, and at actual distances from the valley side, are not too much influenced. In the standard charts the width of the bottom of the valley is normally 1/3 d.

So far only two-dimensional models have been used, and the stress perpendicular to the model plane has been assumed to be the intermediate principal stress, σ_2. Stress measurements are sometimes carried out as a control, mainly where there is reason to believe that the tectonic stresses are unnormal. Also hydraulic splitting tests are sometimes used as a control of the σ_3 = H-lines. For such tests it is important that the boreholes are intersecting natural joints with unfavouralbe directions with regard to the possibilities of leakages from the unlined shaft. The splitting pressure is raised to 20% above the estimated minor principal stress at the actual location.

GEOLOGICAL RESTRICTIONS

The FEM-developed design charts are based on the assumption that the rock mass is homogeneous and continuous, - an assumption which cannot be absolutely correct even for massive Precambrian granites amd gneisses. However, observations and investigations of stress-induced stability problems like rock bursts and popping or spalling rock in a large number of tunnels in fjord and valley sides clearly indicate that the natural jointing of rock masses has only minor influence on the distribution of the virgin stresses. The jointing may, however, have a strong influence on final development of a stability problem as well as on the leakages through the rock mass.

As the permeability of rocks normally is negligible, it is the jointing and the faulting of the rock mass, and in particular the type and amount of joint infilling material, that is of importance when an area is being evaluated. Calcite is easily dissolved by cold, acid water, and gouge material like silt and swelling clay are easily eroded. Crossing of crushed zones or faults containing such materials should therefore preferably be avoided. If this is not possible, a careful sealing and grouting should be carried out. The grouting is the more important the closer leaking joints are to the powerhouse and access tunnels and the more their directions are pointing towards these. The same is also valid for zones or layers of porous rocks or rocks that are heavily jointed or broken.

For pressure shafts in valley sides it should be warned against clay-filled, crushed zones in the actual area as they may have an unfavourable influence on the stress distribution. If they have a strike nearly parallel to the valley side with a steep or medium steep dip towards the valley, they are especially dangerous. Not only may they change the stress distribution, but they may also often give leakages during construction as well as during operation. The hydraulic splitting of the pressure tunnels at Åskora and Bjerka was caused by such unfavourably oriented joints and faults. A careful mapping of all types of discontinuities in the rock mass is therefore an important part of the planning and design of pressure shafts.

During the construction period it is important that changes in all leakages into the shaft or tunnel, even small dripping or seeping leakages, are observed. For the selection of place for unlined, closed surge chambers these observations are of crucial value as points of water leakages are openings, where loss of the compressed air may take place. Core drilling and water pressing tests in the drill holes are thus normally a part of the investigations for the location of these chambers.

LAY-OUT FOR UNDERGROUND HYDROPOWER PLANTS WITH UNLINED WATERWAYS

As a final chapter an example of an underground hydropower plant will be shown and briefly described. Figure 8 shows the simplified plan and cross section of a small hydropower plant with only one turbine. No dimensions are given as the intension is to show a system rather than give details. Similar lay-outs can be found for Norwegian plants with water heads in the range of 200 - 600 m.

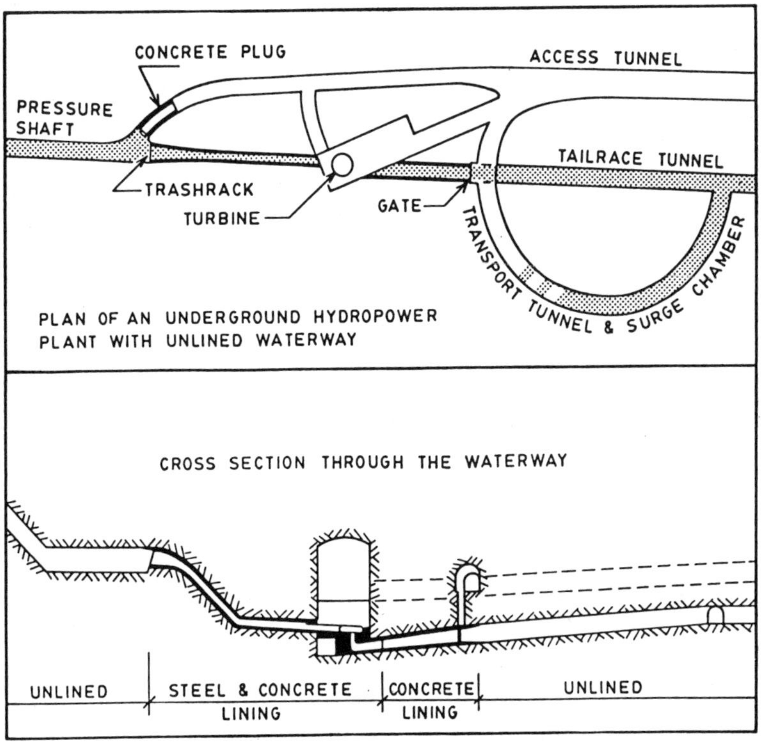

Fig. 8. Plan and cross section of an underground hydropower plant with unlined waterways.

Hopefully the figure is to some extent self-explanatory. It shall, however, be pointed out that when the design charts are used, the dimensionating or critical point will normally be where the unlined pressure shaft ends and the steel-lining starts. This is where the selected σ_3 = H-line should intersect the waterway. The elevation of this point and the length of the steel-lined part will vary with the water head, the size and orientation of the powerhouse, and the geological conditions, - in particular the character and orientation of joints and fissures. Lengths in the range of 30 to 80 m are fairly common.

The access tunnel to the foot of the unlined pressure shaft is finally plugged with concrete and a steel-tube with a hatch cover. The length of this plug is normally 10 - 25 m, depending on water head and geological conditions. Around the concrete plug and the upper part of the steel-lined shaft a thorough high pressure grouting is carried out. This is to avoid leakages into the powerhouse and the access tunnels.

CONCLUDING REMARKS

Experiences from a considerable number of pressure tunnels and shafts, as well as socalled air cushion surge chambers, have been gathered over a long period of time in Norway. These show that, provided certain design rules are followed and certain geological-topographical conditions avoided, unlined rock masses are able to contain water and air under pressures of up to at least 75 bars, equalling 750 m water head. In the future these experiences may be of importance also outside the hydropower industry, for instance for the construction of cheap, unlined storages for different types of gases or liquids under pressure.

REFERENCES

Bergh-Christensen, J., Brudd i ufôret trykktunnel ved Åskora kraftverk. In Broch, Heltzen and Johannessen (ed): Fjellsprengningsteknikk-Bergmekanikk 1974. Tapir, Trondheim, 15.1 - 15.8, 1975.

Bergh-Christensen, J. and Dannevig, N.T., Ingeniørgeologiske vurderinger vedrørende ufôret trykksjakt ved Mauranger kraftverk. Unpubl. rep. Geoteam A/S, Oslo, 1971.

Bergh-Christensen, J. and Kjølberg, R., Investigations for a 1000 metres head unlined pressure shaft at the Nyset/Steggje project, Norway. Int. Symp. Rock Mechanics related to caverns and pressure shafts. Aachen, May 1982 (in print).

Brekke, T.L., Bjørlykke, S. and Blindheim, O.T., Finite element analysis of the Byrte unlined pressure shaft failure. In Brekke and Jørstad (ed.): Large permanent underground openings. Universitetsforlaget, Oslo, 337 - 342, 1970.

Broch, E. and Bergh-Christensen, J., Undersøkelse vedrørende ufôrete trykksjakter. Inst. for Vassbygging, NTH, Trondheim, 1962.

Myrset, Ø., Underground hydro-electric power stations in Norway. In S.M. Bergman (ed): Subsurface space. Pergamon Press, Vol. 1, 691 - 699, 1980.

Norwegian Geotechnical Institute, Oversikt over norske ufôrete tunneler og sjakter. Unpubl. report, 1972.

Rathe, L., An innovation in surgechamber design. Water Power, Vol. 27, 244 - 248, 1975.

Selmer-Olsen, R., Experience with unlined pressure shafts in Norway. In Brekke and Jørstad: Large permanent underground openings. Universitetsforlaget, Oslo 327 - 332, 1970.

Selmer-Olsen, R., Underground openings filled with high-pressure water or air. Bull. Int. Ass. Engineering Geology, Vol. 9, 91 - 95, 1974.

Vogt, J.H.L., Tryktunneler og geologi. Norges Geol. Undersøkelse nr. 93, Oslo, 1922.

ROCK-SUPPORT INTERACTION CALCULATIONS FOR PRESSURE SHAFTS AND TUNNELS

Berechnung der Wechselwirkung zwischen Gebirge und Sicherung bei Druckschächten und Tunnels

Le calcul de l'interaction entre le massif rocheux et le blindage des puits et des tunnels sous pression

E.T.BROWN & J.W.BRAY
Imperial College, London, UK

SUMMARY:
A major factor hindering the detailed application of the method of characteristic lines in underground excavation design is the difficulty of determining realistic rock mass properties and allowing for them in the calculations. A new method of making rock-support interaction calculations for plane strain, axi-symmetric pressure shaft and tunnel problems is presented. This method uses non-linear peak and residual rock mass strength criteria, allows for strain-softening and the development of plastic volumetric strains, calculates the distribution of groundwater pressures by allowing the permeability of the fractured rock mass in the plastic zone to vary with the square of the volumetric strain, and evaluates the influence of water pressure subsequently applied inside the lined excavation.

ZUSAMMENFASSUNG:
Ein Hauptfaktor der die ausführliche Anwendung der Methode der charakteristischen Linien im Untertage Ausgrabung Entwurf verhindert, ist die Schwierigkeit die reele Felsmasse Eigenschaften zu bestimmen und in die Berechnung zu berücksichtigen. Eine neue Methode die die Fels-Unterstutzung Aufeinanderwirkung für ebenen Zwang axialsymmetrische Druckschächte-und Tunnelprobleme berechnet ist dargestellt. Diese Methode wendet nicht-lineare Bruch-und Restfestigkeit Felsmasse Kriteria an, berücksichtigt den Festigkeits abfall und die Entwicklung von plastischen Volumetrischen Formänderungen, berechnet die Verteilung des Grundwasserdrucks bei ermöglichen die Durchlässigkeit der gebrochenen Felsenmässe in die plastische Zone mit dem Quadrat der Volumetrischen Formänderung zu verändern und den Einfluss des nachträglich an der Innenseite der verschalenen Ausgrabung aufgelegenen Wasserdrucks abzuschätzen.

RESUME:
La utilisation de toutes les possibilités de la méthode des characteristiques est empechée par des difficultés au niveau pratique presentées par la détermination de la loi de comportement global du massif fissuré, et par des difficultés au niveau mathématique de tenir compte de ce comportement lors du calcul. On presente ici une nouvelle méthode d'analyse de l'interaction entre une structure de soutènement et le massif, pour le cas de contraintes planes tel qu'un tunnel, et pour le cas axisymmetrique d'un puit. Cette méthode permet l'utilisation des critères non-linéaires de résistance maximale et residuelle, et elle permet de tenir en compte les phenomènes de l'anti-écrouissage et de l'évolution de la dilatation plastique. La variation de la pression d'eau souterraine se calcule a partir de l'hypothèse qu'a l'intérieur de la zone plastique, le pérmeabilité des roches fissurées est proportionelle à la déformation volumetrique au carré, et on tient compte lors du calcul de l'influence de la pression interne sur le paroi de la cavité souterraine.

1. INTRODUCTION

The development of stresses and displacements in the rock surrounding tunnels and shafts and in the lining or support elements has long been studied using ground-support interaction analyses. The use of what is known as the method of characteristic lines or the convergence-confinement method produces ground-support interaction diagrams which show the inter-relationships between the rock mass properties, the in-situ stresses, the type and stiffness of the lining or support and the timing of its installation. The general principles elucidated by this approach are now widely understood and applied in practice, particularly in conjunction with field measurements as in the New Austrian Tunnelling Method (Rabcewicz, 1964).

Despite these advances in general understanding, the basic concepts of ground-support interaction have not, as yet, been incorporated into a widely applied method of making pre-excavation design calculations. This can be attributed, in the main, to two major factors:

(i) the difficulty of adequately predetermining the range of rock mass properties required for use in such calculations; and

(ii) The analytical and computational difficulties associated with solving other than axi-symmetric problems taking into account realistic rock mass properties which generally involve non-linearities and strain-softening post-peak behaviour.

This paper considers the models of rock mass behaviour that have been previously used in rock-support interaction calculations, and proposes a new model of the relevant rock mass properties. The application of this model is illustrated through the solution of an axi-symmetric pressure shaft problem in which the distribution of water pressures throughout the problem domain is taken into account.

2. PREVIOUS SOLUTIONS

Although more complex engineering problems have been solved using numerical methods (e.g. Lombardi, 1980), the differences between models of rock mass behaviour used in rock-support interaction analyses can be conveniently illustrated using a simple axi-symmetric problem. The problem most commonly considered is that of a circular tunnel or shaft or radius r_i, excavated in a homogeneous, isotropic, initially elastic rock mass subjected to an equal all-round in situ stress, p_o (Fig.1). The support system applies a uniform total radial support pressure, p_i. If the stresses induced in the rock mass following excavation exceed its yield strength, a plastic zone of radius r_e will develop around the excavation. The rock outside the boundary defined by r_e is assumed to remain elastic.

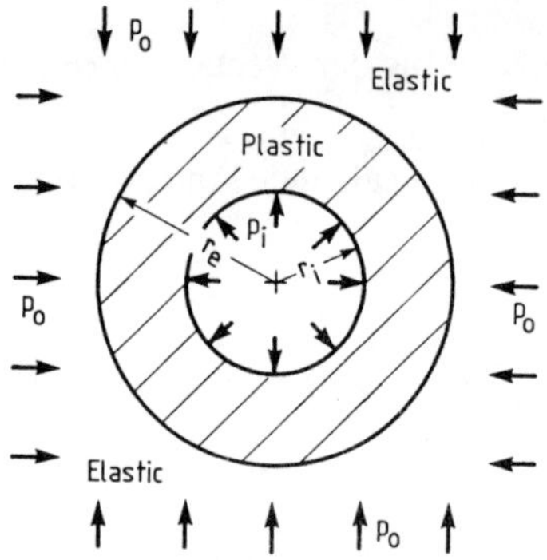

Figure 1: Axi-symmetric tunnel problem without water pressures.

A number of the available solutions to this problem allow for the influence of the proximity of the face (Egger, 1974; Panet, 1976) or construction procedures (Kaiser, 1981) on ground-support interaction. More commonly, plane strain conditions are assumed with all strain increments occurring in the plane of Fig.1. Because of the axial symmetry of the problem, the circumferential and radial direct stresses, σ_θ and σ_r, in the rock mass surrounding the excavation will be the principal stresses σ_1 and σ_3.

The large number of solutions that have been obtained to this and similar problems have been reviewed recently by Brown et al (1982). The various solutions can be distinguished by the manner in which they treat

(i) the strength or yield criterion of the rock mass;

(ii) the post-yield stress-strain behaviour of the rock mass;

(iii) the development of plastic volumetric strains which influence the displacements calculated at the excavation boundary and the extent of the plastic zone.

A great majority of the published solutions, including the earliest (Terzaghi, 1925; Fenner, 1938), use a Mohr-Coulomb criterion, sometimes with a reduced residual strength often characterized by à constant angle of internal friction and a reduced or zero cohesion (e.g. Morrison and Coates, 1955; Hendron and Aiyer, 1972; Egger, 1974; Panet, 1976; Borsetto and Ribacchi, 1979). Daemen and Fairhurst (1971)

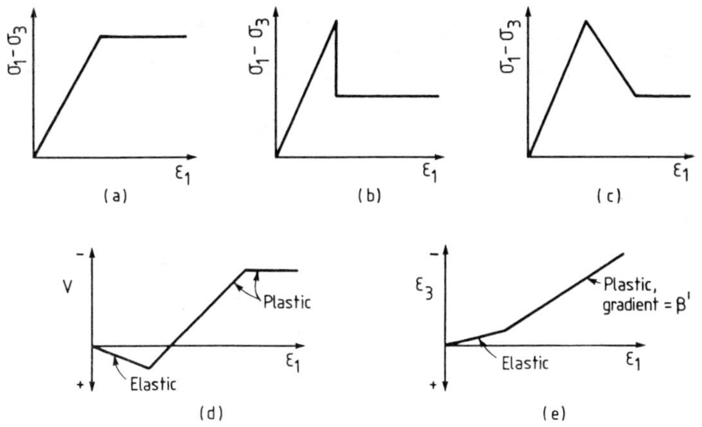

Figure 2: Material behaviour models used in previous solutions.

used a bilinear strength criterion with different peak and residual strengths, while Kaiser (1980) used a rate-dependent Mohr-Coulomb model with different peak and residual strengths. A smaller number of investigators (Hobbs, 1966; Ladanyi, 1974; Hoek and Brown, 1980b; Brown et al, 1982) have used non-linear peak and residual strength envelopes which introduce greater algebraic complexity into the solutions.

Fig.2 summarizes the models of stress-strain behaviour, including plastic volumetric strain, that have been used. The models are presented in terms of the principal stress difference ($\sigma_1-\sigma_3$), major principal (circumferential) strain (ε_1), minor principal (radial) strain (ε_3), and volumetric strain ($v = \varepsilon_1+\varepsilon_3$) developed in the rock mass following excavation. Compressive stresses and contractile strains are taken as positive. In the development of the principal stress difference which produces yield around the excavation, the rock mass is subjected to a stress path which differs from that followed in the standard triaxial compression test widely used to determine rock properties. In the case of a tunnel excavated in a rock mass initially subjected to a hydrostatic stress field, the major principal (circumferential) stress increases and the minor principal (radial) stress decreases as a result of excavation. In the triaxial test, σ_1 increases with σ_3 held constant.

The earliest solutions (Terzaghi, 1925; Fenner, 1938; Kastner, 1949) used an elastic-perfectly plastic stress-strain model (Fig.2a) with zero post-yield volumetric strain. Labasse (1949) was the first to attempt to allow for plastic volumetric strains in the yielding rock mass by estimating an average plastic dilation which was applied at all points in the plastic zone. This concept was later used by several authors (Daemen and Fairhurst, 1971; Lombardi, 1970, 1980; Ladanyi, 1974), but it has the clear difficulty that the plastic dilation must be expected to vary with radius in the plastic zone as the stresses and strain components vary.

The first modification made to the elastic-perfectly plastic stress-strain model was to assume a sudden drop in strength to the residual once peak strength had been attained (Fig.2b). The early solutions obtained using this model (Morrison and Coates, 1955; Hobbs, 1966) took no account of plastic volumetric strains, although Hobbs used different values of the "elastic" constants for the broken and unbroken zones. Subsequent applications of this model used various approaches in the treatment of plastic volumetric strains including the application of the associated flow rule of the theory of plasticity (Hendron and Aiyer, 1972; Ladanyi, 1974; Hoek and Brown, 1980b). Ladanyi (1974) pointed out that indiscriminate application of the associated flow rule can lead to substantial overestimates of dilatation and so applied it over only a limited range of post-peak strain (Fig.2d).

A number of recent solutions allow for strain softening, sometimes perhaps more accurately called strain weakening, of the rock mass, generally using a tri-linear stress-strain model of the type shown in Fig.2c (Daemen and Fairhurst, 1971; Egger, 1974; Panet, 1976; Nguyen Minh and Berest, 1979; Borsetto and Ribacchi, 1979; Brown et al, 1982). Several of these solutions treat plastic volumetric strains by allowing the major and minor principal plastic strains to be linearly related by a variable parameter β' (Fig.2e).

It is well known from experience that the development of stresses and displacements around underground excavations and in linings and supports, can be a time-dependent process. Various attempts have been made to allow for this time dependency in characteristic line calculations (Ladanyi, 1974, 1980; Kaiser, 1980). Although the practical importance of time dependency is acknowledged, its treatment lies outside the scope of the present Paper.

3. MODEL OF ROCK MASS BEHAVIOUR

3.1 Strength criterion

As noted above, most previous solutions have assumed a Mohr-Coulomb strength or yield criterion which gives a linear relationship between σ_1 or $\sigma_1 - \sigma_3$ and σ_3. However, such experimental data as are available, suggest that strength criteria for jointed rock masses are generally non-linear (Jaeger, 1970; Raphael and Goodman, 1979). The determination of an appropriate strength criterion for a given rock mass remains one of the classic problems in rock mechanics. In a recent study of this problem, Hoek and Brown (1980a; 1980b) proposed the empirical non-linear peak strength criterion

$$\sigma_1 = \sigma_3 + (m\sigma_c\sigma_3 + s\sigma_c^2)^{\frac{1}{2}} \quad (1)$$

where σ_1 and σ_3 are the major and minor principal stresses at peak strength, σ_c is the uniaxial compressive strength of the intact rock material, and m and s are constants that depend on the nature of the rock mass and the extent to which it had been broken before being subjected to the stresses σ_1 and σ_3. The parameters m and s vary with rock type and with rock mass quality as measured by Barton, Lien and Lunde's Q factor or Bieniawski's Rock Mass Rating (RMR).

In the broken or plastic zone, the parameters m and s will be reduced to m_r and s_r with the residual strength of the broken rock mass being given by

$$\sigma_1 = \sigma_3 + (m_r\sigma_c\sigma_3 + s_r\sigma_c^2)^{\frac{1}{2}} \quad (2)$$

The strength criterion of equations (1) and (2) offers an advantage over other approaches to the determination of in-situ rock mass strength in that it is based on one simple material property (σ_c) and rock mass quality data that may be systematically evaluated during the investigation and early construction phases of an underground project.

3.2 Stress-strain behaviour

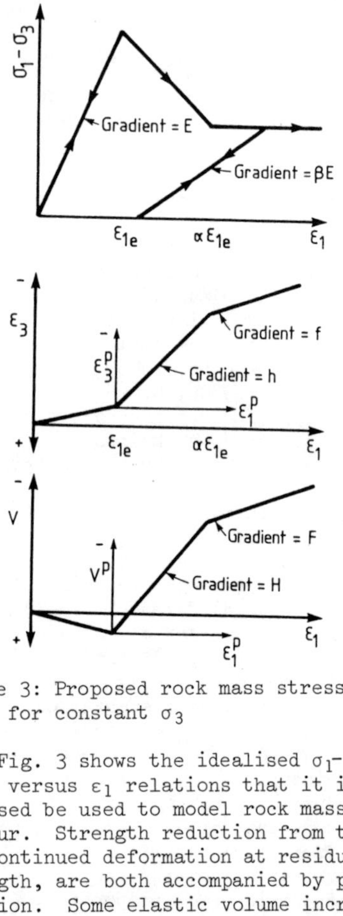

Figure 3: Proposed rock mass stress-strain model for constant σ_3

Fig. 3 shows the idealised $\sigma_1 - \sigma_3$, ε_3 and v versus ε_1 relations that it is proposed be used to model rock mass behaviour. Strength reduction from the peak and continued deformation at residual strength, are both accompanied by plastic dilation. Some elastic volume increase will also occur when the stresses are reduced. This effect, whose magnitude will be influenced by changes in elastic moduli occurring when the rock mass is broken, is not evaluated explicitly, but is subsumed in the gradients of the post-peak ε_3 vs ε_1 and v vs ε_1 curves. Thus, the strain components $\varepsilon_1{}^p$, $\varepsilon_3{}^p$ and v^p are total post-peak rather than plastic strain increments. During unloading and re-loading in the post-peak regions, it is assumed that no hysteresis occurs.

Experimental data are required to

determine the parameters α,β,f,h,F and H which may vary with σ_3. Such data exist for intact rock material but are very sparse for jointed rock. However, data such as those obtained for intact rock by Cook (1981), Crouch (1970), Elliott (1982) and Ladanyi and Don (1971), and for models of jointed rock by Brown (1976) and Michelis (1979), provide evidence of the validity of the model of Fig.3 and permit values of the required parameters to be determined. The approach used here assumes that, on the scale of the problem, the rock mass behaves isotropically, and so overall, rather than purely local, rock mass parameters are being sought.

An alternative to the use of experimentally determined parameters in defining the post-peak volumetric strains is to estimate them using the associated flow rule of the theory of plasticity. There is limited evidence available to suggest that the dilation rate at peak stress in dense, brittle rocks or in tightly interlocked aggregates, can be predicted closely using the associated flow rule (Gerogiannopoulos and Brown, 1978; Ladanyi and Don, 1971). It is not clear, however, that the associated flow rule applies to heavily fractured and poorly interlocked rock masses. Indeed, analyses of data obtained by Brown (1974) and Michelis (1979) suggests that, in some such cases, the flow rule will be non-associated. This means that the resulting plastic volume changes will be less than those predicted using the associated flow rule.

4. ANALYSIS OF AN AXI-SYMMETRIC PRESSURE SHAFT PROBLEM

4.1 Boundary conditions and assumptions

A circular shaft of radius r_i is excavated in a rock mass initially subjected to an equal all-round far field stress, p_o, in the plane normal to the shaft axis. The shaft is then lined with concrete after some convergence has occurred. The internal and external radii of the lining are a and b, respectively. After a water pressure, p_a, is applied inside the shaft, the total radial inter-action pressure between the rock and the concrete is p_b.

The rock around the shaft may fracture to a radius r_e following excavation, but linear elastic behaviour of the lining is assumed throughout. The weights of the lining and of the fractured rock around the shaft are ignored. Compressive stresses, contractile normal and volumetric strains, and outward radial displacements are taken as positive.

Conditions of axial symmetry are assumed from which it follows that

$$\varepsilon_\theta = -\frac{u}{r} \qquad (3)$$

$$\varepsilon_r = -\frac{du}{dr} \qquad (4)$$

$$\frac{d\sigma_r}{dr} = \frac{\sigma_\theta - \sigma_r}{r} \qquad (5)$$

$$u_\theta = 0$$

$$\tau_{r\theta} = 0$$

$$\gamma_{r\theta} = \gamma_{\theta z} = 0$$

where u is the radial component of displacement, z is the axial direction, u_θ is the tangential component of displacement, τ denotes shear stress, and γ denotes shear strain.

Plane strain conditions are assumed so that

$$\varepsilon_z = \gamma_{rz} = 0$$

and

$$v = \varepsilon_\theta + \varepsilon_r \qquad (6)$$

At a radius $r_g(>r_e)$ from the shaft centreline, the ground-water pressure is assumed to be fixed at p_{wg}. When the shaft is empty, water will drain into the shaft. When the shaft is filled with water under pressure p_a, the direction of flow will normally be reversed. In order to calculate the distribution of ground-water pressures, p_w, within the elastic and plastic zones around the shaft, it is necessary to make some assumptions about the variation in the permeability of the rock mass in these two zones.

Assume that, as a result of overstressing, a set of parallel fractures of average spacing d, and average aperture e, are introduced into the rock mass which had an initial isotropic permeability, k_o. The new permeability in the direction of the fractures may be written as

$$k = k_o + \frac{g\, e^3 n}{12\nu} \qquad (7)$$

where $n(=1/d)$ is the number of fractures per metre in the new set and ν is the kinematic viscosity of the permeating fluid.

If there are N such sets of fractures introduced into the rock mass, the total volumetric strain, relative to the initial rock at zero differential stress, will be

$$v = v_e - N\, n\, e \qquad (8)$$

where v_e is the elastic volumetric strain

induced in the initial rock mass. Equations (7) and (8) may be combined in two alternative ways to give

$$(k - k_o) = \frac{g}{12\nu n^2} \left(\frac{v_e - v}{N}\right)^3 \quad (9)$$

$$\text{or } (k - k_o) = \frac{ge^2}{12\nu} \left(\frac{v_e - v}{N}\right) \quad (10)$$

Thus, if n is constant, $(k-k_o)\alpha (v_e-v)^3$; if e is constant, $(k-k_o)\alpha (v_e-v)$. When the peak strength of the rock mass has been exceeded and strain is continuing in the strain-softening and residual zones, it is to be expected that both n and e will increase. Accordingly, it is assumed as an approximation that $(k-k_o)\alpha(v_e-v)^2$. It is further assumed that in the broken zone, under elasto-plastic plane strain conditions, v_e is negligible, so that plastic volumetric strains have an over-riding effect and $(k-k_o)\alpha v^2$. Letthe constant of proportionality be ηk_o, so that it is assumed that in the plastic zone

$$k = k_o(1 + \eta v^2) \quad (11)$$

4.2 Groundwater pressure distribution

Using Darcy's law, the groundwater pressure gradient at any radius r, is given by

$$\frac{dp_w}{dr} = \frac{\gamma_w Q}{2\pi kr} \quad (12)$$

where Q is the rate of flow in m^3 per metre length of shaft and is positive when the flow is directed inwards. Integrating between the limits r = a and $r = r_g$ gives

$$p_{wg}-p_a = \frac{\gamma_w Q}{2\pi k_o}\left\{ l n\left(\frac{r_g}{r_e}\right) + \int_{r_i}^{r_e}\left(\frac{k_o}{kr}\right)dr + l n\left(\frac{b}{a}\right)\right\} \quad (13)$$

it having been assumed that the concrete lining has the same permeability, k_o, as the initial rock mass. The integral on the right hand side of equation (13) is equal to $\int_{r_i}^{r_e} \frac{1}{(1+\eta\ v^2)r}\, dr$ and may be evaluated by numerical integration once the distribution of plastic volumetric strains within the plastic zone has been determined. Having evaluated this integral, the quantity $\frac{\gamma_w Q}{2\pi k_o}$ may be determined using equation (13).

The groundwater pressure at any radius r in the plastic zone is then given by

$$p_w=p_a + \frac{\gamma_w Q}{2\pi k_o}\left\{ \int_{r_i}^{r}\left(\frac{k_o}{kr}\right)dr + l n\left(\frac{b}{a}\right)\right\} \quad (14)$$

4.3 Stresses and displacements in the plastic zone associated with excavation and lining.

The solution must account for the possible existence of three different zones around the shaft:

(a) an elastic zone remote from the shaft;

(b) an intermediate plastic zone in which the stresses and strains are associated with the strain-softening portion of Fig.3; and

(c) an inner plastic zone in which the stresses are limited by the residual strength of the rock mass.

At the boundary between the elastic and plastic zones, the principal stresses and strains are denoted by $\sigma_{re}, \sigma_{\theta e}, \varepsilon_{re}, \varepsilon_{\theta e}$. An effective stress form of the peak rock mass strength criterion, equation (1), gives the relation between the stresses on this boundary,

$$\sigma_{\theta e}-\sigma_{re} = \{ m\sigma_c(\sigma_{re}-p_{we}) + s\sigma_c{}^2\} \quad (15)$$

Using the boundary conditions $\sigma_r = \sigma_{re}$ at $r = r_e$ and $\sigma_r = p_o$ at $r = \infty$, the equation of equilibrium, equation (4), can be solved to give the stresses in the elastic region as

$$\sigma_\theta = p_o + (p_o-\sigma_{re}) \left(\frac{r_e}{r}\right)^2 \quad (16)$$

$$\sigma_r = p_o - (p_o-\sigma_{re}) \left(\frac{r_e}{r}\right)^2 \quad (17)$$

from which we get

$$\sigma_{\theta e} - \sigma_{re} = 2(p_o - \sigma_{re}) \quad (18)$$

Substitution from equation (18) into equation (15) leads to the result

$$\sigma_{re} = p_o - M\sigma_c \quad (19)$$

and

$$\sigma_{\theta e} = p_o + M\sigma_c \quad (20)$$

$$\text{where } M = \tfrac{1}{2}\left\{ \left(\frac{m}{4}\right)^2 + m\left(\frac{p_o-p_{we}}{\sigma_c}\right) + s\right\}^{\frac{1}{2}} - \frac{m}{8} \quad (21)$$

The radial strain produced at the elastic-plastic boundary by the reduction of σ_r from p_o to σ_{re} is

$$\varepsilon_{re} = - \frac{(p_o - \sigma_{re})}{2G}$$

$$\text{or } \varepsilon_{re} = - \frac{M\sigma_c}{2G} \quad (22)$$

where G is the initial shear modulus of the rock mass. For plain strain conditions, $\varepsilon_{\theta e} = - \varepsilon_{re}$, and so

$$\varepsilon_{\theta e} = \frac{M\sigma_c}{2G} \quad (23)$$

In the strain-softening zone, Fig.3 gives

$$\varepsilon_r - \varepsilon_{re} = - h(\varepsilon_\theta-\varepsilon_{\theta e}) \quad (24)$$

where $\varepsilon_r = \varepsilon_3$ and $\varepsilon_\theta = \varepsilon_1$. Combining equations (4) and (24) gives the differential equation

$$\frac{du}{dr} = -h\frac{u}{r} - (h-1)\varepsilon_{\theta e} \tag{25}$$

Integrating equation (25) gives the radial displacement as

$$u = -\left(\frac{h-1}{h+1}\right)r\,\varepsilon_{\theta e} + C_1 r^{-h} \tag{26}$$

The constant C_1 may be evaluated by using the result from equation (3), $u = -r_e\,\varepsilon_{\theta e}$ when $r = r_e$. Thus, it is established that, within the strain-softening zone,

$$\varepsilon_\theta = -\frac{u}{r} = (h-1) + 2\left(\frac{r_e}{r}\right)^{h+1}\frac{\varepsilon_{\theta e}}{h+1} \tag{27}$$

$$\text{and}\quad \varepsilon_r = -\frac{du}{dr} = (h-1) - 2h\left(\frac{r_e}{r}\right)^{h+1}\frac{\varepsilon_{\theta e}}{h+1} \tag{28}$$

The residual strength is reached when $\varepsilon_\theta = \alpha\,\varepsilon_{\theta e} = \varepsilon_{\theta R}$. By substitution in equation (27), it is found that the radius of the boundary between the strain-softening and residual zones is

$$r_R = r_e\left\{\frac{2}{(h+1)\alpha-(h-1)}\right\}^{\frac{1}{(h+1)}} \tag{29}$$

and that

$$\varepsilon_{rR} = (h - 1 - \alpha h)\varepsilon_{\theta e} \tag{30}$$

Similarly, in the residual zone,

$$\frac{du}{dr} = -f\frac{u}{r} - (\varepsilon_{rR} + f\varepsilon_{\theta R}) \tag{31}$$

which, on integration and evaluation of the constant of integration, leads to

$$\varepsilon_\theta = -\frac{u}{r} = \left\{(\varepsilon_{rR}+f\,\varepsilon_{\theta R})+(\varepsilon_{\theta R}-\varepsilon_{rR})\left(\frac{r_R}{r}\right)^{f+1}\right\}.\frac{1}{(f+1)} \tag{32}$$

and

$$\varepsilon_r = -\frac{du}{dr} = \left\{(\varepsilon_{rR}+f\,\varepsilon_{\theta R})-f(\varepsilon_{\theta R}-\varepsilon_{rR})\left(\frac{r_R}{r}\right)^{f+1}\right\}.\frac{1}{(f+1)} \tag{33}$$

It is assumed that for any general point in the plastic region,

$$\sigma_\theta - \sigma_r = \{\bar{m}(\sigma_r - p_w)\,\sigma_c + \bar{s}\,\sigma_c^2\}^{\frac{1}{2}} \tag{34}$$

$$\left.\begin{aligned} \text{where } \bar{m} &= m + \frac{(m_r-m)\,(\varepsilon_\theta-\varepsilon_{\theta e})}{(\alpha-1)\varepsilon_{\theta e}} \\ \bar{s} &= s + \frac{(s_r-s)\,(\varepsilon_\theta-\varepsilon_{\theta e})}{(\alpha-1)\varepsilon_{\theta e}} \end{aligned}\right\} r_e > r > r_R \tag{35}$$

$$\text{and}\quad \left.\begin{aligned}\bar{m} &= m_r \\ \bar{s} &= s_r\end{aligned}\right\} r \leqslant r_R \tag{36}$$

This approach will not necessarily give a linear stress-strain curve in the strain-softening zone as shown in Fig.3.

Using equation (34), the equilibrium equation may be written as

$$\frac{d\sigma_r}{dr} = \frac{\sigma_\theta - \sigma_r}{r} = \frac{\{\bar{m}(\sigma_r-p_w)\sigma_c + \bar{s}\,\sigma_c^2\}^{\frac{1}{2}}}{r} \tag{37}$$

$$\text{where } \bar{m}_a = \tfrac{1}{2}(\bar{m}_{j-1} + \bar{m}_j) \tag{39}$$

$$\text{and } \bar{s}_a = \tfrac{1}{2}(\bar{s}_{j-1}) + \bar{s}_j) \tag{40}$$

The solution for $\sigma_{r(j)}$ is obtained as

$$\sigma_{r(j)} = b - \sqrt{b^2 - a} \tag{41}$$

$$\left.\begin{aligned} \text{where } a &= \sigma^2_{r(j-1)} - 4c\{\tfrac{1}{2}\,\bar{m}_a\sigma_c(\sigma_{r(j-1)}-p_{w(j)} \\ &\qquad -p_{w(j-1)}) + s_a\,\sigma_c^2\} \\ b &= \sigma_{r(j-1)} + c\,\bar{m}_a\,\sigma_c \\ \text{and } c &= \left[\frac{r_{j-1} - r_j}{r_{j-1} + r_j}\right]^2 \end{aligned}\right\} \tag{42}$$

The radial stress on the outer boundary of the first annulus where $r = r_1 = r_e$, is given by equation (19). By successisvely incrementing the radius r, successive values of $\sigma_{r(j)}$ can be calculated from equations (41) and (42). Equation (37) can then be used to calculate the corresponding values of σ_θ. The fact that water pressure, rock mass fragmentation and strength are coupled, means that the above numerical integration to solve for σ_r and that for groundwater pressure (equations 13 and 14) must be carried out alternately in a sequence of successive approximations.

If required, the solutions for $\varepsilon_r, \varepsilon_\theta$ and u may also be obtained using a finite difference procedure as described by Brown et al (1982) for the case of an axi-symmetric tunnel problem without water pressures.

The characteristic line for the rock mass, or the relationship between the internal support pressure (p_i in Fig.1) and radial convergence, may be determined from the result of the calculations described above. For this purpose, it is most convenient to tabulate the results as values of r/r_e, u/r and σ_r. To find the value of r_e for a given value of support pressure, p_i, find the value of σ_r in the table which equals p_i, and calculate r_e from the corresponding value of r/r_e putting $r = r_i$. Points on the characteristic line are obtained by putting $p_i = \sigma_r$, calculating corresponding values of u_i from $(u/r)\,r_i$, and putting $\delta_i = -u_i$.

4.4 Stresses and displacements in the concrete lining

The stresses and displacements in the concrete lining are given by

$$\sigma_\theta = C + D/r^2 \tag{43}$$

$$\sigma_r = C - D/r^2 \tag{44}$$

$$u = -\frac{1}{2G_c}\{(1-2\nu_c)Cr + \frac{D}{r}\} \tag{45}$$

$$\text{where } C = (b^2p_b - a^2p_a)/(b^2-a^2) \tag{46}$$

$$D = (p_b - p_a)\, a^2b^2/(b^2-a^2) \qquad (47)$$

and G_c and ν_c are the shear modulus and Poisson's ratio of the concrete.

For the case of no internal water pressure ($p_a = 0$), the characteristic line for the concrete lining is given by

$$\delta_i = \delta_{io} + \frac{p_i}{k_c} \qquad (48)$$

where δ_{io} = convergence permitted before the lining was installed,

$$k_c = \frac{2G_c(b^2-a^2)}{\{(1-2\nu_c)b^2 + a^2\}b} \qquad (49)$$

= lining stiffness

The value of δ_{io} must be chosen so that the circumferential stress, σ_θ, on the inner wall of the lining is not excessive.

4.5 The effect of an internal water pressure

It is assumed that as the internal water pressure, p_a, in the shaft is raised and lowered, the rock mass will be unloaded and loaded without hysteresis as indicated in Fig.3. It has also been assumed that the concrete lining has a permeability equivalent to that of the initial rock mass and so a new distribution of groundwater pressures will be established within the rock mass. In order to evaluate the new distribution of stresses and displacements following application of p_a, it is necessary to be able to model the stress-strain behaviour of the fractured rock mass around the shaft taking account of the influence of water pressure.

Assume initially that a single set of parallel fractures of average spacing d and inclined at an angle ψ to the circumferential direction is induced by the stress concentration around the shaft. Let the increments of stress, groundwater pressure and strain arising from the imposition of p_a be $\bar{\sigma}_r, \bar{\sigma}_\theta$, $\bar{p}_w$, $\bar{\varepsilon}_r$ and $\bar{\varepsilon}_\theta$. If k_n and k_s are the normal and shear stiffnesses of the stress-induced fractures, then it may be shown that the strain increments associated with deformation of these fractures are

$$\bar{\varepsilon}_\theta' = \frac{1}{k_n d}(\bar{\sigma}_\theta-\bar{p}_w)\sin^2\psi + \frac{1}{d}\left(\frac{1}{k_s} - \frac{1}{k_n}\right)(\bar{\sigma}_\theta-\bar{\sigma}_r)\sin^2\psi\cos^2\psi \qquad (50)$$

and

$$\bar{\varepsilon}_r' = \frac{1}{k_n d}(\bar{\sigma}_r-\bar{p}_w)\cos^2\psi + \frac{1}{d}\left(\frac{1}{k_s} - \frac{1}{k_n}\right)(\bar{\sigma}_r-\bar{\sigma}_\theta)\sin^2\psi\cos^2\psi \qquad (51)$$

A non-zero shear strain component, $\gamma_{r\theta}'$, will also result, but this must vanish under conditions of axial symmetry. To achieve this, assume that there is a second set of stress-induced fractures which mirror image the first. This also results in a doubling of the normal strain increments given by equations (50) and (51).

The value of ψ is unknown. Since ψ will be influenced by the discontinuities and microfractures initially present in the rock mass, its value is difficult to establish in the general case. For convenience, ψ will be taken to be a random variable, in which case $\bar{\varepsilon}_\theta'$ and $\bar{\varepsilon}_r'$ can be replaced by their average values

$$\bar{\varepsilon}_\theta'' = \frac{2}{\pi}\int_0^{\pi/2} \bar{\varepsilon}_\theta'\, d\psi = \frac{1}{k_n d}(\bar{\sigma}_\theta-\bar{p}_w) + \frac{1}{4d}\left(\frac{1}{k_s} - \frac{1}{k_n}\right)(\bar{\sigma}_\theta-\bar{\sigma}_r) \qquad (52)$$

$$\bar{\varepsilon}_r'' = \frac{2}{\pi}\int_0^{\pi/2} \bar{\varepsilon}_r'\, d\psi = \frac{1}{k_n d}(\bar{\sigma}_r-\bar{p}_w) + \frac{1}{4d}\left(\frac{1}{k_s} - \frac{1}{k_n}\right)(\bar{\sigma}_r-\bar{\sigma}_\theta) \qquad (53)$$

To these components must be added the strains produced in the initial rock mass by the stress increments $\bar{\sigma}_r$, $\bar{\sigma}_\theta$ and $\bar{p}_w$. Thus the total strain increments in the plastic zone resulting from the application of p_a are found to be

$$\bar{\varepsilon}_\theta = \frac{1}{2G}\{(1-\nu)\bar{\sigma}_\theta - \gamma\bar{\sigma}_r\} + \frac{1}{k_n d}(\bar{\sigma}_\theta-\bar{p}_w) + \frac{1}{4d}\left(\frac{1}{k_s} - \frac{1}{k_n}\right)(\bar{\sigma}_\theta-\bar{\sigma}_r) \qquad (54)$$

and

$$\bar{\varepsilon}_r = \frac{1}{2G}\{(1-\nu)\bar{\sigma}_r - \nu\bar{\sigma}_\theta\} + \frac{1}{k_n d}(\bar{\sigma}_r-\bar{p}_w) + \frac{1}{4d}\left(\frac{1}{k_s} - \frac{1}{k_n}\right)(\bar{\sigma}_r-\bar{\sigma}_\theta) \qquad (55)$$

which gives

$$\varepsilon_\theta - \varepsilon_r = \frac{1}{2G_f}(\bar{\sigma}_\theta-\bar{\sigma}_r) \qquad (56)$$

$$\text{where } G_f = \left\{\frac{1}{G} + \frac{1}{d}\left(\frac{1}{k_n} + \frac{1}{k_s}\right)\right\}^{-1} \qquad (57)$$

= shear modulus of fractured rock.

For axial symmetry, the strain compatibility equation takes the form

$$\frac{d\bar{\varepsilon}_\theta}{dr} = \frac{\bar{\varepsilon}_r - \bar{\varepsilon}_\theta}{r}$$

Substituting the previous expressions for $\bar{\varepsilon}_\theta$ and $\bar{\varepsilon}_r$, and making use of the equilibrium equation, eventually leads to

$$\frac{d}{dr}(\bar{\sigma}_\theta + \bar{\sigma}_r) = \lambda_o \cdot \frac{d\bar{p}_w}{dr} \qquad (58)$$

where

$$\lambda_o = \frac{4(G-G_f)}{(3+\frac{k_n}{k_s})G - \{(1+2\nu)-(1-2\nu)\frac{k_n}{k_s}\}G_f} \qquad (59)$$

Generally, k_n and k_s will be of the same order of magnitude. If, for simplicity, they are assumed to be equal, equation (59) reduces to

$$\lambda_o = \frac{G - G_f}{G - \nu G_f} \quad (60)$$

Equation (58) may be written in finite difference form and solved giving

$$\bar{\sigma}_r(j) = \{\sigma_r(j-1) + 2\lambda_2\bar{\sigma}_\theta(j-1) + \lambda_1\lambda_2\}/(1+2\lambda_2) \quad (61)$$

$$\sigma_\theta(j) = \lambda_1 - \bar{\sigma}_r(j) + \bar{\sigma}_\theta(j-1) + \bar{\sigma}_r(j-1) \quad (62)$$

$$u(j) = \frac{-r_j}{2G}\{(1-\nu)\sigma_\theta(j) - \nu\sigma_r(j) + (\frac{G}{G_f} - 1)(\sigma_\theta(j) - p_w(j))\} \quad (63)$$

where

$$\lambda_1 = \left\{\frac{2G - G_f(j) - G_f(j-1)}{2G - \nu(G_f(j) + G_f(j-1))}\right\}(\bar{p}_w(j) - \bar{p}_w(j-1)) \quad (64)$$

$$\text{and } \lambda_2 = (r_j - r_{j-1})/r_j + r_{j-1}) \quad (65)$$

It is assumed that no further structural change occurs in the rock surrounding the shaft when the shaft water pressure is applied. The value of G_f is therefore determined by the state of strain occurring before the shaft is pressurised. The value of G_f in the residual zone is taken to be βG, assuming that $\nu = \nu_f$. In the strain-softening zone, G_f is taken to vary linearly with ε_θ according to

$$G_f = G\{1 + \frac{(\beta-1)(\varepsilon_\theta - \varepsilon_{\theta e})}{(\alpha-1)\varepsilon_{\theta e}}\} \quad (66)$$

Equations (61) to (66), when used in conjunction with equations (13) and (14) for groundwater pressures, allow us to proceed in a stepwise manner to determine the changes in stress and displacement at all points due to the increment in shaft water pressure. However, a method of successive approximation is required to ensure that the value of $\sigma_{\bar{r}}(j)/\bar{u}(j)$ at the inner boundary ($r=r_i$) accords with the radial stiffness of the lining.

5. NUMERICAL EXAMPLE

The solution described in Section 4 has been programmed for use with a micro-computer. This program was used to solve a hypothetical pressure shaft problem based on conditions likely to apply in a project such as the Drakensberg Pumped Storage Scheme described by Bowcock et al (1976).

A vertical shaft of radius r_i=3m is excavated to a maximum depth of 400m where there is an equal all round horizontal stress of p_o=27 MPa. At a radius of r_g=150m from the shaft centre-line, the groundwater pressure remains constant at p_{wg}=2.3 MPa. The mudstone and siltstone rock mass is of fair to good quality with m=0.65, s=0.002, σ_c=40 MPa, m_r=0.20, s_r= 0.0001, E=20 GPa, ν=0.20, α=3.5, β=0.5, f=1.2 and h=3.0. The permeability of the rock mass in the plastic zone is $k=k_o(1+10^5 v^2)$ where k_o is the permeability of the rock mass in its initial condition and v is the volumetric strain of the rock mass in the deformed state.

The concrete lining has an inner radius of a=2.75m, an outer radius of b= r_i=3.0m, a uniaxial compressive strength of σ_{cc}=35 MPa and elastic constants E_c= 25 GPa and ν_c=0.25. Its permeability is the same as that of the initial rock.

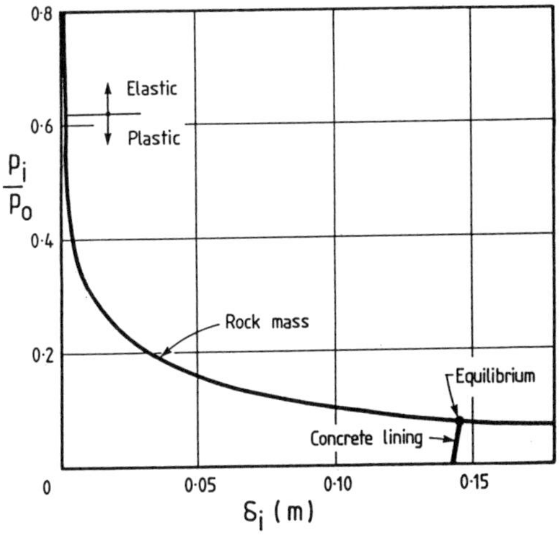

Figure 4: Rock-support interaction diagram for sample problem.

Figure 4 shows the calculated characteristic line for the rock mass showing the development of convergence, δ_i, as the internal support pressure, pi, is reduced from p_o during construction. Say that the amount of free convergence permitted before the lining is installed is 0.1434m. The radial stiffness of the lining is calculated as k_c = 794.47 MPa/m, and equilibrium between lining and rock mass is reached at $\frac{p_i}{p_o}$ = 0.0735 and δ_i = 0.1459m. In this condition, with zero internal water pressure, the maximum circumferential stress at the inner surface of the lining is given by equation (43) as $\sigma_{\theta max}$= 24.84 MPa. Thus the factor of safety against compressive failure of the concrete is 35.0/24.84 = 1.41. The radius of the corresponding elastic-plastic boundary is r_e = 16.024m where

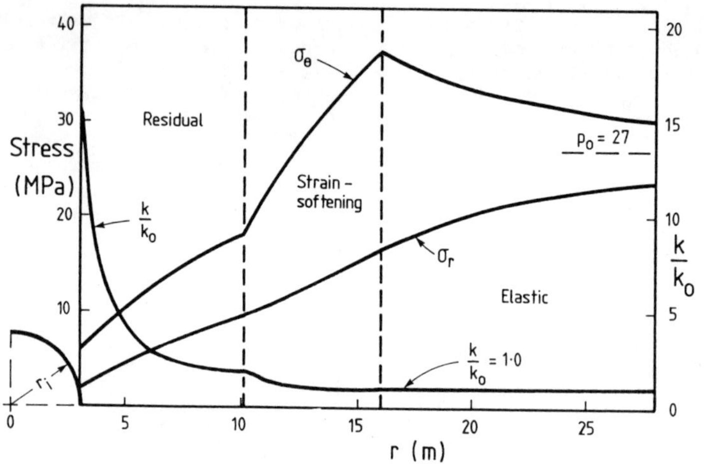

Figure 5: Distribution of radial (σ_r) and circumferential (σ_θ) stresses and permeability ratio (k/k_o) in the rock mass surrounding the pressure shaft in sample problem.

σ_{re} = 16.73 MPa.

Fig. 5 shows the calculated variations of the stresses σ_r and σ_θ in the rock mass, and of the permeability ratio k/k_o, with radius r from the shaft centre-line. The residual zone extends to r_R = 10.146m and the strain-softening zone to r_e = 16.024m. Thereafter the stresses in the rock mass are elastic as given by equations (16) and (17). The permeability ratio drops rapidly in the residual zone from a value of 16.0 on the excavation boundary and approaches unity at the elastic-plastic boundary.

An internal water pressure of p_a = 4.6 MPa is now applied under operational conditions. This produces a new radial rock-support interaction pressure of p_b = 4.93 MPa and a new stress at the elastic-plastic boundary (which remains at r_e = 16.024m) of σ_{re} = 16.88 MPa. The circumferential stress on the inner surface of the lining is reduced to $\sigma_{\theta max}$ = 8.76 MPa, and the convergence at the rock-lining interface is reduced by 0.002m to 0.144m.

6. CONCLUSIONS

It has been shown how more complex and realistic models of rock mass properties than those used hitherto, including an assumed distribution of groundwater pressures in the broken or plastic zone, can be incorporated into the solution of an axi-symmetric pressure shaft problem. The plane-strain solution presented permits the determination of the stresses and displacements in the lining and within the rock mass surrounding the shaft, the variation of permeability and of groundwater pressures within the plastic zone, the extent of the residual and strain-softening zones, and the resulting rock-support interaction diagram. The effects of reloading the fractured rock mass by internal water pressure within the shaft have also been assessed. The solution presented can be readily implemented using a micro-computer.

In order that this approach can be developed into a routine design tool, it is necessary that the present solutions be generalized to allow for non-uniform in situ stress fields and more complex excavation geometries. This will require the use of numerical methods such as the finite element method in place of the closed-form and simple finite difference approach that could be used in the analysis presented herein. In this case, some of the simplifications made in the present analysis for computational ease need not be made.

7. REFERENCES

Borsetto, M. & R. Ribacchi 1979, Influence of the strain softening behaviour of rock masses on the stability of a tunnel. In W. Wittke (ed.), Proc. 3rd Int.Conf. on Numerical Methods in Geomechanics, Rotterdam, A.A. Balkema, 2:611-620.

Bowcock, J.B., J.M. Boyd, E. Hoek & J.C. Sharp 1976, Drakensberg pumped storage scheme - rock engineering aspects. In Z.T. Bieniawski (ed.), Exploration for Rock Engineering, Cape Town, A.A. Balkema, 2: 121-139.

Brown, E.T. 1976, Volume changes in models of jointed rock, J. Geotech. Engng Div., Am. Soc. Civ. Engrs 102 (GT3): 273-276.
Brown, E.T., J.W. Bray, B. Ladanyi & E. Hoek 1982, Characteristic line calculations for rock tunnels. Submitted to J. Geotech. Engng Div., Am. Soc. Civ. Engrs.
Cook, N.G.W. 1981, Stiff testing machines, stick slip sliding, and the stability of rock deformation. In Mechanical Behavior of Crustal Rocks: The Handin Volume, Washington D.C., The American Geophysical Union, p.93-102.
Crouch, S.L. 1970, Experimental determination of volumetric strains in failed rock, Int. J. Rock Mech. Min. Sci. 7(6): 589-603.
Daemen, J.J.K. & C. Fairhurst 1971, Influence of failed rock properties on tunnel stability. In G.B. Clark (ed.), Dynamic Rock Mechanics, New York, AIME, p. 855-875.
Egger, P. 1974, Gebirgsdruck im Tunnelbau und Stützwrikung der Ortsburst bei Uberschreiten der Gebirgsfestigkeit, Proc. 3rd Congr. Int. Soc. Rock Mech., Denver, 2B: 1007-1011.
Elliott, G.M. 1982, A further investigation of a yield criterion for rock, Ph.D. thesis, Univ. of London (in preparation).
Fenner, R. 1938, Untersuchungen zur Erkenntnis des Gebirgsdrucks, Glückauf 74: 681-695, 705-715.
Gerogiannopoulos, N.G. & E.T. Brown 1978, The critical state concept applied to rock, Int. J. Rock Mech. Min. Sci. 15(1): 1-10.
Hendron, A.J. & A.K. Aiyer 1972, Stresses and strains around a cylindrical tunnel in an elasto-plastic material with dilatancy, Tech. Rep. No.10, U.S. Corps of Engineers, Omaha, Nebraska.
Hobbs, D.W. 1966, A study of the behaviour of broken rock under triaxial compression, and its application to mine roadways, Int. J. Rock Mech. Min. Sci. 3(1): 11-43.
Hoek, E. & E.T. Brown 1980a, Empirical strength criterion for rock masses, J. Geotech. Engng Div., Am. Soc. Civ. Engrs 106(GT9): 1013-1035.
Hoek, E. & E.T. Brown 1980b, Underground excavations in rock, London, The Institution of Mining & Metallurgy.
Jaeger, J.C., The behaviour of closely jointed rock. In W.H. Somerton (ed.), Rock mechanics - theory and practice, New York, AIME, p. 57-68.
Kaiser, P.K. 1980, Effect of stress history on the deformation behaviour of underground openings. In Underground Rock Engineering - Proc. 13th Canadian Rock Mech. Symp., Montreal, CIM, p. 133-140.
Kaiser, P.K. 1981, A new concept to evaluate tunnel performance - influence of excavation procedure, Proc. 22nd U.S. Symp. Rock Mech., MIT, p. 264-271.
Kastner, H. 1949, Uber den echten Gebirgsdruck beim Bau tiefliegender Tunnel, Osterreich Bauzeitschrift 10(11).
Labasse, H. 1949, Les pressions de terrains dans les mines de huiles. Partie 2 - Les pressions de terrains autour des puits, Revue Universelle des Mines, 9e Serie V(3): 78-88.
Ladanyi, B. 1974, Use of the long-term strength concept in the determination of ground pressure on tunnel linings, Proc. 3rd Congr. Int. Soc. Rock Mech., Denver 2B: 1150-1156.
Ladanyi, B. 1980. Direct determination of ground pressure on tunnel lining in a non-linear viscoelastic rock. In Underground Rock Engineering - Proc. 13th Canadian Rock Mech. Symp., Montreal, CIM, p. 126-132.
Ladanyi, B. & Nguyen Don 1970, Study of strains in rock associated with brittle failure, Proc. 6th Canadian Rock Mech. Symp., Montreal, p. 49-64.
Lombardi, G. 1970, Influence of rock characteristics on the stability of rock cavities - Part 2, Tunnels and Tunnelling 2(2): 104-109.
Lombardi, G. 1980, Some comments on the convergence-confinement method, Underground Space 4(4): 249-258.
Michelis, P.N. 1979, A critical state approach to the yield and deformation of crystalline rock in the brittle, ductile and transitional regions, Ph.D. thesis, Univ. of London.
Morrison, R.G.K. & D.F. Coates 1955, Soil mechanics applied to rock failure in mines, Can. Min. Metall. Bull. 48(523): 701-711.
Nguyen Minh, D. & P. Berest 1979, Etude de la stabilité des cavités souterraines avec un modèle de comportement elastoplastique radoucissant, Proc. 4th Congr. Int. Soc. Rock Mech., Montreux 1: 249-256.
Panet, M. 1976, Analyse de la stabilité d'un tunnel creusé dans un massif rocheaux en tenant compte du comportement après la rupture, Rock. Mech. 8 (4): 209-223.
Rabcewicz, L.V. 1964, The New Austrian Tunnelling Method, Water Power 16(11): 453-457, 16(12): 511-515, 17(1): 19-24.
Raphael, J.M. & R.E. Goodman 1979, Strength and deformability of highly fractured rock, J. Geotech. Engng Div., Am. Soc. Civ. Engrs 105 (GT11): 1285-1300.
Terzaghi, K. 1925, Erdbaumechanik auf Bodenphysik-alischer Grundlage, Vienna, Deuticke.

DESIGN AND SUPERVISION OF UNLINED HYDRO POWER SHAFTS AND TUNNELS WITH HEAD UP TO 590 METERS

Gestaltung und Kontrolle während des Füllens von Druckschächten und Tunnels bei einem Wasserdruck von 25 bis 59 bar in unausgekleideten Bergmassiven

Dimensionnement et supervision du remplissage des puits et des tunnels sous pression sans soutènement d'une hauteur de refoulement supérieure à 590 m

B.BUEN & A.PALMSTRØM
Ing.A.B.Berdal A/S, Norway

SUMMARY:
Experience has proved careful design, supervision and control during filling of pressure shafts and tunnels necessary to prevent costly and unforeseen repairs and production losses.

To prevent hydraulic splitting in unlined pressure tunnels and shafts, the internal water pressure must be less than the minimum principal stress. Today, the theoretical design is usually done by using finite element methods. Vital for a successful design is the use of engineering judgement. In every case the theoretical models must be modified according to the geological and topographical features.

During construction of the plant, registration of water inflows and mapping of relevant geologic features is done in the tunnels and shafts. This makes identification of permeable zones possible. In critical areas pore pressure measurements are used to determine the necessity of sealing.

In the process of filling the shafts and tunnels, leakage control is done. The tunnel system is filled in steps of 100-150 m in order to carry out the leakage measurements.

Summary of design, supervision and leakage measurements is given for 6 hydropower plants with water pressure on unlined rock in the range of 25-59 bar.The main rock types represented are granite, gneiss, michaschist and phyllite. The coefficient of rock mass permeability calculated from the measurements varies from 10^{-8} to 10^{-9} ms^{-1}.

ZUSAMMENFASSUNG:
Gewonnenende Erfahrungen haben vorsichtige Gestaltungen, Uberwachung und Kontrolle während des Auffüllens von Druckschächte und Tunnels notwendig gemacht um kostspielige und unvorhersehene Reparaturen und Produktionsverluste zu vermeiden.

Um hydraulische Aufspaltung in unausgekleideten Drucktunnels und -Schächte zu vermeiden, muss der innere Wasserdruck kleiner sein als die kleinste Hauptspannung. Heute wird die theoretische Gestaltung hauptsächlich unter Verwendung der begrenzten Elementmethode durchgeführt. Wichtig für die gelungende Gestaltung ist die Anwendung von technischer Urteilskraft. In jedem Fall müssen die theoretischen Modelle die geologische und Topographische Struktur angepasst sein.

Die Registrierung von Wassereinfliessen und Kartierung von relevanten geologischen Daten muss während des Baus durchgeführt werden. Dadurch ist die Identifikation der eksistierenden und potentiellen Wasserdurchlässigen Zonen möglich. In kritischen Gebiete müssen Porendruckmessungen vorgenommen werden um eventuelle Abdichtungsmassnahmen zu beschliessen.

Während des Einlassens von Wasser in Schächte und Tunnels müssen Dichtigkeitsprüfungen vorgenommen werden. Die Tunnels werden im Abschnitte von 100 bis 150 Meter gefüllt um die Prüfungen durchführen zu beschliessen.

Dies Erfahrungsmaterial ist von Konstruktionsarbeiten, Kontrollen und Dichtigkeitsmessungen bei 6 Wasserkraftanlagen mit Wasserdruck von 25 bis 59 Bar in unausgekleideten Bergmassiven gewonnen. Die Hauptbestandteile des Massivs waren Granit, Gneis, Glimmer und Fylite. Die Durchdringlichkeit der Steinmasse zeigte einen aus der Messungen ausgerechneten Koeffezient von 10^{-8} bis 10^{-9} ms^{-1}.

RESUME:

L'experience a prouvé qu'une composition soigneuse avec surveillance et contrôle durant le remplissage des puits et des tunnels de pressions sont de première nécessité pour prévenir des reparations couteuses et imprévues, ainsi que des pertes de production.

Pour empêcher la dispersion hydraulic dans des puits et des tunnels non revêtus, il faut que la pression d'eau initiale soit moins forte que le minimum de la contrainte principale. Pour la composition théorique on se sert aujourd'hui le plus souvent de méthodes d'éléments définitives. Vitale pour une composition réussie est, qu'il faut s'appuyer sur l'expertise des ingénieurs. Dans tous les cas il est de première nécessité que les modèles théoriques sont modifiées en strûcte conformité avec des traits géologiques et tropographiques.

Durant la période de la construction de l'usine, le régistrement du débit entrant d'eau et de la cartographie des traits géologiques relevants a été fait en dedans les tunnels et les puits - procédé lequel a rendu possible l'identification de zones perméables, existantes et potentielles. Dans des domaines critiques, des mesures de pore-pression servent à déterminer la nécissité d'une couche de fermeture.

Durant le procès de remplissage des puits et des tunnels, on a fait le côntrole des fuites. Le système de tunnels a été rempli graduellement sur une mesure de 100 à 150 m les pas, pour être à même de mésurer des fuites.

Les résultats sommaires de l'etude des compositions de la surveillance et des fuites ont été donnés pour 6 usines hydrauliques avec une pression d'eau sur de roche non revêtu, dans un ordre de 25 à 59 bar.

Les types ordinaires de roches représentés sont granitte, gneis, micaschiste et phyllitte. Le coefficient de permeabilité obtenu par la calculation des mesures qui ont été faites dans de roche varie de 10^{-8} à 10^{-9} m/s.

1. INTRODUCTION

Characteristic for large parts of the Norwegian topography are the steep valleys close to high mountain plateaus containing lakes and rivers. With such features a great amount of hydro-electrical power plants are constructed as high pressure plants. These plants are characterized by the power station being situated in the valley close to the slope and with a pressure shaft and a headrace tunnel to the reservoir.

The conventional high pressure power plants were constructed with steel lined pressure shafts or steel pipes on the surface. From the middle of the 50'ies, however, a new design with unlined pressure shafts or unlined pressure tunnels was introduced as shown on Fig. 1 and 2, which gave great reductions in the construction costs and time. The solution involves that high water pressure is introduced directly on the rock mass. This new stress situation around the tunnel results in possibilities for deformations and great leakages to the surface.

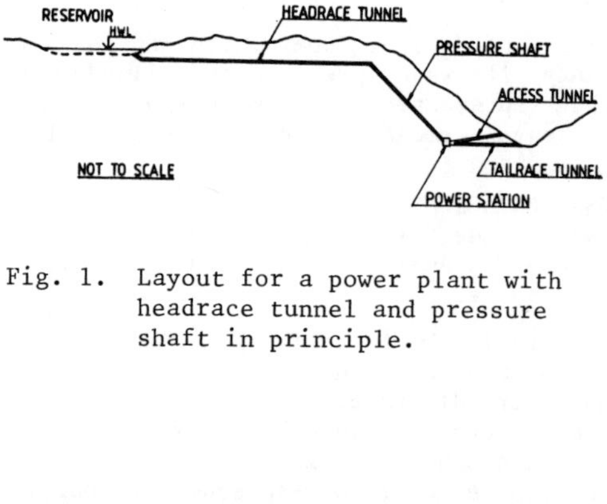

Fig. 1. Layout for a power plant with headrace tunnel and pressure shaft in principle.

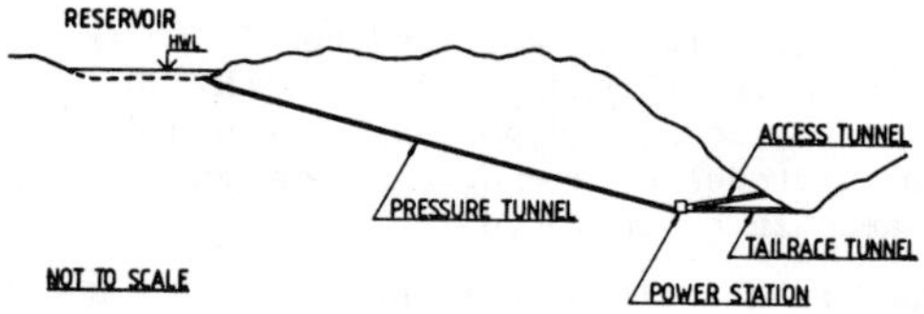

Fig. 2. Layout for a power plant with pressure tunnel in principle.

Unforeseen deformations and/or great uncontrollable water leakages have occurred at Norwegian power plants as late as 1968, 1970 and 1971 during filling up of the water system. Most of the leakages occurred 1-3 days after the tunnels were filled, with insufficient rock cover and/or unfavourable fractures being the main reasons, Ref. (2).

A safe construction of unlined high pressure shafts and tunnels is therefore highly dependant upon a design based on sufficient rock cover with regard to the rock mass quality, together with a planned supervision during construction and the first filling up of the pressure system.

2. DESIGN

At first when the unlined high pressure shafts were introduced an evaluation based on a simple equilibrium state of stress was used. The principle for this was that the weight of the rock mass overburden should exceed the water pressure in the shaft at any point. In Fig. 3 experience gained from 45 unlined Norwegian power plants is compared with the calculation criterion mentioned.

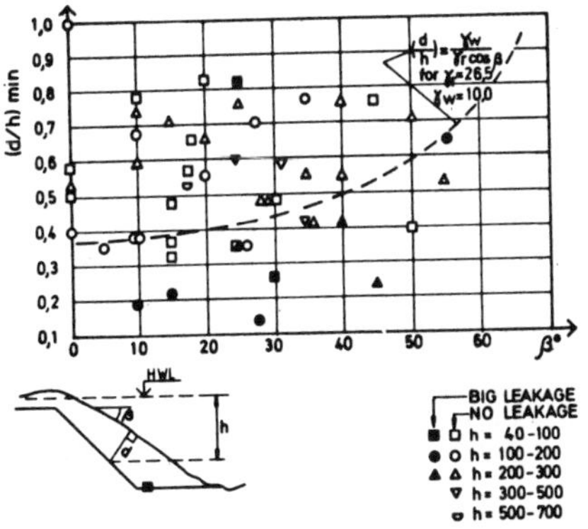

Fig. 3. Unlined tunnels and shafts compared to the "overburden" criteria of design, Ref. (2).

A better basis for design of the unlined high pressure shafts/tunnels became available in 1972 when a method based on finite element analysis of two-dimensional models was introduced, Ref. (4). The main criterion for this model is that the inner water pressure in the shaft/tunnel shall not exceed the minimum principal rock stress. An example of one of these models is shown on Fig. 4 where the design of the pressure shaft of Leirdøla power plant is shown. The critical line Ho/H is for Leirdøla 0,7. The unlined pressure shaft is placed inside this critical line with a safety factor of F = 1.4.

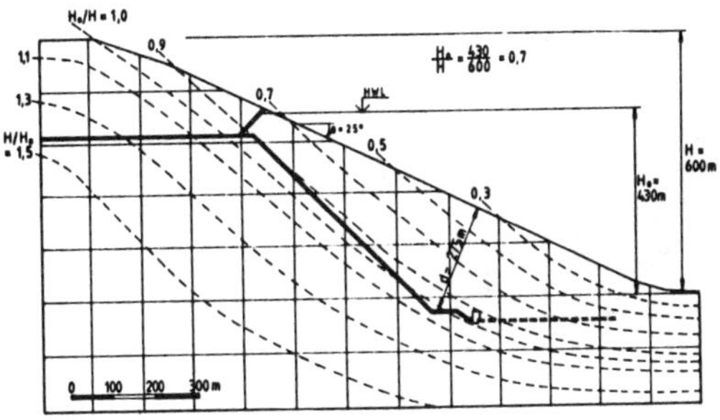

Fig. 4. Model based on finite element methods applied on Leirdøla power plant, Ref. (4).

An understanding of the influence of both the geological and topographical features combined with the calculation criteria is a condition for the engineers evaluation of the safe design of the unlined pressure shaft/tunnel.

3. INFLUENCE FROM A PRESSURE SHAFT UPON GROUNDWATER FLOW AND LEAKAGE

Before excavation of the power plant the ground water in a valley side will flow almost parallel to surface on its way down to the bottom of the valley, Fig. 5A. In moderately jointed rock masses our measurements indicate a mean coefficient of permability $K=10^{-8}-10^{-9}$ m/s^{-1} which equals 0,003-0,3 m/year. In jointed permeable zones the permeability can be considerably larger.

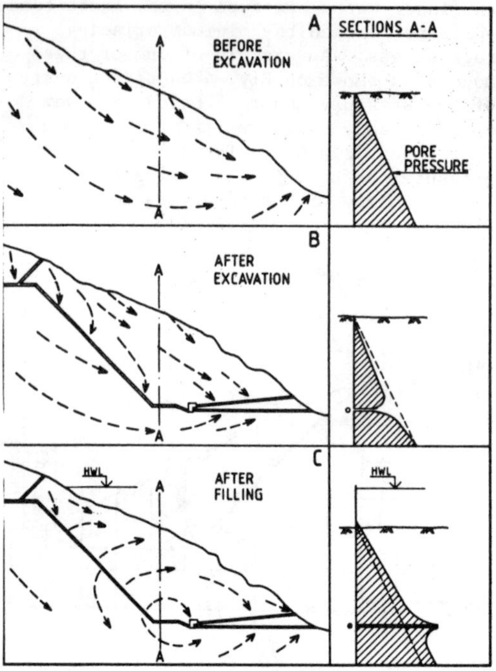

Fig. 5A, B and C. Idealized flow in a homogeneous and isotropic rock massif before and during excavation and after filling.

During and after excavation of the shaft/tunnel pores and joints around it are being drained, and water flows into the shaft/tunnel. A simplified flow sketch for a homogeneous and isotropic condition is shown on Fig. 5B, where it can be seen that most of the leakage water comes from the upper part of the valley side. A considerable reduction of the pore pressures will occur in the rock masses surrounding the shaft/-tunnel. In more permeable rock masses this can result in a lowered water table as indicated on Fig. 5B. This will, however, most often take much longer time than the construction of the power plant.

After the shaft/tunnel has been filled up, Fig. 5C, the water will flow out from it and towards the valley side. Close to the shaft/tunnel the flow will be almost perpendicular to its surface, but further out the flow will be more influenced by the topography. The situation shown in Fig. 5C will cause a small leakage into the shaft at its upper part. When moving down the shaft the leakage out from the shaft will increase with the head. As shown, the water pressure drops significantly within a short distance from the shaft. This has been verified at Skjomen power plant by pore pressure measurements, Ref. (5). The elevation of the ground water level is highly dependant upon the rock mass permeability. As described in the following, any permeable zones will strongly influence on the idealized situation and will result in a more complicated flow net.

Important features of a permeable zone are:

1. The composition and structure of it, mainly its conductivity.

2. The orientation of the zone with regard to the topography, i.e. the valley side.

3. The head in the shaft/tunnel where the zone is found.

The conductivity of a zone can vary from almost zero in clay seams to almost infinity in open water channels in calcite zones. For the evaluation of the sealing works in the shaft/tunnel it is important to have a measure of the degree of the conductivity of the zone. This can best be found by observations of the zone the first days after it has been penetrated. Experience has shown that the leakage from many zones has dropped significantly after a short time because the nearby ground water reservoir has been emptied. If observations are done too late after the zone has been "opened", this can result in underestimates of the necessary sealing works and high leakages.

The orientation and position of the zone in the shaft/tunnel can be even more important than its structure. To illustrate this four different cases of permeable zones are shown in Fig. 6 where the gradient and hence the leakage can vary a lot.

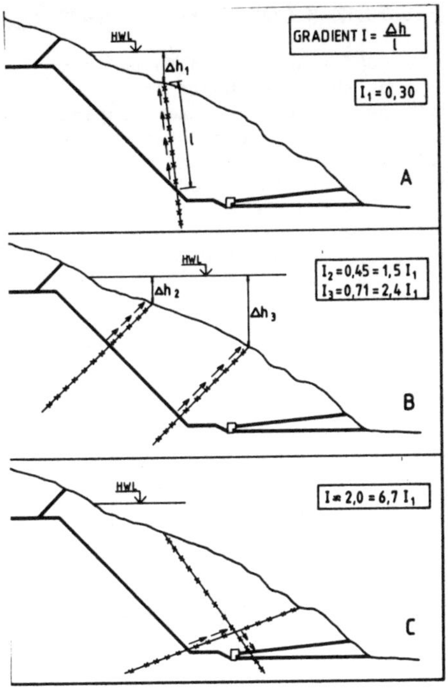

Fig. 6A, B and C. The influence of orientation and position on the leakage potensial of permeable zones.

A most unfavourable situation arises when two zones happen to intersect as shown in Fig. 6C, giving short flow distance down to access- and tailrace tunnel. The gradient can then be 6-7 times larger than a single zone cutting the shaft in example 6A. These examples stress the importance of well planned investigations and evaluations of unlined pressure shafts and tunnels before filling and the need for a careful control during the first filling of the system.

4. SEALING WORKS IN UNLINED PRESSURE TUNNELS AND SHAFTS

Potential leakage zones in tunnels and shafts must always be sealed. Sealing is usually done by means of grouting, using a pressure slightly higher than the static head in the tunnel. Shotcrete lining or cast in place concrete lining is as a rule used only for stability purposes. A special sealing method by using rock bolts, shotcrete and reinforcement has been used together with grouting of open, permeable zones.

Figure 7 shows theoretical flow lines and equipotentials for flow from a tunnel situated below a horizontal ground surface. It is evident that a rapid pressure drop takes place over a short distance out from the tunnel wall. This points to the necessity of concentrating the sealing effort to where it is most effective: close to the tunnel surface.

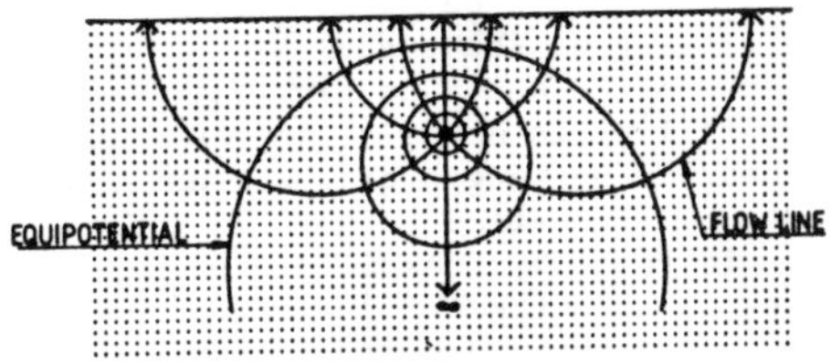

Fig. 7. Theoretical flow from an opening below a horizontal surface.

A simplified calculation of waterflow through an idealized channel, Fig. 8 illustrates the effect of sealing, here assumed achieved by grouting.

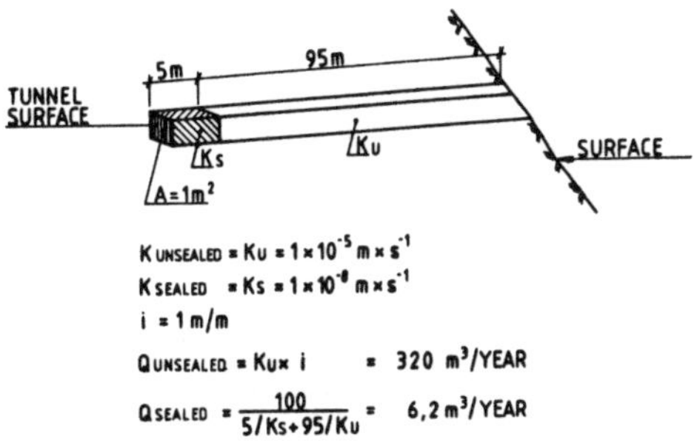

Fig. 8. Simplified channel flow from tunnel to surface.

5. MEASUREMENTS DURING CONTROLLED FILLING OF THE PRESSURE SYSTEM

A large and rapid change in the pore pressure and water flow is introduced within a short time during filling of an unlined tunnel/shaft. The big pressure gradients being set up may result in possibilities for transport of the material in faults and fractures. If local stress anomalies occure deformation also may take place. A well planned control and a low filling-rate will reduce such abrupt change in the stress situation around the shaft/-tunnel.

With the term controlled filling is meant that the water leakages out into the rock masses are being measured during filling of the tunnel system by making pauses as shown on Fig. 9. The rate of filling is normaly limited to 10 m per hour. The length of the measuring periods usually varies between 12 and 24 hours. In this way, possible big leakages may be detected and the tunnel system can be emptied before extensive damages are created.

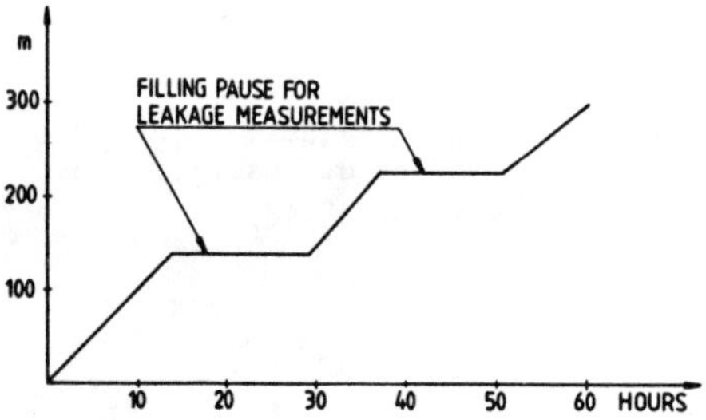

Fig. 9. Filling and measuring programme.

Measurement of the leakage out of a tunnel system or a shaft is indirectly done by registrating the change in water level on a manometer. When the area of the water surface and the leakage through bulkheads and gates are known, the net water leakage going into the rock can be calculated.

6. RESULTS FROM LEAKAGE MEASUREMENTS

The measured leakage from a tunnel is large during the first hours of a measuring period, but decreases rapidly and usually reach a steady state after 12 to 24 hours, depending on the joint volume that has to be filled. Typical leakage curves are shown on Fig. 10. The curves represent 4 different high pressure hydro schemes during various stages of the filling.

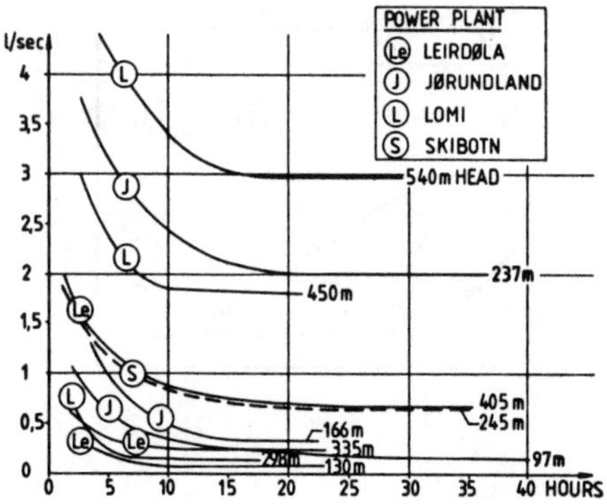

Figure 10. Flow rate curves for 4 different tunnels and shafts at different heads.

The leakages are all small as evident from Fig. 10 and also table 1. This is due mainly to the low mass permeability of the rock itself, but also to the careful sealing of pervious zones.

Predictions on mass permeability of the rock and leakage from the tunnel systems were done for the last two hydro power plants listed in table 1. The predictions were based on measurement of water leaking into the tunnel system before filling, and on assumed or measured pore pressures. As evident in table 1 the predictions were fairly accurate.

TABLE 1. Summary of layout, geology and leakage control results from six hydro power plants.

POWER PLANT		MAX HEAD ON UNLINED ROCK IN BAR	LAYOUT	GEOLOGY	PREDICTED LEAKAGE IN $l \cdot s^{-1}$	MEASURED LEAKAGE IN $l \cdot s^{-1}$	CALCULATED MASS PERMEABILITY IN $m \cdot s^{-1}$
JØRUNDLAND	1971	28	2,0 km pressure tunnel	precambrian granite and gneiss	-	1	$1 \cdot 10^{-9}$
SKJOMEN	1973	36	2,6 km pressure tunnel	precambrian granite	-	1-2	$3 \cdot 10^{-9}$
BORGUND	1974	25	2,9 km pressure tunnel	precambrian gneiss	-	3-4	$1 \cdot 10^{-8}$
LEIRDØLA	1978	45	0,6 km pressure shaft	precambrian gneiss	-	0,9	$1 \cdot 10^{-8}$
LOMI	1979	59	0,7 km pressure shaft	ordovician mica schist and phyllite	1-5	3-6	$5 \cdot 10^{-8}$
SKIBOTN	1980	44	4,0 km pressure shaft	ordovician mica schist	2-10	10-18	$3 \cdot 10^{-8}$

The mass permeabilities given in the table 1 are based on measured water leakage from the tunnel and on measured or assumed pore-pressures in the rock. The calculations are based on equation 1, Ref. (1) which give the volumetric leakage rate from an underground opening of length L.

$$Q = \frac{2\pi \cdot k_m \cdot L \cdot g \cdot P_r}{\mu \cdot \ln(2D/r)}$$

Where
- Q = volumetric flowrate
- k_m = equivalent mass permeability
- g = acceleration due to gravity
- P_r = excess pressure in opening of radius r
- μ = viscosity of liquid
- D = depth of center of opening below surface

7. CONCLUSIONS

The solution with unlined pressure shafts and tunnels is both cost- and time saving. Unexpected adverse geological conditions have, however, in the past been the cause of extensive repairs and loss in production in several hydro power schemes. This proves the necessity of thorough planning and control during all phases of construction. The main points in this process are listed below.

- Collecting of existing geological information and supplementary field mapping.
- Core drilling, permeability testing and observations of groundwater level.
- Assessment of stability for the pressure shaft or -tunnel with respect to geology and topography.
- Mapping of geology, potential leakage zones and registration of water leaking into the shaft or tunnel during construction.
- Testing and control of permeability and pore pressure in the most critical leakage zones.
- Assessment of necessary sealing works and estimate of water losses from the tunnel system in operation.
- Controlled stepwise filling of the tunnel system and calculation of the real water losses.

In finishing we would like to point out that the rentability of investments in sealing works is good. With todays energy prices it is astounding what a leakage as small as 1 ls^{-1} can amount to in lost production over the years in a high pressure hydro power plant.

LITERATURE

1. BARTON, N. 1972: Estimation of leakage rate and transport time for fluid flow from underground openings in jointed rock. Report 54203, Norwegian Geotechnical Institute, Oslo.

2. NGI, 1972: Oversikt over norske uforede tunneler og sjakter med vanntrykk over 100 m samt enkelte andre med lavere trykk. (In Norwegian). Report 54402, Norwegian Geotechnical Institute, Oslo.

3. NGI, 1974: Uforede tunneler. Spesielle problem ved store tverrsnitt. (In Norwegian). Report 54202-2, Norwegian Geotechnical Institute.

4. BJØRLYKKE, S, SELMER-OLSEN, R, 1972: Nødvendig overdekning i dalsider ved fjellrom med høyt innvendig vann- eller lufttrykk. (In Norwegian). Report no. 6, Department of Geology, Technical University of Norway.

5. BUEN, B. 1973: Ingeniørgeologiske forundersøkelser ved Skjomen Kraftverk. (In Norwegian). Fjellsprengningsteknikk - Bergmekanikk, Tapir, Trondheim.

6. SELMER-OLSEN, R. 1969: Experience with unlined pressure shafts in Norway. International symposium on large underground openings, Oslo 1969.

LINING DESIGN FOR PRESSURE SHAFTS AND TUNNELS OF CIRCULAR CROSS SECTION

Berechnung der Auskleidung von Druckschächten und Druckstollen mit kreisförmigem Querschnitt

Dimensionnement des puits et des galeries sous pression de section circulaire

N.S.BULYCHEV
Tula Polytechnic Institute, USSR
J.E.PUERTO & I.N.BULYCHEV
Leningrad Mining Institute, USSR

SUMMARY:
The method of designing the multilayer monolithic and prefabricated-monolithic linings of pressure tunnels and shafts of circular cross section, taking into account the work of linings combined with the rock mass, is considered in the paper. The linings of tunnels and shafts together with the surrounding mass are considered generally as multilayer deformable system. This method permits design of the lining for the internal head, external hydrostatic pressure, rock pressure, including tectonic original field of stresses and seismic actions induced by earthquakes. The method of designing takes into account the cracking in the concrete of linings and the surrounding rock mass under the effect of internal head. The procedure of optimum designing the lining subject to internal head is developed.

ZUSAMMENFASSUNG:
Im Vortrag wird eine Berechnungsmethode für mehrlagige monolitische und vorgefertigt-monolitische Auskleidungen von Druckstollen und Druckschächten mit rundem Querschnitt behandelt, bei der die Zusammenarbeit der Auskleidungen mit dem Gebirgsmassiv berücksichtigt wird. Der Stollen- und Schachtausbau wird zusammen mit dem umgebenden Massiv im allgemeinen als ein mehrlagiges verformbares System betrachtet. Die Methode ermöglicht es, eine Auskleidungsberechnung für Innendruck, hydrostatischen Aussendruck, Gebirgsdruck, darunter bei tektonischem Anfangsspannungsfeld, die durch das Erdbeben hervorgerufen werden, durchzuführen. Die Berechnungsmethode berücksichtigt die Bildung von Rissen im Beton und im umgebenden Massiv. Es ist eine Methodik für die Projektierung der Auskleidung für den Innendruck entwickelt worden.

RÉSUMÉ:
Dans le rapport est exposée la méthode de calcul des revêtements à plusieurs couches, monolithes et préfabriqués-monolithes, pour les galeries et puits en charge de section transversale circulaire , qui tient compte du travail commun des revêtements avec le massif rocheux. Le revêtement des galeries et puits d'ensemble avec le massif ambiant est considéré, dans le cas général, comme un système déformable à plusieurs couches. La méthode permet le calcul d'un revêtement pour la poussée intérieure, la pression hydrostatique extérieure, la pression de terrain, compte tenu aussi du champ de contrainte tectonique initial, et pour les effets dus aux séismes. La méthode de calcul prend en considération la formation de fissures dans le béton et le massif ambiant sous la poussée intérieure. Une méthode de l'étude de projet optimale de revêtement travaillant sous la poussée intérieure a été élaborée.

1 INTRODUCTION

High-pressure tunnels and shafts, as well as underground storage vaults for gas and oil, are usually built with linings of complex multiple-layer design, consisting of layers of steel, reinforced and prestressed concrete, tubing and other items. The complications are due to the high requirements made to such structures and the special features of their performance. Owing to their high cost it is of great importance to design such linings as precisely as possible, thereby reducing expenses in their construction.

The proposed method of designing the linings of pressure tunnels and shafts is based on the general method of designing multiple-layer sectional rings (Bulychev and Olovyanny, 1973) and deals with the lining and the surrounding rock massif as a single deformable system. Such an approach, typical for a new branch of the engineering sciences, the mechanics of underground structures (Bulychev, 1982), in which rapid advances are being made in the USSR at the present time, enables the bearing capacity of the massif to be taken into account to the maximum extent.

The design method is applicable for an arbitrary number of layers of a multiple-layer lining, including periodically nonhomogeneous layers containing annular stiffening ribs (flexible or rigid reinforcing members, tubing, etc.). The method imposes no restrictions on the thickness and mechanical characteristics of the layer materials. Design calculations can be carried out for linings subject to internal pressure, external hydrostatic pressure, rock pressure (including an anomalous tectonic initial stress field) and seismic action due to earthquakes (Bulychev, 1979). The method takes into account the formation of cracks in the concrete and surrounding massif due to the internal pressure. A procedure has been worked out for optimal lining design for structures subject to internal pressure.

Computer programs have been developed for lining design.

2 THE THEORETICAL BASIS OF THE METHOD

The lining design method is based on the general method used for the design calculations of multiple-layer elastic rings, subject to external and internal loads, specified by Fourier series (Fig. 1) The essence of the method consists in determining the stresses on the contact surfaces between the layers by means of recursion formulas and load transmission factors (Bulychev and Olovyanny, 1973). This approach excludes the need to formulate and solve systems of equations corresponding to the conditions of the contact surfaces between the layers, as required in the existing methods of multiple-layer lining design.

The following relations are used in designing pressure tunnels and shafts.

The stresses on an arbitrary contact surface between the layers due to the external load are

$$p_{(i)} = p_{0(i)} + p_{2(i)} \cos 2\theta ; \qquad q_{(i)} = q_{2(i)} \sin 2\theta , \tag{1}$$

where $p_{(i)}$ are the radial stresses on the contact surface, and $q_{(i)}$ are the tangential stresses on this surface.

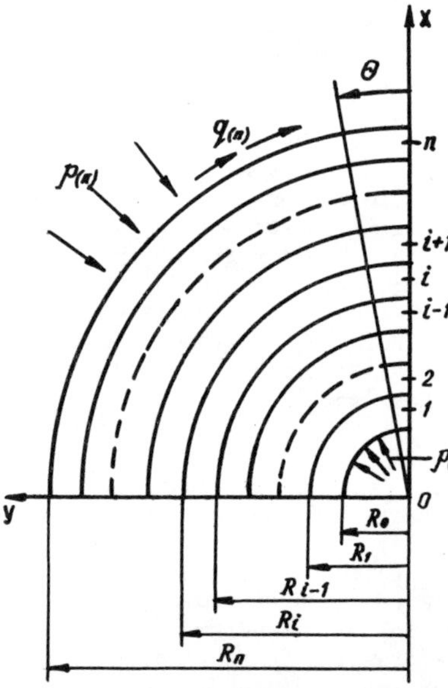

Fig. 1. Basic design layout for a multiple-layer elastic ring.

The stresses on two adjacent contact surfaces are expressed by the relations:

$$p_{0(i-1)} = p_{0(i)} K_{0(i)} ; \tag{2}$$

$$p_{2(i-1)} = p_{2(i)} K_{11(i)} + q_{2(i)} K_{12(i)} ; \quad (3)$$

$$q_{2(i-1)} = p_{2(i)} K_{21(i)} + q_{2(i)} K_{22(i)} ,$$

where $K_{0(i)}$, $K_{11(i)}$, ..., $K_{22(i)}$

are factors of external load transmission (term coined by Prof. N.S. Bulychev) through the i-th layer. These factors are determined by means of recursion formulas (Bulychev, 1979; Bulychev, 1982).

The expression for the factor of transmission of uniform loads is of the form

$$K_{0(i)} = \frac{d_{1(i)}}{d_{2(i)} + \chi_0 \left(d'_{1(i-1)} - K_{0(i-1)} d'_{2(i-1)} \right)} , \quad (4)$$

where

$$d_{1(i)} = c_i^2 (\varkappa_i + 1) ;$$

$$d_{2(i)} = 2 c_i^2 + \varkappa_i - 1 ;$$

$$d'_{1(i)} = c_i^2 (\varkappa_i - 1) + 2 ;$$

$$d'_{2(i)} = \varkappa_i + 1 ;$$

$$\chi_0 = \frac{G_i}{G_{i-1}} \cdot \frac{c_i^2 - 1}{c_{i-1}^2 - 1} ;$$

$$c_i = \frac{R_i}{R_{i-1}} ; \quad \varkappa_i = 3 - 4 \mu_i ;$$

and G_i and μ_i are the shear modulus and Poisson's ratio of the material of the i-th layer.

The factors of external load transmission are determined by equation (4) consecutively for all the layers, beginning with layer 2. Here $K_{0(1)} = 0$. Then, employing equations (2) and (3), the contact stresses are determined for all the layers, beginning with the outer one.

Calculations concerning the action of internal loads are carried out by means of the following relations that are similar to those given above:

(5)

$$p_{0(i)} = p_{0(i-1)} K^*_{0(i)} ;$$

$$K^*_{0(i)} = \frac{d'_{2(i)}}{d'_{1(i)} + \chi'_0 \left(d_{2(i+1)} - K^*_{0(i+1)} d_{1(i+1)} \right)} , \quad (6)$$

where

$$\chi'_0 = \frac{G_i}{G_{i+1}} \cdot \frac{c_i^2 - 1}{c_{i+1}^2 - 1} .$$

The factors of internal load transmission are determined consecutively for all layers, beginning with the $(n-1)$ -th layer. Here $K^*_{0(n)} = 0$.

Upon simultaneous action of both external and internal loads the stresses on the contact surfaces between the layers are added together.

In a design with nonhomogeneous layers having periodical annular insertions of a more rigid material (ribs, Fig. 2a), such layers are dealt with in determining the load transmission factors as being quasi-homogeneous with an equivalent shear modulus:

$$\bar{G} = \frac{G_a \cdot a + G_b \cdot b}{a + b} , \quad (7)$$

where G_a and G_b are the shear moduli of the rib and interrib materials, respectively, and a and b are the width of the ribs and the distance between them (Fig. 2b).

The stresses on the external surface of the nonhomogeneous layer at the contact surface between the ribs and interrib material (Fig. 2b), under uniform external load, are determined by the following relations

$$p_a = \bar{p}_0 \left(1 + \rho \frac{h}{a} \right) ;$$

$$p_b = \bar{p}_0 \left(1 - \rho \frac{h}{b} \right) . \quad (8)$$

where $\bar{p}$ is the average stresses on the contact surface;

$$p = A\left(1 - \bar{K}_0 \frac{d_2'}{d_1'}\right); \tag{9}$$

$$h = a + b;$$

$$A = \frac{a}{h} \cdot \frac{1 - \chi_b}{\chi_b + \frac{a}{b}};$$

$$\chi_b = \frac{G_b}{G_a};$$

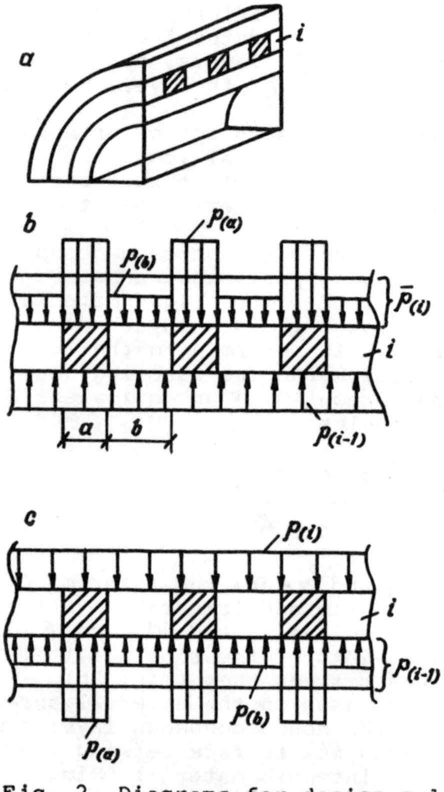

Fig. 2. Diagrams for design calculations for a nonhomogeneous layer: *a* – general view of a lining with a nonhomogeneous layer; *b* – design layout for linings subject to external load; *c* – design layout for linings subject to internal load.

where $\bar{K}_0$ is the average factor of load transmission through a nonhomogeneous layer dealt with as a quasi-homogeneous one.

The stresses on the inner surface of a nonhomogeneous layer, under uniform internal load (Fig. 2c) are determined by the expressions

$$p_a = \bar{p}_0\left(1 + p'\frac{h}{a}\right);$$
$$p_b = \bar{p}_0\left(1 - p'\frac{h}{b}\right), \tag{10}$$

where

$$p' = A\left(1 - \bar{K}_0^* \frac{d_1}{d_2}\right); \tag{11}$$

Upon known stresses on the outer and inner contours of the layer, as described by expressions (1), the normal tangential stresses are found by the equations:

At $r = R_{i-1}$:

$$\sigma_\theta = p_{0(i)} m_1 - p_{0(i-1)} m_2 - \left(p_{2(i)} n_1 - q_{2(i)} n_2 - p_{2(i-1)} n_3 + q_{2(i-1)} n_4\right) \times \cos 2\theta; \tag{12}$$

and at $r = R_i$:

$$\sigma_\theta = p_{0(i)} m_1' - p_{0(i-1)} m_2' + \left(p_{2(i)} n_1' - q_{2(i)} n_2' - p_{2(i-1)} n_3' + q_{2(i-1)} n_4'\right) \cos 2\theta, \tag{13}$$

where $m_1, \ldots, n_4'$ are influence factors given in the pertinent works (Bulychev, 1979; Bulychev, 1982):

$$m_1 = \frac{2c^2}{c^2 - 1}; \; m_2 = m_1 - 1; \; m_1' = m_2; \; m_2' = m_1 - 2.$$

3 DESIGN OF MULTIPLE-LAYER LININGS SUBJECT TO INTERNAL PRESSURE

Given in Fig. 3 is the basic design layout of an underground structure in which the outer, n-th layer models the rock massif. This layout is applicable to vertical workings (shafts) and to horizontal workings

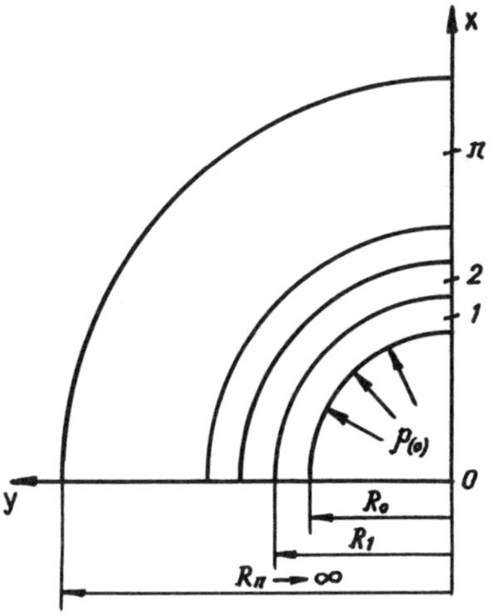

Fig. 3. Basic design layout for a pressure tunnel or shaft.

provided their depth is at least three times their transverse dimensions.

Lining design calculations are to be carried out in the following order. First the load transmission factors are found by equations (6). The factor of load transmission through the $(n-1)$ -th layer is found by the equation

$$K^*_{o(n-1)} = \frac{d'_{2(n-1)}}{d'_{1(n-1)} + 2\,\frac{G_{n-1}}{G_n}\left(c^2_{n-1} - 1\right)} \cdot \quad (14)$$

Next, equation (5) is used to find the stresses on the contact surfaces between the layers, and equations (12) and (13) to find the normal tangential stresses.

If in a certain concrete layer the tensile stresses exceed the strength of its material and cracks are formed, the load transmission factors are determined with crack formation taken into account. Let us consider a two-layer lining, consisting of an inner layer of steel and an outer layer of concrete. Assume that radial tension cracks are formed in the concrete layer and in a certain zone of the rock massif surrounding the working as a result internal pressure. In this case, four layers can be distinguished in the design layout: 1 -- steel, 2 -- concrete, 3 -- crack-formation region in the massif, and 4 -- the massif proper. The load transmission factors are determined by the equation:

$$K^*_{o(1)} = \frac{\varkappa_1 + 1}{4G_1(c_1^2 - 1)}\left[\frac{c_1^2(\varkappa_1 - 1) + 2}{4G_1(c_1^2 - 1)} + \frac{1-\mu_2^2}{E_2}\ln c_2 + \frac{1-\mu_3^2}{E_3}\ln c_3 + \frac{1}{2G_4}\right]^{-1}, \quad (15)$$

where E_i is the modulus of deformation of the material of the i-th layer.

4 DESIGN OF LININGS SUBJECT TO EXTERNAL HYDROSTATIC PRESSURE

The pressure is assumed to be uniform if the static pressure head is at least three times the transverse dimensions of the working. At the surface of contact with the watertight layer, there is a jump in radial stresses equal to the hydrostatic pressure p_w .

In the special case when the watertight layer is the outer layer of a multiple-layer lining, the basic design layout shown in Fig. 4 is applied. The load on the contact surface between the lining and the massif is replaced by an equivalent load p_{eq} applied at infinity:

$$p_{eq} = p_w \frac{2}{\varkappa_n + 1} \cdot \quad (16)$$

The factor of load transmission through the outer rock layer is determined by the equation

$$K_{o(n)} = \frac{\varkappa_n + 1}{2\frac{G_n}{G_{n-1}} \cdot \frac{1}{c_{n-1}^2 - 1}\left(d'_{1(n-1)} - K_{o(n-1)} d'_{2(n-1)}\right)}. \qquad (17)$$

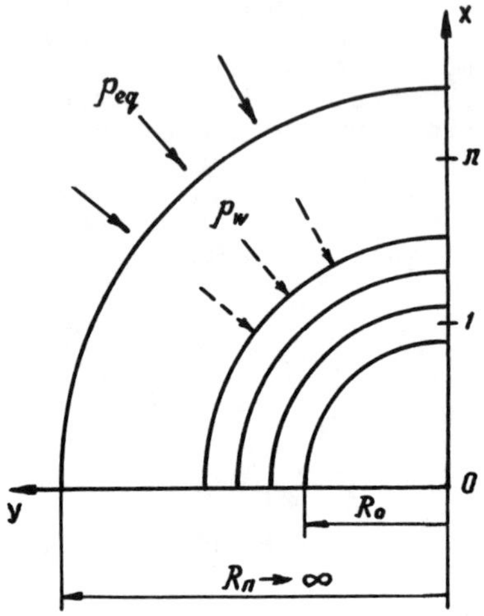

Fig. 4. Basic design layout for linings subject to external hydrostatic pressure.

The design calculations are carried out in the following order. First, all the load transmission factors are determined by equations (4) and (17), then the stresses on the contact surfaces by equation (2) and, finally, the normal tangential stresses in each layer by equations (12) and (13).

5 DESIGN OF LININGS SUBJECT TO ROCK PRESSURE

These design calculations take into account the additional ("removable") stresses due to the construction of the working.

Removable stresses $\sigma^{(1)}$ are related to the initial stresses in the undisturbed massif by the equation

$$\alpha^* \sigma^{(1)} = -\alpha^* \sigma^{(0)}, \qquad (18)$$

where α^* is a factor taking into consideration the amount that the installed lining lags behind the uncovered rock in the working, i.e. the distance from the end of the already installed lining to the end of the already driven working. This factor can be determined on the basis of field measurements (Fotiyeva and Bulychev, 1979).

The total stresses are

$$\sigma = \sigma^{(0)} + \sigma^{(1)}. \qquad (19)$$

The design calculations procedure can be applied to take into account gravitational or tectonic fields of initial stresses in the rock massif. In the particular case of a gravitational field, the stresses are determined by the relations

$$\sigma_x^{(0)} = \gamma H;$$
$$\sigma_y^{(0)} = \lambda \gamma H, \qquad (20)$$

where γ is the weight of the rock per unit volume, H is the depth and λ is the coefficient of lateral pressure.

Depending upon the construction techniques used for the working, the additional stresses are applied in the design layout either to the surface of contact between the lining and the massif or to the inner surface of the lining.

In the former case, a basic design layout similar to that shown in Fig. 4 is made use of. Stresses at the line of contact of the lining with the massif are replaced by equivalent stresses applied at infinity:

$$p_{eq} = p_{o(eq)} + p_{2(eq)} \cos 2\theta, \qquad (21)$$

where

$$p_{o(eq)} = \alpha^* \gamma H \frac{1+\lambda}{\varkappa_n + 1};$$

$$p_{2(eq)} \cong \alpha^* \gamma H \frac{1-\lambda}{12\varkappa_n}(3\varkappa_n + 1).$$

Next the load transmission factors are found and the stresses on the contact surfaces between the layers are determined by equations (2) and (3).

In the latter case (additional stresses applied to the inner surface of the lining), a basic design layout similar to that shown in Fig. 3 is used. The additional (tensile) stresses applied to the inner contour of the lining are described by expressions (1), where

$$p_0^{(1)} = -\alpha^* \gamma H \frac{1+\lambda}{2};$$
$$p_2^{(1)} = -\alpha^* \gamma H \frac{1-\lambda}{2}; \qquad (22)$$
$$q_2^{(1)} = \alpha^* \gamma H \frac{1-\lambda}{2}.$$

Next the load transmission factors $K^*_{0(i)}$, $K^*_{11(i)}$, ..., $K^*_{22(i)}$ are found, and then the additional stresses on the contact surfaces between the layers by equation (5) and the equations

$$\begin{Bmatrix} p_{2(i)}^{(1)} \\ q_{2(i)}^{(1)} \end{Bmatrix} = \begin{bmatrix} K^*_{11(i)} & K^*_{12(i)} \\ K^*_{21(i)} & K^*_{22(i)} \end{bmatrix} \times \qquad (23)$$
$$\times \begin{Bmatrix} p_{2(i-1)} \\ q_{2(i-1)} \end{Bmatrix}.$$

The total stresses on the contact surfaces between the layers are the sum of the initial and removable stresses. In particular, for a uniform component of the loads, the stresses on an arbitrary contact surface between the layers are

$$p_{0(k)} = \alpha^* \gamma H \frac{1+\lambda}{2}\left(1 - \prod_{i=1}^{k} K^*_{0(i)}\right). \qquad (24)$$

Further design calculations of the linings are clear from the aforesaid.

6 DESIGN OF LININGS SUBJECT TO THE SEISMIC ACTION OF EARTHQUAKES

Design calculations are carried out according to the principles established by Fotiyeva and Bulychev (1981). The problem of designing linings to withstand two kinds of elastic waves -- longitudinal and transverse -- is dealt with in the quasi-static formulation. This is due to the length of the waves, which substantially exceeds the transverse dimensions of the underground structures.

The basic design layout is an elastic plane loaded at infinity. The magnitudes of the stresses depend upon the parameters of the elastic waves.

In application to the design of multiple-layer linings, the basic design layout is similar to that shown in Fig. 4. The stresses at infinity are described by expression (21), where

$$p_{0(eq)} = \frac{P}{2(1-\mu_n)}; \qquad (25)$$

$$p_{2(eq)} = \frac{P}{2(1-\mu_n)}\sqrt{(3-4\mu_n)(1-2\mu_n)}; \qquad (26)$$

$$P = \frac{1}{2\pi} k_s \gamma C_1 T_0 .$$

Here k_s is the seismicity coefficient, depending upon the anticipated earthquake intensity, C_1 is the velocity of propagation of longitudinal seismic waves, and T_0 is the period of natural oscillations of the rock particles.

If the lining is subject simultaneously to various loads and action, the stresses in the elements of the lining are added together.

REFERENCES

Bulychev, N.S. 1979, Design of multiple-layer circular linings for hydraulic structures subject to static and seismic action, in Advances in the design and construction of underground hydraulic engineering structures, Collection of scientific works of the Hydroproject Institute, Moscow, p. 24-31 (in Russian).

Bulychev, N.S. & A.G. Olovyanny 1973, Concerning the design of sectional rings, J. Structural Mechanics and Design, No. 5, p. 28-30 (in Russian).

Bulychev, N.S. 1982, Mechanics of underground structures, Moscow, Nedra Publishers (in Russian).

Fotiyeva, N.N. & N.S. Bulychev 1979, Using data of full-scale measurement in lining design for underground structures, Proc. IV Congress of Intern. Soc. for Rock Mech., Montreux, Switzerland, vol. 1, p. 387-392.

Fotiyeva, N.N. & N.S. Bulychev 1981, Principles of tunnel design for seismic regions, Proc. 10th Intern. Conf. on Soil Mech. and Found. Eng., Stockholm, Sweden, vol. 1, p. 291-292.

ÉTUDE DU COMPORTEMENT MÉCANIQUE DU ROCHER, PAR ESSAI HYDRAULIQUE HAUTE PRESSION, POUR DES PUITS DE CHUTE VERTICAUX

Use of high-pressure hydraulic testing for the investigation of the mechanical behaviour of rock in vertical gravity wells

Durchführung von Wasserabpressversuchen zur Untersuchung des mechanischen Verhaltens vom Gebirge in Bezug auf vertikale Schächte

THIERRY DOUCERAIN
Electricité de France, Paris

SUMMARY

In the context of investigations undertaken for the design of an energy transfer pumping station, a high-pressure hydraulic test was used on a shaft with a depth of 300 m which was made in the gravity-well zone.

This test was intended to confirm that the geomechanical characteristics of the bedrock foundation would permit the construction of hydraulic connective structures without the use of steel linings.

The test first of all included the identification (by means of a conventional Lugeon-type test) of very permeable zones and their treatment with cement-slurry injections.

The application of pressures up to approximately 50 bars in the last 150 m of the shaft showed the following :

- the efficiency of the cement injections,
- slight elastic opening of fissuration,
- retention of the overall tightness of the bedrock under high pressure.

This type of test therefore makes it possible to avoid encasing the structures under pressure. A concrete lining complemented by injection should suffice to insure the tightness of the structure.

ZUSAMMENFASSUNG

Im Rahmen der Erkenntnisse zur untersuchung einer Energie-übertragungsanlage durch Pumpen ist eine Wasserdruckprobe in einem 300 m tiefem Bohrloch durchgefürhrt worden, das im Gebiet der Fallaschächte eingebaut ist.

Diese Probe sollte zur Uberprüfung dienen, dass die geomechanischen Eigenschaften des Gründungskörper den Einsatz der hydraulischen verbindungsbauwerke unter Druck ohne Dichtungsstahlpanzerung ermöglichen.

Die Probe berstand in erster Dinie aus der Markierung (durch traditionnelle Prüfung nach Lugeon) und der Verfestigung der stark wasserdurchlässignen Zonen mit Zementschlämmeinjektion.

Der Einsatz von Drucken bis ungefähr 50 bar auf den letzten 150 m des Bohrlochs zeigte :

- die Wirksamkeit der Verfestigung durch Zementschlämmeinjecktion
- eine leichte elastische Offnung des.Rissbildung.
- das Beibehalten bei Hochdruck der Gesamtdichtigkeit des Gründungskörpers.

Diese Versuchsart erlaubte somit die Panzerung der Druckbauwerke nicht vor auszusehen. Eine Betonauskleidung ergänzt durch Injektionsbehandlung sollte eine ausreichende Dichtigkeit der Bauwerke gewährleisten.

RESUME

Dans le cadre des reconnaissances entreprises pour l'étude d'une station de transfert d'énergie par pompage, il a été mis en oeuvre un essai hydraulique haute pression, dans un forage profond de 300 m, implanté dans la zone des puits de chute. Cet essai était destiné à vérifier que les caractéristiques géomécaniques du massif de fondation permettent la mise en place des ouvrage de liaison hydraulique en charge, sans blindage métallique d'étanchéité. L'essai a d'abord comporté le repérage (par essai classique de

type Lugeon) et le traitement par injection au coulis de ciment des zones à forte perméabilité. La mise en oeuvre, sur les cent cinquante derniers mètres du forage, de pressions atteignant environ 50 bars, à montré :
- l'efficacité du traitement par injection au ciment,
- une légère ouverture élastique de la fissuration,
- la conservation, à haute pression, de l'étanchéité globale du massif.

Ce type d'essai a donc permis de ne pas prévoir le blindage des ouvrages en charge. Un revêtement en béton complété par un traitement par injection devrait suffire à assurer l'étanchéité des ouvrages.

1. INTRODUCTION

Dans le cadre de son programme de grand Equipement, Electricité de France envisage d'installer une Station de Transfert d'Energie par Pompage à REDENAT. La S.T.E.P. sera installée en bordure occidentale du Massif Central sur la Dordogne (Corrèze).

Le schéma hydraulique de cet aménagement est précisé sur la figure 1.

La réalisation des ouvrages de liaisons hydrauliques en pression et en souterrain doit obéir à un double objectif :

- d'une part une sécurité totale,
- d'autre part une réalisation au moindre coût.

Ces impératifs conduisent à profiter des qualités géomécaniques du massif rocheux (résistances mécaniques et étanchéité hydraulique) dans lequel les ouvrages souterrains sont creusés de façon à éviter de mettre en place un blindage métallique d'étanchéité.

Pour s'assurer que le massif rocheux dans la zone des puits de chute, présente les caractéristiques géomécaniques nécessaires, il a été mis en oeuvre un essai hydraulique à haute-pression dans un forage de reconnaissance implanté dans la zone des puits.

MISE EN OEUVRE DE L'ESSAI

Le forage de reconnaissance se développe verticalement sur une hauteur de 300 mètres.

2.1. Contraintes inhérentes à l'essai

La mise en oeuvre des essais H.P. a été en premier lieu, limitée à la partie du massif rocheux qui subira les sollicitations hydrauliques maximales, soit sur les cent cinquante derniers mètres du forage. De plus, elle comportait un certain nombre de contraintes techniques conduisant à :

- d'une part, limiter le nombre d'essais H.P. La partie inférieure du sondage a été divisée en 3 tranches de 50 m de hauteur, situées respectivement aux cotes suivantes par rapport au terrain naturel :
  . tranche 1 : de - 150 à - 200 m,
  . tranche 2 : de - 200 à - 250 m,
  . tranche 3 : de - 250 à - 300 m.
- d'autre part, veiller à ce que les débits absorbés au cours des essais H.P. ne dépassent pas les possibilité de la pompe (débit maximal = 30 m3/h). Cet impératif a conduit à réaliser à l'avancement des essais de type Lugeon sur des tranches de 10 m de hauteur permettant de localiser et traiter par injections

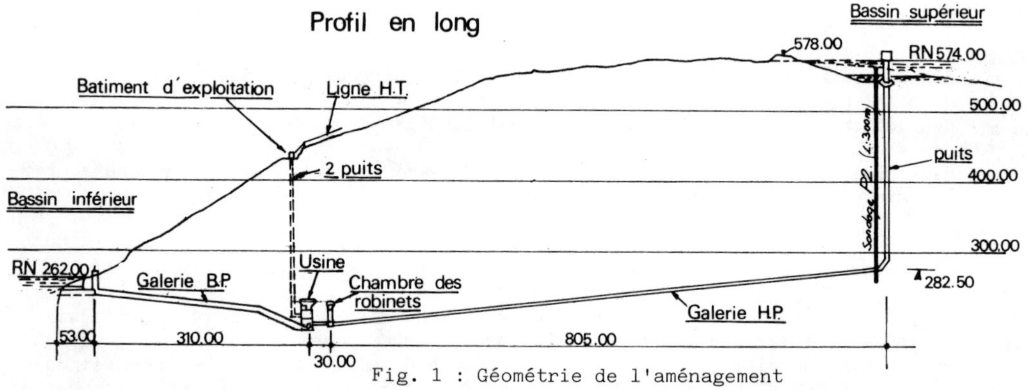

Fig. 1 : Géométrie de l'aménagement

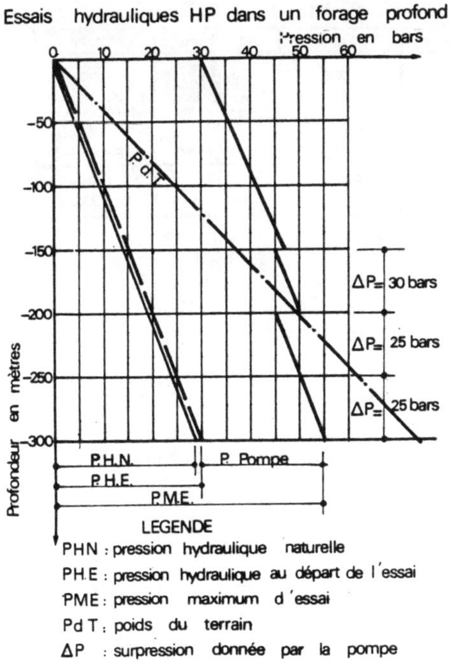

Fig. 2 : Diagramme de pression

avant de reprendre le forage, les zones à fortes absorptions.

2.2. Schéma de mise en pression

La pression maximale développée en tête du forage à été fixé à

- 30 bars pour la tranche n° 1,
- 25 bars pour les tranches n° 2 et n° 3.

Compte-tenu de la hauteur de la nappe dans le massif, la pression totale s'exerçant sur chaque tranche d'essai a été, par souci de sécurité, très supérieure aux sollicitations hydrauliques que devra encaisser le massif. La pression totale pour chaque tranche est (figure 2) :

- tranche n° 1 : entre 45 et 50 bars (pression moyenne 47,5 bars),
- tranche n° 2 : entre 45 et 50 bars (pression moyenne 47,5 bars),
- tranche n° 3 : entre 50 et 55 bars (pression moyenne 52,5 bars).

Sur chaque tranche, l'essai H.P. proprement dit met en oeuvre 2 types de sollicitations (voir sur fig. 3, l'exemple de la tranche 2) ;

- d'une part, 3 cycles de chargement - déchargement,
- d'autre part, après le dernier cycle, un palier de longue durée où la pression maximale est maintenue pendant 16 heures.

2.3. Réalisation du forage d'essai

Le forage a été effectué à la couronne diamantée et au double carottier sur toute la hauteur, en utilisant les diamètres suivants :

- du T.N. à la cote - 10 m : Ø = 170 mm,
- de - 10 à la cote -150 m : Ø = 146 mm,
- de -150 à la cote -200 m : Ø = 131 mm,
- de -200 à la cote -250 m : Ø = 116 mm,
- de -250 à la cote -300 m : Ø = 101 mm.

Pour éviter au cours de l'essai H.P. tout risque de fuite par contournement de l'obturateur, le forage a été tubé, et le tube scellé au terrain, au-dessus

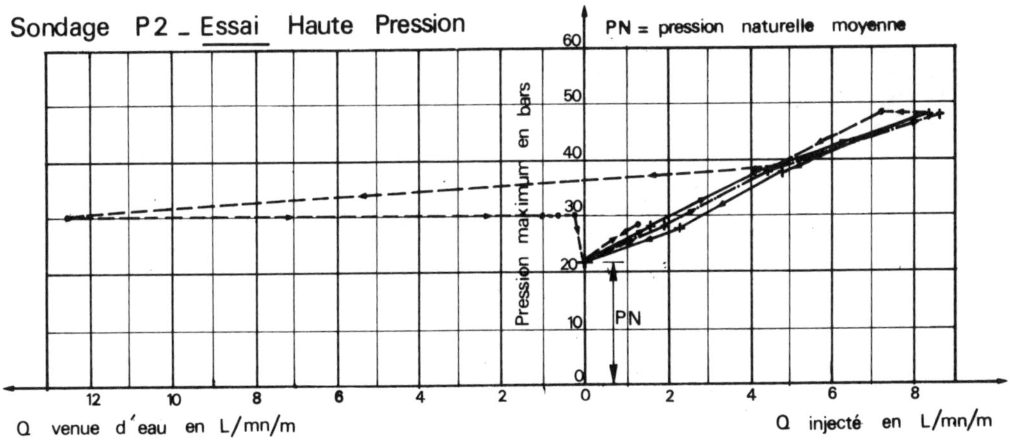

Fig. 3 : Schéma de mise en pression sur la tranche 2

de la tranche testée ; la mise en pression s'effectue directement à partir de la tête du forage.

3. RESULTAT

3.1. Géologie

Le massif rocheux est constitué par du granite de Millevache. Ce granite est fissuré ; une altération particulière apparait irrégulièrement le long de certaines cassures, sous la forme d'un remplissage argileux.

3.2. Essais Lugeon

La figure 4 montre l'évolution en fonction de la profondeur de la perméabilité du matériau (donnée en unité Lugeon) Ce graphique appelle les remarques suivantes :

- entre - 15 m et - 50 m de profondeur la perméabilité décroit de 13 UL à 0,5 UL. Cette diminution traduit la fermeture des discontinuités avec la profondeur ;
- entre - 50 m et - 300 m la plupart des absorptions s'élèvent à 1 ou 2 Lugeon. Ces débits correspondent à des fissures jointives ou rebouchées par des minéraux de recristallisation ;

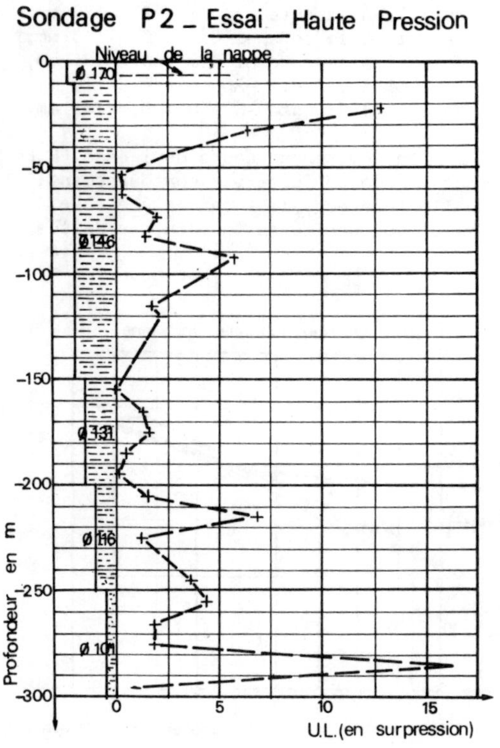

Fig. 4 : Evolution de la perméabilité

Tableau 1

Tranche	1er cycle	2ème cycle	3ème cycle
1	0,025 P = 20 bars	0,073 p = 30 bars	0,05 p = 30 bars
2	0,4 p = 5 bars	0,34 p = 25 bars	0,34 p = 25 bars
3	0,15 p = 10 bars	0,32 p = 25 bars	0,15 p = 25 bars

P : Surcharge due à la pompe

- en 3 points cependant, les absorptions sont plus élevées (supérieures à 5 UL)
  - . de - 90 à -100 m de profondeur (6 UL),
  - . de -210 à -220 m de profondeur (7,5 UL)
  - . de -280 à -290 m de profondeur (15 UL à 9 bars).

Ces débits révèlent l'existence d'une fissuration ouverte susceptible de compromettre l'essai H.P., comme le montre la tranche située entre - 280 et - 290 m de profondeur, où il a été impossible d'atteindre 10 bars. Le traitement de cette zone par injection d'un coulis à base de ciment a été réalisé.

Cette première phase de mesure montre que le matériau présente des caractéristiques de perméabilité le plus souvent faible.

Le but de l'essai haute-pression est alors de vérifier :

- d'une part, l'efficacité de l'injection réalisée sur la fissure ouverte rencontrée,
- d'autre part, qu'il ne se produit pas, à des pressions supérieures à 10 bars, une ouverture irréversible ou non des fissures les plus jointives.

3.3. Essai haute-pression

3.3.1. Cycles de mise en charge

Cette première phase a montré :

- qu'il ne se produit aucune ouverture irréversible ou non des fissures les plus jointives, ni de la fissure ouverte repéré sur la tranche 2 entre - 210 et - 220 m de profondeur, dont le traitement par injection n'avait pas été réalisé (voir fig. 3).
- sur la tranche 3, un comportement parfaitement linéaire et réversible.

Ces mesures permettent de calculer, pour chaque maximum de cycle, le rapport débit absorbé (en l/m/mn) par la surpression en bars en tête du forage (voir tableau 1) (analogue en dimension à une perméabilité).

Ce résultat met en évidence l'efficacité du traitement par injection réalisé sur la tranche 3, puisque sa perméabilité globale est plus faible que celle de la tranche 2.

Un examen plus détaillé du tableau montre cependant, sur les tranches 1 et 3 une augmentation de la perméabilité entre le premier et le deuxième cycle, suivie d'une baisse au cours du troisième cycle.

Ce phénomène peut s'expliquer par :

- d'abord une légère ouverture élastique de la fracturation augmentant la perméabilité globale du massif,
- puis une mise en charge progressive des discontinuités initialement fermées limitant les débits absorbés.

L'ensemble de ces observations montre que le comportement mécanique du matériau est satisfaisant. Il fallait toutefois s'assurer de la conservation de ces propriétés lorsque la charge hydraulique est maintenue constante pendant plusieurs heures.

3.3.2. Cycles longue durée

Le maintien pendant 16 heures d'une surpression atteignant 30 bars (pour la tranche 1) et 25 bars (pour les tranches 2 et 3) confirme les résultats obtenus au cours des cycles chargement - déchargement On n'observe pas d'ouverture de la fracturation. Au contraire, il apparait, sur

Tableau 2

Tranche	ΔP en bars	Débit au début du palier en l/minute/mètre	Débit à la fin du palier en l/minute/mètre
1	30	1,9	1,5
2	25	8,4	7,3
3	25	3,5	3

Tableau 3

Tranche	Seuil de surpression	Volume restitué
1	15 bars	528 l
2	15 bars	3800 l
3	10 bars	115 l

chacune des tranches une diminution du débit absorbé (voir tableau 2 et sur figure 5 l'exemple de la tranche 2).

3.3.3. Phase de redescente

Au cours de la dernière phase d'essai (consistant à redescendre la pression par paliers jusqu'à l'arrêt de la pompe) il a éte constaté sur chaque tranche une restitution de volume apparaissant à partir d'un certain seuil de surpression (voir tableau 3).

Ce phénomène appelle les remarques suivantes :

- il n'apparait qu'après un palier de longue durée et traduit vraisemblablement un phénomène d'emmagasinement dans certaines fractures plus ou moins jointives.
- La restitution apparait à des pressions très voisines d'une tranche à l'autre.
- Les volumes restitués sont cependant variables. On note en particulier que le volume restitué est beaucoup plus faible sur la tranche 3.

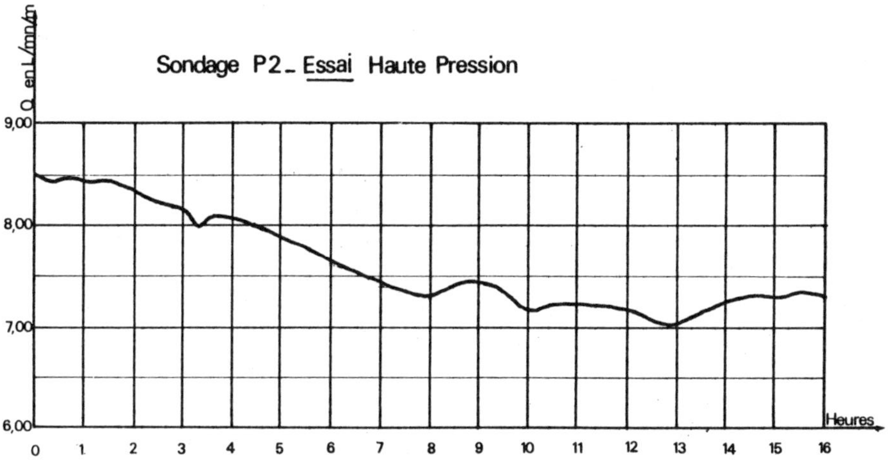

Fig. 5 : Evolution du débit absorbé au cours du temps sur la tranche 2.

4. SYNTHESE DES RESULTATS

4.1. Perméabilité globale

Le maintien pendant plusieurs heures d'une surcharge tend à instaurer un régime d'écoulement permanent où les valeurs de charge sont constantes et les débits pratiquement stables.

Ces valeurs permettent d'estimer la perméabilité globale du massif. On trouve ainsi :

- tranche 1 (de -150 à -200 m) 1,6 d'équivalent UL,
- tranche 2 (de -200 à -250 m) 7,3 d'équivalent UL,
- tranche 3 (de -250 à -300 m) 3,0 d'équivalent UL.

Ces résultats apportent un certain nombre d'enseignements :

- l'étanchéité globale du matériau est, sous fortes pressions, conservée,
- La présence d'une fissure ouverte non traitée entre - 210 et - 220 m n'a pas été préjudiciable du point de vue mécanique, mais confère néanmoins à la tranche 2 une perméabilité sensiblement plus élevée,
- enfin, les résultats obtenus sur la tranche 3 montre l'efficacité d'un traitement par injection au coulis de ciment.

4.2. Palier de longue durée

Chacun des paliers réalisé a mis en évidence une baisse sensiblement continue des débits injectés. Cette baisse peu s'interpréter par les considérations suivantes.

L'injection en continu se propage en premier lieu dans les fissures ouvertes puis gagne progressivement les fissures plus ou moins fermées. Les contraintes de compression s'exerçant sur les lèvres de ces fissures provoquent leur mise en charge progressive, et, en conséqence, une baisse des débits injectés

4.3. Restitution des tranches

La description précédente permet d'expliquer le phénomène de restitution de volume d'eau constaté après chacun des paliers longue durée. En effet, elle met en évidence un phénomène différé d'emmagasinement d'un certain volume d'eau, du à deux facteurs :

- la compressibilité du liquide injecté,
- la compressibilité du terrain sous la charge développée.

La baisse de pression dans le sondage se répercute, lors de la redescente, avec un certain retard dans le réseau de fissures plus ou moins jointives ; elle provoque une détente de l'ensemble solide liquide qui se traduit par l'expulsion du volume de liquide emmagasiné.

L'application numérique suivante permet d'évaluer l'importance de chacun de ces deux facteurs et donc d'illustrer l'interprétation tentée. Ce calcul comprend deux étapes :

- détermination du volume de massif intéressé par l'essai,
- calcul de la quantité d'eau emmagasinée dans ce volume.

Volume de roche intéressé

En admettant que le régime d'écoulement instauré à la fin du palier est proche d'un écoulement en milieu poreux, le rayon d'action est donné par :

$$R = 1{,}5\sqrt{\frac{Tt}{S}}$$

T : transmissivité de l'aquifère
t : durée de l'injection (16 heures)
S : porosité (= 1 %)

Tranche	1	2	3
R en m	13,00	27,70	17,70

Calcul de la quantité d'eau emmagasinée

On admet que le volume de massif intéressé par l'essai est une sphère de rayon R et on appelle V1 et V2 les quantités emmagasinées dans cette sphère par compressibilité respective du terrain et de l'eau. On a, sous une surpression ΔP

$V1 = mv \times p \times 4/3\, \pi R^3$ (avec mv coéfficient de compressibilité du massif)

$V2 = n\beta \times p \times 4/3\, \pi R^3$ (n étant la porosité et β le coéfficient de compressibilité de l'eau).

Les valeurs des différents paramètres sont :

. $mv = 5 \times 10^{-6}$/bar
. $\beta = 1/22\ 000$/bar
. Δp sera prise égale à la valeur de surpression où commence à apparaitre la restitution.

Le tableau 4 rassemble l'ensemble des résultats obtenus :

Tranche	Δ p en bars	V1 en litres	V2 en litres	V1 + V2 en litres	V mesuré en litres
1	15	690	60	750	528
2	15	6670	600	7270	3800
3	10	1160	105	1265	115

Ce calcul, sans prétendre à une rigueur incontestable, fournit un certain nombre d'enseignements :

- les volumes restitués calculés et mesurés pour chacune des tranches 1 er 2 peuvent être considérés comme comparables compte-tenu des hypothèses prises en compte pour effectuer le calcul.
- dans ce cas, on peut expliquer le volume important restitué par la tranche 2 par le fait qu'elle est globalement plus perméable que la tranche 1, et qu'ainsi le volume de roche intéressé par l'essai est plus grand.
- une différence importante apparait entre les valeurs calculée et mesurée de la tranche 3. Cette dernière est par contre très proche de la valeur calculée en ne tenant compte que de la compressibilité de l'eau. Il est vraisemblable que le traitement par injection réalisé sur une partie de la tranche 3, a rigidifié le massif, et donc diminué sa compressibilité ; ce phénomène peut également expliquer la parfaite réversibilité constaté sur cette tranche au cours des cycles de chargement

5. APPLICATION AU PROJET

Le sondage profond peut être considéré comme représentatif au point de vue géologique (pétrographie, fracturation, altération) du massif rocheux où seront creusés les puits des galeries haute-pression.

Il en résulte que les essais hydrauliques H.P. exécutés sur le sondage profond situé dans la zone d'implantation des 3 puits de chute, permettent de tirer pour le projet étudié les enseignements suivants :

- le granite constituant la fondation rocheuse est sain sur pratiquement toute la hauteur du forage. Les diverses zones fracturées et mylonitisées recoupées par le sondage ne devront pas présenter de difficultés majeures pour les travaux d'excavation.
- la perméabilité de la fondation est très bonne entre 1,6 et 7,5 d'équivalent Lugeon sous 47,50 bars. Ce résultat a une double application ; il donne en effet la possibilité :
  - . d'estimer l'ordre de grandeur des venues d'eau auxquelles il faudra faire face pendant les travaux d'excavation (exhaure des puits).
  - . d'envisager de ne pas prévoir le blindage des puits de chute. Un revêtement en béton, complété par un traitement du terrain par injections devraient être suffisants pour assurer l'étanchéité des ouvrages.

DESIGN OF MONOLITHIC LININGS FOR UNDERGROUND STRUCTURES SUBJECT TO INTERNAL PRESSURE AND TO SUBSURFACE WATER PRESSURE

Berechnung der monolithischen Auskleidung von Untertagebauwerken bei Wirkung des Innen- und Aussenwasserdrucks

Calcul des soutènements monolithiques des structures souterraines sujets à la pression intérieure et extérieure de l'eau souterraine

N.N.FOTIYEVA
Tula Polytechnic Institute, USSR

SUMMARY:
The design procedures for closed monolithic linings of underground structures of arbitrary cross-section as well as for complex of parallel interaction circular workings of considerable extent subject to internal head and to external pressure of subsurface water are considered in the paper. The above-mentioned problems were solved using the theory of analytic functions of complex variable, the apparatus of conformal mapping, complex rows and the properties of Cauchy intergrals. The algorithms for calculations were obtained and the programmes for electronic computers of EC type were worked out. The design procedures are illustrated by the examples of calculations of the linings of workings of large cross-section. There are shown some dependences of the stresses and forces in the linings on their geometric characteristics and on the relations of the moduli of deformation for the materials of linings and rock mass.

ZUSAMMENFASSUNG:
Im Vortrag werden Berechnungsmethodiken für geschlossene monolitische Auskleidungen der Untertagebauwerke mit beliebigen Querschnitt sowie für einen Komplex paralleler, einander beeinflussender Rundgrubenbaue bedeutender Länge auf Wirkung des Innen- und des Aussendrucks von Grundwasser dargelegt. Die angegebenen Aufgaben sind unter Nutzung der Theorie der analytischen Funktionen der komplexen Veränderlichen, des Apparates der konformen Abbildungen, der Komplexreihen und der Eigenschaften der Koschi-Integrale gelöst. Es sind Berechnungsalgorithmen erhalten und Programme für Rechenmaschinen der Baureihe EC entwickelt worden. Die Methodiken werden an Beispielen der Auskleidungsberechnungen für Grubenbaue mit grossen Querschnitt illustriert und einige Abhängigkeiten der Spannungen und Kräftein Auskleidungen von ihren geometrischen Characteristiken und vom Verhältnis der Verformungswerte der Auskleidungsmaterialen und des Gesteins dargelegt..

RÉSUMÉ:
Dans le rapport sont exposées les méthodes de calcul de la résistance à la poussée intérieure et à la pression extérieure des eaux souterraines des revêtements monolithes continus dans des ouvrages souterrains de sections quelconque, ainsi que dans un ensemble d'ouvrages souterrains de section circulaire et de longueur considérable, parallèles et s'affectant les uns aux autres. Les problèmes mentionnés sont résolus en appliquant la théorie des fonctions analytiques d'une variable complexe, l'appareil de représentations conformes, des séries complexes et les propriétés des intégrales de Cauchy. On obtenu des algorithmes de calcul et élaboré des programmes pour les calculateurs électroniques de la série EC. Les méthodes sont illustrées par des exemples de calcul des revêtements pour des ouvrages de grande section, et par quelques courbes de variation des contraintes et efforts dans les revêtements en fonction des caractéristiques géométriques de ces derniers, et du rapport entre les modules de déformation des revêtements et du rocher.

1 INTRODUCTION

This paper proposes procedures for designing closed monolithic linings for underground structures of arbitrary cross section, as well as for designing a set of parallel workings, of circular cross section, interacting with one another and of substantial extent, all subject to the action of internal pressure and to the external pressure of subsurface water. The basis of this procedure is the treatment of the lining and the rock massif as a single deformable system. This enables the bearing capacity of the surrounding rock massif to be taken into account to the maximum extent in the design calculations. Formulated and solved for this purpose are the corresponding plane contact problems of elasticity theory for a ring of arbitrary shape (having a single axis of symmetry), reinforcing a hole in a linearly deformable medium having other deformation characteristics, and for a multiply connected piecewise-homogeneous region, i.e. a medium weakened by an arbitrary number of reinforced circular holes arranged in any manner (in the general case, the holes may be of different radii and have reinforcing rings of various thicknesses, made of various materials). Discussed in the paper is the loading of the linings by internal uniformly distributed pressure. For a series of parallel workings this internal pressure may be different in each working (certain of the workings being empty). Also treated is the case of a jump (discontinuity) in normal stresses at the surface of contact between one or several linings and the massif, this jump being equal to the subsurface water pressure, which varies linearly along the height of the lining.

2 DESIGN OF LININGS OF ARBITRARY SHAPE SUBJECT TO INTERNAL PRESSURE

Considered here is the plane contact problem of elasticity theory concerning the equilibrium of a ring of arbitrary shape (with a single axis of symmetry) in a linearly deformable homogeneous isotropic medium. This ring, whose material is characterized by its modulus of deformation E_1 and Poisson's ratio ν_1, functions together with the medium, whose characteristics are E_0 and ν_0, i.e. at the line of contact L (the basic design layout is given in Fig. 1) the conditions of continuity of the stress and displacement vectors are complied with.

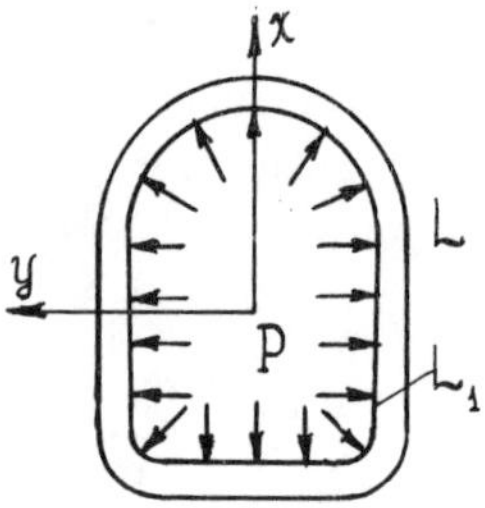

Fig. 1

The inner contour L_1 of the ring is loaded by the uniformly distributed pressure $-p$. The structure is assumed to be deep underground; the influence of the day surface is ignored. This introduces no appreciable error into the calculations provided that the depth exceeds the maximum transverse dimension of the working by more than three times.

The problem is solved on the basis of a further development of the method proposed by Sheremetyev (1949) and the application of the theory of analytic functions of a complex variable, the apparatus of conformal mapping and the properties of Cauchy-type integrals.

Carrying out conformal mapping of the exterior of a circle of radius $R_1 < 1$ onto the exterior of the inner contour L_1 of the lining cross section in such a way that the unit circle Γ becomes the line of contact L, making use of a rational function of the type

$$z = \omega(\zeta) = R\left(\zeta + \sum_{\nu=1}^{n} q_\nu \zeta^{-\nu}\right), \qquad (1)$$

and introducing the complex potentials $\varphi_0(\zeta)$ and $\psi_0(\zeta)$, which are regular outside of the circle of unit radius, as well as the potentials $\varphi_1(\zeta)$ and $\psi_1(\zeta)$, regular in the ring of radius $R_1 \leq r \leq 1$, associated with the stresses of the known formulas of Muskhelishvili (1966), the boundary conditions of the problem being considered are obtained for the transformed region. They are of the form:

$$\frac{\varkappa_0}{\mu_0}\bar{\varphi}_0\left(\frac{1}{\sigma}\right)-\frac{1}{\mu_0}\left[\frac{\bar{\omega}\left(\frac{1}{\sigma}\right)}{\omega'(\sigma)}\varphi_0'(\sigma)+\psi_0(\sigma)\right]=$$
$$=\frac{\varkappa_1}{\mu_1}\bar{\varphi}_1\left(\frac{1}{\sigma}\right)-\frac{1}{\mu_1}\left[\frac{\bar{\omega}\left(\frac{1}{\sigma}\right)}{\omega'(\sigma)}\varphi_1'(\sigma)+\psi_1(\sigma)\right], \quad (2)$$

$$\bar{\varphi}_0\left(\frac{1}{\sigma}\right)+\frac{\bar{\omega}\left(\frac{1}{\sigma}\right)}{\omega'(\sigma)}\varphi_0'(\sigma)+\psi_0(\sigma)=$$
$$=\bar{\varphi}_1\left(\frac{1}{\sigma}\right)+\frac{\bar{\omega}\left(\frac{1}{\sigma}\right)}{\omega'(\sigma)}\varphi_1'(\sigma)+\psi_1(\sigma), \quad \text{at } \Gamma \quad (3)$$

$$\bar{\varphi}_1\left(\frac{R_1}{\sigma}\right)+\frac{\bar{\omega}\left(\frac{R_1}{\sigma}\right)}{\omega'(R_1\sigma)}\varphi_1'(R_1\sigma)+\psi_1(R_1\sigma)=-p\bar{\omega}\left(\frac{R_1}{\sigma}\right)+C, \quad (4)$$

where $\sigma=e^{i\theta}$ is a point of unit circle Γ, $\varkappa_i=3-4\nu_i$ and $\mu_i=E_i/2(1+\nu_i)$ (where $i=0,1$).

After multiplying equation (3) by $\varkappa_1/\mu_1$ and subtracting equation (2), as well as multiplying equation (3) by $1/\mu_1$ and adding the product to equation (2), and then dividing both obtained equations by $(1+\varkappa_1)/\mu_1$, the following is obtained at circle Γ:

$$s\bar{\varphi}_0\left(\frac{1}{\sigma}\right)+\ell\left[\frac{\bar{\omega}\left(\frac{1}{\sigma}\right)}{\omega'(\sigma)}\varphi_0'(\sigma)+\psi_0(\sigma)\right]=$$
$$=\frac{\bar{\omega}\left(\frac{1}{\sigma}\right)}{\omega'(\sigma)}\varphi_1'(\sigma)+\psi_1(\sigma), \quad (5)$$

$$t\bar{\varphi}_0\left(\frac{1}{\sigma}\right)+d\left[\frac{\bar{\omega}\left(\frac{1}{\sigma}\right)}{\omega'(\sigma)}\varphi_0'(\sigma)+\psi_0(\sigma)\right]=\bar{\varphi}_1\left(\frac{1}{\sigma}\right), \quad (6)$$

where the notation

$$t=\frac{1+\varkappa_0\beta}{1+\varkappa_1},\quad d=\frac{1-\beta}{1+\varkappa_1},\quad \ell=1-d,$$
$$s=1-t,\quad \beta=\frac{E_1(1+\nu_0)}{E_0(1+\nu_1)}. \quad (7)$$

has been introduced. Boundary condition (4) remains the same and is combined with conditions (5) and (6).

Next, the complex potentials $\varphi_0(\zeta)$ and $\psi_0(\zeta)$, regular outside of circle Γ, including an infinitely distant point, are represented in the form of the series

$$\varphi_0(\zeta)=\sum_{\nu=1}^{\infty}a_\nu\zeta^{-\nu},\quad \psi_0(\zeta)=\sum_{\nu=0}^{\infty}b_\nu\zeta^{-\nu}, \quad (8)$$

whereas the potentials $\varphi_1(\zeta)$ and $\psi_1(\zeta)$, regular inside the ring, are represented in the form of the summations

$$\varphi_1(\zeta)=P_1(\zeta)+P_2(\zeta),$$
$$\psi_1(\zeta)=Q_1(\zeta)+Q_2(\zeta), \quad (9)$$

where $P_1(\zeta)$ and $Q_1(\zeta)$ are functions that are regular within the unit circle. Therefore, they can be expanded into the series

$$P_1(\zeta)=\sum_{\nu=0}^{\infty}c_\nu\zeta^{\nu},\quad Q_1(\zeta)=\sum_{\nu=0}^{\infty}d_\nu\zeta^{\nu}, \quad (10)$$

and $P_2(\zeta)$ and $Q_2(\zeta)$ are functions that are regular outside a circle of radius $R_1<1$, including an infinitely distant point, and are expressed by the equations

$$P_2(\zeta)=\sum_{\nu=1}^{\infty}l_\nu\zeta^{-\nu},\quad Q_2(\zeta)=\sum_{\nu=1}^{\infty}f_\nu\zeta^{-\nu}. \quad (11)$$

Owing to the geometric and force symmetry with respect to vertical axis Ox, all the coefficients in the series expansions, including those in equation (1), are real.

After multiplying conditions (5) and (6) by the Cauchy kernel $(1/2\pi i)\,d\sigma/(\sigma-\zeta)$ and integrating them term by term along the contour Γ, taking point ζ to the located consecutively outside and inside Γ, it proves possible to express the sought-for complex potentials $P_2(\zeta)$, $\psi_0(\zeta)$, $Q_1(\zeta)$ and $Q_2(\zeta)$ in terms of the potentials $P_1(\zeta)$ and $\varphi_0(\zeta)$. After substituting these potentials into boundary condition (4), the problem is reduced to the treatment of a simply connected region, i.e. an infinite plane with a hole on whose exterior the exterior of a circle of radius $R_1<1$ is mapped with the boundary condition

$$\bar{P}_1\left(\frac{R_1}{\sigma}\right)+\frac{\bar{\omega}\left(\frac{R_1}{\sigma}\right)}{\omega'(R_1\sigma)}P_1'(R_1\sigma)+Q_1(R_1\sigma)+\bar{P}_2\left(\frac{R_1}{\sigma}\right)+$$
$$+\frac{\bar{\omega}\left(\frac{R_1}{\sigma}\right)}{\omega'(R_1\sigma)}P_2'(R_1\sigma)+Q_2(R_1\sigma)=-p\bar{\omega}\left(\frac{R_1}{\sigma}\right)+C. \quad (12)$$

Substituting the expressions for the constituent complex potentials into condition (12), multiplying this condition by the Cauchy kernel $(1/2\pi i)\,d\sigma/(\sigma-\eta)$ and integrating it term by term along contour Γ, taking point η to be located consecutively outside and inside Γ, two functional equations are obtained with respect to the unknown potentials $P_1(\eta)$ and $\varphi_0(\eta)$. After expanding all the terms of one of the functional equations into series in terms of negative powers, and those of the other functional equation into series in terms of positive powers of the variable η, and equating the coefficients in the right- and left-hand sides for the same powers of η, an infinite system of linear algebraic equations is obtained with respect to the unknown coefficients c_ν and a_ν of the expansion of potentials $P_1(\eta)$ and $\varphi_0(\eta)$ into series. This infinite system, after retaining r and s members, respectively, in the series, takes the form:

$$\sum_{\nu=1}^{r} c_{m,\nu} c_\nu + \sum_{\nu=1}^{s} a_{m,\nu} a_\nu = d_m \qquad (m=1,2,\ldots,r),$$

$$\sum_{\nu=1}^{r} c'_{m,\nu} c_\nu + \sum_{\nu=1}^{s} a'_{m,\nu} a_\nu = d'_m \qquad (m=1,2,\ldots,s). \tag{13}$$

The coefficients of the matrices in system (13) and the free terms are determined in accordance with the characteristics of the lining material and of the rock massif, as well as from the coefficients of mapping function (1), by means of formulas given by Fotiyeva (1974). Also given in this work are the fomrulas for determining the stresses in the lining.

The obtained algorithm (at $n = 4$, $r = 4$ and $s = 6$, which are quite sufficient to obtain the accuracy required for all practical purposes) was programmed for an electronic computer by formula translating language (FORTRAN). The program was worked out by Engineer A.N. Kozlov.

Given below as an illustration are the results obtained in designing a lining of vaulted shape, 17 m high and with a 14.5 m span, having the following initial data: lining thickness $\delta = 0.8$ m, ratios of the moduli of deformation of the lining material and rock $E_1/E_0 = 0.8$; 2.0 and 3.0, Poisson's ratios $\nu_1 = 0.15$ and $\nu_0 = 0.25$.

The stress and force diagrams for the lining are given in Fig. 2, where the normal contact stresses σ_ρ/p, bending moments M/p and longitudinal forces N/p are shown. Curves 1, 2 and 3 indicate the stresses and forces, respectively, at values of E_1/E_0 increasing from 0.8 to 3.0.

3 DESIGN OF LININGS OF NONCIRCULAR SHAPE SUBJECT TO SUBSURFACE WATER PRESSURE

Consideration is given here to the plane contact problem of elasticity theory with boundary conditions that indicate a jump (discontinuity) in normal stresses at the line of contact L. This jump is equal to the water pressure, which varies along the height of the lining. The inner contour L_1 is free of external forces.

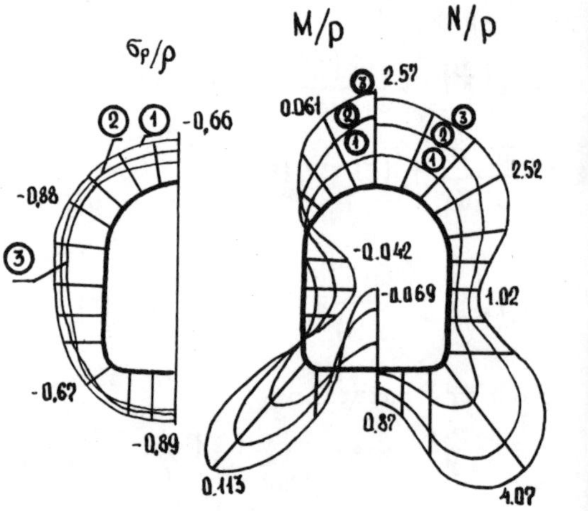

Fig. 2

Taking into account the fact that the external load has a nonzero principal vector, boundary conditions (2) and (3) acquire the additional terms

$$A_1(\sigma) = -\frac{1}{\mu_0} \cdot \frac{\gamma R^2 F}{2\pi(1+\varkappa_0)} \cdot \frac{\bar{\omega}\left(\frac{1}{\sigma}\right)}{\omega'(\sigma)} ,$$

$$A_2(\sigma) = \frac{\gamma R^2}{2} \left[\frac{F}{1+\varkappa_0} \cdot \frac{\bar{\omega}\left(\frac{1}{\sigma}\right)}{\omega'(\sigma)} + \sum_{\kappa=1}^{n+1} \alpha_\kappa \sigma^{-\kappa} + \sum_{\kappa=0}^{2n} \beta_\kappa \sigma^{\kappa}\right], \tag{14}$$

where

$$F = 1 - \sum_{\nu=1}^{n} \nu q_\nu^2 , \tag{15}$$

R is the average radius of the lining, γ is the unit weight of the water and the coefficients α_κ and β_κ are given in the book by Fotiyeva (1974).

Further solution of the problem in the same way as for internal pressure finally yields a system (13) of linear equations, but with other free terms that depend on the kind of load applied. The equations for determining the stresses are also changed. The calculations for designing a lining of arbitrary cross section, subject to subsurface water pressure, are also included in the electronic computer program. Given below in Fig. 3 are the diagrams of bending moments M, $\kappa N{\cdot}m$ and longitudinal forces N, κN in the same lining of vaulted shape at $E_1/E_0 = 2$, height of the subsurface water level (from the origin of coordinates) $H = 25$ m (full lines) and $H = 40$ m (dashed lines).

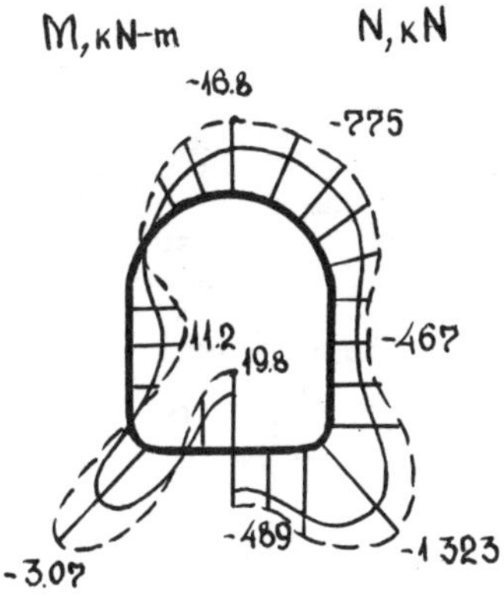

Fig. 3

4 DESIGN OF THE LININGS OF A SET OF CIRCULAR WORKINGS, INTERACTING WITH ONE ANOTHER, SUBJECT TO INTERNAL PRESSURE

Under consideration is the plane contact problem of elasticity theory for a multiply connected piecewise-homogeneous medium, i.e. a medium weakened by a finite number N of arbitrarily arranged circular holes of different radii, reinforced by elastic rings of various thicknesses and made of different materials. The basic design layout is given in Fig. 4.

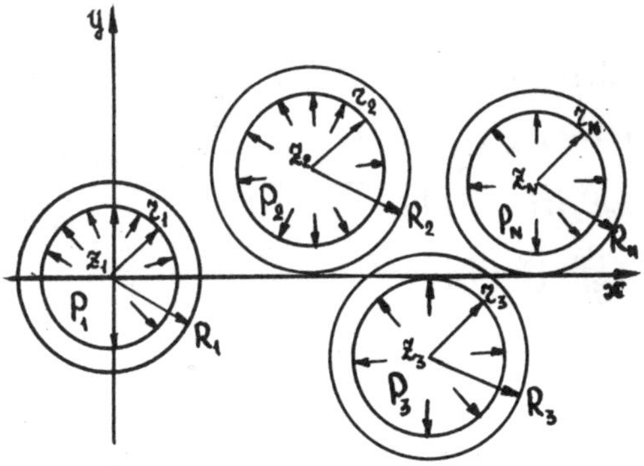

Fig. 4

The rings, of materials with the characteristics E_m and ν_m (where $m = 1, \ldots, N$), function together with the surrounding medium (modulus of deformation E_0 and Poisson's ratio ν_0) and are loaded at their inner contours L_m uniformly by the pressure $-p_m$ (where $m = 1, \ldots, N$).

The solution of the given contact problem was obtained on the basis of a development of the method proposed by Sherman (1951) and is a generalization of the solution for two identical parallel tunnels (Fotiyeva, 1979).

The complex potentials $\varphi_0(z)$ and $\chi_0(z)$, characterizing the stressed state of the medium, are introduced together with the complex potentials $\varphi_m(z)$ and $\chi_m(z)$ (where $m = 1, \ldots, N$), determining the stressed state of the rings reinforcing the holes. Here the potentials $\chi_j(z)$ (where $j = 0, \ldots, N$) are related to $\varphi_j(z)$ and $\psi_j(z)$ by the equations

$$\chi_j(z) = z\varphi_j'(z) + \psi_j(z). \tag{16}$$

Then the equations for determining the stresses (Muskhelishvili, 1966) take the form

$$\sigma_x^{(j)} + \sigma_y^{(j)} = 4\,\mathrm{Re}\,[\varphi_j'(z)],$$
$$\sigma_y^{(j)} - \sigma_x^{(j)} + 2i\tau_{xy}^{(j)} = \tag{17}$$
$$= 2\left[(\bar{z}-z)\varphi_j''(z) - \varphi_j'(z) - \chi_j'(z)\right].$$

The boundary conditions of the boundary value problem in the theory of analytic functions of a complex variable for determining the potentials $\varphi_j(z)$ and $\chi_j(z)$ (where j = 0, 1, ..., N) are written in the form

$$\varphi_0(t) + (t-\bar{t})\overline{\varphi_0'(t)} + \overline{\chi_0(t)} = \varphi_m(t) + \tag{18}$$
$$+ (t-\bar{t})\overline{\varphi_m'(t)} + \overline{\chi_m(t)}, \qquad \text{at } L_m$$

$$\varkappa_0\varphi_0(t) - (t-\bar{t})\overline{\varphi_0'(t)} - \overline{\chi_0(t)} =$$
$$= \frac{\mu_0}{\mu_m}\left[\varkappa_m\varphi_m(t) - (t-\bar{t})\overline{\varphi_m'(t)} - \overline{\chi_m(t)}\right], \tag{19}$$

$$\varphi_m(t) + (t-\bar{t})\overline{\varphi_m'(t)} + \overline{\chi_m(t)} = \tag{20}$$
$$= -p_m(t-z_m) + C_m \quad \text{at } L_m' \ (m=1,\dots,N).$$

After adding together conditions (18) and (19), subtracting condition (19) from (18), multiplied by $\varkappa_0$, at L_m (where m = 1, ..., N), the following is obtained:

$$(1+\varkappa_0)\varphi_0(t) = M^{(m)}\varphi_m(t) + \tag{21}$$
$$+ N^{(m)}\left[(t-\bar{t})\overline{\varphi_m'(t)} + \overline{\chi_m(t)}\right],$$

$$(1+\varkappa_0)\left[(t-\bar{t})\overline{\varphi_0'(t)} + \overline{\chi_0(t)}\right] =$$
$$= M_1^{(m)}\varphi_m(t) + N_1^{(m)}\left[(t-\bar{t})\overline{\varphi_m'(t)} + \overline{\chi_m(t)}\right], \tag{22}$$

with the notation

$$M^{(m)} = 1 + \varkappa_m\beta_m, \quad N^{(m)} = 1 - \beta_m,$$
$$M_1^{(m)} = \varkappa_0 - \varkappa_m\beta_m, \quad N_1^{(m)} = \varkappa_0 + \beta_m, \tag{23}$$
$$\beta_m = E_0(1+\nu_m)/E_m(1+\nu_0).$$

The complex potentials $\varphi_0(z)$ and $\chi_0(z)$, characterizing the stressed state of the medium and regular outside the circle L_m (where m = 1, ..., N), including an infinitely distant point, can be represented in the form of the series

$$\varphi_0(z) = \sum_{m=1}^{N}\sum_{k=1}^{\infty}\alpha_k^{(m)}\left(\frac{z-z_m}{R_m}\right)^{-k},$$
$$\chi_0(z) = \sum_{m=1}^{N}\sum_{k=1}^{\infty}\beta_k^{(m)}\left(\frac{z-z_m}{R_m}\right)^{-k}. \tag{24}$$

Complex potentials $\varphi_m(z)$ and $\chi_m(z)$ (where m = 1, ..., N), indicating the stressed state of the rings and regular, respectively, in the regions $r_m \le r \le R_m$, are expanded into a Laurent series:

$$\varphi_m(z) = \sum_{k=-\infty}^{\infty} a_k^{(m)}\left(\frac{z-z_m}{r_m}\right)^{k},$$
$$\chi_m(z) = \sum_{k=-\infty}^{\infty} b_k^{(m)}\left(\frac{z-z_m}{r_m}\right)^{k}. \tag{25}$$

The coefficients of series (24) and (25) are complex quantities in the general case of arbitrarily arranged centres of the holes.

Next, expansion (25) is substituted into boundary condition (20) at circles L_m' and the condition is multiplied by the Cauchy kernel $(1/2\pi i)\,dt/(t-z)$. The expression thus obtained is integrated with its conjugate condition term by term along the totality of the contours L_m' (where m = 1, ..., N) at z outside of L_m' . After equating the coefficients in the right- and left-hand sides for the same powers of the expression $(z-z_m)/r_m$, two infinite systems of linear equations are obtained with respect to the unknown coefficients $a_k^{(m)}$, $b_k^{(m)}$, $a_{-k}^{(m)}$ and $b_{-k}^{(m)}$ (where k = 1, ..., ∞ and m = 1, ..., N). Next, boundary conditions (21) and (22) and their conjugates are multiplied by the Cauchy kernel $(1/2\pi i)\,dt/(t-z)$ and integrated term by term along the totality of contours L_m (where m = 1, ..., N). For this purpose the functions $\varphi_0(t)$, $(t-\bar{t})\overline{\varphi_0'(t)}$, $\overline{\chi_0(t)}$, $\varphi_j(t)$, $(t-\bar{t})\overline{\varphi_j'(t)}$ and $\overline{\chi_j(t)}$ are first represented on the arbitrary contour L_j (where $j \ne m$) in the form of series in terms of the powers $(t-z_j)/R_j$, making use of the expansion

$$\left(\frac{t-z_m}{R_m}\right)^{-k} = \delta_{j,m}^{-k}\sum_{\nu=0}^{\infty}C_{-k}^{\nu}\,\varepsilon_{j,m}^{\nu+k}\left(\frac{t-z_j}{R_j}\right)^{\nu},$$
$$\left(\frac{t-z_j}{r_j}\right)^{k} = \delta_j^{\,k}\left(\frac{t-z_j}{R_j}\right)^{k}, \tag{26}$$

where

$$\delta_{j,m} = \frac{R_j}{R_m}, \quad \varepsilon_{j,m} = \frac{R_j}{z_j - z_m}, \qquad (27)$$

$$\delta_j = \frac{R_j}{z_j},$$

and $C^{\nu}_{-\kappa}$ is the number of combinations of $-\kappa$ taken ν at a time.

After integrating conditions (21) and (22), as well as their conjugates, and then equating the coefficients in the left- and right-hand sides for the same powers of the variables in the obtained equations, four more infinite systems of linear equations are obtained with respect to the unknowns $\alpha_\kappa^{(m)}$, $\beta_\kappa^{(m)}$, $a_\kappa^{(m)}$, $b_\kappa^{(m)}$, $a_{-\kappa}^{(m)}$ and $b'_{-\kappa}{}^{(m)}$ (where $\kappa = 1, \ldots, \infty$ and $m = 1, \ldots, N$). Thus, there are 6 systems of equations which, after being shortened and after quite complex and cumbersome transformations, can be reduced to two systems, supplemented by two separate equations with respect to the unknowns $\alpha_\kappa^{(m)}$ and $\beta_\kappa^{(m)}$ (where $\kappa = 1, \ldots, n$ and $m = 1, \ldots, N$). After separating the real and imaginary parts, $4nN$ linear algebraic equations are obtained with respect to the real and imaginary parts of $\alpha_\kappa^{(m)}$ and $\beta_\kappa^{(m)}$. The remaining unknowns, $a_\kappa^{(m)}$, $b_\kappa^{(m)}$, $a_{-\kappa}^{(m)}$ and $b_{-\kappa}^{(m)}$ are expressed in terms of $\alpha_\kappa^{(m)}$ and $\beta_\kappa^{(m)}$. The equations for the stresses in the j-th lining are obtained by substituting the corresponding series into relation (17) and transforming to polar coordinates. The forces in the cross sections of each lining are determined by means of the normal tangential stresses at the outer and inner contours, using the ordinary formulas of structural mechanics.

The design algorithm, worked out on the basis of the obtained solution, was programmed for an electronic computer. The program was designed by Engineer A.N. Kozlov. The results of design calculations for the linings of three parallel pressure tunnels are given below as an illustration. The initial data are: $R_1 = R_2 = 5.5$ m, $R_3 = 3.25$ m, $r_1 = r_2 = 4.5$ m, $r_3 = 2.25$ m, $x_1 = 0$, $x_2 = 22$ m, $x_3 = 33$ m, $y_1 = 0$, $y_2 = 12$ m, $y_3 = 0$, $E_0 = 1.5$ GPa, $\nu_0 = 0.27$, $E_1 = E_2 = E_3 = 29$ GPa, $\nu_1 = \nu_2 = \nu_3 = 0.15$, $p_1 = p_2 = 0.9$ MPa and $p_3 = 0$.

The diagrams of bending moments in the linings ($M \cdot 10^{-1}$, kN-m) are given in Fig. 5; those of the longitudinal forces ($N \cdot 10^{-1}$, kN) are given in Fig. 6.

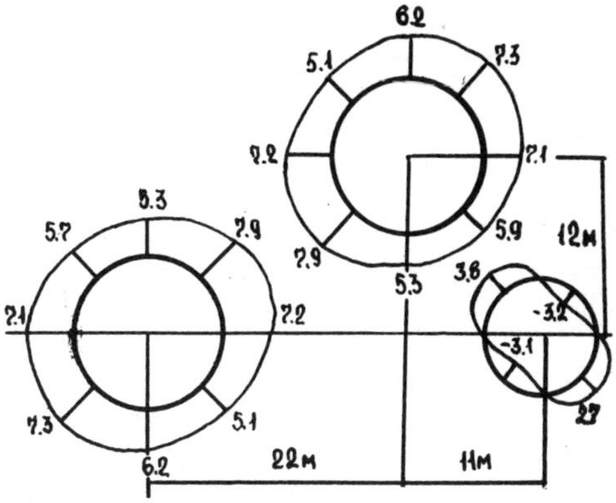

Fig. 5

5 DESIGN OF LININGS OF STRUCTURES SUBJECT TO SUBSURFACE WATER PRESSURE

The procedure for designing the linings of parallel circular tunnels subject to the pressure of subsurface water was worked out by solving the contact problem of elasticity theory for a medium weakened by reinforced circular holes under the conditions that the inner contours L'_m (where $m = 1, \ldots, N$) of the rings are not subject to external forces, and at the outer contours L_m (where $m = 1, \ldots, N$) the normal stresses σ_r are subject to a discontinuity equal to the water pressure.

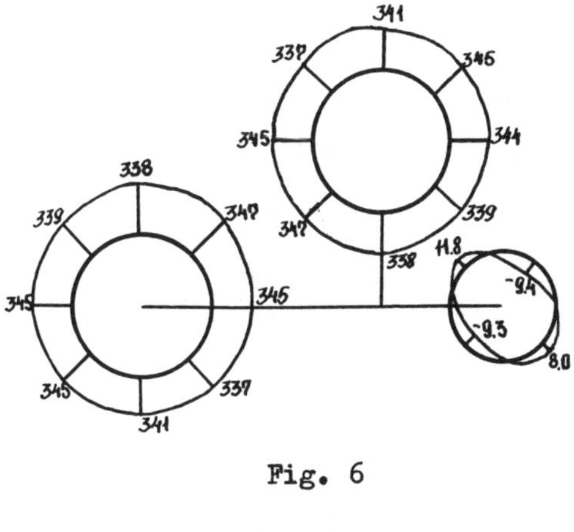

Fig. 6

Table 1

θ°	Moments and forces in the lining cross sections					
	1		2		3	
	$M \cdot 10^{-1}$, kN–m	$N \cdot 10^{-2}$, kN	$M \cdot 10^{-1}$, kN–m	$N \cdot 10^{-2}$, kN	$M \cdot 10^{-1}$, kN–m	$N \cdot 10^{-2}$, kN
0	-3.2	-14.3	-4.0	-14.5	-4.6	-9.7
45	-1.9	-12.9	-1.2	-12.7	-2.4	-8.7
90	-1.5	-12.3	-0.78	-12.1	0.71	-7.6
135	-2.2	-13.0	-1.9	-12.9	-2.1	-8.6
180	-2.6	-14.2	-3.3	-14.4	-6.1	-10.3
225	-2.2	-14.9	-1.8	-14.8	-1.0	-9.0
270	-1.4	-15.0	-0.94	-14.8	0.53	-8.8
315	-1.7	-14.8	-1.07	-14.6	-2.9	-9.7

This problem is solved in the same manner as the preceding one, but with the corresponding complications due to the nonzero value of external forces applied to each contour L_m (where $m = 1, ..., N$). This leads to the appearance of additional terms in the right-hand sides of boundary conditions (18) and (19), and to certain changes in the final formulas for determining the stresses. Dealt with as an example is the preceding case of three parallel tunnels, but with their centres located on a straight line and with the level of the subsurface water at the height H = 30 m above the line of centres. The values of the moments M , kN-m and the forces N , kN are listed in Table 1.

It should be noted in conclusion that the design procedures, algorithms and computer programs that have been worked out enable multivariant calculations to be carried out rapidly and efficiently for practical purposes. They are being employed at the present time in designing various items of underground construction.

6 REFERENCES

Fotiyeva, N.N., 1974, Lining Design for Tunnels of Noncircular Cross Section, Moscow, Stroiizdat Publishers (in Russian).

Fotiyeva, N.N., 1979, Lining Design for Closely Spaced Pressure Tunnels with their Interaction Taken into Account, Collection of Scientific Papers of the Hydroproject Institute on "Improvements in Design and Construction of Underground Water-Development Structures", Moscow, p. 24-31 (in Russian).

Muskhelishvili, N.I., 1966, Certain Basic Problems of Mathematical Elasticity Theory, Moscow, Nauka Publishers (in Russian).

Sheremetyev, M.P., 1949, Stretching an Infinite Plate with a Fixed-in Ring, whose Region, together with the Region of the Plate, is Mapped on a Circle by Means of a Rational Function, Scientific Annals of the Lvov University, vol. 12 (in Russian).

Sherman, D.I., 1951, On the Stresses in a Plane Ponderable Medium with Two Identical Symmetrically Located Circular Holes, Journal: Applied Mathematics and Mechanics, vol. 15, Issue 6, p. 751-761 (in Russian).

INVESTIGATION OF THE ACTIVE TUNNEL SUPPORTING SYSTEM'S EFFECT ON THE SURFACE SETTLEMENTS

Untersuchung der Wirkung des aktiven Tunnelauskleidungssystems auf die Oberflächensetzungen

Analyse de l'effet du système de soutènement actif des tunnels sur les tassements en surface

G.GRESCHIK
Institute for Geodesy & Geotechnics / FTV /, Budapest, Hungary
L.PÁLOSSY & P.SCHARLE
Hungarian Institute for Building Science / ÉTI /, Budapest

SUMMARY:
The tunnelling changes the state /conditions of equilibrium, kinematic conditions etc./ of the surrounding soil in a finite region. This results in settlements of the surface. In urban area as it is the case of the Budapest metro too, the settlements must be limited for protecting the buildings against damages. One possibility for decreasing the surface settlements is to use an active /pressed against the soil/ supporting system. The method applied at the Budapest metro is presented. The results of a FEM calculation show the beneficial effect of the active supporting system on the surface settlements.

ZUSAMMENFASSUNG:
Der Tunnelbau verä-ndert den Zustand /Gleichgewichtszustand, kinematischen Zustand usw./ der umhüllenden Erdmasse in einem endlichen Bereich. Dadurch entstehen Setzungen an der Oberfläche. In Stadtgebieten, wie es auch der Fall bei der Metro in Budapest ist, die Setzungen müssen wegen dem Schutz der Gebäude beschränkt werden. Eine Möglichkeit für Herabminderung der Bodensetzungen ist die Verwendung eines aktiven Tunnel-Stütz-Systems /gegen die Erde gepresst/. Die bei der Budapester Metro verwendete Methode wird vorgeführt.

RÉSUMÉ:
La construction des tunnels modifie l'état /l'état d'équilibre, l'état cinématique, etc./ du sol environnant dans une région finie. Ce qui fait le tassement de la surface du sol. Dans les régions urbaines ce qui est le cas aussi du métro de Budapest, les tassements doit être limites pour proteger les bâtiments contre dommages. Une possibilité pour réduire les tassements c'est la construction avec un système de soutènement actif /pressé contre le sol/. Une méthode appliquée aux Métro de Budapest est presentée.

1. INTRODUCTION

The tunnelling changes the state of the surrounding soil in a finite region. The constructing process results in a change

- in the initial conditions of equilibrium,
- in the initial kinematic conditions, that means the state of rest,
- and sometimes in the physical properties of the soil /e.g.dewatering, watering, grouting, etc./.

According to the construction method applied, to the soil conditions /and to many other factors/, the field of displacements may be quite different, but may be artificially influenced.

In urban areas it is very important to know the permissible settlements or deflection of the surface for avoiding damages of the buildings standing over the area of tunnelling.

To protect the buildings against damages due to the settlements, there are two general ways:

1. Passive way. - Protection is carried out on the surface. In this case buildings are reinforced by different construction methods /e.g. underpinning, tieing the elements or cutting in blocks etc./ for making them capable to bear the effects of settlements.

2. Active way. - Protection is carried out at the deep level by choosing the appropriate construction method. One of these is the active supporting system /temporary supports or final structure are pressed against the soil/rock surface/ suited to the tunnelling method. There are at least two possibilities here:

- In the case of shield tunnelling, the lining is pressed against the surrounding soil /e.g. it was used for running tunnels at the London Underground, Leningrad and Moscow Metros/
- In the case of constructing large underground cavities /e.g. metro stations etc./ by the mining method, active temporary supporting systems are used /e.g. active temporary supporting system was used at construction of parts of a metro station in Paris/.

2. CONSTRUCTION OF THE BUDAPEST METRO

2.1 The Budapest metro lines

Budapest was the first city on the European continent where an underground line was put into operation in the year 1896. After a long period lasted with a lot of political and financial difficulties, an up-to-date second line was completed in 1970 and 1972 in two sections. The length of the operating rapid transit underground network is 27 km and consist of three lines. This third line is progressing by the cut and cover method now.

Nearly some 60 % of the new lines run on the deep level and 15 stations of the 25 are the same. In the 1950's and 1960's the shield tunnelling of cast iron segments and the cast-in-place concrete construction for smaller structures were for both station and running tunnel construction applied. The stations were constructed of three larger tunnels in the 1950's and early 1960's. In the second half of the 1960's a new construction, the so called Budapest type station had been developed. There are five parallel tunnels of the same diameter intersecting each other /Fig.1/. Along the intersection line the construction is by the top and bottom beams and between them standing columns /spacing 4 m/ supported.

2.2 Geology

The ground conditions are different on the two sides of the Danube, sharing the city in two parts. The Buda side is hilly up to 400 m above river level. On the left bank of the river The Great Hungarian Plain joints to the town and the landscape is flat on the Pest side. There the gravel and sand of the Pleistocene and Holocene terraces of the Danube and some intercalated silt and peat laminae cover by a thickness of 10..15 the inclined Oligocene, Miocene and Pliocene clayey strata. The groundwater communicates there with the Danube and provides an unbroken water-table under the surface. As the inclined Tertiary strata approach and are overlain by the saturated terrace gravel, the permeable strata are replenished by water from the Pleistocene aquifer.

2.3 The deep level stations and settlements on the surface

Because of the planned high speed traffic, the curves of the lines are of greater radii than 500 m. The surface street and road network especially in the historical part of the city does not allow a horizontal alignment for construction by cut and cover method with those curves. The second and third level is unfavourable because of the saturated gravelly and sandy strata in which the groundwater flows to the Danube.

The most advantageous vertical alignment is therefore that of, leading the track in separate tubes in the Tertiary clayey sediments. While constructing the stations of the Budapest type surface settlements were observed of the order of decimetre raising a lot of difficulties. It could be found, that the repeated change over of the different provisional supports resulted in increased stresses in some zones that caused compression of the surrounding soil and hence the surface settlements. From the very beginning of applying this type of station, technological modifications were introduced, and at the end a special kind of supporting segment was developed, by which the shifting was totally eliminated.

The early construction method was as follows:

To make possible the excavation for the top and bottom beams, parts of the previously constructed running tunnel rings were removed and serving a provisional support to the upset rings the segments were erected in new positions again. The remaining overbreak was filled up with grouting. The reinforced concrete beams were in pilot tunnels /drifts/ constructed meanwhile on every 4 m a steel-tube-column was set in a raise. After having the parallel roof arches simultaneously completed, the bulk excavation followed and the construction activity was by the setting in of the invert arches finished.

To simplify the construction process and to reduce the number of changes in the stress distribution of the surrounding soil, new "hollow" supporting steel segments were introduced to avoid the readjusting of cast iron tunnel segments. The top and bottom beams were now completed without disassembling the tunnel ring. The pilot tunnels have steel supports and shotcrete lining instead of having a provisional support of timbering or cast-in-place concrete.

There are two settlement-moulds shown on Fig. 2. The station "Klinikák" was built by the earlier multiplied-change-over technology, and the station "Arany János" with the " "hollow" supporting elements. The maximum of the settlements is less than the half of the previous case. The depth and cover are nearly the same in both cases. About 10 m Pleistocene gravel and sand overlies a cover of clay with a thickness of about 5 m.

2.4 The active supporting system applied

In accordance with the endeavour several attempts had been made to substitute a much more safe construction method for the problematic one. The active supporting system served good results at the both tests for separate objects, one of them at the "Arany János" metro station. This method offers the additional advantage of relieving from stress the working face due to the erection of actively operated supporting units. The working areas are provisionally supported by single props or powered hydraulic frames. Corresponding to the magnitude of the primary stresses, they can be preliminary set under load /or the same: erected/. By this way the strata surrounding the openings can be prevented from being displaced toward the openings and the surface from being subsided.

Permanent structures of the lining will be built in continuously under protection of the provisional supporting elements in a way that proper contact is established between them and the surrounding strata as soon as the work of construction is started.

The application of the method is illustrated on Fig.3.

3. NUMERICAL INVESTIGATION OF THE ACTIVE SUPPORTING SYSTEM'S EFFECT

In the followings we are describing the numerical investigation performed for a construction alternative of a deep level station of the Budapest-Metro.

The cross section of the typical five tunnel type station is shown on Fig.1. The tunnels are built by shield method and lined by cast iron segments. The inner part is constructed by mining method. The reinforced concrete beams supported by columns are built in drifts and finally among them are built the concrete arches. A great part of the settlements was produced during the construction of the beams and column rows. For decreasing the surface settlements an alternative method of the construction was projected. According to this version, the column rows /with the bottom and top beam/ would have been constructed in one bigger drift with a steel supporting structure pressed against the soil.

For seeing the difference between the effect of the usual and the active supporting system, the surface settlements were calculated by the finite elements method. In the computer program the finite region was assembled of quadrilateral isoparametric elements. The constitutive law implemented made it possible to take the nonlinear elastic behaviour of the material by incremental loading into consideration. In this case our main purpose was to compare the two kind of the field of displacements and so for simplicity we considered the elastic behaviour of the soil as a linear one.

Figure 4. illustrates the computed finite region consisting of two characteristic soil layers, the upper sand, sandy gravel and the lower clay ones. Inside of the clay layer there are four drifts /this means a state during construction of the station/.

The material characteristics used for the calculation were the followings /the horizontal and vertical directions are denoted by the indices 1 and 2./

	γ_0 kN/m³	K_o	$\nu_1 = \nu_2$	E_2 MPa
Sand, sandy gravel	17,0	0,35	0,25	20
clay	20,0	0,45	0,30	60

where

γ_0 - specific weight of the soil
K_o - coefficient of earth pressure at rest,
ν - Poisson's ratio
E_2 - Young's module in vertical direction,

$$E_1 = \frac{K_o}{\nu_2 + K_o \nu_1} E_2$$

The base for the comparison of displacements was the extreme case when excavation of the drifts was done without any support. The initial loads of the drifts are shown on Fig. 5/a. The field of displacement as a result of the calculation is drawn on Fig. 5/b.

In the second case the drifts are supported in vertical direction /Spring constant 10^4 kN/m/ and pressed against the soil at each node by a force of 150 kN /about 60 % of the total weight at the top/. The initial loads of the drifts are shown on Fig. 6/a and the displacements on Fig.6/b.

Comparison of the surface displacements shows the great effect of the active tunnel supporting system. The calculated maximal displacement on the surface was in the first case abou 13 mm, in the second one about 3 mm. This means, that e.g. when the active stressing was about 60 % of the total weight, the maximal surface settlement has decreased to about less than 1/4.

This result shows the importance of choosing the appropriate construction method and the appropriate statical and kinematical boundary conditions during the construction period, especially when surface settlements were required to be as small as possible.

4. CONCLUSIONS

Large tunnel sections can be constructed at relatively shallow depth even in adverse ground conditions without producing subsidences damging the surface, by using supports with active units. This method offers the additional advantage of relieving from stress the working face due to the erection of actively operated supporting units /as hydraulic props/ and a working area with practically unlimite width advancing frontally can be established. /Kesserü & al/ This proposition was realized at constructing an object of the Budapest metro. The application proved all the awaited advantages.

5. REFERENCES

Greschik, Gy. 1976. Geotechnische Probleme beim Bau der U-Bahn in Budapest, Rock Mechanics, Suppl. 5. 223-229 /1976/.

Kesserü, Zs., Greschik, Gy., & al, 1978, The potentialities inherent in using new methods and complex systems of construction for preventing the occurance of subsidences when establishing sub--surface large openings, Proc.of International Tunnel Symposium '78 Tokyo, B-3-9-1...13.

Greschik, Gy. 1979. Provisional support, primary and permanent lining at the construction of the stations of the Budapest Underground, Proc. of 4th.Int. Conf. of ISRM. Montreux, 425-430.

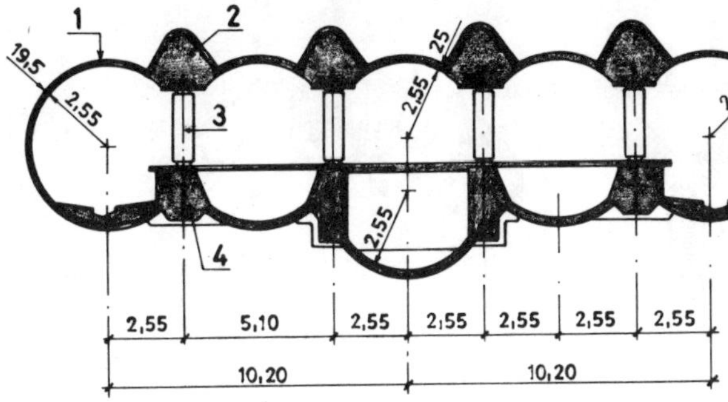

1. running tunnel (cast iron segments)
2. top beam (reinforced concrete)
3. column (thick-walled steel pipe with concrete core)
4. bottom beam (reinforced concrete)

Fig.1 Cross section of the Budapest type /fivetunnel/ metro station

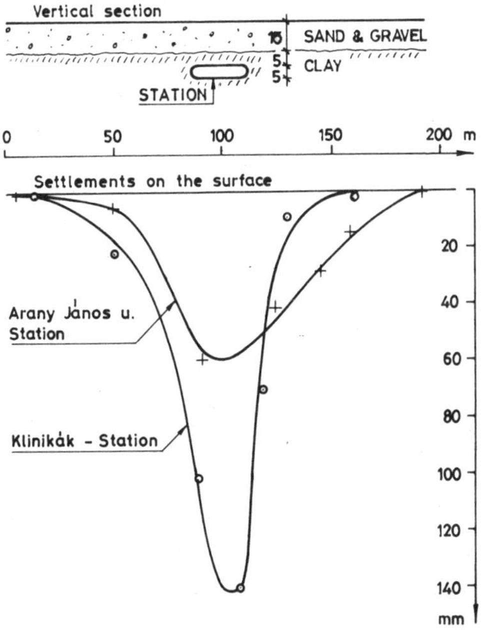

Fig.2 Settlements over similar „Budapest" -type metro stations, built by different construction methods

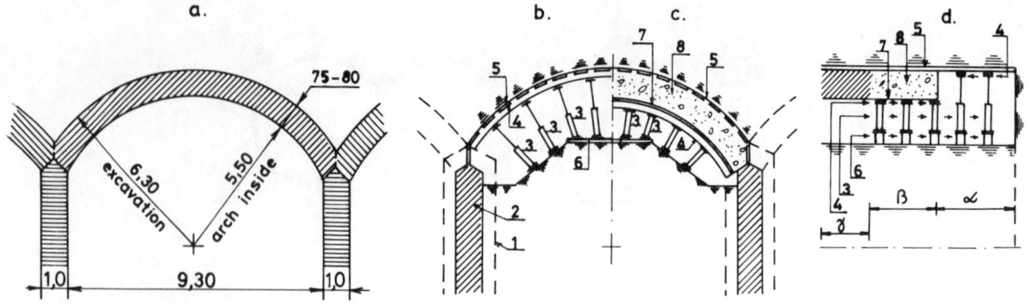

a. sketch of the structure
b. preliminary support by hydraulic props
c. support of the formwork by hydraulic props
d. the steps of constructing the roof arch after completing the side walls
α. excavation and supporting the soil by steel ribs and lagging, prop spacing 1 m
β. supporting the formwork of steel-plate-waterproofing and steel ribs
γ. completed roof arch, bulk excavation

1. lagging and ribs remained in earth after completing the side walls
2. side wall
3. hydraulic prop (active load capacity 300 kN, erected length 2240 mm; stroke 850 mm; type HBT 004-30 f; material: Aluminium; mass 52 kg; product: Hungarian, Balassagyarmati Fémipari Vállalat)
4. steel rib
5. lagging
6. bottom sill
7. steel-plate-waterproofing serving as formwork too
8. structural concrete

Fig.3 Section detail of a treble-arched structure constructed by the active supporting system as part of the applied German tunnelling method

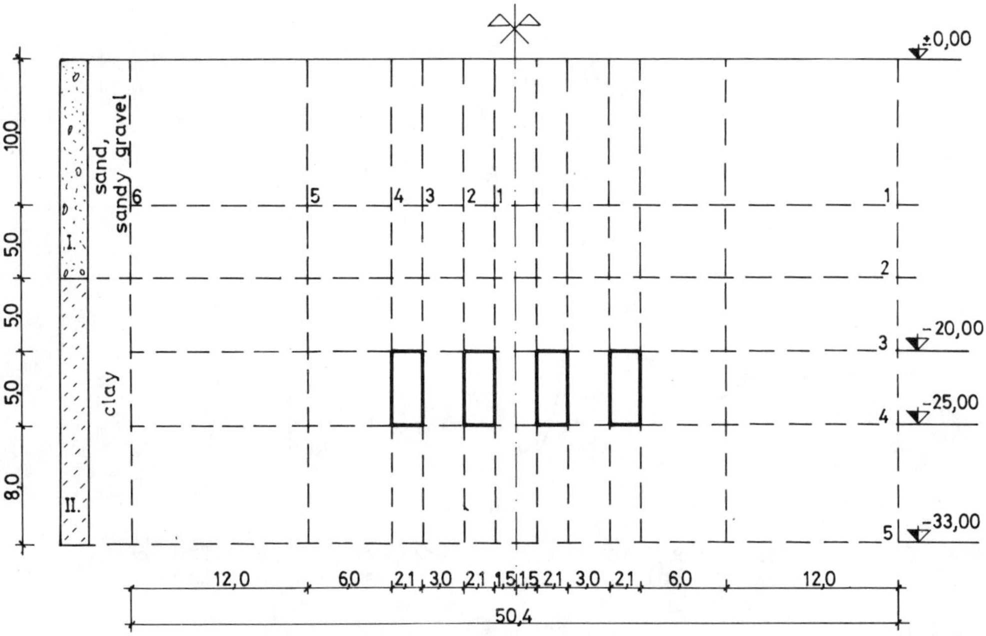

Fig. 4 Mesh around the drifts for calculation of the displacements

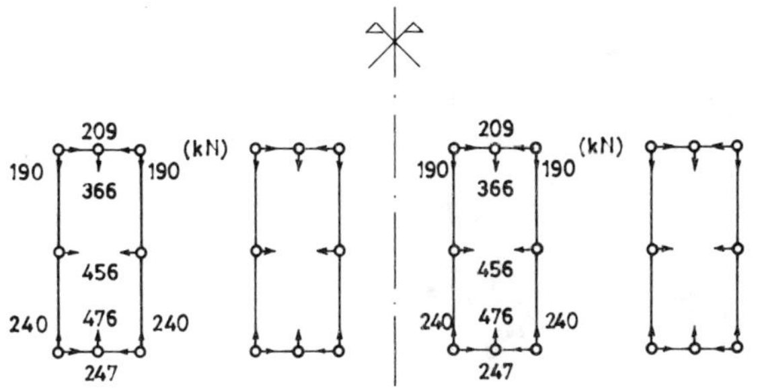

Fig. 5/a Initial loads on the sides of the drifts

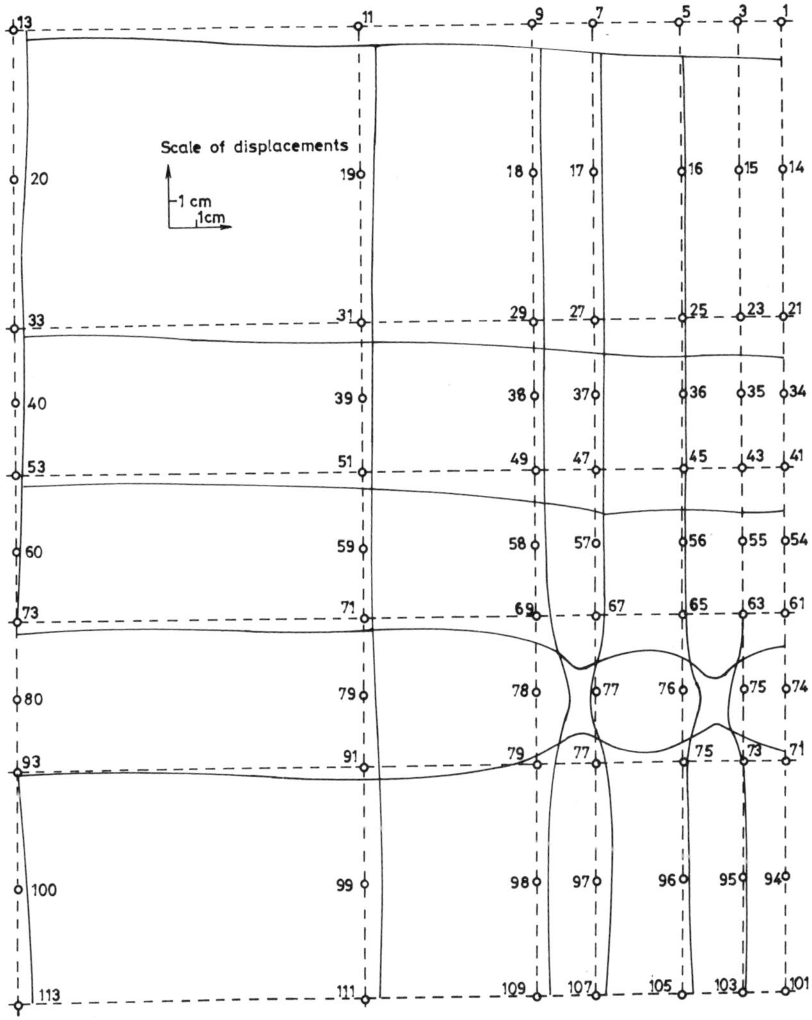

Fig. 5/b Field of displacements, when drifts are excavated

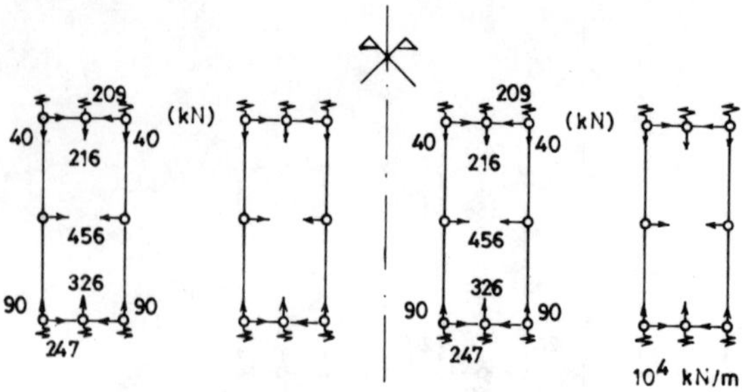

Fig. 6/a Initial loads /decreased by the active force/ on the sides of the drifts

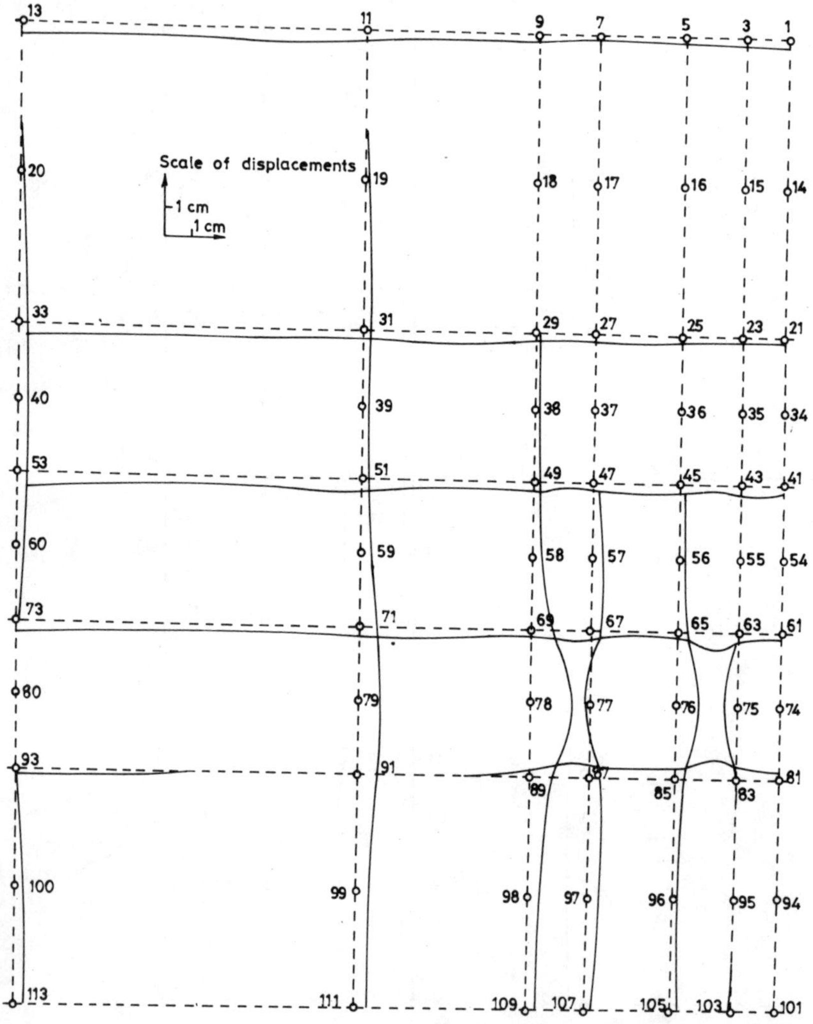

Fig.6/b Field of displacements, when drifts are excavated, supported and pressed /vertically/ against the soil

EVALUATION OF CLASSIFICATION SYSTEMS FOR TUNNELS IN NON-SQUEEZING GROUND CONDITIONS

Auswertung von Klassifikationssystemen für Tunnel in nicht druckhaftem Gebirge

Évaluation des systèmes de classification des tunnels dans les terrains non comprimés

J.L.JETHWA, A.K.DUBE & B.SINGH
Central Mining Research Station, Dhanbad, India
BHAWANI SINGH & R.S.MITHAL
University of Roorkee, India

SUMMARY:
Several classification systems have been developed during the last four decades to predict rock pressures for tunnel support design. Most of these systems are based on correlations of rock mass quality with capacity of supports used in corresponding tunnel sections. As such, these systems are likely to be conservative. It is, therefore, desirable to evaluate these classification systems by measuring actual rock loads on supports during the construction stages of tunnels. In view of the above, two tunnels located in the lower Himalayan region of India have been instrumented. Vertical and horizontal rock pressures estimated from different classification systems have been compared with the short-term observed values at four test-sections to support the use of the Q-system of Barton.

ZUSAMMENFASSUNG:
In den letzten vier Jahrzehnten wurden mehrere Klassifikationssysteme zur Vorhersage des Gebirgdrucks für Tunnelauskleidungen entwickelt. Die meisten dieser Systeme setzen die Gebirgsqualität mit der Kapazität der Tragglieder im betreffenden Tunnelabschnitt in Beziehung. Es ist anzunehmen, dass diese Systeme zu sehr auf der sicheren Seite liegen. Es ist daher wünschenswert, diese Klassifikationssyteme durch Messungen des tatsächlich vorhandenen Gebirgsdrucks auf die Tragglieder während des Bauphasen des Tunnels zahlenmässig zu bestimmen. Unter Berücksichtigung des oben Gesagten wurden in zwei Tunnel in der unteren Himalaya Region Indiens Messinstrumente eingebaut. Der nach den verschiedenen Klassifikationssystemen abgeschätzte vertikale und horizontale Gebirgsdruck wurde mit Werten aus Kurz-Zeit-Beobachtungen aus vier Testbereichen verglichen um die Anwendbarkeit des Q-Systems nach Barton zu stützen.

RÉSUMÉ:
Durant ces quatre dernières décades, plusieurs systèmes de classification ont été développés pour prévoir des pressions rocheuses au moment du dimensionnement des soutènements des tunnels. La majorité de ces systèmes s'appuie sur des corrélations entre la qualité de la masse rocheuse et la capacité des soutènements utilisés en comparant les sections des tunnels. De tels systèmes paraissent être conservateurs. Il est donc souhaitable d'évaluer ces systèmes de classification en mesurant les charges actuelles des roches sur les soutènements pendant les phases de construction des tunnels. C'est à cette fin que deux tunnels situés dans une région relativement basse de l'Himaya en Inde, ont été équipés. Des pressions rocheuses verticales et horizontales ont été estimées à partir des differents systèmes de classification et comparées aux valeurs observées pendant de courtes durées dans quatre sections d'essai afin de soutenir l'application du système "Q" de Barton.

1 INTRODUCTION

Rock pressure has been catagorised as loosening, squeezing, swelling and creep pressures. Out of these, the present study is restricted to the loosening pressure only which is defined as the probable weight of the rock mass likely to fall out from the roof upon the supports. Basically, two approaches are prevailent to determine the loosening pressure for tunnel support design. In the first

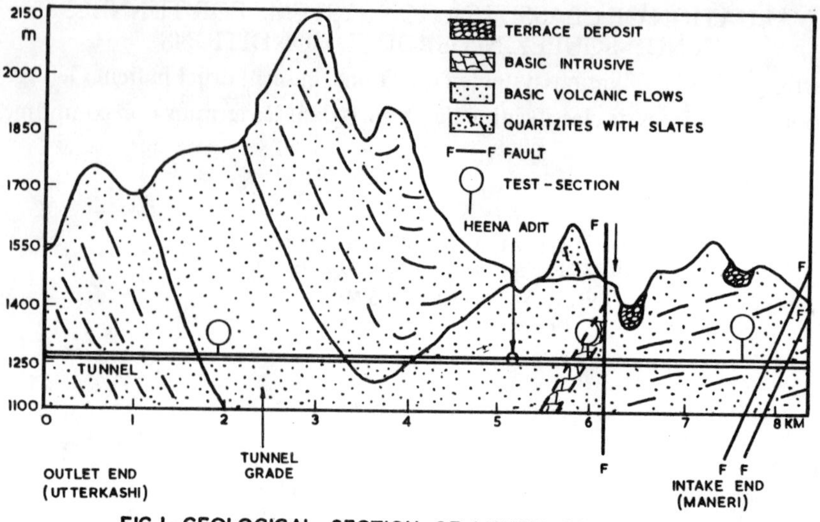

FIG.1 - GEOLOGICAL SECTION OF MANERI-BHALI TUNNEL

approach attempts have been made to correlate the description of rock mass with supports used. This is essentially an empirical practice and several classification systems have been developed along these lines. The second approach is based on instrumentation. This is called 'build as you go' philosophy and is useful only during the construction stage. Classification systems are often used at the design stage. In view of the lack of adequate instrumentation it has not been possible so far to evaluate the various classification systems and the choice of a particular system has often been made on adhoc basis.

An attempt has, therefore, been made in the present study to evaluate the various classification systems. Rock pressures predicted from these systems have been compared with the observed values in order to identify a suitable approach for tunnel support design under non-squeezing rock conditions. The case histories of Maneri-Bhali and Salal Hydel tunnels have been chosen for this purpose.

2 GEOLOGY

Regional geology of the two tunnels with brief description of the schemes are given in the following paragraphs.

2.1 Maneri-Bhali hydel tunnel

The Maneri-Bhali hydel project envisages the construction of a 41m high concrete dam across river Bhagirathi near Maneri village to divert the river into a 8.55 km long tunnel having a finished diameter of 4.75 m. A surface powerhouse is being constructed near the town of Uttarkashi to generate 93 MW of power. The tunnel is being excavated from four faces by conventional method and supported by steel ribs.

The project lies in middle Himalayas and the tunnel crosses hilly terrain with peaks rising to a height of 2150 m. The rock masses belong to the Garhwal group and consist of quartzites interbedded with slates, meta volcanics and basic intrusives (Fig. 1). The rock masses have been folded into a syncline and show a large variation in their dip and strike. The general strike is due NW-SE and the dip is 30°-40° due NE-SW. The tunnel makes an angle of 25° with the strike.

2.2 Salal hydel tunnel

A 2.5 km long tail race tunnel with a finished hourse-shoe section of 11.0 m diameter is being excavated by conventional methods and supported by steel ribs.

The tunnel is projected through the dolomites of the great limestone series of pre-Cambrian age. It passes below a hill under a maximum cover of 630 m. The predicted geological cross-section of the tunnel is shown in Fig. 2. The dolomites are intersected by three sets of closely

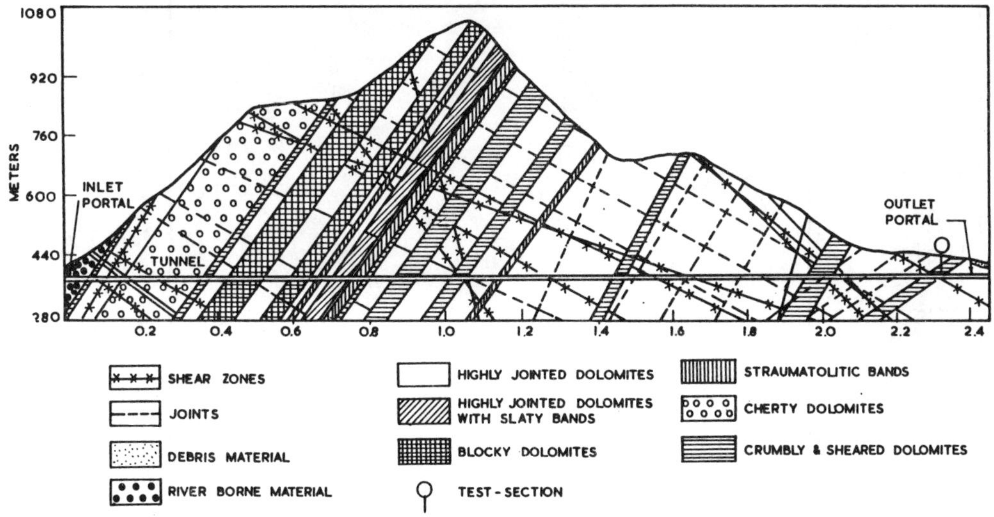

FIG.2 - GEOLOGICAL SECTION OF SALAL HYDEL TUNNEL

spaced joints. The bedding joints are dipping at 45°-55°due North. The transverse joints are dipping at 70°-80° due West and the cross joints are dipping at 30°-40° due South. The tunnel makes an angle of 20°-65° with the strike of these formations. Several shear jones are also present. The thickness of these shear zones vary from a few centimeters to a couple of meters and are filled with crushed calcareous matter. The joints are generally tight except at a few locations where hill water has found access.

3 CLASSIFICATION OF ROCK MASSES

The rock masses of the Salal and the Maneri-Bhali hydel tunnels have been classified by Jethwa et al (1976, 1978). These classifications are given in Tables 1 and 2 respectively.

Table 1. Rock mass classification for Salal hydel tunnel (after Jethwa et al 1976)

Joint Spacing (cm)	Type of Rock Mass
30-100	cherty and blocky dolomites
5-30	highly jointed dolomites
<5	crumbly and sheared dolomites

4 COMPARISON OF OBSERVED AND PREDICTED ROCK PRESSURES

A total of four tunnel sections have been chosen for comparing the observed rock pressures with predicted values. Three of

Table 2. Rock mass classification for Maneri-Bhali hydel tunnel

Joint Spacing (cm)	Type of Rock Mass
>70	massive
30-70	moderately jointed
30-70 with single shear	moderately sheared
30-70 with multiple shears	highly sheared

Table 3. Wall factor (Q_w) for estimating wall rock pressure (p_h) after Barton et al (1975)

Range of Q	Wall Factor Q_w
>10	5.0 Q
0.1-10	2.5 Q
<0.1	1.0 Q

Table 4. Comparison of predicted and observed rock pressures for tunnels in non-squeezing rock conditions

NAME OF TUNNEL, ROCK MASS DESCRIPTION, ESTIMATED PARAMETERS AND OBSERVED TUNNEL-WALL DISPLACEMENTS	PREDICTED ROCK PRESSURES IN kg/cm^2 FROM CLASSIFICATION SYSTEMS OF: TERZAGHI	DEERE et al.	PROTODYAKONOV	BARTON et al.		WICKHAM et al.	OBSERVED ROCK PRESSURE (kg/cm^2)		PERIOD OF OBSERVATION (Months)	REMARKS
	p_v	p_v	p_v	p_v	p_h	p_v	p_v	p_h		
MANERI-BHALI HYDEL TUNNEL										
1. Moderately fractured quartzites, $a=2.4m$, $h=225m$, $\gamma=2.5$ gm/cc, RQD = 75%, Q=3-6, RSR=68, f=8	0.3 to 0.7			0.5 to 0.7	0.2 to 0.4					Steel ribs, stable
$u_a/a = 0.06\%$	(0.5)	0	0.2	(0.6)	(0.3)	0.3	0.6	0	2	
2. Foliated meta basics, $a = 2.4m$, $h = 550m$, $\gamma = 2.5$ gm/cc, RQD = 82%, Q = 3.4-6.8, RSR = 68,	0.3 to 0.7			0.5 to 0.7	0.2 to 0.4					Steel ribs, stable
$f = 10$, $u_a/a = 0.05\%$	(0.5)	0	0.1	(0.6)	(0.3)	0.3	0.8	0	2	
3. Sheared metabasics, $a = 2.4m$, $h = 350m$, $\gamma = 2.5$ gm/cc, RQD = 60%, Q = 0.3-3.3, RSR = 45	0.8 to 2.6	0.0 to 1.6		1.8 to 2.0	0.4 to 1.4					Steel ribs, stable
$f = 9$, $u_a/a = 0.4\%$	(1.7)	(0.8)	0.1	(1.9)	(0.9)	1.1	2.0	0	3	
SALAL HYDEL TUNNEL										
4. Highly jointed dolomites, $a = 6.0m$, $h = 110m$, $\gamma = 2.8$ gm/cc, RQD = 30-40%, Q = 1.2-1.7, RSR = 58	1.7 to 5.5	0.0 to 3.0		1.0 to 1.2	0.5 to 0.7		0.8 to 1.4			Steel ribs, stable
$f = 7$	(3.6)	(1.5)	0.5	(1.1)	(0.6)	1.4	(1.1)	-	1.5	

a = tunnel radius; h = height of cover; γ = unit weight; RQD = rock quality designation; Q = Barton's rock mass quality; RSR = Wickham's rock structure rating; f = Protodyakonov's strength factor; u_a = tunnel-wall displacement; p_v = rock pressure in vertical direction; p_h = rock pressure in horizontal direction; average values in brackets.

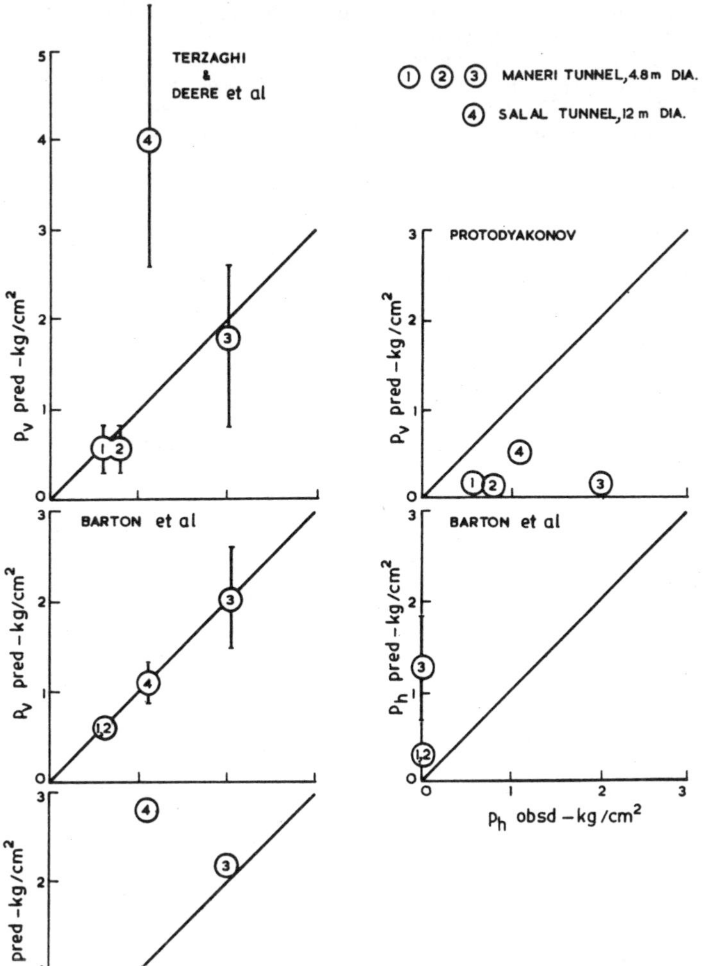

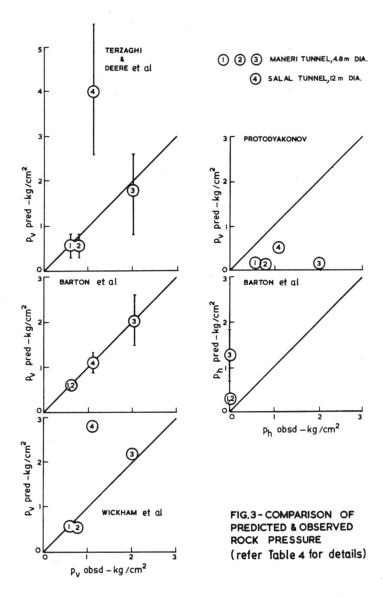

FIG.3 - COMPARISON OF PREDICTED & OBSERVED ROCK PRESSURE (refer Table 4 for details)

these are from the Maneri-Bhali tunnel and the fourth is from the Salal tunnel. The classification systems of Terzaghi (1946), Deere et al (1969) Protodyakonov (1963), Barton et al (1974, 1975) and Wickham et al (1972) have been used to estimate the rock pressures. The method of Lauffer (1958) modified by Pacher, Rabcewicz and Golser (1974) and the geomechanical classification system of Bieniawski (1973, 1975) have not been considered because these approaches suggest a support system for a given set of rock conditions without giving the actual values of rock pressures. Details of these classification systems are not included here due to limitations of space.

The geological details required for estimating Terzaghi's category of rock mass, Protodyakonov's strength factor (f), Barton's rock mass quality (Q) and the rock structure rating (RSR) of Wickham et al were collected at sites with the help of geologists of the Geological Survey of India. The Q-values have been multiplied by a factor of 5 to estimate short-term rock pressures. Similarly, the wall rock pressure (p_h) has been obtained from appropriate wall factors (Q_w) given in Table 3.

The rock conditions have been described as non-squeezing because the tunnel-wall displacements were less than 1 percent of the radius of the openings. The Maneri-Bhali tunnel has been called a small tunnel and the Salal tunnel has been considered a large tunnel. The predicted rock pressures have been compared with the observed values in Table 4 and Fig. 3. The build up of rock pressure in steel ribs was observed with hydraulic load cells developed at the Central Mining Research Station, Dhanbad. Both rock loads and displacements stabilized within three months.

The following trends emerge from Fig. 3 and Table 4:

1. The empirical approaches of Terzaghi (1946) and Deere et al (1969) provide reasonable estimates of rock pressure for a small tunnel. On the other-hand, these methods provide higher estimates for the large tunnel.

2. The method of Prokdyakonov (1963) is unsafe for the small as well as the large tunnel.

3. The Q-system of Barton et al (1974, 1975) provides vertical rock pressures almost equal to the measured values both for the small and the large tunnel. However, the predicted horizontal short-term rock pressures are greater than the measured values.

4. The RSR method of Wickham et al (1972), is safe for the small tunnel but provides higher predictions for the large tunnel.

It may be seen from the above that the classification systems of Terzaghi (1946), Deere et al (1969) Protodyakonov (1963) and Wickham et al (1972), which imply that the rock pressure is directly proportional to the size of the tunnel, do not provide estimates close to the observations. On the contrary, the Q-system of Barton et al (1974, 1975), which suggests that the rock pressure is independent of the tunnel size, provides reasonable predictions at least for the vertical rock pressure in the cases of both small and the large tunnel.

5 CONCLUSIONS

The limited field data suggests that the Q-system of Barton et al (1974,1975) provides reasonably reliable values of short-term vertical rock pressure for steel supported tunnels excavated by conventional method under non-squeezing rock conditions.

6 REFERENCES

Barton,N.,R.Lien and J.Lunde 1974, Engineering classification of rock masses for the design of tunnel supports. Rock Mechanics. Vol.6,No.4, pp.189-236.

Barton,N.R.Lien and J.Lunde 1975, Estimation of support requirements for underground excavations. Proc. Sixteenth Symp. on Rock Mech. Univ. of Minnesota, Minneapolis, U.S.A., pp. 163-177.

Bieniawski,Z.T. 1973, Engineering classification of jointed rock masses. Trans. S.Afr. Inst. Civil Engrs. Vol.5, pp. 335-342.

Bieniawski, Z.T.1975, Case studies prediction of rock mass behaviour by the geomechanical classification. 2nd Australia-New Zealand Conf. on Geomechanics. Brisbane. pp. 36-41.

Deere, D.U., R.B.Peck, J.W.Monsees and B.Schmidt 1969, Design of tunnel liner and support system. Univ. of Illinois, Report prepared for office of High Speed Ground Transportation, U.S.Dept. of Transport, Contract No. 3-0152.

Jethwa,J.L., A.K.Dube and B.Singh 1976, Assessment of rock pressure and support requirements for tail race tunnel of Salal Hydro-electric Project. C.M.R.S. Report. Dec. 1976.

Jethwa,J.L., A.K.Dube and B.Singh 1978, Rock mechanics instrumentation for tunnels in India. Tunnels and Tunnelling. September, pp. 63-66.

Lauffer,H. 1958, Gebirgsklassifizierung fur den stollenbau. Geologic and Bauwesen. Vol. 24, No.1, pp.46-51.

Pacher,F.,L.Rabcewicz and J.Golser 1974, Zum derseitigen stand der gebirgsklassi fizierung in stollenund tunnelbau. Proc. XXII Geomechanics Colloquium. Salzburg. pp. 51-58.

Protodyakonov, M.M. 1963, Firmness coefficient for estimation of rock loads. Personal Communication with Beas Design Organisation, New Delhi.

Terzaghi,Karl 1946, Rock defects and load on tunnel supports. Introduction to Rock Tunnelling with Steel Supports by Proctor, R.V. and T.L.White, Commercial Shearing and Stamping Co., Youngstown, Ohio, U.S.A.

Wickham,G.E., H.R.Tiedman and E.H.Skinner 1972, Support determinations based on geologic predictions. 1st North American Rapid Excavation and Tunnelling Conference, Chicago. Vol. 1. Am. Inst. of Min. Met. and Pet. Engrs. Inc., New York.

PERFORMANCE OF A SHAFT IN WEAK ROCK (BEARPAW SHALE)

Tragverhalten eines Schachtes in weichem Gebirge

Performance d'un puits dans un rocher doux

P.K.KAISER, C.MACKAY & N.R.MORGENSTERN
University of Alberta, Edmonton, Canada

SUMMARY
The performance of a 235 m deep circular shaft with a finished diameter of 4.3 m, excavated by conventional shaft construction techniques in clay shale, was monitored by measuring the rock mass displacement field, the rock stress changes which occurred during the shaft advance, and the stress build up in the cast-in-place concrete liner. The project, the local geology and the instrumentation program is described. The field observations are discussed with particular emphasis on their interpretation to determine the in situ stress field.

ZUSAMMENFASSUNG
Ein 235 m tiefer, kreisförmiger Schacht mit einem Durchmesser von 4,3 m wurde mit konventioneller Bauweise in weichem Tonschiefer erstellt. Das Verhalten des Gesteines und des Schachtausbaues wurde durch Messungen der Felsverschiebungen mit Mehrfach-Messankern, der Felsspannungsänderungen während des Schachtvortriebes und der Dehnungen im Betonring beobachtet. Das Projekt, die lokale Geologie sowie die Messeinrichtungen sind beschrieben und die Auswertung der Messresultate ist erläutert. Spezielles Gewicht wurde dabei vor allem auf die Bestimmung des ursprünglichen Spannungsfeldes gelegt.

RESUME
La performance d'un puits circulaire d'une profondeur de 235 m et d'un diamètre de 4,3 m, creusé suivant les techniques conventionnelles de construction de puits en schiste argileux, a été étudiée par le mesurage du camps de déplacement de la masse rocheuse, les changements de contrainte du roc pendant la construction du puits, et la progression des contraintes sur le revêtement en béton. Le project, la géologie locale et le programme d'instrumentation sont décrits. Les observations sur le terrain sont interprétées pour déterminer le champs de contraintes en place.

1 INTRODUCTION

The design of underground openings in the soft and weak bedrock underlying large areas of the prairie provinces of western Canada has been primarily empirical and the dimensioning of the opening supports is often based on rules developed for comparable rock types in other parts of the world. Their applicability to the local conditions has never been proven and little quantitative data has been collected to describe accurately the rock properties and to evaluate the performance of existing openings. This inhibits more rational design and construction procedures.

The sinking of a vertical shaft at Kipp near Lethbridge in southern Alberta provided an excellent opportunity to collect shaft performance data for the rational design of future adits to this coal mine. For this purpose, it was necessary to determine the *in situ* stress field, to observe the deformations near the opening, to determine the rock mass deformation properties, to determine the strength properties by laboratory tests, and to monitor the load development on the support to verify lining design.

In this paper, we present a brief overview of the project with a qualitative description of the performance of the shaft. This is followed by a detailed interpretation of observations made to evaluate the existing field stresses at the site.

2 PROJECT DESCRIPTION

The prospective mine is located approximately ten kilometers north-west of Lethbridge, on the southern edge of the Alberta Plains (Figure 1). The mine is being developed by Petro Canada Exploration Inc. to exploit part of the bituminous coal of the extensive Lethbridge Coal Field. Several coal mines have operated in this area since the early 1880's but most mines have been inactive over the last two decades. Recent increases in world coal prices make underground mining in this area viable and one additional major project is presently under development nearby.

The shaft with a finished diameter of 4.32 m was sunk by Thyssen Mining Construction of Canada Ltd. between February and November, 1980 using conventional shaft sinking methods. The bedrock was excavated by drilling and blasting 1.8 to 2.4 meter deep, half floor benches. The shaft was lined with a cast-in-place concrete lining with variable thickness depending on the overbreak. The specified thickness was

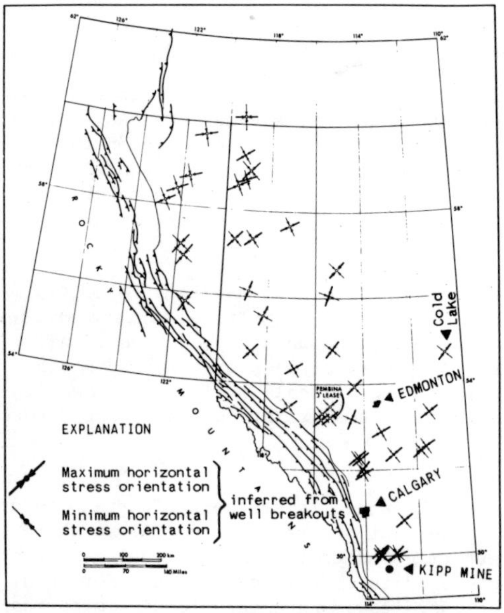

Figure 1 Site location and inferred directions of horizontal principal stresses (after Gough and Bell, 1981).

300 mm for the first 70 m, 400 mm to a depth of 130 m and 500 mm, 600 mm, 700 mm to depths of 175 m, 220 m and 235 m, respectively. The lining construction generally followed one to two shaft diameters behind the shaft bottom. Ready-mix concrete with a specified strength of 35 MPa was poured behind segmental slipforms. Shaft sinking through the bedrock progressed at a rate of about 3 to 4 meters per day. Except during 4-day work stoppages, the rock was seldom unsupported for more than 16 to 20 hours.

3 GEOLOGICAL SETTING

The regional geology of southern Alberta was studied by Russell and Landes (1940). Crawford (1947) investigated the geology and structure of the Lethbridge Coal Field. Sediments of Upper Cretaceous age underlie the Lethbridge area to depths of several hundred meters. The Lethbridge Coal is located in the uppermost beds of the non-marine Oldman Formation, the youngest formation of the Belly River group. Conformably overlying the Oldman Formation is the marine Bearpaw Formation. The surficial deposit at the shaft location consists of about 60 meters of glacial clay till with a 6 meter thick saturated basal

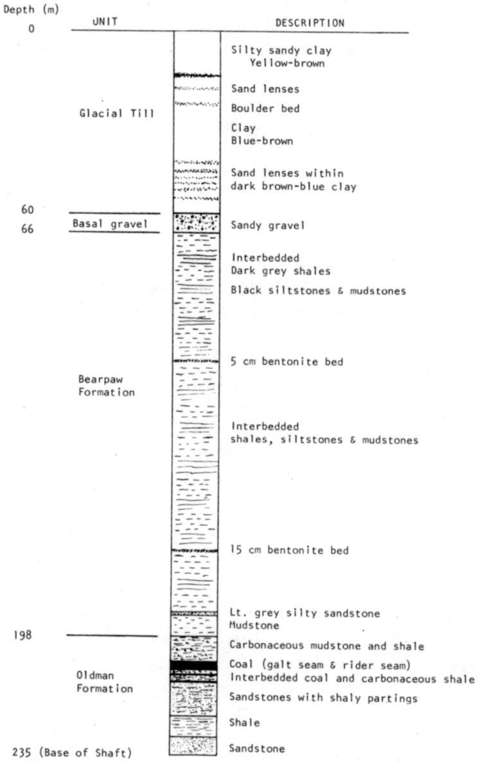

Figure 2 Bedrock profile at shaft location near Kipp, Alberta.

sand and gravel deposit at the bedrock interface. A stratigraphic section is shown in Figure 2.

The Oldman Formation is composed of intercalated and interbedded lightcolored sandstones and clay shales with frequent coal beds in the upper member. The Bearpaw Formation is 132 meters thick near the shaft and consists of alternating beds of sandy and shaley mudstones of between 15 and 30 meters in thickness. The shales are blocky, dominantly dark gray to black, claystones or mudstones with occasional fissle beds. The sandstones are fine-grained argillaceous and poorly indurated (Byrne and Farvolden, 1959). Both formations were formed from detrital sediments deposited in non-marine and marine environments respectively. Montmorillonite, formed from deposits of volcanic ash, is found throughout the bedrock sequence as pure bentonitic clay beds or as the dominant clay mineral in some beds of fine grained rock.

The structural features present in the Upper Cretaceous deposits in this area were largely formed during the Laramide Orogeny in the Tertiary, which produced widespread uplift, crustal shortening and thrust faulting in the Rocky Mountains with renewed uplift in the Sweetgrass Arch east of the mine site (McCrossan and Glaister, 1966). The bedrock structure near Lethbridge consists of a series of gentle, low amplitude anticlines and synclines trending northwest-southeast and plunging gently to the northwest (Crawford, 1947). Associated with these folds are a number of normal and thrust faults which are traceable over several kilometers, or local faults which are identified on mine plans. A major fault zone, the Monarch Fault zone, is located approximately ten kilometers west of the mine site and consists of a series of near vertical to west dipping (20°) thrust faults striking N25°E to N20°W (Crawford, 1947). Orthogonal cleavage has developed in the coal with the major cleavage orientated N50°E and the minor cleavage N40°W.

4 *IN SITU* STRESS FIELD

The regional stress field in Alberta was inferred by Gough and Bell (1981) from an extended study of breakouts in oil wells, hydraulic fracturing of oil fields, rock mass permeability trends and fractures developed during steam injection into oil sand of the Clearwater Formation. The maximum and minimum predicted principal stress directions are shown on Figure 1 indicating unequal horizontal stresses, with the larger stress oriented northeast-southwest or nearly perpendicular to the thrust faults of the Rocky Mountains. Gough and Bell (1981) conclude from well breakouts observed at depths of about 1000 to 2500 m that the strike-slip stress field, with the intermediate principal stress vertical, and the thrust stress field with the minor principal stress vertical, are most likely in Alberta. Furthermore, evidence from fracturing at shallow depths of less than 500 m suggests that the stress field is of strike-slip type, with the major principal stress approximately NE-SW, the minor principal stress NW-SE, and the intermediate principal stress vertical. Fracture data from the Cold Lake heavy oil deposit seem to indicate that the vertical stress corresponds to the expected overburden pressure and that the minimal stress ratio K_o (min) is about 0.8 (NW-SE). The maximum K_o-value could not be determined from the available information but the maximum horizontal stress would be oriented NE-SW.

During drilling of horizontal holes for the extensometers at 180 m depth spalling (20 to 30 mm wide and 10 to 15 mm deep) occurred on opposite ends of the vertical borehole diameter in all three boreholes (N, SW and SE) as far as observable in a 76 cm borehole and definitely to a depth of in excess of 3 to 4 m measured from the shaft wall. With an overburden pressure of about 4.2 MPa at this depth and a tangential stress concentration factor near a bore hole extending from a circular shaft of between 2 to 3 (far from the shaft wall) and 4 to 6 (near the shaft wall) the maximum unconfined rock strength must be less than 8.4 to 25.2 MPa. The fact that the rock quality at this elevation was relatively poor and that spalling occurred in all three holes leads us to the conclusion that the maximum field stress ratio K_o(max) cannot be significantly in excess of unity. If we assume K_o(min) ≥ 0.8 and K_o(max) ≤ 1.3 the resulting horizontal stress ratio N would be greater than or equal to 0.62.

The data to follow will provide some evidence in support of this prediction. However, it must be pointed out that many other geological processes may have significantly altered the local stress field and that the conditions at the shaft may not correspond with the regional stress pattern. For example, in the late Tertiary uplift of the Sweetgrass Arch, located east of Lethbridge, could have caused a local alteration of the shallow bedrock stresses and account for the normal faults observed in several coal mines. In addition, the *in situ* stresses may have been influenced by regional uplift during erosion of several hundred meters of bedrock during the Eocene (Scott and Brooker, 1968), Pleistocene glaciation and deglaciation, as well as by horizontal stress release during formation of a major valley in the proximity of the site.

5 PROPERTIES OF THE BEARPAW FORMATION

A limited number of samples were collected from a clayey mudstone bed in the Bearpaw Formation by drilling horizontal 150 mm holes into the shaft wall at a depth of 91 m. Eight NX-size samples (54 mm) of intact rock, cut parallel to the bedding plane, were tested in multistage triaxial tests at confining pressures between 1.4 and 13.6 MPa. A summary plot of the failure stress conditions is shown in Figure 3. The following average rock properties were determined from these tests:

Unconfined compressive strength: 8 to 14 MPa

Internal friction angle: 33°
(from linearized failure envelope between 0 and 6 MPa confining pressure)

Deformation modulus from:
-constant, intermediate strain rate tests 1.9 to 2.2 GPa
(axial strain rate = 5.5×10^{-6}%/sec)
-variable strain rate tests 1.1 to 1.7 GPa
(with axial strain rates varying between 4.8×10^{-8} and 1.7×10^{-4}%/sec)

Swelling tests showed negligible swelling potential. The *in situ* rock mass properties are not known in detail but RQD values, determined from three drill holes in the immediate vicinity, varied over a wide range from average values of between 60 to 100% for the blocky beds and 0 to 25% for heavily fractured beds.

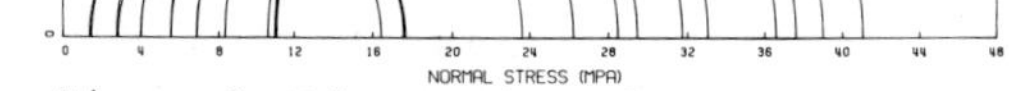

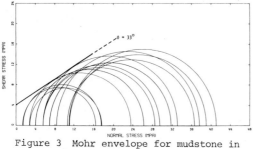

Figure 3 Mohr envelope for mudstone in Bearpaw Formation (91 m depth)

6 INSTRUMENTATION AND TESTING IN THE SHAFT

An attempt was made to determine the *in situ* stress field at a depth of 91 meters (14 m below the bedrock surface) using the USBM-overcoring technique. Because of limited time, only four tests could be executed in one horizontal borehole orientated at N50°W. Accordingly, the entire stress field could not be determined but the stress ratio was found to be below unity with a vertical stress near overburden stress. These tests were, nevertheless, considered a success because they showed that the USBM-overcoring technique can be used in massive units of clay shales or mudstones.

The following instrumentation was installe at three levels in the Bearpaw shale:

111 m depth:
3 mechanical multi-point extensometers;
16 vibrating wire embedment gauges in concrete liner;
1 piezometer;

152 m depth:
3 radial and
4 tangential vibrating wire borehole stress change gauges;
8 embedment gauges in concrete liner;
1 piezometer;

180 m depth:
3 multi-point extensometers;
8 embedment gauges in concrete liner.

All instruments were supplied by the IRAD-Gauge Company and installed during four-day work shutdown periods. The locations of the embedment gauges and the IRAD stress change gauges are shown in Figures 4 and 5.

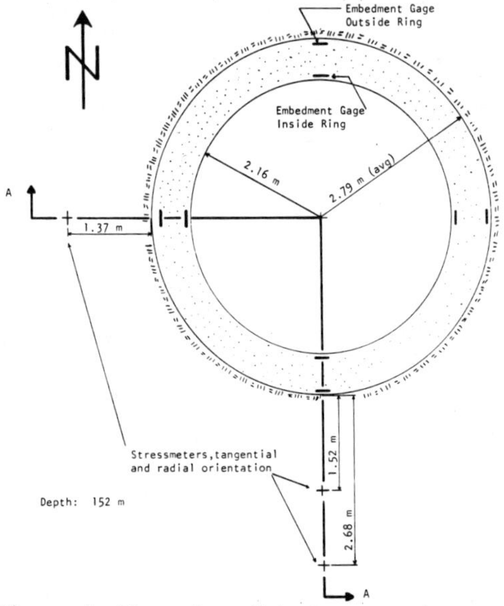

Figure 4 Plan view of instrumentation at elevation 152 m

The stress change gauges were installed 10 m ahead of the shaft bottom in steeply incline holes at elevation 152 m. The embedment gauges were positioned during pouring of the concrete lining at the same level. The inside embedment gauges were placed about 15 cm from the slipform or the rockwall (two each at the north, east, south and west wall). The five-point mechanical extensometers were installed as shown in Figure 6 and extended through the lining. Unfor-

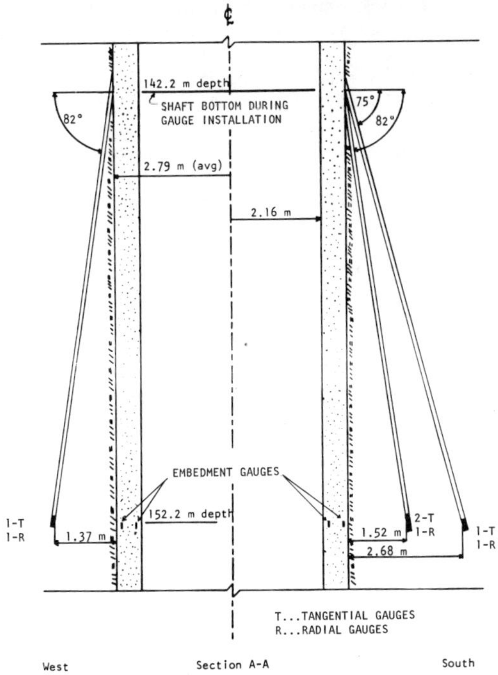

Figure 5 Section view of stress change gauge and embedment gauge installation at 152 m depth

tunately, longterm measurements were only possible on one extensometer because of damage during blasting and pouring of concrete, or because access was impossible after shaft advance. The vibrating wire piezometers were installed immediately behind the liner. None of the piezometers measured significant pressure and it was concluded that no water pressure built up below the bedrock surface.

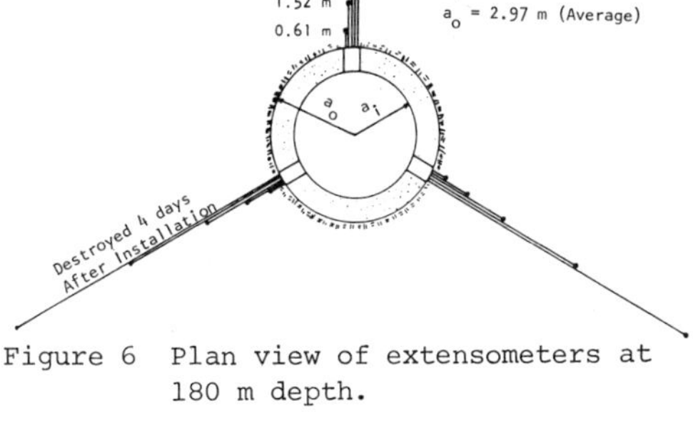

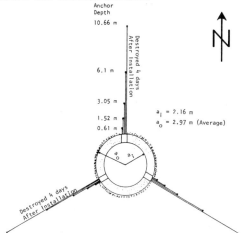

Figure 6 Plan view of extensometers at 180 m depth.

7 OBSERVED SHAFT PERFORMANCE

7.1 Rock Stress Change

Figure 7 presents the data recorded during the advance of the shaft from two tangential and one radial stress change gauge installed 1.52 m from the shaft wall (see Figure 4). No stress change was observed more than one diameter below the shaft bottom. The percentage of the total uniaxial stress changes observed at 55 m from the shaft bottom, before the shaft bottom passed the gauges and before the liner was installed is tabulated in Table I for all gauges. It is of interest to note that the radial stress change occurs almost instantaneously at the shaft bottom and that the tangential stress changes develop slowly to reach the maximum only after more than 7 to 10 diameters from the face. This behaviour corresponds with that predicted by finite element modelling (Kaiser and Hutchinson, 1982). On average

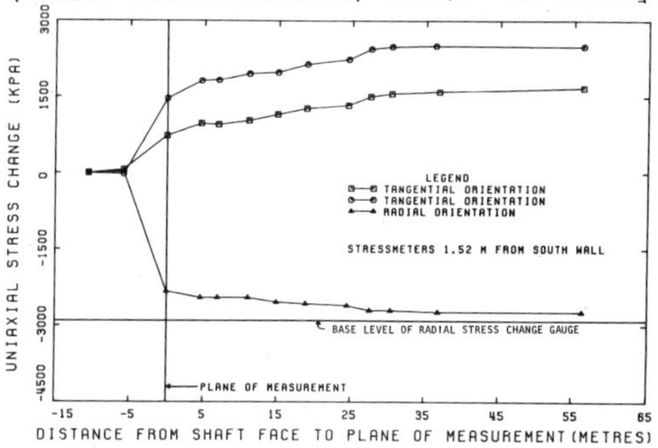

Figure 7 Uniaxial stress change at 1.52 m from shaft wall (152 m depth)

Table I. Radial and tangential rock stress change

Instrument Location	South r=4.31m	South r=5.47m	West r=4.16m
Radial Stress Change:			
a) ahead of face	85%	76%	74%
b) before liner installed at about 10 m	90%	87%	78%
Tangential Stress Change:			
a) ahead of face	42% 59%	72%	43%
b) before liner installed at about 10 m	63% 79%	78%	50%

78% of the radial rock stress change but only 54% of the tangential rock stress change occurred ahead of the shaft bottom while on average 85% radial and 68% tangential stress change was observed before liner installation. Accordingly, the rock stresses changed by less than 7% radially and less than 14% tangentially during the period when the rock mass deformations were recorded by extensometers installed at the face. Hence, the total accumulated rock mass displacements are approximately ten times as large as the ones measured. The stress change gauges are still being read every 2 to 3 months after more than one and a half years and the long term performance will be reported on some other occasion.

7.2 Multipoint Extensometers

Figure 8 presents data from two extensometers at the lower (180 m) level. These instruments were measured for the first 57 and 70 hours after installation until the liner was poured. If it can be assumed that the rate of rock mass stress change at this elevation is comparable to the one observed at 152 m depth, then the measured displacements only reflect 7 to 14% of the total displacements. The magnitude of the displacement measured at the north wall extensometer is very small at depth and close to the measuring accuracy. Nevertheless, the non-symmetric response suggests that the rock mass is anisotropic or that unequal horizontal stresses exist. It is also evident from the rapid increase in displacements near the shaft wall that loosening of a blast damaged zone of less than 0.75 m in thickness causes increased movements near the shaft surface particularly in the area where little radial rock mass straining is recorded at depth (North wall).

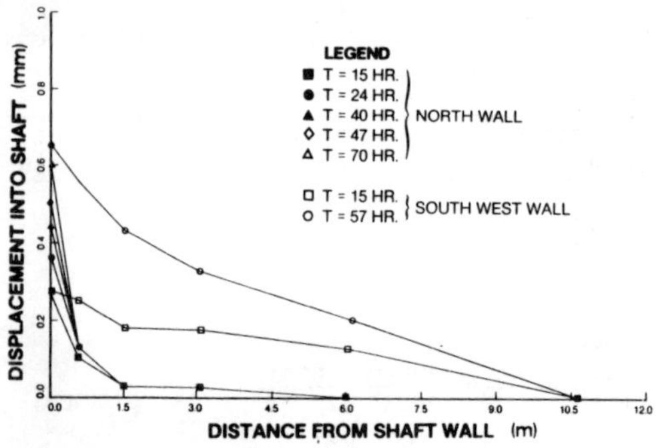

Figure 8 Extensometer readings from two sets at 180 m depth

At the upper level (111 m) the extensometers responded more evenly with about twice as much recorded movement. We believe that this increased movement is related to a difference in the total rock mass stress change that occurred during the measuring period (possibly resulting from less blast related rock damage of higher quality rock ahead of the face or less stress-shielding b the lining).

Long-term measurement showed about 0.5 mm of extensional displacement near the shaft wall between 0 and 250 hrs after pouring of the concrete liner. This movement corresponds to the predicted radial displacement caused by shrinkage of the concrete liner.

7.3 Straining of the Concrete Liner

The locations of the embedment gauges are shown in Figure 4 for the 152 m level but the same configuration was used for all other levels. On average, zero straining or even extensional straining was observed at all but the lowest instrumented ring at 180 m depth. Accordingly, no support pressure was recorded up to a depth between 152 and 180 m. The measurements at the 180 m level are summarized in Figure 9 for all 8 gauges (compression negative). If a concrete modulus of E_C = 30 GPa is assumed, the ultimate tangential compressive stresses vary between a minimum of 0.9 MPa and a maximum of 6.7 MPa. The strain distribution again indicates that the liner must be loaded unequally resulting in bending stresses which reduce the hoop stresses on the outside, at the north and south measuring points, and inside at the gauges on the east and west wall. Opposite but consistent behaviour is observed at the other gauges. The trend of the maximum load must be east-west or close to it. This corresponds well with the principal stress direction predicted from the regional field stress study summarized in Section 4.

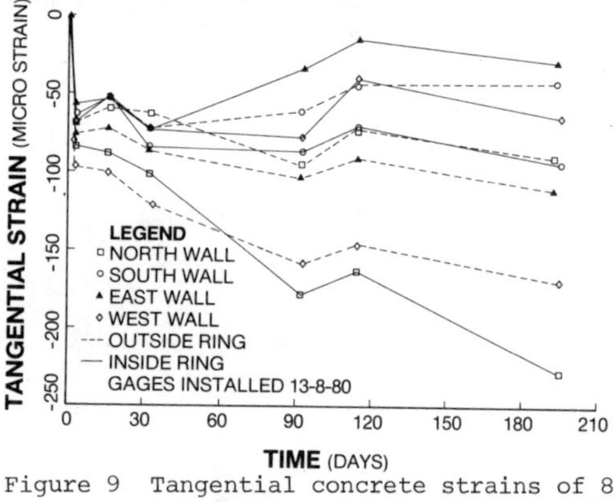

Figure 9 Tangential concrete strains of 8 embedment gauges at 180 m depth

Because the piezometers did not measure any water pressure at the upper two levels, it is reasonable to assume that the lining stresses result exclusively from rock pressure.

8 INTERPRETATION OF MEASUREMENTS TO DETERMINE THE *IN SITU* STRESS FIELD

For the initial evaluation of the measurements presented here it was assumed that the rock mass behaves like an isotropic, elastic continuum. The existence of a blast-damaged rock zone near the wall of the shaft was considered by increasing the opening size slightly and effectively assuming that the damaged rock contributes little to the rock support except transmitting radial liner pressure after sufficient compaction has resulted during wall convergence. By variation of the three stress parameters, magnitude and orientation of the maximum principal stress as well as principal horizontal stress ratio N, the best fit stress field was determined from the stress change gauges (Pariseau, 1978), from the extensometers and from the concrete embedment gauges.

8.1 Stress Change Gauges at 152 m

The least scatter of results was achieved if the tangential stress change data was considered independent of the radial stress change data. Reasonably good data with little orientation dependence could be fitted as long as the principal stress direction was east-west, plus or minus 25°. It was found that, for these stress directions, the horizontal stress ratio N could vary widely between 1.0 and 0.5 without causing significant variations in magnitude of the major principal stress. The major principal stress calculated from measurements taken after 55 m shaft advance was 5.28 MPa ± 0.75 MPa. Assumption of a blast damaged zone of 0.3 to 0.5 m depth, considered to be reasonable, resulted in a reduction of this stress by approximately 20% to 4.25 ± 0.6 MPa. With a vertical stress equal to the overburden stress of 3.6 MPa the stress ratio is equal to $K_o(max) = 1.18 \pm 0.17$. The horizontal stress ratio N could not be determined conclusively, but if it is assumed that the regional field stress condition prevails with $K_o(min) = 0.8$, N would be 0.68 ± 0.09.

Fitting of measurements from the radial stress change gauges was less successful with standard deviations in excess of ±30%. Best fit was reached for N=1 with an average principal stress of 6.75 MPa or 5.35 MPa if a blast damaged zone was considered. The resulting uniform K_o of between 1.49 and 1.88 appears to be too high, particularly for stresses in the NW-SE direction. The results of these radial gauges were disregarded even though no definite explanation for their unexpected behaviour could be found. It should be pointed out, however, that only three radial stress gauges were installed and that malfunctioning of one gauge would significantly distort the results.

Figure 10 shows the predicted stress change distribution for N = 0.6, a maximum field stress (called SIGMA-H(MAX)) of 4.25 MPa (east-west) and 0.3 m blast damage zone. The observed stress changes, normalized to the assumed maximum field stress, are shown on the same figure for comparison. Excellent agreement can be observed for three of the four tangential gauges. Excessive radial stress change was observed on the south wall whereas insufficient radial stress change was recorded on the west wall. Nevertheless, we believe that the assumed parameters are reasonable because of their consistency with other instrument records.

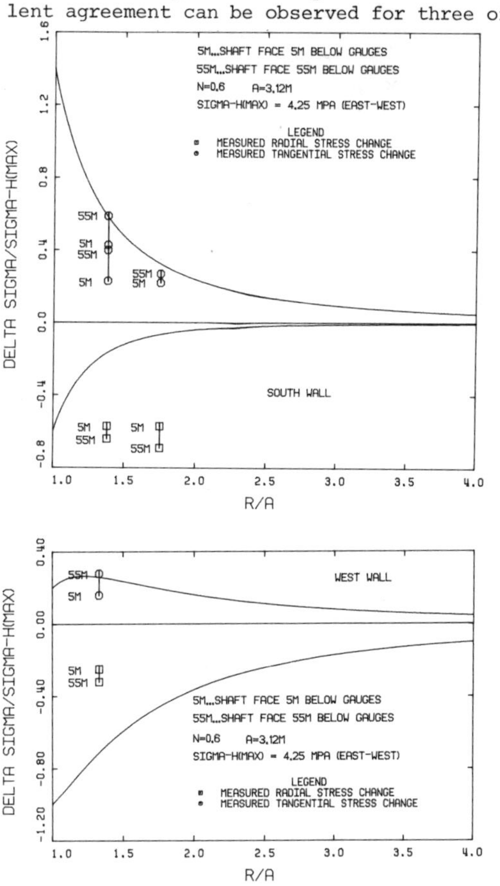

Figure 10 Predicted and measured stress change distribution at 152 m depth; shaft radius A was increased by 0.3 m to account for blast damage effect.

8.2 Multi-point Extensometers

The extremely low strains recorded at the north-extensometer at the 180 m level

(Fig. 8) is indicative of either little stress change during the measuring period, high deformation modulus or unequal horizontal stresses. Variation of the stress field parameters for best fit converged on a principal, horizontal stress ratio of about N=0.6 (S80°W to S70°W). The predicted and measured displacement, determined according to Kruse (1970) and adjusted for zero relative movement at the extreme anchor is shown on Figure 11. The measured displacements are plotted on this normalized graph by assuming E = 1.5 GPa and that 15% of the stress change occurred during the measuring period. Reasonable agreement between observations and prediction confirms the selected parameters. The effect of near surface loosening can be detected clearly from this figure. It is of interest to note that major loosening only occurs at the north wall where higher tangential stresses exist according to the inferred stress field. This nonsymmetric loosening may explain the excessive radial stress drop measured near the south wall.

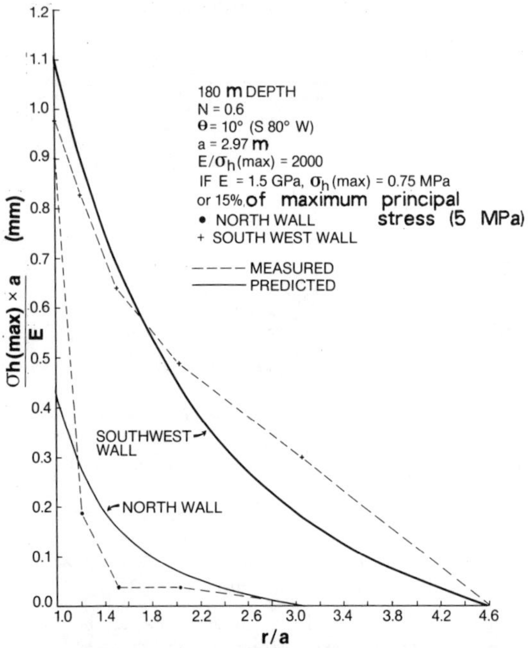

Figure 11 Predicted and measured rock displacements at 180 m depth.

8.3 Lining Strain Measurements

As indicated earlier the strain distribution measured at the 180 m level (Figure 9) shows that the liner must be loaded by unequal horizontal loads. Figure 12 presents the predicted tangential strain distribution calculated for the no-slip case by the relative stiffness method (Einstein and Schwartz, 1979) as a function of the orientation of the minimum principal stress for N=0.6. The concrete strains were divided by a percentage (M) of the assumed maximum horizontal field stress of 5.0 MPa for this presentation. The five curves correspond to the predicted strains at the liner surface (inside and outside wall), at the center of the liner, and at the assumed location of the embedment gauges (inside and outside ring). A concrete modulus of 30 GPa and M=100% was assumed to plot the predicted strains per unit maximum field stress. The total tangential stress change recorded after liner installation at the 152 m level was on average 32% (Table I). For the presentation of the strains measured at the 180 m level after 200 days it was assumed that 29% of the maximum field stress was experienced by the liner (M=29%). The measured strains are plotted for a range of maximum principal stress orientations between S90°W and S70°W, hence θ=0° to 20° for the north and south wall and θ=70° to 90° for the east and west wall.

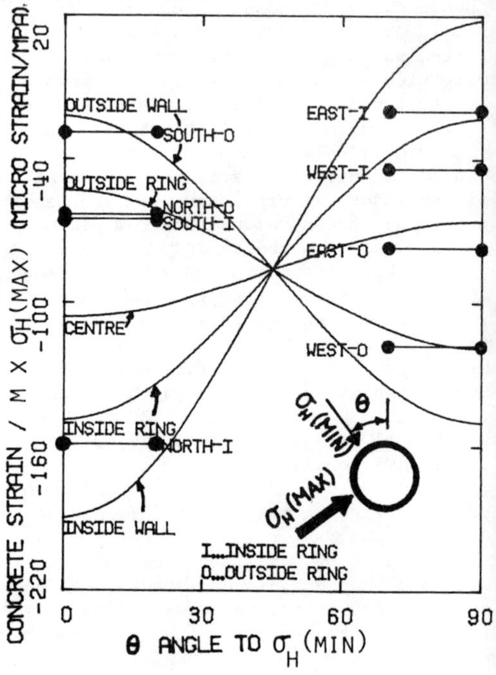

Figure 12 Predicted and measured concrete strains at 180 m depth; assuming N=0.6.

Best agreement is possible for a major principal stress oriented east-west ±20° because of the small curvature in the predicted strain curves. Some scatter of data must be expected because of variable liner thickness due to overbreak and variable concrete modulus. Considering the effect of these parameters, it can be seen from Figure 12 that almost all recorded strains are close to the predicted. There is only one exception, the south-inside gauge.

8.4 Summary

The interpretation of the various types of instruments installed from the shaft indicates that the local stress field is consistent with the regional stress field, that the major principal stress is in the order of 1.2 times the overburden pressure, approximately oriented S70°(±20)W, and that the most likely horizontal stress ratio N is 0.65 ± 0.1. The assumption of elastic rock mass response seems adequate for this site.

9. CONCLUDING REMARKS

The space provided for this paper does not permit presentation of a more complete interpretation of this data for the evaluation of the liner performance and to discuss optimal support design based on the field observations. It is, however, of interest to note that the described instrumentation program provides all necessary information to use the convergence-confinement method for such a design.

Figure 13 shows the schematic ground-convergence and support-action curves for the ground condition observed at the Kipp Mine and for a point on the north or south and east or west wall. The maximum and minimum horizontal stress can be determined from the under-excavation of the rock stress change gauges. The ground-convergence curve can be predicted from the deformations determined from the extensometers and by checking with the laboratory test data. The rock stress change gauges can be used to find the convergence ahead of the face and before the liner installation point. The convergence due to loosening and shrinkage is measured by the extensometers and the liner stress can be predicted by calculating the support interaction point or by determination from the measurements of the concrete embedment gauges. The Factor of Safety of the support can then be calculated by comparison of the liner capacity and the actual liner stresses. For the concrete liner used at the 180 m level the calculated Factor of Safety against localized yielding is in excess of 5 as long as no water pressure build-up or longterm creep results in additional loading of the liner. A thin shotcrete cylinder of less than 10 cm in thickness would theoretically be sufficient to support the rock if it was installed at the same distance, two shaft diameters, from the shaft bottom.

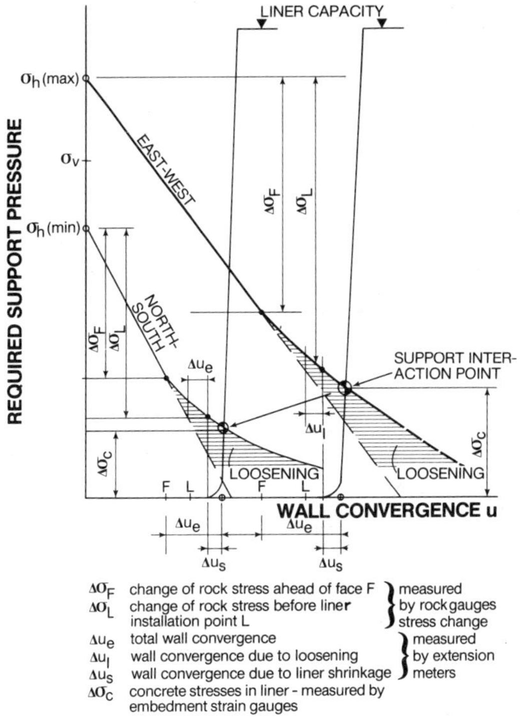

Figure 13 Schematic convergence-confinement diagram

This case history illustrates the usefulness of the combination of rock stress change and rock displacement measurements. Only consideration of all components of the described instrumentation program provided sufficient information to determine the ground-support interaction relationship. The value of extensometer or convergence measurements can be greatly increased if they can be related to stress change measurements.

10. ACKNOWLEDGEMENTS

This research project has been funded through a research contract with Petro Canada Exploration Inc., Calgary, and was supplemented by funds from the National Sciences and Engineering Research Council of Canada. The execution of the field instrumentation program was successful because of the excellent cooperation of the employees of Thyssen Mining Construction of Canada Ltd. and because of the dedication of our senior technician, G. Cyre.

11. REFERENCES

Byrne, P.J.S. and R.N. Farvolden, 1959. Clay Mineralogy and Chemistry of the Bearpaw Formation of Southern Alberta, Alberta Research Council, Bulletin, No. 4, 44 pp.

Crawford, I.D., 1947. The Geology and Structure of the Lethbridge Coal Field. M.Sc. Thesis, Department of Geology, University of Alberta, Edmonton, Alberta, 133 p.

Einstein, H.H. and C.W. Schwartz, 1979. Simplified Analysis for Tunnel Supports, J. Geotechnical Engineering Division, ASCE Proceedings, Vol. 105, GT4, pp. 499-518.

Gough, D.I. and T.S. Bell, 1981. Stress Orientations from Oil-Well Fractures in Alberta and Texas. Canadian Journal of Earth Science, Vol. 18, pp. 635-645.

Kaiser, P.K. and D.E. Hutchinson, 1982. Effects of Construction Procedures on Tunnel Performance. 4th Int. Conf. Numerical Methods in Geomechanics, Edmonton, (in press).

Kruse, G.H., 1970. Deformability of Rock Structures, California State Water Project. Determination of the *In-Situ* Modulus of Deformation of Rock, ASTM STP 477, Am. Soc. Testing and Materials, pp. 58-88.

McCrossan, R.G. and R.P. Glaister, Editors, 1966. Geological History of Western Canada, Alberta Society of Petroleum Geologists, 2nd Ed., 232 pp.

Pariseau, W.G., 1978. A Note on Monitoring Stress Changes *In Situ*. Int. J. Rock Mechanics and Mining Sciences & Geomechanics Abstracts, Vol. 15, No. 4, pp. 161-166.

Russell, L.S. and R.W. Landes, 1940. Geology of the Southern Alberta Plains, Geological Survey of Canada, Memoir 221, 223 pp.

Scott, J.S. and E.W. Brooker, 1968. Geological and Engineering Aspects of Upper Cretaceous Shales in Western Canada, G.S.C. Paper 66-37, 75 p.

ZUR SPANNUNGSERMITTLUNG IN SCHACHTAUSKLEIDUNGEN BEI VERBUNDAUSBAU

Evaluation of stresses in linings of shafts in composite constructions

Détermination des contraintes dans les soutènements des puits des constructions composites

JOACHIM KLEIN

Bergbau-Forschung GmbH, Essen, Bundesrepublik Deutschland

SUMMARY:
Nowadays the lining of shafts in coal mining is built in reinforced concrete for water bearing non-stable stratum. For great depth often a steel / reinforced concrete composite construction method is used. The non-rock connected shaft lining is predominantly loaded by the hydrostatic outside pressure of the asphalt mass in the gliding joint. In the following report especially the different stress distributions in the composite section are shown as a function of idealization (plane stress or plane strain) of the static system. The shaft lining stress analysis for concentric rings is set against the simplified n-calculation with ideal cross-section including remarks for further design. Although it is not a pressure shaft in geomechanical terminology, the result and its interpretation is also representative with vice versa sign of pressure direction. By extension with additional concentric rings the non-rock connected shaft lining may be transformed in a hollow cylinder bedded in elastic continuum.

ZUSAMMENFASSUNG:
Die tragende Auskleidung von Schächten im Bergbau in nichtstandfestem wasserführender Deckgebirge erfolgt heutzutage in Stahlbeton. Bei grossen Teufen wird oftmals ein Stahl-/Stahlbetonverbundausbau gewählt. Der vom Gebirge getrennte Schachtausbau wird im wesentlichen durch des hydrostatischen Aussendruck der Asphaltgleitfuge belastet. In dem vorgestellten Beitrag wird insbesondere der unterschiedliche Spannungsverlauf im Verbundquerschnitt in Abhängigkeit von der Idealisierung des statischen Systems (ebener Spannungszustand oder ebener Verzerrungszustand) dargestellt. Hierbei wird die Schachtauskleidungsberechnung nach dem System der konzentrischen Ringe der vereinfachten Berechnung mit dem ideellen Querschnitt (n-Verfahren) gegenübergestellt und Hinweise zur weiteren Bemessung gegeben. Wenngleich es sich nicht um einen Druckschacht in geomechanischer Terminologie handelt, ist das Ergebnis und seine Interpretation auch bei umgekehrtem Vorzeichen der Druckrichtung repräsentativ. Durch Erweiterung mit zusätzlichen konzentrischen Ringen lässt sich der nicht gebirgsverbundene Schachtausbau in einen, im elastischen Kontinuum gebetteten, Hohlzylinder überführen.

RÉSUMÉ:
Le revêtement portant des puits dans l'exploration des mines dans un terrain de recouvrement aquifère non-stable se fait de nos jours en béton armé. Dans les grandes profondeurs, une construction composite en acier-/béton armé est souvent choisie. Le puits aménagé, qui est séparé du terrain, est chargé principalement par la pression hydrostatique externe du joint glissant en asphalt. Cet exposé présente notamment l'orientation des contraintes dans la section transversale de la construction composite en fonction de l'idéalisation du système statique (état de contraintes plan et état de déformation plan). Avec cela, le calcul du revêtement du puits d'après le système des anneaux concentriques du calcul simplifié est comparé à la section transversale idéale (Procédé-n) et des indications pour la suite du dimensionnement sont données. Même s'il ne s'agit pas, dans la terminologie géomécanique, d'un puits sous pression, le résultat est représentatif, son interprétation, même dans le cas de signes renversés de la direction de la pression, l'est aussi. Par un élargissement au moyen d'anneaux concentriques additionnels, le puits aménagé lequel est détaché du terrain, peut être transformé en un cylindre creux reposant sur un milieu élastique.

Die Auskleidung von Schächten des Steinkohlenbergbaus im nicht standfesten wasserführenden Gebirge erfolgt heutzutage in Stahlbeton. Hierbei sind nicht nur die Richtlinien (1) teilweise an Hochbaunormen orientiert, sondern auch die Bauverfahrenstechnik dem Bauwesen entsprechend. Die vorab im Gefrierverfahren geteuften Schächte werden durch den Einbau einer Asphaltgleitschicht insbesondere gegen spätere Abbaueinwirkungen flexibel gehalten. Ein dünner Stahlblechmantel zwischen Stahlbetonausbau und Gleitschicht sorgt für die Dichtigkeit des Systems. Der innen liegende bewehrte Betonring dient je nach Ausbildung der statischen Aufnahme von Wasser- und Gebirgsdrucklasten. Bei flachen Schächten reicht die Stahlbetonauskleidung gegen die anstehenden Lasten in der Regel aus, während bei großen Teufen zusätzlich ein innerer tragender Stahlmantel eingebracht wird. Man spricht bei entsprechender Schubsicherung von einem Verbundausbau, wobei es gilt, die spezifischen Trageigenschaften der verwendeten Materialien am Gesamttragverhalten zu berücksichtigen.

1. EINLEITENDE BETRACHTUNGEN

Die Festlegung der notwendigen Wanddicken erfolgt in der statischen Berechnung nach (1) unter Ansatz gewisser Belastungsannahmen. Wesentlich ist der Hauptspannungszustand im System, der sich unter gleichförmigem Horizontaldruck einstellt. Wie sich zeigen läßt (Bild 1), ist der Anteil des ungleichförmigen Horizontaldrucks spannungsmäßig für dickwandige Hohlzylinder von untergeordneter Bedeutung, da nur bis 10 % des gleichförmigen Außendrucks berücksichtigt werden. Gleichsam verlieren die Spannungsformeln bei $p_1 > 0.1\ p_o$ bedingt durch die in (2) gemachten Linearisierungen ihre Berechtigung. In den nachstehenden Untersuchungen wird ausschließlich ein gleichförmiger Außendruck in Rechnung gestellt.

Insbesondere die Tangential- oder auch Umfangsspannung genannt ist ihrer Größe nach für die Dimensionierung des Schachtausbaus von

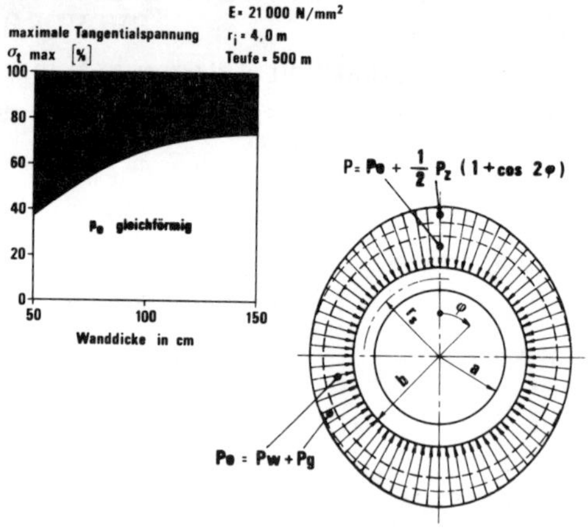

Bild 1: Belastungsannahmen

Wichtigkeit. Gemäß (1) wird sie mit

$$\sigma_t = -\frac{p_o\ r_a}{F}\ (1 + \frac{y}{r_s}) \qquad (1)$$

linearisiert angegeben und ergibt einen im Querschnitt vom Innen- zum Außenrand geradlinig abfallenden Spannungsverlauf. Für dünnwandige Ausbauzylinder im Verhältnis $\frac{b}{a} < 1.2$ ist dies sachgerecht, bei dickwandigen Hohlzylindern zeigt der in Wirklichkeit parabolische Kurvenverlauf an der Außenseite höhere Randspannungen. Bei tiefen Schächten mit Verhältnissen des Außendurchmessers zum lichten Innendurchmesser von z.B. 8,40 m/6.00 m = 1.4 > 1.2 werden die nach Gleichung 1 ermittelten Spannungen am Außenrand unterschätzt. Bei derart dicken Wänden verlieren die in (2) gemachten stabilitätstheoretischen Überlegungen gegenüber festigkeitsmechanischen Aspekten an Bedeutung.

Ähnliches gilt auch für die Beschreibung der ideellen Querschnittsfläche des Verbundausbaus. Mehrheitlich wird das n-Verfahren zur Bestimmung der in Stahl und Beton vorherrschenden Spannungen angewandt. Hierbei wird davon ausgegangen, daß das Hooke'sche Gesetz im Bereich der Gebrauchsspannungen für alle Materialien gültig sei. Diese lineare Beziehung nimmt für den Stahl bekanntlich folgende Form an.

$$\sigma_e = E_e \quad \varepsilon_e \tag{2}$$

Darin ist σ_e die Stahlspannung ε_e die zugehörige Stahldehnung, E_e der Elastizitätsmodul des Stahls. Nimmt man ebenfalls für den Beton im rissefreien Zustand (Spannungszustand I) linear-elastisches Verhalten an, dann gilt für den Verbund, (da an der Berührungsfläche die Dehnungen des Stahls überall gleich den Dehnungen des umgebenden Betons sein müssen)

$$\varepsilon_e = \varepsilon_b \tag{3}$$

oder gemäß Gleichung (2)

$$\sigma_e = n \cdot \sigma_b \tag{4}$$

wenn die dimensionslose Zahl

$$n = \frac{E_e}{E_b} \tag{5}$$

eingeführt wird. Die Formel 4 sagt aus, daß die Stahlspannungen an irgendeiner Stelle des Querschnitts beim Spannungszustand I aus den in Richtung der Stahleinlagen verlaufenden Betonspannungen der gleichen Faser bestimmt werden können. Demnach braucht man bei Anwendung dieser Verfahren die Aufmerksamkeit im wesentlichen nur noch den Betonspannungen zu widmen (die Stahlspannungen lassen sich leicht durch Multiplikation mit n im Querschnittsniveau ermitteln).

Die Richtlinien zur Berechnung von Schachtauskleidungen in nicht standfestem Gebirge (1) geben für den Spannungsnachweis unterschiedliche E-Modulverhältnisse zwischen 7 und 15 an. Streng genommen ist die Spannungsermittlung nach dem n-Verfahren nur für eindimensionale statische Systeme gültig; Schachtauskleidungen sind jedoch mehrdimensionale Systeme. Zwar wird sinnvollerweise das Kontinuum durch ein zweidimensionales Problem idealisiert, doch der in Wirklichkeit dreiachsige Spannungszustand ist davon nicht berührt. Bei mehrdimensionalen Strukturen spielt nämlich neben dem Elastizitätsmodul auch das Verhältnis der Dehnung zur Querkürzung eine wesentliche Rolle. Die hieraus korrelierende Poisson'sche Konstante m ist

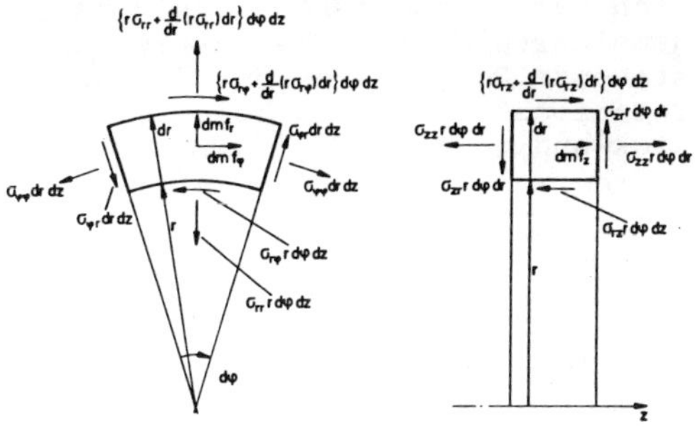

Bild 2: Gleichgewichtsbedingungen

ebenfalls eine werkstoffabhängige Zahl und liegt für Metalle im allgemeinen zwischen 3 und 4, bei Beton ist 6 oder 10 gebräuchlich. Häufiger wird noch der Reziprokwert von m, die Poissonzahl oder die Querdehnungszahl $\nu = 1/m$ gebraucht. Es ist erkennbar, daß eine andere Proportionalität zwischen den Querdehnungszahlen von Stahl und Beton als bei den E-Moduli vorliegt; dies ist insbesondere für die ebene Idealisierung bei Verbundausbauten bedeutsam.

2. SPANNUNGSANALYSE VON VERBUNDAUSBAUTEN

Bei ebenen axialsymmetrischen Problemen der Elasto-Statik sind die zu betrachtenden Spannungs- und Verzerrungszustände, zu deren Beschreibung (3) vorteilhaft Zylinderkoordinaten benutzt werden, voraussetzungsgemäß unabhängig von ϕ und z. Unter Beachtung dieser Bedingung ergeben sich die Gleichgewichtsbedingungen der an einem Volumenelement (Bild 2) angreifenden Kräfte wie folgt:

$$\frac{1}{r}\frac{d}{dr}(r\,\sigma_{rr}) - \frac{1}{r}\sigma_{\phi\phi} + \rho f_r = 0 \tag{6}$$

$$\frac{1}{r}\frac{d}{dr}(r\,\sigma_{r\phi}) + \frac{1}{r}\sigma_{r\phi} + \rho f_\phi = 0 \tag{7}$$

$$\frac{1}{r}\frac{d}{dr}(r\,\sigma_{rz}) + \rho f_z = 0 \tag{8}$$

Mit den Beziehungen zwischen den Verschiebungen und den Verzerrungen eines Körperelements ergeben sich nach Einsetzen in das verallgemeinerte Hooke'sche Gesetz nachstehende Formänderungen für das rotationssymmetrisch belastete dickwandige Rohr:

$$\varepsilon_{rr} = \frac{du_r}{dr} = \frac{1}{E}\left(\sigma_{rr} - \nu\,(\sigma_{\phi\phi} + \sigma_{zz})\right) + \alpha\,(T - T_o) \tag{9}$$

$$\varepsilon_{\phi\phi} = \frac{u_r}{r} = \frac{1}{E}\left(\sigma_{\phi\phi} - \nu\,(\sigma_{zz} + \sigma_{rr})\right) + \alpha\,(T - T_o) \tag{10}$$

$$\varepsilon_{zz} = c = \frac{1}{E}\left(\sigma_{zz} - \nu\,(\sigma_{rr} + \sigma_{\phi\phi})\right) + \alpha\,(T - T_o) \tag{11}$$

Für isotherme Formänderungen, wie hier betrachtet, ist $T = T_o$. Mit den Gleichungen 6, 9, 10 und 11 ist die Problemklasse der ebenen Spannungs- ($\sigma_{zz} = o$) bzw. Verzerrungszustände ($c = o$) erfaßt.

Die vordergründige Frage, ob das System der Schachtauskleidung als ebenes Spannungs- oder Verzerrungsproblem zu betrachten ist, hängt in erster Linie von der konstruktiven Ausbildung ab. Beim ebenen Spannungszustand wirken bekanntlich alle auftretenden Spannungen in den Querschnittsebenen des langgestreckten Bauwerkes, aber senkrecht zu den Querschnittsebenen werden keine Spannungen übertragen. Dieser Spannungszustand kann auftreten, wenn senkrecht zur Schachtachse verlaufene offene Ringfugen die Kontinuität der Auskleidung und damit eine Spannungsübertragung in der Längsrichtung verhindern. Beim ebenen Verzerrungszustand erfolgen alle Verschiebungen in einer Schachtebene. Um diesen Zustand zu erzwingen, sind senkrecht zu den Querschnittsebenen Spannungen notwendig, und es liegt ein dreiachsiger Spannungszustand vor. Wenngleich keine der beiden Idealisierungen dem wahren mehraxialen Spannungszustand vollends gerecht werden, scheint für den längskontinuierlichen Verbundausbau der ebene Verzerrungszustand zutreffender. Parallel dazu werden nachstehend die Ergebnisse für den ebenen Spannungszustand diskutiert. Daß die Spannungen, die senkrecht zu den Querschnittsebenen wirken, wie in (4) geschrieben, meist nicht von Interesse sind, dem kann generell nicht zugestimmt werden. Vielmehr nimmt gerade die mittlere Hauptspannung im Hinblick auf das bruchmechanische Verhalten und somit auch auf die Bemessung überhaupt, eine besondere Rolle ein. Diesbezügliche Hinweise werden in der Schlußbetrachtung noch gegeben. Richtig ist, daß oftmals nur der Einfachheit halber der ebene Spannungszustand gewählt wird. Soweit es sich im Falle eines dickwandigen Rohres um ein System aus einem Werkstoff handelt, sind die Unterschiedlichkeiten nur in der Deformationsaussage zu finden. Bei Verbundwerkstoffen bedingt die Kompatibilität der Verformungen an den Übergangszonen verschiedener Materialien entsprechend korrelierende Spannungen. Die Herleitung der Spannungsgleichungen erfolgt beispielhaft an einem dreigliedrigen Stahl/Stahlbeton/Stahlausbau der im vollen Verbund trägt und unter Außendruck steht.

Wenngleich es sich nicht um einen Druckschacht in geomechanischer Terminologie handelt, ist das Ergebnis und seine Interpretation auch bei Innendruck gültig. Durch Erweiterung mit zusätzlichen konzentrischen Ringen, läßt sich der hier vorgestellte gleitende Schachtausbau in einen im elastischen Kontinuum gebirgsverbundenen überführen.

Im Fall des ebenen Verzerrungszustandes ($\varepsilon_{zr} = \varepsilon_{z\phi} = \varepsilon_{zz} = o$) gelte also:

1.) Gerades, kreiszylindrisches Rohr konstanter Wanddicke
2.) keine volumenhaft angreifenden Kräfte $f_r = o$
3.) Randbedingungen:

$$r = r_i \;:\; \sigma_{rr} = p_o = o$$

$$r = r_3 \;:\; \sigma_{rr} = -p_3 \neq o$$

so daß aus (11) folgt

$$\sigma_{zz} = \nu\,(\sigma_{rr} + \sigma_{\phi\phi}) \tag{12}$$

Nach Einsetzen und Umformen der entsprechenden Gleichungen ergibt sich für σ_{rr} die Eulersche Differentialgleichung:

$$r^2 \frac{d^2}{dr^2} (r\sigma_{rr}) + r \frac{d}{dr} (r\sigma_{rr}) - r\sigma_{rr} = o \tag{13}$$

die mit dem bekannten Lösungsansatz

$$r \sigma_{rr} = c\, r^n \tag{14}$$

die allgemeine Lösung mit den freien Konstanten liefert:

$$\sigma_{rr} = \frac{C_1}{r^2} + C_2 \quad \text{bzw.} \quad \sigma_{\phi\phi} = -\frac{C_1}{r^2} + C_2 \tag{15}$$

Für den inneren Stahlring mit der noch unbekannten Außenlast p_1 ergeben sich folgende Spannungen und Verformungen:

$$\sigma_{rr} = -p_1 \left(\frac{1 - (\frac{r_i}{r})^2}{1 - (\frac{r_i}{r_1})^2} \right) \tag{16}$$

$$\sigma_{\phi\phi} = -p_1 \left(\frac{1 + (\frac{r_i}{r})^2}{1 - (\frac{r_i}{r_1})^2} \right) \tag{17}$$

$$u_r = \frac{r}{E_1} (-p_1) \left(\frac{1 - 2\nu_1^2 - \nu_1 + (\frac{r_i}{r})^2 (1+\nu_1)}{1 - (\frac{r_i}{r_1})^2} \right) \tag{18}$$

Die elastische Lösung für den Betonbereich in der Mitte wird von den weiterhin unbekannten Belastungen p_1 (innen) und p_2 (außen) beherrscht:

$$\sigma_{rr} = (-p_1) \frac{r_1^2}{r^2} \left(\frac{r_2^2 - r^2}{r_2^2 - r_1^2} \right) - p_2 \frac{r_2^2}{r^2} \left(\frac{r^2 - r_1^2}{r_2^2 - r_1^2} \right) \tag{19}$$

$$\sigma_{\phi\phi} = p_1 \frac{r_1^2}{r^2} \left(\frac{r_2^2 + r^2}{r_2^2 - r_1^2} \right) - p_2 \frac{r_2^2}{r^2} \left(\frac{r^2 + r_1^2}{r_2^2 - r_1^2} \right) \tag{20}$$

$$u_r = p_1 \frac{r_1^2}{E_2 (r_2^2 - r_1^2) r} \left\{ r_2^2 (1+\nu_2) + r^2 (1-\nu_2-2\nu_2^2) \right\}$$
$$- p_2 \frac{r_2^2}{E_2 (r_2^2 - r_1^2) r} \left\{ r^2 (1-\nu_2-2\nu_2^2) + r_1^2 (1+\nu_2) \right\}$$

oder verkürzt geschrieben:

$$u_{r_m} = p_1 A_m - p_2 B_m \tag{21}$$

Die letzten vier Gleichungen sind genereller Natur, d.h. für den Außenring aus Stahl oder auch weitere Ringe ergeben sich analoge Gleichungen aus 19 bis 21; es müssen nur die korrespondierenden Belastungsgrößen und Radien eingesetzt werden.

Für die Verschiebungen in den einzelnen konzentrischen Ringen gilt, allgemein:

$$u_{r_i} = p_o A_i - p_1 B_i \tag{22}$$

$$u_{r_m} = p_1 A_m - p_2 B_m \tag{23}$$

$$u_{r_a} = p_2 A_a - p_3 B_a \tag{24}$$

Die Gleichheit der Verschiebungsgrößen an den Übergängen des Verbundausbaus bedingt:

$$u_{r_i} \; (r_1 = \text{rechts}) = u_{r_m} \; (r_1 = \text{links}) \tag{25}$$

$$u_{r_m} \; (r_2 = \text{rechts}) = u_{r_a} \; (r_2 = \text{links}) \tag{26}$$

oder im Fall des Außendrucks $p_3 = p$ und ohne Innendruck $p_o = o$.

$$-p_1 B_{ir} = p_1 A_{ml} - p_2 B_{ml} \tag{27}$$

$$p_1 A_{m_r} - p_2 B_{m_r} = p_2 A_{a_l} - p B_{a_l} \tag{28}$$

Hiermit stehen 2 Bestimmungsgleichungen für die noch unbekannten Zwischendrücke p_1 und p_2 zur Verfügung, die sich errechnen zu:

$$p_1 = -p \left\{ \frac{B_{al} \cdot B_{ml}}{A_{mr} B_{ml} - A_{ml} B_{mr} - B_{ir} B_{mr} - A_{ml} A_{al} - B_{ir} A_{al}} \right\} \tag{29}$$

$$p_2 = -p \left\{ \frac{B_{al} A_{ml} + B_{al} B_{ir}}{A_{mr} B_{ml} - A_{ml} B_{mr} - B_{ir} B_{mr} - A_{ml} A_{al} - B_{ir} A_{al}} \right\} \tag{30}$$

Die Koeffizieneten A .. und B .. lassen sich durch Einsetzen der geometrischen Position und den jeweils relevanten Steifigkeitsparametern ermitteln. Für das nachstehende Beispiel wurden die Beziehungen in einem EDV-Programm auf der Siemens-Rechenanlage der Bergbau-Forschung GmbH implementiert. Neben der Berechnung des jeweiligen Spannungszustandes kann zusätzlich eine Optimierung in bezug auf die erforderlichen Wanddicken ausgeführt werden.

Der ebene Spannungszustand läßt sich durch modifizierte Materialparameter aus dem ebenen Verzerrungszustand herleiten, indem

$$\nu^* = \frac{\nu}{1+\nu} \tag{31}$$

und

$$E^* = E\,(1 - \nu^{*2}) \tag{32}$$

gesetzt wird. Da die formalen Spannungsbeziehungen der einzelnen konzentrischen dickwandigen Rohre erhalten bleiben, ändern sich für den Spannungszustand nur die Verschiebungsgleichungen für den Innenring explizit zu:

$$u_r = - \frac{p_1 r}{E_1 \left(1 - \left(\frac{r_i}{r_1}\right)^2\right)} \left\{ \left(\frac{r_i}{r}\right)^2 \left(1 + \nu_1\right) + 1 - \nu_1 \right\} \tag{33}$$

und den mittleren Ring bzw. weitere Ringe bei zyklischer Vertauschung der Indizes ergibt sich:

$$u_r = p_1 \frac{r_1^2}{E_2 (r_2^2 - r_1^2)\, r} \left\{ r_2^2 (1+\nu_2) + r^2 (1-\nu_2) \right\}$$

$$- p_2 \frac{r_2^2}{E_2 (r_2^2 - r_1^2)\, r} \left\{ r^2 (1-\nu_2) + r_1^2 (1+\nu_2) \right\} \tag{34}$$

3. BEISPIEL UND SCHLUSSBETRACHTUNG

Zur Verdeutlichung der unterschiedlichen Spannungs-Verformungsverläufe wurde die im Bild 3 dargestellte Verbundschachtauskleidung unter 1,3-fachem hydrostatischen Außendruck in 580 m Teufe berechnet. Vergleichend wird die linearisierte Berechnung mittels n-Verfahren im Bild 4 mit eingezeichnet. Das Verhältnis der Elastizitätsmoduli wird in allen Fällen konstant zu n = 10 angenommen, während die Poisson-Verhältnisse für entsprechende Baustoffe zu 0, 0.5 und 1.0 untersucht werden.

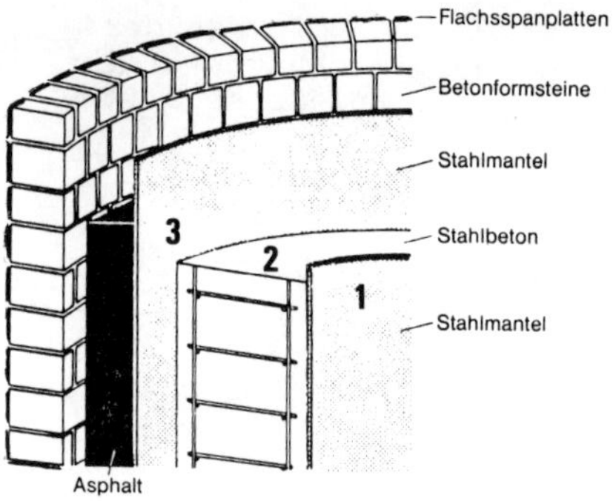

Bild 3: Schachtverbundauskleidung

Es zeigt sich, daß mit der vereinfachten Berechnung nach (1) jeweils im Außenblech rd. 5 % zu geringe Tangentialspannungen ermittelt werden; im Falle inkompressibler Materialien (Bild 4c) sich ein um 20 % hohes σ_θ ergibt. Erwartungsgemäß zeigen die Radialspannungen keine großen Differenzen in Abhängigkeit von der gewählten ebenen Idealisierung. Bei der absoluten Verschiebung erweist sich der ebene Spannungszustand als Modell mit den größeren Deformationen in der Schachtebene. Interessanterweise verhält sich die Zunahme der Radialverformung in Abhängigkeit von der Konstellation der Werkstoffparameter zonenweise unterschiedlich. Ist für die verwendeten Materialien keine Querkontraktion anzusetzen (Bild 4a) ergeben sich bekanntlich für den ebenen Spannungs- bzw. ebenen Verzerrungszustand dieselben Resultate. Dem realen Fall des Stahl-Beton-Stahl-Querschnitts kommt zweifellos der Fall (Bild 4b) am nächsten. Unterschiedliche Elastizitätsmoduli würden aber auch zu größeren Variationen in den Spannungsgrößen führen. Beachtenswert ist, daß z.B. bei Vorgabe eines Stahlquerschnitts die übrigen Abmessungen direkt von den gegebenen Materialkennwerten abhängen und zur optimalen Ausnutzung des Werkstoffes nicht mehr frei wählbar

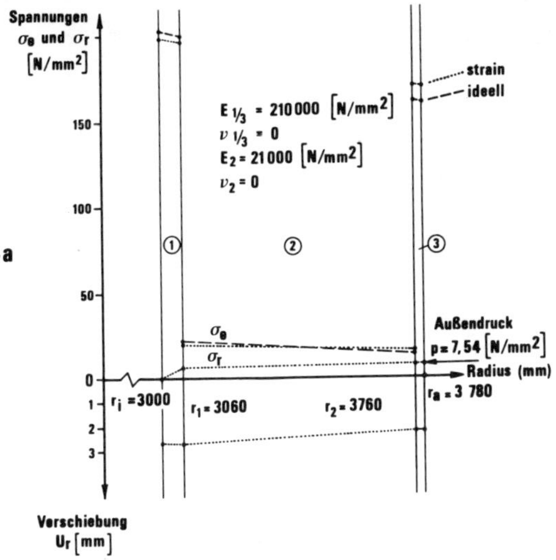

4a

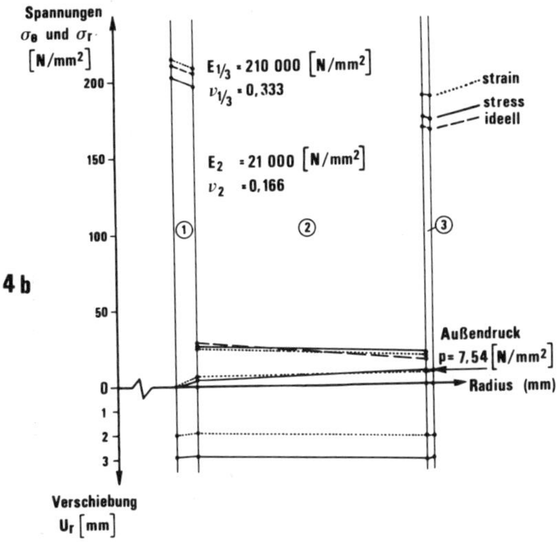

4b

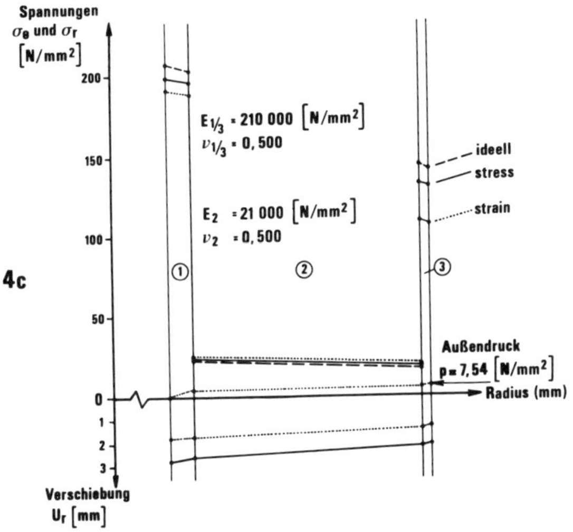

4c

sind. Mögen die Größe der Spannungsdifferenzen in diesem Fall auch nicht so bedeutsam sein, sollte sich der konstruktive Ingenieur über die qualitativen Unterschiede, die sich in Abhängigkeit von der Idealisierung und der jeweiligen Wandstärke des Systems ergeben, bewußt sein.

Insbesondere dann, wenn die Spannungsanalyse zur weiteren Bemessung herangezogen wird, spielt je nach Bruchspannungskriterium die Frage der auftretenden Spannungen eine entscheidende Rolle. Wie in (5) gezeigt, liefert die Beschreibung der Endflächen (offener oder geschlossener Hohlzylinder bzw. als ebener Verzerrungszustand), jeweils unterschiedliche Ergebnisse für die mittlere Längsspannung σ_z. Werden ausschließlich deviatorische Fließbedingungen wie z.B. das Tresca-Kriterium herangezogen, ist selbst bei unterschiedlichen Endflächenbedingungen und teilplastifizierten Rohren eine eindeutige Lösung möglich. Für Vergleichsspannungskriterien, die das gesamte Spannungstripel berücksichtigen, ergeben sich entsprechend der Endflächenhypothese unterschiedliche Fließgrenzen, wobei die Spannungsberechnung für Teilplastifizierung in der Regel numerische Lösungsalgorithmen bedingt. Mit diesen Hinweisen wird deutlich, daß für eine optimale Dimensionierung eines aus mehreren Werkstoffen bestehenden Verbundausbaus die problemgerechte Idealisierung des statischen Systems 'Schachtverbundauskleidung' von vornehmlicher Bedeutung ist.

Quellennachweis

1. Link, H., H.O. Lütgendorf und K. Stoß: Richtlinien zur Berechnung von Schachtauskleidungen in nichtstandfestem Gebirge. Essen 1976, S. 13-17

2. Link, H.: Zur Spannungsermittlung in Schachtauskleidungen. GHH Sterkrade AG 1959, Reihe Bergbau, Heft 29, S. 5-7

3. Lehmann, T.: Elemente der Mechanik II: Elastostatik. Stuttgart 1975, S. 256-263

4. Kastner, H.:
Statik des Tunnel- und Stollenbaus .
Berlin . Heidelberg . New York 1971,
S. 37-40

5. Hill, R.:
The Mathematical Theory of Plasticity.
Oxford 1950, S. 106-114

A METHOD OF DESIGNING PRESSURE TUNNEL LININGS WITH ALLOWANCE MADE FOR RHEOLOGICAL PROCESSES

Eine Entwurfsmethode für Druckstollenauskleidungen mit Berücksichtigung von rheologischen Vorgängen

Une méthode de dimensionnement des soutènements des galeries forcées par le procédé rhéologique

V.L.KUBETSKY
Civil Engineering Institute, V.V.Kuibyshev, Moscow, USSR

SUMMARY:
The paper presents a method of calculating the stress-strain state of single-layer and multilayer pressure tunnel linings subjected to inner hydrostatic pressure, with allowance made for rheological properties of rocks and materials of the lining. The method offers a possibility to easily obtain calculation formula for determination of the stress-strain state with due regard for creep of divers structures, provided there exists a corresponding elastic theory solution. Some problems pertaining to description and determination of the creep parameters of rocks and building materials are discussed as applied to calculations of pressure tunnels for inner hydrostatic pressure. It is shown that the pressure tunnel linings are advisable to build of materials having higher than usual creep.

ZUSAMMENFASSUNG:
Es wird die Berechnungsmethode des Spannungsverformungszustandes ein- und mehrschichtiger Verkleidungen von Stautunneln vorgestellt, bei der Einwirkung des inneren hydrostatischen Druckes, unter Berücksichtigung der reologischen Eigenschaften des Berggesteins und des Konstruktionsmaterials der Verkleidung. Der Lösungsweg beruht auf dem einfachen Austausch der Elastizitätskonstanten der entsprechenden Lösung nach der Elastizitätstheorie, gegen in der Zeit veränderliche Moduls. Zur Anwendung in den Berechnungen der Verkleidungen von Stautunneln auf den inneren hydrostatischen Druck, wurden Fragen zur theoretischen Beschreibung und Deffinierung der Parameter des Kriechzustandes von Berggestein und der Konstruktionsmaterialien betrachtet. Es wird angeführt, dass es sinnvoll ist, bei der Herstellung der Verkleidungen von Stautunneln, Materialien mit erhöhten Kriecheigenschaften zu verwenden.

RESUME:
On y présente la méthode de l'état de contrainte-déformation du tunnel sous l'action de la pression intérieure hydrostatique. Dans les calculs on se rend compte des propriétés réologiques des roches et des matériaux de construction de revêtement. L'application de la méthode permet d'obtenir assez simplement les fonctions pour la définition de l'état de contrainte des constructions de différents types compte tenu du phénomène de fluidité s'il existe une solution de la théorie d'élasticité. On a envisagé les problèmes de la description théorique la définition des caractéristiques de la fluidité des roches et des matériaux de construction dans le cas de la pression intérieure hydrostatique dans les tunnels. Ont fait voir la nécessité de l'utilisation des matériaux spéciaux qui possèdent une fluidité développée pour la construction des tunnels.

I. INTRODUCTION

An analysis of pressure tunnel linings behaviour has shown that their stress-strain state changes considerably with time. One of the main factors influencing the stress state of such structures is the creep of surrounding rock and concrete. Due to the fact that in designing the pressure tunnel linings there exist a possibility to take into account the bearing capacity of the surrounding rock mass, the allowance for the rheological processes is of a considerable practical importance, Kubetsky (1970). This problem is of a comples character, and to improve the reliability of the calculated stress-strain state of underground structures in question it is necessary to perfect the methods of investigating the rheological properties of rock types and materials as well as the methods of analysing the stress-strain state of the structure and the rock mass with due regard for the rheological processes.

2. RHEOLOGICAL PROPERTIES OF ROCKS.

Construction of an underground structures leads to essential changes of the original natural stress state of the rock massif. As a result in different areas of the massif surrounding the structure a complex stress state arises, which is characterized by the Nadai-Lode parameter, μ_σ, ranging from -I to +I:

$$\mu_\sigma = \frac{2\sigma_2 - \sigma_1 - \sigma_3}{\sigma_1 - \sigma_3} \qquad \text{(I)}$$

where $\sigma_1 > \sigma_2 > \sigma_3$ - principal stresses.

Available experimental data show that in general the rheological properties of rocks are significantly influenced by the mode of the stress state and its intensity. Hence, in calculating the stress-strain state of underground structures it is necessary to observe the condition of correspondence of the stress-state mode, which is taken into account in determining the mechanical properties of the rock mass, to the stress state arising in the rock mass as a result of its joint work with the underground structure.

In this connection it is necessary to carry out a sufficiently complete investigation of the rheological properties of rock subjected to stresses of different modes. The problem is complicated by the fact, that in many cases it is practically impossible to prepare and test a representative specimen using standard three-axial instruments because of the natural heterogeneity and fissuredness of the rocks.

A new method is suggested which makes it possible to investigate regularities of the rheological properties of fissured and heterogeneous rocks in their natural condition subjected to stresses of different modes. In essence the method approaches the potentialities of three-axial tests. It is based on applying to a rock massif or monolith of a ring load which may be normal tensile or compressive, or tangential one. The investigations are carried out at different stress states characterized by the parameter, μ_σ, ranging from +I to -I; this gives a possibility to solve many problems pertaining to the field of underground construction. The theoretical and experimental substantiations of the method are given in the papers by Kubetsky (1978, 1980, 1981), Kubetsky, Kozionov (1981).

In the majority of practical cases the pressure tunnels are of axisymmetric shape, and their loading with an inner hydrostatic pressure takes place after complete stabilization in time of the stress-strain state of the surrounding rock mass disturbed by the construction of the tunnel. Thus, using the principle of independence of action of forces, it is possible to consider the stress state of the rock massif and the lining, and its changes in time, as a result of action of the inner hydrostatic pressure only. An analysis of the additional stress state in the rock massif caused by the inner hydrostatic pressure has shown that this is characterized by the parameter μ_σ =0, which corresponds to a condition approximating pure shear. Thus, for the purpose of designing the pressure tunnel linings for an inner pressure it is necessary, when determining the rheological properties of the rocks, to carry out tests at stress states characterized by the parameter μ_σ =0. With a sufficient accuracy such stress state can be obtained by applying a ring tangential load to the surface of the rock massif.

An analysis of data obtained from investigations of the rheological properties of different rocks at stress states characterized by the parameter μ_σ =0 has

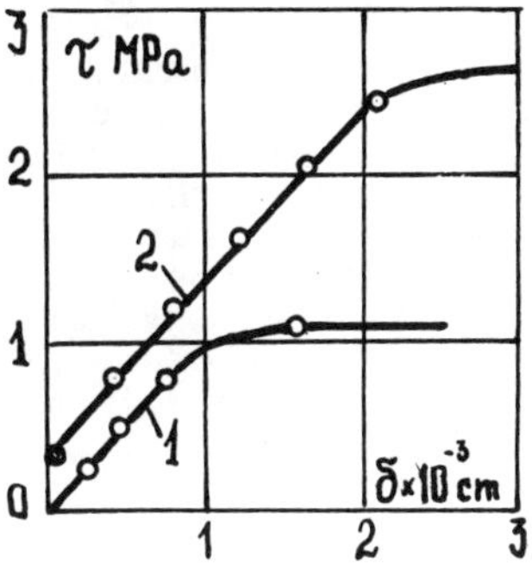

Fig.I.Dependence of horizontal displacements of the rock mass surface, δ, on value of the mean tangential stress,
I - Mudstone, 2 - Tuff.

shown that, in general, the dependence between stresses and strains is of a non-linear character for different moments of time (Fig.I).

However, if the level of stresses is lower than the long-term strength limit, the deformation of rocks with time is of a damping character, thus, with a sufficient accuracy, the creep process may be described with the aid of the Boltzman-Volterra theory of hereditary creep, the Volterra operator characterizing creep deformation of the rock subjected to pure shear being obtained from the formula

$$G_t^{-1}\{Y(t)\} = G_o\left[Y(t) + \int_o^t L(t-t_o)\, Y(t_o)\, dt_o\right] \quad (2)$$

where G_t - time operator; $Y(t)$ - given function of co-ordinates and time; G_o - arbitrary instantaneous shear modulus; t - time.

An analysis of experimental data, Kubetsky, Kozionov (1980), has shown that a good correspondence to the experimental data is achieved by approximating the creep kernel, $L(t - t_o)$, with the aid of the following relation:

$$L(t-t_o)=\lambda_\tau \theta_\tau G_o \cdot e^{-\lambda_\tau(t-t_o)} + A\, T_\tau\left[T_\tau + (t-t_o)\right]^{-2} \quad (3)$$

where λ_τ, θ_τ, T_τ - creep parameters; G_∞ -shear modulus at $t \rightarrow \infty$;

$A = G_o G_\infty^{-1} - G_o \theta - 1$

The creep parameters of the investigated rock types at the stress state characterized by the parameter μ_σ =0 are given in Table I.

Creep parameters of a number of rocks determined with the use of data obtained by field plate tests, are given in the paper by Kubetsky (1979).

As it will be shown in the following, when solving a certain class of problems, relation (2) can be simplified as follows:

$$G'_t = G_o(1 + l_t)^{-1} \quad (4)$$

$$l_t = G_o\, \theta_\tau\, (1 - e^{-\lambda_\tau t}) + A\, t\, (T_\tau + t)^{-1} \quad (5)$$

where G'_t -shear modulus varying with time.

In the paper by Kubetsky (1973) it was shown that, with a sufficient for practical purposes accuracy, when determining the stress-strain states of the pressure tunnel linings, with allowance made for creep, the Poisson's ratio, ν, for the surrounding rock massif may be considered constant in time. Under this condition the relation between the operators of the deformation modulus, D_t, and the shear modulus may be described as wollows:

$$D_t^{-1}\{Y(t)\} = \left[2(1+\nu)\, G_t\right]^{-1} \left[Y(t) + \int_o^t L(t-t_o)\, Y(t_o)\, dt_o\right] \quad (6)$$

or in a simplified form -

$$D'_t = 2(1+\nu)\, G'_t \quad (7)$$

where D'_t -deformation modulus varying in time.

Table I. Greep Parameters.

Rock	Limestone	Tuff	Marl	Mudstone
$\Delta\tau$ MPa	0.25-1.25	0-1.5	0.25-0.80	0.25-0.75
G_o 10^3MPa	2.4	2.7	0.40	1.09
G_∞ 10^3MPa	1.3	1.2	0.10	0.49
λ_τ Day^{-1}	60	38	53	36
θ_τ 10^{-5}MPa	9.7	11	9.2	33.5
T Day	0.39	0.4	0.87	0.46

$\Delta\tau$ -interval of action of the tangential stress at which creep parameters were determined.

It should be emphasized that, in general, relations (6) and (7) can be correctly used, provided the investigated rock massif is at a stress-strain state characterized by the parameter $\mu_\sigma = 0$.

In the USSR, in calculating the pressure tunnel linings for an inner pressure, the thrust-of-earth coefficient, k, or the specific thrust coefficient, k_o, is taken as a characteristic of deformability of the surrounding rock, the radius of the excavation being assumed to be equal to 100cm, Zurabov, Bugayeva (1962). It is assumed that k is a coefficient of proportionality between the inner hydrostatic pressure, P, at any point along the excavation contour, and the radial displacement, u, at the same point -

$$P = k\ u \tag{8}$$

$$k_o = k\ r\ 10^{-2} = D(1 + \nu)^{-1}\ 10^{-2} \tag{9}$$

where D- deformation modulus of the rock.

When allowance is made for creep of the surrounding rock massif with the use of relations (7) and (9), it can be shown that

$$k_{ot} = 0{,}02\ G_t \tag{10}$$

or in a simplified form -

$$k'_{ot} = 0{,}02\ G'_t \tag{11}$$

where K_{ot} - time operator; K'_{ot} - coefficient of specific thrust varying with time.

Relations (2), (4), (6), (7), (10) and (11) can be used in calculations of stress-strain states of the pressure tunnel linings caused by inner pressure, with allowance being made for creep.

3. CREEP OF CONCRETE

An analysis of experimental data obtained in investigating the creep of concrete at different stress states, Arutiunian (1972), Alexandrovsky (1973) et al, has made it possible to conclude that in designing underground structures the hereditary theory of ageing with the creep kernel, suggested by Alexandrovsky (1973), can be successfully used for an analytical description of creep of concrete and its deformation in time. In the majority of practical cases, however, the filling up of a tunnel, as well as creation of an inner pressure in a pressure tunnel, and consequently the loading of the lining, takes place a considerable period of time after the completion of the lining. This enables the designeer to assume that under such conditions the elasticity modulus of concrete is constant in time, i.e. the concrete is assumed to be "old" enough; thus, the calculations of the stress-strain state of the pressure tunnel linings can be carried out with the use of the linear hereditary creep theory formulae -

$$E_{1t}^{-1}\{Y(t)\} = E_1^{-1}\left[Y(t) + \int_o^t N(t - t_o)\ Y(t_o)\ dt_o\right] \tag{12}$$

$$N(t - t_o) = E_1\left[\gamma\ \psi_o\ e^{-\gamma(t - t_o)} + \alpha\ \Delta_o\ e^{-\alpha(t - t_o)}\right] \tag{13}$$

where E_{1t} -time operator; E_1 -elasticity modulus of concrete; $N(t - t_o)$ -creep kernel of concrete; γ day; α day; ψ_o MPa^{-1}; Δ_o MPa^{-1} -creep parameters of "old" concrete.

In the papers by Arutiunian (1972) and Alexandrovsky (1973) it was shown that the Poisson's ratio, ν_1, of concrete may be considered constant in time. Similarly to (4) and (7), relation (12) can be simplified for solving a certain class of problems in the following way -

$$E'_t = E_1\ (1 + n_t)^{-1} \tag{14}$$

$$n_t = E_1(\psi_o\ e^{-\gamma t} + \Delta_o e^{-\alpha t}) \tag{15}$$

where E'_{1t} -deformation modulus of concrete varying with time.

4. STRESS-STRAIN STATE OF SINGLE-LAYER LININGS WITH ALLOWANCES MADE FOR CREEP OF CONCRETE AND ROCK

The investigation of the stress-strain state of pressure tunnel single-layer linings subjected to uniformly distributed inner pressure, P(t), with the use of the linear hereditary creep theory and exponential creep kernels of concrete and rock is described in the papers by Kubetsky (1970), (1973).

To considerably simplify the calculation formulas, and to use a possibility of applying the creep kernels of concrete and rock much better describing the properties of these materials, a new approximate method for solving the problem is suggested which ensures an accuracy sufficient for practical purposes. The approximate method, just as the strict solution, is based on the Volterra's principle: this makes possible using a similar solution of the problem by the theory of elasticity, the elasticity constants being sustituted by the corresponding time operators in the final results only, Rabotnov (1973). In the proposed approximate method, however, the elasticity constants are substituted not by the time operators, but by the corresponding variable in time moduli. For instance, the relation binding the relative creep deformation, $\varepsilon(t)$, of concrete or rock with the stress $\sigma(t)$ at the uniaxial stress state, is taken in the following form:

$$\varepsilon(t) \approx \sigma_t E^{-1}\left[1 + \int_{\tau}^{t} M(t - t_o)\, dt_o\right] = \sigma(t) \cdot (E_t')^{-1} \qquad (16)$$

then

$$(E_t')^{-1} = E^{-1}\left[1 + \int_{o}^{t} M(t - t_o)\, dt_o\right] \qquad (17)$$

where $M(t - t_o)$ -creep kernel; E -elasticity modulus of concrete or the modulus of instantaneous deformation of rock; E_t' -deformation modulus varying in time. Such approach was used in obtaining formulae (4), (7), (11) and (14).

Using the general approach to the solution of the problem described in the paper by Kubetsky (1970), together with the approximate expressions for the time operators, characterizing creep of concrete and rock, and the Volterra's principle, the tangential tensile stress, σ_θ, along the inner contour of the lining at $r = r_o$, and its variation in time at a constant pressure in the tunnel, $P(t) = P_o = \text{const}$, may be expressed in the following way

$$\sigma_\theta(t) = P_o\left[r_o^2 + r_1^2(1 - 2B)\right] \cdot d^{-1} \qquad (18)$$

$$B = 2r_o^2\left[b + c\left(\frac{1 + l_t}{1 + n_t}\right)\right]^{-1} \qquad (19)$$

where $b = (1 - \nu_1)\, r_1^2 + (1 + \nu_1) \cdot r_o^2$; $c = 0{,}5\, E_1 G_o^{-1} d$; $d = r_1^2 - r_o^2$; r_o r_1 - inner and outer radii of the lining respectively.

In Table 2 variations with time of the stress state of a lining, calculated in accordance with the strict solution, Kubetsky (1970), are compared with the approximate solution (17). These calculation were carried out by Nguen The Fung (1980).

Table 2. Variation of σ_θ/P in time.

Time (days)	0	1	3	20	100	∞
strict solution	1,38	2.010	1.85	1.23	0.95	0.94
Approximate solution	1.38	2.009	1.88	1.34	0.97	0.94
Error %	0	0.46	0.82	5.96	2.40	0

An analysis of the calculation results given in Table 2 has shown that, at a constant inner pressure in the tunnel, the error caused by the use of the approximate solution (17) is not inconsistant with the usual accuracy in practical engineering calculations.

Provided the pressure in the tunnel, $P(t)$, increases according to some arbitrary law to its maximum gradually, relation (18) will take the following form -

$$\sigma_\theta(t) = P(t)\left[r_o^2 + r_1^2(1 - 2B)\right] \cdot d^{-1} \qquad (20)$$

where $P(t)$ - given function for the variation of pressure in the tunnel.

An analysis of results obtained for particular calculation cases at a gradual rise of pressure in the tunnel with the use of the strict solution, Kubetsky (1970), and with the use of the approximate solution according to formula (20) has shown that the error can reach 30%, which depends on the rate of rise of pressure in the tunnel. When the rate of rise of pressure in the tunnel decreases, the error in determining $\sigma_\theta(t)$ diminishes. Calculations have shown that, when the rising of pressure to its maximum lasts more than one or two months, the error, as compared to the strict solution, will not exceed 4% to 10%, which is dependent on the creep properties of the lining and rock: under this condition formula (20) may be recommended for practical use. An analysis of real rates of pressure elevation in tunnels for a number of particular cases has shown that this process can sometimes last several months or even years. If it is the case, the difference between the results obtained by the strict and approximate solutions may be neglected. It will be noted that an allowance made for graduality of pressure rise in a tunnel may lead to a considerable decrease of the maximum stresses in the lining, and this decrease under certain circumstances may reach 30% to 50%.

5. STRESS-STRAIN STATE OF MULTILAYER STRUCTURES

An analysis of different designs of pressure tunnel linings used in current hydrotechnical practice, and an analysis of data pertaining to mechanical properties of rock masses surrounding the structure, have shown that in general it would be more rational to use a calculation scheme where the surrounding rock mass and the lining are considered as a single multilayer structure.

Such calculation scheme makes it possible to take into account both the diversity of the structures and the heterogeneity of the rock mass, surrounding the excavation, caused by disturbances of the rock in the process of driving the tunnel as well as by unloading and grouting of the ground; this also enables the designer to calculate the stress state of each element of the multilayer structure, with due regard for the creep, using recursion relations. A solution of the problem with the use of the elasticity theory obtained by Bulychev (1979) was used as a basis for constructing the calculation scheme of the multilayer

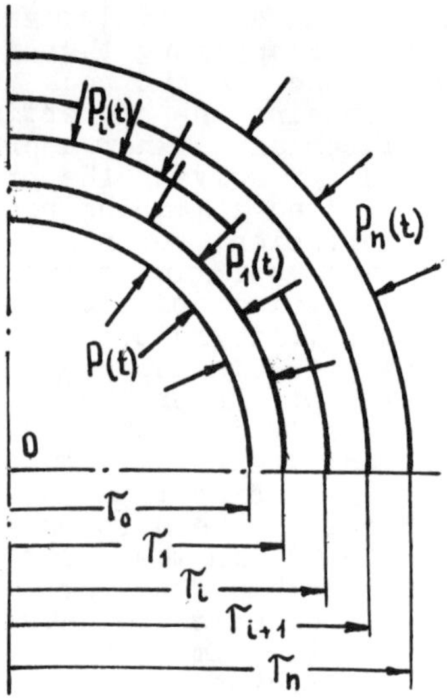

Fig.2. Calculation scheme for a multilayer structure.

structure, some refinements having been introduced allowing for creep and peculiarities of the pressure tunnels. The calculation scheme for the multilayer structure is shown in Fig.2.

To derive the calculation formulae, the condition of equality of pressures and radial displacements at the interface of the layers was adopted:

$$P_{i+1}(t) = P_i(t) \qquad (21)$$

$$U_{i+1}(t) = U_i(t) \qquad (22)$$

where $U_i(t)$ - radial displacement at the contact surface of the i-th layer.

Stresses and displacements in the i-th layer were determined by means of the following formulae:

$$\left.\begin{matrix}\sigma_{\theta i}(t)\\ \sigma_{ri}(t)\end{matrix}\right\} = P(t)\, d_i^{-1}\left\{[r_{i-1}^2 - K_i(t)\, r_i^2] \pm [1 - K_i(t)]\, r_{i-1}^2 r_i^2 r^{-2}\right\} \prod_{j=1}^{i-1} K_j(t) \qquad (23)$$

$$U_i(t) = P(t)\left\{r[r_{i-1}^2 - K_i(t)\, r_i^2](1-\nu_i) + [1-K_i(t)]\, r_{i-1}^2 r_i^2 r^{-1}(1+\nu_i)\right\} d_i E_{it}^{-1} \cdot \prod_{j=1}^{i-1} K_j(t) \qquad (24)$$

$$K_i(t) = 2 r_{i-1}\left\{b_i + m_i(t)\, d_i\, d_{i+1}^{-1}\, [a_{i+1} + \nu_{i+1} d_{i+1} - 2K_{i+1}(t)\, r_{i+1}^2]\right\}^{-1}$$

where $K_i(t)$ - load transfer coefficient; $\bar{E}_{it}$ -deformation modulus operator for the i-th layer; $m_i(t) = E_{it} E^{-1}_{(i+1)t}$; $a_i = r_i^2 + r_{i-1}^2$;

$$b_i = (1 - \nu_i) r_i^2 + +(1 + \nu_i) r_{i-1}^2 \; ; \; d_i = r_i^2 - r_{i-1}^2 \; .$$

In general, determining the stress-strain state of multilayer structures by the theory of linear hereditary creep requires deciphering of expressions consisting of a product of operators characterizing creep properties of different layers, which is associated with certain difficulties. A number of particular solutions with the purpose of determining the stress-strain state of reinforced-concrete linings having one-layer and two-layer reinforcement, with consideration given for the weakend layer of the rock mass around the tunnel, has been obtained by Nguen The Fung (1980) with participation and consultation of the author of this paper. It seems to be more profitable, however, to use, as in the case of one-layer linings, the approximate approach discussed above, which will result in simplifying the derivation of calculation formulae for divers structures. An analysis of calculation results for a number of the most widely used multilayer pressure tunnel linings has shown that the approximate approach provides an accuracy sufficient for practical purposes. This makes it possible to determine accurately enough the stress-strain state of nearly any axisymmetric pressure tunnel lining using arbitrary laws describing creep of the lining material and the surrounding rock mass, provided there exists a corresponding solution of the problem by the elasticity theory, in which elastic constants are substituted by the relevant time moduli varying in time.

The approximate approach can be successfully used both for determining the stress-strain state of a lining with consideration given for creep caused by the inner pressure, and for estimating the effects of prestressing the structure by some method (for instance, by grouting the ground) providing a uniform precompression of the rock and the structure itself. A comparison of the strict solution results, Kubetsky (1977), with the approximate solution shows that the error in this case does not exceed 5%.

Calculations have shown that creep of rock masses influences unfavourably the stress-strain state of the pressure tunnel linings. It should be taken into account, however, that, in practice, designing of the structures in question is, as a rule, made with the use of diminished parameters characterizing the rocks, and their values are nearly equal to, or even less than the values of G_∞ or E_∞. Due to this, when correctly applied, in the majority of cases consideration for creep does not result in incresed thickness of the lining or incresed percentage of reinforcement.

6. CONCLUSIONS

An analysis of theoretical solutions has shown that in construction of tunnels and shafts it is expedient to use for linings special materials characterized by higher than usual creep. The use of such materials offers a possibility to considerably reduce weight of the linings by transferring a part of the applied load to the surrounding rock mass without disturbing its integrity. This factor can be used to the highest degree, if the pressure in the tunnel grows gradually.

7. REFERENCES

Alexandrovsky, S.V. 1973, Designing of concrete and reinforced-concrete structures for temperature and moisture effects with allowance made for creep, p.432. Stroyizdat, Moscow. (in Russian).

Arutiunian, N.Kh. 1972, Creep of ageing materials. Creep of concrete p.155-202. Mekhanika v SSSR za 50 let. V.Z. "Nauka". Moscow. (in Russian)

Bulychev, N.S. 1979, Designing of hydrotechnical tunnel multilayer circular linings for static and seismic loads, p.17-23. Sbornik nauchnykh trudov Gidroproekta.

Sovershenstovanie proektirovaniya i stroitelstva podzemnykh gidrotekhnicheskikh sooruzhneniy, Moscow. (in Russian).
Zurabov, G.G., O.E. Bugaeva, 1962, Hydrotechnical tunnels of water power stations, p.719. Gosenergoizdat. Moscow.
Kubetsky, V.L. 1970, Investigation of stresses in pressure tunnel linings with regard to creep of concrete and surrounding rock mass, p.447-452. II Congress of the ISRM, Beograd.
Kubetsky, V.L. 1973, Some aspects of creep description of fissured rock and their application to the design of pressure tunnels, p.72-86. Proceedings of Civil Engineering Institute, N115, Moscow. (in Russian).
Kubetsky, V.L. 1977, Investigation of the stress state of the rock massif and the tunnel structure caused by grouting, p.81-89. Proceedings of Civil Engineering Institute, N 140, Moscow. (in Russian).
Kubetsky, V.L. 1978, Rock strength investigation method, p.295-299. Proceedings of the I.G.S.Conference "Geocon", India, New Delhi.
Kubetsky, V.L. 1979, Certain laws of creep in fissured rock and semirock, p.215-219. IV Congress of the ISRM. Switzerland.
Kubetsky, V.L. 1980, Investigation of in-situ rheological properties of fissured rocks, p.95-107. Proceedings of Civil Engineering Institute, N 179, Moscow. (in Russian).
Kubetsky, V.L. 1981, Determining mechanical properties of fissured rocks and semirocks as applied to underground construction problems, Gidrotekhnicheskoe stroitelstvo, N 4, p.27-31 (in Russian)
Kubetsky, V.L. & V.A. Kozionov, 1981, Investigation of rheological properties of fissured semirocks, p.105-112. Proceedings of International symposium on Weak Rock. Tokyo, Japan.
Nguen The Fung, 1980, Advancing the method of pressure tunnel linings designing with due regard for creep of rock and concrete. Dissertation for Cand.Sc.(Eng)., Civil Engineering Institute, Moscow, p.196. (in Russian)
Rabotnov, Yu.N. 1977, Elements of hereditary mechanics of solids, p. 383. "Nauka", Moscow. (in Russian)

SOME RESULTS OF RESEARCH ON LINING PRESTRESSING FOR THE PRESSURE TUNNEL OF A PUMPED STORAGE HYDROELECTRIC PLANT

Forschungsergebnisse zur Vorspannung von Druckstollenauskleidungen eines Pumpspeicherwerks

Quelques résultats de recherches sur les soutènements précontraints dans les galeries d'amenée

B.KUJUNDŽIĆ, K.IVANOVIĆ & O.MARKOVIĆ
Jaroslav Černi Institute of Water Resources Engineering, Belgrade, Yugoslavia
Ž.NIKOLIĆ
Energoprojekt, Belgrade, Yugoslavia

SUMMARY:
The type of lining chosen for this plant (now under construction) was non-reinforced concrete with pressure grouting. The tunnel is driven by a Robbin's mole. Pressure grouting has the following aims: to prestress the lining and the rock mass, to reduce heterogeneity and anisotropy effects of the rock mass, and to decrease its permeability. The paper presents the following: data on the tunnel, stress analysis of the lining-rock mass system, the design concept with prestressing by pressure grouting, the methods used for rock mass investigation and testing the lining on pilot stretches, an overview of the results. The conclusions arrived at are generally applicable to pressure tunnels; in particular, an analytical-experimentaldesign methodology for tunnels with pressure grouting is formulated.

ZUSAMMENFASSUNG:
Als Lösung zur Sicherung der Undurchlässigkeit und Stabilität der Druckstollen eines Pumpspeicherwerkes (in Ausbau) wurde eine vorgespannte Auskleidung angenommen. Der Ashub erfolgt mit einer Maschine Typ "Robbins". Der Zweck der Spannungsinjektierung besteht im folgenden: Vorspannung der Tunnelauskleidung und der Felsmasse, Verminderung des Einflusses der Nichthomogenität und der Anisotropie der Felsmasse, sowie Verminderung deren Wasserdurchchlässigkeit. In der Arbeit sind die Daten über dem Tunnel gegeben, Spannungsfeld im System "Belag - Felsmasse" analisiert, Konzeption der technischen Lösung mit Vorspannung mittels Spannungsinjektierung dargestellt, die angenwandten Methoden der Erforschung der Felsmasse und der Untersuchung der Betonauskleidung auf speziellen Versuchsstrecken beschrieben, sowie eine zusammenfassende Übersicht der erhaltenen Ergebnisse gegeben. Die erhaltenen Schlussfolgerungen haben für Druckstollen eine allgemeine Gültigkeit. Insbesondere wurde eine analytisch - experimentelle Methode der Projektierung solcher Tunnele formuliert, wenn die Spannungsinjektierung angenwandt wird.

RÉSUMÉ:
Comme solution d'impermeabilitié et de la stabilité d'une galerie en charge d'une centrale hydraulique de pompage (en construction) on a adopté un revetement en béton non armé avec des injections de précontrainte. L'exavation est faite avec une machine du type Robbins. Le but des injections de précontraintes en est: la précontraintes du revêtement et de la roche, diminuer l'influence d'heterogénéité et d'anisotropie de la masse rocheusse ainsi que diminuer la perméabilité. On présante des données sur la galerie, on analyse l'état des contraintes dans le systeme "revêtement - masse rocheusse", on fait voir la conseption de la solution technique avec la précontraintes par injection, on décrit les méthods appliquées dans les essais de la masse rocheusse et du revêtement en béton sur des secteurs d'essais et on donne une revue sommaire des résultats obtenus. Les conclusions ont un caractere génerale pour les galeries en charges; avec un apercu particulier sur la formule de la méthode analytico - expérimentale de projet des galeries avec l'application des injections de précontrainte.

1. INTRODUCTION

The basic tasks of design and design investigation for the pressure tunnel were:

1. to determine the nature and scope of geotechnical investigations which must be carried out before and during construction
2. to determine lining dimensions and pressure grouting parameters
3. to determine the nature and scope of tests to verify the effects of pressure grouting.

The analyses which enabled the final design choice and laid the groundwork for solving the problems encountered, as presented in this paper, and which in particular enabled the formulation and application of an analytical-experimental methodology for solving the problems associated with this kind of lining, are the result of team work involving staff of the Department of Structural and Geotechnical Engineering of the Jaroslav Černi Institute and of Energoprojekt.

2. DATA ON THE TUNNEL

Both from the constructional and the operational aspect the two-way tunnel is the most important feature of a pumped storage plant. The length of the tunnel is 8 km, 5.6 km through Triassic limestone, and 2.4 km through marl and marly limestone. It is of circular cross-section, with an excavated diameter of 7.0 m, an insided diameter of 6.3 m and a lining thickness of 35 cm.

The maximum internal hydrostatic pressure ranges from 8.0 bar at the intake to 11.0 m at the surge tank. The hydrodynamic maximum at the surge tank is 2.5 bar, so that the maximum total pressure ranges from 8.0 to 13.5 bar.

The "coefficiant of boldness", $2a.p_u$, is 6.3 x 135 = 850.

The tunnel is excavated by a Robbins mole. Immediately behind the advancing mole prefabricated reinforced concrete footwall elements are laid, to provide a bed for the central track for transporting excavated material and the outer tracks for cranes and lining concreting and grouting gear. In the center of the footwall is a drainage duct. The length of the prefabricated elements is about 1/4 of the tunnel circumference and their thickness 35 cm like the rest of the lining which is subsequently cast in situ (Fig. 3).

3. DESIGN CONCEPT

3.1 Philosophy

The design philosophy was based on the following general axioms:

1. The basic function of a pressure tunnel is to enable a certain flow rate of water under the operating conditions of the plant. To fulfill this function the tunnel must be watertight, its lining stable, and with the specified roughness of the inside surface.
2. In the broader sense the lining consists of: the concrete or reinforced concrete, the surrounding rock mass, and all the works carried out to guarantee watertightness and stability of the tunnel and its lining (rock improvement, grouting, waterproofing, etc.). The most important component of the lining, in this wider sense, is the surrounding rock mass around the tunnel, since its properties (permeability and mechanical characteristics) are the principle determinants of the lining design concept.
3. If the rock mass around the tunnel is impermeable, or its permeability is within permissible limits, the concrete lining does not have to fulfill the function of watertightness, and apart from its hydraulic function only has to fulfill the condition of stability.
4. Insofar as the surrounding rock mass is permeable, i.e. its permeability is greater than engineering and/or economic criteria allow, the concrete lining, with supplementary works if necessary (grouting, sealing, etc.) must also ensure the watertightness of the tunnel. An alternative solution is to make the rock mass impermeable by grouting, in which case the concrete lining loses its impermeability function.

Referring to these axioms, the following philosophy was formulated:

1. On the 2.4 km stretch of the tunnel through marl and marly limestone the concrete lining does not have to be watertight since any water leaking through it will not be lost from the upper reservoir.
2. On the 5.6 km stretch through Triassic limestone, which is for the most part fissured and karstified and therefore permeable, watertightness must be provided by the concrete lining and supplementary works, since any water leaking through it would be permanently lost. The possibility of acheiving sufficient impermeability of the rock mass by grouting was rejected as infeasible, principally because of the nature of the fissuring and the predicted karstic phenomena.

For this stretch three lining alternatives

were examined: conventional concrete lining, concrete prestressed by grouting through boreholes or the TIWAG system, and steel lining.

3. The steel lining alternative was rejected on economic grounds.

4. Prestressing by the TIWAG system was rejected as too difficult, requiring very careful work and a well-rehearsed grouting team, and because grouting of the rock mass would not be sufficiently effective to acheive radical consolidation and hence the desired prestressing of the lining.

5. A through analysis was made of the remaining two alternatives, from which it was concluded that the best would be a concrete lining prestressed by pressure grouting of the rock mass through boreholes.

3.2 Stress Analysis

A detailed stress analysis of an unreinforced concrete lining was made using Lame´s theory of a thick tube and varying the modulus of deformation of the rock mass D_s, the modulus of tensile deformation of the concrete E_{bz}, the temperature difference $\Delta t°$, and the lining thickness per unit internal water pressure d. It showed the following:

(1) Temperature influences which may be realistically expected heavily reduce the strength of the lining and may annual it at high values of E_{bz}, regardless of the value of D_s. In this respect a particular problem is the realistic estimation of E_{bz}.

(2) Increasing the lining thickness does not appreciable increase its strength.

(3) The situation will in reality be even more unfavorable because of the heterogeneity and anisotropy of the rock mass and the heterogeneity of the concrete lining, which were not taken into account in the analysis.

(4) Reinforcing of the lining would acheive only a relatively small improvement, and that more theoretical than practical, only for low internal pressures, while at high pressures it would not help even theoretically.

The above conclusions can be generalized in the statement that for hydraulic tunnels of large diameter and high internal pressure an ordinary or reinforced concrete lining cannot be used where the tunnel traverses permeable rock.

3.2.2 Concrete lining prestressed by pressure grouting

The factors taken into account by this stress analysis were: modulus of elasticity of the concrete E_b, deformation modulus of the rock mass D_s, internal water pressure p_u, and cooling of the concrete lining $\Delta t°$ (the influence of cooling of the rock mass was substituted by the additional cooling of the lining).

The analysis did not take into account the rheological behaviour of the rock mass, concrete and hardened grout. Since the analytical treatment of these factors is extremely complicated, and having in view the existence of other factors like anisotropy and heterogeneity of the rock mass around the opening and the secondary stress state in the zone around the tunnel, the view was taken that these factors had to be analyzed experimentally on pilot stretches during construction of the tunnel. The results of these tests enable verification and possible correction of the pressure grouting parameters to render them consistent with the stress analyses already carried out. Thus the position was taken that in the present state of the art the problem of prestressing is best attacked by a combined analytical-experimental method of determining the design parameters.

In the stress analysis of the concrete lining prestressed by grouting, the design axiom was that the compressive stressing remaining in the lining after relaxation should be sufficient to exceed the most unfavorable possible combination of loading and lining cooling effects. Therefore the basic aim of the analysis was to estimate the necessary prestressing after relaxation as a function of the relevant parameters.

The basic aim of the in situ tests was to determine the optimum pressure grouting parameters, from both the engineering and the economic aspect, to acheive the required compressive prestressing of the lining.

To simplify the presentation, compressive stresses in the concrete lining are expressed in terms of the necessary tangential strains induced by pressure grouting. The criterium of minimum required strain means that the strain of the concrete lining remaining after relaxation of the concrete and grouted rock mass be such that the corresponding compressive stressing in the concrete should not fall below zero for the most unfavorable combination of internal water pressure and cooling of the lining.

For given lining dimensions (inside

radius $\underline{a}$ = 3.15 m, thickness $\underline{d}$ = 35 cm) the required tangential strain $\bar{\varepsilon}_\varphi$ depends on the internal pressure p_u, the deformation modulus of the rock mass D_s the modulus of elasticity of the concrete E_b, and the lining temperature drop $\Delta t°$ (Fig. 1).

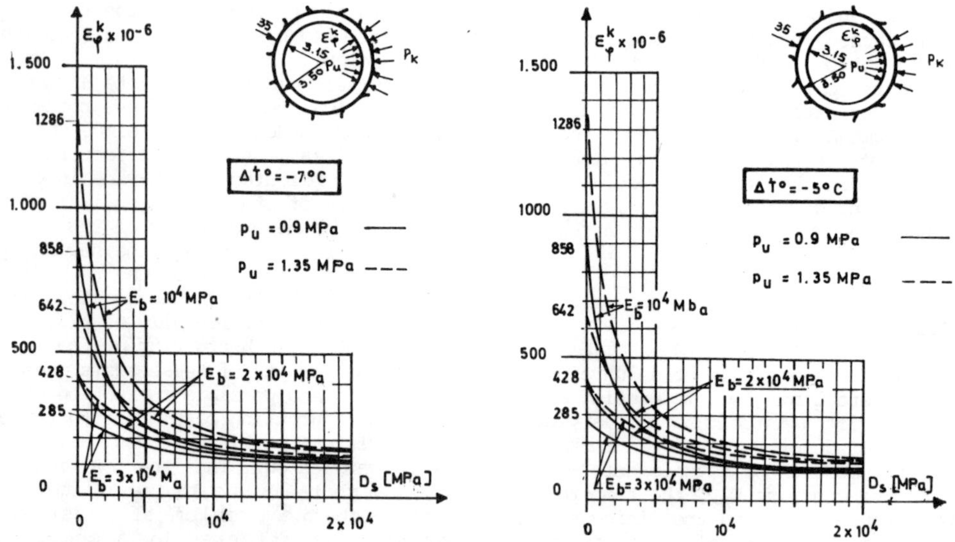

Fig.1 Diagrams of required strains ε_φ^k for p_i=0.9 and 1.35 MPa; $E_b=10^4$, 2×10^4 and 3×10^4 MPa and (a) $\Delta t°$ =-7°C; (b) $\Delta t°$ = -5°C

In contrast to the case of an ordinary concrete lining, where the deformation behaviour of the concrete is expressed in terms of the tensile deformation modulus E_{bz}, in the case of prestressing the compressive modulus of deformation E_b on the descending load line must be used.

The principles and source data for the stress analysis are the same as for a non-reinforced lining except that E_b is used instead of E_{bz}, and the necessary tangential strain ε_φ^k is introduced.

Figure 1 shows diagrams of the required tangential strain for the cases of $E_b=2.10^4$ MPa, p_i=0.9 and 1.35 MPa, as a function D_s and with Δt=-5° and -7°C. Similar analyses were also carried out for $E_b=3.10^4$ and 4.10^4 MPa.

The influence of lining thickness on ε_φ^k was also investigated analytically. It was found that it increases with increasing thickness, the more so the greater the deformation moduli of the rock mass and the greater the magnitude of $\Delta t°$.

From the above analyses the following conclusions were drawn:

(1) For values of $D_s > 10^4$ MPa the magnitude of ε_φ^k depends much more on $\Delta t°$ than on E_b.

(2) At low values of D_s, ε_φ^k depends more on E_b than on $\Delta t°$.

Although these conclusions are derived from a theory which idealizes the concrete and the rock mass (as isotropic, homogeneous and elastic), the consequences of this idealization are less unfavourable than in the case of an ordinary lining. Even under the most unfavourable assumption that pressure grouting has not reduced the degree of anisotropy and heterogeneity of the rock mass, which is unlikely, the superimposed moments, in combination with the prestressing pressure, will only induce eccentric compressive forces in the lining, which is for concrete much more favourable than eccentric tensile forces which rock mass anisotropy and heterogeneity would induce in an ordinary concrete lining.

Furthermore, pressure grouting gives an opportunity to check the quality of the lining works as regards leakage: defects in the concrete can be discovered and made good. In this respect horizontal construction joints are not the problem, but segregation zones in the concrete, which are made good by grouting or other measures, and circumferential construction joints between concrete stretches, which can be sealed.

All the above considerations, and the results of tests carried out so far, indicate that the choice of a concrete lining prestressed by grouting was the right one, both in economic and engineering terms, and that this design concept is generally valid for pressure tunnels, though it calls for further development and research to get still beter results.

4. PRINCIPLES OF PRESTRESSING BY PRESSURE GROUTING

The grout is forced under very high pressure (20-30 bar or more) into a zone of the rock mass around the tunnel opening through boreholes, inducing additional stresses of the desired magnitude. These stresses are transferred on the one hand to the deeper-lying rock mass, and on the other to the concrete lining, subjecting it to compressive prestressing /2/, /3/, /4/.

Grouting is carried out on batches of 44 boreholes at once, eleven on each of four cross sections on a stretch of 10 m.

Apart from prestressing of the lining and of the rock mass itself, the following effects are also achieved in the rock mass: consolidation, cancellation of permanent deformations, augmentation of the modulus of deformation, reduction of anisotropy and heterogeneity, homogenization of the stress pattern around the tunnel, and a considerable reduction in permeability.

Figure 2 shows the borehole pattern used on pilot stretches PD-1 through PD-4. It may be seen that the 5 m holes were not drilled perfectly radially. This was not possible because of the form of the drilling gantry and the fixed position of the two rigs on it.

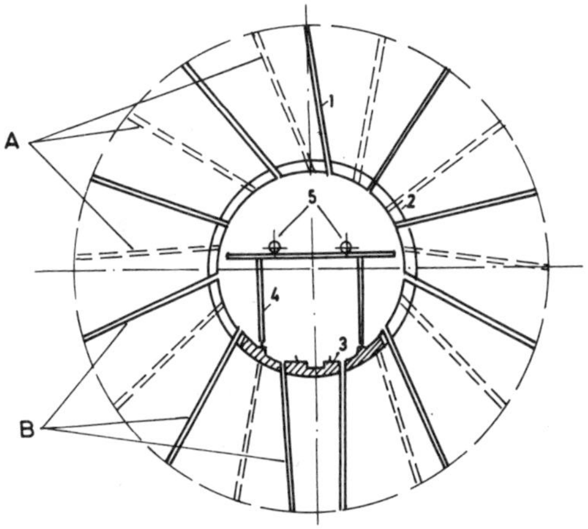

Fig.2 Pressure grouting layout (1)-borehole; (2)- cast concrete in telescopic shuttering; (3)-prefabricated footwall elements; (4)- gantry; (5)- drill rigs. (A) Odd numbered cross section; (B) Even numbered cross section.

Since the Robbin's mole used for driving the tunnel leaves a very regular and smooth circular cross section, the "Kieser effect" was taken into account, i.e. it was expected that the grout would also penetrate in between the lining and the rock mass, thus prestressing the concrete by the high grouting pressure acting directly on the extrados of the lining. This would make for more uniform loading of the lining during grouting, and enabled contact grouting as a special operation to be dispensed with, thus making the whole procedure more economical.

High-pressure grouting thus acheives two prestressing effects: prestressing of the rock mass around the tunnel, and the Kieser effect, i.e. direct prestressing of the concrete lining by grouting mortar penetrating under high pressure into the concrete-rock interface. The former of these two effects is discussed in ref./2/.

The Kieser effect is illustrated in Fig. 3. The pressure of the grout in the rock-concrete interface is transferred to the rock mass on one side and the lining on the other, exerting a prestressing force on it.

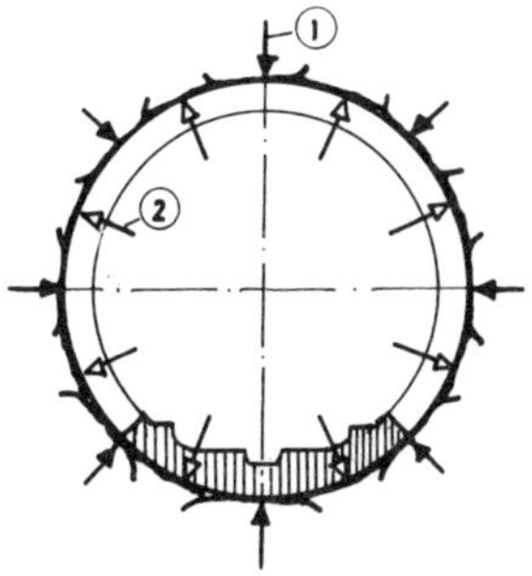

Fig.3 - Prestressing of the tunnel lining by direct action of the grouting pressure at the rock-lining interface; (1) pressure on the lining (2) pressure on the rock mass.

In view of the relative complexity of the lining type chosen, the investigation programme included experimental testing during construction on several pilot stretches (PD's). The purpose of these tests was primarily to verify the lining prestressing effect achieved by the pressure grouting, and also to yield data which would allow correction of the grouting procedure parameters (grout consistency, grouting pressures, borehole depth, sequence of stretches, capacities, etc.) to get better results.

The results of investigations are itemized in the following sections.

Table I Survey of Rock Mass Investigation Methods

Purpose	Method	Amount	Remarks
1. Engineering-geological classification of the rock mass in the parameters of jointing, bulk porosity, permeability, velocity v_p, etc.	1.1 Engineering-geological mapping of the working 1:100	whole length of the tunnel	
	1.2 refraction seismics	whole length of the tunnel	
	1.3 resistivity survey	whole length of the tunnel	
2. Determination of the stress state in the rock mass (primary, secondary and tertiary stresses)	2.1 TLM stress release method	70 measurements in 10 borehole	
	2.2 Tincelin-Mayer method	4 points	Subsequently abandoned
	2.3 Ultrasonic - hole logging - cross holing	16 holes, 132 m, 3 hole pairs, 18 m	
3. Determination of rock mass deformability in quasi-homogeneous zones and the influence of consolidative and high--pressure grouting on deformability and permeability	3.1 Flat jack method - before grouting - after grouting	 6 points 2 points	
	3.2 microseismic surveying around the flat jacks	6 points	
	3.3 substitute test chamber method (at locations of PD's)	3 sites	
	3.4 radial jack method before and after consolidative grouting	2 sites	Subsequently abandoned

Table II Survey of Measurements on Pilot Stretches

Q u a n t i t y	Method (instrument)	No. of meas. points in a cross section	No. of PD's on which applied
1. Tangential strain on the lining extrados	1.1 electroacoustic extensometer (J.Černi)	7+1	5
	1.2 resistance extensometer (Toshiba)	7+1	3
2. Tangential strain on the lining intrados	2.1 mechanical deformmeter	8	6
	2.2 resistance extensometer (Toshiba)	7+1	2
3.Average strain of cast concrete lining	3.1 circumference change with a steel tape passing over a spool whose length is read on a mechanical deflectometer /4/	1	8
4. Radial convergence	4.1 weight-principle device - J-Černi	4	5
	4.2 spring-principle device (Interfels,Austria)	4	3
5. Contact pressure at the rock-lining interface	5.1 pressure cells and manometer (J.Černi)	7	4
6. Rock mass deformation	6.1 quadruple rock extensometer, length 10 m (Toshiba)	3	2

5. INVESTIGATIONS

5.1 Investigations for Choice of Route

The engineering-geology of the formations to be traversed by the tunnel, especially as regards large-scale structural dislocations and karstification, was such that special-purpose investigations were necessary to enable the tracing of the optimum route for it. To this end extensive photogeological, refraction seismic, resistivity, and engineering-geological surveys were carried out. Their results were used to make corrections to the route originally proposed /6/.

5.2 Investigations for the Detailed Design

5.2.1 Concept

Data for the detailed design on the rock mass over the whole 8 km of the tunnel could not obtained by prior investigations, but only during the actual driving of the tunnel, especially because of the great thickness of the overburden.

This approach was also favoured by the fact the excavation by a mechanical mole causes relatively little perturbation of the rock mass, and produces a tunnel of rather regular geometry.

Therefore the investigation concept adopted was that data on the general structural and mechanical properties of the rock mass would be obtained after the excavation of approximately the first 1000 m of tunnel. Prior general engineering-geological surveys had shown that relative to the entire stetch of limestone to be traversed, the first 1000 m would be at least sufficiently representative to ensure that the overall concept would not be subsequently jeopardized.

It was therefore possible to partition the rock mass into quasi-homogeneous zones in all the parameters relevant to the design, although the relative proportions of different classes could not be extrapolated to the full 5600 m of the limestone stretch. As regards the relative proportions of different quasi-homogeneous zones, it was known the situation improved with depth.

As regards investigations directly related to the lining construction, the principle of full-scale pilot stretches was adopted. The first pressure grouting was therefore to be carried on the PD's.

The rock mass along the tunnel route could be roughly divided into "good" and "bad" parts. For the given batch pressure grouting configuration, the PD investigations were therefore required to answer the following questions: (1) - is permanent prestressing of the lining feasible? (2) - will it be necessary to wash out crack fill in good or bad rock parts; (3) - what is the optimum borehole depth for different engineering-geological categories of rock mass; (4) - what grouting parameters give the best results (grout consistency, pumping pressure, minimum necessary quantity of grout, grouting termination criterion, etc.) for different engineering-geological categories of rock mass; (5) - how does grouting influence neighbouring segments of the tunnel. It was estimated that the information required could be obtained with a total of eight PD's.

5.2.2 Investigation methods

In conformity with the concept explained above, the investigations were divided into two basic groups:

(1) investigations of the rock mass

(2) investigations of the lining (coacting with the rock mass).

Group (1) includes: detailed engineering-geological mapping of the working, refraction seismic surveying in the tunnel, resistivity surveying in the tunnel, investigation of virgin stresses and rock mass deformability.

Group (2) includes: measurement of contact pressures at the rock-lining interface, measurement of tangential strains, measurement of changes in lining circumference and of radial convergence. All measurements in this group are carried out on pilot stretches before, during and after their grouting.

Tables I and II show the sequencing of measurements and tests, their extent and purpose.

As regards the investigation of rock mass deformability, the initial programme /5/ envisaged application of the radial jack method, which faithfully mimics the behaviour of the rock mass under internal hydrostatic pressure thanks to the identity of contour conditions with those in the tunnel itself. However, it was not feasible to excavate an exploratory gallery for these tests in the same way as the tunnel would be executed. Because of the possible departure from similarity, and the fact that the test chamber method on a full was chosen, the radial jack method was abandoned.

In connection with the measurements on

PD-1 through PD-4, it should be noted that the basic idea in deciding the layout of the instruments was that on three of the pilot stretches tests would be carried out by the so-called "Substitute Test Chamber Method", in which water is forced under pressure into the rock-lining interface before high-pressure grouting.

Apart from the measurements on pilot stretches, which showed that the necessary stressing of the lining could certainly be acheived by pressure grouting, the following measurements during and after grouting to check its effect were also envisaged: (1) measurement of circumference change; (2) strain release from the lining.

Measurement of circumference changes

Prestressing was monitored during pressure grouting by measuring the circumference change of the cast lining, as was done on the Reisach-Rabenleite plant /4/. This method proved an excellent way of checking the prestressing during the grouting but impractical for long-term measurements because the whole setup is very sensitive to external influence such as mechanical shocks during manipulation of the grouting rig. It could not therefore be used to measure stress relaxation as a function of time. Circumference measurement was applied on only 11 profiles.

Strain release from the lining

For reliable verification of the existence of the required induced normal stresses in the tangential direction in the concrete lining after completion of all the time-dependent processes both in the lining and in the rock mass, an original method was developed, known as "strain release" (see Fig. 4). Its principle is the measurement of strain release during and after slotting of the lining above and below a strain gauge stuck to the intrados in the tangential direction.

Strain release as a function of the slotting process is plotted in Fig. 10. It was found empirically that it is not necessary to cut the concrete right through to the rock, but that a depth of about 20 cm is sufficient.

The method was calibrated at sites in pilot stretches where the stresses were known; the agreement was excellent.

6. RESULTS OF INVESTIGATIONS IN THE TUNNEL

Here we present only results obtained up to the end of 1981, with the emphasis on

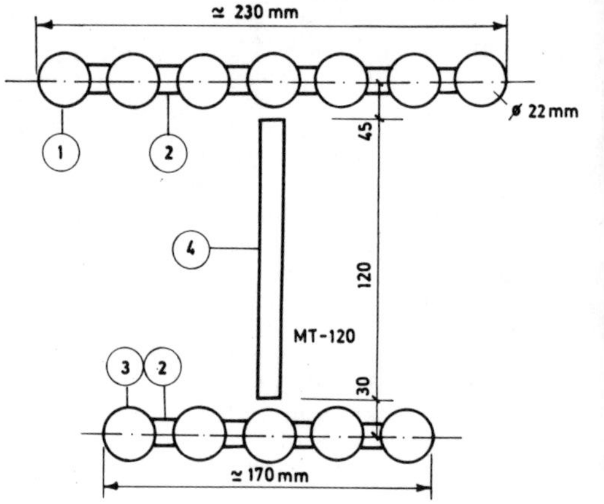

Fig. 4 Strain release setup (1) upper holes; (2) chiselling between holes; (3) lower holes; (4) strain gauge.

lining tests since they, as already explained, were the only way of confirming the correctness of the design concept and verifying the functionality of the lining before putting the tunnel into use.

6.1 Investigation of the Rock Mass

Of the investigations envisaged, the following have been carried out so far:

- engineering-geological mapping over the whole length of the excavated tunnel;
- refraction seismic surveying over one third of the excavation in Triassic limestone;
- resistivity surveying over a greater part of the excavation;
- pre-grouting flat jackk tests at all six of the planned sites;
- post-grouting flat jack tests at three sites;
- tests by the substitute test chamber method at the first measuring site;
- polar microseismic surveying around three flat jacks;
- investigation of virgin stresses by the TLM method at 21 points in three boreholes;
- ultrasonic hole logging and cross--holing.

The remaining planned investigations are now under way.

By the engineering-geological mapping of the working the rock mass has been partitioned into five basic quasi-homogeneous engineering-geological zones: (1) Compact rock mass - class C; (2) Compact, slightly damaged - class C_o; (3) Structurally damaged - class S_o; (4) Fractured - class F_o; (5) Breccoidal with clay bonding - class B_o.

Mixtures of classes are also frequently encountered, e.g. $C + C_o$, $C_o + S_o$, $S_o + F_o$, etc. /6/.

6.2 Results of Investigations on Pilot Stretches

Investigations of stresses and strains in the lining on pilot stretches in the Triassic limestone have been completed at all eight sites envisaged. The results confirm the viability of the design concept.

The performance of the instruments during pressure grouting was better than expected. All those in operation during grouting followed changes in grouting pressure very faithfully. This is evident from Fig.5, which shows the tangential strain on the extrados ε_φ^e as a function of time, and Fig. 6, which shows all the readings at measuring site 2 of PD-1 as a function of time both during and after grouting.

The performance of the instruments on other pilot stretches was similar.

From the radial diagrams of measured values influenced by pressure grouting it may be seen that the lining was prestressed over its whole circumference and that these influences were retained after grouting. In no case was tension induced in the lining, and the strains were often off the scale of the measuring instruments. Figure 7 shows radial diagrams of intrados strain at different grouting pressures on pilot stretch PD-1 located in very good rock, and Fig. 8 the tangential strains on the intrados and extrados after grouting on PD-5, in a zone of faults which the tunnel traverses obliquely over a distance of some 30 m.

Generally speaking, the measurements to date on eight pilot stretches have established the following:

(1) The grouting configuration used (batch grouting on 4 cross sections at intervals of 2.5 m with 11 holes per cross section) reliably produces permanent prestressing of the lining in practically all quasi-homogeneous zones of the rock mass traversed by the tunnel.

(2) Most of the stress relaxation in the lining takes place within the first month after grouting. It does not exceed 30%.

(3) The average consumption of dry material per unit area of tunnel perimeter ranges from 500 to 850 kg/m², or 1100 to 1870 kg/m of tunnel length.

(4) The instruments on one stretch of lining indicate that the lining stress-strain state is also influenced by the

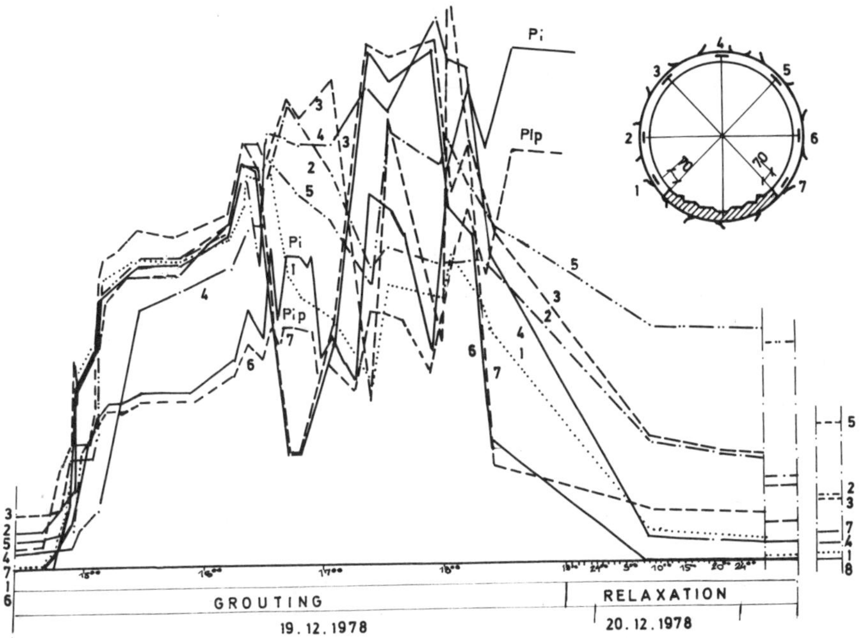

Fig. 5 ε_φ^e as a function of time on PD-1: p_i - pressure in the main grouting line; p_{ip} - pressure in the nearest grouting cross section; (1), (2), (3), ... - values of ε_φ^e at points 1, 2, 3, ...

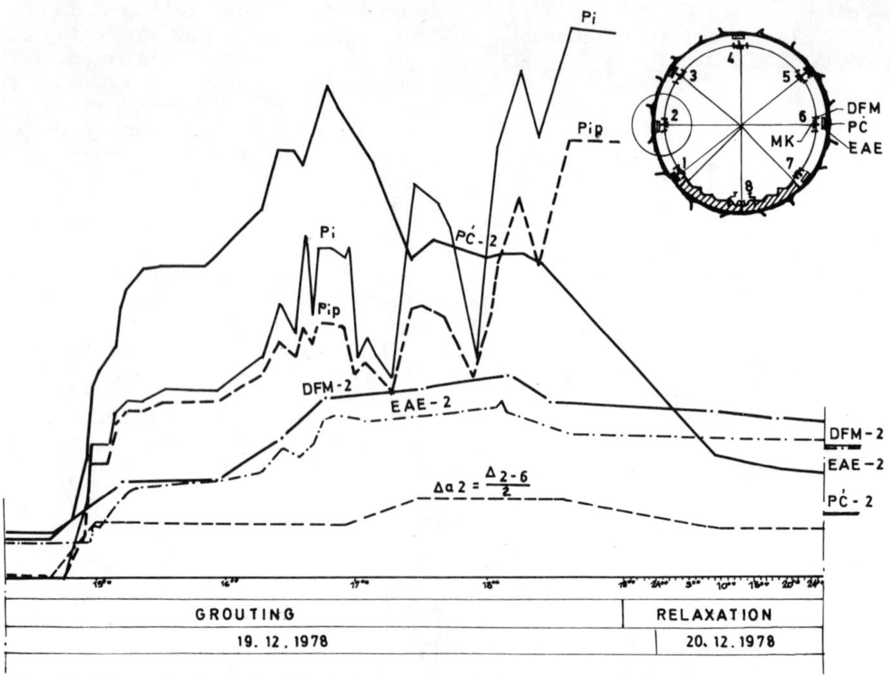

Fig. 6. Time graphs of all readings at measuring site 2 of pilot stretch PD-1: DFM - deformeter; EAE - electroacoustic extensometer; PC - pressure cell; p_i and p_{ip} as in Fig. 5

grouting of neighbouring stretches.

(5) During the grouting of one 10 m stretch of tunnel the grout may penetrate to 30 m or more along the tunnel.

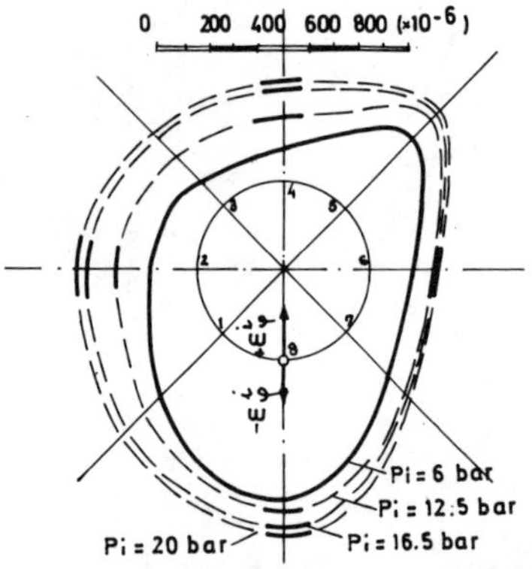

Fig. 7. Radial diagrams of ε_p^i on PD-1

(6) The water/cement ratio of the grout essentially influences the prestressing effect. The thickest grout with which prestressing can be achieved is:

- 1:1.5 for stretches in rock of low deformability
- 1:1 for stretches in rock of higher deformability

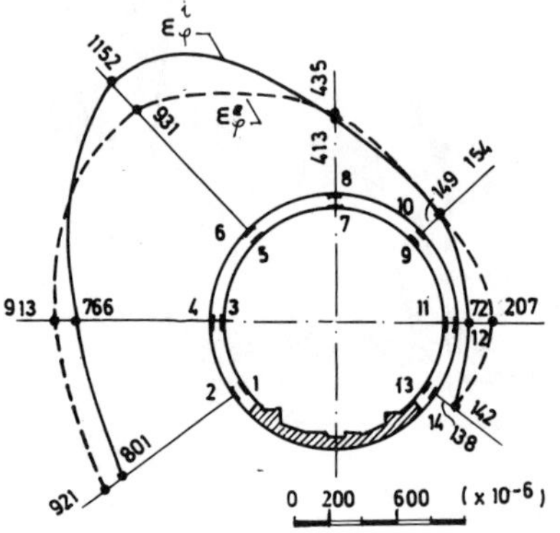

Fig. 8. Radial diagrams of ε_φ^i and ε_φ^e on PD-5

(7) Prestressing of the lining is acheived principally at the rock-lining interface. Grouting of the rock mass produces a supplementary effect, and the effects described under item 3 of this paper are also acheived.

(8) At grouting pressures over 25 bar failure of the lining may occur.

(9) Fault zones must be grouted at least twice.

(10) The grouting sequence must be from the ends inwards over a long reach, as shown in Fig. 9.

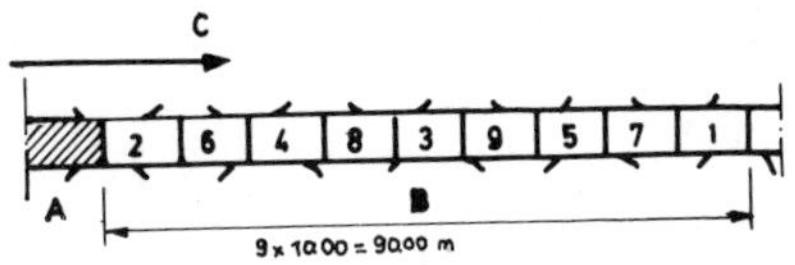

Fig. 9. Sequence of grouting on a 90 m reach in 10 m stretches: A- already grouted; B- now being grouted; (1), (2), (3), ... (9) - sequence of grouting

6.3 Results of Verification Tests

6.3.1 Circumference change

Verification by measuring circumference changes on 11 cross sections /4/ during pressure grouting established that on stretches through low-grade rock (classes under 4 and 5 in section 5.1) one grouting was not sufficient to acheive a satisfactory degree of prestressing. Because of site conditions it was not possible to follow up stress relaxation in the lining and rock mass by circumference measurements. In the light of the specific constructional requirements it was decided systematic checking of grouting performance should not be made by circumference measurements but by measuring strain release, with the condition that where insufficient prestressing of the lining was discovered, regrouting should be carried out with prestressing monitoring during the grouting.

6.3.2 Strain release

Figure 10 shows the evolution of strain release from the lining during a batch of tests carried out one year after pressure grouting. The strain releases measured are compared with the required values (Fig.1). In this way the success of grouting was systematically checked according to predefined criteria. Insufficiently stressed zones were regrouted until the criteria were satisfied.

About 200 tests of this kind are envisaged, taking in more than one third of the grouting stretches in the part through Triassic limestone. To date over 100 have been carried out, and only a few insufficiently stressed stretches were discovered. Two 10 m stretches have since been satisfactorily prestressed by regrouting. Figure 11 shows strain measurements on these two stretches immediately after regrouting. Prior to regrouting the value of ε_φ^i found by the strain release method was 90×10^{-6}.

6.4 Analysis of the Success of Lining Prestressing

Measurements made to date (end of 1981) on pilot stretches PD-1 through PD-5 have established the following average strains in the concrete lining induced by pressure grouting:

- PD-1 350 microstrains;
- PD-2 650 "
- PD-3 600 "
- PD-4 300 "
- PD-5 300 "

The investigation programme envisages measurements by the substitute test chamber method on three representative pilot stretches to estimate D_s, and hence to experimentally verify the success of pressure grouting. So far one such measurement has been made. From its results, by means of a specially developed method, the moduli of deformation of the rock mass have been estimated for the whole length of the tunnel /7/. This method makes use of the correlation between D_s and v_p determined by refraction seismic surveying in the tunnel /8/, /9/. To be on the safe side, the estimated D_s values were intentionally reduced, because of the lack of a sufficient number of test chamber measurements.

The results of these operations are presented in Table III. The required strains $\varepsilon_\varphi^\kappa$ have been taken from Fig. 1 for the case of $\Delta t = -7°C$, $p_u = 0.9$ MPa and $E_b = 2 \times 10^4$ MPa.

The ratio $\varepsilon_\varphi^s / \varepsilon_\varphi^\kappa$ from Table III clearly shows that the prestressing of the lining was satisfactory. It may also be interpreted as a safety factor, which is nowhere less than 1.7.

Although the investigations have not yet been completed, we can already conclude with certainty that the design and testing philosophy was well-founded, that the methodology was correct, and that the overall effort invested in solving the problems of this particular tunnel has provided a basis for defining general principles for hydraulic pressure tunnels prestressed by pressure grouting, embodied in what we have termed the analytical-experimental method.

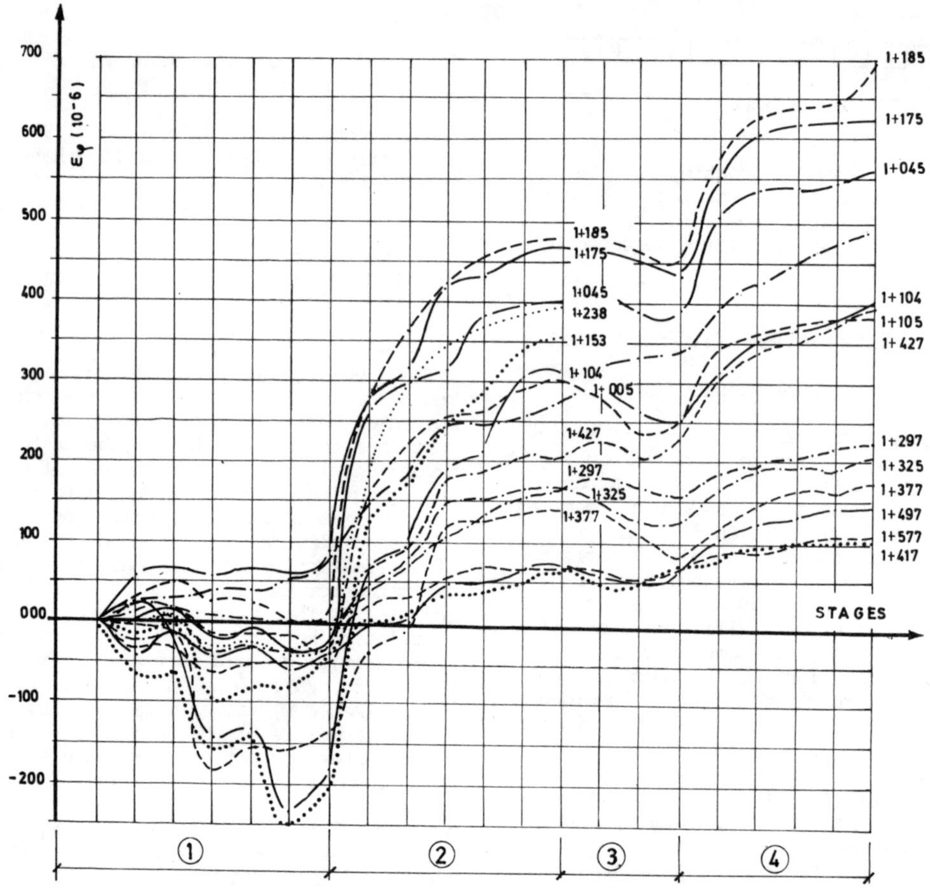

Fig. 10. Evolution of strain release in the lining (1) - drilling upper holes (see Fig. 4); (2) - chiselling between upper holes; (3) drilling lower holes; (4) - chiselling between lower holes

Table III

Pilot stretch	Mean measured strain ε_φ^s x (10^{-6})	D_s (MPa)	Required strain $\varepsilon_\varphi^\kappa$ x 10^{-6}	$\frac{\varepsilon_\varphi^s}{\varepsilon_\varphi^\kappa}$	σ_b (MPa) for $E_b = 2.10^4$ MPa
PD-1	350	11 000	150	2.18	7
PD-2	650	5 000	220	2.45	13
PD-3	600	6 000	200	3,00	12
PD-4	300	13 000	140	2.14	6
PD-5	500	2 000	290	1.72	10

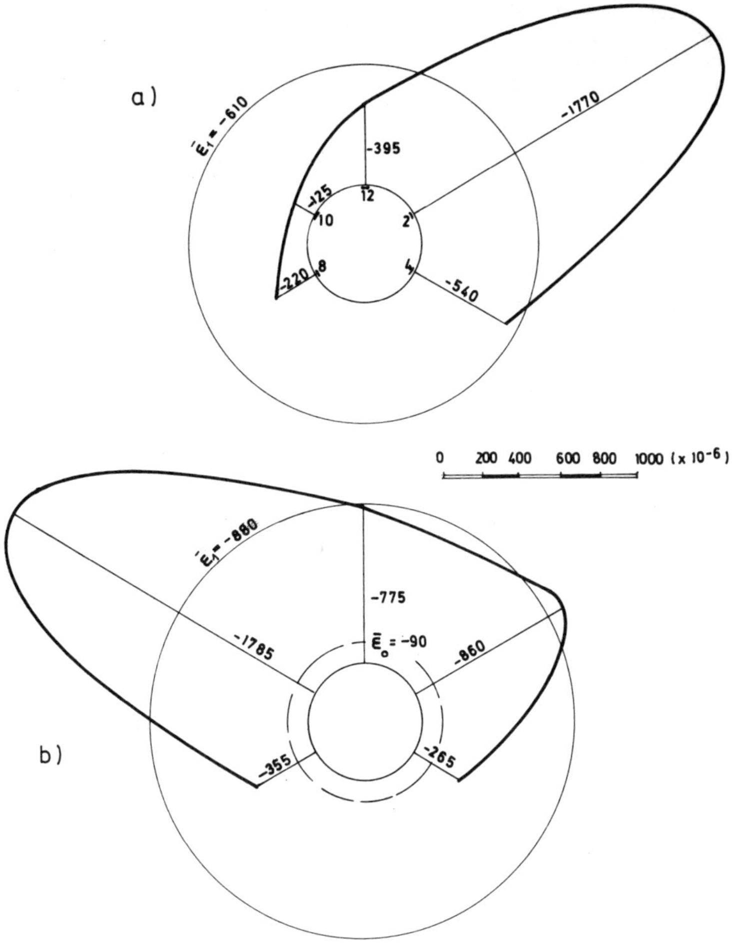

Fig. 11 Results of regrouting: (a) at chainage 5+251; (b) at chainage 5+261; $\tilde{\varepsilon}$ - average strain; ε_o - before regrouting; ε_1 - after regrouting

REFERENCES

/1/ Group of authors: Iskustva dosadašnjih istraživanja u dovodno-odvodnom tunelu reverzibilne hidroelektrane, (Experience from Investigations on the Two-Way Tunnel of a Pumped Storage Plant), Saopštenja, 5. jugoslovenski simpozij o mehanici stijena i podzemnim radovima, (Proceedings of the 5th Yugoslav Symposium on Rock Mechanics and Underground Workings), Split, 1980.

/2/ Kujundžić, B.: Hidrotehnički tuneli sa nearmiranim betonskim oblogama, velikih prečnika sa velikim unutrašnjim pritiscima, (Large-Diameter High-Pressure Hydraulic Tunnels Lined with Unreinforced Concrete), 4. jugoslovenski simpozijum o mehanici stena i podzemnim radovima, (Proceedings of the 4th Yugoslav Symposium on Rock Mechanics and Underground Workings), Kosovska Mitrovica - Zvečan, 1977.

/3/ Group of authors: Sadejstvo stenske mase, betona i lima u tunelima i oknima pod pritiskom reverzibilnih hidroelektrana, (Load-Sharing between Rock Mass, Concrete and Steel in Pressure Tunnels and Shafts of pumped Storage Hydroelectric Plants), Zavod za konstrukcije i geotehniku Instituta za vodoprivredu "Jaroslav Černi" Posebna izdanja, knjiga

23, Belgrade, 1980.

/4/ Glötzl F.: Umfangsmessung während der Vorspannung von Beton-Druckstollen, Das Pumpspeicherwerk Reisach-Rabenleite, Energieversorgung Ostbayern AG, Regensburg, Regensburg, 1957.

/5/ Kujundžić B.: Program istražnih radova za dovodno-odvodni tunel reverzibilne HE, (Investigation Programme for the Two-Way Tunnel of a Pumped Storage Plant), Zavod za konstrukcije i geotehniku Instituta za vodoprivredu "Jaroslav Černi", Belgrade, 1976, Stručna dokumentacija (Internal Documentation).

/6/ Obradović J.: Inženjersko geološka istraživanja za dovodno-odvodni tunel reverzibilne HE sa osvrtom na stanje razvoja i glavne principe inženjerske geologije, (Engineering-Geological Investigations for the Two-Way Tunnel of a Pumped Storage Plant with Special Reference to the State of the Art and Principles of Engineering Geology), Saopštenja, 5. jugoslovenski simpozij o mehanici stijena i podzemnim radovima, (Proceedings of the 5th Yugoslav Symposium on Rock Mechanics and Underground Workings), Split, 1980.

/7/ Marković O.: Program utvrdjivanja kriterijuma za izbor lokacija na kojima će se vrüiti oslobadjanje dilatacija u dovodno-odvodnom tunelu RHE, (How to Determine Criteria for the Location of Strain Release Tests in a Pressure Tunnel), Zavod za konstrukcije i geotehniku Instituta za vodoprivredu "Jaroslav Černi" Belgrade, 1982, Stručna dokumentacija, (Internal Documentation).

/8/ Kujundžić B., Grujić N.: Correlation between static and dynamic investigations of rock mass in situ, Proceedings of the First Congress of the ISRM, Lisabon, 1966, Vol. I.

/9/ Kujundžić B., Petrović Lj.: Korelacija statičkih i dinamičkih karakteristika deformabilnosti krečnjačkih stenskih masa,(Correlation between Static and Dynamic Deformability Characteristics of Limestone Rock Masses), Saopštenja, V jugoslovenski simpozij o mehanici stijena i podzemnim radovima, (Proceedings of the 5th Yugoslav Symposium on Rock Mechanics and Underground Workings), Split, 1980.

LOAD-SHARING BY ROCK MASS, CONCRETE AND STEEL LINING IN PRESSURE TUNNELS AND SHAFTS

Zusammenwirkung des Gebirges, des Betons und der Stahlpanzerung in Druckstollen und Druckschächten

Interaction de la roche, du béton et du soutènement en acier dans les galeries et les puits sous pression

B.KUJUNDŽIĆ
Jaroslav Černi Institute of Water Resources Engineering, Belgrade, Yugoslavia
Ž.NIKOLIĆ
Energoprojekt, Belgrade, Yugoslavia

SUMMARY:

The problem of designing and construction of water tunnels and pressure shafts of large diameters under high internal pressures is encountered more and more in contemporary water power engineering. The paper presents results of investigations concerning the following problems of coaction of steel sheet lining, concrete and rock mass, for cases of steel lining application: methodology of the rock mass investigations, general theoretical aspects of the rock mass - lining coaction, statical analyses of the "steel sheet - concrete - rock mass" system, trial testing of adopted solutions and observation of ready - made linings. Conclusions of interest to practice were drawn, with the basic attitude that under given conditions, solutions may be implemented involving full coaction of the rock mass in accepting internal water pressures.

ZUSAMMENFASSUNG:

Im zeitgemässen hydroenergetischen Bauwesen wird das Problem der Projektierung und des Ausbaus von Druckstollen und Druckschächten mit grossen Durchmessern und grossen Innendrücken immer deutlicher. Im Bericht werden Ergebnisse der Zusammenwirkung der Felsmasse, des Betons und des Stahlpanzerung behandelt, und zwar für Falle, bei denen eine Anwendung des Stahlauskleidung in Frage kommt: Methodologie der Erforschung der Felsmasse, algemeiner theoretischer Aspekt der Zusammenwirkung zwischen der Auskleidung und der Felsmasse, statische Analyse des Systems "Stahe - Beton - Felsmasse", Prüfung der angenomenen Lösungen, sowie die Beobachtung der ausgeführten Auskleidungen. Es werden für die Praxis interessante Schlussfolgerungen gezogen, deren Grungstellungnahme darin besteht, das man, unter gewissen Bedingungen, Lösungen anwenden kann, bei denen auf volle Zusammenwirkung der Felsmasse bei der Aufnahme der Innendrücke gerechnet wird.

RÉSUMÉ

Dans l'utilisation actuelle des forces hydrauliques se pose de plus, en plus le problème du projet et de la construction des galeries et des puits de grands diametres et soumis à de grandes charges internes. Dans le travail on montre les résultats des recherches des questions suivantes se rapportant à l'interaction de la tôle, du beton et de la roche dans les cas de considération de l'application du revêtement en acier et cela comme suit: méthodologie des essais de la masse rocheuse, aspect théorique général de l'intéraction du revêtement et de la roche, le calcul statique du système "tôle - béton - masse rocheuse", essais des solutions adoptées et auscultation des revêtements en exploitation. On tire des conclusions d'interêt pour la pratique avec une attitude générale que, sous quelques conditions, on peut adopter les solutions dans les quelles on compte sur une pleine interaction de la masse rocheusse dans l'action des charges internes.

1. INTRODUCTION

This paper presents results and conclusions drawn from and extensive study entitled "Load-sharing by Rock Mass, Concrete and Steel in Pressure Tunnels and Shafts of Pumped Storage Plants" carried out by the Structural and Geotechnical Engineering Department of the Jaroslav Černi Institute of Water Resources Engineering, for the Corporate Electricity Company of Belgrade. The authors were B. Kujundžić (study director), Ž. Radosavljević, K. Ivanović, O. Marković, Ž. Nikolić, M. Manojlović and Lj. Petrović. This condensed review presents the overall philosophy development, design concepts, the rock mass investigations necessary and modes of presentation of the results, a general discussion of the coaction of lining and rock mass, stress analysis of the steel-concrete-rock mass system, pilot tests of the lining during design and construction, testing and observation of the finished lining, and a final summing up.

2. GENERAL

Constantly accelerating economic growth demands ever more electricity and hence ever greater investment in power systems. Load peaks are a crucial problem whose solution may be sought either in trying to discourage peak consumption by making it more expensive than off-peak electricity, or by rendering the system capable of handling load peaks. This latter solution usually means building hydroelectric plants, and lately especially pumped storage plants, as standby or backup sources.

However, as the ratings of thermal and nuclear plants go higher and higher to meet the ever increasing power demands, so the chances of a large-scale dropout become greater. This means that the hydros also have to have high installed power which can be brought into play at short notice.

The trend towards hydroelectric plants of ever greater power naturally means large-diameter pressure tunnels and shafts, and large reservoirs, usually crested by high dams, making for a high hydrostatic pressure. Hence one of the problems which has to be solved is that of designing and constructing large diameter tunnels and shafts to withstand high internal pressure.

The problem of load-sharing by rock mass, concrete and steel lining is an important aspect of this problem. The basic function of the lining is to ensure impermeability and stability of the tunnel or shaft under operating conditions. This can be achieved most economically by taking the maximum advantage of the relevant properties of the rock mass. Therefore a thorough knowledge of the properties of the rock mass traversed by the tunnel is of prime importance.

To be able to take the coaction of the rock mass into account in design calculations for steel linings the following conditions must be fulfilled: reliable data on its engineering-geological and mechanical characteristics must be available; all cavities around the lining must be well filled by grouting; the thickness of the overburden must satisfy certain criteria.

Steel linings are very expensive and should therefore be used, in principle, only when no other type, usually concrete, is suitable.

In supply tunnels of hydroelectric plants, where the internal hydrostatic pressure can be up to 10 bars exceptionally even 15-20 bars, steel lining is in principle used on sections traversing permeable rock masses of very low modulus of deformation (faulted and very clayey zones, caverns, etc.), and on stretches with insufficient overburden, regardless of the deformation characteristics (portal sections, etc.)whenever the internal pressure is too high to allow the use of concrete lining. In dimensioning a steel lining for these cases, the coaction of the rock mass and lining in taking the water pressure load is not taken into account.

In pressure shafts, which are subject to much higher maximum hydrostatic and dynamic pressures, of the order of tens of bars, steel lining is also used in sections through permeable rock mass wherever the internal pressure may exceed the strength of other types of lining. Load-sharing with the rock mass is taken into account providing that the above conditions are satisfied and the mechanical characteristics of the rock are satisfactory.

3. LINING DESIGN

The prime considerations in choosing the type of lining for a pressure tunnel or shaft must be above all the quality, i.e. deformability of the rock mass, its permeability, the magnitude of the internal pressure, and the tunnel or shaft diameter. A number of types of lining is available, which can be roughly divided into: conventional concrete, steel, and prestressed.

Conventional concrete linings may be plain or reinforced, single- or double-layer and with or without special proofing. As linings with special proofing have not yet been thoroughly verified in practice, they should be used with due caution. Generally speaking, in pressure tunnels steel lining will be used in the case of large diameter and high internal pressure, where the tunnel traverses weak or heavily damaged rock.

A costly steel lining will only be used when no other lining will do. Therefore a basic prerequisite for making the choice of lining is a knowledge of the limits of application of other types.

In pressure shafts steel linings are the rule. The steel sheet, concrete and rock mass share the internal hydrostatic and hydrodynamic pressure load. A special case is that of a concrete lining sheathed in thin steel sheet as waterproofing.

Prestressing may be used both with conventional concrete linings and with steel linings. In the case of concrete linings two types of prestressing are used. One is mechanical prestressing by any of various methods (Kunz, Dyckerhoff and Widmann, VSL, etc.), the other is prestressing by means of grouting, either between the lining and the rock, or directly into the rock mass around the tunel through boreholes (Kieser--Berger, TIWAG, etc.). Grouting can save steel in the case of steel linings: usually the contact between steel and concrete is grouted, with the shaft either empty or under pressure (TIWAG, Kiessling, etc.).

4. ROCK MASS INVESTIGATIONS

For a proper analysis of the coaction of rock mass, concrete and steel data must be obtained on the engineering-geological and hydrogeological properties of the rock mass for each specific case, and especially its deformation characteristics, primary and secondary stress state, and the groundwater conditions.

The choice of methods for investigating rock masses must take into account the fact that they are in principle discontinuous, heterogeneous, anisotropic and stressed.

Deformability. This is investigated by in situ tests. It is expressed in terms of quantitative mechanical characteristics which are directly introduced into the stress calculations for the lining. In situ tests yield: the modulus of deformation D, the modulus of elasticity E, and Poisson's ratio . Apart from these static characteristics, as correlation parameters in setting up a deformability model the following dynamic characteristics are also used: the velocities of elastic waves v_p and v_s, and the dynamic modulus of elasticity E_{dyn}.

The static methods of deformability testing most often used include: test chambers, radial jacks, probe dilatometer, and flat jack. The best method in this case is the radial jack, which allows the same stress state to be induced as will be produced by the actual structure (tunnel or shaft), and it is much simpler and cheaper than the test chamber method. This latter method is used in special cases, particularly when it is necessary to investigate not only the rock but also the lining during the design stage. The probe dilatometer method is appropriate in the case of vertical pressure shafts. The flat jack method has been the most used to date so that there is now a considerable body of data which enables a creative application of the principle of analogy in comparing a specific lining design with other alternatives applied previously under comparable engineering-geological conditions.

The above methods only give data about the rock mass stress-deformation behaviour at a specific number of points. Generalization of these values to the rock mass as a whole is enabled by combined static-dynamic methods. By applying refraction seismic and cross-hole methods along the route of the tunnel or shaft, the rock mass can be divided up into a number of zones quasi-homogeneous in a certain parameter, usually v_p or E_{dyn}. By making comparative dynamic tests using microseismic methods at the points where the static methods have been applied, correlations of the form $D = D(v_p)$ can be set up. Thus for a zone which is quasi-homogeneous in the dynamic parameter v_p, the corresponding value of D can be estimated. This procedure ultimately yields a deformability model of the rock mass, which provides a basis for design.

Virgin stresses. The investigation of virgin stresses for the purposes of pressure tunnel and shaft design has two principle tasks. The first is to estimate primary stresses, and hence the coefficient of lateral pressure . A knowledge of this coefficient is essential for a static stress analysis of the lining.

The second task is to investigate secondary stresses, i.e. the stress state induced in the neighbourhood of the working after excavation. This information is essential when weighing the pros and cons of steel and other types of lining, principally concrete prestressed by pressure grouting.

The most suitable methods for investigating virgin stresses are: strain gauges in boreholes (TLM-site-laboratory method), the Tincelin-Mayer method, and microseismics: ultrasonic hole logging and ultrasonic cross-holing.

The Groundwater Situation. This must be explored because external water exerts a load which has to be taken into account in the lining stress analysis. This influence is particularly important with steel linings, especially with regard to the possibility of lining buckling, but it also has to be considered with other types of lining with a certain degree of permeability, with which a steel lining has to be compared in economic terms.

The jointing of the rock mass is explored by engineering-geological methods, usually mapping, while hydrogeological methods are used to identify zones of different groundwater level (usually by means of piezometers) and to estimate rock mass permeability.

5. PRESENTATION OF ROCK MASS INVESTIGATION RESULTS IN FORMS MOST HELPFUL TO THE DESIGNER

The lining of a pressure tunnel of shaft, especially a steel lining sharing the inside pressure load with concrete and rock mass, calls for especially cautious design. While the steel and concrete are artificial materials with rather well-defined and known mechanical characteristics, the rock mass is in all respects widely variable both from case to case and from place to place in the same structure.

Thus in design estimates regarding local and overall stability and safety the behaviour of the rock mass is the most sensitive factor. Therefore great attention must be paid to the quality and reliability of those characteristics of the rock mass which figure in the stress-strain analysis of the lining.

Apart from the need for reliable, accurate and comprehensive measurements, it is also very important to present these results in forms which will give the designer maximum assistance.

The ultimate aim of the rock mass investigations is to divide up the rock mass into so-called quasi-homogeneous zones, within which its properties can be treated as being constant, and to associate with each such zone numerical values of the characteristics relevant to the design of the structure.

A methodology for acheiving this aim has been developed by Kujundžić (2). The measurement results are presented to the designer in the form of: engineering-geological sections (EGS), the integral engineering-geological section (IEGS), engineering-geological models (EGM) and geotechnical models (GM).

An EGS is plotted for each of the relevant parameters measured or observed, as: lithogenetic composition and fabric, jointing, weathering, groundwater, velocity of propagation of elastic waves, resistivity, virgin stresses, deformability, etc. The EGS's in fact simply display the measurements and observations plotted on different sections through the rock mass. For pressure tunnels and shafts these are usually longitudinal vertical sections along the tunnel or shaft.

The IEGS presents a synthesis of all the parametric EGS's for a given section after they have been analyzed and integrated into a logical and consistent whole.

EGM's are set up in the parameters relevant to design of the lining, such as: deformability, virgin stresses, groundwater These models provide an appropriately simplified representation of the rock mass as a natural medium and show its quasi-homogeneous zones.

GM's show the rock mass divided up into zones within which certain works or rock improvements will have to be carried out: excavation, grouting, rock bolting, drainage, gunniting, etc. Grouting for water tunnels and shafts may be contact, bonding, consolidation, sealing or stressing.

The EGS's, IEGS's, EGM's and GM's should be accompanied by written reports which include interpretations of the graphics, conclusions and observations concerning the properties of the rock mass, regular phenomena which have been noted, and guidelines for design and construction of the lining.

6. GENERAL ASPECTS OF THE COACTION OF LINING AND ROCK MASS

A steel lining involves three basic elements steel plate, secondary concrete lining, and the surrounding rock mass. If the working is not stable, a fourth element is usually included, primary lining (concrete, gunnite, etc.) whose primary function is to ensure stability of the opening after excavation and before the steel and secondary concrete lining is emplaced. A steel lining, whether ordinary or prestressed, is the most complicated type of lining for pressure tunnels and shafts. To make a reliable static stress analysis its behaviour during various stages of execution must be known. The final stress-

-strain state of the lining depends on the constructional history and the associated evolution of stressing: from this aspect we differentiate the following stages and influences in the history of the tunnel: excavation, primary lining, emplacement of steel lining, secondary concrete lining, loading by external groundwater, loading by internal pressure, grouting and prestressing, temperature influences, etc.

Research has shown that if a primary lining is emplaced, rheological processes in the rock mass and primary lining lead to the development of pressures at their contact. This on the one hand gives rise to pressures in the primary lining, opposing the tendency of the rock mass to close the opening (convergence), and on the other hand to radial pressure in the rock mass which makes for a more favourable stress state in it.

The next stage in the behaviour of the lining does not begin until the steel begins to take up the load exerted by internal hydrostatic pressure. Then all three components, the steel, the secondary concrete lining and the rock mass(and the primary lining if executed) share the load induced by internal pressure, each of them with an elastic or quasi-elastic behaviour at first. The first break point occurs when the tensile strength of the concrete in the secondary lining is exceeded and cracks appear, whereafter the concrete behaves only as a buffer between the steel and the rock mass.

Further augmentation of the water pressure in the tunnel leads to cracking of the rock mass. This occurs when the compressive stress reserve in the rock mass is exceeded by the normal stress in the tangential direction, leading to cracking and the opening of existing joints. At this stage the load-sharing role of the rock mass decreases, and more and more of the load is taken up by the steel. In off-loading the rock does not behave as an elastic medium, while the cracked concrete lining follows the strain of the rock mass. Thus the concrete and rock retain permanent deformations after the first hydrostatic loading. The steel, on the other hand, returns elastically to its original dimensions, leaving a gap between it and the concrete. When the pressure rises again the steel must first deform until this gap closes, and during this time it is taking all the load. After closure of the gap the rock mass begins to take a share of the load. Once it has cracked the concrete lining becomes merely a buffer between steel and rock. In the second and subsequent loading cycles the rock mass behaves approximately as an elastic medium and the cycles stabilize.

The appearance of a gap between steel and concrete can be prevented by pressure grouting of the steel-concrete interface. In this case, before the first loading cycle the steel is under tangential pressure stress. Off-loading does not lead to the formation of a gap; the permanent deformation of the rock mass only causes a reduction of the initial stress, but this still remains positive. In subsequent load cycles the load is shared by steel and rock right from the beginning.

7. STATIC STRESS-STRAIN ANALYSIS OF THE STEEL-CONCRETE-ROCK MASS SYSTEM

The stress-strain analysis of a composite structure of this kind is complicated. It must take into account the following factors: rock mass deformability, heterogeneity and anisotropy, virgin stresses, estimated cracking of the concrete and rock, the gap between concrete and steel or concrete and rock mass, temperature changes, prestressing (of steel, concrete and rock mass).

A stress-strain analysis of a prestressed lining must take into consideration stress relaxation due to creep of the concrete and rock mass, shrinkage of the concrete, and shrinkage and creep of the hardened grout around the tunnel or shaft. It can be very considerable, sometimes even more than 65% of the initial stress in the lining right after grouting, and even as much as 80% of the initial stress in cases where the rock mass has low deformation characteristics.

The analysis must also treat the problem of the minimum thickness of the overburden. For this purpose Radosavljević's criterion is recommended.

The problem of twin tunnels, i.e. of the minimum spacing between two or more tunnels or shafts may have to be solved. Their spacing must be such that it is greater than the sum of the perturbed zones created around neighboring openings. In practice it has been found that this is usually about 30 m.

Stress analysis procedures for the lining itself can be roughly divided into three types. The first is analytical, based on the direct application of Lame's theory of thick tubes, the second is graphical, using the Lauffer-Seeber method (3) with strains measured *in situ* (usually by the radial jack method), while the third involves the method of finite elements and is the most universal since it can directly take into account factors such as anisotropy, heterogeneity, prestressing and jointing of the rock mass. However, regardless of the method used, reliable input data are a sine qua non, especially data referring to the mechanical characteristics of the rock mass.

For dimensioning steel linings the following approaches may be encountered in practice:

a. The lining thickness is determined with reference only to the internal water pressure, assuming no load-sharing action of the rock mass. Maximum stresses are within permitted limits for the steel. The problem of stability of the lining under load from external water is solved by stiffening or by anchoring the steel into the concrete.

Though this is considered a conservative approach it is still widespread, chiefly advocated by the steel manufacturers.

b. The lining thickness is determined with reference to the internal water pressure, taking the coaction of the rock mass into account as an augmentation of the stress limits for the steel, up to 90% of the elastic limit. The boiler formula is used. The problem of lining stability under external water pressure is solved by stiffening or anchoring the steel.

This is a less conservative approach, and is used when conditions obtain for the coaction of the steel with the rock mass and concrete, but if such coaction should fail, the lining will not burst.

c. The optimum lining thickness is determined with reference to both internal and external water pressure. In calculations concerning the internal pressure load the coaction of the rock mass is taken into account, as are the influences of temperature changes and gaps between steel, concrete and rock. The problem of stability under load from external water is solved as under a. and b.

This approach is the soundest both from the engineering and the economic aspect, but all the prerequisites for estimating load-sharing by the rock mass must be satisfied.

8. LINING TESTS

If approach c. is taken, it is sound engineering to require qualitative and quantitative proof of the coaction of the lining and rock mass in sharing the internal pressure load. This is achieved by making lining tests both during design and during construction.

The purpose of these tests is to verify the viability of the design concept, to determine the stress-strain state in the lining and rock mass, and to enable the setting up of a rheological model of the rock mass. The following quantities are measured: radial strains in the rock mass, contact radial stresses between lining and rock mass and between concrete and steel lining, tangential strains or stress in the concrete or steel and concrete lining, convergence of the lining intrados, and behaviour of the concrete.

These tests are carried out in special test chambers during design and on pilot stretches, usually during construction. The synthesis of different measurements in a test chamber should demonstrate both qualitatively and quantitatively the existence and degree of load-sharing between the steel or concrete and the rock mass.

Test chamber investigations should be made early on during the design phase. However, the problem of locating a test chamber in a representative environment arises. It can be satisfactorily solved if the tests are designed and implemented according to the principle of "from the general towards the particular".

The tests are made during pressure grouting, under hydrostatic pressure, and after evacuation of the test chamber.

While test chamber investigations yield basic design data, tests on pilot stretches are carried out, as a rule, during the execution of the main construction jobs, and only in cases where pressure grouting of the rock mass or its interface with the concrete or the steel--concrete interface is envisaged. Their only purpose is to check the effect of grouting and determine optimal grouting parameters.

Measurements on pilot stretches are made during pressure grouting, and subsequently to evaluate stress relaxation in the lining.

It is usual to present the results of test chamber and pilot stretch measurements in both graphical and tabular form.

Graphically the results are presented as time graphs, first for each individual gauge, then averaged values from different kinds of measurement, and finally time graphs for all the readings made at one point. Radial diagrams are also given, plotting quantities measured with one kind of gauge over a cross section of the tunnel or shaft under given characteristic circumstances or at certain time intervals.

The tables give the results of each individual reading, and average values for the same readings. The results are presented for different values of characteristic parameters (e.g. grouting pressure) and characteristic time intervals (relaxation).

9. TESTING AND OBSERVATION OF THE FINISHED LINING

Testing of the finished lining is carried out in three main cases: before it is put into use, during use, and at the time of maintenance on spection.

Testing before the tunnel of shaft is put into operation is obligatory. It yields data on the behaviour of the structure as a whole, allows a safety estimate to be made, and ties in all the partial tests made during construction with the overall behaviour. It is also a prerequisite for allowing the structure to be put into regular use.

Many investigations, both in Yugoslavia and abroad, have demonstrated a high degree of load-sharing between steel/concrete lining and the rock mass, often reducing the stress in the steel by 70-90% of that in the corresponding free tube.

Testing of the finished lining includes measurement of strain in the concrete and steel of the lining, concrete-rock contact pressure, radial strain, i.e. changes in the diameter of the tunnel or shaft and of the rock zone engaged in load-sharing, water and rock temperature, internal water pressure, and groundwater pressure insofar as there is any possibility of it affecting the lining. Apart from these measurements, which are carried out at specific cross sections, in the case of pressure shafts measurements are also made to determine shaft volume change, from data on the amount of water put into it during pressure testing. In tunnels without steel lining the leakage rate is also measured.

Testing during operation has not yet achieved obligatory status, though it can yield valuable information on the behaviour of the lining.

Such tests confirm the existence of coaction between steel, concrete and rock mass and that this coaction is maintained during operation, although no sufficiently long-term measurements have been made to completely quantify it. Long-term testing of this kind can provide an insight into the efficacy of various rock improvement procedures.

Observations during a maintenance inspection provide qualitative information. Defects observed may be interpreted by tying in these observations with geological data and the results of mechanical and geophysical investigations of the rock mass. Defects associated with the steel of the lining are usually found to be a consequence of insufficient earlier investigation of the rock mechanics, structure and fabric, and/or insufficient rock improvement measures.

Efficient testing and observation has to be properly designed and programmed in the light of the specific features of the structure, specifying characteristic measuring points, appropriate equipment, and all the quantities which have to be measured.

10. SUMMING UP

The basic aim in designing a pressure tunnel or shaft is to acheive the necessary operating safety at minimum expense and the optimum time of construction. From this point of view the problem of load--sharing between rock mass, concrete and steel is one aspect of the more general problem of economical design, especially as regards saving in steel.

The linings of pressure tunnels and shafts, especially those with a steel linning in which the internal pressure load is shared by steel, concrete and rock mass, call for cautions design. While the steel and concrete are artificial materials whose mechanical characteristics are usually well-known, the rock mass is a natural medium whose composition, fabric, state and properties vary within wide limits from case to case and from place to place in the same working.

Hence in the composite structure "steel--concrete-rock mass" it is the last which is the most sensitive as regards its influence on local and overall stability and safety. Therefore great attention must be paid to the quality and reliability of those characteristics of the rock mass which figure in the stress analysis. It must not be forgotten that pressure tunnels and shafts are linear structures, so that a failure at only one point will put the entire system out of action.

However, today we have at our disposal a reliable methodology for the in situ experimental determination of all the necessary rock mechanical characteristics.

Given that the input data for the stress analysis, especially the mechanical characteristics of all componente of the composite "steel-concrete-rock mass" system, can today be determined to a satisfactory accuracy, and that calculation methods for such composite structures are available which enable a large number of diverse parametric influences to be taken into account, and on the other hand that tests on finished pressure tunnels and shafts to demonstrate a high degree of land-sharing between the lining and the rock mass, i.e. reduction of the stress on the steel, it follows that in designing linings of this kind the coaction of the rock mass should be taken into account.

At present there is no general methodology based on well-defined indices or characteristics for weighing the pros and cans of steel lining (steel-concrete-rock) in a given pressure tunnel or shaft. The methodology for choosing the lining is indirect and reduces to comparative design of steel and other types of lining, in particular prestressed concrete using various prestressing procedures. The final choice is then made by an engineering and economic comparison of the different alternative designs.

The behaviour of a finished lining and the load-sharing between it and the rock mass can be demonstrated by tests. For pressure tunnels and shafts these tests are usually done in test chambers and on pilot stretches.

Test chamber investigations yield data for the designer. They should be carried out early on in design. The measurements are made firstly during pressure grouting or any other prestressing procedure, secondly under internal hydrostatic pressure, and thirdly after evacuation of the chamber.

Tests on pilot stretches are usually made during construction, but only if pressure grouting or some other prestressing procedure is to be used. The tests should yield data on the degree of load-sharing between lining and rock as a function of time, and elements for the determination of any correction of the construction technology which may be necessary.

Considerable importance should also be attached to tests on the finished lining before it goes into use, and later on during operation and during maintenance inspection.

By prudent combination of experimental investigations of the rock mass early on in design, tests on the lining during construction (pilot stretches), and verificatory tests on the finished lining before the tunnel or shaft goes into use, constantly paralleld with calculations and adaptation of the mathematical models, one can confidently opt for a "steel-concrete--rock" design counting on full load-sharing by the rock mass.

REFERENCES

1. Group of authors: Sadejstvo stenske mase, betona i lima u tunelima i oknima pod pritiskom reverzibilnih hidroelektrana, (Load-sharing by Rock Mass, Concrete and Steel in Pressure Tunnels and Shafts of Pumped Storage Plants), Department of Structural and Geotechnical Engineering of the Jaroslav Černi Institute of Water Resources Engineering, Belgrade, 1980.
2. Kujundžić B.: Sadržina i metodika izrade inženjerskogeoloških preseka i inženjerskogeoloških i geotehničkih modela, (Engineering Geological Sections and Engineering Geological and Geotechnical Models: What They Consist of and How to Make Them) Saopštenja sa IX kongresa Jugoslovenskog komiteta za visoke brane, (Proceedings of the 9th Congress of the Yugoslav Committe on Large Dams), Zlatibor, 1973.
3. Lauffer H., G. Seeber: Die Bemessung von Druckstollen-und Druckschachtauskleidungen für Innendruck auf Grund von Felsdehnungsmessungen, Österreichische Ingenieur - Zeitschrift, 1962, Heft 2.

Prof. Branislav Kujundžić, Department of Structural and Geotechnical Engineering, Jaroslav Černi Institute of Water Resources Engineering, Belgrade

Života Nikolić, Design Office, Hydraulic Engineering Department, The Energoprojekt Company, Belgrade

THE ELASTO-PLASTIC THEORY APPLIED TO PRESSURE TUNNELS

Die Anwendung der Elastizitäts- und Plastizitätstheorie auf Druckstollen

La théorie élasto-plastique appliquée aux galeries forcées

LU JIAYOU

Water Conservancy & Hydroelectric Power Scientific Research Institute, Beijing, China

SUMMARY:
In calculating the stresses in the lining of a pressure tunnel with circular cross-section, it is generally assumed that the deformability of rock masses follows the theory of elasticity. However, this assumption does not often consist with the real characteristics of rock masses. In-situ deformation tests have shown that the rock masses yield the law of anisotropic elasto-plastic media. In some cases, the anisotropic behaviour does not obviously express and the rock masses can be approximately treated as the isotropic elasto-plastic media. This paper presents a method dealing with the calculation of the lining stresses considering the elasto-plastic stress-strain relationship based on some in-situ test results. The rock masses are treated as the linear strain hardening media. The critical interior water pressure for creating the plastic deformation of rock masses is given. It is also discussed how to determine the mechanical parameters of rock masses.

ZUSAMMENFASSUNG:
Bei der Berechnung der Spannungen für die Auskleidung eines Druckstollens mit kreisförmigem Querschnitt wird allgemein angenommen, dass die Verformungen des Gebirges der Elastizitätstheorie folgen. Diese Annahme stimmt jedoch oft nicht mit den wirklichen Verhältnissen im Gebirge überein. In-situ Verformungsmessungen haben gezeigt, dass das Gebirge dem Stoffgesetz des anisotropen, elasto-plastischen Mediums folgt. In einigen Fällen zeigt sich kein offensichtlich anisotropes Verhalten und das Gebirge kann annäherungsweise wie ein isotropes elasto-plastisches Medium behandelt werden. Diese Arbeit stellt eine Methode vor, die sich mit der Ermittlung der Spannungen in der Auskleidung aus elasto-plastischen Spannungs-Dehnungs-Beziehungen beschäftigt, die auf Ergebnissen von in-situ Tests basieren. Das Gebirge wird wie ein sich linear verfestigendes Medium behandelt. Der für die Entstehung der plastischen Verformungen verantwortliche kritische Wasserinnendruck wird angegeben. Weiterhin wird das Problem der Ermittlung der mechanischen Gebirgskennwerte diskutiert.

RÉSUMÉ:
Dans le calcul des contraintes dans le revêtement d'une galerie sous-pression, on suppose que la déformation des massifs rocheux suit la théorie d'élasticité. Cependant, cette hypothèse ne s'applique pas toujours aux caractéristiques réelles des massifs rocheux. Des essais de déformation in-situ ont montré que les massifs rocheux répondent à la loi des substances élasto-plastiques anisotropes. Dans quelques cas, le comportement anisotrope ne s'exprime pas d'une façon évidente et les massifs rocheux peuvent être traités approximativement comme les milieux élasto-plastiques isotropes. Cette étude présente une méthode qui traite du calcul des contraintes dans le revêtement en considérant la relation contrainte-déformation élasto-plastique basée sur quelques résultats d'essais in-situ. Les massifs rocheux sont traités comme les substances durcies à déformation linéaire. La pression d'eau interne critique pour produire la déformation plastique des massifs rocheux est donnée. Aussi s'agit-il d'une discussion sur la façon de déterminer les paramètres mécaniques des massifs rocheux.

I. Introduction

Concerning with the theory applied to the calculation of the stresses in pressure tunnel lining with circular cross section, it is generally assumed that the rock masses are elastic media. The contact force between the rock masses and lining follows Winkler's law. But a lot of in-situ rock mechanics tests show that the rock masses are not pure elastic media and the isotropic linear elastic theory can only be applied in a few cases.

The mechanical behaviors of rock masses are very complicated. It is not only affected by the micro-structure and mineral crystals, but also by the macro-structural planes, such as faults, joints and beddings. In hydraulic engineering, the later is more important than the former and strongly affects the deformation and strength characteristics of rock masses. It is the reason, that both the in-situ elastic modulus and yeilding stresses are lower than that obtained from the laboratory tests using rock samples.

The deformation of a discontinuity under normal stresses should approach a certain limit. The discontinuity should be compacted under compression until it no longer affects the total deformation of the rock masses, while it should get apart as the tension stress exceeds its tensile strength. Its shearing deformation is a function of both shearing and normal stresses. The stratified rock masses with parallel planes of discontinuities behaved as composite materials show their anisotropic characters strongly. In contrary, if there havn't any major fault and the joints and fractures exsist in a crissed-cross pattern, the rock masses can be treated as the isotropic media without serious errors.

At present time, there are two mechanical approaches to the rock masses: (1) In the cases of exsisting major faults, the deformation and strength characteristics of rocks and discontinuities should be considered seperately, and stress analysis should be done by using finite element method; (2) In the cases of absence of major faults in the rock masses, the homogenous continued medium mechanics should be applied as usual. If the rock masses deformed more or less similar to the isotropic media, as above mentioned, it appears to be able to solve some problems analytically.

The in-situ test results represent the relationship between the boundary forces and the overall displacement of certain geological element. This kind of stress-deformation relationship expresses a physical mean in the statistical aspects. The mechanical model based on such relationship is equivalent to a pseudo-homogenous medium. Calculating the stress field within the rock masses by using such model must induce some errors, even serious errors at individual points, but it can give the values of boundary displacements due to given boundary forces with certain degree of accuracy, and seems to be suitable to analyze the interaction between rock masses and structures in the fields of stress analysis of pressure tunnel lining.

II. Constitutive equation of rock masses

As above mentioned, the rock masses are the anisotropic elasto-plastic media. It is difficult to obtain the rigorous analytical solution and need to make some simplification according to the rock mechanics tests and the stress level of the lining. There are two most important cases needed of consideration; (1) anisotropic linear elasticity; (2) isotropic elasto-plasticity. Present paper mainly deals with the later case. A alternative method for analyzing the lining stresses based on the typical stress-strain relationship (see Fig. 1) from in-situ test results[2-4] treated as the linear hardening materials have been suggested[5].

Assume the yeilding of the rock masses follows the Von Mises' criterion, which can be expressed in terms of the octahedral shearing stresses as follow:

$$K = \frac{\sqrt{6}}{6} \tau_0 \qquad (1)$$

where

$$\tau_o = \frac{1}{3}\sqrt{(\sigma_1-\sigma_2)^2+(\sigma_2-\sigma_3)^2+(\sigma_3-\sigma_1)^2} \quad (2)$$

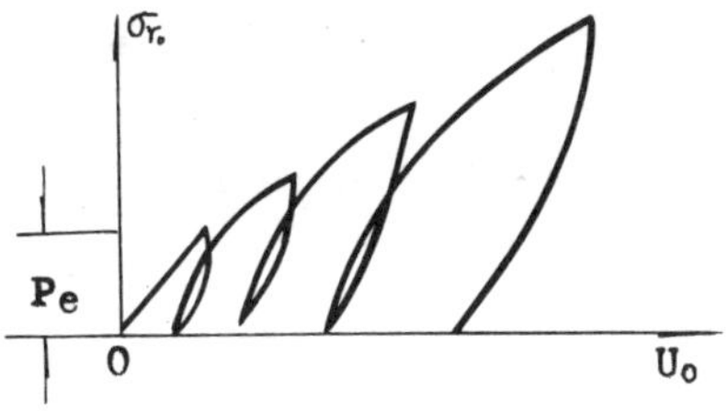

Fig. 1 The typical stress-strain curve of rock masses

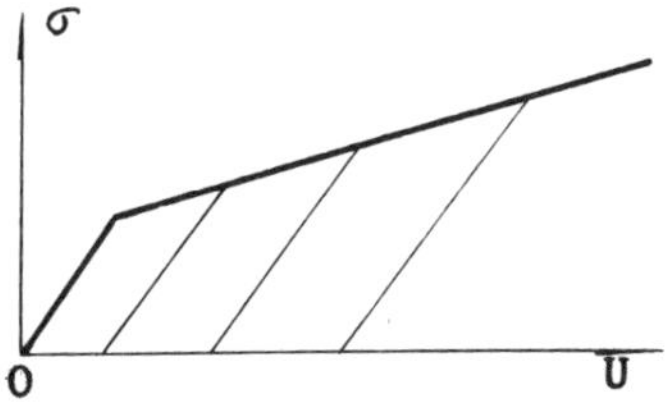

Fig. 2 Idealized stress-strain curve.

The total strain of rock masses in plastic region consists of elastic strain and plastic strain. The elastic strain follows Hook's law, and the relationship between plastic stress increment and strain increment can be expressed as:

$$\left.\begin{aligned} d\varepsilon_x^p &= \frac{F(\tau_o)}{3\tau_o}\left[\sigma_x - \frac{1}{2}(\sigma_y - \sigma_z)\right]d\tau_o \\ &\cdots\cdots \\ d\gamma_{xz}^p &= \frac{F(\tau_o)}{\tau_o}\tau_{xz}\,d\tau_o \end{aligned}\right\} \quad (3)$$

where

$$F(\tau_o) = f'(\tau_o)$$

the linear hardening stress-strain relationship can be expressed as (see Fig. 3):

$$f(\tau_o) = \frac{\tau_o - K_e}{N} \quad (\tau_o \geqslant K_e) \quad (4)$$

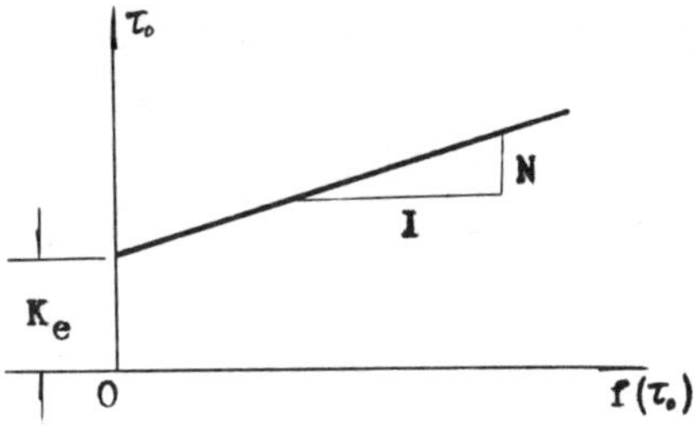

Fig. 3 The linear strain hardening parameters.

For in-sitn water pressure test of circular cross-sectional tunnel, r_o represents the radius of testing tunnel, P_e the pressure at elastic limit. Poisson's ratio ν is determined by test results on rock samples, the other mechanical parameters of rock masses can be determined by using expressions (5) to (8).

modulns of elasticity:

$$E = \frac{\sigma_{r_o}(1+\nu)r_o}{u_o} \quad (\sigma_{r_o} < P_e) \qquad (5)$$

elastic limit:

$$K_e = \frac{\sqrt{6}}{3}P_e \qquad (6)$$

The boundary stress and deformation of the tunnel. (when $\sigma_{r_o} \geqslant P_e$):

$$\left.\begin{aligned} \sigma_{r_o} &= \sqrt{6}\left[(K_e-\beta)\frac{t^2}{2r_o} + \beta\left(\frac{1}{2} + \ln\frac{t}{r_o}\right)\right] \\ u_o &= \frac{\sqrt{6}(1+\nu)K_e t^2}{2Er_o} + \frac{\sqrt{6}(1+\nu)(1-2\nu)\beta}{E} \times \\ &\times \left[\left(\frac{t^2}{r_o} - r_o\right) - r_o \ln\frac{t}{r_o}\right] \end{aligned}\right\} \quad (7)$$

Then the radius of plastic zone t and constant β can be calculated from expression (7) by trial and errors method. Because

$$\beta = \frac{K_e E}{4N(1-\nu^2)+E} \qquad (8)$$

then N can be determined from expression (8). The derivation of expression (7) will be given in the next paragraph.

III. The elasto-plastic analysis of circular cavity

The elastic strain in plastic region can be expressed as:

$$\varepsilon_r=\frac{1+\nu}{E}\left[(1-2\nu)\sigma_r-\nu\sqrt{6}\tau_o\right] \quad (9)$$

$$\varepsilon_\theta=\frac{1+\nu}{E}\left[(1-2\nu)\sigma_r-(1-\nu)\sqrt{6}\tau_o\right] \quad (10)$$

and plastic strain:

$$\varepsilon_r=-\frac{\sqrt{6}}{4}f(\tau_o) \quad (11)$$

$$\varepsilon_\theta=\frac{\sqrt{6}}{4}f(\tau_o) \quad (12)$$

The equation of equilibrium:

$$\frac{d\sigma_r}{dr}+\frac{\sigma_r-\sigma_\theta}{r}=0 \quad (13)$$

It can be rewritten as:

$$\frac{d\sigma_r}{dr}=\frac{\sqrt{6}\tau_o}{r} \quad (14)$$

From expressions (9) to (14) and (4), get:

$$r\frac{d\tau_o}{dr}+2\tau_o-\frac{2K_eE}{4N(1-\nu^2)+E}=0 \quad (15)$$

Solve the differential equation (15), get:

$$\tau_o=\frac{D}{r^2}+\beta \quad (16)$$

from expressions (14) and (16), get:

$$\sigma_r=-\frac{\sqrt{6}D}{2r^2}+\sqrt{6}\beta\ln r+C \quad (17)$$

$$\sigma_\theta=\frac{\sqrt{6}D}{2r^2}+\sqrt{6}\beta(1+\ln r)+C \quad (18)$$

where C and D are integration constants.

Boundary conditions are (see Fig. 4).

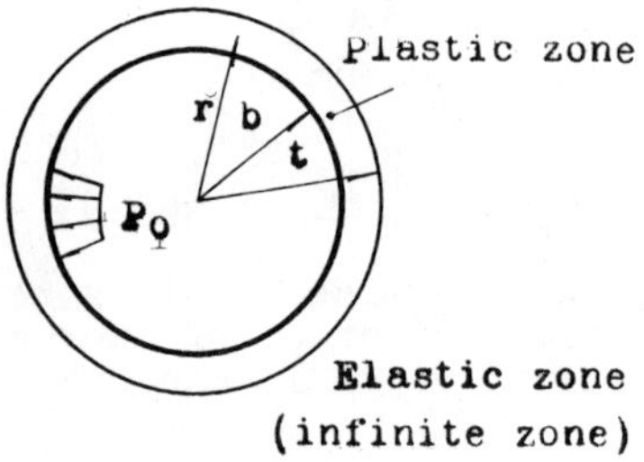

Fig. 4 The elastic and plastic region around a circular cavity.

$$\left.\begin{aligned} &\text{at } r=\infty,\ \sigma_r=0,\\ &r=b,\ \sigma_r=-P_o\\ &r=t,\ \sigma_\theta-\sigma_r=\sqrt{6}K_e\\ &r=t,\ \sigma_r=\frac{AE}{(1+\nu)(1-2\nu)}-\frac{BE}{(1+\nu)t^2}\end{aligned}\right\} \quad (19)$$

where A and B are also integration constants.

The solution of stress and deformation in plastic region ($b\leq r\leq t$) can be expressed as follows:

$$\left.\begin{aligned}\sigma_r&=-\frac{\sqrt{6}(K_e-\beta)t^2}{2r^2}-\sqrt{6}\beta\left(\frac{1}{2}-\ln\frac{r}{t}\right)\\ \sigma_\theta&=\frac{\sqrt{6}(K_e-\beta)t^2}{2r^2}+\sqrt{6}\beta\left(\frac{1}{2}+\ln\frac{r}{t}\right)\end{aligned}\right\} \quad (20)$$

$$u=\frac{(1+\nu)\sqrt{6}K_et^2}{2Er}+\frac{(1+\nu)(1-2\nu)}{E}\times$$
$$\times\left[\frac{\sqrt{6}}{2}\beta\left(\frac{t^2}{r}-r\right)+\sqrt{6}\beta r\ln\frac{r}{t}\right] \quad (21)$$

that in elastic region ($t\leq r<\infty$):

$$\left.\begin{aligned}\sigma_r&=-\frac{\sqrt{6}K_et^2}{2r^2}\\ \sigma_\theta&=\frac{\sqrt{6}K_et^2}{2r^2}\end{aligned}\right\} \quad (22)$$

$$u=\frac{\sqrt{6}(1+\nu)K_et^2}{2Er} \quad (23)$$

IV. Stress analysis of tunnel lining

The stresses of tunnel lining can be calculated by the thick-walled tube equation in theory of elasticity:

$$\sigma_{or}=\frac{P_ia^2-P_ob^2}{b^2-a^2}+\frac{a^2b^2(P_o-P_i)}{(b^2-a^2)r^2} \quad (24)$$

$$\sigma_{o\theta}=\frac{P_ia^2-P_ob^2}{b^2-a^2}-\frac{a^2b^2(P_o-P_i)}{(b^2-a^2)r^2} \quad (25)$$

where, the contact force P_o between rock mass and lining is solved by compatible condition:

$$P_o=\frac{2P_i(1-\nu_o)a^2}{(1-2\nu_o)b^2+a^2}-\frac{\sqrt{6}E_o(1+\nu)(1-a^2/b^2)}{2E(1+\nu_o)[(1-2\nu_o)b^2+a^2]}\left[K_et^2-\right.$$
$$\left.-(1-2\nu)\beta\left\{b^2\left(1+\ln\frac{t}{b}\right)-t^2\right\}\right] \quad (26)$$

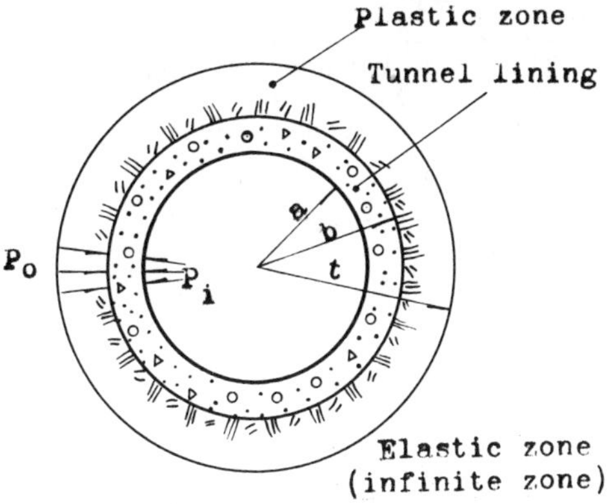

Fig. 5 The lining of a prussure tunnel.

Combining the first expression of equation (20) with equation (26) and given t=b, the critical interior water pressure P_i^* for creating the plastic deformation of rock mass is obtained:

$$P_i^* = \frac{\sqrt{6}\,K_e}{4(1-\nu_0)}\left[\frac{E_0(1+\nu)}{E(1+\nu_0)}\left(\frac{b^2}{a^2}-1\right)+(1-\nu_0)\frac{b^2}{a^2}+1\right] \quad (27)$$

in expression (26) and (27), E_0 and ν_0 are elastic modulu and poisson's ratio of lining material.

V. Stress state of lining during unloading and reloading

The relationship of stress and strain during unloading can be treated as pure elastic. At first, according to unloading $-\Delta P_i$ the $-\Delta P_0$ is found.

$$\Delta P_0 = \frac{2\Delta P_i(1-\nu_0^2)E}{(1+\nu)E_0\left(\frac{b^2}{a^2}-1\right)+(1+\nu_0)E\left\{(1-2\nu_0)\frac{b^2}{a^2}+1\right\}} \quad (28)$$

Then, the increment of stress and deformation in plastic regiou can be solved.

$$\Delta\sigma_r = \frac{2\Delta P_i(1-\nu_0^2)Eb^2}{\left[(1+\nu)E_0\left(\frac{b^2}{a^2}-1\right)+(1+\nu_0)E\left\{(1-2\nu_0)\frac{b^2}{a^2}+1\right\}\right]r^2} \quad (29)$$

$$\Delta\sigma_\theta = \frac{-2\Delta P_i(1-\nu_0^2)Eb^2}{\left[(1+\nu)E_0\left(\frac{b^2}{a^2}-1\right)+(1+\nu_0)E\left\{(1-2\nu_0)\frac{b^2}{a^2}+1\right\}\right]r^2} \quad (30)$$

$$u = \frac{-2\Delta P_i(1+\nu)(1-\nu_0^2)Eb^2}{\left[(1+\nu)E_0\left(\frac{b^2}{a^2}-1\right)+(1+\nu_0)E\left\{(1-2\nu_0)\frac{b^2}{a^2}+1\right\}\right]r} \quad (31)$$

the residual stress and deformation are as follows:

$$\left.\begin{aligned} \sigma_r^r &= \sigma_r + \Delta\sigma_r \\ \sigma_\theta^r &= \sigma_\theta + \Delta\sigma_\theta \\ u^r &= u + \Delta u \end{aligned}\right\} \quad (32)$$

Put $-P_i$ and $-P_0$ into expressions (24) and (25) to instead of P_i and P_0, the elastic stress increments $\Delta\sigma_{0r}, \Delta\sigma_{0\theta}$ can be obtained. The residual stresses in lining

$$\left.\begin{aligned} \sigma_{0r}^r &= \sigma_{0r} + \Delta\sigma_{0r} \\ \sigma_{0\theta}^r &= \sigma_{0\theta} + \Delta\sigma_{0\theta} \end{aligned}\right\} \quad (33)$$

If the lining have lost contact with the rock masses after emptying, the tunnel lining does not subject to rock resistence in the initial stage and acts as a thick-walled tube. Before the lining contacts the rock masses once again, the stress distribution is rather complicated. It is known that this is possibly the most dangerous case, especially in the top of lining. It may be the reason of producing longitudinal cracks.

VI. Numerical example

A circular-sectional pressure tunnel with radius b = 2.5 m; the mechanical parameters of rock masses: E = 2 X 10^{-5} kg/cm^2, ν = 0.3, K_e = 6 kg/cm^2, N = 10^4 kg/cm^2; The interior radius of lining a=2m, the outer radius is b.

The mechanical parameters of lining material: E_0= 2 X 10^5 kg/cm^2, ν_0 = 0.15.

Interior water pressure	r	Theory of elasticity		Present paper	
kg/cm^2	m	σ_θ kg/cm^2	σ_r kg/cm^2	σ_θ kg/cm^2	σ_r kg/cm^2
11.8	2	13.4	-11.8	13.4	--11.8
	2.5	8.5	-7.4	8.5	-7.4
18	2	20.4	-18	23.6	-18
	2.5	13	-11.3	16.3	--10.5

(1) According to (27), $P_i^* = 11.8$ kg/cm^2

(2) The interior water pressure equal to the critical pressure,

$P_i = P_i^* = 11.8$ kg/cm^2

$P_o = 7.35$ kg/cm^2, according to theory of elasticity

$P_o = 7.35$ kg/cm^2, according to present paper.

(3) The interior water pressure $P_i = 18$ kg/cm^2 exceeds the critical pressure

$P_o = 11.3$ kg/cm^2, according to theory of elasticity

$P_o = 10.5$ kg/cm^2, according to present paper.

(4) The stress distribution in the lining in both cases is listed in the following Table.

(5) As the interior water pressure decreased from 18 kg/cm^2 to zero, the residual stresses in lining are

at

$r = 2$ m, $\sigma_\theta^r = 3.2$ Kg/cm^2,

$\sigma_r^r = 0$,

$r = 2.5$ m, $\sigma_\theta^r = 3.3$ Kg/cm^2,

$\sigma_r^r = 0.8$ Kg/cm^2.

It means that there is 0.8 kg/cm^2 radially residual tensile stress at the boundary between lining and rock masses.

(6) If the lining depart from the rock masses after unloading,

when $P_i = 18$ kg/cm^2, $U_b = 0.026$cm.

The elastic recovery after unloading is $\Delta u_b = 0.018$ cm.

The residual displacement is $U_b^r = 0.008$ cm. In practice, the gap between lining and rock masses does not symmetrically distribute, at bottem $U_b^r = 0$ and at top $U_b^r = 0.016$ cm.

(7) Reloading. Before the lining touches the rock masses again, the contact forces equal to zero. When the lining touches the rock masses again, the contact force is about $P_i = 5.6$ kg/cm^2, which is estimated by using the symmetrical equation. Put $P_i = 5.5$ kg/cm^2

at

$r = 2$ m, $\sigma_\theta = 2.5$ Kg/cm^2

$r = 2.5$ m, $\sigma_\theta = 19.6$ Kg/cm^2

These values are estimated to be 1.06 and 1.2 times of the tangential stresses induced by the maximum interior water pressure during first loading respectively according to present paper, or 1.2 and 1.5 times respectively according to theory of elasticity.

Conclusion

Because of the complicacy of the mechanical behavior of rock masses, the in-situ test is needed for large diameter and high pressure tunnel. The calculating method suggested in this paper suitable for the isotropic elasto-plastic medium. In desiging linings by using the given method the stresses should be calculated not only based on the maximum design load during first loading, but also need to check the cases of unloading and reloading. Possibly the most unfavorable situation must appear during reloading when a gap exists between the lining and the rock after unloading.

References

1. **Галеркин, Б.Т., Напряженное состояние цилиндрической трубы в упругой среде, Галеркин Сопрание Сочинений, том, 1, Цзд. АН СССР, 1952, 311-317.**
2. Huang Renfu. et Al. Some Problems on In-situ Determination of the Deformability of Rock Masses, Journal of Hydraulic Engineering, No. 4, 1963 (In Chinese).
3. Kastner, H. Statik des Tunnel-und Stollenbaues, Springer-Verlag, 1962.
4. Jaeger, C., Rock Mechanics and Engineering, Cambridge University Press, 1972.
5. Phillips, A., Introduction to Plasticity, Ronald Press Co., 1956.
6. Prager, W. and Hodge, P. G., Theory of Perfectly Plastic Solids, John Wiley, 1951.
7. Lu Jiayou, Calculation Method of Stresses in Pressure Tunnel Lining Allowing for the Characteristics of Rock Mass Deformations, Chinese Journal of Geotechnical Engineering, 1982, to be published (In Chinese).

HIGH PRESSURE TUNNEL SYSTEMS AT SIMA POWER PLANT
Hochdruckstollensysteme beim Kraftwerk Sima
Systèmes de tunnels à haute pression de la centrale électrique de Sima

Ø.MYRSET
Norwegian State Power System, Oslo
R.LIEN
Norwegian Geotechnical Institute, Oslo

SUMMARY

The article describes geologic conditions, investigations performed and design criteria for unlined high pressure tunnels and air cushion chambers. The economic advantages of unlined pressure tunnels for the upper portion of the head instead of steel lined shafts all the way to the top are discussed. Further, the paper discusses the decision of adopting the air cushion chamber solution for the Lang-Sima system. Problems related to establishing access to unlined high pressure tunnels are also described.

ZUSAMMENFASSUNG

Der Artikel beschreibt geologische Verhältnisse, durchgeführte Erkundungen und massgebende Kriterien für die Ausführung von nicht ausgekleideten Hochdruckstollen und Luftkissenkavernen im Fels. Wirtschaftliche Vorteile bei ungekleideten Druckstollen statt gepanzertes Ausbau einer oberen Stufe des Gefälles wird behandelt. Weiterhin wird der Beschluss beim Kraftwerk Lang-Sima eine Luftkissenkaverne zu verwenden diskutiert. Probleme, die mit der Etablierung von Zutritt zu ungekleideten Hochdruckstollen verbunden sind, werden auch diskutiert.

RESUME

L'article décrit les conditions géologiques, les reconnaissances de terrain et les critères de désign pour tunnels de haute pression non-revêtus et pour chambres à coussin d'air. Les avantages économiques des tunnels non-revêtus pour la portion supérieure de la tête d'eau relativement aux tunnels revêtus d'acier tout le long de la perte de charge sont discutés. L'article décrit en plus les raisons du choix de chambres à coussin d'air pour le complexe Lang-Sima. Les problèmes relatifs à l'accès aux tunnels non-rêvetus sous haute pression sont aussi discutés.

1 GENERAL DESCRIPTION

The Sima project started in 1920 when Osa Fossekompani A/S began building a power station in Osa, in the municipality of Ulvik, Hardanger. Work was however discontinued then. During World War II, the Germans, planning an aluminium plant in Osa, resumed the work. After a short time the project stopped once more.

In 1962, the State Power System made a fresh start at the project and extended considerably the area covered. In 1973, a reduced plan for development of Eidfjord North was adopted by the Norwegian Parliament Stortinget. The plant was named the Sima Power Plant.

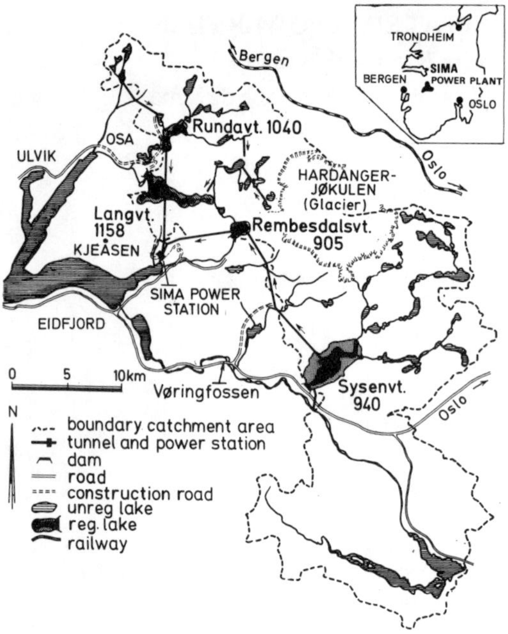

Fig. 1 Sima Power Plant area.

1.1 The Sima Power Plant is today (1982) the largest in Norway

The power station's four generating sets have a total output of 1120 MW and the annual output of power is about 2800 GWh (2800 million kWh). The entire power works cost 2000 million kroner, exclusive of interest during the construction period.

The Sima power station uses water from two geographically separate areas and properly speaking consists of two stations, Lang-Sima and Sy-Sima, installed in one generating hall.

1.2 Ground conditions are favourable

Below 1000 meters, the Sima region consists of Precambrian rocks, mostly gneiss and granite, covered locally by phyllites of Cambro-Silurian age.

Loose material from the late Quarternary age is found on hillsides and valley bottoms. Exposed bedrock occurs frequently in the mountainous area.

1.3 Lang-Sima

The upper parts of the Sima River system, inclusive of Austdøla, are diverted to Langavatn. Langavatn, one of the intake basins, gave rise to the abbreviated name Lang-Sima. Langavatn is dammed up by rock-fill dams. The reservoir has 48 metres of working storage and top water level at 1158 metres above sea level. Norddøla is diverted to Rundavatn, the other intake basin. Rundavatn is dammed up to 1040 metres above sea level by a rockfill dam.

The two Lang-Sima generating sets can run alternately on water from Langavatn or Rundavatn.

From the intakes, the water is carried to the valve chamber at Kjeåsen through one common, unlined tunnel, 8 kilometres long with a cross-sectional area of 30 square metres. The Kjeåsen area is 600 metres above sea level. The maximum water pressure in the unlined section of the supply tunnel is 525 m.

Instead of a conventional surge shaft in the water supply system, a comparatively new concept was selected, the so-called air cushion chamber. The air volume is approximately 5000 cu. metres with 48 atm. maximum air pressure. The pressure, maintained by compressors, is monitored continuously. From the valve chamber at Kjeåsen, the water is led to the power station through a steel-lined shaft.

1.4 Sy-Sima

Water from Bjoreio is diverted to the main storage in Sysenvatn, which has 66 metres of working storage and a top water level 940 metres above sea level. Sysenvatn is the origin of the abbreviation Sy-Sima. The Sysen dam is also a rockfill dam, with an impervious core of moraine material. With its 3.6 million cu. metres of fill, the dam is one of the largest in Norway. The crest of the dam is 1100 metres long and is easily seen from Highway 7 across the plateau.

Water is carried from Sysenvatn to Rembesdalsvatn through a 14 kilometres long tunnel, with a cross-sectional area of 35 sq. metres.

Rembesdalsvatn is the intake basin for Sy-Sima. Drawing from Sysenvatn can maintain a high water level during most of the generating period. Rembesdalsvatn has 45 metres of working storage and a top water level 905 metres above sea level.

A tunnel 7 kilometres long with a sectional area of 52 sq.metres leads from Rembesdalsvatn to the valve chamber at Kjeåsen. Maximum water pressure in the unlined tunnel to Sy-Sima is 300 metres. The surge shaft in this supply tunnel also serves as the intake for the Åsåni river.

1.5 Pressure shafts with a total steel lining weight of 7500 tons

From Kjeåsen, the water is carried down to the power station in two steel-lined pressure shafts, one for Lang-Sima and one for Sy-Sima. Each of the shafts divides into two branches at the bottom. The gradient of the 850 metres long shafts is 1 : 1.

The Lang-Sima shaft has an internal diameter of 3.4 metres at the top and 2.75 metres at the bottom. At its thickest, the lining is 78 mm. Corresponding figures for Sy-Sima are 3.9 - 3.0 metres in diameters and 68 mm thickness. The total steel weight is 7500 tons.

1.6 The power station - a large underground chamber

The machine hall situated in Simadalen, about 3 kilometres from Eidfjord, has a 700 metres long access tunnel. The excavated chamber is 200 metres long, 20 metres wide and 40 metres high. High stresses in the rock caused so-called rock burst. To secure the underground rooms against rock fall, 20,000 steel bolts were used in the power station and adjacent tunnels. The total length of these bolts amounted to 100 kilometres. Conditions in the rock made it natural to choose a very compact power station layout.

Lang-Sima's two generating sets operate with two gross heads - 1152 metres (Langavatn) and 1034 metres (Rundavatn). Each set has a vertical Pelton turbine with 5 jets and a 250 MW generator.

Each of Sy-Sima's two 310 MW generating sets have a 5-jet vertical Pelton turbine. Up to the time of writing (1982), these are the world's largest Pelton turbines as far as output is concerned.

2 INVESTIGATIONS CARRIED OUT AND USE OF RESULTS

In the area of the Sima Power Plant, bedrock is exposed nearly everywhere in valley sides and on mountain plateaux. In this situation, favourable for geological field observations, only geological mapping was performed as preinvestigation. Experience with tunnels and underground chambers in the Precambrian gneissic rocks in the area indicated conditions favourable for tunnelling and excavation of large underground chambers.

The main problems concerned firstly the high stresses in rock masses especially near the valley bottoms, where rock burst phenomena could easily be observed on the surface (mountain heights up to 1500), and secondly weakness zones (faults) with gouge material containing swelling clay. Since few faults were observed, little or no lining of tunnels was expected necessary. However, heavy rock burst problems were expected in the power station and in the tunnels around it. Generally speaking, these observations were confirmed afterwards.

After tunnelling started, geological tunnel mapping was performed continuously. In the access tunnel to the Power Station and in the valve chamber at Kjeåsen (Fig. 2 and 5) rock stress measurements were carried out (Mining Department, The Norwegian Institute of Technology, Trondheim, Norway). Stress measurements were also done in the proposed location of the air cushion chamber. Table 1 shows the stress measurements made:

Table 1. Principal stresses measured.

Location	Principal stresses (MPa)		
	σ_1	σ_2	σ_3
Power station			
Access tunnel	19.5	9.5	3.2
Kjeåsen valve chamber	10.0	6.7	4.8
Air cushion chamber	13.0	10.0	6.8

The data in Table 1 were used to find a proper orientation of the power station and reevaluate the necessary lining for the roof and walls. In addition, the data also enabled one to place the cone-shaped end of the steel lining for Sy-Sima and Lang-Sima according to the criterion that water pressure on unlined rock should not exceed the minimum principal stress (σ_3). The air cushion chamber should also follow the same criterion i.e. internal air pressure less than (σ_3). (Broch and Selmer-Olsen, 1982).

The design of unlined pressure tunnels and especially air cushion chambers needs to consider carefully the permeability of the rock. The rock at the cone-shaped end of the steel lining was of very good quality both for Sy-Sima and Lang-Sima and no water leakage into the tunnel was registered. This was found satisfactory, but due to a fault zone in the rock, the steel lining for Sy-Sima had to be extended such that it ran over the fault zone.

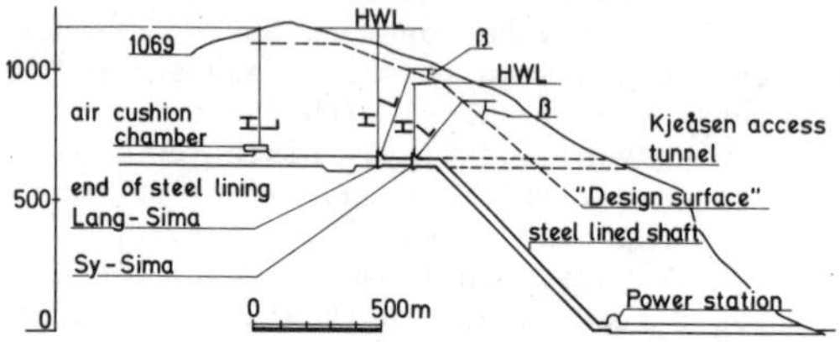

Fig. 2 Longitudinal section of the Sima Power Plant. See Table 2.

In the area of the air cushion chamber, extensive core drilling and permeability tests were performed to check the imperviousness of the rock mass. As mentioned before, the air cushion chamber site was first of all selected at a location with sufficiently high minimum principal stress (σ_3), but at the same time at a location where a minimum of air leakage could occur. The site chosen showed no water leakage into the tunnel and the rock surface was dry. The permeability tests showed practically no water flow with pressures up to 60 bars. It was concluded that no injection work was necessary.

2.1 The overburden criterion for unlined high pressure tunnels seems to give a safe design

Figure 2 illustrates the overburden criterion used at NGI for the design of unlined high pressure tunnels and air chambers: the weight component of the overburden normal to the surface should exceed the water pressure. With reference to Fig. 2, the criterion can be expressed by the formula

$$L \cdot \cos\beta \cdot \gamma_r \geq H \cdot \gamma_\omega$$

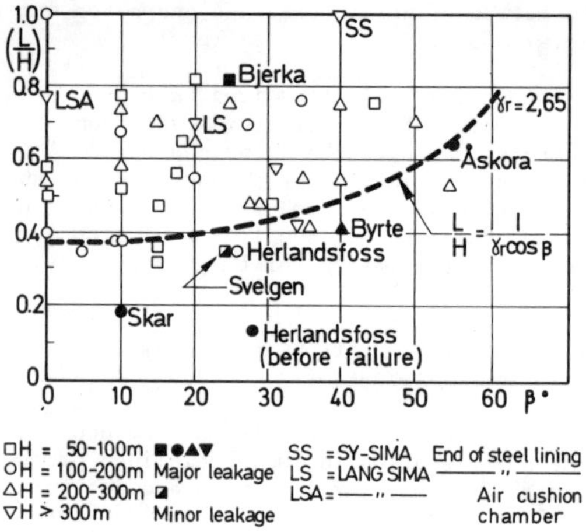

Fig. 3 Diagram for the ratio overburden/ water head versus inclination of "Design Surface".

Particular attention should be paid to unfavourable joint sets or fault zones and to special topographical conditions. For instance, edges or any important convex formation should not be considered as overburden, and a line for the so-called "Design Surface" should be drawn. See Fig. 2. In the case of the Sima Power Plant this simple criterion agrees well with the results of more sophisticated finite element analyses, described by Broch and Selmer-Olsen (1982).

Table 2 applies the overburden criterion to the Sy-Sima and Lang-Sima pressure tunnels. Figure 3 presents the results from the analysis of 43 high pressure shafts and tunnels. The dashed curve indicates equilibrium between water head (H) and overburden (L) measured normal to the "Design Surface". The Sy-Sima and Lang-Sima data are also plotted in the diagram. The distance above the dashed curve can be regarded as an apparent safety factor (F).

Lang-Sima has been in operation for 2 years and Sy-Sima for 1 year. Inspection after the emptying the Lang-Sima system showed no sign of deformations that could cause either water or air leakage (Johansen and Vik, 1982).

Table 2. Data for the overburden criterion at Sy-Sima and Lang-Sima. See Fig. 2.

Location	H, water press. (m of water)	L, overburden⊥ to surf, (m)	L/H	Slope angle β^o	Min. Ratio L/H after diagram	Apparent F
Sy-Sima						
Cone-shaped end of steel lining	300	300	1.0	40	0.5	2.0
Lang-Sima						
Cone-shaped end of steel lining	520	362	0.7	20	0.4	1.75
Air cushion	490	≈400	≈0.8	0	0.38	≈2.0

3 ECONOMICAL ADVANTAGES OF UNLINED TUNNELS

Preparatory work on the project started in 1973. The major part of the work took place during the second half of the seventies. Lang-Sima started operation in early 1980 and Sy-Sima in early 1981, both with nearly full storage. A representative starting date can thus be taken as mid-1980.

The costs for the whole power project amounted to about 2,000 million current kroner, exclusive of interests. In reference to an average building index, this amount corresponds to 2,400 million 1980-kroner. If one includes 7% per year in interest over the period the capital is invested, the costs reach 2,800 million kroner (in 1980, 5 Norwegian kroner = US $ 1.00). The total is approximately distributed as follows: 45% on the regulation area (dams and diversion tunnels), 35 to 40% on the power station and 15 to 20%, or more precisely 500 million kroner, on the supply systems (from the power station wall to the intake).

It is of interest to study the distribution of costs within the sypply systems. One can begin with the unit costs for the most important parts of the project. These unit costs are given as total costs at the time of the starting date, mid-1980. (The same applies to capitalized energy loss.) For both the building and installation works, investment tax (about 13%), local and central joint costs (auxil. constructions and operations, administration, etc.) and an interest rate of 7% have been added to the direct costs. (It is approximately correct to distribute the joint costs proportionally. If one increases the quantity of direct works in one location, the contribution of the auxiliary constructions and operations will also increase. In the opposite case, the direct work will go slower, thus increasing the direct costs). Together these added costs result in total costs in terms of 1980-kroner, approximately double the current direct costs.

In the calculation of capitalized energy loss due to friction in the supply systems, the winter power (about 2/3 of yearly production), is considered produced essentially at maximum output. The capitalized value of the energy loss at this output is taken as 2.50 kr/yr kWh. These assumptions can depart to some degree from the bases used for dimensioning 10 years ago.

Table 3 lists for Sy-Sima the costs and capitalized value of the energy loss per metre length of shaft or tunnel. The table compares steel-lined and unlined shaft/tunnel sections. In the unlined tunnel, the stabilization costs are low. On the 7-km stretch from the cone-shaped end of steel lining to the Rembesdalsvatn intake, about 1% of the length is lined with concrete. In the Lang-Sima supply tunnel, the same favourable rock conditions prevail in the selected tunnel alignment.

Table 3 provides data for the shaft at El. 40. The steel lining from El. 40 and upwards is designed for a "standard" transfer of the loads to the rock (about 50%). Below this elevation, the load transfer ability is reduced by the excavated rock at the power station. The steel thickness increases from 39 mm at E. 40 to 68 mm at the bottom (El. 0).

As shown in Table 3, the costs for the steel-lined part of the Sy-Sima supply system amount to about eight times the cost per metre length of the unlined tunnel. The ratio between the value of the energy loss is even larger. The cost differences in Lang-Sima follow the same trends. Even if the cross-sections in Lang-Sima are somewhat smaller over the whole length; the water pressure necessitates a larger steel thickness. The combined steel weight of 7500 tons, is therefore distributed approximately evenly between the two shafts.

Table 3. Sy-Sima supply system. Illustration of costs and capitalized energy loss in kroner/metre length of steel-lined and unlined tunnel.

1 System part/ Location	2 Technical data, dimensions	3 Cost kr/m	4 Value of energy loss kr/m	5 Total (3 + 4) kr/m
Steel-lined shaft, El. 40	Shaft area = 12 m^2 Concrete = 5 m^3/m Lining ∅ = 300 cm Steel weight = 3000 kg/m	90,000	40,000	130,000
Steel-lined shaft, El. 600	Shaft area = 18 m^2 Concrete = 6 m^3/m Lining ∅ = 390 cm Steel weight = 3000 kg/m	90,000	10,000	100,000
Steel-lined tunnel, from El. 600 to end of steel lining	Tunnel area ≃ 22 m^2 Concrete = 10 m^3/m Lining ∅ = 390 - 400 cm Steel weight = 3000 kg/m	90,000	10,000	100,000
Unlined tunnel, from end of lining to intake	Area = 52 m^2	11,000	2,000	13,000

Inclusive of various complementary mechanical equipment at Kjeåsen (for instance valves), the steel-lined parts of the supply systems cost about 250 million kroner, and amount to the same cost as the unlined sections: about 15 km of supply tunnels with accesses, shafts, air cushion chamber and supplementary mechanical equipment.

Since the economical advantages of using unlined tunnels are so important, persistent efforts have been made in the last 20 to 30 years to replace the lined tunnel concept with unlined constructions. This evolution is shown in Fig. 4 The figure gives the scheme used in the 1970s (alternative 1),

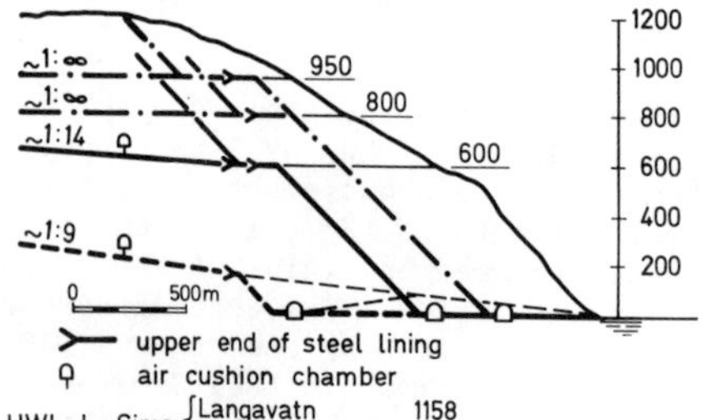

Fig. 4 Alternatives for building of Sima power station (intake - outlet).
Alt. 1 Carried out in the 1970s ———
" 2 Typical for the 1950s ·—·—
" 3 Possible in the 1980s -----

the solution applicable to a design carried out in the 1950s (alternative 2), and the potential solution for a design made during the 1980s.

With alternative 2, the steel lining for Sy-Sima is taken up to El. 800 and to El. 950 for Lang-Sima. In addition to the access and work area at El. 600, the same must also be established at the higher elevations. The length of the supply tunnel remains unchanged, but the station could be moved 300 m outward, due to the steel lining system past Kjeåsen. It also gives a reduction in tunnel length at the power station level.

Table 4 gives costs and capitalized energy loss per metre length for the tunnels leading to the power station. The head loss in the tailrace tunnel is equalized to a change in turbine level (Pelton turbine).

An estimate of the cost for alternative 2 indicates an 80 million kroner additional cost relative to alternative 1. In addition, the capitalized energy loss would have increased.

The economical consequences of the different methods of carrying water from the intake to the outlet can be illustrated by a comparison of costs plus capitalized energy loss per metre along the horizontal alignment (using average energy loss for the shafts).

Table 4. Tunnels leading to power station. Illustration of costs and capitalized energy loss in kroner/m length.

1 Tunnel	2 Technical data, Equipment, Dimensions	3 Cost kr/m	4 Value of energy loss	5 Total (3+4) kr/m
Access	Area = 48 m^2 with roadway, light system Monitoring cables, ventilation equipment	17,000		17,000
Cable	Area = 22 m^2, 4x3 units 400 KV cables	29,000	2,000	31,000
Tailrace	Area = 110 m^2	19,000	3,000	22,000
Total		65,000	5,000	70,000

For the Sima project, the following costs apply:

- unlined tunnels = 25,000 kr/m
- steel-lined shafts = 300,000 kr/m
- tunnels leading to the station = 70,000 krs/m.

If the Sima power development was planned today, one should seriously consider alternative 3, shown in Fig. 4. (A power complex in operation consists entirely of unlined systems with air cushion for water heads up to 780 m.)

The station is receded 600 m in the rock. Sy-Sima is also in this case designed with air cushion. With this alternative, the monetary savings relative to a surge shaft solution are larger than the value of lost energy from the River Åsåni (included in alternative 1, Fig. 4). The significant savings come from a reduction in length of the steel-lined section, - for example, the steel weight reduces from 7500 to 2500 tons - and from the elimination of the access and work area at Kjeåsen.

On the whole, the costs of alternative 3 are estimated as 180 million kroner less than the costs for alternative 1. The energy loss is also smaller, even when the 17 Gwh inflow energy from Åsåni is not used. In addition, constraints on the environment will be reduced and the regulation stability of the station improved.

Relative to alternative 1, alternative 3 presents some significant advantages. The reduction in costs corresponds however, to no more than 6 or 7% of the entire power plant costs. The "savings" would be quickly lost if a mishap would shut down the power station operation for some time. Since the alternative 3 solution lies on the borders of today's experience and technology, advanced and thorough field investigations and tests should be conducted before finalization of the design.

4 SURGE SHAFT OR AIR CUSHION CHAMBER

4.1 General technical and economical factors

Compared to surge shafts, air cushion chambers will generally prove more economical the higher the water pressure, since the surge shafts must be taken up to the highest regulated water level and transport costs during construction and stabilization increase with shaft length.

The air cushions in use up to now require longer operation interruption than surge shafts during revision of the supply system. This question concerns essentially the choice of compressor capabilities. It is difficult to establish the reduction in quality of a power complex as a function of length of interruptions in operation. One should investigate the expected need for revisions (inspections, emptying of sand trap, repairs after a stone fall, etc), the stations operation time, the storage possibilities, etc.

With air cushion chambers, the station generally acquire a better regulation stability than technically and economically feasible with surge shafts, but it is again difficult to translate this advantage to monetary quantities.

The air cushion solution involves however, a risk factor: in case of mishap, it is possible that the air blows out through the supply system. The design therefore incorporates some safety measures that ensure that such an accident will probably not occur.

Instrumentation and compressors for the air cushion chambers require supervision and maintenance, whereas experience with surge shafts has shown them as maintenance-free. The power consumption during filling and refilling of air is believed today to represent a relatively modest quantity.

4.2 Conditions at Sima

As shown in Fig. 5, Sy-Sima is designed with surge shafts, which also serve for water transport from the River Åsåni. The air cushion solution has therefore not been investigated at Sy-Sima. At Lang-Sima, design of an air cushion chamber was selected after the supply tunnel had been driven through its actual position. At this stage, possible stabilization with water curtains and semi-cylindrical steel lining was considered. Preparatory work was done to position water curtains in case air leakage would become unacceptably large.

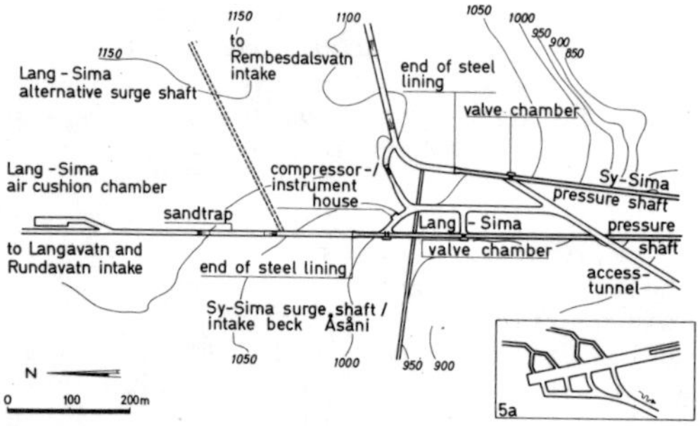

Fig. 5 Plan of Kjeåsen surge chamber with valves, accesses, etc. (circa El. 600).

Fig. 5a Power station with branched pipes, tailrace, access and cable tunnels (circa El. 0).

The air cushion is dimensioned for 5000 cubic metres at a pressure of 48 atm (or 240,000 cubic metres at 1 atm), which correspond to the operating conditions for the highest regulated water level at Langavatn. For uniform operations under lowest regulated water level at Rundavatn (El. 1013), the air cushion increases in volume to 7000 cubic metres. Because of the need for additional safety, a total volume of 10,000 cubic metres was provided, inclusive of the access tunnel. The rock in the chamber was stable and impervious and no stabilization was necessary.

The compressor and the instrument housing were placed right outside the disassembly chamber, about 600 m from the air cushion. The air duct (for filling and emptying), the measurement duct, the measuring cables and the water duct (for placement of a water curtain eventually) were placed in a small concrete culvert in a corner of the tunnel.

The compressor for the main filling is mobile and is assumed to be used to fill the air cushion of two neighbouring power plants. It has a capacity of 20 l/min (about 29,000 cubic metres/day) up to a maximum pressure of 30 atm (which corresponds to the water level in the supply tunnel at El. 960). It follows that the chamber has sufficient volume for air filling at this pressure. For the refilling operation three compressors are installed, each 1.5 cu.m/min capacity (corresponding to 6000 cu.m/day) up to a maximum pressure of 50 atm.

The time used for filling up the unlined supply system in the case of a surge shaft, is determined by the rate at which one wishes to transfer the load to the rock: about 100 m water pressure/day corresponds to 5 days necessary for filling. The air cushion alternative equipped with the previously mentioned compressor capacity, requires 10 days theoretically. This time can be reduced to 5 days by doubling the capacity of the main compressor.

The total costs involved in the air cushion chamber concept amount to 8 million kroner, of which 40% goes to construction costs. The total cost per unit metre for the connection between the air cushion and the compressor/instrument housing reaches approximately 5000 kroner of which 20% goes to construction works. The surge shaft, 800-m long with cross-sectional area of 20 m^2, costs 16 million kroner, inclusive of stabilization work (there is however, some uncertainty involved with the extent of the stabilization work). The savings with an air cushion chamber solution are thus about 8 million kroners.

Air leakage has proved very small; the power consumption to the compressor is thus modest. It has not been necessary to use the water curtain. The installation of a semi-cylindrical steel lining would have cost 10 million additional kroner. In the event that the execution of the higher galleries reveals unsatisfactory rock quality for air cushion chamber, one would at this point change to a surge shaft solution.

5 ACCESS TO SUPPLY SYSTEM WITH HIGH WATER PRESSURE (> 150 m)

5.1 Choice of layout

a) Dismountable part of supply pipe or
b) Access at upstream end of steel lining

The need and requirements of the access to the tunnel depend on the conditions and characteristic of the supply system. A distinctive access is advantagous construction-wise when the construction sequence of the supply tunnel must follow a critical path. A layout with distinctive access facilitates entrance to the system while in operation. The choice of access layout must consider the geological conditions in the proposed area. A distinctive access increases the extent of unlined rock surface/spaces exposed to maximum water pressures. Among the 50 unlined supply systems in the Norwegian power works with water pressure from 150 to 750 m, the large majority is designed with a distinct access (steel-lined).

In the Sima power complex, Lang-Sima has a 340-cm diam. dismounting pipe-part as access to the unlined tunnel, whereas Sy-Sima has a distinctive access to the unlined tunnel through a port (see Fig. 6). The positioning of the transition between the steel-lined and unlined sections in the supply system should be based on geological and economical considerations and should not be considerably influenced by the access itself. The cost for the port layout at Sy-Sima (exclusive of the work for the separate access tunnel), amounts to 1.5 million kroner, 2/3 of which concern the steel construction.

Figure 6 presents for Lang-Sima a hypothetical access solution similar to the solution used in Sy-Sima. Because of the higher hydrostatic pressure at Lang-Sima the port layout would have cost in this case 2.5 million kroner. In addition, the access tunnel itself would have been about 100 m longer than in the case of a disassembly chamber, corresponding to an increase in cost of about one million kroner. The elimination of the disassembly chamber should lead to savings of one million kroner, mainly because of the reduction of steel weight by about 50 to 60 tons as a

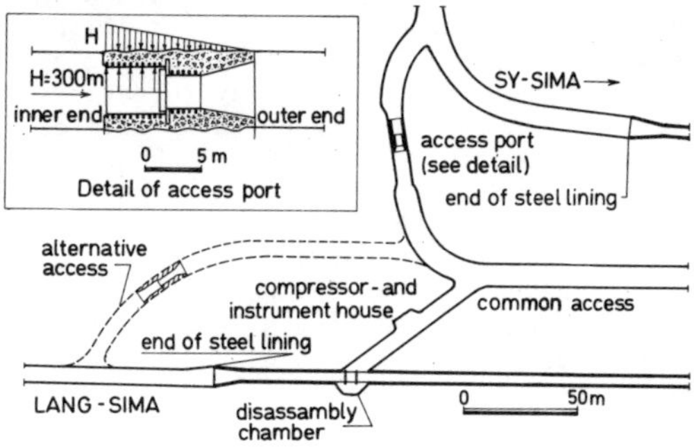

Fig. 6 Plan of Kjeåsen access system

result of the increase in load transfer to the rock without the presence of the chamber. The increase in costs from the building of a distinctive access will therefore amount to about 2.5 million kroner.

The sum must be viewed in light of various construction and operation advantages. Mounting, concreting, injection work, upstream the disassembly chamber, ca. 50 m, took a total of about 12 weeks. The experience acquired at Sy-Sima indicates that a port layout at Lang-Sima would require about 8 weeks or a reduction in the construction time of one month. The Sy-Sima access will also facilitate transport during operation, for example in the case of emptying of sand traps, rockfall in tunnel, etc.

The Lang-Sima access design was preferred partly because the cost difference had been evaluated as larger, partly because of some uncertainties with respect to the rock conditions. The disassembly room could however, have been placed nearer the cone-shaped end of steel lining. (The costs would not change, but the construction time would have been reduced). The distance from unlined tunnels exposed to water pressure is here significantly longer than used for access ports (see below), due to the disassembly chamber.

5.2 Realization of access layout placed upstream of the steel lining

As mentioned before, the Sy-Sima layout is the most used access design in Norwegian water power projects. The localization of the access tunnel should consider the nature of the rock, distance to other tunnels or caverns in the area, especially on the water side. When concrete lining is required based on the conditions along the access tunnel alone, - and the situation is often such - the length of the lining generally covers 4 or 5% of the hydrostatic pressure; in one case, the lining covered only 2.5% of the water head. Rock quality and the tunnel cross-section are decisive factors for the choice of the length of the concrete and steel lining. The amount of injection work depends on both the rock permeability and the length chosen. For deep injection, pressures up to the water pressure are used, but generally never higher than 30 bars.

Leaks occur mostly at the concrete - rock boundary, but in locations with a relatively short steel-lining on the air side, the water comes through in the weaker concrete lining. Leakage has rarely been measured larger than 5 l/s. It is often necessary to inject several times until the leakage decreases to an acceptable level, dependent on the risk involved and the economy (for example value of leak water).

The selection of the port location along the concrete lining varies from the inner to outer end of the lining and it seems to depend on the owner or consultant. Most often, about half of the length of concrete lining is steel-lined. A pipe is often preferred. The port opening is as large as 340 cm in diameter, or 270 x 300 cm^2 in the case of rectangular openings.

Figure 6 shows the main dimensions of the access layout used at Sy-Sima. The port opening 260 x 260 cm^2 was used. The port is constructed such that the load is transferred to the four sides. The hydrostatic pressure is approximately 300 m, with maximum fluctuation 20% higher. The port is placed about halfway in the concrete lining. There exists some minor weakness zones in the rock, but with the concrete work and injection, the leakages were brought down to a modest value (< one l/s).

If the design had been carried out today, one would have moved the port with steel lining a little towards the outer end of the concrete lining and increased the opening at the inner end. One would then obtain a better seal between concrete and rock. This assumes that the steel lining is watertight. One should pay special attention to the assembly weld right inside the port. Placement of the port at the inner end of the concrete lining would present a disadvantage with respect to leakage, as it could lead to a water trickle at this location, which results in a higher inward water pressure on the concrete construction.

ACKNOWLEDGEMENTS

The authors acknowledge Eng. Stein Sandvær from The Norwegian State Power System, for preparing the drawings, Dr. Suzanne Lacasse from Norwegian Geotechnical Institute (NGI) for translation and review of the paper and Mrs Kirstin Eggestad from NGI for the layout and preparation of the manuscript.

REFERENCES

Broch, E. and R. Selmer-Olsen 1982, The development of unlined pressure shafts and tunnels in Norway. To be publ. in: International Society for Rock Mechanics. Symposium on Rock Mechanics related to Caverns and Pressure Shafts. Aachen 1982

Johansen, P.M. and G. Vik 1982, Experience and measurements from air-cushion surge chambers in Norway. To be publ. in: International Society for Rock Mechanics. Symposium on Rock Mechanics related to Caverns and Pressure Shafts. Aachen 1982

Lien R. 1972, Oversikt over norske uforete tunneler og sjakter med vanntrykk over 100 meter samt enkelte andre med lavere trykk. (Review of Norwegian unlined tunnels and shafts with water pressure above 100 m). Norwegian Geotechnical Institute, Oslo. Internal report, 54402. 23p.

Myrset, Ø. 1980, Underground hydro-electric power stations in Norway. International Symposium (on) Subsurface Space. Rockstore '80. Stockholm 1980. Proceedings, Vol. 2, pp. 691-699.

Selmer-Olsen, R. 1974, Underground openings filled with high-pressure water on air. International Association of Engineering Geology. Bulletin, No. 9, pp. 91-95.

Smith, P.T. 1974, The Eidfjord hydro development in western Norway. Water Power, Vol. 26, No. 7, pp. 239-245.

Terzaghi, K. 1962, Stability of steep slopes on hard unweathered rock. Géotechnique, Vol. 12, No. 4, p. 251-270. Also publ. as: Harvard soil mechanics series, 69. Norwegian Geotechnical Institute. Publication, 50.

CERTAIN PECULIARITIES OF ROCK PRESSURE MANIFESTATION IN ARPA-SEVAN TUNNEL CONSTRUCTION

Einige Besonderheiten des Spannungszustandes im Gebirge beim Bau des Arpa-Sevan Tunnels

Quelques particularités de l'état des contraintes du terrain pendant la construction du tunnel d'Arpa-Sevan

G.M.PETROSIAN, A.A.SIMONIAN & A.A.SANAGUIAN

Yerevan Tunnel Laboratory of the Georgian Research Institute of Energo-Technical Construction, Tbilisi, USSR

SUMMARY:
The present paper reports the results of combined investigations of rock pressure manifestation and of rock mass stresses and deformation as well as the engineering measures on tunneling in complicated geotechnical situations. Investigations were carried out under natural conditions in the course of years, at the same time a cycle of the rock laboratory tests was performed. The pressure intensive manifestations laws operating deep down under the surface were found due to the investigation results. During the tunnel construction they allowed to realise new lining designs providing the rock mass stability, high rates of tunneling and the operation reliability of the underground construction.

ZUSAMMENFASSUNG:
Im Vortrag sind Ergebnisse einer komplexen Untersuchung der Erscheinungen des Bergdrucks, des Gesteinzustandes bei Spannung-Verformung sowie die ingenieurtechnischen Massnahmen zum Tunnelvortrieb unter äussert komplizierten geotechnischen Bedingungen gezeigt. Die Untersuchungen wurden unter Naturbedingungen jahrelang vorgenommen. Das schloss jedoch keinen Zyklus der Laborprüfungen des Gesteins aus. Nach den Ergebnissen der komplexen Untersuchungen sind die Gesetzmässigkeiten einer intensiven Druckerscheinung in den grossen Tiefen festgestellt werden. Sie ermöglichten u.a. während des Tunnelbaus eine neue Ummantelungskonstruktion zu realisieren die jeweilige Stabilität des Gesteins, hohe Schnelligkeit des Vortriebs und Sicherheit des unterirdisches Bauwerks im Betrieb absicherte.

RESUME:
L'exposé fait état des résultats des investigations complexes de la pression des roches, de l'état de contrainte et de déformation des massifs rocheux, ainsi que de la technique de percement du tunnel dans des conditions géotechniques fort compliquées. Les recherches s'échelonnant sur plusieurs années ont été menées dans des conditions naturelles, sans exclure, pour autant, tout un cycle d'essais des roches en laboratoire. Les résultats des recherches complexes ont permis d'établir les lois régissant les manifestations intensives de la pression en grande profondeur. Ces lois ont permis de trouver, au cours de la construction du tunnel, une nouvelle forme de blindage assurant la stabilité du massif rocheux, une vitesse de percement accrue et la fiabilité de fonctionnement de l'ouvrage souterrain.

1 INTRODUCTION

Up to the end of the 50s the waters of the highland lake Sevan stored in the course of centuries were used for irrigation and power needs of Armenia. It reduced its level by 18m. In order to preserve the flora and fauna of the lake Sevan basin, of this pearl of nature, in the period between the 60s and the 80s a number of irrigation and power measures were realised, the river Arpa diversion to the lake Sevan being one of them.

The construction complex for diverting the river Arpa to the lake Sevan is presented as follows. Due to the 47 m high barrage on the river Arpa, a water storage is created with available capacity of 25 mln m^3. From the storage the water is directed to the lake Sevan through two powerless (pressureless) tunnels with 48.3 km of total length. On its way the tunnel includes the waters of the tributary Elegis. The tunnel capacity along the tributary Elegis is 18 m^3/sec and after it it is 25 m^3/sec. The diverted flow volume is defined as 250 mln m^3.(Hydraulic Power Engineering of Armenia, 1979).

2 GEOTECHNICAL CONDITIONS

The Arpa-Sevan tunnel route passes through large rock masses presented by separate lithologic and stratigraphical formations. Upper Cretaceous conglomerates, sandstones, limestones and porphyrites forming the anticlinal fold nucleus of Hayotsdzor (Armenian Valley) synclinarium serve as the basis for the whole complex of the highland rocks. Within the diversion route boundaries they occur than the tunnel level mark and are crossed by separate fragments of other tunnels. The upper part of the complex is presented by volcanogenic-sedimentary rocks of the Middle Eocene, mainly by tuff stone of various bedding, by tuffites, and by tuff aleurites with porphyrite subordinate interlayers. Thickness of this formation lies within 200 - 2000 m. Volcanogenic rocks of the Upper Eocene, Miocene and Pliocene formations also occur in the described deposits. They are presented by porphyrites and andesites, by their tuffs and tuffobrecias, by pumice-liparite tuffs of psephitic structure intermitted with members of andesite tuff-brecias, with tuffite lentils, with dark-brown clays and with clayey conglomerates. Within the described region intrusive rocks are presented by granodiorites. Their intrusive bodies in the form of stocks and sills broke through the thickness of volcanogenic-sedimentary rocks and occurred all along the tunnel route.

Volcanogenic-sedimentary Eocene rocks are highly dislocated and folded, with numerous cracks and breaking zones due to the rock hydrothermal changes.

It was just in these zones that underground waters of different temperature and mineral composition found their way out at separate points. In doing so, spring-like waters escaping through the craks with the temperature less than 10°C were distributed along the tunnel route, their total discharge being no more than 670 l/sec. The termal underground mineralized waters occurred along the tunnel route with their total discharge 80-100 l/sec. and the temperature within 20°C - 46°C. Mineral waters escaped usually accompanied by a carbon dioxide outburst which reached 60-100 l/sec.

Prediction of the rock geothermal regime along the diversion route was principally correct, except for the zones connected with the Quarternary volcanism activity where the registered temperatures were 5°-6°C higher than it had been supposed to be according to the geothermal gradient calculations.

In 1974 the tunnel opened a large deep-seated rapture of overfault type, namely, the Hankavan-Sunik fracture which occurred at 650-1340 m from the surface and which was 1200-1500 m long in the working section. Before that the geological maps of the republic had not indicated fractures of this type in the region under design for the diversion. The present paper shows how the engineering difficulties which appeared in the tunnel construction due to the fracture mentioned above could be overcome.

3 NATURAL INVESTIGATIONS AND CONSTRUCTION METHODS

Tunnel No.1, 13.7 km long, was driven by four counter faces, two of them were opened additionally from the mine 190 m deep. Tunnel No.2 was driven by seven counter faces, five of them were opened additionally from three mines 350-661 m deep. The cross-section of the tunnel has mainly a pan-like shape with dimensions 10.4 m^2 and 12.3 m^2. The tunnels were mainly driven by drilling and blasting over the whole of the section.

Lining construction types I-XIII were used depending on the rock physical and mechanical properties as

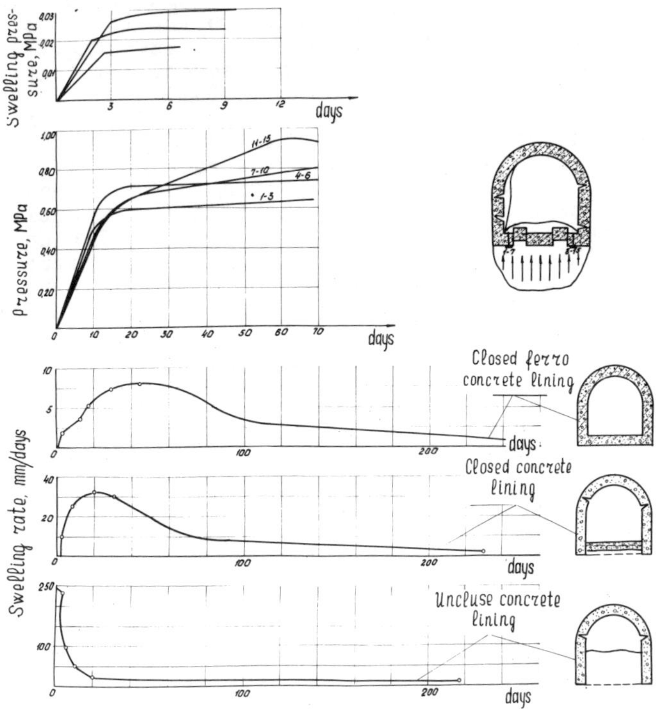

Fig.1.

well as on the rock pressure value. Lining construction types I-III have a levelling functions and not a carrying one, other types are carriers, types XI-XIII being heavy; these latter types were worked out in the process of tunnel 2 construction and were realised when driving a section 1500 m long between the faces No.8 and No.9 within the limits, of the Hankavan-Sunik fracture.

The rocks of this fracture opened by the tunnel in the face No.9 were presented by crumpled andesite brecias in the state of dark-brown Miocene clays, due to weathering. The Miocene clay member thickness exceeded 4 m. From the very first moment these clays were intensively pressed out into the working with the rate 0.3 - 0.2 m/day, later in the course of 10 days this rate decreased to 0.08 m/day. Being pressed out from the bottom, the clays were periodically removed by conventional technical means. But with the clay thickness increase the situation grew more and more complicated. Attempts to stop swelling when constructing a closed concrete lining, and further a powerful ferroconcrete lining with 60 cm of the reverse vault thickness did not arrive to the desired results. The tunnel fragment 32 m long was completely destroyed (see Fig.1). Special instrumental investigations in the nature (Petrosian, 1977) showed that in 200 days after the clays were opened, the swelling reached 2.5 m., 70% of these deformations taking place during the first 20 days (Fig. 1).

The contacting normal pressures were measured by 15 dynamometric sections introduced into the bottom of the ferroconcrete lining (Petrosian, 1977). The measurements showed that these pressures were changing within 0.6-0.92 MPa before the lining was completely destroyed (Fig. 1). During the lining destroyment pressures up to 1.3 MPa were registered.

The detailed laboratory study of the physical and mechanical properties of the fracture rocks showed that at 13% of natural humidity their compressive strength was changing within 3.1-4.3 MPa.

The rocks being water sharply decrease their strength which is equal to 0.97 MPa on the average. The laboratory study of swelling showed that even in the disconsolidated state the swelling pressure of Miocene clays does not exceed 0.03 MPa (Fig.1). Therefore, this rock tendency for the intensive pressing out cannot be explained by swelling phenomenon.

These powerful deformations took place due to the clay overtension under the thick rock mass. Every day tensions existing at the depth of the tunnel occurrence were measured ba the dynamometric section method (Zavriev, Petrosian, 1977). The measurements showed that the every day tensions were changing within 15.3-16.8 MPa, i.e. they exceed the ultimate strength of the Miocene watersaturated clays more than 15 fold. When driving the tunnel, the natural equilibrium was violated and, that is why, the plastic rocks of the fracture were observed to fill intensively in the working. It should be noted that the attempts to by-pass the fracture and to change the tunnel route were not successful, for the Miocene clays were met everywhere.

In this connection, using the Italian method of the irrigation tunnel driving on the river Fortor (G.Baldovin, 1973) it was decided to apply the following technology of the tunnel construction: the working was opened by 2 m an errector mounted a prefabricated lining of metal tubbings. The prefabricated ring was supposed to take up 70% of load before the inner ferroconcrete jacket 50 cm thick was ready to operate. It was constructed in 8-10 days, i.e. when the pressure growth started to stabilize. The metal tubbings started to deform in 3-4 days after their mount, there appeared cracks, and the assembling bolts in the ring broke. Sometimes the deformation process developed so quickly that they did not manage to close the lining ring.

Instrumental observations over the process of the load and deformation growth showed the following (Fig. 2,A):

the contacting normal pressures over the lining outline are statically unbalanced and are distributed according to the law described by the expression (see Fig.2,A). Some papers also confirm this law (Petrosian, 1980);

the maximum pressure vector was orientated in the direction perpendicular to the rock stratification;

the contacting normal pressures over the combined lining outline are stabilized for 100-120 days after the stiff lining construction, 80% of load being already realised during the first 12-20 days of observations.

At the same time investigations showed with 99.9% of probability that the maximum pressure on the stift combined lining may reach 2.8 MPa and the minimum one is 1.28 MPa, with the average pressure being equal to 2.0 MPa. In this case the combined lining inner outline shift did not exceed 30-35 mm, according to our instrumental investigations.

The problem of resisting the clay intensive pressure seemed to be solved and realised correctly from the technical point of view. But in this case the tunnel driving rate would not actually exceed 8-12 m/month. If taking into account that ground waters with a stabilized discharge of 250-400 l/sec flooded the working and that the driving from the face No.8 in the fracture zone was accomponied by the gas frequent outburst and the rock swelling, the Arpa-Sevan tunnel construction would come to its end many years if new technical solutions were not found.

Long-lasting investigations in the tunnel were prompting that to provide the high rate of driving under these conditions it was necessary to create a new type of lining which from the very moment of its construction should possess a high carrying and a definite yielding capacity so that the rock mass could be relieved of the intensive deformations in the time.

A collective of authors (Petrosian, 1980) worked out and introduced a precast lining with the carrying capacity up to 4.0 MPa and with yielding gaskets, it was made of ferroconcrete blocks and satisfied the requirements stated above. The lining ring was yielding due to the four gaskets 4 mm thick between the block ends (Fig.2,B).

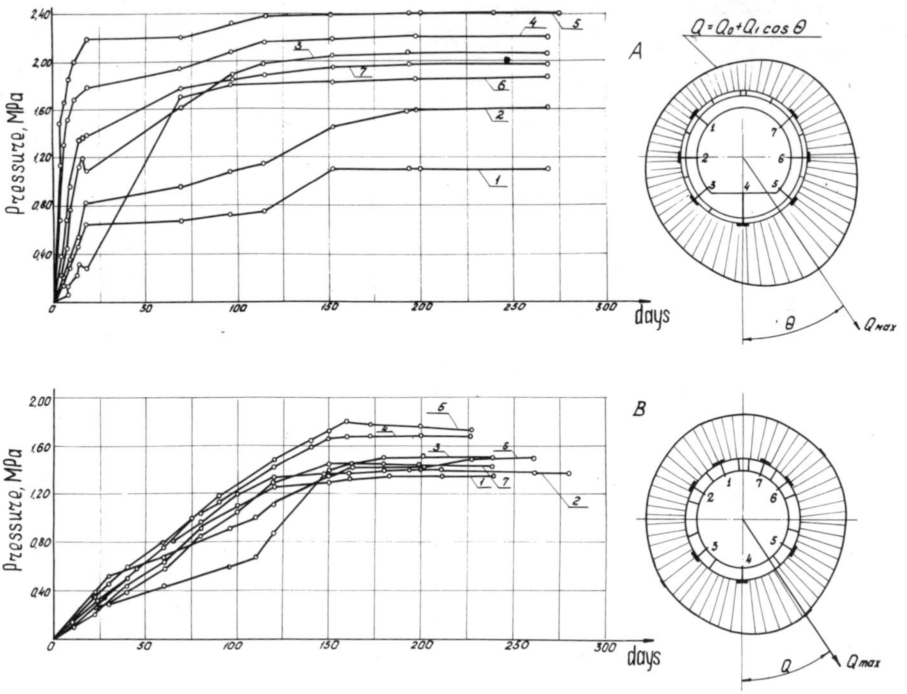

Fig.2

Being affected by the Miocene clay intensive shifts the multi-layer gaskets between the blocks compressed, hence the block lining ring compressed too by 12-14 cm on the whole within the first 20-28 days after their mounting, while the fracture rocks relieved of the intensive pressure.

Instrumental observations over the clay mass and the block lining interaction during the new technology application showed the following (Fig.2,B):

irregularity of normal contacting pressures over the block lining outline at the moment of their stabilization is principally small;

the maximum pressure reaches 1.8 MPa, the minimum one - 1.33, while the average pressure is equal to 1.46 MPa;

the main loads are already realised on the 150 day from the moment of the lining mounting, the lining being compressed by 15-16 cm.

The combined investigation showed the application of linings with limited yielding not to change the direction of the maximum pressure vector, but to decrease considerably the distribution irregularity of the normal contacting pressures over the outline.

Thus, application of the precast block linings with yielding gaskets provided stability and safety of the tunnel driving under very hard geotechnical conditions, the driving rate being 40-10 m/month. The fracture zone was driven through by the precast block lining and now the tunnel is successfully operating.

4 REFERENCES

Hydropower of Armenia, 1979, M., Vneshtorgizdat.

Zavriev G.P., Petrosian G.M. et al., 1977. Weak Rock Swelling in Tunnel Construction. Proceedings of the Georgian Research Institute of Hydropower Construction, v.4.

Zavriev G.P., Petrosian G.M. et al., 1977. Experimental Methods of Rock Pressure Definition in Clayey

Rocks. Proceedings of the Georgian Research Institute of Hydropower Construction, v.5.

Baldovin G. et al., 1973. Tunnel Construction in Highly Swelling Clays. Proceedings of the 8th International Congress on Ground Mechanics and Fundament Building, v.2.

Petrosian G.M., Simonian A.A. 1980. Statistic Analysis of the Radial Pressure Distribution Irregularities over the Lining Outline of Tunnels Constructed in Clayey Rocks. Proceedings of the Georgian Research Institute of Hydropower Construction, v.7.

Petrosian G.M., Simonian A.A. 1980. Tunnel Supporting Constructed in Unstable Rocks, "Mine Construction", No.3.

ERFAHRUNGEN BEIM BETRIEB DES DRUCKSTOLLENS FÜR DAS SPEICHERKRAFTWERK ROSSHAUPTEN AUS FELSMECHANISCHER SICHT

Rock mechanical experiences operating the pressure tunnel of the pumped storage plant Rosshaupten

Expériences de mécanique des roches relatives au fonctionnement des galeries forcées de la centrale de pompage Rosshaupten

R.RAPP

Bayerische Wasserkraftwerke AG, München, Bundesrepublik Deutschland

SUMMARY

The high-pressure-tunnel for the hydroelectric plant Roßhaupten was built in 1951/52. The 424 m long hydraulic tunnel has an internal diameter of 8,35 m. The final lining of the hydraulic tunnel covers a length of 245m, after the prestressing procedure, with core ring lining according to Kieser/Berger. The geology of the surrounding mountains is characterized by the almost vertically strata of the tertiary, oligocene molasse. The strata runs almost parallel to the tunnel axis.Excavation and supporting were used in several stages according to the modified Belgian Tunnelling construction method with Kunz'equipment. Within the 245 m Tunnel length with core ring lining, 81 measuring transmitters were installed in three measuring cross sections, and the measured values acquired in a fixed telemetering device. The measuring transmitters were builtin in accordance with the state of construction, depending on their task. The measuring method was particularly intensively carried out during the construction and initial operation of the seasonally regulated reservoir. The inspection period covers almost 8 years. In the report, the measurement results are compared with the theoretical tests and the method evaluated.

ZUSAMMENFASSUNG

Der Triebwasserstollen für das Kraftwerk Roßhaupten wurde in den Jahren 1951/52 gebaut. Der 424 m lange Stollen hat einen lichten Durchmesser von 8,35 m. Auf eine Länge von 245 m erfolgte die endgültige Sicherung des Stollens nach dem Vorspannverfahren mit Kernringauskleidung nach Kieser/Berger. Die Geologie des anstehenden Gebirges ist durch die nahezu senkrecht einfallenden Schichten der tertiären, oligozänen Molasse gekennzeichnet. Die Schichten streichen nahezu parallel zur Stollenachse. Ausbruch und Sicherung erfolgten in mehreren Teilen nach der modifizierten belgischen Bauweise mit Kunz'scher Rüstung. In der 245 m langen Stollenstrecke mit Kernringauskleidung wurden in drei Meßquerschnitten 81 Meßgeber installiert und die Meßwerte in einer stationären Fernmeßeinrichtung erfaßt. Die Meßgeber wurden je nach Aufgabe entsprechend dem Baufortschritt eingebaut. Die Meßwerterfassung wurde insbesondere während der Bauausführung und Inbetriebnahme des Jahresspeichers intensiv betrieben. Der Überwachungszeitraum umfaßt nahezu 8 Jahre. Im Bericht werden die Meßergebnisse den theoretischen Untersuchungen gegenübergestellt und das Verfahren bewertet.

RESUME

La galerie des eaux motrices de la centrale électrique de Roßhaupten a été construite en 1951/52. Cette galerie longue de 424 mètres a un diamètre intérieur de 8,35 m. Le blindage définitif de la galerie sur une longueur de 245 m a été réalisé conformément au procédé de précontrainte avec un revêtement annulaire selon Kieser/Berger. La géologie du terrain en place est caractérisée par les couches plongeantes quasi verticales de la molasse tertiaire, oligocène. Les couches sont presque parallèles à l´axe de la galerie. Le percement et le blindage ont étéeffectuées d´après le mode de construction belge modifiéavec l´échafaudage de Kunz. 81 indicateurs de mesure ont été installés dans trois sections de mesure à l´intérieur de la galerie longue de 245 m à revêtement annulaire. Les valeurs mesurées sont enregistrées dans un dispositif de télémesure stationnaire. Les indicateurs de mesure ont été installé en fonction de la tâche à remplir conformément à l´avance des travaux. L´enregistrement des valeurs mesurées a été effectué de manière intensive notamment pendant la réalisation des travaux. La période de contrôle s´étend sur un espace de temps de 8 ans environ. Les résultats de mesure dans le rapport sont comparés aux analyses théoriques et le mode opératoire est analysé.

1. VORBEMERKUNGEN

Der Triebwasserstollen für das Kraftwerk Roßhaupten mit einer Ausbauleistung von 48 MW wurde im Zusammenhang mit dem 41 m hohen Erdstaudamm in den Jahren 1951/52 gebaut. Triebwasserstollen haben die Aufgabe, über möglichst lange Zeiträume störungsfrei und nur mit geringen Gefällsverlusten zu arbeiten. Für einen reibungslosen und damit wirtschaftlichen Kraftwerksbetrieb ist diese Bedingung unbedingt zu erfüllen, da Ersatzstollen meistens nicht vorgesehen sind und im Bedarfsfalle auch nicht kurzfristig hergestellt werden können. Welch große Schäden mit all ihren negativen Folgeerscheinungen auftreten können zeigt sich z.B. am Umleitungsstollen der Mollaro-Sperre am Noce; dort sind nach zweijähriger Betriebszeit bei größten Wassergeschwindigkeiten von 12 m/s die Betonsohle zerstört und der anstehende Fels bis auf eine Tiefe von 3,2 m ausgefräst worden. Im Falle Tarbela sind durch zu große Fließgeschwindigkeiten bekanntlich erhebliche Schäden entstanden, deren Sanierung aufwendige bauliche Maßnahmen zur Folge hatte. Zur Beseitigung von Schäden an Triebwasserstollen sind meist aufwendige Untersuchungen der Schadensursache, die Erarbeitung von Sanierungskonzepten und die Schadensbehebung selbst vorzunehmen. Die maximale Fließgeschwindigkeit in verkleideten Druckstollen soll bei sandfreiem Wasser im allgemeinen 3 bis 6 m/s betragen. Die bei höheren Wassergeschwindigkeiten auftretenden Probleme sind hauptsächlich folgende:

1. Mechanische Beanspruchung des Betons vor allem an Umlenk- und Ablösungsstellen infolge Unterdruck, der im Grenzfall zu Kavitation führen kann.
2. Mechanische Beanspruchung durch mitgeführte Schwerstoffe
3. Dynamische Kräfte bei Richtungsänderungen des Wassers infolge der zeitlichen Impulsänderung
4. Zusatzbelastung infolge hydrodynamischer Drücke bzw. Unterdrücke

Um Kavitationsschäden am Beton zu vermeiden, soll der Unterdruck an keiner Stelle den Wert von 0,6 bis 0,7 bar überschreiten. Druckstollen erfordern bekanntlich eine Auskleidung, die bei den auftretenden Wasserinnendrücken dauernd rissefrei bleiben soll, da Wasseraustritte unter hohem Druck neben betrieblichen Nachteilen zu Auswaschungen im Gebirge mit hieraus resultierenden Gebirgsbewegungen führen und gegebenenfalls den Bestand des Stollens gefährden können. Die Bandbreite der auftretenden Beanspruchungen sowohl vom Gebirge her als auch durch den Kraftwerksbetrieb sowie ungünstige Überlagerungen dieser Kraftwirkungen sind so genau wie möglich zu ermitteln.

2. DER DRUCKSTOLLEN DES KRAFTWERKS ROSSHAUPTEN

2.1 Allgemeines

Aus Zweckmäßigkeitsgründen wurden dem Hauptstollen zeitlich gesehen vor allem zwei Aufgaben übertragen. Während der Bauzeit des Erddammes diente er als Umleitungsstollen für das Lechwasser; nach Inbetriebnahme des Speicherkraftwerkes hat er die Aufgabe des Triebwasserstollens übernommen. Diese unterschiedlichen Betriebszustände stellten entsprechend verschiedene Anforderungen an den Stollen. Als Umleitungsstollen mußte ein maximaler Abfluß von rund 500 m³/s mit einer Fließgeschwindigkeit von v = 9,3 m/s abgeführt werden, dabei ist aber nur ein Innendruck von rund 0,5 bar aufgetreten. In seiner jetzigen Funktion ist der Abfluß im Regelfall auf die Schluckfähigkeit der Turbinen mit 2 x 75 m³/s begrenzt, dafür tritt ein Innendruck von 3,6 bar auf. Die Fließgeschwindigkeit beim Ausbauabfluß beträgt rund 2,8 m/s. Neben dem Gebirgs- und Kluftwasserdruck war bei der Beanspruchung der Stollenauskleidung auch der Geschiebetrieb zu berücksichtigen.

Die dynamischen Druckverhältnisse in den verschiedenen Betriebszuständen wurden sowohl berechnet als auch durch Druckstoß- und Abschaltversuche ermittelt. Mit den Versuchen sind vor allem die berechneten Druckverhältnisse und die Laufzeit der Druckwelle im 70,46 m langen und ca. 750 to schweren Verteilerdruckrohr überprüft worden.

2.2 Gebirgsbeschaffenheit

Die Geologie des Gebirges ist durch die nahezu senkrecht einfallenden Schichten der tertiären, oligozänen Molasse bestehend aus Mergel, Steinmergel, Sandstein und einigen Konglomerateinschlägen aus Nagelfluh gekennzeichnet. Das Streichen der Schichten erfolgt nahezu parallel zur Stollenachse. Die Felsüberlagerung beträgt über Stollenfirste i.M. 19 m, darüber ist eine Lockergesteinsüberschüttung von rund 10 m. Der Abstand bis zur Talflanke beträgt rund 65 m. Die Gesteinsfestigkeit der anstehenden Schichten hat Werte die mit 50 bis 100 MN/m² ermittelt wurden.

2.3 Ausführungsplanung und Baudurchführung

Aus technisch-wirtschaftlichen Gründen wurde ein Triebwasserstollen mit einem lichten Durchmesser von 8,35 m gewählt, wobei auf eine Länge von 245 m die endgültige Sicherung des Stollens mit dem Vorspannverfahren mit Kernringauskleidung nach Kieser/Berger erfolgte. Als Alternativlösung zur rissefreien Aufnahme des Innendruckes wäre eine 2,25 cm starke Stahlauskleidung erforderlich gewesen. Bei Normalstau beträgt der hydrostatische Innendruck 3,6 bar; der Gebirgswasserdruck rund 2,5 bar.

Der Bemessungsdruck zur Vorspannung der unbewehrten Betonröhre unter Berücksichtigung der Einflüsse aus Schwinden und Kriechen, sowie der Forderung, daß bei voller Beanspruchung der Innenring keine Zugspannungen aufzunehmen hat, wurde mit 8 bar festgelegt, wovon 6 bar für die Vorspannung wirksam wurden (Bild 1). Der Ausbruch erfolgte in mehreren Teilen nach der modifizierten belgischen Bauweise mit Kunz'scher Rüstung (Bild 2). Die vorläufige Sicherung wurde unmittelbar nach dem Ausbruch eingebaut. Die endgültige Sicherung der 245 m langen Strecke besteht aus einer 35 cm starken, unbewehrten Betonschale, die Trennung zwischen vorläufiger und endgültiger Sicherung übernehmen Verpreßringformsteine. Die Vorspannung wurde mittels eingepreßtem Zementmörtel in 5 m-Abschnitten hergestellt. Zur Erhöhung des Widerstandes gegen Abrieb durch Geschiebetrieb erhielt die Sohle eine 6 cm dicke Hartbetonschicht. Aus Voruntersuchungen und Berechnungen

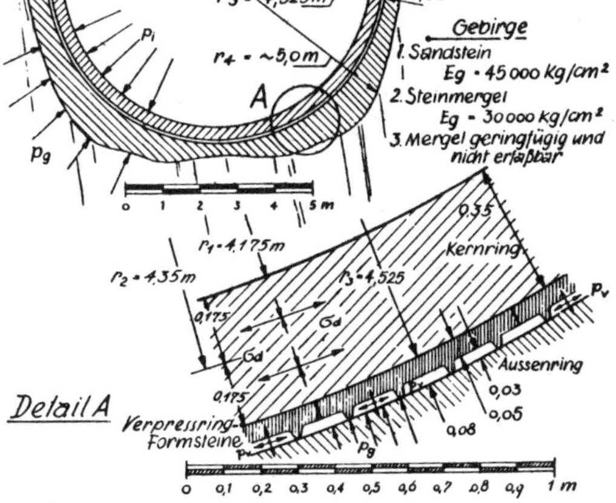

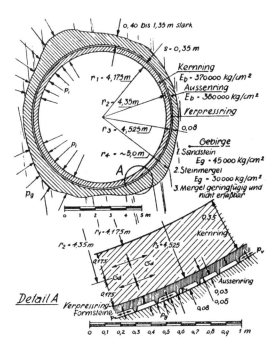

Bild 1: Bezugsgrößen des Hauptstollens für rechnerische Auswertung

ergaben sich folgende Forderungen für den Vortrieb und die Sicherung:

a) Der Ausbruch soll besonders im Bereich der Ulmen möglichst vorsichtig und erschütterungsfrei mit geringen Abschlagstiefen durchgeführt werden.

b) Aufgrund der geologischen Gegebenheiten ist mit Ablösungen einzelner Schichtpakete zu rechnen. Zur Verhinderung von Niederbrüchen ist eine Querträgerzimmerung vorzusehen.

c) Die Sicherung soll dem Ausbruch in geringem Abstand folgen.

d) Ein rascher Ringschluß sollte angestrebt werden.

Die nach diesen Richtlinien durchgeführten Vortriebsarbeiten einschließlich Sicherung und Herstellung der Innenschale des gesamten Stollens jedoch ohne Vorspannarbeiten konnten in 10 Monaten abgewikkelt werden.

3. MESSUNGEN UND BEOBACHTUNGEN AM DRUCKSTOLLEN

3.1 Meßeinrichtungen

In der 245 m langen Stollenstrecke mit Kernringauskleidung wurden in 3 Meßquerschnitten 81 Meßgeber installiert und die Meßwerte in einer stationären Fernmeßeinrichtung erfaßt. Die Meßgeber und die stationä re Fernmeßeinrichtung wurden von der Fa. Maihak geliefert. Für die Abfrage von Meßwerten standen folgende Meßgeber zur Verfügung:

- 18 Geber zur Ermittlung des Fel widerstandes, womit die Kraftwirkungen zwischen Gebirge und Sicherung erfaßbar werden.
- 54 Geber zur Bestimmung der Betondehnung im Außenring. Verpreßring und Kernring
- 3 Geber zur Bestimmung der Wasserstände im Gebirge.

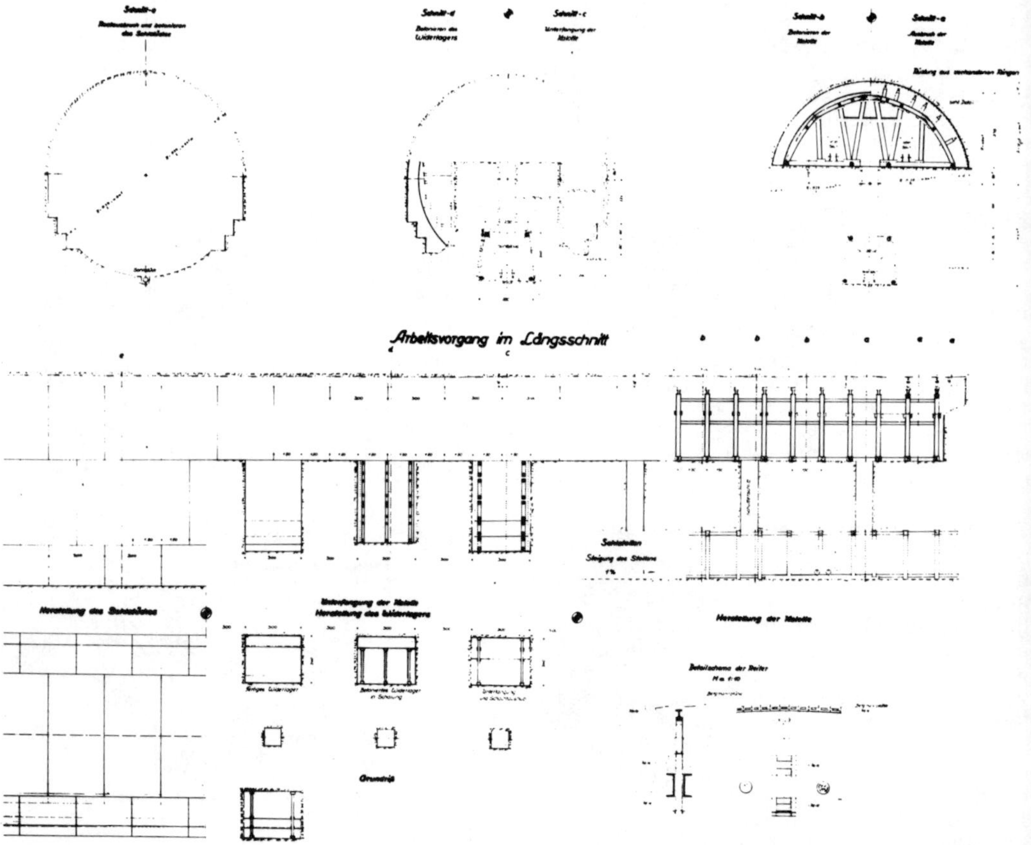

Bild 2: Phasen für Ausbruch und Sicherung

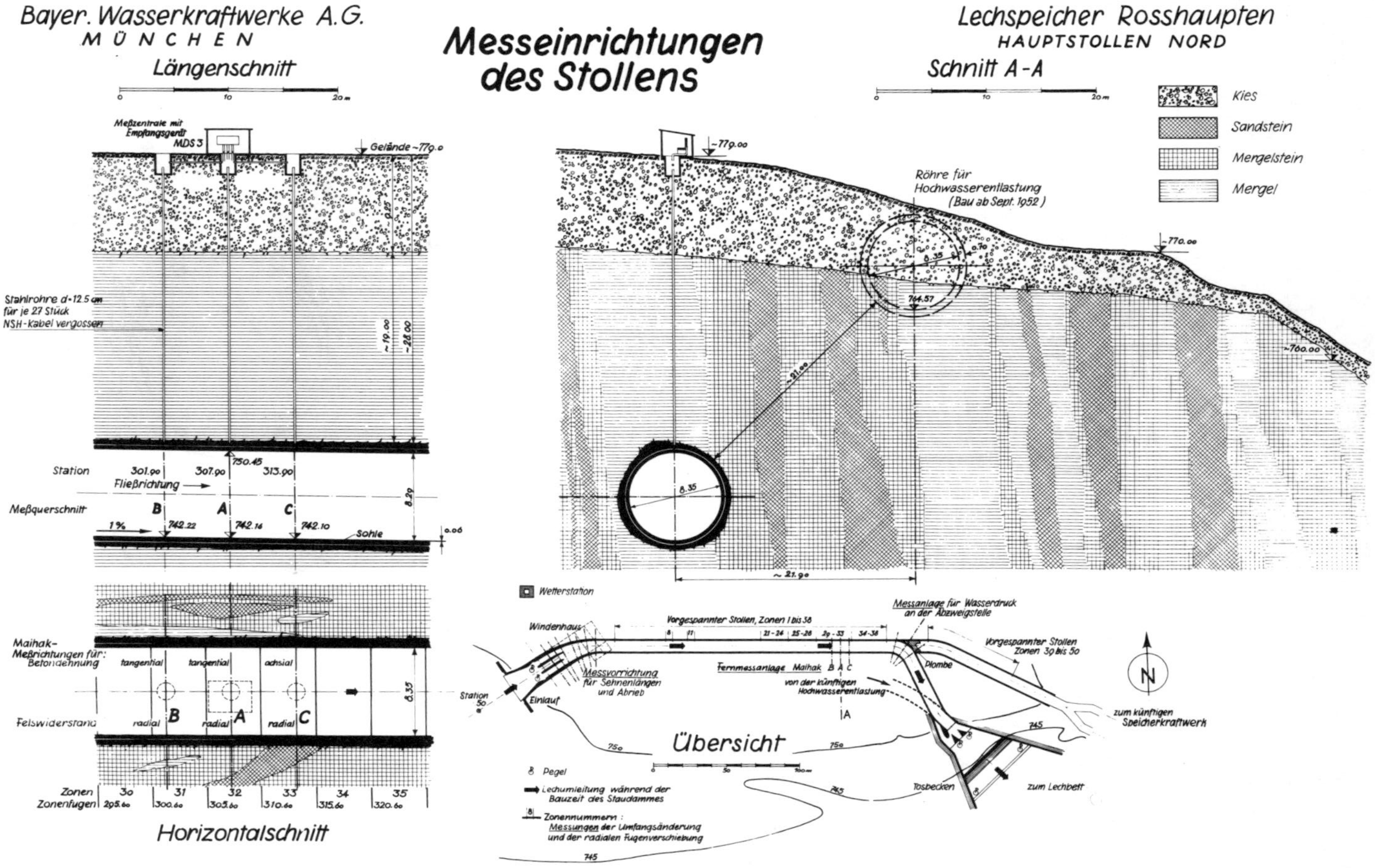

Bild 3: Übersicht der Meßeinrichtungen des Stollens

Eine Übersicht der Meßeinrichtungen des Stollens, der Meßzentrale mit Kabelführung, sowie der örtlichen Gegebenheiten zeigt Bild 3. Die Anordnung der Meßgeber in den Meßquerschnitten ist in Bild 4 dargestellt.

Zusätzlich wurden während der Vorspannung geodätische Messungen zur Ermittlung der radialen Verschiebungen durchgeführt. Mit Hilfe dieser Verformungsmessungen konnten die bei der Vorspannung aufgetretenen Bewegungen der Innenlaibung des Kernrings ermittelt werden. Die Messungen haben wichtige Erkenntnisse über den Aufbau der Vorspannung gebracht und waren eine wertvolle Hilfe bei der Durchführung dieser Arbeiten.

3.2 Meßergebnisse

Über die Ergebnisse der Messungen am Stollen Roßhaupten während der Bauausführung, beim Probestau, bei der Inbetriebnahme und der anschliessenden Betriebsdauer von nahezu zwei Jahren, in der auch Druckstoßversuche durchgeführt wurden, ist schon in mehreren Veröffentlichungen berichtet worden (2, 3, 4). Das Ergebnis sämtlicher Messungen vom Zeitpunkt des Einbaues der Meßgeber bis zum April 1959, das ist ein Beobachtungszeitraum von rund 8 Jahren, ist im Bild 5 dargestellt. Hierin sind auch die Bauvorgänge und die verschiedenen Funktionen des Stollens aufgezeichnet.

Auf die Beanspruchungen des Stollens während des 8-jährigen Beobachtungszeitraumes wird anschließend kurz eingegangen.

- Einflüsse aus Temperatur

Die Temperatur im Beton bzw. im Gebirge war in der Zeit der Lechumleitung sowohl von der Wasser- als auch von der Lufttemperatur beeinflußt. Während des anschließenden Betriebs sind die Einflüsse der jeweiligen Temperatur des Betriebwassers ausschlaggebend. Die Vorspannung des Kernrings im März 1952 erfolgte bei einer mittleren Temperatur von etwa 9°C. Bei der statischen Berechnung der endgültigen Sicherung wurde ein Δ t von $\pm$7°C angesetzt. Im Beobachtungszeitraum nach Inbetriebnahme des Stollens wurde eine niedrigste Temperatur von ca. + 5°C und eine höchste Temperatur von ca. + 13°C gemessen. Der Differenzbetrag lag damit noch weit unter dem angenom-

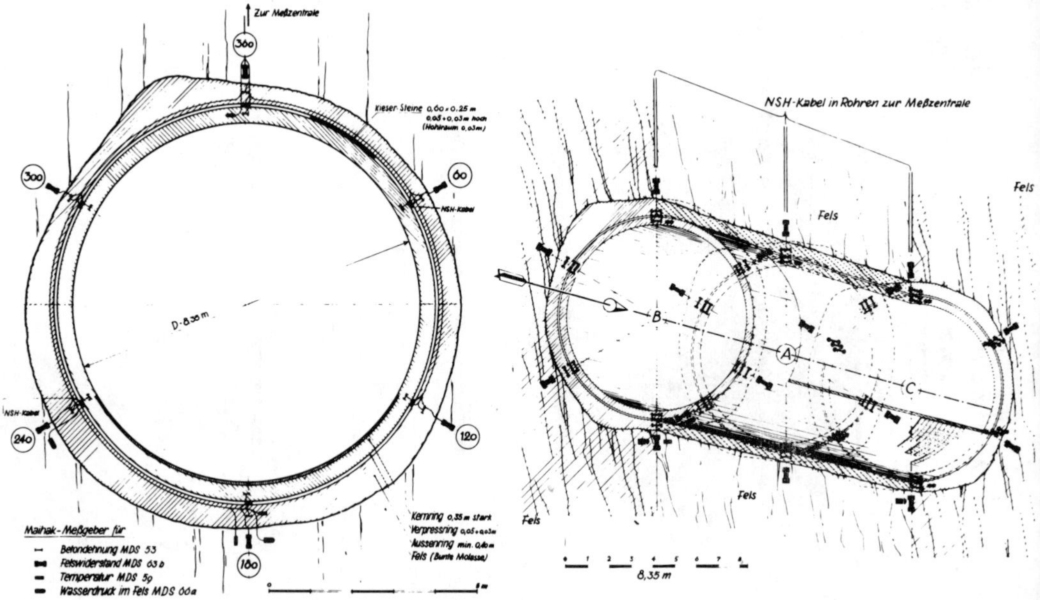

Bild 4: Anordnung der Meßgeber

menen Betrag von 14°C. Eine Temperaturzunehme von 1°C erzeugt eine Erhöhung der tangentiellen Felsspannung um σ = - 0,03 MN/m².

- Einflüsse aus Außenwasserdruck

Um den Einfluß des für den Stollen wirksamen Wasserdrucks ermitteln zu können, muß der Außenwasserdruck mit dem Innenwasserdruck überlagert werden. Im Betriebszustand ist der Innenwasserdruck immer größer als der Außenwasserdruck. Der maximale Überdruck liegt etwa bei 1,5 bar. Bild 5 zeigt weiter eine sofortige Reaktion der Betondehnungsgeber auf Veränderungen des Innenwasserdruckes. Die Veränderung des Außenwasserdrukkes ist vom jeweiligen Stauspiegel im Speicherbecken und den anstehenden geologischen Verhältnissen abhängig. Insbesondere Schichtung und Klüftung können hier abschnittsweise sehr unterschiedliche Wirkungen bringen.

- Wirkung der Vorspannung und des Felswiderstandes

Während die Vorspannung verhältnismäßig stark auf äußere Einflüsse wie Temperatur und Wasserdruck reagiert, zeigt der Felswiderstand einen weniger ausgeprägten und gedämpften Verlauf. Im Beobachtungszeitraum hat sich die aufgebrachte Vorspannung nicht wesentlich verändert. Es kann davon ausgegangen werden, daß sie auch heute noch wirksam ist. In diesem Zusammenhang sei vermerkt, daß anläßlich einer Stolleninspektion im Jahre 1980 keine Veränderungen im Stollen, die auf ein Abklingen der Vorspannung hinweisen, festgestellt worden sind. Ein weitgehend elastisches Tragverhalten der Stollenauskleidung kann daher unterstellt werden. Aus dem Verlauf des Felswiderstandes, der im Laufe der Zeit abgenommen hat, möchte auf eine gewisse Konsolidierung des Gebirgskörpers geschlossen werden.

In nachfolgender Tabelle werden die Ergebnisse von Berechnung und Messung gegenübergestellt. Bei der Berechnung waren u.a. auch die geologischen Verhältnisse zu berücksichtigen. Hiernach war im Sohl- und Firstbereich wegen der nahezu senkrecht anstehenden Schichten ein anderer Bettungsmodul als im Ulmenbereich anzusetzen.

4. ABSCHLIESSENDE BEURTEILUNG

Durch die meßtechnische Überwachung beim Bau und Betrieb des Stollens Roßhaupten konnte der Nachweis erbracht werden, daß die gewählte und ausgeführte Bauweise praktisch allen Anforderungen gerecht wird. Zusammenfassend kann man feststellen, daß die durch Einbeziehen der mittragenden Wirkung des Gebirges ein wirtschaftliches Verfahren für den Stollenbau gewählt worden ist. Der Triebwasserstollen Roßhaupten erfüllt alle an ihn gestellten Aufgaben und gewährleistet einen reibungslosen Kraftwerksbetrieb.

5. QUELLENNACHWEIS

(1) GSAENGER A.: Beanspruchung von Beton und Betonbauwerken unter Einwirkung von hohen Wassergeschwindigkeiten; beton H.9/1962, S. 405/412 Beton-Verlag GmbH Düsseldorf

(2) FROHNHOLZER J.: Messungen am Hauptstollen des Lechspeichers Roßhaupten; Bayerische Wasserkraftwerke AG München, März 1953

(3) FROHNHOLZER J.: Maihak-Dauer-

Tabelle: Vergleich der Spannungen im Innenring zwischen Rechnung und Messung

Spannungen gemessen am 30.9.1954

	Zentriwinkel v. Scheitel d =	60°	120°	180°	240°	300°	360°	Dim.
Spannungen	Rechnung σ =	0	-10,4	-2,8	+2,8	-10,4	-1,0	MN/m²
	Messung σ =	-3,5	-11,1	-4,7	-0,7	-15,9	-4,5	MN/m²

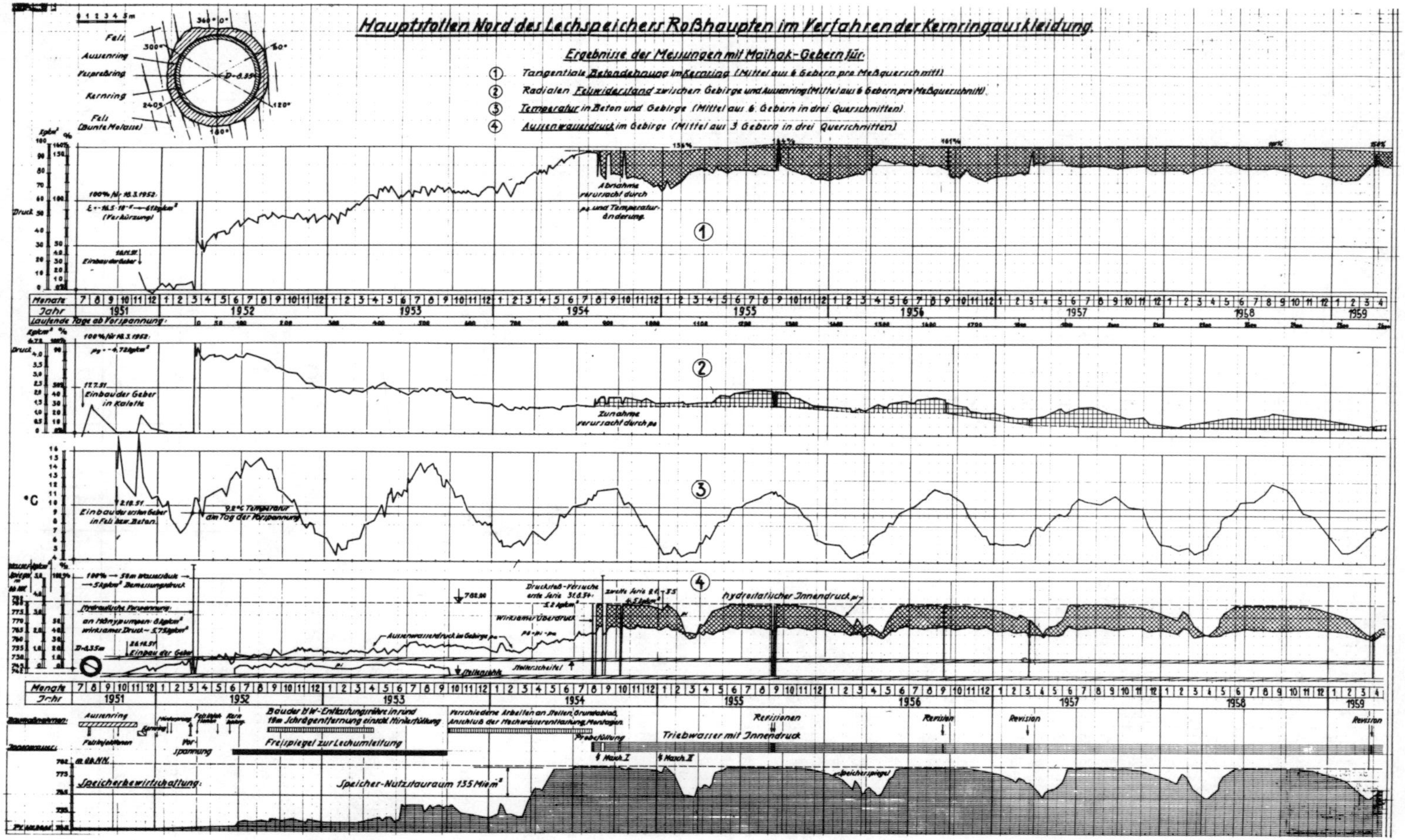

Bild 5: Auswertung der Meßergebnisse

messungen zum Verfahren der Kernringauskleidung beim Hauptstollen Roßhaupten; DIE BAUTECHNIK 32. Jahrgang, S. 368 bis 376, Heft 11 - November 1955
(4) FROHNHOLZER J.: Meßtechnische Überwachung des Verfahrens der Kernringauskleidung für Druckstollen mit Maihak-Gebern; DIE BAUTECHNIK 1953, S. 300
(5) HETZEL K.: Vorgutachten über den für das Speicherwerk Roßhaupten geplanten Triebwasser- und Grundablaß-Stollen vom 4. Dez. 1950
(6) FROHNHOLZER J.: Der Speicher Roßhaupten als Hauptglied für den Rahmenplan des Lechs; Die Wasserwirtschaft 43. Jahrgang, Heft 7 u. 8, April und Mai 1953
(7) CONRADI E.: Druckstoß- und Abschaltversuche im Kraftwerk Roßhaupten; Die Wasserwirtschaft 5/1969, S. 121 bis 126
(8) HAIMERL; L.A.: Das Speicherkraftwerk Roßhaupten - Schweizerische Bauzeitung, 79. Jahrgang, Heft 10 u. 11 1961
(9) GIESECKE J.: Einsatz spezieller Betone für Sanierungsmaßnahmen am Tarbela-Staudamm; Bauingenieur 56/1981; S. 437 bis 440
(10) NN.: Another year of repairs for Tarbela; World Water, December 1978, P. 12
(11) CHAO, P.C.: Tarbela designers aware of dangers; World Water, August 1981, P. 5
(12)NN.: Tarbela Desingers "were warned about cavitation dangers"; World Water,March 1981, P. 6
(13) NN.: Tunnel collapse slows Victoria dam drive; World Water, September 1981, P. 7
(14) Bericht der BAWAG über die Stollenbegehung am 14. und 15. April 1980
(15) MÜLLER: Hauptstollen des Lechspeichers Roßhaupten, Vergleich zwischen Rechnung und Messung; nicht veröffentlichter Bericht der BAWAG München, März 1956
(16) MÜLLER L.: Der Felsbau, 3. Band - Tunnelbau - F. Enke-Verlag Stuttgart (1978)
(17) HETZEL K.: Tunnel- und Stollenbau; F. Schleicher Taschenbuch für Bauingenieure, 2. Auflage (1955)
(18) WITTMANN: WASSERKRAFTANLAGEN-Triebwasserleitungen; F. Schleicher Taschenbuch für Bauingenieure 2. Auflage (1955)
(19) BÖSS P.: Berechnung der Leistungsfähigkeit des Umleitungsstollens beim Speicher Roßhaupten; Wiss. Ausarbeitung v. 3.12.50 unveröffentlicht
(20) MARKL S., PONTOW KH.: Untertagebauten, W. Ernst u. Sohn 1968

GALERIES FORCÉES PRÉCONTRAINTES ET CHAMBRES D'ÉQUILIBRE POSTCONTRAINTE ACTIVE DE REVÊTEMENTS EN BÉTON

Prestressed pressure tunnels and surge shafts – Active post-tensioned concrete linings

Vorgespannte Druckstollen und Schächte – Aktive Vorspannung von Betonauskleidungen

PIERRE E.ROELLI
Losinger SA, Berne, Suisse

SUMMARY:
For thirty years, prestressed concrete has undergone a period of turbulent development. Bridges, tanks and silos, flat slabs, off-shore oil platforms and ships are realized in prestressed concrete. In lining pressure tunnels and shafts, the tendency to move from steel to concrete can be seen.
This new mode of construction, not very well known at this moment by the project engineers of hydroelectric power schemes, is an interesting alternative to the classical steel linings for medium to large diameters (2.5 m to 30 m) and in the medium hydraulic pressure range (2.5 to 3.0 MN/m2 without rock participation). The active post-tensioned concrete linings are particularly suitable in case of an important inner pressure which cannot be taken by the surrounding rock, by too poor rock covering of the galery or with bad rock conditions. The post-tensioned concrete lining is also able to take entirely the place of steel lining. The active post-tensioned lining is economical (10 % to 30 % cheaper than the classical solutions), quickly executed, pratically without maintenance and is not exposed to buckling caused by sudden dewatering. A description of a special anchorage unit specially designed for the described structures, the construction procedure and some practical examples are the topics of this paper.

ZUSAMMENFASSUNG:
Seit dreissig Jahren erlebt der vorgespannte Beton eine Zeit stürmischer Entwicklung. Es ist selbstverständlich, dass Brücken, Reservoirs und Silos, aber auch Flachdecken im Hochbau heutzutage in Spannbeton realisiert werden; diese Technik kommt auch für Flughafenpisten, Offshore-Oelplattformen und sogar Schiffe zur Anwendung. Eine ähnliche Tendenz zeichnet sich auch auf dem Gebiet der Auskleidung von Druckstollen und -schächten ab.
Die vorgespannten Druckstollenverkleidungen, den projektierenden Ingenieuren des hydraulischen Fachgebietes noch wenig bekannt, sind eine interessante Alternative zu den klassischen Stahlpanzerungen für mittlere und grosse Durchmesser (von 2.5 bis 30 m) und mittlere Betriebsdrücke (2.5 bis 3.0 MN/m2 ohne Felsmitwirkung).
Die aktiv durch Einzelspannglieder vorgespannten Betonverkleidungen sind anwendbar, wenn der Betriebsinnendruck für die Felsumhüllung zu hoch ist, wenn die Felsüberlagerung ungenügend ist, oder wenn die Felsqualität schlecht ist; darum ist eine aktiv vorgespannte Druckstollenverkleidung ohne weiteres im Stande, eine klassische Stahlpanzerung zu ersetzen. Diese Verkleidungsart ist besonders wirtschaftlich (10 % bis 30 % billiger als die klassischen Lösungen), schnell gebaut, praktisch ohne Unterhalt (kein Korrosionsschutz zu erneuern); keine Beulgefahr infolge Kavitation oder plötzlicher Entleerung ist ein zusätzlicher Vorteil des Systemes. Eine Beschreibung einer speziell entwickelten Spannverankerung für diese Anwendung, die Ausführungsphasen sowie die Erwähnung von ausgeführten Druckstollen und Schächten werden in diesem Vortrag präsentiert.

RESUME:
Le développement et la généralisation de l'emploi du béton précontraint ont connu un essor fulgurant ces dernières décénnies. Les ponts bien sûr, les réservoirs et silos, ainsi que les dalles et radiers de bâtiment sont réalisés en béton précontraint. Cette technique est même appliquée aux pistes d'aéroports, aux plateformes off-shore d'exploitation pétrolière et aux coques de navires.
Dans le même contexte, les revêtements de puits et galeries forcées des complexes hydro-électriques font appel maintenant au béton précontraint. Cette technique de construction, encore peu connue parmi la plupart des ingénieurs projetant des complexes hydro-électriques, représente une alternative intéressante et ayant fait ses preuves face aux classiques blindages en acier en ce qui concerne les moyens et grands diamètres (de 2.50 m à plus de 30 m) et les pressions moyennes (jusqu'à 2.5 - 3.0 MN/m2 sans participation de la roche).
Les revêtements précontraints activement par câbles d'acier à haute résistance entrent en ligne de compte lorsque la pression hydraulique intérieure de la galerie est trop forte pour l'enveloppe rocheuse environnante, lorsque le recouvrement de la galerie est insuffisant ou que la qualité de la roche est médiocre; à ce titre la précontrainte est en mesure de jouer totalement le rôle d'un blindage classique en acier; contrairement à d'autres systèmes, elle ne sert pas seulement à améliorer l'étranchéité de revêtements de galerie en béton non armé ou munis d'armature passive sujets à la fissuration. La galerie précontrainte activement par câbles s'impose pour des motifs économiques (de 10 % à plus de 30 % plus avantageuse que les solutions blindées classiques), sa rapidité d'exécution, son entretien inéxistant (pas de protection antirouille à renouveller) et son insensibilité au risque de claquage provoqué par cavitation ou sous-pression lors de vidanges subites ou par sollcitation de pression d'eau extérieure. Une description d'un système d'ancrages spécialement conçu pour les galeries, l'énumération des opérations nécéssaires à la réalisation des revêtements précontraints, la présentation de quelques exemples pratiques complètent cet exposé.

1 INTRODUCTION

Depuis la fin de la seconde guerre mondiale, le béton précontraint a connu un développement spectaculaire à cause principalement d'une activité débordante dans le domaine du génie civil et de la construction ces trois dernières décénnies; l'intêret de cette technique est aussi dû à des raisons économiques car on assiste de plus en plus à la réalisation de structures en béton précontraint au dépend de constructions en acier.

Les ponts de courtes et moyennes portées, les grands réservoirs pour stockage de solides, liquides et de gaz, les dalles à longue portée et fortes surcharges dans le bâtiment et les constructions industrielles, les pistes d'aéroports, les grandes plateformes pétrolières off-shore en Mer du Nord, même les coques de bateau font appel au béton précontraint.

Une tendance identique se profile pour les revêtements de galeries sous pression et les chambres d'équilibre des complexes hydroélectriques.

Ces dernières années, plusieurs exemples d'exécution en Italie et en Suisse ont démontré que les revêtements en béton précontraint sont économiquement très compétitifs et techniquement irréprochables; ils représentent ainsi une alternative intéressante aux traditionnels blindages en ancier.

2 TYPES DE REVETEMENTS DE GALERIES

Un trop faible recouvrement rocheux, une trop forte pression hydraulique intérieure ou une importante perméabilité de la roche requièrent un renforcement du revêtement de la galerie. Les galeries de dérivation ou de fuite et les chambres d'équilibre soumises à des pressions moyennes sont particulièrement bien adaptées à une exécution en béton précontraint. Les puits de descente qui subissent à leur partie inférieure des pressions considérables seront par contre classiquement blindés, pour autant que la participation de la roche ne puisse être prise en compte. Avant de parler spécifiquement des galeries forcées précontraintes, nous ferons ci-après une énumération succincte des divers types de revêtements usuels de galeries en charge; généralement, les revêtements de galerie sont adaptés aux conditions de l'enveloppe rocheuse environnante. Il en résulte que les galeries ne sont pas revêtues de la même façon sur toute leur longueur, mais au contraire, chaque tronçon verra l'application d'un système particulier. Nous pourrons, par exemple, classer ces revêtements selon les critères qui nous interessent en deux groupes principaux, soit:

- les revêtements sans précontrainte
- les revêtements avec précontrainte

2.1 Revêtements sans précontrainte

Un recouvrement suffisant de la galerie, une roche de bonne qualité pauvre en fissures et failles et un environnement imperméable appellent un revêtement en béton non armé d'épaisseur moyenne qui sera de plus post-injecté au niveau du contact entre le béton et la roche. Cette classique manière de procéder pour les galeries soumises à des pressions moyennes et se trouvant dans un milieu favorable sert surtout à améliorer le profil hydraulique de la galerie.

Cependant, malgré des méthodes de bétonnage continues supprimant les joints de travail, une imperméabilité suffisante ne peut être garantie dans toutes les conditions géologiques rencontrées et des fuites d'eau localisées se produisent aux points faibles où se sont formées des fissures. Pour palier à ces inconvénients, on a alors recours au béton armé en garnissant les coffrages de corbeilles d'armature passive plus ou moins importantes. Malheureusement, une armature passive, si massive soit-elle, est sous-employée car les fers ne travaillent qu'au taux de résistance effective à la traction du béton avant la fissuration. On n'arrive par ce moyen qu'à répartir les fissures et non à les empêcher, ce qui de plus peut être problématique pour la protection de l'armature contre la corrosion.

Le stade suivant est bien sûr le blindage en acier qui forme une enveloppe résistante et étanche contre la pression d'eau agissant à l'intérieur de la galerie. On a recours à ce mode de revêtement lorsque la couverture rocheuse est insuffisante et lorsque la pression intérieure atteint des valeurs considérables, surtout dans les puits de descente. Même si la stabilité de l'enveloppe rocheuse environnante est suffisante, le blindage acier représente la solution technique classique la meilleure dans le domaine des hautes pressions de service. Le blindage acier est par contre onéreux et des mesurer particulières sont à prendre lorsque agit une pression d'eau à l'extérieur ou qu'un risque de claquage existe en cas de vidange subite de la conduite; on est parfois amené à dimensionner un blindage en acier contre des influences extérieures plus défavorables que la pression intérieure.

2.2 Revêtements précontraints

A cause de la faible résistance nominale du béton aux contraintes de traction, (béton armé ou non), on a cherché à empêcher la fissuration des revêtements en béton en appliquant depuis assez longtemps déjà un système de précontrainte passive. L'effet de précontrainte est obtenu en s'appuyant sur l'enveloppe rocheuse environnante pour introduire un état de compression aussi durable que possible dans le revêtement de béton. Un recouvrement rocheux minimal est requis ainsi qu'une certaine qualité de l'enveloppe environnante qui doit supporter des pressions d'injection considérables lors de la mise en contrainte. Les systèmes les plus usités sont autrichiens: le système de murage Kieser et le système d'injection Tiwag. Ces prodédés de précontrainte passive se caractérisent par une mise en pression à l'aide de lait de mortier injecté derrière le revêtement, ou dans une couche intercalaire. Faisons remarquer que la précontrainte ainsi provoquée dans le revêtement doit être initialement particulièrement forte pour compenser en partie les pertes dûes au fluage de la roche de support qui est par définition de qualité insuffisante. En additionnant les pertes au fluage et au retrait du revêtement lui-même, l'effet de précontrainte a tendance à s'amenuiser avec le temps. Pour remedier à cet inconvénient, on construit maintenant des revêtements de ce genre en double bétonnage et en intercalant entre deux plusieurs couches de feuilles synthétiques armées et soudées afin d'améliorer l'étanchéité en cas de fissuration.

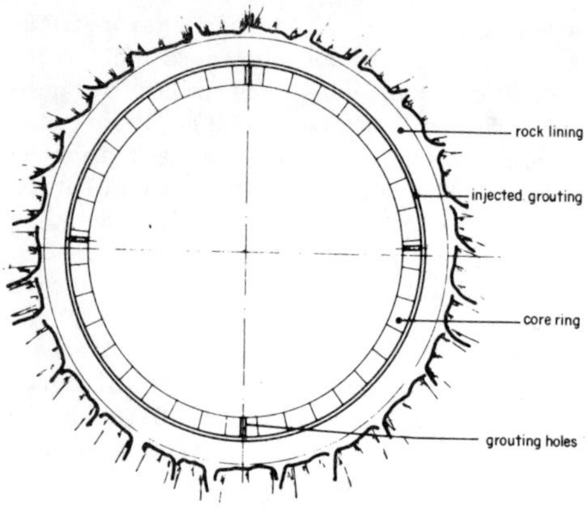

Fig. 1 Methode du murage du Dr. Kieser. Construction à l'aide de blocs de maçonnerie intérieurs

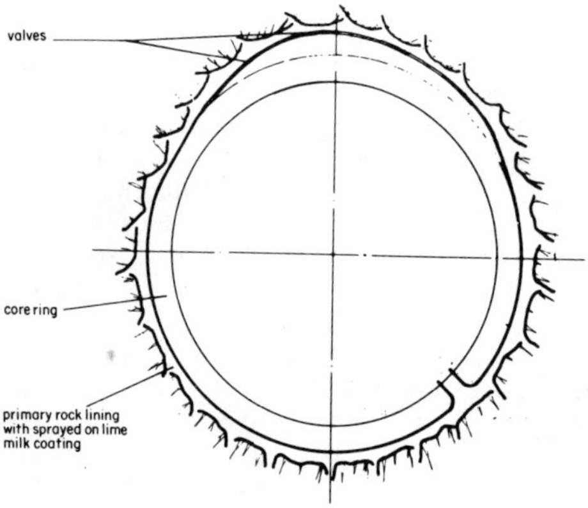

Fig. 2 Méthode de pressage par injection de TIWAG

Si les techniques de précontrainte passive mentionnées ci-dessous sont utilisées sous certaines conditions techniques particulières, ce sont par contre des conditions purement économiques qui ont conduit à étudier le remplacement des blindages classiques en acier par des revêtements en béton ayant recours à la précontrainte active à l'aide de câbles ou fils d'acier à haute résistance. Cette méthode, assez récente, s'est révèlée très fonctionnelle notamment à cause de son prix de revient, de sa rapidité d'exécution et de son entretien inéxistant en service.

La précontrainte est engendrée par des câbles circulaires posés dans ou autour du revêtement; une participation de la roche à la reprise de la pression hydraulique intérieure peut éventuellement être prise en compte, une injection de remplissage exécutée après mise en tension garantissant le contact avec l'enveloppe rocheuse environnante.

Parmi les premières applications de précontrainte active par fils d'acier, citons un tronçon de galerie forcée de l'usine électrique de Kaprun en Autriche où des éléments préfabriqués et précontraints de 3.20 m de diamètre et 300 mm d'épaisseur furent posés par segment sur une longueur de 1316 m en 1944; le procédé d'enroulage de fils d'acier système Wayss & Freitag assurait la précontrainte.

En 1957, la firme Dyckerhoff et Wydman a précontraint une portion de puits du complexe hydroélectrique de Lünersee en Autriche. Il s'agissait d'un ouvrage d'une longueur de 200 m, d'un diamètre intérieur variant entre 5.64 m et 6.28 m et dans lequel règnait une pression intérieur de 1.2 MN/m2. Pour la première fois, on a appliqué des unités de précontrainte circulaires et séparées de la même façon que pour les réservoirs et silos. Les barres de précontrainte sont ancrées dans des contreforts aménagés en saillie à l'intérieur du profil. Trois barres, chacune sur une ouverture de 120

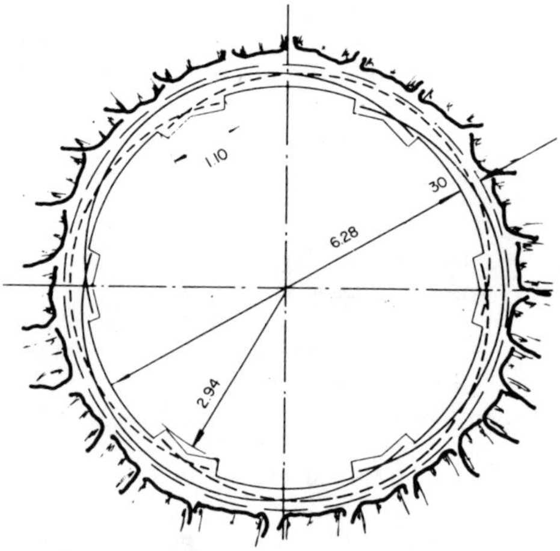

Fig. 3 Précontrainte active à l'usine de Lünersee. Système Dyckerhoff & Wydmann

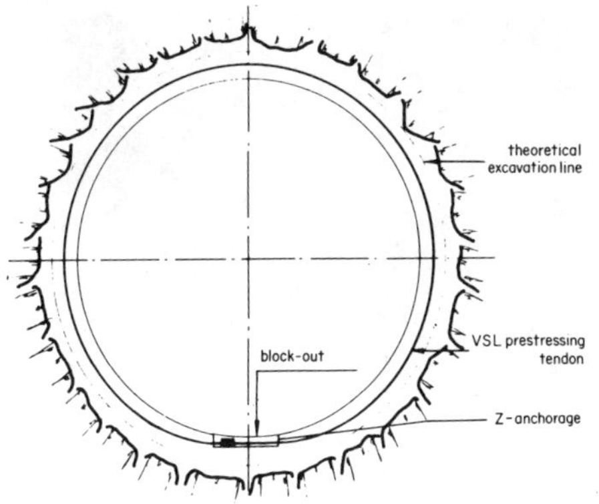

Fig. 4 Précontrainte active système VSL

degrés, ferment un anneau. Une post-injection pratiquée entre roche et revêtement parachevait l'ouvrage. Ces deux méthodes de précontrainte active ainsi que plusieurs autres procédés n'ont pas connu d'applications ultérieures.

3 PRECONTRAINTE DE GALERIES VSL

Le système de précontrainte active VSL par câbles séparés appartient lui aussi à la même famille: il se base sur le développement de câbles circulaires qui agissent comme des cercles de tonneaux; les ancrages intermédiaires, en principe une pièce pour chaque câble annulaire à 360 degrés, ne requièrent aucun contrefort d'ancrages apparent.

Lors de la mise en tension du câble qui a lieu selon le principe de fonctionnement d'une boucle de ceinture, l'ancrage se meut à l'intérieur d'une niche parallèlement au câble sans aucun appui sur le béton.

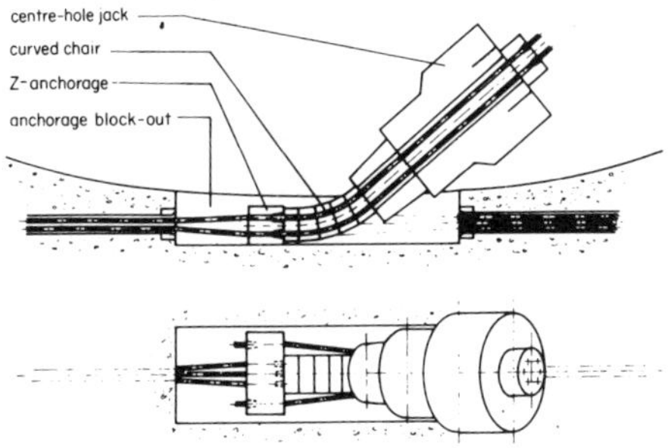

Fig. 5 Mise en tension d'un ancrage intermédiaire VSL

Le câble est formé d'un faisceau de torons d'acier à haute résistance enfermé dans une gaine métallique injectée après mise en tension; de plus en plus, afin de simplifier les opérations et garantir une friction très réduite des torons lors de la mise en tensions, on a recours à des torons graissés enrobés dans une peau de polyéthylène, le tout étant directement noyé dans le béton. La protection contre la corrosion est irréprochable, la sécurité de l'ouvrage à la rupture n'en est que fort peu affectée et les opérations de post-injection des gaines de câble sont supprimées. Deux types d'ancrage intermédiaires sont actuellement utilisés:

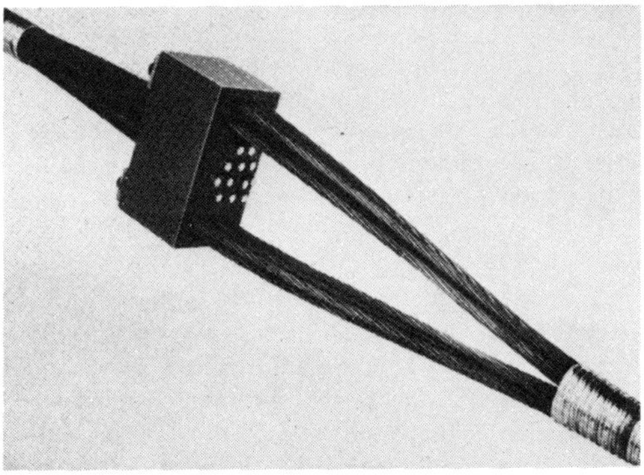
Fig. 6 Ancrage intermédiaire VSL type Z

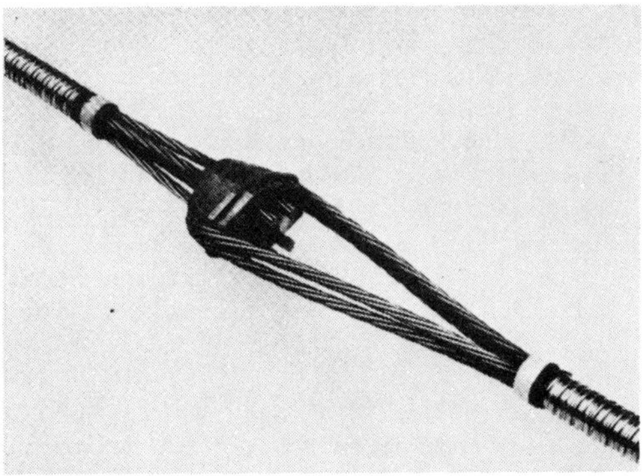
Fig. 7 Ancrage intermédiaire VSL type ZU

La capacité à la rupture de chaque unité de câble varie entre 370 kN (2 torons de 0.5") et 3600 kN (12 torons de 0.6", section dyform). Pour les très grands diamètres comme les grandes chambres d'équilibre, une unité à 22 torons de 0.6" est disponible (rupture à 6600 kN). La mise en tension est assurée à l'aide d'une chaise de dérivation et d'un vérin hydraulique à évidement central.

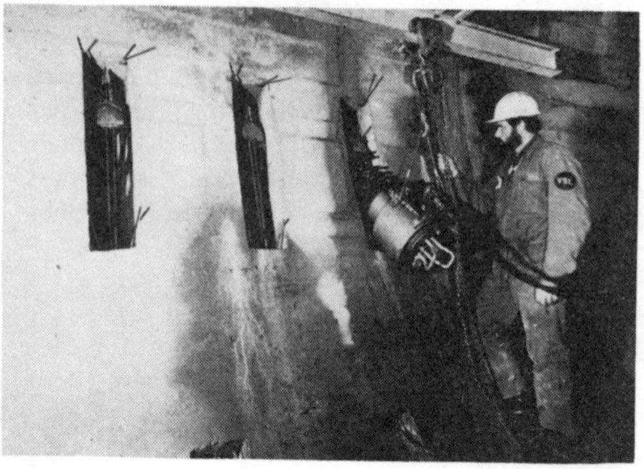

Fig. 8 Mise en tension d'un câble annulaire

Les étapes de construction d'un revêtement en béton précontraint se déroulent comme suit, après excavation du profil:

a) Giclage d'une solution de poudre calcaire hydraulique contre la roche pour éviter l'adhérence à la paroi du revêtement lors de sa mise en contrainte. Lorsque des problèmes de drainage particuliers surgissent notamment lors de la construction de puits verticaux, une feuille d'isolation en matière synthétique structurée peut être intercalée entre la roche et le béton du revêtement.

b) Pose d'ancrages courts par adhérence, environ une pièce pour 2 m2 de paroi rocheuse. Dans des conditions particulières, il est possible d' avoir recours à des profilés métalliques circulaires en lieu et place des ancrages.

c) Sur les têtes d'ancrage ou les profilés circulaires, fixation de fers ronds longitudinaux servant de supports aux câbles annulaires de précontrainte.

d) Pose des câbles préfabriqués et des coffrages de niches d'ancrage en polystyrol expansé ou coffret boismétal.

Fig. 9 Câbles et coffrages de niches dans une galerie de grand diamètre

Fig. 10 Portion de galerie avant le bétonnage

e) Mise en place d'une couche intérieure d'armature passive servant à la répartition des efforts longitudinaux lors de la mise en tension des câbles de précontrainte.

f) Bétonnage à l'aide des coffrages classiquement utilisés dans les galeries; le béton devra répondre aux critères suivants:

- une résistance nominale à la compression sur cube égale ou supérieure à 30 N/mm2 est requise; la qualité du béton est déterminée par l'épaisseur du revêtement et la concentration de précontrainte. A cause de la construction voûtée, des contraintes admissibles de compression assez élevées pourront être considérées.

- en plus des critères de résistance, le béton devra être imperméable et bien se comporter contre les influences mécaniques et chimiques. La plasticité du mélange devra en outre être suffisante pour permettre sa mise en place par pompage.

- ces exigences en partie contradictoires sont remplies en recourrant à une granulométrie convenable des agrégats, une proportion de 400 à 500 kg de ciment par m3 de béton, un facteur eau/ciment de 0.4 et un plastifiant adéquat. Une quantité de ciment élevée joue un rôle secondaire, les effets de retrait du béton étant bien moindres dans le bétonnage des galeries que pour les structures à l'air libre.

- un revêtement de galerie n'est que fort peu exposé aux changements de température, au gel et à l'eau salée. Par contre, les effets de cavitation et la composition chimique de certaines eaux requièrent un vibrage-compactage soigné, un facteur eau/ciment

Fig. 11 Mise en tension des câbles dans la galerie de dérivation de Piastra-Andonno. Longueur 11.4 km, 29'000 câbles, 400 câbles mis en tension par jour

faible et des agrégats du béton exempts de composants ultra - fins. Nos expériences ont montré un excellent comportement des ouvrages réalisés au point de vue durabilité.

g) Mise en tension des câbles de précontrainte, éventuellement injection des gaines.

h) Post-injection à basse pression entre le revêtement et le rocher au moyen de manchons plastiques disposés dans l'armature avant bétonnage. Cette injection sert à combler les éventuels interstices qui se serait formés lors de la mise en tension de la structure.

i) Remplissage des niches d'ancrage par injection à basse pression d'un mortier spécial adéquat.

Après cette suite d'opérations qui peuvent être menées par diverses équipes les unes à la suite des autres, la galerie est prête à entrer en fonction.

Un revêtement de galerie précontraint activement selon le procédé mentionné présente plusieurs avantages:

- L'acier de précontrainte utilisé ayant une résistance à la rupture pouvant être cinq fois supérieure à l'acier des blindages classiques, il en résulte une économie substantielle. Notons que l'épaisseur requise pour un revêtement précontraint n'est que rarement supérieure à celle d'un blindage en acier pourvu de son remplissage périphérique en béton; les frais d'excavation restent donc dans la plupart des cas semblables.

- Mentionnons que les galeries forcées sont le plus souvent aménagées dans des zones montagneuses difficiles d'accès; les matériaux utilisés sont facilement transportables et ne posent pas les problèmes qui surgissent lors de l'acheminement de viroles de blindage de grand diamètre qui de plus doivent être assemblées par soudage sur place.

- L'avantage de l'utilisation d'une quantité réduite d'acier peut jouer un rôle non négligeable dans les pays non-producteurs. Une comparaison des coûts entre blindage et précontrainte est régie par les fluctuations du marché de l'acier, par la situation géographique du chan-

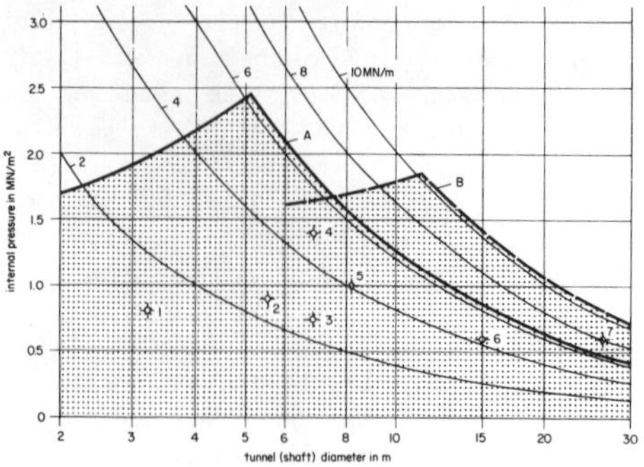

Fig. 12 Domaine d'application des revêtements précontraints; courbe A: câbles sans contreforts d'ancrage / courbe B: câbles avec contreforts d'ancrage. Diagramme conçu sans participation de la roche à la reprise de la pression hydraulique

tier et des problèmes logistiques s'y rattachant. Notre expérience nous démontre que les économies vont de 10% à plus de 30% lors de comparaisons de prix de revient avec une solution classique.

- A cause des importants délais de fabrication, la planification d'une galerie blindée classique doit être entreprise à long terme. Une solution précontrainte par contre est réalisable dans des délais très courts et peut être constamment adaptée à la qualité de roche rencontrée lors des travaux d'excavation du profil.

Fig. 13 Câbles circulaires de précontrainte dans la chambre d'équilibre de Suviana Brasimone

Fig. 14 Galerie de dérivation à la sortie du barrage d'Oberaar, Forces Motrices de l'Aar supérieure. Avant le cachetage des niches d'ancrage

- Grâce à l'absence de fissures des structures précontraintes, une excellente durabilité et résistance à la corrosion caractérise ce mode de construction. Le béton possède la faculté de se "récupérer" après une importante surpression sans qu'il en résulte des dommages, car la précontrainte active referme les fissures après une surcharge accidentelle.

- Aucun risque de claquage dû à la cavitation, une vidange soudaine ou une pression d'eau extérieure ne peut affecter ce genre de revêtement.

4 EXEMPLES DE REALISATION

Les premières applications pratiques du système ont vu la réalisation des chambres d'équilibre des centrales de San Fiorano et Suviana Brasimone en Italie.

Une intéressante réalisation fut celle qui eut pour cadre la centrale de Piastra-Andonno en Italie: en 1973, une galerie de dérivation de 11,4 km de longueur revêtue de béton non armé était sujette à de très importantes pertes d'eau causées par une fissuration générale. Le maître d'oeuvre, ENEL, opta pour une réfection totale du revêtement en béton précontraint; le cahier des charges stipulait une perte maximale de 7.5 litres par seconde et par km sous 0.8 MN/m2. Le blindage en acier ne fut pas retenu pour des raisons de durée des travaux, la précontrainte réduisant par contre cette durée de 50 %. Le tronçon de 11,4 km fut revêtu en 12 mois; les pertes effectives en services n'atteignent que 1.25 l/s/-km.

Depuis lors, plusieurs ouvrages ont été réalisés en béton précontraint. Citons des portions de galerie de dérivation et de fuite de la centrale de pompage-turbinage du Grimsel en Suisse: diamètre intérieur 6.80 m, pression de service 7.5 à 1.4 MN/m2, sans participation de la roche à la reprise de la pression hydraulique intérieure.

En Italie, lors de la construction de l'usine de pompage-turbinage de Chiotas-Piastra (ENEL) implantée près du col de Tende, on a aussi eu recours au revêtement précontraint pour la réalisation de la tête des puits de descente.

Une portion de galerie de dérivation, une chambre annulaire horizontale d'amortissement, un puits principal, un puits pièzométrique et les raccords reliant ces structures ont été précontraints et forment un ensemble monolithique.

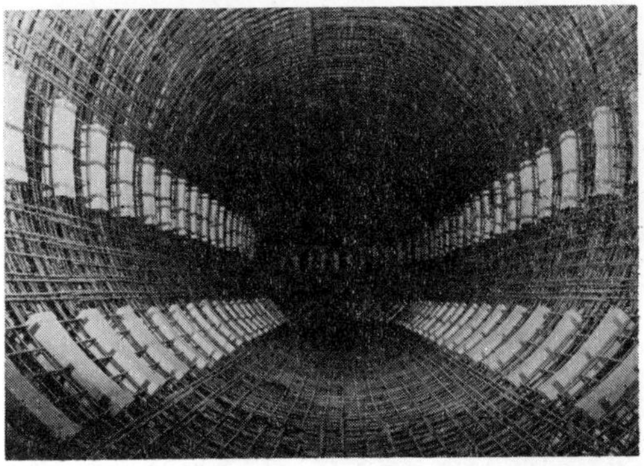

Fig. 16 Centrale de Chiotas-Piastra: Chambre annulaire horizontale avant le bétonnage; coffrages de niches d'ancrage en polystyrol expansé

5 CALCUL D'UNE GALERIE PRECONTRAINTE

Le revêtement de la galerie forme une coque appuyée dans le rocher, lequel participe ainsi comme enveloppe solidaire avec le béton précontraint. L'influence d'une zone sur l'autre ne peut être dé-

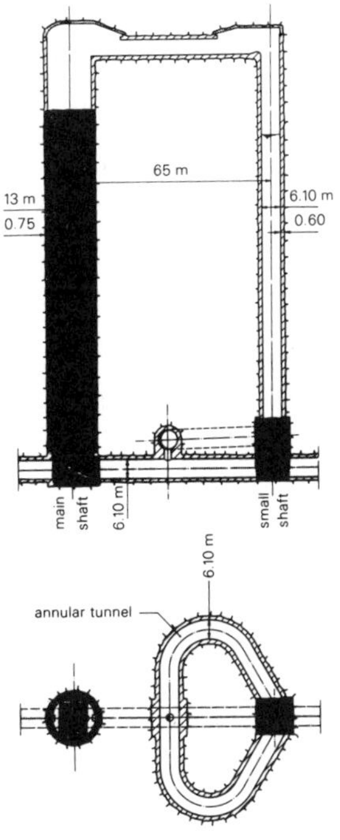

Fig. 15 Centrale de Chiotas-Piastra: Complexe précontraint à l'entrée des puits de descente

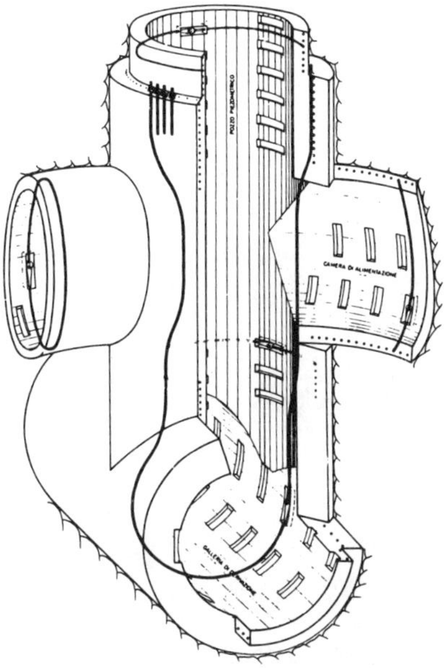

Fig. 17 Grand raccord précontraint équipé de câbles à ancrages multiples; jonction entre deux galeries et un puits vertical, diamètre intérieur 6.10 m. (Centrale de Chiotas-Piastra, ENEL)

Fig. 18 Détail de câblage et d'armature du raccord de la fig. 17

finie qu'avec une analyse du système mixte rocher-béton sur lequel agissent les diverses charges considérées. C'est pourquoi il faudra définir avant le dimensionnement propre du revêtement si la structure de l'enveloppe rocheuse environnante et le recouvrement de la galerie permettent une participation à la reprise de la pression intérieure. La précontrainte par unités de câbles autonomes est dans ce cas très flexible; en jouant sur l'espacement et la taille des câbles, il est possible de moduler en tout point la force annulaire de retenue

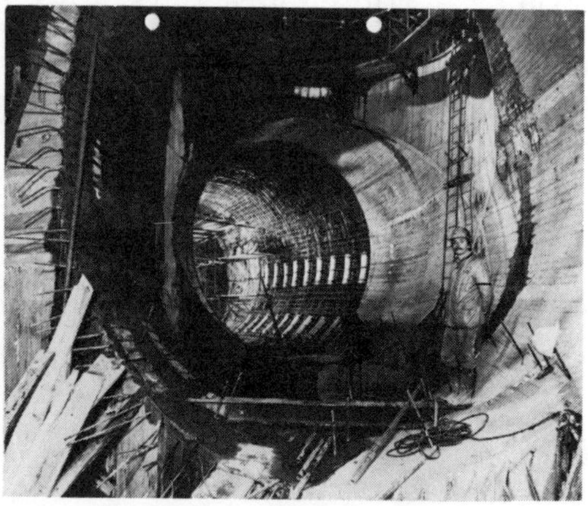

Fig. 19 Centrale de Chiotas-Piastra: Portion de galerie précontrainte diam. 6.10 m en cours d'exécution

engendrée par la précontrainte et de s'adapter aux caractéristiques rocheuses du moment rencontrées lors de l'excavation.

5.1 Sollicitations du revêtement

Avant tout, la galerie est bien sûr soumise à la pression hydraulique intérieure qui engendre donc des efforts de traction annulaire et des déformations dans le revêtement qui sont aisément calculables par des méthodes simles. De plus agissent aussi:

- pression hydraulique extérieure éventuelle
- pression de la roche
- retrait et fluage de revêtement
- température
- poids propre

Ces influences, suivant leur importance et les conditions d'utilisation seront considérées dans le calcul.

5.2 Précontrainte

La force de déviation du câble, $u = \frac{P}{r_V}$, s'oppose à la pression intérieure pi qui tend à "ouvrir" le revêtement; il faudrait ainsi un câble parfaitement circulaire et sans frottements pour obtenir une force de précontrainte P constante en tout point:

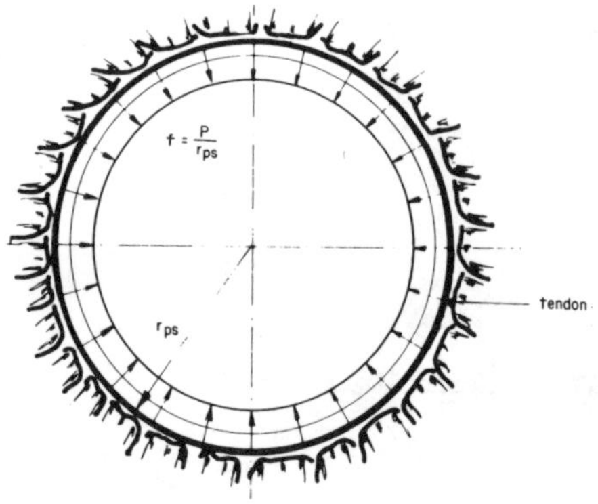

Fig. 20 Profil de câble idéal, force de déviation constante sur le pourtour

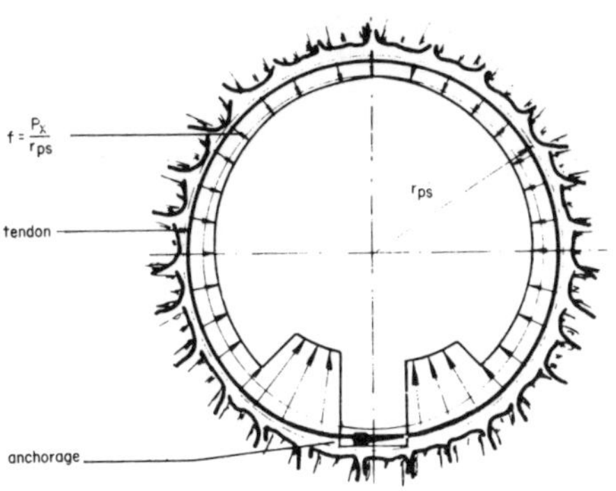

Fig. 21 Profil effectif du câble et force de précontrainte réelle engendrant les forces de déviation

En réalité, la force P varie à cause du frottement du câble lors de la mise en tension et le rayon r_v est modifié à proximité de l'ancrage pour l'engagement du vérin; il en résulte des forces de dérivation différenciées et des moments fléchissants secondaires.

La force de précontrainte et calculable le long du câble grâce à la formule de Coulomb:

$$P_x = P_o \cdot e^{-(\mu\alpha + kx)}$$

On admettra les coefficients de friction suivants:

	μ	k
- gaine conventionnelle:	0.19	$1 \cdot 10^{-3}$
- toron enrobé graisse et polyéthylène:	0.06	$1 \cdot 10^{-3}$

Pour le toron enrobé de polyéthylène, la perte par friction à l'opposé de l'ancrage (déviation de 180°) n'est que de 18% par rapport à la force au vérin en admettant une longueur de câble moyenne. Cette basse friction offre une appréciable économie d'acier par rapport au câble en gaine conventionnelle. Le recul des clavettes lors du blocage des torons dans la tête d'ancrage n'a qu'une influence locale. En ce qui concerne les pertes de précontrainte à long terme, l'utilisation généralisée d'acier à basse relaxation ainsi que la mise en tension de la structure après un délai raisonnable permet de limiter celles-ci à environ 10%.

Le changement d'excentricité du câble au niveau de l'ancrage engendre dans les structures épaisses des moments fléchissants parasitaires qui peuvent être simplement calculés par la méthode du centre de gravité élastique ou par programme-computer. Lors de la planification de la galerie forcée de Piastra-Andonno, on réalisa une portion de tunnel-test en grandeur nature de 10 m de longueur. Après mise en tension des câbles de précontrainte, il s'avéra que les mesures de déformation relevées sur le modèle correspondaient fort bien avec le théorie.

L'influence des moments parasitaires dûs à la variation de la force de précontrainte et à la variation d'excentricité des câbles peut être réduite dans de fortes proportions en décalant les ancrages des câbles successifs et en appliquant des contre-excentricités adéquates aux câbles par rapport au centre de gravité de la section du revêtement; on obtiendra ainsi une force de précontrainte globale quasiment constante et les moments parasitaires juxtaposés n'auront qu'une influence minime sur les contraintes du béton, soit environ 1 % à 3 % de la compression centrée.

L'enveloppe rocheuse formant support et les surprofils résultants d'excavation à l'explosif ont une influence sur le revêtement précontraint dans le proportions suivantes:

- La précontrainte engendre des forces normales et des moments fléchissants qui déforment le revêtement radialement; comme le rocher forme appui, le tube précontraint ne peut se mouvoir librement mais sera retenu dans diverses zones de l'enveloppe rocheuse. Le modèle de calcul d'un tube libre ne correspond pas tout à fait à la réalité.

Fig. 22 Conduite-test pour le projet Piastra-Andonno (ENEL)

- A moins que la galerie ne soit creusée par un tunnelier mécanique genre "Robbins" le profil obtenu par minage ne sera pas circulaire et régulier.

Afin d'étudier l'influence de ces facteurs, une étude à été menée par l'Institut de Mécanique des Roches de l'Ecole Polytechnique Fédérale de Zürich à l'aide du programme aux éléments finis "STAUB".

Plusieurs sections de galeries précontraintes ont été calculées; des conditions d'appui multiples, des surprofils, plusieurs positions d'ancrages ont été simulés et nous ont permis de tirer les enseignements suivants:

- L'effet de support de la roche dépendant de la position des ancrages et des variations d'excentricité des câbles a tendance à réduire les moments parasitaires induits:

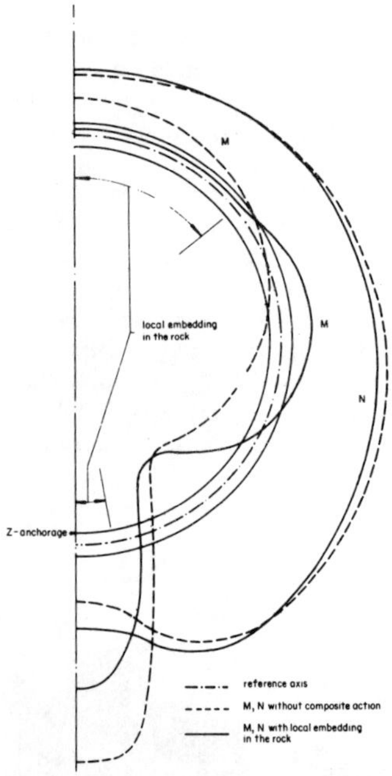

Fig. 23 Diagramme des forces agissantes avec et sans influence de la roche

- Les surprofils, même importants, ont peu d'influence (d'ailleurs positive) sur les moments secondaires. La compression centrée dûe à la précontrainte décroit localement de même naturellement que la traction engendrée par la pression intérieure.
- Une campagne de mesures conduite sur le site à l'aide de distomètres et d'extensomètres a confirmé les déformations calculées par ordinateur.
- Une comparaison entre différents calculs d'une portion de galerie déterminée, soit par programme aux éléments finis, programme coque simplifié ou encore par calcul à la main par la méthode des forces a montré que les résultats obtenus oscillaient dans une fourchette de 10 % au maximum.

Pour clore cet aperçu de la calculation mentionnons encore que l'influence de l'épaisseur du revêtement sur la répartition des contraintes est à étudier pour les revêtements particulièrement massifs et que la distribution longitudinale des contraintes engendrées par la précontrainte obéit aux lois de la théorie des poutres élastiquement appuyées.

6 CONCLUSION

Nous insisterons sur le concept de précontrainte active de ce mode de construction; en effet, la force de précontrainte induite, après déduction d'environ 10 % de pertes à long terme, reste continuellement active pour résister à la pression hydraulique intérieure.

Cet exposé a pour but de faire connaître un aspect relativement nouveau de l'application de la précontrainte à l'aide de quelques considérations théoriques, pratiques et économiques démontrées par quelques exemples d'exécution; notre intention est d'informer l'ingénieur spécialiste qu'il est possible de s'écarter des chemins très traditionnels en réalisant des structures à la fois économiques et durables.

NEUE ENTWICKLUNGEN IM DRUCKSTOLLENBAU

New ways for the construction of pressure tunnels

Nouveaux développements dans la construction des galeries forcées

G.SEEBER
Institut für konstruktiven Wasserbau & Tunnelbau, Universität Innsbruck, Österreich

SUMMARY:
The actual tendency to exploit our energy resources as thoroughly as possible lead to a Renaissance in the development of hydro power and also gave rise to new inspirations in the field of pressure tunnel design. Dams are always getting higher and capacities of power plants are steadily increasing. This required new and improved lining systems for the corresponding pressure tunnels, in order to cope with the increased stresses. One possibility of controlling the higher pressures are prestress techniques; a further improvement can be achieved by a combination with a plastic sheet. Finally, for highest pressures like those ocurring in pressure shafts, the only possibility left is a steel lining. Modern design methods basing on in-situ measurements reduce the thickness of the lining to such an extent, that the practicable minimum thickness would be sufficient for the largest part of a pressure shaft. Specific measures have to be taken to support the external rock water pressure.
In all these cases mechanical excavations provided better conditions for the construction works as well as for the static effectiveness of the linings.

ZUSAMMENFASSUNG:
Der gegenwärtige Trend zu möglichst vollkommener Ausnutzung der vorhandenen Energiereserven führte zu einer Renaissance im Wasserkraftbau und gab auch der Entwicklung des Druckstollenbaues neue Impulse. Die immer höher werdenden Talsperren und die steigenden Leistungen der Kraftwerke erforderten bei den Druckstollen neue und verbesserte Auskleidungssysteme, um den erhöhten Beanspruchungen gerecht zu werden. Eine Möglichkeit zur Beherrschung höherer Drücke bieten Vorspannverfahren; eine weitere Verbesserung bringt eine Kombination mit einer Kunststoffolie. Schließlich bleibt bei höchsten Drücken, wie sie in den Druckschächten auftreten, nur mehr die Möglichkeit einer Stahlpanzerung. Moderne Bemessungsmethoden, basierend auf in-situ Messungen, reduzieren die Wanddicke dermaßen, daß für den größten Teil eines Druckschachtes die Minimalwanddicke ausreichen würde. Zur Aufnahme des Gebirgswasserdruckes sind dann eigene Maßnahmen erforderlich.
In allen Fällen ergaben sich durch den mechanischen Ausbruch bessere Bedingungen sowohl für die bauliche Ausführung als auch für die statische Wirksamkeit der Auskleidung.

RESUME:
La tendance actuelle visant à une exploitation très radicale de nos ressources énergétiques mena à une renaissance dans l´évolution de l´énergie hydro-électrique et aussi donna de nouvelles impulsions pour le développement des galeries en charge. Comme l´hauteur des barrages monte de plus en plus et les puissances des usines hydro-électriques augmentent continuellement, il fallut des nouveaux et améliorés systèmes de revêtement pour les galeries en charge, afin de satisfaire aux efforts élévés. Une possibilité de contrôler les pressions plus fortes ce sont des méthodes de précontrainte; une amélioration supplémentaire peut être obtenue par une combinaison avec une feuille en matière plastique. Enfin, en ce qui concerne les pressions les plus fortes qui se manifestent dans les puits en charge, il ne reste que la possibilité d´un blindage en acier. Les méthodes modernes de dimensionnement, basant sur des mesures "in situ", réduisent l´épaisseur du revêtement tellement que pour la partie la plus longue d´un puits en charge l´

epaisseur minimale serait suffisante. Afin de supporter la pression d'eau du terrain, des mesures spéciales doivent être prises.
En tous ces cas les excavations par moyens mécaniques menèrent aux meilleures conditions, non seulement pour l'exécution des traveaux, mais aussi pour l'effectivité statique du revêtement.

1 ALLGEMEINES

Der gegenwärtige Trend zu möglichst vollkommener Ausnutzung der vorhandenen Energiereserven führte auch zu einer Renaissance im Wasserkraftbau und gab der Entwicklung des Druckstollenbaues neue Impulse. Die immer höher werdenden Talsperren und die steigenden Leistungen der Kraftwerke erforderten bei den Druckstollen neue und verbesserte Auskleidungssysteme, um den erhöhten Beanspruchungen standhalten zu können. Ein Maß für die Größe der Beanspruchung eines Druckstollens ist die Umfangszugkraft $Z = p_i \times r_i$, die in Abb. 1 für einige hochbeanspruchte Druckstollen dargestellt ist.

Abb. 1: Einige Beispiele vorgespannter Druckstollen und Druckschächte

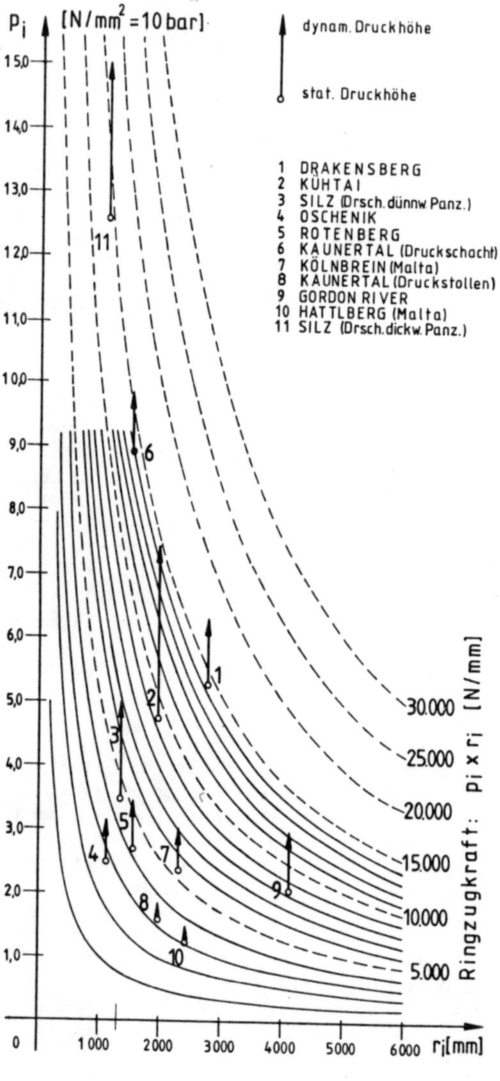

Einfache Betonauskleidungen können selbst bei bestem Gebirge nur relativ geringe Drükke rissefrei aufnehmen. Auch Stahlbewehrungen bringen wenig im Verhältnis zum Aufwand. Große technische und wirtschaftliche Erfolge konnten mit der Anwendung von Vorspannverfahren bei Betonauskleidungen erzielt werden. Eine weitere Verbesserung und damit eine große Erweiterung des Anwendungsbereiches brachte die Kombination des Spaltinjektionsverfahrens (zur Vorspannung) mit einer Dichtungsfolie. Damit wird auch die Sicherheit bei eventuell verlorener Vorspannung wesentlich erhöht. Auch im Bereich höchster Drücke, der den Stahlpanzerungen vorbehalten bleibt, brachten neue, hochfeste Stahlsorten, kombiniert mit Vorspannung und Bemessungsverfahren, welche auf in-situ Messungen aufbauen, weitere wirtschaftliche Vorteile.

Unabhängig von der direkten Entwicklung der Auskleidungssysteme ergaben sich aber auch vom Ausbruchsverfahren her neue und wesentliche Aspekte: Der mechanische Ausbruch mittels Stollenfräse brachte eine gewaltige Verbesserung der Gebirgsverhältnisse am Ausbruchsrand sowie große ausführungstechnische und statische Vorteile infolge der glatten kreiszylindrischen Profilform.

2 AUSKLEIDUNGSARTEN, IHRE ANWENDUNGSBEREICHE UND -KRITERIEN

Der schematische Höhenplan gem. Abb. 2 zeigt die üblichen Verhältnisse für einen Hochdruck-Triebwasserweg mit den Bereichen der verschiedenen Auskleidungssysteme (Seeber 1975 und 1981, Walch 1926, Kieser 1960, Wanner 1975).

2.1 Unausgekleidete Druckstollen

Obwohl man "keine Auskleidung" schwerlich als Auskleidungssystem bezeichnen kann, muß der unausgekleidete Druckstollen in diesem Rahmen doch kurz besprochen werden, da die Entwicklung auch hier Fortschritte erzielte. Unausgekleidete Druckstollen waren bisher nicht nur deshalb selten, weil es besonders

Abb. 2: Schematischer Höhenplan eines Hochdruck-Triebwasserweges

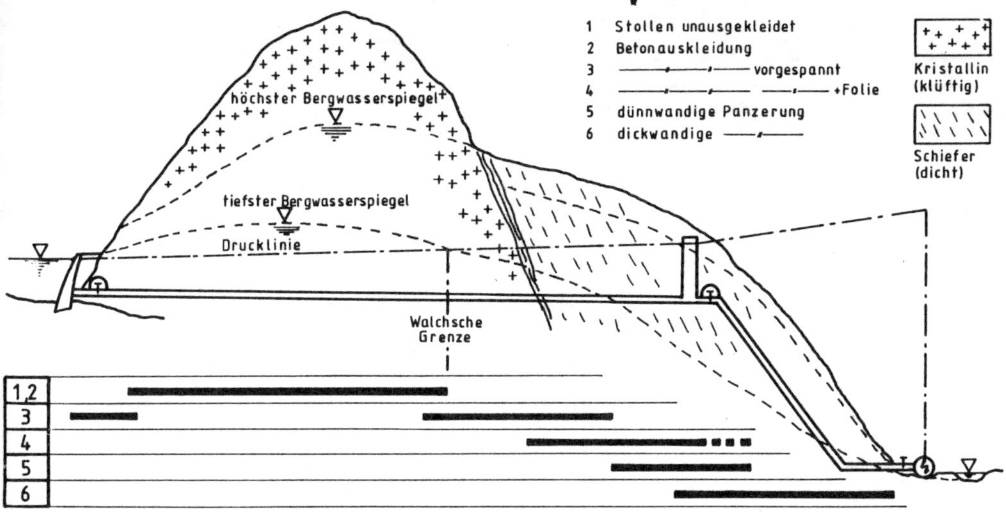

in den Alpen wenig standfeste und dichte Gebirgsmassive gibt, sondern weil zum Ausgleich der erhöhten Reibungsverluste ein unausgekleideter Druckstollen mit etwa dem 1,5-fachen Durchmesser ausgebrochen werden muß. Durch den mechanischen Vortrieb wird die Felsoberfläche so glatt ausgebrochen, daß die notwendige Durchmesservergrößerung nur mehr rd. 17% beträgt. Außerdem wird das Gebirge praktisch nicht mehr gestört, sodaß die Standfestigkeit um etwa zwei Klassen verbessert wird. Nebenbei hängt die Größe des Durchmessers meist mehr von der gerade zur Verfügung stehenden Fräse ab, sodaß diese hydraulisch geforderte Vergrößerung des Durchmessers wirtschaftlich nicht zum Tragen kommt (Pircher 1980, Lauffer/Seeber 1961). Es ist daher zu erwarten, daß in Zukunft wesentlich mehr Druckstollen unverkleidet bleiben werden.

In diesem Zusammenhang muß auf einen sehr wichtigen Umstand hingewiesen werden: Das Gebirge muß nicht unbedingt ganz dicht sein, damit keine Wasserverluste auftreten. Es genügt, wenn der Kluftwasserspiegel höher liegt als der Betriebswasserspiegel.

2.2 Einfache Betonauskleidungen

Liegt also ein Druckstollenabschnitt hinter der sogenannten Walch'schen Grenze (Walch 1926), so braucht er bei standfestem Gebirge nicht ausgekleidet zu werden. Bei nicht standfestem Gebirge genügt eine einfache Betonauskleidung. Ihre Funktion ist die Abstützung des Gebirges und die Verringerung der Reibungsverluste. Bei mechanischem Vortrieb genügt unter Umständen schon eine wenige Zentimeter starke Spritzbetonauskleidung, deren Stärke den Standfestigkeitsverhältnissen angepaßt werden kann. Bei Schalbetonauskleidungen sollte jedoch auf jeden Fall durch Kontaktinjektionen im First ein sicherer Kontakt zwischen Gebirge und Auskleidung hergestellt werden.

2.3 Vorgespannte Betonauskleidungen

Diese werden dann erforderlich, wenn weder ein dichtes Gebirge noch ein entlastender Bergwasserdruck vorhanden ist. Durch das Schwinden und die Abkühlung des Betons entsteht eine Kontraktion von rd. 0,2‰. Bei Innendrücken über rd. 5 bar müssen daher Risse auftreten, da das Gebirge gar nicht zur Mitwirkung kommen kann. Eine Gebirgsmitwirkung von Anfang an wird jedoch erreicht, wenn der Betonring z.B. durch eine Spaltinjektion (Abb. 3) gegen das Gebirge vorgespannt wird (Wanner 1975, TIWAG). Das Zusammenwirken von Betonring und Gebirge unter der Wirkung des Injektionsdruckes und des Innendruckes kann in einem Diagramm gem. Abb. 4 anschaulich dargestellt werden.

Voraussetzung für die Anwendbarkeit und die Erhaltung der Vorspannung ist, daß die kleinste primäre Gebirgsspannung mit Sicherheit größer ist als der Vorspann- bzw. der Innendruck. Normalerweise ist die Horizontalspannung σ_H die kleinere und damit maßgebende Spannung.

Setzt man

$$\sigma_H = \lambda\, \sigma_v = \lambda\, \gamma_f\, H_f \geqq \gamma_w\, H_w$$

so wird

$$H_f \geqq H_w \frac{\gamma_w}{\lambda\, \gamma_f}\ ; \quad \text{mit } \gamma_f = 2{,}5, \quad \lambda = 0{,}4$$

wird

$$\underline{H_f \geqq H_w}$$

Abb. 3: Das TIWAG-Spaltinjektionsverfahren

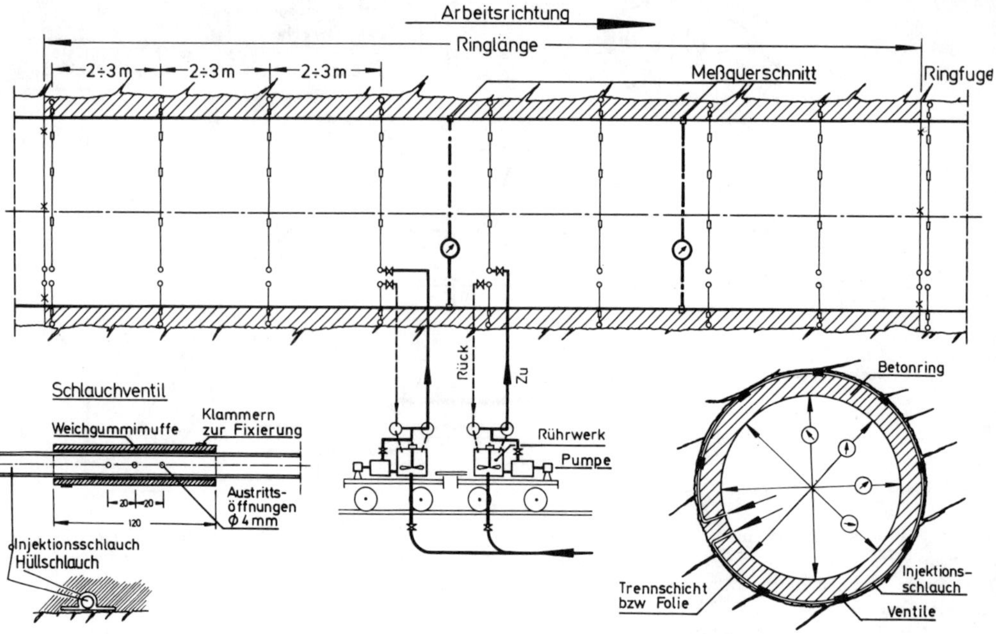

Abb. 4: Schematisches Bemessungsdiagramm für vorgespannte Betonauskleidungen von Druckstollen

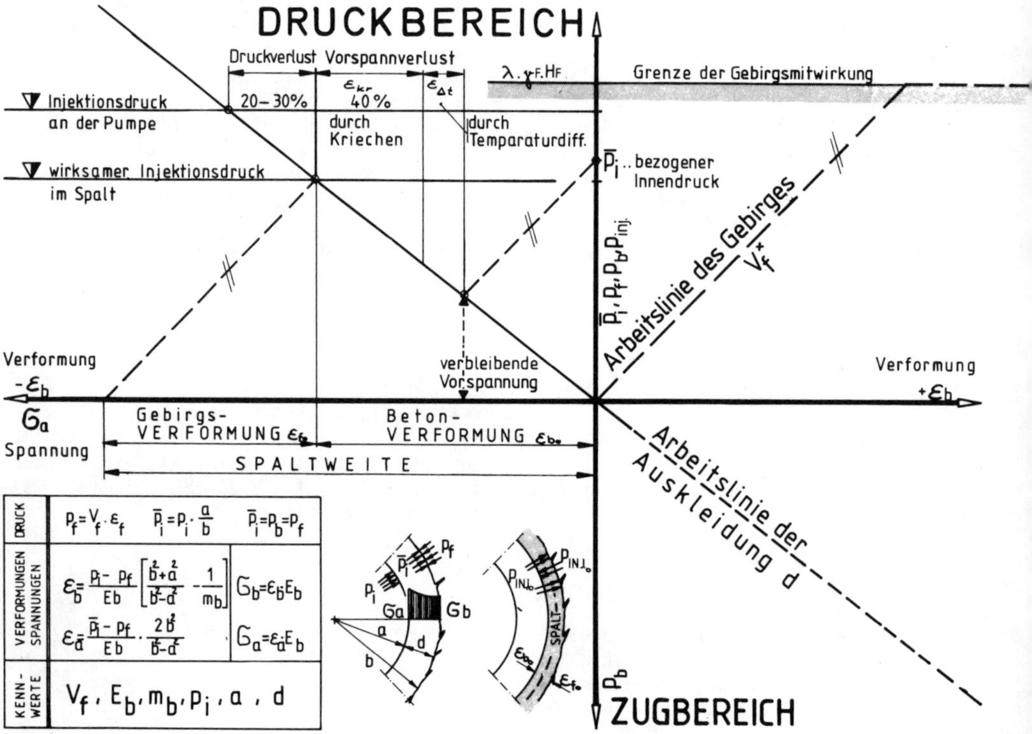

Die Überlagerungshöhe muß also mindestens der Druckhöhe entsprechen. Dies ist die äußerste Grenze der Anwendbarkeit und ist nur dann vertretbar, wenn die Horizontalspannung sicher vorhanden, d.h. meßtechisch erfaßt ist. Wegen der großen Unsicherheit in der Annahme der Horizontalspannung erscheint es jedoch zweckmäßig, einen Sicherheitsfaktor von 2 einzuführen. Dabei ist zu beachten, daß jener Stollenabschnitt, für den eine solche vorgespannte Betonauskleidung in Frage kommt (Abb. 2), im vorderen Bereich schon recht oberflächennahe und unter Umständen im schmalen Bergrücken liegt, wo nur mehr mit geringen Horizontalspannungen gerechnet werden kann (Seeber/Demmer/Finger 1979).

Die Grenze des Anwendungsbereiches ist daher oft sehr unsicher. Verhindert man aber einen Wasseraustritt infolge eventuell auftretender Risse durch eine Dichtfolie, so wird nicht nur der Wasserverlust vermieden, sondern vor allem auch gefährliche Folgewirkungen wie Felsgrundbruch. Es ist daher in erster Linie die Sicherheit, die durch den Einbau einer Dichtfolie erhöht wird.

Die Beanspruchung einer solchen Dichtfolie in einem Druckstollen ist jedoch wesentlich anders und viel größer als bei einer Isolierung wie etwa in einem Verkehrstunnel: Die Dichtfolie wird durch den hohen Wasserdruck gegen die rauhe Fels- bzw. Spritzbetonunterlage gepreßt, in welcher sich noch dazu Risse öffnen, die von der Folie überbrückt werden müssen.

2.4 Vorgespannte Betonauskleidungen mit Dichtfolie

Die geringe Zugfestigkeit des Betons verlangte bisher eine so große Vorspannung, daß unter Innendruck keine Zugspannungen auftreten. Die relativ hohe Festigkeit moderner Kunststoff-Folien überbrückt Risse mit einer Rißweite etwa gleich der Foliendicke bis zu sehr hohen Drücken. Dies schafft nun die Möglichkeit, im Grenzfall die Gebirgsmitwirkung nicht nur bis zur Größe der kleinsten Primärspannung heranzuziehen, sondern auch noch einen Teil des passiven Widerstandes bzw. der inneren Reibung auszunützen. Um aber eine kompakte und möglichst elastische Verbindung des Verbundsystems Betonring - Gebirge zu behalten, sollte dieses Auskleidungssystem grundsätzlich auch nur soweit eingesetzt werden, als die damit verbundene Vorspannung erhalten werden kann - wenn auch bei einem örtlichen Vorspannverlust noch keine Undichtheit entstehen würde.

Die Kriterien für die Anwendbarkeit sind deshalb etwas komplexer:

- Bei einem weichen, kriechfähigen Gebirge sollte die vorhin erwähnte Bedingung $H_f > H_w$ eingehalten werden. Im Bemessungsdiagramm gem. Abb. 4 wäre die Gebirgsarbeitslinie bei $p_f = \lambda\ \gamma_f\ H_f$ zu begrenzen. Allerdings kann bei einem weichen Gebirge meist mit einem höheren Seitendruckbeiwert gerechnet werden.
- Ein festeres Gebirge wird bei geringen Überlagerungshöhen eher eine geringe Horizontalspannung aufweisen, dafür aber auch eine geringere Nachgiebigkeit. Eine Belastung über $p_f = \lambda\ \gamma_f\ H_f$ ist zulässig bis etwa $\lambda = 1$, d.h. $p_f = \gamma_f\ H_f$, solange die Deformationen nicht zu groß werden.

Hiefür gilt das Kriterium, daß ein einziger diametraler Riß nicht größer werden sollte als etwa die Hälfte der Wanddicke der Folie.

Die Bedingung lautet:

$$s = 2u = 2R\ \frac{p_f}{V_f^+} \leqq \alpha\ .\ t \rightarrow$$

$$p_f \leqq \frac{\alpha . t . V_f^+}{2R}\ ;$$

s	Rißweite
u	Radialverschiebung
t	Wanddicke der Folie
$V_f^+ = V_f \cdot \frac{m}{m+1}$	Verformungsmodul
$\alpha = 0{,}5$	Ein Reduktionsfaktor, abhängig von der Materialfestigkeit; durch Spaltdruckversuche zu bestimmen.

Zieht man das Gebirge soweit zur Mitwirkung heran, sollte es selbstverständlich sein, die Gebirgsmitwirkung auch meßtechnisch durch geeignete Versuche zu erfassen.

Die Frage des Kriechens und der Alterung des Folienmaterials ist zwar noch nicht endgültig geklärt, doch sind die Bedingungen für eine lange Lebensdauer im Stollen sicher sehr günstig: Es gibt weder UV-Strahlung noch extreme Temperaturen, die eine rasche Alterung herbeiführen könnten. Die durch die Spaltinjektion satt gebettete Folie kann im Normalfall nicht ausweichen und wird durch den Wasserdruck auch nicht übermäßig belastet, sodaß die Gefahr des Kriechens keine allzu großen Probleme aufwerfen dürfte. Die Fähigkeit der Folie, einen eventuellen Riß im Unterlagsbeton zu überbrükken, muß allerdings versuchsmäßig nachgewiesen werden.

Als Folienmaterial wurde bisher sowohl Polyvinylchlorid (PVC) als auch Polyäthylen (PE) eingesetzt, wobei hinsichtlich der Versprödung Polyäthylen wohl vorzuziehen sein dürfte. Sehr günstig wirkt sich eine Vliesunterlage aus einem Polypropylen-Vlies aus; Sie bildet einen wirksamen Schutz gegen mechanische Beschädigungen an der rauhen Unterlage (Fels, Spritzbeton), erhöht die Fähigkeit der Folie zur Rißüberbrückung und bringt eine gute Möglichkeit für die - eventuell auch flächenhafte - Befestigung der Folie. Da das Vlies jedoch als sperrender Filter für die Spaltinjektion wirkt, muß es an der Rückseite mit einer dünnen Folie kaschiert werden.

Der rauhe Felsausbruch beim konventionellen Vortrieb erforderte eine sehr hohe Dehnfähigkeit des Folienmaterials. Aus diesem Grunde konnte nur ein sehr weicher Kunststoff und auch nur eine relativ geringe Wanddicke (< 3 mm) verwendet werden. Bei dem sich nun rapide durchsetzenden mechanischen Vortrieb fällt diese Forderung weg, und es können dickere und festere Folien eingesetzt werden, wie zuletzt beim Kraftwerk Langenegg der Vorarlberger Kraftwerke AG. Dadurch wird auch das Risiko der Beschädigung während des Baues stark reduziert. Das glatte, kreiszylindrische Profil verbessert ganz wesentlich die Bedingungen sowohl für die Applikation der Folie und deren mechanische Beanspruchung, für die Durchführung der Spaltinjektion, als auch für die statische Wirkung des Betonringes.

Dieses wirtschaftliche Auskleidungssystem ist daher bestens geeignet für die Übergangsstrecke von einer Panzerung zu einer Betonverkleidung, sowie für den Einsatz in Druckschächten bis in den mittleren Druckbereich.

Da dieses Auskleidungssystem zum Unterschied zu einer Stahlpanzerung weitgehend beulsicher ist, kann die Trasse ohne Schwie rigkeiten so tief ins Gebirge verlegt werden, daß die nötige Primärspannung erreicht wird.

Die Technologie des Systems kann heute als weitgehend ausgereift angesehen werden. Schwierigkeiten ergaben sich bisher nur beim Einbau in Schrägschächten, wo sämtliche Arbeitsgänge von einem Schrägaufzug aus erfolgen müssen.

2.5 Stahlpanzerungen

Der höchste Druckbereich in Druckschächten bleibt nach wie vor den zugfesten Stahlpanzerungen vorbehalten. Der Einsatz hochfeste Sonderstähle und eine weitgehende Ausnutzun der Gebirgsmitwirkung gem. Abb. 5 führen da

Abb. 5: Bemessungsdiagramm für Druckschachtpanzerungen mit Grenzbedingungen

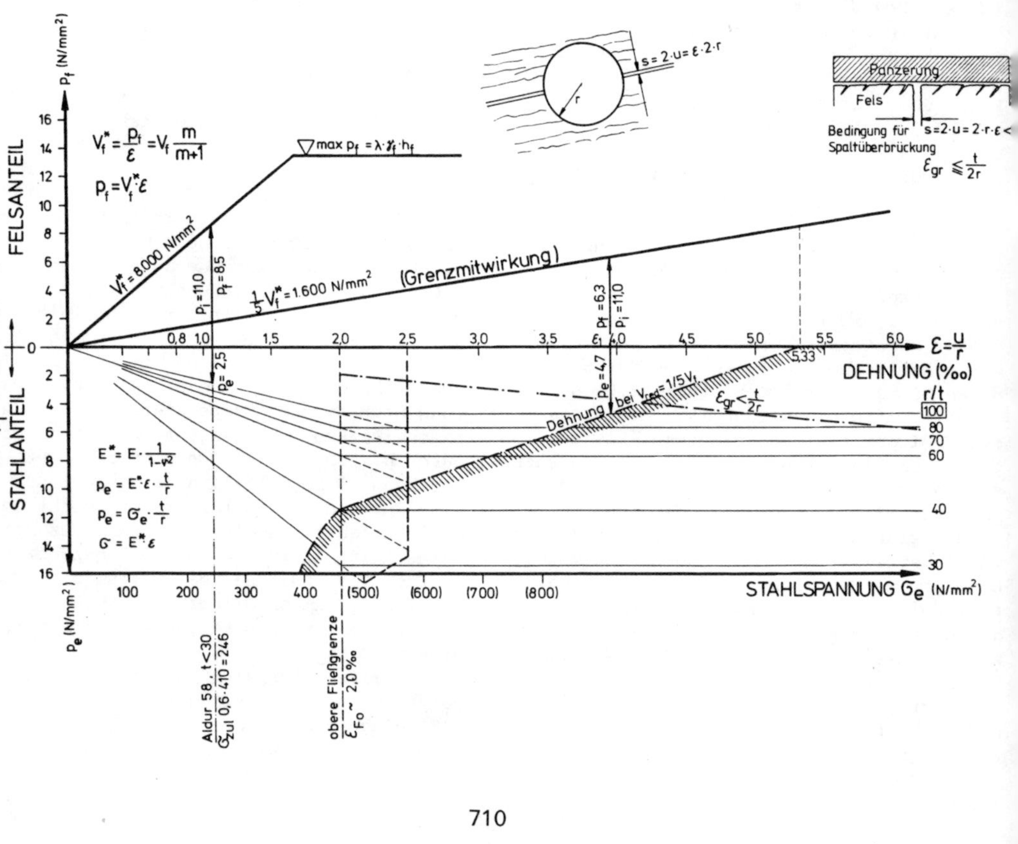

zu, daß heute meist nur mehr der unterste Bereich eines Druckschachtes auf Innendruck zu bemessen ist.
Abb. 6 zeigt die mögliche Innendruckaufnahme einer Panzerung mit einer minimalen Wanddicke von 1/100 R_i für zwei Stahlsorten mit Streckgrenzen von 400 bis 580 N/mm^2 in Abhängigkeit vom Verformungsmodul des Gebirges.

Abb. 6: Mögliche Innendruckaufnahme einer Panzerung mit Minimalwanddicke in Abhängigkeit von Stahlqualität und Verformungsmodul des Gebirges

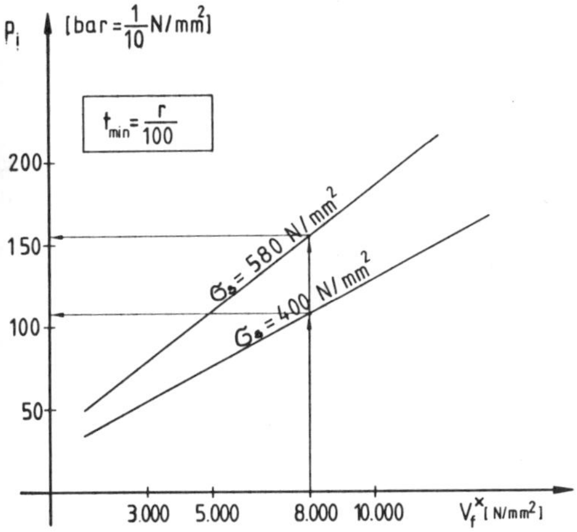

Eine derart hohe Ausnutzung der Gebirgsmitwirkung ist natürlich nur zulässig, wenn bestimmte Kriterien erfüllt sind (Seeber 1975):
- Der vom Gebirge zu tragende Innendruckanteil p_f darf nicht größer werden als die senkrecht zur Panzerung wirkende, kleinste Komponente der Primärspannung.
- Für den Fall, daß die Gebirgsmitwirkung örtlich absinkt, muß nachgewiesen werden, daß bei einer möglichen Grenzmitwirkung ein diametraler Riß im Hinterfüllbeton nicht größer wird als etwa die Blechdicke.
- Um das sofortige Mittragen des Gebirges zu erreichen, muß der bekannte Spalt zwischen Panzerung und Beton durch Injektionen verpreßt werden.

Die unter diesen Bedingungen möglichen geringen Wanddicken haben jedoch den Nachteil einer geringen Beulfestigkeit gegenüber dem Bergwasser- und dem Injektionsdruck (Bild 7). Dies führt zu einer Diskrepanz in der Trassenwahl:
Aufgrund der Bedingung 2 wäre eine möglichst tief im Berg liegende Trasse günstig. In Hinblick auf einen niedrigen Bergwasserdruck sollte die Trasse wieder möglichst seicht liegen. In begrenztem Ausmaß

Bild 7: Eingebeulte Druckschachtpanzerung

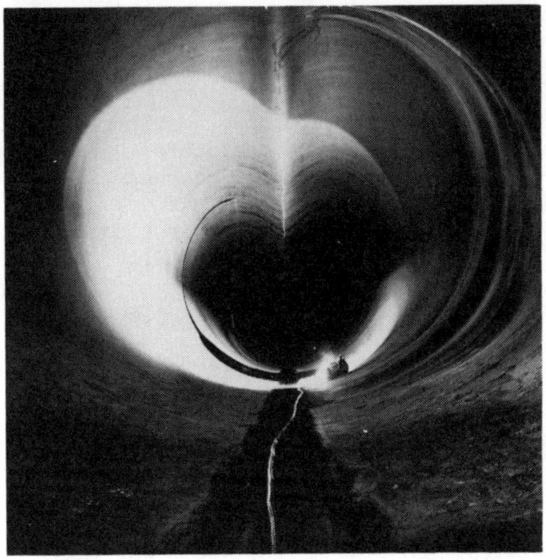

ist eine Erhöhung der Beulfestigkeit durch konstruktive Maßnahmen wie Ringversteifungen, Schubpratzen und Dübel möglich, doch bringen diese auch beachtliche Mehrkosten (Amstutz 1969, Montel 1960). Am Rande sei erwähnt, daß es jüngst der "Arbeitsgruppe Beulversuche" gelungen ist, aufgrund einer Serie von Beulversuchen die Berechnung der wirtschaftlichen Dübelversteifung auf eine sichere Basis zu stellen (Finger/Wieser 1980).

Vielfach erweist es sich wirtschaftlicher und bautechnisch günstiger, beim "glatten Rohr" zu bleiben und die Wanddicke auf den Außendruck zu bemessen.

Als technisch interessante und wirtschaftliche Lösung erwiesen sich dünnwandige Rohre mit einem Beton-Innenring, wie sie bereits im Schrägschacht des Wasserschlosses des Kaunertal-Kraftwerkes verwendet wurden (Lauffer 1966). Die Vorfertigung gestattet die Anwendung hoher Betonqualitäten von B 500 bis B 600, sodaß die Betondicke und damit die Gewichte relativ nieder gehalten werden können. Die Rohre widerstehen hohen Bergwasserdrücken und können mit hohen Injektionsdrücken hinterpreßt und vorgespannt werden. Infolge des Beton-Innenringes erübrigt sich der teure Korrosionsschutz. Der Einbauvorgang ist derselbe wie bei dickwandigen Panzerrohren, sodaß der Bauablauf nicht umgestellt werden muß.

Der Einsatz solcher Rohre gestattet auch die Wahl einer tief liegenden Trasse, die wiederum der meist anschließenden vorgespannten Betonauskleidung mit Dichtfolie entgegenkommt.

3 ANWENDUNGSBEISPIELE

3.1 Kraftwerksgruppe Sellrain-Silz der Tiroler Wasserkraftwerke AG

Die 760 MW-Kraftwerksgruppe umfaßt zwei Kraftwerksstufen: Eine Oberstufe Kühtai mit dem 60 Millionen m^3-Jahresspeicher Finstertal und dem 300 MW-Pumpspeicherwerk (Schachtkraftwerk) Kühtai sowie eine Hauptstufe mit dem 460 MW-Kraftwerk Silz.

3.1.1 Druckschacht der Oberstufe Kühtai

Die besonderen Betriebszustände der beiden je 150 MW starken Pumpturbinen bewirken im Druckschacht Kühtai eine überdurchschnittlich große dynamische Druckerhöhung bis etwa 70% des statischen Druckes. Dies brachte für die Betonauskleidung dieses Druckschachtes eine extrem hohe Belastung: maximaler statischer Innendruck rd. 480 m WS, maximaler dynamischer Druck rd. 740 m WS. Die Trassierung erfolgte so, daß einerseits der innere, mit Beton auszukleidende Abschnitt tief genug im Berg lag, andererseits für den maschinellen Ausbruch und die nachfolgenden Arbeiten eine günstige Neigung bei einer möglichst kurzen Länge gegeben war (Abb. 8) (Pircher 1980).

Auf rd. 300 m erhielt die Flachstrecke des Druckschachtes eine Panzerung, wobei die letzten 35 m als Übergangsstrecke dünnwandig mit einem Betondruckring ausgeführt wurden; ab hier war die Überlagerung groß genug für die Anwendung einer vorgespannten Betonauskleidung mit einem Durchmesser von 4 m. Im Bereich des unteren Krümmers und auch noch rd. 200 m in den Schrägschacht hoch war das Gebirge (Schiefergneis) teilweise gestört, weshalb hier auf 400 m Länge zusätzlich eine Dichtungsfolie angeordnet wurde. Trotz des hohen Innendruckes wurde versucht, die Wanddicke so dünn als möglich zu halten, um eine möglichst hohe Elastizität des Betonringes zu erreichen. Ein Injektionsdruck von 30 bis 45 bar erzeugte in der 30 cm dicken Betonauskleidung eine Druckspannung hart an der Grenze der Druckfestigkeit des Betons. Um die Vorspannung voll auszunützen, wurde der Injektionsdruck den jeweiligen tatsächlichen, an Proben ermittelten Festigkeitswerten angepaßt.

Eine ganz wesentliche Verbesserung der Ve hältnisse erbrachte der maschinelle Vortrie Auf der relativ glatten Felsoberfläche ließen sich die Injektionsschläuche wesentlich besser verlegen; der Betonring erhielt wege seiner gleichmäßigen, geringen Wanddicke und der exakten kreiszylindrischen Form kau Biegespannungen und ließ sich deshalb auch höher belasten.

Ebenso vorteilhaft war natürlich auch die glatte Felsoberfläche für die Anbringung der 3 mm starken PVC-Folie, die auf einem kaschierten Polypropylen-Vlies verlegt wurde. Zusätzlich angebrachte Injektionssperren aus Vliesstreifen verhinderten ein allzu weites Vorauseilen der Zementmilch. Die gute Gängigkeit des Spaltes zwischen kaschiertem Vlies und Fels erlaubte das Einpressen der Zementmilch über einfache, in die Folie eingeschweißte Rohrstutzen.

Abb. 8: Höhenplan der Oberstufe Kühtai

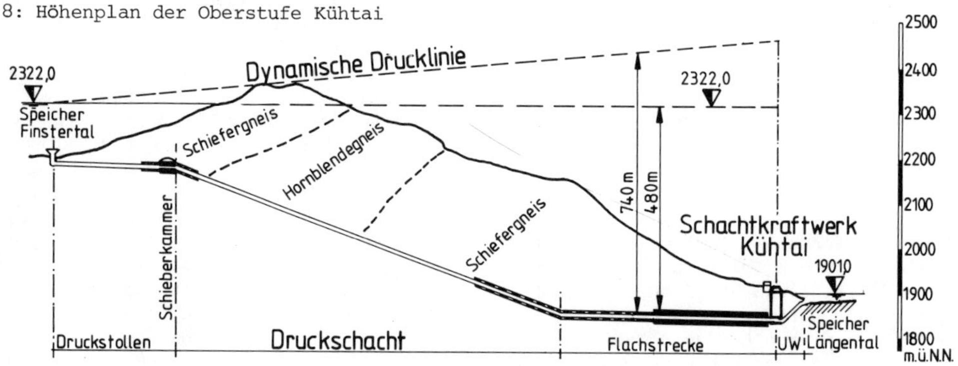

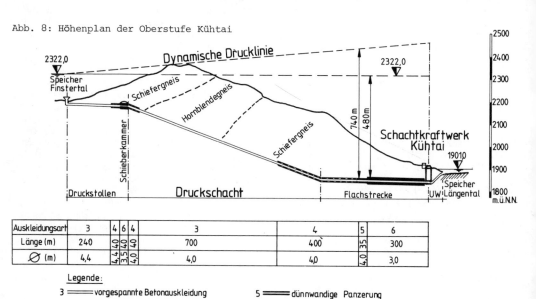

Auskleidungsart	3	4	6	4	3	4	5	6
Länge (m)	240	40	40	40	700	400	35	300
Ø (m)	4,4	4,4	3,5	4,0	4,0	4,0	4,0	3,0

Legende:

3 vorgespannte Betonauskleidung

4 vorgespannte Betonauskleidung mit Folie

5 dünnwandige Panzerung

6 dickwandige Panzerung

Der Druckschacht ist nun bereits seit Herbst 1980 in Betrieb und hat seine Bewährungsprobe bestens bestanden. Bei der Druckprobe zeigte sich für den ganzen 950 m langen, betonverkleideten Abschnitt ein Wasserverlust von lediglich rd. 1,6 l, der im Laufe des ersten Betriebsjahres aufgrund der Anhebung des Kluftwasserspiegels etwa auf die Hälfte zurückging.

3.1.2 Druckschacht der Hauptstufe Silz

Trotz der enormen Druckhöhe dieses Druckschachtes von rd. 1250 m statischem und 1500 m dynamischem Druck - er ist derzeit einer der höchstbeanspruchten Druckschächte der Welt - kann die Stahlpanzerung nur im untersten Teil auf Innendruck voll ausgenützt werden. Durch die hohe Dehnfähigkeit der modernen Rohrleitungs-Sonderstähle kann das Gebirge in weit höherem Maße als bisher zum Mittragen herangezogen werden. Dies führte zu so geringen Wanddicken, daß der mögliche Bergwasserdruck nicht mehr aufgenommen werden könnte. Um diesem Problem auszuweichen, war ursprünglich vorgesehen, den obersten Druckschachtabschnitt oberhalb Fenster Mais (Innendruck bis rd. 500 m) ähnlich wie den Druckschacht Kühtai mit einer vorgespannten Betonauskleidung mit Dichtungsfolie auszukleiden. Die Ergebnisse eines Versuches in einem 30 m langen Versuchsstollen im Fenster Mais waren an und für sich befriedigend, doch zeigte eine Arbeitsplanung, daß zum Unterschied zu horizontalen Druckstollen oder dem flach geneigten Druckschacht Kühtai die Befestigung der Folie und die nachfolgenden Arbeitsgänge von einem Schrägaufzugwagen aus äußerst schwierig würden. Außerdem muß im Schrägschacht mit einer vergrößerten Verletzungsgefahr gerechnet werden. Die TIWAG entschloß sich daher, hier jenes System anzuwenden, das sich schon im Schrägschacht des Kaunertal-Kraftwerkes bewährt hatte. Die dünnwandigen Rohre mit einem Durchmesser von 2,90 m wurden vor dem Einbau in einem Betonwerk mit einem 10 cm dicken Innenring aus hochfestem Beton B 500 versehen, der durch Vorwärmen des Stahlrohres leicht vorgespannt wurde. Die Verbundrohre wurden in 6 m-Schüssen zur Einbaustelle gebracht. Die Montage, Hinterbetonierung mit Gußbeton und Spaltinjektion erfolgte dann im Schacht auf diesselbe Weise, wie bei den Panzerrohren des unteren Schachtabschnittes, sodaß keine Umstellung des Arbeitsablaufes erforderlich wurde. Lediglich der 40 cm schmale Ring des Schweißnahtbereiches mußte nachträglich noch ausbetoniert werden.

Der hochfeste Beton-Innenring erlaubte eine Spaltverpressung über die üblichen

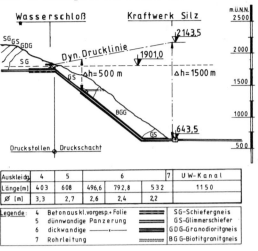

Abb. 9: Höhenplan der Hauptstufe Silz

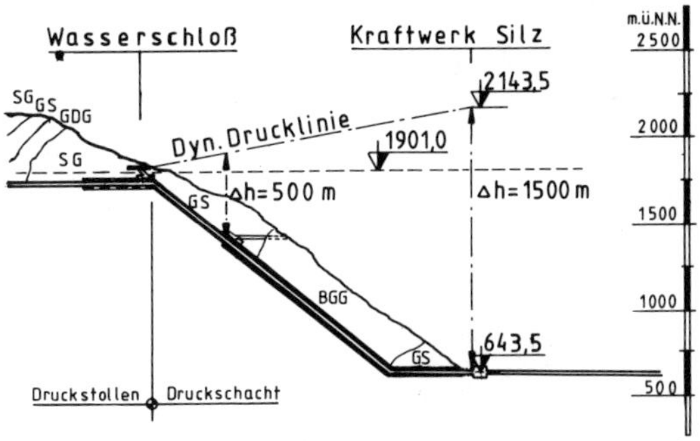

Auskleidg.	4	5	6			7	UW-Kanal
Länge [m]	403	608	496,6	792,8	532		1150
Ø [m]	3,3	2,7	2,6	2,4	2,2		

Legende:		
4	Betonauskl. vorgesp. + Folie	SG-Schiefergneis
5	dünnwandige Panzerung	GS-Glimmerschiefer
6	dickwandige	GDG-Granodioritgneis
7	Rohrleitung	BGG-Biotitgranitgneis

am Rohr befestigten Injektionsleitungen mit einem Druck von 30 bis 40 bar, sodaß der Innenring eine weitere Vorspannung erhielt, die ein Reißen unter Innendruck verhindert. Infolge des hohen Injektionsdruckes wird das Gebirge nicht nur vorbelastet, sondern über die bei diesem Druck im Hinterfüllbeton auftretenden Radialrisse gut verpreßt und verfestigt. Gegenüber der Folienauskleidung ist dieses System vollkommen unproblematisch beim Einbau im Steilschacht und letzten Endes auch nicht wesentlich teurer.

3.2 Pumpspeicherwerk Drakensberg der Electricity Supply Commission of South Africa/Projektant Gibb Hawkins & Partners

Dieses 1000 MW-Kraftwerk hat eine Doppelfunktion. Es pumpt Wasser aus dem Tugela River in Natal auf das rd. 500 m höher gelegene Hochland von Johannesburg, dem Quellgebiet des Vaal, um dessen Wasserführung zu verbessern. Der größte Teil des in den Sterkfonteinspeicher hochgepumpten Wassers wird jedoch zur Erzeugung von Spitzenstrom wieder zum Kilburnspeicher abgearbeitet (Abb. 10) (Van der Walt/Graber 1977, Bowcock 1979).

Die beiden Druckstollen mit je 5,5 m Durchmesser erhalten einen statischen Innendruck von 530 m WS, der infolge des Druckstoßes bis auf 620 m WS ansteigen kann. Das Gebirge ist aus horizontal gebankten Sandsteinen und Mergeln aufgebaut, die zum Teil sehr dicht und fest (E = 16000 N/mm^2), zum Teil aber auch stärker gestört und erodierbar erscheinen. Es mußte deshalb eine

Abb. 10: Übersicht über das Pumpspeicherwerk Drakensberg (Südafrika)

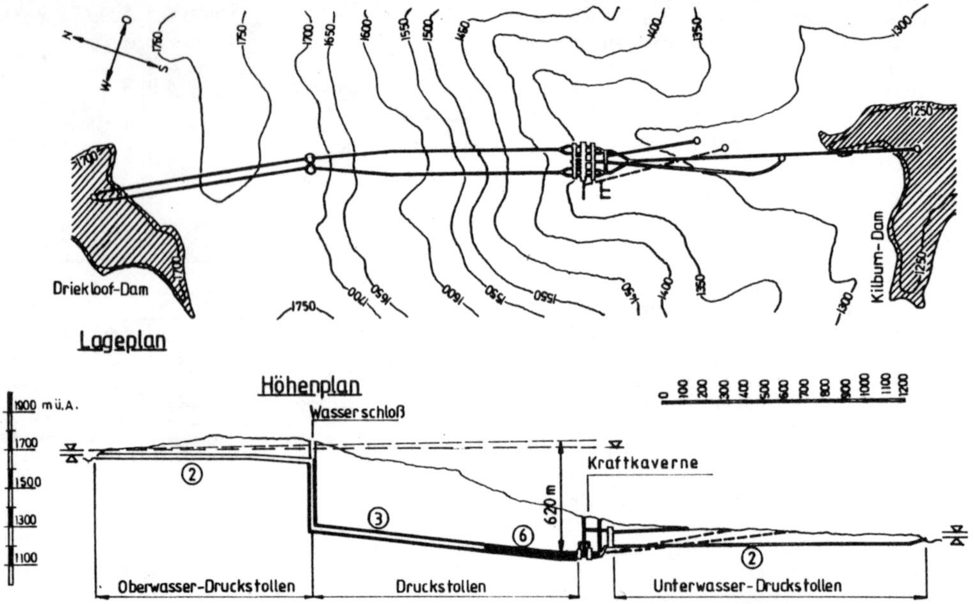

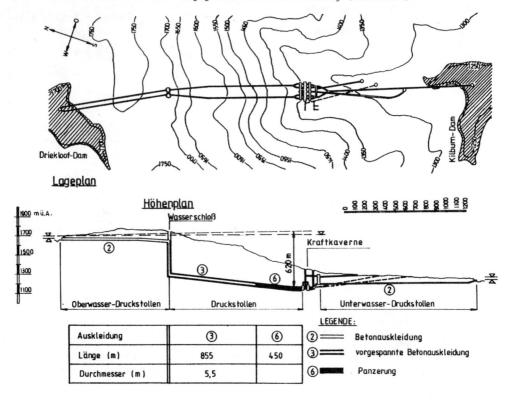

Auskleidung	③	⑥
Länge (m)	855	450
Durchmesser (m)	5,5	

LEGENDE:

② Betonauskleidung

③ vorgespannte Betonauskleidung

⑥ Panzerung

Auskleidung gewählt werden, die auch unter diesen hohen Drücken dicht bleibt. Als wirtschaftlichste Lösung wurde hiefür nach eingehenden Untersuchungen anstelle einer stark bewehrten eine vorgespannte Betonauskleidung in Erwägung gezogen. Diese konnte jedoch bei der relativ geringen Überlagerungshöhe nur gewagt werden, weil in vielen und sorgfältigen Messungen des natürlichen Spannungszustandes auch eine Horizontalspannung etwa in der selben Höhe wie die Vertikalspannung nachgewiesen werden konnte. Inzwischen war bereits der Ausbruch für die 75 cm dicke Betonauskleidung (innen Kreis-, außen Hufeisenprofil) erfolgt. Die nun vorgegebene, etwas zu große Wanddicke erforderte für die Vorspannung unter Berücksichtigung der Vorspannverluste einen extrem hohen Injektionsdruck von rd. 80 bar, ein Druck, der bisher noch nicht für Injektionsvorspannungen angewandt worden war. Die Betonspannung liegt dabei nahe an der Bruchgrenze des Betons B 300. Diese Zusammenhänge zeigt sehr deutlich das Bemessungsdiagramm gem. Abb. 11.

Das leicht hufeisenförmige Ausbruchsprofil wurde zwar mit Spritzbeton relativ gut ausgeglichen, doch brachten schon geringe Abweichungen von der theoretischen Kreisringform infolge der beträchtlichen Spaltweite und der großen Wanddicke so hohe Biegespannungen, daß an einigen Stellen die Bruchgrenze überschritten wurde. Die Durchmesserkonvergenz betrug bis über 15 mm, im Mittel etwa 8 mm. Die vorhandene Bewehrung verhinderte in diesem Fall aber das Ausbrechen größerer Betonkegel, wie dies schon öfters geschah, sodaß die Risse innerhalb der Bewehrung blieben. Damit brachte sie der im Vorspannbereich arbeitenden Mannschaft einen zusätzlichen Schutz.

Der erste Druckstollen ging Mitte Januar 1981, der zweite Ende September 1981 unter Druck. Die Dichtheit entsprach voll den Erwartungen und die eingebauten Meßgeräte zeigten ein rein elastisches Verhalten der vorgespannten Betonauskleidung.

Zusammenfassend kann zu diesem Druckstollen gesagt werden, daß hier sowohl von der Betonbeanspruchung als auch von der Gebirgsmitwirkung mehr oder weniger die Grenzen des derzeit Möglichen erreicht wurden. Es muß hier aber auch erwähnt werden, daß dieser Erfolg nur möglich war infolge des hervorragenden Einsatzes aller an der Projektierung und an der Ausführung beteiligten Ingenieure und Mannschaften.

Abb. 11: Bemessungsdiagramm für den
Druckstollen Drakensberg

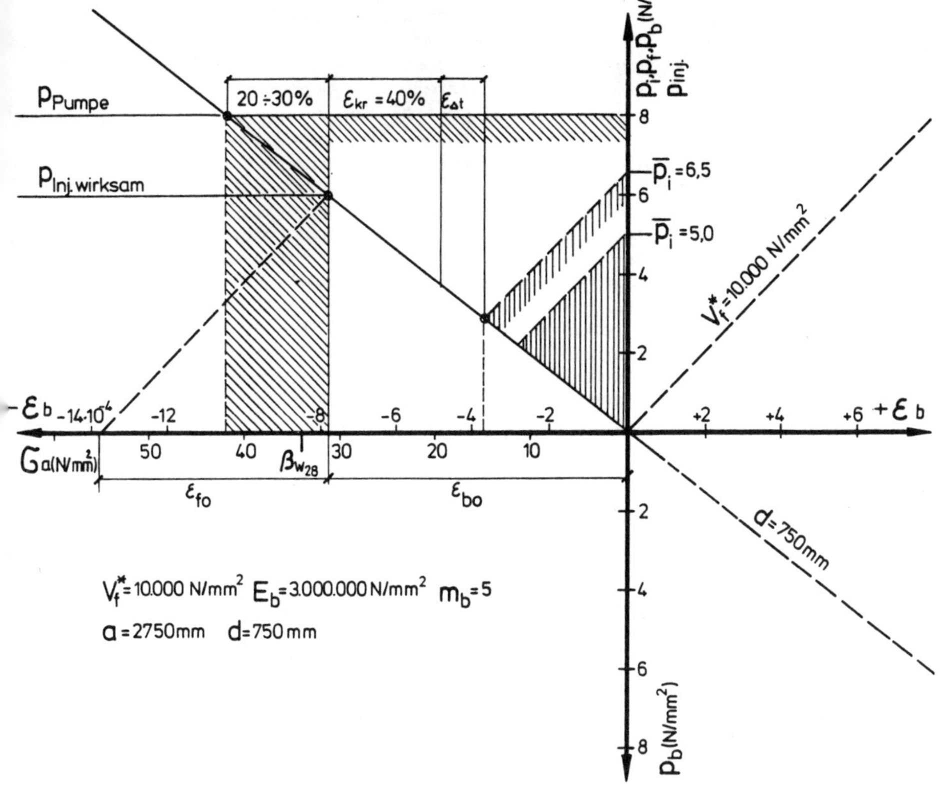

Abb. 12: Höhenplan des KW Langenegg

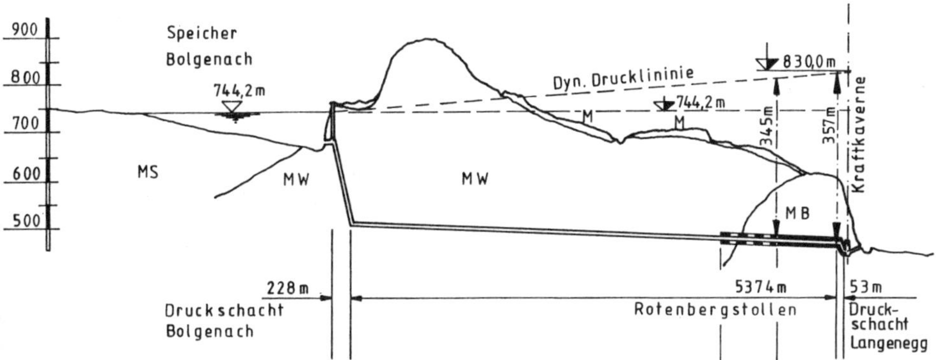

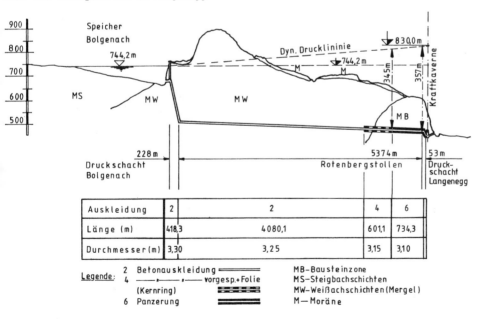

Auskleidung	2	2	4	6
Länge (m)	418,3	4080,1	601,1	734,3
Durchmesser (m)	3,30	3,25	3,15	3,10

Legende:
2 Betonauskleidung ═══
4 —⁓—⁓— vorgesp. + Folie (Kernring)
6 Panzerung

MB – Bausteinzone
MS – Steigbachschichten
MW – Weißachschichten (Mergel)
M – Moräne

3.3 Kraftwerk Langenegg der Vorarlberger Kraftwerke AG/Projektant Vorarlberger Illwerke AG

Der Druckstollen des Kraftwerks Langenegg, der Rotenbergstollen, wurde so trassiert, daß der größte Teil des 5,37 km langen Stollens so tief im Berg liegt, daß infolge der Primärspannung und der Dichtheit des Gebirges (Mergel) eine einfache Betonauskleidung gewählt werden konnte. Allerdings mußte dafür auf ein Wasserschloß verzichtet werden, was zu einer gewissen Betriebseinschränkung führte, die jedoch bewußt in Kauf genommen wurde (Abb. 12).

Der Stollen, der mit einer Fräse im unteren Bereich durch Sandsteine, anschließend durch Mergel vorgetrieben wurde, steht unter einem maximalen Innendruck von rd. 350 m WS (Innerhofer 1977).

Im Anschluß an die Stahlpanzerung des untersten Abschnittes kam in einer rd. 600 m langen Übergangsstrecke in durchlässigen Sandsteinen eine vorgespannte Betonauskleidung mit einer dickeren (5 mm) Folie zum Einsatz. Infolge der glatten Auflagerfläche konnte auch ein wesentlich festeres und widerstandsfähigeres Material (PE) verwendet werden. Unmittelbar hinter der Fräse wurde auf den Sohlstreifen der Folie sofort ein Sohltübbing mit den Schienen verlegt, sodaß alle weiteren Arbeitsvorgänge und Transporte über dieses Gleis erfolgen konnten.

In Verbindung mit dem heute bei Druckstollen und besonders bei Druckschächten üblichen mechanischen Ausbruch eröffnet die Anwendung dieser widerstandsfähigen Folien die Möglichkeit für den Einsatz wirtschaftlicher vorgespannter Betonauskleidungen auch in Druckschächten bis zu relativ hohen Innendrücken.

4 LITERATURHINWEISE

Amstutz, E. 1969, Das Einbeulen von Schacht- und Stollenpanzerungen, Schweizer Bauzeitung 28

Bowcock, J.B. 1979, Drakensberg Pumped Storage Scheme, Tunnels & Tunnelling 1/2

Finger, W. & Wieser, H. 1980, Zur Aufnahme des Außendruckes bei Stollenpanzerungen - Neue Lösungen und ihre rechnerische Erfassung, Der Bauingenieur 55

Innerhofer, G. 1977, Stress Measurements of the Rock Mass in the Headrace Tunnel Langenegg, Proc. of the International Symposium on Field Mechanics, Zürich

Kieser, A. 1960, Druckstollenbau, Wien, Springer Verlag

Lauffer, H. 1966, Die Druckschacht- und Druckstollenpanzerungen des Kaunertalkraftwerkes, Der Bauingenieur 2

Lauffer, H. 1968, Vorspanninjektionen für Druckstollen, Der Bauingenieur 7

Lauffer, H. & Seeber, G. 1961, Design and Control of Linings of Pressure Tunnels and Shafts, Based on Measurement of the Deformability of the Rock, Bericht R.91, 7. ICOLD-Kongreß, Rom

Lauffer, H. & Seeber, G. 1966, Die Messung der Felsnachgiebigkeit mit der TIWAG-Radialpresse und ihre Kontrolle durch Dehnungsmessungen an der Druckschachtpanzerung des Kaunertalkraftwerkes, Sitzungsberichte des 1. Kongresses der ISRM, Band II, Lissabon

Montel, R. 1960, Formule semi-empirique pour la détermination de la pression extérieure limite d'instabilité des conduits métalliques lisse noyés dans du béton, La Houille Blanche 5

Pircher, W. 1980, Erfahrungen im Fräsvortrieb bei der Kraftwerksgruppe Sellrain-Silz, Rock Mechanics, Suppl. 10

Seeber, G. 1975a, Die Sicherheit von Druckschachtpanzerungen, ÖIZ 5

Seeber, G. 1975b, Neue Entwicklungen für Druckstollen und Druckschächte, ÖIZ 5

Seeber, G. 1981, Möglichkeiten und Grenzen im Druckstollenbau, Schweizer Ingenieur und Architekt 29

Seeber, G. & Demmer, W. & Finger, W. 1979, Die Schäden im Hattelberg-Druckstollen als Folge eines außergewöhnlichen Primärspannungszustandes, ISRM, Montreux

TIWAG, Verfahren und Einrichtung zum Auskleiden von Druckstollen, Österreichisches Patent Nr. 265 980 und Auslandspatente

Van der Walt, N.T. & Graber, B.W. 1977, Drakensberg Pumped Storage Scheme, Proc. of the 10th World Energy Conference, Istanbul

Walch, O. 1926, Die Auskleidung von Druckstollen und Druckschächten, Berlin, Springer Verlag

Wanner, H. 1975, Einsatz von Tunnelvortriebsmaschinen im kristallinen Gebirge, Diss. Nr. 5594, ETH Zürich

Adresse des Verfassers:
o.Univ.-Prof.Dipl.-Ing.Dr.techn. Gerhard Seeber, Vorstand des Instituts für Konstruktiven Wasserbau und Tunnelbau, Universität Innsbruck, Technikerstraße 13, A-6020 Innsbruck, Austria

ROCK ENGINEERING ASPECTS OF THE CONCRETE LINED PRESSURE TUNNELS OF THE DRAKENSBERG PUMPED STORAGE SCHEME

Felsmechanische Gesichtspunkte bei den betonausgekleideten Druckstollen der Pumpspeicheranlage Drakensberg

Aspects en mécanique des roches des galeries sous pression à soutènement en béton de la centrale de pompage Drakensberg

JOHN C.SHARP
Rock Engineering Consultant, Jersey, UK
LOU P.GONANO
Golder Associates, Seattle, Washington, USA

ABSTRACT

The rock engineering aspects of the concrete lined pressure tunnels for the Drakensberg Pumped Storage Scheme covering investigation, design and construction are described. The scheme has an operating head of some 500m and is located in a near horizontally bedded sedimentary rock formation containing relatively weak argillaceous strata. Detailed investigations included a test chamber, hydrofracture testing and in-situ stress measurements. The test chamber was fully instrumented and tested to determine the lining/rock response up to internal pressures of the same order as the overburden stress. Design criteria were developed for the permissible extent of the concrete linings with respect to overburden criteria, the long term rock support characteristics and the general behaviour of the composite lining/rock structure. Controlled excavation and support procedures for the tunnels are described. Lining prestressing using interface grouting was carried out to minimise the potential for cracking and inhibit deterioration of the rock due to the frequent pressure fluctuations within the waterway. The behaviour of the lining during watering up was monitored and compliance with the design model observed.

RESUME

Une description est donnée des aspects géotechniques des tunnels de pression revêtus de béton pour le Projet de réservoir d'eau pompée de Drakensberg, couvrant les investigations, les études et la construction. Le projet a une hauteur d'eau disponible de quelques 500 m et il est situé dans une formation presque horizontale de roche sédimentaire en strates contenant des couches argileuses relativement faibles. Les investigations de détail comprenaient une chambre d'essai, des tests d'hydrofracture et des mesures d'efforts sur place. La chambre d'essai entièrement équipée d'appareils de mesure fut essayée pour déterminer la réponse du revêtement et de la roche jusqu'à des pressions internes du même ordre que celles dues aux terrains susjacents. Des critères d'étude ont été développés en vue de l'étendue permissible des revêtements de béton quant aux critères de terrains susjacents, des caractéristiques de support de la roche à long terme et de la tenue générale de la structure composée de revêtement et roche. Les méthodes d'excavation contrôlée et de support des tunnels sont décrites. Une précontrainte du revêtement au moyen de coulis interfacial fut effectuée pour minimiser le potentiel de fissuration et opposer la détérioration de la roche due aux fréquentes fluctuations de pression dans les tunnels. La tenue du revêtement durant la mise en eau fut observée et la conformité avec le modèle de l'étude respectée.

UBERSICHT

Die Beschreibung befaßt sich mit den gesteinstechnischen Aspekten der betonverschalten Druckstollen für das Drakensberg Bewässerung und Energiespeicherungsprojekt und behandelt Forschung, Entwurf und Konstruktion. Das Projekt hat ein Druckgefälle von ca. 500 m und befindet sich in fast horizontal gelagertem Sedimentgestein mit relativ schwacher Tonschicht. Detaillierte Untersuchungen einschließlich Bau einer Testkammer, Hydrobruchversuche und Messung der Spannungen an Ort und Stelle wurden durchgeführt. Die mit kompletter Instrumentierung ausgerüstete Kammer wurde getestet, um die Verschalung/Gestein-Reaktion auf Innendrücke bis zur Überlastgrenze zu ermitteln. Konstruktionskriterien für den zulässigen Umfang der Betonverschalung wurden entwickelt, die Überbelastung, die langzeitigen Tragfähigkeiten des Gesteins und das Verhalten der Verschalung/Gesteinstruktur allgemein berücksichtigten. Gesteuerte Ausschachtungen und Abstützverfahren werden beschrieben. Um die Möglichkeit des Spaltens zu verringern und den Verfall des Gesteins durch häufige Druckschwankungen zu hemmen, wurde eine Vorspannung der Verschalung mit Grenzflächenverguß durchgeführt. Das Verhalten der Verschalung während des Wasserauffüllens wurde uberwacht und Übereinstimmung mit dem Entwicklungsmodell konnte festgestellt werden.

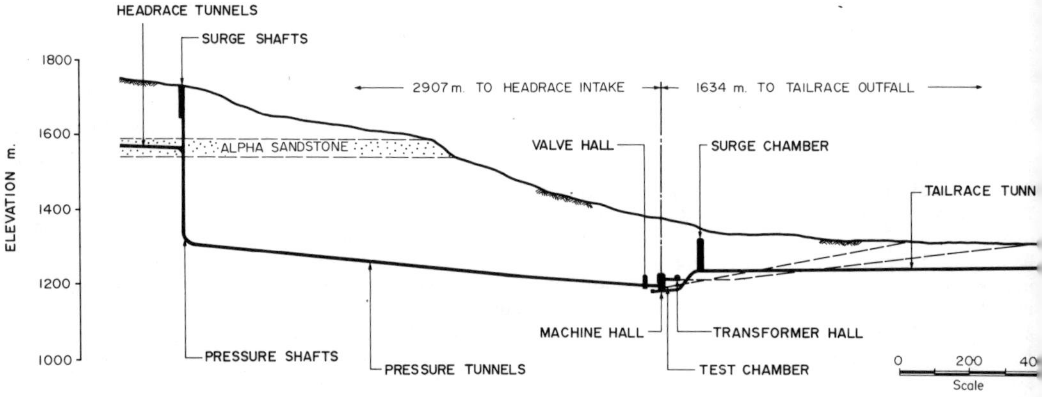

FIGURE 1 PARTIAL CROSS SECTION THROUGH SCHEME ALIGNMENT SHOWING PRESSURE SHAFTS AND TUNNELS AND TEST CHAMBER LOCATIONS

1 INTRODUCTION

The Drakensberg Pumped Storage Scheme is a dual purpose scheme designed for both energy storage and water supply purposes. The scheme is located in a near horizontally bedded sedimentary rock formation with an overall alignment length of some 4,5 km comprising headrace tunnels, surge and pressure shafts, pressure tunnels (penstocks) power station complex and tailrace tunnel. The general arrangement of the pressure tunnels in relation to the other scheme components is illustrated on Figure 1.

The interbedded sandstone and siltstone rock mass is relatively deformable and the more argillaceous (muddy) units are susceptible to deterioration if not adequately protected.

The twin 5,5m internal diameter concrete lined pressure tunnels are some 850 m long and slope at a grade of 1 in 10. The maximum operating head is up to 500 m and a comparison with other schemes in terms of rock deformability is given on Figure 2.

The lack of suitable precedent for high head concrete lined tunnels in relatively weak, sedimentary strata called for detailed investigation measures covering the support characteristics of the rock and the susceptibility of the rock to hydrofracture as well as special design considerations for the lining structures.

The paper is arranged in six parts as follows :

- Pressure Tunnel Layout and Geology
- Prototype Investigations (Penstock Test Chamber)
- Rock Mass Characteristics along Tunnel Alignment
- Tunnel Excavation, Support and Final Lining
- Observed Response
- Conclusions

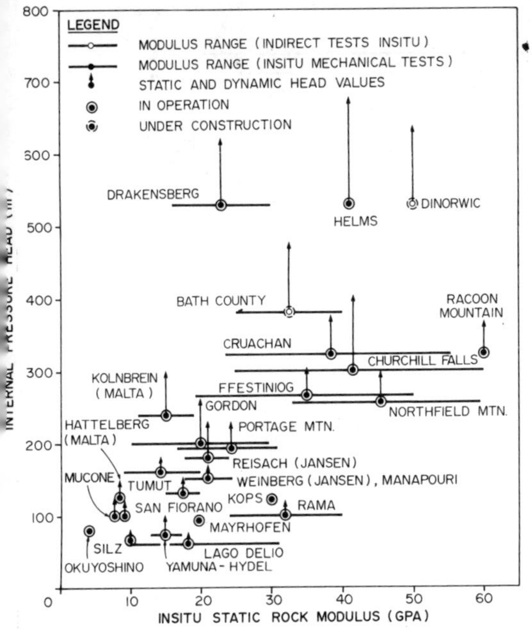

FIGURE 2 COMPARISON OF INTERNAL PRESSURE AND ROCK MODULUS FOR HIGH HEAD PRESSURE TUNNELS

2 PRESSURE TUNNEL LAYOUT & GEOLOGY

The general arrangement of the pressure shafts and tunnels is shown on Figure 1. From the bottom of the shafts, the concrete lined tunnels extend for a distance of about 1,1 km after which the tunnels are steel lined to the machine hall.

The vertical shaft arrangement was favoured in the near horizontally bedded strata after careful study of several alternatives including inclined and surface penstocks.

The pressure tunnels were located at the lowest elevation consistent with geological, hydraulic and construction considerations. To achieve the maximum possible cover upstream of the power station and thus minimise the length of steel lining, the ruling minimum grade of 1 in 20 was adopted as far as the drainage tunnel. Upstream of this location (which is close to the end of the steel lining), a maximum grade of 1 in 10 was dictated by efficient excavation and lining methods.

The rocks through which the pressure tunnels pass form part of the Middle and Lower Beaufort Series of the Karoo system. The rocks consist primarily of interbedded sandstones and siltstones (including muddy siltstones) with occasional thin seams of mudstone and carbonaceous materials. The rocks are characterised by their greenish grey/bluish grey colouring and some components of volcanic origin are evident within the sediments (Bowcock et al., 1976; Golder Associates, 1977a).

Bedding is the dominant structure over the tunnel alignment, individual bed thicknesses varying from a few millimetres to several metres. Although major sandstone units occur at the site these do not occur within the vertical interval of the pressure tunnels. The bedding planes are the most significant structural weaknesses and can be slikensided or micaceous.

Faults occur over the pressure tunnel alignment and these in part have had an influence on the tunnel layout. The faults typically comprise a brecciated zone some 0,1 to 0,5 m in width and have associated sympathetic shears and jointing.

Dykes which are generally competent and of limited width (less than 0,5 m) also cross the tunnel alignment. The dyke margins may be fractured and hence permeable compared with the generally impermeable rock mass.

Jointing over the tunnel alignment is generally limited to specific zones, often in the vicinity of faults.

3 PROTOTYPE INVESTIGATIONS

A prototype trial section of the concrete lined pressure tunnels was constructed in the form of a test chamber and tested to determine the short and long term behaviour under internal pressure conditions. The objectives of the test programme were the determination of the maximum extent of the concrete linings with respect to minimum overburden conditions (location of transition to steel; hydrofracture potential in the rock), the structural deformability of the concrete/rock structure and the long term operating behaviour. A high potential cost saving could result from the use of concrete linings in the shafts and tunnels instead of steel.

The test chamber was located in an area representative of the poorer rock conditions expected over the main tunnel alignment.

3.1 Chamber Construction and Grouting

The chamber was constructed as part of the exploratory works in the period May 1975 to May 1976 and involved excavation and rock support, in situ casting of the lining in stages and cavity and consolidation grouting.

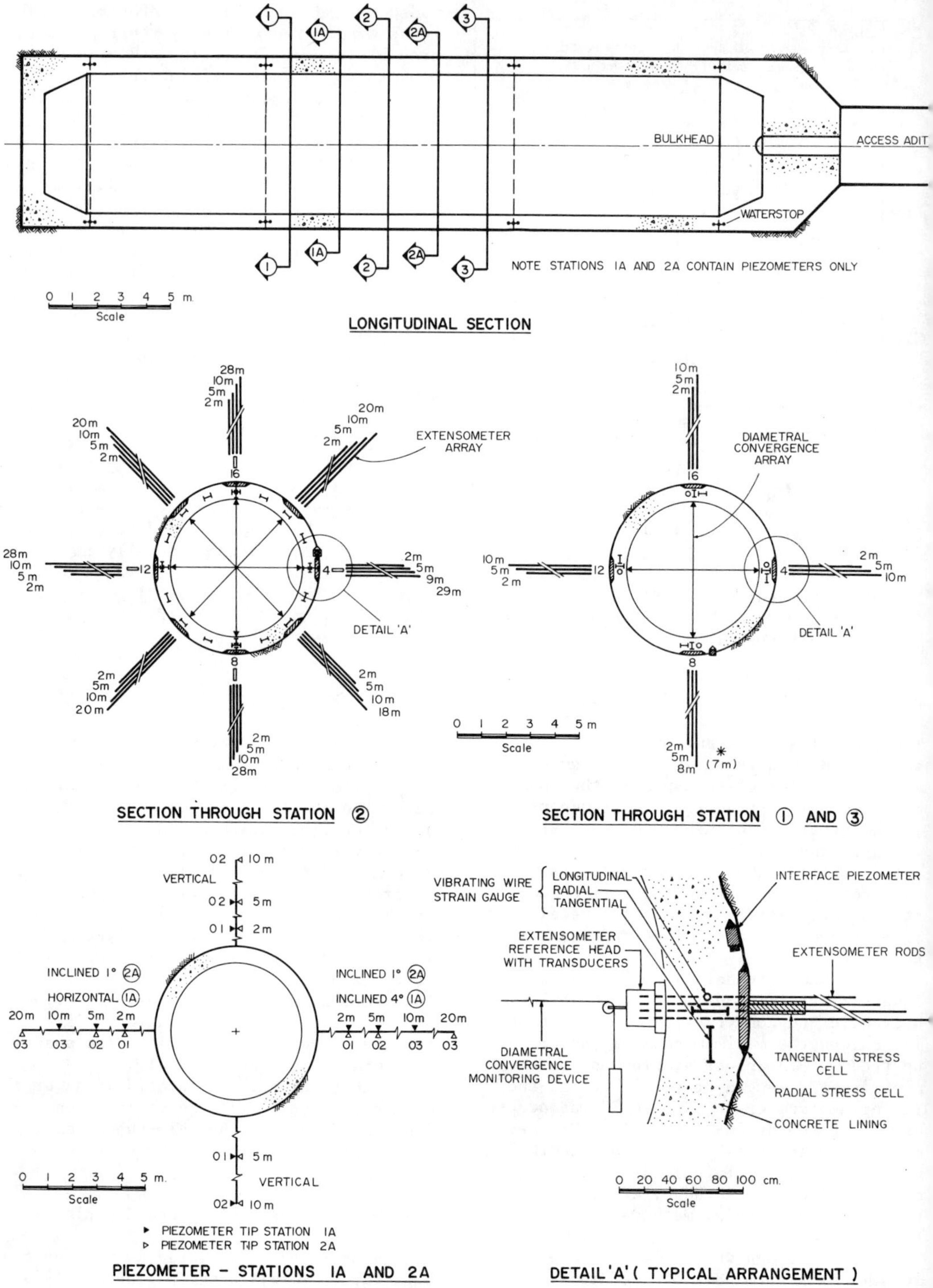

FIGURE 3 TEST CHAMBER LAYOUT AND INSTRUMENTATION ARRANGEMENTS

The chamber comprised 3 x 10 m long bays each 5,5 m internal diameter with a nominal lining thickness of 0,6 m as shown on Figure 3. Construction was designed to duplicate as closely as practicable the anticipated methods for the pressure tunnels.

The rock was subjected to extensive borehole grouting measures that produced a relatively high (40% application factor) and markedly non-uniform tangential prestress in the lining as indicated on Figure 4.

3.2 Chamber Instrumentation

A comprehensive array of instruments including convergence monitors, vibrating wire strain gauges, extensometers, stress cells and piezometers was built into the central bay of the chamber during construction to measure the stress-deformation response of the concrete and rock. Typical instrumentation layouts are shown on Figure 3. All instrumentation was designed to operate under pressures up to 7,5 MPa and yielded valuable results, except for the extensometers.

The instrumentation was designed to gain a fundamental appreciation of the behaviour of the lining/rock structure and thereby permit meaningful predictions of operating conditions for the variety of head, rock type and overburden cover along the alignment of the pressure tunnels.

The monitoring in order of eventual benefit can be summarised as follows :

- Diametral convergence/divergence measurements (3 sections ; 8 arrays)
- Strain measurements using embedded vibrating wire strain gauges (tangential (24), radial (12), longitudinal (12)
- Water pressures behind the lining and in the surrounding rock mass (20 hydraulic piezometers)
- Stresses across the lining/rock interface (mercury filled stress cells : 16 radial, 4 tangential)

3.3 Chamber Test Programme

A programme of testing to measure the structural response under short term, sustained and transient internal pressure loading was carried out between December 1976 and July 1977.

Cyclic pressurization stages with 1 MPa pressure increases to a proposed maximum of 5 MPa were carried out. Owing to increased leakage above 4 MPa, the maximum attainable pressure with the available pumping capacity was 4,2 MPa.

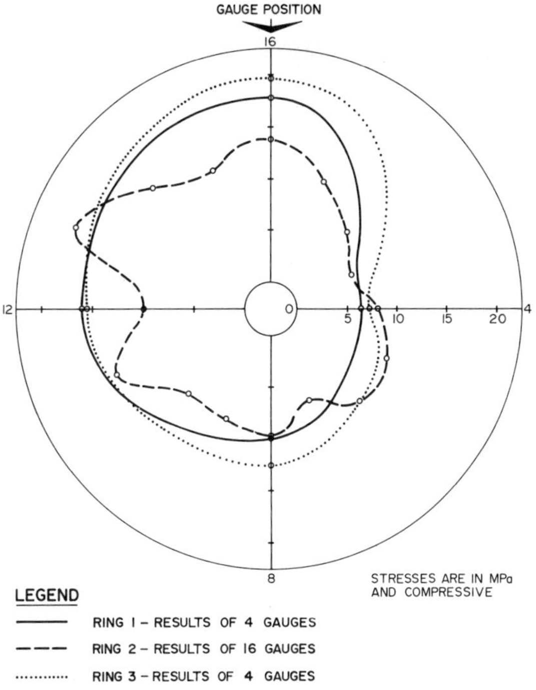

FIGURE 4 TEST CHAMBER - TANGENTIAL LINING STRESSES PRODUCED BY HIGH PRESSURE GROUTING

Dewatering of the chamber was carried out prior to and following the 4,0 and 4,2 MPa tests to assess any cracking of the lining. The overall test programme is shown on Figure 5.

Post-testing investigations extending over two and a half years in the form of measurements of the lining deformations (due to creep and loss of prestress), direct in situ measurements of lining prestress and laboratory creep tests on concrete and rock core were also performed. Lining prestress measurements were carried out using large diameter overcoring of 200 mm gauge length rosettes at eight locations around the lining circumference.

The test results were used to establish a preliminary creep model for the tunnels to predict long term stress conditions.

3.4 Associated Deformability Testing

As part of the test chamber programme, large scale plate bearing tests (500 ton) were conducted in an adit parallel to the chamber to determine the modulus conditions around the chamber periphery (Bowcock et

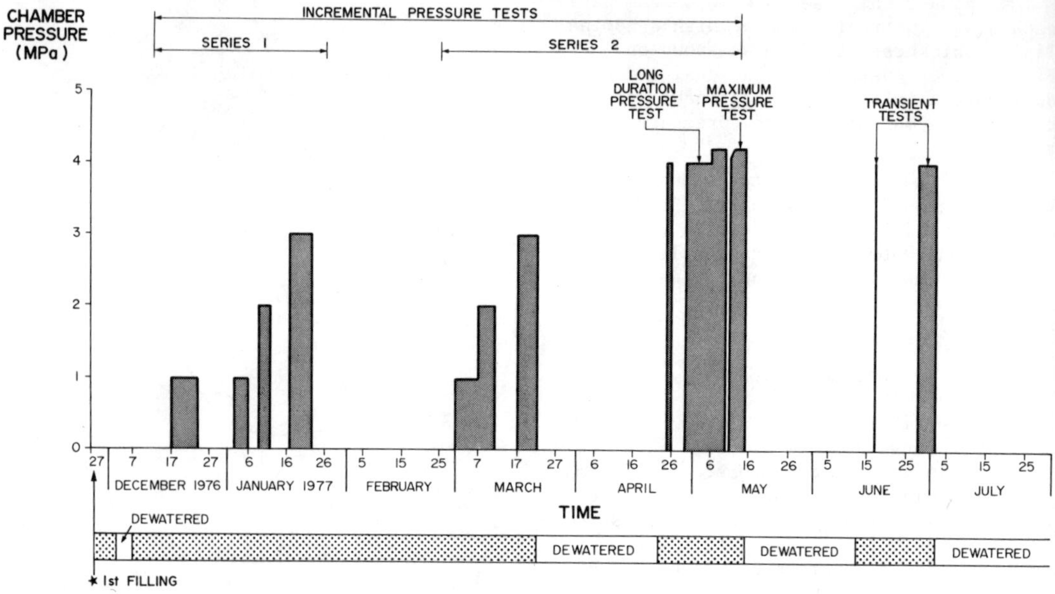

FIGURE 5 TEST CHAMBER PROGRAMME

al 1976). In addition laboratory tests were undertaken on the complete range of rock types at different orientations to determine the degree of anisotropy.

Values for the undisturbed rock mass moduli obtained from 14 plate bearing tests were 18 GPa and 25 GPa normal and parallel to the bedding. Laboratory modulus values from a large number of tests gave corresponding average values of 22 GPa and 31 GPa. The difference is attributed to occasional minor jointing and the effect of larger scale layering or bedding.

The loading response of the undisturbed rock is approximately linear elastic with minimal creep and permanent deformation. The surface zone disturbed by excavation exhibits a modulus 10 to 15 per cent of that of the undisturbed rock.

3.5 Associated In-situ Stress Measurements

Stress conditions in the vicinity of the test chamber were determined using triaxial strain cells and the borehole overcoring technique. Owing to the bedded, anisotropic nature of the rock, additional laboratory evaluations were carried out to produce representative strain-stress conversion factors for use in the evaluation. (Gonano and Sharp, 1982).

The inferred vertical and horizontal stresses at the test chamber were as follows :

σ_v = 3,9 MPa = 1,2 x theoretical overburden
σ_h = 6,3 MPa, perpendicular to the tunnel axis

A stress ratio, K of 1,6 was thus inferred.

3.6 Test Chamber Results

Deformation. Deformation data, as yielded by diametral closure measurements and VW strain gauges, indicated a near-linear response of vertical diametral expansion to chamber pressure for short term loading. Horizontal expansions were less than the vertical, clearly indicating an "ellipsing" profile, exaggerated at higher pressures by a reduced rate of horizontal expansion.

Tangential strain rates measured in the chamber lining were in good agreement with those inferred from closure measurements. The ellipsing type of radial displacements were reflected in a concentration of strain change in the springline area of the lining.

The magnitude and sense of the three orthogonal lining strains were compatible with a model of the chamber expanding circumferentially whilst subject to increasing radial strain, indicating radial compression of the lining and surrounding rock.

A distinct trend in the change in deformation behaviour with increasing chamber pressure was noticed. The ellipsing pattern became more pronounced and individual readings showed a greater divergence from the mean. Above 3 MPa, the long term deformability showed a distinctive departure from proportionality with chamber pressure.

Crack patterns observed corresponded well with inferred deformations.

Stress Changes. Radial stress cell measurements indicated an initial radial stress transfer at the lining/rock contact of approximately 50% of chamber pressure. The apparent increase in radial stress transfer at higher pressures (3 MPa and above) was due to hydraulic connections to several cells. Proportionality of radial stress changes with chamber pressure increments in reliable cells indicated a composite action between the lining and rock (no change in radial stress transfer characteristics).

Tangential stress at the lining/rock interface decreased during internal pressurization. However, at higher pressures (2 MPa in the case of springlines instruments), hydraulic connections occurred, rendering the readings invalid.

Water Pressure and Leakage. Piezometric pressures in rock surrounding the chamber increased steadily with chamber pressure.

The response of piezometers in the horizontal plane was greater than that of gauges above and below the chamber. This behaviour probably reflected the directional permeabilities of the rock and the influence of hydrofracturing.

Pumping rates necessary to maintain chamber pressure increased sharply between 2 and 3 MPa and reached a maximum of 90 litres/min at 4,2 MPa.

3.7 Data Evaluation

An evaluation of the data from the test program indicated three pressure dependent ranges of behaviour as illustrated on Figure 6 :

- a linear elastic deformational response up to a pressure equivalent to 60 percent of overburden.
- a slightly non-linear elastic response above 60 percent of overburden caused by cracking of the lining and localized hydrofracturing of the rock.
- unstable hydrofracturing on a large scale in the rock at internal pressures close to, or in excess of, the overburden pressure together with significant cracking of the lining.

Design criteria for the service and potential failure conditions were established from these data on the basis that the maximum internal pressures would not extend the lining beyond the elastic range.

In the elastic response range, the stress-strain behaviour can be analysed in some detail. At higher internal pressures, the model of behaviour is less explicit and is based primarily on observation.

Stress and strain conditions created by the application of internal pressure were deduced from convergence, vibrating wire strain gauge and stress cell readings. Whilst the short term response of the instruments was generally linear with increasing pressure, variability of conditions both longitudinally and circumferentially was noticeably greater at 4 MPa than at 3 MPa and below. This increase in variability was mainly due to variable loading effects following lining cracking and leakage.

Variability of piezometric response in the rock was observed at pressures above 2 MPa and was attributed to the discrete nature of fissuration in the low permeability bedded rock (connecting some gauges and not others) and hydrofracturing at the springline areas.

The observed variabilities in instrument readings reflected to a large degree, real variations in material properties and structural conditions under load. The influence of these variabilities on lining performance, particularly cracking of the lining at high internal pressures, is fundamental to the lining design.

The following types of evaluation were carried out :

- Closed form elastic solutions : A detailed investigation of the distribution in space and with time of the statistically averaged data for the 0 - 3 MPa pressure range. This ensured that the general pattern of stress, strain and deformation behaviour was correctly assessed. The responses during both high pressure grouting and internal pressurisation were analysed.
- Numerical simulation of the stress, strain and deformation behaviour : Correct simulation was achieved by trial and adjustment to fit the measured behaviour during the elastic response range (0 - 3 MPa). Particular attention was paid to modelling the anisotropic response.

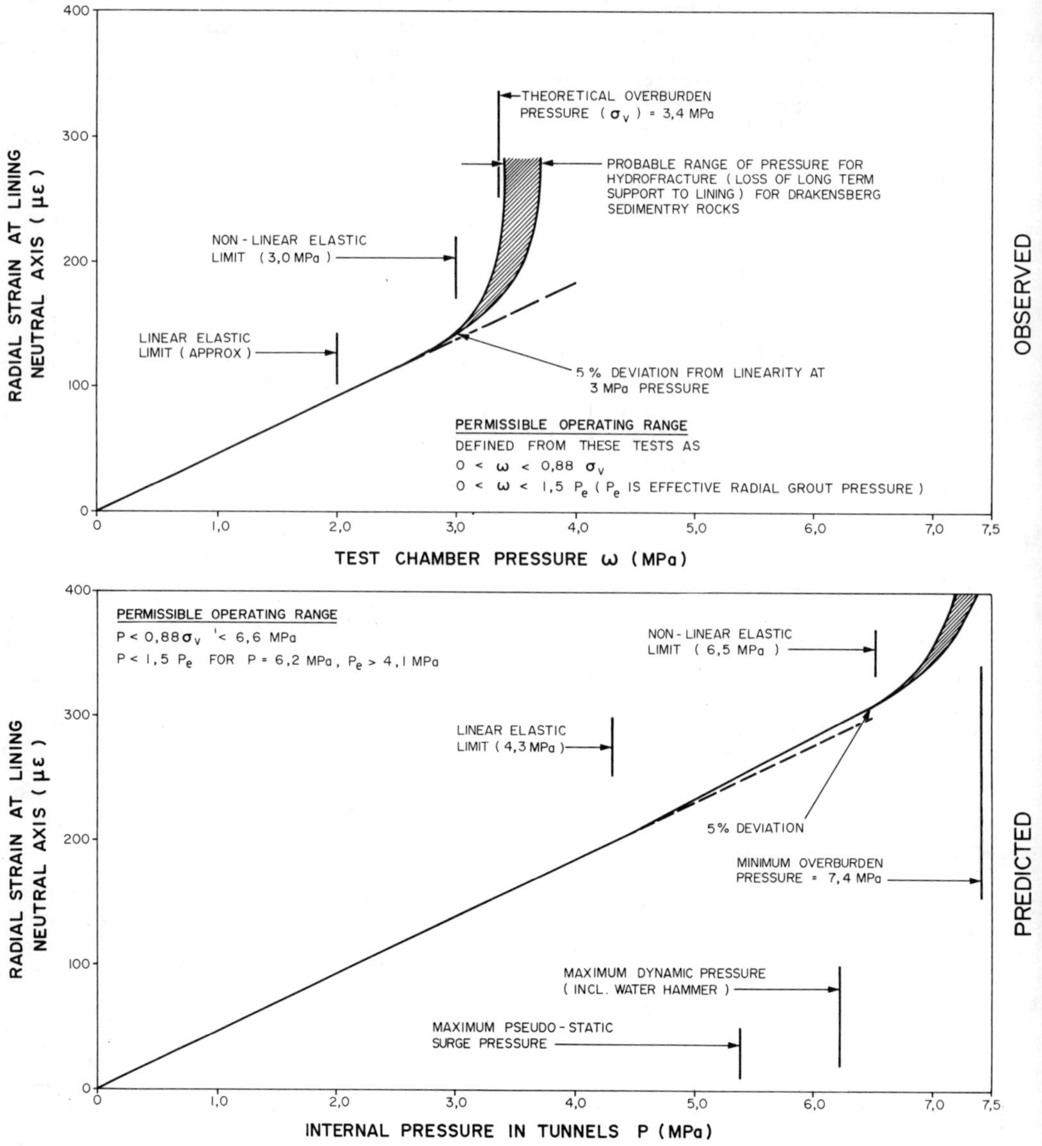

FIGURE 6 TEST CHAMBER OBSERVATIONS AND PREDICTED BEHAVIOUR FOR PRESSURE TUNNELS

- Advanced deformation characteristics : Non-linear and irreversible effects at pressures above 3 MPa and the effect of hydrofracturing were studied.
- Sustained loading characteristics : An evaluation of deformation behaviour under sustained loading.
- Transient response : A study of the effects of rapid pressure changes.

3.8 Deformability Criteria - Rock Support

The observations over the range of elastic response (0 - 3 MPa) were used to derive deformability criteria for the lining/rock structure.

A tunnel deformability model for the pressure tunnels was developed incorporating the effects of modulus anisotropy, excavation, grouting and stress conditions. Data from associated deformability testing were also used to formulate the model. A comparison of instrument results (convergence, radial rock stresses and tangential lining strains) confirmed the existence of modulus anisotropy (E_h/E_v = 1,3) as determined from the plate bearing tests.

The resulting deformability model, shown on Figure 7, was used as the basis for predicting expected stress changes in the pressure tunnel linings due to internal pressurisation.

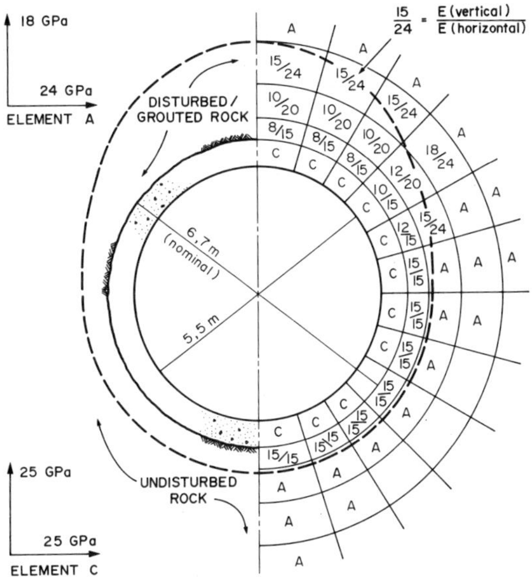

FIGURE 7 SCHEMATIC CROSS SECTION SHOWING TUNNEL DEFORMABILITY MODEL

3.9 Advanced Deformation Behaviour

The non-linear response of the lining/rock structure at the higher chamber pressures was associated with a number of physical phenomena, each of which was considered in the design of the prototype tunnels. These included stress redistribution around the lining, cracking of the lining, asymmetrical deformations, leakage of water and hydrofracture effects.

The advanced deformation behaviour, associated with inadequate prestress in the lining and rock, was considered to be an unacceptable condition for the operational state due to cracking of the lining and hydrofracture effects in the rock mass.

The onset of the non-linear and non-elastic (unstable) response regimes was interpreted mechanistically in terms of the local and regional stress conditions. Dimensionless parameters relating internal pressure, effective grout pressure and overburden stress to the observed behaviour of the test chamber were derived to allow extrapolation for the design of the pressure tunnels under both service and failure states.

The onset of hydrofracture occurred at a chamber pressure of approximately 3 MPa. The hydrofracture was apparently initiated in the vicinity of the springlines and developed in the zone of disturbed rock immediately adjacent to the lining. In this zone, the rock had negligible tensile strength and the permeability characteristics were related primarily to the level of the minimum principal stress.

Despite cracking in the lining, average deformability of the structure increased only slightly. In all tests, over the pressure range 0 - 4 MPa, average tangential stresses in the lining were compressive. Notwithstanding cracking and the developments of external water pressure in the rock, the lining appeared to act integrally with the rock. Apparent inconsistencies in the behaviour were attributed to the high variabilities of initial prestress and induced lining stresses.

The rock mass has extremely low porosity and the influence of pore water pressures (effective stress concept) on deformability was not found to be significant, except locally at the springlines where a more destressed and permeable zone existed.

Below 4 MPa chamber pressure, induced radial stresses in the rock were everywhere greater than the chamber pressure and thus leakage of water did not directly affect the radial reaction offered to the lining.

Advanced deformation behaviour was related to the presence of water in bedding planes at pressures close to the minimum principal stress. The adverse effects of the resultant hydrofracture condition were cracking of the lining, fissuration of the rock along bedding and a resultant deformation pattern that was considered to be unacceptable in terms of the lining service requirements. The advanced deformation observations provide a well defined limit to the range of elastic response.

The ratio of internal design pressure to minimum regional stress was used as a principal guide parameter for estimating the elastic range under the different stress conditions associated with the pressure tunnels.

3.10 Overburden Criteria

The test chamber observations were used to establish an adequate factor of safety against hydrofracture and so determine the permissible extent of the concrete linings in relation to overburden cover. Hydrofracture effects could lead to both unacceptable leakage into the rock and result in aerial jacking as well as cracking and structural distress to the lining.

The chamber observations indicated localised hydrofracture developing above 3 MPa internal pressure with significant hydrofracture effects at sustained internal pressures close to the inferred vertical stress of 3,4 MPa. Enhanced vertical deformation of the lining structure at sustained high pressures was attributed to the formation of an extended zone of hydrofracturing at the springlines.

The apparent sensitivity of the rock to hydrofracturing is attributed to the relatively weak bedding partings and the orientation of the bedding in relation to the minimum principal stress (close to vertical).

3.11 Sustained Loading Characteristics

Sustained loading conditions were evaluated for 3 and 4 MPa internal pressures.

At 3 MPa, chamber expansion with time was circumferentially uniform and attributed to creep in both the lining and the rock. Radial stresses at the lining/rock contact remained constant with time. Creep magnitudes deduced were in agreement with the general behaviour derived by calculations and observations elsewhere.

The repeatability of loading response and the small magnitude of creep confirmed that at 3 MPa pressure the rock and lining behaved elastically and that cracking of the lining and water pressures in the rock were not significant.

Under the 4 MPa internal pressure maintained for 15 days, chamber behaviour was markedly different from that at 3 MPa. Time-related deformations were significant and asymmetrical circumferentially. The vertical deformations increased by 50% of the initial values and were attributed to the preferential horizontal development of large-scale hydraulic jacking.

3.12 Transient Loading Characteristics

Simulation of the rapid loading and unloading likely to be experienced under service conditions was attempted to check for any deviations from the static loading response. Loading rates of 4 MPa in 1½ hours and unloading from this pressure in less than one minute were achieved.

Changes in lining, rock and groundwater conditions for the rapid application of internal load were immediate and in accordance with previously determined elastic moduli. Apart from longer term creep effects, the full response to the sudden application of pressure occurred essentially in the time span of loading. This included groundwater response at the piezometer locations.

The responses to unloading from 4 MPa in time periods of 1 minute and 1½ hours were very similar. Such response was characterised by immediate and proportional variations in lining convergence and strain such that long-term stable conditions were achieved at the completion of unloading.

During unloading, an immediate and significant reduction in external water pressure immediately outside the lining occurred due to elastic stress redistribution in the rock and contraction of the lining. A conservative estimate for design purposes of the immediate pressure reduction due to elastic rebound was 25% of the internal pressure change. A lag of the order of many hours was observed in the decay of residual water pressures.

The post-unloading reductions in water pressure were not reflected in changes in lining displacements indicating that the external water pressures were effective over only a small area of the lining.

Because groundwater pressure changes and lining displacements on loading were immediate, the effective water pressure/flow relationship through the lining/rock was dependent upon whether the structure was being loaded or unloaded. The difference in loading/unloading characteristics could thus lead to cumulative deformation effects from repeated cycles of sharply fluctuating pressures.

3.13 Preliminary Long Term Creep Estimates

A particularly important requirement with respect to the design for service conditions is the provision of adequate long term prestress in the lining/rock structure. Long term predictions were obtained from additional post-testing investigations and an evaluation of the creep characteristics of the concrete.

Overcoring stress measurements on the lining inner surface some 2½ years after grouting indicated that a significant degree of prestress had been retained. An average residual surface tangential prestress of some 10 MPa was measured compared with an estimated 11,5 MPa at the time of grouting.

These stresses were in reasonable agreement with those determined from a collective evaluation of creep behaviour based on laboratory measurements and long term lining strain observations.

The observed loss of 15% prestress is relatively small and is related to the extended grouting period (47 days) in which some portion of the creep occurred before maximum prestress was achieved. Because creep decays in an exponential manner from the start of grouting, the losses subsequent to the completion of grouting were less than if a very short grouting duration had been used.

A fundamental model of creep behaviour for the particular conditions of the pressure tunnel lining/rock interaction was developed from the ongoing observations on the test chamber and from concrete and rock material tests. This model, defined in Figure 8, was used for initial estimates of the long-term stress state of the linings under the various construction, prestress and internal pressure conditions along the tunnels.

Design aspects for long-term creep effects included :

- evaluation of creep magnitude (including temperature effects)
- required long-term stress conditions for the tunnels, based largely on test chamber performance.
- estimates of the initial prestress requirements using the structural creep model (Figure 8) and appropriate material creep parameters.
- formulation of equivalent convergence requirements for high pressure grouting

Creep of the concrete was found to be the most significant source of prestress loss. After allowing for the elastic effect of internal pressurization, the 50-year lining prestress in the pressure tunnels was estimated to be in the range 30 - 40% of the initial average prestress. Further creep studies are reported by de Witt 1982

3.14 Conclusions

Through the use of internal water pressure loading representative of service conditions it has been possible to simulate realistically two important sets of conditions in the test chamber which form the basis of the structural design of a

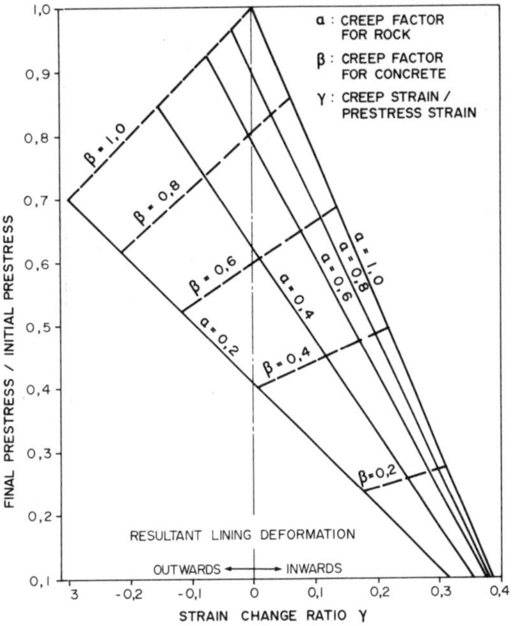

FIGURE 8 STRUCTURAL CREEP MODEL BASED ON TEST CHAMBER RESULTS

rock supported pressure tunnel :

- Actual service operational conditions for which the main requirements are the provision of stable lining conditions through the maintenance of an elastic response to the imposed loads;
- Potential failure conditions for which a suitable margin of safety must be provided. By subjecting the test chamber to structural failure, reliable estimates of safe working conditions have been established.

4 ROCK MASS CHARACTERISTICS ALONG ALIGNMENT OF TUNNELS

The general geological conditions have been described in Part 2. An initial appreciation of the geology was obtained from air photo interpretation, surface mapping and several deep boreholes. Detailed geological investigations were carried out in two phases :

- exploratory adits and boreholes at the downstream end of pressure tunnels
- mapping of the pressure tunnel excavations

The purpose of the adits and boreholes was to determine the possible extent of the concrete lined tunnels and achieve an optimum location for a cut-off zone designed to prevent the leakage of high

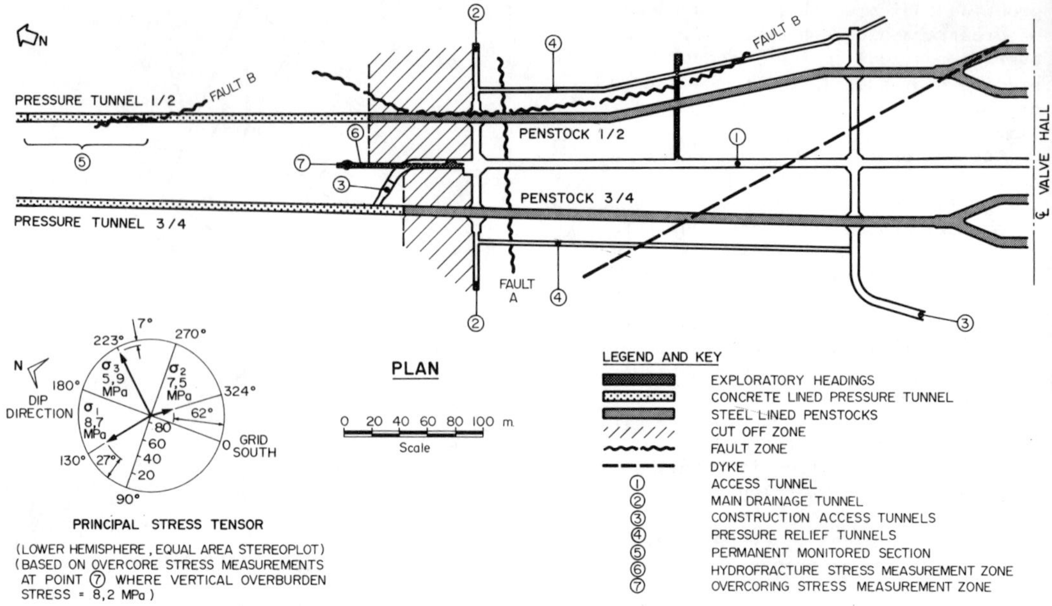

FIGURE 9 PRESSURE TUNNELS DOWNSTREAM SECTION - LAYOUT, GEOLOGY AND STRESS CONDITIONS

pressure water southwards towards the steel-lined penstocks and the Power Station Complex. The investigation identified several major faults, illustrated on Figure 9, which influenced the final location of the cut-off zone and the alignment of tunnel 1/2.

During driving of the pressure tunnels other faults were intersected notably Fault B subparallel to tunnel 1/2.

4.1 In situ Stress Measurements

In situ stress measurements were made at the downstream end of the pressure tunnels using a similar procedure to that described in Section 3.4.

The average stress conditions are given on Figure 9. A ratio of horizontal to vertical stress, K, of 0,9 was observed, significantly lower than that at the test chamber location (1,6).

The reduction in horizontal stresses normal to the pressure tunnel axis was attributed to the presence of faulting in the area (Golder Associates 1977b) as well as a reduction in K with depth. The measured vertical stress was approximately equal to the minimum theoretical overburden stress of 7,4 MPa normal to the ground surface.

4.2 Hydrofracture Testing

Hydrofracture tests were performed in boreholes drilled normal to the bedding in the area indicated on Figure 9.

The tests indicated that the bedded rock has minimal resistance to hydrofracturing. Initiation of cracking and propagation of water occurred along bedding planes at pressures approximately 100 to 110 percent of the vertical overburden stress above the measurement point. This behaviour occurred in preference to fracturing normal to the minimum principal stress direction and is attributed to the lack of jointing and the low or zero tensile strength of the bedding planes. Where jointing was intercepted in the test boreholes, the flow of water and the development of induced permeability increased gradually with pressure.

4.3 Permeability Testing

Permeability measurements were carried out on all rock units encountered along the tunnel alignment. Measurements were also made of the permeability of significant structural features that might influence the effectiveness of the cut-off. Some tests were carried out at elevated pressures to simulate the effect of high pressure water in the rock and thus to determine the pressure dependent permeability characteristics.

Permeabilities for all strata were found to be very low (generally less than 10^{-7} m/sec) and virtually independent of pressure. Permeabilities of the encountered faults were also relatively low, the most significant being Fault A with a zone permeability up to 10^{-4} m/sec at pressures in excess of 2 MPa.

4.4 Rock Deterioration Studies

The pressure transients associated with pumped storage operation can induce onerous loading conditions on the rock, particularly if the lining cracks and the cracks extend into the rock. Mechanisms which could lead to a long-term deterioration of rock support include :

. softening/swelling of the intact rock
. crack propagation in the rock as a result of transient water pressures
. erosion and transport of disaggregated rock through the lining.

In an attempt to define limiting conditions under which deterioration would not occur, laboratory tests were carried out on the range of rock types encountered to determine their swell potential at different moisture contents when subjected to water at varying pressures. Erosion tests on both naturally and artificially fractured specimens were also conducted.

The studies indicated that to maintain the support capacity of the rock in the long term, cracking of the lining and rock and resultant softening of the rock under cyclic loading conditions should be minimised. This was achieved by the adoption of lining prestressing to produce an essentially crack free lining and compressive stress conditions within the rock long term. Steel reinforcement was also incorporated in the lining as an extra safeguard to distribute any cracking that might occur.

4.5 Overburden Criteria and Extent of Concrete Linings

The minimum overburden cover permissible, which governs the extent of the concrete lined sections, was evaluated on the basis of the following :

. Precedent practice
. Test chamber performance
. In situ stress conditions and hydrofracture characteristics
. Weak, bedded nature of the rock

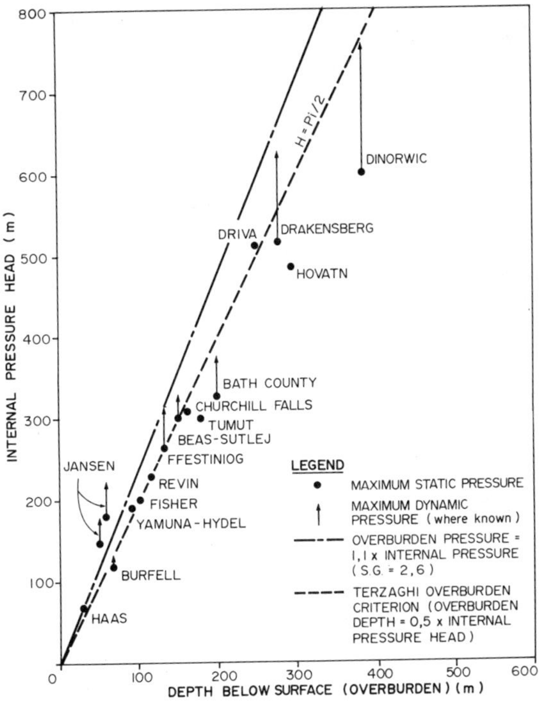

FIGURE 10 MINIMUM OVERBURDEN CRITERIA FOR VARIOUS PROJECTS

. Maximum static, surge and dynamic pressures within the waterway.

Unless the lining can be made completely watertight, which was not practicable at Drakensberg owing to the high internal pressures and relatively deformable rock, the maximum pressure in the tunnel should be lower than the overburden stress by a reasonable factor of safety to prevent the development of aerial jacking and uncontrolled leakage. The maximum internal surge pressure was applied in this criterion since the duration of the dynamic pressure pulse was insufficient to develop jacking or injection over a significant zone.

The minimum overburden criteria adopted for a number of relatively high head tunnels are compared on Figure 10. Precedent practice has incorporated a minimum overburden ratio (overburden stress/internal pressure head) of about 1,1. This ratio has been widely applied to more conventional hydro stations but not necessarily to pumped storage where frequent large transients occur.

The results of the Test Chamber indicated that hydrofracture along bedding (the initial development of aerial jacking) occurred at or close to the overburden stress under sustained pressure conditions. These findings were attributed directly to the weak, bedded nature of the rock and the possible influence of an elevated horizontal stress field giving rise to reduced tangential compression at the spring lines.

The investigation of in situ stresses indicated that the measured vertical stress was not less than the minimum overburden stress based on depth normal to the ground surface. The hydrofracture testing has indicated a somewhat higher value of vertical stress equivalent to the theoretical overburden based on the vertical depth below ground surface. (Based on the scale of the measurement technique, values from the hydrofracture tests are likely to be more representative than values obtained from the overcore measurements).

The weak, bedded nature of the rock mass was found to control the orientation of potential hydrofracture planes and thus the vertical stress, although not the minimum value, was used for design purposes. The sensitivity of the bedded rock to hydrofracture at stresses close to overburden was notable.

On the basis of the above considerations, a minimum ratio of theoretical vertical overburden stress to surge pressure of 1,2 was adopted. This value incorporates both the dominant effect of the bedded strata and the sloping topography. The value was applied at the drainage gallery location (see Figure 9) since leakage of high pressure water outside the short length of steel linings through the cut-off zone could potentially occur.

For the final layout adopted, somewhat higher values have resulted from the influence of fault locations (notably Fault 'A') on the choice of the drainage tunnel location.

The ratio of vertical overburden stress/internal pressure head applicable to the upstream end of the steel and the drainage tunnel location are as follows :

	Surge Head	Dynamic Head
End of Steel Pressure Tunnel 1/2	1,46	1,21
End of Steel Pressure Tunnel 3/4	1,41	1,16
Penstock Drainage Tunnel	1,29	-

5 TUNNEL EXCAVATION, SUPPORT AND FINAL LININGS

5.1 Basic Considerations

The high head conditions and the low modulus of the rock require that deformations of the tunnels in service be minimised as far as possible. To achieve this objective, particular attention was paid to excavation and support of the tunnels to minimise disturbance around the excavation profile.

Although extensive grouting measures were adopted, pressure grouting to restore the low modulus of rock disturbed by poor excavation practice was not considered reliable.

5.2 Excavation Procedures

Tunnel excavation was carried out using conventional drill-and-blast methods proceeding from the downstream end. Three meter rounds were drilled using a four-boom hydraulic jumbo. Near faults and intersections and in areas of poor crown conditions, reduced round lengths were adopted.

Blasting was carried out using both smoothwall and presplit techniques, the latter being adopted in the poorer ground conditions. These techniques combined with accurate drilling and well balanced charges produced a high standard of excavation with a large percentage of half-barrels evident and few signs of disturbance to the rock. Only nominal scaling was usually necessary except where faults and joints intersected the crown and haunches of the tunnel.

5.3 Support Design and Procedures

Support of the tunnel excavations was designed in accordance with the long term objective of retaining maximum rock stiffness.

Tensioned rock reinforcement using two speed resin grouting was placed over the roof and haunch areas to within 1m of the advancing face. Where poorer geological conditions were encountered (faulting/jointing) additional reinforcement was specified. Typical patterns are shown on Figure 11.

Shotcrete using the dry mix method was applied to the crown, haunch and sidewalls of the tunnels to prevent deterioration of the argillaceous strata. Mesh was incorporated into the shotcrete only where

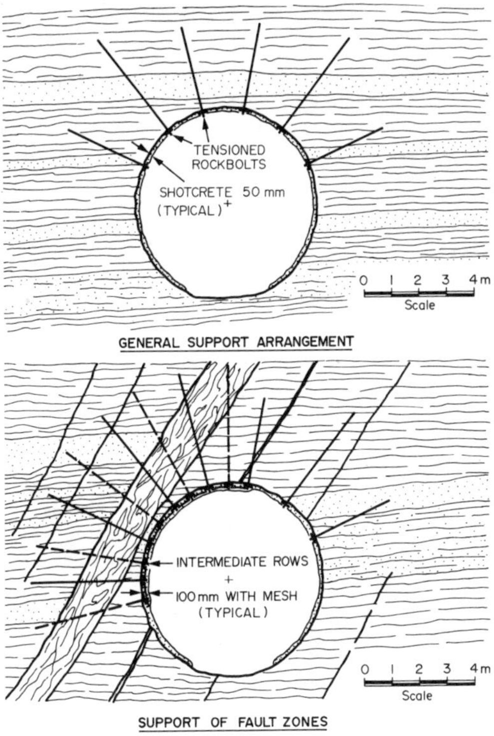

FIGURE 11 PRESSURE TUNNELS - TYPICAL EXCAVATION SUPPORT

major faults were intersected. Shotcrete was generally held slightly back from the face to prevent damage from blasting and debonding on silty or micaceous bedding planes.

Monitoring to check for satisfactory stability conditions in the advancing tunnels was carried out using convergence and extensometer measurements. Typical diametral convergence values were of the order of 5mm resulting from ongoing excavation of the face and indicated well controlled, near elastic stress relaxation. Convergence values normal to faults which were subparallel to the tunnel were typically 10 - 15mm and indicated (from extensometer data) loosening to a greater depth.

5.4 Final Profiles

The excavated profiles conformed reasonably well with the nominal shape except in areas where major geological structures were encountered. After excavation of each tunnel was completed, the cross-sectional profiles were upgraded to produce a more uniform lining thickness in order to improve the efficiency of the interface prestress grouting. The use of sliping and shotcrete backfill over some 40% of the tunnel circumference produced smooth and uniform profiles with no areas greater than 2m x 2m extending more than ± 100mm from the average tunnel radius of 3,3m.

5.5 Lining Construction

The reinforced concrete linings were some 550 - 600mm thick and cast in monolithic 12m bays. To achieve the required degree of prestress in the final linings, the TIWAG interface system was adopted in preference to the borehole consolidation arrangement used for the test chamber. As well as the inherent simplicity and practicality of the method, it was expected that more uniform stress conditions could be achieved.

Prior to lining casting, a debonding film was applied over the shotcrete surface. Circumferential grout injection tubes split into upper and lower sections and equipped with manchettes at 1,5m intervals were spaced at 2,4m centres along the tunnels.

Full details of the lining design and interface grouting arrangements are given in Eastwood and de Witt, 1982.

5.6 Cavity and Consolidation Grouting

Grouting of the rock around the tunnel linings and the lining interface was carried out to achieve the following main objectives :

- Improvement of the modulus of disturbed rock zones.
- Prestressing of the concrete lining and surrounding rock.

Modulus improvement was directed particularly to those areas where faults may have led to loosening at depth, a condition not adequately covered by the test chamber or the resulting tunnel deformability model.

Cavity and in effect low pressure consolidation was carried out over the length of the tunnel through arrays of six 2m long holes at 3m centres. Grouting pressures up to 1,5 MPa were used.

Over fault zones or zones where significant jointing had been observed, comprehensive water tests were performed to determine the degree of potential loosening at depth. Measured permeabilities were low and subsequent high pressure consolidation grouting using 3m long holes and 5 MPa nominal pressures recorded only limited takes.

In spite of these specific treatment measures, prior to interface grouting, non-uniform conditions remained, particularly in the vicinity of major faults as evidenced by the variable takes during the interface injections.

For consolidation of the rock immediately adjacent to the lining, reliance was placed upon the interface technique. Injection of grout into the rock at up to 8 MPa and preloading of the rock from the interface would both result in improved modulus conditions.

6 PRESSURE TUNNEL OBSERVED RESPONSE

6.1 Monitoring Arrangements

The pressure tunnel design was based primarily on the test chamber performance. In order to check the extrapolation of these observations to the pressure tunnel location and service conditions, monitoring of the pressure tunnels was performed in two principal stages as follows :

- Monitoring of interface grouting - lining stressing operations.
- Monitoring of long term performance in service.

Evaluation of the interface grouting system using relatively high grout pressures was based initially on measurements made at an instrumented lining section containing embedded and surface vibrating wire strain gauges and diametral convergence arrays. Subsequent routine measurements and control of the grouting operation were based largely on four line, diametral convergence arrays over the entire length of both tunnels. Average convergences of 7mm were achieved resulting in an initial tangential pre-stress of 20 - 25 MPa. Significant variability of prestress was observed around the tunnel circumference similar to that existing in the test chamber. Full details of the monitoring system and results are given by Eastwood and de Witt, 1982.

Checking of the long term performance of the tunnel linings is being carried out using a permanently monitored section as shown on Figure 9. This section contains remotely monitored embedded instrumentation similar to that installed in the prototype test chamber.

6.2 Initial Watering Up

Initial watering up (pressurisation) of tunnel-shaft 1/2 occurred over a 12 day period in January and February 1981. Filling was controlled to allow observations of lining behaviour and leakage to be made with increasing pressure.

Leakage rates from tunnel-shaft 1/2 were initially up to 0,5 litres/second decreasing with time as the linings and surrounding rock became fully saturated. The very low rate of overall leakage and the lack of seepage observed at the drainage tunnel (see figure 9) are indicative of the low permeability of the rock and the efficacy of the grouting procedures.

Strain changes observed in the lining at the permanent monitored section are shown on Figure 12. The response was extremely linear with pressure indicating overall elastic behaviour of the lining/rock structure as required by the design assumptions. A strain change rate of 40 microstrain/MPa was observed compared with some 50 microstrain/MPa for the test chamber. In relation to the deformability model (see Figure 7) conditions have been stiffer than expected, particularly bearing

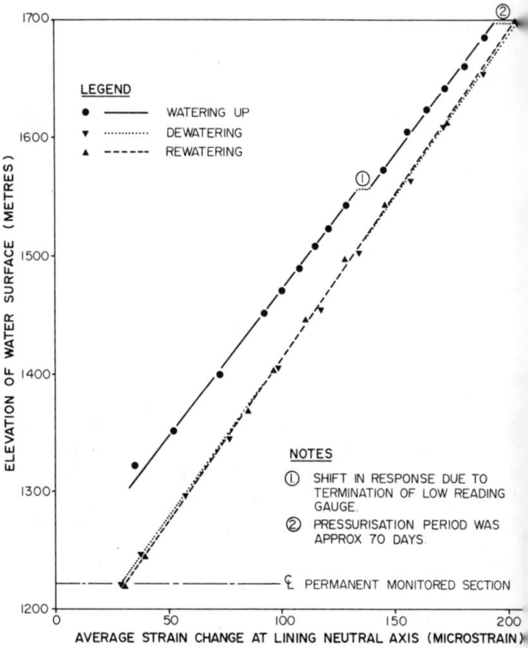

FIGURE 12 PRESSURE TUNNELS PERMANENT MONITORED SECTION - OBSERVED RESPONSE WATERING UP DEWATERING REWATERING

in mind the relatively adverse geological conditions at the permanent monitored section, owing to the presence of faulting. An overall rock modulus of some 20 GPa was inferred compared with 16 GPa for the test chamber.

6.3 Dewatering and Rewatering

Dewatering of tunnel 1/2 to permit inspection occurred some 3 months after initial pressurisation and commissioning. The lining strain response is shown on Figure 12 and indicates an expected linear response slightly stiffer than that for the initial watering up (37 microstrain/MPa).

Rewatering, which was carried out after a few days, produced a very similar strain response to dewatering as shown on Figure 12. An overall leakage test of tunnel-shaft 1/2 gave a leakage rate of 0,005 litres/second some two orders of magnitude less than that observed during initial watering up.

7 CONCLUSIONS

Construction and testing of a chamber in relatively weak argillaceous rocks has permitted a full understanding of the likely behaviour of high head concrete lined tunnels in such rock conditions. Representative loading, using water under pressure, was important in the correct determination of response, particularly at elevated pressures.

Expected deformability criteria for the lining/rock structure have been reliably assessed for use in the pressure tunnel design. The chamber and associated testing have allowed failure conditions for the lining to be reliably established for bedded rock which has been shown to be sensitive to hydrofracture effects.

Careful control of tunnel excavation and support has led to minimal disturbance to the rock profile and ensured that the maximum stiffness in the rock has been retained long term. High pressure grouting primarily by the interface method has led to improved stiffness of the lining/rock structure as well as imparting significant compressive stresses to resist cracking.

Observations of the tunnels during initial pressurisation and operation have confirmed the validity of extrapolating the test chamber results to elevated pressures and have thus substantiated the design assumptions.

ACKNOWLEDGEMENTS

The authors wish to thank the Electricity Supply Commission of South Africa for permission to publish this paper and Gibb Hawkins and Partners and Golder Associates for the material which has been used in its preparation. They also wish to acknowledge the extensive contribution of their many colleagues whose work is reported here.

REFERENCES

Bowcock, J.B. Boyd, J.M. Hoek, E. & J.C. Sharp 1976, Drakensberg Pumped Storage Scheme - Rock Engineering Aspects in Proc. Symposium on Exploration for Rock Engineering, Johannesburg.

Eastwood, M.T. & M.J. de Witt 1982, Concrete Waterway Linings for Drakensberg Pumped Storage Scheme (in press).

Golder Associates 1977a, Drakensberg Main Contract Design Report : Geology Vol I - VI.

Golder Associates 1977b, Drakensberg Main Contract Design Report : In Situ Stress Measurement Vol IX.

Gonano, L.P. & J.C. Sharp 1982, Measurement of In Situ Stresses in a Weak, Bedded Rock Mass (in press).

de Witt, M.J. 1982, Stress Relaxation in a Prestressed Concrete Pressure Tunnel Lining.

A FINITE ELEMENT MODEL FOR EXCAVATION, LINING AND LINING PRESTRESSING OF WATER POWER PLANT TUNNELS

Ein Finite-Element-Modell für den Ausbruch, die Auskleidung und die Vorspannung von Wasserkraftwerksstollen

Un modèle d'éléments finis pour le forage, le soutènement et la précontrainte des galeries des centrales hydroélectriques

DAN STEMATIU
Civil Engineering Institute, Bucharest, Romania
FLORIN LĂCĂTUŞ & RADU POPESCU
Water Power Design Institute, Bucharest, Romania

SUMMARY:
A rational design of the support and lining structures can be achived only if the load sharing capacity of the rock mass is taken as far as possible into consideration.
The proposed finite element model reproduces the structure-rock interaction phenomena. The rock mass can be nonhomogeneous and anisotropic and is considered to show viscous behaviour. The lining prestressing performed by grouting the surrounding rock with cement grout under high pressure is considered.
In the first part of the paper the performances of the mathematical model are analysed in terms of the numerical results and the field measurements for two Romanian water power tunnels. In the second part of the paper, detailed discussions of the lining prestressing parameters are given.

ZUSAMMENFASSUNG:
Eine rationelle Aufstellung von Aussteifungs- und Vermantelungsarbeiten der hydrotechnischen Stollen kann man nur dann durchführen, wenn man die Übernahmefähigkeit des Felsengesteines von äußeren Beanspruchungen in Betracht zieht.
Das vorgeschlagene mathematische Modell gibt Wechselwirkungserscheinungen zwischen der Struktur und dem Gesteinsmassiv wieder. Das Felsengestein kann ungleichartig und anisotrop sein, und man nimmt an, daß es ein dichtflüssig-elastisches Verhalten aufweist. Die Vorspannung der Verkleidung wird durch Einspritzen des umgebenden Felsengesteines mit Zementmilch unter Druck durchgeführt.
Im ersten Teil der Arbeit werden die Leistungen des vorgeschlagenen mathematischen Modells aufgrund des Vergleiches von Berechnungs- und Messungsergebnissen analysiert, die für zwei hydrotechnische, in Rumänien ausgeführte Stollen durchgeführt werden. Im zweiten Teil der Arbeit werden die Parameter, von denen die Vorspannung der Verkleidung abhängt, ausführlich behandelt.

RESUME:
Une étude raisonnable des travaux d'étoyage et de revêtement des galeries hydrotechniques n'est possible que si l'on envisage la capacité des roches de résister aux efforts extérieurs.
Le modèle mathématique proposé reproduit les phénomènes d'interaction entre la structure et le massif rocheux. La roche peut être non homogène et anisotrope et on lui attribue un comportement visco-élastique. La

précontrainte du revêtement est réalisée par l'injection de la roche avoisinante de lait de ciment sous pression.
Dans la première partie de l'ouvrage on analyse les performances du modèle mathématique proposé sur la base de la comparaison entre les résultats des calculs et ceux des mesures effectués pour deux galeries hydrotechniques mises en oeuvre en Roumanie. Dans la seconde partie de l'ouvrage on présente en détail les paramètres dont dépend la précontrainte du revêtement.

1 INTRODUCTION

For water power plant tunnels a rational design of the support and lining structures can be achived only if the load sharing capacity of the rock mass is taken as far as possible into consideration.

An elastic support structure, according with NATM principle, has the purpose of transforming the rock surrounding the tunnel profile from a load-exerting into a load-carrying member of the system. The lining structures of the pressure tunnels with large internal pressures are designed function of the amount of the pressure load which can be transfered to the rock mass. Basically, both unreinforced and reinforced concrete linings are quite unsuitable for one of the most important tasks, namely the prevention of water losses because of their low tensile strength. Consequently, a so-called passive prestressing is promoted, where the prestressing is produced by surrounding rock, as support or active element. In the last decades, for many pressure tunnels the prestress has been applied by grouting the surrounding rock mass and forcing the cement grout under high pressure into the rock cracks and discontinuities. The final lining stresses are dependent of the prestressing reduction due to the concrete creep, of the viscous flow of the rock mass and of the pressure rising schedule.

The proposed mathematical model, based on the finite element concept, takes into account all these structure - rock interaction phenomena. The behaviour of tunnel support and lining structures is analysed for plane strain conditions. The three-dimensional effects of the tunnel face advancing are taken into considerations by introducing the "equivalent initial stress" artifice. The rock mass can be nonhomogeneous and anisotropic, and is considered to show viscous behaviour associated with the deviatoric deformations during the excavation process, and with the radial deformations under the internal pressure loading. The rock bolting effects are reproduced by changing the elastic properties of the surrounding rock and introducing a radial anisotropy. The shotcrete placement effects are reproduced by introducing a ring of finite elements with in time increasing Young modulus, according to shotcrete grow in strength. The tunnel lining prestressing process is reproduced by considering the grout pressures as a hydrostatic state of residual stresses and then evaluating the lining stressing due to the residual stress relief. The time-dependent behaviour of both rock and lining is considered by the plastic flow of the concrete lining and by the rock stress relaxation.

The performances of the mathematical model are analysed in terms of the numerical results and field data for two Romanian water power tunnels. In the second part of the paper, detailed discussions of the lining prestressing parameters are given.

2 MATHEMATICAL MODEL

The finite element method under plane strain conditions is considered. The quadrilateral plane strain elements are used,having the incompatible displacement modes included at the element level (Bathe, Wilson 1976). The finite element mesh comprises the tunnel and the surrounding rock mass and the displacements of the mesh boundaries, at 4...8 diameters distance from the tunnel axis, are constrained. The initial stress state given by the overburden load or by in situ stresses is considered to be constant over the finite element mesh. The rock elastic properties are specified in accordance with the rock type and the distance from the tunnel axis, reproducing the crushed and the stress released zones of the rock mass (Stănucă 1976).

2.1 Material models

The time-dependent rock behaviour is simulated by means of the Kelvin's rheological models. During the excavation process the viscous behaviour of the rock mass is related to the deviatoric deformations (Ghaboussi, Gioda 1977). The parallel coupling of the spring and of the dashpot reproduces the viscous shear deformations and the serial coupled spring reproduces the instantaneous shear deformation (figure 1). Both dashpot and springs are assumed to have linear, time independent characteristics. The volumetric ground deformations are considered to follow the linear elastic behaviour. The viscous and elastic shear components are computed using a step-by-step time incremental analysis, assuming a constant stress $\tau(t)$ over each time step, equal to the stress defined at the end of the preceeding step:

$$\gamma_e(t+\Delta t) = \frac{\tau(t)}{G_1}$$

$$\gamma_v(t+\Delta t) = \gamma_v(t)\exp(-\frac{G_2}{\eta}\Delta t)+ \qquad (1)$$

$$\frac{\tau(t)}{G_2}\left[1-\exp(-\frac{G_2}{\eta}\Delta t)\right]$$

A simple procedure that allows the determination of the creep model constants is presented by Ghaboussi and Gioda.

Under the internal pressure loading the viscous behaviour of the rock mass is related to the radial deformations ε_r. The Kelvin model is similar to the one presented in figure 1 but the elastic and viscous parameters become E_1,

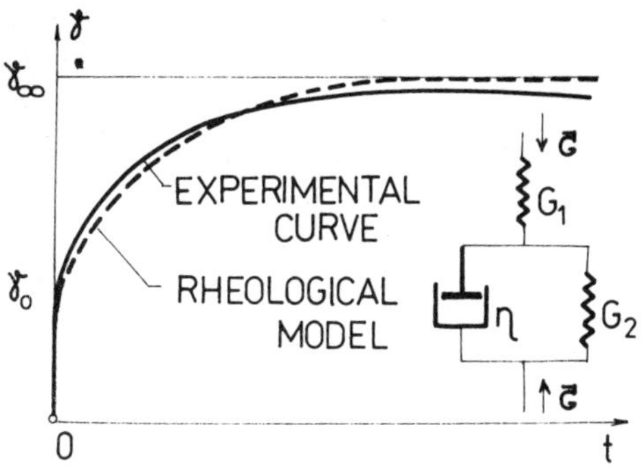

Figure 1. The rheological model for the viscous behaviour of the rock mass (after Gaboussi and Gioda 1977).

E_2 and η_r. The same step-by-step procedure with constant radial stress $\sigma_r(t)$ over each time step is accepted:

$$\varepsilon_{e,r}(t+\Delta t) = \frac{\sigma_r(t)}{E_1} \qquad (2)$$

$$\varepsilon_{v,r}(t+\Delta t) = \varepsilon_{v,r}(t)\exp(-\frac{E_2}{\eta_r}\Delta t)+$$

$$\frac{\sigma_r(t)}{E_2}\left[1-\exp(-\frac{E_2}{\eta_r}\Delta t)\right]$$

The time dependent shotcrete behaviour is related to the in time increasing Young modulus $E_s(t)$ in accordance with the shotcrete grow in strength. At the time t_i after the shotcrete placement, the Young modulus has the value:

$$E_s(t_i) = E_{so}\left[1-\exp(-kt_i)\right], \qquad (3)$$

where E_{so} is the final elasticity modulus and k depends on the shotcrete recipe.

The time dependent lining concrete behaviour is related to the plastic flow under the tangential compressive stresses $\sigma_t(t)$. As-

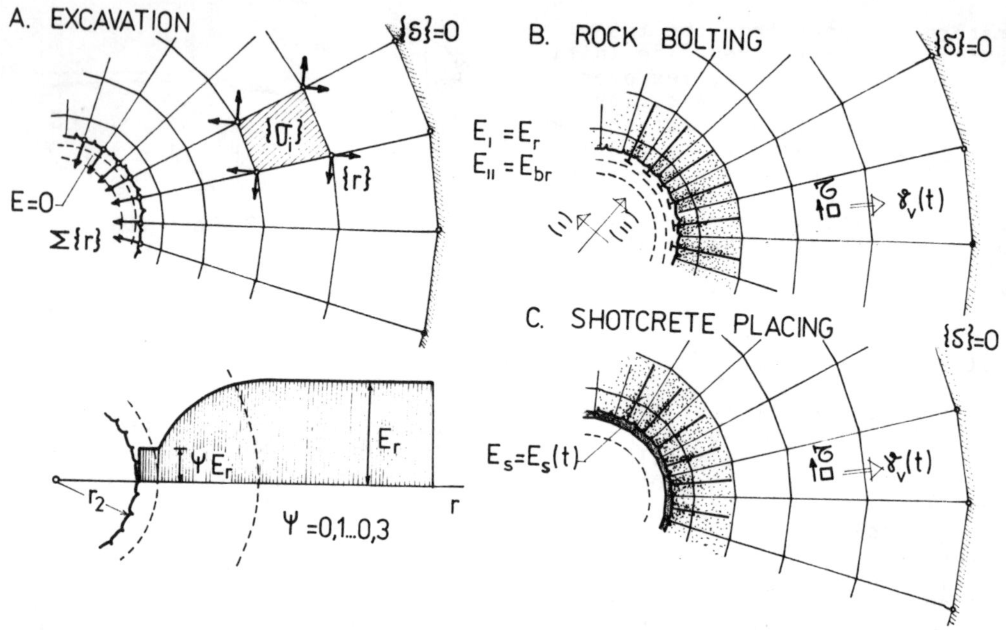

Figure 2.The excavation,rock bolting and shotcrete placement algorithm.

suming a constant stress $\sigma_t(t)$ over the time increment Δt, the creep deformation can be determined in accordance with the experimental relationship obtained for the concrete arches under uniform external pressure (Straub 1960):

$$\varepsilon_c(t+\Delta t) = 56.7 \times 10^{-10} \times \left[a\,\sigma_t(t)\right]^{1.3}(t+\Delta t)^{0.4} \quad (4)$$

where a = 0.0689 and σ_t is expressed in daN/cm^2. There is no plastic flow under the tangential tensile stresses.

2.2 Excavation, shotcreting and lining modelling

The usual finite element procedures are accepted (figure 2). The rock mass is divided into 16 zones, each zone being characterized by a certain ratio R_E between the Young modulus at the given time step and the Young modulus of the initial state. The stiffness matrices of the rock zones are previously asambled using the Young moduli of the initial state. When the total stiffness is asambled, the zone stiffness matrices are multiplied with the "activity" ratio R_E. During the excavation process the finite elements of the excavating zone become inactive and the activity ratio R_E = 0. At the shotcrete placement the corresponding zone becomes an active one and the activity ratio R_E is time dependent, in accordance with the in time increasing shotcrete modulus given by the relationship (3). At the concrete lining placement the corresponding zone becomes an active one, but with a constant value of the activity ratio R_E. Following the same procedure the heading in stages as well as the partial aplying of the support structures can be modeled.

2.3 Rock stress relief and relaxation modelling

At the moment of the tunnel face excavation an analysis is performed to make the peripheral plane of the tunnel a stress-free surface, by releasing the initial stresses $\sigma_i = (\sigma_o \, \sigma_v \, o)$. The equivalent nodal forces:

$$R_e = -\Sigma \int_V B^T \sigma_i \, dV \qquad (5)$$

become the external load and the total stiffness matrix K_E is defined in accordance with the innactive excavated zone (figure 2,A). The equilibrium equation

$$K_E \, \delta_e = R_e \qquad (6)$$

gives the elastic displacements δ_e and the stress relief $\Delta\sigma_e = EB^e\delta_e$. The new stress state is $\sigma_o = \sigma_i - \Delta\sigma_e$.

The development of the time-dependent viscous displacements and the rock stress relaxation are determined by using the step-by-step time incremental analysis. For the time step Δt the viscous shear deformation $\gamma_v(t+\Delta t)$ is given by the relationship (1) and then the viscous strain vector ε_v is computed assuming a constant volumetric strain $(\varepsilon_x + \varepsilon_y)_{\Delta t} = (\sigma_x + \sigma_y)_{t+\Delta t}$. The strain increment $\Delta\varepsilon_v = \varepsilon_v(t+\Delta t) - \varepsilon_v(t)$ is used to evaluate the equivalent nodal forces

$$\Delta R_v = -\Sigma \int_V B^T E \, \Delta\varepsilon_v \, dV \qquad (7)$$

which become the external load. The equilibrium equation

$$K_E \, \Delta\delta_v = \Delta R_v \qquad (8)$$

gives the viscous displacement increments $\Delta\delta_v$ and the stress relaxation within the rock mass $\Delta\sigma_v = E\,(B\,\Delta\delta_v - \Delta\varepsilon_v)$.

2.4 Progress of the tunnel face modelling

The tunnel face advancing introduces a three-dimensional behaviour of the deformation phenomenon as displacements develope in accordance with the progress of the tunnel face. The radial displacements along the tunnel axis are shown in figure 3,A, for a circular in shape tunnel driven in an elastic ground. One can notice the displacements of a given cross section (say s-s) develope during the tunneling process, and if the rate of advancing is constant the displacements shows a time-dependent evolution (figure 3,B). For the choosen cross section S-S the initial stress, can be considered as a time-dependent stress, given by the approximate relationship (Sakurai 1978):

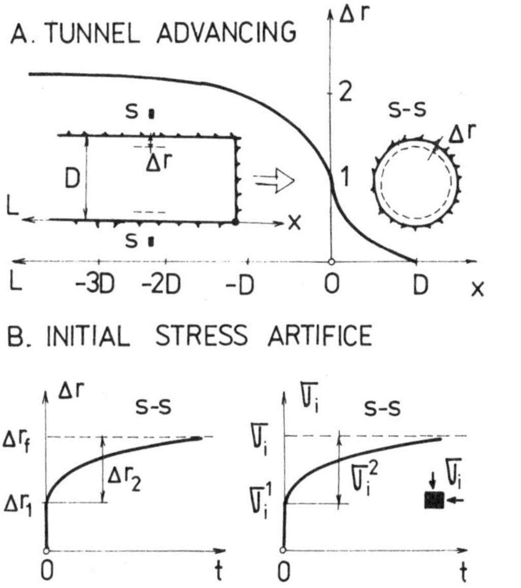

Figure 3. The "equivalent initial stress" procedure (after Sakurai 1978).

$$\sigma_i(t) = \sigma_i^1 + \sigma_i^2 \left[1-\exp(-t/f)\right] \quad (9)$$

where f is a parameter function of the advansing rate. The initial stress in relationship (9) is considered the "equivalent initial stress". For a medium quality rock with $\mu \leq 0{,}3$, the usual proportions are $\sigma_i^1 = 0.3\,\sigma_i$ and $\sigma_i^2 = 0.7\,\sigma_i$. Using that equivalent initial stress artifice the tunnel behaviour in a given cross section can be analysed under the plane strain condition if at each time step Δt the viscous displacement analysis - relationships (7) and (8) - is made after a stress relief analysis - relationships (5) and (6) - where the initial stress σ_i is replaced by $\Delta\sigma_i = \sigma_i(t+\Delta t) - \sigma_i(t)$.

2.5 Rock bolting modelling

Within the finite element zone affected by the rock bolting the elastic properties are changed. A radial anisotropy is considered, the Young moduli along the bolting direction being given by:

$$E_{br} = E_r A_r + E_b A_b \quad (10)$$

where E_r and E_b are the Young moduli of the rock mass and of the bolts respectively, and A_r and A_b are the rock and the bolt areas corresponding to a unit radial area (figure 2,B). The total stiffness matrix is reevaluated and the development of viscous displacements is determined following the same procedure as in the section 2.3. After the shotcrete placement the total stiffness matrix is reevaluated in accordance with the in time changing of the shotcrete Young modulus given by relationship (3) (figure 2,C).

2.6 Lining prestressing modelling

The tunnel lining is considered to be applied after the rock stress relaxation has been completed. The rock grouting, with cement grout under high pressure which penetrates behind the tunnel lining into the surrounding rock mass, has two distinctive effects: rock mass consolidation and tunnel lining prestressing.

In order to evaluate the prestressing effect, within the finite elements located in the grouted zone, a residual hydrostatic stress state is considered, as beeing equal to the grout pressure p acting at the element level The grout pressures are determined by a steady flow seepage analysis, specifying as boundary conditions the grouting pressure along the injection drillings and zero pressure at the finite element mesh boundaries. The residual stresses, given by the grout pressure acting into the rock mass cracks and fissures, are then released. The equivalent nodal forces:

$$R_p = -\sum \int_V B^T\, p\, dV \quad (11)$$

become the external load and the total stiffness matrix K_L comprises the lining and the rock mass finite element zones (figure 4,A). The usual procedure:

$$K_L\, \delta_g = Rp$$
$$\sigma_l = EB\, \delta_{g,\text{lining}} \quad (12)$$

gives the grouting displacements δ_g and the lining prestressing stresses σ_l.

The δ_g displacements bring about at the same time a decreasing of the grouting stresses $\Delta p_i = p - \sigma_m$, where $\sigma_m = 0.5 \times (\sigma_x + \sigma_y)$ and σ_x, σ_y are the stress normal components of the stress tensor $\sigma = E\,B\,\delta_g$, rock. As during the grouting process the grout pressures are kept constant, the additional pressure Δp_i is again replaced by the equivalent nodal forces ΔR_i, acting at the finite element nodes where $\Delta p_i > 0$:

$$\Delta R_i = -\sum \int_V B^T \Delta p_i\, dV \quad (13)$$

and the additional prestressing stresses $\Delta\sigma_{li}$ are determined from relationships (12). There is an iterative process, and the new equilibrium state is reached when the additional stresses $\Delta\sigma_{li}$ become insignificant.

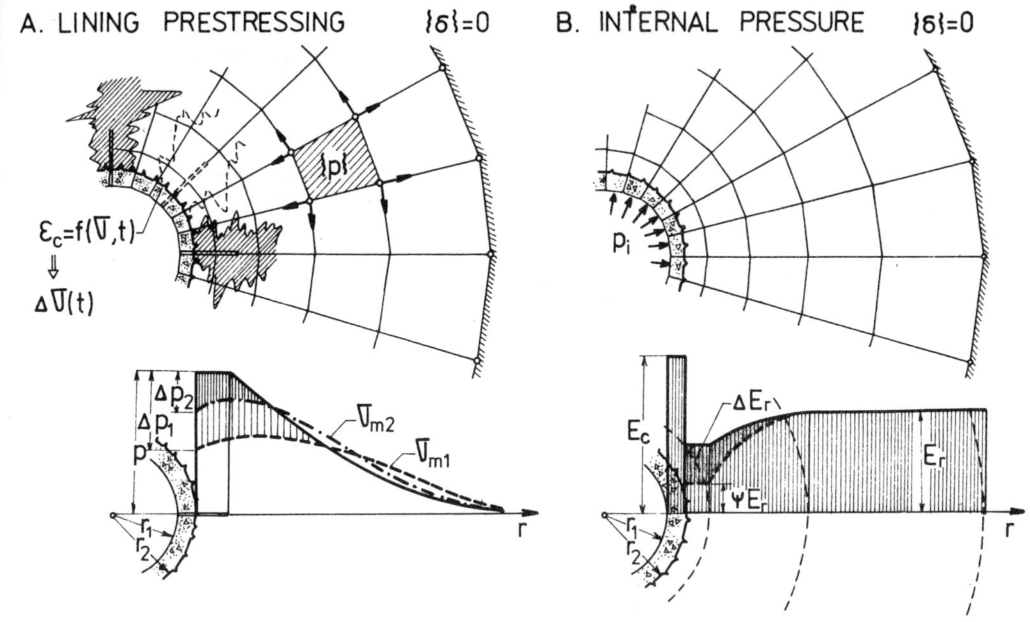

Figure 4. The lining prestressing and pressure loading algorithm.

At the grout hardening, the rock elastic properties of the grouted zone are improved (figure 4,B). It is assumed that Young modulus of the surrounding rock is 1.5 up to 2.5 times as large as the one of the original disturbed rock.

The lining prestressing effects undergo an in time decreasing due to the lining concrete creep. In the analysis, at each time step Δt the creep deformation $\Delta\varepsilon_c$ is computed in accordance with the relationship (4) and then using the relationships (7) and (8) the resulting displacements $\Delta\delta_c$ bring the reduction of the lining pre-stressing stresses $\Delta\sigma_1 = E_c \times (B\,\Delta\delta_c - \Delta\varepsilon_c)$.

2.7 Rising of the internal pressure modelling

The internal pressure, step-wise applied, acts as an uniform load on the lining intrados (figure 4,B). After each pressure step Δp a stress relaxation takes place as a consequence of the time-dependent viscous deformation of the rock mass. The same step-by-step time incremental procedure is used, as described in section 2.3. The strain increment $\Delta\varepsilon_v$ in relationship (7) is now given by the viscous flow equations (2).

3. EXCAVATION AND ELASTIC SUPPORT SIMULATION

In order to verify the mathematical model capableness, several excavation and support placement analyses have been performed.
A circular in shape tunnel,driven in a homogeneous, isotropic rock mass has been considered. The tunnel diameter is 6.0 m, and the rock properties as well as the discretization mesh are given in figure 5. The same figure presents some of the numerical results of the performed analyses. One can notice the effect of the rock bolting and of the shotcrete placement on the in time development of the radial displacements. The shotcrete axial thrust presents a slow increase in the first days, in accordance with the reduced Young modulus, and then reaches a quasi-constant value as the radial displacements stabilize. The radial stress σ_r and the tangential stress

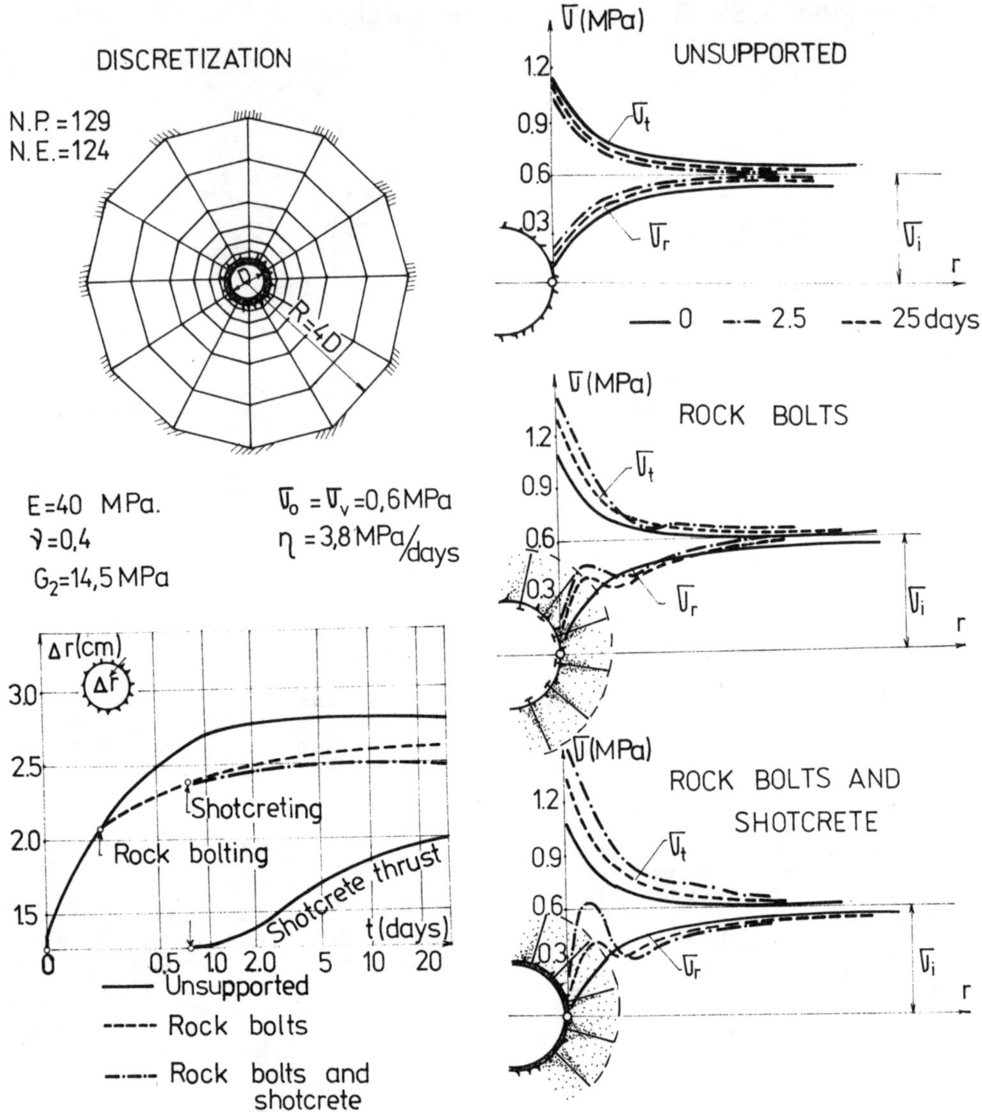

Figure 5. The modelling of the excavation and support instalation for a circular tunnel driven in a homogeneous, isotropic rock.

σ_t distributions within the rock mass show the well known pattern in the case of the unsupported tunnel. The rock bolting and the shotcrete placement especially bring about a significant time-dependent increase of the radial stresses within the bolted rock ring. Thus the load-carrying rock ring is revealed.

The tailrace tunnel of the Sasciori water power plant has been chosen for the next analysis in order to compare the numerical results with the field measurements. The tunnel cross section has a horseshoe shape, the rock mass is nonhomogeneous and anisotropic, prevailing the weak sandstones and the conglomerates (figure 6). The excavation is completed in three succesive stages. The discretization mesh reproduces the tunnel geometry, the excavation phases and the rock anisotropy in accordance with the field schistosity. The analysed cross section correspondes to a measurement section, provided for convergence measurements and extensometer readings as is shown in figure 7.

The comparison between the analysis results and the field data is presented in figure 7. The rock mass properties have been selected in accordance with some field tests and based on the interpretation of the field data: E_1 = 200 MPa, E_2 = 100 MPa, G_1 = 40 MPa, G_2 = 100 MPa, η = 150 MPa/day, σ_o = 0.55 MPa, σ_v = 1.1 MPa. For lack of significant field tests no distinction has been made between the sandstone and conglomerate properties. The 4 m base length extensometer measurements are in a good agreement with the numerical results when the extensometer anchoring is made

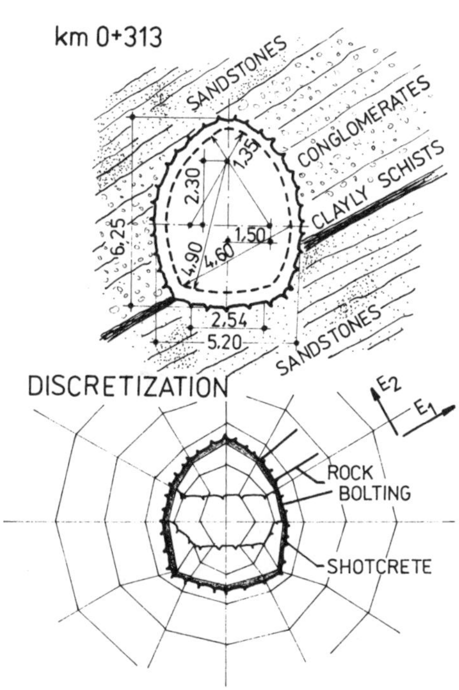

Figure 6. The analysed cross section for Sasciori tailrace tunnel.

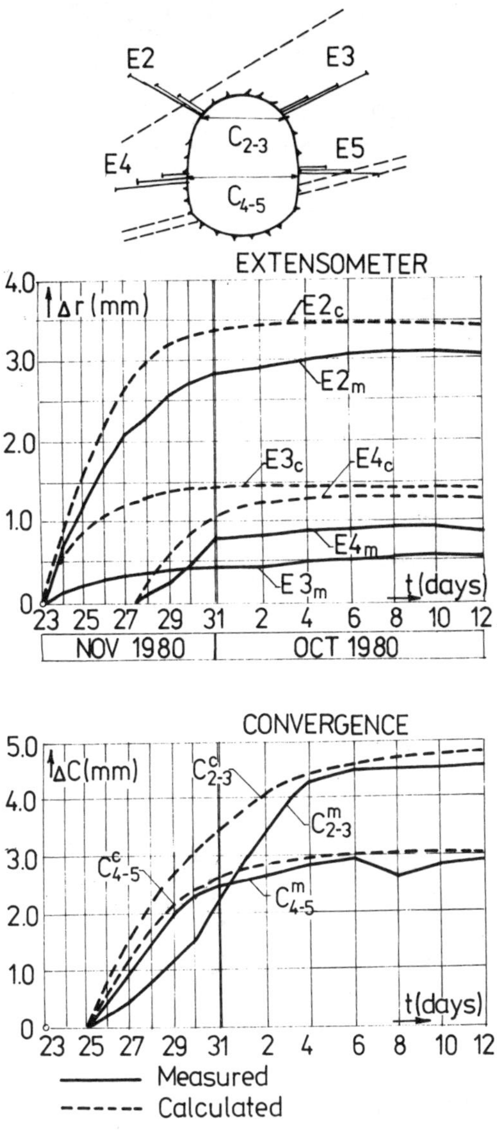

Figure 7. Numerical results and field measurement for Sasciori tailrace tunnel.

within the sandstones, and presents significant differences when the anchoring point is placed within the conglomerates. The convergence movement measurements are in a very good agreement with the analysis results, validating the model capableness to reproduce the global behaviour.

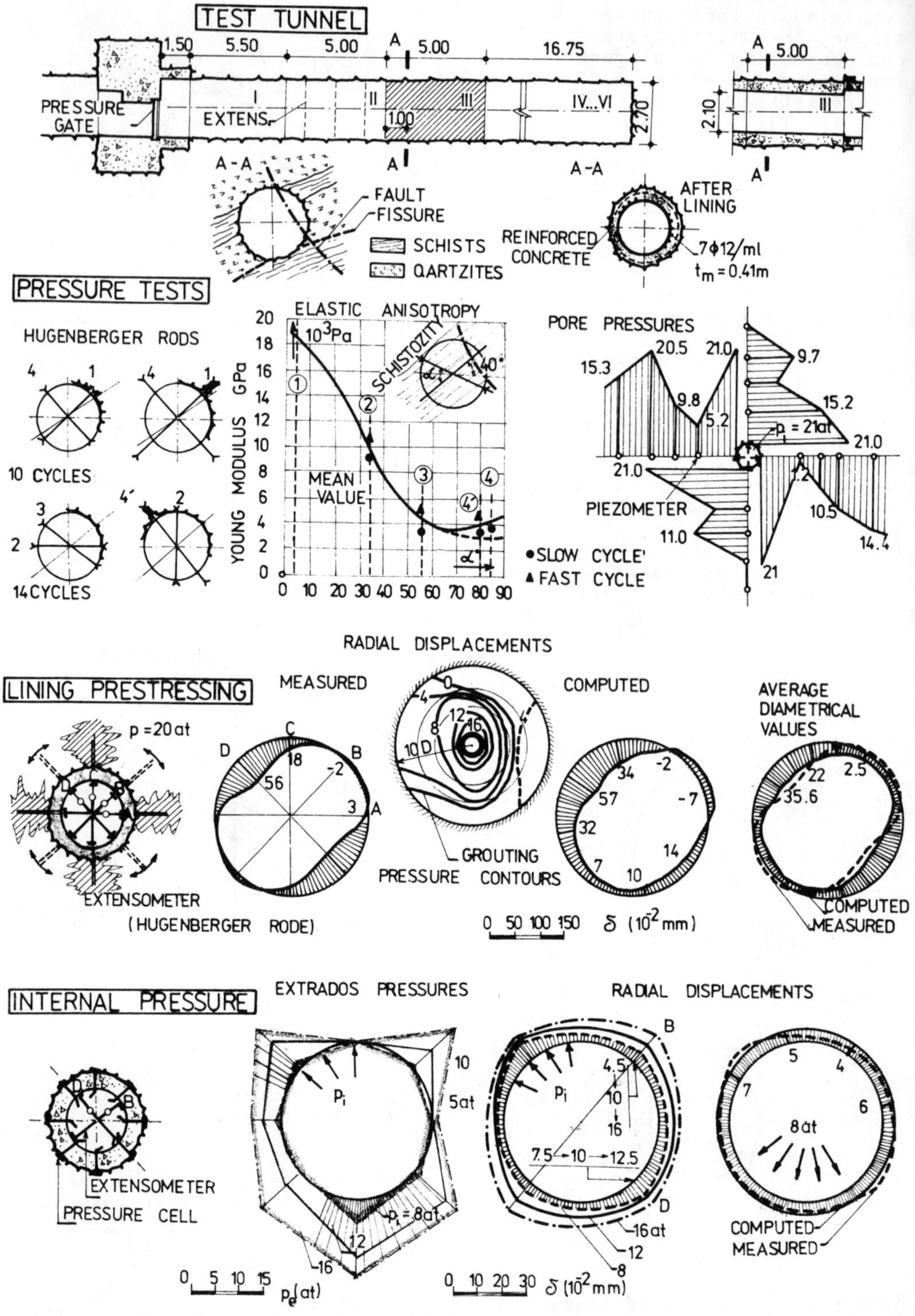

Figure 8. Numerical results and field measurements for the test tunnel.

4 PRESTRESSING AND PRESSURE LOADING SIMULATION

The performances of the mathematical model are discussed on the basis of the comparison between the field measurements and the analysis results obtained for a test tunnel driven in the vecinity of the headrace tunnel and the pressure shaft of the Lotru power plant. The tunnel dimmensions, the geological situation and the main field data and numerical results are shown in figure 8.

The analysed cross section A-A is located within the tunnel section III, driven in a zone of schists and quartzites with a schistosity orientation at about 40° from the horizontal plane. A well marked fault, normal oriented to the schistosity, crosses the tunnel line. After the preliminary tests performed in the unlined tunnel, a reinforced concrete lining have been installed.

The elastic and permeability properties of the rock mass have been determined on the basis of the internal pressure tests realized in the unlined tunnel. The Hugenberger rode readings for 24 pressure rising cycles have furnished the Young moduli along the different directions from the schistosity plane (Vlăduţ, Gane 1979). The Young moduli variation function of the measurement directions have allowed the defining of the anisotropy ratio E_1/E_2 = 19 000 MPa/4000 MPa = 4.75. The piezometer readings at different locations within the rock mass have furnished the pore pressures for several internal pressures and have rendered evident a permeability anisotropy due to the schistosity and mainly due to the crossing fault.

The lining prestressing due to the surrounding rock grouting has been indirectly determined, by measuring the diametrical deformations of the lining intrados. The injection drillings, of 1.5 m depth, are located along the two normal diameters, alternating from one grouting plane to the other. The grouting pressure was 20 at and the average diametrical deformations showed a maximum value of 0.56 mm normal orientated related to the rock mass schistosity (figure 8). A prestressing modelling analysis has been performed for the same test tunnel. The elastic and anisotropy properties of the rock mass are those determined on the basis of the internal pressure tests carried out in the unlined tunnel. The grout pressures within the rock mass are accepted to be the same with the water pore pressures determined during the above mentioned tests. The grout pressure contours drawn in accordance with this assumption are shown in the figure 8. The analysis results render evident a nonuniform distribution of the radial displacements, with the maximum values located at the left zone of the tunnel crown, due to the elastic and permeability anisotropy. The comparison between the average values of the computed diametrical displacements and the field measured values shows a good agreement. The displacement patterns are the same and the mean differences do not exceed 25%.

For the lined tunnel subjected to the hydrostatic water pressure, the field measurements have furnished the diametrical displacements and the water pressures acting on the lining extrados. One can notice that internal pressures less than 8 at do not lead to significant leakages of water into the surrounding rock, the extrados pressures are negligable and the radial displacements are in accordance with the elastic anisotropy. When the internal pressure exceed 8...10 at the extrados pressures are of the same order of magnitude with the internal ones, and their nonuniform distribution leads to a different pattern of the radial displacements. The internal pressure modelling analysis has been performed for an internal pressure of 8 at, in order to obtain a significant comparison. The field data and the numerical results are in a very good agreement.

As a whole, the presented comparisons validate the proposed mathematical model and render evident the model capableness to reproduce the lining - rock mass interaction phenomena for pressure tunnels driven in nonhomogeneous and anisotropic ground.

5 PRESTRESSING PARAMETERS

In lining of pressure tunnels and shafts driven in weak grounds and subjected to large internal pressures, the prestressed concrete lining can be a complete and economical substitute for the traditional steel lining. In Romania, as in some other European countries, the prestressing is usually performed by grouting the surrounding rock mass with cement grout under high pressure, which penetrates into the rock fissures and cracks. As against the Kieser and TIWAG methods, where the prestressing is applied through the agency of a hydraulic pressure acting in a cavity between the core ring and the supporting rock, the rock mass

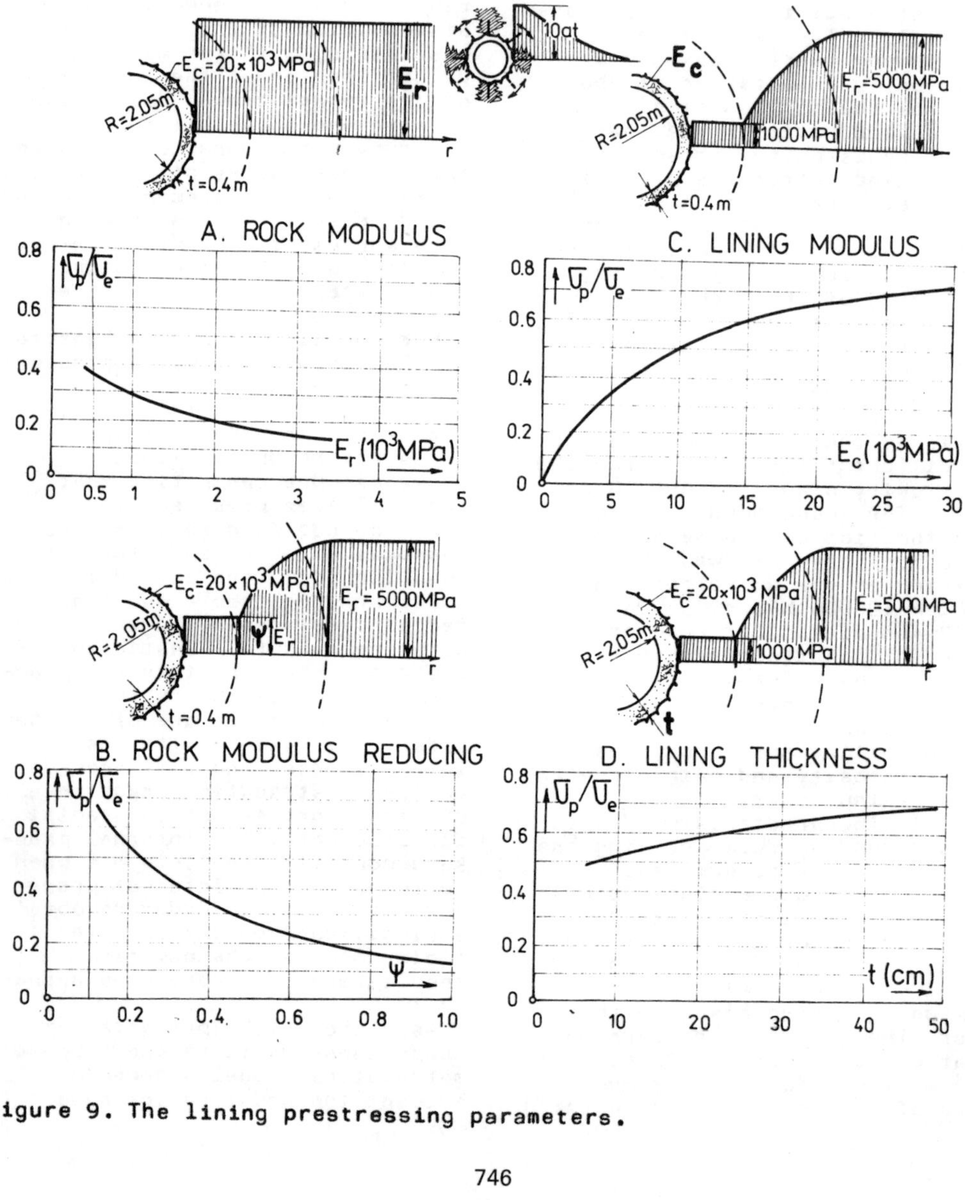

Figure 9. The lining prestressing parameters.

becomes the active element of the prestressing process. However, the traditional design methods evaluate the prestressing stresses considering the tunnel lining subjected to an extrados pressure equal to 0.3...0.6 of the grouting pressure. The 40...70% reduction of the grouting pressure is taken on empirical basis, disregarding the rock properties and the lining design. In the followings, the prestressing effects in accordance with the rock and lining parameters are analysed, on the basis of the proposed mathematical model. In order to refer the numerical results to the traditional design method the prestressing effects are expressed as a ratio between the computed stresses σ_p and the stresses σ_e given by an extrados pressure equal to the grouting pressure.

The figure 9 shows the analyses results obtained in the case of a circular pressure tunnel, with an internal diameter of 4.1 meters, driven in a homogeneous isotropic rock.

If the surrounding rock is undisturbed during the tunneling process, as it hapends in the case of the fullface boring, the prestressing effects significantly depend on the rock Young modulus (figure 9,A). The weaker the rock mass the larger the lining prestressing. When the rock modulus $E_r \geqslant 5000$ MPa the prestressing effects are less than 10% of the theoretical ones, given by the extrados acting pressures.

If the drilling and blasting tunneling method is used, a ring of disturbed rock surrounds the tunnel section. The Young modulus of the disturbed rock mass decreases to ψE_r, where $\psi < 1$ (Stănucă 1976). The prestressing effects depend on the rock disturbance degree, increasing when the surrounding rock modulus decreases (figure 9,B). It follows the lining prestressing by rock grouting is very adequate for the blasting excavated tunnels, where the rock grouting leads also to the rock mass consolidation.

The elapsed time between the lining concreting and the prestressing process can be expressed by the Young modulus of the lining, which increases with the concrete age (figure 9,C). One can notice the prestressing effects are reduced if the rock grouting is realized at short time intervals after the lining instalation, due to the reduced stiffness of the lining. As a consequence, the rock grouting is recomanded to be performed after 40...60 days since the lining concreting in order to acquire the desired prestressing.

The lining thickness affects also the prestressing effects (figure 9,D). The stiffer the lining, the larger the lining prestressing. However, the thickness variation in the usual lining thickness range does not affect significantly the prestressing effects.

The influence of the elastic and permeability anisotropy is discussed on the basis of the analyses results presented in figure 10. For the same circular pressure tunnel a certain schistosity has been considered. The corresponding permeability anisotropy is $K_2 = 100\,K_1$ and several degrees of elastic anisotropy are assumed. The grout pressure contours and the resulted radial displacements, liner thrusts and bending moments are presented. One can notice that when the elastic anisotropy is reduced ($E_1/E_2 < 1.5$) the radial displacements and the prestressing stresses are in accordance with the grout pressure pattern. When the elastic anisotropy increases, the radial displacements are larger at the tangency points between the tunnel lining and the schistosity plane. The lining stresses and bending moments change accordingly.

6 CONCLUDING REMARKS

6.1 The proposed mathematical model reproduces the support structure - rock mass interaction and the tunnel lining - rock mass interaction during the tunneling, prestressing and tunnel loading processes.

6.2 The comparison between the analyses results and the field measurements performed for the

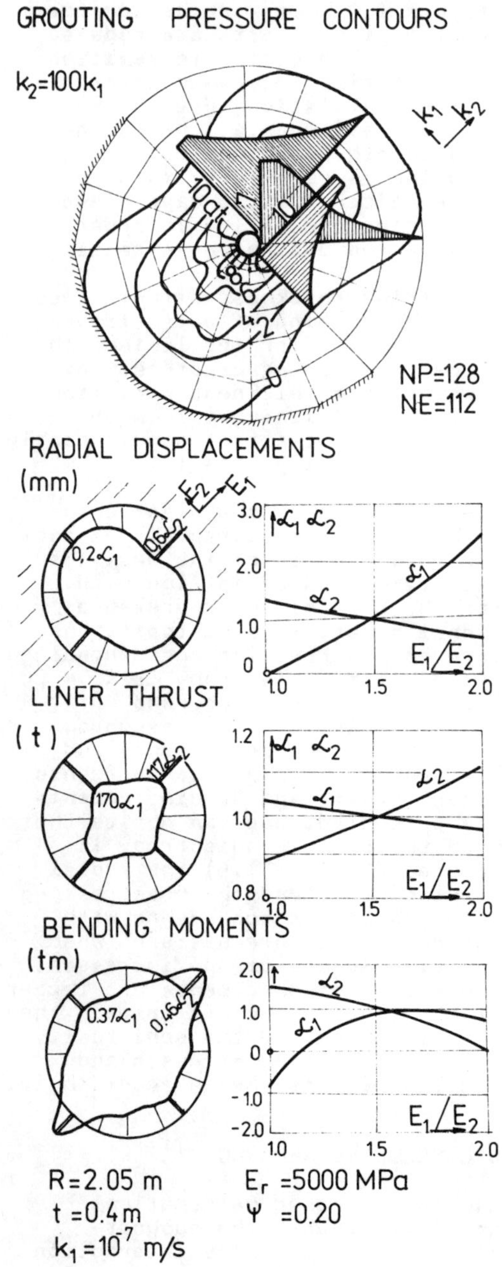

Figure 10. The influence of the elastic and permeability anisotropy on the prestressing effect.

Sasciori tailrace tunnel and the Lotru test tunnel render evident the capableness of the model.

6.3 When the lining prestressing is performed by grouting the surrounding rock with cement grout under high pressure the rock mass becomes the active element of the prestressing process. As against the Kieser and TIWAG methods the prestressing effects depend on the rock elastic properties, on the rock disturbance degree, on the lining age and thickness and on the rock mass anisotropy.

7 REFERENCES

Bathe, K.J. and Wilson, E.L. 1976, Numerical methods in finite element analysis, Prentice Hall, New Jersey.

Stanuca, A. 1976, Contributions to rock - tunnel lining interaction for pressure tunnels (in Romanian), PhD thesis,Civil. Eng.Inst.of Bucharest.

Ghaboussi, I. and Gioda, G. 1977, On the time-dependent effects in advancing tunnels,Int.Journ. for Numerical and analytical methods in geomechanics, Vol.1, No.3.

Straub, L. 1960, Plastic flow in concrete arches, Journ.ASCE - Struct.Div.vol.8.

Sakurai, S. 1978, Approximate time dependent analysis of tunnel support structures considering progress of tunnel face, Int. Journ.for Numerical and analytical methods in geomechanics, Vol.2, No.2.

Vladuţ, I.T. and Gane, S. 1979, Field measurements for a test pressure tunnel, Report to ISPH-Bucharest.

DETERMINATION OF OPTIMAL SHAPE OF UNDERGROUND OPENINGS AT HIGH INTERNAL PRESSURE AROUND ITS CONTOUR

Bestimmung der optimalen Hohlraumform bei hohem Innendruck

Détermination de la forme optimale des cavités souterraines de pression interne élevée autour de leurs contours

N.P.VLOKH & A.V.ZOUBKOV
Institute of Mining, Sverdlovsk, USSR

SUMMARY:
It is suggested to provide the underground structures, which are designed for a high internal pressure of gas or water, an elliptical form in cross section where the minor axis of an ellipse must coincide with the direction of actoin of the greatest compression in a rock mass. The relationship for a ratio of ellipse axes against stresses, acting in a rock mass, rock strength and internal pressure is presented. It is recommended to determine the stresses in a rock mass during tunnel construction by measuring it when driving an exploration drift along the path of a tunnel. A method of stress determination in a rock mass based on the use of stress change at the face of a driven opening is presented.

ZUSAMMENFASSUNG:
Es ist vorgeschlagen, den Untergrundbauten die sich unter hohem Innendruck von Wasser und Gas befinden, elliptische Form im Schnitt zu geben, wobei kleine Ellipsachse mit der Richtung des maximalen Zusammanpressens im Gebirge zusammenfallen soll. Es ist die Abhängkeit des Verhältnisses der Ellipsachsen von Spannungen im Gebirgsmassiv, der Gebirgsfestigkeit und des Innendruckes gegeben. Es ist sinnvoll, die Gebirgsspannungen beim Tunnelbau während der Erkundungsarbeiten auf der Tunneltrasse zu bestimmen. Es ist die Methode der Bestimmung der Gebirgsspannungen gegeben, in der die Veränderungen der Spannungen in der Sohle des durchgeführten Streckes berücksichtigt sind.

RESUME:
Pour les chantiers sousterrains, soumis a de fortes pressions d'eau et de gaz, les auteurs preconisent une forme ellipsoidale dont le petit axe de l'ellipse coinciderait avec la propagation de la pression maximale de la masse rocheuse. A ete formulee la correlation entre les contraintes dans la masse rocheuse, la durete de la roche, les pressions internes et les axes de l'ellipse. Il serait interessant d'evaluer les contraintes dans la masse rocheuse lors de l'avancement d'une galerie de prospection suivant le trace du tunnel. Les auteurs proposent egalement la methode de determination des contraintes dans la masse rocheuse resultant de la variation des contraintes au front de taille d'une galerie an avancement.

The stability of underground openings largely depends on its shape, determination the parameters of which at high internal pressure is based upon the knowledge of values and directions for the principal normal stresses in a rock mass (σ_1^m and σ_2^m).

In order to determine these stresses it is recommended to use deformational analytical methods, this causing the need in the Knowledge of elasticity moduli of a rock in a piece (E_k) and in mass (E_m).

The results of the research work carried out in the Institute of Mining under the Ministry of Ferrous Metallurgy of the USSR confirm the point that all hard rocks are elastic both in a piece and in mass. Therefore the methods from the theory of elasticity can be used in the solution of problems in the field of rock mechanics. It has been found also that moduli of elasticity in a rock mass are defined as $E_m = (0.5 - 0.9)E_k$.

The method based on the use of deformation of an opening during its excavation has been developed in the Institute for the operative determination of stresses in a rock mass within large base (or area of measurements). For the case of a circular opening the formulas for determination of stresses are given by

$$\sigma_{1,2}^m = \frac{E_m}{D}\left(\frac{\Delta U_I + \Delta U_{III}}{2(A+B)} \pm \right.$$

$$\left. \pm \frac{1}{2(A-B)}\sqrt{(\Delta U_I - \Delta U_{III})^2 + [2\Delta U_{II} - (\Delta U_I + \Delta U_{III})]^2}\right),$$

$$\theta = \frac{1}{2} arctg \frac{2\Delta U_{II} - (\Delta U_I + \Delta U_{III})}{\Delta U_{III} - \Delta U_I},$$

where $\Delta U_I = U_I - U_I' - \sigma_o C \frac{D}{E_m}$;

$$\Delta U_{II} = U_{II} - U_{II}' - \sigma_o C \frac{D}{E_m};$$

$$\Delta U_{III} = U_{III} - U_{III}' - \sigma_o C \frac{D}{E_m};$$

$$A = 3(1-\mu^2) - K_{\parallel} + K_{\perp}\cdot\mu;$$

$$B = -(1-\mu^2) - K_{\perp} + K_{\parallel}\cdot\mu;$$

$$C = -K_o(1-\mu^2);$$

U_I, U_{II}, U_{III} - dimension of an opening in section, respectively, in horizontal direction, vertical direction and at an angle of 45° to both when the face is away from this place at a distance of over one opening's diameter (D);

U_I', U_{II}', U_{III}' - the same dimension but when the face coincide with the area of measurements;

μ - the Poisson's ratio of a rock

D - diameter of an opening;

σ_o - stresses in a rock mass along the axis of an opening (may be measured on the wall of an opening).

$K_{\parallel} = 1.67$, $K_{\perp} = -0.08$, $K_o = -0.38$ at $\mu = 0.2$.

$K_{\parallel} = 1.57$, $K_{\perp} = -0.07$, $K_o = -0.46$ at $\mu = 0.3$

$K_{\parallel} = 1.50$, $K_{\perp} = -0.08$, $K_o = -0.53$ at $\mu = 0.4$

θ - an angle which determine the direction of action of σ_1^m and which is taken from the horizontal direction (I-I) in a clockwise manner.

Providing that vertical and horizontal stresses on the wall of an opening are additionally determine with an account for the determined deformations of an opening during its excavation one can get the values of σ_1^m, σ_2^m, θ and E_m.

It is recommended to carry out these experiments in an exploratic drift which has been driven along the path of a tunnel and can be consequently worked out to full planned cross section.

It is desirable at high internal pressure to provide the tunnels ar shafts in an elliptical form where the major axis of an ellipse must be directed perpendicularly to the direction of action of the greates compression in a rock mass (σ_2^m).

The ratio of semi-axes of an ellipse can be found from the follow ing expression:

$$\frac{a}{b} \geq \frac{2(\gamma - 1)}{\gamma + \lambda - 1 - \frac{[\sigma]_p}{\sigma_2^m}} \geq$$

$$\geq \frac{1 + \gamma - \lambda - \frac{[\sigma]_p}{\sigma_2^m}}{2(\gamma - 1)},$$

where a, b-are the major and minor semi-axes of an ellipse, respectively;

$$\gamma = \frac{P}{\sigma_2^m} ;$$

$$\lambda = \frac{\sigma_1^m}{\sigma_2^m} ;$$

P-is the internal pressure;
$[\sigma]_p$-is the tension strength of a rock.

In this case the tension stresses around the tunnel contour do not exceed $[\sigma]_p$ and the costs of supporting the opening will be at minimum, i.e. it will be sufficient to cover the walls of an opening around its contour with a hydroisolating material.

A rectangular-elliptical opening having the same height to width ratio as an elliptical one will sustend less pressure and the values of maximum stresses around the contour of such an opening during its excavation (without internal pressure) can be 1.2-2 times higher than those for an elliptical one. An elliptical opening has therefore certain advantages over an rectangular-elliptical one both from the point of view of providing greater internal pressure and less stresses during its excavation.

The reciprocal solution of the formula 1 provides the possibility to find the deformation arising during the excavation of an opening and to determine the probability of squeesing the tunnelling machine with the cutting wheel designed for boring to full cross section.

THE INFLUENCE OF HISTORY OF WATER LOAD ON TUNNEL STRESSES

Der Einfluss der Belastungsgeschichte aus Wasserdruck auf die Tunnelspannungen

L'influence de la charge provenant de la poussée d'eau antérieure sur les contraintes du tunnel

ZHANG YOUTIAN & ZHANG WUGONG

Water Conservancy & Hydroelectric Power Scientific Research Institute, Beijing, China

SUMMARY:
The influence of history of water load on tunnel stresses is discussed from the point that water load on tunnel is seepage body force, corresponding calculation method is proposed and an engineering project designed by this method is given as an example.

ZUSAMMENFASSUNG:
Die Wasserbelastung eines Tunnels ist eine Feldkraft. Von diesem Standpunkt aus wird der Einfluss der Geschichte der Wassrbelastung auf die Spannungen des Tunnels diskutiert. Eine entsprechende Berechnungsmethode wird vorgeschlagen. Eine nach dieser Methode konstruiertes Projekt wird als Beispiel angegeben.

RÉSUMÉ:
La charge d'eau provenant du tunnel constitue la force volumétrique. Le texte discute, à partir de ce point de vue, l'histoire de la charge d'eau ainsi que son influence à l'égard de la pression du tunnel. On a présenté la méthode de calcul correspondante et donné des exemples de travaux conçus d'après cette méthode.

1. INTRODUCTION

The water load is generally considered as an inchangeable load acting on the boundaries of the lining in tunnel design. This simplification being unable to reflect the actual condition of water load on tunnel often leads to a conservative or unsafe design.

Tunnel is a structure in rock mass with concrete lining as usual. Both rock mass and concrete are porous media. Water Percolating through these media forms a potential field $H(x_1, x_2, x_3)$ of seepage body forces, which act at every point of the field with three components:

$$X_i = -\gamma \frac{\partial H}{\partial x_i} \quad (i=1,2,3) \qquad (1)$$

where γ —— specific gravity of water, $H=\frac{p}{r}+Z$, p —— water pressure, Z —— the relative elevation of the point above the datum line.

Strictly speaking, water load should be considered as body forces in tunnel design. Only in the case of impervious lining, such as steel plate, or suddenly filling of the tunnel water load can be treated as boundary forces. For a tunnel, body force is the general form of water load, and the boundary force is only a special form of it. This is an important characteristic of water load on tunnel.

The seepage potential H is governed by Laplace's equation

$$\frac{\partial^2 H}{\partial x_1^2} + \frac{\partial^2 H}{\partial x_2^2} + \frac{\partial^2 H}{\partial x_3^2} = 0 \qquad (2)$$

in which H must satisfy boundary conditions.

From this point of view it implies that the process of tunnelling and lining will change the boundary conditions. Seepage potential field will be changed according to the change of boundary conditions even though the water head remains unchanged. Consequently the water load also varies in pace with various stages during tunnel construction so it has its own loading history. This is another important characteristic of water load acting on tunnel[1].

2 SEEPAGE FORCE AS THE WATER LOAD ON TUNNEL

The permeability factor of intact rock is very small, being in order of 10^{-7}-10^{-10}cm/s, but permeability factor of rock mass is considerably greater (about 10^3-10^6 times) than that of intact rock[2][3]. This remarkable difference is caused by joints, cracks and fractures in rock mass with a width of 1 mm or sometimes greater than 10 mm. Fractures in rock mass connected with each other will form seepage passages for water. Fractures usually appear in groups. Each group of fractures has almost the same orientation, so the rock mass shows evidently the anisotropic permeability. As the permeability of fractures is much greater than that of intact rock, we can approximately assume that the intact rock is impervious. Supposing the seepage flow in fracture is evenly distributed throughout the rock mass as a whole, we get a model of anisotropic homogeneous permeable medium. In general, the velocity vector at a point in space of anisotropic seepage potential field does not coincide with potential gradient and form an angle with it. The velocity vector $\bar{V}$ can be expressed as

$$\bar{V} = -\bar{\bar{K}}\,\bar{J}\,, \qquad (3)$$

where J —— hydraulic gradient and $\bar{\bar{K}}=K_{ij}$ (i,j=1,2,3) —— permeability tensor[4].

Since K_{ij} is equal to K_{ji}, the number of independent elements of permeability tensor is only 6 for three dimensional flow and 3 for two dimensional flow.

Let x_1, x_2, x_3 be the Cartesian coordinates, then formula (3) can be written as

$$\begin{Bmatrix} V_1 \\ V_2 \\ V_3 \end{Bmatrix} = -\begin{Bmatrix} K_{11} & K_{12} & K_{13} \\ K_{21} & K_{22} & K_{23} \\ K_{31} & K_{32} & K_{33} \end{Bmatrix} \begin{Bmatrix} J_1 \\ J_2 \\ J_3 \end{Bmatrix} \qquad (4)$$

Putting (4) into the continuous equation of flow we obtain partial differential equation

$$\sum_{i=1}^{3} \frac{\partial}{\partial x_i} \sum_{j=1}^{3} K_{ij} \frac{\partial H}{\partial x_i} = 0 \qquad (5)$$

If K_{ij} are constants within the domain in consideration, formula(5) can be written as

$$\sum_{i=1}^{3} \sum_{j=1}^{3} K_{ij} \frac{\partial^2 H}{\partial x_i \partial x_j} = 0 \qquad (6)$$

In accordance with variational principle, solving of formula (6) is actually a problem of finding the extremal of functional

$$f(H) = \frac{1}{2} \iiint \sum_{i=1}^{3} \sum_{j=1}^{3} K_{ij} \frac{\partial H}{\partial x_i} \frac{\partial H}{\partial x_j} dx_1 dx_2 dx_3 \qquad (7)$$

Now we can find the solution of seepage potential field and then the corresponding stress distribution by using finite element method without any difficulty.

An example is given hereafter to illustrate the features of tunnel stress distribution under the seepage force of water load.

There is a circular hydraulic tunnel 5 m in diameter with concrete lining 0.7 m in thickness. Underground water table located at 50 m above tunnel axis. Modulus of deformability is 50000 kg/cm^2 for rock mass and 200000 kg/cm^2 for concrete; Poisson's ratio is 0.25 for rock mass and 0.167 for concrete. Let K_R express the permeability factor of rock mass and K is that of concrete. Tunnel stress distribution under water load were found for various K_R/K by using FEM. Fig. 1 represents the relationship of σ_t' and σ_n' with K_R/K, where σ_t' is the tangential stress of lining at its inner edge, and σ_n' is the normal stress at the boundary between the lining and rock mass.

From Fig. 1 some characteristics of tunnel stress distribution due to seepage force may be described as follows:

a, The tangential stress of lining is determined mainly by water head but affected slightly by value K_R/K.

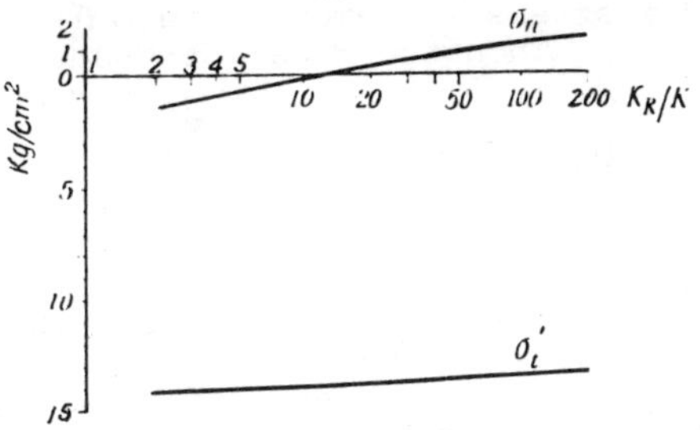

Fig. 1 Relation between stresses and the ratio K_R/K

b, If there are drainages behind lining (corresponding the case $K_R/K=0$) σ_n' and σ_t' get their maximum negative (compressive) values. It means that the tangential stress of lining can not be relieved by drainage.

c, σ_n' is positive when K_R/K is small but negative when K_R/K is large. The tensile stress at the contect surface will be lowered or relieved at all by using drainage system.

3 HISTORY OF WATER LOAD

3.1 Three typical histories of water load

A, Original underground water table is below the bottom of excavating contour of the tunnel, so the seepage potential field will not change during tunnelling. When lining is completed, the underground water table rises up to a certain level above the top of tunnel because seepage water flows down stream from the resevoir put into performance after the tunnel has completed (Fig. 2).

B, Tunnel is located underneath the river bed. The seepage potential field varies not only during tunnelling, but also after lining in spite of the underground water level remains the same (Fig. 3).

C, The underground water table is higher than the top line of excavation. Owning to lack of adquate water supply, water level suddenly falls down after excavation. When the lining is completed the water table rises back to a certain level due to reduce of seepage flow into the tunnel (Fig. 4).

3.2 The influence of water load history on tunnel stress distribution

Analysing the typical case B (Fig. 3) as an example, we can realize that water load history plays an important role. After tunnel is excavated, seepage potential field H_1 is formed but the underground water table remains the same because of abundant water supply. Under the seepage force $\frac{\gamma \partial H}{\partial x_i}$ rock mass deforms due to

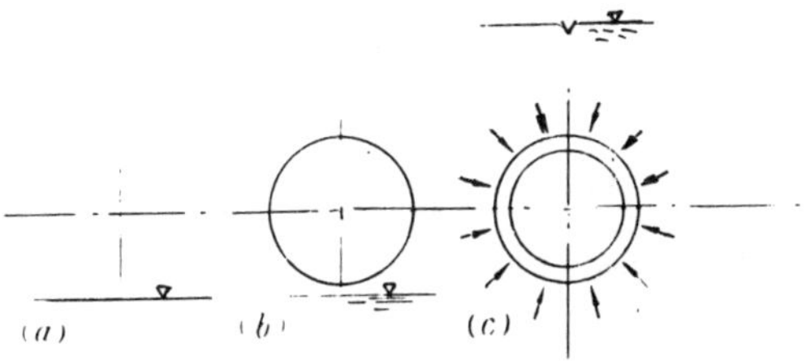

Fig. 2 Typical case A

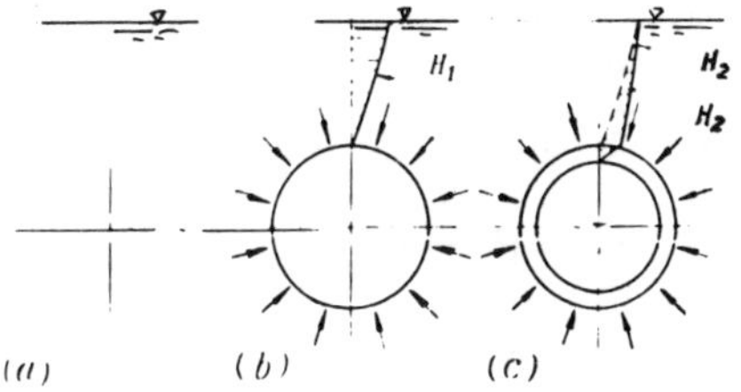

Fig. 3 Typical case B

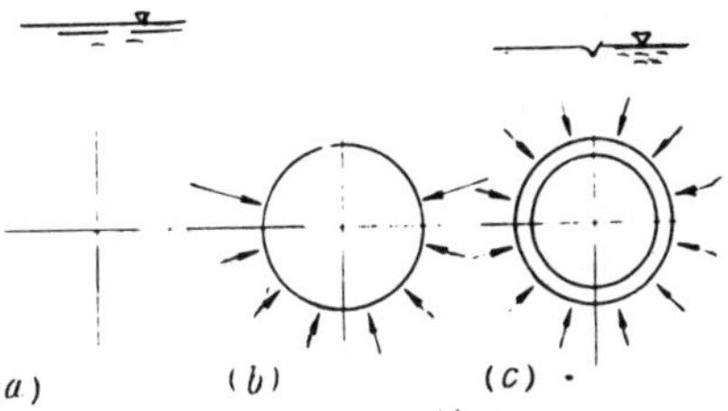

Fig. 4 Typicla case C

excavation. Since the fractured rock mass usually has a good permeability, the steady-state seepage flow will be formed i.e. the deformation process will be ceased before the begining of lining. After lining is completed seepage potential fields varies from H_1 to

H_2 because boundary conditions are changed. It is quite clear that the lining bears only seepage forces due to $\Delta H=H_2-H_1$ rather than H_2. There are only small tensile stresses in lining since the seepage force corresponding to ΔH is in selfequilibrium. But the typical case A (Fig.2) is different at all. The increment of seepage potential H is $\Delta H=H_2$, under the seepage forces of which lining bears considerable compressive stress. Typical case C is similar to B, the only difference lies in the fact that underground water table also changes in different stage.

3.3 The procedures of calculation

When the history of water load is taken into account, the procedures of tunnel stress calculation are described as follows.

Let H_o express the original seepage potential in rock mass, which can be neglected in calculation since the gradient of H_o is usually quite small. New boundary condition forms after the tunnel had been excavated and seepage potential field varies from H_o to H_1. The potential increment is

$$\Delta H_1 = H_1 - H_0 \qquad (8)$$

Stresses in surrounding rock mass produced by ΔH_1 is σ_{R1} Obviously, the stress of lining $\sigma_{L1}=0$ in this period as it has not yet been completed.

A new seepage potential field H_2 is established after lining, the potential increment is

$$\Delta H_2 = H_2 - H_1 \qquad (9)$$

Stress increment in rock mass and lining are $\Delta\sigma_{R2}$ and σ_{L2} respectively under the action of ΔH_2. The total stresses in this period are

$$\left.\begin{aligned} \sigma_{R2} &= \sigma_{R1} + \Delta\sigma_{R2} \\ \sigma_{L2} &= \sigma_{L1} + \Delta\sigma_{L2} \end{aligned}\right\} \qquad (10)$$

Seepage potential field H_3 is set up after filling of the tunnel. The increment is

$$\Delta H_3 = H_3 - H_2 \qquad (11)$$

The stress increments are $\Delta\sigma_{R3}$ $\Delta\sigma_{L3}$ Then the final stresses are

$$\left.\begin{aligned} \sigma_{R3} &= \sigma_{R2} + \Delta\sigma_{R3} \\ \sigma_{L3} &= \sigma_{L2} + \Delta\sigma_{L3} \end{aligned}\right\} \qquad (12)$$

When seepage potential field is continuous to fluctuate, we can extend the above mentioned formulas into a more general form

$$\Delta H_n = H_n - H_{n-1} \qquad (13)$$

$$\left.\begin{aligned} \sigma_{Rn} &= \sigma_{n(n-1)} + \Delta\sigma_{Rn} \\ \sigma_{Ln} &= \sigma_{L(n-1)} + \Delta\sigma_{Ln} \end{aligned}\right\} \qquad (14)$$

Formulas (13) and (14) can be conveniently compiled into a FEM program.

Now we again use the above mentioned example to describe the influence of different histories of water load.

Suppose $K_R/K=50$, $H_o=50$ m. Fig. 5a gives the tangential stresses of tunnel when the history of water load follows the typical case B, and Fig. 5b gives that of typical case A.

Fig. 5a and 5b show clearly that the tunnel stress distributions corresponding to different histories of water load are quite different in spite of the same final loading condition. Consequently, one ought to analyse tunnel stresses according to its real history of water load if he wants to work out a correct design.

4 STRUCTURAL MEASURES FOR IMPROVING WORKING CONDITION OF TUNNEL

4.1 Drainage

As the water load acts as the seepage body force. It is necessary to adopt some structural measures to change the seepage potential field for improving working condition of tunnel. Drains are one of the effective measures most preferable in practice.

For tunnel in typical case A, if ratio K_R/K is greater than a

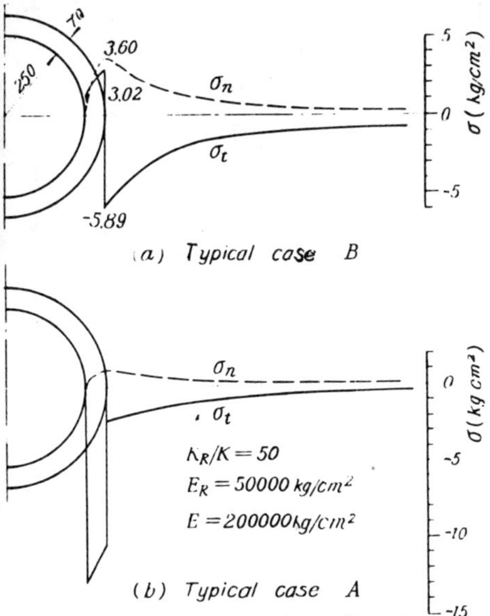

Fig. 5 Stress distribution

certain value, normal tensile stresses will appear in contact boundary between lining and rock mass. This situation is of serious concern for tunnel of typical case B. The rock mass does not share any part of water load once tensile stresses exceed the bonding strength between lining material and rock mass. Drainage system set up in rock near lining can decrease or eliminate these tensile stresses. For tunnel in typical case C, water level at period c can be lowered by drainage, so that the increment of seepage potential force, i.e. the load acting on lining will be decreased.

4.2 Grouting

Rock grouting techniques are used not only to increase the modulus of deformability, but also to decrease the permeability of rock mass, consequently the working condition of tunnel lining are improved as well. Grouting can be used for all three typical cases. Particularly for case B, if consolidation grouting behind the working face is done prior to excavation, when tunnel being dug ahead the stability of rock mass is considerably improved, at the same time, the history of water load becomes more favorable thus decreasing the tangential stresses of lining to a certain extent.

4.3 Rock bolts

It is too expansive to pump large quantity of seepage water if water can not flow out by gravity. Under such circumstances rock bolts can be used instead of drainage. One end of the bolt is fixed in rock and the another end-in lining. If the bonding between lining and rock is destroyed by high tensile stresses, then tensile stresses may be assumed to be taken by bolts and its strength may reach yield stregth σ_T. The lining can be calculated as a separated structure from rock (Fig. 6). The bending moment inside lining can be decreased to minimum by reasonable arrangement of rock bolts.

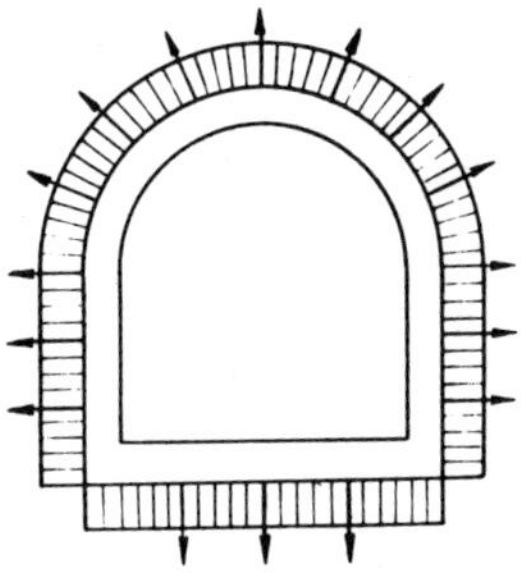

Fig. 6 Sketch for calculating stresses of tunnel lining

4.4 Injection of pressure water between rock and lining

For tunnel of typical case B outer water load is almost fully taken by rock mass because of influence of history of water load. In the case of pressure tunnel, outer water pressure can not compensate inner water pressure on lining, so that high tangential tensile stresses will occur in lining and cause cracks. If we want to decrease the tensile stresses in lining, a better way is to make lining separated from rock mass before inner water pressure applies, so that outer water pressure can act directly on lining. Separating lining from rock by using high pressure water injection is a more effective measure in practice.

5 A DESIGN EXAMPLE

Three siphonal tunnels crossing the Yellow River at 70 m beneath the river bed are planed to use in a diversion project. The three parallel tunnels have same circular sections of 9.5 m diameter, same lining of 1 m thickness and equal spacing of 31 m center to center. Tunnels will be located in fractured limestone. The underground water is interconnected with the river water. The water level of the river above tunnel axis is 81.21 m high, the inner water pressure head is 69.26m. For the sake of safety excavation will be done after grouting behind the working face. The remained thickness of consolidated rock mass after excavation is about 5 m (Fig.7).

A series of calculations using the above mentioned method has been made, the typical result of which is shown in Fig. 8.

The history of water load on tunnels is similar to the typical case B. Before applying the inner water pressure there are small tangential tensile stresses in lining. When the tunnels are put into operation, although the outer water head is greater than the inner water head, the lining stresses are not compressive as expected. On the contrary, the tensile stresses are as large as σ_t = 20.1 kg/cm^2, which is beyond the ultimate tensile strength of concrete, so that the method making the lining separate from rock mass by using high pressure water injection is recommended.

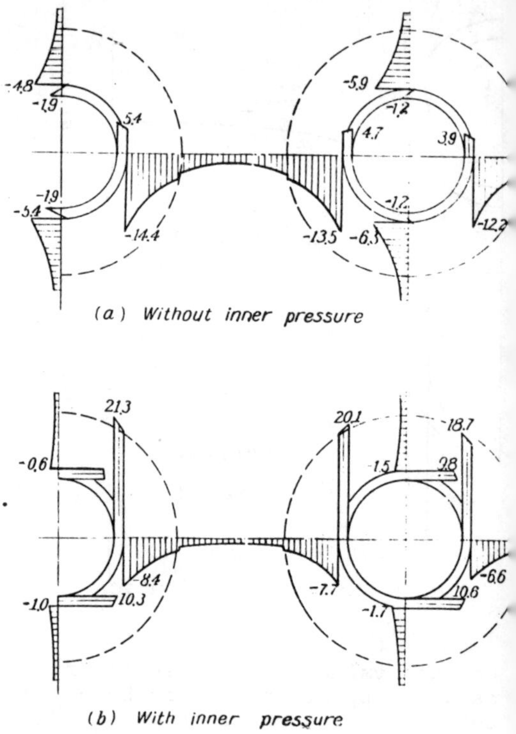

Fig. 8 Stress distribution

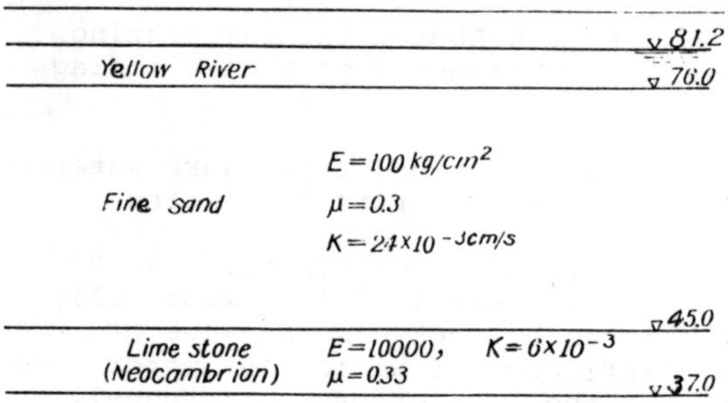

Fig. 7 Sketch for tunnels

6 REFERENCES

Zhang, Y., Zhang, W. 1981, Static Calculation of Water Load Acting on Tunnels, Journal of Hydraulic Engineering, No 3, Beijing, (In Chinese).

Jaeger, C., 1979, Rock Mechanics and Engineering, Combridge.

Stagg, K. G., Zienkiewicz, O. C., 1972, Rock Mechanics in Engineering Practice, New York.

Ромм, Е. С., 1966, Фильтрационные свойства трещиноватых горных пород, Москва.

* 4 *

LIMITATION OF THE APPLICABILITY OF TUNNEL BORING MACHINES AS SEEN FROM THE ROCK MECHANICAL POINT OF VIEW

Einsatzgrenzen von Tunnelvortriebsmaschinen aus felsmechanischer Sicht

Limites d'emploi de foreuses pour le creusement du tunnels, du point de vue de la mécanique des roches

ERFAHRUNGEN MIT TUNNELBOHRMASCHINEN IN STÖRZONEN - EINFLUSS AUF BOHRGESCHWINDIGKEIT UND AUSNUTZUNGSGRAD

Experiences with tunnel boring machines in fault zones – Influence on penetration rate and utilization

Expériences avec des machines à forer les tunnels dans des zones instables – Influence sur la vitesse de pénétration et sur l'utilisation

U.BECKMANN & Th.KRAUSE
Technische Universität Braunschweig, Bundesrepublik Deutschland

SUMMARY:
The use of tunnel boring machines (TBM) increased in the last 1o years by several hundred per cent. Positive records of more than one thousand meters advance per month contrast with disillusioning negative records of only a few meters advance/month in fault zones. The influence of these zones on penetration rate and utilization is shown in seven case histories. A dependence of the daily advance rate from the length and quality the fault zone can be recognized. The requirements resulting from these experiences for Engineers, TBM-manufacturers and site managers are pointed out.

ZUSAMMENFASSUNG:
Der Einsatz von Tunnelbohrmaschinen (TBM) hat sich in den letzten 1o Jahren um mehrere Hundertprozent gesteigert. Positiven Rekordleistungen von mehr als tausend Meter Vortrieb pro Monat stehen ernüchternde Negativrekorde von nur wenigen Metern Vortrieb/Monat in Störzonen gegenüber. An sieben exemplarischen Fällen wird der unterschiedliche Einfluß dieser Zonen auf die Bohrgeschwindigkeit und den Ausnutzungsgrad aufgezeigt. Eine Abhängigkeit der täglichen Vortriebsgeschwindigkeit von der Länge und Qualität der Störzone ist erkennbar. Die sich aus diesen Erfahrungen ergebenden Forderungen an den ausschreibenden Ingenieur, an die Maschinenhersteller und an die Bauausführenden werden zusammengefaßt aufgestellt.

RESUME:
L'usage des tunneliers s'est intensifié pendant les 1o derniers ans de plusieurs cent pour cent. Des records positifs de plus que mille mètres d'avancement par mois contrastent avec des records négatifs et désillusionnants de seulement quelques mètres par mois dans des accidents géologiques. L'influence de ces accidents sur la vitesse de pénétration et sur l'utilisation est décrit dans sept cas exemplaires. Une dépendance de la vitesse d'avancement par jour de la longueur et de la qualité des accidents géologiques est reconnue. Les exigences qui résultent de cettes expériences pour les ingénieurs projetants, pour les producteurs et pour les ingénieurs organisateurs sont soumises.

1 EINFÜHRUNG

Moderne Tunnelbohrmaschinen (TBM) werden seit 1952 gebaut. In den Anfangsjahren wurden sie nur zögernd eingesetzt. Der Durchbruch gelang ihnen Ende der sechziger Jahre. Bis 1969 waren weltweit nur 182 km Tunnel mit TBM aufgefahren, seit 197o wird jedoch ein schnell wachsender Anteil gebohrt. Bis April 1981 waren insgesamt 438 Tunnel (Bild 1) mit einer Länge von 1 483 km gebohrt. Die technischen Geburtswehen dieser Maschinen sind heute Geschichte. Fälle des totalen Versagens - die früher häufiger auftraten - werden immer seltener.

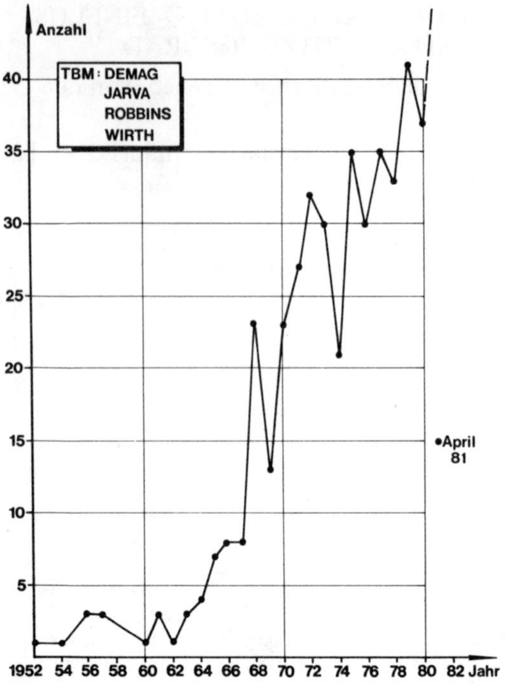

Bild 1 Anzahl der weltweiten TBM-Vortriebe. Die Projekte sind im Jahr des Anbohrens gezählt.

Nach wie vor gibt es aber zwei Hauptprobleme:

1. Zu lockeres Gestein
2. Zu hartes Gestein

Auswirkungen von zu lockerem Gestein auf Stillstände durch Sicherungsarbeiten, den Ausnutzungsgrad, die Bohrgeschwindigkeit und damit auf die durch die beiden letztgenannten Einflußgrößen bestimmte tägliche Vortriebsleistung einer TBM werden an den folgenden Beispielen aus Störzonen gezeigt.

Hierbei werden unter dem Begriff Störzonen tektonisch verursachte Brüche oder Bruchzonen im Gebirge verstanden, in denen der Gesteinsverband unterbrochen und eine Gleitverschiebung der beiden gegenüberliegenden, zum Bruch parallelen Trennflächen erkennbar ist (Verwerfung bzw. Verschiebung).

Die Beispiele stammen von verschiedenen Maschinen mit 3,5 m Durchmesser. Die Bilder enthalten nur Aufzeichnungen von Tagen, an denen mehr als 1 m gebohrt wurde, die Auswirkungen der Störungen werden daher nicht voll offenbart. Stillstandtage werden jedoch ergänzend im Text angeführt. Die Sicherungsarbeiten wurden in allen Beispielen mit Ankern, Stahlbögen und -blechen ausgeführt, Spritzbeton wurde nicht eingesetzt.

2 BEISPIELE

Beispiel 1 (Bild 2a)

Kurze, leichtere Störung (40° Streichen zur Achse, senkrechtes Einfallen, 4 m mächtig) in einer Sandstein-Tonstein Wechsellagerung. Die tägliche Vortriebslänge sank in der Störung auf 2 m bzw. 8 m ab und ging danach wieder auf die durchschnittliche Höhe von ca. 25 m zurück. Die Bohrgeschwindigkeit ging am ersten Tag auf ca. 50 % zurück. Der Ausnutzungsgrad der Maschine sank wegen der Gebirgssicherung - 3,5 m hinter der Ortsbrust - auf 5 bzw. 15 %. Für die ca. 10 m lange Störzone wurden 2 Tage benötigt. Stillstandtage gab es keine. Ein durch den Versatz im First angeschnittener, nachbrüchiger Tonstein verursachte weiterhin Stillstände durch Sicherungsarbeiten; er lief nach ca. 50 m schleifend aus.

Beispiel 2 (Bild 2b)

Die Störung mit mehreren Metern Versatz brachte anstelle eines Sandsteins einen zerrütteten Tonstein in die obere Stollenhälfte. Sehr ausgeprägt war hier die Zunahme der Bohrgeschwindigkeit am Anfang der Störung, auch der hohe Bohrgeschwindigkeitswert (5m) rechts im Bild kündigt eine erneute Störung an. Der tägliche Vortrieb lag zwischen 2,1 m und 7,3 m bei Ausnutzungsgraden von 6-8 %. Ein zweiter Versatz nach 26 m brachte härteren Sandstein fast vollflächig in den Querschnitt zurück, nur wenige Zentimeter Tonstein verblieben im First. Für die 26 m lange Störung wurden fünf Arbeitstage benötigt. Sicherung: nach 3,5m.

Beispiel 3 (Bild 2c)

Eine ca. 45 m lange Störung in einem Tonstein kündigte sich durch die Zunahme der Bohrgeschwindigkeit an. Die tägliche Vortriebsleistung ging von knapp 40 m zunächst auf 16 m, dann auf 2 m bzw. 6 m herunter, um über 14 m und 25 m schließlich den Ausgangswert wieder zu erreichen. Auch hier ist an zwei Tagen eine Verringerung der Bohrgeschwindigkeit zu erkennen. Die Stillstände

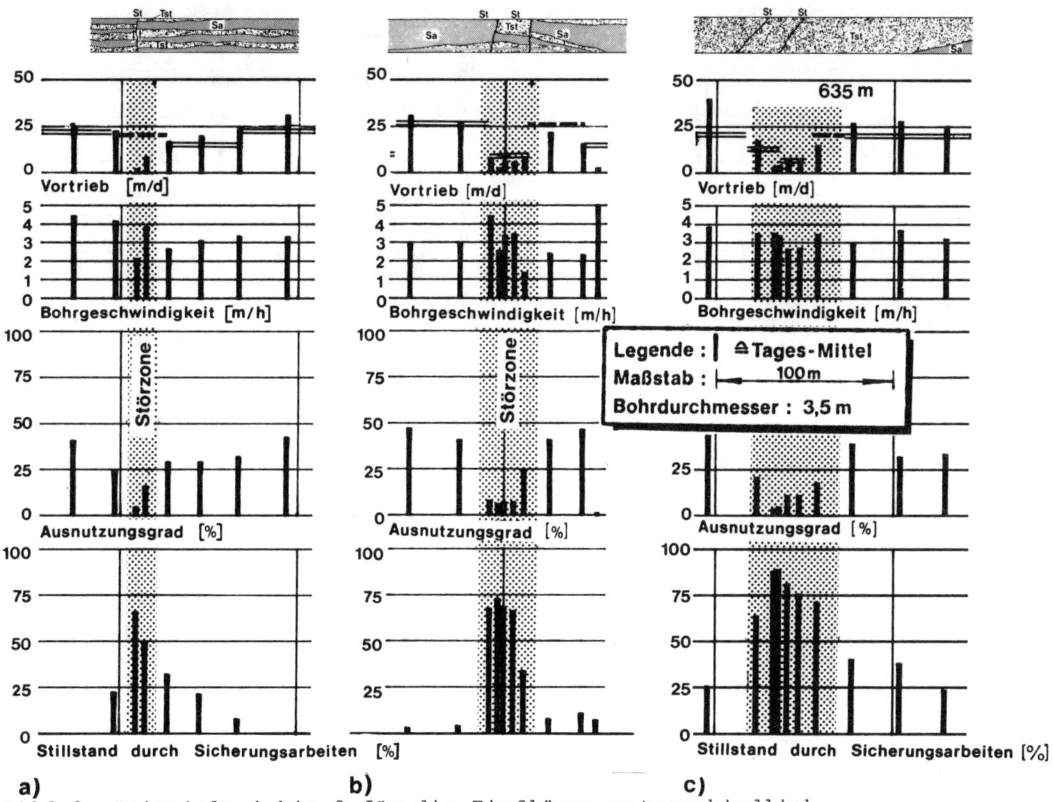

Bild 2 Beispiele 1 bis 3 für die Einflüsse unterschiedlich breiter Störzonen (10 m, 26 m, 45 m).

durch Sicherungsarbeiten waren mit bis zu 88 % sehr hoch, obwohl die Sicherung schon 3,5 m hinter dem Bohrkopf eingebaut wurde. Die Störung wurde in sieben Tagen bewältigt, auch hier kam es nicht zu einem ganztätigen Stillstand.

Beispiel 4 (Bild 3a)

Ein Versatz von ca. 35 m brachte anstelle eines Sandsteins einen Tonstein in den Querschnitt. Die Störung kündigte sich durch Zunahme der Bohrgeschwindigkeit an, ein anschließender starker Rückgang der Bohrgeschwindigkeit und des Ausnutzungsgrades lag im Zentrum der Störung. Dort war sie mit grusigem, weichem Material gefüllt, das die Maschine verschüttete. Fünf volle Sicherungstage wurden benötigt, bevor die Maschine wieder bohren konnte (diese Tage sind im Bild nicht dargestellt). Für die ersten 50 m der Störung wurden 14 Arbeitstage benötigt. Die Auswirkungen der Störung in dem Tonstein geringer Festigkeit waren auch auf den weiteren 50 m noch sehr stark, der Einfluß nahm erst dann langsam ab. Sicherung: nach 3,5 m.

Beispiel 5 (Bild 3b)

In dem ersten, ca. 100 m langen Stollenabschnitt lagen zwei Störungen mit 15 m bis 20 m Länge, dazwischen stand stark geklüfteter, sehr gebrächer Tonschiefer in der oberen Stollenhälfte an, der auf einem flach fallenden, harten Kalkstein gelagert war. Infolge Kompaktionsdruck und einer Verschiebung auf dem Kalkstein war der Tonschiefer stark entfestigt. Für diese 100 m wurden 57 Arbeitstage benötigt, davon gingen 8 durch störungsbedingten Maschinenausfall und 21 Tage ausschließlich für Sicherungsarbeiten verloren.

Am Ende der zweiten 100 m wurde eine weitere Verwerfung von 30 m Länge angefahren. Für diesen Bereich wurden 29 Arbeitstage mit 19 Still-

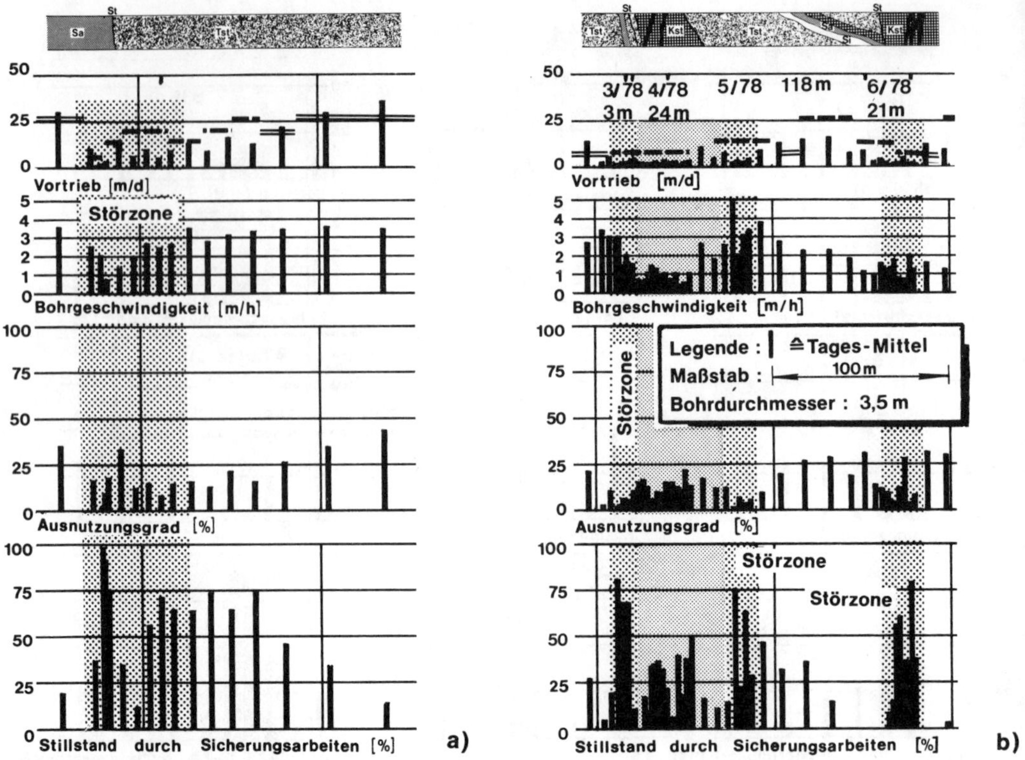

Bild 3 Beispiele 4 und 5 für ausgedehntere Störzonen unterschiedlicher Qualität. a) 50 m lange Störzone mit anschließendem ca. 50 m langen, stark zerklüfteten Bereich. b) Störungen über insgesamt 200 m Stollenlänge.

standtagen für Sicherungsarbeiten benötigt. In diesem Beispiel konnte - TBM bedingt - erst 14 m hinter der Ortsbrust gesichert werden.

Beispiel 6 (Bild 4)

In diesem 85 m langen Störungsbereich lagen sechs Verwerfungen (2 - 4 m Versatz), die anstelle des vollflächig anstehenden Sandsteins ständig wechselnde Sandstein/Tonstein-Anteile in den Querschnitt gebracht hatten. Zwischen Sandstein und dem zerrütteten Tonstein lag noch eine etwa 1 m dicke Schicht aus weichem, verwittertem Siltstein, der an den Verwerfungen breiig war. Hohe Wasserzuflüsse von 7000 l/min erschwerten die Arbeiten.

Die TBM begann abzusinken, als der weiche Siltstein/Tonstein in der Sohle anstand. Ursache hierfür war einmal das Eigengewicht der Maschine, aber teilweise auch die Ablenkung des gewölbten Bohrkopfes durch den härteren Sandstein im First. Vor einer 14-tägigen Weihnachtspause war der Bohrkopf 27 cm abgesunken, hinterher 60 cm. Die TBM wurde zurückgezogen und bohrte sich dann auf einer betonierten Sohle wieder vor. Das Anheben der Maschine dauerte neun Arbeitstage.

Insgesamt wurden für die ersten 22 m 20 Arbeitstage benötigt. Im restlichen Störungsbereich waren bis zu 2 m tiefe Ulmen- und Firstnachbrüche das Hauptproblem. Obwohl die TBM weiter - aber in geringerem Masse - zum Absacken neigte, konnte dies durch die Maschinensteuerung beherrscht werden. Für die gesamte Störzone wurden 37 Arbeitstage benötigt, die Sicherung wurde in diesem Beispiel 3,5 m hinter der Ortsbrust eingebaut.

Beispiel 7 (Bild 5)

Dieser ca. 215 m lange Störungsbereich bestand nicht aus einer grossen Störung, sondern aus einer Fol-

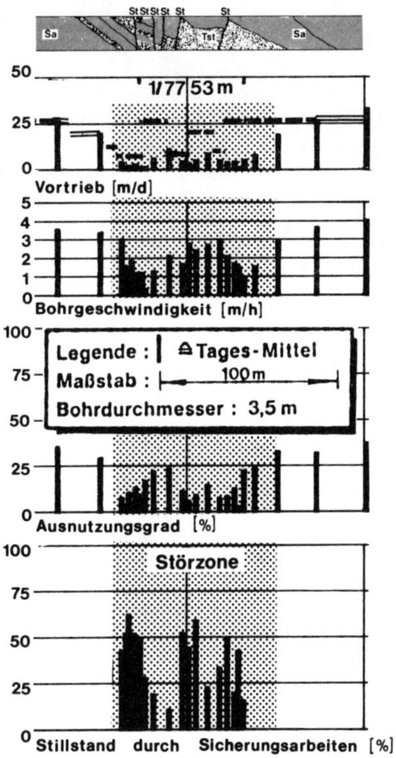

Bild 4 Beispiel für eine 85 m lange Störzone mit sechs Verwerfungen und hohem Wasserzufluß

ge von kleineren Störungen in Verbindung mit einem Tonstein von geringer Festigkeit, der infolge Verschiebung spiegelglatte Schichtflächen (Harnische) besaß. Zu Beginn lagen die Tagesleistungen noch bei 8 m, wechselten dann zwischen 2 m und 16 m stark hin und her und gingen schließlich auf Werte zwischen 1 m und 3 m herunter. In einem Monat konnten nur 19 m, im nächsten nur 14 m vorgetrieben werden. An nur 30 Tagen (bei 65 Arbeitstagen) wurde im April bis Juni gebohrt. 31 Tage gingen mit Sicherungsarbeiten und Freiräumen der TBM verloren, vier mit störungsbedingten TBM-Ausfällen. Danach blieb die TBM völlig stecken, sie war total verschüttet und mußte händisch überfirstet werden (Bild 6a). Da eine horizontale Erkundungsbohrung für einen weiteren Bereich die gleichen schlechten Verhältnisse erwarten ließen - die Bohrung mußte sogar verrohrt werden - wurden weitere 57 m Stollen im Handvortrieb (s. Lücke der Aufzeichnung im Bild 5 und s. Bild 6b) aufgefahren, bis wieder einigermaßen standfestes Gestein angetroffen wurde.

Auch in diesem Beispiel ist die Bohrgeschwindigkeit bis zu 50 % geringer als normalerweise. Insgesamt wurden für die 215 m Vortrieb über 8 Monate benötigt, allerdings einschließlich zweier Horizontalbohrungen (ca. 170 m). Wie im Beispiel 4 war auch hier der Sicherungseinbau erst 14 m hinter dem Bohrkopf möglich. Dies erwies sich als äußerst nachteilig. Hinzu kam, daß der Bohrkopfbereich nur über eine sehr enge Mannrutsche erreichbar war. Die Maschine füllte nahezu den gesamten Tunnelquerschnitt aus. Ein anderes Vorarbeiten als über der Maschine war daher praktisch nicht möglich. Der eingebaute Dachschild schützte zwar die Maschine vor Nachbrüchen beim Bohrbetrieb, lockerte aber durch die Maschinen-Vibration beim Bohren das auf ihm liegende Gebirge zusätzlich auf und verstärkte so die Nachbrüche.

Für die aufgeführten Beispiele läßt sich eine gewisse Abhängigkeit der täglichen Vortriebsgeschwindigkeit von der Störungslänge erkennen (Bild 7). Es ergeben sich allerdings auch Abweichungen, die durch die unterschiedliche Qualität der Störung bedingt sind. Ähnliche Abweichungen finden sich bei den wenigen, in der Literatur geschilderten Fällen. Bei ihnen spielen zusätzlich noch unterschiedliche Maschinen-Konstruktionen und der TBM-Durchmesser eine Rolle. Die am häufigsten erzielte Tages-Vortriebsgeschwindigkeit in Störungen bis ca. 80 m Länge liegt für Durchmesser bis ca. 6 m bei ca. 1 m/Arbeitstag. Erst bei wenigen, neueren Maschinen werden Werte bis 6 m/Arbeitstag genannt (z.B. Schoknecht, 1978; Stapel, 1981).

3 AUSWIRKUNG VON STÖRZONEN

Aus den eigenen Beispielen und Beobachtungen in anderen Vortrieben können zusammenfassend folgende Auswirkungen festgestellt werden:

1. Früherkennung

Störzonen kündigen sich an. Ihre Nähe ist über eine Zunahme der Bohrgeschwindigkeit i.d.R. erkennbar, da die Nachbarbereiche der Störzone meist stärker geklüftet sind.

2. Ausnutzungsgrad

Störzonen können den Ausnutzungsgrad

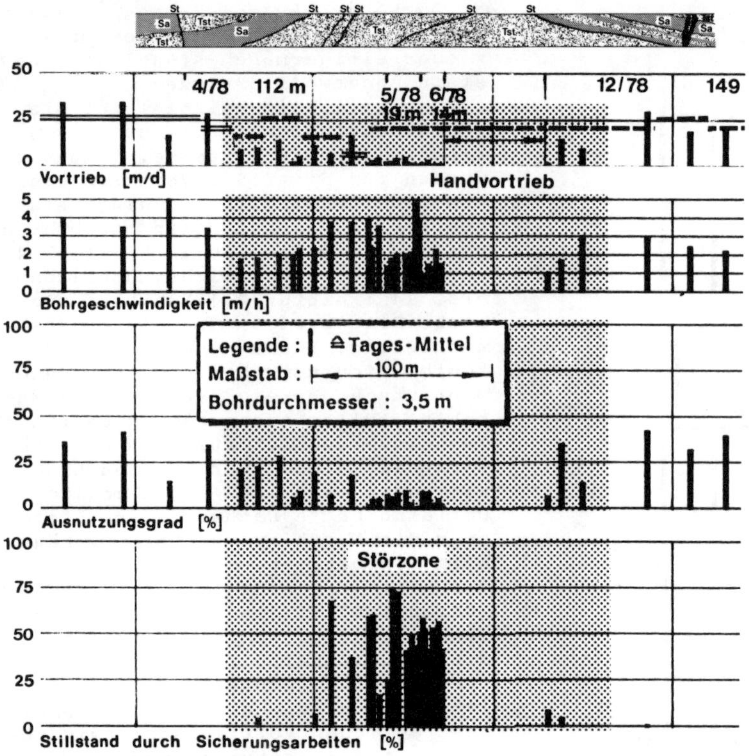

Bild 5 Beispiel für einen ca. 215 m langen Störungsbereich, der teilweise konventionell aufgefahren werden mußte.

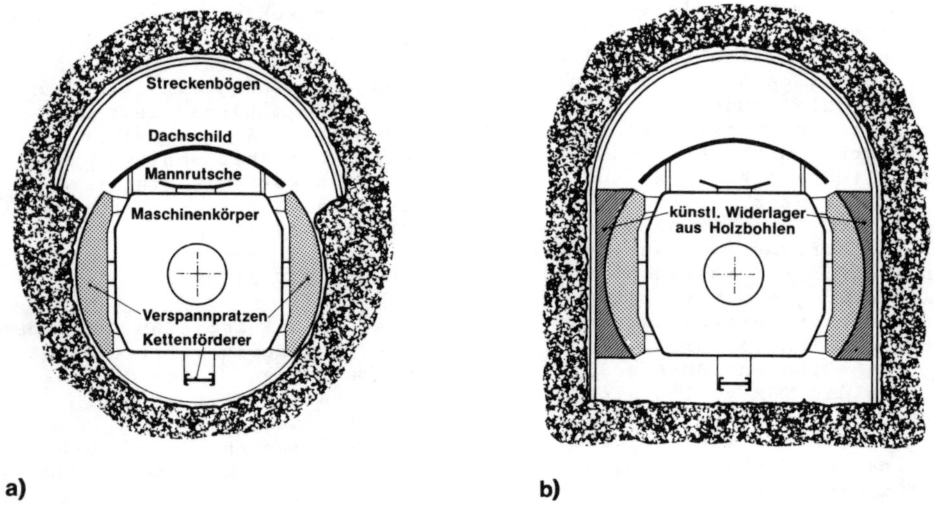

Bild 6 Überfirstung der TBM a) und konventioneller Vortrieb vor der Maschine b)

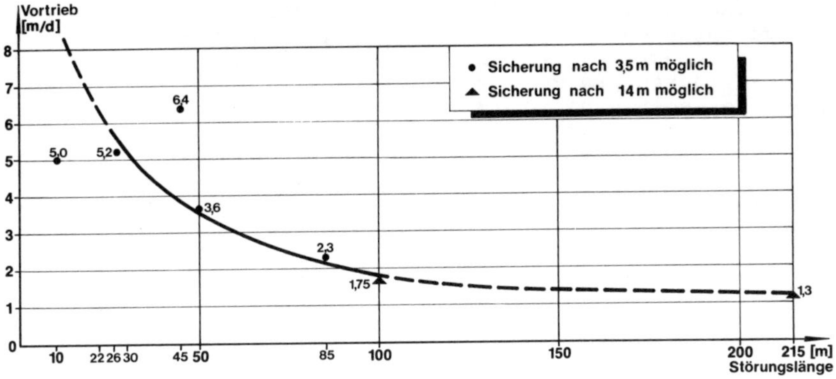

Bild 7 Abhängigkeit des täglichen Vortriebes von der Störungslänge

einer TBM wegen der erforderlichen, umfangreichen Sicherungsarbeiten drastisch bis auf wenige Prozent verringern. Je länger Störzonen sind, desto häufiger werden auch ganze TBM-Stillstandtage. Wesentliche Ursache des hohen Zeitaufwandes ist oft die stark eingeschränkte Zugänglichkeit des Querschnitts im TBM-Bereich.

3. Bohrgeschwindigkeit
Störzonen erfordern häufig eine Verringerung des Andrucks. Stark zerschertes Gebirge muß schonend gebohrt werden, um Nachbrüche möglichst gering zu halten. Häufig sind die Verspannmöglichkeiten eingeschränkt und müssen künstlich (Beton, Hartholz) hergestellt werden. Sie erlauben nur einen verringerten Andruck. Dieser macht sich nicht nur in der Störzone selbst, sondern auch im Übergang zu festerem Gestein bemerkbar. Der Bohrkopf selbst bohrt dann bereits wieder in härterem Gestein, die Verspannung befindet sich aber noch im Bereich des weichen Materials der Störzone und ist nur eingeschränkt verspannbar.

4. Vortriebsgeschwindigkeit
Störzonen verringern die sich aus der Bohrgeschwindigkeit und dem Ausnutzungsgrad ergebende Vortriebsgeschwindigkeit auf bis zu 5 bis 10 % der normalen Tages-Mittelwerte. In längeren Störzonen (>100 m) kann die Vortriebsgeschwindigkeit bis auf einen Mittelwert von 1 m/Arbeitstag heruntergehen. Dieser Wert ist häufig auch nur in kürzeren Störzonen erreicht worden, besonders wenn diese mit lockergesteinsähnlichem Material (z.B. Mylonit) gefüllt sind.

5. Richtungsstabilität
Störzonen erschweren das Einhalten der Sollachse. Häufig sackt die Maschine in dem weichen Füllmaterial ab, besonders wenn Wasserzuflüsse das Material zusätzlich erweicht haben. Verstärkt wird dies Absacken durch hohe Auflasten auf dem Dachschild infolge von Nachbrüchen bzw. Druckhaftigkeit.

6. Beschädigungen
Störzonen können Beschädigungen an der TBM verursachen. Sie entstehen sowohl am Bohrkopf als im Maschinenbereich durch herabfallende, größere Gesteinsbrocken. Auch ein Verklemmen bzw. Blockieren des Bohrkopfes ist möglich, wenn grobstückiges Haufwerk nicht von den Bohrkopfschaufeln aufgenommen werden kann und zwischen Ortsbrust und Bohrkopf eingeklemmt wird. Es muß dann von Hand entfernt werden.

7. Handvortrieb
Störzonen können die vorübergehende Einstellung des Bohrbetriebs und einen händischen Vortrieb erzwingen. Bei letzterem wird die Maschine häufig mehr zum Hindernis als zum Schutz- oder Hilfsmittel. Ein händischer Vortrieb bedeutet härtesten und gefährlichen Einsatz für die Vortriebsmannschaft, er hat eine zusätzlich leistungsmindernde Auswirkung auf ihre Moral.

8. Aufgabe
Störzonen können im Extremfall die völlige Aufgabe des Bohrvortriebs notwendig machen. Die Maschine muß dann zurückgezogen und der Vortrieb bergmännisch beendet werden.

4 FORDERUNGEN AN DIE AUSSCHREIBUNG

Wegen der möglichen, erheblichen Auswirkungen von Störzonen auf die Gesamtwirtschaftlichkeit eines Vortriebs, muß ihre Erkundung einer der Schwerpunkte des ingenieurgeologischen Untersuchungsprogramms sein. Diese möglichst lückenlose Vorauserkundung hat deswegen eine besondere Bedeutung, weil von ihr zwei Grundsatzentscheidungen abhängen:

1. Einsatz einer Tunnelbohrmaschine ja/nein
2. Festlegung der technischen Konzeption einer TBM

Es müssen daher bei der ingenieurgeologischen Erkundung die größten Anstrengungen unternommen werden, Störzonen vorab zu erkennen und zutreffend zu beschreiben. Die Anwendung einer weiterentwickelten Fotogeologie könnte hier u.a. in Zukunft zu einem zuverlässigen Hilfsmittel werden. Zur Beschreibung der Störung gehören:

- Mächtigkeit (Breite)
- Fallen und Fallrichtung bzw. Streichen zur Tunnelachse
- Versatz

Das Ausmaß des Versatzes läßt Rückschlüsse auf den Grad der Störung zu. Aus Breite, Fallen und Streichen ergeben sich die Längen, auf denen sich die Störung ganz oder teilweise im Tunnelquerschnitt befindet. Schon geringe Abweichungen der Breite und/oder der Streichrichtung ziehen bei flachen Streichen ein Vielfaches an Störungslänge im Tunnel nach sich (Bild 8).

Die Abrechnung des Vortriebs in Störzonen kann auf zwei Arten vollzogen werden:

- Gebirgsgüteklasse
- Selbstkostenerstattung

Bei kürzeren Störungen (bis ca. 30 - 50 m) kann die Leistungsvergütung noch innerhalb einer entsprechenden, TBM-geeigneten Gebirgsklasse abgewickelt werden (z.B. Beckmann/Simons, 1982). Hiermit werden auch die Randbereiche der Störungen entsprechend ihren Schwierigkeiten zutreffend erfaßt. Für längere Störzonen (>ca. 50 m) wird eine längenmäßig gestaffelte (50 - 100 m; >100 m) Sonderregelung auf Selbstkostenerstattungsbasis pro Tunnelmeter vorgeschlagen, die auch vorab in der Ausschreibung festgelegt werden sollte. Für Störungen, die bei der Erkundung nicht oder nur teilweise erkannt wurden, deren Antreffen aber für möglich gehalten wird, ist der Grad der Wahrscheinlichkeit ihres Antreffens anzugeben. Anbieter sollten davon ausgehen dürfen, daß mit Störungen oder Störungsdimensionen, die in der Ausschreibung völlig unerwähnt bleiben, auch nicht zu rechnen ist. Dies gilt besonders für längere Störungen, die die weiter oben genannten Grundsatzentscheidungen beeinflussen.

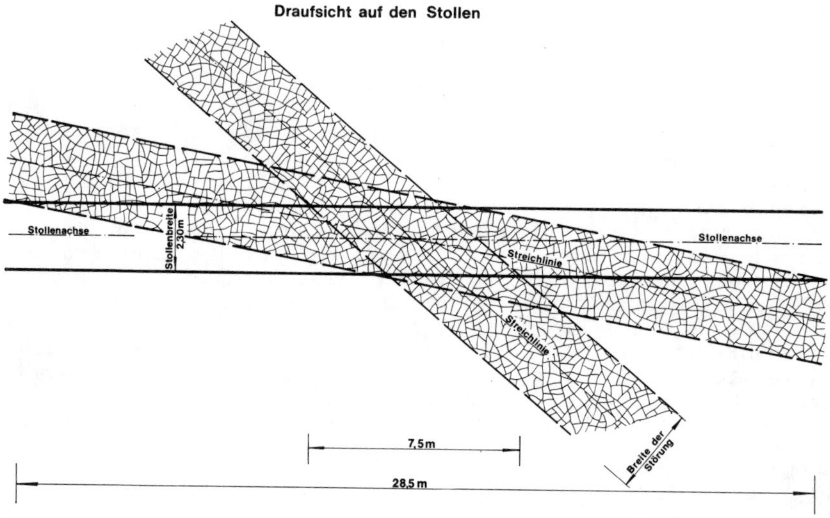

Bild 8 Leichte Veränderungen in der Streichrichtung ergeben besonders bei flachen Winkeln ein Vielfaches an Störungslängen im Tunnel.

5 FORDERUNGEN AN DIE TUNNELBOHRMASCHINEN

Aus den bisher gemachten Erfahrungen ergeben sich einige grundsätzliche Forderungen an Tunnelbohrmaschinen, um mit ihnen flexibel auf bestimmte, immer wieder vorkommende Gebirgsverhältnisse reagieren zu können. Es muß aber betont werden, daß Flexibilität nicht Universalität bedeuten darf: nicht jede Maschine muß alles haben bzw. können. Aufgrund der gegebenen Randbedingungen für jedes einzelne Projekt muß stets neu untersucht werden, ob sich eine Maschine zum Auffahren eignet, welcher Art ihre Konstruktion sein muß und welche Kompromisse beim Einsatz von Gebraucht-Maschinen noch vertretbar sind.
Es ergeben sich folgende Forderungen:

1. Schutzschild

Ein Schutzschild muß die Maschine im vorderen Bereich vor nachbrechendem Gebirge schützen - im Extremfall rundum -, bis die vorläufige Sicherung eingebracht werden kann. Er muß auch verhindern, daß Gebirgsbrocken zwischen Maschine und Bohrkopf fallen und letzteren festklemmen.

2. Frühzeitige Gebirgssicherung

Die Gebirgssicherung muß möglichst direkt hinter dem Bohrkopf bzw. Staubschild - im Extremfall rundum - möglich sein. Gerade in Gebirge mit extrem kurzen Standzeiten hat dies eine hohe Bedeutung. Dieser Arbeitsbereich muß sicher geschützt und gut zugänglich sein. Es muß entsprechendes Hilfsgerät für die Sicherungsarbeiten in diesem Bereich auf der Maschine installiert sein, wie z.B. eine Bogen-Versatzeinrichtung und Ankerbohrgeräte. Die Sicherungsarbeiten müssen bei laufendem Bohrbetrieb möglich sein.

3. Aktive Verbesserung der Gebirgs-Standfestigkeit

Die eleganteste Methode, Störungen zu durchörtern, ist sicher ein frühzeitiges Verbessern der Gebirgs-Standfestigkeit. Erfolgreich praktiziert wurde bereits eine fächerförmige Vorausinjektion als "Gebirgs-Schutzschild" (Hövelhaus/Henneke, 1979). Ist ein Injizieren nicht möglich, wäre eine künstliche "Gebirgs-Bewehrung" auf ähnliche Art denkbar. Die erforderlichen Bohrungen müssen mit einem bzw. mehreren lafettenartig auf der TBM montierten Bohrgeräten möglich sein (s. Punkt 2).

4. Antransport von Sicherungsmaterial

Sicherungsmaterial und Arbeitsmittel müssen durch eine geeignete Transportvorrichtung vom anliefernden Transportmittel durch die Maschine bis zum Einbauort transportiert werden können. Körperlicher Einsatz des Personals sollte hierbei weitestgehend vermieden werden. Ein ausreichender Einsatzvorrat von Sicherungsmaterial muß auf der Maschine zwischengelagert werden können. Auch dessen An- und Abtransport muß in der oben beschriebenen Weise möglich sein.

5. Abtransport von Ausbruch- bzw. Nachbruchmaterial

Der Abtransport von Ausbruch- bzw. Nachbruchmaterial muß unabhängig vom Bohrbetrieb auch dann laufen können, wenn dieses Material händisch gelöst wurde. Hierzu gehört, daß vor dem Bohrkopf gelöstes Material durch diesen hindurch abgefördert werden kann, ohne daß der Bohrkopf bewegt werden muß (z.B. vorgezogenes Förderband). Nachbruchmaterial von der Sicherungsplattform muß direkt auf das Förderband geladen werden können.

6. Abstützung des Bohrkopfes

Eine großflächige Abstützung nach unten und seitlich möglichst dicht am Bohrkopf muß in der Lage sein, dessen Einsinken in weichem Material weitgehend zu verhindern. Eventuell muß dies durch eine aufwärtsgerichtete Gegenkraft unterstützt werden, die in der Lage ist, den Bohrkopf hochzudrücken.

7. Abweiser am Bohrkopf

Durch Abweiser am Bohrkopf soll verhindert werden, daß sich größere Gesteinsbrocken dort verklemmen. Anfallende Brocken verbleiben solange im Schneidraum, bis sie durch die Meißel weit genug verkleinert worden sind.

8. Schlammpumpe

Für Störungen mit weicher Füllung und hohem Wasserzufluß ist der Einbau einer Schlammpumpe erforderlich, da der Schlamm nicht über ein Förderband abgefördert werden kann.

6 FORDERUNGEN AN DIE BAUSTELLENORGANISATION

Bei entsprechender Vorbereitung und Einstellung auf eine Störzone lassen sich allzu drastische Leistungseinbußen verhindern. Daraus ergibt sich folgende Forderung an die Baustellen-

Organisation:
Vorbereitete Verfahrenskonzepte
Eine Tunnelbohrmaschine und ihre Mannschaft muß jederzeit darauf vorbereitet sein, in der Ausschreibung beschriebene, jedoch örtlich nicht vorhersehbare Störungen anzubohren. Hierzu gehören klare Verfahrenskonzepte für das notwendige Vorgehen und das ständige Bereithalten des erforderlichen Materials und Geräts zur Gebirgssicherung bzw. für eine künstliche Verspannungsunterstützung.

Werden die aufgestellten Forderungen im Bedarfsfalle soweit wie notwendig erfüllt, sind auch Störzonen größerer Ausdehnung keine unüberwindlichen Hindernisse mehr, sie sind mit wirtschaftlich vertretbarem Aufwand durchfahrbar. Bei neueren Tunnelbohrmaschinen sind die genannten Forderungen häufig schon - zumindest teilweise - im Grundsatz verwirklicht, Verbesserungen sind aber noch möglich. Werden die aufgestellten Forderungen nicht berücksichtigt, werden auch in Zukunft Tunnelbohrmaschinen in Störzonen teilweise oder ganz scheitern.

7 LITERATUR

Beckmann, U. Einflußgrößen auf den Einsatz von Tunnelbohrmaschinen. Diss. TU Braunschweig (in Vorbereitung).

Beckmann, U./Simons, H. Tunnel boring machine payment on the basis of actual rock quality influence. Tunnelling '82, London, The Institution of Mining and Metallurgy.

Hövelhaus, H.-W./ Henneke, J. Maschineller Gesteinsstreckenvortrieb. Glückauf 115 (1979) Nr. 9, 403 - 410.

Nicholson, K. Coping with difficult ground on the full face mechanised tunnel drives at Kielder Tunnels and Tunnelling (1979) June, 55 - 57.

Schoknecht, H. Schachtanlage Victoria 1/2 in Lünen. Unser Betrieb, Deilmann-Haniel (Dez. 1978) Nr. 22.

Stapel, A.G. In die Tunnelröhre von morgen geguckt. Bauwirtschaft 19. Nov. (1981) H. 46/47, 1677-1686.

PRE-INVESTIGATION AND GEOLOGICAL FOLLOW-UP OF A TBM PROJECT IN AUSTRIA

Geologische Voruntersuchungen und die Projektverfolgung in einem Tunnel in Österreich

Investigations préliminaires et suite d'un projet de tunnel en Autriche

ERNST BUECHI
University of Berne, Switzerland
ERIC KARNELO
Atlas Copco Jarva AG, Thun, Switzerland

SUMMARY:
The pre-investigation of geological conditions for a tunnel boring machine project is of great importance as difficult conditions, either very hard rock or too soft and decomposed rock can result in a slow down of the performance and an increase of the cost. This can be difficult to accept both for the contractor and the owner of the tunnel.
It is described how the pre-investigations have been made on a project in Kärnten, Austria, and how the follow-up has been made in cooperation between the owner, contractor and the supplier of the TBM.
Different new ideas have been tried to improve the testing of the rock and the information of the rock mass.

ZUSAMMENFASSUNG:
Die geologischen Voruntersuchungen sind von grosser Bedeutung für eine Tunnelfräsmaschine. Entweder sehr harte Gesteinspartien oder schlechte gebräche Verhältnisse können zur Verminderung der Maschinenvortreibsleistung führen und dadurch zu erhöhten Baukosten. Dies kann zu vertraglichen Schwierigkeiten zwischen Bauherr und Unternehmer führen.
Es wird beschrieben, wie die Voruntersuchungen für ein Projekt in Kärnten, Oesterreich ausgeführt wurden und wie die eigentliche Projektverfolgung verlief, in enger Zusammenarbeit mit Bauherr, Unternehmer und dem Maschinenhersteller. Verschiedene neue Methoden wurden untersucht um die Aussagekraft einzelner Testverfahren zu verifizieren.

RESUME:
Les analyses géologiques précédentes sont de très grande importance pour un tunnelier. D'une part les zônes extrèmement dures ou d'autre part des zônes mylonitisées avec très peu de résistence conduisent à une diminuation de la performance de la machine et y inclus une augmentation des frais. Cela provoque souvent des problèmes entre le propriétaire et l'entrepreneur.
Les analyses précédentes sont déscrites pour un projet à Kärnten, Autriche. Et puis on décrit les travaux et les tests qui sont faits pendant et après le travail du tunnelier en collaboration avec le propriétaire, l'entrepreneur et le constructeur de la machine. Plusieurs nouvelles méthodes ont été testées concernant leur valeur pour des prédictions de la performance et les frais d'un tunnelier.

1. THE WOELLA TUNNEL

The Woellabach is a part of an extension of the hydropower plant Innerfragant in the Fragant Power Project Group belonging to Kärntner Elektrizitäts-Aktiengesellschaft (Kelag) with headoffice in Klagenfurt, Austria.

The tunnel is 6770 m long with a diameter of 3.5 m and will bring the water from the Woella stream to the plants in the valley. Two smaller streams will also be taken in by short diversion tunnels. One of them is also made by TBM why the total length driven will be 7200 m. The contractor responsible for the

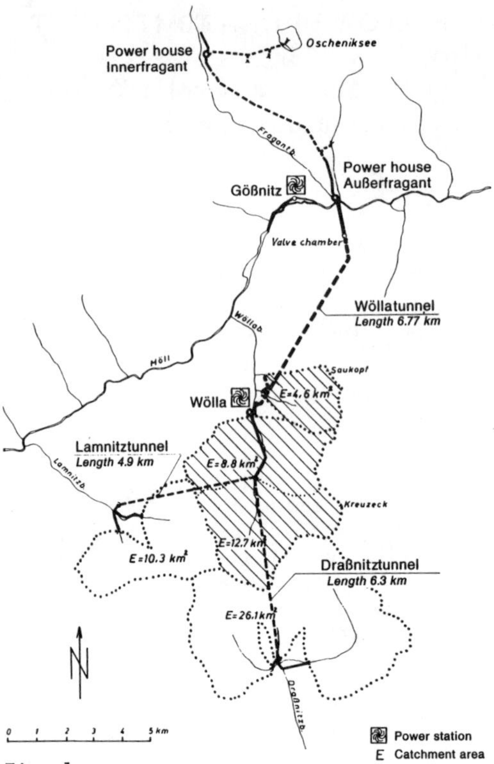

Fig. 1
Fragant Power Project Group - Kreuzeck Intake Area

tunnelling project is Ilbau in Spittal/-Drau, Austria, see Fig. 1.

2. BASIC GEOLOGICAL INFORMATION

A general geological report for this project was prepared by a consulting geologist for the owner company Kelag including a geological map 1:10'000, a geological profile for the tunnel line, a detailed mapping for a main shear zone and a description for the petrographic and the tectonic situation in this area, see Fig. 2. Later on, three variants of tunnel lines with further geological descriptions were available. At the beginning all descriptions were based to a conventional method. After a decision to use a TBM (it was the first project for Kelag and for Ilbau to operate with a TBM) for the contract a classification in 7 classes was prepared. It is including different rock qualities and their influence on the tunnelling with a TBM and the corresponding need for rock support, similar to DETZELHOFER, (1979).

The tunnel passes through the rocks of the "zentralalpinen Altkristallins", mainly composed of paragneissis, chlorite-mica-schists, with amphibolitic pegmatite and amphibolitic lenses. The whole complex is modified by intensive tectonic and diaphthoretic events.

For the predictions of the TBM performance (advance rate and cutter consumption) the Atlas Copco Jarva company tested 12 rock samples for calculations with the prediction formula of the Colorado School of Mines (FUN DEN WANG OZDEMIR, SNYDER, 1978) in combination with experiences in similar rock conditions (uniaxial Compressive Strength, Point Load Test, Cerchar Abrasivity Index, petrographic thin section analysis).

Later on, in collaboration with the University of Luela (S) a further

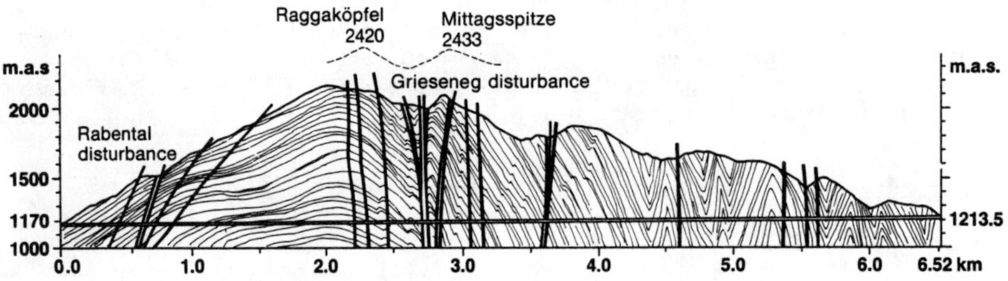

Fig. 2
Wölla Tunnel - Longitudinal Section

prediction for the advance rate for the whole project was given, based on indentation tests, (HANDEWITH 1972)).

3. DESCRIPTION OF THE TUNNEL BORING MACHINE (TBM)

Based on the geological investigation an Atlas Copco Jarva TBM Mark 12-035 was chosen. The machine got a "T" type clamping system which gives good space around the machine in the relatively small tunnel size (3.5 m). See Fig. 3.

This system also includes two front grippers and a front lift leg which makes it possible to pass soft rock with less problems. The cutter head is also enclosed with a rotating crown shield to hinder blocky ground to stall the head. It was later proven that all these measures helped by passing bad zones and caving ground.

To avoid that the machine could be torque limited in the softer rock the power for the cutterhead was chosen extra high, 4 motors of 150 kW.

The cutter head is fitted with 22 single disc cutters (disc Ø 40 cm)

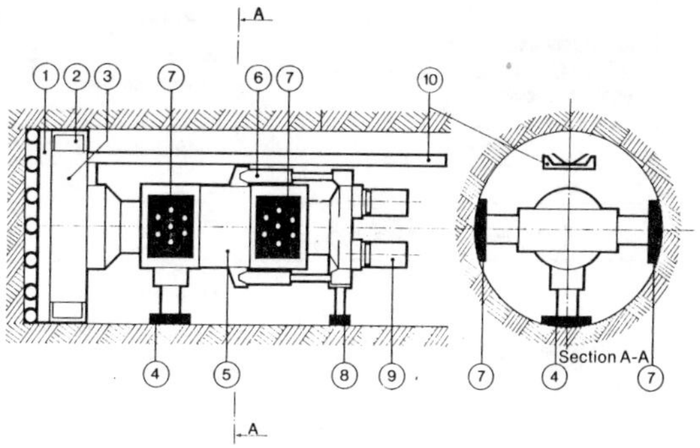

Component location

1. Cutter head and cutters
2. Muck bucket
3. Muck rings
4. Front lift leg (1)
5. Main body
6. Thrust cylinder
7. Clamp legs (4)
8. Reset legs (2)
9. Electric drive motor
10. Primary conveyor

Fig. 3

and a 4 disc center cutter (disc Ø 30 cm).

Rockbolting is possible with stoper rock drills behind the front part of the machine where also the pre-manufactured rail segments are installed.

Owner Company: KELAG	Constructor Company: ILBAU	Manufacturer of TBM: ATLAS COPCO JARVA	Institute CERAC	University of Luela
- Geological mapping of the tunnel 1) - Petrography	- Shift reports 2) - Continuous monitoring TBM thrust, amps, rate of penetration - Core drilling	- Equipment for core drilling 3) - Rock mechanics: uniaxial CST PLT CAI - Structural and mineralogical analysis - Cutter change report - Cutter wear report	- Mini Disc-Test 4) - Field indentation test 5)	- Geophysical methods 6) - Indentation Test 7)

1) including classification with regard to rock type, crack and joint frequency, direction and type
2) prepared and proposed by Atlas Copco Jarva AG, see Fig. 4
3) installation of a Pixie 20 on TBM back up equipment, 8 cm core diameter
4) DUBUGNON, JANACH, 1981
5) similar to Modified Schmidt Hammer, JANACH, MERMINOD, 1982
6) SUNDIN, 1981
7) HANDEWITH, 1972

Atlas Copco **Schicht-Rapport**	Baustelle: Wölla	Datum: 05.10.81
	Maschinenführer:	Schicht: Tag

Position		Vortrieb Meter	Stundenzähler 807.9		Leistung m/h
Start	Ende		Schicht	Total	
2924.-	2946,-	22 m	5,7	813,6	3,9

Richtungskontrolle

Bezeichne mit
O beim Start
× beim Ende

von Schicht

vordere

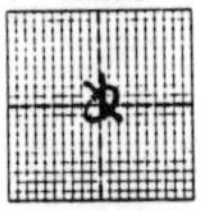

hintere

Code für Unterbruch

MD	Mechanischer Defekt der Maschine	CI	Kühlungsdefekt
BC	Förderband Maschine	MM	Maschinenwartung
EL	Elektr. Defekt auf der Maschine	TC	Meisselwechsel
HY	Hydr. Defekt auf der Maschine	TI	Meisselkontrolle

LB Schichtpause

MR	Keine Lehrwagen	CE	Kühlung extern
BB	Förderband Nachläufer	PS	Elektrische Zufuhr
CP	Wagenwechselvorrichtung	LA	Laser, Vermessungen
VT	Ventilation	MS	Materialzufuhr
DS	Entstaubung	RT	Holz unter Anpressplatte
TR	Geleise und Leitungen	GS	Ausbau

Fräsen		Umsetzen		Stop		Ursache für Unterbruch Code oder Klartext	Druck Vorschub	Amp. Fräskopf
Uhrzeit	Min.	Uhrzeit	Min.	Uhrzeit	Min.			
				0600	45	TI Wartung		
0645	25	0710	3				90	170
0713	35	0748		0748		TC 3Stück	100	160
0945	23	1008	6				125	180
1014	23	1047	4				125	160
1051	21	1112	5				125	170
1117	21	1136	4				100	170
1140	20	1200		1200		LB	90	170
1300	4	1304	3					
1307	16	1323	3				80	180
1326	19	1345	3				80	180
1348	15	1403	7			MR	70	150
1411	17	1428	5				80	180
1433	5			1438		MR	100	170
1447	12	1459	6					
1505	16	1521	9			MR	100	170
1530	16	1546		~~1549~~			110	180
1549	15			1604		MR	80	170
1612	5	1617	3				7	
1620	19	1639	4				70	170
						Total / Total Durchschnitt		

Bemerkungen:

Hydraulik-Anlage				Zufuhr Schmierfett	Temperatur Hauptlager	Unterschriften	
Amp. 1. Pumpe	Amp. 2. Pumpe	Temperatur	Zufuhr Hydrauliköl			Atlas Copco	Kunde
52	21	80	145	45 bar			

Fig. 4

4. Specifications - Atlas Copco Jarva TBM MK 12-035

Bore Diameter	3.5 m
Cutter head - Horsepower	600 kW
- Rotational Speed	10.6 rpm
- Thrust	635 tons
- Torque	540 kNm
- Stroke	1.2 m
- Motors	4 x 150 kW
Clamp Leg Gripper Force	1,900 tons
Clamp Leg Configuration	"T" Design
Muck Handling Capacity	6 m/hour
Maximum Hydraulic System Pressure	172 bar
Number of Cutting Discs	26
Cutter Diameter	39.4 cm
Total Machine Power	882 kVA
Total Machine Length	11.6 m
Total Machine Weight	150 tons

5. PLANNED FOLLOW UP FOR THE PROJECT

On a planning meeting the distribution of the work for a very ambitious and detailed follow up was discussed and decided according to the following diagram. At this time the analysis of different methods is still going on. The final reports and results will be available within this group.

6. GEOLOGICAL RESULTS

A general comparison of the predicted and the effective geological tunnel profile shows a good correspondence. The only main difference was the shear zone of Griesenegg. Predicted was a zone of about 250 m with poor rock quality and several mylonites.

In reality it was splitting up to several discontinuities, which had only little influence on the mining procedure.

The rock mechanical analysis shows a large range of each parameter within to the different rock types.

The utilization of shift reports and the continuous monitoring of thrust, torque and instantaneous penetration rate in combination with a detailed geological mapping gives a lot of possibilities for analysis. Variations in rock

	CST (MPa) *1	PLT (MPa) *2	CAI (0.1 mm) *3
Gneiss	160-220	7.5-11.0	3.4-4.8
Schist	60-140	4.0- 6.5	2.2-3.1
Pegmatite, Aplite	180-220	7.0- 9.0	4.2-4.6
Amphibolite	180-260	9.0-12.0	3.4-3.8

*1 Compressive strength test, core diameter 22 mm, length 44 mm, polished ends and dried at 104 °C

*2 Point load test (indirect tensile strength), all measurements on fresh broken rock samples (no cores)

*3 Cerchar abrasivity index

type and in rock mass properties can be studied, providing a lot of information of the influence on the TBM performance.

The smooth tunnel wall presents excellent conditions to observe deformations and rock falls resulting from the local rock pressure situation. These observations are so impressive that on the one hand an overestimation may result. On the other hand a flexible shotcrete lining is possible to combine with a reasonable rock bolting, to avoid an unnecessary systematical lining.

7. ORGANIZATION AND TBM PERFORMANCE

The crew consists of 7 men in the tunnel, working 11 hours each shift seven days a week, enabling a very high utilization of the machine.

With this organization and a very good teamwork within the crews the performance has been extremly good. The assembly started on July 7, 1981 and the whole tunnel, including the diversion tunnel of 551 m, resulting in a total length of 7250 m, was ready in the first week of March 1982.

Advance Rates until January 16, 1982

Meter per	Best	Average
Hour	6	3.8
Day	63	34.0
Week	345	226.0
Month	1265	942.0

The utilization of the TBM (boring and resetting) has been over 60 % of total working time. This must be regarded as unusually good taking also in consideration that the work was going on continuously with no maintenance shifts or stops over weekends and holidays. Only over Christmas the whole jobsite was closed.

8. FLEXABILITY OF A TBM

The main tunnel of this project was planned to be mined with a TBM and to be finished in March 1982. From this tunnel two short tunnels should be done by drill and blast for the water intake of the two rivers: "Klenbach" and the "Gronbach".

By the reason of the very high advance rate of the TBM and because of the experience, that even in poor rock conditions the Atlas Copco Jarva TBM was able to advance twice as fast as with the conventional method, the construction company Ilbau decided to mine the tunnel for the water intake of the "Klenbach" (551 m) with the TBM too. In a curve of 329 m radius and 70° the machine turned to the right, see Fig. 5. On January 15th, after 23 working days, partly in poor and weathered rock conditions, the machine broke through to the surface. A great advantage was, that this could be done without any preparations from outside for the tunnel portal.

In only two days the TBM with the back-up system was drawn back for 314 m taking off the rails and cleaning the tunnel floor. In the following 9 days the new starting chamber was prepared by drill and blast to continue in the direction of the main tunnel. In another 4 days the machine was drawn back to the branching point, pushed over to the left and walked into the starting chamber. On February 1, only 15 days after the break through and a total interruption of 38 working days on the main tunnel the TBM could continue to finish the project on March 4.

This is a good example that also a TBM can be used in a flexible way, if the machine is adapted for different rock conditions and with a gripping sys-

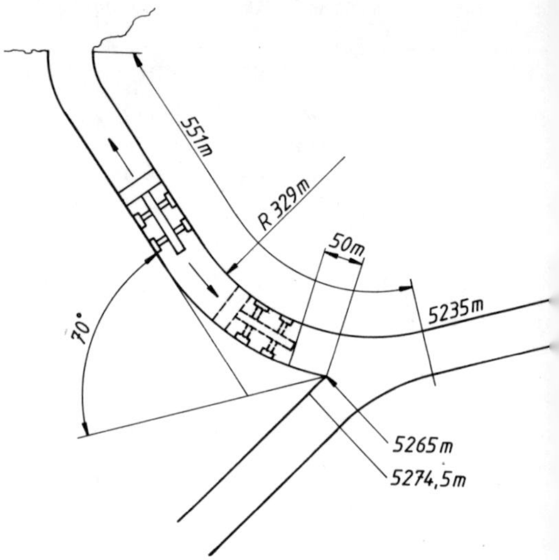

Fig. 5

tem, that allows that the machine can walk itself. The management must, however, also have the courage to test unconventional ideas.

9. CONCLUSIONS

Today a number of prediction systems exist based on different rock parameters combined with experience like Colorado School of Mines, NTH Trondheim (Blindheim), Handewith Indentation (Ingersoll Rand), giving all fairly good results in homogeneous rock. A good system for predicting the influence of the rock mass like anisotropy, schistosity, fracture frequency, however, is still lacking. The result in the Woella tunnel was better than anticipated mainly because of the influence of jointing and other weakness planes.

In the NTH method a way of considering the fracture frequency is included in a more systematic way. It is, however, very difficult to use this in advance (for prediction) and has its greatest advantage in explaining why the result with a TBM was different from what could be expected. Once a tunnel is made the fracture frequency can be checked easier.

The experience from the Woella tunnel has given some ideas how a system could be built up which is easier to use in advance. Those ideas will be followed up on other projects.

The experience of this TBM project has proven that a good pre-investigation is still of great importance. It has, however, also been demonstrated how difficult it is to predict the influence on the tunnel level of shear zones and faults that can only be observed on the surface, especially if the overburden is great. The geophysical methods tested have not yet made it possible to give a better prediction. They have, however, at least indicated the fault zones in a good way and more work should be done to improve such methods.

The pre-investigation is most important for finding zones with bad rock and great water inflow, as most hard rock today is not hindering the TBM and can be bored with economical speed and costs. The TBM can, however, also be prepared and adapted for bad rock conditions decreasing this influence on the TBM performance. It is, however, difficult to find the right balance in the design, as a machine that can cope well with both, very hard and very soft rock, is not really ideal for any of these conditions.

The only way to come any further in understanding the problems and improvement of the machines is the detailed follow up of projects. We think that the cooperation between the owner of the tunnel, the contractor, research institutes and the manufacturer of the machine that has been used in this project is an example how it could be done.

We therefore like to thank Dr. Wellacher and Dr. Litscher from Kelag, Dir. Gasser and Ing. Zdraleck from Ilbau for making this study and report possible.

10. BIBLIOGRAPHY

Blindheim, O.T., Dahl Johannsen, E. 1981, "Fullprofilboring av Tunneler" Prosjektrapport 1.79, Trondheim, Universitetet i Trondheim.

Detzelhofer, H. 1979, 25 Jahre Gebirgsklassifizierung nach "Lauffer" im Wandel der Stollenbautechnik, Oesterreichische Wasserwirtschaft 31, p. 181 ff.

Dubugnon, O., Janach, W. 1981, "Mini-Rollenbohrwerkzeug zur Leistungsvorhersage von Tunnelbohrmaschinen", Düsseldorf, Int. Kongress "Tunnel 81".

Handewith, H.J. 1972, "Suggested tunnel investigation criteria for rock boring machines" IngersollRand Comp., Lawrence Division, Seattle. Presented at the 8th Canadian Rock Mech. Symposium, Toronto 1972, pp 177 - 186.

Janach, W., Mérminod, A. 1982, "Rock Abrasivity Test with a Modified Schmidt Hammer, Int. J. Rock Mech. Min. Sci. & Geomech. Vol. 19 pp. 43 to 45, 1982.

MASCHINELLES AUFFAHREN VON HORIZONTALEN TUNNELSTRECKEN GRÖSSEREN DURCHMESSERS MIT TUNNELBOHRMASCHINEN AN BEISPIELEN IN FRANKREICH, GUATEMALA UND DER SCHWEIZ

Mechanical driving of horizontal-type tunnels with large diameter, by means of tunnel boring machines, taking as examples France, Guatemala and Switzerland

Creusement mécanique de tunnels horizontaux à grand diamètre au moyen de tunneliers, exemples de la France, du Guatemala et de la Suisse

M.EISTERT
Wirth GmbH, Erkelenz, Bundesrepublik Deutschland

SUMMARY:
The WIRTH GmbH manufactures full-face-tunneling machines and enlarging machines. Full diameter- and enlarging machines for tunnel projects with large diameter are compared economically and technically. It is shown how the tunnel diameter and the technical rock data affect the design of the tunnel boring machines. By means of various job sites the technical improvement of the WIRTH tunnel boring machines is explained.

ZUSAMMENFASSUNG:
Die WIRTH GmbH fertigt Vollschnitt- und Erweiterungstunnelbohrmaschinen. In einem wirtschaftlichen und technischen Vergleich werden Vollschnitt- und Erweiterungsmaschinen für Tunnel-Projekte mit großem Durchmesser gegenübergestellt. Der Einfluß des Tunneldurchmessers bzw. der Gesteinsdaten auf die technische Auslegung der Tunnelbohrmaschinen wird aufgezeigt. Verschiedene Baustelleneinsätze erläutern die technische Weiterentwicklung der WIRTH-Tunnelbohrmaschinen.

RESUME:
La Soc. WIRTH GmbH fabrique des tunneliers pleine section et d'élargissement. Les machines pleine section et d'élargissement pour les projects des tunnels aux grands diamétres sont comparées économiquement et techniquement. L'influence du diamétre de tunnel et/ou des caractéristiques du rocher sur la conception technique des tunneliers est indiquée. Plusieurs emplois sur les chantiers de forage expliquent l'amélioration technique des tunneliers WIRTH.

1. EINLEITUNG

Im Tunnelbau gewannen vollmechanische Vortriebsmethoden in den letzten Jahren gegenüber den konventionellen bergmännischen Methoden zunehmend an Bedeutung. In der Entwicklung des vollmechanischen Tunnelvortriebs konnten in den letzten 10 - 15 Jahren erhebliche Fortschritte erzielt werden, an denen auch unsere Firma maßgeblich beteiligt war.

Seit 1967 baut WIRTH Tunnelbohrmaschinen für Hartgesteinformationen. Zur Zeit bietet WIRTH Vollschnittmaschinen bis zu einem Bohrdurchmesser von 8 m und Erweiterungsmaschinen bis 12 m Bohrdurchmesser an. Kennzeichnend für das Erweiterungssystem ist, daß zunächst im Zentrum ein Pilotstollen mit verhältnismäßig kleinem Durchmesser - mindestens jedoch 3,30 m - aufgefahren wird, der als Richtstollen für den anschließenden Einsatz der Erweiterungsmaschine dient. Das Schema beider Maschinentypen ist auf Bild 1 dargestellt.

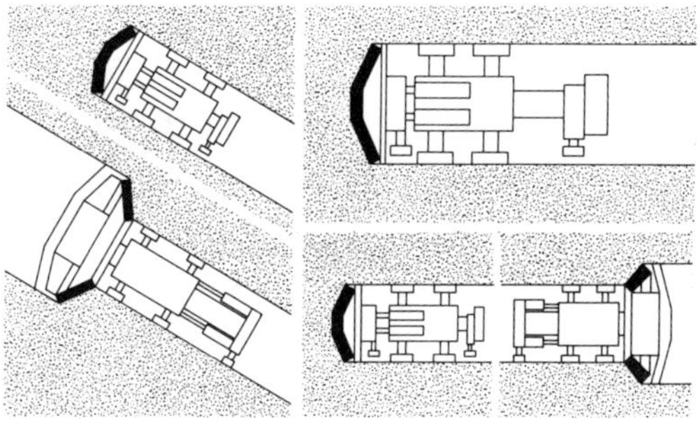

Bild 1 Schema Vollschnittmaschine - Erweiterungsmaschine

Beide Maschinentypen bestehen im wesentlichen aus Bohrkopf, Innenkelly mit Antrieb, Außenkelly mit Verspannelementen sowie nachgeschalteten Ver- und Entsorgunseinrichtungen. Die Innenkelly wird in der gegen das Gebirge verspannten Außenkelly geführt und schiebt den elektrisch oder hydrostatisch angetriebenen Bohrkopf gegen das Gebirge. Die Vorschubzylinder stützen sich gegen die Außenkelly ab. Bei der Vollschnittmaschine wird die Außenkelly gegen das gebohrte Profil verspannt, bei der Erweiterungsmaschine in der Pilotbohrung.

Da auch bei den Erweiterungsmaschinen der volle Restquerschnitt des Tunnels in einem Arbeitsgang abgebohrt wird, sind sie als Besonderheit der Vollschnittmaschinen aufzufassen und nicht als Teilschnittmaschine, deren wesentliches Merkmal ein im Verhältnis zum aufzufahrenden Querschnitt kleiner, horizontal und vertikal verfahroder schwenkbarer Schneidkopf ist.

2. EINFLUSS DES TUNNELDURCHMESSERS

Im Zusammenwirken von Tunnelbohrmaschine und Gebirge ergeben sich mit wachsendem Durchmesser einige gegenläufige Gesetzmäßigkeiten:

- Die erforderliche Vorschubkraft der Tunnelbohrmaschine wächst linear, das zur Drehung des Bohrkopfes erforderliche Drehmoment quadratisch mit dem Durchmesser.

  Die aus Vorschubkraft und Drehmoment resultierenden Reaktionskräfte müssen über die Verspannung sicher in das Gebirge eingeleitet werden. Vollschnittmaschinen verspannen sich gegen die gebohrte Tunnelwand, diese erfährt dadurch eine große zusätzliche Belastung. Erweiterungsmaschinen verspannen sich im Pilotloch; dadurch bleibt das Endprofil unbelastet.

- Mit wachsendem Durchmesser verringert sich bei sonst gleicher Gebirgsklasse die Standzeit des ungesicherten Hohlraums, gestörte Zonen werden stärker wirksam. Wenn die Standzeit des Gebirges nicht für den Durchgang der Tunnelbohrmaschine ausreicht, sind unmittelbar hinter dem Bohrkopf bereits Sicherungsmaßnahmen erforderlich, die die Vortriebsleistung mindern können.

- Mit wachsendem Durchmesser muß die Drehzahl des Bohrkopfes verringert werden, da die Bahngeschwindigkeit der Rollenbohrwerkzeuge einen maximalen Wert von 1,5 - 2 m/s nicht überschreiten darf. Di Nettobohrgeschwindigkeit ist eine linear Funktion von Drehzahl des Bohrkopfes und Eindringtiefe (penetration) der Werkzeug Da zudem bei Vollschnittmaschinen jede Schneidbahn nur einfach bestückt werden kann, sinkt bei diesen Maschinen die Nettobohrgeschwindigkeit bei sonst gleichen Parametern mit wachsendem Durch messer. Dadurch wird die Notwendigkeit von Sicherungsarbeiten im Maschinenbereich weiter erhöht.

3. VERGLEICH VOLLSCHNITTMASCHINE-ERWEITERUNGSMASCHINE

Erweiterungsmaschinen erlauben eine besser Anpassung an unterschiedliche Bohrdurchmesser als Vollschnittmaschinen. Der Grund liegt darin, daß alle Erweiterungsmaschine sich im Vorbohrloch verspannen. Somit sind bei gleichem Pilotdurchmesser keine Änderungen am Maschinenkörper, sondern nur Änderungen am Bohrkopf erforderlich. Eine Vollschnittmaschine kann im Bohrdurchmesse mit technisch vertretbaren Mitteln um etwa 70 - 100 cm geändert werden (neuer Bohrkopf, Änderung der Verspannung). Eine solche Änderung kostet etwa 20 - 25 % des Maschinenneuwertes. Eine Erweiterungsmaschine kann dagegen um max. 3 - 4 m im Bohrdurchmesser geändert werden, eine solche Änderung kostet nur etwa 10 - 15 % des Maschinenneuwertes. Der durch nachträglichen Umbau maximal mögliche Bohrdurchmesser wird durch die in der Maschine ursprünglich installierte Leistung und die Parameter des zu bohrenden Gesteins begrenzt.

Das Erweiterungssystem ermöglicht eine vielseitigere Nutzung der Maschineneinheiten gegenüber einer Vollschnittmaschine Trotz dieses Vorteils erfordert es im Vergleich zu einer gleichgroßen Vollschnittmaschine keine größeren Investitionen. Ein Kombination aus Vollschnittmaschine zum Bohren des Pilotstollens und einstufiger Erweiterungsmaschine mit eigener Energieversorgung ist sogar geringfügig preiswerter als eine gleichgroße Vollschnittmaschine. Der Durchmesser der Pilotmaschine liegt in einem Bereich, der sehr häufig bei begehbaren Servicestollen, Wasserüberleitungsstollen und Schrägschächten für Wasserkraft- und Belüftungsanlagen vorkommt. Zusammen mit der Erweiterungsmaschine für große Querschnitte unterschiedlichster Durchmesser erschließt diese Maschinenkombination also ein weites Einsatzspektrum.

)as Auffahren eines Pilotstollens bietet über den beschriebenen wirtschaftlichen /orteilen hinaus folgende technische Vor-.eile:

- Aufschluß über eventuell unbekannte geologische Details
- Vereinfachte Wetterführung
- Möglichkeit präventiver Sicherungsmaßnahmen vom Pilotstollen aus
- Freier Querschnitt hinter dem Bohrkopf für Ausbau oder Betonierungsarbeiten
- Steigerungsmöglichkeit der Bohrgeschwindigkeit der Erweiterungsmaschine im Vergleich zu gleichgroßer Vollschnittmaschine. Da das die Bohrgeschwindigkeit bestimmende Bohrkopfzentrum entfällt, können die Schneidbahnen mehrfach bestückt werden.

:um heutigen Zeitpunkt stellt unserer leinung nach die Erweiterungsmaschine lie einzige Lösungsmöglichkeit dar, Schrägschächte mit Durchmessern größer 4 m und ;teigungen bis zu 45° maschinell aufzu-:ahren.

)ie Einsatzgrenze von Erweiterungsmaschinen ist dann erreicht, wenn bereits im 'ilotbohrloch in großem Umfang ein aufwendiger Ausbau erforderlich ist, da dieser 'on der Erweiterungsmaschine weggebohrt verden muß. Kleinere Störzonen könnten :. B. mit Hilfe einer unbewehrten Spritzbetonsicherung überwunden werden. Eine andere Möglichkeit wäre der Einsatz von geklebten Kunststoffankern, die vom Pilotstollen aus in der für den Endquerschnitt erforderlichen Länge gesetzt werden. Die überlänge wird dann später von der Erweiterungsmaschine weggebohrt.

. BOHRWERKZEUGE

ie Wirtschaftlichkeit des maschinellen unnelvortriebs wird maßgeblich von den erkzeugkosten beeinflußt. Alle unsere aschinen können mit standardisierten Disen- oder Warzenrollenbohrwerkzeuge ausgeüstet werden, die im eigenen Werk in Serie efertigt werden (Bild 2). Um die Bohrwerkeuge leicht wechseln zu können und um die rsatzteilhaltung zu erleichtern, sind alterungen und Lager untereinander ausauschbar. Zur Erhöhung des Bohrfortschritts st der Andruck je Werkzeug in den letzten ahren immer weiter gesteigert worden, Kontruktion und verwendete Materialien der ollenbohrwerkzeuge wurden entsprechend eiterentwickelt und erlauben heute einen ndruck bis zu 250 kN je Werkzeug. Gleicheitig konnte die Standzeit der Lager und Disken in den letzten Jahren ständig gesteigert werden, so daß die Werkzeugkosten je m^3 Festgestein trotz des gestiegenen Preisindexes gesenkt werden konnten. Je nach Festigkeit und Gehalt an abrasiven Mineralien können heute in der Regel für Dolomite, Kalkstein, Gneise, kristalline Schiefer Bohrwerkzeugkosten zwischen 5 und 40 DM/m^3 Festgestein angenommen werden.

Bild 2a Diskenrolle WIRTH ED-LWG IV

Bild 2b Warzendiskenrolle WIRTH WD4-LWG VI

5. EINSATZBEISPIELE

Im nachfolgenden möchte ich Ihnen über einige Einsätze von WIRTH-Tunnelbohrmaschinen mit einem Bohrdurchmesser von mehr als 5 m berichten. Als Maschinenhersteller beschränke ich mich in meinen Ausführungen auf die Vorstellung der Maschinenkonzeption, die auf den jeweiligen Baustellen zum Einsatz kamen.

5.1. Baustelle Pueblo Viejo Quixal, Guatemala

Im Rahmen des Kraftwerkbaues Pueblo Viejo Quixal in Guatemala mußte ein 16 km langer Druckstollen mit 5,64 m Durchmesser aufgefahren werden. Das geologische Gutachten wies auf der Stollentrasse Sandstein, Schiefer, Kalkstein, Dolomit und Mergel aus, einzelne Zonen sollten nur bedingt standfest sein. Wir erhielten 1977 den Auftrag, zwei baugleiche Tunnelbohrmaschinen zur Ausführung dieses Vorhabens zu liefern.

Beide Maschinen erhielten einen stufenlos regelbaren hydraulischen Antrieb. Dadurch ist es möglich, für jede geologische Formation durch Variation von Drehzahl und Vorschubkraft ein Optimum hinsichtlich des Bohrvorgangs zu erreichen. Die regelbare Drehzahl des Bohrkopfes erlaubt ein verhaltenes Bohren in gestörten Zonen. Dadurch wird die Gefahr des Verkeilens des Bohrkopfes durch hereinbrechende Gesteinsbrocken verringert. Außerdem wird die Bohrgutaufnahme durch das Schaufelwerk bei großen Wasserzuflüssen erleichtert. Beide Maschinen wurden mit einem Bohrkopfmantel versehen, der den Bohrkopf und das Kratz- und Schaufelwerk vor nachbrechendem Felsmaterial schützt. Der Mantel ist über Hydraulikzylinder mit der Innenkelly verbunden und dient gleichzeitig als vordere Abstützung der Maschine. Das hat den Vorteil, daß - falls erforderlich - bereits unmittelbar hinter dem Bohrkopf ein Stahlringausbau eingebracht werden kann. Der Abstand zwischen Kaliberkante Bohrkopf bis zum ersten Ausbauring beträgt nur ca. 1600 mm. Um das Einbringen des Ausbaues bzw. die Durchführung von anderen Sicherungsmaßnahmen zu erleichtern, wurden hinter dem Bohrkopf verstellbare Arbeitsbühnen angeordnet (Bild 3).

Bild 3 TB V-564 H, Blick auf Bohrkopfmantel, verstellbare Arbeitsbühnen, Vorschubzylinder bei Hubbeginn

Bild 4 TB V-564 H, Montage der Maschine auf der Baustelle

Zu Bohrbeginn - Juni 1978 - war vorgesehen, daß jede Maschine ca. 8000 m auffahren sollte. Die erste Maschine wurde jedoch nach 5100 m durch einen Fließsandeinbruch während eines Schichtwechsels verschüttet und nicht mehr geborgen. Für die zweite Maschine wurde der Losabschnitt auf 11.400 m verlängert. Sie erreichte am 18.4.1981, also nach 34 Monaten, das Losende und hat damit die z. Zt. längste durchgehende Bohrung mit einer WIRTH-Maschine aufgefahren. Trotz dieser guten Gesamtleistung zeigen die Baustellenberichte hohe Stillstandzeiten, die durch Sicherungsarbeiten bedingt waren. Diese Erkenntnisse führten zu einer grundlegenden Weiterentwicklung der Tunnelbohrmaschinen, die ich Ihnen am Beispiel unserer Maschinen TB IV und TBS V erläutern möchte.

5.2. Baustelle Le Pouget, Frankreich

Die TB IV-505, die ich Ihnen als nächstes vorstelle, wurde 1980 für das Auffahren eines Druckstollens von 5,05 m Durchmesser für das Kraftwerk Le Pouget im Südwesten von Frankreich gebaut. Die Stollentrasse verlief zwar vorwiegend durch gut bohrbaren Gneis, es mußten jedoch auch einige gestörte Zonen durchfahren werden.

Der Bohrkopfmantel dieser Maschine kann während des Vortriebs mechanisch im Durchmesser geringfügig verkleinert werden. Hierdurch wird die Gefahr des Festklemmens des Mantels in druckhaftem Gebirge verringert. Bei dieser und allen anderen beschriebenen Maschinen ist der Bohrkopfmantel in Vorschubrichtung gesehen über Hydraulikzylinder (Schleppzylinder) mit dem nicht drehenden Bohrgutzylinder verbunden, der Bestandteil der Innenkelly ist. Dadurch ist eine Verwinklung zwischen Mantel und Maschine möglich, wodurch die Kurvengängigkeit verbessert wird.

Bild 5 TB IV-505 H, Blick in den Arbeitsraum hinter dem Bohrkopf

Die Vorschubzylinder wurden zwischen Hinterkante Außenkelly und Innenkelly zurückverlegt und sind als Zugzylinder ausgebildet. Das über der Innenkelly liegende Förderband und die Belüftungslutte können bei Stillstand des Bohrkopfes hydraulisch bis zur ersten Verspannebene zurückgefahren werden. Da der Bohrkopfmantel gleichzeitig als vordere Abstützung der Maschine dient, ist der Raum zwischen Hinterkante Bohrkopf und Vorderkante Außenkelly nur noch durch den Vierkant der Innenkelly ausgefüllt. Bild 5 zeigt sehr deutlich den im Vergleich zu bisherigen Maschinenkonstruktionen großen Freiraum, der für Sicherungsarbeiten und die dafür erforderlichen Einrichtungen (Bohrlafette etc.) genutzt werden kann. Die hintere Abstützung und der Nachläufer wurden in Portalausführung konzipiert. Dadurch werden der Zugang zum Arbeitsraum hinter dem Bohrkopf für das Personal bzw. der Materialtransport wesentlich erleichtert.

Bild 6 TB IV-505 H, Gesamtansicht von der Maschinenrückseite

5.3. Schachtanlage Lohberg, Deutschland

Ab unserem Maschinentyp TB V, d.h. ab einem Durchmesser von ca. 5,50 m, ist es möglich, das Maschinenförderband im Innenraum der Innenkelly anzuordnen. Bei dieser Lösung entfällt die Unterbrechung des Bohrbetriebes bei Sicherungsarbeiten, die bei den kleineren Maschinen ein Zurückschieben des über der Innenkelly angeordneten Förderbandes erforderlich machen. Sicherungsarbeiten und Bohren sind jetzt in noch größerem Maße gleichzeitig möglich und führen zu einer Steigerung der Vortriebsleistung des Gesamtsystems. Bild 7 zeigt unsere Streckenvortriebsmaschine TBS V-650, bei der diese Anordnung zum ersten Mal verwirklicht wurde. Bei dieser Maschine wurden besonders die Belange des Steinkohlenbergbaus berücksichtigt, das Grundkonzept dieser Maschine wird jedoch auch bei unseren Tunnelbohrmaschinen für den Ingenieurtunnelbau Anwendung finden.

Zur Ortsbrustsicherung beim Meißelwechsel besitzt der Bohrkopf dieser Maschine einen Frontschild, der mittels Hydraulikzylinder um max. 800 mm aus dem Bohrkopf heraus gegen die Ortsbrust gefahren werden kann. Im Bereich der Firste können von der Rückseite des Bohrkopfes aus Lanzen durch den Bohrkopfmantel gesteckt werden, die als zusätzlicher Firstschutz dienen.

Bild 8 TBS V-650 E/Sch Frontansicht der Maschine

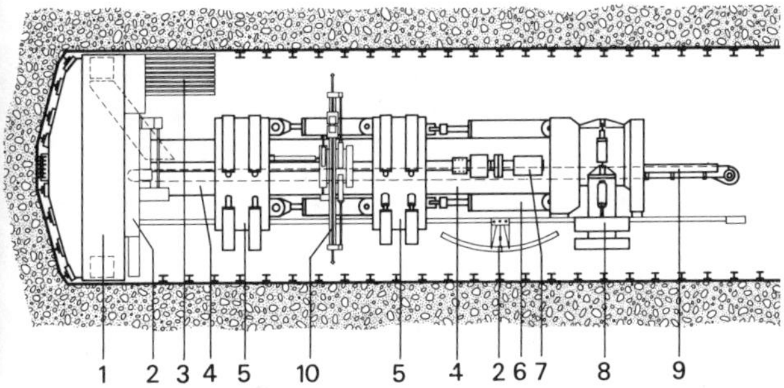

1. Bohrkopf mit hydraulisch verstellbarem Mantel
2. Ausbausetzvorrichtung und Transportsystem
3. Bohrkopfmantelverlängerung
4. Innenkelly
5. 2-teilige Außenkelly mit Spannschilden und Verstellzylinder
6. Vorschubzylinder
7. Bohrkopfantrieb
8. hintere Abstützung
9. Förderband
10. Ankerbohrgerät

Bild 7 TBS V-650 E/Sch Schnittzeichnung

Der Durchmesser des Bohrkopfmantels kann mittels Hydraulikzylinder um max. 15 cm verringert werden. Nach hinten ist der Mantel mit Schlepplanzen so weit verlängert, daß mit Hilfe einer Ausbausetzvorrichtung noch im Schutz des Mantels Ausbauringe vormontiert und verspannt werden können. Die Bogensegmente werden mittels zwei unter der Außenkelly installierten Einschienenhängebahnen zu der Ausbauvorrichtung gebracht. Zunächst werden die Segmente in einem an der Bohrkopfrückwand im Schutz des Bohrkopfmantels angebrachten Speicherrad zu einem kompletten Ring vormontiert. Transport, Einbau und Spannen des vormontierten Ausbauringes können bereits während des Bohrens durch einen Hubbock mit integrierter Spannvorrichtung vorgenommen werden. Dieser ist auf der Innenkelly zusammen mit der Ausbaubühne längsverschiebbar angeordnet.

Bild 9 TBS V-650 E/Sch Seitenansicht

Die Außenkelly ist in Längsrichtung in zwei Hälften geteilt, die über Hydraulikzylinder verbunden sind, so daß der Abstand der Verspannebenen zueinander verändert werden kann. Durch diese Anordnung und die Ausbildung der Spannschilde ist es möglich, unmittelbar hinter dem Bohrkopf einen Ringausbau mit beliebigem Bauabstand einzubringen, der bis auf 75 cm reduziert werden kann. Das Konzept der Maschine läßt es zu, zwischen den Außenkellyhälften Bohrlafetten zu installieren, die unabhängig vom Bohrvorgang der Vortriebsmaschine Ankerlöcher im First- und Sohlbereich in einer Ebene bohren, die senkrecht zur Vortriebsrichtung steht.

5.4. Kerenzerstraßentunnel, Schweiz

Der Tunnel mit dem größten Durchmesser, der bisher mit WIRTH-Tunnelbohrmaschinen aufgefahren wurde, ist zur Zeit am Walensee in der Schweiz im Bau.

Im Zuge der Bauarbeiten für die schweizer Autobahn N 3 wurde im Februar 1979 am Walensee mit dem Bau eines 5,67 km langen Tunnels begonnen, der die Richtungsfahrbahn der N 3 Richtung Chur unter dem Kerenzerberg aufnimmt, während für den Verkehr in Richtung Zürich die bestehende Nationalstraße ausgebaut wird.

Die ganze Tunnelstrecke ist in erster Linie aus geologischen Gründen in zwei Baulose aufgeteilt. Auf dem 3039 m langen Los Gäsi wird mit Tunnelbohrmaschinen ein Kreisprofil von 11 m Durchmesser und 95 m² Querschnitt aufgefahren. Hierbei sind auf den ersten 2,2 km standfeste Kreidekalke, die örtlich mit Mergelschichten durchsetzt sind zu durchfahren, anschließend standfester Kalkfels, teils gebräche Zementsteinbrekzie. Das andere Los wird in konventioneller Bauweise in einem Maulprofil aufgefahren, da dort größere Stör- und Lockerzonen angetroffen werden.

Bild 10 Kerenzerstraßentunnel, Montage des Erweiterungsbohrkopfes Ø 11 m

Den Zuschlag für das Los Gäsi erhielt eine Arbeitsgemeinschaft von 7 namhaften schweizer Baufirmen, die den Tunnel von einem Pilotstollen aus mit der WIRTH-Erweiterungseinheit TBE 350/770 und TBE 770/1100 H auffährt, die bereits im Sonnenbergtunnel mit Erfolg gebohrt hatte. Für diesen Einsatz wurden die Maschinen wie folgt umgebaut:

- Vergrößerung des Bohrdurchmessers von 10,46 auf 11,00 m
- Verstärkung des Bohrkopfantriebs für die Stufe 7,70/11,00 m
- Eigenes Hydraulikaggregat für jede Stufe, um parallelen Bohrbetrieb zu ermöglichen

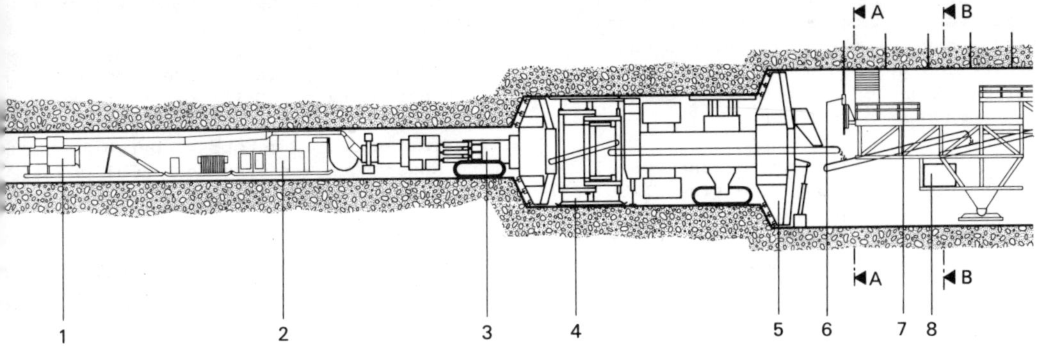

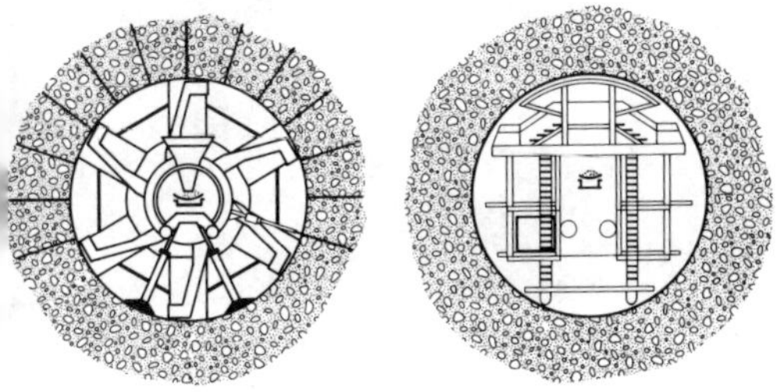

Schnitt A - A Schnitt B - B

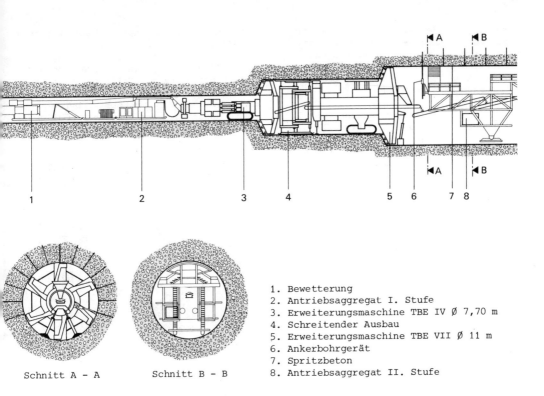

1. Bewetterung
2. Antriebsaggregat I. Stufe
3. Erweiterungsmaschine TBE IV Ø 7,70 m
4. Schreitender Ausbau
5. Erweiterungsmaschine TBE VII Ø 11 m
6. Ankerbohrgerät
7. Spritzbeton
8. Antriebsaggregat II. Stufe

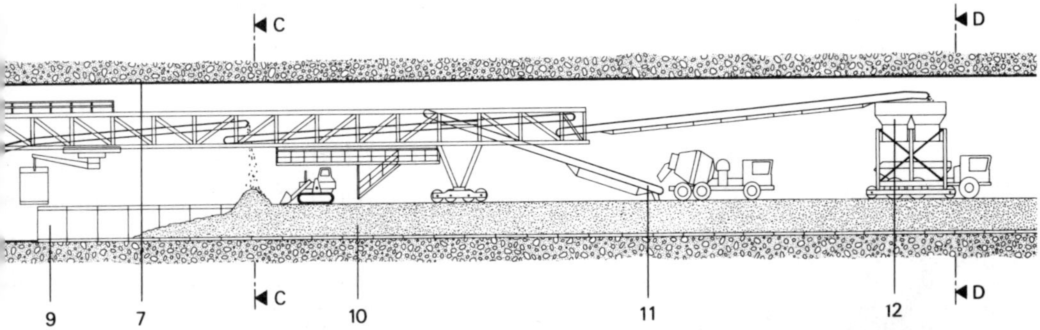

9. Sohltübbings
10. Fahrbahnauffüllung
11. Spritzbetonanlieferung
12. Bohrgutumschlag

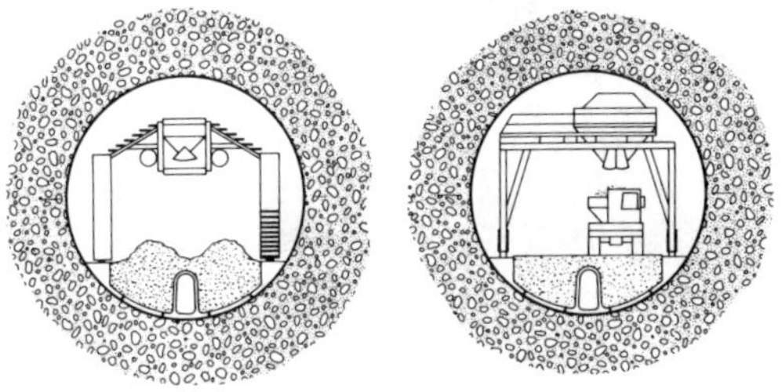

Schnitt C - C Schnitt D - D

Bild 11 Zweistufige Pilotbohrlocherweiterung Kerenzerstraßentunnel, Längs- und Querschnitt

Direkt hinter der 2. Erweiterungsstufe wurde von der Arge ein gut durchdachtes Nachlaufsystem mit Arbeitsbühnen und maschinellen Einrichtungen für die unmittelbar dem Ausbruch folgenden Sicherungs- und Ausbaumaßnahmen angeordnet.

Zum Auffahren des Pilotstollens von 3,50 m Durchmesser stand der Arge eine WIRTH TB-II sofort zur Verfügung, so daß bereits gut 2 Monate nach der Auftragsvergabe der Anschlag des Pilotstollen erfolgte.

Das gesamte Arbeitsschema der Erweiterungseinheit ist aus der Längs- und Querschnittdarstellung in Bild 11 ersichtlich. Die Einrichtungen für Bewetterung, Hydraulik- und Stromversorgung sowie Führerstand und die Verspann- und Führungseinrichtung der ersten Erweiterungsstufe auf 7,70 m Bohrdurchmesser sind im Pilotloch angeordnet. Dahinter folgt der Bohrkopf für 7,70 m Durchmesser, ein hydraulisch gesteuerter Schreitausbau zur Sicherung der Firste sowie wiederum Verspann- und Führungseinrichtung der zweiten Stufe für 11,00 m Bohrdurchmesser im Bohrloch von 7,70 m Durchmesser. Unmittelbar hinter dem Bohrkopf für 11,00 m Durchmesser steht der gesamte Querschnitt für folgende Arbeiten zur Verfügung:

- Felssicherung mit Ankern, Baustahlgewebe und Spritzbeton
- Einbau des Sohlgewölbes aus Fertigteilen mit integriertem begehbaren Drainagestollen
- Auffüllen der Sohle mit Ausbruchmaterial

Bild 13 Kerenzerstraßentunnel, Durchfahrung der Lüftungszentrale, Blick in Bohrrichtung

In dem dort anstehenden Gebirge wurden ausschließlich Diskenrollen verwendet. Die Pilotbohrmaschine war mit Zweiringdisken Typ WIRTH LWG II, die Erweiterungsbohrköpfe mit Einringdisken LWG III bestückt. Anfänglich gab es Verschleißprobleme mit den Kaliberrollen des 11 m Kopfes. Durch konstruktive Änderungen war es jedoch möglich, die Standzeit dieser Rollen auf 300 m zu steigern.

Bild 12 Kerenzerstraßentunnel, Durchfahrung der Lüftungszentrale, Blick auf den Nachläufer

Der mittlere Bohrfortschritt der Erweiterungseinheit betrug knapp 10 m/d, die maximale Tagesleistung lag bei ca. 24 m/d. Gegenüber dem Vortrieb des Sonnenbergtunnels konnte die Vortriebsleistung somit fast verdoppelt werden. Diese Leistungssteigerung ist sowohl auf die Erhöhung der reinen Nettobohrleistung als auch auf den gut organisierten Ausbaubetrieb zurückzuführen. Ein Vortrieb von durchschnittlich 10 m pro Tag bedeutet:

- 850 m^3 Festgestein lösen, transportieren und teilweise wieder einbauen
- 57 St Anker setzen
- 174 m^2 Armierungsgewebe verlegen
- 287 m^2 Spritzbeton in Stärken von 3 - 7 c[m] aufbringen
- 22 St Sohltübbinge verlegen

Die guten Erfahrungen beim Sonnenbergtunnel mit diesem Vortriebssystem und die sofortig[e] Verfügbarkeit der vorhandenen Maschinen waren mitbestimmend für diesen Wiedereinsatz. Heute würden wir auf Grund unserer technischen Erfahrung und Weiterentwicklungen für solche Vorhaben eine einstufige Erweiterungskombination anbieten, wie sie Bild 14 zeigt. Hierbei sollte der Durchmesser des Pilotstollens etwa 40 % des Enddurchmessers betragen. Bei einer einstufigen Erweiterungskombination lassen

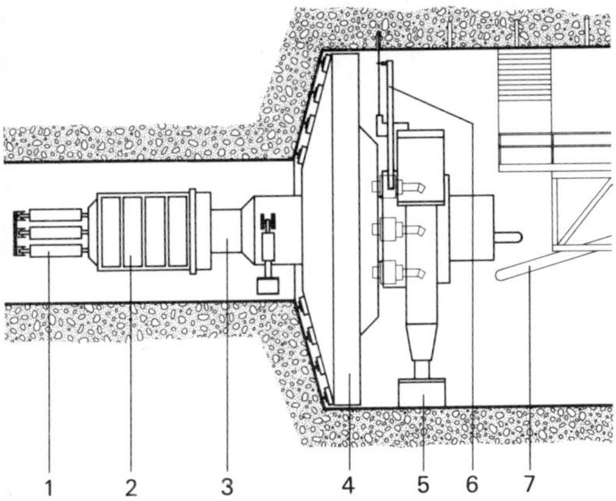

1. Vorschubzylinder
2. Außenkelly mit Verspannung
3. Innenkelly
4. Bohrkopf mit Antrieb
5. Abstützung
6. Ankerbohrgerät
7. Nachläufer mit Förderband

Bild 14 Einstufige Pilotbohrlocherweiterung

sich vorläufige Sicherungsmaßnahmen zwischen den Erweiterungsstufen einsparen, die beim Einsatz der zweistufigen Kombination bisweilen erforderlich waren. Diese neuen Erweiterungsmaschinen werden mit einer Außenkelly entsprechend unseren Vollschnittmaschinen gebaut.

6. ZUSAMMENFASSUNG

Anhand einiger Baustelleneinsätze habe ich Ihnen die Konzeption unserer Tunnelbohrmaschinen erläutert. Wie aus den vorgestellten Beispielen ersichtlich, haben Vollschnitt- sowie Erweiterungsmaschinen ihre Einsatzberechtigung. Die Entscheidung für die eine oder die andere Variante muß nach sorgfältiger Abwägung aller technnischen und wirtschaftlichen Gesichtspunkte getroffen werden.

Tabelle 1 Technische Daten der beschriebenen Tunnelbohrmaschinen

Baustelle		Pueblo Viejo Quixal	Le Pouget	Lohberg	Kerenzerstraßentunnel Pilotbohrung	1. Stufe	2. Stufe
Tunnelbohrmaschine		TB V H	TB IV H	TBS-V E/Sch	TB II H	TBE IV H	TBE VII H
Bohrdurchmesser	m	5,64	5,05	6,50	3,50	3,50/7,70	7,70/11,00
Drehzahl	min^{-1}	0 - 6	0 - 7	5	0 - 12	0 - 5,5	0 - 4
max. Drehmoment*	kNm	800	630	1390	260	750	1440
Antriebsleistung	kW	4 x 160	3 x 200	6 x 132	3 x 132	3 x 160	5 x 160
max. Bohrandruck	kN	6350	5000	8600	4400	6800	6800
max. Vorschubgeschw.	m/h	3,2	3,2	3,2	3,9	3,2	3,2
Bohrhub	mm	1200	1250	1500	1200	1500	1500
max. Verspannkraft	MN	23	13	22	12	18	18
Inst. Gesamtleistung	kW	640	650	850	460	786	910
Disken-	Art	1-Ring	2-Ring	1-Ring	2-Ring	1-Ring	1-Ring
Bohrwerkzeuge	Anzahl	37	35	51	26	50	46

* maximales Drehmoment am Bohrkopf bei maximaler Drehzahl

UNTERTAGEBAU MIT TEILSCHNITTMASCHINEN, DERZEITIGER EINSATZBEREICH UND ENTWICKLUNGEN ZU DEREN ERWEITERUNG

Underground excavation with roadheaders, range of application and possibilities of further development

Exploitation souterraine à l'aide de machines à attaque partielle, domaine d'emploi actuel et développements pour son élargissement

K.GEHRING
Voest-Alpine AG, Zeltweg, Österreich

SUMMARY:
The paper shows, by using examples of roadheader installations for underground excavations, the principal methods under use today. The preliminaries, necessary conditions and limits for the application of this type of machines are discussed in their technical as well as in their economical influence. The potentials of development, distinguishing these machines form the end of the paper, this recognising of new fields of adaptation and the combination with new methods of rock disintegration.

ZUSAMMENFASSUNG:
Der Artikel gibt - an Hand von Einsatzbeispielen - eine Überblick über den Anwendungsbereich von Teilschnittmaschinen im Stollen und Tunnelbau. Die Voraussetzungen, Bedingungen und Grenzen des Einsatzes dieser Maschinen werden sowohl in technischer als auch in wirtschaftlicher Hinsicht diskutiert. Die Entwicklungsmöglichkeiten, die diese Maschinentype besitzt, sowie die Weiterentwicklung von Vortriebsverfahren bilden den Schluss, wobei noch neue Einsatzgebiete und die Kombination mit neuen Technologien des Gesteinsabbaues angesprochen werden.

RESUME:
L'article montre quelques exemples d'application des machines de creusement à l'attaque ponctuelle dans les excavations souterreines. Les présuppositions, les conditions et les limites de l'application de ces machines sont discutées d'un point de vue technique et économique. Les possibilités de dévéloppement que possèdent ces machines ainsi que la mise au point de futures méthodes de creusement constituent la fin de l'article, tout en abordant des domaines s'application nouveaux en combinaison avec des technologies nouvelles de désintégration de roches.

EINLEITUNG

Wenn man bedenkt, daß seit der Einführung der Teilschnittmaschinen (oder exakt Schneidkopfmaschinen) im Westen insgesamt ca. 500 Einheiten in der Bauindustrie für die untertägige Auffahrung von Stollen und Tunneln verkauft wurden und von diesen zur Zeit weltweit ca. 300 Maschinen noch im Einsatz stehen, so wird die Bedeutung dieser Maschinentype am besten durch folgende Ziffern belegt: Man kann annehmen, daß die durchschnittliche Löseleistung/Mbh - quer durch alle Maschinenklassen - bei ca. 20 fm3 liegt und die Maschinenausnützung im Durchschnitt zumindest 20 % der verfügbaren Arbeitszeit beträgt, so ergibt sich daraus, daß jährlich zumindest 7,2 Millionen fm3 Gestein mit diesen Maschinen gelöst wird. Dies entspricht - um die Ziffer zu veranschaulichen - einem Tunnel mit 80 m2 Querschnitt und 90 km Länge. Dabei sind in diesen Zahlen die im Ostblock eingesetzten Maschinen nicht berücksichtigt. Da die Entwicklung dieser Maschinentype aber ihren Ausgang im Ostblock nahm, muß angenommen werden, daß auch in diesen Ländern Schneidkopfmaschinen nicht nur im Bergbau, sondern in erheblichem Maße auch in der Bauindustrie eingesetzt sind.

1. DERZEITIGER STAND DER ENTWICKLUNG

1.0 ALLGEMEINES

Von den Haupttechnologien zur Auffahrung untertägiger Hohlräume - Sprengvortrieb, Tunnelbohrmaschinen Schildvortrieb mit und ohne mechanische Löseeinrichtungen sowie Teilschnittmaschinen wurden die Teilschnittmaschinen als letzte entwickelt und als letzte für die Anwendung im Stollen-u. Tunnelbau herangezogen.
Das bedeutet, daß sowohl maschinentechnisch als auch verfahrenstechnisch im Vortrieb mit Teilschnittmaschinen die größten potentiellen Entwicklungsreserven liegen. Dieser Artikel hat das Ziel, den derzeitigen Stand der Technologie der Auffahrung untertägiger Hohlräume mit Teilschnittmaschinen (kurz TSM) zu umreißen, die Voraussetzungen, Bedingungen und Grenzen für deren Einsatz darzulegen, bestehende Entwicklungsnischen aufzuzeigen sowie Ansätze für die Weiterentwicklung der Maschinen- und Verfahrenstechnik - bezogen auf den Stollen- und Tunnelbau - zu diskutieren.

1.1 ÜBERSICHT ÜBER DEN STAND DER MASCHINENTECHNIK.

Zur Zeit sind drei Hauptkonstruktionsprinzipien auf dem Markt vertreten:
a) Fräslader
b) TSM mit Längsschneidkopf
c) TSM mit Querschneidkopf
Die Vor-und Nachteile der einzelnen Konstruktionsprinzipien sind in der Fachliteratur in umfangreicher Form besprochen worden.(MENZEL, FRENYO, 1981, GEHRING 1981).
Wenn man Sonderkonstruktionen für Rohrvortrieb ausklammert, liegen die Maschinengewichte zwischen 8 u. 140 t, die Antriebsleistungen zwischen 20 und 300 KW am Schrämkopf. Besitzen die leichteren Maschinen weitgehend elektrische Einzelantriebe, so wird mit zunehmender Antriebsleistung die Versorgung der Antriebe durch ein zentrales Hydraulikaggregat typisch. Ausgenommen bleibt der Antrieb des Schrämkopfs, der praktisch ausschließlich elektrisch erfolgt.
Neben den üblicherweise sehr kompakt gebauten Maschinen geht eine Sonderentwicklung in Richtung von Maschinen, die aus einem Stand sehr große Profile schneiden können. Dies können einseits Spezialkonstruktionen für diese Anforderungen sein, daneben ist als wichtige Entwicklung der Anbau von Schrämaggregaten an Bagger (mit und ohne zusätzliche Ladeeinrichtung, die am Bagger fix montiert ist) zu sehen.

Tabelle 1. Gesteinsverhältnisse u. Betriebsergebnisse von Einsatz einer F6-A Bewässerungsstollen Carcassone).

Art des Gesteins	Mergel	Kalksandstein
σ_D (N/mm2)	17-21	60-117
σ_Z (N/mm2)	o,7-1,1	3,0-4,3
s_{rund} (mm)	5,92	0,65
Theoretische Schneidleistung (fm3/h)	14	1,5
Tatsächliche Schneidleistung (fm3/h)	15,12	1,17
F_{schim}	0,011	0,030
Theoretischer Meißelverbr. (Stück / fm3)	0,003- 0,004	0,4-0,7
Tatsächlicher Meißelverbr. (Stück / fm3)	0,0041	1,1

1.2.Übersicht über den Stand der Verfahrenstechnik

1.2.0 Allgemeines

Bestehende Bauverfahren wurden - wenn die Eignung vorlag - so zugeschnitten, daß sie die für den Einsatz von TSM erforderlichen Voraussetzungen schufen. Daneben ging die Maschinenentwicklung in Richtung Anpassung an bewährte Vortriebsverfahren.

Generell werden beim Einsatz von TSM folgende Verfahren angewendet:
- Vollprofilvortrieb
- Kalotten-Strossenbauweise mit lang vorgesetzter Kalotte
- Kalotten-Strossenbauweise mit kurz vorgesetzter Kalotte
- Kernbauweise

Beim Kalotten-Strossen-Vortrieb mit lang vorgesetzter Kalotte sowie bei der Kernbauweise kann der Einsatz einer TSM auf den Kalottenbereich

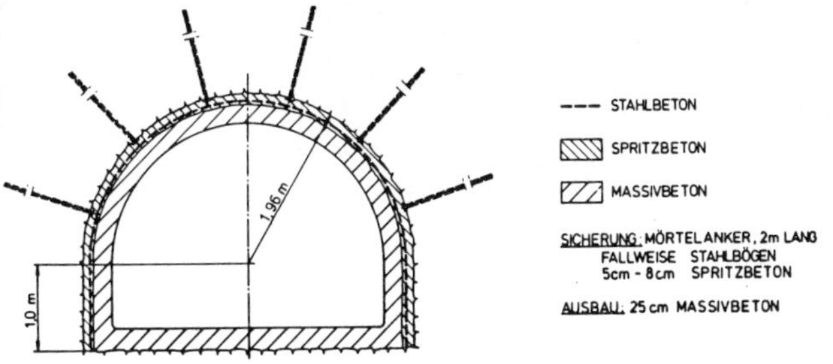

Abb. 1 Bewässerungsstollen Carcassone, Regelprofil

beschränkt bleiben, die Strosse wird - bei Großprofilen auch in mehreren Abschnitten - durch andere Verfahren wie z.B. Reißen mit Schubraupen, Lockerungssprengen udgl. abgebaut.
Im folgenden sollen die Verfahren jeweils an Hand eines Beispiels kurz beschrieben werden:

1.2.1. Vollprofilvortrieb

Dieser bedingt, daß die Profilgröße maximal die Reichweite der Maschine erreicht. Generell ist das Verfahren daher - bei den heutigen Maschinenreichweiten - auf Querschnitte bis ca. 45 m2 Ausbruchsfläche limitiert, wobei üblicherweise nur Hufeisenprofile geschnitten werden können. Das Schneiden von Kreisprofilen sowie von größeren Querschnitten erfordert Sonderkonstruktionen.
Als Beispiel sei der Einsatz eines Alpine Miners F6-A bei einem Bewässerungsstollen in der Nähe von Carcassone dargestellt werden. Die wichtigsten Werte für diese Auffahrung sind in Tab. 1 zusammengestellt. Der Stollen besitzt Hufeisenquerschnitt. Überwiegend lagen tonige Mergel vor, nur über einen kurzen Abschnitt war Kalksandstein zu durchfahren, der die Kapazität der Maschine hinsichtlich max. schneidbarer Festigkeit überstieg. Ein Regelquerschnitt ist in Abb.1. zu sehen.

1.2.2 Kalotten-Strossenbauweise mit lang vorgesetzter Kalotte

Diese Bauweise ist in all jenen Fällen einzusetzem. wo die Höhenreichweite der TSM unter der geplanten Höhe des Ausbruchsquerschnitts liegt. Fehlende seitliche Reichweite kann durch seitliches Überstellen der TSM in der Kalotte ausgeglichen werden.
Da bei dieser Bauweise der Sohlschluß relativ weit hinter der Ortsbrust erfolgt und die Form einer Kalotte zudem statisch ungünstig ist, ist eine Voraussetzung für diese Bauweise festes Gebirge, das mit Hilfe einer entsprechend dimensionierten Hohlraumsicherung die Deformationen innerhalb eines zulässigen Bereiches hält - wobei dieser Bereich fallweise durchaus die gleiche Größenordnung wie beim Sprengvortrieb erreichen kann. Bei entsprechend verformungsumempfindlichen Gebirge ist die Anwendung dieser Bauweise auch mit sofort

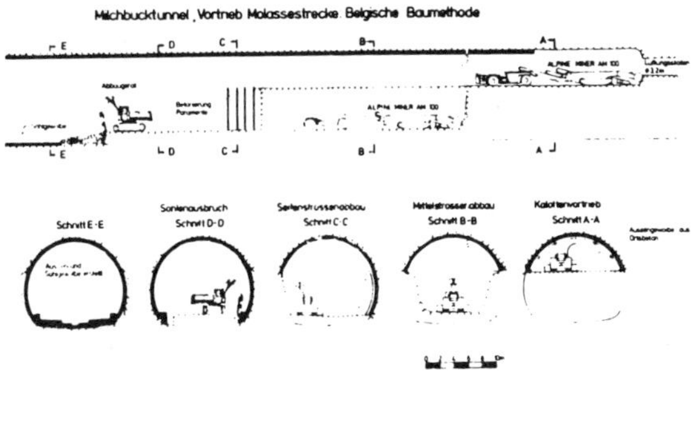

Abb. 2 Kalotten-Strossen-Vortrieb mit lang vorgesetzter Kalotte(am Beispiel Milchbucktunnel Zürich)

Abb. 3 Einsatz Alpine Miner AM 100 bei Kalottenvortrieb Milchbucktunnel

nachgezogener Betonschale möglich. Bei dieser Variante ist wichtig, daß durch entsprechende Kerben im Fels am Fuß der Kalottenschale ein möglichst guter Lastabtrag sichergestellt ist. Dies ist inbesondere eine Voraussetzung dafür, daß beim Strossenabbau während der Wegnahme der Felsstützung bis zum Einbau der Betonschale im Strossenbereich keine schädlichen Setzungen der Kalottenschale auftreten.

Abb. 2 zeigt als Beispiel für eine derartige Bauweise die Auffahrung des Milchbucktunnels in Zürich. Bei diesem Projekt ist ein Alpine Miner AM 100 eingesetzt. Als Sonderform dieser Bauweise wurde hier einerseits die Kalotte vorlaufend ganz durchgebrochen und erst anschließend mit der Strossenauffahrung begonnen. In der Kalotte wurden vorab 3 Vorstollen mit einer

Tabelle 2. Gesteinsverhältnisse u. Betriebsergebnisse vom Einsatz einer AM 100 (Milchbucktunnel Zürich Kalottenvortrieb)

Gestein	Mergeliger Standstein
σ_D (N/mm2)	32-42
σ_Z (N/mm2)	2,3-2,5
s_{rund} (mm)	2,32-3,35
Theoretische Schneidleistung (fm3/h)	38-50
Tatsächliche Schneidleistung (fm3/h)	41,7
F_{schim}	o,o41-o,2o
Theoretischer Meißelverbrauch (Stk./fm3)	0,07-0,13
Tatsächlicher Meißelverbrauch (Stk./fm3)	0,068

Tunnelbohrmaschine aufgefahren. Tab. 2 zeigt die wesentlichen Betriebsergebnisse aus dem Kalottenvortrieb. Der Strossenabbau ist derzeit bis auf rd. 100 m beendet.

1.2.3 Kalotten-Strossenbauweise mit kurz vorgesetzter Kalotte

Diese Bauweise wird bei größeren Querschnitten (über etwa 30 m2), schlechten Gebirgsverhältnissen (druckhaft, rollig) und hier insbesonere im städtischen Bereich angewendet.
Das Prinzip besteht darin, daß die

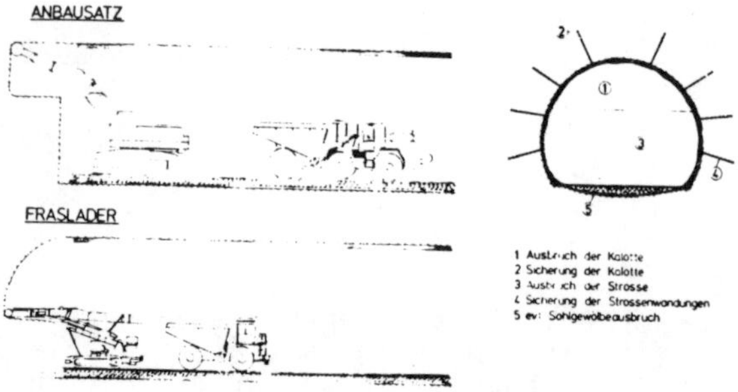

Abb. 4 Kalotten-Strossen-Vortrieb mit kurz vorgesetzter Kalotte.

Abb. 5 Schrämbagger 100 KW beim Kalottenschnitt (Straßentunnel Triest)

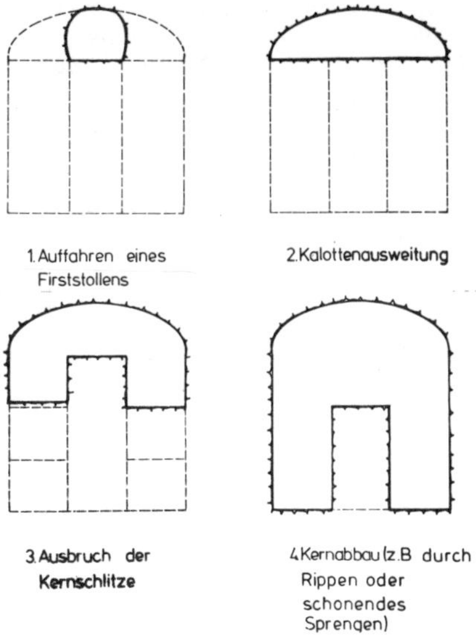

Abb. 6 Kernbauweise, Prinzipskizze

TSM (oder ein Bagger mit TSM-Anbausatz) auf der meist fertig betonierten Sohle des Tunnels steht und zuerst im Kalottenbereich etwa 2-3m vorschneidet. Das gelöste Material wird durch eigene Fördereinrichtungen (z.B. unter dem Schrämarm laufender Kratzförderer) oder durch die Bewegung des Schrämkopfes unter gleichzeitigem Verfahren der TSM aus dem Kalottenbereich entfernt und auf der Sohle entweder durch die Ladeeinrichtung (bei Komplettmaschinen) oder durch eigene Ladegeräte aufgenommen. Anschließend wird die Kalotte sofort gesichert. Erst anschließend erfolgt der Strossenabbau (evtl. mit Herstellung eines Sohlgewölbeausbruchs u. anschließend Sicherung des Strossen- und Sohlbereichs.

1.2.4 Kernbauweise

Kernbauweise kann in unterschiedlicher Abfolge der Teilausbrücke bei größeren und Größtquerschnitten angewendet werden. Dabei ist sie sowohl bei sehr strengen Toleranzen für Oberflächensetzungen im Verkehrstunnelbau (insbesondere bei schlechtem Gebirge) als Alternative zu 1.2.3 anwendbar als auch für die Auffahrung untertägiger Großhohlräume (z.B. Krafthauskavernen,untertägige Speicher udgl.)

Im ersteren Fall wird zumeist von zwei Ulmstollen ausgehend der Randbereich des Hohlraumes ausgebrochen und ausgebaut, wobei abschnittsweise von unten nach oben gearbeitet wird. Dieses Verfahren bedingt sehr kom-

Tabelle 3. Gesteinsverhältnisse und Betriebsergebnisse vom Einsatz AM50 bei den Mönchsberg-Parkgaragen.

Gestein	durchschnittliche	beste	schlechteste (feste Einlagerungen)
	Verhältnisse		
σ_D (N/mm2)	15-50	8,3-20	150
σ_Z (N/mm2)	2,0-4,3	1,5-2,0	71
s_{rund}	1,1	5,2	0,4
Theoret. Schneidl. (fm3/h)	10	34	-
Tatsächl. Schneidl. (fm3/h)	8	40	-
F_{schim}	0,10	0,046	0,72
Meißelverbrauch (Stk./fm3)	0,03-0,10	0,025	-
Tatsächl. Meißelverb. (Stk./fm3)	0,08	0,030	

pakt gebaute Maschinen und ist - wegen der geringen Vortriebsleistung bei gleichzeitig schlechter Maschinenausnützung sicherlich nur bei kurzen Tunnelbauten eine wirtschaftliche Alternative, da hier die Möglichkeit des kurzfristigen Überstellens der Maschine zwischen verschiedenen Angriffspunkten möglich ist.
In festerem Gebirge wird die Auffahrung von der Kalotte her begonnen, wobei anschließend die seitlichen Schlitze geschrämt werden.

Tabelle 3 ergibt eine Zusammenstellung wichtiger Einsatzdaten von diesem Projekt, in Abb. 7 ist eine AM 50 beim Auffahren eines Kernschlitzes dargestellt. (KOEHLER,1975)

2. EINSATZBEDINGUNGEN

2.0. Allgemeines

Stärker als jedes andere Bauprojekt sind Projekte des Untertagebaus mit bestimmten Technologien nur unter bestimmten Randbedingungen herstellbar. Während diese Bedingungen z.B. beim Hochbau vorher genau festgelegt werden können und mit an Sicherheit grenzender Wahrscheinlichkeit eine Änderung während der Bauausführung nicht zu erwarten ist, trifft dieser Umstand auf den Stollen- und Tunnelbau nur sehr beschränkt zu. Insbesondere die geotechnischen Randbedingungen eines Projekts können nur in einem Umfang durch Voruntersuchungen ermittelt werden, der das Risiko des Bauausführenden groß bleiben läßt. Daneben sind aber auch die Wechselwirkungen Projektausgestaltung - Verfahrenstechnik nur beschränkt kalkulierbar, d.h. ein Untertagebauwerk, dessen Endzustand durch die Verwendung genau definiert ist, ist kostenmäßig schwer erfaßbar. Je nach angetroffenen Verhältnissen können die Kosten zur Erreichung dieses Endzustands sehr stark variieren. Unter diesen Gesichtspunkten soll nun der Einsatz von TSM - auch in Relation zu anderen Verfahren - diskutiert werden.

2.1.0 Geotechnische Voraussetzungen

Wie bei allen mechanischen Verfahren ist der TSM-Vortrieb stark von den angetroffenen Gebirgsverhältnissen abhängig. Sind dies beim Vortrieb mit Tunnelbohrmaschinen pri-

Abb. 7 Herstellen der Kernschlitze mit Alpine Miner AM 50 bei den Parkgaragen Mönchsberg.

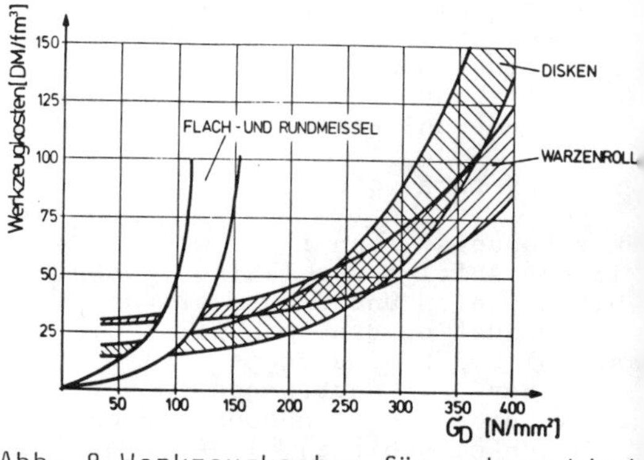

Abb. 8 Werkzeugkosten für unterschiedliche Werzeugformen in Abhängigkeit von der einaxialen Gesteinsfestigkeit.

mär Werte der Stabilität der Hohlraumwandung (fallweise auch der Ortsbrust)(WANNER, 1979), so ist eine TSM zwar bezüglich Gebirgsqualität wesentlich anpassungsfähiger, ihre Leistung wird aber wesentlich stärker von der Gesteins-bzw. Gebirgsfestigkeit beeinflußt.
Ab einer bestimmten Festigkeit - die abhängig von Art der TSM und installierter Leistung am Schrämkopf ist, ist deren Einsatz überhaupt nicht mehr möglich. Dabei liegen die Höchstwerte - selbst bei den stärksten am Markt befindlichen TSM - bei max. 40 % der max. mit Tunnelbohrmaschinen durchörterten Festigkeiten. (MORGEN, 1980, GEHRING, 1981, OBERMAIER, 1980).
Dazu kommt, daß die Verschleißkosten aufgrund des unterschiedlichen Beanspruchungsmechanismuses (gleitende Reibung-sollende Reibung) mit zunehmender Festigkeit und Abrasivität ebenfalls sehr stark divergieren Um daher das Risiko beim Einsatz einer TSM möglichst gering zu halten, ist es erforderlich, die Werte für Festigkeit und Abrasivität entlang der späteren Tunneltrasse möglichst kontinuierlich zu kennen.
Da alle gängigen Aufschlußverfahren nur punktuelle Aufschlüsse liefern, ist zur Erfüllung obiger Forderung neben der meßtechnischen Auswertung von Gesteinsproben auch ein Studium des geologischen "backgrounds"erforderlich.

2.2.1 Voraussetzungen von Seiten des Projekts

Von Seiten des Projekts ist erforderlich, daß auf die Besonderheiten des Einsatzes von TSM Bezug genommen wird. Als Beispiel: TSM-Einsatz kann zu einer entsprechenden Änderung der Regelprofile führen, da die Auflockerungen im Bereich der Hohlraumwandung, die bei Sprengvortrieb auftreten, entfallen und daher die Sicherung geringer dimensioniert werden kann, zumindest in den besseren Gebirgsklassen.
Wichtig von Seiten des Projekts ist auch der Bauzeitplan. Zu enge Termine für den Baubeginn können einen TSM-Einsatz unmöglich machen. Allerdings sind die Lieferzeiten für TSM wesentlich niedriger als für andere Einrichtungen des mechanischen Vortriebes.

2.2 Bedingungen für TSM-Einsatz

2.2.0 Technische Bedingungen

Als wesentliche technisch-organisatorische Bedingungen für TSM-Einsatz sind zu nennen:
- ausreichende Verfügbarkeit von elektrischer Energie aus dem Netz, wobei hier ersatzweise mit Dieselgeneratoren gearbeitet werden kann.
- entsprechend eingerichtete Werkstätte mit ausgebildetem Personal
- die relativ geringe Korngröße des Haufwerks ist zulässig
- gesicherte Ersatzteilversorgung
- Lösung des Staubproblems (Vorstollen, Absaugung)
- evtl. Integration der Sicherungsarbeiten in den Maschinenbereich, v.a. bei beengten Platzverhältnissen.

Dazu kommen - von Projekt zu Projekt unterschiedlich - die Möglichkeiten eine wechselseitige Anpassung von

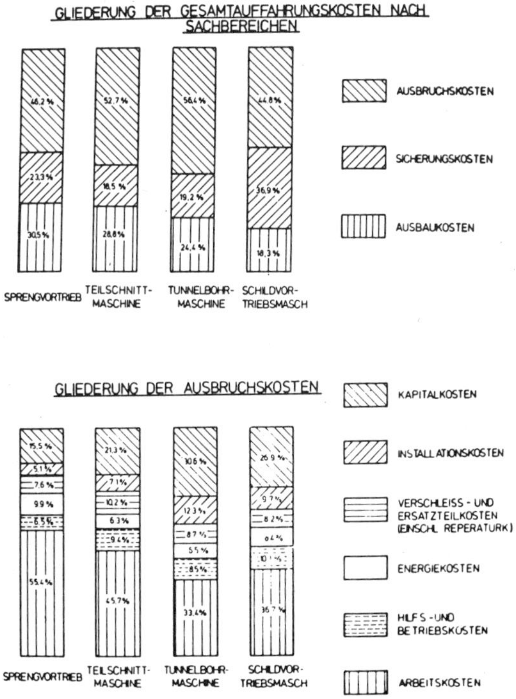

Abb.9. Kostengliederung für die Hauptverfahren zur Auffahrung untertägiger Hohlräume

Verfahrenstechnik mit TSM und den vorliegenden Randbedingungen, wie z.B. Art, Umfang und Ort der Sicherungsarbeiten, Abförderung des Haufwerks usw.

2.2.1 Wirtschaftliche Bedingungen

Hier sind als wesentlichste Faktoren zu nennen:

- die Investitionskosten für eine TSM stehen in einem vertretbaren Verhältnis zu den Gesamtkosten des Projekts, alternativ kann bei geringerem Projektumfang der Mieteinsatz einer Maschine in Betracht gezogen werden.
- Gesamtkosten für das Projekt - hier insbesondere die Summe der Kosten für Ausbruch, Sicherung, und Ausbau sind gegenüber konkurrierenden Verfahren niedriger. Als Beispiel dazu zeigt Abb. 9; vergleichsweise die Verteilung der Kosten für die Verfahren Sprengvortrieb, Tunnelbohrmaschine, Schildvortriebsmaschine und Teilschnittmaschine, sowohl nach Ausbruchs-, Sicherungs- und Ausbaukosten als auch nach Investitionskosten, Arbeitskosten, Verschleiß- und Ersatzteilkosten, Energiekosten und Betriebsmittelkosten aufgegliedert. Diese Aufgliederung ist auf gleiche Projektgröße sowie gleiche Randbedingungen aufgebaut.
- Bei allen Wirtschaftlichkeitsüberlegungen ist aber auch der vorhandene, meist abgeschriebene Gerätepark der Fa. zu berücksichtigen. Derartige Kostenvergleiche werden hinfällig, wenn für einzelne Verfahren Restriktionen (z.B. ganzes oder teilweises Sprengverbot) o. besondere Präferenzen (z.B. kreisrunde Stollen mit glatten Wandungen im Wasserkraftwerksbau) bestehen. Weiters sind die lokalen Lohnkosten von erheblichem Einfluß. In Ländern mit hohem Lohniveau einerseits sowie in Ländern mit starkem Mangel an qualifizierten Mineuren andererseits ist ein deutlich begünstigender Trend für mechanische Verfahren und damit auch für TSM gegeben.

2.3 Grenzen der Einsatzmöglichkeit

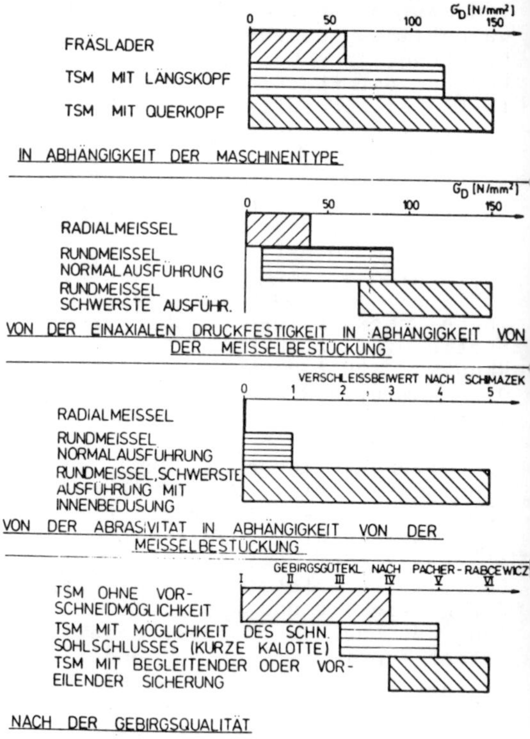

Abb. 10. Technische Grenzen für den Einsatz von Teilschnittmaschinen nach verschiedenen Kriterien.

ist dargestellt, welche Bereiche durch die heute auf dem Markt befindlichen Vortriebsmaschinen bzw. auf diesen Maschinen angeordneten Schneidsysteme und Werkzeuge abgedeckt werden können. Wie zu zeigen sein wird, liegen diese Grenzen - soweit es den Stollen- und Tunnelbau betrifft - erheblich über den Werten, die im freien Wettbewerb gegenüber anderen Verfahren als wirtschaftliche Grenzwerte anzusehen sind (GEHRING,1980, MCFEAT-SMITH, FOWELL, 1979)

2.3.1. Wirtschaftliche Grenzen

Wie schon in Abschnitt 2.2.1 angeschnitten, ist eine wirtschaftliche Abgrenzung des Einsatzes praktisch nur für jedes Projekt gesondert möglich. Abb. 11

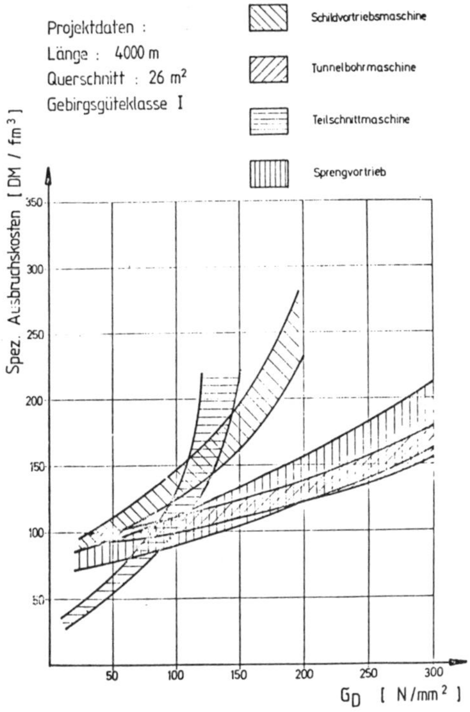

Abb. 11 Spez. Ausbruchskosten für die Hauptverfahren zur Auffahrung untertägiger Hohlräume (in Abhänigkeit von der einachsialen Gesteinsdruckfestigkeit).

zeigt für eine Auffahrung unter bestimmten Randbedingungen, daß etwa zwischen 60 und 75 N/mm2 einaxialer Gesteinsdruckfestigkeit die Wirtschaftlichkeitsgrenze des TSM-Vortriebes liegt, wenn keine Restriktionen vorliegen. Wenn die Betonmehrkosten durch Überprofil beim Sprengvortrieb miteingerechnet werden so müssen die genannten Werte etwa um 10 N/mm2 höher angesetzt werden. Der verringerte Sicherungsaufwand insgesamt ist in gesundem Gebirge bei diesen Festigkeiten nur schwer kalkulierbar,es kann aber - je nach Gebirgsklasse-eine Einsparung von 5-40 % des Sicherungsaufwandes erwartet werden, wobei hier Kosten für geringeres Überprofil nicht berücksichtigt sind.
Wie eine Reihe von TSM-Einsätzen in der Praxis zeigt,liegen sie fast durchwegs unter den oben genannten Festigkeitswerten. Dies ist zusätzlich dadurch bedingt, daß die Verschleißkosten je nach Gestein das zwei- bis dreifache derjenigen beim Sprengvortrieb betragen.

3. ENTWICKLUNGSMÖGLICHKEITEN FÜR TSM

3.0 Allgemeiner Trend

Zur Zeit sind bei TSM folgende Entwicklungstrends feststellbar:
- höhere Antriebsleistungen am Schrämkopf
- zentrale, innenliegende Zweikettenförderer
- Hummerscherenladeeinrichtung o. ähnliche Konstruktionen
- Erhöhung des Anteils an Gußkonstruktion
- zunehmende Anwendung von Schrämarmen, die wahlweise mit Längs- und Querschneidköpfen ausgerüstet werden können
- Verringerung der Bodenpressung unter dem Raupenfahrwerk
- expandier- bzw. knickbare Ausleger
- Übergang zur Zentralschmierung
- Verbesserung der Profilkontrolle um das Überprofil zu reduzieren und letztlich die TSM fernsteuerbar zu machen.

Von bestehenden Maschinentypen lassen solche die besten Chancen auf dem Markt erwarte, die in möglichst vielen der genannten Punkte bereits durch möglichst vielfältige Einsätze in der Praxis entpsrechend an die heutigen Anforderungen angepaßte Bauteile besitzen.

3.1 Beseitigung von Schwachstellen

3.1.0 Maschine

Hier sind je nach Maschinentype und Hersteller deutlich unterschiedliche Anforderungen zu stellen. Dies zeigt sich in den Verfügbarkeitswerten, die zwischen ca. 65 % für nicht ausgereifte Konstruktionen und über 90 % für erprobte Maschinentypen liegen. Die oberen Werte liegen in der gleichen Größenordnung, wie sie ausgereifte Tunnelbohrmaschinen oder Bohrwägen besitzen.

3.1.1 System

Vortriebssysteme mit TSM sind zur Zeit noch durch folgende Schwachstellen gekennzeichnet:

- hoher Staubanfall, der insbesondere bei größeren Querschnitten u. quarzhältigem Gestein Entstaubungsleistungen erforderlich machen würde, die die Grenze der leistungsstärksten auf dem Markt befindlichen Entstauber überschreiten
- schwierige Überstellbarkeit von Maschinen, insbesondere was den elektrischen Anschluß betrifft. Dadurch wird das Arbeiten einer TSM an verschiedenen Orten, das aufgrund der heute üblichen hohen "Marschgeschwindigkeiten" der Maschinen prinzipiell möglich wäre, auf den Bereich der doppelten Schleppkabellänge (max. 400 m) beschränkt
- die bisher verwendeten Anbaugeräte (Ankerbohr- und Setzeinrichtungen Sprenglochbohreinrichtungen, gewisse Formen der Zwischenförderung) sind noch nicht bei allen Firmen ausgereift. Ein wesentlicher Bestandteil der NÖT, der Spritzbeton, ist bisher noch nicht in das Vortriebssystem integriert worden.

Wichtig wäre daher die Lösung folgender Probleme:

- Entstauber mit höherem Wirkungsragd, die evtl. in Systembauweise auf der Maschine möglichst und die Absuagmengen anpassungsfähig und trotzdem mobil sind
- elektrische Schnellverbindungen, die den Sicherheitsanforderungen untertage einerseits und den hohen installierten Leistungen andererseits gerecht werden
- Weiterentwicklung der von der Maschine her einbringbaren Sicherungsmaßnahmen. Hier ist - insbesondere bei kleinen Querschnitten - die Integration der Spritzbetonarbeit erforderlich.

Um eine gute Systemabstimmung zu erreichen, wäre eine möglichst frühzeitige Kontaktnahme Maschinenlieferant – Auftragnehmer anzustreben. Dem stehen die oft sehr kurzen Fristen für Anbotslegung und Baubeginn entgegen. Daher müßten solche Vorab-Gespräche bereits mit den planenden Stellen geführt werden.

3.1.2 Verfahren

Das Hauptproblem bei allen beschriebenen und angewandten Verfahren liegt darin, daß die Maschinenausnützung sehr niedrig bleibt. Sie liegt im Duchschnitt zwischen 15 % und 30 % und kann nur unter besonders günstigen Randbedingungen auf Werte über 40 % angehoben werden. Dem stehen z.B. bei Tunnelbohrmaschinen Ausnützungswerte entgegen, die 60 % und mehr der verfügbaren Arbeitszeit betragen können.

Das Problem liegt darin, daß zur Zeit jede Sicherungsmaßnahme, die im Maschinenbereich erfolgt, einen Maschinenstillstand bedingt. Dabei beträgt üblicherweise die Sicherungszeit das mehrfache der Ausbruchszeit. Hier sind die - teilweise bereits begonnenen - Entwicklungen

- TSM in Messerschild integriert
- TSM mit Einrichtung zum Versetzen von Betontübbingen
- Spritzbetonautomat auf TSM

sicher Schritte, die eine Verbesserung der Situation bringen können.

Bisher wurden Vortriebsverfahren nur für den Einsatz von TSM adaptiert. Es ist aber sicher auch die Möglichkeit gegeben, speziell auf die Erfordernisse einer TSM zugeschnittene neue Verfahren zu entwickeln.

3.2 Neue Einsatzgebiete für TSM

Neben den bisher beschriebenen Verfahren des Untertagebaus mit TSM erscheinen folgende weitere Einsatzmöglichkeiten gegeben bzw. wurden bereits praktisch genützt:

- Schachtabteufen mit TSM, die auf einer Schraubenlinie rückwärts schneidet
- TSM mit Abfangvorrichtung, um Neigungen größer als ± 20° aufzufahren
- von anderen Geräten (z.B. Tieflöffelbagger) unabhängige Grabenfräsen mit eigener Lade- und Fördereinrichtung

Hier bleibt dem Einfallsreichtum des Bauingenieurs sicher noch ein reiches Feld.

3.3 Kombination mit neuen Technologien

Es sollen hier nur Möglichkeiten angerissen werden, die sich aufgrund der technologischen Entwicklung der Gesteinszerstörung anbieten könnten:

- Komination von Schneidmeißeln mit Hochdruckwasserdüsen (Vorversuche aus den USA und der Schweiz liegen dazu vor) z.B. DUBUGNON, 1981.
- Meißel mit Eigenschwingung oder unterstützt durch Ultraschall (hier wird sicherlich das Materialproblem für Meißel und Meißelhalter schwierig zu lösen sein)
- Abkehr von den heute verwendeten Formen der Radial- und Rundmeißel (hiezu laufen Versuche in der CSSR)
- Verwendung von Rundmeißeln auf Teilschnittmaschinen (hiezu wird eine Abspannung der Maschine) und eine Zwangsführung des Schrämarms erforderlich werden.

Alle hier genannten Verfahren sind bereits durch Patente abgedeckt. Trotzdem muß erwartet werden, daß bis zur Marktreife solcher Technologien noch zumindest 5 Jahre vergehen werden.

4. AUSBLICK

Wie dargelegt wurde, hat die noch relativ junge Teilschnittmaschine sich bereits heute einen beträchtlichen Marktanteil gesichert. Es kann angenommen werden, daß mit der weiteren Ausreifung dieser Maschinen ihre Konkurrenzfähigkeit gegenüber anderen Geräten zum Ausbruch untertage noch erheblich steigen wird, Voraussetzung dafür wird nicht zuletzt eine möglichst einge Zusammenarbeit zwischen Planern, Baufirmen und Maschinenherstellern sein. Nur dieser Rückfluß der vor Ort genommenen Erkenntnisse wird es ermöglichen, den gestellten und immer steigenden Anforderungen an Teilschnittmaschinen möglichst nahe zu kommen.

5. LITERATURVERZEICHNIS

Dubugnon, B. 1981, An experimental Study of Water assisted Drag Bit Cutting of Rocks (nicht veröffentlicht)

Gehring, K. 1979, Anpassung von Teilschnittmaschinen an durch Gebirge und Bauwerk vorgegebene Bedingungen, Proc. 4th ISRM-Congress, Balkema, Rotterdam

Gehring, K. 1980, Besonderheiten geologisch - geotechnischer Voruntersuchungen beim Einsatz von Teilschnittmaschinen,Proc. 4. Nationale Tagung über Felsmechanik, Aachen, S. 115 - 133.

Gehring, K. 1981, Solution to Problems with Roadheader Installation in Tunnelling Projects, Proc. 1981 RETC, S. 1045 - 1061

Gehring, K. 1981, Technische und wirtschaftliche Abgrenzung der Einsatzbereiche von Verfahren zur Auffahrung untertägiger Hohlräume, Vortrag TU Karlsruhe (Veröffentlichung in Vorbereitung).

Mc. Feat - Smith, I. & R.J. Fowell 1979, The Selection and Application of Roadheaders for Rock Tunnelling, Proc. 1979 RETC, S. 261 - 277.

Köhler, H. 1975, Die Mönchsberg-Parkgaragen Nord und Mitte,Porr-Nachrichten 64, S. 8 - 18

Matusek, Z. & Vasek, J. 1976, Untersuchungen über den Einsatz von Streckenvortriebsmaschinen zum Nachreißen von Gestein, Glück Auf -FH 1976, S. 199 - 204

Menzel, W. & Frenyo, 1981, Teilschnitt-Vortriebsmaschinen mit Längs- u. mit Querschneidkopf, Glück Auf 117/5, S. 284 - 287

Morgen, W. 1980, Kritische Betrachtungen über die Einsatzkriterien maschineller Flöz- und Gesteinsstreckenvortriebe und deren Wirtschaftlichkeit im Vergleich zu Sprengvortrieben, Nobelhefte 46, S. 121 - 129

Obermaier, H. 1980, Roadheader Technologie bites into the 80s. Tunnels and Tunnelling, Vol. 12/4, S. 17 - 22

Wanner, H. 1979, Deciding on the Excavation Method for a Tunnel - From the Geologist`s Point of View, Underground Space, Vol. 3, S. 293 - 296

RECENT TRENDS IN TUNNELING TECHNIQUES USING WATER JETS - A REVIEW

Neue Entwicklungen im Tunnelbau durch den Gebrauch von 'water-jets' - Eine Rückschau

Récentes tendances dans les techniques de forage des tunnels par l'emploi de 'water-jets' - Révision

K.S.JANAKIRAM
Department of Science & Technology, New Delhi, India
B.C.SYMALA RAO
Indian Institute of Science, Bangalore

SUMMARY:
In the last decade, with the demand for utilization of natural resources for power developments, the use of water jets for rock cutting, tunneling and mining has found extensive application. In comparison to excavation by means of blasting, water jets have the advantage that the excess excavation beyond the planned cross section is marginal and that the load sharing capacity of the rock mass is retained. By inducing cavitation in the water jets, which increase the cutting capability, hard rock tunneling is possible by fitting an array of water-jet nozzles to a conventional tunnel boring machine. In this paper the several features and techniques of liquid jet cutting with special reference to tunnels and caverns are discussed. The characteristic features of the erosion caused on rocks and minerals with the variation of several parameters are presented. The state of art of the cutting techniques in the last decade is presented.

ZUSAMMENFASSUNG:
Im letzten Jahrzehnt hat mit der Notwendigung natürliche Quellen zur Energiegewinnung heranzuziehen, der Gebrauch des "water jets" in Bezug auf die Schneidbarkeit von Fels, als auch im Tunnel- und Bergbau erheblich an Bedeutung gewonnen. Im Vergleich mit den herkömmlichen Ausbruchsmethoden haben "water jets" den Vorteil, daß der Mehrausbruch gegenüber dem planmäßigen Querschnitt außerordentlich gering ist und die Festigkeit des Gebirges erhalten bleibt. Indem eine Kavitation im "water jet" erzeugt wird, steigt die Schneidfähigkeit und es ist auch möglich, harte Gebirge durch die Kombination einer konventionellen Tunnelbohrmaschine mit einer Reihe von "water jet"-Düsen zu lösen. In diesem Beitrag werden verschiedene Arten und Techniken von flüssigkeitsgestützten Schneideverfahren in Bezug auf Tunnel- und Kavernenbauten diskutiert. Charakteristische Besonderheitem beim Lösen von Gesteinen und Mineralien mit einer Variation der verschiedenen Kennwerte werden vorgestellt. Außerdem wird die Entwicklung der Schneidetechniken im letzten Jahrzehnt dargestellt.

RESUME:
Pendant cette dernière décade, à cause de la demande d'utilisation des ressources naturelles pour des développements de l'énergie, l'usage des "water jets" dans le découpage des roches, le forage des tunnels et l'exploitation des mines a trouvé une application intensive. Comparativement à l'excavation au moyen d'explosif, les "water jets" présentent l'avantage de réduire les débordements hors du profil prévu et de préserver la portance du terrain. En produisant une cavitation dans les jets d'eau, ce qui accroît leur capacité de découpage, l'équipement d'une foreuse de tunnel conventionnelle d'une gerbe de pulvérisateurs de jets rend possible le forage des tunnels dans les roches dures.

Les différentes caractéristiques et techniques relatives au découpage au jet de liquide sont discutées dans cet exposé avec une référence spéciale aux tunnels et aux cavernes. Cet exposé présente egalement les traits caractéristiques de l'érosion des roches et des minéraux qui en résulte ainsi que la variation de plusieurs paramètres. De plus, la situation de l'art des techniques de découpage y est rapportée.

1. INTRODUCTION

In the last two decades man's search for the optimum utilization of natural resources for power development has increased fivefold. The increase in world population and expectation for the improvement in the quality of life, has led to an increased demand for energy. Among the sources of energy, the utilization of Hydro-potential caters to a larger percentage. Further, the majority of mineral wealth and fossil energy of the world is located at depth and this requires increased volumes of rocks to be penetrated each year in order to satisfy the world's demand. All the potential energy resources must therefore be exploited if the energy crunch is to be reduced to an uncomfortable squeeze. Almost all these resources are in hilly terrains and the case of Development of Hydropower tunneling is extremely important.

From time immemorial, rock has been broken by either the impact of a relatively sharp-edged tool against the rock, or by the dragging of a relatively sharp-edged tool across the rock surface. In recent years relative sophistication has been achieved in drilling rigs and its components.

Since inception rock drilling has undergone relatively very little revolutionary changes. The method of breaking the rock essentially remains the same i.e. the drilling of holes within the rock surface, the holes filled with explosives and ignited, thus breaking relatively large volumes of rock. However, evolutionary changes have been observed in the fact that the drilling equipment has become larger and more sophisticated. However, a better control of the environmental features such as noise, dust and hazards to the mining operator have not been achieved substantially. Novel systems developed usually requires a lead time of 10 to 20 years between conception and widespread adaptation. In the geotechnical field, water jet cutting technology, is in the state of major evaluation (1-9).

Mining and cutting with continuous water jets were first developed in the 19th Century in conncection with the discovery of gold bearing ore in silt deposits. Later by increasing the pressures these were tried for coal mining. Probably the Russians were the first to use water jets (1930) to cut harder materials while boring the tunnels for the Moscow subway. Further these were tried in drilling oil rigs which has received the highest attention in this decade.

The utility of jet cutting and drilling rigs is a highly demanded in mines where it is necessary to drive access tunnels and shafts from the surface to the deposit. Conventional methods where the drill and blast techniques are used are extremely slow in operation and cyclic by nature. Recent technological advances have included the development of continuous tunnel boring machines, outside drilling heads capable of grinding out holes with diameters upto 12 ft. These are massive equipments and for economic operations they are used for lenghts exceedings 5,500 meters of length. This paper reviews the present and proposed uses of continuous and pulsed water jets for tunneling, mining, demolition purposes and machining and lining of inner surfaces of tunnels.

2. MECHANISM OF JET CUTTING

The mechanism of Jet cutting can be explained in several ways depending on the type of nozzles - whether it is an ordinary nozzle or cavitation induced nozzle and the type of target - whether a rock or a metal. However, to an extent the mechanism of erosion of rock with a water jet is explained by the fracture phenomena of an elastic brittle material. Erosion can also be explained by the following: as all rocks are permeable there is a possibility that water penetrates the voids between grains and thus exposes the grain to hydraulic forces which make them come off. The condition for breakage is the net hydraulic force on a grain must overcome the cohesive forces between the grains. If the rock is dry and when a jet hits it an upper limit to the rate at which a crater can grow is the rate at which the water can penetrate the pores. Parameters controlling flow of liquid through porous media are of interest. If the pressure is so low that the hydraulic forces on the grain do not overcome cohesive forces between the grains, the water penetrates the rock and a zone of water propogates into the rock. If the pressure is large enough to let the hydraulic forces spell the grains off, the acting pressure profile caused by the jet always acts against a varying rock face which is dry. The water zone should lie some distance ahead of the crater as the position of the Water Zone is an upper limit of the position of the crater.

With intermittent on pulsed jets, the shots at higher pressures tended do drill holes through the blocks rather than break them. This is due to the instantaneous attack on the rock samples without any applied loading cracked along their weakest plane, usually the bedding plane. The rock surface subjected to high uniaxial stress over a short instant cracked in a plane parallel to the applied stresses irrespective of the direction of the natural plane of weakness.

Rehbinder (10) has proposed a simple model of erosion of rock with a water jet which explains qualitatively some effects of erosion cutting in rocks that are impossible to explain with mechanical stresses and fractures i.e. the rock properties are important in erosion cutting than those of mechanical cutting. In mechanical cutting a parameter like compressive strength is of great importance. Permeability and grain size may be considered with sufficient accuracy. The tensile strength of the rock is closely related to the threshold pressure. The permeability becomes significant as long as the diameter of the jet is greater than two times the diameter of the biggest grains of the rock.

Investigators have reported (11-14) that in case of jets with a combination of cutters, the load exerted on the rock is shearing action with purely mechanical breaking (pressing/ squeezing action). The static forces required for the functioning of cutting discs can be reduced proportionally to the compressive strength/tensile strength ratio of the rock. Cutting efficiency of a high pressure water jet is attributable to the energy transfer through an extremely small contact surface between the water jet and the rock surface; which corresponds to the cross section of the water jet. The transfer of cutting efficiency of the water jet is by a factor of 1500 higher than that of cutting discs.

The rock destruction efficiency can be expressed in terms the specific energy, i.e. the Energy required to excavate an unit volume of the rock surface. This energy is dependant on the particular rock and the type of destruction method employed. The specific energy mainly depends on the nozzle size, the jet pressure, the fluid medium, the traversing and the rock properties. For a fixed nozzle size, the variation in jet pressure and traversing rate define a family of curves for specific energy in terms of the above mentioned parameters. From these curves an optimum operating condition based on energy efficiency can be obtained for specified conditions. For stationary targets the specific energy decreases with increasing pressure. For traversing targets the specific energy increases with increasing specific pressure and for a fixed test declines with increasing traversing rate to an optimum value dependant on pressure level, traversing rate (for fixed nozzle size) and stand-off distance. The higher the pressure the larger the value of optimum traversing rate. The energy efficiency of multipass jetting decreases as the depth of the Kerf increases. Hence for optimum energy utilization jetting into an existing Kerf should be avoided.

3. DESIGN CONSIDERATIONS

Several investigators (15, 16, 17) have pursued the application of high pressure water jets in relation to the mechanical disc cutters for underground tunneling. Hoshino (8) has reported laboratory investigation using high pressure water jets to assist mechanical disc cutters. It has been predicted that more than twice the advance rate may be achieved for hard rock tunneling. Field samples of rock were tested initially and the tunnel boring machine was designed and constructed. Water jet assisted tunnel boring has been found to be technically feasible and economically advantageous. The design consists of the use of cutter and the jet interactions to reduce cutter forces and cutter wear and to improve tunneling advance rate and thereby reduce the tunneling cost.

It is highly desirable to have a mechanical boring machine which has the capacity to function with or without the water jet equipment. The water jet equipment should be designed such that it can be turned off whenever maintenance or repairs are required without affecting the mechanical tunnel boring. It should be possible to maintain the jet rig during regular machine service time or during the tunnel boring, without affecting the penetration. The water jets in front of the cutter should be well protected from the impact and abrasion of the tunnel face rock. The equipment should be compact and safety preconditions should be incorporated in the design and the plumbing system so that any failure of the pressure system will not cause hazards. The power requirement of the water pumping system should be reasonable that the available line power supply could be made use of directly.

The design and fabrication of a jet cutting rig can be grouped as

I) design of the traversing body,

II) the design of the tower which carries the suivel and power system for the nozzle movement,

III) the design of a step motor system for the incremental feeding of the nozzle,

IV) a platform capable of travelling back and forth at a slow speed with limit switches.

The several design parameters that are important are the jet pressure, traverse speed, number of nozzles, nozzle diameter and nozzle rotational speed. These could be suitably varied to obtain optimum performance of the water jet. For combined jet and cutter machines the three types of patterns are I) jet under the cutters II) jets between the cutter and III) jets both under and between the cutters; which would improve the advance rate and reduce the cutter wear. Jets placed across the entire cutter face at strata-gic points will greatly aid in improving the performance. The jet nozzle should be designed to take advantage of the cutter housing structure as much as possible. For a constant cutter spacing the kerf depth cut by water jets, either under the cutter or between the cutters tend to reduce the thrust required on the cutter. The deeper the water kerf, the lower the thrust requirement and thereby a reduction in the cutter load. The interaction between the water jet and mechanical rock cutting can be suitably managed for an optimized performance. Several basic investigations have revealed that use of additives for the liquid jet increases the cutting efficiency. The high molecular liquid polymer increases substantially the viscosity of water. The hydrocarbons present in the additives have a lubricating effect and reduces the frictional resistance, increases the flow speed with less wear of the materials, less mist formation, improve energy utilization and a narrover confinement of the jet.

4. POTENTIALS AND LIMITATIONS OF THE JET CUTTING TECHNOLOGY

High pressure water jets have been investigated for their ability to economically cut and break the materials that have proven difficult for conventional methods. High pressure water jet technique can be automated so that it can be operated by one man, does not damage the surrounding materials and eliminates tool wearing expenses. Experimental cutting of concrete has indicated that significant improvements in cutting rates over conventional saw methods can be achieved. Other benefits are, reduced dust levels, minimal nozzle wear compared to saw blade life, safe cutting regimes and a potential for reduced noise levels.

Around the world, at several laboratories continuous water jets are being used to augment the performance of tunnel boring machines which use cutters to disintegrate the rock into small chips a few inches across. The rate of advance and the life of disc roller cutters is limited due to the abrasion and enormous thrust required to force the cutters into rock face. Henneke and Bauman (2) have conducted tests which indicated that water jets permit a reduction in forward thrust one and half times and a corresponding reduction in weight of the boring machine.

Environmetally the water jet is an acceptable tool. Its noise level and the amount of dust it creates is much lower than a jack hammer. By combining the cutter discs with high pressure water jets, the advantages are: the importance in tunneling advance time, rotational speed of the drilling head and the increase in the advance force. The water jets improve the efficiency of mechanical drilling tools and reduces the feed forces required for breaking the rock. In case of coal mining the conventional tunneling machines are approaching technological and economical limits i.e., the bulky dimensions, heavy weights and mounting services. With the use of jets, the feed could be reduced by 50%, the weight of tunneling or full face equipment could be reduced substantially.

In comparison with the conventional drilling bits and erosion bits the efficiency of jet cutting is quite high and the time taken to cut a unit area is reduced by 35 - 40%. Erosion bits in combination with nozzles can drill 2 to 3 times faster than conventional bits. Bits such as diamonds, drag blades or roller cones can be used in conjunction with multiple nozzles to obtain greater efficiencies. The drill bit is provided with two operators along its length - one vertical and one angled nozzle and the bit is connected to a high pressure piping. A purposeful and well confined action of water jets on the central section of the drilling head yields better results. A load release could be brought about for the cutting discs in the peripheral area depending upon the intensity of cutting. An effective cooling of the bits and discs and simultaneous high flushing rate of the tunnel floor to remove the drillings and debris could be achieved substantially. The grooving depth has been found to be increased upto 70% or pressure reductions upto 40%, by using additives in the pressorized water. The water jets have erogonomic advantages in terms of controlling the dust by the very fine pulverised water jets at the tunneling head and in the drilling section. The pulverized jets absorb the dust almost to 100% so that the dust extraction devices could be done away with.

Water jets are highly useful in the installation of roof bolts inside tunnels and in the construction of underground power stations. These are more advantageous over mechanically anchored bolts. In case of water jet blasting, where notches are made in rocks by super high pressure jets, the direction oft blasting force can be controlled. This helps in less damage to the surrounding rock, and control of blasting force at the perimeter zone minimises the fissured zone in the surrounding rock. This method reduces the number of loose parts of rock which are hazardous and the rock surface remains smooth after blasting. Further, the volume of over break and the amount of charge in the shot holes at the perimeter thereby saving considerable costs. High pressure liquid jets when used in conjunction with the conventional tunneling machines have the following potential technical advantages.

a) Less bulky equipment and low feed requirement

b) Easier mounting, dismantling and transportation

c) Reduced wear of the drilling tools,

d) Efficient dust suppression and elimination of sparks and

e) Economic viability.

5. TYPES OF EQUIPMENTS

Water jet cutting equipments can be classified under the following headings:

a) Continuous jet drilling rigs

b) Pulsed or intermittent jet drilling rigs

c) Combined cutter and high pressure jets

d) Water jet blasting.

The basic requirements of a continuous water jet rig are a high pressure pump, nozzles of suitable profiles and control mechanism. The cutting capabilities of the jets could be increased by having cavitation inducers in the nozzle (14). The jets could be traversed across the area of tunneling. The nozzle diameters and the pressures upto 1000 Mpa. In case of pulsed or intermittant jet drilling rigs, high pressure air compressors and snap acting intensifiers are made use of for thrusting water columns and droplets at high pressure on the rock and the surface is loaded periodically. Measurements have indicated that intermittant pressures of the order of 5000 mpa are obtained. However the initial investment over these test rigs are still quite expensive. In this the basic studies have been going on in several research institutions (18, 19, 20). The recent research investigations related to the constructive aspects of the cavitation phenomena introdruced in jet cutting technology seem to a drastically change the scene in the design and fabrication of tunneling and cutting contrivances.

The combined cutter and high pressure jets with suitable orientation of the cutters and the jets have ushered a new era in the design and fabrication of mining, tunneling and drilling equipments. These possess an average increase in advance ratio of 50 to 60%, which leads to overall cost savings of 14 to 25%. By having dual nozzles and rotating them during tunneling operations, a substantial increase in the cutting rate could be obtained. The combination of cutting discs and high pressure jets consists of water jets on either sides of the drilling tool, cut grooves and free surfaces into the rock where as the nib left in between the grooves will be removed by the shearing action of the cutting discs.

The water jet blasting is characterized by making notches using super high pressure jets so that the direction of blasting force can be controlled. During blasting with lined shot holes which are loosely charged, cracks grow to the neighbouring shot holes to decrease the expansion in other directions. The addition of notches to the shot holes causes cracks to grow in the direction of notches because the shock wave and the high gas pressure from the blasting act mainly in this direction.

A greater detail of these equipments has not been brought out at this stage and only the salient features and a broad picture is depicted.

6. CONCLUSIONS

In view of the world facing a severe energy crisis, the technology of tunneling, drilling, mining and cutting using liquid jets has opened a new era in the optimised exploitation of the natural resources. Though this field is the laboratory stage, the day is not far off when the entire conventional types of tunneling and mining would be replaced by the liquid jet cutting contrivances.

REFERENCES

1 Vijay, M.M. and Briverlay, J.H. 1978, Cutting Rocks and Other Materials by Cavitating and Non-Cavitating Jets, Proc. Fourth Int. Symp. on Jet Cutting Technology, Paper C5, pp. 51 to 66

2 Lothar Baumann and Heneke, J. 1980, Attempt of Technical-Economical Optimization of High Pressure Jet Assistance for Tunneling Machines, Proc. Fifth Int. Symp. on Jet Cutting Technology, Paper C4, pp. 119 to 139

3 Conn. A.F., 1979 Elevated Ambient Pressure Effects on Rock Cutting by Cavitating Fluid Jets, Proc. Fifth International Conference on Erosion by Solid an Liquid Impact, pp. 68-1 to 68-8

4 Lichtarourier, A. and Scott, P.J., Erosion Testing with Cavitating Jet, Proc. Fifth International Conference on Erosion by Solid and Liquid Impact, pp. 69-1 to 69-8.

5 Summers, D.A., The Potential Application of Water Jets in Geotechnical Excavation, Proc. Fifth Int. Conference on Erosion by Solid and Liquid Impact, pp. 71-1 to 71-7.

6 Bertin, E.F. et. al, A New Technique in the Application of High Speed Water Jet, Proc. Fifth Int. Conf. on Erosion by Solid and Liquid Impact, pp. F2-15 to F2-22.

7 Daniel, I.M. 1976, Experimental Studies of Water Jet Impact on Rock and Rocklike Materials, Proc. Third Int. on Jet Cutting Technology, pp. B3-27 to B3-46.

8 Hoshino, K. et. al, 1976, The Development and the Experiment of the Water Jet Drill for Tunnel Construction, Proc. Third Int. Symp. on Jet Cutting Technology, pp. E4-41 to E4-48.

9 Rehbinder, G., 1976, Some Aspects on the Mechanism of Erosion of Rock with a High Speed Water Jet. Proc. Third Int. Symp. on Jet Cutting Technology, pp. E1-1 to E1-20.

10 Burhnell, D.J. and Symmers, D.A., 1976, Preliminary Experimentation of the Design of the Water Jet Drilling Device, Proc. Third Int. Symp. on Jet Cutting Technology, pp. E2-21 to E2-28.

11 Fun Den Wang, 1976, Water Jet Assisted Tunnel Boring, Proc. Third Int. Symp. on Jet Cutting Technology, Paper E6.

12 Labus, T.J., Energy Requirements for Rocl Penetration by Water Jets, Proc. Third Int. Symp. on Jet Cutting Technology, pp. E3-29 to E3-40.

13 Janakiram, and Symala Rao, B.C., 1978, 'Some Observations on Velocity and Frequency Effects in Liquid Impact Erosion using Plain and Cavijets, CAVITATION FORUM, Am. Soc. of Mechanical Engineers.

14 Leach, S.J. and Walker, G.L., 1966, 'The Application of high speed liquid jets to cutting', Some Aspects of Rock Cutting by High Speed Water Jets', Trans.

Royal Soc. London, U.K., Vol. 260, 1966.

15 Teuro Yahiro, 1974, On the Characteristics of High Speed Water Jet in the Liquid and its Utilization on Induction Grouting Method, KICT, Japan, Report No. 16.

16 Teuro Yahiro, et. al, 1975, The Development and Application of a Japanese Grouting System, Water Power and Dam Construction, Feb., 1975.

17 Janakiram, K.S. and Syamala Rao, B.C., 1978, 'Studies on the Characteristics of Erosion With Plain Jets and Jets with Cavitation Inducers', Journal of Testing and Evaluation, Am. Soc. for Testing and Materials, Vol. 6, No. 6, November.

18 Janakiram, K.S. and Syamala Rao, B.C. 1982, 'Studies on Erosion due to Impingement of Jets with Cavitation Inducers,' International Water Power and Dam Construction, London, January.

19 Moodie, K. and Taylor, G., 1974, 'A review of current work on the cutting and fracturing and rocks by high pressure water jets, Proc. Fluid Power Equipment in Mining, Quarrying and Tunneling, I. Mech. Eng., U.K., paper C22/74.

ZUKUNFTSWEISENDE ENTWICKLUNGEN VON VOLLSCHNITTMASCHINEN AUFGRUND VON ERFAHRUNGEN BEI EINSÄTZEN IM BERGBAU

Future-oriented development of full-section tunnelling machines based on experience gained in the mining industry

Développements orientés vers l'avenir d'engins de forage à pleine section basé sur les expériences gagnées dans les mines de houille

CLAUS MASSON

E.Heitkamp Berg- und Bautechnik GmbH, Herne, Bundesrepublik Deutschland

ZUSAMMENFASSUNG

Seit dem ersten Leistungseinsatz von Vollschnittmaschinen im Steinkohlenbergbau hat eine erhebliche technische Weiterentwicklung stattgefunden. Durch Veränderungen in der Bohrkopfform, der Verlagerung der Diskenmeißel, der Verkürzung der Maschinenkonstruktion im Bohrkopfbereich und der Entwicklung neuartiger Ausbausetzvorrichtungen konnte das wichtigste Ziel erreicht werden, nämlich in Gesteinen extrem unterschiedlicher Festigkeit und Standsicherheit auch während der Durchfahrung geologischer Störungen eine hohe und regelmäßige arbeitstägliche Vortriebsleistung zu erreichen. Dieses ist besonders zu bewerten, wenn man berücksichtigt, daß im Steinkohlenbergbau ständiger Ausbau sofort im Maschinenbereich mit Mattenverzug und Ausbauringen mit geringeren Ringabständen von üblicherweise 75 cm zur Standsicherheit der Gesteinsstrecken und zur Sicherheit der Vorortbelegschaft unumgänglich notwendig und von der Bergbehörde vorgeschrieben ist.

SUMMARY

Since full-section tunnelling machines were first brought into use in coal mining their further technical development has been considerable. By means of alterations to the form of the drill point, the repositioning of the disk's chisels, the shortening of the machine in the area of the drill point and the development of new forms of lining arrangements it has been possible to achieve the most important objective, namely the accomplishment of a consistanty high tunnel driving performance during a working day in rocks of widely differing strength and stability as well as while driving through geological faults. This is of particular value, when it is taken into account that in coal mining permanent lining immediately in the vicinity of the machine is absolutely necessary and required by the authorities, mesh lagging and steel ring lining with a small ring spacing, usually of 75 cm, being used to secure the rock areas and ensure safety of the personnel at the working face.

RESUME

Depuis le premier emploi productif des machines à attaque globale dans l'exploitation des mines de houille, une évolution technique considérable a eu lieu. Les transformations dans la forme de la tête de foration, le déplacement des molettes à disque, le raccourcissement de la construction des machines dans le domaine de la tête de foration et le développement de nouveaux engins de pose de soutènement ont permis d'atteindre le but le plus important, c'est-à-dire de parvenir par un usage quotidien à une puissance de creusement élevée et réguliere dans les terrains de résistance et de stabilité extrêmement différentes, également pendant la traversée des zones géologiques instables. Cette performance doit être particulièrement appréciée, quand on considère que, dans l'exploitation des mines de houille, l'autorité des mines prescrit un étaiement stable dans le domaine immédiat des machines à l'aide de bandage en treillis et de cintre dont les plus petits écartements sont habituellement de 75 cm, indispensable à la stabilité des galeries au rocher et à la sécurité du personnel sur place.

1. Einfluß der Forderung nach sofortiger Hohlraumsicherung auf die Maschinenkonzeption

Die im Bergbau unabdingbare Forderung der sofortigen Hohlraumsicherung durch Stahlringausbau und Mattenverzug unmittelbar hinter der Ortsbrust setzt einen ausreichend großen freien Raum im Maschinenbereich voraus, um die notwendigen Ausbauarbeiten ausführen zu können. Dieser war damals am ehesten bei einer Maschine gegeben, die nur ein seitliches Abspannpaar besaß gegenüber den sonst üblichen zwei oder sogar vier Abspannpaaren in Form eines Andreaskreuzes. Der Vortrieb wurde dadurch behindert, daß die Abspannung zwischen den Ringen gegen das Gebirge erfolgen mußte. Ringabstände von in der Regel nur 100 cm und sogar weniger verlangten eine besonders sorgfältige Fahrweise der Maschine. Die Abstände der Ausbauringe mußten sauber eingehalten werden und diese selbst mußten genau bankrecht gestellt werden. Die Durchführung der einzelnen Fahroperationen der Vortriebsmaschine stellten dabei häufig nicht erfüllbare Anforderungen an die Maschinenführer.

Um den Wunsch nach immer geringeren Abständen der Ausbauringe erfüllen zu können, mußten die Abspannplatten schmaler werden, dabei durfte der spezifische Anpreßdruck gegen das Gebirge nicht so hoch werden, daß dieses möglicherweise zerdrückt wurde. Daher entwickelte man - vor allem bei den einpaarigen Seitenabspannungen - eine Platte mit senkrechter großer Rille. Damit konnte der Ausbauring überfahren werden, indem sich das Ringprofil in diese Rille legte.

Ein möglichst großer freier Raum hinter dem Bohrkopf wurde nicht nur zur Durchführung der Ausbauarbeiten beansprucht. Neben ausreichendem Platz für vier bis fünf Arbeiter mußte hier auch die Ausbausetzvorrichtung Platz finden. Diese bestand zunächst aus einfachen Taschen, in die die Kalottensegmente eingefädelt wurden, nachdem das Sohlensegment von Hand in die geforderte Position gebracht worden war. Als Ausbauprofil konnten zunächst nur sehr leichte GI-Profile eingesetzt werden, die von zwei Leuten noch von Hand bewegt werden konnten. Als Verbindung dienten einfache Laschen, die in an die Enden der Segmente angeschweißte Taschen gesteckt wurden, eine Konstruktion, die außerordentlich labil gegen Knickung war. Die Ausbautätigkeit war dabei sehr zeitaufwendig und verursachte ständige Wartezeiten bei der Bohrarbeit. Inzwischen wurden jedoch Erektoren entwickelt, die eine Ringmontage aus beliebig vielen Einzelsegmenten in allen Profilen - auch Rinnenprofilen - von einem Montagestand aus in kurzer Zeit ermöglichen, ohne daß Bohrstillstände entstehen. Es können schwerste Profile Anwendung finden, da die Handarbeit nahezu ausgeschaltet ist. Die Segmente werden heute über Bänder aus dem hinteren Maschinenbereich bis an den Montageort gefahren und dort von hydraulischen Hubeinrichtungen in die Montageposition im Erektor gebracht, ohne daß nennenswerte körperliche Kraft anzuwenden wäre. Das erste Segment wird im Erektor durch eine Schraube befestigt. Die nachfolgenden Segmente werden aus der Montageposition durch motorisches Drehen des Erektors dem im Erektor eingespeisten vorhergehenden Segment angepaßt und angeklemmt. Lediglich die von Hand eingefügten Verbindungselemente der einzelnen Segmente werden mit Schlagschraubern ebenfalls von Hand angezogen. Ist der Ring komplett eingebaut, werden die Klemmverbindungen gelöst, der Ring wird hydraulisch aus dem Erektor gedrückt und mit einem Nachspannzylinder hydraulisch gegen das Gebirge verspannt. Die Ausbausetzvorrichtung wird heute direkt hinter dem Bohrkopf in einem kurzen Vollschild untergebracht. Die Ausbauarbeit erfolgt im Schutze von Dachschilden, die eine Länge von ca. 2,50 m haben. So wird sichergestellt, daß zu keiner Zeit die Firste freiliegt und ein Gebirgsniederbruch im Maschinenbereich nicht erfolgen kann.

Kommt es zu höheren Gebirgsdrücken auf den Schild, die verursacht sein können durch Konvergenzen oder Gebirgsauflockerung, werden Schlepplanzen an die Schildenden montiert, die auf bereits gestellte Ausbauringe aufliegen und die Gebirgslasten auf diese übertragen.

Um Gebirgsniederbrüche auch zwischen Bohrkopf und Ortsbrust so gering wie möglich zu halten, wurden die ursprünglich parabolisch geformten Bohrköpfe völlig abgeflacht, so daß heute von der Ortsbrust bis zum ersten gestellten Ausbauring nur noch ein max. Abstand von 2,50 m verbleibt. Dabei zeigte sich jedoch, daß die Maschinenführung im Bohrkopfbereich erschwert wird und sich vor allem auf die Kalibermeißel und deren Lager Querkräfte durch leichte taumelnde Bewegungen des Bohrkopfes auswirken, die einen erheblich höheren Verschleiß oder sogar Bruch zur Folge haben. Der schmale Spannschild hinter dem Bohrkopf ist jetzt also nicht mehr in der Lage, den vorderen Maschinenteil während des Bohrens zu fixieren. Daher wird man in Zukunft von einem total abgeflachten Bohrkopf, der die Stabilisierung der Ortsbrust begünstigen sollte, bei einer einpaarigen Maschinenabspannung wieder abgehen müssen.

Wegen der wachsenden Teufen im westdeutschen Steinkohlenbergbau (1200 m und mehr sind inzwischen der Normalfall) und der größer werdenden Bohrdurchmesser (in Zukunft dürfte aus wettertechnischen Gründen der Durchmesser 7,0 m und mehr betragen) steigt die Problematik der Gebirgskonvergenzen. Damit gewinnt auch die Forderung nach frühzeitigem Ausbau mit hoher Frühtragfähigkeit an Bedeutung.
Eine weitere Verringerung des Abstandes Ortsbrust-Ausbau kann nur erreicht werden, wenn der Schild hinter dem Bohrkopf weiter verschmälert wird. Bei den Maschinen mit einpaariger Abspannung dient diese Einrichtung aber gleichzeitig als vordere Maschinenabstützung und Verspannung zum Zwecke der Stabilisierung und Richtungsgebung der Maschine und ist daher nicht ohne weiteres zu verkürzen. Er müßte im Gegenteil aus den eben genannten Gründen bei Wahl eines flachen Bohrkopfes noch verbessert werden. Bei besonders großen Frühkonvergenzen bereits im Bereich des Bohrkopfes hat sich außerdem gezeigt, daß der als Abstützung und Verspannung dienende Bohrkopfschild eingeklemmt wird, die Maschine nicht mehr bewegt werden kann und von Hand wieder freigespitzt werden muß.
In konsequenter Verfolgung des Zieles eines möglichst frühen Ausbaues bleibt daher aus heutiger Sicht zwangsweise nur die Rückkehr zur zweipaarigen Maschinenverspannung. In diesem Fall hat der Schild hinter dem Bohrkopf außer der Schutzfunktion für die Ausbaubelegschaft gegen hereinbrechendes Gebirge keine weiteren maschinentechnischen Funktionen. Die doppelte seitliche Verspannung der Maschine erlaubt es auch, den abgeflachten Bohrkopf mit den genannten Vorteilen beizubehalten. Außerdem hat sie den Vorteil, daß bei begrenzten seitlichen Gebirgsausbrüchen wenigstens von einem Abspannpaar ein ausreichendes Widerlager gefunden wird, um den notwendigen Andruck des Bohrkopfes zu gewährleisten. Bei nur einer Abspannung entstehen in derartigen Situationen zwangsläufig Maschinenstillstände für die notwendige seitliche Verfüllung, die am schnellsten durch Mörteltrockenmischung, in Jutesäcken verpackt, erfolgt, die nach Einbringen in den Hohlraum durchfeuchtet werden.
Das System der doppelten Verspannung findet auch deswegen in jüngster Zeit wieder Anwendung, weil vor allem die deutschen Maschinenhersteller aufgrund der Einsatzerfahrungen im letzten Jahrzehnt, die sie gemeinsam mit den Maschinenbetreibern in hervorragender Zusammenarbeit machen konnten, wesentlich leichtere, den technischen Bedürfnissen und Beanspruchungen entsprechend aber völlig ausreichende Konstruktionen anbieten mit dem entsprechenden Platzgewinn im Maschinenbereich. Die größer gewordenen Bohrdurchmesser begünstigen die Entwicklung. Alle vorgenannten Erfahrungen und Überlegungen sind in der Konzeption der letzten im Steinkohlenbergbau zum Einsatz gekommenen Maschinen vereinigt. Der durch die Doppelabspannung verringerte freie Arbeitsraum wurde dadurch besser ausgenutzt, daß der Antransport der einzelnen Ausbauelemente bis zur Einbaustelle nicht über sondern unter der Maschine mit Hilfe einer Einschienenhängebahn in Paketen erfolgt und die Einspeisung der Ringsegmente in den Erektor von der Sohle aus vorgenommen wird. Dadurch wurde soviel Raum gewonnen, daß zwischen den Abspannelementen noch Platz für die Montage von Ankerbohrgeräten blieb, um die geforderte Systemankerung neben einem planmäßigen Ringausbau zu gewährleisten.
Mit der Forderung nach einer Systemankerung als Ausbauform neben einem systematischen Ringausbau ist in neuester Zeit der Platzbedarf im Maschinenbereich zur Einrichtung von Ankerbohrmaschinen noch größer geworden.
Um den vollen Kreisquerschnitt abbohren zu können, werden vor und hinter den Abspannplatten je zwei Bohrlafetten mit Arbeitsbühnen installiert. Mit den vorderen Bohreinrichtungen werden Firste und halbe obere Kalotte, mit den beiden hinteren Einrichtungen die untere Kalottenhälfte und die Sohle abgebohrt, so daß die Ankerung des gesamten Kreisquerschnittes möglich ist.

2. Entwicklung von Bohrkopf und Meißel

Die Gründe für die Entwicklung von einer konischen zu einer flachen Bohrkopfform mit ihren Vor- und Nachteilen wurden bereits erwähnt. Als Bohrwerkzeug wurde inzwischen von allen Maschinenherstellern im Normalfall ein Einringdiskenmeißel gewählt, der für alle Gesteinsarten sowohl hinsichtlich der Löseleistung als auch in bezug auf den Verschleiß als günstigste und wirtschaftlichste Konstruktion eingesetzt wird. Abstände der Schneidbahnen von 80 bis 100 mm sind die Regel. Bei extrem harten oder zähen Gesteinen kann dieser Abstand auf 40 bis 50 mm heruntergesetzt werden. Dieses ist zu erreichen einmal durch Erhöhung der Meißelzahl auf dem Bohrkopf, was bei großen Bohrdurchmessern unproblematisch ist. Bei geringeren Durchmessern unter 4,5 m kann diese Lösung schwierig werden, weil der Platzbedarf für die Installation der Meißelhalterungen auf dem Bohrkopf nicht verfügbar ist. Hierfür ist vor allem von den deutschen Maschinenherstellern ein Zweiringdiskus in nur einer Lagerung entwickelt worden, mit dem diese geringen Schneidbahnenabstände erreicht werden können. Durch Verbesserung der Diskenlager und der Halterungen am Bohrkopf können die auftretenden hohen Lagerkräfte gut beherrscht werden.

Bisher wurden die Meißel in auf den Bohrkopf aufgeschweißte Halter eingesetzt. Im Falle von Ausbrüchen aus der Ortsbrust geraten dann immer wieder große Brocken zwischen Meißelwerkzeug und Bohrkopf und bewirken den Abriß von Halterungen bzw. den Bruch von Meißeln.
Werden die Meißel zu weit abgefahren bzw. brechen Meißel ab, stoßen die Halterungen gegen die Ortsbrust und werden deformiert oder zerstört. Daher verlegt man in einer neueren Entwicklung die Halterungen in Meißeltaschen, die in den Bohrkopf eingelassen sind. Als Nachteil dieser Lösung zeigte sich, daß vor allem klebendes Bohrklein die Taschen zubrikettiert und die Meißel sich dann nicht mehr drehen. Daher werden in Zukunft diese Vertiefungen nicht mehr so extrem sein können bzw. die Taschen muldenförmig auszubilden sein, um diese Erscheinung zu verhindern.
Ein weiterer Vorteil der in den Bohrkopf eingelassenen Meißel ist, daß die Meißellager nach hinten zu öffnen sind. Dadurch ist es möglich, den Meißelwechsel nicht mehr vor der Ortsbrust sondern aus dem hinteren Bohrkopf vorzunehmen. So werden die Wechselzeiten erheblich herabgesetzt. Ein weiterer wichtiger Vorteil dabei ist, daß die Meißelkontrolle und der Meißelwechsel von einem geschützten Stand erfolgen können und nicht mehr aus dem Bohrraum zwischen Bohrkopf und ungeschützter Ortsbrust ausgeführt werden müssen. Zu letzterem erfolgten für Maschineneinsätze im Steinkohlenbergbau strenge Sicherheitsauflagen, nachdem ein bedauerlicher tödlicher Unfall durch Steinfall aus der Ortsbrust erfolgte. Es besteht jetzt für die noch laufenden älteren Maschinen die Anordnung, daß die Ortsbrust vor dem Betreten des Bohrraumes gesichert werden muß. Bei den bis Ende 1981 zum Einsatz gekommenen Maschinen kann diese Forderung nur durch Notlösungen erfüllt werden. Diese bestehen darin, daß in der Firste zwei Hydraulikzylinder gegen die Ortsbrust aus dem Bohrkopf herausgefahren werden. An diese Zylinder wird ein Netz gespannt, unter dem der Meißelwechsel erfolgt. Weitergehend ist die Lösung, nach der bei zurückgefahrener Maschine eine Stahlplatte, die während des Bohrvorganges am Bohrkopf anliegt, durch vier Hydraulikzylinder gegen die Ortsbrust gefahren wird und damit ein weitgehend zuverlässiger Ortsbrustverbau erzielt wird.

Sehr interessant ist ein Forschungsvorhaben des Steinkohlenbergbauvereins, das mit Mitteln des BMFT gefördert wird. Zur Unterstützung der Gesteinslösung durch Diskenmeißel werden Hartwasserstrahlen mit einem Druck bis zu 5000 bar gegen die Ortsbrust gerichtet, die das Gebirge bis zu 2 cm tief aufkerben. Vorteile dieses Verfahrens sind: höhere Vortriebsleistunge wesentlich geringerer Meißelverschleiß mit weniger Stillstandszeiten für Meißelwechse reduzierter Staubanfall im Bohrraum, besse Meißelkühlung und Verringerung der Temperaturen im Bohrraum.

Dieser Punkt ist vor allen Dingen für den Steinkohlenbergbau von Wichtigkeit, da in Teufen von 1000 m bereits Gebirgstemperaturen von 50° und mehr herrschen und die Gefahr der Verpuffung bei Auftrete von Methangas gemindert wird. Ein derartiger Vorfall hat erst in jüngster Zeit zu einem beträchtlichen Maschinenschaden geführt mit einem für die Reparatur zu erwartenden Stillstand von mind. 6 Monaten und Schadenskosten von mehr als 6,5 Mio. DM.

3. Entwicklung in den nachgeschalteten Einrichtungen

Im Gegensatz zu Tunnelvortrieben werden im Steinkohlenbergbau die Abwetter aus den Maschinenvortrieben den übrigen Grubenwettern wieder zugeführt, die noch zur Bewetterung weiterer Betriebe verwendet werden. Sie müssen daher weitestgehend entstaubt werden. Aus dieser Notwendigkeit wurden in den letzten 10 Jahren Entstaubungsan-

lagen entwickelt, die im Dauerbetrieb einen Entstaubungsgrad von 98 - 99 % erreichen. Neue nicht brennbare Filtermaterialien in Kerzen- oder Taschenform erzielten bei genügend hohem Wetterdurchgang und erträglichen Kompressionsverlusten diesen hohen Reinigungsgrad, so daß die zunächst eingesetzten Naßentstaubungsanlagen sehr bald abgelöst und auf Trockenentstauber übergegangen werden konnte. Gegenüber der ursprünglichen Filterschlammbeseitigung stellt heute die Feinststaubbeseitigung in Säcken kein Problem mehr dar.
Trotz guter Durchgangsleistungen von 200 bis 250 m^3/min staubbelasteter Luft je Filtereinheit werden die Geräte der Forderung nach kompakter und wartungsfreundlicher Bauweise gerecht. Bei Entgasungen des Gebirges muß eine ausreichende Spülung des Bohrraumes mit Frischwettern erfolgen, da bei einem Methangehalt der Wetter von über 1 % die automatische elektrische Abschaltung des Vortriebssystemes erfolgt. Zukunftsaufgabe wird es sein, Filtereinrichtungen mit noch höherem Entstaubungseffekt und geringeren Druckverlusten auch bei höheren Wettergeschwindigkeiten zu entwickeln.

Die in jüngster Vergangenheit in den großen Teufen aufgetretenen Gebirgskonvergenzen haben selbst die schwersten im Bergbau üblichen nachgiebigen Ausbauringe deformiert bzw. im Durchmesser derartig verringert, (bei einem Bohrdurchmesser von 6,5 bis auf 5,5 m), daß die nachgeschalteten Einrichtungen von der Maschine nicht mehr mitgezogen werden konnten. Diese Einrichtungen werden in der Regel auf Bühnen an Einschienenhängebahnen verfahren, die an den Ausbauringen befestigt werden. Die Gesamtlänge eines derartigen Gerätezuges hat aufgrund der Notwendigkeit der Mitführung von Elektro- und Hydraulikeinrichtungen für die Maschine und die Beladebänder,die Entstaubungsanlagen, die Wetterkühleinrichtungen und die Kabelspeicher eine Länge von 200 bis 250 m erreicht. Die zu befürchtenden Konvergenzen haben nun dazu geführt, daß die einzelnen Aggregate nicht mehr auf den Bühnen in Baugruppen nebeneinander, sondern hintereinander aufgestellt werden, wodurch die Einrichtungszüge sich auf über 300 m verlängern. Gewonnen wurden dadurch seitlich angebrachte Fahrwege, die bei größeren Konvergenzen abgeklappt werden, so daß ein reibungsloser Durchgang durch die Strecken auch bei extremen Durchmesserverringerungen durch Gebirgskonvergenzen möglich ist.

ROCK MECHANICAL VIEWPOINT ON EXCAVATION OF PRESSURE TUNNEL BY TUNNEL BORING MACHINE

Gebirgsmechanische Betrachtung über den Ausbruch eines Druckstollens mittels Tunnelbohrmaschine

Aspect mécanique de la roche dans l'excavation d'une galerie forcée à l'aide d'une machine à forer

T.NISHIDA, Y.MATSUMURA, Y.MIYANAGA & M.HORI
Electric Power Development Co. Ltd., Tokyo, Japan

SUMMARY:
In a project of Shimogo pumped storage hydro power station of 1,000 MW, a tunnel boring machine was employed to excavate the inclined pressure tunnel of the penstock. The tunnel has been completed with 5,8 m diameter and at 37° inclination angle. This performance was the first success in Japan in the excavation of an inclined tunnel by TBM. The surrounding rock is little loosened by the excavation if TBM is employed. The thickness of the loosening zone generated in the circumferential area of the tunnel was measured by a technique of seismic prospecting in the field. From the results, the thickness was found to be 0.3 m at most, which was relatively small in comparison with that caused by the conventional blasting method. Consequently, for the sake of the reduction of the loosening zone by the use of TBM, a design of the steel lining in the penstock has become economical. The cost of the steel lining was reduced by about 17% compared with a cost required for a case when the conventional blasting method would be employed.

ZUSAMMENFASSUNG:
Im Rahmen des Bauprojektes für das Shimogo Pumpenspeicherwerk mit einer Kapazität von 1.000 MW wurde eine Tunnelbohrmaschine eingesetzt, um einen schrägen Druckstollen für die Turbinenleitung auszubrechen. Der Stollen wurde mit einem Durchmesser von 5,8 m und einem Gefälle von 37° fertiggestellt. Diese Leistung repräsentierte in Japan den ersten Erfolg für den Ausbruch eines Schrägstollens unter Verwendung einer Tunnelbohrmaschine (TBM). Das umgebende Gestein wird durch den Ausbruch nur wenig aufgelockert, wenn eine Tunnelbohrmaschine benutzt wird. Die Dicke der im Umfangbereich des Stollens entstandenen Auflockerungszone wurde mit Hilfe einer seismischen Untersuchungstechnik gemessen. Die Ergebnisse zeigten, dass die Dicke maximal 0,3 m betrug. Dieser Wert ist relativ klein verglichen mit der durch das herkömmliche Sprengverfahren verursachten Auflockerung. Die Verwendung der Tunnelbohrmaschine ermöglicht somit eine Verkleinerung der Auflockerungszone und folglich eine wirtschaftlichere Stahlauskleidung in der Turbinenleitung. Die Kosten der Stahlauskleidung wurden um ca. 17% reduziert, verglichen mit den erforderlichen Kosten in einem Fall, wo das herkömmliche Sprengverfahren benutzt wird.

RESUME:
Pour le projet de l'usine de pompage de 1,000 KW, une perceuse de tunnels fut utilisée pour l'excavation de la galérie forcée inclinée et de la conduite forcée. La galerie terminée avait un diamètre de 5,8 m et un angle d'inclinaison de 37°. Ceci fut le premier succès, au Japon, d'excavation d'une galerie inclinée à l'aide d'une machine à percer les tunnels (TBM). Les roches se trouvant aux alentours sont quelque peu désagrégées si la machine TBM est utilisée pour l'excavation. L'épaisseur de la zône de désagrégation provoquée dans la périphérie du tunnel fut mesurée selon une technique de prospection sismique. D'après les résultats de cette prospection l'épaisseur maximum était de 0,3 m, valeur relativement faible comparé à celles obtenues en utilisant la méthode sautage conventionnelle. Par conséquent, afin de réduire la zône de désagrégation à l'aide de la machine TBM on est arrivé à une conception économique du revêtement d'acier de la conduite forcée. Le coût du revêtement d'acier est environ 17% moins cher que le coût d'un revêtement lorsque la méthode de sautage conventionnelle est utilisée.

1 INTRODUCTION

In Shimogo pumped storage hydro plant project, a tunnel boring machine (hereinafter called "TBM" for short) was successfully employed to excavate an inclined pressure tunnel of penstock. The use of TBM has brought fairly good tunnelling performances even in poor geological conditions. In order to investigate geotechnical properties of the rock and to obtain basic data applied for a design of the steel lined pressure tunnel, a series of laboratory tests on rock specimens and field tests on intact rocks has been carried out.

Throughout the accomplishment of tunnelling by TBM and the rock mechanical investigation in this project, the authors try to find a correlation between geotechnical properties of rock and performances of TBM such as velocity of advance, thrust force and torque.

Furthermore, the authors pay attention to a fact that an excavation by TBM would not so much loosen a base rock surrounding the tunnel, compared with a case by a conventional blasting method. This fact has been proved in the field by a technique of seismic prospecting. Such this advantage obtained by the use of TBM from a viewpoint of rock mechanics has been considered into analytical design concerning the steel lining. As a result, some saving on the steel lining in thickness was attained in the final design.

2 OUTLINE OF THE PROJECT

2.1 General

A pumped storage hydro plant project is under construction at Shimogo in Fukushima prefecture located at about 200 km north of Tokyo. Waterway, connecting in between upper and lower reservoirs, is approximately 3.5 km in total length, and effective head to be obtained is about 400 m. The expected electric power is to be 1,000 MW. A construction of the project has started in April, 1978, and starting of electric generation will be scheduled for July, 1984.

One of main topics in the construction of this project is that TBM was employed to excavate the penstock firstly in Japan. The penstock is composed of two lines of pressure tunnel as shown in Fig. 1. Further, as seen in a longitudinal section of the penstock in Fig. 2, it is designed such that the upper penstock inclines at 37° and the lower penstock inclines at 51°. The former, of which length is approximately 500 m, has been excavated by means of TBM. On the other hand, the section of the lower penstock has been excavated by a conventional blasting method with supporting system by using rock bolts and shotcrete.

2.2 Geology

Geology in a region around the penstock and the underground power station is highly complicated, as shown in Fig. 2. The rocks are mainly composed of fine grained sandstone, accompanied with some layers of coarse grained sandstone and chert. Geological boundaries of these rock formations are generally sheared and faulted to some extent. Further, igneous rocks of rhyolite, granite porphyry and porphyrite have penetrated into these weak zones, and have formed thin layers.

Due to the high complexity of previous geologic process, the rocks are more or less factured and, spacing of cracks is therefore quite short. RQD ranges from 5 to 20% throughout all kinds of the rocks.

The lower penstock and the power station are placed within a block of diorite which has been formed by penetrating the original bedrock of sedimentary rocks. The diorite is comparatively competent and, not so much fractured. RQD in this region is about 50% in average.

3 TUNNELLING PERFORMANCE OF TBM

3.1 Type of machine

At present, there are about 20 types of TBM on the market, each having special design features. A common characteristic of all types is that each machine is generally designed or modified for the specific project on which it is to be used. Therefore, a selection of machine must be decided in consideration of type of rock to be drilled, stability of tunnel after drilling, diameter of tunnel, environmental conditions and so on.

In the present project, it was taken into account in selecting a type of TBM that a machine must be available to be applied both for soft and hard rocks. In addition, such a machine, of which drilling manner does not harm a tunnel stability, since the base rock is considerably fractured and faulted. Finally, the machine of Wirth (Federal Republic of West Germany) made, has been selected and purchased after sufficient inquiries. The drilling manner by this machine is such that a pilot tunnel

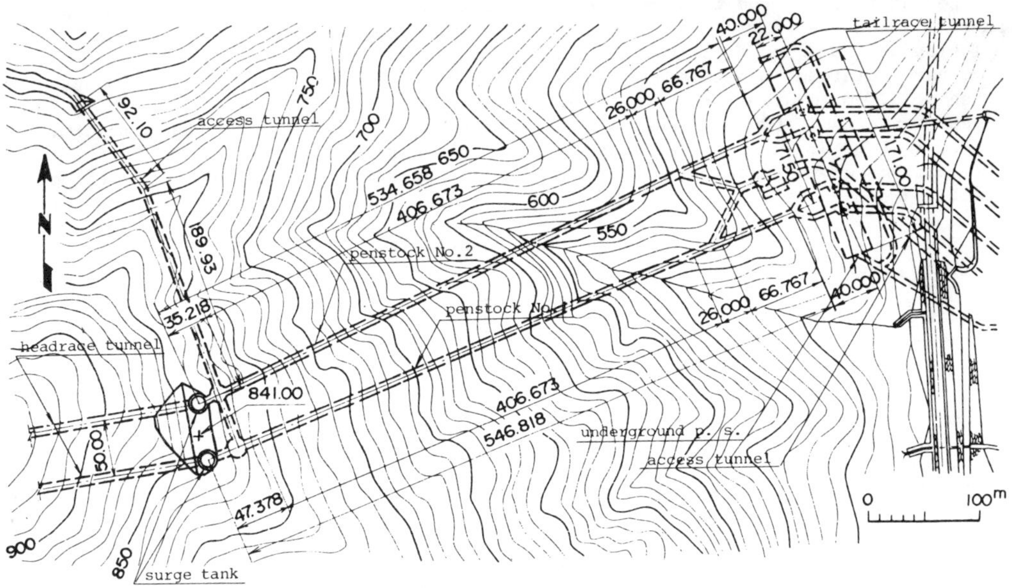

Fig. 1. Plan of penstock

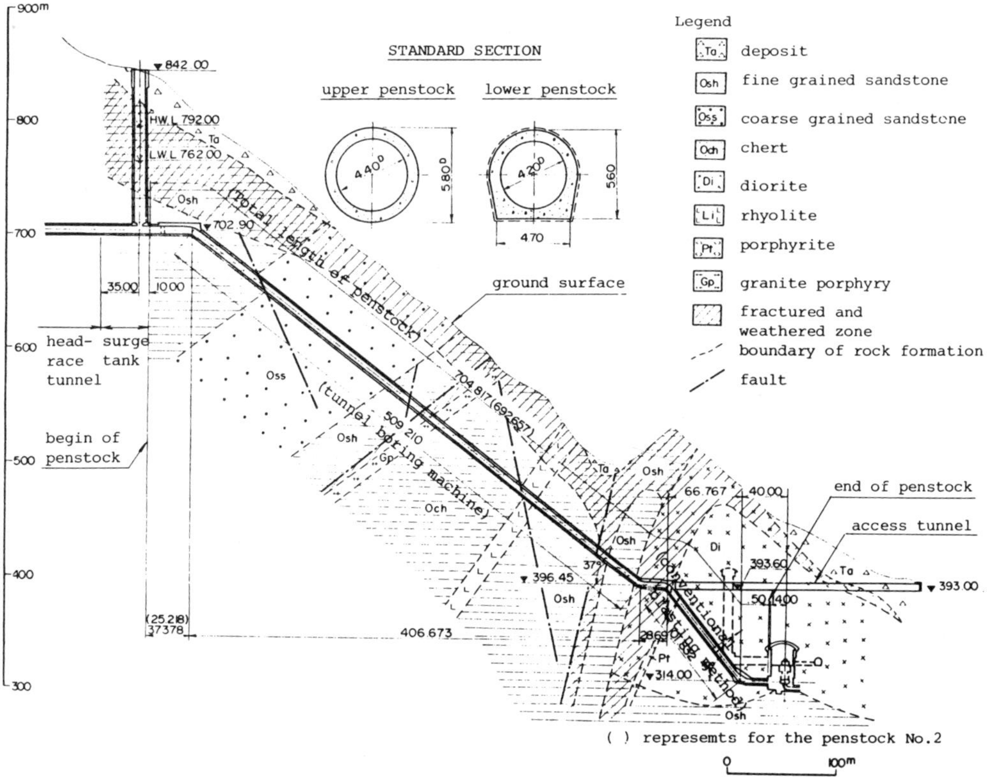

Fig. 2. Geology in a region around the penstock

is opened at first by the pilot machine with a drilling diameter of 3.3 m. After completion of the pilot drilling, the tunnel is then enlarged to obtain a complete section of 5.8 m in diameter by the reaming machine. Features of the machines are sketched in Fig. 3. Further, main design specifications of the machine are listed in Table 1.

3.2 Actual progress

The excavation of the upper penstock by TBM was started in May, 1979 and, completed at the end of 1980. It took for about 20 months of period. The pilot drilling was accomplished at first in order of No. 1 and No. 2 penstock. Successively, the enlargement of the pilot drilling was followed by the reaming machine in both tunnels of No. 1 and No. 2 penstock.

An average velocity of advance became to be 5.0 m/hr and 3.2 m/hr throughout the pilot drilling and the reaming, respectively. It may be realized that these average velocities are fairly close to the maximum values as listed in Table 1. It might be said therefore that the tunnelling performance of TBM was quite good on a point of the progress of the excavation. In addition, defacement of disk cutters on the boring head was not marked throughout. These facts may be due to a reason that the rock to be excavated has a relatively low compressive strength. Another reason is that the rock could be easily chipped by the drilling performance with small thrust force and torque, because it was heavily fractured.

A total number of the cutters which have been replaced throughout, was 49 sets for the pilot machine and, 101 sets for the reaming machine. A rate of replacement of the cutter per unit volume of the rock to be excavated becomes to be approximately 0.006 sets/m^3.

3.3 Reinforcement on the excavated surface

Damages in the surrounding base rock due to the excavation by TBM was negligibly small in general, because the machine did not inflict harmful shock onto the rock. The excavated surface was therefore actually stable. Only in a few portions where the rock was strongly fractured, however,

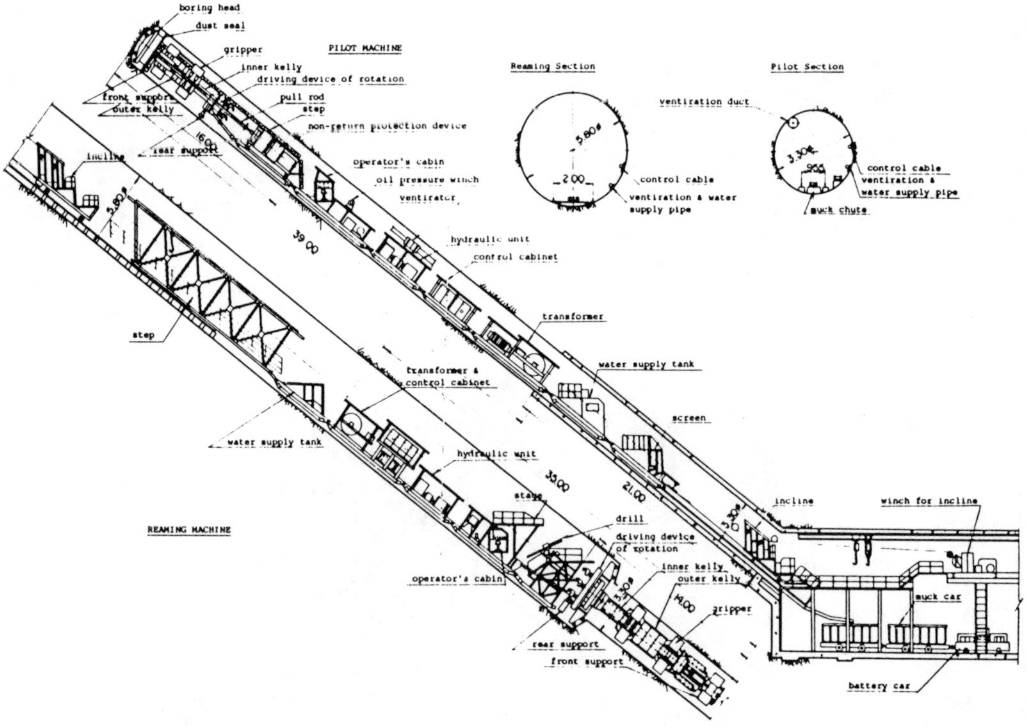

Fig. 3. Profile of pilot and reaming machines

a minor collapse was experienced, occurring mainly near the tunnel face.

In the pilot drilling, a reinforcement on the excavated surface was scarcely needed, because of the drilling with a small section. A resin spray was only conducted in a part of ceiling of the tunnel. In case when a fracture zone was encountered, it was specially treated with reinforcement by means of rock bolt and timbering frame. The rock bolt to be used was 1.0 m in length and 22 mm in diameter. Both of them was specially ordered to be made of glass-fibre. Because, in the following reaming stage, they should be drilled as the surrounding rock all together.

In the reaming stage, a reinforcement was performed in whole section for a protection of the excavated surface. In most section except fracture zone, a resin spray with a few millimeter in thickness was conducted around the whole surface of the tunnel. It was quite effective for a purpose to protect a thin layer near the surface from collapsing. A shotcrete was also employed with 5 cm in thickness instead of the resin spray, in case when the surface was wet by the underground water. In the fracture zone, steel rock bolt of 2.0 m in length and steel timbering frame were used.

Throughout the reinforcement in the reaming stage, it was conducted by the resin spray in 75% of the total section, 20% by the shotcreate and 5% by means of rock bolt and timbering frame.

4 ROCK MECHANICAL CONSIDERATION ON TUNNELLING BY TBM

4.1 Geotechnical properties of rock

Various tests were carried out in the laboratory and the field to investigate geotechnical properties of rock to be excavated. In the laboratory, the following tests were performed; measurement of ultra-sonic wave velocity, Shore hardness, uniaxial compression test and Brazilian test. The test specimen was prepared from the rock core taken from the tunnel by using a boring machine. The specimen used for the uniaxial compression test and the measurement of ultra-sonic wave velocity is 56 mm in diameter and 112 mm in length. For the other tests, it is the same diameter and 56 mm of the length. A sampling position is indicated in Fig. 4. The obtained test results are summarized in Table 2, in which notations mean as fol-

Table 1. Specification of the tunnel boring machine

Specification	Pilot machine	Reaming machine
Type	TBII 300/330	TBEII-330/580-612H-(717H)
Drilling diameter	ϕ3.0 ∿ 3.3 m	ϕ5.8 ∿ 6.1 m (7.1 m)
Total length	39 m	35 m
Stroke	1.2 m	1.5 m
Velocity of advance	0 ∿ 5.6 m/hr. (infinitely variable)	0 ∿ 3.9 m/hr. (infinitely variable)
Maximum thrust	440 ton	550 ton
Maximum torque of head	26 ton-m	72 ton-m
Rotation of head	0 ∿ 12 rpm (infinitely variable)	0 ∿ 6 rpm (infinitely variable)
Weight	130 ton	190 ton
No. of center cutter	1 set (1 disk cutter x 5)	none
No. of cutter (outer zone)	19 sets (2 disk cutters)	20 sets (2 disk cutters)
Area of gripper	80 cm x 90 cm x 8 = 57,600 cm^2	front 150 cm x 70 cm x 4 = 42,000 cm^2 rear 173 cm x 95 cm x 4 = 65,740 cm^2
Bearing force of gripper	1,130 ton	1,600 ton

lows; γ_d: dry density, V_p: velocity of P-wave, V_s: Velocity of S-wave, E_d and ν_d: dynamic modulus of elasticity and Poisson's ratio calculated from the wave velocities, E_s and ν_s: static modulus of elasticity and Poisson's ratio determined from stress-strain curve of the uniaxial compression test, σ_c: uniaxial compressive strength, S_t: tensile strength and H: Shore hardness.

Based on two important engineering properties of the rock, the uniaxial compressive strength and the modulus of elasticity, the test results are plotted in Fig. 5 by the way of Deere and Miller's classification (Stagg and Zienkiewicz (1974)). The strength distributes in wide range from the category of high strength to very low strength, but the strength of fine grained sandstone is classed into the D category except a few results. On the other hand, it is noted that rhyolite belongs in strength category B and C. The reconsolidated fault breccia possesses a very low strength, the E category.

Concerning the modulus of elasticity, all results concentrate on the boundary between the ranges of M and L, that is, the ratio of the modulus to the uniaxial compressive strength is to be nearly 200:1.

After the pilot drilling has been completed in No. 1 and No. 2 penstock, a bore hole jack test was carried out to obtain a deformation modulus of the base rock. The equipment used for this test is the same type as Goodman's jack. A borehole to be prepared was 66 mm in diameter and about 1.5 m in depth from the surface, which was drilled in a radial direction of the tunnel. The test position and the result are shown in Fig. 4. It is noted that the modulus is in a range between 3 x 10^4 to 7 x 10^4 kgf/cm^2 for all kinds of

Table 2. Results on rock properties

Penstock	Sampling Position	Type of rock	γ_d gf/cm^3 (av.)	Ultra-sonic wave velocity V_p km/sec	V_s km/sec	E_d 10^5kgf/cm^2	ν_d	E_s 10^5kgf/cm^2	ν_s	σ_c kgf/cm^2	S_t kgf/cm^2	H (av.)
No. 1	TD 32 m	Fine grained sandstone	2.45	3.87	2.01	2.6	0.32	0.67	0.23	320	38	55
	115 m	Rhyolite	2.53	5.32	2.97	5.8	0.27	2.3	0.19	1,600	123	85
				5.29	2.97	5.7	0.27	2.1	0.19	1,650		
	190 m	Porphyrite	2.57	4.43	2.36	3.8	0.30	1.9	0.20	830	101	88
				4.10	2.21	3.4	0.29	1.6	0.23	650		
				4.38	2.51	4.1	0.26	1.3	0.25	770		
	227 m	Granite porphyry	2.57	2.76	1.50	1.5	0.29	0.59	0.27	190	55	65
				3.75	1.97	2.6	0.31	0.71	0.21	350		
	240 m	Reconsolidated fault breccia		2.53	1.22	1.0	0.35	0.21	0.27	150	19	41
				2.19	1.30	1.0	0.23	0.24	0.29	130		
	360 m	Coarse grained sandstone	2.58	5.23	2.97	5.9	0.26	1.7	0.20	1,260	128	88
				4.19	2.20	3.3	0.31	1.5	0.21	870		
				5.18	2.94	5.7	0.26	1.8	0.18	1,250		
	433 m	Fine grained sandstone	2.57	3.54	1.87	2.4	0.31	0.76	0.22	420	48	58
				4.13	2.19	3.3	0.30	0.59	0.22	360		
				3.71	2.15	3.1	0.25	0.63	0.21	440		
No. 2	TD 180 m	Fine grained sandstone	2.44	3.84	2.00	2.7	0.31	1.1	0.22	490	25	65
				3.75	1.92	2.5	0.32	2.1	0.23	280		
	260 m	Granite porphyry	2.45	4.28	2.24	3.5	0.31	1.6	0.21	880	32	40
	282 m	Fine grained sandstone	2.51	3.89	2.00	2.8	0.32	0.59	0.30	110	35	49
				3.92	2.11	3.0	0.30	1.2	0.29	210		
				3.81	1.96	2.7	0.32	1.1	0.26	230		
	305 m	Fine grained sandstone	2.42	2.87	1.35	1.3	0.36	0.19	0.28	150	14	50
	320 m	Fine grained sandstone	2.44	2.54	1.22	1.0	0.35	0.73	0.28	180	39	63
	350 m	Coarse grained sandstone	2.55	4.70	2.67					360	58	87
	400 m	Rhyolite	2.59	5.17	2.95	5.7	0.26	1.9	0.23	890	90	85
				5.19	2.98	5.9	0.26	1.8	0.18	1,200		
				5.79	2.97	5.8	0.26	1.9	0.19	1,600		
	470 m	Coarse grained sandstone	2.60	4.24	2.20	3.4	0.32	0.85	0.18	310	110	70
				4.45	2.53	4.4	0.26	0.88	0.21	330		

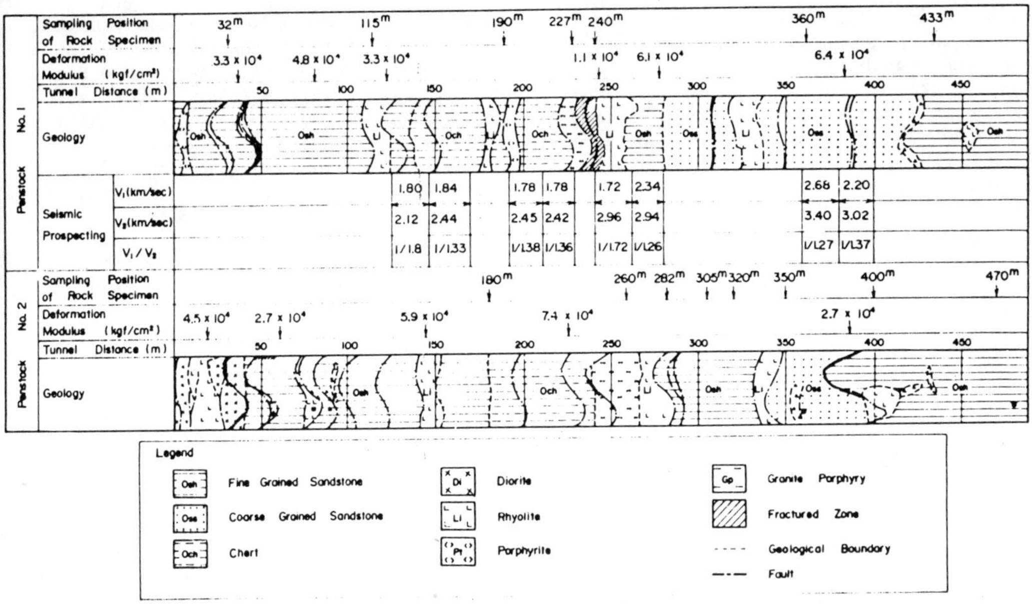

Fig. 4. Geological conditions and results of field tests

rock, except the result measured within the fracture zone in No. 1 penstock. There, it shows 1.1 x 10^4 kgf/cm^2.

Comparing the deformation modulus of base rock with the static modulus of elasticity measured from the intact rock at these corresponding test positions, it is noted that the latter is two to seven times of the former.

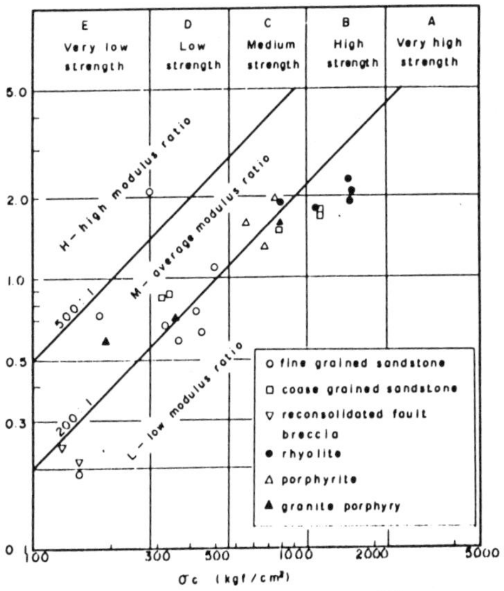

Fig. 5. Engineering classification for the rocks

4.2 Loosening of rock by tunnelling

In general, when a tunnel is excavated, the rock in the circumferential area may be loosened in some degree. This loosening is relevant to method of tunnel excavation, amount of dynamite to be used for blasting and shape of tunnel in cross-section as well as geological conditions. From theoretical and experimental point of view, however, this is not definitely understood yet.

In the present project, it was tried that the loosening of rock was experimentally investigated by a technique of seismic prospecting. The test was performed in the upper penstock No. 1 which was excavated by TBM. For a comparison, the same test was also done in the tailrace tunnel of the present project. This tunnel is a standard horseshoe shaped cross-section of 5.1 m in diameter and 25 m^2 in the area of cross section. The excavation was carried out by drill and blast method. Initially, the tunnelling has been progressed with a conventional method using H-150 steel timbering for the support. Then, the tunnelling was changed to so-called new Austrian tunnelling method (N.A.T.M. in short form) by means of rock bolts (5 to 6 bolts per section) and shotcrete with 5 cm in thickness. Geology in this zone is composed of alternative layers of fine grained sandstone and shale.

The test procedure of the seismic prospecting is schematically explained in Fig. 6 for a case performed in the upper penstock, which is the same as for the case in the tailrace tunnel. A seismic pickup is fixed to the rock in a line along the longitudinal axis of the tunnel with an interval of 2 m. A hit by a large mallet is then applied at a point close to an end pickup, and the travelling wave is observed by the oscillograph. Another hit is also applied at the other end in the same way for the analysis described below.

In the upper penstock, the test was carried out in some typical sections as shown in Fig. 4. An example of time-distance curve is shown in Fig. 7. Wave velocities in the rock mass of the first layer, V_1, and the second layer V_2, can be calculated from the curve. The first layer means a circumferential area near the excavated surface, which can be regarded as a loosenning zone from a sense that the rock in this zone is yielded by shear failure and/or tensile fracture due to initial stress relief and tunnelling disturbances. On the other hand, the second layer can be regarded as an original base rock behind the surface layer, which would not be affected by the tunnelling. According to Fig. 7, V_1 is obtained to be 1,780 m/sec and V_2 is 2,450 m/sec. Furthermore, it is known that the boundary between the first and the second layers exists in the depth of 0.5 m at most, generally less than 0.3 m in a mid section.

The similar time-distance curve obtained in the tailrace tunnel is shown in Fig. 8 for both cases in the conventional method and N.A.T.M., respectively. In the former, V_1 and V_2 are 880 m/sec and 4,000 m/sec, respectively. The thickness of the loosening zone is in the range between 0.5 m to 1.3 m. While, in the latter, those velocities are comparatively same as the above in the magnitude. The thickness of the loosening zone, however, is relatively thinner compared with that for the conventional method, being in a range from 0.3 m to 0.6 m.

A comparison of these test results provides two distinct features concerning the loosening in the surrounding rock.

1. The thickness of the loosening zone resulted from TBM excavation is negligibly small. On the contrary, an apparent and thick zone will be caused by other blasting method.

2. In TBM excavation, a wave velocity in the loosening zone does not reduce so much from the original velocity of the base rock. In other words, a ratio, V_1/V_2, is in a range between 1/1.2 to 1/1.7 as shown in Fig. 4. While, for the blasting method, the velocity in the loosening zone remarkably reduces from the original velocity of the base rock. The ratio is therefore in a range from 1/4.5 to 1/6.8.

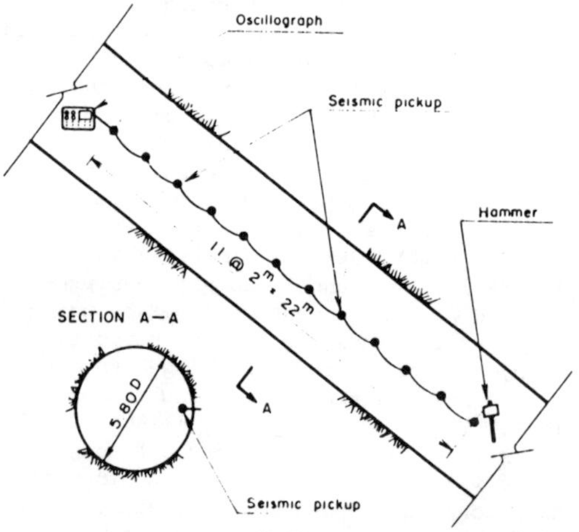

Fig. 6. Schematic diagram of seismic prospecting

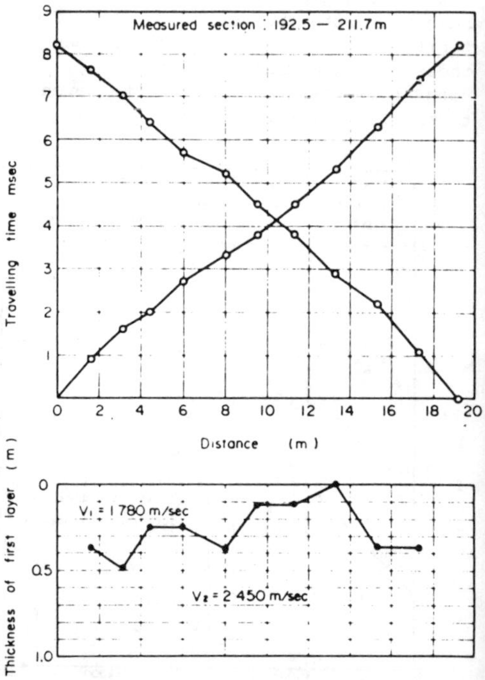

Fig. 7. Typical results of time-distance curve and thickness of loosening zone (upper penstock)

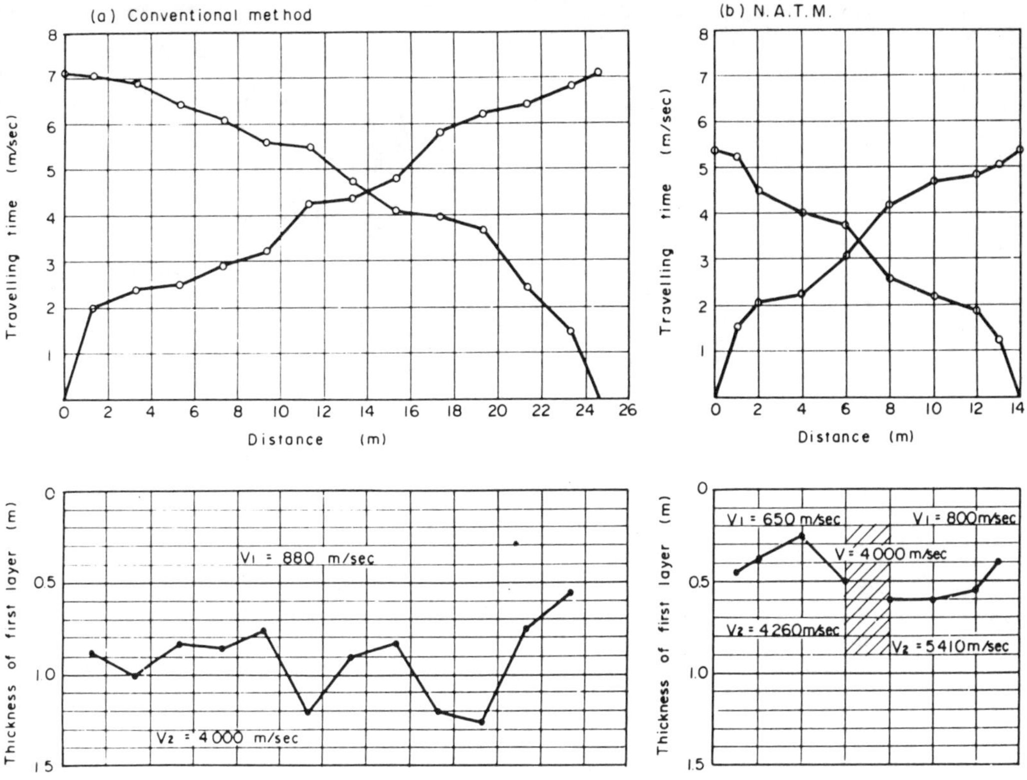

Fig. 8. Typical results of time-distance curve and thickness of loosening zone (tailrace tunnel)

4.3 Correlation between geotechnical properties of rock and operation of TBM

The tunnelling performance of TBM may be quantitatively evaluated from the velocity of advance, thrust force and torque acting to the boring head during the operation. For simplicity, the discussion is limited to the pilot drilling, hereinafter.

Based on the investigation of TBM excavations which have been experienced in the past in Japan, Ikeda and Nishimatsu (1981) reported that the velocity of advance was closely related to the geotechnical properties of rock and could be expressed in terms of the index of discontinuity and the uniaxial compressive strength by the equation as follows;

$$V = 5.07 - 1.33 \log k^3\sigma_c \qquad (1)$$

where V: the velocity of advance (m/hr), σ_c: the uniaxial compressive strength of rock (kgf/cm^2) and k: the index of discontinuity which is defined by the ratio of elastic wave velocity in a mass of base rock to that in the intact rock. As example in the present project, according to the test results on P-wave velocity in the intact rock at the sampling positions of 190 m and 360 m in No. 1 penstock, and the velocity in the base rock, V_2, at the corresponding position shown in Fig. 4, the value of k is calculated to be 0.57 and 0.70, respectively. Taking the uniaxial compressive strength of the rock into account, the term of $k^3\sigma_c$ in the above equation becomes therefore to be 139 and 386. Consequently, the velocity of advance can be evaluated from Eq. (1), and it is obtained as 2.2 m/hr and 1.6 m/hr, respectively. As described previously, the average velocity of advance in the pilot drilling was 5.0 m/hr. Consequently, it may be said that the machine used in this project has been considerably improved in recent years. And, it is also concluded that the machine was very acceptable to the geological conditions in this present case.

The torque and the thrust force of the

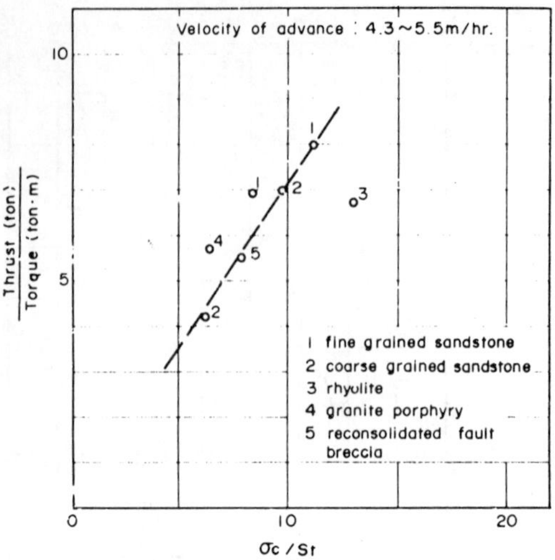

Fig. 9. Relationship between tunnelling performance and rock properties

boring head were recorded during the operation of TBM. Both of them changed in a wide range, namely, from 10 to 23 ton·m and from 30 to 200 ton, respectively. It is found out from consideration on these actual results, however, that a ratio of the thrust force to the torque falls into a relatively narrow range from 4 to 8. On the other hand, a ratio of the uniaxial compressive strength σ_c to the tensile strength S_t was also obtained for each kind of rock formation, and compared with the ratio above mentioned, as shown in Fig. 9. Although there have been obtained only a few data for a purpose of such this consideration, it may be noted that there exists a linear relationship between these two ratios.

5 DESIGN OF STEEL LINING IN PRESSURE TUNNEL

5.1 Analytical design procedure

A magnitude of tensile stress of steel lining when subjected to hydraulic pressure is determined by various conditions, for instances, deformation characteristics of the surrounding base rock, thickness of concrete layer, magnitude of hydraulic pressure and thickness of steel lining. It has been also known that the loosening zone of rock in the circumferential area of the tunnel affect the resultant lining stress. An analytical investigation is conducted to study the influence of the

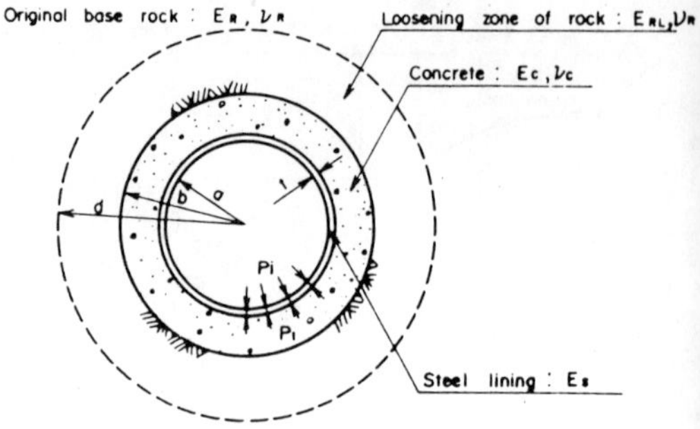

Fig. 10. Analytical conditions on design of steel lining

loosening zone on the lining stress. It was carried out under a simplified condition to modify the tunnel excavated by TBM as illustrated in Fig. 10. In the figure, p_i denotes the internal hydraulic pressure and p_l the reactive pressure against the lining.

A ratio of p_l to p_i implies a proportion of hydraulic pressure partly supported by the base rock, and is referred to as a bearing rate of pressure on rock to be denoted by λ. It can be therefore defined as

$$\lambda = \frac{p_l}{pi} \qquad (2)$$

The lining stress can be given by the following equation;

$$\sigma = \frac{a}{t}(1 - \lambda)pi \qquad (3)$$

where, σ means the lining stress and, t the thickness of the lining.

Based on the theory of multiple thick cylinder and, assuming that the concrete layer can not transmit a tensile stress in the tangential direction, the bearing rate of pressure on the rock can be expressed by a function of material constants of the rock, concrete and steel lining. It is then deduced as follows;

$$\lambda = \frac{C_1C_2}{C_1C_2 + (C_2C_3 - C_4)t'} \qquad (4)$$

where, the constants, C_1, C_2, C_3 and C_4, are given by

$$C_1 = \frac{E_{RL}}{E_R}$$

$$C_2 = \frac{(\frac{d}{b})^2 + 1}{(\frac{d}{b})^2 - 1} - \nu_R + (1 + \nu_R)C_1$$

$$C_3 = C_1\frac{E_S}{E_C}\ln\frac{b}{a} + \frac{E_S}{E_R}\left\{\frac{(\frac{d}{b})^2 + 1}{(\frac{d}{b})^2 - 1} + \nu_R\right\}$$

$$C_4 = 4\frac{E_S}{E_R}\frac{(\frac{d}{b})^2}{\{(\frac{d}{b})^2 - 1\}^2}$$

and

$$t' = \frac{t}{a}$$

In the above equations, E_{RL}, E_R, E_S and E_C represent the elastic modulus of each constitutive materials as shown in Fig. 10. ν_R means the Poisson's ratio of the rock.

5.2 Effect of loosening zone on design of steel lining

In order to know an effect of loosening zone on the design of steel lining, Eq.(4) is now calculated by using definite values to be employed in the actual design. In the calculation, the following values have been taken; a = 220 cm, b = 290 cm, E_S = 2.1 x 10^6kgf/cm^2, E_C = 2.1 x 10^5kgf/cm^2, E_R = 5.0 x 10^4kgf/cm^2, ν_R = 0.3 and t = 2.5 cm. However, it has not so far been well known how much the elastic modulus of loosened rock is reduced from that of the original base rock. With reference to the results of the seismic prospecting described beforehand, it may be supposed that a decrease in the elastic modulus is in a range of 40 to 60%. Therefore, the value of E_{RL}/E_R is taken as two cases of 0.4 and 0.6 in the calculation.

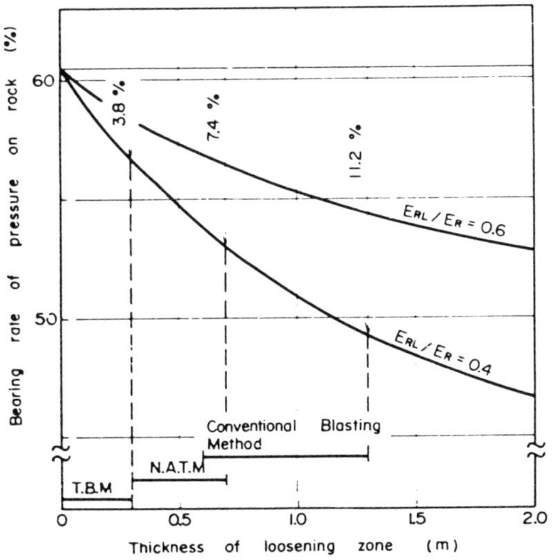

Conditions of Calculation

a = 220 cm　　b = 290 cm

Es = 2.1 x 10^6 kgf/cm²　　Ec = 2.1 x 10^5kgf/cm²

ER = 5.0 x 10 kgf/cm　　ν_R = 0.3

ERL/ER = 0.4

Fig. 11. Effect of loosening zone on the bearing rate of pressure on rock

Fig. 11 shows a variation of λ, the bearing rate of pressure on rock, with the thickness of loosening zone surrounding the tunnel. It is noted that λ decreases in the thickness, and that as the value of E_{RL}/E_R becomes to be smaller, λ decreases more rapidly with the thickness of loosening zone. As previously mentioned, the thickness of loosening zone is dependent upon a tunnelling method to be employed. A possible range of the thickness, which have been supposed from the field measurement by using the technique of seismic prospecting, is represented in the figure for each tunnelling method of TBM excavation, N.A.T.M. and conventional method. As a conclusion, in case when TBM is employed to excavate the pressure tunnel, it is possible to take a larger value of the bearing rate with amount of at most 7.4% (56.7% for TBM - 49.3% for conventional method) in designing the steel lining, on the basis of the case when the conventional method is employed. This fact results in an economical design. A saving of the steel lining to be expected is computed based on the results shown in Fig. 11 and Eq.(3). The obtained result is summarized in Table 3.

In the original design of the steel lining, the loosening zone caused by a tunnelling has been supposed to be approximately 2 m, and a total weight of the steel lining prepared for the section of the upper penstock was 3,500 ton. Since then, taking the actual experimental results about the loosening zone into account, the design was improved. In the final design, a total weight of the steel has decreased to 2,900 ton. The steel of 600 ton in weight was therefore saved, and the saving rate has become to be 17.1%.

6 CONCLUSIONS

Throughout the excavation of the penstock by TBM, a comprehensive investigation on tunnelling performance has been carried out from a viewpoint of rock mechanics.

Table 3. Saving of steel lining by excavation method

Excavation method	TBM	N.A.T.M.	Conventional method
Thickness of loosening zone	0 ∿ 0.3 m	0.3 ∿ 0.7 m	0.6 ∿ 1.3 m
Bearing rate of pressure on rock: λ	60.5 ∿ 56.7%	56.7 ∿ 53.1%	53.9 ∿ 49.3%
Decrease in λ	0 ∿ 3.8%	3.8 ∿ 7.4%	6.6 ∿ 11.2%
Saving rate of steel lining	22 ∿ 15%	15 ∿ 7.5%	9.1 ∿ 0%

The advantages by the use of TBM was considered in the design of steel lining. The main conclusions in this paper are as follows;

1. Although the rock was finely fissured and fractured in some degree, no serious trouble of tunnelling has happened in the excavation. The tunnelling performance was satisfactorily good, and has become the first success in Japan in the excavation of an inclined tunnel by TBM.

2. A ratio of the thrust force to the torque acting on the boring head is likely related to the geotechnical properties. It is found in this study that there may exist a linear relationship between the ratio of thrust force to torque and the ratio of uniaxial compressive strength to tensile strength of rock.

3. The surrounding rock is not almost loosened by the excavation if TBM is employed. The thickness of the loosening zone generated in the circumferential area of the tunnel was measured by a seismic prospecting, and it was at most 0.3 m in case of TBM and in a range from 0.6 to 1.3 m for the excavation by blasting.

4. For the sake of the reduction of loosening zone by the use of TBM, a design of steel lining in the penstock becomes to be economical. The cost of the steel linning was saved by about 17% in comparison with a cost required for the case of blasting method.

7 REFERENCES

Ikeda, K. & Y. Nishimatsu, The effect of geotechnical properties of rock formation on the productivity of tunnel boring machine, J. Jap. Soc. Eng. Geology. 22-2: 1 - 5 (in Japanese).

Stagg, K.G. & O.C. Zienkiewicz, Rock mechanics in engineering practice, P. 1-12. London, John Willey & Sons.

THE APPLICATION OF TUNNEL BORING MACHINES TO BAD ROCK CONDITIONS

Die Anwendung von Tunnelbohrmaschinen bei schlechten Gesteinsverhältnissen

L'usage de machines à forer dans de mauvaises conditions des roches

R.J.ROBBINS
The Robbins Co., Kent, Washington, USA

SUMMARY:
High speed tunnelling rate and the ability to advance the tunnel heading while creating little disturbance to the stability of rock formations are two of the most important advantages in the use of full face tunnel boring machines. However, if a machine does not accomplish both of these objectives better than conventional drill and blast methods, it may be a liability to the job.
The major reasons for the misapplication of TBM's stem from a lack of understanding on the part of owners, contractors and manufacturers of two things: 1. what ground conditions will be encountered as the tunnel advances 2. what features should be incorporated in the machine to seccessfully cope with these geologic conditions.
The selection may depend on the degree ot instability expected in the ground and the rate at which failure will occur. The rate of failure in overstressed rock is proportional to the ratio of the rock stress to the apparent rock mass strength.
Water may or may not be present and in many locations such as Spain, The U.S.S.R. and the U.S.A. good advance rates have been maintained while boring through high water in flow at the face. However, at these same locations when the water washed in large quantities of fine or crushed material from fault zones or unconsolidated layers the heading advance was completely stopped.

ZUSAMMENFASUNG:
Hohe Bohrgeschwindigkeit und die Faehigkeit, die Ortsbrust mit geringer Stoerung des Gebirges vorzutreiben, sind zwei der wichtigsten Vorteile in der Anwendung von Vollschnitt-Tunnelbohrmaschinen. Wenn eine Maschine jedoch diese beiden Ziele nicht besser erreichen kann als traditionelle Bohrungs- und Sprengmethoden, koennte sie das Projekt negativ baeinflussen.
Die Hauptgruende fuer Fehlanwendung der Tunnelbohrmaschinen liegen in dem Missverstaendnis von zwei Problemen seitens der Besitzer, Unternehmer und Fabrikanten: 1. welche Gesteinsverhaeltnisse werden waehrend des Tunnelfortschrittes vorgefunden 2. welche Merkmale sollte die Maschine aufweisen, um diese geologischen Verhaeltnisse erfolgreich zu meistern.
Die Wahl kann auf dem im Boden erwarteten Unbestaendigkeitsgrad und der Versagungshaeufigkeit beruhen. Die Versagungshaeufigkeit in ueberbeanspruchtem Gestein ist proportional zu der augenscheinlichen Gesteinsmassenstaerke.
Gute Fortschrittsgrade sind mit oder ohne Wasser beim Durchbohren von an der Vorderseite vorbeifliessendem Hochwasser unter anderem in Spanien, Russland und den Vereinigten Staaten seit laengerer Zeit erzielt worden. Wenn das Wasser in solchen Gebietan jedoch grosse Mengen von feinen oder zerdrueckten Substanzen aus Verwerfungen oder nicht kompakten Lagen hereinbringt, wird der Tunnelvortrieb vollstaendig zum Halt gebracht.

RESUME:
Le forage à grande vitesse et la possibilité d'avancer une galerie, en même temps causant seulement une perturbation négligeable à la stabilité de formations rocheuses, sont les deux avantages les plus importants avec l'usage de plein-face foreuses. Néanmoins, quand une machine n'achève pas ces deux buts mieux que les méthodes traditionelles de forage, le projet peut en souffrir.

Il faut chercher la raison principale d'une mauvaise application de foreuses mécaniques dans un manque de compréhension de deux choses de la part des propriétaires, entrepreneur et fabricants: 1. quelles seront les conditions de terrain que l'on va rencontrer quand la galerie avance 2. quelles sont les caractéristiques à incorporer dans la machine pour Le choix peut se faire selon le degré l'instabilité attendu dans le sol et la fréquence des fautes. Cette fréquence de fautes dans une roche surcompressée est proportionelle au rapport entre la tension de la roche et la résistance apparente de la masse des roches. Il peut y avoir de l'eau ou non, mais de bons taux d'avance ont été maintenus en beaucoup d'endroits, par example en Espagne, en Union Soviétique et aux Etats Unis, avec le forage où de très fort écoulements d'eau était présent à la face. Toutefois, l'avance de la galerie était complètement arrêté aux mêmes endroits, quand l'eau entrainait de grandes quantités de matériaux fins ou concassés originant dans des zones de faille ou dans des couches non-consolidées.

Tunnel boring machines, especially full-face machines for boring rock formations have been used on more challenging jobs as the capability of these machines has developed over the years.

1 ADVANTAGES

The major advantage of tunnel boring machines (TBMs) has been speed in advancing the heading. Other advantages which may be critical in some applications are reduced section of the tunnel resulting from elimination of overbreak; smooth wall excavation; relatively undisturbed rock formations; early and simple installation of tunnel supports; more uniform rock restraint due to more continuous contact between the supports and the rock; and in the case of some machine designs the ability to restrain caving in of the face by continuous breasting support while the excavation takes place continuously.

2 LIMITATIONS

Opposing these advantages are a number of factors which, if misunderstood, can more than offset the advantages and turn the improperly applied machine into a serious loss of time and capital for all parties concerned. Among them is the sensitivity of this equipment to geologic conditions which were unanticipated when the tunnel job was planned or the inability of some types of TBMs to adapt to changing geologic conditions.

Tunnel boring machines have achieved world record tunnel advance rates of up to 2000 M in one month under ideal geologic conditions. Unfortunately some of the features which permit these advances make the machines especially susceptible to background with unstable rock conditions. Machines which advance at a sustained rate of six meters per hour are designed with large bucket openings and with maximum space provided for the flow of cut rock at the tunnel face, through the cutterhead and on the machine conveyor. These features are not desirable for tunnelling through unstable rock which caves in at the face ahead of the cutters. Such a machine in unstable ground usually excavates a cavern ahead of the face which progresses upward to form a chimney. As the machine progresses forward this caved chimney will be filling with broken rock from above, and this completely unstable moving debris will now surround the forward part of the machine.

If tunnel ribs, wire mesh, lagging and perhaps shotcrete are immediately applied, it may be possible to support the crown and walls of the tunnel, but these supports may not be able to provide adequate reaction against the grippers if backed by loose and broken rock. Thus the difficulties at the face are transferred to the area behind the face and then to the gripper area. This is illustrated in Figure 1.

The result is that the high speed open type of machine is now either at a complete standstill or progressing very slowly. The principal advantage of using the machine is no longer realized, especially if progress is slower than it would be with conventional drill and blast methods or hand mining methods.

One such machine, illustrated in figure 2, bored at world record rates achieving 2.1 km of bored and supported tunnel in one month. The job was the Oso Tunnel in Colorado, U.S.A. The rock was shale of moderate strength (300 to 400 kp/cm2). A best day record (24-hour period) of 127.7 meters was achieved. This required boring at an average penetration rate of seven meters per hour for more than 18 hours out of a 24-hour day.

In spite of these spectacular achievements the tunnel took 7-1/2 months longer to complete than should have been necessary.

This was the result of the machine encountering a zone of less than 300 M of unexpected bad ground. The contractor had expected to bore 8,113 m of 3.1 M diameter tunnel in a fairly good quality shale requiring only rock bolts and steel straps for primary rock support. The tunnel was to be lined with 240 mm of poured-in-place concrete as a final lining. After boring 362 M of shale in less than one month they broke into a zone of glacial debris including boulders, water, clay and other valley fill material. The machine bored forward as far as possible, using steel ribs and wood lagging with wire mesh as a primary support. After a few days of this, progress came to a halt and they began the job of withdrawing the machine. The glacial material followed the machine as it was backed out of the tunnel, and when hand mining resumed with the use of channel spiling over steel ribs and full breasting of the face, it took weeks to advance back to the point from which the machine had been removed.

This handmining procedure continued throughout the fall, winter and spring until they again reached the shale forma-

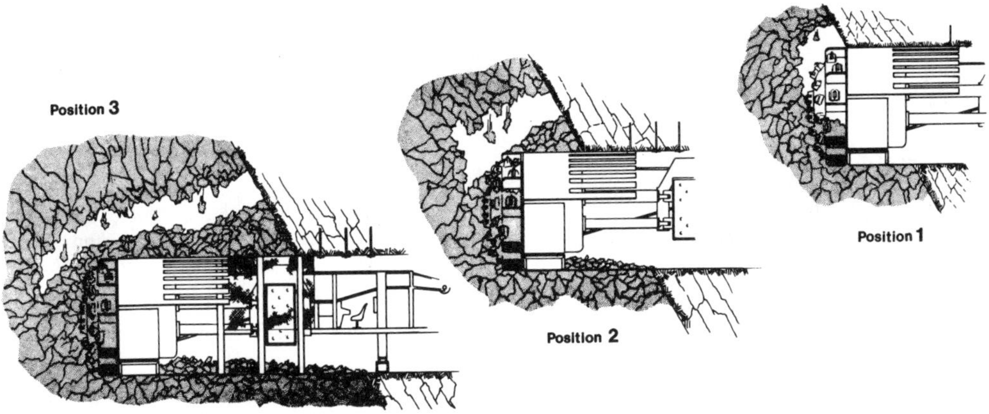

Figure 1

Figure 2

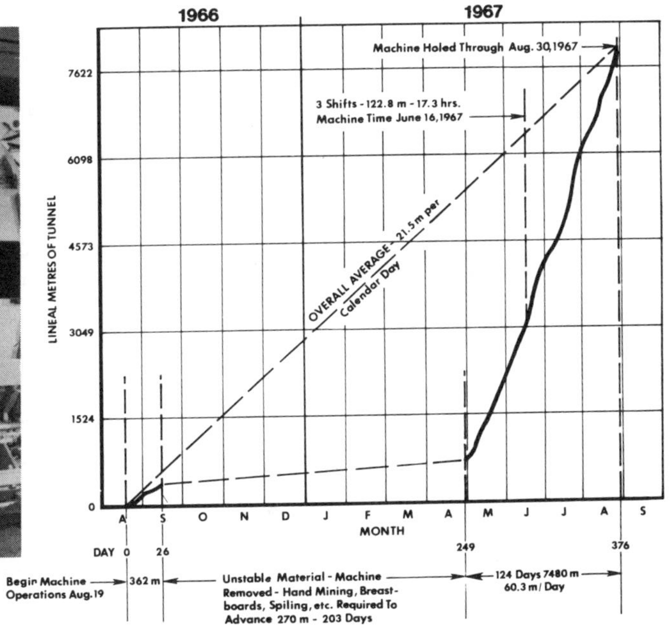

OSO TUNNEL MACHINE - PROGRESS CHART
Source. U. S. DEPARTMENT OF THE INTERIOR REC-ERC-74-7

Figure 3

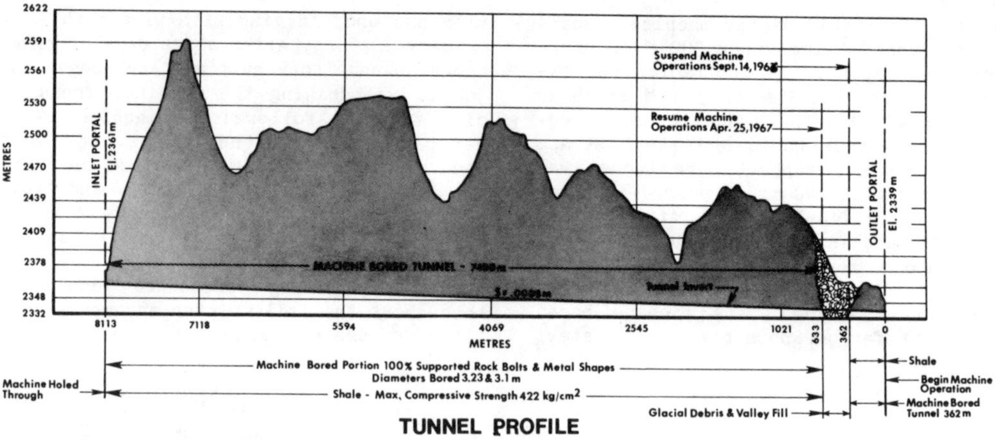

TUNNEL PROFILE

Figure 4

tion. Average progress through the unexpected geologic conditions was 1.33 M per day. The machine bored the remaining 7,480 M at an average rate of 60.3 M per day.

Figures 3 and 4 show graphically the progress of the machine on this job.

3 SPECIAL FEATURES

In order to overcome the difficulty in dealing with unstable rock conditions, machines have been developed with features which help control the flow of broken rock. As might be expected these features act to reduce the machine's high-speed performance in good rock conditions.

Resolving this conflict requires an understanding of the tradeoffs in machine design features and performance and perhaps even more importantly, a good advance knowledge of what to expect from geologic formations to be bored. The more uncertain one is as to how the rock will react to a tunnel being bored through it, the more one is driven to select a conservative set of features which will minimize imagined difficulties. This will most certainly result in a reduction of advance rates when boring good rock.

3.1 Geologic difficulties

Geologic conditions listed below have presented special problems to tunnel boring machines:

- Overstressed rock
- Unstable rock and mixed face conditions
- Water inflow
- Squeezing ground

These conditions are often found to occur in combination with one another. This tends to complicate tunnelling, and it may be difficult to identify which geologic condition is creating the most serious problems.

3.2 Overstressed rock conditions

Rock may be overstressed in some locations of relatively low stress if the rock has a low strength. A high-strength granite or gneiss will be able to support much higher in situ rock stresses from either high overburden or residual techtonic stress before failure, but when this rock fails it exhibits much the same type of failure as a weak rock under much lower stress. Very high-strength brittle rock such as quartzite may burst violently or fall in thin slabs in rapid succession, whereas in the lower-strength rocks cracks propagate more slowly. Both rock types, however, become cracked or sheared when overstressed to the point of failure with slabs falling from the walls and crown of the tunnel close behind the tunnel face. The cracks progress forward as the machine bores, maintaining the same spaced relationship with the tunnel face, assuming no change in the quality or strength of in situ rock.

If a sheared or fractured zone is encountered the rock behaves as though it had a much lower strength even though individual unbroken pieces of rock may be quite strong. At this point the apparent strength of the rock mass as a whole will become the factor which controls the degree of instability.

3.3 Rate of failure

An important factor in mechanical tunnelling through bad rock is the speed at which the heading can be advanced. Unless the rock has a very low cohesion, it will fail gradually. The rate of failure will be dependent on a number of factors; among them:

- Strength of the individual rock fragments
- Surface flatness or texture of joints and cracks
- Openness of joints or cracks
- Presence of a lubricant such as clay or water in the fissures
- Orientation of major sets of joints in relation to rock stresses

All of these factors considered together determine the effective strength of the rock mass.

The rate of failure will in general be proportional to the ratio of the effective rock strength to the magnitude of the unbalanced rock stress. Thus in a cohesionless rock mass made up of weak rock fragments, with voids or low friction platy minerals, such as chlorite or graphite on the joint surfaces, the rate of failure can be expected to be moderately fast even at low levels of rock stress. The failure will be rapid in this rock if high rock stresses are present.

If the rate of failure is fast the rock will begin to cave at the face while it is being cut. Rock will fall out of the face into the space around the projecting cutters. Voids will develop ahead of the machine, but in many types of rock the natural locking together of the rock particles by the arching shape of the tunnel crown and the transition to the gage or outer cutters from face cutters can keep the rock intact at the periphery of the bore.

When machine tunnelling, high advance rates can be achieved in these poor rock conditions due to the rock fractures. It is often possible to advance to the point where the tunnel shield or the primary support can be installed before the rock has a chance to loosen or fall away.

For this reason it is important that a system of supports be used which can be installed quickly without holding up progress of the machine and which can be installed as close to the face as possible.

Some tunnel contractors hold the opinion that if the job contains difficult ground with unstable rock their chance of completing the work on schedule will be greater with a TBM than with conventional drill and blast methods. Experience with both methods in conditions where the time can be predicted to cross a known fault zone have shown the value of moving quickly through bad ground.

3.4 Unstable understress rocks

Highly fractured rock may present special problems when it is encountered in an understressed state. This is the case in Melbourne, Australia, where the Melbourne and Metropolitan Board of Works has driven many kilometers of machine bored tunnels for sewer and water supply purposes in diameters ranging from about 2.7 M to 4.5 M. Similar difficult rock conditions were encountered by the Melbourne Underground Rail Loop Authority (MURLA) as they constructed the new Melbourne Subway System.

The rock is a loose, highly fractured and weathered silirian mudstone and sandstone which has been intruded by basaltic dykes which indurated and fractured the sedimentary rocks. The basalt then weathered, in some places altering completely to a plastic clay which is shot through the sedimentary rock.

The major problem here is that the excavations take place at a shallow depth. There is not sufficient cover to consolidate this broken and weathered material, which sometimes acts like a pile of poorly stacked bricks. The engineers for the Rail Loop Authority decided that two principles must be followed to safely construct their 7.1 M diameter metro tunnels:

1. They must install primary supports (which were steel arches for the upper half of the tunnel and concrete segments for the lower half) so close to the tunnel face that there was no room for a shielding system. In other words, they felt that rapid installation of a permanent primary support immediately behind the cutters to accept the gravity-induced ground load was the surer way to avoid ground loosening and street settlement than to catch the ground with a shield and install the supports at the rear where the ground load would be transferred from a shield tail to the permanent supports.

2. They recognized the hazard of loose rock falling out of the crown and face of the tunnel as it was being cut, and the chance for a large void to develop above and ahead of the machine. They chose to use shotcrete as the means to stabilize this condition. This also required a machine with an open area just behind the cutterhead and above the cutterhead support in place of a shield, so that the men with shotcrete guns could spray the rock immediately as it was beginning to cave

above the cutterhead.

A novel technique that was used to permit installation of steel arches as close to the face as possible was to place them at an incline leaning forward from the feet, which were placed on the last installed set of precast concrete invert segments to the crown, where they were held temporarily in place by cantilevered needle beams until they were jacked against the rock and secured to the previously installed steel arch with tie rods. Figure 5 shows this type of support.

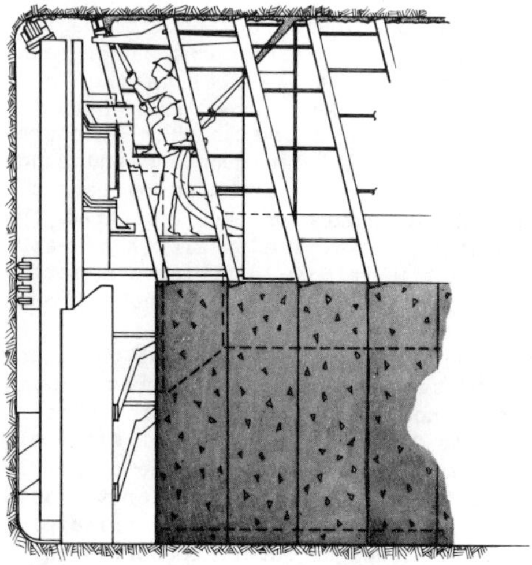

Figure 5

3.5 Shields in unstable rock conditions

Use of a shield is the first solution that occurs to most tunnel engineers when faced with a job dominated by unstable rock conditions. By now quite a bit of experience has been gained using shielded TBMs in rock tunnelling where precast concrete segments are the rock support and final lining. These tunnels have been used for hydroelectric power, both in pressure tunnels and open flow head race tunnels, and for other uses such as sewers, subways, water supply and irrigation tunnels in Europe, South America and the United States.

In 1972 a special type machine was developed for this type of work which provides the possibility of combining advantages of the security of shield tunnelling and precast segments with the rapid advance rates of a conventional hard rock TBM. It also offers the additional advantage of flexibility in selection of any type of primary support desired in lieu of concrete segments or advancing in good rock with no supports at all.

This is the double telescoping shield machine, one example of which is shown in Figure 6. The principal advantage of this design is that the concrete lining segments can be assembled in the tail section of the rear shield while the machine and the front shield are boring forward. During this boring period the telescoping zone between the two shields is expanding but remains closed to caving rock from the outside. If the ring of segments is erected without difficulty this can be accomplished in the same time required for the machine to advance the length of one ring, usually from 0.6 to 1.5 meters.

During the boring, the thrust and torque reaction from the cutterhead and front shield propulsion system is reacted by grippers set into the rear shield. When the boring cycle and ring erection are complete the rear shield is retracted to the front shield closing the telescoping section. The machine in Figure 6 is shown in the retracted position.

In case the machine is passing through a zone of very bad ground which cannot provide sufficient gripping reaction for the machine thrust, then the progress of the machine is stopped as it would be with a conventional single shield while a ring of segments is installed within the tail of the rear shield. This ring of segments together with all those set behind provides the cutting thrust reaction through the primary (forward) and secondary (rear) sets of propulsion cylinders.

The cutterhead shown on the machine in Figure 6 contained some unique features never before used and designed specifically to be effective in very unstable rock. The face of the cutterhead consists of a series of concentric rings of grill bars which are mounted very close to the rock face as it is being cut by the cutters (2.5 to 3.5 cm). The position of these grill bar rings does not permit the cut material to fall down the face to the bottom where it is customarily picked up by peripheral buckets. Therefore, this cutterhead has buckets which extend radially inward to pick up the broken rock immediately as it is cut.

The grill bars are provided to close the normal space provided between the cutterhead and the rock which fills with material when the rock in an unstable face cave. This avoids a large unsupported area at the face and the development of voids and chimneys from caving rock.

Figure 6

The cutters protrude only a short distance beyond the grill bars. If a large boulder or massive rock fragment caves against the cutterhead it is held more or less in place in its original position by the grill bars which are rotating and rubbing against it, while at the same time the cutters chip away at it to break the rock into small chips. On recent designs of this type head the cutters are changeable from the inside of the cutterhead, as are the bucket lips. Therefore, no person is required to go in front of the cutterhead for cutter or bucket lip repair, exposing themselves to the danger of caving rock. The cutters can also be inspected and replaced without retracting the machine from the face. This is especially important while the grill bars are supporting broken rock at the face.

A section drawing through a cutterhead of this type is illustrated in Figure 7.

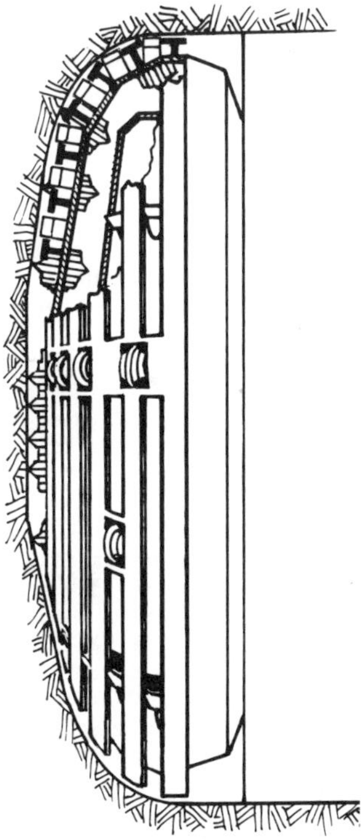

Figure 7

3.6 Water inflow

Water flowing into the tunnel in large quantities is probably the major cause of serious difficulties in tunnelling. However, machines have bored successfully in conditions of high water inflow and give good promise of being the most sure method to make reliable progress under such conditions. Conventional drill and blast methods have serious problems when high water inflow is encountered. This is especially true if the rock is fractured and unstable, requiring breasting at the face.

The major problems associated with water in machine tunnelling are the accumulation of fine material in the tunnel invert and spillage from the machine conveying system. Even in good rock a tunnel borer creates a large amount of fine crushed rock by the action of the cutters. This fine rock is normally picked up and carried out by the buckets and conveyor by being mixed with large chips. With high water flow at the face the fines are washed out of the mixture and flow around the front support to accumulate in the tunnel invert. The buckets also pick up water and dump it onto the conveyor belt, which often spills over the side, washing more fines into the tunnel invert.

As a result of this accumulation of fines, the installation of tunnel supports, both concrete segments and steel ribs, becomes more difficult. The invert must be mucked out by hand, usually with shovels or hand trowels, before the supports can be installed.

The most severe condition associated with water is the case where inflowing water carries with it fine material from within the rock. This can be fault gauge material in the form of clay, sand and fine rock particles, or it may be simply an uncemented sand layer or lense in a sedimentary rock. Material carried in with the flowing water has in some tunnels accumulated in such quantities that it has nearly filled the entire tunnel, completely immersing the machine under water-deposited sand.

3.7 Squeezing ground

Rock which is overstressed to the point that it will fail as the machine bores forward will not stop its stress relief by redistribution of the stresses around the tunnel periphery until the interior dimensions of the bored tunnel have been reduced to provide for the necessary lowering of the stress level of the rock around the tunnel to values which the rock can support. In highly overstressed rock, i.e., rock in which the unbalanced in situ stress is high in relation to the effective rock mass strength, the movement inward will be considerable. In some cases this could theoretically mean complete closure of unrestrained or unsupported rock before the stresses are brought into equilibrium.

Cutterheads on shielded tunnel boring machines are designed to cut a slightly larger-size tunnel than the outside diameter of the shield. This provides clearance for steering and moving the shield. In the case of double telescoping shield machines, clearance is required for steering both shields and for retracting the second shield forward. In squeezing rock this clearance can close up as the rock walls move inward. In most cases of squeezing rock the rate of failure and movement of the rock is quite apparent since the rock closes around the rear part of the shield tail first. If the machine continues to move ahead rapidly it may find itself temporarily ahead of the closure and free of squeeze. However, if there is a problem installing a ring of segments which holds up progress even for twenty or thirty minutes, or perhaps a simple hydraulic component failure or cutter which must be repaired, the ground moves in relentlessly to grasp the tail shield, then the forward shield, in a powerful grip.

This is one condition in which the double telescoping shield described in section 3.5 above is particularly vulnerable. This type of machine is necessarily quite long due to the two overlapping shields with all the equipment contained in each. The extra length requires extra time for that length of tunnel to be bored, hence more chance for the inward squeezing. The safest solution to such a problem, when faced with the advance knowledge that such a condition of squeeze is likely to exist, is to give up the advantage of erecting lining during boring. If a simple single shield is used, particularly a short shield with short rings of segments, the rock loads can be transferred quickly to the lining. Such a shield should be of heavy construction and have a slight conical taper, larger at the front than at the rear. If the tail is machined to a thinner section at the rear, close-fitting segments can be used without providing for a large gap resulting from the overcut of the cutters, the conical taper, a thick shield tail and an internal clearance for the segments. High-pressure shield thrust cylinders and a well reenforced concrete segment design can also do a great deal to keep a shield machine from becoming stuck in squeezing ground.

A tunnel designer or a contractor who must make a selection of whether to use a TBM on a bad rock job, especially if one suspects the possibility of squeezing ground, can readily see the importance of analyzing the many types of machines with different features from which to select. Many of the machine features described above can be interchanged from one type of machine to another.

If faced with the possibility of squeezing ground one should also consider the use of a machine similar to that used in Melbourne, Australia, as described in section 3.4. With this machine the rock loads never pass through the machine (except at the cutterhead while cutting the rock). They are supported immediately by the shotcrete and steel rib system. For squeezing rock a yielding type steel rib could be utilized, hence we have a continuous excavation and support system with many similarities to the New Austrian Tunnelling Method (NATM).

3.8 A universal machine

As mentioned earlier, when high water inflows are encountered in crushed faulted rock or very weak sediments they tend to carry into the tunnel large quantities of sandy material which create perhaps the most difficult condition for the tunnel engineer to face. The rock through which the tunnel is passing at that moment becomes similar to a soil tunnel for an urban subway in a loose gravel or underconsolidated sand. These are conditions which would point to the use of a slurry-type tunnel boring shield or perhaps a soil pressure balanced type machine.

These machines provide complete shielding and a sealed lateral bulkhead across the shield in front of which the cutterhead operates in a pressurized environment, usually underwater, to counteract the water pressure in the ground. The area within the rear of the shield and throughout the rest of the tunnel is in free atmospheric air. This type of machine, which has been used very extensively in Japan and to a limited extent in Europe, provides an interesting possibility to solve the problems of a hard rock TBM which must pass through wet fault zones where the conditions deteriorate to become similar to subacqueous soil tunnelling.

Figure 8 illustrates the concept of a machine which incorporates the features of a shielded hard rock TBM together with those of a slurry-type machine for subacqueous soil conditions. Such a machine must be able to bore hard unfractured rock in dry or wet conditions. Depending on the amount of water flowing from the face, the

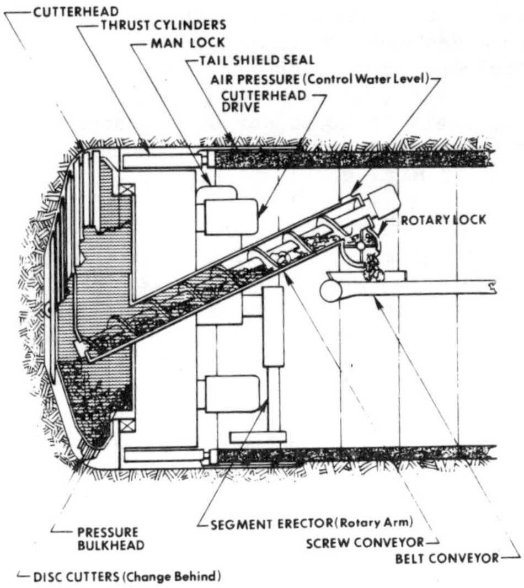

Figure 8

bulkhead and conveying system would be left open to permit drainage or would be closed so as to contain the water to the face or to provide a collection point for pumping.

An invert segment and steel arch combination of supports could be used, or only invert segments bolted to the tunnel invert in very good rock conditions will provide the thrust and torque reaction.

In very bad rock full concrete segmental lining would be used which could be sealed against the inner surface of the shield tail. This then provides the possibility to completely close the bulkhead, and with use of an appropriate muck removal system, the machine can be used as a slurry or soil pressure balanced type machine.

Many tunnels have sufficient occurrence of hard rock plus badly faulted rock with high water flows. Perhaps such a tunnel will some day soon provide the opportunity to demonstrate the advantages of a machine which could handle all these conditions with a good assurance of steady advance rates.

Conclusion

Although the sciences of geologic exploration, geophysics and rock mechanics have provided an ever increasing understanding of what to expect from the materials in the earth's crust, and how they may behave in various circumstances, it seems quite unlikely that techniques will ever be developed to predict clearly and accurately what the tunnelling conditions will be before a designer or builder must choose his methods of excavation and support. This will remain a particularly difficult and risky field of construction and engineering, especially where tunnels pass under areas of high cover or highly stressed ground.

It may be more feasible, and indeed may prove to be more realistic, to expect that adaptable tunnel boring machines will be developed which can cope with the varying and unknown conditions of deep rock tunnelling than to expect, in the same time period, development by the geotechnical fraternity of information which can be accurately interpreted by tunnel builders.

DIE BEEINFLUSSUNG DER VORTRIEBSGESCHWINDIGKEIT VON VOLLSCHNITTMASCHINEN MIT DISKENMEISSELN DURCH DIE GEBIRGSANISOTROPIE

The influence of the anisotropy of the rock mass on the rate of advance of a full-face tunneling machine with disc cutters

L'influence de l'anisotropie d'un massif rocheux sur la vitesse de creusement d'un tunnelier à attaque globale avec des molettes à disque

H.-P.SANIO & H.K.KUTTER
Ruhr Universität, Bochum, Bundesrepublik Deutschland

SUMMARY:
Cuttability and drillability of rock are similarly affected by geological structural features as are strength and deformability of a rock mass. The results of wedge penetration tests and disk cutting experiments on rocks with a distinctive strength anisotropy clearly show that anisotropy and discontinuities have to be fully taken into account for realistic predictions of the rate of penetration of a full-face tunnelling machine. A simplified procedure, assuming continuity and isotropy, would lead to wrong predictions. This is demonstrated on Ruhr Sandstone, a rock of only slight strength anisotropy. There the rate of advance of a full-face tunnelling machine in a direction normal to the bedding can be 1.3 times higher than in the direction parallel to it. An important mechanical parameter for the prediction of such differences is the tensile strength of the rock, particularly its degree of anisotropy.

ZUSAMMENFASSUNG:
Ähnlich wie die Standfestigkeit und Verformbarkeit des Gebirges wird auch dessen Lösbarkeit massgebend durch die Beschaffenheit des geologischen Gefüges beeinflusst. Durch Ergebnisse von Keileinpressversuchen und Schneidversuchen mit Diskenmeisseln in Gesteinen mit ausgeprägter Festigkeitsanisotropie wird gezeigt, daß eine vereinfachende Betrachtungsweise, die das Gebirge als homogen und isotrop annimmt, in anisotropen Gesteinen keine realistischen Vortriebsprognosen für Vollschnittmaschineneinsätze ermöglicht. Selbst in Gesteinen mit nur schwach ausgeprägter Festigkeitsanisotropie, wie zum Beispiel Ruhrsandstein, kann die Nettobohrgeschwindigkeit einer Vollschnittmaschine bei einem Tunnelvortrieb senkrecht zur Schichtung um den Faktor 1,3 grösser sein als parallel dazu. Ein wichtiger mechanischer Parameter zur Abschätzung solcher Unterschiede ist die Gesteinszugfestigkeit und deren Anisotropie.

RESUME:
La fragmentation ou forabilité d'un massif rocheux dépend en grande partie des qualités de la structure géologique analogue à la stabilité et déformabilité de le massif rocheux. Les résultats des essais avec un coin et avec des molettes ont démontré qu'il n'est pas vrai de faire des prévisions réalistes concernant la progression quotidienne avec un tunnelier "pleine section" en roche anisotrope basées sur la supposition que la roche est homogène et isotrope. Même dans des roches n'ayant qu'une très faible anisotropie de la résistance comme, par exemple le "Ruhrsandstein" (le sable de la Ruhr), la vitesse de creusement nette d'un tunnelier "pleine section" peut s'élever 1,3 lors de la progression de creusement du tunnel verticalement par rapport à un creusement parallel à la stratification. La résistance de la roche à la traction et sa anisotropie sont paramètres méchaniques très important pour l'estimation de telles différences.

1 EINFÜHRUNG

Die Leistungsfähigkeit und Wirtschaftlichkeit von Vollschnittmaschinen wird, abgesehen von Aspekten rein baubetrieblicher oder technischer Natur, hauptsächlich durch die Geologie der aufzufahrenden Tunnelstrecken bestimmt. Neben der Gesteinsart bewirken insbesondere Ausmaß und Orientierung von Klüftung und Gesteinsanisotropie Unterschiede im Werkzeugverschleiß und in der erreichbaren Bohrgeschwindigkeit. Außer dem Bruchvorgang unter der Einwirkung einer Meißelschneide wird auch die Verspannbarkeit der Maschine vom Gesteinsgefüge positiv oder negativ beeinflußt. Obwohl diese Tatsache seit langem bekannt ist (Blindheim 1979, Wanner 1975) wird das Gebirge für Bohrbarkeitsprognosen häufig immer noch als homogen und isotrop betrachtet. Mit Hilfe einfacher, die Gefügeorientierung nicht berücksichtigender Festigkeitsparameter, wie z.B. einaxiale Druckfestigkeit oder Scherfestigkeit, werden Vorhersagen der Vortriebsleistung von Vollschnittmaschinen getroffen (Roxborough, Phillips 1975, Wang et.al. 1978). Dieses Vorgehen kann in vielen Fällen durchaus befriedigende Ergebnisse liefern, aber auch, angesichts einer Vielfalt von geologischen Parametern, deren Einfluß auf die Bohrgeschwindigkeit einer Vollschnittmaschine heute noch nicht sicher beurteilt werden kann, zu ungenauen oder falschen Aussagen führen.

Um hier zu einer besseren Kenntnis der Wechselwirkung zwischen Vollschnittmaschine und Geologie zu gelangen, wird in diesem Beitrag anhand von einigen interessanten Versuchsergebnissen gezeigt, wie sich die Anisotropie der mechanischen Gesteinseigenschaften auf die Werkzeugbelastung und die Nettobohrgeschwindigkeit von Vollschnittmaschinen auswirkt. Es handelt sich hierbei um Ergebnisse von kontrollierten Schneidversuchen mit Diskenmeißeln und Keileindringversuchen im Labor, die im Rahmen eines Forschungsvorhabens über den Einfluß des geologischen Gefüges auf die Wirkungsweise von Vollschnittmaschinen im Streckenvortrieb ermittelt wurden.

2 VERSUCHSBEDINGUNGEN

2.1 Versuchsgesteine

Die Auswahl der Versuchsgesteine erfolgte hauptsächlich unter dem Gesichtspunkt, daß ein möglichst weiter Bereich verschiedener Festigkeiten und Anisotropiegrade vertreten sein sollte. Neben hauptsächlich verwendeten Sandstein- und Tonschieferproben aus dem Ruhrkarbon wurden für die Keileindringversuche auch verschiedene alpine Gneise sowie Kalkstein-, Marmor-, Diabas- und Granitproben benutzt.

Die im Rahmen dieses Beitrages vorgestellten Ergebnisse wurden an den drei in Tabelle 1 zusammengestellten Gesteinen ermittelt. Die beiden mit K und S gekennzeichneten Sandsteine unterscheiden sich hauptsächlich durch ihren Verwitterungsgrad. Beide weisen einen Quarzgehalt von ca 70 % auf und sind stratigraphisch dem unteren Oberkarbon zuzuordnen. Der Gneis stammt aus Sondrio (Tessin, Schweiz)und ist tertiären Alters. Sein Quarzgehalt beträgt ca 45 %.

Tabelle 1. Die wichtigsten mechanischen Kennwerte der Versuchsgesteine.

Gestein	$\sigma_{C\perp}$	$\sigma_{C\parallel}$	$Is50_{\perp}$	$Is50_{\parallel}$	$v_{\perp}$	$v_{\parallel}$
	MPa	MPa	MPa	MPa	km/s	km/s
Sandstein K	149	149	6,7	4,7	3,6	4,1
Sandstein S	177	153	11,9	9,8	3,6	4,2
Gneis	173	133	7,4	3,6	2,7	4,1

σ_C : einaxiale Gesteinsdruckfestigkeit

Is50: auf einen Standardkerndurchmesser von 50 mm normierter Punktlastindex

v : Kompressionswellengeschwindigkeit aus dem Durchschallungsversuch

$\parallel$: Index zur Kennzeichnung, daß der betreffende Wert bei Belastung oder Durchschallung parallel zu Schicht- oder Schieferungsflächen gewonnen wurde

$\perp$: Index zur Kennzeichnung, daß der betreffende Wert bei Belastung oder Durchschallung senkrecht zu Schicht- oder Schieferungsflächen gewonnen wurde

2.2 Keileindringversuchsstand

Mit der in Abb.1 schematisch gezeigten Versuchseinrichtung wurden Untersuchungen über das Bruchverhalten von anisotropen Gesteinen bei Belastung der Gesteinsoberfläche mit keilförmigen Stempeln durchgeführt. Hierbei wurde die Raumlage der Anisotropieflächen (Schichtung, Schieferung) systematisch bezüglich der Keileindringrichtung variiert. Das Ziel dieser Versuche war, die für den Bruchvorgang wichtigen Gesteinsparameter herauszustellen und relevante Indexversuche zur Abschätzung der Bohrbarkeit des Gesteines mit Rollenmeißeln zu entwickeln.

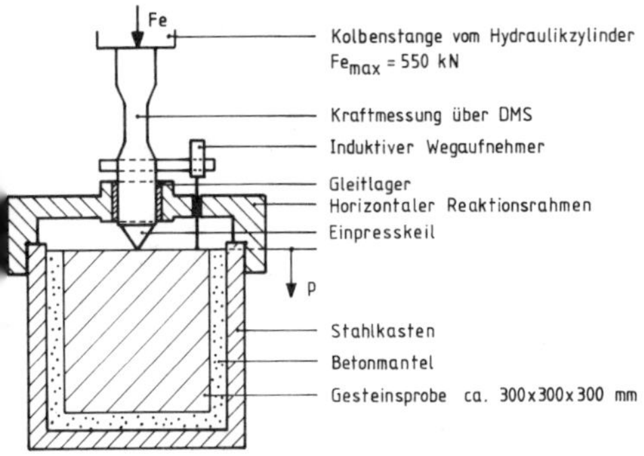

Abb.1 Schematische Darstellung des Keileindringversuchsstandes

Technische Merkmale dieser Versuchsanlage:

- Normal- und Quersteifigkeit > 10^6 N/mm
- kontinuierliche Kraft- und Wegaufzeichnung
- anpreßkraftgesteuerte Versuche mit einer Maximallast von 550 KN
- Probe zum Schutz gegen Aufspaltung während der Versuche in einem Stahlkasten mit Beton eingegossen
- Eindringtiefen bis zu 10 mm in jedem Gestein realisierbar
- verschiedene Keilgeometrien verwendbar. Für die hier beschriebenen Untersuchungen wurde ein scharfkantiger Keil mit einer Breite von 30 mm und einem Öffnungswinkel von 90° verwendet.

2.3 Schneidversuchsstand

Aufbauend auf den Ergebnissen der Keileindringversuche wurde mit der anschließend beschriebenen Versuchsanlage der Einfluß der Festigkeitsanisotropie auf die Schneidbarkeit des Gesteines mit Rollenmeißeln untersucht. Für diese Versuche wurde ein fabrikneuer Diskenmeißel mit Einfachschneide, 70° Keilwinkel und einem Durchmesser von 350 mm benutzt. Die Abbildungen 2 und 3 zeigen schematisch die verwendete Versuchsanlage.

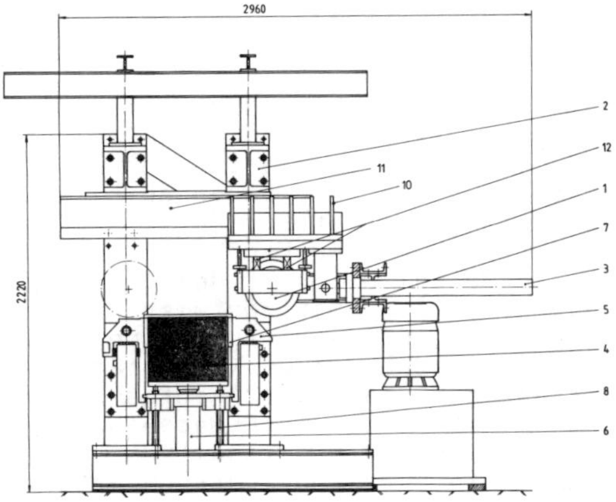

Abb.2 Seitenansicht des Schneidversuchsstandes

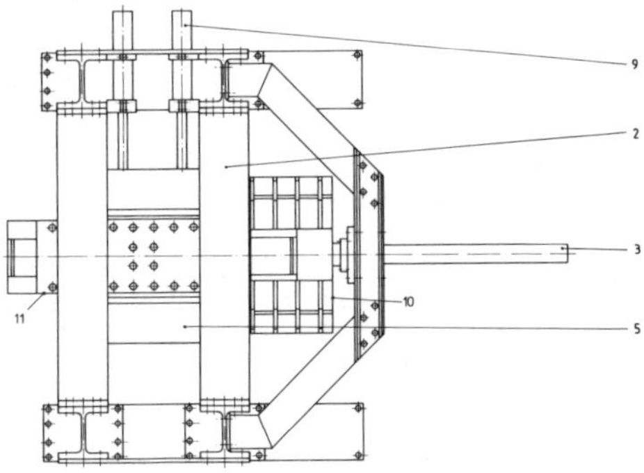

Abb. 3 Aufsicht des Schneidversuchsstandes

Die auf den Meißel (1) wirkenden Kräfte werden durch eine fest vorgegebene Penetration bestimmt. Die mittleren Normal- und Querkräfte können bis zu 150 KN und die mittleren Rollkräfte bis zu 75 KN betragen. Kurzfristige höhere Spitzenbelastungen sind zulässig. Die gemessenen Steifigkeiten betragen normal 10^6 N/mm und lateral 10^4 N/mm. Die maximal mögliche Rollgeschwindigkeit des Meißels beträgt 400 mm/s.

Die Gesteinsproben (4) mit einer Abmessung von 500x400x400 mm werden in einen Probenkasten (5) eingebaut und lagenweise mit dem Meißel abgearbeitet. Die Einstellung der Penetration erfolgt mit Hilfe des Vertikalzylinders (6) und die Einstellung des Schneidbahnabstandes über die beiden Horizontalzylinder (9). Innerhalb des Kastens wird die Probe mittels Druckkissen (7) biaxial verspannt und über Gewindestangen (8) vertikal fixiert. Der Kasten selbst wird mit Arretierungsstangen und vier großen Muttern gegen seitliches Verschieben gesichert. Der über Schlitten (10) und Laufbett (11) geführte Meißel wird mit dem Vorschubzylinder (3) in horizontaler Richtung über die Gesteinsprobe bewegt. Hierbei werden die Werkzeugkräfte vom Reaktionsrahmen (2) aufgenommen und mit Hilfe der Kraftmesseinrichtung (12) dreidimensional registriert. Die Meßdatenerfassung erfolgt mit einem x-y Schreiber sowie on-line über analog-digital Wandler und Kleincomputer, der auch die Auswertung der Daten übernimmt.

Nach jeder Änderung der Versuchsparameter oder beim Anschnitt eines neuen Gesteinsblockes wird die Probenoberfläche mit den aktuellen Versuchsparametern so lange abgetragen, bis sich ein quasi-stationärer Zustand bei den Werkzeugkräften einstellt. Zur Vermeidung von systematischen Verfälschungen der Versuchsergebnisse werden Randschneidspuren sowie Ein- bzw. Auslaufbereiche des Meißels in jeder einzelnen Bahn bei der Auswertung der Versuchsdaten nicht berücksichtigt.

2.4 Definition der verwendeten Parameter

In den folgenden Kapiteln werden die anschließend aufgeführten Bezeichnungen verwendet:

F : Werkzeugkraft am Rollenmeißel oder Einpreßkeil in KN

MD : Häufigkeit mit der die zugeordnete Lastfunktion ihren Mittelwert auf 1 m Meißelrollstrecke durchsetzt in m^{-1}

R : Siebdurchgang in %

p : Penetration in mm

S : Schneidbahnabstand in mm

β' : Bezogen auf eine Tunnelvortriebsmaschine mit flachem Bohrkopf ist β' der Schnittwinkel zwischen Schichtung oder Schieferung und Ortsbrust. (vgl. Abb.4)

α' : Winkel zwischen momentaner Schnittrichtung eines einzelnen Meißels und der Streichrichtung von Schichtung oder Schieferung auf der Ortsbrust. (vgl.Abb.4)

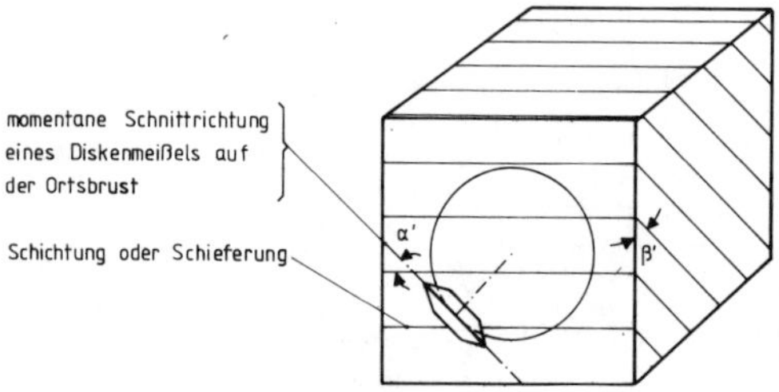

Abb.4 Definition der Winkel α' und β

Zur weiteren Untergliederung werden die zuvorgenannten Bezeichnungen bei Bedarf wie folgt indiziert:

e : Meßwert ist der Einpreßkraft im Keileindringversuch zugeordnet

E : Meßwert ist der Eindringkraft im Schneidversuch mit Diskenmeißeln zugeordnet

90 : Meßwert wurde bei einer Gefügeflächenorientierung von $\beta' = 90^0$ ermittelt

0 : Meßwert wurde bei einer Gefügeflächenorientierung von $\beta' = 0^0$ ermittelt

m : Kennzeichnung von Kraftmittelwerten

p : Kennzeichnung von Maximalkräften

R,Q: Kennz.v.Roll- und Querkräften

3 KEILEINDRINGVERSUCHE

Preßt man einen keilförmigen Stempel in eine Gesteinsprobe, so ist der Beginn des Eindringvorganges dadurch gekennzeichnet, daß im Bereich der Keilspitze infolge hoher Druckspannungskonzentrationen die Mineralkomponenten und der Mineralverbund des Gesteines zerstört werden. Hierdurch bildet sich eine Zone aus pulverisiertem Gestein, deren Ausdehnung sich mit wachsender Penetration vergrößert. An der Berandung dieser sogenannten "plastischen Zone" wirken hohe radiale Druckspannungen, die sich vermutlich mit steigender Eindringtiefe, bedingt durch eine zunehmende Einengung des pulverisierten Gesteinsbereiches, vergrößern. In dieser ersten Phase des Keileindringvorganges wird der Betrag der Einpreßkraft von der Druckfestigkeit des Gesteines bestimmt.

Durch die an der Grenze der plastischen Zone angreifenden Spannungen werden im umliegenden noch unzerstörten Gestein weiterreichende Bruchvorgänge ausgelöst, die zur Abtrennung von Gesteinsscherben, der sog. Chips, führen. Dies bewirkt einen Abbau der Druckspannungen innerhalb des pulverisierten Gesteinsbereiches und führt aus Gleichgewichtsgründen zu einer Reduzierung der Eindringkraft Fe. Bei weiterem Einpressen des Keiles wiederholen sich die zuvor beschriebenen Vorgänge und die Krafteindringkurven erhalten ihre charakteristische sägezahnartige Form (Abb.5).

In der Literatur findet man unterschiedliche Ansichten darüber, ob für das Lösen der zuvorgenannten Chips Scher- oder Zugspannungen verantwortlich sind. Die meisten bisher bekannten theoretischen Überlegungen hierzu gehen von dem Gedanken aus, daß die Abtrennung der Chips durch Scherbrüche entlang ebener oder gekrümmter Gleitflächen erfolgt (Roxborough, Phillips 1975, Wang et.al.1978, Pariseau 1971, Benjumea, Sikarskie 1969). Andere Autoren sind der Auffassung, daß diese Modellvorstellung zur Beschreibung der ablaufenden Bruchvorgänge weniger geeignet ist und vertreten die Ansicht, daß hauptsächlich durch Zugspannungen erzeugte Risse das Lösen der Gesteinsscherben bewirken (Farmer, Glossop 1980). Die eigenen Versuchsbeobachtungen bestätigen sehr eindeutig die Richtigkeit des Zugbruchkonzeptes, denn die Bruchflächen der Chips sind stets rauh und zeigen häufig deutlich sichtbare "plume structures", aber nie Schervorgänge bestätigende Schleifspuren. Zudem besteht, wie die Ergebnisse in diesem Kapitel zeigen, ein offensichtlicher Zusammenhang zwischen der Zugfestigkeit und der Resistenz des Gesteines gegen das Eindringen eines Keiles.

Geht man davon aus, daß die innerhalb der plastischen Zone wirkenden radialen Druckspannungen tangential zur Berandung des pulverisierten Gesteinsbereiches orientierte Zugspannungen induzieren, so wird die Chipbildung in dem Moment erfolgen, wo diese Zugspannungen die Gesteinszugfestigkeit überschreiten. Ist die

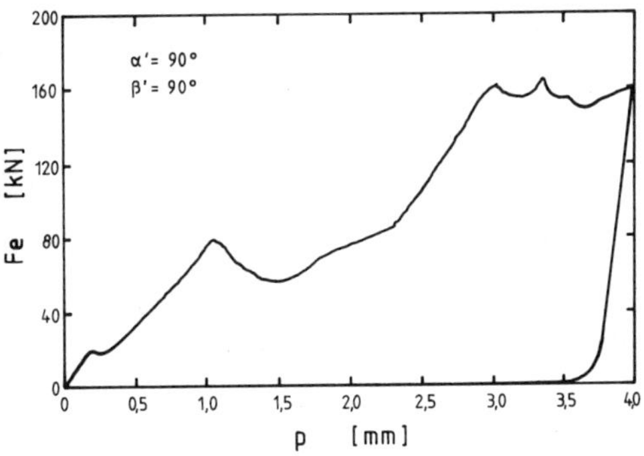

Abb.5 Typische Krafteindringkurve aus einem Einpreßversuch in Sandstein K

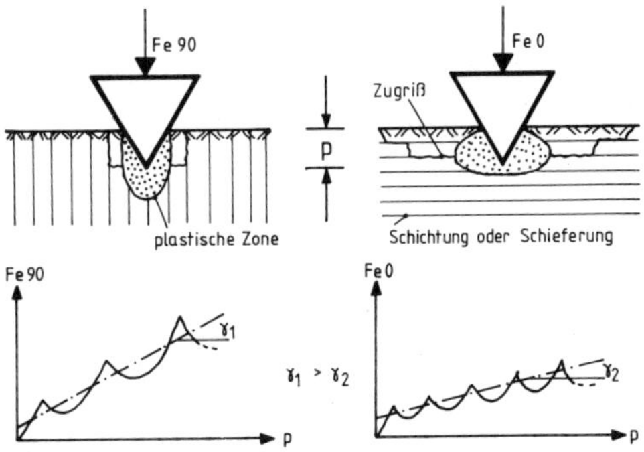

Abb.6 Mechanik des Keileindringvorganges in anisotropem Gestein

Gesteinszugfestigkeit niedrig, so können sich aus Gleichgewichtsgründen auch keine hohen Druckspannungen in der plastischen Zone aufbauen und die Eindringkraft bleibt klein. Führt man Keileindringversuche in anisotropen Gesteinen durch, so werden demzufolge die Einpreßkräfte immer dann niedrig sein, wenn die durch das Eindringen des Keiles erzeugten Zugspannungen normal zu nahe der Gesteinsoberfläche verlaufenden Schicht-, Schieferungs- oder Kluftflächen wirken (Abb.6).

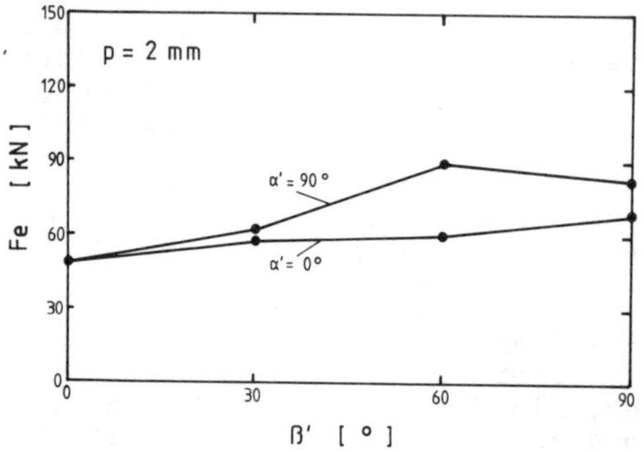

Abb. 7 Anisotropieabhängigkeit der Keileindringkraft für Sandstein K

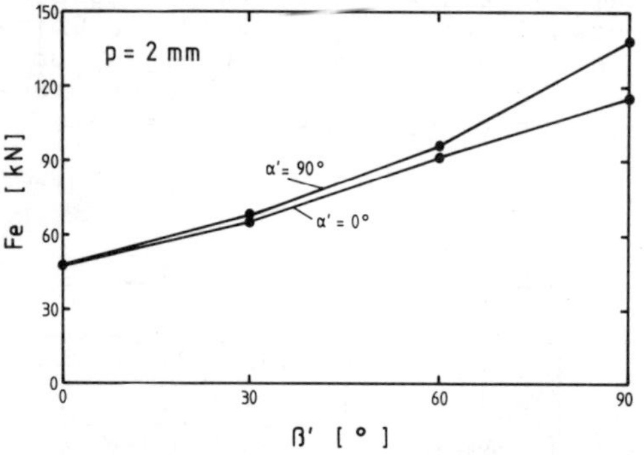

Abb. 8 Anisotropieabhängigkeit der Keileindringkraft für Gneis

Die Abb.7 und 8 zeigen einige interessante Ergebnisse der Keileindringversuche für Sandstein K und Gneis. Die eingetragenen Datenpunkte sind jeweils Mittelwerte aus 6-7 Einzelversuchen.

Wie erwartet ist Fe immer dann besonders klein, wenn sich die chiperzeugenden Zugrisse parallel zu Schwächeflächen im Gestein ausbreiten können ($\beta' = 0^{\circ}$). Erfolgt hingegen die Rißausbreitung überwiegend senkrecht zu vorhandenen Schicht- oder Schieferungsflächen, so wird Fe besonders groß ($\beta' = 90^{\circ}$). Wie die folgende Tabelle 2 zeigt, existiert ein deutlicher Zusammenhang zwischen der Zugfestigkeitsanisotropie, hier ausgedrückt durch die entsprechenden Punktlastindexwerte, und dem Keileindringverhalten. Fe90 ist hierbei jeweils das arithmetische Mittel der bei $\beta' = 90^{\circ}$ und einer Penetration von 2 mm gemessenen Einpreßkräfte und Fe0 der entsprechende Wert bei $\beta' = 0^{\circ}$.

Tab.2 Zusammenhang zwischen Festigkeitsanisotropie und Keileindringverhalten

Gestein	$\sigma c\perp/\sigma c\parallel$	$Is50\perp/Is50\parallel$	Fe90/Fe0
Sandstein K	1,0	1,4	1,4
Gneis	1,3	2,1	2,7

Da man heute vielfach davon ausgeht, daß die Druckspannungen innerhalb der plastischen Zone der einaxialen Druckfestigkeit entsprechen (Roxborough, Phillips 1975, Wang et.al. 1978), ist in Tabelle 2 zum Vergleich auch das Verhältnis der senkrecht und parallel zu Schicht- und Schieferungsflächen gemessenen einaxialen Druckfestigkeiten angegeben.

Interessanterweise korreliert das Verhältnis von Fe90 zu Fe0 nur schlecht mit der entsprechenden Anisotropie der einaxialen Druckfestigkeiten. Betrachtet man hierzu noch einmal Abb.6, so erkennt man, daß längs der Berandung der plastischen Zone kein konstanter Winkel zwischen den radial wirkenden Druckspannungen und den Anisotropieflächen besteht. Demzufolge wird in analoger Weise auch die Größe der jeweils maßgeblichen Druckfestigkeiten schwanken. Da nun aber die Keileindringkraft stets mit den über die Oberfläche der plastischen Zone integrierten Spannungen im Gleichgewicht stehen muß, scheint es fraglich, ob sich in anisotropen Gesteinen einer bestimmten Keileinpreßrichtung überhaupt eine maßgebliche einaxiale Druckfestigkeit zuordnen läßt.

Zusammenfassend läßt sich aufgrund der mechanischen Ähnlichkeit zwischen dem Keileindringvorgang und dem Schneidvorgang mit Diskenmeißeln folgern, daß anisotropiebedingte Unterschiede der Nettobohrgeschwindigkeit einer Vollschnittmaschine besser durch richtungsabhängige Zugfestigkeiten als durch entsprechende einaxiale Druckfestigkeiten beschrieben werden können.

4 SCHNEIDVERSUCHE

Der Bohrfortschritt einer Vollschnittmaschine mit Diskenmeißeln ist erst dann gewährleistet, wenn zwischen benachbarten Meißelspuren ein vollständiger Gesteinsabtrag stattfindet. Die hierbei ablaufenden Bruchvorgänge sind grundsätzlich die gleichen wie im Keileindringversuch, d.h. ein ständiger Wechsel zwischen Phasen der Gesteinszertrümmerung und Phasen der Chipbildung bewirkt ein Oszillieren der Werkzeugkräfte (Abb.9).

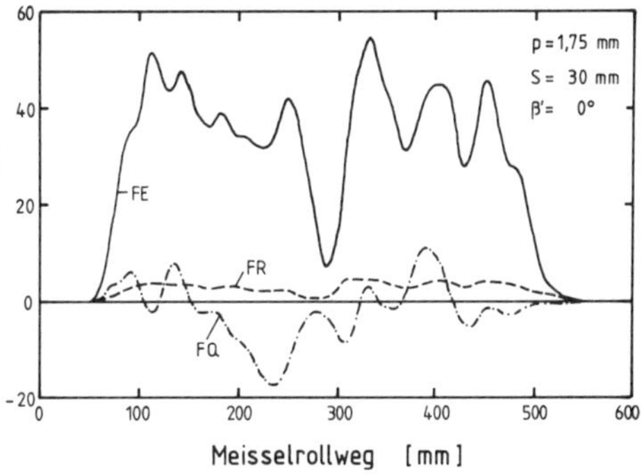

Abb.9 Schreiberaufzeichnung eines Schneidversuches in Sandstein S

Je nach Penetration, Spurabstand, Gesteinsart und Gefügeflächenorientierung kann aber der durch die Chipbildung erzeugte Ausbruch zunächst so gering sein, daß der Gesteinsabtrag zwischen den Schneidbahnen nicht sofort, sondern erst nach mehreren Bohrkopfumdrehungen erfolgt. Dies wurde bei den Schneidversuchen dadurch berücksichtigt, daß für jede gewählte Kombination der Versuchsparameter mindestens vier und teilweise sogar bis zu zehn Lagen (entsprechend den Bohrkopfumdrehungen) durch den Meißel abgetragen wurden.

Da die Schneidversuche nicht mit konstanter Anpreßkraft, sondern mit fest vorgegebener Eindringtiefe durchgeführt wurden, entsprechen die anschließend angegebenen Penetrationswerte somit der Bohrkopfpenetration einer Vollschnittmaschine mit steifem Bohrkopf. Dies bedeutet, daß mit Hilfe der im Labor gemessenen Werkzeugkräfte eine realistische Abschätzung der Vortriebsgeschwindigkeit von Vollschnittmaschinen möglich ist, wenn die mechanischen Gesteinseigenschaften im Labor und unter Tage vergleichbar sind. Für den hier untersuchten Ruhrsandstein sind die Voraussetzungen für eine Übertragbarkeit der Laborergebnisse auf den in-situ Fall sehr gut, da Sandsteinbereiche im Ruhrkarbon erfahrungsgemäß homogen und wenig zerklüftet sind.

4.1 Gesteinsanisotropie - Nettobohrgeschwindigkeit

Die Abb.10 und 11 zeigen einige der wichtigsten experimentell ermittelten Abhängigkeiten, die sich mit der Nettobohrgeschwindigkeit einer Vollschnittmaschine in Verbindung bringen lassen. In den Diagrammen ist die Beeinflussung der mittleren, normal zur Probenoberfläche gemessenen Eindringkraft durch Penetration, Spurabstand und Gesteinsanisotropie ersichtlich. Jeder eingetragene Datenpunkt wurde aus mindestens 20 Einzelversuchen ermittelt.

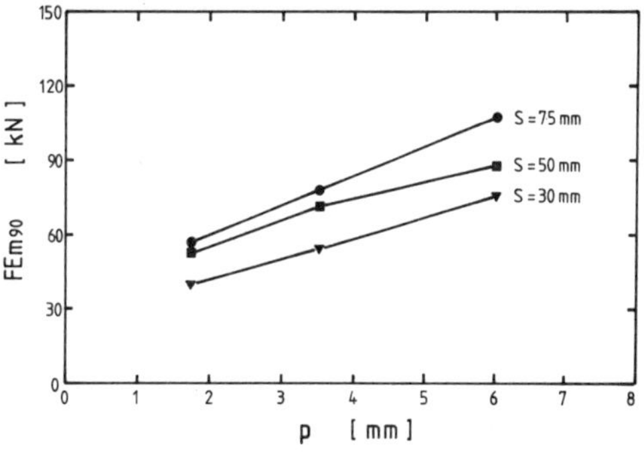

Abb.10 Mittlere Eindringkräfte in Sandstein S bei einer Meißelrollgeschwindigkeit von 300 mm/s

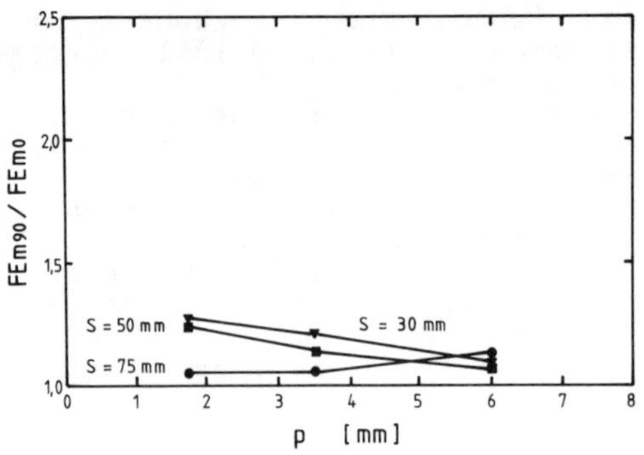

Abb.11 Anisotropieabhängigkeit der Eindringkräfte in Sandstein S bei einer Meißelrollgeschwindigkeit von 300 mm/s

Man erkennt, daß FEm mit steigender Eindringtiefe und steigendem Schneidbahnabstand zunimmt. Bei ungünstiger Gefügeflächenorientierung ($\beta' = 90^{0}$) sind die mittleren Eindringkräfte zwischen 1,1 und 1,3 mal größer als bei günstiger ($\beta' = 0^{0}$). Dieses Ergebnis korrelliert gut mit der Punktlastanisotropie des untersuchten Sandsteines von 1,2 und bestätigt die Resultate der Keileindringversuche deutlich.

Aus Abb.11 geht hervor, daß die Beeinflussung von FEm durch die Gesteinsanisotropie offenbar je nach Spurabstand und Penetration unterschiedlich stark ist. Vernachlässigt man dies in erster Näherung und nimmt unabhängig von S und p ein konstantes Verhältnis von FEm90 zu FEm0 an, so können die Schneidversuchsergebnisse auf halb theoretischem, halb empirischem Wege für Ruhrsandstein wie folgt mathematisch approximiert werden:

$$p = \left[\frac{FEm}{K(\beta')}\right]^2 \cdot \frac{1}{D \cdot S} \qquad (1)$$

$K(\beta')$: anisotropieabhängiger Festigkeitsparameter

D : Durchmesser des Meißels

Ausgehend von den Kurven in Abb.10 scheint ein quadratischer Zusammenhang zwischen FEm und p zunächst nicht ganz gerechtfertigt zu sein. Bedenkt man jedoch, daß bei der Penetration p = 0 auch die Eindringkraft FEm = 0 sein muß, so wird der Ansatz einer allgemeinen Exponentia funktion für die Beziehung zwischen FEm und p verständlich.

Mit Hilfe von Zusammenhang (1) kann nun die Anisotropieabhängigkeit der Nettobohrgeschwindigkeit einer Voll schnittmaschine für Ruhrsandstein abgeschätzt werden. Geht man hierzu davon aus, daß bei maximalem Bohrkopfandruck gerade die Kraft FEm90 pro Meißel zur Verfügung steht, so kann die Maschine damit bei günstig Raumlage der Schichtung ($\beta' = 0^{0}$) di Bohrkopfpenetration p_I und bei ungünstiger Raumlage der Schichtung ($\beta' = 90^{0}$) die Bohrkopfpenetration p_{II} erreichen. Berücksichtigt man, daß bei einem Tunnelvortrieb senkrecht zur Schichtung die Penetratio p_{II} auch schon mit einer geringeren Andruckkraft pro Werkzeug (FEm0) er reichbar ist, so ergibt sich aus Be ziehung 1:

$$\frac{p_I}{p_{II}} = \left[\frac{FEm90}{FEm\ 0}\right]^2 \qquad (2)$$

Die Schneidversuchsergebnisse liefern ein durchschnittliches Verhält nis FEm90/FEm0 von 1,15. Eingesetzt in (2) ergibt sich hieraus, daß die Nettobohrgeschwindigkeit einer Voll schnittmaschine im untersuchten Ruh sandstein bei einem Vortrieb senkrecht zur Schichtung ca 32 % größer ist als parallel dazu.

Dieses Ergebnis ist vor allem des wegen interessant, weil diese doch beträchtliche Beeinflussung der Net tobohrleistung durch die Gesteinsan isotropie für einen gemeinhin als näherungsweise isotrop angesehenen Ruhrsandstein ermittelt wurde. Der Vergleich mit den Resultaten der Keileindringversuche zeigt, daß in Gesteinen mit ausgeprägterer Festig keitsanisotropie wie z.B. Gneis ode Tonschiefer noch wesentlich größere anisotropiebedingte Schwankungen de Vortriebsleistung einer Vollschnitt maschine möglich sind.

4.2 Gesteinsanisotropie - Werkzeugbelastung und Bruchgutbeschaffenheit

Um die Beanspruchung der Rollenbohr werkzeuge einer Vollschnittmaschine realistisch beurteilen zu können, werden nicht nur Informationen über die Belastungsmittelwerte benötigt, sondern vor allem Angaben über Spitzenbeanspruchungen und die Häufigkeit ihres Auftretens. Hierbei ist die maximale Größe aller Kraftkomponenten wichtig, d.h. nicht nur Roll- und Eindring- sondern auch Querkraftspitzen sind von Interesse, letztere besonders auch wegen ihres Beitrages zur Momentenbelastung des Lagers. Ergebnisse diesbezüglicher Messungen im Rahmen der Schneidversuche mit Diskenmeißeln sind in den Abb. 12, 13, 14 und 15 zusammengestellt.

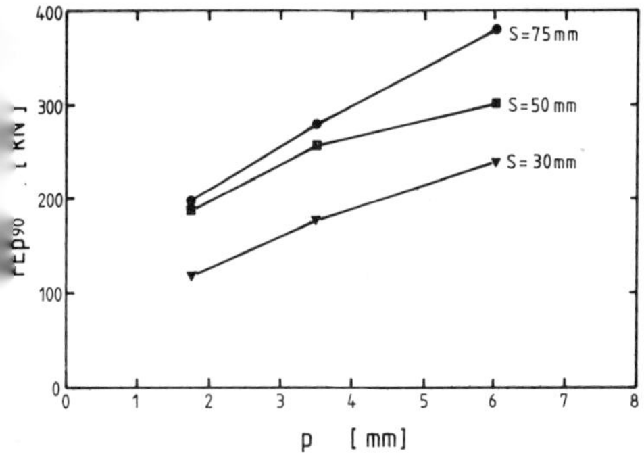

Abb.12 Maximale Eindringkräfte in Sandstein S bei einer Meißelrollgeschwindigkeit von 300 mm/s

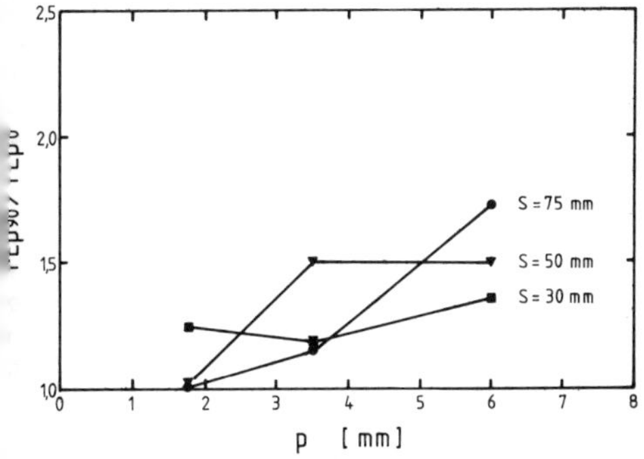

Abb.13 Anisotropieabhängigkeit der maximalen Eindringkräfte in Sandstein S bei einer Meißelrollgeschwindigkeit von 300 mm/s

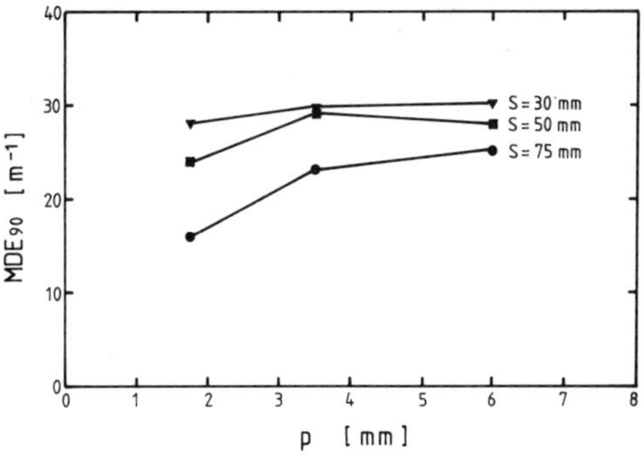

Abb. 14 Mittelwertdurchgänge der Eindringkraft pro Meter Meißelrollstrecke in Sandstein S. Meißelrollgeschwindigkeit 300 mm/s

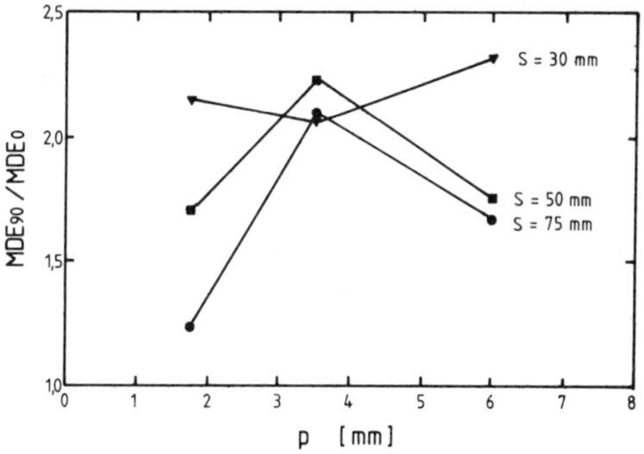

Abb.15 Anisotropieabhängigkeit der Mittelwertdurchgänge der Eindringkraft pro Meter Meißelrollstrecke in Sandstein S. Meißelrollgeschwindigkeit 300 mm/s

Man erkennt, daß die Maximalwerte der Eindringkraft einen ähnlichen funktionalen Zusammenhang zu S und p aufweisen wie die zugehörigen Mittelwerte (Abb.12). Die Spitzenlasten sind für alle untersuchten Spurabstände und Penetrationen etwa 3,5 mal so groß wie die entsprechenden Kraftmittelwerte. Die maximalen Roll- und Querkräfte ergeben sich überschlägig zu:

$FRp \approx 1/12 \ FEp$

$F_{Qp} \approx 1/3 \; F_{Ep}$

Diese sehr stark vereinfachten Angaben sind nicht ganz frei von systematischen Fehlern, weil die Anisotropieabhängigkeit der Spitzenlasten nicht mit der der Kraftmittelwerte übereinstimmt (vgl.Abb.11 mit Abb. 13). Die Ursachen hierfür sind jedoch vermutlich weniger mechanisch bedingt, sondern mehr auf die relativ große Streuung der Maximallasten zurückzuführen. Dennoch ist auch hier ein sehr starker Einfluß der Festigkeitsanisotropie auf die Werkzeugbelastung deutlich erkennbar.

Aus Abb.14 entnimmt man, daß die Eindringkraftfunktion ihren zugehörigen Mittelwert bei ungünstiger Gefügeflächenorientierung ($\beta' = 90^{\circ}$) zwischen 15 und 30 mal pro Meter Meißelrollstrecke durchsetzt (vgl. Definition von MD in Abschnitt 2.4). Bei einer angenommenen maximalen Meißellaufstrecke von 100 km bis zum notwendigen Austausch infolge Verschleiß muß ein Rollenbohrwerkzeug im Ruhrsandstein demnach je nach Spurabstand zwischen $1{,}5 \cdot 10^{6}$ und $3{,}0 \cdot 10^{6}$ Lastwechsel aushalten. Eine für die Lebensdauer eines Rollenbohrwerkzeuges sicher nicht unwichtige Tatsache ist, daß sich die Anzahl der Lastwechsel bei günstiger Orientierung des Trennflächengefüges ($\beta' = 0^{\circ}$) unter Umständen auf weniger als die Hälfte reduziert (Abb. 15).

Eine weitere Auswirkung der Festigkeitsanisotropie macht sich bei der Größenverteilung des Schneidgutes

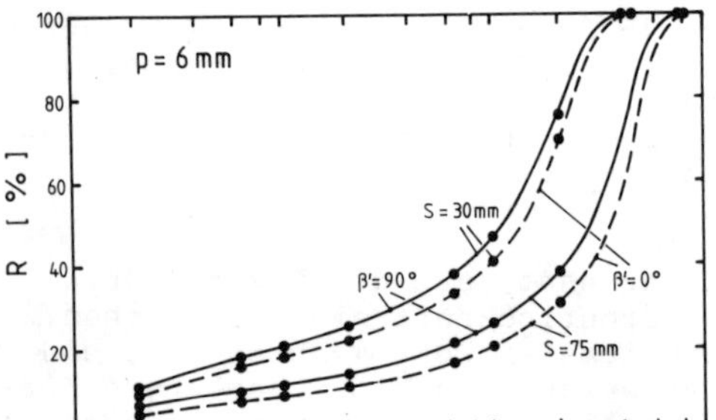

Abb.16 Kornverteilung des Bruchgutes in Sandstein S bei einer Meißelrollgeschwindigkeit von 300 mm/s

bemerkbar. Die in Abb.16 aufgetragenen Kornverteilungskurven des bei einer Penetration von 6 mm erzeugten Schneidgutes zeigen eine deutliche Verschiebung zu größeren Scherben bei einer Abtragung parallel zum Trennflächengefüge und umgekehrt ein höherer Anteil an Feinteilen bei einer schichtnormalen Abtragung.

5 SCHLUSSFOLGERUNGEN

1. Die Nettobohrgeschwindigkeit von Vollschnittmaschinen wird signifikant durch das Vorhandensein von Schwächeflächen im Gestein und deren räumliche Orientierung beeinflußt. Selbst in nur schwach anisotropen Ruhrsandsteinen (mit einer Anisotropie der Punktlastfestigkeit $Is50_{\perp}/Is50_{\parallel}$ = 1,2) kann die Nettobohrgeschwindigkeit einer Vollschnittmaschine bei einem Tunnelvortrieb senkrecht zur Schichtung 1,3 mal größer sein als parallel dazu. In anderen Gesteinen mit stärker ausgeprägter Anisotropie wie z.B. Tonschiefer od Gneis ($Is50_{\perp}/Is50_{\parallel}$ = 2,1) kann dieses Verhältnis der Vortriebsgeschwindig keiten auf 2,7 oder teilweise noch größere Werte ansteigen. Einschränkend muß hierzu allerdings gesagt werden, daß die Gebirgseigenschafte unter Tage in der Regel durch mehr als ein mechanisch wirksames Trennflächensystem bestimmt werden. In intensiv geklüfteten Gebirgsbereich tritt deshalb ein richtungsabhängiger Einfluß von Schichtung und Schi ferung auf die Bohrgeschwindigkeit einer Vollschnittmaschine nicht meh so klar hervor wie im Labor.

2. Auch die Belastung der Rollenbohrwerkzeuge einer Vollschnittmaschine hängt stark von der Raumlage des Trennflächengefüges im Gebirge ab. Ortsbrustparallele Schwächeflächen im Gestein reduzieren die mittleren und maximalen Werkzeugkräfte. Zur Verdeutlichung ein kurzes Zahlenbeispiel:

Moderne im Ruhrbergbau eingesetzt Vollschnittmaschinen haben heute Schneidbahnabstände zwischen 70 und 80 mm und verfügbare Nettoandruckkräfte pro Werkzeug von etwa 100 KN Hiermit kann im Ruhrsandstein bei schichtparalleler Auffahrung eine Penetration von etwa maximal 6 mm erreicht werden. Ein Vergleich der bei dieser Penetration zu erwartenden Werkzeugkräfte ergibt, daß dies bei einem Tunnelvortrieb parallel zur Schichtung um ca 70 % größer sind als bei einer Auffahrung senkrecht dazu.

3. Zusätzlich zum Betrag der Werkzeugbelastung wird auch deren Dynamik stark von der Orientierung der Schwächeflächen beeinflußt. Die Dynamik der Meißelbeanspruchung verringert sich mit der Abnahme des Winkels zwischen Schwächefläche und Ortsbrust. Für das unter 2. aufgeführte Maschinenbeispiel würde sich beim Wechsel vom schichtnormalen zum schichtparallelen Auffahren eine Zunahme der Häufigkeit der Be- und Entlastungswechsel von ca 70 % ergeben.

4. Letztlich ergibt sich über die Anisotropieabhängigkeit von Werkzeugbelastung und Frequenz der Belastungswechsel auch eine erhebliche Abhängigkeit des Werkzeugverschleisses von der Schichtorientierung. Mit zunehmender Höhe der Belastungsspitzen und ansteigender Zahl der Lastwechsel bei Annäherung an eine schichtparallele Auffahrung nimmt vermutlich im gleichen Maße, wenn nicht sogar noch stärker, auch der Werkzeugverschleiß zu.

Aus 1.bis 4. folgt, daß die reinen Vortriebskosten pro Qubikmeter gelösten Gesteins bei Vollschnittauffahrungen im Ruhrsandstein mit abnehmendem Schnittwinkel zwischen Tunnelachse und Schichtung zunehmen. Eine Nichtbeachtung der Gesteinsanisotropie kann also selbst in nur schwach anisotropen Gesteinen wie Ruhrsandstein zu Fehleinschätzungen der Wirtschaftlichkeit eines Vollschnittmaschinensystems führen.

ANMERKUNGEN

Die hier berichteten Untersuchungen sind ein Teilergebnis eines längerfristigen Forschungsunterfangens, das zu Beginn vom Bundesministerium für Forschung und Technologie und seit April 1981 von der Deutschen Forschungsgemeinschaft finanziell getragen wurde. Die Schneidversuche mit Diskenmeißeln wurden von M.J.Oly durchgeführt.

Literaturübersicht

Benjumea, R., Sikarskie, D.L. 1969, A note on the penetration of a rigid wedge into a nonisotropic brittle material, Int. J. Rock Mech. Min. Sci. 6 4 : 343-352

Blindheim, O.T., Dahl Johansen, E., Johannessen, O. 1979, Criteria for the selection of fullface tunnel boring or conventional tunnelling, Proc. 4th Int. Congr. Rock Mech., Montreux, 1 : 341-346

Farmer, I.W., Glossop, N.H. 1980, Mechanics of disc cutter penetration, Tunnels & Tunnelling, July : 22-25

Pariseau, W.G. 1971, Wedge indentation of anisotropic geologic media, Dyn. Rock Mech., 12. Symp. Rock Mech., Univ. of Missouri, Rolla, 1970, AIME, New York : 529-546

Roxborough, F.F., Phillips, H.R. 1975, Rock excavation by disc cutter, Int. J. Rock Mech. Min. Sci. & Geom. Abstr. 12 12 : 361-366

Wang, F.D., Ozdemir, L., Snyder, L. 1978, Prediction and verification of tunnel boring machine performance, Euro Tunnel, Basle, Switzerland, Febr.28 - March 3, Technical Conference, 4 : 50 S

Wanner, W.J. 1975, Einsatz von Tunnelvortriebsmaschinen im kristallinen Gebirge.Abhängigkeit des Vortriebes von geologisch-petrographischen Bedingungen, Dissertation, ETH Zürich : 157 S

EINSATZBEISPIELE FÜR DEN VORTRIEB MIT TEILSCHNITTMASCHINEN UNTER SCHWIERIGEN RANDBEDINGUNGEN

Applications of selective cutting machines for roadheading in difficult strata conditions

Exemples d'emploi de machines à attaque partielle dans de difficiles conditions du terrain

EBERHART UNGER
Westfalia Lünen, Lünen, Bundesrepublik Deutschland

SUMMARY:
The continuing growth of the use of Selective Cutting Machines for driving roadways and tunnels in both civil engineering projects and in coalmines, as well as for mining minerals by the pillar and chamber method has attracted much interest during the past years. As compared with full-facers, roadheaders of this type have the advantage that they are independent of the shape of the cross-section. Owing to the excellent manoeuvrability of the machine small curves and roadway junctions can be negotiated. Two recent applications of Selective Cutting Machines open up new possibilities in the successful use of adequately modified versions of this type of machine even in difficult strata conditions. The results obtained with the Boom Cutter Loader "Luchs" in the drivage of a sag pipe crossing under the Rhine river with only a small cover where large quantities of carbonated water were encountered were a great success. Equipped with auxiliary equipment the Boom Cutter Loader type used on this project operated efficiently even on a section with a gradient of 60% to the rise. Another application of a "H-Luchs" was to drive tunnels for the Munich underground system by using the New Austrian Tunnelling Method. Here the Selective Cutting Machine proved to be capable of heading even large cross-section tunnels from a static central position.

ZUSAMMENFASSUNG:
In den letzten Jahren haben Teilschnittmaschinen sowohl im Tiefbau für das Auffahren von Stollen und Tunneln als auch im Bergbau für das Auffahren von Strecken bzw. bei der Mineralgewinnung im Örter- oder Kammerbau zunehmend an Bedeutung gewonnen. Gegenüber Vollschnittmaschinen haben Teilschnittmaschinen den Vorteil, von der Querschnittsform unabhängig zu sein. Aufgrund der Beweglichkeit dieser Maschinen lassen sich enge Kurven und Streckenabzweige gut bewältigen. Zwei Einsatzbeispiele mit Teilschnittmaschinen zeigen Möglichkeiten auf, wie durch Modifizierung der Geräte auch schwierige Randbedingungen bewältigt werden können. Der Einsatz eines Fräs-Laders "Luchs" beim Auffahren eines Dükers unter dem Rhein mit geringer Überdeckung und bei grossem kohlensäurehaltigen Wasseranfall war ein voller Erfolg. Die aufzufahrende Steigungsstrecke von 60% Steigung hat der Frä-Lader mit Hilfe einer Zusatzeinrichtung ebenfalls gut bewältigt. Ein anderer Einsatz mit dem "H-Luchs" im Müchener U-Bahn-Bau hat gezeigt, dass mit Teilschnittmaschinen auch grosse Querschnitte in der NÖT aus dem Stand bearbeitet werden können.

RESUME:
Au cours de ces dernières années, les machines ponctuelles sont devenues importantes sur le secteur des travaux publics pour le creusement de galeries et de tunnels, et sur le secteur des mines pour le traçage de voies et pour l'abattage de minéraux dans des exploitations par piliers longs abandonnés ou par chambres et piliers. La machine ponctuelle s'emploie dans toute section - quelle que soit sa forme - ce qui est un avantage par rapport à la machine pleine section. Les machines très mobiles prennent facilement des courbes serrées et des branchements de la voie. Deux exemples d'utilisation prouvent que des machines ayant subi les modifications nécessaires peuvent travailler dans ces conditions difficiles. On a utilisé avec succès une fraise-chargeuse "Lynx" pour le creusement d'une traversée sous le Rhin, avec faible couche de recouvrement et avec importantes venues

d'eau carbonatée. A l'aide d'un dispositif auxiliaire, la fraise-chargeuse a pris aisémen la rampe montante de 60%. Une autre application du "Super-Lynx" pour la construction d'un ligne de métro à Munich a démontré que les machines ponctuelles peuvent couper sans se déplacer de très grandes sections suivant la nouvelle méthode autrichienne.

1. AUSWAHL DER VORTRIEBSVERFAHREN

Unterschiedliche Hohlräume werden auf verschiedene Weise zu unterschiedlichen Zwecken geschaffen. In erster Linie bestimmen der vorgesehene Verwendungszweck, der dafür erforderliche Querschnitt mit dem dazugehörigen Ausbau und die vorhandene Gesteins- oder Bodenart die Auswahl des Vortriebsverfahrens und der optimalen Vortriebseinrichtung. Faktoren von ständig wachsender Bedeutung sind bei jeglicher Art des Vortriebs der Umweltschutz und die Humanisierung der Arbeitswelt. Beides führt z.B. dazu, daß bei der Herstellung von unterirdischen Verkehrswegen und Kanalisationsanlagen in bebauten Gebieten ein mit Erschütterungen, Lärm- und Staubentwicklung verbundenes Verfahren nicht angewendet werden darf. Von den Vortriebseinrichtungen sind hier als Beispiele genannt:

Der Schildvortrieb als geschlossener Handschild oder vollmechanischer Schild,
der Messerschild mit teil- oder vollmechanisiertem Abbau,
der Rohrvorpreßbetrieb mit mechanisierter Gewinnungs- und Ladearbeit,
der Vortrieb mit Teilschnittmaschinen und
der Sprengvortrieb mit nachgeschalteter Lade- und Abfördereinrichtung.

2. TEILSCHNITTMASCHINEN

In den letzten Jahren haben Teilschnittmaschinen sowohl im Tiefbau für das Auffahren von Stollen und Tunneln als auch im Bergbau für das Auffahren von Strecken bzw. bei der Mineralgewinnung im Örter- oder Kammerbau zunehmend an Bedeutung gewonnen.

Gegenüber Vollschnittmaschinen, die in der Regel nur kreisrunde Querschnitte herstellen können, haben Teilschnittmaschinen den Vorteil, von der Querschnittsform unabhängig zu sein. Sie bringen in der Regel zwar nicht so hohe Gewinnungsleistungen wie eine Vollschnittmaschine, erlauben aber dafür eine partielle Bearbeitung der Ortsbrust. Aufgrund der Beweglichkeit dieser Maschinen lassen sich enge Kurven und Streckenabzweige

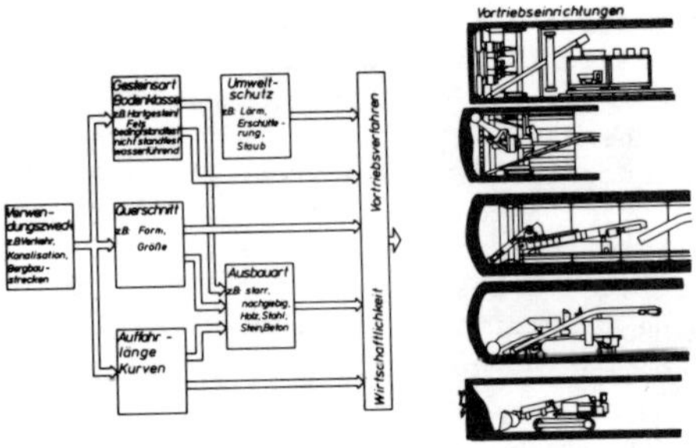

Bild 1: Kriterien für die Auswahl der Vortriebsverfahren und Vortriebseinrichtungen

gut bewältigen. Parallelstrecken sind mit nur einem Gerät im Wechselbetrieb aufgefahren worden. Bei wechselnder Geologie und bei großem Anfall von Wasser und Schlamm haben Teilschnittmaschinen ihre Bewährungsprobe gut bestanden.

Es wird vorausgesetzt, daß die heute auf dem Markt gängigen Maschinen bekannt sind. Aus diesem Grund soll an dieser Stelle auf eine eingehende Besprechung der Geräte verzichtet werden. Es sei jedoch de

Hinweis gestattet, daß sich die Teilschnittmaschinen in vier Gruppen einteilen lassen:

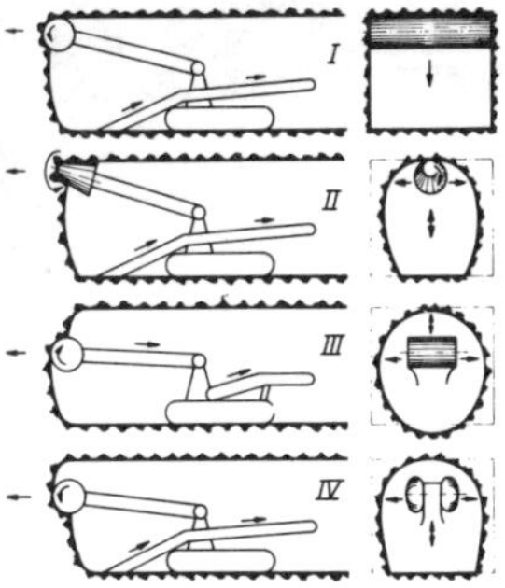

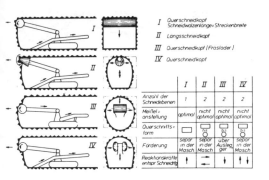

I Querschneidkopf Schneidwalzenlänge = Streckenbreite
II Längsschneidkopf
III Querschneidkopf (Fräslader)
IV Querschneidkopf

	I	II	III	IV
Anzahl der Schneidebenen	1	2	2	2
Meißelanstellung	optimal	nicht optimal	nicht optimal	nicht optimal
Querschnittsform	▭	▭ bis ○	▭ bis ○	▭ bis ○
Förderung	separ. in der Masch.	separ. in der Masch.	über Ausleger	separ. in der Masch.
Reaktionskräfte entspr. Schneidrtg.	↑	→ ←	↓	↑ ↓

Bild 2: Darstellung der Teilschnittmaschinen

1. Querschneidkopfmaschinen, wobei die Länge der Schneidwalze der Streckenbreite entspricht.
2. Längsschneidkopfmaschinen oder Pinselmaschinen.
3. Querschneidkopfmaschinen; Fräs-Lader, bei denen die Abförderung des gelösten Gutes über den Schneidarmausleger erfolgt.
4. Querschneidkopfmaschinen mit 2 axial angeordneten Schneidrädern.

In jahrelanger Erfahrung hat sich herausgestellt, daß bei Teilschnittmaschinen dem axialen Schneidprinzip der Querschneidkopfmaschinen gegenüber dem radialen Schneidprinzip der Längsschneidkopfmaschinen vor allem in festen Gebirgsformationen der Vorzug zu geben ist. Bei diesen Geräten werden die resultierenden Kräfte aus dem Schnittdruck in vertikaler Richtung über den Maschinenkörper auf die Sohle abgesetzt. Dadurch sind keinerlei zusätzliche Stützelemente erforderlich. Bei den Teilschnittmaschinen ist besonders Wert darauf zu legen, daß nicht nur die Lösearbeit, sondern vor allem auch die Ladevorgänge durch oder über die Maschine einwandfrei und betriebssicher bewältigt werden. Hier gilt der Leitsatz: "Jede Maschine ist so gut wie ihre Ladeeinrichtung selbst".

Wie vorher bereits erwähnt, sind für den wirtschaftlichen Einsatz einer Teilschnittmaschine neben der Gewinnbarkeit des Gebirges viele Gesichtspunkte zu berücksichtigen, auf die hier nicht näher eingegangen werden soll. Deshalb sei als Anhaltspunkt für die Einsatzmöglichkeit der unterschiedlichen Typen der Maschine kurz folgender Hinweis auf die einaxiale Druckfestigkeit des Gebirges gegeben, ohne damit endgültig beurteilen zu wollen, ob eine schneidende Gewinnungsmaschine wirtschaftlich einzusetzen ist.

Die Fräs-Lader im Leistungsbereich bis 50 kW im Schneidkopf lassen sich bei Druckfestigkeiten bis 3000 N/cm^2 ohne weiteres einsetzen. Die Maschinen im Leistungsbereich bis 100 kW (darunter die Fräs-Lader Luchs und H-Luchs) können bis 8000 N/cm^2 ohne weiteres wirtschaftlich arbeiten. Teilschnittmaschinen mit 200 kW Leistung im Schneidkopf und mehr können bis 10 000 N/cm^2 Druckfestigkeit arbeiten. Bei günstigen Gebirgsverhältnissen kann der Einsatz der zuletzt genannten Maschinen auch bei höheren Druckfestigkeiten noch wirtschaftlich sein.

3. EINSATZBEISPIELE

Einige Einsatzbeispiele mit den Teilschnittmaschinen Luchs und H-Luchs sollen die Möglichkeiten aufzeigen, wie durch Modifizierung der Geräte auch schwierige Randbedingungen bewältigt werden können.

3.1 Fräs-Lader Luchs

Beispielhaft ist der Einsatz mit einem Fräs-Lader Luchs beim Auffahren des Rhein-Dükers Koblenz-Ehrenbreitstein, der von der Arbeitsgemeinschaft Philipp Holzmann AG, Zweigniederlassung Koblenz, Bilfinger & Berger-Bau-AG, Niederlassung Koblenz, und Hochtief AG, Zweigniederlassung Koblenz, als Sondervorschlag angeboten und gebaut wurde.

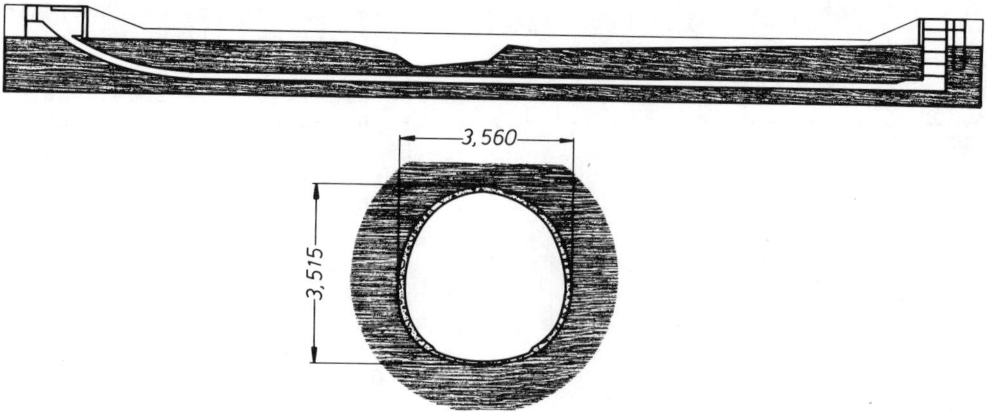

Bild 3: Streckenführung mit Querschnitt

Die Länge des Dükers beträgt etwa 375 m, wobei ca. 310 m unter dem Flußbett liegen. Die Mindestüberdeckung des Tunnels lag bei 3 m unter der Rheinsohle. Unter dem Rhein steigt der Düker gleichmäßig mit 2 ‰. Auf dem linken Rheinufer zum Hochpunkt beträgt die Steigung bis zu 60 %. Der Ausbruchquerschnitt des Tunnels, ein Maulprofil, betrug ca. 10 m². Kompakter Tonstein mit nicht erkennbaren Schichtungen und Tonschiefer mit deutlicher Schichtung und klaren Trennflächen waren zu durchörtern. Kohlensäurehaltiges Wasser fiel auf der gesamten Tunnelstrecke an. Als Gebirgssicherung erhält der Stollen während der Vortriebsarbeit eine 10 cm starke bewehrte Spritzbetonschale.

Die ersten 42 m des Stollens wurden im gebirgsschonenden Sprengvortrieb aufgefahren mit Abschlagslängen von 1,5 m. Beim Sprengen wurde der Gebirgsverband gestört und stellte im Bereich des Rheingrabens mit nur **3 m** Überdeckung ein hohes Risiko dar. Angefahrene Kamine liefen aus, bevor die Spritzbetonsicherung eingebrach werden konnte. Im folgenden Sprengbetrieb wurden weitere Großklüfte an gefahren. In den Störzonen trat regelmäßig kohlensäurehaltiges Wasser aus, was zu Verbrüchen führte.

Gesteinsuntersuchungen zeigten, da mit einer Teilschnittmaschine vom Typ Fräs-Lader Luchs der Fels gelös werden konnte. Aus diesem Grunde en schloß man sich zur schonenden Gebirgslösung, d.h. den Vortrieb durc Fräsen mit einem Fräs-Lader Luchs weiter durchzuführen.

Bild 4: Blick in den Stollen mit Laserrichtstrahl

Die Fräs-Lader verwirklichen das Prinzip des gleichzeitigen Lösens, Ladens und Förderns in besonders anschaulicher Weise, da alles, was von der Fräswalze gelöst wird, über den Schneidarm abtransportiert werden kann. Eine getrennte Ladeeinrichtung ist deshalb nicht erforderlich. Das macht die Geräte sehr wendig. Die Ladearbeit auch bei einem Unterschnitt der Sohle ist einwandfrei. Herabgefallenes Gut nimmt die Schneidtrommel wieder auf und erlaubt ein sauberes Freischneiden der Streckensohle.

Bild 5: Fräs-Lader Luchs; Laden und Abfördern des Haufwerks in der Strosse eines S-Bahn-Tunnels

Der Tonschiefer war infolge seiner ausgeprägten Schieferung fräsbar. Auftretende Quarzbänke und kalzitische Einlagerungen behinderten den Fräsbetrieb nicht.

Die im Stollen angefallene Wassermenge, 10 m hinter der Ortsbrust gemessen, betrug bis zu 14 l/s und der gesamte Wasseranfall am Stollenmundloch 105 l/s. Ein Umrüsten der E-Motoren und Aggregate des Fräs-Laders Luchs auf die Schutzart EP 56

Bild 7: Wasserandrang im Tunnel

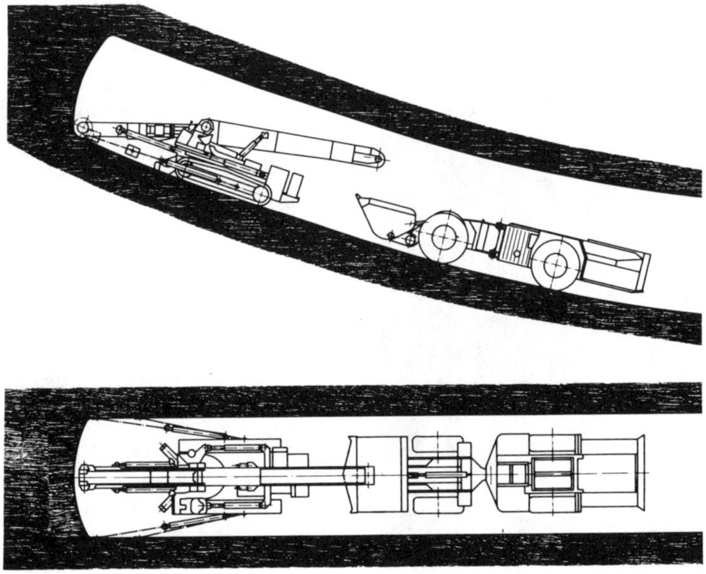

Bild 6: Fräs-Lader mit Klettervorrichtung in der Steigungsstrecke

war erforderlich, d.h. die E-Motoren sind bei vorübergehender Überflutung geschützt. Kompakter Tonstein war im Bereich der Steigungsstrecke zu durchörtern. Gesteinsuntersuchungen, bei der Fachhochschule des Landes Rheinland-Pfalz (Abt. Koblenz) durchgeführt, zeigten schwankende Druckfestigkeitswerte von 7800 N/cm² bis 25 000 N/cm². Die hohen Druckfestigkeiten erfordern eine zeitweilige Umstellung des Fräsvortriebs auf Sprengvortrieb.

Der zum Lösen des Gesteins erforderliche Anpreßdruck von ca. 4 t wird bis zu 25 % Steigung von dem Fräs-Lader selbst übernommen. Da in der Steigungsstrecke die Steigung bis zu 60 % betrug, wurde eine Zusatzausrüstung erforderlich, um die Teilschnittmaschine gegen Abrutschen zu sichern. Eine Klettervorrichtung - bestehend aus 2 Hydrozylindern von 10 t Zugkraft, 2 Hobelketten mit Schäkeln und Ankerplatten - wurde installiert. An den vor der Ortsbrust gesetzten 2 Felsankern wurden die Ankerplatten befestigt. Die beiden an der Maschine befestigten Hobelketten mit den integrierten Hydraulikzylindern waren an den Anker platten angeschlagen. Damit war ein ausreichende Haltekraft für die Maschine auch während des Schneidens gewährleistet. Die beim Vortrieb an getroffenen Gebirgsverhältnisse bezüglich Festigkeit und schleißschar fer Mineralien waren für eine Teilschnittmaschine an der obersten Grenze oder gar darüber. Durch die nicht erkennbaren geologischen Störungen, die in Form mit Schlamm und Kies gefüllten Trichtern auftraten, war der Einsatz einer Teilschnittmaschine Luchs gerechtfertigt. Mit kürzeren Abschlagslängen, die sofor mit Spritzbeton versiegelt wurden, konnten Nachbrüche verhindert werde

Bild 8: Fräs-Lader mit Klettervorrichtung in der Steigungsstrecke

Der Einsatz von Rundschaftmeißeln Typ U47, brachte Meißelverschleißkosten von 15,- bis 17,- DM/fm³. In Anbetracht der vorherrschenden schwierigen Gebirgsverhältnisse ein noch brauchbares Ergebnis.

An dieser Stelle sei der Hinweis gestattet, daß der Einsatz von Teil schnittmaschinen nicht von der installierten Leistung im Schneidkopf sondern von den auf dem Markt vorhandenen und angebotenen Schneidwerkzeugen abhängig ist. Hier sind die Hersteller von Schneidwerkzeuge aufgerufen, die Entwicklung weiter zu forcieren und möglicherweise mit neuen Technologien und Werkstoffen die Einsatzgrenzen von Teilschnittmaschinen zu erweitern.

Bei der Gesamtlänge des Tunnels von 360 m wurden 70 m im Sprengvortrieb und 290 m im Fräsbetrieb aufgefahren. Die Vortriebsleistungen beim Fräsbetrieb betrugen bis zu 20 m/Woche, wobei die effektive Vor triebsleistung 67 cm/h betrug.

Bei diesem kombinierten Schieß- und Fräsbetrieb hat sich gezeigt, daß trotz hoher Verschleißkosten der Schneidwerkzeuge am Fräs-Lader Luchs der Einsatz einer Teilschnitt maschine noch wirtschaftlich sein kann. Außerdem sei erwähnt, daß diese Bauweise eine Sicherheit für die Mineure ergab. Trotz großer erwähnter geologischer Probleme ist während der gesamten Vortriebsarbeit kein einziger Unfall aufgetreten.

3.2 Fräs-Lader H-Luchs

Ein weiterer interessanter Einsatz mit einem Fräs-Lader H-Luchs wurde beim U-Bahn-Bau in München durchgeführt. Es handelt sich um das Baulos 6, Odeonsplatz, der U-Bahn-Linie 5/9, welches von der Arbeitsgemeinschaft Bilfinger & Berger-Bau-AG, Hochtief AG, Dykerhoff & Widmann AG durchgeführt wird.

schnitt beim 2gleisigen Tunnelstück von ca. 300 m Länge beträgt rd. 80 m². Im eingleisigen Bereich liegt der Querschnitt bei 36 - 38 m², wobei die Länge etwa 500 m beträgt.

Mit dem Fräs-Lader H-Luchs, der in wesentlichen Bauelementen dem Luchs gleicht, jedoch so konzipiert ist, daß über eine Zwischenbühne größere Höhen und Querschnitte aus dem Stand geschnitten werden können, lassen sich diese vorhandenen Unregelmäßigkeiten einwandfrei bewältigen. Diese Teilschnittmaschine H-Luchs ist so konzipiert, daß auch bei verhältnismäßig großen Querschnitten die NÖT durchführbar ist.

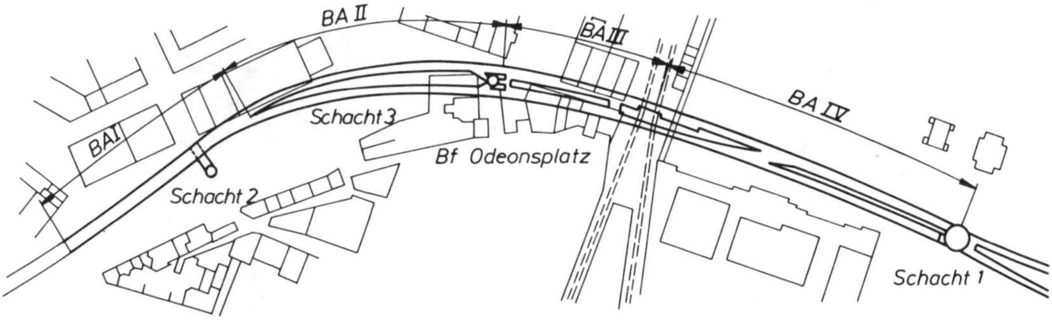

Bild 9: Streckenplan

Das Bauwerk ist gekennzeichnet durch einige Aufweitungen mit Trompeten und zusätzlichen sprunghaften Aufweitungen. Das Unterfahren eines bestehenden U-Bahnhofes und das Erstellen eines neuen U-Bahnhofes gehörte mit zur Baumaßnahme. Der Quer-

Der H-Luchs hat keine separate Ladeeinrichtung. Das gelöste Gut wird direkt über den Schneidarm, der als

Bild 10: Fräs-Lader H-Luchs

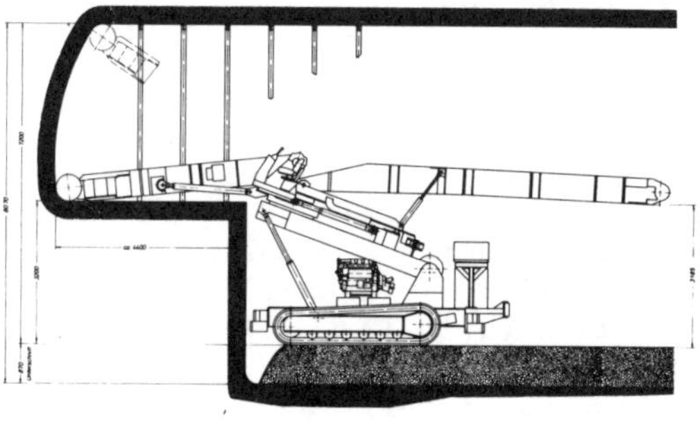

Bild 11: H-Luchs in den Neuen Österreichischen Tunnelbauweise (NÖT)

Kratzförderer ausgebildet ist, abtransportiert. Damit besteht die Möglichkeit, beim Kalottenvortrieb das gelöste Gut sofort abzufördern und über den Heckausleger auf Fahrzeuge auszutragen. Nachdem die Kalotte etwa 3 - 4 m vorgezogen ist, kann im Wechsel jeweils Kalotte und Restausbruch bauabschnittsweise gefräst und gesichert werden. Die Maschine ist außerdem in der Lage, einen Unterschnitt von 0,8 - 1,3 m herzustellen. Damit waren

Bild 12: Fräs-Lader beim Ausschneiden der Kalotte

die Voraussetzungen geschaffen, bei diesem schwierigen Bauvorhaben alle Querschnitte aus dem Stand mit der Maschine bearbeiten zu können. Ein schneller Ringschluß und entsprechende Versiegelung mit Spritzbeton waren auch bei diesen großen Querschnitten gegeben (Bild 12).

Der H-Luchs, mit einem zusätzlichen Dieselmotor ausgerüstet, ist in der Lage, schnell seinen Einsatzort zu wechseln, d.h. man kann mit einem Gerät 2 Tunnelröhren gleichzeitig im Wechselbetrieb bearbeiten (Bild 13 u. 14).
Nach dem Umsetzen wird der Stromanschluß hergestellt, und die Teilschnittmaschine ist wieder einsatzbereit. Die Umsetzzeiten und Ausbrucharbeiten sind dann so abgestimmt, daß sie mit den in der

Bild 13: Umsetzen des Fräs-Laders H-Luchs in die zweite Strecke

Bild 14: Einfahren des H-Luchses in die zweite Strecke

zweiten Tunnelröhre stattfindenden Sicherungsarbeiten übereinstimmen. Damit ist ein optimaler Vortrieb aus der Sicht der Teilschnittmaschine gewährleistet. Bei den ein- und zweigleisigen Strecken sind Vortriebsleistungen von 4 m/Tag/Tunnelröhre erreicht worden. Das Kriterium für die Vortriebsleistung liegt bei den Sicherungsarbeiten. Maschinenmäßig sind bei dem anstehenden Boden aus Schluff und Mergel mit Druckfestigkeiten von 2500 - 3000 N/cm^2 und eingeschlossenen Sandsteinbänken mit dem H-Luchs 40 - 50 fm^3/h reiner

Schneidzeit möglich. Abschläge von 1 m Bauabstand sind schon in 30 Minuten erzielt worden.

Beim großen Tunnelquerschnitt von 80 m² ist erstmals die "Zweizellige Bauweise" zum Tragen gekommen. Diese Bauweise ist dadurch gekennzeichnet, daß der Gesamtquerschnitt in zwei Teilquerschnitten, in Tunnelachse versetzt, aufgefahren wird.

Bild 16: Blick in den Tunnelquerschnitt, zweizellige Bauweise

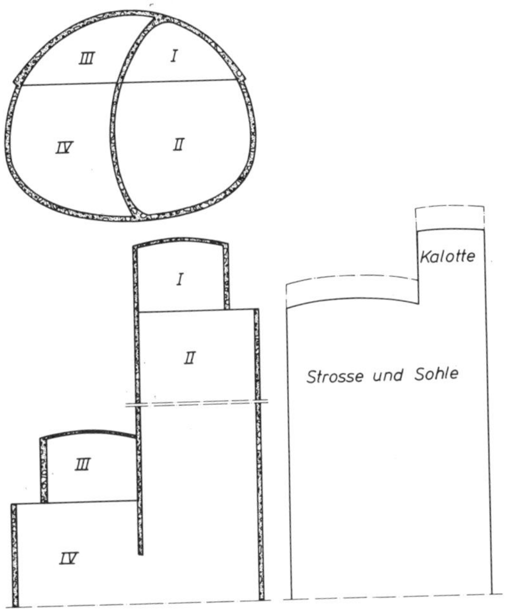

Bild 15: Aufteilung des Gesamtquerschnittes und Ablauf des Abbauvortriebes

Bild 17: Ausschneiden der Kalotte im dritten Abschnitt

Zuerst wird die Kalotte, die etwa 3 - 4 m vorgezogen ist, ausgefräst, an der Außenwand mit Matten verzogen und mit Spritzbeton versiegelt, hiernach die Strosse und Sohle nachgeschnitten und ebenfalls an der endgültigen Tunnelwand mit Matten verzogen und mit Spritzbeton gesichert. Während der Sicherungsarbeiten in dem vorlaufenden Querschnitt wird der H-Luchs umgesetzt und der zweite Teilquerschnitt, ca. 10 - 15 m nachlaufend, ausgefräst. Auch hier wird

Bild 18: H-Luchs beim Abschrämen der Betonstütze

wieder der Kalottenbereich etwa 3 - 4 m vorgezogen. Die aus dem ersten Teilquerschnitt hergestellte Spritzbetonsicherung, als Stütze dienend, wird mit der Teilschnittmaschine weggeschnitten. Damit kann in der Firste der Kalotte der Anschluß mit Mattenverzug und Spritzbeton endgültig hergestellt werden. Der weitere Arbeitsablauf bezieht sich auf den Restausbruch des zweiten Teilquerschnitts und der Verbindung des letzten Stücks mit Matten und Spritzbeton.

Bei diesem komplizierten Bauvorvorhaben hat sich gezeigt, daß die Teilschnittmaschine H-Luchs auch unter schwierigen Bedingungen einsetzbar ist. Aufgrund der Beweglichkeit dieser Maschine sind Abzweige, Aufweitungen und Übergänge ohne Schwierigkeiten aufgefahren worden. Geologiebedingt wird die Maschine demnächst erstmals in einem Tunnelteilstück unter Druckluft eingesetzt.

4. QUELLENVERZEICHNIS

Freytag, L. 1980, Streckenvortrieb mit Geräten und Einrichtungen der Westfalia Lünen, Referat am 3. Juni 1980 in Ostrava/CSSR, Westfalia Lünen, Lünen.

Leyendecker, Willy 1981, Tunnel unter dem Rhein zur Aufnahme von Versorgungs- und Entsorgungsleitungen, Mitteilungsblätter der Tiefbau-Berufsgenossenschaft, Heft 8/1981: 538-556, München.

* 5 *

ROCK MECHANICAL PROBLEMS IN ASSOCIATION WITH UNDERGROUND STORAGE

Felsmechanische Probleme im Zusammenhang mit der untertägigen Speicherung

Problèmes de mécanique des roches en relation avec le stockage souterrain

WP-CAVE FOR DRY UNDERGROUND STORAGE OF HIGH-LEVEL NUCLEAR WASTE

WP-Cave für trockene unterirdische Lagerung hoch radioaktiver Abfälle

Cave-WP pour le stockage souterrain à sec de déchets hautement radioactifs

BENGT Å.ÅKESON
Chalmers University of Technology, Gothenburg, Sweden
STEN G.A.BERGMAN
Stocksund, Sweden
K.IVAR SAGEFORS
WP-System AB, Stockholm, Sweden

SUMMARY

The WP-CAVE concept for long-term storage of spent nuclear fuel in an isolated rock cavern has been further developed. Installations and operations have been suggested for horizontal and vertical transportation and for remote handling and final emplacement of 10 years old spent fuel. The fuel assemblies are stored in the same condition as on their removal from the reactor (no encapsulation). The displacements and stress redistributions in the rock mass during the excavation and construction of a WP-CAVE have been calculated by use of the finite element method. The conclusion is that no extensive cracking due to tensile stresses or spalling due to excessive compressive stresses should be expected.

ZUSAMMENFASSUNG

Das Konzept WP-CAVE für die Einlagerung von gebrauchtem Kernbrennstoff in einer isolierten Felskaverne ist weiterentwickelt worden. Einrichtungen und Bedienungsverfahren werden für horizontale und vertikale Transporte und für Fernsteuerung und endgültige Unterbringung von 10-jährigem gebrauchtem Kernbrennstoff vorgeschlagen. Die Brennstoffelemente werden in demselben Zustand eingelagert wie sie aus dem Reaktor ausgenommen worden sind (kein Einkapseln). Die Verschiebungen und Spannungsumlagerungen in der Felsenmasse während des Ausbaues einer WP-CAVE sind mit der Methode der finiten Elemente berechnet worden. Die Schlussfolgerung ist dass keine umfassende Rissbildung wegen Zugspannungen oder Abplatzung infolge grosser Druckspannungen zu erwarten sind.

RESUME

Le concept de WP-CAVE pour le stockage de longue durée de combustible nucléaire usagé dans une caverne rocheuse isolée a été développé. Des installations et des operations ont été suggérées pour des transports horizontaux et verticaux et pour le pilotage à distance et l'emplacement final du combustible nucléaire de dix ans d'âge. Les batteries de combustible usagé sont stockées dans les mêmes conditions qu'à leur enlèvement du reacteur (pas d'enrobement). Les déplacements et les redistributions de tensions dans la masse rocheuse pendant l'excavation et construction d'une WP-CAVE ont été calculés par la méthode des éléménts finis. La conclusion est qu'aucune formation étendue de fissures due à des contraintes de tension et qu'aucun écaillement par des tensions de compression excessive ne sont attendues.

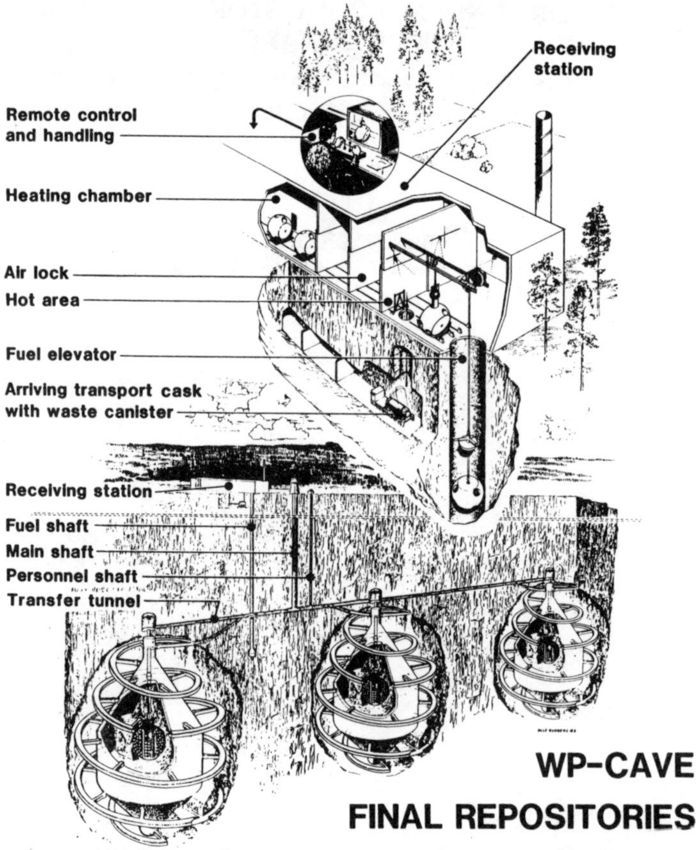

Fig. 1. Group of three (or more) WP-CAVEs and joint receiving station for spent nuclear fuel. Depth to centre of repository is 300 m. Diameter of central ball-filled cavern is 40 m. Surrounding clay barrier (watertight bentonite-quartz compound) has thickness 5 m. Its distance from cavern wall is 40 m. Cylindrical heat stack in porous cavern enhances natural convection of enclosed air (which evens out temperature peaks). Helical tunnel with horizontal adits is used during excavation only.

In receiving station, each concrete ball arrives on a rail-bound wagon and each waste canister in a radiation-shielded transport cask on a truck. Ball is slowly preheated before being remotely loaded with three waste canisters and being remotely lowered through fuel shaft to horizontal transfer tunnel.

One WP-CAVE can accommodate nuclear waste with a total initial thermal power of 300 kW. This means a storing capacity of one year's unreprocessed spent nuclear fuel (about 350 tons) from 12 nuclear 1000 MWe reactors when assuming 10 years of interim storage from time of removal of spent fuel from reactor.

Maximum bulk temperature of circulating air and maximum surface temperature of metal canisters in sealed and abandoned cavern have been calculated to be 200 °C and 330 °C, respectively. These maxima will be reached 10-15 years from time of deposition of waste and closure of cavern. Maximum temperature of clay barrier will be about 40 °C (after 50 years). Maximum increase of temperature at ground surface above WP-CAVE will be less than 1 °C.

Central cavern of WP-CAVE has been estimated to stay completely dry during about 1000 years. No groundwater flow through repository will occur within 100 000 years or more. WP-CAVE has been designed to permit easy retrieval of stored waste for a period of 200 years from time of deposition of waste-carrying balls in heat stack (and sealing of cavern and barrier). No monitoring from outside is needed at any time.

1 INTRODUCTION

The WP-CAVE storage facility (fig. 1) has been developed since 1976, see Åkesson, Bergman & Sagefors (1979, 1980, 1981). It

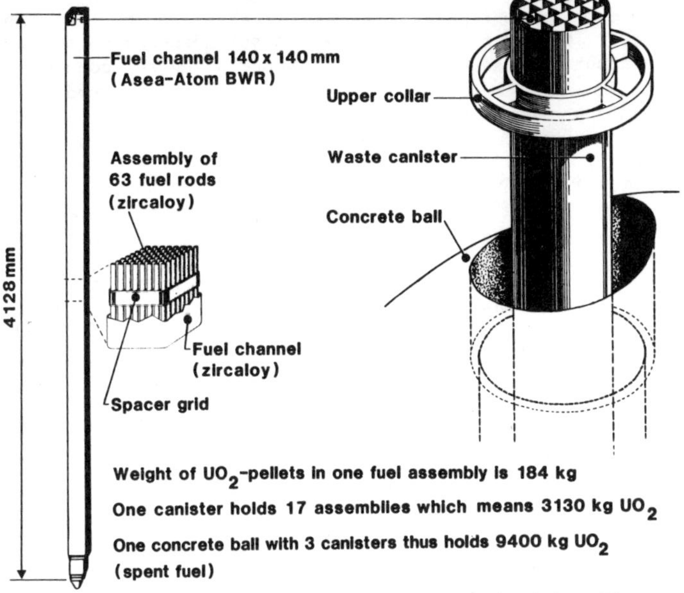

Fig. 2. Assemblies of spent nuclear fuel are taken directly from interim storage (for instance, from Swedish central storage facility CLAB) and are placed (after drying) in a specially designed cylindrical canister having a closed lower end and an open upper end. Fuel channels may or may not accompany assemblies in canister. Filled canister (with a provisional upper end cap) is transported to WP-CAVE receiving station where upper and lower collars are remotely mounted and fastened. Canister is then remotely inserted into hole of concrete ball (fig. 3) with collars resting on seating ledges (not shown).

One canister measures 4300 mm by 900 mm. It holds 3100 kg of spent nuclear fuel with initial thermal power 2.7 kW (10 years old fuel). One loaded canister weighs about 8 tons.

Fuel assemblies of BWR type have been considered in this example. Another canister design will be required for fuel assemblies of PWR type (cassette with 7 compartments instead of 17, etc).

intends to solve two of the most important technical problems met with in any scheme for underground disposal of nuclear wastes: how to keep the store dry for a long enough time and how to dispose of the residual heat during the first decades and centuries. Excessive moisture and heat would lead to corrosion of waste canisters unless a very heavy encapsulation were used. Further, the WP-CAVE admits of an easy retrieval of stored wastes during the first 200 years.

Because of the engineered clay barrier, which completely surrounds the central cavern of the sealed and abandoned repository, no rock "free from fissures" is needed for WP-CAVE. It has also been designed to withstand future fault movements and earthquakes. No monitoring from the outside is required at any time. Fig. 1 shows three WP-CAVEs and the pertinent text recapitulates some of the details. Further information can be found in the three reports referred to above where also the method of excavation and construction is accounted for.

The present report contains two parts: the first one discusses the transportation, handling and emplacement of the spent nuclear fuel, and the second summarizes rock mechanical calculations for the construction stages performed by use of the finite element method.

2 ABOVEGROUND TRANSPORTATION

The fuel elements are assumed to have been provisionally stored for 10 years after their removal from the nuclear reactor (for instance, at the Swedish central storage facility CLAB). In order to fix the ideas, the Asea-Atom fuel assemblies for boiling water reactors (BWR) will here be considered. At the interim storage, 17 assemblies of 63 fuel rods (in the as stored condition) are remotely placed in a specially manufactured open cylindrical canister as shown in fig. 2. One such canister will thus hold about 3100 kg of spent UO_2-pellets.

One loaded canister can now be placed in a standard transportation cask for nuclear fuel, see reports by KBS (1977, 1978) and Westinghouse (1979). The total weight of one loaded cask may be 80 tons. A special vehicle carries the cask to the receiving station of the WP-CAVEs. It is noted that the sealed cask is filled with inert gas of reduced pressure and has been designed to absorb and shield radiation, transmit and dissipate heat and withstand possible mechanical shocks.

3 CONCRETE BALLS

The manufacturing of the concrete balls has previously been discussed, see references. The balls will be made from reinforced heat-resistant concrete and they will be heat treated and cured. Fig. 3 shows a design of such balls adapted to the fuel elements and waste canisters in fig. 2. Each ready ball is placed on a rail-bound wagon in a supporting structure which can be tilted as shown in fig. 1. The ready balls are preheated.

4 RECEIVING STATION

Conventional arrangements with air locks and hot cell handling are applied at the receiving station, see fig. 1. The transport cask is raised to an upright position and a shielding sleeve is connected to its upper end before the lid of the cask is opened. The canister with its spent fuel assemblies (fig. 2) is hoisted into the hot cell space and the two collars are slipped onto the canister and fastened. The canister is then lowered into one vertical hole of a tilted concrete ball (fig. 3).

The next two arriving waste canisters are placed in the other two holes of the same concrete ball being tilted into new positions. Finally, the concrete ball with its three canisters is lifted from its support on the wagon, moved horizontally and lowered into the fuel shaft. Provisional shielding lids cover the upper and lower ends of the three holes of the ball.

Remote handling is needed during all the operations described above. Conventional decontamination will be required for the hot area before it can be reentered by operating personnel.

5 UNDERGROUND TRANSPORTATION

The fuel elevator in fig. 1 takes the loaded concrete ball down to a horizontal transfer tunnel connecting with the shafts of the WP-CAVEs. The ball is placed in a radiation-shielded box on a new rail-bound wagon. A central concrete wall divides the tunnel into two parallel parts. The concrete balls with their radioactive waste are transported on one side of the wall under surveillance by personnel from the other side. No serious contamination of the transportation space is foreseen.

In the space just above the specific WP-CAVE under loading the ball is lifted by a new traversing unit, the lids are removed and the ball is lowered into its final position in the heat stack in the central cavern as shown in fig. 4. Remote handling by use of TV-cameras is again necessary. A three-legged hydraulic unit as shown in fig. 4 may provide the exact positioning of the ball. Empty concrete balls shall be placed in the lowermost layer and also on top of the five or six layers of loaded balls in the heat stack.

The vertical shaft of the ball-filled

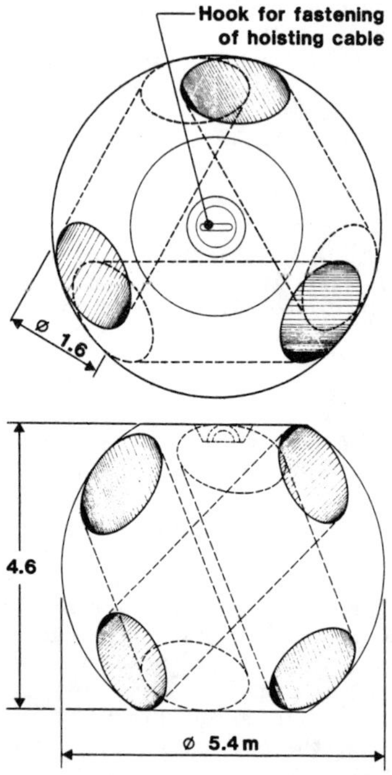

Fig. 3. Plan view and side view of concrete ball to be loaded with three waste canisters (fig. 2) in its three sloping holes (non-concurrent). If ordinary solid reinforced concrete is used, dead weight of one ball will be about 130 tons. Other solutions leading to a lighter ball may be possible. Each loaded canister with collars weighs about 10 tons.

WP-CAVE can now be sealed and the repository abandoned for ever. During the following 200 years, the sealing may be broken, the cavern reopened and the concrete balls with the spent fuel be retrieved (perhaps for reprocessing of the fuel by use of some today unknown technology). The procedure described above should then be applied in reverse.

6 ROCK MECHANICAL CALCULATIONS

A finite element calculation of displacements and stresses has been performed for the construction Stages 3, 4 and 6 of WP-CAVE as defined by Åkesson, Bergman & Sagefors (1979, 1980). The excavation starts from below. After Stage 3, the lower conical part of the 5 m wide slot for the clay barrier (fig. 1) has been excavated and successively back-filled with a compacted bentonite-quartz compound. After Stage 4, the vertical cylindrical part of the slot has been excavated and back-filled. Also the central cavern (diameter 40 m) has now been excavated. After Stage 6, the excavation and back-filling of WP-CAVE are complete.

The initial stresses (in situ stresses in the virgin rock mass) are taken as a vertical compression σ_{vi} balancing the overburden $\rho g h$ (ρg=27 kN/m^3) and a cylindrical horizontal compression

$$\sigma_{hi} = (6.0 + 0.05\ h\ (\text{metres}))\ \text{MPa}$$

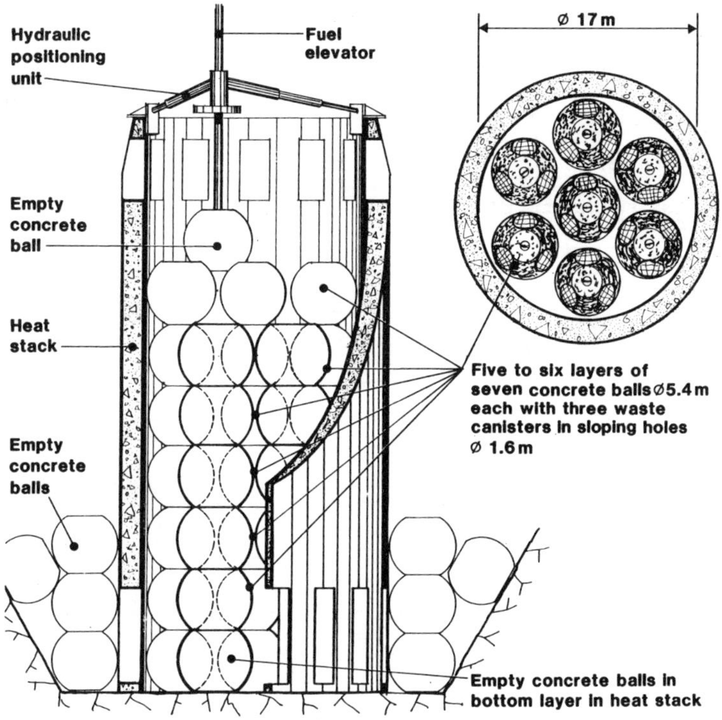

Fig. 4. Heat stack and concrete balls in central cavern of WP-CAVE (fig. 1). Displayed design is for 350 tons of spent nuclear fuel which is 10 years old at time of deposition. Balls outside stack are empty (and non-retrievable). They have been placed during construction of cavern and stack. Their functions is to prevent a mechanical collapse of cavern (as caused by compressive thermal stresses in rock wall, or by an earthquake). They shall permit a natural convection (downward) of heated air coming out from stack.

Balls inside stack are retrievable within first 200 years. After this period of time a gradual collapse of balls, stack and cavern (which will not affect integrity of clay barrier) can be accepted since residual heat production from stored nuclear waste will then have decayed to a small fraction of its initial value (300 kW).

After 100 years, sealing may be broken and repository reopened also for purpose of filling interior of cavern and stack with dry bentonite powder (or some other substance then available) thus creating an additional barrier for migrating radioactive particles.

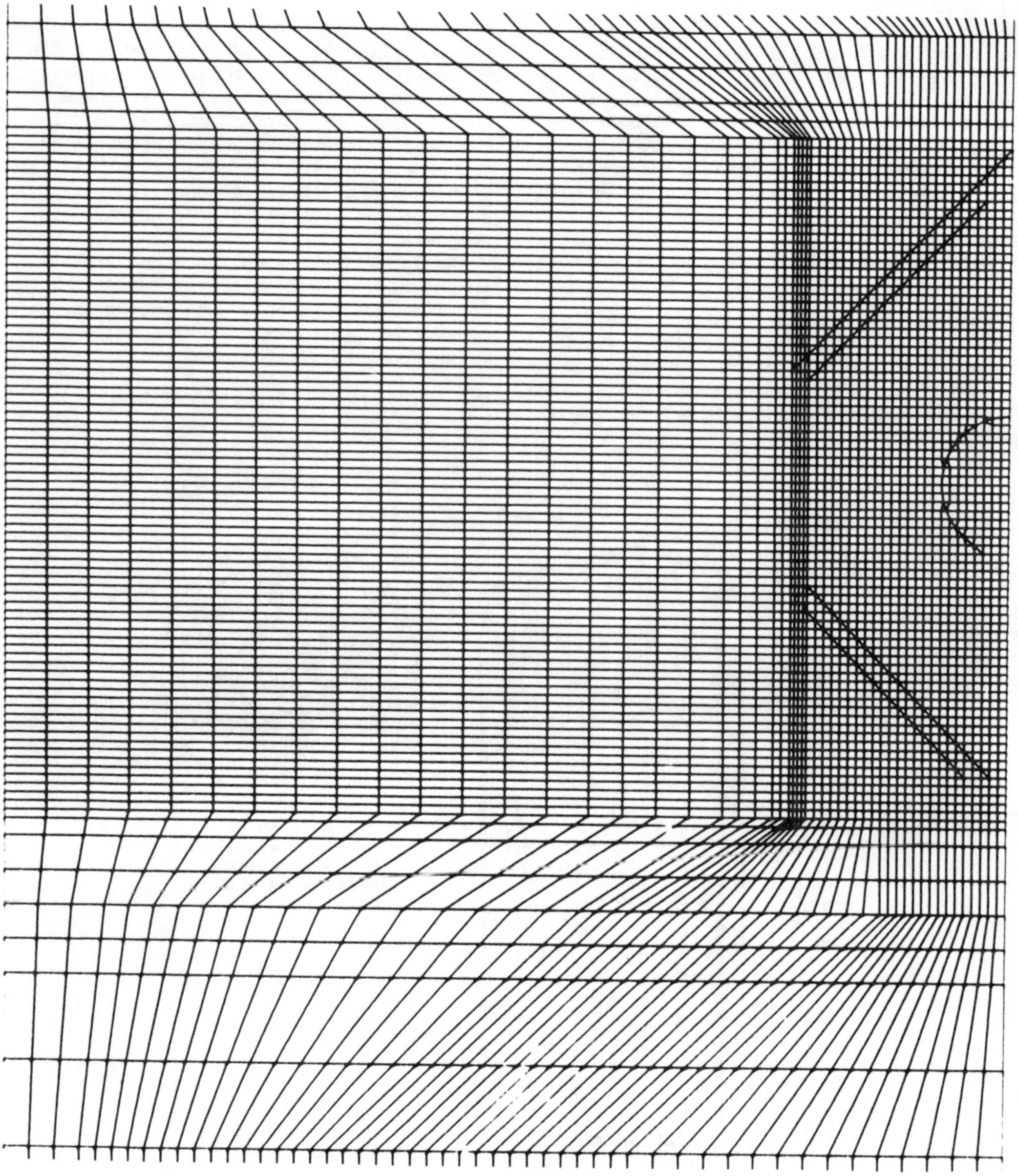

Fig. 5. Central portion of finite element mesh (partially distorted and supplemented rectangular mesh) used in calculation of displacements and stress redistributions during successive excavation (from below) of one WP-CAVE. Rotational symmetry is assumed. Left half of vertical plane through axis of symmetry is shown. Total number of nodes is 52×100=5200. Total number of elements (ring-shaped) is 51×99+99=5148. Cross-section of smallest rectangular element is 1.25×2.50 m^2. Total rock mass considered in calculation is a cylinder of radius 300 m and depth 595 m.

Future location of central cavern and slot for clay barrier can be seen (some rectangular elements have been subdivided into two triangular elements for adaption to sloping walls). Depth to centre of cavern is 300 m. Homogeneous isotropic precompressed (vertically and horizontally) linearly elastic material is assumed. During excavation, left boundary nodes are free to move vertically (but not horizontally). Bottom boundary nodes are free to move horizontally (but not vertically).

where h is the depth below ground. This uniform two-way compression σ_{hi} has been experimentally observed in the Näsliden mining project in northern Sweden, see Leijon, Carlsson & Myrvang (1981).

The centre of the cavern is located at the depth 300 m (the initial vertical and horizontal compressive stresses at this level thus being 8 MPa and 21 MPa, respectively). The total width and height of the rock mass body inside the slot are 120 m and 167.5 m, respectively.

7 ROCK MASS PROPERTIES

In this first approximate investigation, the rock mass and the back-fill will be modelled as homogeneous isotropic linearly elastic media. No swelling pressure of the clay material will be considered (it will not have developed as yet). Assumed values of the modulus of elasticity and the Poisson ratio are (r=rock mass, cl=clay barrier)

E_r = 40 GPa $\qquad \nu_r$ = 0.20

E_{cl} = 400 MPa $\qquad \nu_{cl}$ = 0.20

The same density is assumed for the rock mass and the clay barrier (ρ=2700 kg/m^3, g=10 N/kg).

8 CALCULATION MODEL

Rotational symmetry is presupposed, and a cylindrical rock mass body of radius 300 m and depth 595 m is considered. Ring-shaped finite elements with quadrilateral cross-sections are used. The shape functions for the displacement field are bilinear, or equal to those obtained through an isoparametric transformation of the bilinear rectangular element, see Cook (1981).

The finite element mesh chosen is reproduced in fig. 5. For the cylindrical rock mass body mentioned, the nodal displacements are horizontally locked (but vertically free) at the cylindrical boundary surface and vertically locked (but horizontally free) at the lower base surface. The calculations were performed by the Luleå University Computing Group for Rock Mechanics (P. Jonasson) with a new module (axisymmetric stress state) of the BEFEM code, see Groth (1981).

9 DISPLACEMENTS AND STRESSES AFTER STAGE 3

A zero initial displacement state and a nonzero initial stress state as described above formed the starting point for the calculations. The rock material (E_r, ν_r) in the lower conical part of the slot was replaced by the clay material (E_{cl}, ν_{cl}). This new structure was 'loaded' with the initial stresses of the remaining rock mass (no initial stresses in the part of the clay barrier now constructed). Thereby the successive excavation and successive back-filling were considered reasonably well approximated as to the gross behaviour of the rock masses within and around WP-CAVE. Local stress concentrations at the excavation front are as usual hard to estimate and no special regard was paid to them when choosing the finite element mesh.

Figs. 6, 7 and 8 display parts of the calculated and plotted displacement and stress fields. It is seen how the release of the initial compressive stresses in the excavated slot makes its two faces converge (fig. 6) and how this convergence will compress the clay material. The assumed relative stiffness (E_{cl}/E_r=0.40/40=1/100) is found (fig. 7) to be sufficiently high to prevent the creation of large tensile vertical stresses (which would have meant extensive horizontal cracking) in the lower part of the inner rock mass body. Also the circumferential confinement of this body is seen (fig. 8) to be enough to prevent the formation of large tensile hoop stresses (which would have meant extensive radial cracking).

The calculated stress concentrations (though inaccurate) at the excavation front are deemed to be of a magnitude which will cause no problems. Practical experience of this situation has been gained from ordinary cut and fill mining of much wider slots (20 m instead of 5 m).

The lack of calculated large tensile stresses indicates that the calculation model applied here (isotropic linearly elastic material) should provide a rather good approximation of the real behaviour of the rock mass and clay barrier. The moderate 'precompression' of the clay barrier (unswollen) after Stage 3 is only to be welcomed.

10 DISPLACEMENTS AND STRESSES AFTER STAGE 6

The calculated displacements and stresses after Stage 3 were used as initial values below. The rock material (E_r, ν_r) in the central cylindrical part of the slot was replaced by the clay material (E_{cl}, ν_{cl}) and all the finite elements in the central cavern were removed (attributed zero stiffness). This new structure was 'loaded' with the initial stresses of the remaining rock mass and with the initial stresses of the lower conical part of the clay barrier. Displacements and stresses were calculated (not shown here) after this Stage 4 and stored. Some vertical tensile stresses were observed after Stage 4 in a volume throughout the inner rock mass body

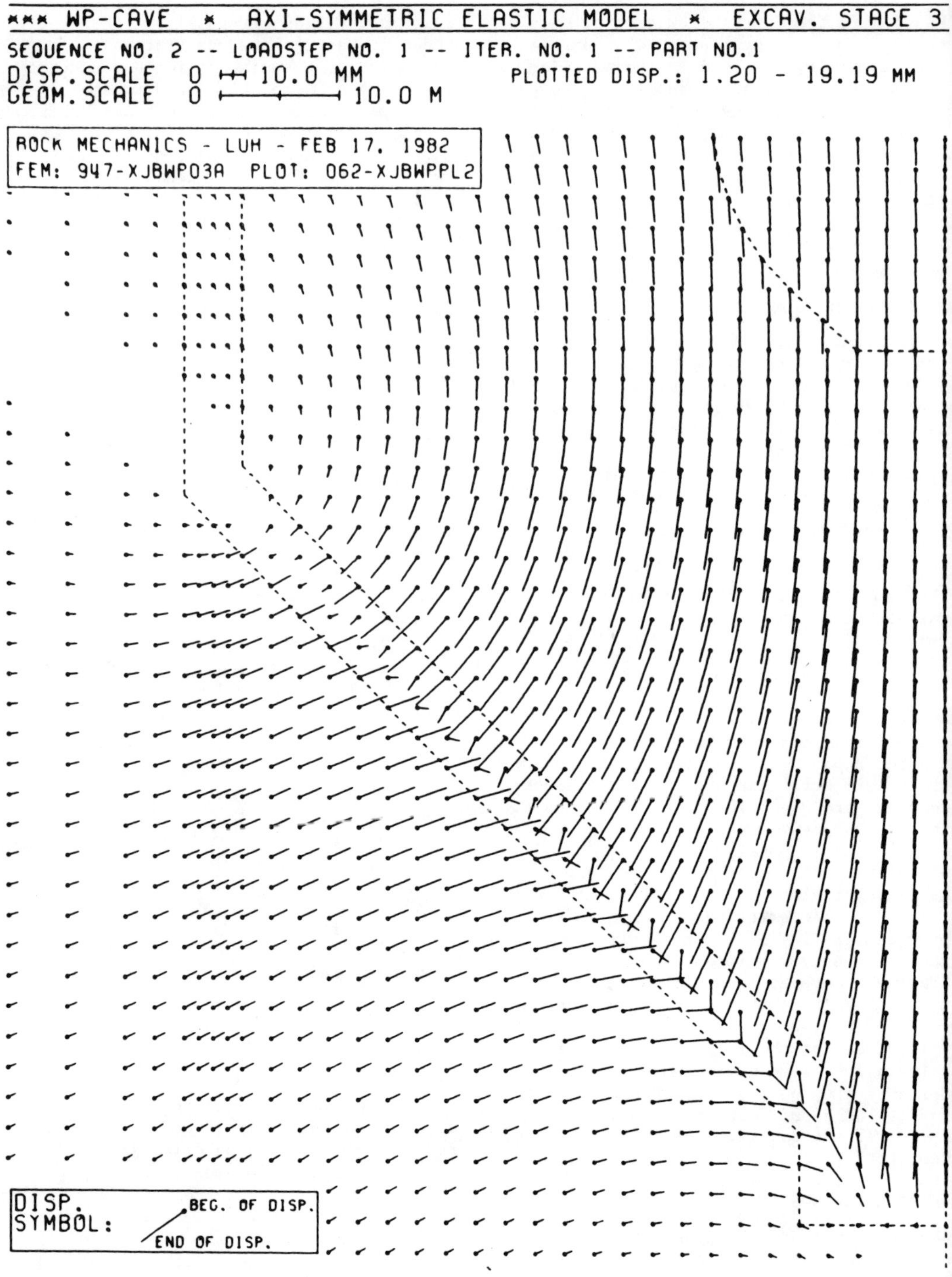

Fig. 6. Calculated magnitude and direction of nodal displacements in lower part of WP-CAVE (fig. 5) after excavation and backfilling of lower conical slot for clay barrier (Stage 3). Release of compressive initial stresses in slot during excavation is seen to make slot faces converge (as expected). Maximum vertical settlement of inner rock mass body is seen to be 18 mm.

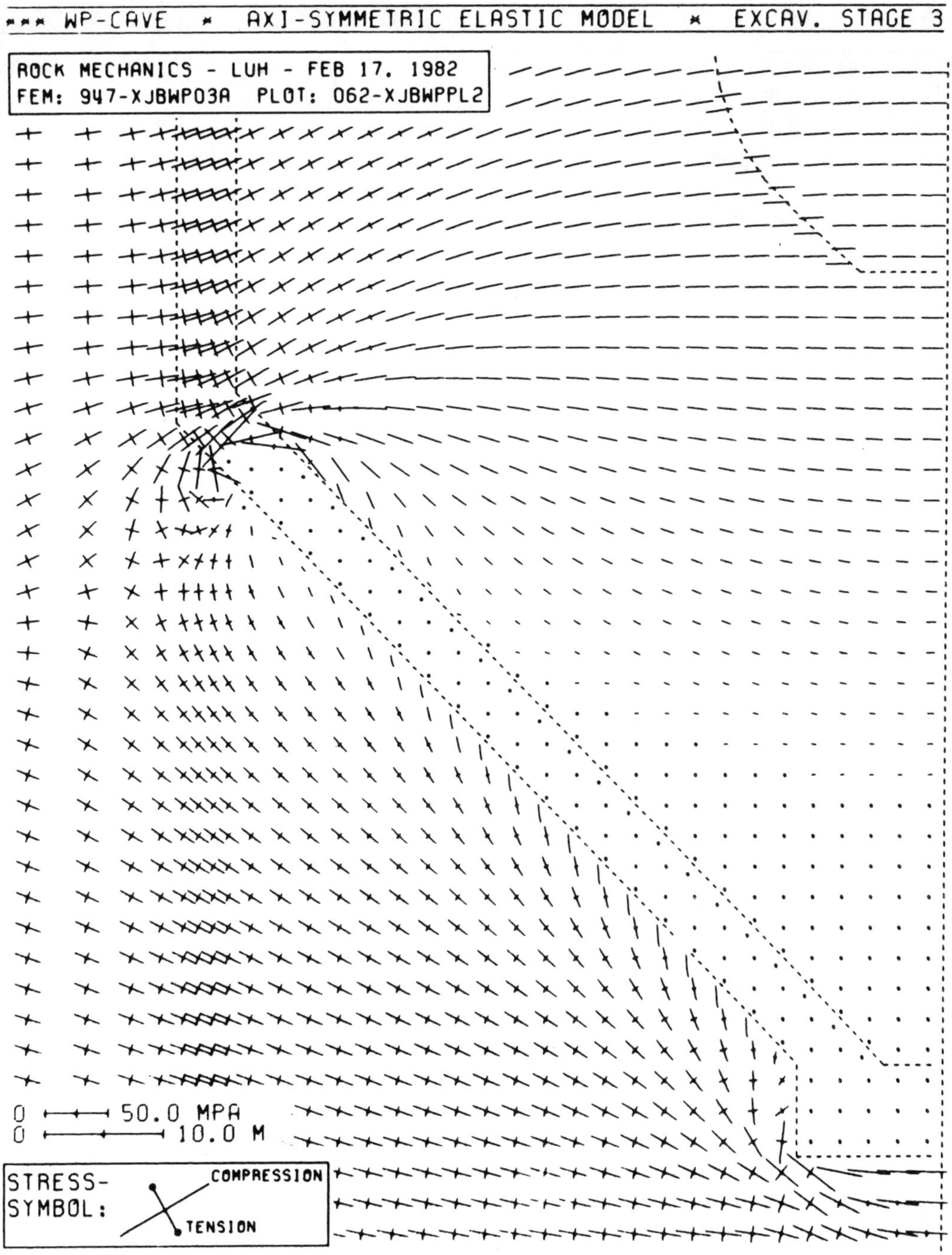

Fig. 7. Calculated magnitude and orientation of principal stresses (including initial stresses) in vertical plane of lower part of WP-CAVE (fig. 5) at midpoint of finite elements after excavation and back-filling of lower conical slot for clay barrier (Stage 3). Maximum compressive stress is seen to be 62 MPa. Only small tensile stresses are found (they are not visible in plot but can be read from printed output). Note that figs. 7 and 8 are complementary to each other.

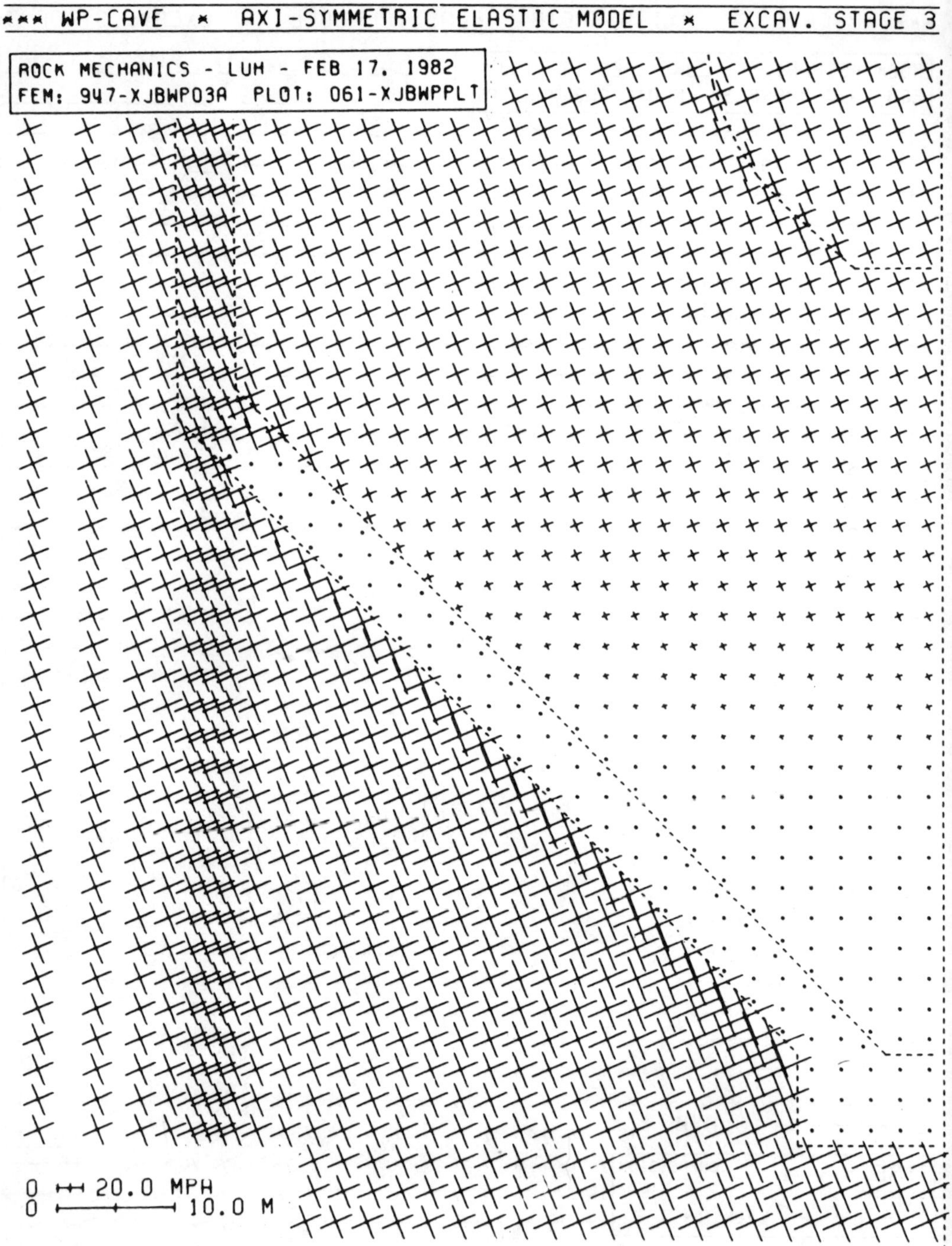

Fig. 8. Calculated magnitude of hoop stresses (including initial stresses) in lower part of WP-CAVE at midpoint of finite elements after excavation and back-filling of lower conical slot for clay barrier (Stage 3). Maximum compressive hoop stress is seen to be about 50 MPa (a doubling of initial value of hoop stress). No tensile hoop stresses are found. Magnitude of crosses (rotated for clarity) indicates magnitude of hoop stresses (acting perpendicularly to plane of figure).

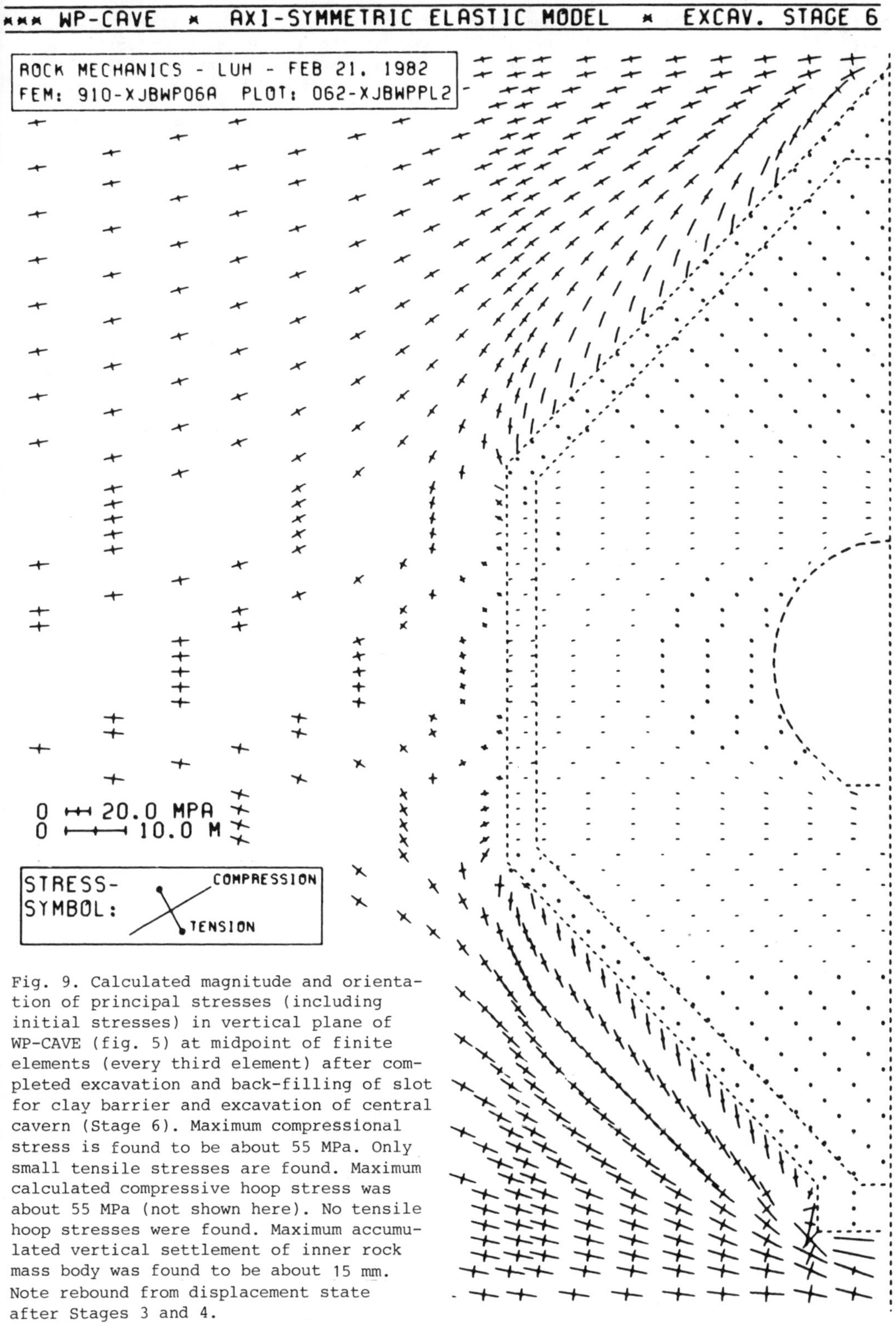

Fig. 9. Calculated magnitude and orientation of principal stresses (including initial stresses) in vertical plane of WP-CAVE (fig. 5) at midpoint of finite elements (every third element) after completed excavation and back-filling of slot for clay barrier and excavation of central cavern (Stage 6). Maximum compressional stress is found to be about 55 MPa. Only small tensile stresses are found. Maximum calculated compressive hoop stress was about 55 MPa (not shown here). No tensile hoop stresses were found. Maximum accumulated vertical settlement of inner rock mass body was found to be about 15 mm. Note rebound from displacement state after Stages 3 and 4.

at the level of the upper end of the cylindrical slot.

Finally, the above displacements and stresses (after Stage 4) were used as initial values for the last step of the calculations where the rock material (E_r, ν_r) in the upper conical part of the slot was replaced by the clay material (E_{cl}, ν_{cl}). Fig. 9 shows one plotted result from this calculation of the displacement and stress fields after Stage 6.

Only small tensile stresses were found after Stage 6 which once more justifies the calculation model used. The small compressive horizontal stresses (2-3 MPa) seen in the inner rock mass and in the clay barrier should be altogether beneficial for the stability of the central cavern. A limited horizontal cracking (opening-up of existing horizontal fissures) in the inner rock mass is predicted by the present analysis.

The calculated maximum vertical settlement and radial expansion of the inner rock mass are about 15 mm (a rebound as compared to Stage 3) and 20 mm, respectively. These are deemed to be very reasonable values. The total inward movement of the outer rock mass is maximally 23 mm along the cylindrical part of the slot. The level of the calculated compressive hoop stresses (50-60 MPa) in the outer wall of the slot is such that no serious problems with spalling should occur.

On the whole, the present finite element calculations confirm the rough estimates previously made about settlements and stresses, see Åkesson, Bergman & Sagefors (1979, 1980). The lay-out of WP-CAVE is judged to be rather favourable from the rock mechanical point of view. The problems predicted for the excavation and caused by the settlement of the inner rock mass would rather seem to be less than those commonly encountered in standard upward cut and fill mining under the same in situ stress conditions.

11 CONCLUDING REMARKS

A sequence of proposed installations and operations for the transportation, handling and emplacement of 10 years old spent nuclear fuel in WP-CAVE has been described. Rock mechanical calculations by use of the finite element method have been carried out for the construction stages of WP-CAVE. These calculations demonstrate a rather favourable geometrical shape of the slot for the clay barrier and of the central cavern. The conclusion so far is that no serious problems should be expected during the construction and operation of WP-CAVE.

It might be added here that the estimated cost of the WP-CAVE storage facility as described above is 1.1 mil of a US dollar per kWhe produced by the nuclear reactors. It might also be stated once more that a free site selection in good quality rock mass (granite, etc.) is made possible by WP-CAVE - it will require no rock volume which has been preinspected to be 'free from fissures'.

12 REFERENCES

Åkesson, B.Å., S.G.A. Bergman & K.I. Sagefors 1979, WP-CAVE for underground disposal of high-level nuclear waste. WP-System AB, 104 30 Stockholm, 52 pp.

Åkesson, B.Å., S.G.A. Bergman & K.I. Sagefors 1980, WP-CAVE - A new concept for underground high-level nuclear waste repository, Subsurface Space, Proceedings of the International Symposium Rockstore '80, Stockholm, vol. 2, pp. 791-800 (includes references to previous reports).

Åkesson, B.Å., S.G.A. Bergman & K.I. Sagefors 1981, Caves for safe long-term storage of nuclear wastes, Tunnels & Tunnelling, vol. 13, no. 11, pp. 13-15 (see also vol. 13, no. 10, p. 5, and vol. 14, no. 1, pp. 13-18).

Bärring, J., H. Johansson, P. Olowson & P. Swenzén 1981, Placing nuclear fuel elements in a dry final repository (in Swedish). Department of Mechanical Engineering (Division of Solid Mechanics), Chalmers University of Technology, Gothenburg, 52 pp.

Cook, R.D. 1981, Concepts and applications of finite element analysis, 2nd ed. Wiley, New York, 558 pp.

Groth, T. 1981, Description and applicability of the BEFEM code. In O. Stephansson & M.J. Jones (eds.), Application of rock mechanics to cut and fill mining (Proceedings of a conference at The University of Luleå in June 1980), pp. 204-208, The Institution of Mining and Metallurgy, London.

KBS (Nuclear Fuel Safety Project) 1977 & 1978, Handling of spent nuclear fuel and final storage of vitrified high level reprocessing waste (vols. I to IV), and Handling and final storage of unreprocessed spent nuclear fuel (vols. I and II). Stockholm, 436 & 508 pp.

Leijon, B., H. Carlsson & A. Myrvang 1981, Stress measurements in Näsliden mine. In O. Stephansson & M.J. Jones (see above), pp. 162-168.

Westinghouse 1979, Spent fuel handling and packaging program (E-MAD facility, Jackass Flats, Nevada). Westinghouse Advanced Energy Systems Division, 111 pp.

ZUR ENTWICKLUNG VON RECHENMODELLEN ZUR ABSCHÄTZUNG DER THERMOMECHANISCHEN AUSWIRKUNGEN EINES ENDLAGERS FÜR RADIOAKTIVE ABFÄLLE IM SALZGEBIRGE

Evaluation of the thermomechanical response in a repository for radioactive wastes in a salt dome by the development of computing models

Développement de modèles de calcul pour l'estimation des effets thermomécaniques d'un dépôt définitif pour les déchets radioactifs dans un terrain salifère

G.ALBERS & C.EHLERT
Rheinisch-Westfälische Technische Hochschule Aachen, Bundesrepublik Deutschland

SUMMARY:
In the Federal Republic of Germany it is provided to dispose of the radioactive wastes from nuclear power plants in a repository within a salt dome. Because of the radioactive decay heat the salt dome will be heated, which a. o. results in thermal stress-strain-fields. Therefore the mechanical integrity and the maintenance of the barrier-function of the rock has to be ensured by use of suitable calculational models.
The problematic nature of such models is explained by describing the German concept for the ultimate storage facility for high-level radioactive wastes (HAW) and the principal calculational strategy. Furthermore the actual state of model development and some calculational results are presented.

Zusammenfassung:
In der Bundesrepublik Deutschland ist zur Beseitigung des bei der friedlichen Nutzung der Kernenergie anfallenden radioaktiven Abfalls dessen Endlagerung im Salzgebirge vorgesehen. Aufgrund der radioaktiven Nachzerfallswärme wird das Salzgebirge aufgeheizt, was u. a. zum Aufbau von Thermospannungs- und Thermodehnungsfeldern führt. Die Gewährleistung der Integrität und damit der Barrierenfunktion des Gesteins ist mittels geeigneter Rechenmodelle nachzuweisen.
Die Problemstellung wird anhand des deutschen Endlagerkonzepts für hochradioaktiven Abfall (HAW) und der grundsätzlichen Rechenstrategie erläutert. Anschließend werden der derzeitige Stand der Modellentwicklung und mittels ausgewählter Beispiele einige Rechenergebnisse vorgestellt.

RESUME:
En République Fédérale d'Allemagne il est prévu de faire le stockage final des déchets radioactifs, qui sont causé par l'utilisation de la puissance nucléaire, dans un dépôt final dans des formations salines diapiriques. Le dome de sel est échauffé de la chaleur de décroissance des nucléides radioactifs. Cela mène à la formation des tensions et déformations thermiques. L'intégrité et l'indemnité de la barrière géologique doit être prouvée par l'emploie des modèles numériques appropriés.
Le caractère problématique de ces modèles est discuté à l'exemple de la conception allemande pour le stockage final des déchets de haute activité (angl.: HAW) et à la stratégie fondamentale de la calculation numérique. Ensuite la situation actuelle de la developpement des modèles pour la calculation numérique et quelques résultats de calculation sont présentés.

1 EINLEITUNG

Die friedliche Nutzung der Kernenergie ist in den letzten Jahren Gegenstand z. T. harter öffentlicher Auseinandersetzung geworden. Die Kritik konzentriert sich zunehmend auf die - zur Rückgewinnung des noch spaltbaren Materials - geplante Wiederaufarbeitung abgebrannter Brennelemente und besonders auf die Beseitigung des anfallenden radioaktiven

Abfalls. Während auf die Wiederaufarbeitung notfalls verzichtet werden könnte, ist die Beseitigung der Abfälle zwingend notwendig.

Ziel der Beseitigung der radioaktiven Abfälle ist es, letztere während des Zeitraums ihrer Radiotoxizität von der Lebenssphäre des Menschen fernzuhalten. Nachdem zahlreiche Vorschläge (z. B. Versenkung im Meer, Abschuß in den Weltraum) diskutiert wurden, wird nunmehr weltweit die Endlagerung in geologischen Formationen als die beste Möglichkeit angesehen. Als Wirtsgestein wird dabei u. a. in der Bundesrepublik Deutschland Salzgestein bevorzugt, da es die a priori an das aufnehmende Gestein zu stellenden, qualitativen Forderungen unter Sicherstellung der Barrierenfunktion am besten erfüllen dürfte (Venzlaff (1978)). Andere Konzepte (Granit, Ton) werden meist von solchen Ländern (Schweden, Belgien) untersucht, die nicht über ausreichende Salzlagerstätten verfügen.

Die Barrierenfunktion des Salzgesteins kann neben geologischen Instabilitäten (vgl. z. B. Dtsch. Geol. Ges. (1980)) durch den Eingriff in das natürliche System beeinträchtigt werden. Durch die Erstellung von Grubengebäuden, besonders aber durch die Aufheizung des Gebirges infolge der Nachzerfallswärme der eingebrachten radioaktiven Spaltprodukte werden Thermospannungs- und Thermodehnungsfelder erzeugt. Diese thermomechanischen Zusatzbelastungen könnten bei Überschreiten von Grenzwerten die Integrität des Salzstocks gefährden.

Die hohen Sicherheitsanforderungen an ein solches Endlager erfordern die hinreichend genaue Vorhersage der zu erwartenden thermomechanischen Auswirkungen, wobei wegen des zu betrachtenden großen Zeitraums (z. B. 10 000 Jahre) der Berechnung mittels geeigneter Modelle besondere Bedeutung zukommt. Darüberhinaus können Vorausberechnungen wertvolle Hinweise bezüglich einer optimalen Auslegung eines Endlagers geben.

Am Lehrauftrag Leistungsreaktoren wurde vor ca. 20 Jahren mit der Entwicklung von Rechenmodellen zur Ermittlung der zu erwartenden Temperaturverteilungen in einem Endlager für radioaktive Abfälle begonnen. Seit einigen Jahren wird parallel zu dieser inzwischen als nahezu abgeschlossen zu betrachtenden Entwicklung an der Erstellung eines Recheninstrumentariums (MAUS-Mechanical Analysis of Underground Storage) zur Spannungs- und Verformungsanalyse gearbeitet.*

Ziel des Vortrags ist es, die damit verbundene Problematik anhand des deutschen Endlagerkonzeptes und der grundsätzlichen Rechenstrategie zu erläutern. Anschließend werden der derzeitige Stand der Modellentwicklung und mittels einiger ausgewählter Beispiele erste Rechenergebnisse vorgestellt.

2 PROBLEMSTELLUNG

Die radioaktiven Abfälle werden je nach ihrer Radiotoxizität anhand der drei Kategorien leicht-, mittel- und hochaktiv unterschieden und für jede Kategorie ist eine spezifische Konditionierung und Lagerung der Abfälle vorgesehen (DWK (1977)). Da der größte Teil der freigesetzten Wärme aus dem hochradioaktiven Abfall (HAW: high-level radioactive waste) stammt, werden die folgenden Ausführungen - soweit sie das Endlagerkonzept betreffen - auf die Abfallkategorie beschränkt.

Unter der Voraussetzung, daß die abgebrannten Brennelemente wieder aufgearbeitet werden, soll der wärmefreisetzende HAW nach dem deutschen Endlagerkonzept in zylindrische Borosilikatgläser eingebunden werden. Die Glaskörper werden in Edelstahl-Kokillen (Durchmesser 20-40 cm, Höhe: 1 m) eingebracht, welche schließlich in das Endlager transportiert werden.

Eine denkbare Anordnung eines Endlagers in einem Salzstock ist in Abb. 1 qualitativ wiedergegeben. Der mehr oder weniger homogene Salzstock ist von verschiedenen Neben- und Deckgesteinen umgeben und enthält in einer möglichst homogenen Steinsalzpartie das eigentliche Endlager. Letzteres besteht aus einem Streckensystem, von welchem aus Bohrlöcher niedergebracht werden, die ihrerseits die Kokillen mit dem HAW aufnehmen (vgl. Einzelheit A in Abb. 1). Nach der Verfüllung der Bohrlöcher werden diese versiegelt und die entsprechende Strecke sukzessive mit Salzgruß verfüllt.

Bei Beachtung der Abb. 1 und des beschriebenen Endlagerkonzeptes wird deutlich, daß im wesentlichen

a.) der Endlagerstandort

b.) die Endlagerauslegung

die thermomechanischen Auswirkungen im Salzstock bestimmen. Nach der Festlegung eines Endlagerstandortes sind die spezifischen Salzstockeigenschaften (z. B. Salzstockgeometrie, thermomechanische Stoffdaten) vorgegeben. Demgegenüber kann die Endlagerauslegung (z. B. Spaltproduktkonzentration im Abfallgebinde, Bohrlochlänge, Bohrlochabstand) in gewissen Grenzen frei gewählt und

---

*Die Arbeiten wurden im Auftrag des Kernforschungszentrums Karlsruhe und der Gesellschaft für Strahlen- und Umweltforschung in Zusammenarbeit mit der Kommission der Europäischen Gemeinschaften durchgeführt.

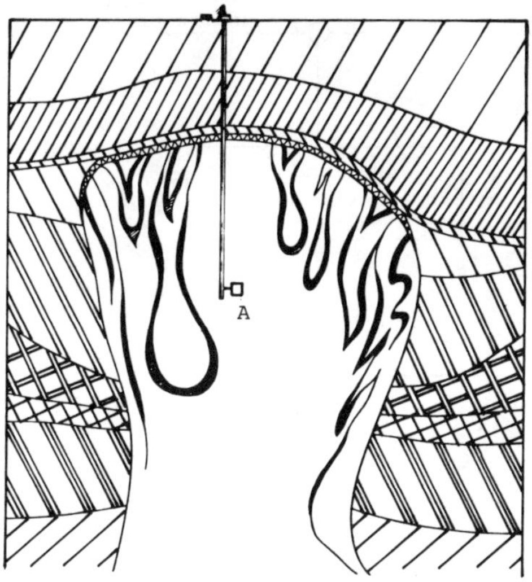

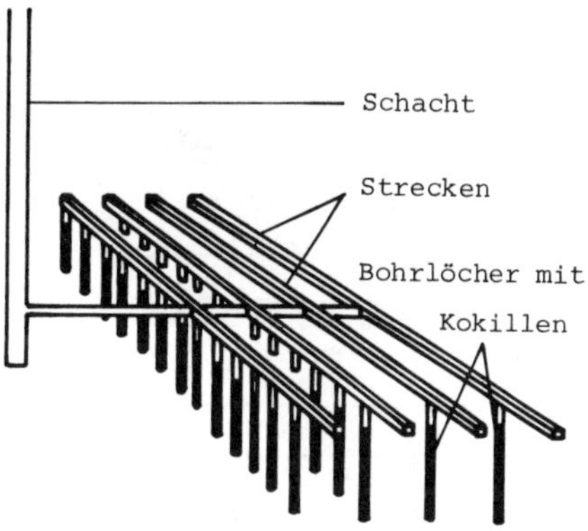

Abb. 1: Eine denkbare Anordnung eines Endlagers für hochradioaktiven Abfall (HAW) in einem Salzstock.

somit indirekt Einfluß auf die sich nach der Einlagerung einstellenden Temperatur-, Spannungs- und Dehnungsfelder genommen werden. Als Beispiel dafür sind in Abb. 2 die maximalen Salztemperaturen dargestellt, die sich nach Ploumen (1980 b) bei unterschiedlichen Anfangswärme(stab)leistungen, Bohrlochlängen

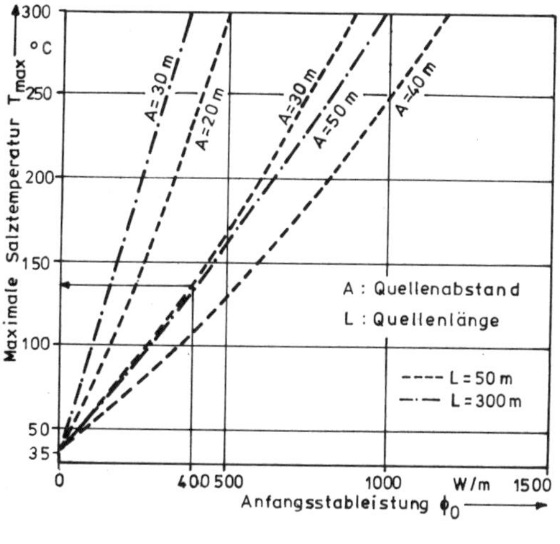

Abb. 2: Maximale Endlagertemperaturen in Abhängigkeit verschiedener Endlagerungsparameter.

und -abständen für HAW-Kokillen mit einem Durchmesser von 20 cm einstellen.

Zusammenfassend ergibt sich aus obigen Überlegungen die in Abb. 3 gezeigte prinzipielle Vorgehensweise bei der Spannungs- und Verformungsanalyse.

Ausgehend von den speziellen Eigenschaften des Endlagerstandortes und den vorgegebenen Endlagerauslegungsdaten werden zunächst die orts- und zeitabhängigen Temperaturfelder ermittelt. Anschließend erfolgt die Berechnung der thermomechanischen Belastungen, wobei die spezifischen Standort- und Auslegungsdaten sowie die nun bekannten Temperaturverteilungen hinreichend genau erfaßt werden müssen.

Die bei der Spannungs- und Verformungsanalyse erhaltenen Ergebnisse sind anhand geeigneter Sicherheitskriterien zu beurteilen. Werden die vorzugebenden Sicherheitskriterien erfüllt, so ist die Rechnung beendet; andernfalls sind die Endlagerspezifikationen in einem quasi-iterativen Prozeß solange zu variieren, bis die thermomechanischen Belastungen den vorgegebenen Sicherheitskriterien genügen.

Es muß ausdrücklich betont werden, daß die Ergebnisse der Spannungs- und Verformungsanalyse nur ein Kriterium für die Endlagerauslegung darstellen. Andere, die Endlagerspezifikationen beeinflußende Kriterien (z. B. Chemie, Laugenmigration) sind jedoch nicht

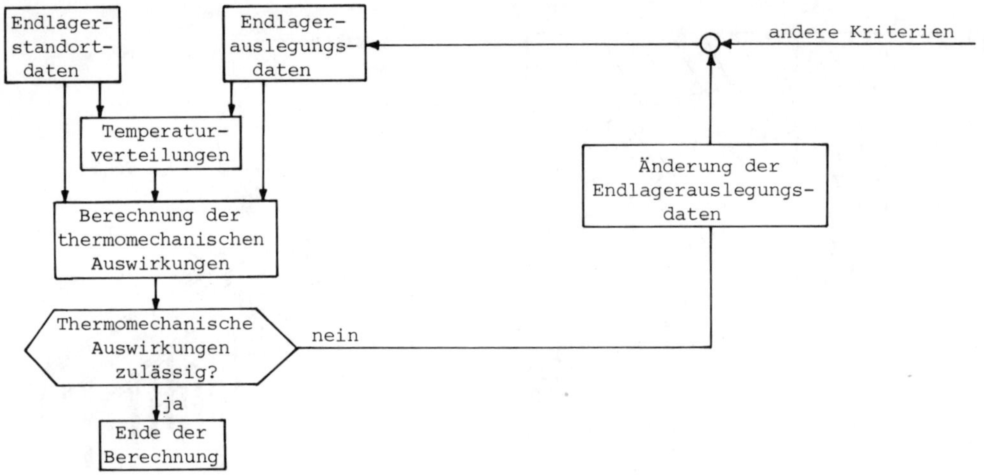

Abb. 3: Flußdiagramm zur Berechnung der thermomechanischen Auswirkungen in einem Salzstock nach der Endlagerung von HAW.

Gegenstand der hier beschriebenen Arbeiten und werden daher nicht weiter berücksichtigt.

3 ANFORDERUNGEN AN DIE RECHENMODELLE UND DERZEITIGER ENTWICKLUNGSSTAND

Die wesentlichen Anforderungen an die Rechenmodelle - wie sie sich aus der prinzipiellen Vorgehensweise entsprechend Abb. 3 ergeben - und der derzeitige Entwicklungsstand von MAUS sollen im folgenden etwas detaillierter beschrieben werden. Hierzu erscheint es zweckmäßig, die wesentlichen Eingangsgrößen für die Spannungs- und Verformungsanalyse

- Endlagerauslegungsdaten
- Temperaturverteilung
- Endlagerstandortdaten

getrennt zu charakterisieren und durch Gegenüberstellung des jeweiligen Entwicklungsstandes Tendenzen für zukünftige Modellerweiterungen aufzuzeigen.

3.1 Endlagerauslegungsdaten

Für die Entwicklung von Rechenmodellen ist die Kenntnis des qualitativen Charakters der Endlagerauslegung von Bedeutung, nicht aber die Kenntnis eines konkreten, quantitativ festgelegten Konzepts. Unter diesem Aspekt wird die Endlagerauslegung im wesentlichen durch

- die Endlagergeometrie
- die Abfallzusammensetzung
- die eingebrachten Fremdmaterialien

bestimmt.

Das Rechenmodell muß den verschiedenen Grundgeometrien (z. B. Bohrloch, Strecke) und deren Kombination (Anordnung im Endlager) gerecht werden, weshalb die Methode der Finiten Elemente als Basis für die Programmentwicklung ausgewählt wurde. Zur Zeit existieren von MAUS Versionen des ebenen Spannungs- und des ebenen Dehnungszustands sowie eine rotationssymmetrische. An die Implementierung dreidimensionaler Elemente ist gedacht, jedoch erscheint aufgrund der hohen Rechenzeiten und damit hohen Rechenkosten eine Anwendung nur in wenigen, besonders interessierenden Fällen sinnvoll.

Die Abfallzusammensetzung bestimmt den zeitabhängigen Wärmeeintrag und die Bestrahlung des umgebenden Materials. Die Wirkung des ersten Aspektes wird bei der Ermittlung der Temperaturverteilung (s. Kap. 3.2) berücksichtigt und die Rückwirkung auf die Spannungs- und Dehnungsfelder mittels der temperaturabhängigen Formulierung der Stoffgleichungen (s. Kap. 3.3) erfaßt. Ein möglicher, lokal begrenzter Strahlungseinfluß auf das Deformations- und Festigkeitsverhalten von Steinsalz wird im Rechenmodell zur Zeit nicht berücksichtigt.

Die Art der eingebrachten Fremdmaterialien (z. B. Kokillen-Material, Versatzmaterial) ist durch geeignete Materialgesetze zu simulieren. In Kap. 3.3 wird ausführlich das für Steinsalz abgeleitete und in MAUS implementierte Stoffgesetz beschrieben. Es kann davon ausgegangen werden, daß dieses Gesetz (oder Teile desselben) das Verhalten der meisten Fremdmaterialien qualitativ mit einschließt. Eine Ausnahme stellt z. B. das Versatzmaterial dar, welches aufgrund seines Porenvolumens zunächst auch irreversibel komprimiert wird. Dieser Effekt wurde jedoch bei der Formulierung des Materialgesetzes für Steinsalz - weil er dort nicht relevant ist - nicht berücksichtigt (vgl. Kap. 3.3), so daß entsprechende Weiterentwicklungen notwendig sind und zur Zeit durchgeführt werden.

3.2 Temperaturverteilungen

Eine der wesentlichen Eingangsgrößen für die Spannungs- und Verformungsanalyse ist die sich infolge der Wärmeproduktion des HAW einstellende Zeit- und ortsabhängige Temperaturverteilung im Salzgebirge und den übrigen Gebirgsbildnern. Erhöhte Gebirgstemperaturen wirken sich unmittelbar über die thermische Dehnung und mittelbar über die Änderung der Stoff- und Festigkeitseigenschaften der Gesteine auf die Spannungs- und Verformungsfelder aus.

Seit Anfang der sechziger Jahre werden daher Forschungs- und Entwicklungsarbeiten zur Erstellung eines geeigneten Recheninstrumentariums zur Bestimmung der Temperaturfelder durchgeführt. Die entwickelten Programme basieren auf der Finite-Differenzen-Methode oder dem Grobmaschenverfahren, wobei letzteres einer speziellen Form der Finiten-Elemente-Methode entspricht. Da die thermischen Stoffwerte ihrerseits mehr oder weniger starke Temperaturabhängigkeit aufweisen, müssen nichtlineare Gleichungssysteme gelöst werden. Abgesehen von der notwendigen Anpassung an zu untersuchende Spezialfälle (z. B. Nachrechnung von Versuchseinlagerungen) kann die Programmerstellung als abgeschlossen betrachtet werden. Ein informativer Überblick über die Grundlagen und Anwendung der Programme findet sich in Ploumen (1977, 1979, 1980 a, 1980 b).

Für die Verwendung der errechneten Temperaturverteilungen als Eingangsgrößen für MAUS ist eine entsprechende Kompatibilität zwischen den Programmen zu gewährleisten. Zu diesem Zweck wurde ein Algorithmus zur räumlichen und zeitlichen Interpolation erstellt.

3.3 Endlagerstandortdaten

Die Höhe der zu erwartenden Thermospannungen und -dehnungen und der Grad der durch sie entstehenden Integritätsgefährdung hängen wesentlich von den thermomechanischen Eigenschaften des Gesteinssystems ab. Abb. 1 ist zu entnehmen, daß letzteres i. a. aus verschiedenen standortspezifischen Materialien, welche zudem geometrisch kompliziert zueinander angeordnet sein können, aufgebaut ist. Es ist daher zweckmäßig, daß Gesteinssystem in verschiedene Teilbereiche aufzuteilen und zumindest die wesentlichen Gebirgsbildner in Geometrie und Stoffverhalten explizit zu berücksichtigen.

Die sich aus dieser Vorgehensweise ergebenden geometrischen Verhältnisse lassen sich durch Verwendung Finiter Elemente theoretisch beliebig genau nachbilden. Analog zu Kap. 3.1 wird jedoch auch hier der Detaillierungsgrad durch die beschränkte Rechnerkapazität und besonders durch die hohen Rechenkosten beschränkt, weshalb zur Zeit nur zweidimensionale Rechnungen sinnvoll erscheinen.

Zur Beschreibung des Stoffverhaltens des Gesamtgebirges ergibt sich aus der oben beschriebenen Aufteilung des Gebirges in verschiedene Materialzonen die in Abb. 4 gezeigte Vorgehensweise.
Das Stoffverhalten des Gesamtgebirges wird durch Stoffgesetze für die verschiedenen, homogen vorausgesetzten Materialzonen und das Stoffverhalten an den Grenzflächen zwischen zwei benachbarten Materialien beschrieben. Diese Unterscheidung ist notwendig, da die bei Spannungs- und Verformungsanalysen i. a. zugrundegelegte Kontinuumstheorie an den Grenzflächen möglicherweise nicht mehr zutrifft, wenn z. B. das Öffnen einer Kluft oder das gegenseitige Abgleiten benachbarter Materialien auftritt. Werden infolge der thermomechanischen Belastungen

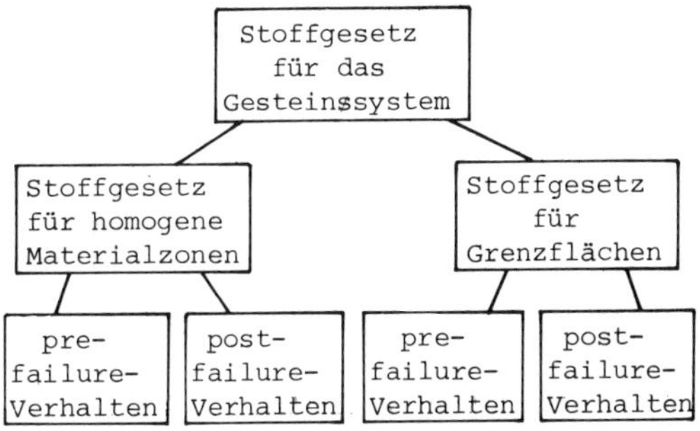

Abb. 4: Zur Modellierung des Stoffverhaltens des Gesamtgebirges.

Elastisches Verhalten	Kompressionsmodul K = konst. Schubmodul $G(T) = C_1 \; (1 - C_2(T - 273\ K))$ linearer thermischer Ausdehnungskoeffizient α = konst.
Plastisches Verhalten	$\varepsilon^{pl}_{eff} = C_3 \left(\frac{\sigma_{eff}}{1bar}\right)^{C_4} (1 - C_5(T - 273\ K))^{C_6}$
Visko-plastisches Verhalten	$\dot{\varepsilon}^{vpl}_{eff} = \dot{\varepsilon}^{sec}_{eff} \left(1 + < C_7 - \frac{\varepsilon^{vpl}_{eff}}{C_8\ \dot{\varepsilon}^{sec}_{eff}} >\right)$ mit $\dot{\varepsilon}^{sec}_{eff} = C_9 \frac{G(T)}{T} \left(\frac{\sigma_{eff}}{G(T)}\right)^{C_{10}} \exp\left(-\frac{C_{11}}{T}\right)$ und < > = < > wenn < > größer oder gleich 0.0 < > = 0.0 wenn < > kleiner als 0.0
Visko-elastisches Verhalten	$G(t-t_o;T) = C_{12} \; (1 - C_2(T - 273\ K)) + \sum_{j=13}^{14} C_j \exp\left[-\frac{t-t_o}{\tau_j/\varphi(T)}\right]$

Abb. 5: Stoffgesetz für Steinsalz

gebietsweise die gültigen Festigkeitsgrenzen überschritten, so ändert sich das Stoffverhalten in diesen Gebieten. Daraus folgt die Notwendigkeit, jeweils noch zwischen dem Bereich unterhalb von Festigkeitsgrenzen (pre-failure-Bereich) und oberhalb von Festigkeitsgrenzen (post-failure-Bereich) zu unterscheiden. Ziel der Entwicklung eines umfassenden Rechenmodells muß es sein, diese Verhaltensweise richtig wiederzugeben.

Ausgehend von dieser Zielvorstellung wurde zunächst ein auf der Kontinuumstheorie aufbauender Algorithmus zur Erfassung der Stoffgesetze für homogene Materialzonen im pre-failure-Bereich erarbeitet und in MAUS implementiert (Ehlert (1981)). Das zugrundegelegte Stoffverhalten wurde im wesentlichen entsprechend dem von Steinsalz ausgelegt. Es läßt sich durch die Merkmale "elastisch-plastich, viskoelastisch-viskoplastisch, temperaturabhängig" charakterisieren. Die formelmäßigen Zusammenhänge für die einzelnen Stoffgesetzteile sind in Abb. 5 zusammengestellt.

Wie Abb. 5 zu entnehmen ist wird der elastische Anteil durch einen konstanten Kompressionsmodul K und einen temperaturabhängigen Schubmodul G(T) beschrieben. Der plastische Dehnungsanteil wird durch eine Potenzfunktion abhängig von der effektiven Spannung (σ_{eff}) und der Temperatur (T) repräsentiert. Das viskoplastische Stoffgesetz erfaßt das primäre und sekundäre Kriechen, wobei im wesentlichen σ_{eff}, T und die akkumulierte viskoplastische Dehnung eingehen. Die sekundäre Kreichgeschwindigkeit gehorcht dabei einer Arrhenius-Funktion.Zur Berücksichtigung des viskoelastischen Verhaltens kann der elastische Schubmodul G(T) durch eine Relaxationsfunktion für Schub ersetzt werden, wobei die Zeit (t) und die Temperatur (T) als Variablen eingehen.

Die in Abb. 5 angegebenen Konstanten (C_1... ... C_{14}) müssen der standortspezifischen Salzart angepaßt werden; das Stoffgesetz dürfte jedoch qualitativ gültig bleiben und aufgrund seiner Komplexität auch das Materialverhalten der meisten anderen Gebirgsbildner qualitativ mit einschließen. Aus diesem Grund wird die Entwicklung von Stoffgesetzen für homogene Teilbereiche im pre-failure-Bereich als vorerst abgeschlossen betrachtet (Ausnahme: Versatzmaterialien; vgl. Kap. 3.1).

Im Mittelpunkt der derzeitigen Modellentwicklungen stehen entsprechend Abb. 4 das post-failure-Verhalten für homogene Materialzonen und die Formulierung eines Stoffgesetzes für Grenzflächen zwischen benachbarten Materialzonen (siehe Lehrauftrag Leistungsreaktoren (1981 a, 1981 b)).

4 THERMOMECHANISCHE BELASTUNG IM NAH- UND FERNFELD EINES ENDLAGERS FÜR HAW

Entsprechend den Ausführungen in Kap. 3 befinden sich die Rechenmodelle zu Spannungs- und Verformungsanalyse in der Entwicklungsphase. Dies erfordert einerseits den Vergleich der verschiedenen Algorithmen durch die Nachrechnung von Benchmark-Problemen und die Verifikation der Modelle durch die Nachrechnung von Experimenten. Andererseits ergibt sich jedoch die Möglichkeit erste Aussagen über die letztlich zu erwartenden thermomechanischen Belastungen in einem Salzstock zu treffen. Hier soll sowohl für den Nah- als auch für den Fernbereich eines Endlagers jeweils ein Beispiel für solche Anwendungsrechnungen vorgestellt werden.

4.1 Thermomechanische Belastung im Nahfeld eines Endlagers für HAW

Der HAW wird nach dem Einschmelzen in Glasblöcke in Edelstahl-Kokillen eingebracht (Kap. 2). Diese HAW-Kokillen dienen einerseits aufgrund ihrer speziellen Form der guten Handhabbarkeit des Abfallgebindes; andererseits dienen sie auch als Barriere gegen die Freisetzung von Radionukliden über einen vorzugebenden Zeitraum (z. B. Betriebsphase des Endlagers). Zur Erfüllung dieser zweiten Aufgabe ist eine entsprechende mechanische Auslegung der Kokillen notwendig, welche wiederum die Kenntnis ihrer Belastung voraussetzt.

Aufgrund des viskoplastischen Fließvermögens von Steinsalz werden die Bohrlöcher zur Aufnahme der Kokillen infolge des Gebirgsdrucks und der Thermospannungsfelder in relativ kurzen Zeiträumen (z. B. 2 Monate) soweit zufließen, daß sich das Salzgestein an die Kokillen anlegt und letztere mechanisch belastet werden.

Diese Belastung der Kokillen wurde unter Berücksichtigung der in Tabelle 1 angegebenen (wichtigsten) Randbedingungen berechnet.

Maximaltemperatur im Steinsalz	140° C
Bohrlochlänge	50 m
Kokillendurchmesser	20 cm
Kokillenwandstärke	0.8 cm

Tabelle 1: Die wichtigsten Randbedingungen des Rechenmodells.

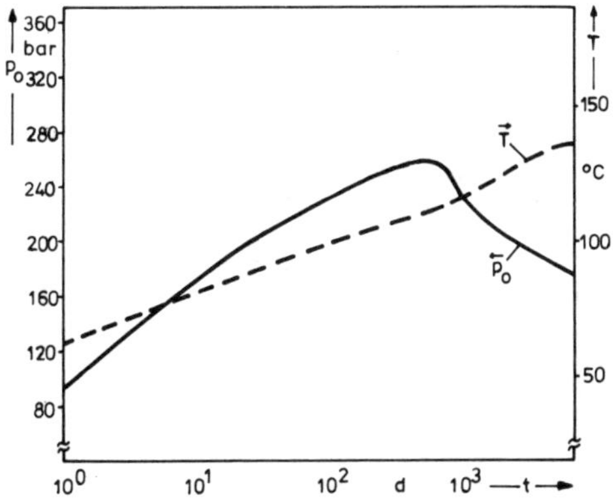

Abb. 6: Zeitlicher Verlauf des Gebirgsdrucks und der Temperatur auf der Kontaktfläche Kokillen-Gebirge

Abb. 6 zeigt die Druckbelastung der Kokillen und die an der Kontaktfläche zwischen Kokillen und Salz herrschende Temperatur als Funktion der Zeit. Der Druckverlauf ist charakterisiert durch:

a.) der Maximalwert von 258 bar wird nach ca. 2 Jahren erreicht.

b.) Mit zunehmender Zeit überwiegt die Relaxation den Spannungsaufbau und die Belastung nähert sich dem lithostatischen Druck, welcher entsprechend einer Teufe von ca. 825 m mit -173 bar als mechanische Randbedingung vorgegeben war.

Es können somit folgende wesentliche Schlüsse für die Auslegung von Kokillen gezogen werden:

- Die maximale Belastung der Kokille beträgt etwa das 1,5 fache des lithostatsichen Gebirgsdrucks.

- Die maximale Belastung tritt noch während der Betriebsphase des Endlagers (nach ca. 2 Jahren) auf.

Setzt man voraus, daß die Kokillen während der Betriebsphase des Endlagers ihre Barrierenfunktion erfüllen sollen, so muß die berechnete Maximalbelastung als Auslegungsgrundlage herangezogen werden.

4.2 Thermomechanische Belastung im Fernfeld eines Endlagers für HAW

Zur Berechnung der thermomechanischen Belastung im Fernfeld eines Endlagers für HAW wurde die relativ komplizierte Geometrie eines Salzstocks (vgl. z. B. Abb. 1) vereinfachend durch ein rotationssymmetrisches Modell - bestehend aus Endlager, Salzstock und Deckgebirge - simuliert (Abb. 7 a). Das Stoffverhalten von Steinsalz wurde durch das in Abb. 5 gegebene Stoffgesetz (ohne Viskoelastizität) beschrieben, wogegen für das Deckgebirge linear-elastisches Verhalten vorausgesetzt wurde. Die Endlagerauslegung erfüllte folgende zwei Hauptgesichtspunkte (des weiteren gelten die Angaben aus Tabelle 1):

a.) Der von 16 Kernkraftwerken (à 1300 MWe) innerhalb von jeweils 25 Betriebsjahren erzeugte Abfall soll aufgenommen werden.

b.) Die unter der vereinfachenden Annahme einer homogenisierten Endlagerzone sich einstellende maximale "Durchschnittstemperatur" soll 100° C betragen.

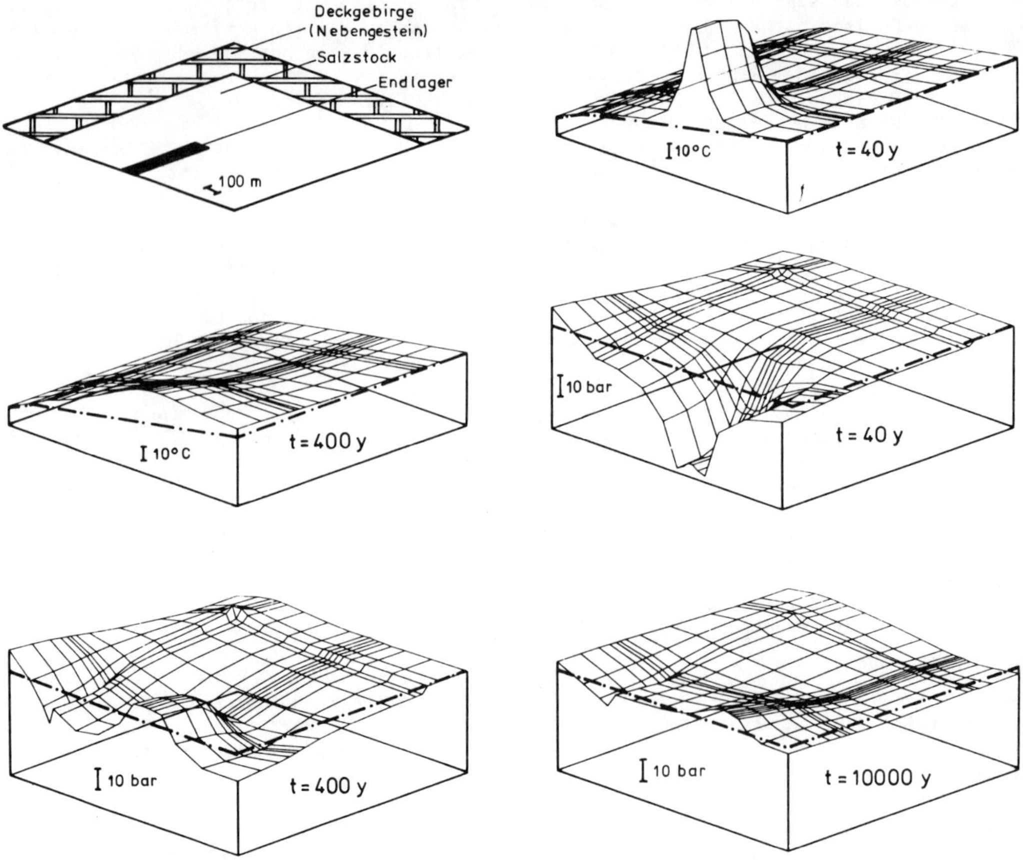

Abb. 7: Struktur des großräumigen Referenzfalls (a) und einige Ergebnisse für die Temperaturverteilung (b-c) und die Änderung der mittleren Spannung (e-f) zu verschiedenen Zeitpunkten (- · - Anfangswerte)

Abb. 7 b und 7 c zeigen die unter diesen Voraussetzungen ortsabhängigen Temperaturverteilungen nach 40 bzw. 400 Jahren. Nach 40 Jahren ergeben sich deutliche Temperaturerhöhungen im unmittelbaren Endlagerbereich, während in einiger Entfernung davon noch die ungestörten Temperaturen (strichpunktierte Linie) vorliegen. Nach 400 Jahren beträgt die maximale Temperaturerhöhung nur noch ca. 40° C ; die Wärmefront ist jedoch bedeutend weiter fortgeschritten. Nach etwa 1000 Jahren stellt sich nach diesem Modell der natürliche Temperaturgradient wieder ein.

Als Beispiel für die Spannungsverteilungen ist in Abb. 7 d bis 7 f die Änderung der mittleren Spannung ($\sigma_m = (\sigma_1+\sigma_2+\sigma_3)/3$; σ_i= Hauptspannungen) gegenüber dem lithostatischen Druck (strichpunktiert), welcher als hydrostatisch angenommen wurde, nach 40, 400 und 10000 Jahren dargestellt. Nach 40 Jahren ist der mittlere Druck auf 130% seines Anfangswertes von -160 bar angestiegen. Mit zunehmender Zeit nimmt die Bedeutung der Spannungsrelaxation zu, so daß der Spannungszustand seinem Anfangswert zustrebt. Durch das gleichzeitige Auftreten von Relaxation und Belastungszunahme kommt es zu einer wellenförmigen Bewegung der Spannungsfront durch das Gebirge. Schließlich kann festgehalten werden, daß die Spannungen sehr viel langsamer als die Temperaturen abgebaut werden (vgl. Abb. 7 f), was auf die irreversiblen Verformungen zurückzuführen ist.

5 ZUSAMMENFASSUNG UND SCHLUSSFOLGERUNGEN

Die Problemstellung und der Entwicklungsstand von Rechenmodellen zur Berechnung der thermomechanischen Auswirkungen eines Endlagers für hochradioaktive Abfälle (HAW) im Salzgebirge werden beschrieben. Desweiteren werden sowohl für das Nah- als auch für das Fernfeld je ein Berechnungsbeispiel vorgestellt. Die wesentlichen Ergebnisse und Schlußfolgerungen aus den bisherigen Untersuchungen lassen sich wie folgt zusammenfassen:

- Die Endlagerauslegungsdaten lassen sich i. a. mit dem entwickelten Rechenprogramm zur Spannungs- und Verformungsanalyse (MAUS) erfassen. Denkbare Erweiterungen liegen z. B. in der Anwendung dreidimensionaler Modelle und in der Formulierung eines besonderen Stoffgesetzes für Versatzmaterialien.

- Die orts- und zeitabhängigen Temperaturfelder können mit den vorhandenen Programmen hinreichend genau als Eingabedaten für die Spannungsberechnung bereitgestellt werden.

- Ein elastisch-plastisches, viskoelastisch-viskoplastisches, temperaturabhängiges Stoffgesetz für homogene Materialien ist formuliert.

- Erste Aussagen über die zu erwartenden thermomechanischen Belastungen können getroffen werden; diese können als Auslegungshilfen (z. B. für die Kokillen) herangezogen werden.

- Derzeitige Arbeiten beschäftigen sich u. a. mit der Simulation des post-failure Verhaltens homogener Materialien und dem Verhalten von Grenzflächen.

- Zur Verfeinerung der Modelle müssen genauere Daten über die verschiedenen Neben- und Deckgesteine durch experimentelle Untersuchungen bereitgestellt werden.

6 LITERATUR

Dtsch. Geol. Ges. (Hrsg.) 1977, Geowissenschaftliche Aspekte der Endlagerung radioaktiver Abfälle Symposium der Dtsch. Geol. Ges. am 19.11. 1979 in Braunschweig, Ferdinand Enke Verlag, Hannover.

Deutsche Gesellschaft für die Wiederaufbereitung von Kernbrennstoffen mbH (DWK) 1977, Bericht über das in der Bundesrepublik Deutschland geplante ENTSORGUNGSZENTRUM für ausgediente Brennelemente aus Kernkraftwerken.

Ehlert, C. 1981, Thermospannungen in einem Endlager für hochradioaktiven Abfall, Dissertation, Aachen

Lehrauftrag Leistungsreaktoren 1981 a, Entwicklung von Rechenmodellen zur Berechnung von instationären Temperatur-, Spannungs- und Dehnungsverteilungen im Nahbereich der eingelagerten hochaktiven Abfälle, Berichte zum Forschungsauftrag gleichen Namens der Kernforschungszentrum Karlsruhe GmbH (unveröffentlicht)

Lehrauftrag Leistungsreaktoren 1981 b, Thermomechanische Belastung eines Salzstocks im Fernfeld einer Einlagerungszone für radioaktiven Abfall, Berichte zum Forschungsauftrag gleichen Namens der Gesellschaft für Strahlen- und Umweltforschung mbH, München (unveröffentlicht)

Ploumen, P., Strickmann, G. 1977, Berechnung der zeitlichen und räumlichen Temperaturverteilung bei der säkulären Lagerung hochradioaktiver Abfälle in Salzstöcken Lehrauftrag Leistungsreaktoren im Institut für Elektrische Anlagen und Energiewirtschaft der RWTH Aachen

Ploumen, P., Strickmann, G., Winske, P. 1979, Untersuchungen zur Temperaturentwicklung bei der Endlagerung hochradioaktiver Abfälle, Teil I: Berechnung der Zeit- und ortsabhängigen Temperaturfelder, Atomwirtschaft - Atomtechnik, 2: 85-91.

Ploumen, P. 1980 a, Numerische Langzeitberechnung dreidimensionaler Temperaturfelder mit Hilfe eines speziellen Finite-Element-Verfahrens am Beispiel der Endlagerung hochradioaktiver Abfälle im Salzgestein, Dissertation, Aachen

Ploumen, P. 1980 b, Temperaturverteilung in einer Salzformation nach der Endlagerung hochradioaktiver Abfälle, in: Proc. Symp. "Geology and Nuclear Waste Disposal" held in Oct./Nov. 1979 at the Institute of Earth Science, Utrecht.

Venzlaff, H. 1978, Tieflagerung radioaktiver Abfälle aus geologischer Sicht, Atomwirtschaft 7/8: 335-338.

SOME GEOTECHNICAL ASPECTS OF UNDERGROUND DISPOSAL OF WASTES

Geotechnische Aspekte bei der unterirdischen Lagerung von Abfällen

Quelques aspects géotechniques du stockage souterrain des déchets

M.A.AZIZ
National University of Singapore

SUMMARY:
Waste is an unavoidable consequence of various human activities. Waste disposal problems have been increasing at an alarming proportion worldwide. Due to strict regulatory controls on dumping of wastes on land and at sea, the subsurface burial of wastes is a disposal alternative.
The underground disposal operation must be carefully engineered to provide long-term protection of groundwater, surface water, air and public health in general.
Subsurface geologic conditions have a major effects on the cost, safety and environmental impacts of underground disposal of wastes.
This paper delineates some salient features of the geotechnical aspects of various options such as subsurface burial, entrenchment, mine storage and deep well storage for the underground disposal of wastes of different types. It also stresses the need for a prudent approach for making the disposal methods safe, economically attractive and environmentally acceptable.

ZUSAMMENFASSUNG:
Abfall ist die unvermeidliche Folge verschiedener Aktivitäten des Menschen. Die hiermit verbundenen Probleme haben inzwischen weltweit ein alarmierendes Ausmaß erreicht. Da das Verkippen von Müll zu Land und See strikten Kontrollen unterworfen ist, bietet sich das unterirdische Lagern von Abfällen als Alternative an.
Eine unterirdische Lagerung von Abfällen verlangt eine besonders sorgfältige Arbeitsweise, damit Probleme bezüglich des Grundwassers, Oberflächenwassers, der Lufthygiene sowie allgemeiner Gesundheitsfragen langfristig vermieden werden. Die geologischen Verhältnisse haben einen maßgeblichen Einfluß auf die Kosten, die Sicherheit und die Umweltbelastung des unterirdischen Abfallagers.
In dieser Arbeit werden einige wesentliche Punkte bezüglich der geotechnischen Beurteilungen der unterirdischen Abfallagerung diskutiert. Es wird dabei auf die verschiedenen Lagerungsmöglichkeiten wie u.a. Vergraben, die Lagerung in Stollen und in Bohrlöchern Bezug genommen. Schließlich wird die Notwendigkeit einer umsichtigen Arbeitsweise hervorgehoben, die auf Abfallagerung abzielt.

RESUME:
Le déchet est la conséquence inévitable de diverses activités humaines. Les problèmes inhérents au stockage des déchets ont atteint une proportion alarmante à l'échelle mondiale. A cause des contrôles réguliers

et stricts qu'exige l'emmagasinage des déchets sur le sol et dans la mer, leur enfouissement souterrain constitue une alternative de stockage.

La méthode d'emmagasinage souterrain doit être étudiée soigneusement afin que la protection des eux souterraines, des eaux superficielles, de l'air et de la santé publique en général soit garantie à long terme.

Les conditions géologiques ont un grand effet sur le coût, la sécurité et les modifications de l'environnement du stockage souterrain des déchets.

Cette étude décrit quelques traits saillants des aspects géotechniques des diverses possibilités d'emmagasinage souterrain de différents types de déchets comme l'enfouissement souterrain, le stockage dans les galeries, dans les mines et dans les puits profonds. Donc, il s'avère nécessaire de procéder à une approche prudente tendant à donner de la sécurité aux méthodes de stockage, à les rendre économiquement attractives, acceptables pour l'environnement.

1 INTRODUCTION

Every country generates a substantial quantity of wastes (solid, semi-solid and liquid-hazardous and non-hazardous) through various human activities creating difficult disposal problems which are increasing at an alarming proportion world-wide. Dumping of wastes on land and into the sea is an economically attractive method but there are strict regulatory controls on such method of waste disposal due to various environmental health problems. Hence, the underground storage of wastes is a disposal alternative.

Disposal of solid wastes and noxious fluids underground, by tipping them down unused mine shafts or pumping them down dumb wells has become of increased interest in many countries (Gray et al 1974, 1976; Tchobanoglous et al 1977; Sikora and Colaccico 1980; Hill et al 1981) as controls on dumping at sea and on the surface become more strict. Underground disposal of wastes can be an acceptable practice where the local geology and hydrology are favourable and where there are rigorous engineering and administrative controls (Galley 1968; Gray et al 1976; Knight et al 1978). The most important aspect geotechnically, is that there must be a negligible rate of groundwater movement near the storage area (Huches et al 1971; Mclean and Gribble 1979). Because geologic conditions have a major effect on the cost, safety and environmental impacts of underground disposal of wastes, geotechnical aspects are an important consideration in the site selection. Cost, safety and environmental impacts of underground disposal of wastes are obviously not independent variables. The design engineer must select an optimum site, based on thorough geologic investigation, for underground disposal of wastes in order to achieve acceptable levels of safety and environmental impacts at a reasonable cost.

In this paper, the author delineates some salient features of the geotechnical aspects of various methods of underground disposal of wastes. Various control measures that can be adopted to abate the pollution of the aquifers and other adverse environmental impacts are also highlighted.

2 GEOTECHNICAL AND OTHER ENVIRONMENTAL CONSIDERATIONS FOR SITE SELECTION

The concept of underground disposal of wastes encompasses more than just simple burial of wastes. Proper geotechnical investigation of the proposed site by the conventional boreholes technique and other appropriate methods is essential in order to gain in-depth knowledge of the site with respect to the type and properties of soils and rocks (Berg 1976; Hirschfeld 1976; USEPA 1981). Main considerations are (1) permeability of soils and rocks, (2) presence of fissures, joints, faults and folds, (3) aquifer location and extent and (4) potential for subsurface migration of leachate and gases from the wastes. Sometimes, specific requirements need to be established such as no location of the burial site within 50 m of a fault, etc. In addition, the following parameters must be considered: (1) volume, physical, chemical and biochemical characteristics of the wastes, (2) hydrogeological characteristics of the site and the surrounding land, (3) quality, quantity and direction of groundwater flow, (4) proximity and withdrawal rates of groundwater uses, (5) land use pattern in the immediate vicinity and the local environment, and (6) potential for environmental health risks.

3 OPTIONS FOR UNDERGROUND DISPOSAL

Various options for underground disposal of wastes include subsurface burial, entrenchment, mine storage and deep well disposal. A number of detailed sources are available to obtain a more thorough understanding of these options from various authors and organizations such as Galley 1968; Merz and Stone 1970; Gray et al 1974, 1976; Tchobanoglous et al 1977; Golueke 1977; Sikora and Colaccico 1980; USEPA 1980, 1981; Hill et al 1981. A brief discussion of each option is presented in the next sections with special reference to the geotechnical aspects based on author's field and laboratory investigations.

3.1 Subsurface burial

Subsurface burial is a common method of solid waste disposal. Well developed methods for design, construction, operation and maintenance of a subsurface burial system are practiced nowadays in many countries where sufficient land is available for the purpose (Merz and Stone 1970; Salvato et al 1971; Finn et al 1975). But countries like Singapore, Hong Kong, and Japan having limited landmass do not generally encourage extensive waste burial. However, studies were carried out in a limited scale to evaluate the effectiveness of the subsurface burial of some specific wastes. From these studies, two contaminants of environmental concern from subsurface burial operation of wastes were found to be important - these are gases and leachate (Aziz 1981). Gases always generate as the organic component of the wastes decomposes anaerobically whereas the leachate generates only when there is an excess of water infiltrating through the buried wastes. The principal gases generated from decomposing wastes are carbon dioxide and methane. Carbon dioxide is the gas of consequence of ground water quality, since the other gases of decomposition are relatively insoluble in water. When the carbon dioxide is dissolved in water, it causes a lowering in pH value, resulting in a corrosive environment and an increase in water hardness (Gray et al 1974; Golueke 1977; Aziz 1981; Hill et al 1981). Leachate, an effluent from a waste containment site, is a liquid of complex nature consisting of organic and inorganic salts, heavy metals, pesticides, toxic chemicals, acids, virus and pathogens. The potential for leachate degradation of groundwater from a waste burial site is directly related to the geological and hydrological characteristics of the site. The geological factors include the soil and bedrock type and conditions of their respective abilities to attenuate or restrict movement of leachate and gases emanating from the disposal site. Hydrological factors include the groundwater location and movement, the amount and intensity of rainfall and the ability to control surface water or drainage. Occasionally, a site situated above the water table in an area of low rainfall, and underlain by impervious clay soils can completely contain leachate and gases. Such ideal conditions are not normally available; therefore, special design features, and/or operational methods must be provided. The desired short-term containment of the leachate and the gases of decomposition of waste can be achieved by lining disposal sites by appropriate sealing materials such as bentonitic clay. (Tchobanoglous 1977; Aziz and Ramaswamy 1980). Gas venting is required irrespective of whether the site is lined or unlined.

3.1.1 Burial of solidified/stabilized wastes

Waste stabilization/solidification is usually a pretreatment process of underground burial that has become popular in many parts of the world to insure safe disposal of wastes containing harmful constituents. Generally, solidification improves the handling and physical characteristics of the wastes whereas stabilization induces a chemical change to produce an insoluble form of waste constituents or places the wastes in a matrix that is insoluble. Treatment processes now available for solidification/stabilization of wastes include cement-based processes, pozzolanic processes, thermoplastic techniques, organic polymer processes, self-cementing processes, and glassification, and production processes of synthetic minerals or ceramics or any other useful products (USEPA 1981; Ronald et al 1981). This is relatively a new technology and there is no universally accepted procedures. In general, the stronger, more impermeable and durable a treated wastes, the more effective will be its containment. Cement-based treated wastes have been reported to have compressive strength around 13,800 kN/m^2 (2,000 lb/sq.in), permeabilities of 7.9×10^{-4} cm/sec, less than 20% weight loss after 12 freezing-thawing cycles and with excellent durability (Ronald et al 1981). Small column leaching test has shown that in cement and bitumen-based systems, the strongest materials have the minimum contaminant loss. Tests have also shown that when solidified stabilized wastes are buried underground, the major factor limiting the loss of material from the monolithic mass is diffusion of the chemical constituents to the surface of the solid. But very little information is currently available on the effective diffusivities of solidified/stabilized industrial and other types of wastes.

Most of the wastes intended for underground disposal have no present value, and hence, treatment for solidification/stabilization represents additional costs which needs to be added to the total cost of disposal. Therefore, a complete economic analysis of the cost of waste collection, transportation, materials, and equipment required for the solidification/stabilization process, and the cost of transporting and subsurface burial of the treated wastes is essential before a decision is made to adopt this system of underground waste disposal.

3.2 Entrenchment

Entrenchment of wastes is in fact a modified landfill procedure in which the waste is placed in trenches and buried. Entrenchment of sewage sludge and nightsoil has been practiced in some countries with beneficial results (shende 1974; Shuval 1977; Rybezynski et al 1978; Sikora and Colacicco 1980) but very little information is available on the direct entrenchment of refuse and other types of wastes. Field studies were carried out on the entrenchment method of waste disposal using urban refuse mixed with food and fruit processing wastes. The experimental trench was 3 m deep and 1 m wide. After placing the wastes in the trench, the top was covered with land-cut materials and well compacted. The site was monitored for 12 months. There was little odour problem and the site was later used for vegetable production (Aziz, 1981). Microbial studies on the soil samples from the entrenchment site showed no sign of pathogenic organisms present after three months. The major environmental concern of the site was the groundwater contamination. Groundwater monitoring of the entrenchment site did not indicate any serious contamination problems. From the limited short-time studies, it is difficult to generalize that there is no possibility of groundwater contamination from this method of waste disposal. In fact, the contamination of groundwater is probable and the magnitude of contamination is site-specific. The success of the method depends upon the imperviousness (absence of fractured rocks) and sufficient depth to groundwater. In fact, the site selected was of intact shale and there was negligible rate of groundwater movement near the site. From the field studies it is observed that the success of the waste entrenchment depends upon the nature of the wastes to be entrenched; site selection after proper geotechnical investigation;efficient collection, transportation and placement of wastes, approved soil cover; restoration of the site afterwards and utilization for agricultural purposes.

Another field investigation was conducted on the entrenchment of wastes in clayey soils. As clayey soils are highly impervious the wastes entrenched in the clayey soils did not pose any problem of odour and groundwater contamination. This method of underground disposal of wastes hold immense potential in areas where exists an extensive deposits of clayey soils.

3.3 Mine storage

Another option for wastes-especially hazardous wastes disposal is packing solidified wastes in nonbreakable containers such as drums, concrete cylinders and special glass cases, transporting these containers down the mine shafts and placing them in prepared chambers. The disposal areas are segregated to contain wastes that are compatible with one another; chambers are filled and sealed off. If the mine is selected properly based on sound geotechnical investigation the containers are expected to have an indifinite life unless they are corroded from inside. The main advantage of this system of underground disposal of wastes is that the waste can be retrieved at a later date if necessary. Salt, potash and gypsum deposits have been identified as having the most potential for the waste storage (Jumikis 1967; Galley 1968; Huches et al 1971; Lindsey 1975; Knight et al 1978; McLean and Gribble 1979). Salt deposits have been found to have many advantages for industrial waste disposal when lying within close proximity of industrial areas because of avoidance of transportation hazards of wastes (Ronald et al 1981).

3.4 Deep well disposal

Deep well disposal involves injection of liquid wastes into subsurface geologic formations by means of wells. The underlying concept of the technique is the isolation of the waste materials from the usuable environment by means of injecting into and confining them to selected geological strata without any other or potential beneficial uses, although there is some evidence of biological treatment in selected situations (Ronald et al 1981). The injection technique can provide a final solution to certain liquid waste problems provided that the disposal strata of low utility exist into which the waste can be injected without undesirable consequences, and that the waste can be permanently confined to the chosen strata.

The technique of deep well disposal is widely used by the petroleum industries both for secondary recovery of oils and for the disposal of brine wastes. Today nearly 1,200 ha-m of brine wastes are injected yearly through many thousands of wells in oil-producing countries. Since 1950s, there has been a steady increase in the use of deep wells for the disposal of other industrial wastes. Over thousands of deep wells containing over many varieties of chemicals are now operating in many industrialized nations of the world (Ronald et al 1981).

Deep well disposal is, of course, not considered as a all-cure for problems related to the disposal of varieties of liquid wastes. Some argue that it is a safe and economical method of waste disposal while others are concerned with groundwater pollution and further use of the aquifer. Some have limitations on the type of wastes that can be disposed of, for example, chlorinated hydrocarbons. In fact, the geologic formation is the prime factor in deep well disposal. Important parameters that must be considered for the underground disposal of wastes by deep well method are uniformity, large areal extent, substantial thickness, high porosity and permeability, low pressure, nature of aquifer (aquifer containing brackish water, salt water or brine, artesian water), separation from fresh wates horizons, adequate overlying and underlying aquicludes, groundwater circulation, geologic structures (fissures, joints, faults and folds) and the compatibility between the mineralogy and the fluids of the geologic strata and the disposed wastes. Though the capacity of the potential receiving geologic formations is sometimes enormous, but still unrestricted deep well disposal must not be encouraged. Based on sound geotechnical investigation, the indiscriminate use of such formations in any specific area must be controlled which include the awarding the permit and the delineation of parameters such as permissible disposal rates and pressure, types of materials used for construction and tests and monitoring facilities that can ensure the utility and safety of the installation. Some cases of deep well disposal known to have created environmental problems have been reported to be in unsuitable geologic formations or have been poorly engineered and installed for the existing geologic conditions. Actually the success of a deep well disposal method depends on sound geologic investigation of the site, good engineering and construction techniques.

4. CONCLUSIONS

Because subsurface geotechnical conditions have a critical effect on the cost, safety and the environmental impact of the underground disposal of wastes, it is important that broad-scale geotechnical studies be carried out early in the site selection phase of the project. Properly planned, designed, constructed and maintained underground facilities, based on sound geotechnical investigations, for waste disposal can have profound impacts on solving critical waste disposal problems and safeguarding the public health and environmental quality in general. The ultimate goal, is, of course, to make the underground waste dispal systems safe, economically attractive and environmentally acceptable.

5. REFERENCES

Aziz, M.A. and S.D. Ramaswamy 1980, Energy from farm and human wastes. Proc. 2nd Conv. Eng. Inst. Southeast Asian Nations (CEISEAN) on Resource Development, Manila, Feb. 4-6, 1-18.

Aziz, M.A. 1981, Some public health aspects of water supply and wastewater disposal in hot climate countries. Proc. 9th Fed. Con. Australian Wat. & Wast. Assoc., Inst. Engrs. Australia, Perth, April 6-10, 1981.

Aziz, M.A. 1981, Energy and useful by-products from organic wastes. Proc. UNESCO/UPM/FEISEAP Reg. Workshop on Bio-conversion for Fuel Production, Serdang, Malaysia, Oct. 20-24.

Berg, D.R. 1976, Solid waste management of energy complexes. Proc. Eng. Fdn. Conf. Civ. Envr. Eng. Aspects of Energy Com-

plexes, ASCE, 201-210.
Finn, D.G., K.J. Hanley and T.V. Degreare 1975, Use of water balance for predicting leachate generation from solid waste disposal sites. US-EPA, Washington, D.C., Pub. 530/SW-168.
Galley, J.E.(ed.) 1968, Subsurface disposal in geologic basins - a study of reservoir strata. Mem. Am. Ass. Petrol. Geol., 10.
Gray, D.A., J.D. Mather and I.B. Harrison 1974, Review of groundwater pollution from waste sites in England and Wales with provisional guidelines for future site section. Q.J. Eng. Geol., 7: 181-198.
Gray, D.A. et al 1976, Disposal of highly-active solid radioactive wastes into geological formations - relevant geological criteria for the United Kingdom, Rep. Inst. Geol. Sci., 76/12:4.
Golueke, C.G. 1977, Biological reclamation of solid wastes. Rodale Press, Emmaus, P.A. (USA), 1-142.
Hill, R.D., N.B. Shomaker, R.E. Landreth and C.C. Wiles 1981, Four options for hazardous waste disposal. Civ. Eng.-ASCE, 51:82-85.
Hirschfeld, R.C. 1976, The role of geotechnical engineering in land planning. Proc. Eng. Fdn. Conf. Civ. Envr. Eng. Aspects of Energy complexes, ASCE, 65-72.
Huches, G.M., R.A. Landon and R.N. Fairolden 1971, Hydrogeology of solid waste disposal sites in Northeastern Illinois. US-EPA, Washington, D.C., Pub. SW-12d.
Jumikis, A.R. 1967, Introduction to Soil Mechanics. Van Nostrand, Princeton, N.J.
Knight, M.J., J.G. Leonard and R.J. Whiteley 1978, Lucas Heights solid waste landfill and downstream leachate transport - a case study in environmental geology. Bulletin of Int. Assoc. Eng. Geol., F.R. Germany, 18:45-64.
Lindsey, A.W. 1975, Ultimate disposal of spilled hazardous materials. Chem. Eng. 82:23.
McLean, A.C. and C.D. Gribble 1979, Geology for civil engineers, George Allen & Unwin, London, 166-170.
Merz, R.C. and R. Stone 1970, Special studies of a sanitary landfill. US Dept. of HEW, PHs, Washington, D.C.
Rybezynski, W., C. Polprasert and M. McGarry 1978. Appropriate waste treatment for tropical climates. Proc. Int. Conf. Wat. Pol. Cont. Dev. Count. Bangkok. 735-742.
Salvato, J.A., W.G. Wilkie and B.E. Mead 1971, Sanitary landfill - leaching prevention and control, J. Wat. Pol. Cont. Fed., 43:10.
Shende, G.B. 1974, Sewage utilization in agriculture. Inding Farming, 23/11:23-31.
Shuval, H.L. 1977, Public health considerations in wastewaters and excreta reuse for agriculture. Water, Wastes and Health in Hot Climates. R. Feachem, W. McGarry and D. Mara (eds.), John Wiley, London, 365-380.
Sikora, L.J. and D. Colacicco 1980, Entrenchment of sewage sludge - a disposal-use alternative. Civ. Eng.-ASCE, 52:80-82.
Tchobanoglous, G., H.Theisen and R. Eliasen 1977, Solid wastes: engineering principles and management issues: McGraw-Hill, New York, 317-373.
USEPA 1980, Hazardous waste land treatment, Washington, D.C., Report No. SW-874.
USEPA 1981, A guid to the disposal of chemically stabilized and solidified waste. Washington, D.C., Report No. SW-872, PB-81-181-505.

UNLINED COMPRESSED AIR SURGE CHAMBER FOR 24 ATMOSPHERES PRESSURE AT JUKLA POWER PLANT

Unausgekleidetes Druckluftwasserschloss für 24 bar der Jukla Wasserkraftanlage

Chambre à air comprimé sans soutènement, d'une pression de 24 atm. de la centrale électrique de Jukla

J.BERGH-CHRISTENSEN
A/S GEOTEAM, Oslo, Norway

SUMMARY:
The Jukla Pumped-Storage Power Project in Western Norway includes a 6,200 m^3 compressed air surge chamber designed for operational air pressures between 6 bar and 24 bar. The paper describes the site investigations performed as a basis for chamber design.

ZUSAMMENFASSUNG:
Das Pumpenspeicherwerk Jukla in West-Norwegen umfasst auch ein 6,200 m^3 grosses Wasserschloss dass mit komprimierter Luft in Form eines Luftkissens arbeitet, mit einem Betriebsdruck zwischen 6 bar und 24 bar schwankend. Die ausgeführten Felduntersuchungen als Grundlage für den Entwurf der Kammer werden beschrieben.

RESUME:
Le projet pompage-emmagasinement de Jukla à l'ouest de la Norvège comporte une chambre à air comprimé dimensionnée à 6,200 m^3 pour des pressions opératives entre 6 et 24 bars. Le présent article décrit les reconnaissances in situ effectuées en vue du désign de cette chambre.

The use of unlined, pressurized rock cavities has long traditions in Norway. More than 50 hydro electric power plants with unlined pressure shafts and tunnels have been constructed involving water pressures ranging from 150 to more than 500 metres static head.

The traditional high pressure plant comprises a headrace tunnel at near reservoir level, with surge shaft at the downstream end, and a pressure shaft down to the power station.

Recent developments in power plant design has called for the use of deep-lying pressure tunnels. The conventional surge shaft is replaced by deep lying chamber containing a large bubble of compressed air, as indicated in Fig. 1. The air bubble or cushion functions as shock absorber to ensure hydraulic stability of the system.

In 1973 and 1974, the world's two first high pressure air cushion surge chambers were successfully put into operation, at the Driva and Jukla power plants in Norway, thus furnishing practical experience of

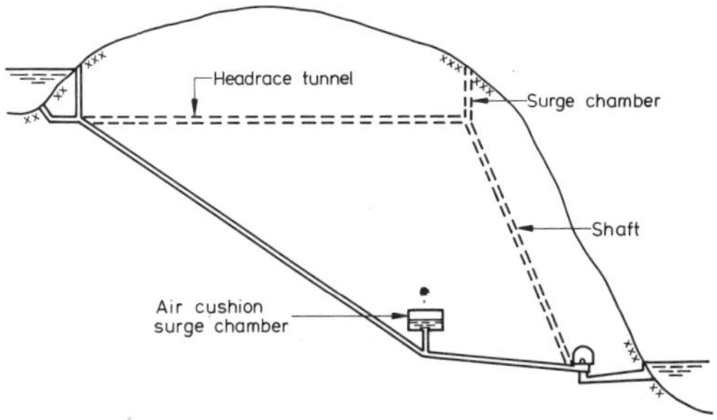

Fig. 1. Utilization of compressed air cushion surge chamber, as compared with conventional shaft design.

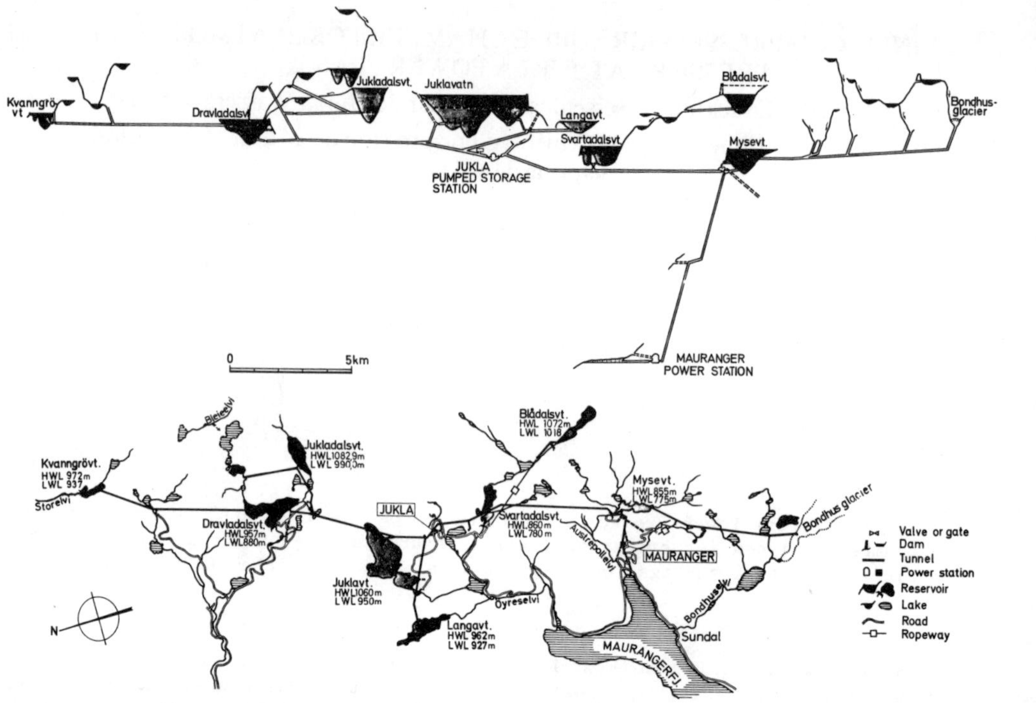

Fig. 2. The Folgefonni Hydro-Electric Power Development Project.

large, unlined rock chambers for gas containment (Rahte 1975, Stokkebø 1972).

The Jukla pumped storage power project, developed and owned by the State Power Board, utilizes run-off from the great Folgefonn glacier in western Norway. It forms part of the Folgefonni power development project as visualized in fig. 2. The Jukla project includes a 6200 m^3 compressed air surge chamber, with operational air pressures varying between 6 bar (kg/cm^2) and 24 bar.

Acting as engineering geological consultant to the State Power Board, A/S GEOTEAM was responsible for site investigations and rock mechanics design evaluations performed prior to and during construction of this chamber.

The investigations were performed in three consecutive phases:

1. Geological mapping of tunnels.

2. Diamond core drilling, pore pressure measurements and air and water leakage tests, and

3. Inspection and control during excavation.

Initially a detailed engineering geological survey in the already completed headrace pressure tunnel was performed. The rock here is Precambrian gneiss showing near horizontal foliation and moderate schistosity. The headrace tunnel crosses a few major swelling-clay gouges calling for local on-face concrete lining support. Except for these zones, the rock is moderately jointed.

Based on the geological survey, a 100 m section of the headrace tunnel, situated 600 m upstream of the power station and with a rock overburden of 340 m, was provisionally selected for detailed investigations. The potential chamber location is indicated in figs. 3 and 4. Here three 40-80 metres deep diamond core drillholes, as well as an 18 metres percussive drill hole were drilled to investigate the rock quality, as visualized in fig. 5. They revealed massive rock with RQD values better than 90 at the proposed chamber location.

Decisive for a feasibility evaluation of an unlined air cushion surge chamber is the rate of air loss to be expected due to leakage through the rock. Theoretical

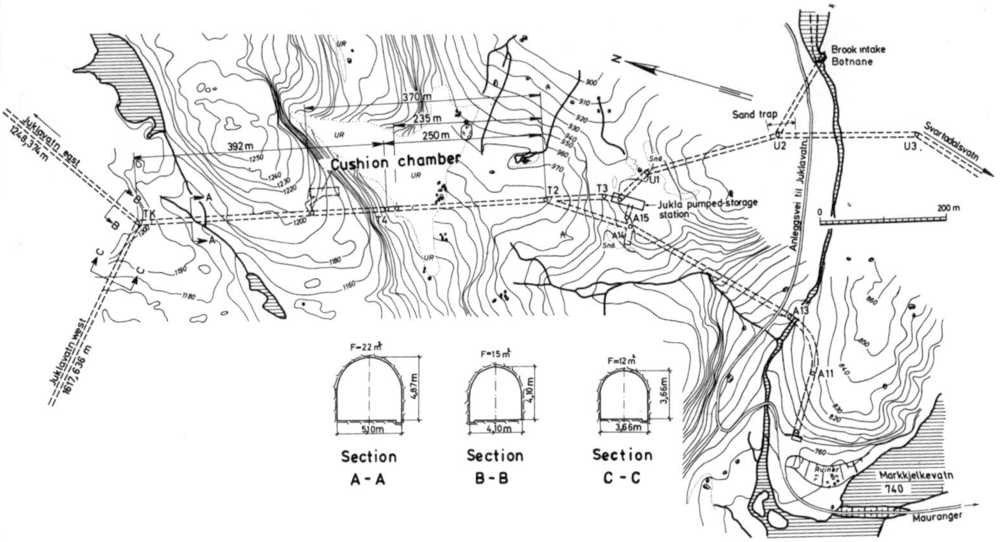

Fig. 3. Plan of Jukla Power Plant.

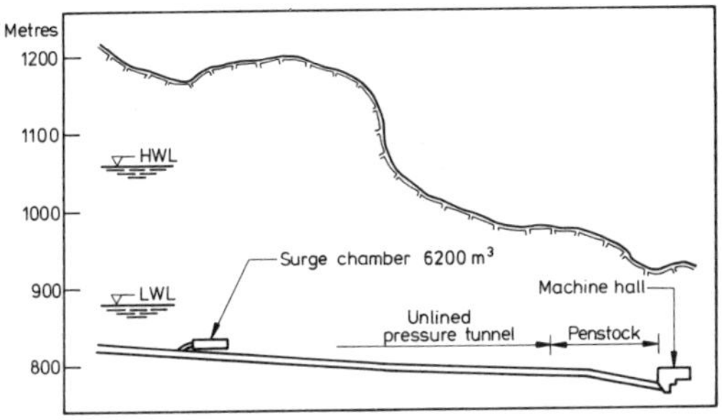

Fig. 4. Jukla Power Plant. Section showing location of air cushion chamber.

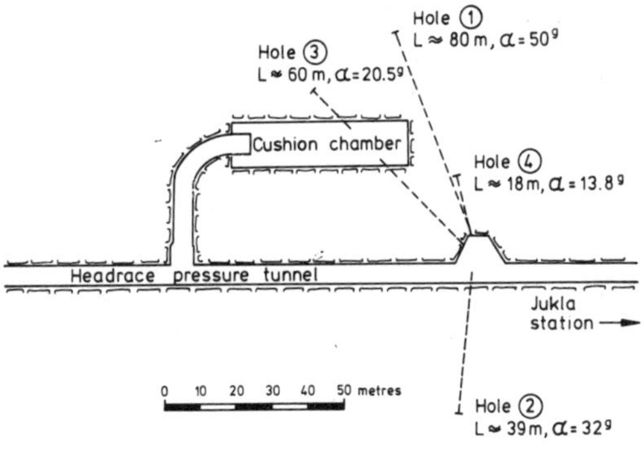

Fig. 5. Exploratory drillings at the chamber site.

studies indicate that such losses are governed by two main factors: - the permeability of the rock mass, and the ratio of chamber gas pressure to pore water pressure in the surrrounding rock.

Pore water pressure in the surrounding rock was continuously recorded during site investigations and the subsequent construction period, and showed a natural pore pressure in the surrounding rock of 17 bar (kg/cm^2), fig. 5.

For assessment of rock mass permeability, in situ air and water pumping tests were performed in two of the diamond core drillholes, employing special test equipment designed and operated by Norwegian Geotechnical Institute personnel. (DiBiagio and Myrvoll, 1972).

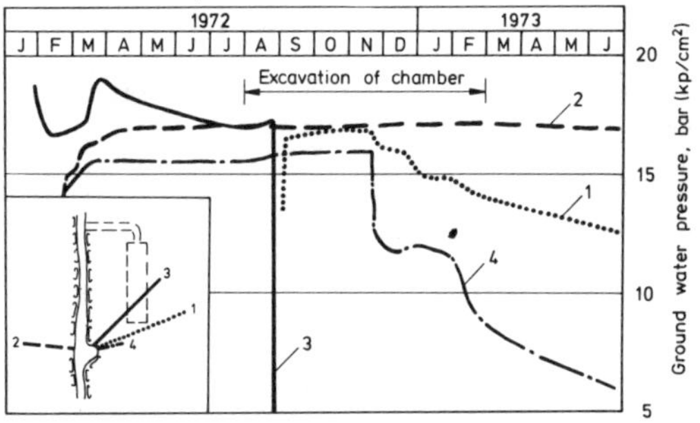

Fig. 6. Pore pressures recorded at the chamber location.

Water pressure tests were carried out at pressures up to 50 bar, using borehole test sections of 67 m and 46 m lengths. At peak pressure, water losses of 360 cm^3 and 30 cm^3 per minute respectively were recorded for the two test sections, corresponding to Lugeon values of 0.0015 and 0.0002. This extremely low rock mass permeability clearly indicated favourable conditions for surge chamber placement.

Air leakage tests were performed in the same borehole test sections as mentioned above. Typical test results are shown in figs. 7 and 8. At peak pressures of 40 bar the recorded air leakage, reduced to equivalent volume at atmosperic pressure and given in normal litres per minute, was 215 and 6 Nl/min respectively for the 67 and 46 m long borehole sections.

Both theoretical evaluations and practical experience indicate that water pressure tests give the most reliable basis for rock mass permeability assessment of potential air leakage problems. Taking into consideration the difference in vicosity of water and air, water permeability test values may be utilized for computation of possible air leakage rates from an underground chamber.

Based on an evaluation of all permeability data, possible air leakages from the surge chamber were calculated to be of the order of 100-500 Nl/minute, and hence well within acceptable limits.

The surge chamber, with a cross section of 128 m^2, length 48 m and a total volume of 6200 m^3, was excavated during the period August 1972 - February 1973. Due to the near horizontal rock schistosity, the roof was permanently secured with grouted rock bolts. No further reinforcement or sealing measures were found necessary.

In May 1974 the compressed air surge chamber was put into operation. The experience so far shows that the site investigations furnished satisfactory basis for leakage evaluation.

During operation of the surge chamber, total air losses of the order of 20-200 Nl/minute have been recorded at working pressures beyond 17 bar. With pressures lower than the recorded ground water head of 17 bar, no appreciable air losses have been recorded. The operational experiences thus confirm the feasibility of using borehole permeability tests as a basis for air loss calculations by pressure chamber design and siting.

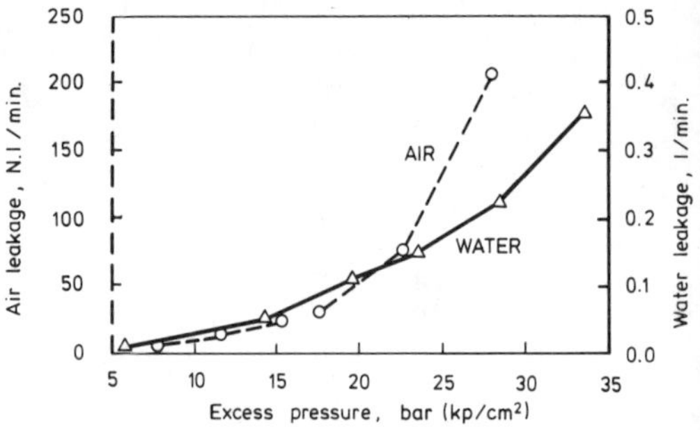

Fig. 7. Borehole 1. Water and air leakage tests.

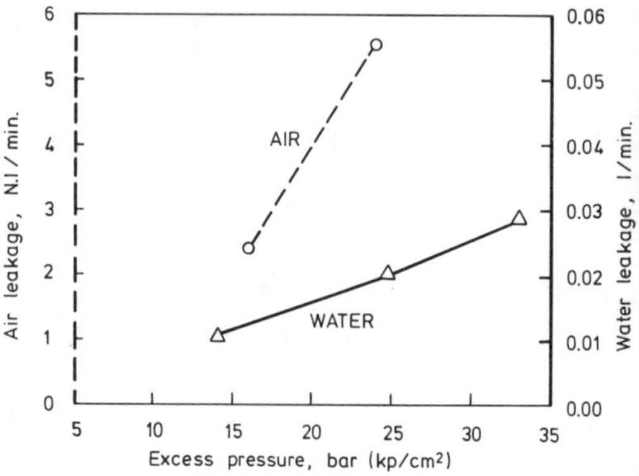

Fig. 8. Borehole 3. Water and air leakage tests.

REFERENCES

Di BIAGIO, E. and MYRVOLL, F. 1972. "In situ tests for predicting the air and water permeability of rock masses adjacent to underground openings." Symp. of the Int. Soc. for Rock Mechanics "Percolation through fissured rock" Stuttgart 1972.

RAHTE, L. 1975. "An innovation in surge chamber design." Water Power, Vol. 13, No. 9, pp. 35-39.

STOKKEBØ, O. 1972. "Jukla pumped-storage project in Norway." Economic Comm. for Europe, Symp. on hydro-electric pumped-storage schemes, Athens 1972.

RECENT DEVELOPMENTS IN UNDERGROUND STORAGE TECHNIQUES

Neue Entwicklungen der Technik für unterirdische Lagerung

Développements récents dans les techniques de stockage souterrain

ÅKE CALMINDER
WP-System AB, Stockholm, Sweden
TORBJÖRN HAHN
Teknisk Databehandling AB, Stockholm, Sweden

SUMMARY:
Changes in the energy situation, as well as safety aspects, have caused new and more stringent demands to be made for the storage of oil. It will become necessary to put an increasing share of the oil storage underground. However, conventional methods for storage of oil, on waterbed in unlined caverns, are not sufficient for all types of products. Vertical, cylindrical caverns can provide better storage conditions for oil products. Simple calculations show that from a rock mechanical point of view, such caverns are preferable because the cylindrical wall and the dome or cone-shaped roof provides more favourable stress conditions at the contour.

ZUSAMMENFASSUNG:
Änderungen der Energisituation wie auch Sicherheitaspekten haben neue und strengere Anspruche für Öllagerung mitgebracht. Dadurch hat es sich notwendig gezeigt einen steigernden Anteil von den Öllagern untertage zu bringen. Konventionelle Methoden für lagerung auf Wasserbett ohne Auskleidung sind aber nicht zufrieden für alle Typen von Ölprodukten. Verticale cylindrische Cisternen können bessere Lagerungsbedingungen für alle Produkte bringen. Einfache elastische FEM-Berechnungen zeigen auch besseren Spannungsverhältnisse auf die Wand und Firste in Verhältnis zu konventioneller Tunnelausformung.

RESUME:
Le changement dans la situation de l'énergie a impliqué des demandes nouvelles et plus rigoureuses pour le stockage d'huile. Mais les méthodes conventionelles pour le stockage souterrain d'huile en couche d'eau dans les cavernes sans revetment étanche, ne sont pas suffisantes pour tous les types d'huile. Les cavernes verticales peuvent offrir de meilleures conditions de stockage pour tous les produits et cette formation est de stabilité meilleure pour las parois rocheuses et le toit rocheux que la formation conventionnelle des tunnels horizontaux.

1. BACKGROUND

The first underground storages for petroleum products on waterbed were made in Sweden about 40 years ago when storing on waterbed in underground tanks was first used, according to the so-called Sentab method. In principle, these storages were made as shown in fig. 1. The bottle-shaped steel tank with back-up concrete, was kept filled to the barrier level by pumping water to and from the bottom of the cavern.

This method was succeeded 30 years ago by a method for storage on waterbed in unlined rock caverns invented by H Edholm. The method is very simple and consequently cheap. As it is also very reliable, with regard to safety of the stored product and the environment, the method

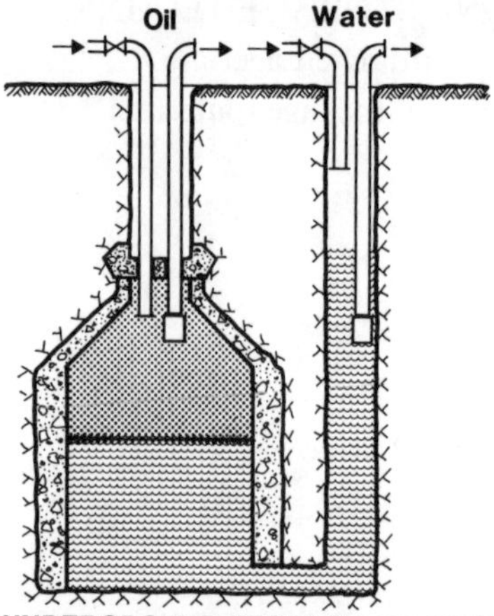

Fig. 1. UNDERGROUND STORAGE ON WATERBED FOR PETROLEUM PRODUCTS ACCORDING TO THE "SENTAB" METHOD

is competitive to this very day for storage of most petroleum types and petroleum products. It also provides good storage conditions for liquified gas. The common principle design is shown in fig. 2.

Up till now, the storage caverns have usually been constructed horizontally, contrary to the Sentab method, with tunnel-shaped caverns with a span up to 20m, depth to 35m and length up to several hundred m. The tunnel-shape was chosen as a consequence of the development of efficient tunnel excavation equipment during the last decades. This design has proven to give safe and cheap operation of the storage. But, experience also shows that storing on large extended waterbeds is not suitable for some petroleum types e.g. heavy crude types inclined to give sludge deposit problems. The large waterbed is unsuitable for storing products sensitive to water such as jet fuels. In fact, jet fuel can be adversely affected by bacteria and fungi, mainly in the oil/water surface, and in such a way as to be disastrous for safety in flight.

New problems can be added to the aforementioned ones due to the petroleum supply and transportation patterns which will apply in the near future.

The shortage of light petroleums will bring more heavy ones onto the

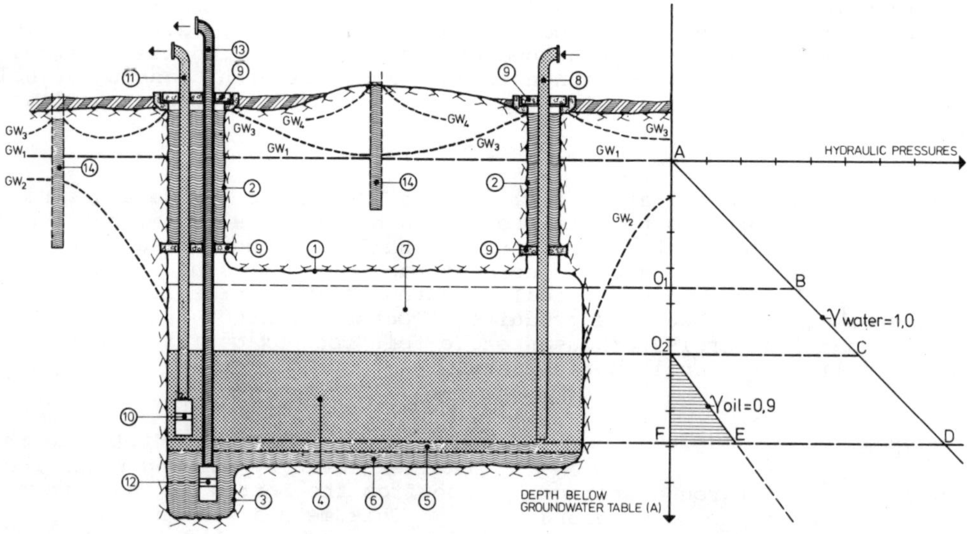

1. ROCK CAVERN
2. WATERFILLED SHAFT
3. PUMP PIT
4. OIL (or liquefied gas)
5. OIL/WATER INTERFACE
6. WATER-BED
7. GASFILLED SPACE
8. INCOMING OIL PIPE
9. CONCRETE BARRIER
10. OIL PUMP
11. OIL DISCHARGE PIPE
12. LEAKAGE WATER PUMP
13. DISCHARGE PIPE LEAKAGE WATER
14. DRILLED HOLES FOR WATER INJECTION

GW. GROUND WATER

Fig. 2. Oil storage on waterbed in unlined rock cavern

market, even very heavy ones with high pour point and considerable tendencies to sludge deposits.

In a few years the IMCO codes for crude oil washing (COW) will be effective for all countries. The crude carriers will then transfer all sludge deposits into the storage tanks (presently often dumped into the sea on the return trip to the export terminal).

These two features, combined, will make horizontal caverns unfit for storage of heavy crudes.

Although the horizontal cavern construction has usually functioned well, there are some obvious drawbacks with this design. The cost for reinforcing fair and weak rock is considerable and such work can interfere badly with the excavation time schedule.

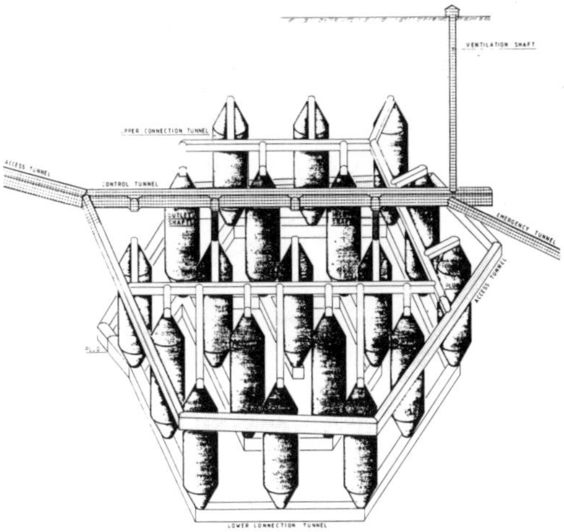

Fig. 4. POLYTANK cavern group

2. THE VERTICAL TANK CONCEPT

All the aforesaid, indicates that there is a need for a NEW design for storage caverns. Vertical, cylindrical caverns seem to suit the functional demands favourably. The Polytank method has re-introduced the vertical tank for storage - as single caverns or several caverns in a group - See figs. 3 and 4.

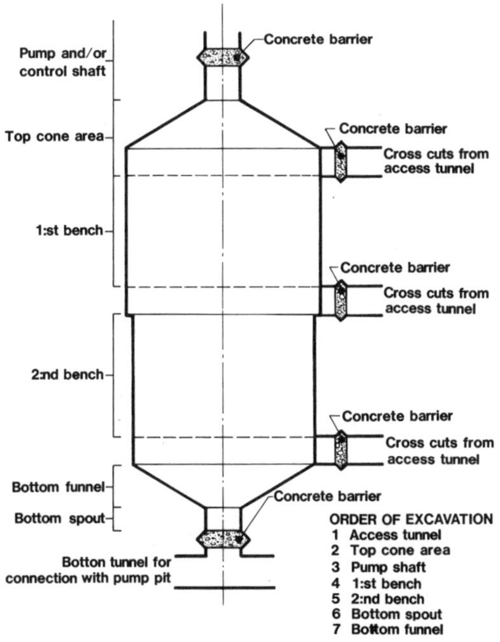

Fig. 3. Principle design for POLYTANK oil storage cavern

3. ROCK MECHANICAL ASPECTS

A simple elastic analysis shows that the very shape of a rock cavern has a considerable influence on the stresses at the contour. The relation between horizontal and vertical virgin stresses is, for a given shape, the most important factor affecting the tangential stresses at the contour. The overall size is not so significant to the stresses.

Fig. 5 illustrates how the tangential stresses at the crown of an eliptical cavern, change with the span when considering different ratios of the vertical and horizontal virgin stresses, σ_v and σ_h.

When σ_h/σ_v is less than 0.5, there will be tensile stresses at the crown when the span is larger than 25m, according to the cross section in fig 5.

For a plane wall (normal for a conventional tunnel for storage) there will be tensile stresses at the wall when $\sigma_h/\sigma_v > 0.5$. This fact has, in combination with unfavourable joint pattern, caused problems in some cases.

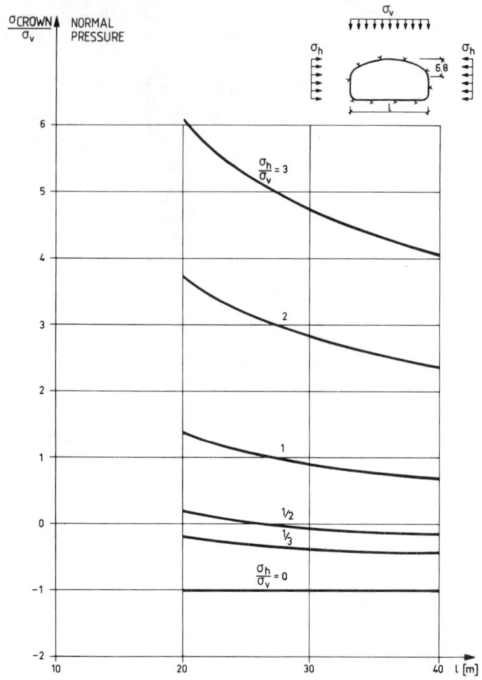

Fig. 5

A diagram showing the horizontal pressure at the crown as a function of the span and the relationship between the horizontal and vertical stresses in the rock mass. The diagram is valid for an eliptical shaped cavern roof.

The rock mass, however, includes a joint pattern of larger or smaller discontinuities. These influence the probability of occurenc of severe joints and combinations of joints increasing with size. Despite this, an elastic analysis is a useful tool when comparing different designs. It can give an idea of which volumes are affected by tensile stresses, which combined with unfavourable joint pattern can lead to stability problems. Mathematical analyses using FEM have been carried out in order to compare the Polytank design with a conventional tunnel. Interactive graphic computer programmes, as a user oriented generation of input data for the FEM programme, made it possible to change the geometry and the FEM-mesh in an easy way.

The stress conditions at the contour for the different ratios σ_h/σ_v = 0, 0.5, 1, 1.5, are illustrated in figs. 6-9

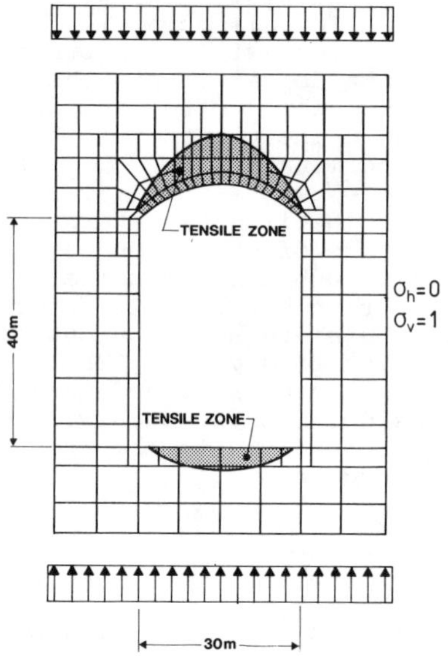

Fig. 6a

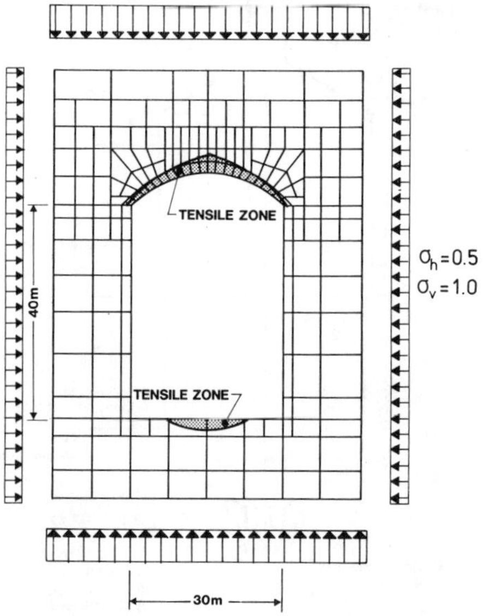

Fig. 6b

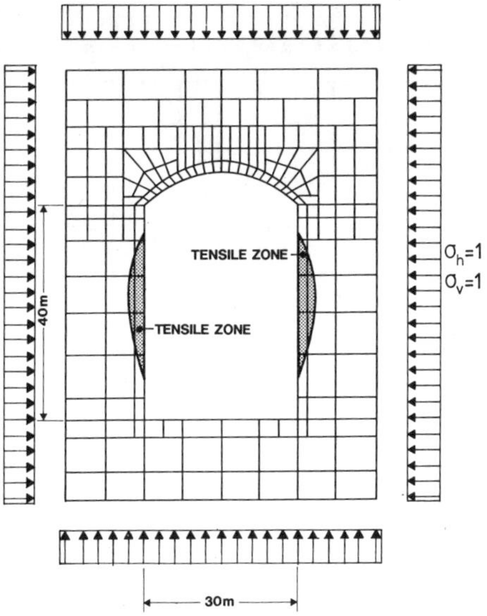

Fig. 6c

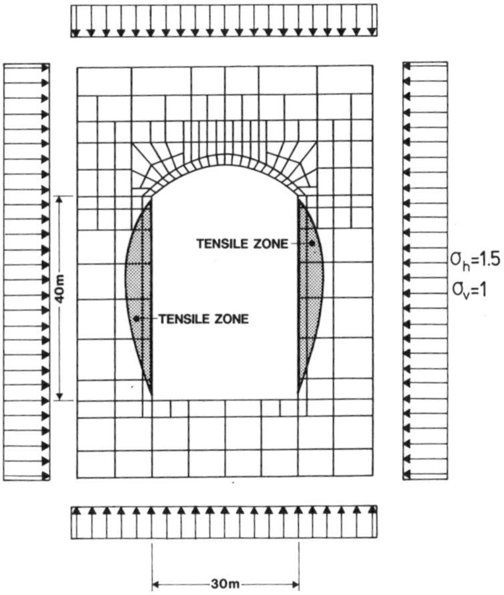

Fig. 6d

Figs. 6a-6d
Stress conditions for different ratios of σ_h/σ_v virgin stress for a conventional tunnel shape.

Thus, for a conventional tunnel, according to figs 6a and b, with 30m span, two dimensional FEM calculations show that there will be tensile stresses at the roof when $\sigma_h/\sigma_v > 0.5$.

When $\sigma_h/\sigma_v > 0.5$ there will be tensile stresses at the plane wall. See figs. 6c and 6d.

By rotation symmetrical calculation of the same cross section, the tensile stresses will be less when only vertical virgin stresses exist and there will be no tension when $\sigma_h/\sigma_v > 0.2$ for the dome-shaped roof. For all loading cases, there will be no tensile stresses at the cylindrical wall. See figs. 7a and 7b.

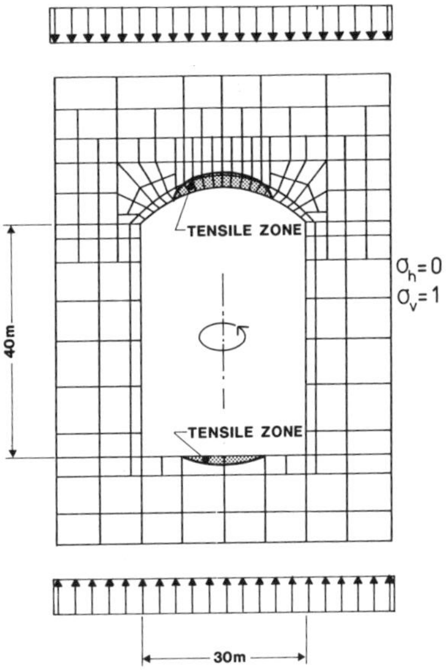

Fig. 7a

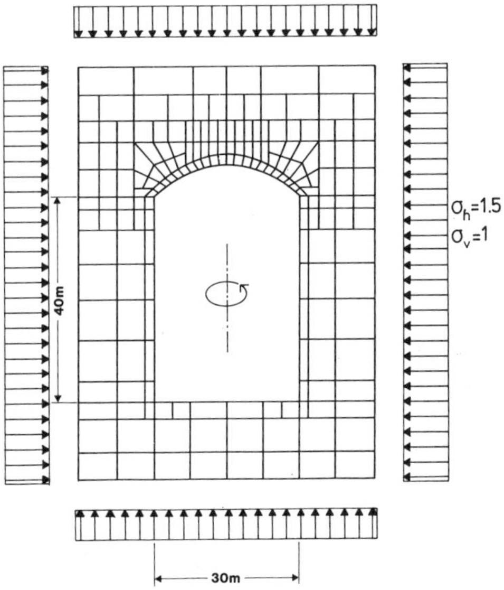

Fig. 7b

The cone-shaped roof, as illustrated in figs. 8a and 8b, will be still more favourable regarding tensile stresses.

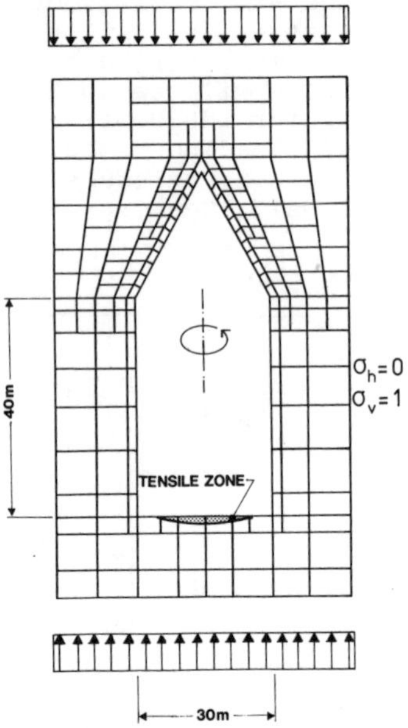

Fig. 8a

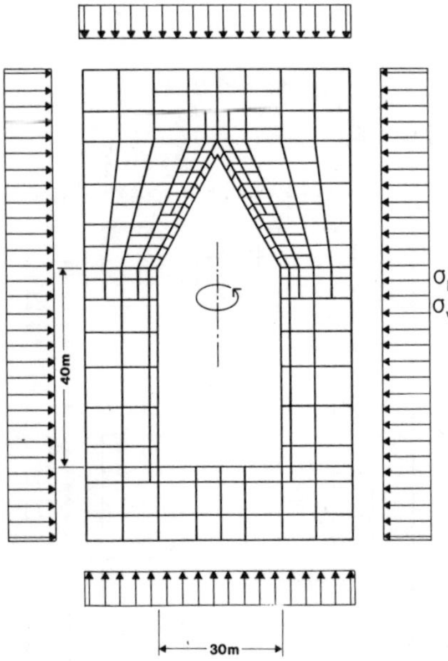

Fig. 8b

Also, the size will affect the stresses less compared to a conventional tunnel.

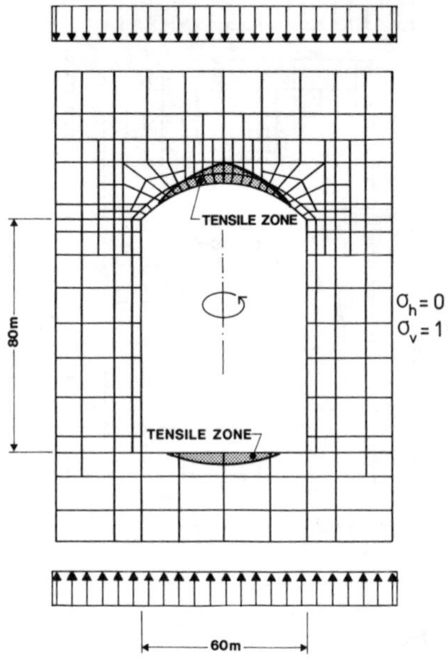

Fig. 9a

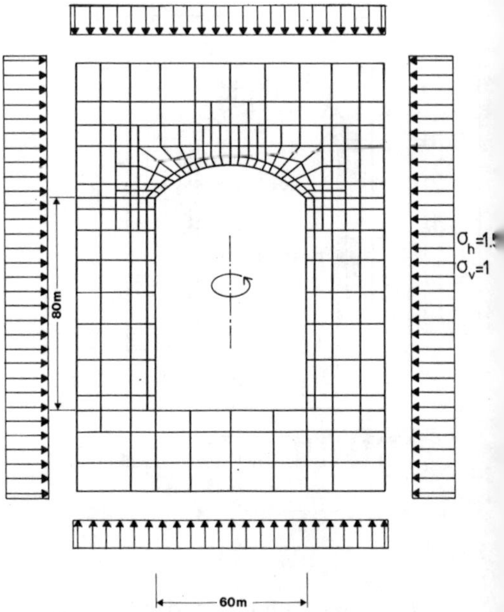

Fig. 9b

In the examples illustrated in figs. 9a and 9b, a span of 60m will make very slight changes to the horizontal stresses. The cone-shaped roof (not illustrated for this span) will not have any tension at the roof, even for the loading case with only vertical stresses.

Thus, when considering rock mechanical aspects of the Polytank design, a number of favourable points can be emphasized as consequences of the cylindrical shape and the cone or dome-shaped roof.

One of these points is stress condition. It seems that different structures of the rock mass will not give as many problems concerning stability as with a conventional tunnel. Therefore, it is quite possible to increase the diameter for many rock conditions.

This larger cross section is of considerable importance economically, especially for storages in weak rock and in the construction of caverns with expensive lining (because the ratio between the cross section area and the circumference is more favourable).

In order to investigate the influences of distances between the cisterns and the relation heights/diameter, model tests were carried out by the Okumura Corp., Japan, by applying uniaxial loads for the model pieces according to fig. 10. The results of these tests are presented in fig. 11 and show that σ is predominantly affected by the distance between the cisterns, and less by the relation h/d, for uniaxial loading.

It must be emphasized, however, that these calculations and model test can only be of use when comparing different designs in general. The final decision as to diameter, top angle of the cone, distance between the cisterns and levels of reinforcement etc. can only be decided when all valuable information about the rock is utilized - geological survey, rock stress measurements, computer analyses (taking the joint pattern and joint properties into account).

4. ASPECTS ON THE GEOPLANNING

A good geological survey of the rock, for vital parts of the Polytank storage, can be obtained with the aid of a core drilled hole along the axis of each conceived cavern. Such drill holes can also be used for rock stress measurements, TV-inspection and possible test pumping and/or water pressure tests. During the excavation, the many excavation fronts in a cavern group offer ex-

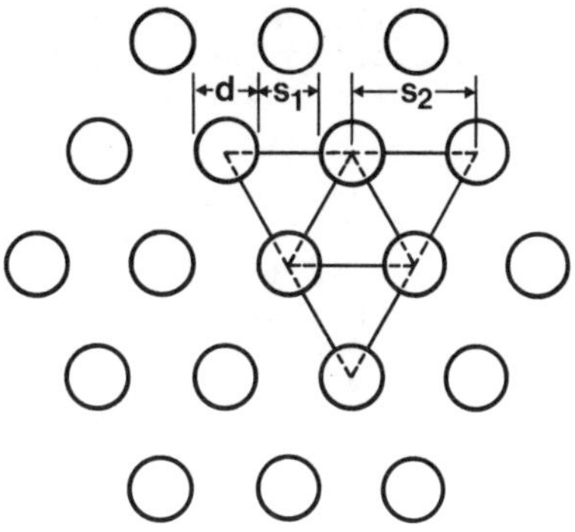

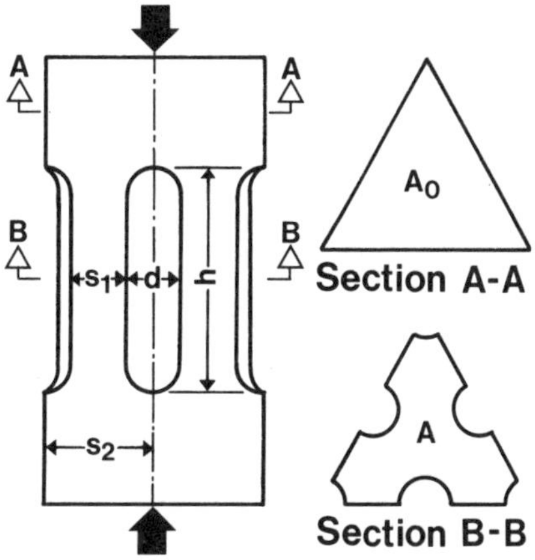

Fig. 10

Test pieces used for physical model tests, Okumura Corp. 1981.

Aspect ratio / Distance ratio		h/d		
		2.0	4.0	6.0
s_1/d (A/A_0)	0.3 (0.46)	0.543	0.523	0.503
	0.5 (0.60)	0.687	0.667	0.647
	0.7 (0.69)	0.785	0.765	0.745
	1.0 (0.77)	0.872	0.852	0.832

Fig. 11

Ratio between failure stress and parameters

cellent possibilities for performance of all types of reinforcement work without disturbing the time schedule.

5. CONSTRUCTION

The return to the use of vertical caverns suits the recent development of bench drilling equipment for holes with a depth of 30-50m. Such holes can be drilled today with an accuracy of ± 15cm. Even taking into account thorough and cautious excavation, the excavation capacity for vertical caverns is very high and construction time for Polytank storages can generally be expected to be less than for storages with horizontal cavern design.

In vertical caverns, disturbances in the bed rock, such as joints, crushed joints and clay dykes, are mostly easy to handle due to the good access to the roof and wall surfaces. With multi-cavern storages, in particular, access is available to many headings. This provides alternatives for excavation in cases of necessary reinforcement work at one or more of these headings. Thus, disturbances will not, or at least only slightly, affect the time schedule for the excavation.

The vertical shape of Polytank is very favourable for concrete or shotcrete lining in cases of weak rock conditions and also where lined and sealed storage caverns are demanded. The sealing is made by plastic lining of the concrete or shotcrete. Sealed caverns are constructed today with limited capacity but, in the future, will be utilized for larger capacities.

A very important advantage of the vertical design is that the caverns can be excavated very carefully which causes less damage to the surrounding rock at the contour. This is due to the fact that no heavy bottom charges are needed for the benches. By using longer holes, the many look-outs of horizontal gallery and bench drillings can be avoided, which also gives better contour.

6. FUNCTIONAL ASPECTS

The vertical Polytank caverns offer good conditions for handling and storage of all types of crude oil and oil products. The funnel design of the bottom makes it easy to collect and pump out even severe sludge deposits from heavy crude oi[l]. A vertical cavern can also be adapt[ed] easily for any change of such crude[s] likely to occur in the future.

The design gives good water separation conditions in the cavern and the water leakage into the cavern will be rapidly collected in th[e] water pit for further transfer to the oil separator. As described earlier, caverns for products sensitive to water will preferably be lined with a plastic lining. The design with bottom in the shape of a funnel with spout makes it easy to empty even big caverns and gives most favourable operating condition for the pumps, because the static head of the product is substantiall[y] higher than the NPSH, (Net Positive Suction Head) for the pump, except for the last few cubic metres of the caverns to be emptied. By installing conventional crude oil washing (COW) devices, as used on crude oil carriers, all types of deposits from heavy products can be handled in Polytank caverns.

A vital feature for the good function of the storage on waterbed is the maintenance of a ground wate[r] table. The compact location of the caverns of a Polytank storage makes it easy to control the ground water conditions. When necessary, the ground water can be controlled by establishing an artificial ground water above and around the storage. This is provided with the aid of a curtain of water filled drill holes around the storage which are fed with water from the water filled access tunnels and from special water supply tunnels. The static he[ad] in this curtain is kept above the level of the head of the original ground water table. To keep the ground water at sufficient static head above the caverns, a special horizontal water injection curtain is made above the top of the cavern[s]. It should be mentioned that underground storages, with very few exceptions, are operated by sinking of the ground water table above and closely around a storage. By establishing such a ground water regime it is assured that there is always an influx of water towards the storage making a safe barrier against the escape of oil to the ground water bed. The pressure of a cone of depression is easily controlled by water level control holes at different points within and around the storage area.

7. ECONOMY

It has been pretended that vertical caverns should be considerably more expensive than horizontal ones. An appreciable number of calculations have shown that, apart from reinforcement costs, horizontal caverns can be slightly cheaper than vertical ones, for storages in good and very good rock. In most cases, however, the difference would be balanced by the higher reinforcement costs for the horizontal alternative. In fair and weak rock, vertical caverns are always likely to be cheaper. This is due to the fact that roof and wall areas to be reinforced are comparatively smaller for vertical caverns than for horizontal ones. Furthermore, the curved walls of the vertical cylinder have better stability than the plane walls of horizontal tunnel shaped caverns.

In fact, the excavation and mucking costs differ very slightly between horizontal and vertical design and between different cavern shapes. As a rule, the difference in construction costs depend on the costs for reinforcement of the caverns. It is difficult to state, even roughly, the costs for underground storage installations but in most cases underground storage installations are somewhat cheaper than aboveground tanks including foundations and impoundments but excluding land costs. Also, lined and sealed rock storages are often cheaper than corresponding aboveground storages.

8. CONCLUSIONS

The Polytank method has many favourable points compared to horizontal caverns:

1. Safe storing of oils inclined to heavy sludge deposits.
2. Good control of oil/water interface conditions.
3. Good protection for products sensitive to air and water.
4. Good operation conditions for heated oil.
5. Better stability due to better stress conditions at the contour.
6. Less reinforcements due to less mantel area per volume unit.
7. Better shape for performance of linings.
8. Less lining area for lined caverns.

9. REFERENCES

Sagefors, I., Calminder, Å. 1980 Polytank Underground Liquid Storage. In Sub-surface Space. Rockstore '80. S.M. Bergman (ed) Oxford & New York, Pergamon Press.

Calminder, Å., 1981 Vertical Pattern for Petroleum Storage in Weak Rock, Tunnels and Tunnelling, 6: 11-14.

Hahn, T., Josefsson, L., Keijer, U. The Finite Element Method in Rock Mechanics. Some aspects in connection with a practical case (in Swedish). Royal Swedish Fortifications Admin. Report 134:4 Eskilstuna '81.

Hahn, T., Keijer, U., Some aspects on how to use numerical analyses in rock design- an application to the design of a cavern with 30m span. SRM Symposium, Aachen '82.

Hiltscher, R., Strindell, L., Rock Stress Measurements as a base when designing large caverns (in Swedish) National Comm. of Rock Mechanics (BEFO) 1976.

BASIC STUDIES ASSOCIATED WITH THE DESIGN OF SALT CAVERNS FOR THE STORAGE OF PRESSURIZED FLUIDS

Grundlagenstudien über den Entwurf von Salzkavernen zum Speichern von Flüssigkeiten unter Druck

Études fondamentales en relation avec la conception des cavernes excavées dans un massif de sel pour l'emmagasinage des fluides sous pression

H.REGINALD HARDY, Jr.
Pennsylvania State University, University Park, USA

SUMMARY:
A recent review of the world literature indicates that the necessary expertise for designing, constructing and stability monitoring of engineering "structures" constructed in salt is at present relatively limited, and additional basic research in a number of areas is necessary. In this regard, since 1975 a research project has been underway at The Pennsylvania State University, involving the design and performance of salt caverns for the storage of pressurized natural gas. During this project studies have been carried out in two specific areas, namely: the development of a better understanding of how salt behaves under conditions of stress and temperature equivalent to those found around a typical pressurized underground cavern, and the development of analytical methods by which the behavior of proposed and operating caverns may be suitably evaluated. The present paper will include an outline of the fundamental concepts involved in the salt cavern storage of natural gas, and a brief review of the laboratory and analytical studies (closed-form and FEM) carried out during the research project.

ZUSAMMENFASSUNG:
Ein kürzlich abgeschlossener Überblick über die Weltliteratur zeigt, daβ die nötige Expertise für den Entwurf, den Bau und die Überwachung der Stabilität von Höhlen die im Salz angelegt wurden beschränk ist, und Grundlagenforschung in einer Anzahl von Gebieten notwendig ist. An der Pennsylvania State University ist seit 1975 ein Forschungsproject über den Entwurf und die Anlage von Salzhöhlen zum Speichern von verflüssigtem Erdgas aktiv. In seinem Rahmen ist auf zwei besonderen Gebieten gearbeitet worden: Der Entwickelung eines besseren Verständnisses des Benehmens von Salz unter Spannungs- and Temperaturzuständen, die denen entsprechen, die in der Umgebung von typischen unter Druck gesetzten Höhlen herrschen, und der Entwickelung von analytischen Methoden, durch die das Verhalten von vorgeschlagenen Höhlen und solchen, die in Betrieb sind, beurteil werden kann. Dieser Vortrag enthält einen Abriβ der Grundlagen der Speicherung von Erdgas in Salzhöhlen und einen kurzen Überblick über Laboratoriumsversuche und analytische Studien, die im Rahmen dieses Forschungsprojektes ausgeführt wurden.

RESUME:
Une révision des informations de sources mondiales confirme l'opinion que l'expertise nécessaire à la conception, la construction et le contrôle de la stabilité des oeuvres de génie réalisés dans un massif de sel est relativement restreinte. A cet effet, un projet de recherches concernant la conception et le comportement des cavernes excavées dans un massif de sel pour l'emmagasinage sous pression du gaz naturel est en marche dupuis 1975 à The Pennsylvania State University. Ce projet s'est penché sur l'étude dans deux domaines particuliers soit; l'étude d'une meilleure connaissance du comportement d'un massif de sel dans l'ambiance de contraintes et de température existante dans un emplacement type de caverne sous pression ainsi que du développement des méthodes analytiques visant une évaluation convenable du comportement de cavernes sous étude ou existantes. Cette communication traitera des idées fondamentales de l'emmagasinage sous pression du gaz naturel dans les cavernes excavées dans un massif de sel. En plus, une revue briève des études en labo et analytiques (équations mathématiques rigoureuses et éléments finis) sera présentée.

1 INTRODUCTION

Extensive research and industrial development in the area of salt cavern storage is presently underway in the USA and elsewhere. In particular, the use of solution mined caverns for the storage of such materials as crude oil, petroleum products, natural gas, and compressed air has accelerated rapidly during the last 10 years. It is apparent, therefore, that in the future the utilization of caverns, from which salt has been extracted by conventional or solution mining techniques, will play a vital role in supporting the world's growing energy and environmental demands.

A recent review of the literature has indicated, however, that the necessary expertise for designing, constructing, and stability monitoring of engineering "structures" constructed in salt is at present relatively limited, and additional basic research in a number of areas is necessary. In this regard, since 1975 a research project has been underway at The Pennsylvania State University, involving the design and performance of salt caverns for the storage of pressurized natural gas. During this project studies have been carried out in two specific areas, namely: the development of a better understanding of how salt behaves under conditions of stress and temperature equivalent to those found around a typical pressurized underground cavern, and the development of analytical methods by which the behavior of proposed and operating caverns may be suitably evaluated.

Various aspects of this project have been presented at Fifth Symposium on Salt held in Hamburg in 1978 (Hardy, 1980A; Hardy and Mangolds, 1980; Hardy et al., 1980). The present paper will include an outline of the fundamental concepts involved in the salt cavern storage of natural gas, and a brief review of the more recent laboratory and analytical studies. It should be emphasized that, although the paper deals specifically with the storage of natural gas the majority of the material presented may be equally well applied to salt caverns used for the storage of pressurized fluids in general.

2 GENERAL ASPECTS OF THE CURRENT PROJECT

2.1 Underground storage of natural gas

As the demand for natural gas increases, the necessity of storing larger and larger volumes of gas underground during periods of low demand has increased markedly. At present three basic types of underground storage are utilized, namely, former gas and oil reservoirs, aquifers, and man-made caverns. The use of man-made caverns for the storage of natural gas has accelerated in recent years. Such facilities include mined caverns and tunnels, and modified mine workings. In such facilities the role of water in limiting the storage pressure of the structure may, at least in some cases, be of less importance than in aquifer and reservoir facilities.

Man-made storage facilities offer the advantage that their dimensions, and often their location, may be conveniently tailored to the storage requirements. Furthermore, in some cases where suitable reservoirs or aquifers are not available, they provide the only available storage capability. Such facilities, since they involve an open cavity rather than a mass of porous rock, are capable of extremely high injection and withdrawal rates. At present solution mined salt caverns are the most widely utilized of the man-made storage facilities. In spite of their numerous advantages they do suffer from one serious limitation, namely, the fact that their structural stability is highly sensitive to the minimum storage pressure level.

Although the storage of liquids in salt caverns was initiated early in the 1920's, it was not until the mid 1960's that such facilities were utilized for the storage of compressed natural gas. The first gas cavern in the United States developed specifically for natural gas storage was constructed in 1970 by the Transcontinental Gas Pipe Line Corporation in the Eminence Salt Dome in Covington County, Mississippi (Anon., 1971). According to a recent A.G.A. survey (Anon., 1980A), as of 1980 there were eight salt cavern facilities in operation in North America utilized specifically for the storage of natural gas. These facilities involve a total of 19 separate storage caverns, and some 27,500 MMscf of natural gas. A recent industrial report (Anon., 1980B) indicates that in North America at present seven additional caverns are in the planning or construction stage. Numerous other salt cavern storage facilities are also in use for the storage of crude oil, petroleum products, and other fluids.

Similar storage facilities are in use in Great Britain, Germany, France, and other foreign countries (Hardy, 1980B). For example, Gaz de France has plans to construct a total of 45 salt caverns at two sites (Etrez and Tersanne) for the storage of natural gas. At present eight of these are completed, 10 are under construction, and a number are in the planning stage. In Germany, one firm, Kaveren Bau- und Betriebs - GmbH (KBB) has in recent years constructed 16 storage caverns for natural gas as well as over 40 other caverns for the storage of compressed air, butane, and crude oil.

2.2 Salt cavern storage concept

Salt caverns for the storage of pressurized natural gas are simply large tanks created underground using solution mining (leaching) techniques. As shown in Figure 1A, when a cavern is being developed in a salt dome or in a pure, thick, bedded salt deposit, only one well is usually drilled. Suitable pipe (casing) is cemented from the top edge of the salt layer to the surface and then a string of smaller piping is hung inside the outer pipe. Using the so-called direct injection technique, fresh water is pumped down the inner pipe into the salt formation, where it dissolves the salt. The resulting brine is then forced up the space between the inner and outer pipes. This brine may be disposed of by selling it to a salt company or by injecting it into a porous rock formation located well below any fresh water reservoirs. By controlling the fresh water flow rate and the bottom-end position of the inner pipe, it is possible to generate a cavern of specific size and geometry. Once the required cavern has been developed, as determined by sonar techniques, the cavern is dewatered by injecting gas through the outer annulus and displacing the brine out of the cavern through the inner pipe. Following suitable integrity evaluation, the cavern is ready for use as a storage facility (see Figure 1B).

One important advantage of salt cavern storage is that since the gas does not have to flow through porous rock into the wellbore, as it does in other types of underground gas storage (reservoirs and aquifers) it can be produced very quickly (high deliverability) when needed and the cavern can be refilled rapidly when demand is less. For "peak shaving," then, salt caverns are ideal since they need not be large to be extremely valuable. They can, however, be built to store large volumes if required and single caverns with volumes of 20×10^6 ft^3 have been constructed.

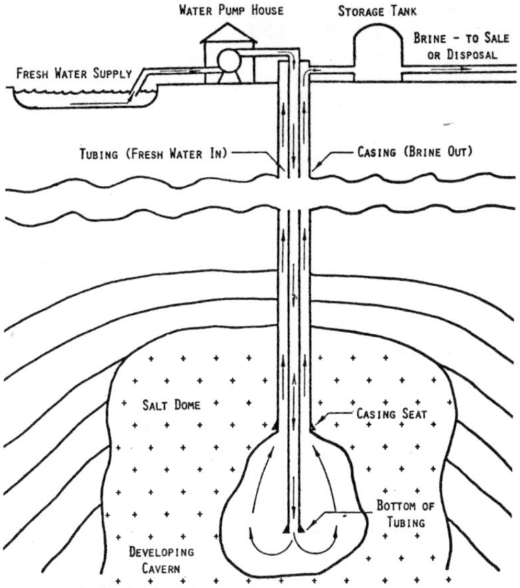

(A) Solution mining operation (after Slater, 1975)

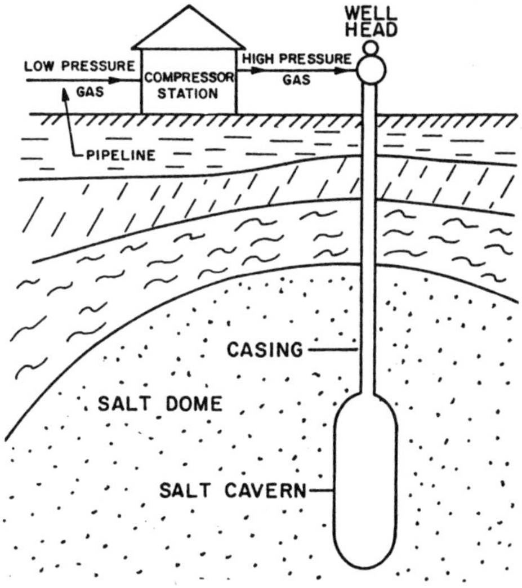

(B) Completed storage cavern

Figure 1. Simplified diagrams illustrating salt cavern development and utilization.

2.3 Rock mechanics considerations

A major concern in the design of storage caverns is structural stability. An excellent review of the general rock mechanics considerations necessary for the development of suitable salt cavern storage facilities has been presented recently by Querio (1980). In terms of the fundamental mechanics principles involved, salt cavern storage involves the storage of a pressurized fluid in a thick-walled underground container, the walls of which are composed of salt. In use this container is loaded internally by the pressure of the stored fluid, and externally by in-situ ground stresses. The mechanical stability of such a container depends on the internal pressure, the in-situ stress field, the geometry of the container, and the mechanical properties of the associated salt. It is important to note that in such a storage facility there is a critical minimum storage pressure as well as a maximum one. This critical minimum pressure level arises due to the fact that over a specific range the pressure exerted by the stored fluid actually helps maintain cavern stability by partially balancing the effects of the in-situ stresses; however, below the minimum critical pressure the in-situ stress field may be sufficient to overcome the "strength" of the surrounding salt causing cavern closure and/or failure.

There are a number of possible types of mechanical instabilities that may occur in solution mined storage caverns during and after their development (Hardy, 1980A). These include subsurface subsidence and subsequent surface subsidence, closure, local fracture and block flow, deep fracturing, and various combinations of the above. It should be emphasized that at present, with the exception of closure, the occurrence of gross instabilities of the type noted are rare; although small scale instabilities of most types probably occur frequently. It is apparent, therefore, that as salt cavern storage becomes more popular, and larger and more sophisticated cavern facilities are contemplated, careful site selection, more rigorous design techniques, and methods of early instability detection will be necessary to insure long-term cavern stability.

Studies to date indicate that salt cavern closure, where the cavern volume effectively decreases as a function of time, is normally due to the presence of high in-situ stress, low cavern pressures, and/or elevated temperatures. Experience has shown that solution mined salt storage caverns normally experience an initial 5-10 percent closure during the first year or so following completion; however, there are cases where closures of 20 percent or more have been observed. Such a situation would certainly have to be defined as a "facility failure." Since cavern closure is a stress dependent instability it is directly related to cavern depth and possibly in some instances to the presence of orogenic stresses. Although such stresses may play an insignificant role in the closure of caverns located in bedded salt deposits, they may well be extremely important in those cases where the caverns are located in salt domes. Unfortunately, the mechanics of salt dome formation and the associated in-situ stress fields are not well known at present.

Based on fundamental rock mechanics considerations and a review of the limited field case histories available for operating caverns, the following factors appear to be of critical importance in the design of salt caverns.

(1) In-situ Stress Field
  - Depth
  - Stress Ratio (K)

(2) Cavern Dimensions
  - Shape (Geometry)
  - Size (Volume)

(3) Cavern Spacing

(4) Storage Pressure Limits
  - Maximum
  - Minimum

(5) Injection-Withdrawal Cycle
  - Pressure Increment
  - Injection/Withdrawal Rate
  - Shut-in Time

(6) Temperature
  - Ambient Salt Temperature (Geothermal Gradient)
  - Temperature Changes Due to Injection/Withdrawal

(7) Mechanical Properties of Associated Media
  - Salt
  - Adjacent Rock

2.4 Possible design approaches

In terms of basic mechanics considerations there are three general approaches to the problem of salt cavern design. These are based on the assumed characteristic behavior of the media involved, namely, elastic, elastic-plastic, or viscoelastic-viscoplastic. A brief outline of each approach follows.

(1) Elastic approach--"Design is based on the fact that the maximum stresses around the cavern do not exceed the yield strength of the salt." Using this approach only the elastic properties and the yield strength of the salt are required. Furthermore, the associated analytical methods are relatively simple, with the necessary finite element programs being commonly available and inexpensive, and closed-form solutions for a number of typical cavern shapes also being available. Although this approach is useful for preliminary analyses, it is too conservative and therefore impractical for actual cavern design. Since the yield strength of salt is relatively low ($100 < \sigma_y < 2000$ psi),

the necessity of maintaining the maximum stresses below the yield strength would require that the stored gas be kept at a relatively high pressure. This in turn would result in limited working gas and an uneconomical storage facility.

(2) Elastic-plastic approach--"Design is based on the fact that the maximum stresses around the cavern, during certain phases of the injection-withdrawal cycle, may exceed the yield strength of the salt and limited plastic (permanent) deformations may occur. However, such stresses should not reach levels where significant time-dependent strain (creep) occurs." Using this approach requires a relatively limited knowledge of the mechanical properties of the salt, namely, the elastic properties, the yield strength, and the plastic deformation characteristics (flow rule). Furthermore, from an analytical point-of-view, although only limited closed-form solutions exist, a number of suitable finite element programs are commonly available and the cost of running these is relatively inexpensive.

Using this design approach operating pressures would depend on the maximum permanent cavern closure that can be tolerated. These may be computed as a function of minimum proposed cavern pressure and are assumed to be independent of time. This approach also makes it possible to compute the dimensions of the plastic zone surrounding the cavern and this data may be utilized as a means of computing cavern spacing in multiple-cavern installations. In general this approach may provide reasonable estimates for a number of parameters needed in cavern design, however, in many cases these may be overly conservative. Furthermore, care must be taken to insure that the maximum stresses do not reach levels where the material begins to deform in a time-dependent manner.

(3) Viscoelastic-viscoplastic approach--"Design is based on the fact that the maximum stresses around the cavern, during certain phases of the injection-withdrawal cycle, may exceed the stress level at which time-dependent deformation occurs." In the present context the term viscoelastic-viscoplastic is considered to include a wide range of material behavior including viscoelastic-plastic, elastic-viscoplastic, and viscoelastic-viscoplastic. Since both laboratory and field studies indicate that salt is in fact a viscoelastic-viscoplastic material, this approach is the most desirable. The associated analysis, however, is highly sophisticated and requires a very detailed knowledge of the properties of the associated salt.

A truly realistic viscoelastic-viscoplastic analysis would require very detailed mechanical property data, including the elastic, viscoelastic, plastic, and viscoplastic properties of the specific salt in which the cavern is to be constructed. At present even the general range of many of these properties are not available, and in some cases suitable standard tests for their evaluation are still under development. Furthermore, in terms of the necessary analytical techniques, although a few highly simplified closed-form solutions have been developed in the present study, in general such a design approach requires the use of relatively complex and somewhat expensive finite element programs. At present, in most cases, these must be considered as research tools rather than design aides, although it is felt with some additional research finite element programs suitable for design could be developed.

Using this design approach operating pressures will depend on the maximum level of volume closure which can be tolerated during a specific period of cavern use (e.g., 10 years). Due to the fact that the salt is considered to be viscoelastic-viscoplastic its behavior will be time-dependent and may also exhibit so-called "memory effects." As a result cavern closure in general will depend not only on the minimum storage pressure level but also on the pressure versus time characteristics of the current, as well as previous, injection-withdrawal cycles.

2.5 Outline of current project

The ultimate goal of the current project is to develop generalized criteria by which the operation of existing salt cavern storage facilities could be optimized and on which the design of future caverns could be based. Unfortunately, due to the relatively limited state-of-the-art available in respect to salt cavern design, the experimental and analytical difficulties encountered, and limitations in the available time and funding, it has not been possible as yet to complete the development of the desired generalized criteria. Nevertheless, the studies to date have made it possible to formulate the basic principles necessary for future development of rational salt cavern design criteria, and have resolved a considerable number of the intermediate problems. Figure 2 presents a block diagram illustrating the various components of the project. Research has been carried out on all components with the exception of No. 7, for which further detailed studies are required.

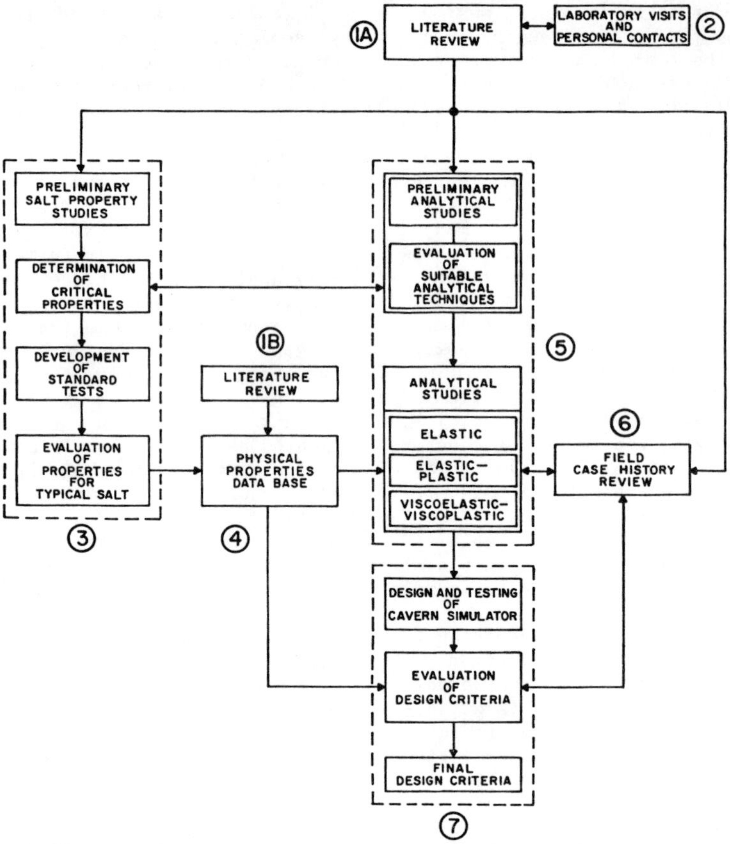

Figure 2. Block diagram illustrating the various components of the overall salt cavern design project. (Component 7 remains to be completed.)

As illustrated in Figure 2, the project has involved theoretical studies to develop suitable methods for analysis of cavern behavior (component 5), and laboratory studies (component 3) in which the basic mechanical behavior of salt were investigated in order to evaluate the necessary parameters for use in these and future analytical studies. These major studies have been supplemented by a detailed review of the associated literature, and the development of extensive personal contacts with other researchers involved in the study of the mechanical behavior of salt and salt cavern design.

A brief outline of the laboratory and analytical studies undertaken during the current project will be presented in subsequent sections of this paper. A full description of these studies is included in a project monograph presently in the final stages of preparation (Hardy, 1982).

3 LABORATORY STUDIES

3.1 General

The rational design of an underground structure is contingent on a thorough knowledge of the essential properties of the construction medium. Salt is one of the more complex of the common geological materials in respect to its response to stress. As a result, a relatively large number of mechanical parameters are required if a realistic design of a structure in salt is to be undertaken. From a laboratory point-of-view, tests on salt present a considerable number of problems not encountered with other geologic materials. During the early stages of the project the majority of the laboratory effort was expended in reviewing the associated literature, isolating the most-critical properties, evaluating methods for salt specimen preparation and specimen strain measurement, and carrying out a variety of preliminary tests.

Details on these preliminary studies have been presented in an earlier paper (Hardy and Roberts, 1977).

Once a decision was made as to the required critical properties, the development of the necessary equipment and procedures for carrying out the associated laboratory tests was initiated. In some cases existing standard techniques could be applied directly; however, in most cases, extensive development work was required. Figure 3 presents a block diagram of the overall laboratory program. As indicated, the necessary physical property data (accessory, elastic, strength, and inelastic properties) were generated by the five major studies shown to the left side of the figure, namely:

(1) General studies--Uniaxial studies to evaluate the elastic properties (Young's modulus and Poisson's ratio) and strength properties (compressive and tensile strength) were carried out. A number of accessory parameters, such as specific gravity, acoustic emission, ultrasonic velocity, etc., were also investigated.

(2) Creep studies--Creep studies were undertaken in order to evaluate a number of the viscoelastic-viscoplastic parameters for salt. A three-phase program was involved.

(3) Yield strength studies--Here acoustic emission, microscopic and other techniques were investigated in an attempt to develop an objective means for evaluating the yield-point in salt. Tests were carried out on both single crystal and polycrystalline specimens.

(4) Residual stress retention studies--Since residual stresses may be important in the analysis of salt cavern stability, particularly in salt domes, experiments were carried out to evaluate if and how residual stresses may be stored in salt. Studies were conducted on artificial salt and on a number of types of natural salt.

(5) Failure criteria studies--Initial analysis of the stress states associated with pressurized caverns loaded under typical in-situ stresses indicated that mixed states of compression (C) and tension (T) may occur. Studies were planned to evaluate the failure criteria of salt under the following states of stress: T-T-C, T-C-C, and C-C-C. These studies, however, were of a low priority, relative to the other four, and to date only preliminary considerations have been given to initiation of the necessary test program.

Since the present paper does not permit a detailed discussion of all phases of the laboratory studies, attention will be focused on selected aspects of the creep and yield strength studies.

3.2 Creep studies

The most common test for determining time dependent response (viscoelastic-

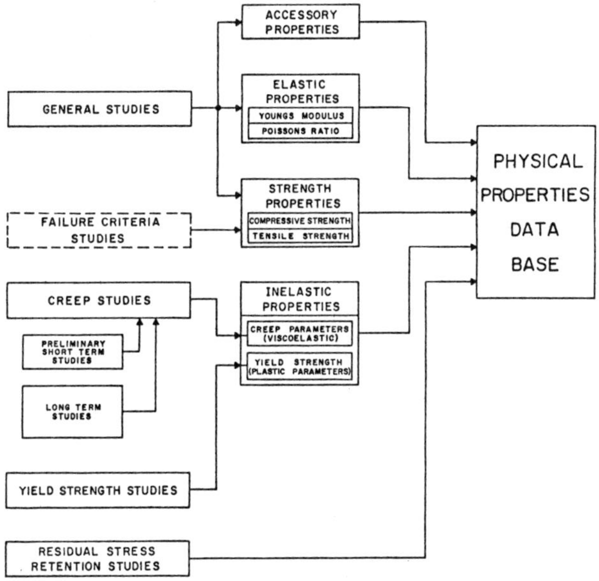

Figure 3. Block diagram of overall laboratory program associated with the salt cavern design project.

viscoplastic character) of a material is the creep test. During this test, a load (either tension or compression) is applied to the material as rapidly as possible, and maintained for a certain time period during which specimen deformations or strains are measured. Such tests may be conducted under uniaxial, biaxial, or polyaxial loading conditions.

In-house laboratory studies to evaluate the creep behavior of salt were initiated during the first year of the current project (1975) and continued until the end of 1981. Although the study of short-term creep in typical hard rocks presents a number of experimental difficulties, these are almost insignificant compared to the problems encountered in carrying out relatively long-term studies on salt. A number of these problems include difficulties associated with specimen preparation and specimen strain instrumentation, the sensitivity of salt to humidity and temperature, and the problems of maintaining creep testing facilities operational over extended continuous periods of time (days to months).

In general laboratory studies associated with the creep behavior of salt have involved a three-phase program, namely:

(1) Phase I--This phase involved the evaluation of various methods of specimen preparation and strain instrumentation, modification of existing testing facilities, and the completion of a series of short-term creep and acoustic emission studies on specimens of artificial salt. These studies were completed in 1977 and a detailed description of this phase is presented in a recent M.S. thesis (Roberts, 1981).

(2) Phase II--The second phase of the creep study involved the development, construction, and calibration of creep testing facilities specifically designed for carrying out long-term creep experiments on salt. This included apparatus for conducting both uniaxial and triaxial creep tests over periods of time up to three months or more. Following completion of the facilities a series of uniaxial creep tests were carried out on specimens of artificial salt and a number of types of natural salt. These studies were completed in early 1979 and a recent M.S. thesis (Bakhtar, 1979) presents a detailed description of this phase of the study.

(3) Phase III--The final phase of the study was initiated early in 1979. It involved initially some redesign of the apparatus developed earlier in Phase II and the relocation of the overall creep testing facility. This was followed by the development of facilities for carrying out tests at elevated temperatures, and the improvement of strain, load, and temperature monitoring facilities. Subsequently, an extensive series of calibration studies were completed and creep tests under uniaxial and triaxial stress were carried out on a range of types of natural salt at room and elevated temperatures.

Figure 4 shows a view of two of the uniaxial creep loading frames and the associated load control rack developed during the Phase II studies. A block diagram of the deformation, strain, and load monitorin facilities utilized during the Phase III studies is shown in Figure 5. Similar facilities were developed for triaxial creep tests.

Figure 4. Uniaxial creep loading frames and associated load control rack.

During the Phase III creep studies a considerable number of very detailed creep tests were carried out on a variety of types of natural salt. These tests were conducted in order to optimize experimental techniques and associated data processing techniques, and to generate various creep parameters for use in later analytical studies. Eight major groups of creep tests were undertaken including incremental and load-unload tests, long-term tests under room and elevated temperature conditions, and a series of short-term comparative tests on six different types of salt. Data from these tests were fitted to various forms of the Burgers model and to a temperature-dependent secondary creep model (Norton's law). Figure 6, for example, illustrates the axial creep strain versus time data obtained for a specimen of type

S12 salt (specimen S12L-01) tested over a total period of 148 days at a uniaxial stress of 1450 psi and a temperature of 117°F. Table 1 presents the associated Burgers model parameters.

A detailed description of the various creep studies carried out during the Phase-I, -II, and -III studies is available elsewhere (Hardy, 1982). A number of general conclusions based on the experimental results obtained from creep tests on natural salt carried out during the Phase III studies are as follows:

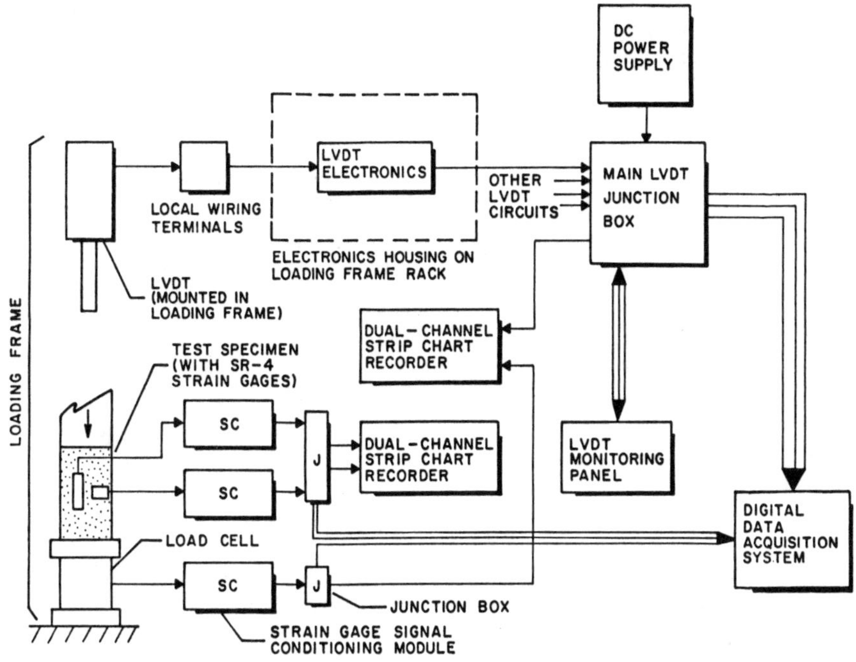

Figure 5. Block diagram of the monitoring system utilized in the Phase III creep studies.

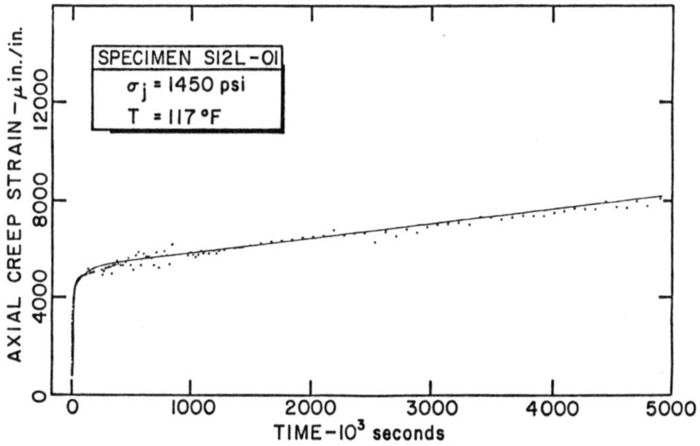

Figure 6. Axial creep strain versus time curve for the first 58 days of a 148 day long-term elevated temperature creep test on specimen S12L-01. (Natural salt type S12; test conducted at a uniaxial compressive stress of 1450 psi and a temperature of 117°F; curve is an n = 3 Burgers model fit to the data.)

Table 1. Burgers model (n = 2 & 3) parameters for specimens S12L-01 (natural salt type S12) based on data obtained during a long-term test under conditions of uniaxial compressive stress and elevated temperature.

Specimen Number	n* -	$\Delta\sigma_j$ psi	σ_j psi	E_1 10^6 psi	N_1 10^9 psi-sec	E_2 10^6 psi	N_2 10^9 psi-sec	E_3 10^6 psi	N_3 10^9 psi-sec	E_4 10^6 psi	N_4 10^9 psi-sec
S12L-01	2	1450	1450	0.64	0.12	0.51	5.96	0.30	2214	-	-
	3	1450	1450	0.82	0.10	0.59	2.44	1.56	138	0.30	2351

*Parameters associated with the generalized Burgers model.

(1) In general, the results of high quality uniaxial creep tests on a range of types of natural salt indicated that the observed creep behavior for these materials could be reasonably well represented by means of the Burgers mechanical model. Sufficient data was not available from triaxial tests to validate the applicability of Burgers model type analysis for such data.

(2) The analysis of short-term creep data for seven different types of salt indicate (at least in terms of the test conditions utilized) that the creep characteristics of salt are highly site specific.

(3) The difficulties encountered in fitting Burgers models to uniaxial creep data was found to increase greatly as the duration of the associated creep experiment increased. This appears to be primarily due to the development of linear or quasi-linear creep behavior, after test durations of approximately 100 x 10^3 seconds, which tends to override the initial non-linear (transient) creep response.

(4) Extremely accurate control of stress and temperature is necessary in both uniaxial and triaxial creep experiments if meaningful data is to be obtained.

(5) In general, it was observed that, under the same stress conditions, larger test specimens exhibit a lower creep rate than smaller ones. In general, the form of the associated "size effect" relationship is unknown. Caution, therefore, should be exercised in comparing creep data obtained from different sized test specimens. However, since the size effect appears to be related to the degree of specimen confinement, such effects may be less critical when specimens are tested under triaxial stress.

(6) If the steady state creep characteristics of a salt are required, creep experiments must be run sufficiently long to insure that the creep strain versus time data is truly linear.

(7) When utilizing creep strain-rate data to evaluate stress and/or time dependency, it is imperative that all data utilized be based on tests conducted over similar periods of time.

(8) In order to obtain more accurate data in regard to the transient creep characteristics of salt it will be necessary to develop a more objective means for computing the instantaneous strain occurring during loading and unloading, and the time (t = 0) at which creep strain first occurs.

3.3 Yield strength studies

As part of the current study, a laboratory investigation was undertaken into several phenomena associated with the plastic deformation of salt (Richardson, 1978). This investigation was conducted for the purpose of developing an objective means of assessing the yield strength of salt for underground cavern design purposes During the first stage of these laboratory tests, single crystal specimens of salt were loaded in uniaxial compression well into the plastic region. Stress-strain behavior, changes in dislocation density, acoustic emission (AE), and permanent strain upon unloading were observed during these tests. In the second stage of the study, these same characteristics were monitored during the deformation of polycrystalline natural salt, and the present discussion will for the most part be limited to the results of tests on this material.

During deformation studies, two different types of tests were utilized, namely, single cycle and load-unload tests. In the former, specimen stress was increased, at either a constant load or a constant strain rate, to a specific stress level and then decreased to zero. The latter, load-unload test had a more complex format. In this type of test the axial deformation was increased at a constant rate from a fixed medium preload to a peak strain level and back to the minimum preload. The specimen was loaded repetitively in this manner, with the peak deformation level being increased by fixed increments for each cycle. In these studies the plastic yield-point was defined as the applied axial stress level at which a permanent strain of 0.2 percent was induced in the test specimen. In this paper this will be referred to here as the 0.2 percent offset-strain yield limit.

Figure 7 is an idealized representation of the load and stroke output characteristic of a load-unload test on a specimen of polycrystalline salt. Single crystal specimens were similarly tested, although their stress-strain behavior differed from that of the natural salt. The following features should be noted on Figure 7:

(i) the minimum preload,
(ii) the peak stress (A) for cycle 2,
(iii) the total strain (B) for cycle 2,
(iv) the permanent strain (C) for cycle 2,
(v) the cumulative total strain (D), obtained by adding the permanent strain from cycle 1 to the total strain (B) from cycle 2, and
(vi) the cumulative permanent strain (E), obtained by adding the permanent strain (C) from cycle 2 to that from cycle 1.

The critical parameter obtained using the load-unload test procedure is the cumulative permanent strain, which represents the offset-strain used to determine the 0.2 percent offset-strain yield limit.

Figure 8 shows typical stress-strain data for a specimen of natural polycrystalline salt (type S4) deformed at a constant rate of 20 μs/sec. It is evident, due to the lack of any obvious inflection, that a yield-point cannot be directly determined from a curve of this type, except by some indirect or arbitrary means.

Six specimens of natural polycrystalline salt (type S4) were subsequently tested using the load-unload method described earlier. An initial test (specimen J-3) provided information on the behavior of type S4 salt under load-unload conditions and enabled a deformation-time program to be established for subsequent tests. Suitable data was obtained from these later tests, and Figure 9 illustrates a typical example of the associated strain versus stress curves. The yield-point values, obtained using the 0.2 percent offset technique, were obtained from the cumulative permanent strain curves and are given in Table 2. The mean yield-point value was found to be 564 psi. Data obtained during the preliminary tests on specimen J-3 were not included here since the deformation-time program utilized differed significantly from that used for the later specimens.

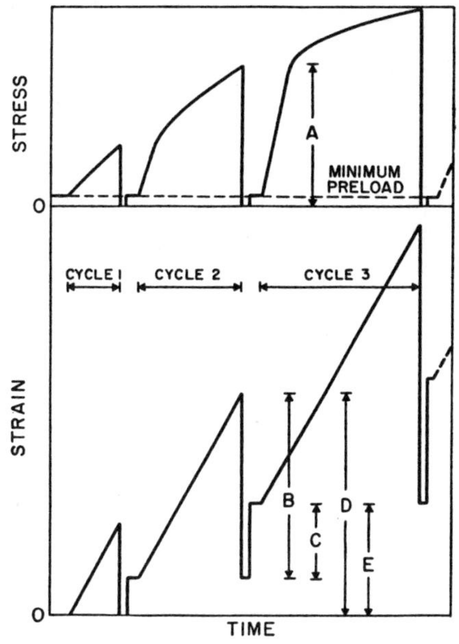

Figure 7. Stress and strain versus time for load-unload test on natural polycrystalline salt. (Only three cycles are shown. Letters indicate important features of cycle-2 as discussed in the text.)

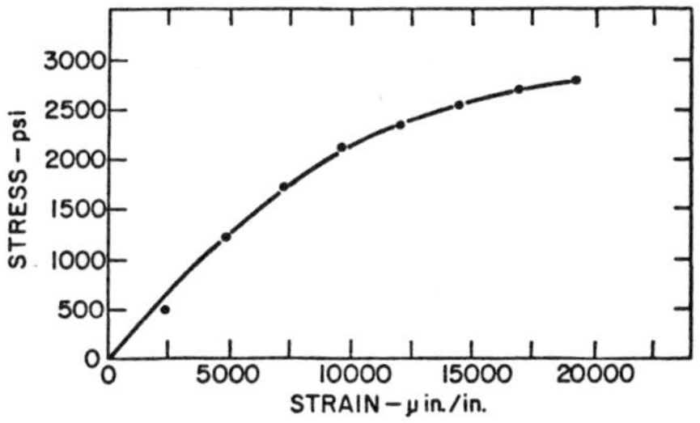

Figure 8. Stress-strain behavior of natural polycrystalline salt (type S4) at a constant strain rate of 20 μs/sec (specimen J-6).

As was observed earlier for single crystal salt, polycrystalline salt was also found to generate AE activity during deformation studies. Figure 10 presents the results of three single-cycle deformation tests, carried out at a constant strain rate of 20 μs/sec, during which AE activity was also monitored. The AE rate data shown was obtained at a total system gain of 94 dB.

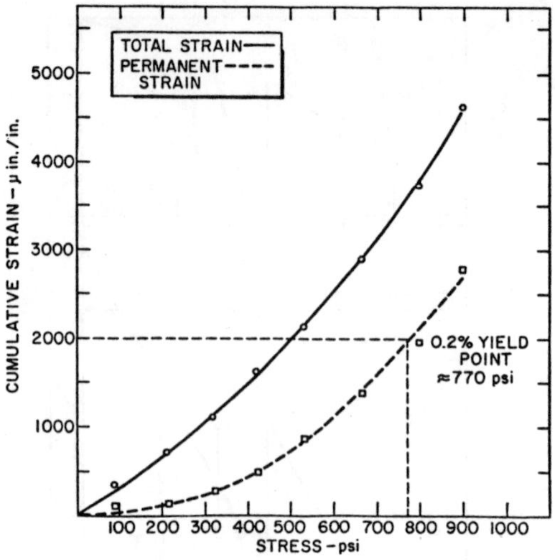

Figure 9. Cumulative total and cumulative permanent strain versus stress data obtained from load-unload tests performed on specimen S-10 (salt type S4) deformed at a strain rate of 20 μs/sec.

Table 2. Yield-point values for natural polycrystalline salt (type S4) under uniaxial compressive stress at room temperature.

Specimen Number	0.2% Yield-Point Stress psi
J-4	440
J-7	405
J-8	405
J-9	800
J-10	770
Mean Value	564
Standard Deviation	203

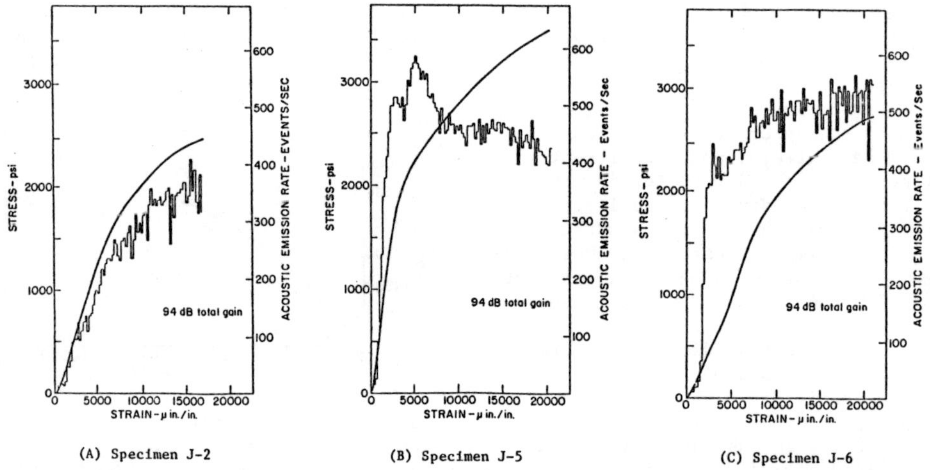

Figure 10. Stress and AE rate versus strain for three specimens of natural polycrystalline salt (type S4) deformed at a constant rate of 20 μs/sec. (Smooth curves denote stress-strain data and irregular curves denote AE rate data; AE data was monitored at a total system gain of 94 dB.)

As noted the AE results for the three tests exhibit wide differences, even though the stress-strain data are generally similar. The results for specimen J-2 (Figure 10A) indicates that the AE rate and the stress both increase at approximately the same rate with increasing strain until the test was terminated at a strain of 18,000 μs. For specimen J-5 (Figure 10B), the rate of increase of the AE rate was more rapid, peaking at about 5000 μin./in., after which it dropped somewhat and then leveled off. Finally in the case of specimen J-6 (Figure 10C), the AE rate was found to increase rapidly for strain levels up to approximately 2500 μin./in. at which point the rate of increase slowed down and continued to slowly decrease until the test was terminated.

Based on the limited studies carried out on polycrystalline salt, the ability of the AE technique to delineate a yield-point appears to be inconclusive. The results shown earlier in Figure 10B, however, appear somewhat encouraging when compared with similar data from single crystal tests, and further studies in this area are required.

A detailed description of the various tests carried out on single crystal and polycrystalline salt during the yield strength studies are available elsewhere (Hardy, 1982; Richardson, 1978). A number of general conclusions based on these tests are as follows:

(1) The uniaxial yield strength of salt single crystals deformed at a strain rate of 13 μs/sec is in the range of 100-200 psi, with the mean for tests on 10 specimens being 132 psi. The yield-point was readily determined from the macroscopic stress-strain behavior.

(2) In the case of salt single crystals, other phenomena show characteristic behavior at the yield-point which could if desired, be used to roughly locate the yield-point. These phenomena include AE rate, dislocation density, and amount of permanent strain remaining upon unloading for various peak-strain levels. One of the phenomena, AE rate, has remote-detection possibilities.

(3) Natural polycrystalline salt appears to have no true yield-point in the sense of a distinct elastic-plastic transition. The onset of plastic deformation in individual crystals of a polycrystalline aggregate would intuitively be expected to exhibit the same physical phenomena at the yield-point as the single-crystal specimens. However, efforts to study these phenomena in polycrystalline salt met with very limited success. Dislocation studies were unsuccessful for technical reasons and AE investigations were inconclusive. It is felt, however, that further more detailed evaluation of the AE technique should be undertaken.

(4) The results of the load-unload test for natural polycrystalline salt suggest a significant amount of permanent strain exists after unloading from even a very small peak load, indicating that a certain amount of plastic flow takes place at near-zero stress levels. The load-unload test could be used to determine an arbitrary, but potentially useful, yield-point by specifying the level of permanent strain necessary to define such a yield-point. In the current studies the 0.2 percent offset-strain convention resulted in a mean yield strength of 564 psi for the natural-polycrystalline salt specimens (type S4) tested.

4 ANALYTICAL STUDIES

4.1 General

The original intention of the analytical phase of the current salt cavern design project was to develop a highly flexible, computer-based "cavern-behavior simulator" that could be programmed to investigate a wide range of conditions associated with the storage of natural gas in salt caverns. From the outset it was clear that such a simulator should involve the use of a suitable finite element program incorporating constitutive relations based on the mechanical and thermal properties of salt. At an early stage in the analytical studies two finite element programs (BOPACE and BUMINES) were obtained and modified for use on the Penn State computer. As the project proceeded, however, it becomes increasingly clear that the development of a practical simulator would not be immediately possible due both to the complexity of the problem and the time and financial restrictions of the project. Rather than proceeding with the development of an overly simplified simulator, with limited application to real field situations, it was, therefore, decided to utilize the available finite element programs to carry out a series of relevant analytical studies, the results of which could later be used as the basis for the development of the desired cavern-behavior simulator.

A block diagram in Figure 11 illustrates the major studies undertaken in the analytical phase of the project. These included a series of three finite element studies, and a study involving the closed-form analysis of two simple cavern shapes.

In review the major analytical studies were as follows:

(1) Elastic studies--In the first series the behavior of three cavern shapes, spherical, tapered cylindrical, and tear-frop were investigated assuming that the salt behaved elastically. Although this assumption is somewhat unrealistic, particularly at high stress levels, the results did provide useful data on the elastic stress distributions existing around the three cavern shapes, and the effects of in-situ stress (related to cavern depth) and cavern pressure.

(2) Elastic-plastic studies--The behavior of a cavern with a circular cross-section was investigated assuming that the salt was an elastic-plastic material. Such a

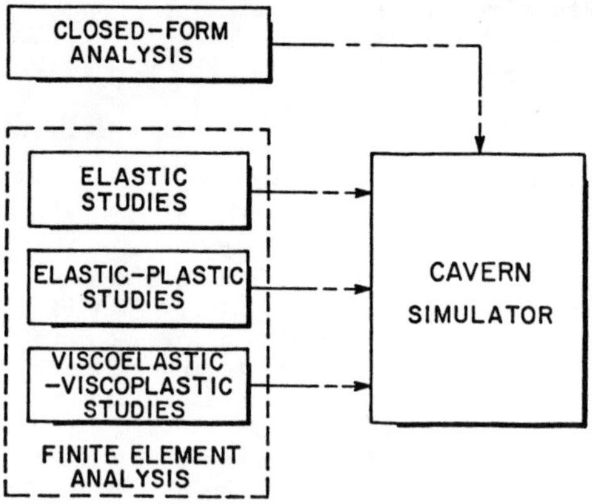

Figure 11. Block diagram illustrating the major studies undertaken in the analytical phase of the current project.

material behaves elastically at low stresses and above a critical stress (yield stress) behaves as a time-independent plastic material. The BOPACE finite element program was utilized for these analyses which provided useful data on stress distribution and cavern closure as a function of such parameters as in-situ stress and cavern pressure. Since material behavior was considered to be time-independent, information on such characteristics as the rate of cavern closure could not be evaluated.

(3) Viscoelastic-viscoplastic studies--In the final series of analytical studies it was assumed that the salt behaves as a viscoelastic-viscoplastic material. Such materials, in general, exhibit elastic, viscoelastic, plastic, and viscoplastic behavior. Two sets of studies were carried out in this series, namely, those based on closed-form and finite element techniques. In the former studies the closed-form stress-strain-time relations were developed for a cylindrical and a spherical cavern assuming that salt behaved as a rigid-viscoplastic material. Using these relations the rate of cavern closure as well as other factors were evaluated for these two cavern shapes as a function of a number of parameters including cavern pressure and temperature. In the latter studies the behavior of three cavern shapes, spherical, tapered cylindrical, and teardrop, were investigated using the BUMINES finite element program. Here the salt was assumed to be an elastic-viscoplastic material. In particular the rate of cavern closure was investigated as a function of cavern pressure.

Only a few examples of the results obtained during the analytical studies will be included in the present paper. However, a detailed presentation of the overall analytical study will be available in an associated project monograph presently in preparation (Hardy, 1982).

4.2 Elastic-plastic analysis

In the elastic-plastic analysis the behavior of a cavern of circular cross-section located at a depth of 6000 feet, as illustrated in Figure 12, was investigated as a function of internal pressure. These studies, carried out by Punwani (1982) using the BOPACE finite element program, assumed a hydrostatic in-situ stress field ($k = 1$) and that the salt had a Young's modulus of 1.1×10^6 psi, a Poisson's ratio of 0.475, and a yield strength of 2000 psi.

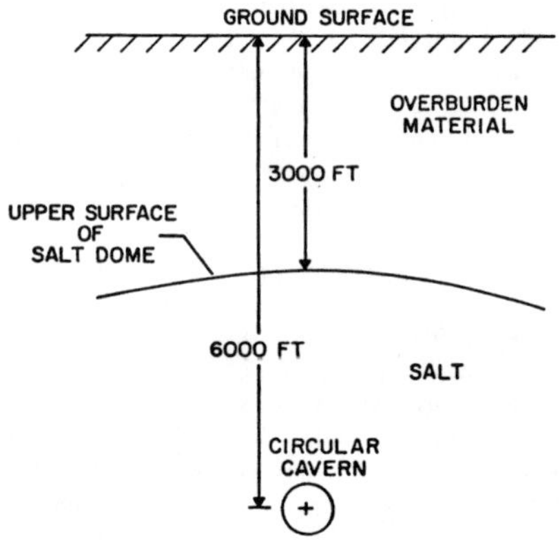

Figure 12. Schematic drawing of circular cavern located at a depth of 6000 feet. (Figure is not drawn to scale.)

A total of eight load cases [increments in the internal cavern pressure (P_i)] were investigated in the course of the final elastic-plastic analysis. The incremental loading-sequence began with the internal cavern pressure (P_i) being approximately equal to the average in-situ stress (P_o = 6000 psi). The cavern pressure was then decreased in a number of increments to a lower value of 1000 psi. Output generated during the analysis was in the form of tabulated data and computer-drawn contour plots. The latter included plots of tangential and radial stress components, effective stress, total effective strain (elastic plus plastic), effective plastic strain, and cavern closure. Figure 13 illustrates a series of effective stress plots for various levels of cavern pressure.

Figure 14 illustrates the associated cavern closure ($\Delta V/V \times 100$) plotted as a function of differential stress ($P_o - P_i$). As noted, there is a significant although small decrease in cavern volume in the initial elastic region (E); however, as the differential stress increases and the material becomes more plastic in nature (region E-P), the degree of cavern closure becomes much more pronounced. At low differential stresses the cavern closure is an approximately linear function of differential stress. However, at higher values of differential stress, the plastic character of the material becomes dominant and the relationship between cavern closure and differential stress becomes increasingly non-linear.

It is important to note that all elastic-plastic analyses carried out in the current study assumed plane strain conditions, although a solution-mined cavern would obviously be best approximated by an axisymmetric solution. Using plane strain conditions, however, the analysis should result in higher effective stresses and deformations than would be obtained using an axisymmetric condition for the same cavern cross-section, thus resulting in a "built-in" safety factor. Unfortunately, the magnitude of this safety factor cannot be simply evaluated.

In review, a number of the more important results of the elastic-plastic analyses are as follows:

(1) As similarly noted in earlier elastic analyses, the maximum effective stresses around the cavern increased with decreasing cavern pressure.

(2) The levels of maximum effective stress determined in the elastic-plastic studies were considerably lower than those determined under similar conditions during the elastic studies.

(3) Initial plastic yield was found to occur in the cavern structure at a differential stress level equivalent to approximately 62.5 percent of the assumed yield strength of the associated salt.

(4) Cavern closure was found to increase with increasing differential stress (i.e., decreasing cavern pressure). In the elastic region this increase was linear, but as cavern pressure decreased further and the plastic character of the material became more dominant, the relationship between cavern closure and differential stress became increasingly non-linear.

(5) At the lowest cavern pressure investigated (1000 psi), a cavern closure of approximately 2.4 percent was observed. This relatively low level of cavern closure is not consistent with the vary large cavern closures reported in the literature.

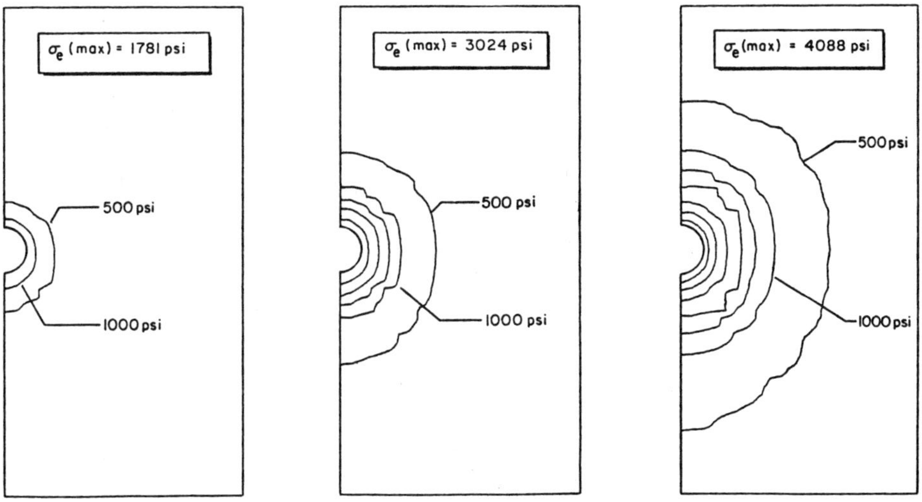

(A) P_i = 5000 psi (B) P_i = 3000 psi (C) P_i = 1000 psi

Figure 13. Effective stress contours associated with the elastic-plastic analysis of a circular cavern for a series of cavern pressures. (Assuming elastic-plastic, strain-hardening material behavior; k = 1.0, cavern depth - 6000 feet; contour interval - 500 psi.)

This appears to reinforce the generally accepted theory that major cavern closure in the field is mainly due to time-dependent inelastic behavior (creep).

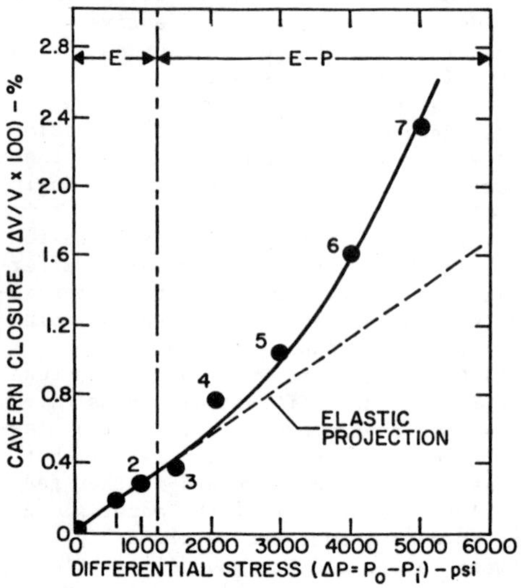

Figure 14. Variation of cavern closure as a function of differential stress. (Elastic-plastic analysis; k = 1.0 and cavern depth - 6000 feet. The symbols E and E-P designate the elastic and elastic-plastic regions, respectively.)

4.3 Viscoelastic-viscoplastic analysis

During the current study both elastic and elastic-plastic analyses were found to provide useful insights into the overall problem of salt cavern design, however, they did not provide a suitable explanation for the large, time-dependent decreases in cavern volume noted in actual field situations. In the final phase of the analytical studies, consideration was first given to assuming that salt behaved in a general viscoelastic-viscoplastic manner. However, due to the analytical complications resulting from this assumption, and the lack of the necessary mechanical property data, it was decided to reduce the complexity of the analyses by assuming that the salt behaved either as a rigid-viscoplastic material (closed-form solutions) or an elastic-viscoplastic material (finite element analysis).

In the associated finite element analysis carried out by Chabannes (1982), the investigation of the closure characteristics of three cavern shapes, spherical, teardrop, and tapered cylinder, as illustrated in Figure 15, were undertaken. The dimensions selected for each cavern shape were such that in all cases the overall cavern volume was approximately 2.53 x 10^6 barrels. In all cases the caverns were assumed to be located in a hydrostatic stress field (k = 1) at a depth of 3000 feet, as shown in Figure 16. The overburden and salt were assumed to have densities of 154.20 and 138.54 lbs/ft^3, respectively.

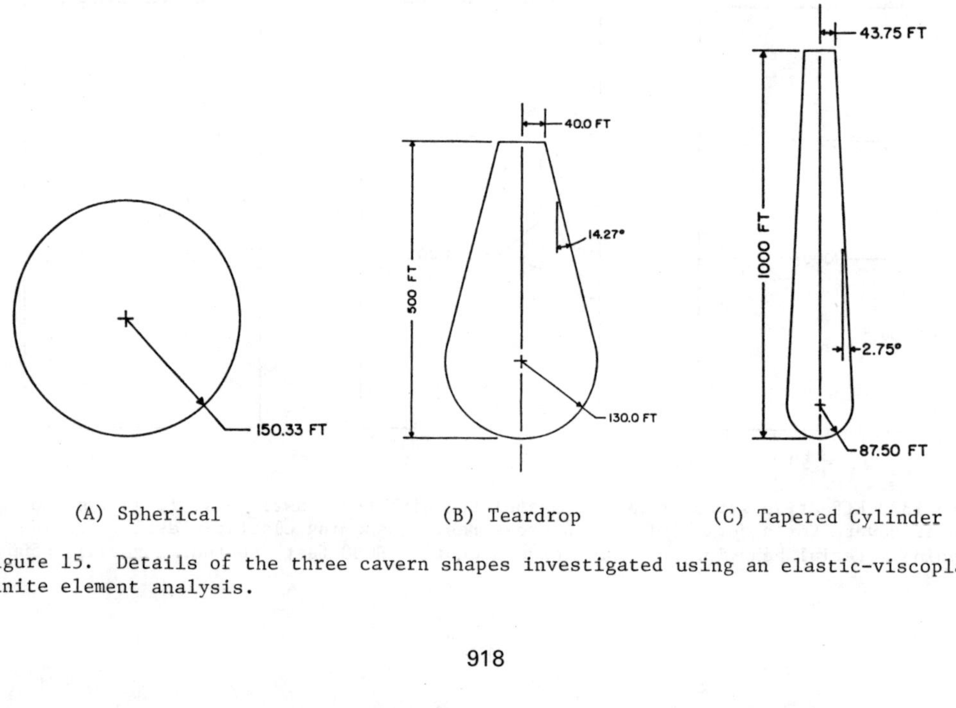

(A) Spherical (B) Teardrop (C) Tapered Cylinder

Figure 15. Details of the three cavern shapes investigated using an elastic-viscoplastic finite element analysis.

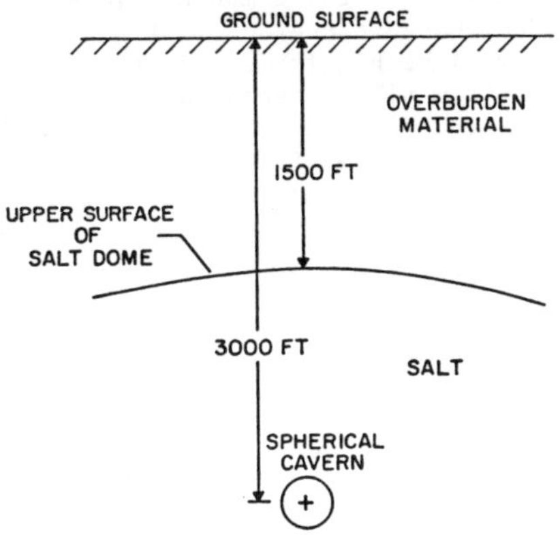

Figure 16. Schematic drawing of a spherical cavern located at a depth of 3000 feet. (Figure is not drawn to scale.)

In order to account for the influence of geothermal gradient in the analyses, the cavern structures were assumed to be at a uniform temperature of 110°F. This temperature was based on a geothermal gradient of 20°F/1000 feet and a mean surface temperature of 50°F. The total strains computed in the finite element analyses were assumed to be the sum of the elastic and viscoplastic (creep) strain components. The elastic strains for all cases were computed based on the assumption that the salt was a homogeneous, isotropic, linear elastic material with a Young's modulus of 1.0×10^6 psi and a Poisson's ratio of 0.4. A temperature-dependent secondary creep law (Norton's law) was used to account for the creep strains, and was of the form:

$$\dot{\varepsilon}_e^c = A \exp(-Q/RT)(\sigma_e/\sigma_c)^n \qquad \text{(Eq. 1)}$$

where $\dot{\varepsilon}_e^c$ is the effective creep strain rate, A and n are experimentally determined constants, Q is the activation energy, R is the universal gas constant, T is the absolute temperature, σ_e is the von Mises effective stress, and σ_c is a constant used to normalize stress. Values used for the various parameters in the current analysis are presented in Table 3, and were developed from available creep data for salt from the Tatum Salt dome, Mississippi (Chabannes, 1982).

The volume closure characteristics as a function of time for the three cavern shapes were analyzed using the BUMINES finite element program. During the study the effects of three different internal cavern pressures, 1000, 2000, and 2700 psi were investigated and the results are shown

Table 3. Values for temperature-dependent secondary creep model parameters for salt from the Tatum Salt dome.

Parameter	Value
A	8.372×10^{-15} in./in./second
n	4.29
Q	11550 calories/mole
R	1.987 calories/mole/°K
σ_c	1 psi

graphically in Figure 17. The data presented are based on the assumption that in all cases the center of the caverns were located at a depth of 3000 feet, and that the material surrounding the caverns was at a uniform in-situ temperature of 110°F. As can be seen the spherical cavern exhibits the minimum closure followed by the teardrop cavern, with the tapered cylindrical exhibiting the greatest closure. For a non-hydrostatic initial stress field ($k \neq 1$), the teardrop cavern would probably be the most suitable. It is not likely, however, that the in-situ stress field in a salt dome would deviate significantly from hydrostatic due to the strong creep characteristics of salt which, over geologic time, would tend to reduce any natural stress differences.

In review, a number of the more important results of the elastic-viscoplastic analyses were as follows:

(1) As indicated in Figure 17 the rate of cavern closure is highly sensitive to the level of the internal gas pressure. Furthermore, even at storage pressures only slightly less than the in-situ stress level (see Figure 17A where $P_o - P_i$ = 300 psi) significant time dependent closure can occur over extended periods of time.

(2) As would be expected for the case of a hydrostatic in-situ stress field, the closure characteristics of a spherical or a teardrop cavern are clearly superior to those of a tapered cylindrical cavern.

(3) The results from the current studies indicate that a secondary creep law will provide a transient volume closure response.

(4) Based on the form of the creep law used in the present study it is apparent that cavern depth should be kept as shallow as possible in order to minimize the influence of in-situ temperature which normally increases with depth. In general an increase in temperature will always lead to a disproportionally larger increase in volume closure.

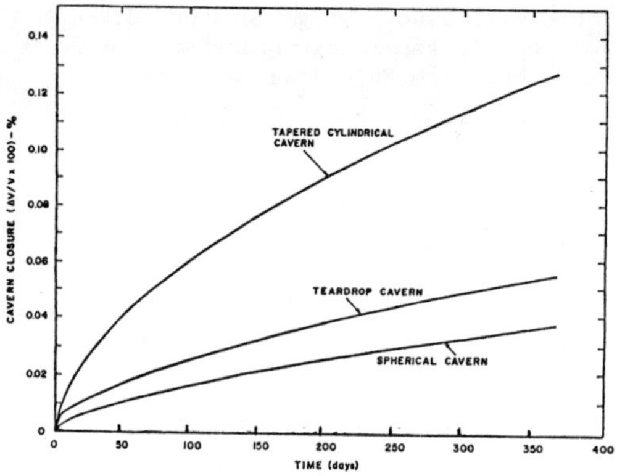

(A) P_i = 2700 psi

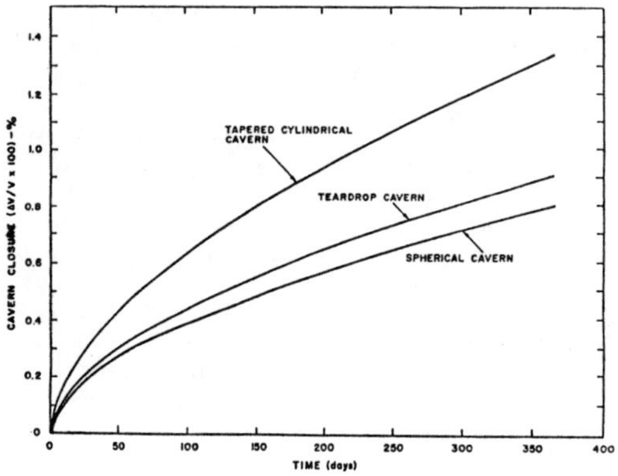

(B) P_i = 2000 psi

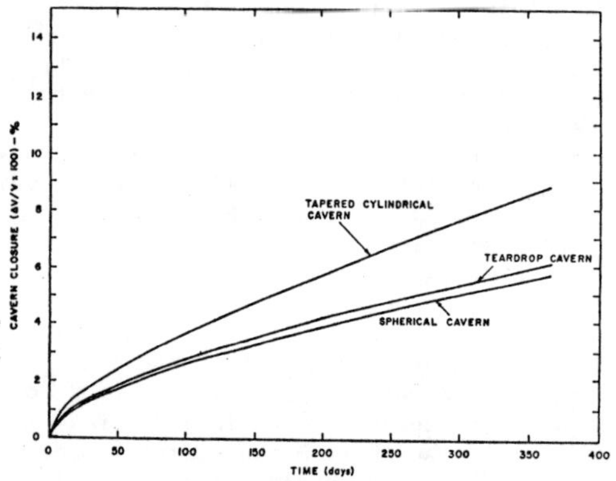

(C) P_i = 1000 psi

Figure 17. Influence of cavern shape on volume closure as a function of time for three different values of internal gas pressure. (Elastic-viscoplastic analysis; cavern depth - 3000 feet and in-situ temperature - 110°F.)

(5) In general the computed time-dependent closure characteristics of a cavern will be highly dependent on the assumed form of the creep law employed. Furthermore, for a specific creep law, closure will be sensitive to the associated creep law parameters.

5 DISCUSSION

In the current paper a brief review of the laboratory and analytical phases of a study underway to develop criteria for the design of salt caverns for the storage of natural gas has been presented. This study has been underway for some seven years and at present a detailed monograph describing the progress to date is in preparation (Hardy, 1982). Results to date have been encouraging, however, due to the complexity of the problem additional research remains to be carried out before fully acceptable design criteria can be developed.

6 ACKNOWLEDGEMENTS

The major funding for the studies described in this report have been provided by the Pipeline Research Committee of the American Gas Association (project PR-12-71). Additional funds, particularly in the latter stages of the study, have been provided by the Department of Mineral Engineering at Penn State. The writer gratefully acknowledges the assistance of Dr. A. J. Campos and Dr. A. W. Khair, Research Associates; E. J. Kimble, Jr., Research Aide; and K. Bakhtar, C. Chabannes, A. Mangolds, M. Mrugala, A. Richardson, and D. Roberts, graduate assistants; all of whom have provided considerable assistance in the project.

7 REFERENCES

Anon., (1971), "Gas Stored in Salt-Dome Caverns," Oil and Gas Journal, February 15, 1971, pp. 67-70.

Anon., (1980A), "The Underground Storage of Gas in United States and Canada," American Gas Association, XU0781, Arlington, Virginia, 25 p.

Anon., (1980B), "Survey of Salt Cavern Storage of Natural Gas in the United States and Canada - 1980," CER Corporation, Las Vegas, Nevada, 32 pp.

Bakhtar, K., (1979), "Development of Long Term Creep-Testing Facilities for Evaluation of Inelastic Behavior in Salt," M.S. Thesis, Department of Mineral Engineering, The Pennsylvania State University, August 1979.

Chabannes, C. R., (1982), "An Evaluation of the Time-Dependent Behavior of Solution Mined Caverns in Salt for the Storage of Natural Gas," M.S. Thesis, Department of Mineral Engineering, The Pennsylvania State University, May 1982.

Hardy, H. R., Jr., (1982), "Theoretical and Laboratory Studies Relative to the Design of Salt Caverns for the Storage of Natural Gas," American Gas Association Monograph, In Press.

Hardy, H. R., Jr., (1980A), "Development of Design Criteria for Salt Cavern Storage of Natural Gas," Proceedings Fifth International Symposium on Salt, Vol. 2, A. H. Coogan and L. Hauber - Editors, Northern Ohio Geological Society, Inc., Cleveland, pp. 13-20.

Hardy, H. R., Jr., (1980B), "Outline of Activities During 1980 Sabbatical Leave," Internal Report RML-IR/80-17, Geomechanics Section, Department of Mineral Engineering, The Pennsylvania State University.

Hardy, H. R., Jr. and A. Mangolds, (1980), "Investigation of Residual Stresses in Salt," Proceedings Fifth International Symposium on Salt, Vol. 1, A. H. Coogan and L. Hauber - Editors, Northern Ohio Geological Society, Inc., Cleveland, pp. 55-63.

Hardy, H. R., Jr. and D. A. Roberts, (1977), "Evaluating the Physical Properties of Salt Associated with Design of Salt Cavities for Natural Gas Storage," Proceedings A.G.A. Transmission Conference (St. Louis, 1977), A.G.A. Cat. No. X50477, pp. T-266 to T-272.

Hardy, H. R., Jr., D. A. Roberts, and A. M. Richardson, (1980), "Application of Acoustic Emission in Fundamental Studies of Salt Behavior," Proceedings Fifth International Symposium on Salt, Vol. 1, A. H. Coogan and L. Hauber - Editors, Northern Ohio Geological Society, Inc., Cleveland, pp. 269-280.

Punwani, S. G., (1982), "On the Non-Linear Structural Analysis of Underground Openings by the Finite Element Method, with Special Reference to Gas Storage in Salt Domes," M.S. Thesis, Department of Mineral Engineering, The Pennsylvania State University.

Querio, C. W., (1980), "Design and Construction of Solution Mined Caverns for LPG Storage," American Chemical Society Symposium on Underground Storage of Liquified Gas, March 1980.

Richardson, A. M., (1978), "An Experimental Investigation of the Uniaxial Yield Point of Salt," M.S. Thesis, Department of Mineral Engineering, The Pennsylvania State University, November 1978.

Roberts, D. A., (1981), "An Experimental Study of Creep and Microseismic Behavior in Salt," M.S. Thesis, Department of Mineral Engineering, The Pennsylvania State University, March 1981.

Slater, G. E., (1975), "Salt Caverns - Multi-Purpose Storage Vessels," Earth and Mineral Sciences, Volume 44, No. 5, February 1975, The Pennsylvania State University, p. 35.

UNDERGROUND OIL CAVERN PROJECT U 20 - U 22 NESTE OY PORVOO WORKS, FINLAND

Unterirdisches Ölkavernen Projekt U 20 - U 22 Neste Oy, Porvoo Werke, Finnland

Projet des cavernes souterraines U 20 - U 22 pour le stockage du pétrole Neste Oy, Raffinerie de Porvoo, Finlande

Y.IGNATIUS, S.JOHANSSON & P.RAVASKA
Neste Engineering, Neste Oy, Espoo, Finland

Summary

At the Porvoo Works of Neste Oy - Finland's national oil company - there are a total of 4,8 million m^3 of underground oil storage in operation at present.
In late 1979 a new cavern project, named U 20 - U 22, was initiated for the construction of an additional 800.000 m^3 of cavern space, for storing oil products. In connection with this project a rock mechanics program was also undertaken. This program includes i.a. extensive site investigations, state of stress determinations in situ, laboratory tests on core samples, rock mechanical calculations, cavern design studies, and design of blasting methods.
In the course of actual construction work rock mass deformations were checked by means of extensometers. Additional state of stress measurements were also carried out, as well as control of the ground water level. Temperature measurements in the rock mass are carried out continously as part of the caverns will hold oil with a temperature of +95°C at a later stage.

ZUSAMMENFASSUNG

Neste Oy - die nationale Ölgesellschaft Finnlands - hat in seinen Porvoo Werken heutzutage Lagerstätten in Felskavernen mit einem Gesamtvolumen von 4,8 Millionen m^3 für Öl im Betrieb.
Die Planung eines neuen Kavernenprojektes für die Lagerung von Ölprodukten, namens U 20 - U 22, wurde am Ende 1979 angefangen. Das Behältervolumen ist 800.000 m^3. Im Zusammenhang mit diesem Projekt wurde ein felsmechanisches Programm unternommen. Dieses Programm enthält u.a. ausgedehnte Bodenuntersuchungen, Bestimmungen vom Primärspannungszustand, Laborversuche von Kernproben, felsmechanische Kalkulationen, Planung von Kavernenkonstruktion und Bestimmung von Sprengungsmethoden.
Deformationsmessungen wurden gemäss aktueller Konstruktionstechnik mit Extensometern durchgeführt. Weitere Messungen des Spannungszustandes sowie die Kontrolle des Grundwasserspiegels wurden auch durchgeführt. Temperaturmessungen des Felsgrundes werden kontinuierlich ausgeführt, weil ein Teil von den Kavernen das Öl später bei der Temperatur von +95°C behalten wird.

Résumé

La compagnie pétrolière finlandaise nationale NESTE OY dispose actuellement à sa raffinerie de Porvoo de 4,8 millions de m^3 de stockage souterrain de pétrole.
Vers la fin de 1979, on a mis en route le projet U 20 - U 22 en vue de la construction d'un stockage souterrain supplémentaire de 800.000 m^3 pour stocker des hydrocarbures. Dans le cabre de ce projet on a aussi mis sur pied un programme de mécanique des roches. Ce programme comprend, entre autres, une étude complète du site, la détermination "in situ" de l'état des contraintes, des essais de laboratoires sur les carottes, des calcul de mécanique des roches, des études conceptuelles de cavernes et l'établissement de méthodes de creusement à l'explosif.
Au cours des travaux actuels de construction, les déformations de la masse rocheuse ont été mesurées à l'aide d'extensomètres. On a aussi procédé à des mesures additionnelles

de l'état des contraintes ainsi qu'au contrôle du niveau de la nappe phréatique. Les mesures de la température de la masse rocheuse ont eu lieu de façon permanente du fait qu'à un stade ultérieur, le pétrole sera stocké dans une partie des cavernes à une température de +95°C.

1. INTRODUCTION

The first unlined underground caverns for oil storage were built in Finland in the early 1960's and those currently in use have a total volume of over 10 million m^3 (60 million bbl). The volume of the biggest unit is somewhat over 1 million m^3 while the smallest units hold about 50.000 m^3 each. Crude oil takes up about 35 per cent of the total storage capacity, with refined products such as butane, gasoline, dieseloil and light and heavy fuel oils taking the remainder.

Neste Oy - Finland's national oil company - produces no oil itself. All crude oil is purchased under long-term contracts. The underground storage facilities located at the company's Porvoo Works (figure 1) represent about half of the total volume of oil caverns in Finland. In the Porvoo works area are located a total of 21 currently operational cavern units. 3,6 million m^3 of the volume is used for storing crude oil, and 1,2 million m^3 is used for storing light and heavy fuel oil, dieseloil, and butane.

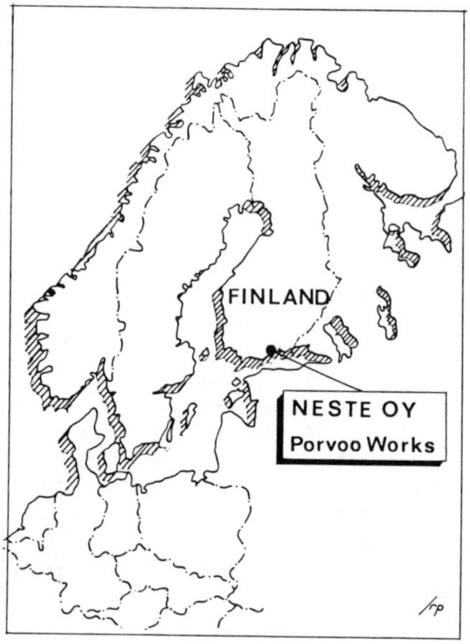

Figure 1 Geographical location of Neste Oy Porvoo works

At the moment all completed installations are working completely statisfactorily and there have been no serious accidents or any environmental pollution.

2. PROJECT DESCRIPTION

Neste's Porvoo Works are located about 50 km east of Helsinki on the southern coast of Finland by the Baltic Sea.

The underground oil storage caverns U 20 - U 22 comprise three separate units, with a total effective volume of slightly over 800.000 m^3. All caverns are designed and constructed for storing of oil products, such as diesel oil, light fuel oil and also heavy fuel oil, the last product having a pumping-in temperature of +95°C, and a specific gravity of 0.98 tn/m^3.

Cavern U 20 comprises two parallel caverns with an access tunnel in the pillar between the caverns, the cavern volume is 200.000 m^3. Cavern U 21 is constructed as three parallel caverns, with an access tunnel in the pillar between caverns U 21 A and U 21 B. The total volume of the cavern unit is 300.000 m^3. Cavern U 22 is similar to cavern U 20, but the effective volume is 300.000 m^3. The main cross section of the caverns varies from 566 m^2 to 585 m^2.

All caverns are operated via a dry pump room located at the bottom level of the caverns and separated from the caverns themselves. Filling and discharge is carried out via pipelines located in a vertical shaft to the ground surface. The lay-out principle is presented in figures 3 and 4.

The inlet flow rate is 4,000 m^3 per hour for each unit, the discharge rate being 3 x 1,000 m^3 per hour for each group of caverns.

Leakage water pumps have a capacity of 2 x 15 m^3 per hour.

In addition, the project also comprised construction of access tunnels, pipe and instrument shafts, temperature and sampling holes, as well as pump pits, concrete plugs, underground ventilation, and instrumentation, with an emergency power station. Under normal conditions the caverns are operated from the remote control centre, located about 2 km from the caverns.

Construction work was initiated in March 1980, and oil fill of the last cavern unit will start in July 1982. Caverns U 20 and U 21 became operational during late 1981.

3. SITE INVESTIGATIONS

3.1. General

The planning and design of an underground oil cavern project must include a careful study of the bedrock. In order to locate and design rock caverns in the most appropriate way with respect to the properties of the rock, it is necessary to ascertain what the rock mass is like at the relevant depth.

To achieve optimum construction economy the bedrock must be utilized fully and the sealing element, the ground water, must be stable in its depth and seasonal variations. Engineering-geological bedrock outcrop mapping in combination with core drillings, in-situ state of stress determinations, and hydrogeological studies as well as laboratory tests and rock mechanical calculations were all carried out in order to determine actual subsurface conditions. (3)

3.2. Geological conditions

The rocks of the study area belong to the

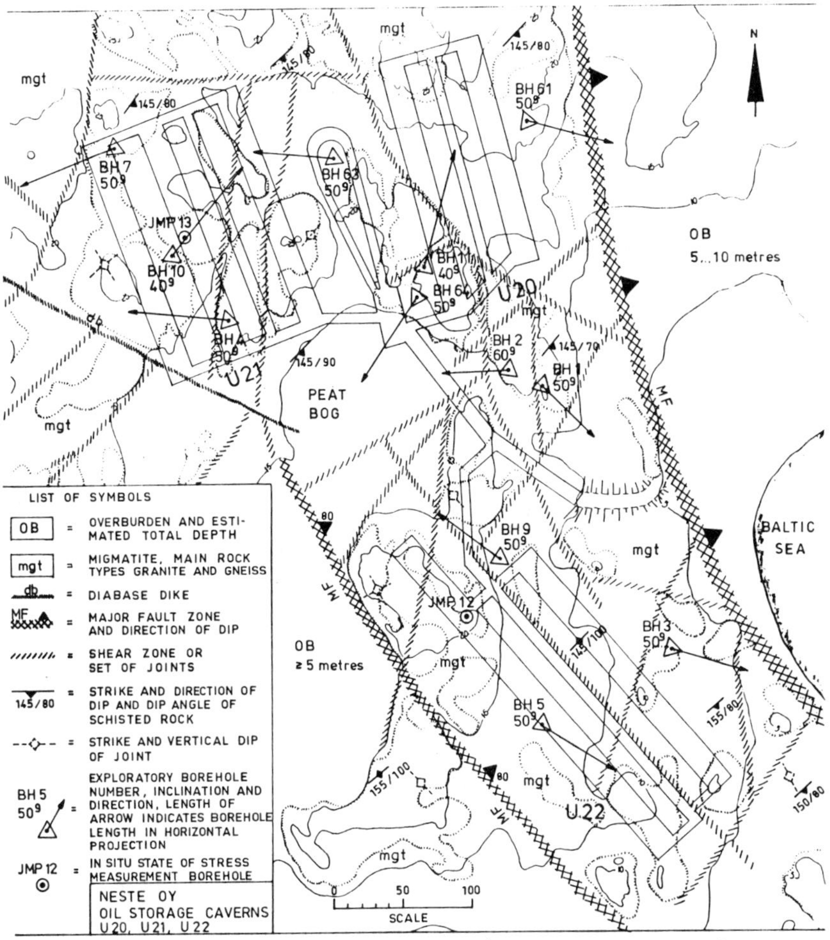

Figure 2 Engineering geological map and drill hole locations.

Svecokarelidic orogenic belt, the folding of which took place in connection with regional metamorphism and plutonism during the Precambrian about 1800 million years ago. A characteristic feature of many Svecokarelidic areas is an abundance of mixed rocks, with two components of different character. The older component is a metamorphic schist or a plutonic rock and the younger component is an igneous looking granitoid rock usually microcline rich granite. The migmatite forming granite with associated pegmatites and aplites penetrate all older rock, forming a great variety of migmatites. (11)

Mica schists and micagneisses are very common and because of migmatization these rock types are commonly microfolded. Microcline granite is another very common rock type in the Porvoo works area. The granite is generally coarse-grained even resembling pegmatite. Dikes and layers of amphibolitic composition, together with metadiabase dikes form the hypabyssal rocks in the area. The strongly fractured metadiabase dikes in particular cause problems in connection with construction works in rock.
Dikes and small massifs of pegmatite (granite) also occur.

The general strike of the Svecofennic belt is quite variable, and the migmatitic micagneisses show great variations in the strike of the foliation. The dips of the schistocity and the foliation are usually vertical or very steep. The migmatized gneisses have been highly plastic and even slight movements have easily caused changes in the attitudes of small folds and beds. (11) The general strike of gneissic rock is 50°...70° (ENE - WSW). The dips are mostly very steep (70°...85°) or vertical. Generally the dip is towards 150° (SSE).

Amphibolite dikes and beds parallel the schistocity of the gneissic rock, while the metadiabase dikes so far observed show no regular stratigraphic pattern. The rock mass of the investigation area is located between two parallel N-S trending major fault zones, the eastern one shown on the map in figure 2, the other one, named "grand canyon", being located about 500 metres west from the mapped area. In addition to these faults the rock mass contains a number of shear zones and strongly fractured zones, and also one significant fault in the vicinity of the construction area. One metadiabase dike cuts the southern end of cavern U 21 C. (see figure 2)

The joint system of the gneissic granite rock consists of two well-defined joint sets, one set corresponding to the strike and dip of the structure of the rock type. The other set has an orientation which is almost perpendicular to the main structure. In addition horizontal and/or gently inclined (inclined at 20°) jointing is met in the superficial parts of the rock mass. The frequency of these joints decreases with increasing depth, and hence they do not cause severe problems in connection with excavation works. The joint frequency of the steep joints in the top-part of the bedrock varies between 1 to 2 joints per linear metre. Joint surfaces are generally rather rough and the infilling (gouge) thickness is less than 10 mm. being normally only 1 to 2 mm. One typical characteristic of the rocks in the Porvoo area is the frequent occurrance of slickensides (chloritized polished and striated joint surfaces), the general dip of which are 50°...90°. These movement surfaces both parallel the strike of the schistocity or cut the schistocity at an angle of 20° to 60°, necessitating often additional reinforcements, in connection with cavern construction works, and also overbreaks in the excavation profile.

3.3. Exploratory drillings

Diamond core drillings comprise the most important method at the site investigation stage. Engineering geological mapping results as well as preliminary cavern planning aspects were both taken into account when the exact locations, directions, and inclinations of the boreholes were determined. (4)

Altogether 11 boreholes, figure 2, were drilled in the site investigations. Coring was done using T-type double tube core barrels of the swivel type, giving 42 mm or 32 mm core samples. Oriented core samples were also sporadically taken. In each borehole water pressure tests, were carried out to ascertain the relative tightness of the fracturing in the bedrock using double and/or single packers. The pressure serial used was 0,3;0,5;0,7;0,5;0,3 MPa for each tested interval and the pressure was kept constant for each pressure for a period of 5 min. The length of each test section tested with double packers was 3 metres. Single packers were used to test the total amount of water forced into the rock for a distance of 30 metres at the bottom part of the holes. Measurements were made

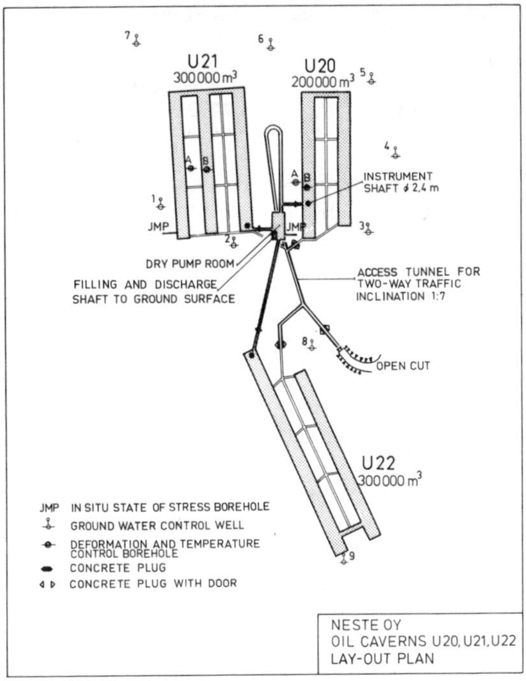

Figure 3 Lay-out of caverns U 20 - U 22

at over 80 levels in all. The results of the tests indicated that the mean water loss value in Lugeon units at the planned cavern levels was less than 1 Lugeon, except for zones with highly fractured rock, where this value reached as much as 5 Lugeon units.

Attention in examining core samples was focused chiefly on the following factors: rock types and their variations, type of jointing and nature of joints, infilling thickness on joint surfaces, number of primary joints, (particularly slickensides and "rust" joints) orientation of the rocks, zones of highly fractured rock, shear zones, and other similar zones of weakness. (3) The reasons for core losses were also examined. The mean RQD value for about 4/5 of the rock mass lay between 80 % and 90 %, while in the fractured and sheared zones representing about 1/5 of the rock mass, the corresponding value was 10 % to 25 %. No major faults could be located at the selected final site for the caverns. The results of the exploratory drillings indicated that the rock mass is rather homogenous and impervious and hence suitable for underground cavern construction.

3.4. In situ rock state of stress measurements

When an opening is excavated in a rock mass part of the existing support is removed. The resulting redistribution of stresses in the vicinity of the opening may create unstable conditions in the remaining rock mass. The stability is dependent on the properties of the rock mass as well as upon the primary stress field existing in the rock mass prior to disturbance by excavation.

It must be borne in mind that in situ state of stress measurements can only present the stress conditions at or close to the point at which the measurements are carried out. A large number of measurements is needed if an accurate picture of the stress conditions is required, which in turn makes the measurements both costly and time consuming.

It was therefore decided to carry out measurements of in situ rock stress only in two drill holes located above the roofs of caverns U 21 and U 22 (see figure 2) and check the results by two additional drill holes: one located, in the topheading part of cavern U 21, and one in the bottom part of the dry pump room, figures 3 and 4.

In the first two measurements Hast´s overcoring method was used. (1) The latter two measurements were done using the improved Leeman method. (8) A total of 21 stress measurements were carried out at different depths in the rock mass.

Interpretation of the surface state of stress measurements indicated that a relatively "weak" horizontal compressive stress field exists in the area, the mean value of the stress in borehole Jmp 12 was σ_1 = 4.5 MPa in a direction almost E-W, the corresponding value in Jmp 13 was σ_1 = 10.5 MPa in a direction almost N-S.

The maximum compressive horizontal stress in the direction of the strike was 20.0 MPa. In the direction perpendicular to the strike the corresponding value was 17.5 MPa. Both values were obtained at a depth of 20 metres in the rock, i.e about 20 metres above the final vault level.

The values obtained by the Leeman method in the excavated space were: drill hole Jmp 1 σ_1 = 10.9 MPa, direction SE - NW and Jmp 2 σ_1=15.1 MPa direction, S - N.

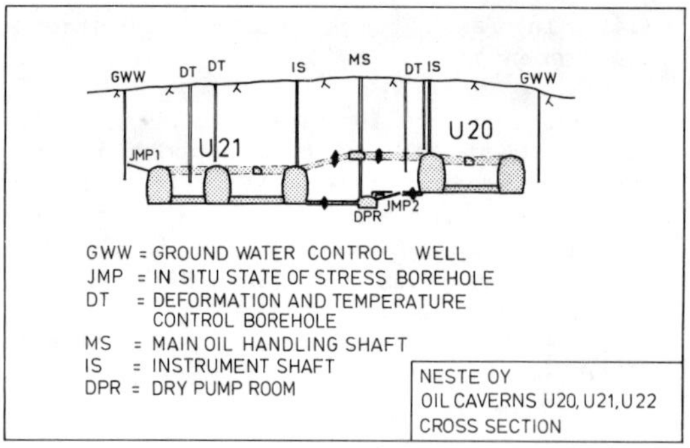

Figure 4 Cross section through caverns U 20 and U 21

Generally in Finland the maximum stress is horizontal or gently inclined. (10) The stress can be calculated from the equation

$$\sigma_{H1} = 8 + 0.060 \times h,$$

where h is the depth from the ground surface and H_1 is the maximum stress in MPa. Correspondingly the vertical stress can be calculated from the equation

$$\sigma_v = 4 + 0.025 \times h.$$

4. LABORATORY TESTING

Laboratory testing on representative core samples was carried out by the Laboratory of Excavation Engineering of the Department of Mining and Metallurgy at the Helsinki University of Technology, in accordance with recommendations by ISRM, and with other international norms and standards in this field.

A summary of test results is presented in Table 1. As can be seen, the mechanical strength properties of the rocks can be considered good to excellent from the point of view of underground construction.

5. ROCK MECHANICAL CALCULATIONS

Even though rock mass characteristics and the primary stress are known, it is impossible mathematically to predict with absolute certainty the changes in the rock mass caused by an excavation. The rock mass is a nonhomogenous materi- al. Bearing this in mind, the results of the finite element calculations (FEM) carried out were used for guidance pur- poses in the design of the cavern pro- files. Stresses and displacements were calculated using three different two-dimensional FEM-models, figure 5, the models being considered elastic and isotropic. Parameters used in the calulations were selected from the results of the laboratory tests and the in situ state of stress measurements. The following parameters were used:

- Dry density 27.0 KM/m^3
- Young´s modulus 24,500 MPa
- Poisson´s ratio 0.25
- Horizonal stress: 0 MPa; 5 MPa; 10 MPa
- Vertical stress: weight of rock mass

From the results of these calculations it could be seen that all three tested models proved suitable for design of the cavern profiles.

In addition to stability calculations, calculations were also made on temperature distribution in the rock mass in relation to time. This was concidered very important as one of the caverns will be filled with oil at +95°C at a later operational stage.

Furthermore different types of ground water flow calculations were carried out, in order to study. the draining effect of access tunnels in the cavern system, as the tunnels outside the concrete plugs in figure 3, will be left unfilled with water during operation.

The effects of an internal fire and explosion creating a pressure of 10 bars was also studied with a mathematical model.

Table 1 Mechanical properties of rocks

Density	
- granite	26.2...26.8 kN/m^3
- gneiss	27.3...28.9 kN/m^3
- pegmatite	25.9...26.5 kN/m^3
Uniaxial compressive strength	
- granite	90 ...120 MPa
- gneiss	100 ...280 Mpa
- pegmatite	50 ...140 MPa
Indirect tensile strength	
- granite	8 ... 10 MPa
- gneiss	9 ... 12 Mpa
- pegmatite	4 ... 8 MPa
Porosity (n)	0.05... 0.5 %
Young´s modulus (E)	45 ...103 GPa
Poisson´s ratio (γ) mean value	0.25
Los Angeles value (crushed material)	$\leq$ 25

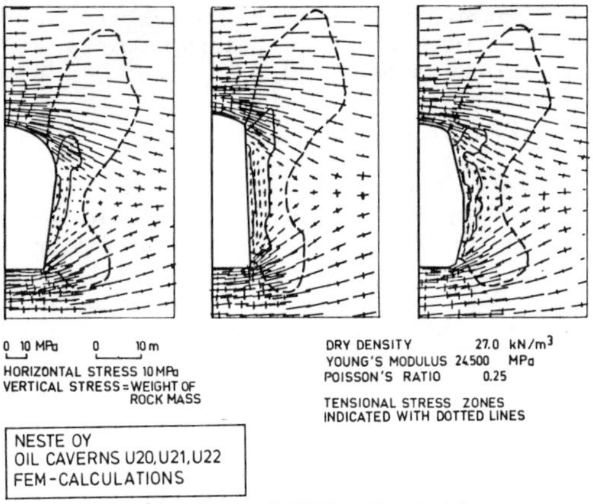

Figure 5 Results of FEM-calculations

6. ENGINEERING DESIGN

6.1. Design criteria

From an operational point of view it was desirable to locate the caverns in the vicinity of the harbour, as the major part of the oil products are transported by coastal tankers forward from the refinery. This factor had to be taken into account in the site selection.

It was further requested that the amount of leakage water into the cavern for hot oil should be less than 0,2 m^3/h or 5 m^3/day.

The caverns were to be designed to withstand an internal fire and explosion pressure of 10 bars and an external pressure of 20 bars, and also the effects of a one ton military bomb.

The life time of the caverns was set at a minimum of 25 years, during which time no blockfalls or cave-ins are allowed that might prevent operation of the caverns. A further task was to design such doors in the concrete plugs to the caverns as would enable entry with motorized excavation and restauration equipment. The diameter of the man-hole in the plug being only 600 mm. The safety distance to caverns U 17 - U 18 was set at a minimum of 50 metres.

From an engineering geological point of view it was of importance to locate the longitudinal direction of the caverns perpendicular to the strike of the schistocity and preferably also parallel to the greatest horizontal measured primary stress. (3)

From earlier experience it was well known that the water conductivity of the joints decreases with increasing depth and that the levels of the cavern vaults should be defined accordingly. The cavern vaults are located at over 40 metres depth below the ground surface and also at least 20 metres below the natural ground water table.

Special attention in the design was paid to permissible blasting vibrations, as the storage caverns were to be excavated partly underneath the tank farm area and also close to two caverns already in operation, U 17 - U 18. Finally, a tight time-schedule for the construction work had to be drawn up as it was requested that 500.000 m^3 of space (caverns U 20 and U 21) should be ready to receive oil before the end of 1981.

6.2. Lay-out and cavern cross-section

One of the most important tasks in the design was to work out a cavern cross-section (profile) that would make it possible to set up a work schedule suited to the mechanics of the bedrock and to the blasting methods and excavation equipment used, as well as to other factors such as reinforcements, transportation of broken rock, ventilation, and naturally the overall time-schedule.

Neste policy is that in addition to the main access tunnel at least two and preferably several topheadings or overhead tunnels should be under excavation simultaneously. Furthermore, possibilities for maintaining and servicing of excavation equipment must be good. At least one vertical shaft shall always be provided for, thereby cutting down the hours otherwise lost in ventilating only via the access tunnel. Based upon previous experience in cavern construction, cross-sections of 500 m^2 to 600 m^2 had proven both stable and economically feasible. (2,5)

Taking the above criteria into consideration the final lay-out of the caverns was prepared figures 3 and 4.

The bidding contractors were given two alternatives for the excavation of the main cavern cross section, figure 6. The selected contractor, a Finnish consortium named Vesto-Elovuori, offered an attractive pricing for alternative B in figure 6 and was contracted for the excavation works. A new era in the excava-

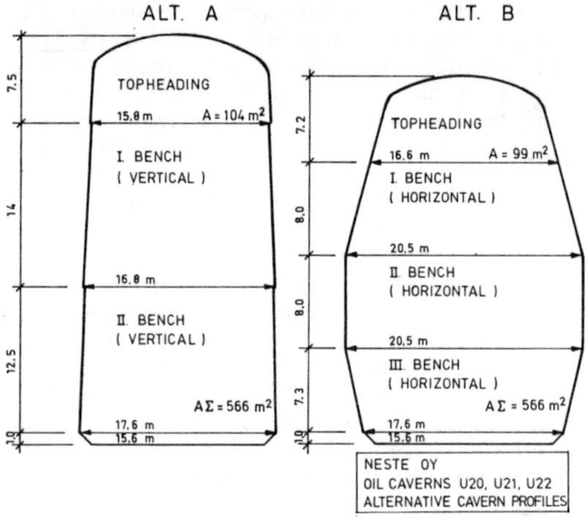

Figure 6 Alternative cavern cross sections

tion of feasible oil storage caverns began. The economic feasibility lies in the fact that the area of the topheading is rather small. As well known excavation of the topheading is both time-consuming and costly when compared to benching. Further advantages lie in the greatly improved work safety it offers especially in scaling and reinforcements, as these works can be done using normal scissor trucks. In high vertical benches, "sky-lift" type trucks must be used, which is both costly and time-consuming.

6.3. Excavation

6.3.1. Open cut and main access tunnel

The strength and intact nature of Precambrian bedrock in Finland has meant that cavern construction methods based on drilling and blasting have retained their position as the most economical methods.

The excavation process was started on the 16th of March 1980, by blasting out the open cut and the inclined main access tunnel leading down to the dry pump room and to the separate cavern units. Due to the large size of the project and because of the pressure of the timetable, the main access tunnel all the way to the instrument centre (figure 3) was constructed for two-way traffic, the cross-section being about 60 m^2. The bottom of the tunnel was paved with asphalt concrete, thereby reducing tyre wear, and also permitting higher driving speeds and increased total work output.

All other tunnels were constructed for one-way traffic with passing points at selected places.

6.3.2. Main caverns

The quality, strength, and stability of an underground oil cavern is determined to a large extent by the prevailing engineering geological conditions, but also on the quality of drilling and charging of explosives in the excavation process. For example, the strike facilitates the loosening of rock, when the schistocity is almost perpendicular to the advance of the excavation, because the tensile strength of the rock in the direction of the throw is at its minimum. The quality of the profile and the stability of the exacavation is generally good. If the longitudinal direction of the excavation cuts the schistocity at a small angle, (less than 30°), overbreaks might easily occur, and the excavation surface is uneven and the stability poorer (9).

Particularly important are the contour holes of the excavation profile. These should be drilled with as small a look-out angle as possible and be kept as far as possible parallel with the longitudinal direction of the caverns. Equally important is the setting out of the positions of the drillholes and the use of the minimum required charge weights. This also leads to considerable savings in the total work. Blasting for underground oil storage caverns is a cutting tool not a bombing operation (7,12).

In the design it was considered important to limit the loose crack (break-up) zone caused by blasting to 0.3 m. Furthermore, acceptable overdrilling was limited to ± 200 mm. The setting out accuracy of drill holes was set at 50 mm. An old truth is that the blasting result cannot be better that the drilling, hence these strict tolerances. A typical drilling and blasting pattern is presented in figure 7. Using these methods, the costs for scaling and additional reinforcements could be minimized.

A normal drifting result was 80 to 100 linear metres of topheading plus about 30 metres of one-way tunnel per week. Each week comprised five work days with two rigs operating triple shifts. The rigs were of the type Atlas Copco Boomer RH 170 fitted with three drilling booms each. Prior to the arrival of the elec-

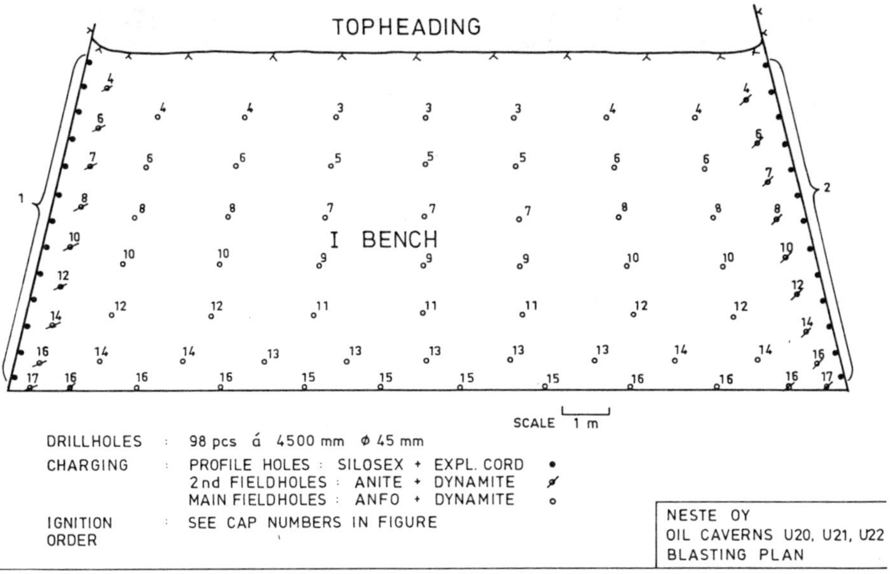

Figure 7 Typical drilling and charging pattern.

tric-hydraulic jumbos two multiboom pneumatic drilling jumbos of Tampella Tamrock manufacture were used.

At the benching stages, each bench being 8 metres high, the bottleneck of the excavation was no longer drilling and blasting, but taking away the broken rock. An average daily excavation capacity of 2,500 to 3,000 m^3 solid rock was well within reach.

Rock removal was carried out using a Cat 988A and a Cat 988B for loading of broken rock on to the off-highway trucks. These were of the type Kochums KL 442 (4) and Kochums KL 420 (8).

6.3.3. Instrument shafts

Each cavern unit is fitted with instruments, for measurements including the oil temperature, the upper oil level and the oil-water interface. Shafts for these instruments were originally designed to be excavated using the long-hole drilling and blasting method. (6)

The contractor chose to carry out shaft excavation using the raise boring method. In two shafts a Dresser 800 Strata Borer was utilized and in one shaft a Tamrock Rhino 1000. The acceptable deviation was set at 10 mm per linear metre of shaft, in two shafts this was achieved, in one shaft a small correction had to be made in the upper part of the shaft.

The advantages of using the raise bore method were several: reinforcements could be considerably reduced or left out, concrete consumption in plugs decreased and no disturbance of the main execavation process occurred. The following penetration effects were achieved in the raise borings:

- pilot hole (Ø 280 mm) 1,80 m/h
- shaft (Ø 1500 mm) Dresser 800 Strata Borer 0,85 m/h
- shaft (Ø 2400 mm) Dresser 800 Strata Borer 0,32 m/h
- shaft (Ø 2400 mm) Tamrock Rhino 1000 0,57 m/h

The depth of each shaft was between 43 m and 45 m. The rock can be classifed as medium hard according to Finnish rock conditions.

6.4. Reinforcements

In earlier oil storage cavern projects at the Porvoo Works, as a rule no systematic reinforcing of the cavern roofs and walls has been carried out. (6) In this cavern project, however, it was decided to reinforce the roofs systematically and also partially the upper parts of the side walls.

This decision was made in order to improve work safety, in order to strengthen the blocky zone around the profile, and in order to avoid block falls in connection with the storing of hot oil.

The bolts used were grouted and untensioned steel bars (25 mm A 400 H steel). The most commonly used length was L = 3200 mm. A 250 x 250 mm steel cover plate, threaded onto the bolt and thereafter shotcreted, adds considerable safety against rockburst caused for instance by sudden increase in temperature. The roofs were systematically bolted c/c 2 m and the upper inwards inclined wall parts at c/c 3 m.

In addition to this, and as a common Neste safety rule, all areas significant from the operational point of view were bolted and shotcrete lined. The thickness of the shotcrete varied between 40 mm and 70 mm. Wire mesh reinforcement was applied when using 70 mm shotcrete.

Further, all auxiliary space where the operating personnel works, as well as the dry pump room, was systematically reinforced by bolting and shotcreting.

Altogether the following amounts of reinforcements were used:

- bolts 25, A 400 H
  L = 3200-6000 mm, 15000 pcs
- shotcrete type K35
  d $\geq$ 40 mm 30000 m^2
- shotcrete " K35
  d $\geq$ 70 mm + mesh 8000 m^2

6.5. Time-schedule

The project decision was made in late 1979, and at the same time the site investigation as well as the basic design was started. Excavation works were started in mid-March 1980, as at that time it could be verified that the selected area was suitable. Construction was carried out in such a way that cavern U 20 was ready to receive oil in mid-October 1981 and cavern U 21 in mid-December 1981. Cavern U 22 has a longer construction time and will be ready for filling at the beginning of July 1982. Excavation works in this cavern were completed on the 15th of February 1982. The overlap in the time-

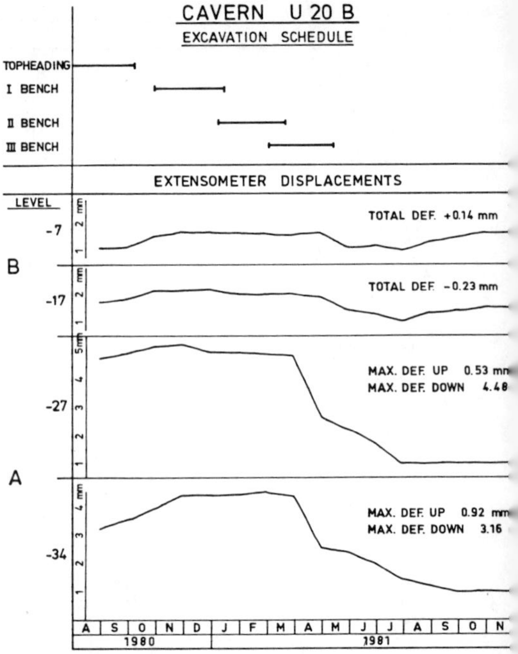

EXTENSOMETERS U20 -7 AND U20 -17 ARE LOCATED ABOVE VAULT OF CAVERN U20B, EXTENSOMETERS U20 -27 AND U20 -34 ARE LOCATED IN THE PILLAR BETWEEN CAVERN U20B AND ACCESS TUNNEL TO DRY PUMP ROOM

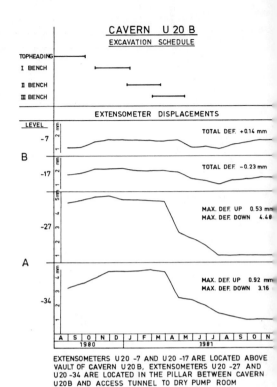

Figure 8 Results of deformation measurements in cavern U 20 B

schedule between excavation works and installation works required special attention in the control of blasting vibrations. Naturally also a vibration monitoring system was established for the control of maximum allowable vibra- tions in the nearby caverns U 17 - U 18, as well as for surface structures.

7. CONTROL MEASURES DURING EXCAVATION

7.1. Deformation measurements.

Deformations were monitored using INTERFELS multiple rod extensometers mounted at various depths in a total of four boreholes, located above the arch of the caverns and in the pillar between two adjacent caverns figure 4. An examp- le of recorded displacements is presen- ted in the graph in figure 8. In the up- per part of the figure are shown the different excavation stages.

The maximum downward deformation in the pillar was 4,5 mm, this being recorded when the bottom bench was excavated. One possible reason for the downward deformation is a number of inclined (dip 60°) gouge filled joints located in the pillar.

The deformations in the arch area of cavern U 20 were very small. All recorded deformations in cavern U 21 were of very small magnitude.

7.2. Ground water control

Regular ground water observations have been carried out at the Porvoo Works in a total of about 30 drilled wells, scattered over the area of underground construction. These observations were started in the early 1970's and are still continuing. Despite the favourable location of caverns U 20 - U 22 in relation to the Baltic Sea, figure 2, a total of 12 new ground water observation wells were drilled in the rock mass surrounding the caverns.

Regular observations at one-week intervals were started on August 1 1980 in these wells. Some graphs of recorded variations are presented in figure 9. As can be seen no serious draw-downs have so far been recorded, which means that the natural supply, from precipitation and the Baltic Sea, has been sufficient to keep the ground water at a high level.

On the other hand it is a well-established fact that the rocks in the Porvoo area are quite impervious, for instance recorded leakage water volumes are rather small (2.4).

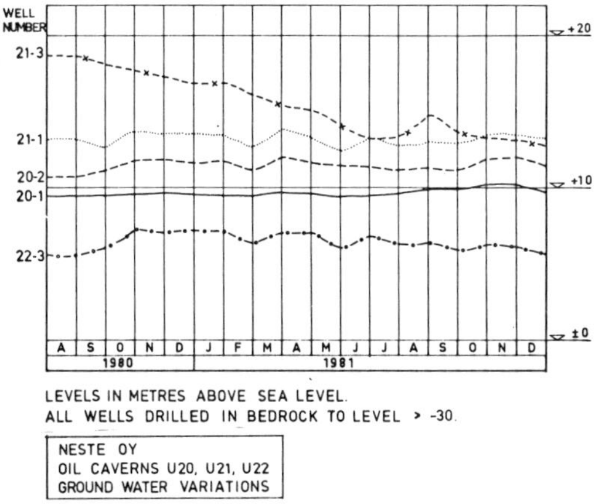

Figure 9 Variations in level of natural ground water table

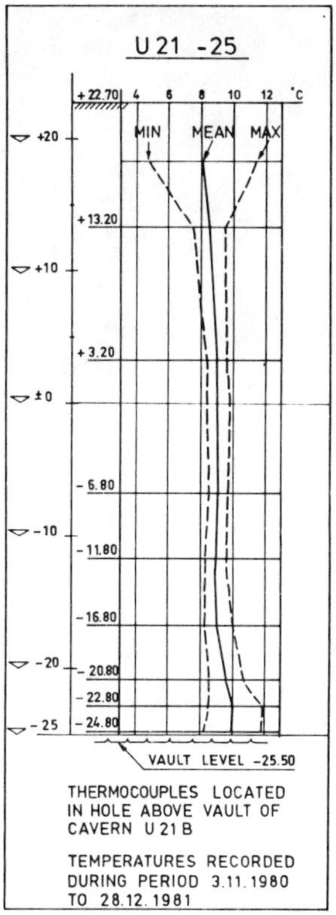

Figure 10 Temperature distribution in rock mass above cavern U 20

In addition to ground water observations, mapping of leakage water occurrences during the excavation process was carried out at regular intervals.

Leakage water amounts recorded in connection with the operation of caverns U 20 and U 21 were as follows at the beginning of February 1982:

- Cavern U 20 3,0 to 3,5 m^3/day
- Cavern U 21 2,8 to 3,0 m^3/day

It should be noted that both caverns are equipped with waterlocks in the concrete plugs, which are continuously supplied with water and that leakage distances to the cavern walls in the surroundings of the plugs are only c. 20 metres.

7.3. Temperature measurements in rock

In order to have an idea of the annual mean temperature in the bedrock surrounding the caverns, a total of 42 thermocouples were installed at different levels in 4 boreholes. The location of

Figure 11 Cavern U 21 B ready to receive oil.

the temperature measuring points is shown in figure 4. The graph in figure 10 illustrates temperatures recorded thus far.

It can be seen that the rock mass temperature becomes very stable at a depth of c. 10 m below the ground surface, which also is close to the level of the ground water surface, figure 9.

These temperature measurements will continue for a period of several years, as it will be of great importance to have a complete picture of the tempera- ture distribution in the rock mass, when oil at + 95°C is stored.

Bibliography

1. Hast N. 1958, The Measurement of Rock Pressure in Mines, Sveriges Geologiska Undersökning, Yearbook 52, SER. C 560, 1 - 183

2. Ignatius Y. 1980 Underground Storage of Oil and Gas Products, Subsurface Space, Volume 1, 53 - 57

3. Johansson S. 1980, Geological surveys for underground oil storage facilities, Underground space, Volume 5, 36 - 39.

4. Johansson S. 1981a Neste Oy´s underground oil storage, Oil and Gas J. Nov. 9. 277 - 286.

5. Johansson S: 1981b Construction and economics of unlined oil caverns, Tunnels & Tunneling, Oct. 1981

6. Koskinen E. and Kangas-Ikkala R., 1968 Underground oil reservoirs of the Neste Oy´s Porvoo plant. Finnish building magazine 1968:4, 172 - 177.

7. Langefors U. and Kihlström B. 1967 The modern technique of rock blasting. Almqvist & Wiksell, Stockholm

8. Leeman E.R. and Hayes D.J. 1966 Technique for determining the complete state of stress in rock using a single borehole. Proceedings 1st ISRM Congress, Vol. II, 17 - 24.

9. Maijala P.V. (Ed.) 1980, The effect of the structural and mechanical properties of rock masses on the kind of ecavation. The Mining and Metallurgical Society of Finland, Work comittee n:o 27. Report, 1 - 80

10. Matikainen R. (Ed.) 1981, Jännitystilamittaukset Suomessa (In situ state of stress measurements in Finland). The Mining and Metallurgical Society of Finland, Sarja A, n:o 64, 1 - 109

11. Simonen A., 1980 The Precambrian in Finland, Geol. Survey of Finland, Bulletin 304

12. Svanholm B-O., Persson P-A., Larsson B, 1977 Smooth blasting for reliable underground openings Proc. of 1st Int. Symp. Storage in Excavated Rock Caverns 573 - 579.

PREDICTION OF AIR LEAKAGES FROM AIR CUSHION SURGE CHAMBERS

Schätzung der Luftverluste bei Schwallkavernen mit Luftkissendämpfung

Prédiction des pertes d'air à partir des puits des chambres d'équilibre à coussin d'air

P.M.JOHANSEN & G.VIK
Norwegian Geotechnical Institute, Oslo

SUMMARY:
The air leaking out of air-cushion surge chambers has to be compensated for by stationary compressors. To predict the air loss, the Norwegian Geotechnical Institute has utilized a method developed by Tokheim and Janbu (1973). The paper presents calculations and measurements made at three sites. The correlation between predictions and observations is reasonable. The observed air losses at the three sites ranged from about $8.3 \cdot 10^{-4}$ m^3/sec (at 10°C and 1 bar) to $3.3 \cdot 10^{-1}$ m^3/sec (at 10°C and 1 bar).
The paper also decribes briefly the 120 000 m^3 air-cushion surge chamber at Kvilldal, West Norway, operating since December 1981.

ZUSAMMENFASSUNG:
Luft die aus eine Luftkissenkaverne sickert muss durch Druckluft ersetzt werden. Zur Vorausschätzung der Luftverluste wurde bei Norwegischer Geotechnische Institut eine von O.Tokheim and N.Janbu entwickelte Metode benutzt. Berechnungen und Messungen für drei Baustellen werden präsentiert und zeigen eine verhältnismässig gute ubereinstimmung zwischen berechnete und gemessene Werte. Die gemessene Luftverluste liegen bei der dichteren Kaverne um 50 l/min (10°C, 1 bar Normalluft), bei der undichteren um 20 000 l/min. Eine kurze Beschreibung von die 120 000 m^3 grosse Luftkissenkaverne des Kraftverkes Kvilldal die seit Dezember 1981 in Betrieb steht, ist auch gegeben.

RESUME:
Les pertes d'air des chambres à coussin d'air sous pression variable doivent être compensées par des compresseurs. Afin de prédire ces pertes, l'Institut norvégien de géotechnique a utilisé une méthode développée par Tokheim et Janbu (1973). L'article présente les calculs et mesures faits à trois emplacements. La corrélation entre prédictions et observations est raisonnable. Les pertes d'air observées aux trois emplacements varient entre environ $8.3 \cdot 10^{-4}$ m^3/s (à 10°C, 1 bar) et $3.3 \cdot 10^{-1}$ m^3/s (à 10°C, 1 bar). En plus l'article décrit brièvement la chambre à coussin d'air de Kvilldal, de dimensions 120 000 m^3, en opération depuis décembre 1981.

1 INTRODUCTION

Developments in tunneling and power plant design have led to the use of deep high-pressure headrace tunnels. In this new design, the traditional surge shaft is replaced by an unlined rock cavern filled partly by water and partly by air. The air-cushion is meant to dampen the pressure oscillations occurring with decreases or increases of the generator input, see fig. 1.

The new design required a method to predict air leakage rates as a basis for selection of compressor capacity. The compressor size depends on the maximum time allowable for chamber filling, and the capacity necessary to compensate for air loss through the rock mass. In Norway, the State Power System, uses mainly mobile compressors for filling up, and stationary compressors to compensate for lost air.

To predict air loss rates, the Norwegian Geotechnical Institute has used a method developed by Tokheim and Janbu (1973) at the department of Soil Mechanics at the Norwegian Institute of Technology. The method is described in detail by Dr.Tokheim and Prof. Janbu elsewhere in this symposium.

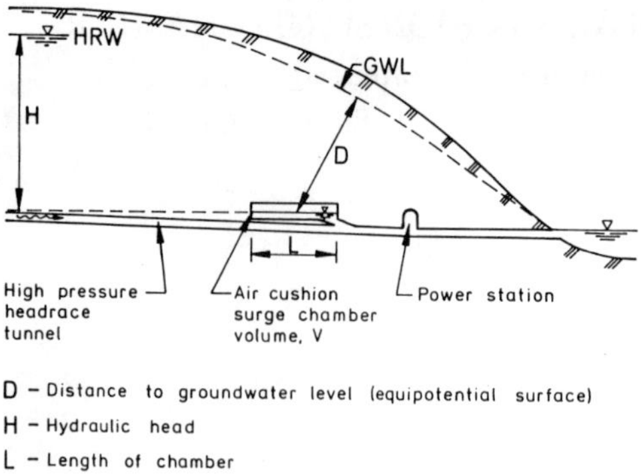

Fig. 1. General layout of a power plant with air-cushion surge chamber.

At three power plant sites, the Norwegian Geotechnical Institute (NGI) conducted the geological investigations necessary to determine the best site possible for the location of air-cushion surge chambers, and predicted the air leakage according to the method of Tokheim and Janbu. The three power plants owned by the Norwegian State Power System are Lang-Sima, Oksla and Kvilldal. At a fourth location, the Nye Osa power plant, relatively large air losses were recorded. The owner, the Energy Authority in the County of Hedemark, provided NGI with permeability measurements which made possible a prediction of the rate of air loss.

2 THEORETICAL BACKGROUND

The Tokheim and Janbu theory formulates the rate of air leakage through water saturated rock mass, Q_{aw}, as follows:

$$Q_{aw} = \psi \cdot Q_a = \psi \cdot \frac{\pi \cdot K \cdot L \cdot p_o}{\mu_a \cdot G} \cdot \left[\left(\frac{p_s}{p_o}\right)^2 - \left(\frac{p_e}{p_o}\right)^2 \right] \quad (1)$$

List of symbols:

- Q_{aw} = Air leakage rate through water saturated rock mass in m^3/s at 10°C and a pressure of $1.0 \cdot 10^5$ Pa.
- Q_a = Air leakage rate through dry rock mass, m^3/s at 10°C and a pressure of $1.0 \cdot 10^5$ Pa.
- ψ = Constant, $0 < \psi < 1$.
- K = Intrinsic permeability, m^2.
- L = Length of chamber, m.
- μ_a = Dymamic viscosity of air $1.76 \cdot 10^{-5}$ kg/m · s.
- G = Geometry factor, depending on the dimensionless parameters r/D and L/D.
- r = Chamber radius (idealized geometry).
- D = Distance from cavern center to equipotential surface (= ground water level).
- p_o = Reference pressure, $1.0 \cdot 10^5$ Pa.
- p_s = Maximum absolute air pressure in the cavern, Pa.
- p_e = Absolute air pressure on the dimensioning equipotential surface. This is usually equal to the ground water level and $p_e = p_o = 10^5$ Pa.

As stated by equation (1), the air flow through the saturated rock mass is reduced with a factor ψ compared to flow through the dry rock mass.

2.1 The value of ψ

Air leakage rate in water saturated rock mass is a function of the dimensions D, r, L and the absolute air pressures p_s and p_e. The mean water gradient, i_m, in the outward direction from the water filled part of the chamber after the surge chamber has been put in operation, is defined according to Tokheim and Janbu:

$$i_m = \frac{p_r}{\gamma_w \cdot D} \quad (2)$$

- p_r = excess pressure of water in the chamber compared to hydrostatic distribution of pore water pressure, Pa.
- γ_w = unit weight of water, 10 kN/m^3.

In the case of air-cushion surge chambers, the gradient i_m, is generally about 0.5 and never more than 1.0 for free drainage to the surface. This implies that ψ rarely exceeds 0.5 (Tokheim and Janbu, 1973). For gradients i_m not too far below 0.5, ψ will presumably lie within the interval 0.1 - 0.5 for usual chamber geometries.

2.2 The value of G

To calculate the value of the geometry factor G, one needs to estimate the geometry of the flow through the rock mass. If the dimension of the excavations is of the same order as the spacing between water filled fissures, three-dimensional flow can be assumed. In the case of anisotropic flow, a two-dimensional model must be considered. In the three-dimensional case the chamber geometry is modelled as a cylinder with spherical ends, and the length, L, is in this case the distance between the sphere centers. For two-dimensional flow the real length is used. Common values of G for three-dimensional flow range between 1.2 - 1.8 and for two-dimensional flow between 3.5 - 5.0.

2.3 The permeability K

The influence of the factors ψ and G on the

Table 1. Measured intrinsic permeabilities at three sites, $K(m^2)$

Measuring method / Site	Lang-Sima Sima power plant Eidfjord, West-Norway	Oksla power plant Odda, West-Norway	Nye Osa power plant Rena, East-Norway
Lugeon test, mean	$5.1 \cdot 10^{-18}$	$3.0 \cdot 10^{-17}$	$9.8 \cdot 10^{-15}$
Lugeon test, median	$4.7 \cdot 10^{-18}$	$3.7 \cdot 10^{-17}$	$6.0 \cdot 10^{-15}$
Water discarge from boreholes	$8.8 \cdot 10^{-19}$	$2.4 \cdot 10^{-18}$	$9.9 \cdot 10^{-15}$
Water flow (+ evaporation) into the chamber	$2.9 \cdot 10^{-19}$	$3.4 \cdot 10^{-18}$	$1.7 \cdot 10^{-15}$
Selected K-value for air leakage calculation	$5.1 \cdot 10^{-18}$	$3.7 \cdot 10^{-17}$	$9.9 \cdot 10^{-15}$

Table 2. Parameters used in leakage calculation.

Parameter, unit / Site	Lang-Sima Sima power plant Eidfjord, West-Norway	Oksla power plant Odda, West-Norway	Nye Osa power plant Rena, East-Norway
D, m	350	450	125
r, m	8.0	8.5	7.0
L_2, m 1)	-	80	70
L_3, m 1)	36	63	56
i_m	0.58	0.11	0.60
ψ	0.50	0.15	0.5
p_s, 10^5 Pa	49	46	20
G_2 1)	-	4.6	3.7
G_3 1)	1.3	1.5	1.7
V, m^3	6200	17000	12500

1) L_2, L_3 and G_2, G_3 denote lengths and geometry factors used in the two- and three-dimensional calculations respectively.

air leakage rate is of the order of 10^1. The intrinsic permeability, K, is the parameter with the largest influence on the air-leakage rate. The geological investigations aim therefore at obtaining a resonable value of the average permeability.

3 SELECTION OF CONSTRUCTION SITE

In Norway, six air-cushion surge chambers have been constructed to date (1982). All the chambers are located in gneissic and granitic rock mass of precambrian age. The quality of this rock is generally very good. Occasionally the rock has discontinuities containing swelling clay or other clay minerals. The hydraulic function of the surge chamber limits the length of the head-race tunnel available to about one km. Within this section, the best site possible is selected after investigations by core drillings and measurements of hydraulic conductivities.

4 DETERMINATION OF K

To increase the confidence in the measured permeability, NGI measures the permeability in three ways:

- Constant head test (Lugeon tests) with stepwise increasing hydraulic heads until the maximum head equals maximum absolute air pressure in the surge chamber.
- Measurement of water flow out of free draining boreholes (if any).
- Measurement of water flow into the excavated cavern, including theoretical evaporation from the cavern walls. The discharge is also measured during excavation.

5 MEASUREMENTS FROM THREE SITES

Table 1 lists the permeabilities measured by the above three methods at the power plants under study and compares measured values of the intrinsic permeability used in prediction of air leakage.

6 PREDICTION OF AIR LEAKAGE

The values listed in Tables 1 and 2 were used in equation (1) for the leakage calculations.

For three-dimensional flow, the following rates of air leakage were predicted (all leakages are measured at 10°C and 1 bar pressure):

Lang-Sima: $Q_{aw} = 3.0 \cdot 10^{-3}$ m³/s (180 l/min)
Oksla: $Q_{aw} = 8.8 \cdot 10^{-3}$ m³/s (530 l/min)
Nye Osa: $Q_{aw} = 1.2$ m³/s (70 m³/min)

In the case of two-dimensional flow, the predicted rates were:

Oksla: $Q_{aw} = 3.6 \cdot 10^{-3}$ m³/s (220 l/min)
Nye Osa: $Q_{aw} = 6.7 \cdot 10^{-1}$ m³/s (40 m³/min)

7 MEASUREMENTS OF AIR LOSSES

The air volume in the chamber is measured by the water level, (and thus the water volume) and the air pressure P. The product $P \cdot V$ is obtained.

Even with good instruments, it is difficult to measure water levels with accuracy better that ± 1 cm. With an area of about 800 to 1000 m², a one-cm increase in water level corresponds to a compressed air loss of 10 m³.

The reported air losses at the three sites are (at 10°C and 1 bar):

Lang-Sima: $Q_{aw} = 7.5 \cdot 10^{-4}$ m³/s (45 l/min), The pressure p_s averaged only 36.3 bars during the measuring period.

Oksla: "Very modest leakage, almost impervious."

Nye Osa: $Q_{aw} = 0.1 - 0.37$ m³/s (6 – 22 m³/min). The air loss varied considerably with water level in the chamber. Based on compressor running time only, the rate of air leakage was increasing. The compressor capacity was however not checked.

The air loss at Lang-Sima, if calculated at actual p_s-value during the measuring period was: Q_{aw}(3-dim.) $= 1.3 \cdot 10^{-3}$ m³/s (80 l/min), with $i_m = \psi = 0.40$.

Table 3 compares the predicted and measured rates of air loss.

Table 3. Predicted and measured rates of air loss, Q_{aw} (m³/s at 10°C and 1 bar).

Site	Lang-Sima (p_s = 36.3 bars)	Oksla	Nye Osa
Calc. 3-dim.	$1.3 \cdot 10^{-3}$	$8.8 \cdot 10^{-3}$	1.20
Calc. 2-dim.	-	$3.6 \cdot 10^{-3}$	0.67
Measured	$7.5 \cdot 10^{-4}$	minimal leakage, almost impervious	0.1-0.37

In view of the accuracy of the water level measurements and since the dimensioning permeability is taken as either the maximum mean or maximum median, the Tokheim and Janbu model is believed suitable for prediction of air leakages.

8 SOME DATA ON KVILLDAL, ULLA-FØRRE, WEST-NORWAY, THE LARGEST POWER STATION AND AIR-CUSHION CHAMBER IN THE COUNTRY.

At Kvilldal, the first of four generators each capable of producing 300 MWh, was put in operation at the end of 1981. The power plant comprises an air-cushion surge chamber with total volume of about 120 000 m³ including access and transportation tunnels. With all generators running, the air volume in the chamber will be about 80 – 95 000 m³ at an absolute pressure of 42 bars.

The chamber is excavated around a rectangular central pillar measuring 84 x 46 m. The cavern has a span of 16 m and the height varies between 17 and 24 m.

The maximum operating pressure in the chamber will be 42 bars. The Norwegian Geotechnical Institute has calculated the rate of air leakage. The predictions are however hampered by the unusual chamber geometry and uncertainties in the pore pressure value. Piezometer installations indicated high pore pressure at chamber depths, thus low mean water gradient i_m and low air losses.

Measurements near the chamber give low pore pressures and therefore higher calculated air losses. The Tokheim and Janbu theory yields a rate of air flow of $1.7 \cdot 10^{-2}$ m³/s (1 m³/min). Until chamber filling is complete, it is difficult to measure air losses, since the water surface is very large (~5000 m²) but measurements during the first months of filling indicate a total air loss of the order of $1.7 - 3.3 \cdot 10^{-2}$ m³/s (1 – 2 m³/min).

9 REFERENCES

Tokheim, O. and N.Janbu 1973, Overslag over luftlekkasjer fra lukkede fordelings-basseng i fjell (Estimates of air leakages from air-cushion surge chambers). Publ. in Lukket fordelingsbasseng med luftpute. Samlerapport. Ed. by Norwegian Institue of Technology. Dept. of Soil Mechanichs, Trondheim, a.o. pp 75 – 113.

Tokheim, O. and N.Janbu 1982, Flow rate from a source or sink located in a semi infinite permeable mass. Paper to be published in International Symposium on Rock Mechanichs related to Caverns and Pressure Shafts, Aachen 1982.

ROCK MECHANICAL PROBLEMS IN ASSOCIATION WITH UNDERGROUND STORAGE ON THE MECHANICAL RESPONSE OF GRANITE TO CONDITIONS ASSOCIATED WITH THE DISPOSAL OF NUCLEAR FUEL WASTE

Über die mechanische Reaktion von Granit im Zusammenhang mit der Beseitigung nuklearer Brennstoffabfälle

Réaction mécanique du granit en relation avec l'élimination des déchets nucléaires

E.Z.LAJTAI
University of Manitoba, Winnipeg, Canada

SUMMARY:
The response of granite to the environment of an underground nuclear fuel waste vault is examined through laboratory experiments using specimens of intact granite. Conventional creep tests and specially designed crack growth experiments suggest that void volume created through microfracture at 140 MPa may be less than one tenth of one percent. At higher stresses, the granite may enter into steady-state creep and eventually fail. Because stresses of this magnitude will either be unlikely or limited to very small areas, the creation of a significantly large high permeability zone in the geological barrier is not expected.

ZUSAMENFASSUNG:
Die Reaktion des Granits zu der Umgebung von Felshohleräumen fuer Atomabfallprodukte wird durch Laborexperimente untersucht, indenen Proben von unversehrten Lac du Bonnet Granit verwendet werden. Normale Kriechversuche und spezial entwickelte Experimente fuer Rissvergroesserungen deuten daraufhin, dass das Gesamtvolumen der Mikrorupturen bei 140 MPa wehniger als ein zehntel Prozent ist. Bei groesseren Druckspannungen von solcher Groesse unwahrscheinlich sind,oder nur in sehr kleinen Flächen vorkommen, wird keine bedeutsam hohe Durchlässigkeitszone in der geologischen Barriere erwarted.

RESUME:
Grâce à des expériences menées en laboratoire, où on utilise des échantillons de granit provenant de la régeion du Lac du Bonnet, Manitoba, on essaie de tester les réactions qu'un dépôt de déchets nucléaires pourrait exercer sur la roche. Selon les tests conventionnels de fluage et des expériences plus spécifiques destinées à mesurer l'extension des fissures, on est porté à croire que le volume du vide crée par la micrófracture à 140 MPa n 'atteint que le dixième d'un pour cent. Sous des compressions plus élevées, le granit peut se déformer lentement et, à long terme, il peut se fracturer. Mais il est peu probable que des contraintes de cette ampleur soient appliquées ou si elles devaient l'être, elles seraient réduites à des secteurs d'une superficie limitée. De ce fait, il y a peu de chances qu'une zone de haute perméabilité d'une étendue considérable se forme dans la roche.

1 INTRODUCTION

The Canadian nuclear fuel waste management program is administered by the Whiteshell Nuclear Research Establishment of Atomic Energy of Canada Limited. Field and laboratory investigations are now under way to locate and then develop an underground waste disposal vault in a hard rock formation of the Canadian Shield. This paper examines the problem of the long-term response of granitic rock to the anticipated environment of a nuclear fuel waste management site. The rock used in the experiments is Lac du Bonnet granite obtained from a quarry near Lac du Bonnet, Manitoba, Canada. An underground research laboratory is now planned for location in the same granite.

2 ANTICIPATED ENVIRONMENTAL CONDITIONS FOR WASTE DISPOSAL VAULTS

Many aspects of the design and construction of the nuclear fuel waste vault have not been finalized yet so that the environmental conditions to which the granite will be subjected during its service-life are still subject to some speculation. Conventional wisdom, however, suggests that the relevant factors include the state of stress, including its time dependence, and the temperature and the chemistry of the groundwater.

2.1 State of Stress

The stress to which the rock in a disposal vault will be subjected is determined by the state of the presently acting tectonic stress (the primary state of stress), the geometry of the underground development, the method of excavation, and the thermal load generated by the radioactive decay of the fuel waste.

There have been a number of measurements of tectonic stresses in the Canadian Shield (Herget, 1980), indicating that in-situ stresses at 1 km depth (the maximum which is now under consideration) may be postulated as follows. The maximum principal stress is horizontal trending easterly with a magnitude of about 45 MPa. The vertical direction coincides with the minimum principal stress direction, its magnitude being equal to the gravitational load, i.e. 25 MPa. The third, the intermediate principal stress is again horizontal with its magnitude varying widely between 25 and 45 MPa.

With its magnitude depending on the general outlay of the underground installations, a concentration of stress occurs at the rock perimeter as the openings are excavated (the secondary state of stress). The magnitude of the stress concentration, is influenced by the construction technique as well. Drilled tunnels in relatively unfractured rock, like the Lac du Bonnet granite, could fully develop the theoretical elastic stress concentrations. Conversely, a conventional construction method using explosives damages the rock walls and consequently shifts the stress concentrations inward into the rock with some loss in magnitude. The stress concentration factor around a single opening ranges typically between one and three. Even after allowing for thermal loading and the effect of overlapping stress fields between intersecting or adjacent developments, a stress concentration factor greater than three to four is unlikely to occur. The maximum secondary principal stress therefore should be no greater than about 150 MPa, which is about one half to two thirds of the uniaxial compressive strength of Lac du Bonnet granite (Lajtai, 1981). Because all three principal primary stresses are compressive and the stress differences are relatively small, no secondary tensile stresses are expected. The minimum secondary principal stress should therefore act perpendicular to the rock walls of the vault and should approximately be zero, since the soft backfill would create little, if any, confining effect. (This could change if the buffer and the backfill were designed to develop an appreciable swelling pressure).

2.2 Temperature

The temperature of the rock will start at its present equilibrium temperature, possibly a few degrees over freezing. It would rise slightly during the construction period, but the major change would occur only after the fuel waste is put in place and the vault is sealed. Assuming that the skin temperature of the containers will be about 150°C, and the average backfill temperature about 100°C, rock temperature should, because of its distance from the containers, be less than 100°C.

2.3 Groundwater

Regardless of the construction technique used, sooner or later the rock will be saturated with groundwater of a composition that may not be much different from what exists at the site before construction is undertaken. In the Canadian Shield, water composition at one kilometer depth may vary widely from that typical of unpolluted drinkable groundwater to a brine richer in dissolved solids than sea water.

The groundwater pressure could range from zero during the construction stage to a much higher value after the disposal vault is backfilled and sealed. The most reasonable assumption is about 10 MPa, i.e. the hydrostatic pressure at 1 kilometer depth. If the rock is tight and the vault is filled completely by fully saturated backfill, thermal expansion could lead to higher pressures. The maximum that could conceivably occur is set by the pressure necessary to open naturally occurring fractures. This should be close to the minimum principal stress or about 25 MPa.

2.4 Time

Perhaps the most important factor in determining rock response in the long term is the length of time during which the high stresses exist. A nuclear fuel waste disposal site is different from all other underground installation by having a life expectancy that is measured in thousands rather than tens of years. The highest stresses will probably exist for hundreds of years, starting with the peaking of temperature only a few tens of years after the sealing of the vault.

3 THE SCIENTIFIC CHALLENGE

The design of a nuclear fuel waste disposal vault is a unique rock mechanics problem for at least two reasons. These are the unusually long service life, and the relatively high service temperature. Both time and temperature play a major role in rock deformation, and more specifically in the creep of rock.

Crack growth and creep in rock is easy to demonstrate when the stress applied is near the compressive strength so that failure occurs within a reasonably short time. In experiments of this type, failure of Lac du Bonnet granite occurs after a total elastic plus creep strain of just over 3,000 $\mu\varepsilon$ (0.3 percent). Presumably the same total strain could be accumulated at a stress far below the compressive strength, but over a longer time period. To reach this, the rock would have to enter steady-state creep, although the rate could be extremely small. Indeed, 3,000 $\mu\varepsilon$ could be accumulated at rates as low as 10^{-13} per second, assuming a thousand year service-life. Measuring experimental rates as low as this is extremely difficult, if not impossible. A rate of 10^{-6} per second may be the lowest rate that can be managed using conventional strain gauge instrumentation. Tests under water are even more difficult because of the additional problem of strain gauge corrosion.

Crack growth is usually considered as a problem of mechanics. Growth can occur, however, while all mechanical parameters are kept constant suggesting that degradation of granite may occur by other means as well. Indeed, the term "stress corrosion" has been coined to suggest that chemical reactions do occur even in relatively short term creep tests. Stress may not even be necessary. In tropical areas, it is just a matter of time before processes of chemical weathering reduce granite to a mixture of clay and sand. The relevance of processes of chemical surface weathering to the environment of a nuclear fuel waste disposal site however is beyond the scope of this paper.

The response of granite to nuclear waste disposal vault conditions is complicated further by the fact that the expected temperature range, say 70 to 100°C, is situated in a range of limited interest. Research in engineering rock mechanics is usually restricted to the +30° to 30°C, while geochemistry works in the 200°C plus temperature range. The Canadian Nuclear Fuel Waste Management Program is now intensifying research in this sofar uncovered temperature range.

4 EXPERIMENTS

The most obvious deformational process at loads substantially below the compressive strength of rocks is creep and crack growth. It is usually assumed that the two are closely related. In a conventional creep test, changes in strain or volume, or both, are measured as a function of time while the load is kept constant.

All the creep and crack growth experiments in this work involved the uniaxial compression of rock. In a number of tests, axial and lateral strains were measured using electronic strain gauges accurate to 1-2 microstrains. The longest test conducted lasted 72 days. All successful tests required, in addition to extreme care in instrumentation, the use of up to 13 strain gauges at least two of which are not subject to stress. These are used to track instrument drift.

The conventional electronic strain gauge instrumentation does not adapt well to the measurement of strain in specimens of granite tested while submerged in water. Techniques to moisture-proof the strain gauges are being tried, but so far no reliable results have been produced. The sensitivity of crack growth and creep to moisture and elevated temperature, was evaluated by using another approach, which was developed in cooperation with B.J.S. Wilkins of Atomic Energy of Canada Limited.

Microcracks grow in planes containing the maximum and intermediate principal stresses. In the uniaxial compression of a rock cylinder, this is any plane that includes the axis of the cylinder. Crack growth therefore should be reflected by a decrease in tensile strength when tension is applied perpendicular to such diametral planes. The actual decrease in tensile strength is related to crack growth; the proportionality factors are not yet known. In an earlier paper (Lajtai, 1981), it was demonstrated that in samples subjected to instantaneous compression, the tensile strength is essentially unaffected below compressive stress of 205 MPa. This is the stress at which the lateral strain, and therefore the crack volume, tends to accelerate, although the first sign of crack growth is demonstrated at less than one-half of this stress. The advantage of tracking crack growth by changes in tensile strength is that it requires no electronic strain gauges, and therefore is relatively easy to use on samples which have been compressively loaded while submerged in water. The disadvantage of the approach is that the measurement of tensile strength is subject to a coefficient of variation of about 10 percent for Lac du Bonnet granite. A meaningful interpretation of the data therefore must include the use of statistics.

To test the power of this approach four identical specimen groups, each containing fourteen 31 mm diameter and 28 mm high cylinders were prepared. Samples in three of the groups were compressed for one week in three identical loading frames, but under three different environments: 1) at room temperature and humidity (cold-dry); 2) at room temperature, but submerged in synthetic granite groundwater (cold-wet); 3) submerged in same water but at 80-90°C (hot-wet). The load for each group was uniaxial compression kept between 140 and 143 MPa. The fourth group was not loaded but used to find the tensile strength of the intact cylinders. After compression all 56 specimens, properly marked, were tested in random order using the Brazilian technique. At all stages great care was taken not to introduce equipment or operator bias.

5 THE RESULTS

The growth of cracks, as a function of stress only, can be derived from a stress-strain diagram that includes the two strain parameters; the axial and the lateral strain. Volumetric strain, and the relative crack volume can be calculated from these. The latter is the difference between the actual volumetric strain and the projected elastic volumetric strain calculated from the elastic modulus E and the Poisson's ratio ν determined from the precracking part of the stress-strain curves. In a typical uniaxial compression test, the axial strain curve (Figure 1) is almost perfectly linear from the beginning to the end (failure) of the test. The lateral strain curve on the other hand shows the first sign of dilatancy at stresses between 50 and 100 MPa with the departure from elastic behaviour accelerating at about

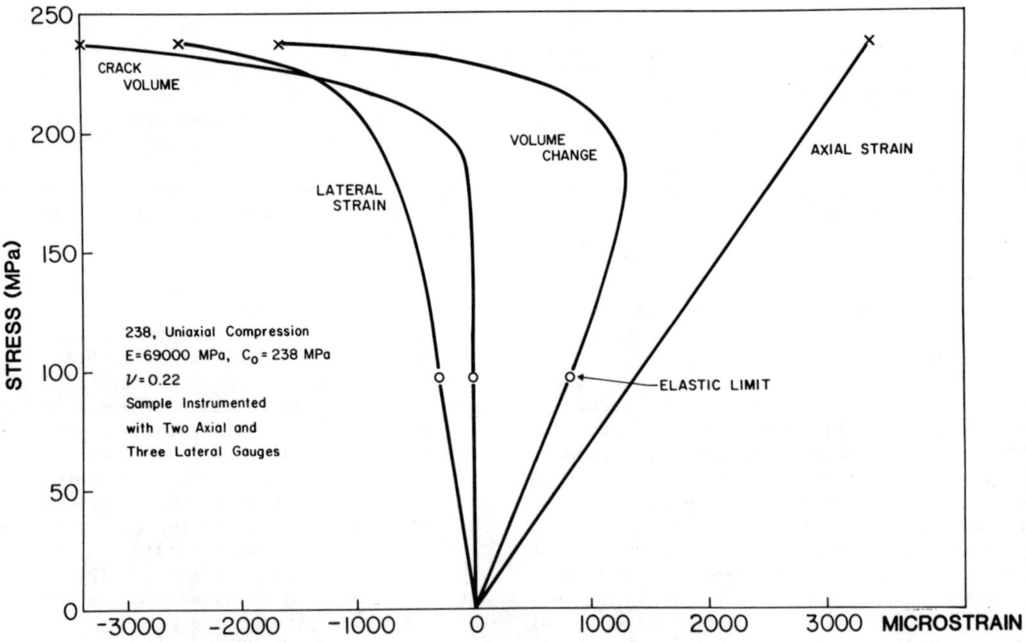

Figure 1. A typical stress-strain diagram describing the response of Lac du Bonnet granite to a test in uniaxial compression.

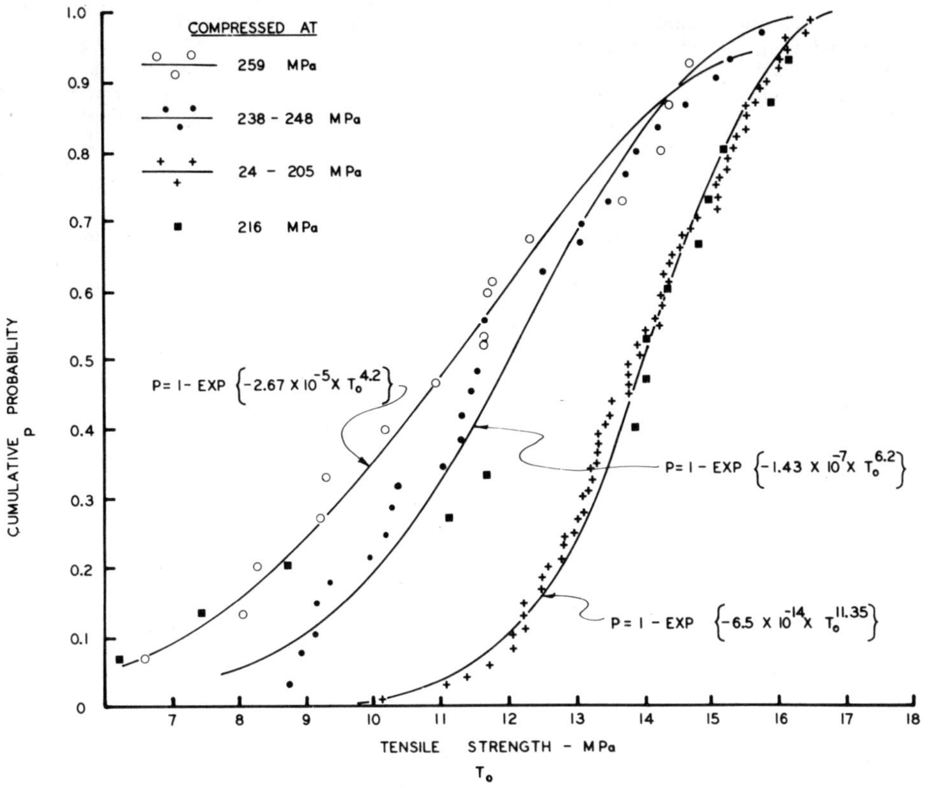

Figure 2. Cumulative probability distribution of tensile strength data from tests of rock specimens previously subjected to uniaxial compression to a stress level set below the compressive strength. The fitted curves are Weibull distributions.

200 MPa. Being controlled by lateral strain, the volumetric strain and the crack volume curves display similar behaviour. This trend in crack growth is reflected in changes in the tensile strength of granite that had previously been subjected to compression. Specimen compressed at less than 216 MPa show no statistically significant change in tensile strength (Figure 2). Above this stress the drop in tensile strength is rapid (the tests used 31 mm diameter, 28 mm high cylinders that have a compressive strength of about 300 MPa).

The time dependence of deformation at room temperature and humidity was investigated through conventional creep tests. In general, the axial strain is independent of time. Figure 3 shows an exception where both the axial and the lateral strains display the characteristic stages of a complete creep curve. This however requires high stresses usually above 200 MPa. More commonly, only the lateral strain is time dependent. Because stresses in the nuclear fuel waste disposal vault are not expected

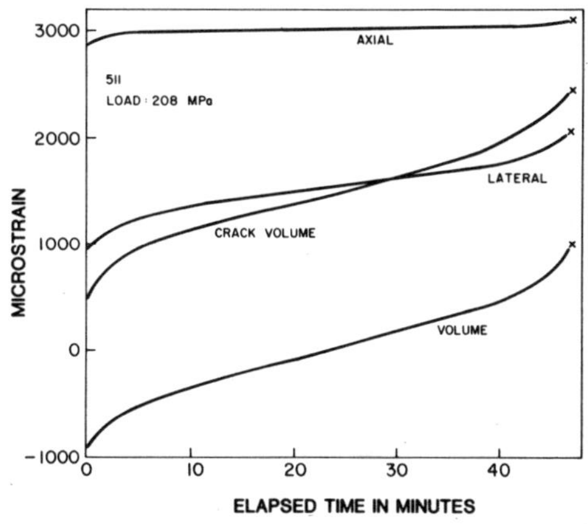

Figure 3. A typical set of creep curves for a high stress test, showing all three stages of time dependent response.

to exceed 150 MPa and probably will be much lower, testing concentrated on creep in the 140-150 MPa range. The longest of the three tests conducted so far lasting a total of 72 days is shown in Figure 4. With the axial strain remaining constant, the lateral strain exhibited a relatively long-term but nonetheless logarithmic creep, as the strain eventually became constant during the last ten days. Small changes in strain are better shown by plotting the strain rate on logarithmitic scale against time (Figure 5). Here the other two tests are included as well. It

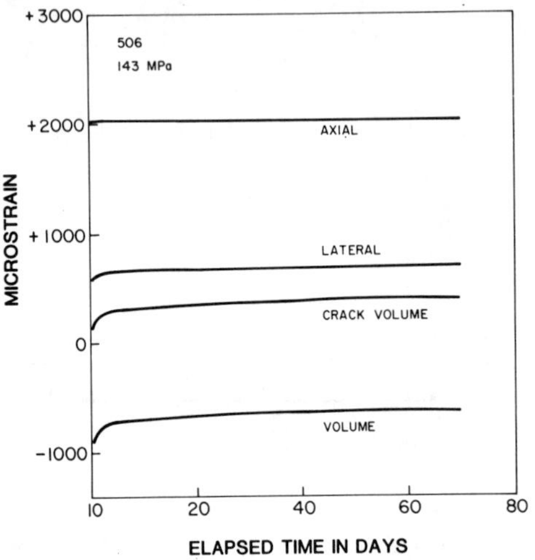

Figure 4. Creep curves for the longest (72 days) test with loading at 143 MPa. Only primary creep was detected.

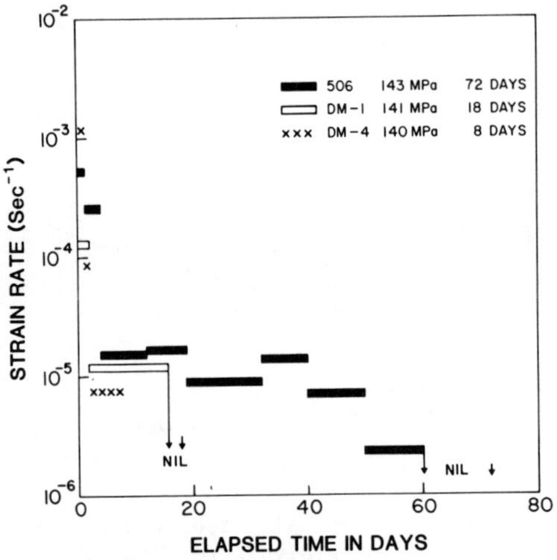

Figure 5. Strain rates obtained from three creep tests at 140-143 MPa.

would appear that at this stress level, an appreciable part of time is spent at an averaged strain rate of 10^{-5}/sec.

The changes in tensile strength of specimen subjected to different environments are shown in Figure 6. The individual data points are included only for the two extreme cases, for the control and wet-hot groups; for clarity, the individual data points belonging to the cold-wet and cold-dry environments were deleted and only the theoretical Weibull curves (Weibull, 1950) are shown. Interestingly, the greatest change occurs at the high-strength tail of the distribution curves; the low strength tail of the distribution appears to be the same for each group.

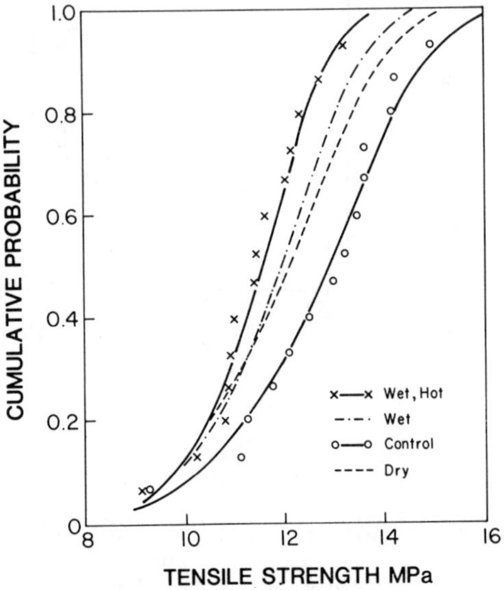

Figure 6. The effect of different environmental conditions on crack growth as measured by the decrease in tensile strength. For the sake of clarity, individual data points are shown only for the two extreme cases. The compressive stress in all three environments was constant at 140 MPa. The curves shown are Weibull fits.

6 DISCUSSION AND CONCLUSIONS

The three creep tests that were conducted between 140 and 143 MPa seemed to undergo only primary creep. The accumulated crack volume, or added fracture porosity were calculated to be 96 (141 MPa), 425 (140 MPa), and 400 (143 MPa) microstrain equivalents. Three data points do not make a statistical sample. By ignoring the low value one may however get the crude estimate of an additional .04 percentage points in fracture porosity as a result of loading at 140 MPa for one week under room temperature and humidity. (To obtain the total porosity expressed as percentage, add the quoted value to the initial porosity of the rock, which has not been measured, but for granite is typically in the 1-5 percent range). Present indications are that at this stress level the rock does not enter into secondary creep, so that the 0.04 percentage points increase in fracture porosity is the most that is expected. This increase corresponds to a decrease in average tensile strength from 12.70 MPa (control group) to 11.94 MPa (cold-dry) for a change of 0.76 MPa or 6 percent. The difference is small, nonetheless it is statistically significant at the 99 percent confidence level. The change from the control to the hot-wet group is from 12.70 to 11.44 for a difference of 1.26 MPa, which obviously is also a significant difference (99.9 percent confidence level). Speculating that the drop in tensile strength is proportional to added fracture porosity, the projected increase in fracture volume for the hot-wet environment at 140 MPa could be around 0.07 percentage points. The assumption implied in this estimate is that in the hot-wet environment creep is still logarithmic. If on the other hand, the specimen in the hot-wet environment entered into secondary creep, fracture porosity would increase until failure. Typical values for added fracture porosity just before failure are in the 0.3 to 0.5 percentage point range.

Among other creep tests conducted at room temperature and humidity but above 140 MPa stress, one at a stress of 147 MPa may have entered into secondary creep. Conversely, several others at higher stress but under 200 MPa, showed only primary creep. It would appear therefore that 140 MPa is probably close to the limit under which no secondary creep and subsequent failure of the rock is expected. This "threshold" stress in the wet-hot environment may be lower. This is still to be investigated.

Although it is most unlikely that a condition of creep failure will ever be approached in the nuclear waste disposal vault under consideration, the consequences of such are still worth considering. If creep failure were to occur, it would take place in a progressive manner as the stress concentration shifts toward the interior of rock following the spalling of the failed rock at the perimeter. The process would continue on until a more stable perimeter producing a smaller stress concentration is established. For the given primary stress field the stress concentration around an ideally shaped opening would be slightly above two, suggesting a stress of no more than 100 MPa. No substantial crack growth is expected at stresses as low low as this. One may therefore conclude that under the worst condition that could develop through the type of crack growth described here, the backfilled vault would be surrounded by a probably discontinuous blanket of fragmented rock. Although the resulting permeability increase is potentially undesirable as it may facilitate the movement of fluids, the fragmentation of rock would not be without some benefit. It would increase the surface area of rock available for the adsorption of undesirable waste products.

7 ACKNOWLEDGEMENTS

The research described in the paper is sponsored by the Whiteshell Nuclear Research Establishment of Atomic Energy of Canada Limited through a research contract with the University of Manitoba. The project officer from WNRE is Gary R. Simmons. Technical assistance was provided by Ed Lemke, Narong Piamsalee and students of the senior class in Geological Engineering. Valerie Ring prepared the manuscript.

8 REFERENCES

Herget, G. 1980, Regional stresses in the Canadian Shield. Proceedings, 13th Canadian Rock Mechanics Symposium, p. 9-16.

Lajtai, E.Z. (in press), Creep and crack growth in Lac du Bonnet granite due to compressive stress. Proceedings, Canadian Fracture Mechanics Conference 5, Winnipeg.

Weibull, W. 1951, A statistical distribution function of wide applicability, Appl. Mech. Rev., 5: 449-451.

FELSMECHANISCHE PROBLEME BEI DER ERRICHTUNG VON SPEICHERKAVERNEN

Rock mechanical problems related to the construction of storage caverns

Problèmes de mécanique des roches dans la construction des cavernes de stockage

M. LANGER
Bundesanstalt für Geowissenschaften und Rohstoffe, Hannover, Bundesrepublik Deutschland

SUMMARY:
Mined cavities are used world-wide as storage facilities for various materials (oil,gas, waste). Thereby, new problems arise for the rock-mechanics engineeer: proof of the long-term tightness, stability analysis of very large caverns which cannot be artificially supported, the influence of considerable changes of temperature on the rock behavior. Recent results of research on rheological (creep-) behavior and on the flow- and failure parameters of rock salt can help to solve these problems. A numerical computer code - ANSALT - to solve engineering problems in evaporite rock has been developed. An extensive concept for the proof of stability of a mine for the final disposal of radioactive wastes in salt rock has been worked out.

ZUSAMMENFASSUNG:
Bei den künstlich geschaffenen Speicherhohlräumen unterscheidet man bergmännisch hergestellte Felskavernen und ausgespülte Salzkavernen. Solche Kavernen werden für die Lagerung verschiedenartiger Stoffe (Öl, Gas, Abfälle) weltweit genutzt. Dabei haben sich auch für den Felsmechaniker neuartige Probleme ergeben: Nachweis der lang-zeitigen Dichtheit, Standsicherheitsanalyse nicht ausbaufähiger großer Hohlräume, Einfluß starker Temperaturänderungen auf das Gebirgsverhalten. Zur Lösung dieser Probleme können neue Forschungsergebnisse zum rheologischen (Kriech-) Verhalten und über Fließ- und Bruchparameter speziell von Steinsalz beitragen. Die Entwicklung eines numerischen Rechenprogrammes - ANSALT - zur Bearbeitung von Ingenieurproblemen im Salzgebirge ist abgeschlossen. Zum Endlagerbergwerk für radioaktive Abfälle im Salzgebirge ist ein umfassendes Konzept für den Sicherheitsnachweis erarbeitet worden.

RESUME:
Dans les cavernes de stockage de construction artificielle, on distinque les cavernes minières, des cavernes salines lessivées. Les cavernes salines furent utilisées dans le monde entier pour l'entrepôt de matériaux divers (pétrole, gaz, déchets). Ce faisant, le spécialiste de la méchanique des roches se heurta à de nouveaux problèmes: mise en évidence de l'étanchéité de long durée, analyse de la stabilité de grandes cavernes dont la fortification n'est pas possible, influence de forts changements de température sur le comportement de la roche. Pour résoudre ces problèmes, de nouveaux résultats de recherche sont en mesure de contribuer au comportement rhéologique et sur les paramètres de coulement et de rupture du sel gemme. Le développement d'un programme numérique de calcul-ANSALT - servant à résoudre les problèmes d'ingénieur est achevé. Un vaste concept pour la preuve de la sécurité a été élaboré pour un stockage définitiv des déchets radioactifs dans la roche saline.

1. EINLEITUNG

Die Einbringung von gasförmigen oder flüssigen Energieträgern (Öl, Gas, Druckluft) oder Produkten der chemischen Industrie (Erdölprodukte u.ä.) in unausgekleideten Hohlräumen unter der Erdoberfläche zur vorübergehenden Lagerung wird als "Untergrundspeicherung" bzw. "unterirdische Speicherung" definiert. Bei der Speicherung ist eine spätere Wiederentnahme des Speichergutes vorgesehen. Im Gegensatz dazu wird die dauerhafte Beseitigung von Stoffen (Abfällen) in den Untergrund mit der Absicht, sich ihrer zu entledigen, als "Deponie" oder "Endlagerung" bezeichnet.

Der für die Lagerung genutzte unterirdische Hohlraum ist entweder natürlich vorhanden (Porenspeicher in klastischen Sedimenten) oder wird künstlich geschaffen (Kavernen). Als natürliche Porenspeicher werden vor allem ausgebeutete Gas- oder Öllagerstätten oder auch wassergefüllte poröse Sedimentschichten (Aquifere) verwendet, die sich über geologische Zeiten hinweg als dicht gezeigt haben.

Bei den künstlich geschaffenen Speicherhohlräumen unterscheidet man bergmännisch errichtete Felskavernen und durch Ausspülen von Salzformationen hergestellte Salzkavernen. In einigen Fällen werden auch aufgelassene Bergwerke oder alte Stollen zu Speicher- oder Deponiezwecken eingerichtet. Im folgenden werden einige felsmechanische Fragestellungen, die sich bei der Planung und Errichtung von Speicherkavernen ergeben, behandelt.

2 GEOTECHNISCHE KRITERIEN FÜR DIE STANDORTAUSWAHL VON SPEICHERKAVERNEN IM FELS

Die Technik, flüssige Speicherprodukte in unausgekleideten Felskavernen zu lagern, setzt ein allseitiges Druckgefälle vom umgebenden Grundwasser zum Kaverneninhalt voraus, da im porösen oder geklüfteten Fels nur das Porenwasser und Kluftwasser den Speicherraum abdichten. Das benötigte Druckgefälle wird dadurch gewährleistet, daß der höchstmögliche Stand des Speichergutes in der Kaverne immer unter dem niedrigsten Grundwasserspiegel gehalten wird. Verluste von Speichergut aber auch Verschmutzung des Grundwassers durch das Speichergut werden durch dieses Druckgefälle ausgeschlossen. Um das erforderliche Druckgefälle aufrecht zu erhalten, muß das der Kaverne zufließende Wasser abgepumpt werden und - nach Durchlaufen einer Kläranlage - einem Vorfluter zugeleitet werden. Tabelle 1 gibt einige Beispiele von Speicheranlagen dieser Art.

Aus den geschilderten Gegebenheiten des Speicherverfahrens lassen sich die geotechnischen Ansprüche, die an den Fels und die Grundwasserverhältnisse gestellt werden müssen, ableiten . Geeignet für die Anlage von Speicherkavernen sind alle Gesteinsfolgen ausreichender Mächtigkeit mit

- einer Eigentragfähigkeit, die den Bau standsicherer Hohlräume der erforderlichen Größe ohne Ausbau (bzw. mit nur geringem Ausbau) ermöglicht
- geringer Durchlässigkeit
- genügend Teufe unter einem Grundwasserspiegel, der nur geringen Schwankungen unterliegt
- günstiger Lage zu einem Vorfluter mit ausreichender Wasserführung.

Durch diese Bedingungen wird erreicht, daß die Kosten für die aufzufahrenden Hohlräume auf ein Mindestmaß beschränkt werden, daß nur geringe Wassermengen abgepumpt und geklärt werden müssen und daß der Vorfluter nicht unzulässig verschmutzt wird.

2.2 Klassifizierung

Nach dem Grad, in dem die dargelegten Anforderungen an Kavernenstandorte sich erfüllen lassen, können unter Berücksichtigung von Erfahrungen aus dem Felshohlraumbau drei Klassen unterschieden werden, z.B. für eine vergleichende Standortbewertung:

Klasse I: Die Anlage von Kavernen ist in der gewünschten Größe (Kavernenquerschnitt von rd. 300 m²) ohne nennenswerte Schwierigkeiten und weitgehend ohne Ausbau möglich.
Klasse II: Das Bauvorhaben läßt sich mit wirtschaftlich vertretbarem Aufwand an Ausbau- und Sicher-

Tabelle 1: Beispiele von Speicheranlagen

Gestein	Granit bzw. Gneis								Kalkstein (Kreide)			
Speicheranlage	SCA Sunsvall	Shell Gothenburg	GLAB Gävle	Laajasalo (Finnland)		GoV Stockholm	KH Karlshomn	BP Göteborg	Lavéra	Vexin	Petit Couronne	
Volumen [m³]	70.000	20.000	100.000 100.000	110.000	170.000	45.000 45.000	110.000	103.400 121.800 125.800	123.000 in 3 Kavernen	130.000	50.000	12.600
Breite [m]	15	15	15	16	18	18	20	20	13	~ 6,40	4	4
Höhe [m]	20	22	23,6	30	30	15	30	30	19,7	~ 8,60	5,5	5,5
Länge [m]	2X110	80	252	233	330	157	2X80	164	162	Stollen-system mit 28 m Achsabst.	Kamer- und Pfeilersystem, Stollen mit 20 m Achsabstand	
Länge [m]			270			159		195	?			
Länge [m]								235	204			
Speichergut		Propan	schweres Heizöl	Öl	Öl		schweres Heizöl	schweres Heizöl	Propan	Propan	Propan	Butan
Teufe unter Gelände (Kavernenfirste) [m]		90	~ 30	~ 45	~ 45				~ 120	130–150	140	140
Zugang		Schrägstollen 15 m² Querschnitt (Schacht)	Schrägstollen 12 ··· 17 % Gefälle	Schrägstollen mit 7 m Breite und 35 m² Querschnitt Schacht für Rohre					Schrägstollen Querschnitt 51 [illegible] Gefälle 13–14 % Schacht ø 3 m		3 Schächte mit 107 cm Rohren	2 Schächte mit 107 cm Rohren

Tabelle 2: Geotechnische Standortbewertung für die Anlage von Speicherkavernen im Fels

Bewertungskriterien	Klasse I	Klasse II	Klasse III
Gebirgszustand	quasi homogen, isotrop	weitgehend homogen, schwach anisotrop	inhomogen, stark anisotrop
Durchtrennungsgrad	sehr gering geklüftet	vereinzelte Großklüfte oder Störungen	mäßig bis stark geklüftet
Verhältnis Gebirgs- zu Gesteinsfestigkeit	annähernd gleich	$\geq$ 50 %	$\geq$ 20 %
Mindestwerte für das Gebirge: Kohäsion c Reibungswinkel φ Zugfestigkeit σ	 $\geq$ 50 bar $\geq 25^{o}$ $\geq$ 4 bar	 $\geq$ 25 bar $\geq 25^{o}$ $\geq$ 2 bar	 $\geq$ 10 bar $\geq 20^{o}$ $\geq$ 0,5 bar
Spannungszustand in einem Seitendruckverhältnis von	$0{,}7 \leq \lambda \leq 1{,}5$	$0{,}3 \leq \lambda \leq 0{,}7$	$\lambda < 0{,}3$ od. $\lambda > 1{,}5$
Auflockerung des Gebirges bis max. Verformung δ	2 m, örtlich durch Ausbruch $\leq$ 30 mm	4 m, örtlich durch Ausbruch $\leq$ 60 mm	8 m, technisch zu begrenzen $\leq$ 100 mm
Wasserzufluß a.d. Gebirge	< 300 m^3/d	< 700 m^3/d	> 700 m^3/d
Wasserzugabe i.d. Gebirge	gering, nur bei Bau	kann erforderlich werden	ist in der Regel erforderlich
Vorfluter, Kapazität " Lage z.Standort	groß unmittelbare Nähe	mittel geringe Entfernung (ca. 1 km)	mäßig bis geeignet größere Entfernung (ca. 10 km)
Realisierbarkeit einer Felskavernenanlage	Anlage in gewünschter Größe ohne besondere Probleme möglich. Weitgehend ohne Ausbau	Ausbau und Sicherheitsmaßnahmen wirtschaftlich vertretbar. Anlage mit kleineren Querschnitten möglich	erhebliche Ausbaumaßnahmen erforderlich kleine Querschnitte Stollen-System

heitsmaßnahmen und für einen beschränkten Kavernenquerschnitt (etwa 50 m²) durchführen

Klasse III: Die Anlage von Kavernen/Stollen (Querschnitt etwa 20 m²) ist grundsätzlich noch möglich, erfordert aber größeren finanziellen und technischen Aufwand.

In Tabelle 2 ist der Versuch unternommen, die für diese Klassifizierung geforderten geotechnischen und hydrogeologischen Standorteigenschaften durch einige Kennwerte quantitativ zu beschreiben. In der Regel können diese Kennwerte (z.B. Durchtrennungsgrad, Gebirgsfestigkeit, natürlicher Spannungszustand,

Wasserzufluß, Kapazität des Vorfluters) durch den Ingenieurgeologen oder Felsmechaniker aufgrund seiner Erfahrung verhältnismäßig sicher geschätzt werden, so daß sie für eine vergleichende Standortbewertung ausreichen. Eine konkrete Standortbewertung (Planungsphase) erfordert jedoch eingehende ingenieurgeologische und hydrogeologische Voruntersuchungen.

3 DIMENSIONIERUNG VON SALZKAVERNEN

3.1 Entwurfskonzept

Steinsalzlagerstätten - insbesondere in den sogenannten Salzstöcken - bieten ideale Voraussetzungen für die Anlage großräumiger unterirdischer Speicherkavernen. Das Salzgebirge ist praktisch undurchlässig für Gase und Flüssigkeiten. Der Grund für diese Dichtigkeit ist die plastische Verformbarkeit von Salzgesteinen in einem weiten Druck-, Temperatur- und Verformungsgeschwindigkeitsbereich, denn diese Fähigkeit verhindert das Aufreißen bzw. Offenbleiben von Spalten und Klüften, auf denen Flüssigkeiten und Gase zirkulieren könnten. Verlust des Speichergutes und Kontamination des Grundwassers ist damit ausgeschlossen. Die Speicherung in Salzkavernen ist jedoch nicht nur eine umweltfreundliche sondern auch eine kostengünstige Methode zur Lagerung insbesondere von Öl und Gas, da nicht nur mit

Tabelle 3: Speicherkavernen in Salzstöcken Nordwestdeutschlands

Lfd. Nr.	Ort	Betriebsges.	Anzahl Kavernen		Teufe m	Füllung
			Betrieb	Planung		
1a	Heide	Dt. Texaco AG	1	-	660- 760	Butan
1b	Heide	Dt. Texaco AG	9	2	600-1000	Rohöl
2	Kiel	Stadtwerke Kiel	1	-	1300-1400	Stadtgas
3	Sottorf	Dt.Shell AG	9	2	500-1200	Rohöl/Heizöl
4	Bremen-Lesum	Mobil Oil AG	6	-	600-1300	Rohöl/Heizöl
5	Neuenhuntorf	EWE	4	-	600- 950	Erdgas
6	Blexen	Untertage-Speicherges. (USA)	4	4	640-1430	Rohöl
7	Etzel	IVG	33	22	800-1600	Rohöl/ Ölprodukte
8	Rüstringen	NWKG	33	3	1100-2000	Rohöl/ Ölprodukte
9	Ohrensen/ Hersefeld	Dow-Chemical GmbH	2	-	800-1100	Äthylen-Propylen
10	Groothusen	Ruhrgas AG	1	-	1800	Erdgas
11	Nüttermoor	EWE	2	-	1350	Erdgas

der Ausspülmethode (solution mining) ein Verfahren zur Verfügung steht, große Lagerkapazitäten zu schaffen, sondern auch auf Grund günstiger mechanischer Eigenschaften das Salzgebirge ohne Ausbau standfest gehalten werden kann. (Sicherheit für die oberirdische Bebauung). Die Gefahr des Zusammenbruchs selbst größter Salzkavernen ist gering, weil das Material den Spannungsspitzen - z.B. bei der Kavernenherstellung - durch bruchlose Kriechverformung ausweicht. So überrascht es nicht, daß zur Zeit weit über 200 Millionen Kubikmeter Speicherraum im Salzgebirge zur Lagerung von Öl, Rohölprodukten, Flüssiggas und Gas weltweit genutzt werden. Einzelne Kavernen liegen dabei in der Größenordnung von 500 000 m^3. Einen Überblick über die Speicherprojekte der Bundesrepublik Deutschland gibt Tabelle 3.

Trotz der generellen günstigen Eigenschaften von Salzgesteinen muß in jedem Einzelfall die Standsicherheit der Kaverne (in Abhängigkeit von Hohlraumgröße und -form)nachgewiesen werden. Dieser Standsicherheitsnachweis muß gegenüber Bruch (Übersteigen der Festigkeit) aber auch gegenüber Fließen (Übersteigen der Fließgrenze) erfolgen, da ein stetige Kriechverformung letztlich - wenn nicht ein entsprechend großer Innendruck z.B. durch das Einlagerungsgut vorhanden ist - zur Schließung der Kaverne oder zumindest zur Gebrauchsunfähigkeit der Kaverne führen kann (Berechnung der Konvergenz). Das Auftreten möglicher tektonischer Spannungen, die Verminderung der Festigkeit an Diskontinuitätsflächen (Trennflächen wie z.B. Tonlöser), mögliche Spannungsumlagerungen an inhomogenen Einlagerungen sind dabei zu berücksichtigen. Gerade im Salzkavernenbau kommt dem rechnerischen Standsicherheitsnachweis eine besondere Bedeutung zu, da die nicht begehbaren gesolten Speicherkavernen weder mit einfachen Mitteln meßtechnisch überwacht noch bei Versagen einzelner Gebirgspartien durch nachträgliche Sicherheitsmaßnahmen stabilisiert werden können.

Die sonst beim Entwurf eines Felshohlraumes übliche intensive Erschließung der Gebirgsverhältnisse und Kontrolle der Standsicherheit durch in-situ-Messungen während der Bauzeit (und danach) ist hier nur sehr eingeschränkt möglich (vgl. Abb. 1). Umso größeres Gewicht kommt dem theoretischen Teil des Konzeptes zur sicheren und wirtschaftlichen Dimensionierung von Salzkavernen zu:

Formulierung eines mechanischen Gebirgsmodelles und des dazugehörigen Berechnungsmodelles; Parameterstudien, Festlegung von Sicherheits- und Versagenskriterien, Berücksichtigung des besonderen Materialverhaltens von Salzgesteinen (Kriechen, Plastizizät).

Durch mehrere Forschungsvorhaben auf dem Gebiet der Salzmechanik konnten dazu in den letzten Jahren durch die Bundesanstalt für Geowissenschaften u. Rohstoffe, Hannover neue Erkenntnisse gewonnen werden (LANGER 1978 und 1981a). Das daraus abzuleitende Stoffmodell für Steinsalz wird im folgenden kurz beschrieben.

3.2 Stoffmodell für Steinsalz

Die Grundlage der theoretischen und experimentellen Behandlung von Deformationsvorgängen in Salzgesteinen ergibt sich aus einer Analyse der Phänomene Kriechen und Plastizität. Übersichten über veröffentlichte Stoffgesetzformulierungen finden sich z.B. bei DAWSON (1979) und LANGER (1981b).

Alle bisher entwickelten Stoffmodelle sind mit unterschiedlichen Nachteilen behaftet. Die phänomenologischen Materialgleichungen, insbesondere die auf der Verfestigungstheorie basierenden Formulierungen geben nur das "curve-fitting" Produkt einer speziellen experimentellen Situation wider, so daß sie ungeeignet erscheinen, auf Verhältnisse übertragen und extrapoliert zu werden, die wesentlich von den Bedingungen des Experimentes abweichen. Die Materialbeschreibung durch rheologische Modelle enthält in der notwendigen Verallgemeinerung eine Vielzahl von Materialparametern, die das inelastische Verhalten beschreiben sollen. Deren experimentelle Bestimmung scheint jedoch ein hoffnungsloses Unterfangen

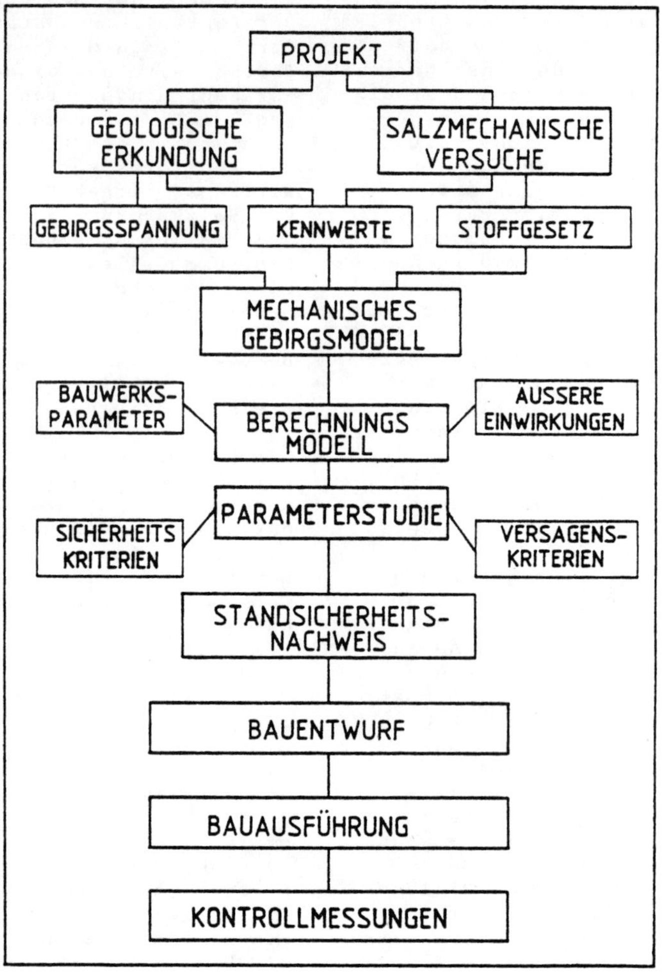

Abb. 1: Entwurfskonzept für die Planung und Errichtung von Speicherkavernen im Salzgebirge

zu sein, zumal geeignete Versuchsmethoden zu einer unabhängigen Bastimmung der Stoffparameter im einzelnen noch nicht entwickelt sind.

Mit der Theorie der Zustands- oder inneren Variablen sowie der Theorie der Stoffe mit Gedächtnis ist ein theoretischer Rahmen vorhanden, thermodynamisch konsistente Materialgleichungen für inelastisches Material, wie Salzgestein es darstellt, zu entwickeln. Dabei sind die bereits zur phänomenologischen Beschreibung des stationären Kriechens verwendeten, auf mikrophysikalischen Deformationsmechanismen basierenden Beziehungen geeignet, zur Identifizierung der Zustandsvariablen beizutragen.

Die letztgenannten Theorien weisen z.Zt. jedoch noch den Nachteil auf, daß die für die Lösung praktischer Ingenieurprobleme notwendige Abstützung der Materialparameter auf experimentelle einfach zu bestimmende Größen nicht vorgenommen werden kann.

Dennoch ist es wichtig, die mikrophysikalischen Verformungsmechanismen zu untersuchen, die zu einem bestimmten Kriechverhalten des Materials führen, um für bestimmte

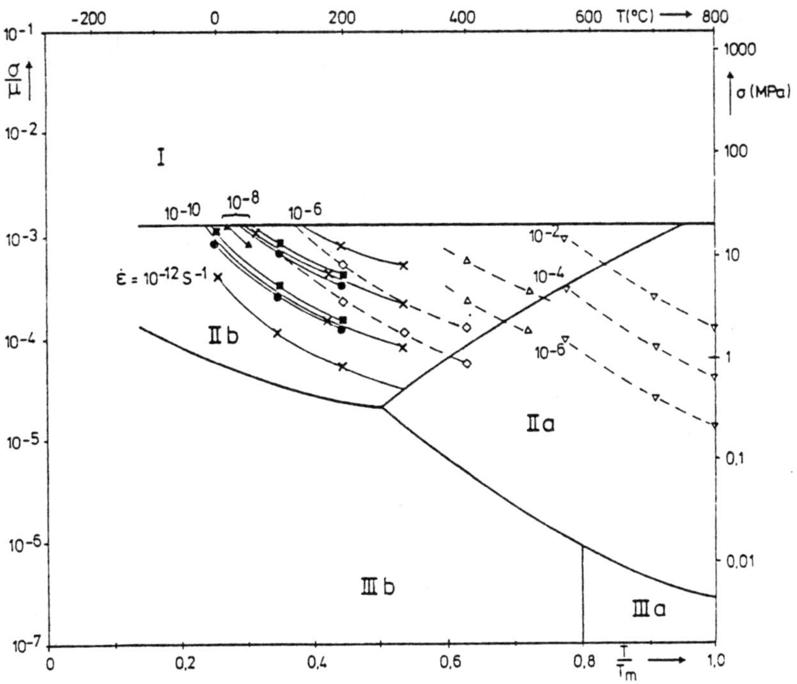

Abb.2: Deformationsdiagramm für natürliches polykristallines Steinsalz (nach ALBRECHT u.HUNSCHE, 1980):

Eingetragen sind die Bereiche der verschiedenen Deformationsmechanismen und $\dot{\varepsilon}$-Isolinien für verschiedene Messungen.

Korngröße: d = 1mm
Schubmodul: μ = 15 GPa
Schmelztemperatur: T_m = 801° C

Durchgezogene $\dot{\varepsilon}$-Isolinien: Aus Messungen an natürlichen Steinsalzproben gewonnene Gesetze. Unterbrochene $\dot{\varepsilon}$-Isolinien: Aus Messungen an künstlichen Steinsalzproben gewonnene Gesetze:

Bereich I: Versetzungsgleiten
Bereich II: Versetzungsklettern
(a. Hochtemperaturkriechen
b. Tieftemperaturkriechen
Bereich III: Diffusionskriechen
(a. Volumendiffusion
b. Kongrenzendiffusion)

Temperatur- und Spannungsbedingungen dazugehörige Stoffgleichungen auf Grund theoretischer Erwägungen abzuleiten. Nur so sind Entscheidungen möglich, inwieweit die für einen bestimmten Zustand experimentell abgesicherten Stoffmodelle auf andere Spannungs- Temperatur- und Verformungsgeschwindigkeitsbedingungen übertragbar sind. Für Steinsalz ist das Wandern von Versetzungen (Versetzungen sind lineare Gitterfehler) im Kristallgitter ein entscheidender Verformungsmechanismus. Das Wandern von Versetzungen kann sich u.a. äußern als Versetzungsgleiten oder Versetzungsklettern. Die auf Verformungsmechanismen bezogene Darstellung von Kriechgesetzen erfolgt in sogenannten Deformationsdiagrammen. Ein solches Deformationsdiagramm für natürliches, polykristallines Steinsalz zeigt Abb. 2.
Auf der Grundlage dieser Überlegungen und eines umfangreichen Versuchsprogrammes (einaxiale und dreiaxiale Kriechversuche unter verschiedenen Spannungs-, Verformungs- und Temperaturbedingungen, Festigkeits- und Kriechbruchversuche unter Variation der Temperatur- und des Spannungsgrades) wurde ein auf die Praxis der Ingenieurarbeiten ausgerichtetes pragmatisches Stoffgesetz für Steinsalz abgeleitet. Die mathematische

Tabelle 4: Stoffmodell für natürliches polykristallines Steinsalz

$$\underset{\sim}{\varepsilon}_{ges} = \underset{\sim}{\varepsilon}^{el} + \underset{\sim}{\varepsilon}^{cr} \mid \underset{\sim}{\varepsilon}^{f} \qquad (1)$$

$$\underset{\sim}{\varepsilon}^{el}_{ij} = -\frac{\nu}{E}\, \underset{\sim}{\sigma}_{kk}\, \delta_{ij} + \frac{1+\nu}{E}\, \underset{\sim}{\sigma}_{ij} + \alpha_t\, \Delta\vartheta\, \delta_{ij} \qquad (2)$$

$$\dot{\underset{\sim}{\varepsilon}}^{cr}_{ij} = \frac{3}{2}\, \frac{\varepsilon^{cr}_{eff}}{\sigma^{cr}_{eff}}\, \underset{\sim}{s}_{ij} \qquad (3)$$

$$\dot{\varepsilon}^{cr}_{eff} = \sqrt{\frac{2}{3}\, \dot{\underset{\sim}{\varepsilon}}_{ij}\, \dot{\underset{\sim}{\varepsilon}}_{ij}} \qquad (4)$$

$$\sigma_{eff} = \sqrt{\frac{3}{2}\, \underset{\sim}{s}_{ij}\, \underset{\sim}{s}_{ij}} \qquad (5)$$

$$\dot{\varepsilon}^{cr}_{eff} = \sum_{i=1}^{3} \dot{\varepsilon}^{cr}_{eff\,i}(S, \sigma_{eff}, \vartheta) \qquad (6)$$

$$\dot{\varepsilon}^{cr}_{eff\,1} = A_1\, e^{\frac{-Q_1}{R\vartheta}} \left(\frac{\sigma_{eff}}{G}\right)^{n_1} \qquad (7)$$

$$\dot{\varepsilon}^{cr}_{eff\,2} = A_2\, e^{\frac{-Q_2}{R\vartheta}} \left(\frac{\sigma_{eff}}{G}\right)^{n_2} \qquad (8)$$

$$\dot{\varepsilon}^{cr}_{eff\,3} = 2\left(B_1\, e^{\frac{-Q_1}{R\vartheta}} + B_2\, e^{\frac{-Q_2}{R\vartheta}}\right) \sinh\left(D \left\langle \frac{\sigma_{eff} - \sigma^{o}_{eff}}{G} \right\rangle\right) \qquad (9)$$

$$\dot{\underset{\sim}{\varepsilon}}^{f}_{ij} = \dot{\lambda}\, \frac{\delta f}{\delta \sigma_{ij}} \qquad (10)$$

$$f = II_s - fkt(I_\sigma, II_{\dot{e}}, \vartheta, m, S) = 0 \qquad (11)$$

$$f = \tau_o - C_1 \sigma_o^{\alpha} \cdot e^{-C_2 \sigma_o (\vartheta - \vartheta_o)^2} \left(1 + C_3 \ln \frac{II_{\dot{e}}}{II^{o}_{\dot{e}}}\right) \qquad (12)$$

Formulierung ist in Tabelle 4 wiedergegeben. Die in Tabelle 5 angegebenen Stoffparameter sind aus einer Vielzahl von Versuchen an verschiedenen Steinsalzgesteinen gemittelte Werte.

Hauptziel von Standsicherheitsrechnungen im Salzkavernenbau ist der Nachweis, daß die durch den Hohlraumausbruch hervorgerufenen Spannungsumlagerungen einen Gleichgewichtszustand annehmen und sich keine unzulässigen Konvergenzen und Schäden während der Nutzungszeit einstellen, d.h. es müssen Spannungs- und Verformungsverteilungen bzw. Verformungsgeschwindigkeitsverteilungen im die Kaverne umgebenden Gebirge unter Berücksichtigung der zeit- und temperaturabhängigen rheologischen Eigenschaften der Gesteine berechnet werden. Ein für die Lösung solcher geomechanischer Problemstellungen besonders geeignetes Rechenverfahren stellt die Finite-Element-Methode dar. Dieses computergerechte numerische Rechenverfahren ermöglicht es, die für die Standsicherheit wichtigen Einflußfaktoren wie Geologie, Betriebsbedingungen, Hohlraumgometrie und Bauverfahren in

Tabelle 5: Stoffparameter für natürliches polykristallines Steinsalz

elastische Kennwerte equ. 2	Bruchkennwerte equ. 12
$E = 25\,000 \pm 5\,000$ MPa	$C_1 = 2.71$
$\nu = 0.25 \pm 0.05$	$C_2 = 1 \cdot 10^{-6}$
$\alpha_t = 0.45 \cdot 10^{-4} K^{-1}$	$C_3 = 0.01$
$G = 9600$ MPa	$\alpha = 0.7$
Kennwerte für stationäres Kriechen equ. 7 und 8	equ. 9
$A_1 = 1.2 \cdot 10^{22} s^{-1}$	$B_1 = 1.5 \cdot 10^{7} s^{-1}$
$A_2 = 1.7 \cdot 10^{14} s^{-1}$	$B_2 = 3.6 \cdot 10^{-2} s^{-1}$
$Q_1 = 27$ kcal mol^{-1}	$Q_1 = 27$ kcal mol^{-1}
$Q_2 = 12.9$ kcal mol^{-1}	$Q_2 = 12.9$ kcal mol^{-1}
$n_1 = 5.5$	$D = 3.5 \cdot 10^{3}$
$n_2 = 5.0$	$\sigma^{o}_{eff} = 20$ MPa

wirklichkeitsnahen Ansätzen zu berücksichtigen. Das FEM-Verfahren ist sowohl für die Berechnung linearer wie nichtlinearer Randwertaufgaben geeignet; insbesondere kann es auf das bei Salzgesteinen so hervorstechende zeit- und temperaturabhängige Stoffverhalten ohne Schwierigkeiten ausgerichtet werden.

Von der BGR ist in Zusammenarbeit mit der Fa. Control Data, Hamburg ein "special purpose" Rechenprogramm ANSALT (Analysis of Nonlinear Thermomechanical Analysis of Rock Salt) entwickelt worden. Basis code for ANSALT ist ANSR II (1979) vom Earthquake Engineering Research Center, Uni California, Berkeley. Eine kurze Beschreibung des Programmes bringt Tabelle 6 (vgl. auch WALLNER, 1981 und 1982).

4 STANDSICHERHEITSNACHWEIS FÜR EIN ENDLAGERBERGWERK FÜR RADIOAKTIVE ABFÄLLE

4.1 Allgemeine Sicherheitsanalyse

Unter Endlagerung wird im folgenden eine wartungsfreie, zeitlich unbefristete und sichere Verwahrung (d.h. dauerhaft getrennt vom Lebensraum) von für diesen Zweck bestimmten Stoffen verstanden. Jedes Endlagerkonzept muß sich daher an der Forderung orientieren, daß die Abfälle solange von der Biosphäre isoliert bleiben, bis die Aktivität der einzelnen Radionuklide auf ein zulässiges Maß abgeklungen ist. Je nach Zusammensetzung der Abfallprodukte bedeutet dies einen Zeitraum irgendwozwischen 10^3 und 10^6 Jahren. Sieht man von der hypothetischen Möglichkeit der Ablagerung im Weltraum einmal ab, so ist Endlagerung nach dieser Definition im Grundsatz nur in geologischen Formationen des tiefen Untergrundes denkbar. Dabei muß der Aufbewahrungsort im Untergrund so gewählt werden, daß der Transport gefährlicher Mengen von Radionukliden in die Biosphäre durch zirkulierende Grundwässer verhindert werden kann. Im Prinzip soll das bei allen Endlagerkonzepten, wie sie von verschiedenen Ländern untersucht werden, durch ein System hintereinandergeschalteter oder ineinandergreifender natürlicher und technischer Barrieren sichergestellt werden (Multibarrierenprinzip), wobei in unterschiedlichen Konzepten technische und natürliche Barrieren unterschiedliches Gewicht haben können (vgl. Abb. 3). In der Bundesrepublik Deutschland ist das Schwergewicht der Forschungsarbeiten schon früh auf eine Endlagerung in den diapirischen Salzstrukturen (Salzstöcke) Norddeutschlands ausgerichtet worden.

Der Sicherheitsnachweis für ein Endlagerbergwerk nimmt die zentrale

Tabelle 6: Rechenprogramm "ANSALT"

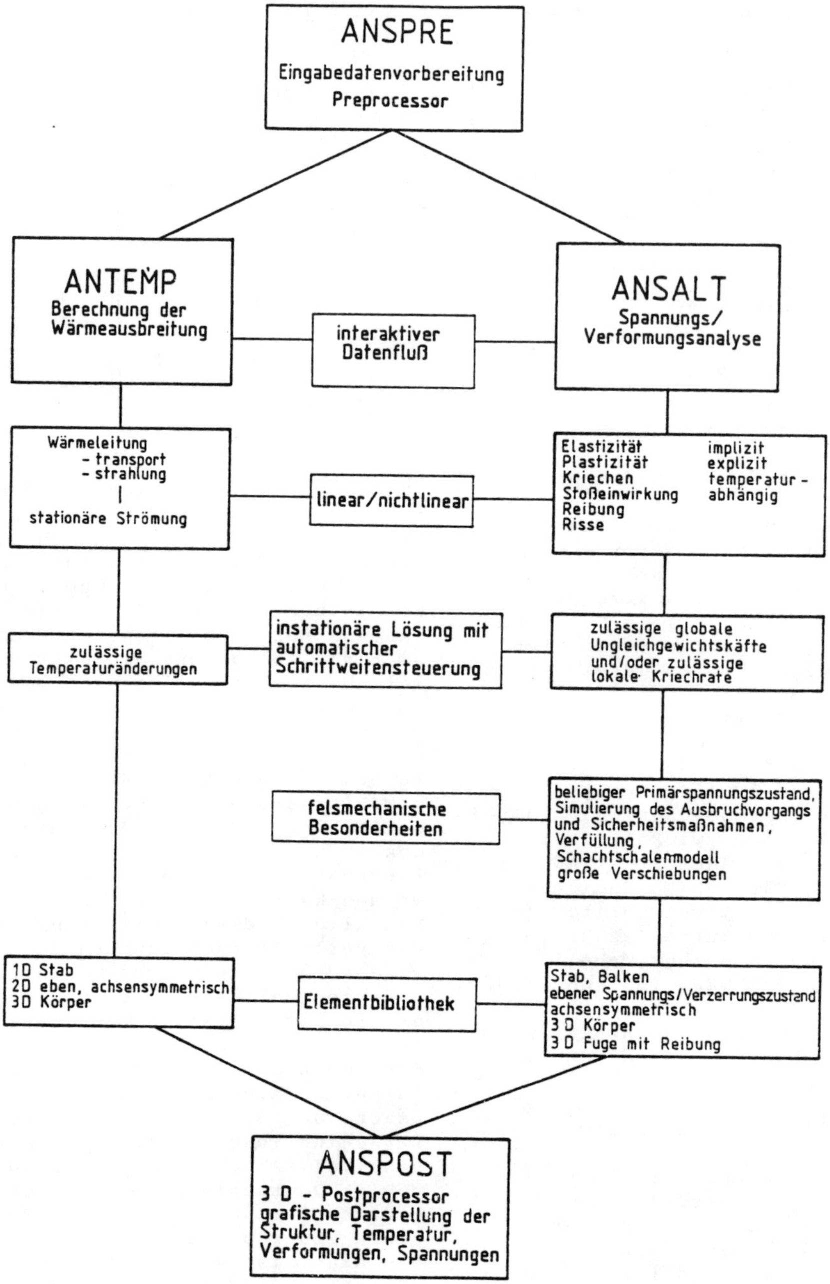

MULTIBARRIERENPRINZIP

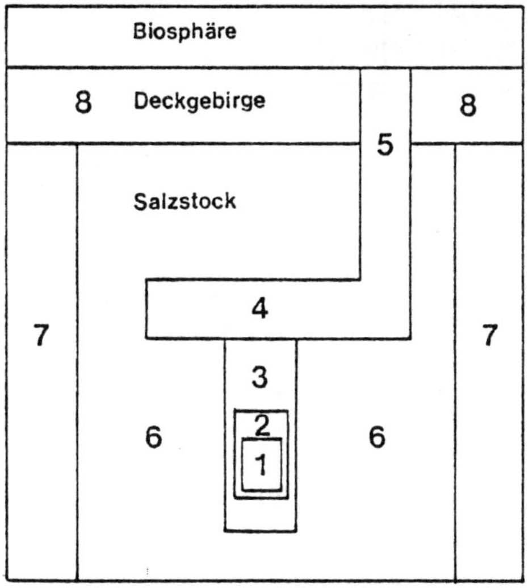

Nr.	Barriere	System
1	Fixierung	T
2	Behälter	T
3	Bohrloch	T/M
4	Grubenbau	M
5	Schacht	M
6	Salzstock	M/G
7	Sedimentgestein	G
8	Lockergestein	G

T : Technisches System
M : Gebirgsmechanisches System
G : Geologisches System

Abb. 3: Multibarrierenprinzip der Endlagerung radioaktiver Abfälle

Stellung in der Gesamtproblematik ein und damit die Frage nach dem Konzept und den Kriterien eines solchen Sicherheitsnachweises. Da bei der Endlagerung im geologischen Medium das Tragverhalten des Gebirges (Endlagerbergwerk), die Schutzwirkung (Barriere) des umgebenden Gesteinskomplexes für lange Zeiten und die geologische Stabilität des Endlagerbereiches (z.B. Salzstock) wesentliche Komponenten sind, kann ein solcher Sicherheitsnachweis nicht rein bauingenieurmäßig definiert werden sondern muß auch geologische Faktoren und Prozesse integrieren; Standsicherheitsbegriffe und Sicherheitsfaktoren des normalen Ingenieurbaus reichen hier nicht aus.

Die Entwicklung eines realistischen und tragfähigen Sicherheitskonzeptes unter der gestellten Forderung nach höchstmölicher Sicherheit stößt auf unüberwindbar erscheinende Schwierigkeiten; denn es stehen Betrachtungsräume (bis zu 1 Million Jahre) zur Debatte, für die selbst erfahrene Geologen kaum Prognosen wagen, und es ist ein Material einzulagern, das für den Felsmechaniker neuartige Gefahrenmomente (Radioaktivität, Wärmeentwicklung) mit sich bringt. Selbst vom Methodischen her fehlt wesentliches Rüstzeug:

- geschlossene Konzepte zum Sicherheitsnachweis von Felshohlräumen und Grubenbauen ähnlich dem Sicherheitskonzept oberirdischer Ingenieurbauten sind bisher nicht entwickelt
- im Rahmen des Sicherheitsnachweises von Kernkraftwerken erarbeitete Methoden auf probabilistischer Grundlage (Risikoanalyse) sind auf geologische Medien nur mit erheblichen Einschränkungen und Modifikationen übertragbar
- die sicherheitstechnische Relevanz der Kopplung geomechanischer und geochemischer Langzeitprozesse ist weitgehend unerforscht.

Auf Grund dieser Gegebenheiten erscheint als einzig sinnvoller Weg, zur überzeugenden Sicherheitsanalyse eines Endlagers zu kommen, folgende Vorgehensweise zu sein, die sich aus dem Prinzip mehrfach angeordneter Barrieren (d.h. Systeme zur Behinderung der Freisetzung von Schadstoffen) bei der Endlagerung ableiten läßt (Multibarrierenprinzip); nämlich (vgl. Abb. 4):

a) getrennte Analyse der Wirksamkeit der einzelnen Barrieren als technische Systeme (Abfallform, Behälter), gebirgsmechanische Sy-

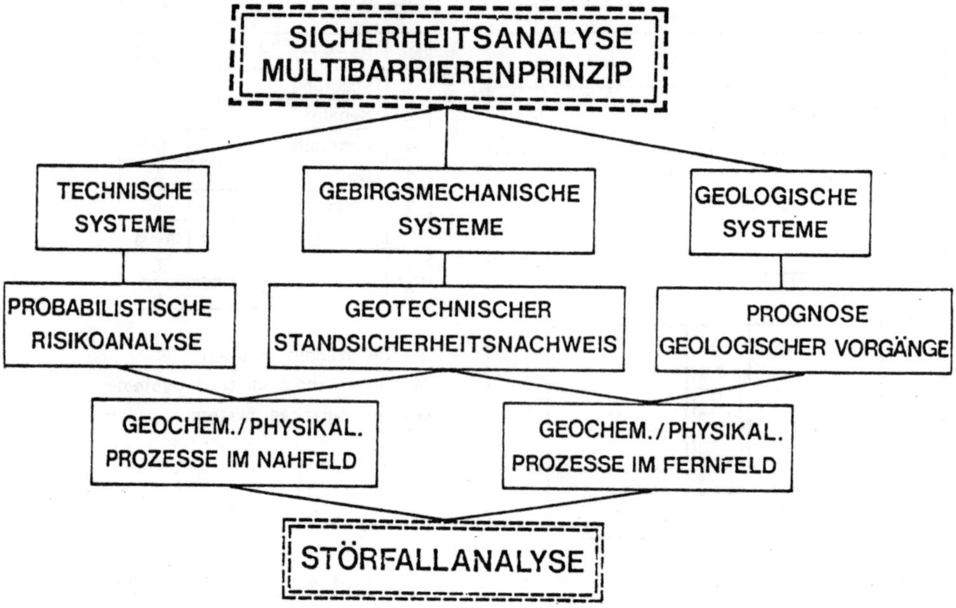

Abb. 4: Sicherheitskonzept der Endlagerung radioaktiver Abfälle

steme (Bohrlöcher, Grubenbaue, umgebendes Salzgebirge) und geologische Systeme (Salzstock, Deckgebirge) mit der systementsprechenden Methodik, also z.B.
- probabilistische Risikoanalyse bei den technischen Systemen
- Standsicherheitsnachweis bei den gebirgsmechanischen (d.h. felsmechanisch/bergbaulichen) Systemen
- Prognosen zukünftiger geochemischer, hydrogeologischer und tektonischer Vorgänge bei den geologischen Systemen

b) Analyse der physikalischen und geochemischen Prozesse, die durch gegenseitige Beeinflussung der Barrieren verschiedener Systeme entstehen, mit Bewertung des Einflusses auf den Transport des Schadstoffes im Nahfeld wie im Fernfeld, also z.B.
- Untersuchung der Korrosion der Behälter im umgebenden Salzgestein und ihre Bedeutung für die Auslaugraten
- Bewertung der geochemischen Langzeitprozesse im Salzgebirge durch Aufheizung und Laugenmigration
- Thermomechanische Berechnung der Salzstockbewegung (Spannungs-Deformationsfelder) in Abhängigkeit von Geometrie und Wärmepotential des Einlagerungsfeldes

c) Zusammenfassende Analyse der Sicherheit des Endlagers durch Identifikation und Bewertung des Zusammenwirkens aller Barrieren bei bestimmten, theoretisch denkbaren Ereignissen (Unfälle, Störfälle), die eine Gefahr der Feisetzungspfaden und sich daraus ergebenden Schadenswirkungen (Störfallanalyse), z.B.
- Wasser- oder Laugeneinbruch
- gebirgsmechanisch bedingter Zusammenbruch des Grubengebäudes
- geologisch/tektonische Katastrophen

Man erkennt, daß felsmechanische Standsicherheitsnachweise für das Endlagerbergwerk, deren Grundlagen im folgenden näher erörtert werden sollen, nur eine Komponente der gesamten Sicherheitsanalyse sind.

4.2 Geotechnisches Sicherheitskonzept

Ein Grubenbauwerk kann als standsicher angesehen werden, wenn folgende Einzelnachweise erbracht werden (ALBRECHT u.a. 1978) für die Bau- und Betriebsphase:
- während und nach der Erstellung des Grubenbaues treten keine unzulässigen Verformungen weder im Hohlraum selbst noch an der Tagesoberfläche auf, die die Funktionsfähigkeiten des Bergwerks bzw. die Sicherheit von Bauwerken übertage beeinträchtigen
- das Tragvermögen des Gebirges wird weder örtlich (lokales Versagen) oder als Ganzes (Zusammenbruch) so erniedrigt, daß sich schlagartige oder allmähliche Verbrüche von Hohlräumen ereignen
-unkontrollierte Laugen- oder Wassereinbrüche bzw. Gasausbrüche werden vermieden

für die Nachbetriebsphase (verfülltes Bergwerk):
- thermische Belastungen führen nicht zu Zersetzungen von Salzmineralen (z.B. Abspaltung von Wasser aus Carnallit), die zu einer Gefährdung oder Minderung der Gebrauchsfähigkeit der Anlage führen könnten
- die Integrität des Salzstockes wird durch Thermospannungen (mögl. Rißbildung) nicht beeinträchtigt
- thermisch induzierte Laugenmigration führt nicht zur Nuklidfreisetzung

Diese Kriterien eines Standsicherheitsnachweises sind durch verschiedene natürliche wie technisch bedingte Faktoren beeinflußt (vgl. Abb. 5). Natürliche Einflußfaktoren sind durch die geologischen Verhältnisse (z.B. inhomogener Schichtenaufbau, Faltungstektonik des Salzstockes, petrographische Zusammensetzung der Salzgesteine), durch den in-situ Spannungszustand, durch mögliche Gas- und Laugenvorkommen, durch temperatur- und zeitabhängige Bruch- und Verformungseigenschaften der Salzgesteine vorgegeben. Technisch bedingte Einflußfaktoren ergeben sich aus der Einlagerung radioaktiver Abfälle (z.B. Wärmeentwicklung, Radioaktivität, physikal./chem. Langzeiteffekte), aus den Auffahrtechniken (z.B. Sprengen, Solen,schneidene Gewinnung) und der Geometrie der Hohlräume (z.B. Hohlraumform u. -größe, räumliche Lage zueinander, Pfeilerform u. deren Größe) und aus den Betriebsbedingungen (z.B. Anordnung der Einlagerungsbohrlöcher, max. zulässige Temperatur befahrener Strecken, Bauzustände, Sicherheitsmaßnahmen), Deshalb kann ein solcher Nachweis im konkreten Fall nur durch Kombination von ingenieurgeologischen Erkundungen, geotechnischen Untersuchungen, felsmechanischen Messungen, felsstatischen Berechnungen, meßtechnischen Überwachungen und bergbaulicher Betriebserfahrung erfolgen. Umfang und Genauigkeit der Erkundungen und Messungen sowie die Sicherheitszuschläge bei den felsstatischen Berechnungen für die jeweiligen Einzelnachweise richten sich nach der Schwere der möglichen Schadensfolgen, die sich aus der Störfallanalyse ergeben. Erkundungen, Messungen und theoretische Berechnungen dürfen dabei nicht isoliert betrachtet werden, sie gehören funktional zusammen und stützen sich gegenseitig (z.B. mechanisches Modell des Gebirges, Parameteranalysen, Kontrolle statischer Berechnungen). Da der endgültige Aufschluß des Gebirges und damit das zweifelsfreie Erkennen der standsicherheitsrelevanten Gebirgsparameter erst beim Auffahren der Grubenbaue erfolgen kann, haben die für den Entwurf (Planungsphase)durchzuführenden Standsicherheitsberechnungen nur prognostischen Charakter. Während der Bauphase läßt sich der Kenntnisstand schrittweise durch meßtechnische Kontrollen der Berechnungsergebnisse und durch Einsatz geophysikalischer Erkundungsmethoden verbessern. Der endgültige Nachweis der Standsicherheit wird so erst während der Bau- bzw. Betriebsphase durch meßtechnische Überwachung und Langzeitkontrollmessungen zu erbringen sein. Zur Bewertung dieser Messungen ist eine begleitende Auswertung der geologischen Spezialaufnahmen und der Vergleich mit Spannungs- /Verformungsberechnungen insofern unerläßlich, als nur so die auf komplexe Gebirgsstrukturen bezogenen Meßwerte richtig interpretiert werden können. Die fortlaufende, den einzelnen Planungs-, Bau- und Betriebsphasen angepaßte Vervollständigung und Überprüfung des Kenntnisstandes zur Standsicherheit ist also wesentlicher Bestandteil des be-

SICHERHEITS-KRITERIEN	NATÜRLICHE EINFLÜSSE	TECHNISCHE EINFLÜSSE	MASSNAHMEN
Verformungen	Geologische Verhältnisse	Hohlraum-geometrie	Geologische Erkundung
Spannungen	Tektonik	Bauverfahren	Geotechnische Untersuchung
Versagensform	Primärspannung	Nutzungsart	Statische Berechnung
Tragvermögen	Mechanische Gebirgskennwerte	Betriebs-bedingungen	Kontrollmessung
Laugeneinbruch	Gas- und Laugenvorkommen	Temperatur	Bergbauliche Maßnahmen

GEOTECHNISCHES STANDSICHERHEITSKONZEPT

Abb. 5: Geotechnisches Standsicherheitskonzept

schriebenen geotechnischen Sicherheitskonzeptes.

5 SCHRIFTTUM

Albrecht, H., Meister, D., Stork, G.-H. & M. Wallner 1978, Zur Frage des Standsicherheitsnachweises von Hohlräumen in Salzgesteinen. 5th Int. Symp. on Salt Vol. I, p- 195-211, Hamburg/ Cleveland

Albrecht, H. & U. Hunsche, Gebirgsmechanische Aspekte bei der Endlagerung radioaktiver Abfälle in Salzdapiren unter besonderer Berücksichtigung des Fließverhaltens von Steinsalz. Fortschr. Miner. 58, 2, p. 212-247, Stuttgart

Autorenkollektiv 1980, Empfehlungen für den Felsbau unter Tage. Taschenbuch für den Tunnelbau, p. 157-239, Essen.

Dawson, P.R. 1979, Constitutive models applied in the analysis of creep of rock salt, Research report Sandia 79-0137, Albuquerque

Langer, M. 1978, Grundzüge einer theoretischen Salzmechanik, 3rd. Nat. Symposium on Rock Mechanics, p. 167-188, Aachen.

Langer, M. 1980, Grundlagen des Standsicherheitsnachweises für ein Endlagerbergwerk im Salzgebirge. 4th Nat. Symposium on Rock Mechanics, Aachen, p. 365-408.

Langer, M. 1981 a, The rheological behaviour of rock salt. Proc. 1. Int. Conf. on the Mechanical Behaviour of Salt, Penn State University, im Druck

Langer, M. 1981b, The mechanical behaviour of halite rock as a basis for the dimensioning of pillars and caverns. Proc. Int. Tunnelbautagung, Düsseldorf im Druck.

Wallner, M. 1981, Analysis of thermomechanical problems related to the storage of heat producing radioactive waste in rock salt, Proc. 1st Conf. on the Mechanical Behavior of Salt, Penn State University, in print

Wallner, M. 1982, Thermomechanical calculations waste repository, im gleichen Band.

THERMOMECHANICAL RESPONSE OF A DISPOSAL VAULT IN A HIGH HORIZONTAL STRESS FIELD

Thermomechanische Beanspruchung eines Abfallspeichers in einem hohen horizontalen Spannungsfeld

Demande thermomécanique d'une voûte de stockage dans un champ de contraintes horizontal élevé

C.F.LEE, K.K.TSUI & A.TSAI
Ontario Hydro, Toronto, Canada

SUMMARY:
An attempt is made to predict the thermomechanical stability of a conceptual disposal vault for immobilized irradiated fuel on the basis of numerical modelling and fieldobservations. For study purposes, it is assumed that the disposal vault would be located in a granitic pluton in the Canadian Shield, at a reference depth of 1 km from the surface. The results of in-situ stress measurements have revealed a state of high horizontal compressive stresses in many parts of the Canadian Shield. Field observations indicate that fracturing and spalling of surficial layers of rock could result if the combination of thermal, in-situ and axcavation stresses exceeds the strength values of the rock. The rock stresses are computed in two steps using the finite element technique. A simulation of the excavation of the disposal vault is first carried out, taking into account the in-situ stresses. This is followed by a detailed analysis of the transient temperatures and thermal stresses generated by the radiogenic heat source at various times during the post-emplacement period.

ZUSAMMENFASSUNG:
Es wird versucht, die thermomechanische Stabilität einer sich noch im Planungsstadium befindenden Aufbewahrungsgrube für bestrahlten Brennstoff durch zahlenmässige Modellierung und Feldbeobachtungen vorauszusagen. Zwecks Untersuchung wird angenommen, dass die Aufbewahrungsgrube in einem granitischen Pluton im "kanadischen Schild" in einer Tiefe von 1 Kilometer liegt. Die Ergebnisse der in-situ Spannungsmessungen haben einen Zustand hoher horizontaler Druckspannungen in vielen Teilen des kanadischen Schildes gezeigt. Feldbeobachtungen zeigen, dass sich Bruchbildung un Abblättern der Oberflächenschichten des Gesteins ergeben könnten, wenn die Kombination von thermischen, in-situ und durch Sprengungen verursachten Beanspruchungen die Widerstandswerte des Gesteins überschreitet. Die Felsbeanspruchungen werden in zwei Schritten mittels der Finite-Elemente-Methode berechnet. Eine Simulation des Ausbruchs der Aufbewahrungsgrube wird zunächst durchgeführt, die die in-situ Beanspruchungen in Betracht zieht. Es folgt eine ausführliche Analyse der Übergangstemperaturen und der Wärmespannungen, die von der radiogenischen Wärmequelle zu verschiedenen Zeiten während der Periode nach der Herstellung erzeugt werden.

RESUME:
On essaye de prédire, sur la base de la modélisation numérique et des observations sur le site, la stabilité thermomécanique d'une caverne de stockage à l'état de la conception, destinée à recevoir le combustible irradié immobilisé. Aux fins de l'étude, on suppose que la caverne de stockage soit située dans un pluton granitique du Bouclier canadien, à une profondeur de référence d'un kilomètre de la surface. Les résultats de mesures in situ des tensions ont démontré un état de tensions compressives horizontales élevées dans plusieurs parties du Bouclier canadien. Les observations faites sur place indiquent que la fissuration et l'écaillement des couches superficielles du rocher pourraient résulter si la combinaison des tensions thermiques, in situ et dues au creusement, dépasse les valeurs de la résistance du rocher. Les tensions du rocher sont calculés en deux étapes, utilisant la technique des éléments finis. D'abord on effectue une simulation du creusement de la caverne de stockage, en tenant compte des tensions in situ; puis on effectue une analyse détaillée des températures transitoires et thermiques générées par la source radiogénique de chaleur, à divers moments pendant la période suivant l'implantation.

1 INTRODUCTION

Of all the alternatives considered for the ultimate disposal of nuclear fuel waste, geologic disposal appears to be the most promising and most extensively studied. The geologic media currently being investigated include crystalline hard rocks, salt and argillaceous formations. By far, the majority of the research programs - including the Canadian program - has been devoted to the study of crystalline hard rocks. Specifically, the Canadian program focusses on the development of a disposal vault in a suitable pluton in the Canadian Shield, which is known for its high degree of stability over geologic times. Four categories of plutonic rocks are being considered, namely, granite, gabbro, syenite and anorthosite, with granite being the most abundant in occurrence. For study purposes, a reference depth of approximately 1 km has been assumed for this disposal vault.

No decision has yet been made on whether to reprocess the irradiated fuel from Canada's CANDU reactors. Hence, the nuclear fuel waste to be disposed of eventually could be in the form of either immobilized irradiated fuel or immobilized reprocessing waste. In the latter case, the plutonium would have been extracted for use in advanced fuel cycles. In either case, heat would be generated as a result of radioactive decay. This paper examines the mechanical effect of radiogenic heat on the rock mass around an irradiated fuel disposal vault. The thermomechanical response of the host rock has been generally recognized as a basic research requirement in the geologic disposal of nuclear fuel waste. In Canada, this has been a subject of investigation since the inception of the Canadian nuclear fuel waste management program. As a matter of fact, one of the few case histories of thermal spalling actually took place in the Canadian Sheild. In the following sections, the paper will give a brief description and interpretation of this case history, followed by some typical results of thermomechanical analyses of a conceptual disposal vault for irradiated fuel. A preliminary assessment of the likelihood of thermomechanical instability in the rock mass adjacent to the vault is also included.

2 THERMAL SPALLING OF CRYSTALLINE ROCKS

The Canadian Shield occupies approximately 50% of the surface area of Canada, being comprised of a variety of crystalline rocks of Precambrian age. A major geomechanical feature of these rocks is their state of high horizontal stress. Figure 1 illustrates the variation of average horizontal stress with depth, as observed in underground mines in the Canadian Shield (Herget 1980). Within the depths where measurements were made, the average horizontal stress appears to be substantially higher than the corresponding vertical value, which generally correlates with the weight of the overlying rocks. These measurements of horizontal stress compared favourably with those reported in Hast (1969) for Scandinavian rocks, as well as with some of the measurements obtained in South Africa and Australia. It should be noted that high horizontal stresses are also observed in the Paleozoic bedrock of Ontario, to the south of the Canadian Shield (Lee 1981). The origin of these high horizontal stresses is not precisely known, although they are believed to be related to the glacial, erosion and tectonic histories of the region (Lee & Asmis 1980).

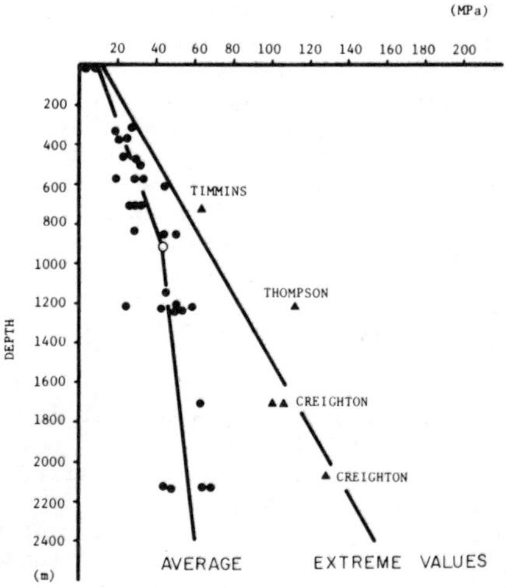

Figure 1 Measurements of average in-situ horizontal compressive stress in the Canadian Shield (after Herget, 1980)

The excavation of a tunnel opening (or a disposal vault) in a horizontal stress field creates a stress concentration effect in the tunnel roof and floor. There is a general increase in the horizontal (or tangential) compressive stresses in these parts of the rock mass around the tunnel opening. The magnitude of this increase depends on the degrees of anisotropy in the in-situ stress system and the deformation properties of the rock, as well as other factors such as the depth of cover and the presence of geologic structures (Lee 1979). If the tunnel is heated, the rock mass tends to expand. The geometric constraint is such that radial expansion can occur much more readily than tangential expansion. In other words, a state of tangential compression would be generated by the thermal load. This would be superimposed onto the combination of in-situ and excavation stresses in the rock mass, thus enhancing the tangential (and horizontal) compressive effect in the roof and the floor. The thermal load can also produce tensile stresses in the walls of the tunnel, along with some radial tension in the roof and the floor in some cases (Tsui & Lee 1980). Thermomechancial failure would occur when the combination of thermal, in-situ and excavation stresses exceeds the strength of surficial layers of rock in compression or tension. The extent of failure would largely depend on the thermal load imposed on the rock.

This apparently was the situation in the exhaust passage of an underground diesel-powered electric generator installaton at North Bay, Ontario, in the Canadian Shield. The passage was horizontal and originally 1.8 m (6 feet) wide by 2.1 m (7 feet) high, located at a depth of approximately 150 m below the surface. The host rock consisted of a competent granitic paragneiss. The in-situ stresses at this depth were not precisely known. Surficial overcoring of granitic outcrop in the area gave an average horizontal compressive stress of 7.59 MPa, based on the USBM borehole deformation gauge (Obert & Stephenson 1975). This is consistent with the magnitude of horizontal compressive stresses commonly found in surficial rocks of the Canadian Sheild, and is indicative of a high horizontal stress regime.

The exhaust gases, at a temperature of approximately 315°C, caused the spalling of 0.6 m of rock from each wall and 1.8 m from the roof (Gray 1975). The cross-section of the diesel-exhaust passage was changed from a rectangle to one with a rounded, elliptical roof. The floor was protected by debris from the roof and walls. The rough surface condition left by blasting during the original mining operation was eventually replaced by a relatively smooth condition. Figure 2 illustrates the spalls as observed in the diesel-exhaust passage. A typical spall was a curved plate averaging about 2.5 cm in thickness and 0.3 - 0.6 m in diameter. The smooth fracture surface by which each spall was separated from the wall was generally parallel to the surface of the opening. Thus, as noted in Gray (1965), "The course of the fracture seemed to be determined mainly by the pattern of thermal stress surrounding the opening, and not by the gneissic structure of the rock". The gneissic foliation in the rock was approximately horizontal. "The many vertical joints did not seem to have affected the course of spall fractures except that joint surfaces formed part of the edge boundaries of some spalls and that discontinuities on the walls occurred where spalls had terminated at joint surfaces" (Gray 1965).

A similar mode of surficial spalling was observed in a smaller test passage (0.76 m by 0.76 m in cross-section and 3 m long), excavated subsequently in the same formation for the purpose of

Figure 2 Spalls in diesel - exhaust passage (after Gray 1965)

Figure 3 Spalls in test passage (after Gray, 1965)

experimental study. Thermocouples were installed in the walls and the test passage was heated by means of the gaseous products of combustion from an oil-fired furnace. Test runs showed that spalling occurred at a surface temperature rise as low as 61°C. One run was continued for 8-1/2 hours and a mass of spalls was produced as shown in Figure 3. The spalls had the same plate-like appearance, but were roughly one-third the size and thickness of those in the diesel-exhaust passage. It was hence evident that the size of the spalls were dependent on the size of the underground opening involved. Again the fracture surfaces appeared to ignore the structure in the rock and to be determined mainly by the pattern of thermal stress (Gray, 1965).

It is apparent from the above case history that a good knowledge of the thermal stress regime would be required in assessing the thermomechancial stability of an underground opening. This would in turn require a knowledge of the thermal loading condition, the boundary and initial conditions, as well as the thermal and mechanical properties of the rock mass within the pertinent range of temperature. The thermal stress regime can be determined either analytically or numerically. Numerical methods are often preferred because of the complexity of the boundary and loading conditions involved. In the following section, a finite element modelling of the thermal stress regime around an irradiated fuel disposal vault is described. The combination of thermal, in-situ and excavation stresses is examined in light of the North Bay experience, for a preliminary assessment of thermomechancial stability.

3 THERMOMECHANICAL ANALYSIS OF A DISPOSAL VAULT

The Canadian concept of geologic disposal includes the construction of a number of long horizontal disposal rooms in parallel at a depth of approximately 0.5 - 1 km below the surface. Figure 4 illustrates the tentative geometric layout of an irradiated fuel (IF) disposal room and the canisters.

At the time of emplacement in a disposal room, the irradiated fuel is assumed to be 10 years out of the reactor core, having an initial thermal power of 269 W per canister. The normalized rate of radiogenic heat decay for each canister is illustrated in Figure 5 below.

The canisters would have at least 1 m of backfill material placed around them at the time of emplacement (Figure 4). The remainder of the disposal room would be left open for 20 years. Two subsequent backfilling and cooling options are being considered: (a) no ventilation after emplacement and initial backfilling, to be following by complete backfilling at 20 years; (b)

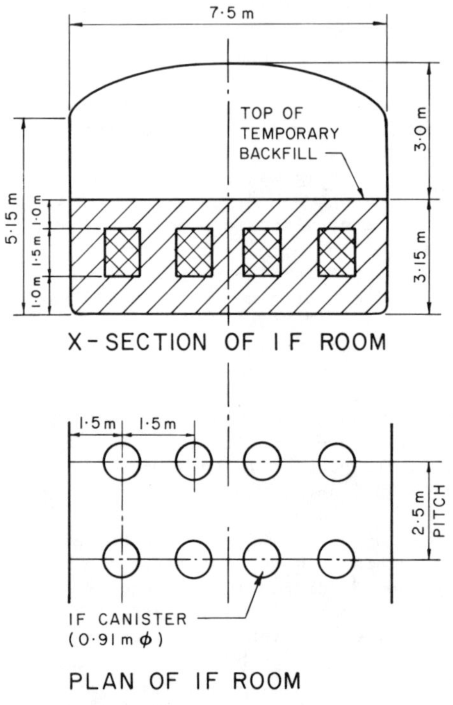

Figure 4 Tentative geometric layout of IF disposal room and canisters

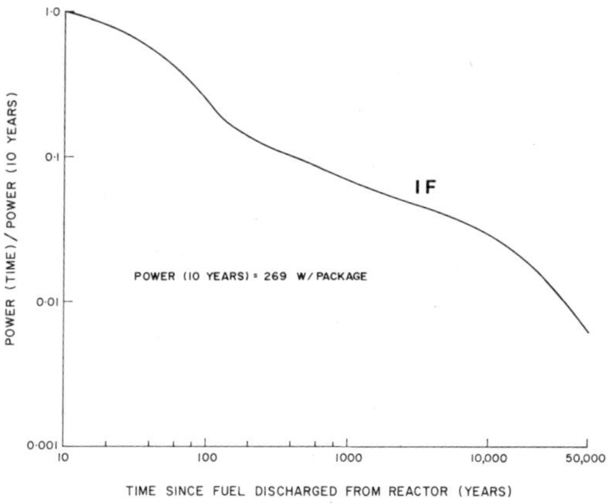

Figure 5 Radiogenic heat decay of irradiated fuel

10 years of ventilation after emplacement, to be followed by final backfilling (Wiles & Mahtab 1980).

Three finite element codes, ANSYS, DOT and SAPIV were used to determine the transient temperatures and thermal stresses generated by the radiogenic heat source. A careful assessment was made of the effects of boundary conditions, element and grid size, time steps, as well as material non-linearity and three dimensionality (Tsui & Tsai 1981; Tsui et al 1982). Figure 6 illustrates the boundary and initial conditions for the analysis of a unit

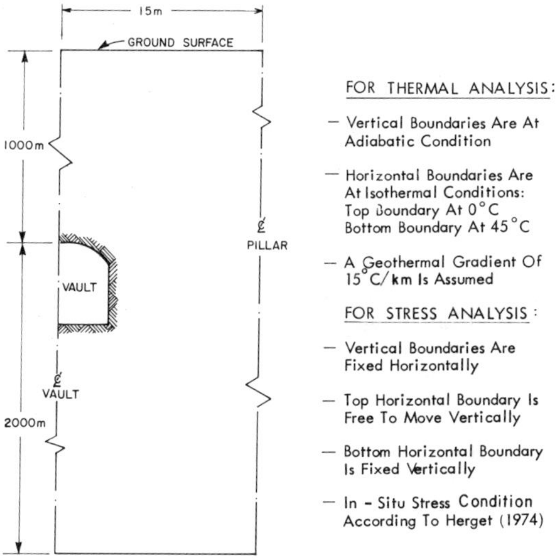

15m
GROUND SURFACE
1000m
2000m
VAULT
℄ PILLAR
℄ VAULT
FOR THERMAL ANALYSIS:
— Vertical Boundaries Are At Adiabatic Condition
— Horizontal Boundaries Are At Isothermal Conditions: Top Boundary At 0°C Bottom Boundary At 45°C
— A Geothermal Gradient Of 15°C/km Is Assumed
FOR STRESS ANALYSIS:
— Vertical Boundaries Are Fixed Horizontally
— Top Horizontal Boundary Is Free To Move Vertically
— Bottom Horizontal Boundary Is Fixed Vertically
— In - Situ Stress Condition According To Herget (1974)

Figure 6 Boundary and initial conditions for analysis

cell in a room-and-pillar configuration. A reference depth of 1 km was assumed for the purpose of the analyses.

Table 1 summarizes the material properties used in the analysis. The host rock was assumed to be a granite.

Table 1 Material properties used in finite element analysis

Property	Unit	Granite	Backfill
Thermal Conductivity	W/m°C	3	2
Specific Heat	J/Kg°C	800	800
Density	Kg/m^3	2800	2000
Young's Modulus	GPa	40	1.45
Poisson's Ratio	--	0.2	0.16
Linear Coefficient of Thermal Expansion	10^{-6}/°C	8	34

Figure 7 illustrates the temperature time-history computed for a given point at the interface between the canister and the initial backfill (Point A in Figure 7). A ventilation cooling period of 10 years is included. Two assumptions of floor to ceiling heat transfer were examined: (i) an adiabetic (or insulated) boundary at the open space perimeter, and (ii) the occurrence of natural convection and radiation in the still air enclosed between the initial backfill and the host rock. In the latter case, this was accomplished by incorporating into the analysis an equivalent thermal conductivity of 15 W/m°C for the still air - an approach suggested in Davis (1979).

There are two striking features in Figure 7. The first is the large difference in temperature rise between the two heat transfer assumptions as they pertain to the still air during the initial 20 years of emplacement. It reflects the important effect of natural convection and radiation in the still air, which is ignored in the adiabatic boundary assumption. These two modes of heat transfer in the still air effectively reduce the peak temperature in the backfill by approximately 25 - 30°C. Their incorportion into the analysis tends to give a more realistic distribution of the transient temperatures around the disposal room. With the commencement of ventilation

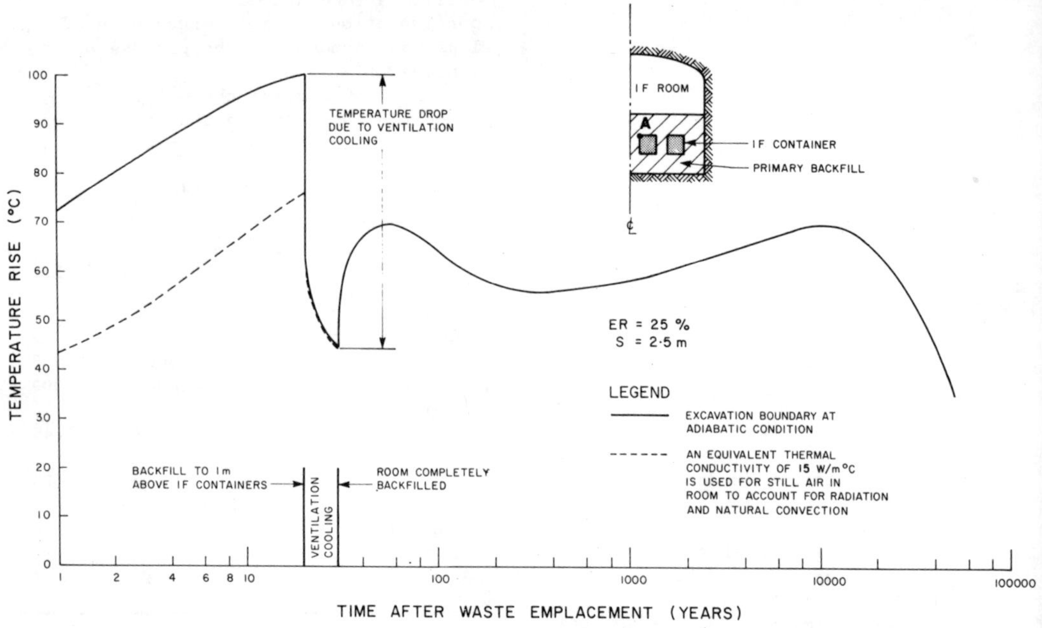

Figure 7 Temperature time-history of point A at canister/backfill interface

cooling at 20 years, the temperature rise drops off drastically, reaching a low of 44°C at 30 years. Complete backfilling takes place at the end of 30 years, thereby, eliminating any heat transfer effect due to the air.

The second striking feature in Figure 7 is the occurrence of a second temperature peak at around 10,000 years. Mayman et al (1980) noted that double peaks or multiple maxima in temperature could occur if the irradiated fuel has several exponentially decreasing heat sources, such as in the case of the irradiated fuel from the CANDU reactors. The areal extent of the underground disposal facility is another important factor. Beyerlein and Claiborne (1980) have shown analytically that a second peak would not occur if the disposal facility is less than 1 km^2 in areal extent. In a smaller facility, the heat generated at the centre can dissipate more readily into the ambient rock mass.

Figure 8 illustrates the spatial distribution of temperature rises at 20 years, immediately prior to the introduction of ventilation cooling. The effect of heat transfer in the still air between the initial backfill and the host rock is included. It can be seen that the maximum temperature rise occurs reasonably close to Point A, the temperature time-history of which is given in Figure 7.

Figures 9 and 10 compare the horizontal stress distribution immediately after excavation and at 20 years after the emplacement of IF. The former represents the combined effect of in-situ and excavation stresses, while the latter also incorporates the thermal stresses at that point in time. The following linear relationships suggested by Herget (1974) for in-situ stresses in the Canadian Shield were used as a first approximation.

Thus, at the disposal vault horizon, the in-situ horizontal stress would be on the order of 48 MPa, with a corresponding vertical value of 28 MPa. Figure 9 clearly illustrates the effect of stress concentration in the roof and at the floor corners due to excavation in a high horizontal field. This stress concentration effect is reinforced by the thermal load, giving combined maximum horizontal compressive stresses of approximately 120 MPa and 150 MPa in the roof and the floor respectively (Figure 10). There is only a small amount of horizontal tension in the wall (Figure 10). Similarly, in examining the computed vertical stress results,

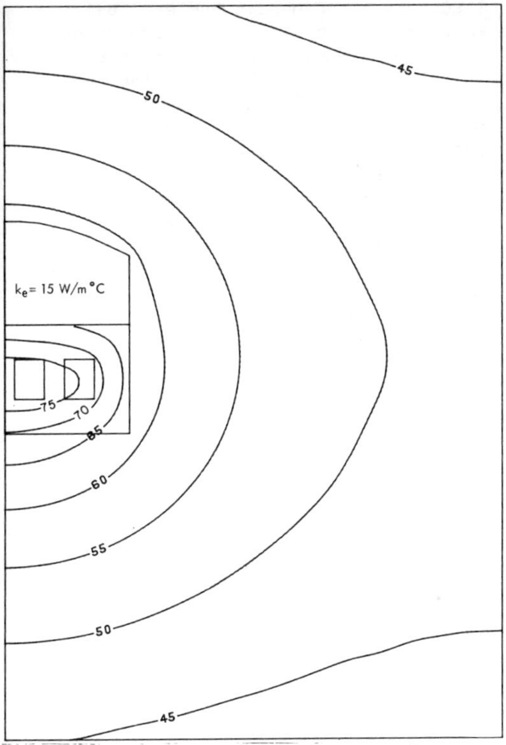

Figure 8 Contours of temperature rise in °C at 20 years

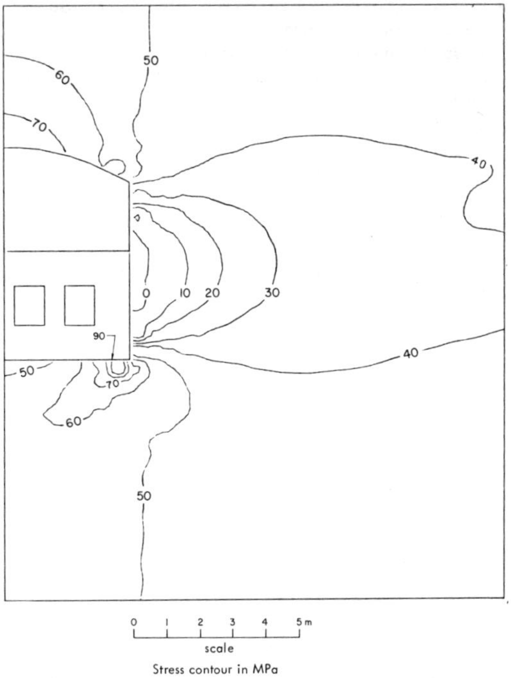

Figure 9 Horizontal stress distribution immediately after excavation

Average horizontal stress in kPa
= 8170 + 41.7 x depth in metres.

Vertical stress = overburden pressure.

the only tension zone that could be detected is a small one which occurs beneath the floor, with relatively low tensile stresses. For a stress distribution such as that given in Figure 10 to produce thermal spalls, a most probable mechanism would be the sub-horizontal splitting of surficial rock layers in the roof parallel to the direction of maximum compression (Fairhurst & Cook 1966), coupled with tensile failure in the wall. This is also consistent with the plate-like appearance of the thermal spalls in the Nortrh Bay case history earlier described. A closer examination of Figure 10 indicates that the compressive stress levels in the roof would be generally lower than the average compressive strength of competent granitic rocks (typically in the range of 150 - 200 MPa). Likewise, the tensile stresses in the wall and the floor are too small to cause any major tension failure around the IF disposal

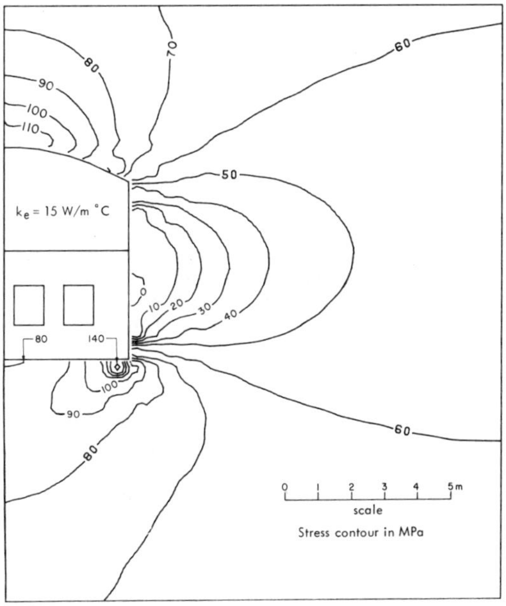

Figure 10 Horizontal stress distribution at 20 years after IF emplacement

room. Thermomechanical instability due to a gross overstressing of the rock mass is hence highly improbable, although some minor surficial fracturing and spalling may still occur, particularly in weak zones of the host rock. This would have a more significant effect on the hydraulic conductivity of the rock mass in the very near-field, than on the stability of the disposal room itself. Work is currently being carried out to assess this effect through a coupling of the near-field hydrogeologic, thermal and thermomechanical regimes. It is anticipated that the results of the coupled anlaysis will be reported in due course.

4 CONCLUSIONS

The thermomechanical stability of an underground opening in rock is determined largely by the combined values of thermal, in-situ and excavation stresses immediately around the opening. While thermal spalling may appear to be a direct consequence of the thermal load, the in-situ and excavation stresses may in some cases account for a major portion of the total stresses generated around the opening. An example of this would be a high horizontal stress field, such as the Canadian Shield. The case history of thermal spalling which occurred in North Bay appears to be a result of sub-horizontal splitting of surficial rock layers in the roof, coupled with tensile failure of the walls. Both of these failure modes are consistent with the stress configuration around a heated opening in a high horizontal stress field. Applying this concept to the assessment of thermomechancial stability around an irradiated fuel disposal vault, it is concluded that the stresses which would be generated are sufficiently low to ensure the overall stability of the disposal vault. Some minor surficial fracturing and spalling may still occur in weak zones of the rock, but the effect would likely be confined to a localized increase in hydraulic conductivity in the very near field of the disposal vault.

5 ACKNOWLEDGEMENTS

The work described here forms a part of Ontario Hydro's technical assistance to the Atomic Energy of Canada Limited (AECL) in the Canadian Nuclear Fuel Waste Management Program. Permission by these two agencies to publish this work is gratefully acknowledged. The authors are indebted to Dr. T.E. Rummery, Dr. K.W. Dormuth and Mr. G.R. Simmons of AECL, and to Messrs. W.G. Morison, J.I. Adams, E.M. Taylor, Dr. R.C. Oberth and Mr. R.A. McEachran of Ontario Hydro for their critical review of the manuscript and their valuable comments. Thanks are also due to Mr. M. Thomas for the preparation of the illustrations, and to the Word Processing Unit of Ontario Hydro for the careful typing of the manuscript.

6 REFERENCES

Beyerlein, S.W. & H.C. Claiborne 1980, The possibility of multiple temperature maxima in geologic repositories for spent fuel from nuclear reactors. Oak Ridge National Laboratory Report, ORNL/TM-7024.

Davis, B.W. 1979, Convection and Thermal radiation analytical models applicable to a nuclear waste repository room. Lawrence Livermore Laboratory Report, UCID - 18103.

Fairhurst, C. & N.G. W. Cook 1966, The phenomenon of rock splitting parallel to the direction of maximum compression in the neighbourhood of a surface, Proc. 1st ICRM, Lisbon, 1:687-692.

Gray, W.M. 1965, Surface spalling by thermal stresses in rocks, Proc. Rock Mech. Symp., Toronto, p. 85-106.

Hast, N. 1969, The state of stress in the upper part of the Earth's Crust, Tectonophysics 8:189-211.

Herget, G. 1974, Ground stress determination in Canada, Rock Mechanics 6:53-64.

Herget, G. 1980, Regional stresses in the Canadian Shield, Proc. 13th Canadian Rock Mech. Symp., Toronto, p. 9-16.

Lee, C.F. 1979, Stress-induced instability in underground excavations, Proc. 19th U.S. Symp. Rock Mech. 1:165-173.

Lee, C.F. 1981, In-Situ stress measurements in southern Ontario, Proc. 22nd U.S. Symp. Rock Mech., p. 435-442.

Lee, C.F. & H.W. Asmis 1980, An interpretation of the crustal stress field in northeast North America, Proc. 20th U.S. Symp. Rock Mech. 1:655-662.

Mayman, S.A., R.G. Charlwood & J.L. Ratigan 1980, Long-term thermal response of a CANDU fuel disposal vault, Atomic Energy of Canada Limited Technical Record #134.

Obert, L. & D.E. Stephenson 1965, Stress conditions under which core discing occurs, Trans, Soc. Mining Eng., AIME, p. 227-235.

Tsui, K.K. & C.F. Lee 1980, Thermo-mechanical stability of heated rock caverns, Proc. 21st U.S. Symp. Rock Mech., p. 183-191.

Tsui, K.K. & A.Tsai 1981, Near-field thermal and stress analyses for immobilized waste and irradiated fuel disposal vaults in crystalline hard rock, Draft Report to Atomic Energy of Canada Limited.

Tsui, K.K., C.F. Lee, A. Tsai & N.L. Harris 1982, Thermomechancial modelling of a nuclear waste disposal vault in crystalline hard rock, Proc. 4th Int. Conf. on Numerical Methods in Geomechanics, Edmonton, Canada.

Wiles, T. & M.A. Mahtab 1980, Irradiated fuel vault: room-and-pillar thermal rock mechanics analyses, Atomic Energy of Canada Limited Technical Record #50.

ROCK MECHANICS DESIGN OF AN UNDERGROUND CANDU NUCLEAR POWER PLANT

Felsmechanischer Entwurf eines unterirdischen CANDU Kernkraftwerks

Dimensionnement d'une centrale électrique nucléaire souterraine de CANDU au moyen de la mécanique des roches

C.F.LEE, K.K.TSUI & H.W.ASMIS
Ontario Hydro, Toronto, Canada

SUMMARY:
This paper outlines the four modes of rock mass instability which have to be considered in designing large excavated caverns for housing the reactors and auxiliary equipment of a 4 x 850 MWe underground CANDU nuclear power plant. The first mode consists of the potential instability of joint blocks in the roof and the walls of the caverns, which is triggered sometimes by the blasting effect. The second mode of instability is caused by an overstressing of the rock mass due to the combination of in-situ and excavation stresses. In the extremely remote event of a loss-of-coolant accident and a sudden release of pressurized steam into the cavern, the third mode of instability, which is thermomechanical in character, would have to be considered. The likelihood and extent of thermomechanical instability can be assessed in an analysis of the transient temperatures and thermal stresses generated in surficial layers of the host rock. Earthquake and near-field rockburst effects contribute to the fourth mode of rock mass instability underground, which is dynamic in character. It is concluded that the four instability modes can be properly accounted for in engineering design, posing no major hazards to the safety of an underground nuclear plant.

ZUSAMMENFASSUNG:
Es wird ein Überblick gegeben auf die vier Arten des Felseninstabilität, die bei der Planung grosser Kavernen zur Unterbringung der Reaktoren und Hilfsanlagen eines 4 x 850 MWe unterirdischen Candu-Kernkraftwerkes, zu betrachten sind. Erstens die potentielle Instabilität der Kluftkörper in der Krone und in den Wänden der Kaverne, die manchmal unter dem Einfluss der Sprengarbeiten hervorgerufen wird. Die zweite Art der Instabilität ist auf eine Überbeanspruchung der Felsenmasse zurückzuführen, die einer Kombination der in-situ und der durch Sprengungen verursachten Beanspruchungen zuzuschreiben ist. Im dem höchstunwahrscheinlichen Fall eines gefährlichen Kühlmittelverlustes end einer plötzlichen Freisetzung von Druckdampf in die Kaverne, käme die dritte Art der Instabilität, die von thermomechanischer Natur ist, in Frage. Die Wahrscheinlichkeit und Grösse der Thermomechanischen Instabilität lassen sich durch eine Analyse der in der Oberflächenschichten des Ursprungsgesteins erstehenden Übergangstemperaturen und Wärmespannungen, bewerten. Die Wirkungen von Erdbeben und möglich naheliegenden Gebirgsschlägen bilden auf die vierte Art der unterirdischen Felseninstabilität, die von dynamischer Natur ist. Zum Schluss wird die Folgerung gezogen, dass die vier Arten der Instabilität in der technischen Planung sachgemäss berücksichtigt werden können, und keine grossen Risiken für die Sicherheit eines unterirdischen Kernkraftwerkes darstellen.

RESUME:
Cette communication donne les grandes lignes des quatre modes d'instabilité de la masse rocheuse, dont il faut tenir compte dans la conception de grandes cavernes abritant les réacteurs et l'appareillage auxiliaire d'une centrale nucléaire souterreine Candu de 4 x 850 MWe. Le premier mode comprend l'instabilité potentielle des ensemble de diaclases dans la voûte et les parois des cavernes, qui est parfois amorcée par les travaux aux explosifs. C'est le surchargement de la masse rocheuse, causé par une combinaison des tensions in-situ et de celles dues au creusement, qui est responsable du deuxième mode d'instabilité. Dans le cas extrêmement peu probable d'un incident dangereux de perte de réfri-

gérant et d'une libération subite de vapeur pressurisée dans la caverne, c'est la troisième mode d'instabilité, de nature thermomécanique, qui serait impliqué. La probabilité et l'ampleur de l'instabilité thermomécanique peuvent être évaluées au moyen d'une analyse des températures transitoires et des tensions thermiques générées dans les couches superficielles du rocher hôte. Le quatrième mode d'instabilité de la masse rocheuse souterraine, qui est de nature dynamique, est causé par les effects des tremblements de terre ou d'éventuels éboulis de roches à proximité. En conclusion, on constate que l'on peut bien tenir compte des quatre modes d'instabilité dans le calcul technique, évitant ainsi des risques importants pour la sécurité d'une centrale nucléaire souterraine.

1 INTRODUCTION

Nuclear power currently provides a significant portion of the electrical energy consumed in many ISRM member nations. Prompted largely by defense and environmental considerations, a number of investigations have been made in recent years on the underground siting of nuclear power plants. These investigations have focussed, in particulár, on the relative merits, cost penalties and technical feasibility of the underground siting option.

This paper highlights the rock mechanics design considerations in a study recently completed by Ontario Hydro, a major Canadian electrical utility which serves the Province of Ontario. The contribution of nuclear energy to Ontario is reflected in the fact that one-third of the electricity currently produced in Ontario comes from nuclear power plants in operation. This figure is expected to rise to one-half by the end of the century.

2 REFERENCE DESIGN

The underground nuclear power plant studied by Ontario Hydro features four 850 MWe CANDU reactor units, housed in large caverns to be excavated in the Precambrian basement rock of granitic gneiss, at a reference depth of approximately 400 m from the surface. The CANDU is a unique Canadian pressure tube reactor design using natural uranium fuel and heavy water as both coolant and moderator. Figure 1 shows the general cross section of this plant. Note that with the exception of the reactor and nuclear components, all other plant components are erected on or near the surface, including the powerhouse. A comprehensive documentation of the study results is given in Oberth et al (1979). In the reference design portrayed in Figure 1, the rock mass would serve as an integral part of the reactor containment system.

3 ROCK MECHANICS DESIGN CONSIDERATIONS

There are two basic design requirements for the rock mass around the proposed reactor caverns, namely, a high degree of watertightness, together with a high degree of stability both during plant operation and under accident conditions. In much of Ontario, Canada, a state of high horizontal in-situ stress has been observed (Lo 1978, Lee 1981). This state of horizontal compression contributed significantly to the watertightness of most of the Paleozoic and Precambrian rock formations of Ontario. The joints and fractures found in such rocks are usually very tight, resulting in rock mass permeabilities of generally well below 10^{-8} m/sec. In the highly improbable event of a plant accident resulting in the release of radioisotopes into the groundwater system, it is expected that molecular diffusion would be the dominant mechanism for the migration of such isotopes away from the reactor cavern. It is generally recognized that molecular diffusion is an extremely slow process, with isotope concentrations tapering off rapidly from the source.

Several factors have to be considered in terms of rock mass stability around the reactor cavern. These include:

(i) Rock mass stability as controlled by joint blocks and fractures around the cavern;

(ii) Rock mass stability as dictated by the stress levels around the cavern;

(iii) Rock mass stability during a hypothetical loss-of-coolant accident, resulting in an injection of steam into the cavern; and

(iv) Rock mass stability during earthquakes.

These factors are dealt with sequentially in the following sections:

3.1 Structurally controlled rock mass instability

The rock mass adjacent to an underground

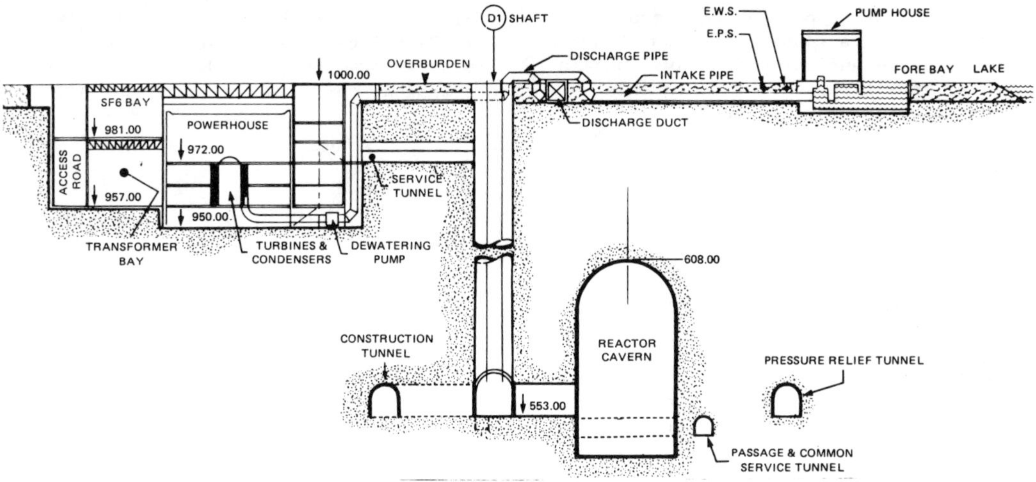

Figure 1 General cross section of underground CANDU nuclear power plant

opening could be locally unstable by virtue of the loose joint blocks and slabs bounded by the surface of the opening and such structural features as joints, fractures, shear zones and faults in the rock mass. The state of equilibrium of such joint blocks and slabs could be affected significantly and instantaneously by blasting. This type of instability may or may not reflect the overall stress configuration around the opening. In general, it could be effectively controlled by limiting the span of the opening, and by providing an adequate amount of rock support (in the form of rock bolts, shotcrete and steel ribs).

For a 4 x 850 MWe underground CANDU plant, four large caverns with principal dimensions of 100 m length x 35 m width x 60 m height would be required to house the reactor components and auxiliary equipment. Stable rock caverns with spans on the order of 27 m had previously been excavated in competent rocks in Canada and Europe. The results of pilot drilling and testing at the construction site of Ontario Hydro's Darlington Nuclear Generating Station, located 65 km to the east of Toronto, indicated that the quality of the Precambrian basement rock (granitic gneiss) and the overlying Paleozoic limestones was excellent (Oberth & Lee 1980). The rock quality designation (RQD) was consistently in the range 90-100% below a depth of 54 m in a 303 m deep test boring. The average joint spacing in the granitic gneiss was in excess of 1 m. The results of single packer tests indicated no measureable absorption of water below a depth of 30 m from the surface, confirming a very tight rock mass with a permeability of less than 10^{-9} m/sec. Pending confirmation by more detailed site-specific investigations, it is anticipated that Precambrian basement rocks with similar qualities to the granitic gneiss at this test site would generally be able to host the proposed reactor caverns, and be self-supporting to a very large extent, requiring only limited mechanical support. Given the high values of RQD and large joint spacing observed in test drilling, it is expected that the pattern of rock bolting (with chain-link wire mesh) shown in Figure 2 would adequately provide the mechanical support

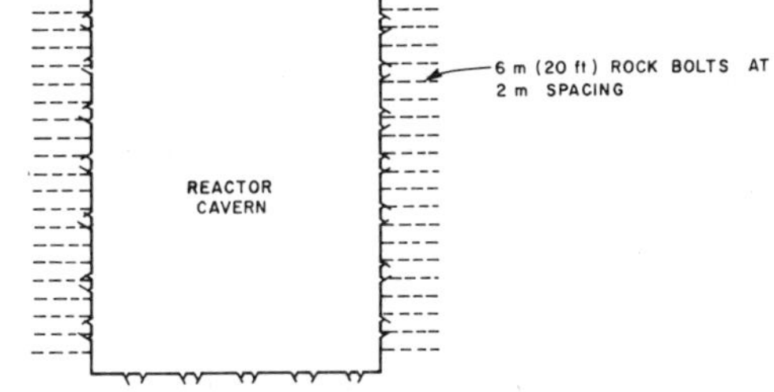

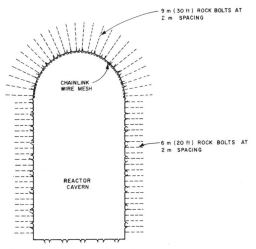

Figure 2 Proposed rock support system for reactor caverns

required. The support system recommended herein is consistent with those used in large underground excavations in similar rock types and of comparable dimensions (eg. Cording et al 1971; Benson et al 1972; Hamel & Nixon 1978).

3.2 Stress controlled rock mass instability

This type of instability refers to a gross overstressing of the rock mass adjacent to the cavern, either in compression, tension or shear. The extent of failure depends on the size of the overstressed zone and hence on the overall stress configuration around the cavern. As such, rock support systems would only have limited success in suppressing deep-seated, stress-induced instability in a rock mass. Among the more effective means of preventing this type of instability would be the optimization of cavern shape and alignment, and, in some cases, the depth of cover as well. The likelihood of its occurrence can be assessed on the basis of in-situ stress measurements and a stress analysis simulating the process of cavern excavation.

Figure 3 illustrates the assessment of stress-induced instability in a high horizontal stress field, following the excavation of a large reactor cavern. It is a plot of the contours of horizontal compressive stress around the cavern, based on an elastic, two-dimensional finite element simulation of cavern excavation. The initial stresses in the rock mass are respectively 22 MPa horizontally and 10 MPa vertically, based on the results of in-situ stress determination using the hydrofracturing method (Haimson & Lee 1979). These results, which indicate a state of high horizontal stress along the entire 303 m depth of the test boring, are consistent with other measurements and observations made in Ontario. They reflect the glacial and tectonic histories of the rock formations under consideration, particularly the effects of continental glaciation and erosion (Lee 1978a; Lee & Asmis 1979). In general, in a high horizontal stress field, the excavation of a tunnel or cavern opening results in concentration of horizontal compressive stress in the roof and the floor of the opening. If these horizontal compressive stresses exceed the compressive strength of the rock, buckling and spalling of surficial layers of the rock may occur, as manifested by case histories (Lee 1978b). Examining the distribution of horizontal compressive stress shown in

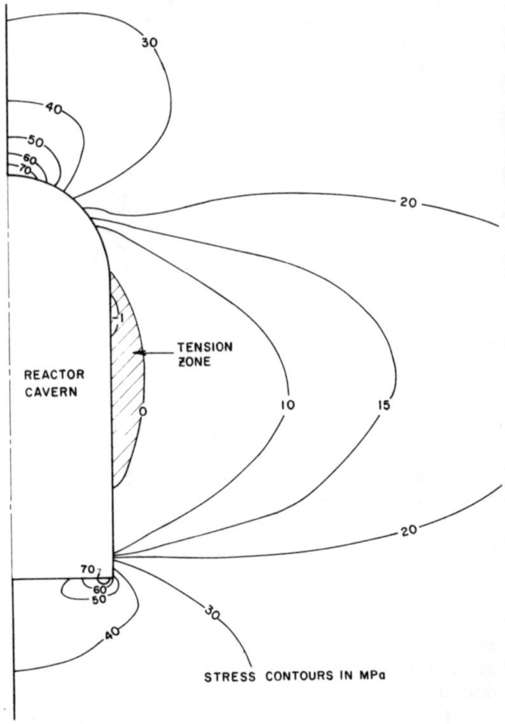

Figure 3 Contours of horizontal stress around the reactor cavern following excavation

Figure 3, it is obvious that the approximately 60 MPa of horizontal compressive stresses in the roof and the floor corners are rather small compared with the average compressive strength of granitic gneiss (150-200 MPa). A state of stress-induced instability in the granitic gneiss around the reactor cavern immediately following excavation is hence extremely unlikely, largely because of the strength of the rock. Similarly, it could be verified from the results of the stress analysis that the tensile and shear stresses would very unlikely exceed the respective strengths of the host rock.

3.3 Thermomechanical stability

The stress distribution shown in Figure 3 represents the combined effect of in-situ and excavation stresses. There are conceivably other effects which could change this stress distribution, such as time-dependent deformation (or creep), thermal loading and earthquakes. Given the stress levels and the strength and deformation properties of the granitic gneiss, the effect of time-dependent deformation is expected to be relatively minor. The case of thermally loading the rock mass, following the extremely remote event of a loss-of-coolant accident and the rupture of a coolant pipe, is dealt with in this section. The effect of seismic loading is examined in Section 3.4

With a sudden release of hot, pressurized steam into the cavern, it is anticipated that the temperature at the face of the rock could rise to as high as 100°C for a period of approximately one day. A state of thermal shock results, with thermal expansion of the rock permitted in the radial direction and prohibited in the tangential direction due to the geometry of the cavern (Lee & Klym 1977). The distributions of temperature and horizontal stress under such an accident condition are illustrated in Figure 4, based on a two-dimensional finite element analysis of the thermal stresses (Tsui & Lee 1980). The stress distribution shown in Figure 4 represents the combined effect of in-situ, excavation and thermal stresses. It can be seen that the horizontal compressive stresses in the roof and the floor corners may increase to approximately 120 MPa, which is still somewhat lower than the average compressive strength of the granitic gneiss (150-200 MPa). A tension zone with relatively small tensile stresses could develop in the walls. Some minor spalling may hence occur in the walls, along with some surficial spalling from the roof locally in weak zones of rock. However, the amount of spalling would be nowhere near those reported in Gray (1965). Precautionary measures which could be applied to enhance the thermomechanical stability of the reactor caverns includes the installation of long bolts or cable anchors (with chain-link wire mesh), the provision of an emergency dousing system, thermal insulation, and the cutting of a small vertical slot in the roof to relieve the tangential compression in surficial layers of rock. A preliminary analysis indicates that such a slot would be effective in reducing the possibility of thermal spalling in both the roof and walls (Tsui & Lee 1980). This would ensure that the stability of the roof is preserved and that an emergency dousing system hung from the roof would function properly.

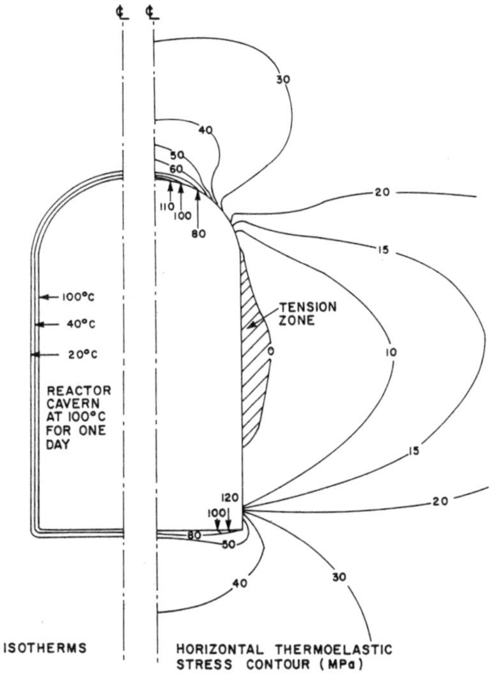

Figure 4 Distributions of temperature and horizontal stress around the reactor cavern after exposure to 100°C for one day

3.4 Dynamic Stability

The seismic qualification of nuclear plant structures and components represents a major factor affecting plant design and plant cost. It is hoped that a significant portion of the cost penalty of underground siting could be offset by the reduction in seismic design criteria associated with underground siting.

Field observations have demonstrated that underground openings are generally more stable than surface structures during a strong earthquake. Dowding & Rozen (1978) studied the response of 71 tunnels to strong ground motions in California, Alaska and Japan. The results indicated that at peak accelerations which caused heavy damage to surface structures, there was only very minor damage to the tunnels. Similar observations have also been made in underground mines. The miners working at depth sometimes do not feel the earthquakes occurring at the surface. The catastrophic earthquake (M8.3) which demolished the City of Tangshan, China on July 28, 1976, and which reportedly claimed the lives of several hundred thousand residents occurred near a major coal field in northern China, the Kailuan coal mine. Practically the entire shift of over ten thousand coal miners working underground at the time of the main shock escaped and returned safely to the surface.

The increased stability of structures with depth during earthquakes can be attributed to two primary factors, namely, the de-amplification of seismic motions with depth and the very large stiffness and high resonant frequencies of tunnels in rock. A finite difference analysis using pulse waves indicated that an attenuation factor of between 1.5 and 2.0 on peak accelerations could be achieved at depths of 300 to 400 m below the surface, for frequency and velocity contents of interest to eastern Canada, and for both vertically and obliquely propagating waves (Asmis 1980). This is consistent with the results of similar analyses carried out by Glass (1973), Yamahara et al (1977) and Allenworth et al (1977). The analyses also indicated that the dynamic stresses generated in the rock mass would only be a very small fraction of the in-situ and excavation stresses. While such a small fractional increase may be sufficient to trigger a rockfall in some cases, it is believed that most rockfalls occurring during earthquakes are more likely controlled by geologic structures and joint blocks rather than by the overall stress configuation. To assess the seismic stability of joints and joint blocks, a finite difference solution was developed during the present study, capable of simulating the displacement of both discrete joints and major joint sets, as well as the loss of joint friction during dynamic excitation (Asmis, 1981). Figure 5 illustrates the displacement pattern generated around a rectangular underground opening intersected by a major shear plane dipping at 40°, assuming the angle of friction along the shear plane to be velocity-dependent and reduced by 40% during a near-field strong rockburst. This method of analyzing the displacement of discrete fractures and joint blocks can be applied to any given site when detailed site-specific information on joint orientation and spacing becomes available. The effect of in-situ and excavation stresses is also incorporated into the analysis. The methodology and input requirements are of sufficient generality to apply to all underground openings which may be subjected to long-term and short-term dynamic effects, including the underground disposal vaults for nuclear wastes.

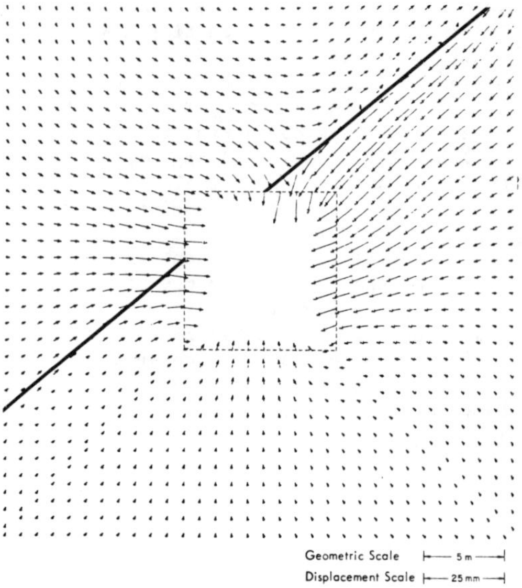

Figure 5 Displacement field around a rectangular opening intersected by a 40° shear plane and subjected to a near-field strong rockburst

4 CONCLUSIONS

The rock mechanics design of large reactor caverns requires a careful consideration of the various modes of rock mass instability which may occur under normal operating conditions and credible accident conditions. These possible modes of rock mass instability include:

(i) Structurally controlled instability of joint blocks following cavern excavation, which could be minimized by the installation of mechancial supports such as rock bolts, shotcrete and steel ribs;

(ii) Stress controlled instability due to an overstressing of the rock mass around the cavern, the extent of which could be assessed in a stress analysis and minimized by optimizing the cavern shape, alignment and depth;

(iii) Thermal spalling of surficial rock layers in the remote event of a sudden release of pressurized steam into the cavern, which could be minimized by such precautionary measures as the installation of long bolts with chain-link wire mesh, an emergency dousing system, thermal insulation and the cutting of a small vertical slot in the roof to relieve surficial tangential compression; and

(iv) Dynamically induced displacements and rockfalls, which could be assessed in a dynamic modelling of joint block movement, and minimized by avoiding major fault zones in underground siting.

Possible approaches which could be utilized to design against these modes of instability are outlined in the paper. It is concluded that all of these instability modes can be properly accounted for in engineering design, posing no major hazards to the safety of an underground CANDU nuclear plant.

5 ACKNOWLEDGEMENTS

The authors are indebted to Messrs. J.I. Adams and E.M. Taylor of Ontario Hydro for their review of the manuscript and permission to publish. The work described here constituted part of Ontario Hydro's Underground Nuclear Power Plant Study, of which Dr. R.C. Oberth was the co-ordinator.

6 REFERENCES

Allensworth, J.A, J.T. Finger, J.A. Milloy, W.B. Murfin, R. Rodeman & S.G. Vandevender 1977, Underground siting of nuclear power plants: potential benefits and penalties, Sandia Laboratories Report SAND 76-0412,NUREG-0255.

Asmis, H.W. 1980, Dynamic response of underground openings in discontinuous rock, Ontario Hydro Report No. 80044

Asmis, H.W. 1981, The dynamic response of caverns in discontinuous rock, Proc 22nd US Symp. Rock Mech. p 252-257.

Benson, R.P., R.J. Conlon, A.H. Merritt, P. Joli-Coeur & D.U. Deere 1971, Rock mechanics at Churchill Falls, Proc. Symp. Underground Rock Chambers, Phoenix, Arizona, p. 407-486.

Cording, E.J., A.J. Hendron Jr. & D.U. Deere 1971, Rock engineering for underground caverns, Proc. Symp. Underground Rock Chambers, Phoenix, Arizona, p. 567-600.

Dowding, C.H. & A. Rozen 1978, Damage to rock tunnels from earthquake shaking, ASCE J. Geotech. Eng. Div. 104 : 229-247.

Glass, C.E. 1973, Seismic considerations in siting large underground openings in rock, Ph.D. Thesis, University of California at Berkeley.

Gray, W.M. 1965, Surface spalling by thermal stresses in rocks, Proc. Rock Mech. Symp., Toronto, p. 85-106.

Haimson, B.C. & C.F. Lee 1979, Stress measurements in underground nuclear plant design, Proc. 1979 RETC, Atlanta, Georgia, 1:122-135.

Hamel, L. & D. Nixon 1978, Excavation of world's largest underground powerhouse, ASCE J. Construction Div. 104:333-351.

Lee, C.F. 1978a, A rock mechanics approach to seismic risk evaluation, Proc. 19th US Synp. Rock Mech. 1:pp 88.

Lee, C.F. 1987b, Stress-induced instability in underground excavations, Proc. 19th US Symp. Rock Mech. 1:165-173.

Lee, C.F. 1981, In-situ stress measurements in southern Ontario, Proc. 22nd US Symp. Rock Mech. p. 435-442.

Lee, C.F. & H.W. Asmis 1979, An interpretation of the crustal stress field in Northeast North America, Proc. 20th US Symp. Rock Mech. 1:655-662.

Lee, C.F. & T.W. Klym 1977, Stability of heated caverns in a high horizontal stress field, Proc. Rockstore 77, Stockholm, 2:441-448.

Lo, K.Y. 1978, Regional distribution of in-situ horizontal stresses in rocks of southern Ontario, Can. Geotech. J. 15:371-381.

Oberth, R.C. and C.F. Lee 1980, Underground siting of a CANDU nuclear power station, Proc. Rockstore 80, Stockholm, 2:701-711.

Oberth, R.C. et al 1979, Underground CANDU power station - conceptual design and evaluation Ontario Hydro Report No. 79374.

Tsui, K.K. & C.F. Lee 1980, Thermomechanical stability of heated rock caverns, Proc. 21st US Symp. Rock Mech. p. 183-191.

Yamahara, H., Y. Hisatomi & T. Morie 1977, A study on the earthquake safety of rock caverns, Proc. Rockstore 77, Stockholm, 2:377-382.

METHODEN ZUR DIMENSIONIERUNG UNTERIRDISCHER SPEICHER VON ERDÖL UND ERDGAS

A method for dimensioning underground oil and gas storage reservoirs

Une méthode de dimensionnement de réservoirs souterrains d'huile et de gaz

R.PARASCHKEWOW & N.NIKOLAEW
Technische Hochschule für Bergbau & Geologie, Sofia, Bulgarien

SUMMARY:
The present paper deals with a strength theory for the triaxial state of stress of rocks in the form $\sigma_1 > \sigma_2 = \sigma_3$, which is based on the combined action of geostatic pressure and internal pressure of the underground construction. An engineering approach for dimensioning storage reservoirs has been developed on the case of triaxial strength of rocks.

ZUSAMMENFASSUNG:
Im vorliegenden Bericht, wird die Festigkeitstheorie im Bezug auf den dreiaxialen Spannungszustand der Gesteine vom Typ $\sigma_1 > \sigma_2 = \sigma_3$ betrachtet, auf der Grundlage der Wechselwirkung des geostatischen Drucks und der inneren Spannung der unterirdischen Konstruktionen. Es ist entwickelt ein Ingenieurverfahren zum Dimensionierung der Speicherungen auf Grund ihrer dreiaxialen Festigkeit der Gesteine.

RESUME:
Le rapport présente une théorie de résistance concernant l'état de contrainte triaxiale des roches en forme $\sigma_1 > \sigma_2 = \sigma_3$, qui se base sur l'action combinée de la pression géostatique et la pression intérieure dans la construction souterraine. Une méthode technique à dimensionnement des réservoirs souterrains a été développée en se basant sur la résistance triaxiale des roches.

Die unterirdische Speicherung von Flüßigkeiten und Gasen (Erdöl, Erdgas, Salzlösungen u.a.) findet immer breitere Anwendung. Die technischen Möglichkeiten und die ökonomische Zweckmäßigkeit vom Aufbau unterirdischen Druckspeicherungen hängen im höchsten Grade von der begründeten Ingenieuranlegung der Anlagen auf Grund der richtigen geomechanischen Beurteilung der natur-technischen Bedingungen ab. Die Erhöhung der Standfestigkeit und Wirtschaftlichkeit der unterirdischen Druckanlagen läßt sich nach verschiedenen Arten erreichen. Besonders effektiv sind aber die Lösungen, bei denen am vollsten die reale Standfestigkeit des Gesteines erfaßt und die Ausnutzung des eigenen Widerstandes und der Tragfähigkeit des Gesteines gesichert wird.

Es ist bekannt, daß bei dem Aufbau unterirdischer Kammerspeicherungen für Erdöl und Erdgas die Zwischenkammerpfeiler einem allseitigen unregelmäßigen Druck ausgesetzt sind. Ihre Standfestigkeit wird aber oft auf Grund der Voraussetzung bestimmt, daß im bedingten durchschnittlichen Querschnitt die Beanspruchung des Gesteines auf einem monoaxialen Druck ausgesetzt ist. Deswegen wird als Festigkeitskriterium der experimentell gefundene Wert der Gesteinsfestigkeit des monoaxialen Drucks R_H ausgenutzt und die Standfestigkeit des Pfeilers als Quotient zwischen der durchschnittlichen Druckspannung und der Festigkeit R_H

$$n = \frac{\sigma}{R_H} > 1 \qquad (1)$$

erfaßt.

Die bekannten analytischen Berechnungsmethoden (von M.Stamatin, H. de La Coopilière, W.S.Romanow, WNIIG u.a.) sind ausführlich und tiefschürfend von Z.Kleczek (Górnictwo, Rock 2,Zeszyt 3,Krakow, 1978) analysiert. Der in den Pfeilerzwischenkammern ausgebildete Druckspannungszustand wird nach der Methode von W.S.Romanow (Abb.1) ausgewertet:

- die vertikale Druckspannung wird nach der Gleichung

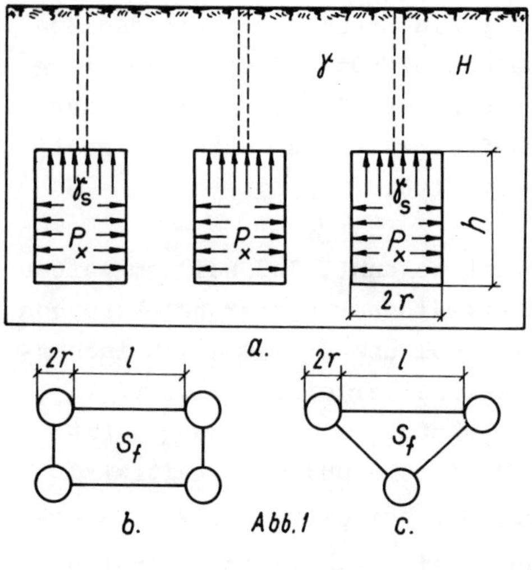

Abb.1

$$\sigma_1 = \frac{\gamma HS - \gamma_s H (S - S_f)}{S_f} + \gamma H ,$$

bestimmt, und (2)

der horizontaleDruck hängt von dem hydrostatischen Druck des Fluidums in der Kammer ab.

$$\sigma_3 = P_x = \gamma_s \left(H + \frac{h}{2}\right) , \qquad (3)$$

Darin bedeutet:

S	-die Gesteinsfläche, die durch einen Pfeiler gestützt wird
S_f	die Fläche des gestützten Pfeilers
H	Abstand von der Erdoberfläche
γ	Mitteldichte des Deckgebirges
h	Höhe der Kammer und des Pfeilers
γ_s	Dichte der gespeicherten Flüssigkeit

Zur Dimensionierung benutzt man das Festigkeitskriterium von Coulon-Moor: $\sigma_1 = \psi \sigma_3 + R_H$ (4) , wobei $\psi = \frac{1+\sin\rho}{1-\sin\rho}$ ist.

Aus der Gleichung (2) und der Abb.1 folgt, daß die Größe des vertikalen Drucks σ_1 von dem Anordnungsnetz der Kammerspeicherungen und dem Verhältnis zwischen den Abmessungen der Kammer und Pfeiler abhängt. Das Festigkeitskriterium (4) erfaßt die zusammengefaßte Widerstandsfähigkeit des Gesteines durch die monoaxiale Druckfestigkeit R_H und den Winkel der inneren Reibung ρ .Die Abhüllungskurve der Moorschen Hauptkreise ist eine Gerade, was eine ständige Erhöhung der Widerstandsfähigkeit des Gesteines mit Vergrößerung der Absolutwerte der Hauptspannungen σ_1 und σ_3 und des Verhältnisses $\frac{\sigma_3}{\sigma_1}$ voraussetzt. Die Ergebnisse aus der Untersuchung der Festigkeit verschiedener Gesteinsarten beim Raumdruckspannung von der Art $\sigma_1 > \sigma_3 = \sigma_2$ stimmen in meisten Fällen (für Hochdrücke) nicht mit den Kriterien (4) überein. Dies könnte mit den Umständen erklärt werden, daß ein Teil der Störungen bei den großen Tiefen den Hochdrücken entsprechen, unter dem Einfluß der hohen Werte der gespeicherten elastischen potentiellen Energie in den Gesteinen "geklebt" und der Einfluß der so genannten Innenreibung vermindert wird.

Tabelle 1

σ_1, kgs/cm^2	$\sigma_3 = P_x$	$m = \frac{\sigma_3}{\sigma_1}$	$\sigma_1 - 2\sigma_3 = A$	$\bar{A}$ mittlere	Art des Materials
1	2	3	4	5	6
1360	0	0	–		
2350	250	0,106	1850		Marmor
3150	500	0,158	2150	2120	
3505	685	0,193	2195		
5550	1650	0,289	2250		
590	100	0,170	390		Kohle
750	200	0,268	350		
980	300	0,306	380	367	
1150	400	0,348	350		
860	150	0,175	560		Mergel
1050	210	0,200	630	606	
1530	450	0,294	630		
1300	100	0,077	1100		künstliches
1420	200	0,141	1020		Material
1780	300	0,168	1180	1080	
1820	400	0,220	1020		

Nach den von den Autoren durchgeführten analytischen Untersuchungem wird die Gesteinsfestigkeit in einem ungleichen dreheaxialen Druckspannungszustand ($\sigma_1 > \sigma_2 = \sigma_3 = P_x$) durch die kritische Größe der zusätzlichen über dem hydrostatischen Druck vertikalen Spannung $\delta\sigma_S$ nach folgender Gleichung bestimmt:

$$\delta\sigma_S = (\sigma_1 - P_x) - P_x = A = const \quad (5)$$

oder

$$\sigma_1 - 2\sigma_3 = A = const \quad (6),$$

wobei A die Raumfestigkeit der Gesteine bei einem Verhältnis zwischen den Extremwerten der Hauptspannungen in den Grenzen

$$0 < m = \frac{\sigma_3}{\sigma_1} < 0,5 \quad (6a)$$

darstellt.

Die auf der Tabelle 1, Spalten 4 und 5 zusammengefassten Ergebnisse von den Untersuchungen verschiedener Autoren zeigen eine zulässige Befriedigung des Kriteriums (6). Die Gesteinszerstörung bei einem ungleichen dreheaxialen Druckspannungszustand ist nur dann in Kraft, wenn der vertikale Druck σ_1 mehr als zweimal den Seitendruck $\sigma_3 = P_x (\sigma_1 \geqq 2\sigma_3 + A)$ übertrifft. Die konstante Festigkeitscharakteristik A des entsprechenden Gesteines drückt die Formänderungsenergiequantität aus, erzeugt von

Tabelle 2

σ_1, Kbar	$\sigma_3 = P_x$ Kbar	$m = \frac{\sigma_3}{\sigma_1}$	$\sigma_1 - 2\sigma_3 = A$	$\bar{A}$	Gestein
1	2	3	4	5	6
8,25	1,0	0,121	6,25		Granit
11,70	2,0	0,172	7,70	6,96	
12,90	3,0	0,232	6,90		(Bulgaria)
14,90	5,0	0,336	4,90		
5,70	1,0	0,175	3,70	3,25	
6,80	2,0	0,284	2,80		Syenit
7,80	3,0	0,358	1,80		USSR
9,80*	5,0	0,501*	-0,20*	-	
12,80*	8,0	0,625*	-3,20*	-	

der zusätzlichen über dem hydrostatischen Druck vertikalen Spannung $\delta\sigma$ (5). Wie aus der Tabelle 2 ersichtlich ist (M.S.Wolarowicz, J.S.Tomaschewskaia,W.A.Budnikow, Mechanika gornih porod pri visokih davleniah, Nauka, Moskwa,1979) wächst in manchen Fällen (bezeichnet mit Sternchen) bei wesentlicher Vergrößerung des Seitenwiderstandes $P_x = \sigma_3$ die Größe des vertikalen Zerstörungsdrucks gering an. Dann widerspiegelt die zusätzliche Erhöhung des Druckes σ_1, beiKennzifferwerten $m = \frac{\sigma_3}{\sigma_1} \geq 0,5$, die so genannte Restfestigkeit der Gesteine und zeugt von der wesentlichen Zerstörung ihrer Verbindlichkeit bis zum Eintreten ihres endgültigen Zerfallens. Im allgemeinen ist die Raumfestigkeit des Gesteines A wesentlich größer als die Festigkeit bei einem monoaxialen Druck R_H [$A = (1,5 + 3) R_H$]. In diesem Fall führt die Dimensionierung der unterirdischen Kammerspeicherungen mit Berücksichtigung des Seitendrucks P_x der gespeicherten Flüssigkeit zu einer Verminderung der Pfeilerabmessungen und zu einem höheren Ausnutzungsgrad der entsprechenden unterirdischen Flächen Bei Einhaltung der bisher verwendeten Bezeichnungen (Gleichungen 1, 2,3) und in Übereinstimmung mit Abb. 1,b (Quadratnetz der Anordnung der Kammerspeicherungen) empfiehlt man, die Dimensionierungen nach folgenden Gleichungen durchgeführt zu werden:

-Größe der vertikalen Hauptspannung σ_1

$$\sigma_1 = \frac{\gamma H(1+\beta)^2 - \pi \gamma_s H r^2}{(1+\beta)^2 - \pi r^2} + \gamma h \quad (7)$$

wobei $\beta = \frac{l}{2r}$

- Größe der horizontalen Hauptspannung σ_3 nach Gleichung (3)

$$\sigma_3 = P_x = \gamma_s \left(H + \frac{h}{2}\right)$$

-Dimensionierungskriterium bei der dreiaxialen Gesteinsfestigkeit nach den Gleichungen (6) und (6a),

$$\frac{\gamma H(1+\beta)^2 - \pi \gamma_s H r^2}{} = 2\gamma_s\left(H + \frac{h}{2}\right) + \frac{\Delta \lambda}{n} \quad (8)$$

wobei λ ein Koeffizient ist, der den Einfluß der Pfeilerform bei einer Netzanordnung der Kammerdruck speicherungen erfaßt und n-Sicherheitskoeffizient, dessen Werte niedrig im Vergleich zu der Dimensionierung bei Berücksichtigung der Widerstandsfähigkeit des Gesteins bei einem monoaxialen Druck R_h zu erfassen sind. Dieses Verfahren sichert eine vollere Erfassung der Trag- und Widerstandsfähigkeit der Gesteine, entsprechend der Ausnutzungsdynamik der unterirdischen Kammerdruckspeicherungen.

FATIGUE CHARACTERISTICS OF ROCKSALT WITH REFERENCE TO UNDERGROUND STORAGE CAVERNS

Ermüdungseigenschaften des Steinsalzes im Hinblick auf Untergrundgasspeicherkavernen

Les caractéristiques de fatigue du sel gemme en liaison avec les cavités souterraines de stockage de gaz

E.K.S.PASSARIS
University of Newcastle upon Tyne, UK

SUMMARY:
The fatigue failure characteristics under low frequency (0.1 Hz) cyclic loading were determined for rocksalt with reference to the operations of underground storage caverns. Results show that rocksalt is significantly weakened by cyclic loading and under uniaxial compression the fatigue limit is 60% of the static strength. The effect of partial unloading and rest intervals as part of the operational procedures of storage caverns was also examined.

ZUSAMMENFASSUNG:
Die Brucheigenscheften unter Wechsellast des Steinsalzes wurden unter Niederfrequenz (0.1 Hz) an Dauerfestigkeitsproben im Hinblick auf Untergrundgasspeicherkavernen gemessen. Resultate zeigen dass Steinsalz bei zyklischer Belastung bedeutsam geschwächt oder ermüdet wird. Bei uniaxialer Kompression is die Dauerfestigkeit 60% der statischen Festigkeit. Die Wirkung der partiellen Entlastungen und der vorrübergehenden ruhezustände in Hinblick auf Speicherkavernen wurde geprüft.

RÉSUMÉ:
Les caractéristiques de la rupture du sel gemme ont été determinés par des essais de fatigue a basse fréquence (0.1 Hz). Les résultats montrent que le sel gemme diminue son comportement sous les effets de fatigue. Pour les essais en compression uniaxiale la contrainte de la rupture après fatigue n'est que de 60% de la contrainte de la rupture originale. Les effets du dechargement parcial et des intervales du repos en liaison avec les operations de cavités du stockage sont aussi examinés.

1 INTRODUCTION

The growth in the use of salt caverns for the storage of gas is becoming more and more impressive and research on this topic assumed a position of increased importance.

In determining the stability of any underground storage facility consideration is given to the effects of gravitational, and possibly tectonic, loading and of loading due to the pressure exerted by the stored gas.

The latter loading is expected to vary in magnitude according to whether gas is being injected into or withdrawn from the salt cavern, thus subjecting the rock mass surrounding the opening to a cyclic stress field. This type of cyclic loading often causes a material to fail at a stress level lower than its determined ultimate strength, a phenomenon called fatigue.

Cyclic fatigue on materials such as metals, polymers, concrete and soil has been investigated in the last decades in an extensive manner. In contrast the fatigue characteristics of rock materials have received a rather limited attention and research in the fatigue of rocksalt in particular is still in its infant stage.

The present paper reports the results of the second phase of a comprehensive experimental study of the fatigue characteristics of rocksalt in connection with the loading conditions related to the operation of gas storage caverns.

Fatigue studies are customarily conducted by subjecting the material under investigation to an application of stress conditions of lower magnitude than the equivalent ultimate strength determined from static tests. Experimental results from fatigue tests are commonly presented in the form of S–N curves where S is a percentage of the ultimate static strength and N is the number of cycles to cause failure at that stress level.

The main objective of the investigation is to provide a better understanding of the fatigue strength of rocksalt by establishing the S–N curves for various loading conditions corresponding to operating pressures of storage caverns. In addition the investigation aims in assessing the extent of any cummulative damage that might be exerted upon a salt storage cavern subjected to a cyclic storage operation.

During the working life of a storage cavern the cyclic changes of internal pressure are followed by corresponding variations of temperature on the cavern surface caused by the adiabatic compression and expansion of the stored gas. The effect of such temperature changes on the fatigue of rocksalt was not investigated during this phase of the experimental programme and all reported tests were conducted under constant ambient room temperature.

2 TESTING PROCEDURE

2.1 Salt Specimens

All tests were conducted on Triassic rocksalt from the Cheshire basin originating from the Meadow Bank Rock Salt Mine operated by Imperial Chemical Industries. Rocksalt in that area is generally restricted to two horizons within the Keuper marls (Poole & Whitman 1966) and shows a considerable variation in composition, colour and texture. The individual halite grains range in size from 2mm to 20mm being more typically large and they vary in shape from being anhedral in the holocrystalline rock to being subhedral or euhedral where mudstone content is higher.

Right-cylindrical specimens of 75mm diameter were cored out of a large salt block by diamond drilling in one direction only, thus reducing substantially the effect of sample variability. Each specimen was initially trimmed to 152mm length using a dry carborundum wheel and subsequently the ends were ground to better than 0.008mm of parallel and to the required length of 150mm.

2.2 Apparatus

The salt specimens were cyclic loaded in an electro-hydraulic Avery universal testing machine which is servo-controlled by an R.D.P. Servocon unit. The testing machine has a capacity of 250 kN which was considered suitable for the testing programme since the highest load required was 140 kN. The Servocon unit incorporates a programmable ramp and a servo-amplifier, the former enabling loading frequencies to be set and the latter employed for the setting of the maximum and minimum stress for each cycle.

The longitudinal strain of the specimens was monitored by means of a D5/500 linear variable differential transformer transducer manufactured by R.D.P. with a working range of ± 12.5mm.

2.3 Experimental Programme

During the first phase of the currently ongoing investigation into the behaviour of rocksalt under cyclic loading, thick-walled cylindrical specimens were subjected to biaxial stress field (Passaris 1972) by internal and external pressurization. The work reported here which forms the second part of the investigation is examining the fatigue characteristics of rocksalt when subjected to uniaxial compressive cyclic loading.

As part of the general requirements of the programme three different types of cyclic tests were conducted:

- uniaxial compressive tests with full unloading and loading stresses varying between 60% and 80% of the ultimate equivalent static strength of salt
- uniaxial compressive tests with partial unloading and loading conditions corresponding to the stresses occuring around gas storage caverns, and
- successive uniaxial compressive tests with full unloading and a loading stress of 70% of the ultimate static strength incorporating a variable rest interval.

It is considered as standard practice in fatigue tests to employ cyclic rates that simulate the expected frequencies occuring in the actual structure. However, if one had, for example, to simulate the loading frequency of a diurnal type gas storage cavern, a single test (depending on the stress level) could last anything between 15 days to perhaps several years. Practical limitations therefore have dictated a loading frequency of 0.1 Hz which allowed, for instance, the longest test in this programme to last no more than 47 hours.

The effect of loading frequency f on fatigue life of rocks seems to be the subject of conflicting interpretations from various workers and certainly further experimental work is required to determine fully its influence. Work by Burdine (1963) indicated that there seems to be no relation between N and f, while experimental evidence from Attewell & Farmer (1973) suggests that N and f are proportional. It was also implied by the latter authors that for a given energy availability the rock would more readily succumb to low-frequency dynamic stresses of higher amplitude than to high frequency dynamic stresses of low amplitude. Consequently since during this test programme the relation between the experimental stress amplitude and the stress amplitude occuring in an actual storage cavern was kept constant, one would expect a reduction in the influence of a different level of frequency.

A total of 54 salt specimens were tested of which five produced results which were rejected as being completely unrepresentative of the overall consistent behaviour of rocksalt. In specific, three failed prematurely due to the presence of extensive discontinuities in the salt specimen and two showed an unusually high strength subsequently linked to their extremely high percentage of marl content.

3 EXPERIMENTAL RESULTS

3.1 Uniaxial Compressive Static Tests

The first task of the experimental work of this phase was to determine the ultimate compressive static strength of the particular rocksalt under investigation.

A total of 13 specimens were tested in uniaxial compression employing various loading rates ranging between 0.5 MPa/min to 260 MPa/min. The experimental results are shown in Fig. 1 where the ultimate static strength in uniaxial compression is plotted against the logarithm of the rate of loading. The graph clearly indicates a peak strength at the loading rate of 3 MPa/min which contradicts the suggestion made by Dreyer (1972) whereby the strength increases monotonically with the rate of loading.

Eventually the value of 31.3 MPa being the mean value of the ultimate strength at the loading rate of 3 MPa/min was accepted as the static strength which could characterize the particular salt under investigation. The reasons behind such a decision were:

- The small variation of the strength at that level
- The fact that the 3 MPa/min rate coincides with the requirements suggested by the Commission of Standardisation of Laboratory and Field Tests of I.S.R.M.

and - That since at 3 MPa/min a peak strength was exhibited the calculation of testing stress levels as percentages of the static strength will be on the safe side when assessing the stability of a gas storage cavern.

3.2 Uniaxial Compressive Cycle Tests with Full Unloading

The stress level capable of causing the failure of rocks under cyclic loading usually decreases exponentially with the number of cycles, eventually reaching a near constant fatigue strength or endurance limit. Below this limit a rock material can be stressed an infinite number of times without failure.

The aim of the cyclic loading tests with full unloading was to determine this fatigue

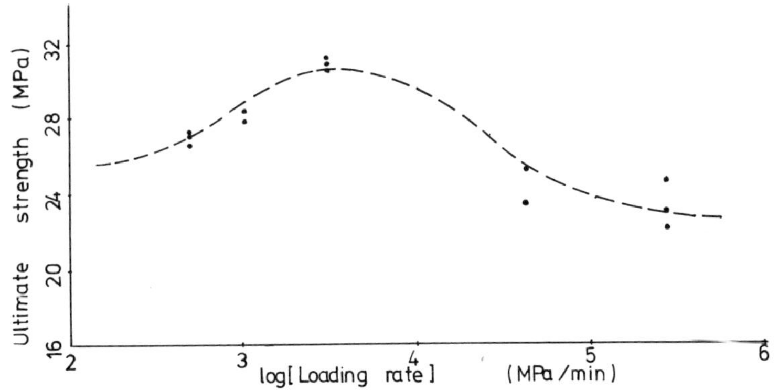

Fig. 1. The effect of loading rate on the uniaxial compressive strength of rocksalt.

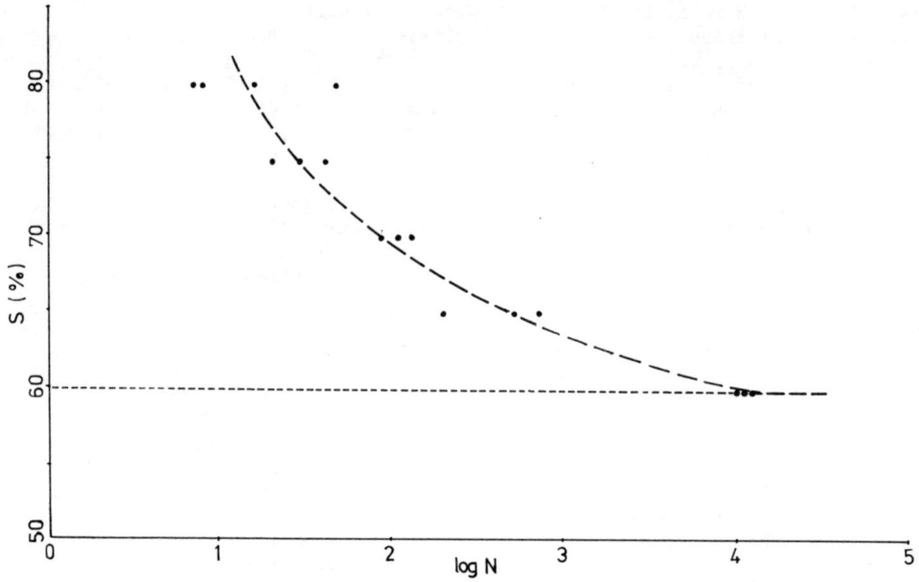

Fig. 2. Fatigue failure results for the test series with full unloading.

strength of rocksalt and for the purpose of this series of tests a limit of 10,000 cycles was introduced beyond which the test was terminated. This figure was employed as it was considered unlikely that an operating gas storage cavern would undergo such a large number of cycles in its working life.

Results from 16 specimens are plotted in the form of S – logN curve as shown in Fig. 2, indicating that a fatigue limit exists at a level of 60% of the ultimate strength, i.e. at a stress of 18.8 MPa.

Computer assisted curve-fitting techniques applied to the results of Fig. 2 indicated that the S-N curve can be expressed in the form of

$$S = 1.91 \times N^{-0.05}$$

This series of tests gave a set of overall consistent results yielding a reliable value for the fatigue strength of rocksalt. The shape of the S-N curve of rocksalt is similar to the type of S-N curves obtained by other workers (Hardy & Chugh 1970, Haimson & Kim 1972) for various geologic materials.

As stated earlier the longitudinal deformation of the specimens was monitored and in order to establish an appreciation of the change of modulus of the salt during the cyclic loading the maximum applied stress was divided by the maximum occuring strain and termed apparent stiffness. A typical change of the apparent stiffness is shown in Fig. 3 for S=0.65 where a sharp drop (caused most probably by closure of microcracks and microvoids) is followed by what seems a steady state region and by a third region with an accelerated decrease leading to failure. Similar reductions in the modulus during fatigue tests have been reported by other workers notably Attewell & Farmer (1973) for dolomite, Haimson & Kim (1972) for white Tennessee marble and Nordby (1958) for concrete.

3.3 Uniaxial Compressive Cyclic Tests with Partial Unloading

In order to render an experimentally determined "fatigue strength" meaningful it is important that it is related to particular loading conditions over a specific life of a structure. In the case of gas storage salt caverns it is often standard practice to assume the maximum and the minimum gas pressure as being equal to 70% and 30% respectively of the equivalent geostatic stress field (Dean 1978, Ottosen & Krenk 1979) which is normally taken as being of isotropic nature.

Employing the closed formed solution used by Hardy (1972) for underground storage caverns assuming an idealized spherical shape in an elastic medium the following loading conditions were calculated:

Depth of cavern (m)	Minimum stress (%)	Maximum stress (%)
540	32	55
575	34	59
650	39	65
690	41	70

pressure.

The above table was formed by assuming that the intermediate principal stress has no effect on the failure of rocksalt, which complies with the Mohr criterion. Furthermore since the angle of internal friction for rocksalt is very small (Vouille et al 1981) it was taken as being zero thus

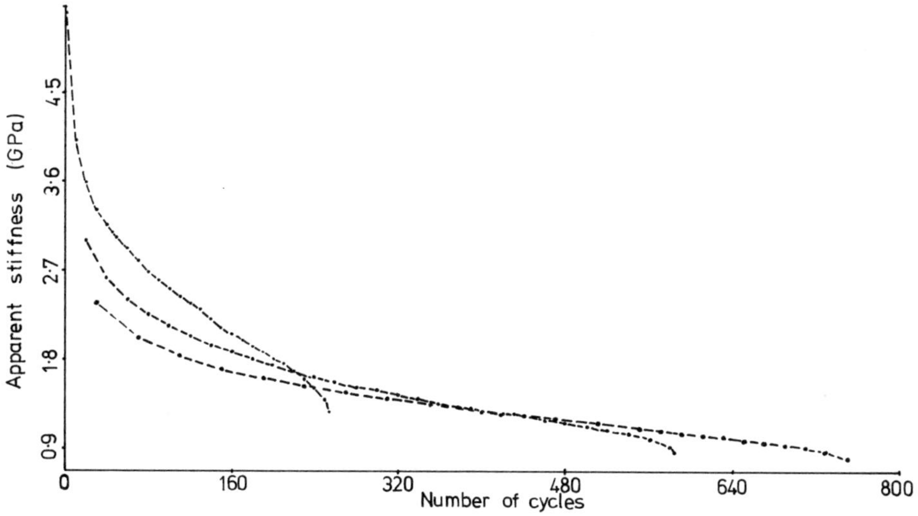

Fig. 3. Reduction of the apparent stiffness at S = 0.65 and full unloading.

where the minimum and maximum stresses are expressed as percentage of the static strength and correspond to an internal gas pressure in the cavern of 70% and 30% respectively of the equivalent geostatic introducing an extra factor of safety.

The S-logN curve for this series of tests exhibited similar trends to those obtained by the full unloading series. However in Fig. 4, where the results of 11 specimens

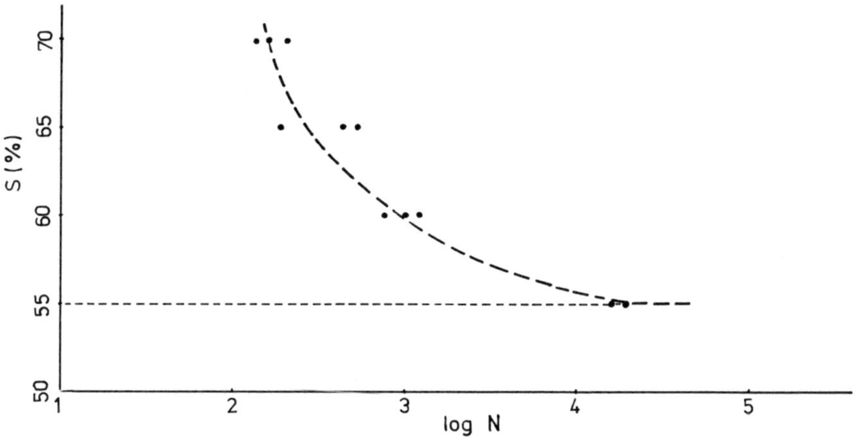

Fig. 4. Fatigue failure results for the test series with partial unloading.

are plotted, one can see that the endurance limit was reduced to 55% of the ultimate static strength. Furthermore by studying Fig. 5 where the apparent stiffness is plotted against N it is clear that the characteristic drop in the initial part of the curve is again present. In addition the third region is more clearly defined compared with the equivalent series incorporating full unloading. It appears therefore that the existance of a minimum non-zero load as opposed to full unloading amplifies the reduction of the apparent stiffness by reducing the strain amplitude thus increasing the number of cycles to failure in the third region.

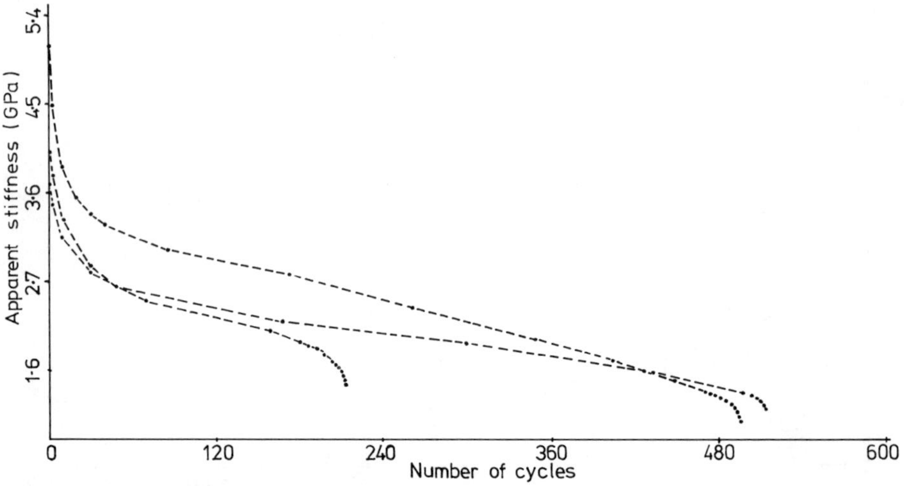

Fig. 5. Reduction of the apparent stiffness at S = 0.65 and partial unloading.

3.4 Uniaxial Compressive Cyclic Tests with Rest Intervals

These tests were performed with a maximum stress level of 70% of the ultimate static strength and full unloading of the specimens. The tests were interrupted after 75 cycles (which corresponds to half the fatigue life of rocksalt at that stress level) and rest periods were introduced prior ro cyclic re-testing to failure.

A total number of 9 specimens were tested in these series and the results are summarized in the following table.

Taking into account that for a maximum stress level of 70% of the ultimate static strength, the full unloading test series resulted in values of N ranging between 126 and 168 (the mean value is 149) the following comments can be made:

- Rest intervals between cycles are beneficial and increase the fatigue of rocksalt
- Short rest periods, i.e. of the order of $\frac{1}{2}$ hour seem to have little or no effect at all. While longer rest periods (ranging between 3 to 16 hours) clearly improve the endurance limit of rocksalt and the longer the rest period the better seems to be the recovery.

Length of rest period (hrs.)	Cycles to failure
$\frac{1}{2}$	163
$\frac{1}{2}$	104
$\frac{1}{2}$	108
3	284
3	155
3	170
16	377
16	240
16	117

The above observations appear to agree with the conclusions of Raithby & Whiffin (1968) who stated that the rest periods have a beneficial effect on the fatigue strength of concrete.

4 CONCLUSIONS

The relationship between the loading rate and the ultimate uniaxial compressive strength of rocksalt is interesting and merits further investigation. The choice of 31.3 MPa as the ultimate static strength used throught the fatigue tests is fully justified as it is on the safe side.

Despite the rather variable nature of rocksalt (Potts et al 1978) the results from the present experimental programme are consistent and therefore yield useful information on its fatigue characteristics and the related effect on the stability of underground gas storage salt caverns.

The fatigue experimental results for rocksalt are similar in nature to those obtained by previous workers for other rock materials and enable an accurate assessment of the fatigue strength to be made. The fatigue limit of rocksalt is 60% of the ultimate static strength in uniaxial compression with full unloading at the end of each cycle (tested to 10,000 cycles).

The introduction of a partial unloading, at the end of each cycle, reduces the fatigue limit of rocksalt to only 55% of its ultimate static strength. Consequently the fact that gas storage caverns are never pressurized to the full geostatic stress is an indication that the endurance limit deduced by fatigue tests with full unloading cannot be used directly in assessing the stability of a storage cavern.

Finally it was shown that rest intervals have a beneficial effect on the fatigue strength of rocksalt which appears to be proportional to the length of the rest period. This indicates that for a given number of storage cycles, gas storage caverns of diurnal type are more prone to fatigue failure compared with the storage caverns used for seasonal demands.

5 REFERENCES

Attewell, P.B. & I.W. Farmer 1973, Fatigue behaviour of rock, J.Rock Mech. Min. Sc. 10:1 - 9.

Burdine, N.T. 1963, Rock failure under dynamic loading conditions, J. Soc. Petrol. Engrs. 3(1): 1 - 8.

Dean, F. 1978, Salt cavity storage, Gas Engng. and Management Sept. 291-305

Dreyer, W. 1972, The science of rock mechanics. Clausthal, Trans Tech publications.

Haimson, B.C. & C.M. Kim 1972, Mechanical behaviour of rock under cyclic fatigue, Proc. 13th Symp. Rock Mechanics, ASCE: 845 - 864.

Hardy, H.R. Jr. 1972, A study to evaluate the stability of underground gas storage reservoirs. Arlington, Virginia, Am. Gas Ass.

Hardy, H.R. Jr. & Y.P. Chugh 1970, Failure of geologic materials under low-cyclic fatigue, Proc. 6th Symp. Rock Mechanics, Montreal.

Nordby, G.M. 1958, Fatigue of concrete - a review of work, J. Amer. Concr. Inst. 30(2): 191 - 219.

Ottosen, N.S, & S. Krenk 1979, Non-linear analysis of cavities in rock salt, Int. J. of Rock Mechanics & Min. Sc. & Geomech Abstracts 19 (4):245 - 252.

Passaris, E.K.S. 1972, Fatigue characteristics of rocksalt concentric bored cylinders, M.Sc. Dissert. Univ. of Newcastle upon Tyne.

Poole, E.G. and A. J. Whitman 1966, The geology of the country around Nantwich and Whitchurch, Geol. Surv. Mem. 122.

Potts, E.L.J., T.W.Thompson, E.K.S. Passaris & S.T. Horseman 1978, An investigation into underground gas storage in brine well cavities, 5th Symp. Salt, Hamburg:105-123.

EXPERIMENTAL STUDY OF ROCKSALT FOR COMPRESSED AIR ENERGY STORAGE

Versuchsstudie an Steinsalz zur Druckluft-Energiespeicherung

Expérimentation du sel gemme pour l'utilisation de l'air comprimé pour le stockage d'énergie

R.L.THOMS & R.M.GEHLE
Louisiana State University, Baton Rouge, USA

SUMMARY:
A combined laboratory and field test program was performed for long-term cyclic load effects on rock salt. Test conditions were selected to simulate compressed air energy storage (CAES) effects on salt surrounding pressurized caverns. Data are presented and discussed for permeability, mechanical response, and hydraulic fracturing of salt related to CAES effects.

ZUSAMMENFASSUNG:
Im Labor und an Ort wurde eine zweifache Teststüdie unternommen, um langfristige Wirkungen der zyklischen Last auf Steinsalz festzustellen. Testverhältnisse wurden ausgewählt, um die Wirkungen von Druckluft-Energielagerung (CAES, d.h. "compressed air energy storage") auf Druckhölhlen umgebendes Salz zu simulieren. Daten werden vorgelegt und diskuttiert in Bezug auf Permeabilität, mechanische Reaktion und hydraulische Zersplitterung in Beziehung mit CAES-Wirkungen.

RESUME:
Un programme expérimental d'études en laboratoire et sur le terrain a été réalisé afin d'analyser les effets à long terme de la pression cyclique sur le sel gemme. Les conditions des experiénces ont été déterminées de facon à simuler les effets de l'utilization de l'air comprimé pour le stockage d'énergie (UASCE) sur le sel gemme se trouvant autour de cavités pressurisées. Les données sont présentées et analysées en fonction de la perméabilité de l'effet mécanique, et de la fracturation hydraulique du sel, liés aux effets de l'UACSE.

1. INTRODUCTION

1.1 Background of compressed air energy storage (CAES) in salt.

Rock salt frequently occurs naturally in a relatively homogeneous and impermeable type of rock formation. Thus formations of both dome and bedded salt have been used for a number of decades as a geological media for storage (geostorage) of gas and liquid hydrocarbons.

The concept of using underground openings in salt for energy storage in the form of compressed air apparently dates back to the late 19th century, according to Aufricht and Howard (1961), as compressed air storage was attempted in a mine near Heilbronn in Germany in 1899. Almost eighty years later the first CAES facility became operational near Huntorf in the Federal Republic of Germany (FRG), and reportedly has been highly successful (Herbst, 1981). This well known facility utilizes two caverns in the underlying Huntorf salt dome as CAES reservoirs (Quast, 1981).

1.2 Test program at Louisiana State University (LSU) for CAES in salt.

The general objectives of the LSU test program were to provide a data base for mechanical response of rock salt under conditions similar to CAES applications, and to formulate stability criteria for CAES reservoirs (caverns) in U.S. salt formations. Results from this program, when completed, should permit efficient design and utilization of CAES caverns in salt over long time periods. This paper deals mainly with data from the test program, and does not include stability criteria which will be presented in a later report.

From the beginning, the LSU test program was designed to include two phases: (1) laboratory tests specialized for CAES, and (2) in situ tests in salt mines. Limited numerical modeling also was performed to couple the two test phases, and for test planning and data analysis. Both test phases will be outlined in this paper, and a summary section will include some general conclusions based on both phases of the CAES test program for salt.

2. LABORATORY TESTS

2.1 Design of laboratory test plan

The novel consideration for CAES reservoirs is the long-term cyclic character of pressure and thermal loadings on the rock salt surrounding the caverns (Thoms and Gehle, 1981a). An extensive amount of literature exists for salt subjected to effects of monotonic loading followed by long-term creep at medium and elevated temperatures. In some cases, relatively few cycles of loading and unloading were performed as part of the initial phases of testing.

The number of parameters that can be varied are significant when simulating time dependent effects for salt caverns subjected only to static loads. Assessing cyclic pressure and thermal load effects on salt for a wide range of conditions over long periods with only one or two general purpose test machines would present a lifetime task. Thus a laboratory was designed and developed with test capabilities particularly applicable to CAES caverns in salt.

To accumulate adequate data from long-term tests, parallel testing in time was essential. Accordingly, six specialized and relatively simple test units were assembled for long-term testing, and one small general purpose test machine was purchased for quick index tests and calibration of field instrumentation.

The long-term test units consisted of four basic elements as indicated in the schematic of Fig. 1: (1) load frame, (2) triaxial (Von Karman) cell and platens, (3) a pair of air-to-oil pressure intensifiers, and, (4) a control unit for two channels of inlet air to the pressure intensifiers. A previous design by Obert (1963) was used as the basis for design of the triaxial cells and selection of a commercially available and relatively inexpensive concrete test machine for the load frames. Pressure intensifiers were also purchased, however the controls unit was designed and fabricated at LSU.

The assembled test units can be used for long-term triaxial testing of 4 x 8 in. (100 x 200 mm) diameter x length cylinders with lateral and axial applied stresses up to

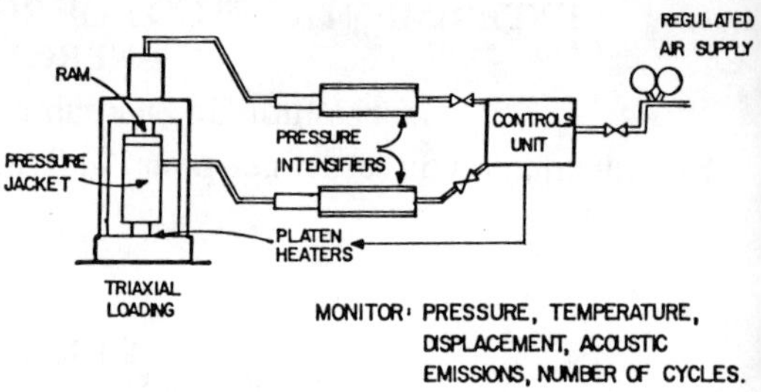

Figure 1. Schematic of long-term test unit

5,000 and 11,250 psi (34.5 and 77.6 MPa) respectively. Constant elevated temperatures up to around 215°F (100°C) also can be applied. Applied pressures and axial displacements of specimens versus time are monitored with electronic devices and recorded on a central data logger. Acoustic emissions from loaded specimens are monitored intermittently or during periods of special interest with an "Acoustic Emissions Technology (AET), Pioneer 5000" unit.

The capacities of the long-term units are adequate for testing salt corresponding to control points around CAES caverns ranging in depth to around 5000 ft (1524 m). Load paths are stress controlled during testing.

A small, constant strain machine manufactured by "Geotest" was purchased for performing index tests. The index tests consisted of the conventional indirect tension or Brazilian test (Jaeger and Cook, p. 169, 1979).

The basic philosophy of testing salt for CAES was to perform a relatively large number of simple index tests, and then progressively fewer of the more complicated (and difficult) tests, but with adequate numbers of tests to span the environment around CAES caverns. Salt from at least four sources was to be subjected to the same suite of tests so that any differences due to salt origin could be studied.

2.2 Test matrix and some typical results

Table 1 is the matrix of uniaxial and triaxial tests performed on salt from a typical source. Each column represents a type of test, with complexity of tests increasing by column from left to right. The time sequence of load phases for each type of test progresses from top to bottom within each column. Load conditions for specimens are indicated by numbers within parenthesis, with upper and lower numbers representing axial and lateral stresses (psi) respectively. The sequence of load phases was selected to subject salt specimens to increasingly strenuous environments, and to attempt to separate cyclic and elevated temperature

Table 1. Matrix of tests for each source of salt.

	Uniaxial Compression	Triaxial Compression	Triaxial Extension
Creep	$\binom{1000}{0}$	$\binom{1500}{500}$	$\binom{750}{2500}$
	$\binom{2000}{0}$	$\binom{3500}{1500}$	$\binom{1000}{3500}$
Cyclic	$\binom{500\text{-}1000}{0}$	$\binom{1000\text{-}5000}{0\text{-}500}$	$\binom{450\text{-}750}{2250\text{-}2500}$
	$\binom{1000\text{-}2000}{0}$	$\binom{3000\text{-}3500}{1000\text{-}1500}$	$\binom{750\text{-}1000}{3000\text{-}3500}$
Cyclic/ Thermal	(100-180)	(100-180)	(80-180)
	(100-180)	(100-180)	(80-180)

effects from well known static creep effects. Thus a typical long-term test incorporated an initial short-term loading to desired load environment, followed by 200-300 hours of static load application, then cyclic load application for similar time periods, followed by application of cyclic loads at elevated temperatures. The test was concluded when either: (1) the specimen failed by separation, or (2) excessive specimen deformation exceeded the capacity of the test cell. In addition to the tests listed in Table 1, 3 Brazilian "quick" index tests were performed on specimens from each source of salt.

From the laboratory test program certain conclusions were reached relative to effects of different types of tests. That is, test data tended to range from "scattered" to more "closely grouped" as types of tests used progressed from Brazilian, uniaxial compression, triaxial extension, and through the triaxial compression tests. Triaxial extension tests were more difficult to perform than other test types, however they were considered the most significant for CAES caverns.

Figures 2 through 5 represent data collected from a suite of index Brazilian tests; an early uniaxial cyclic test (Thoms, Nathany, and Gehle, 1980), and a typical long-term triaxial extension test. Sources of salt and conditions of loading are given in the illustrations.

From Fig. 2 it can be noted that salt from the Huntorf dome yielded closely grouped data that was similar in value to U.S. dome salt. The Red Lake salt was from a deposit in northwestern Arizona.

With reference to Figs. 3-5, it appears that cyclic pressure loads with small amplitudes relative to mean value had little effect on the general trend of salt specimen behavior. The ratios of load cycle amplitude to mean value used in the tests were estimated as reasonable for CAES effects on the basis of a simplified finite element analysis of a "typical" cavern subjected to operating pressures. The behavior of salt under such conditions may be characterized as exhibiting a time dependent "band" of displacement response similar to static creep response, with the displacement response band-width dependent upon the amplitude of applied cyclic pressure loading.

Data for overtest conditions are still not complete, however the triaxial extension tests with axial and lateral stresses of 1000 and 3500 psi (6.9 and 24.1 MPa) respectively have resulted in a number of early failures of specimens. Also, oil leakage through the membranes confining the specimens has been difficult to stop under these load environments.

2.3 Permeability tests.

Laboratory permeability tests on rock salt have been reported previously by Aufricht and Howard (1961) and by Sutherland and Cave (1980). They observed that the permeability of rock salt decreased with confining pressure, and that it also decreased with cyclic load applications.

Apparatus were designed for this study that allowed permeability testing of rock salt specimens in the same pressure cells used for mechanical response tests. Figure 6 is a schematic of the modified cell and enclosed 4 x 4 in. (100 x 100 mm) diameter x length salt specimen. Specimens were tested with constant flow rate of air under triaxial compression conditions. Air pressure values were monitored upstream and downstream of the specimens, along with flow rate, and used to calculate permeability by (Scheidegger, p. 93, 1960),

$$q = -k/\mu \, (p_u^2 - p_d^2) \, / \, (2 \, p_u \, L) \qquad 2.3.1$$

where q = flow monitored downstream of the specimen

k = permeability

μ = dynamic viscosity of air

p_u = pressure upstream

p_d = pressure downstream

L = length of specimen

Figure 7 displays some early results obtained with the laboratory steady-flow apparatus. Test results were consistent with findings of other investigators; and more results will be presented in the final report for this study. With increasing confining pressures the permeability of specimens rapidly decreased to immeasurably small values using the steady-flow technique.

Methods employing the transient form of the flow equation have been used for measurements of permeability for "tight" rocks.

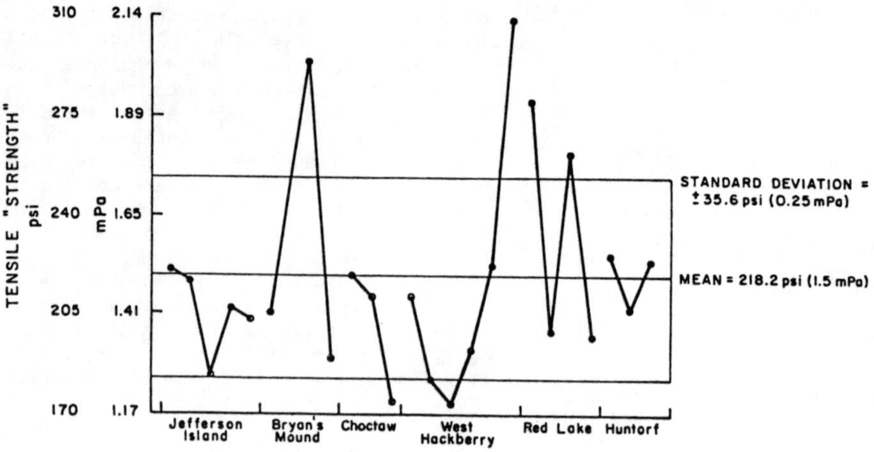

Figure 2. Brazilian test results for salt from different sources.

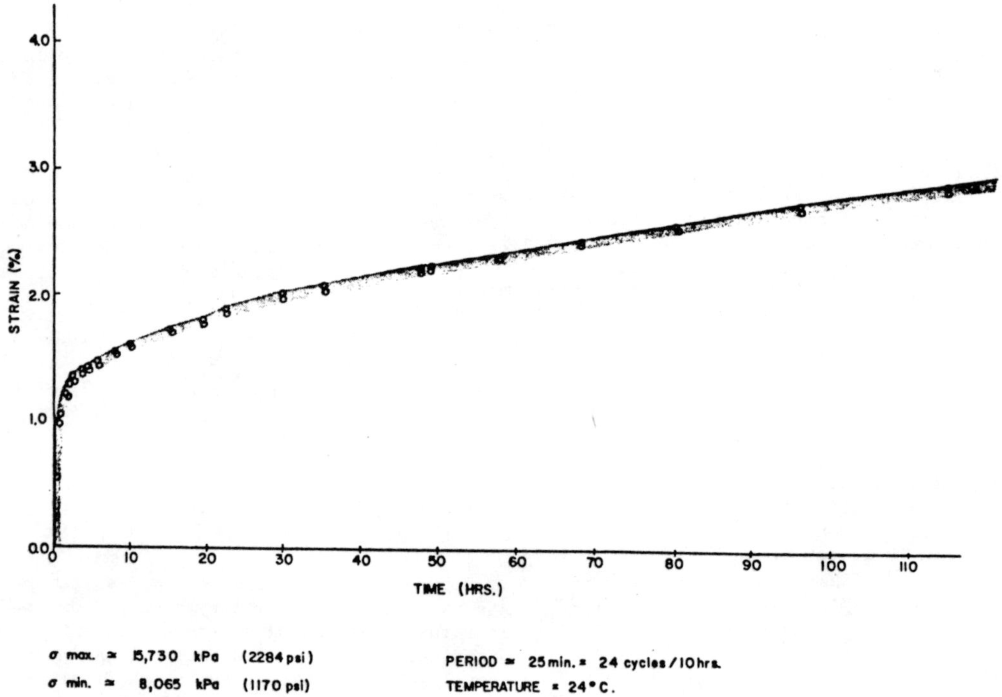

Figure 3. Uniaxial cyclic test on Avery Island dome salt.

A related method has been outlined for the CAES program by numerical (finite difference) solution of the quasi-linear equation governing transient gas flow (Scheidegger, p. 105, 1960),

$$k \frac{\partial^2 (p)^2}{\partial x^2} = c \frac{\partial p}{\partial t} \qquad 2.3.2$$

where p = applied pressure
k = permeability measure
c = effective porosity measure

The method employs a known initial volume (reservoir) of air and applied pressure increment along with numerical solutions (family of curves) of eq. 2.3.2. A monitored pressure decay curve can be fitted to the most similar curve of the numerical solution to obtain a measure of k/c. Separation of k and c requires additional work if a semi-infinite body is used as a specimen, but can be achieved in principle by optical methods if necessary.

Specimen 2 of Fig. 7 was subjected to cyclically applied hydrostatic confining pressures following the steady-flow test. Pressure values were cycled between approximately 1000 and 1500 psi (6.9 and 10.3 MPa), and air flow rates greater than 2 cc/min no longer could be detected after a few (less than ten) cycles. This behavior was consistent with reports by other workers on cyclic load effects on rock salt permeability.

It was noted that permeability values obtained in the laboratory for rock salt were strongly dependent on specimen history. Specimen 2 of Fig. 7 was obtained by the authors by coring with diamond bit in an area of the Jefferson Island mine where floor heave was present. Specimen 1 represents salt in an area where floor heave was not present, however it can be noted that when confining pressures were increased to approximately 1500 psi (10.3 MPa), permeability values for both specimens became essentially the same.

The apparent differences in rock salt permeability illustrated to the authors that laboratory test values of permeability of rock salt should be considered seriously only if the complete history of the specimens are known. Otherwise, fictitiously high values of permeability may be obtained which are not representative of the rock salt mass in an undisturbed confined state. This is particularly true for some types of rock salt that tend to disaggregate readily.

3. IN SITU TESTS

3.1 Design and development of in situ test plans in Jefferson Island mine.

The initial in situ test plan included drilling vertical 4 in. (100 mm) diameter holes vertically into the floor of the Jefferson Island (JI) salt mine, and subjecting the holes to cyclic effective air pressures based on CAES conditions. However the presence of horizontal partings near the floor surface and in the vicinity of the test site caused this concept to be abandoned. Subsequently test holes were slant drilled beneath pillars at angles dipping approximately 45° below the horizontal.

Figure 8 depicts the second in situ test hole configuration. With this configuration the salt around the test holes was essentially undisturbed and confined by the pillar above. Eight holes of 2 in. (50 mm) diameter were drilled approximately parallel to depths of 20 ft (6.1 m) with spacing ranging from 12 to 36 in. (305 to 914 mm). Details of the preparation of the test holes by casing and sealing with standard pipe have been presented previously by Thoms and Gehle (1981a).

Qualitative cross-borehole permeability tests were performed with freon gas, following the work of Aufricht and Howard (1961), who apparently initially performed such tests in salt mines. No detectable amounts of freon flowed through the confined salt between the slant test holes, which contrasted with Aufricht and Howard's findings of significant permeability around holes drilled horizontally into the relatively unconfined salt of pillar faces. In both studies, the test holes were drilled dry to avoid possible glazing and artificial reduction in salt permeability caused by the use of brine as a drilling fluid.

A preliminary air pressurization boreholes test also was performed at the Jefferson Island mine site to check instrument performance; however, the test site was lost with the inundation of the mine on Nov. 20, 1980 (Mine Safety and Health Administration report 1981).

3.2 Development of site and performance of tests in Cote Blanche mine.

A new test site was developed in the Cote Blanche salt mine in south Louisiana with the kind consent and assistance of the mine operators, Domtar Chemical, Ltd. Twelve test holes of 2.5 in. (63.5 mm) diameter were drilled and prepared as depicted in Fig. 8. The indicated borehole caliper device was designed by Charles Powell, consultant; and was installed downhole at a depth of approximately 12 ft (3.7 m). Thereby diametric displacements of the hole in the vertical plane were monitored as tests proceeded. Acoustic emissions (AE)

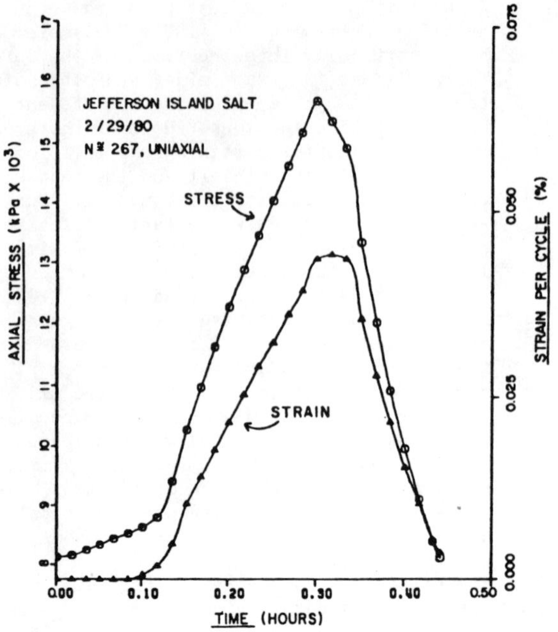

Figure 4. Typical cycle of uniaxial test.

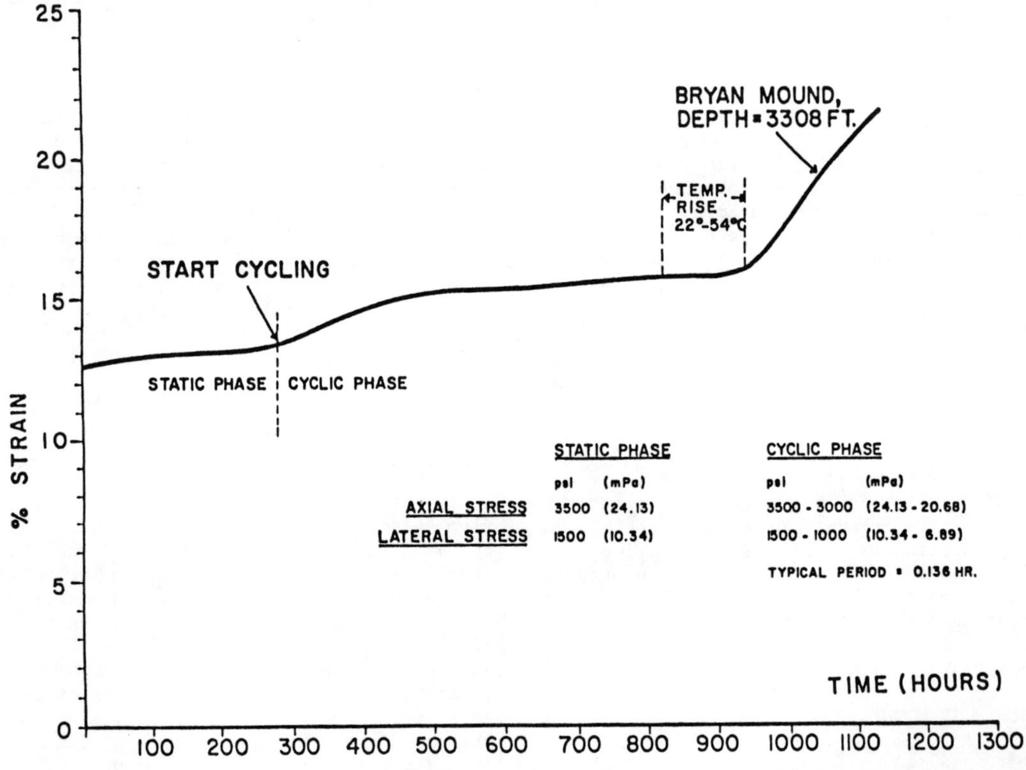

Figure 5. Long-term triaxial extension test with cyclic loads.

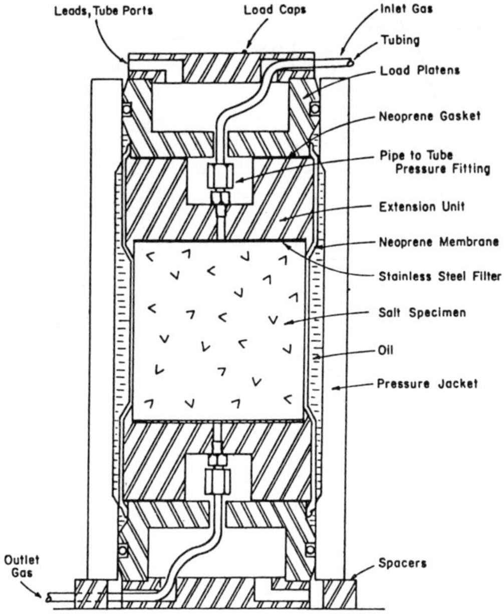

Figure 6. Triaxial cell for permeability tests.

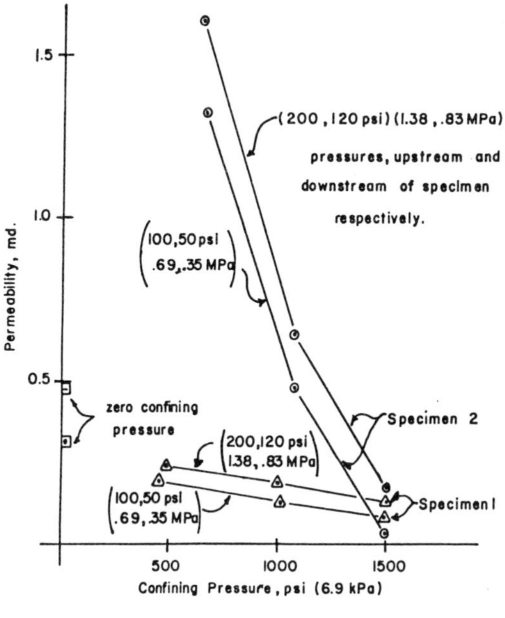

Figure 7. Permeability of dome rock salt.

also were monitored and recorded, along with magnitude of applied hole pressure.

Figure 9 depicts test results obtained from a static/cyclic air pressurization test of one of the boreholes at the Cote Blanche (CB) site. These data indicate the rock around the pressurized hole responded in a way generally similar to laboratory specimens. That is, the long-term behavior was dominated by mean value of applied pressure and was similar to creep of rock salt under static constant load effects. The short-term response was essentially linear to cyclically applied pressures. More detailed analyses of the salt behavior have been presented recently by Thoms and Gehle (1981b).

The shear deformation modulus, G, of the salt under monotonically increasing and cyclic pressures was estimated from the data with the elastic solution for a pressurized borehole. Values obtained for the monotonic and cyclic loading phases respectively were $G = 1.9$ to 2.0×10^6 psi (13 to 13.8 GPa), and $G = 3.5$ to 4.4×10^6 psi (24 to 30 GPa). Values from the cyclic phase thus were larger than previously reported values by a factor of 2 to an order of magnitude. Investigations of these apparently excessive values of deformation modulus are not complete; and possible effects such as instrument cable lengths, recalibration, and lack of fit of the caliper and deformed borehole are still under study at this time.

A series of high pressure tests, with oil as the pressurizing fluid for safety reasons, also was performed at the Cote Blanche site (Gehle and Thoms, 1981). A three-hole configuration and instrumentation were used as indicated schematically in Figs. 10 and 11. With this arrangement it was possible to apply controlled high pressured oil (up to 5000 psi, 34.5 MPa) to the central hole, and monitor diametric displacements and acoustic emissions via the neighboring holes. Test plans included hydro-fracing the three-hole system, and then studying its post-fractured behavior.

Figure 12 depicts data from the test when the first salt hydro-fracing was achieved. These data also were reported previously by Gehle and Thoms (1981). The salt around the central borehole apparently first fractured at a stress slightly less than 2500 psi (17.2 MPa). Significant AE was not observed prior to this pressure level, but became very obvious at the time of fracture and for some time thereafter. Four additional pressurizations were applied, with peak values of 2200-2300 psi (15-16 MPa) attained. Around 5 weeks later, the test hole was again pressurized twice to values ranging around 2300 psi (16 MPa) by vigorous

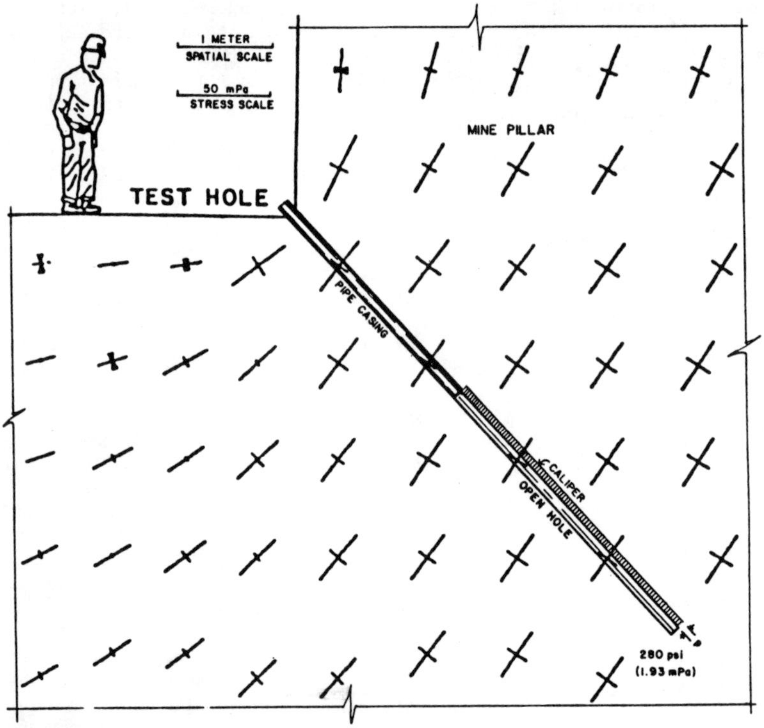

Figure 8. Typical borehole for in situ tests.

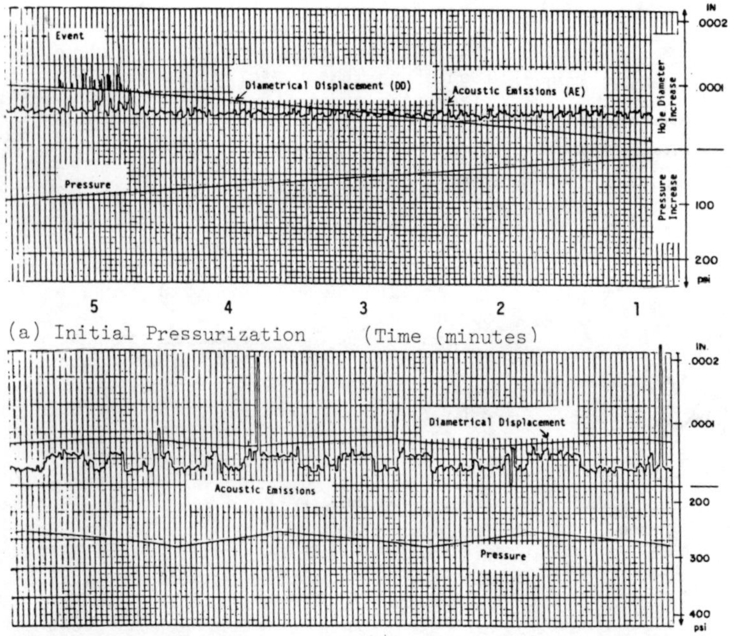

(b) Cyclic Pressurization (Time (minutes)

Figure 9. Air pressurization of borehole in salt mine.

pumping of oil, however on a final third pressure test only 2100 psi (14.5 MPa) oil pressure could be attained.

Three months later, a final pressurization test was performed on the previously fractured three-hole system. The central hole was subjected to cyclic pressures, with minimum and maximum values ranging in four major test stages from: (1) 1400 to 1950 psi (9.7 to 13.4 MPa), (2) 1400 to 1750 psi (9.7 to 12.1 MPa), (3) 1400 to 1700 psi (9.7 to 11.7 MPa), and (4) 1150 to 1500 psi (7.9 to 10.3 MPa). The test was performed over a time period of 4 hours, with the second stage making up the major part of the test.

The main objective of the test was to determine possible leakage through the previously fractured salt for applied cyclic pressure less than the apparent hydro-fracing values. In each of the four test stages, oil flow into the test hole had to be increased with time to maintain the desired peak pressure. At the end of the 4 hours of cyclic loading, the maximum pressure that could be achieved by vigorous oil pumping was 1650 psi (11.4 MPa), which was significantly less than the 1950 psi (13.4 MPa) obtained at the beginning. These results implied a progressive deterioration of the pressure retaining capacity of the salt around the hole due to cyclic loads.

3.3 Estimates of in situ stress by hydraulic fracturing

Estimates can be made of the magnitude of the in situ stress state based on the combination of hole pressure required for fracture and a finite element method (FEM) analysis of relative magnitudes of stress components.

With references to Figs. 8 and 10, the central pressurized hole was assumed to be in a state of plane (y,z) strain, and unaffected by its neighboring holes. For long-term effects, the salt was assumed to be incompressible, i.e., $\nu = 0.5$, and therefore

$$\sigma_x = 0.5\ (\sigma_y + \sigma_z) \qquad 3.3.1$$

From the FEM analysis of Fig. 8 (Gehle, 1980), the ratio of $\sigma y/\sigma z = 2.2$. Note that relative magnitudes of stress were employed; magnitude of σy were estimated from pressure required for fracture.

Using an elastic solution from Jaeger and Cook, p. 389, (1979), and referring to Fig. 10, the fracture will occur in the salt in the x,y plane rather than in the z,x plane provided

$$(\sigma_z+\nu(3\sigma_y-\sigma_x)) < (3\sigma_y-\sigma_x) \qquad 3.3.2$$

Using the plane strain assumption and FEM results previously cited yields,

$$1.02\sigma_y < 2.27\sigma_y \qquad 3.3.3$$

where $\nu = 0.25$ has been employed because of the short-term character of the applied fracturing pressure. The result 3.3.3 implies that salt will fracture in the x,y plane normal to the hole axis. Also, by Jaeger and Cook (1979), fracture initiates for

$$p \geq T + (\sigma_z + \nu(3\sigma_y-\sigma_x)) \qquad 3.3.4$$

where p = fracture pressure in hole
T = tensile strength of salt

From laboratory indirect tension (Brazilian) tests, a reasonable value for T = 220 psi (1.5 MPa), and by previously described mine tests, p = 2500 psi (17.2 MPa). Employing these data and assumptions with eq. 3.3.4 yields,

$$\sigma_y = (2500-220)/1.02 = 2235 \text{ psi } (15.4 \text{ MPa}) \qquad 3.3.5$$

The value of σ_y estimated here is approximately one half the magnitude obtained by the FEM as depicted in Fig. 8. Several explanations are possible, for example; (1) the overburden effects have been partially transferred from the site pillar to the mine abutment zone which is nearby, (2) the term $(3\sigma_y-\sigma_x)$ is excessive in eq. 3.3.4 because it is derived from an elastic solution for stress concentration which is unlikely in plastic rock salt, and (3) the neighboring holes weakened the salt around the central hole and caused it to fail prematurely.

A more nearly ideal hydro-facing test in rock salt would be conducted in a single hole at greater depth, and would employ a continuous monitor of fluid flow rate into the hole for crack propagation study. As noted by Jaeger and Cook (1979), crack propagation, unlike initiation, is independent of material properties and depends only upon the in situ stress state.

3.3. In situ permeability studies

As noted previously, qualitative permeability tests employing possible cross-borehole flow of freon gas were performed in situ. These tests were performed both in the Jefferson Island and Cote Blanche mines in holes drilled horizontally, and in holes drilled slanting beneath pillars. In both mines, significant gas flow was found between holes drilled horizontally to depths of 10 to 15 ft (3 to 4.5 m) into pillar

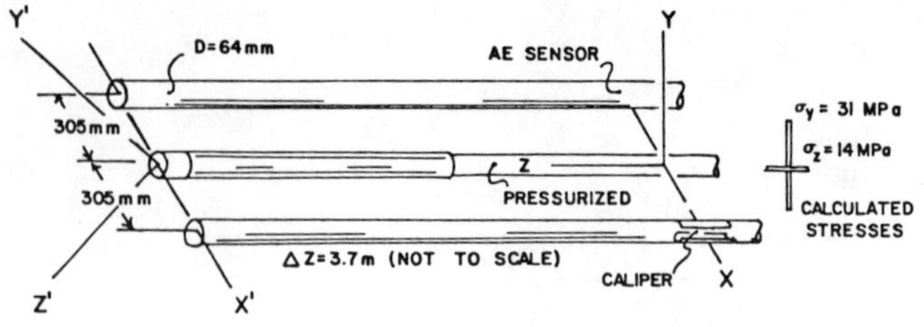

Figure 10. Three-hole configuration for high-pressure oil tests.

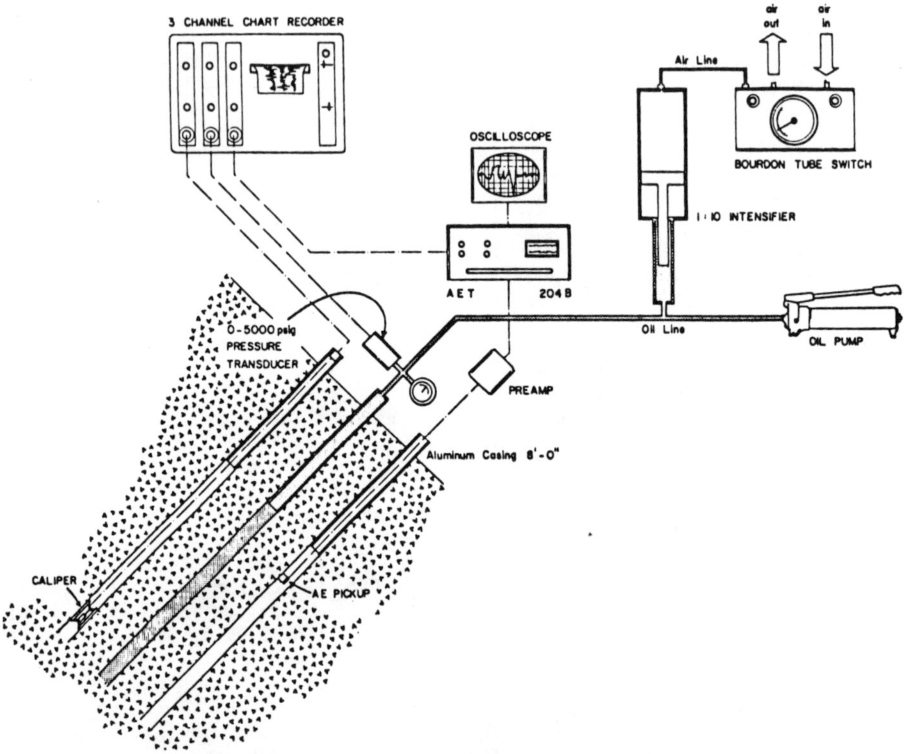

Figure 11. Instrumentation and apparatus for high-pressure oil tests.

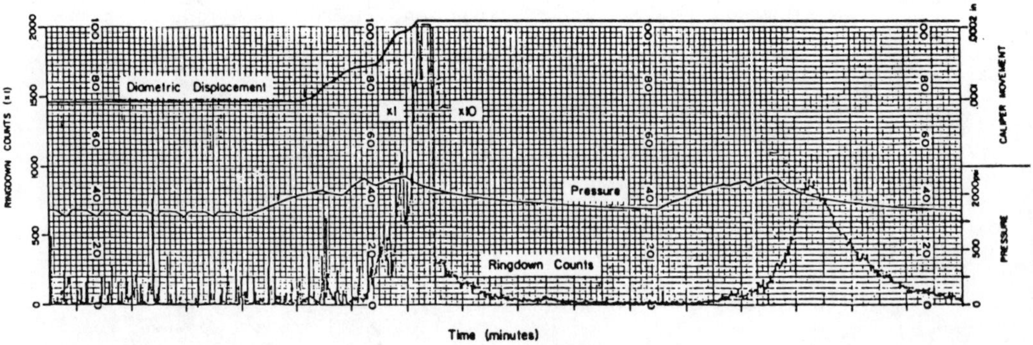

Figure 12. Hydro-fracing data for boreholes in salt.

faces where the salt was relatively unconfined. By contrast, no gas flow could be detected between slant holes with spacing of approximately 12 in. (305 mm) in the Jefferson Island mine. A preliminary test of this type also was performed at the Cote Blanche mine, but will be repeated for a longer time period (4 hours) before this study is concluded.

Quantitative in situ permeability tests in rock salt are more difficult to perform. An exact solution employing bipolar coordinates was derived for cross-borehole flow, assuming gas flow rates could be monitored (Gipson and Thoms, 1981). However, the qualitative test indicated cross-borehole flow rates in confined salt would not be adequate for practical applications.

A transient method was outlined which employed a numerical solution for the radial form of eq. 2.3.2 and a borehole "straddle packer". An initial-design straddle was developed and carried into the Cote Blanche mine for tests in boreholes of 2¼ in. (57 mm) diameter and 60 ft (18.3 m) depth in the floor. Such boreholes are routinely drilled for blasting while bench mining in the Cote Blanche mine. They are available for tests only for limited time periods between drilling and filling with explosives, and thus a reasonably fast permeability test is essential.

The initial-design straddle packer did not perform satisfactorily in the described holes because of gas (air) leakage between the rubber sleeves and the borehole wall. The walls displayed a helical spiral relief pattern due to the action of the two-blade "drag bit" used in drilling, and the packer sleeves apparently were not sufficiently compliant to seal against such a surface. A second-generation packer has been designed which uses materials based on successful packers developed by other workers (Warne, et al. 1979), however the limited time period remaining in this study may preclude its implementation.

4. SUMMARY AND CONCLUSIONS

The planning, development, and implementation of a test program for compressed air energy storage has been described. Conclusions reached from this study now follow.

Laboratory and in situ cyclic tests yielded generally consistent qualitative results, with long-term creep behavior related to mean values of load, and short-term displacements following applied cyclic pressures in an approximately linear response.

Rock salt appears relatively insensitive to small amplitude cyclic pressure loads within ranges anticipated for CAES applications. This includes caverns to depths of around 3000 ft (900 m). Elevated temperatures remain the major influence in accelerating salt creep. It thus appears reasonable to estimate CAES cavern behavior under regular operating conditions on the basis of data obtained from static creep tests at room and at elevated temperatures. Rapid unloading of deep caverns over a large pressure range is a special case for further study.

Permeability data for rock salt in the laboratory and in situ are strongly dependent on degree of confinement, extensional strains, and generally the history of the salt being tested.

Hydraulic fracturing of storage reservoirs in salt does not make them useless for static and limited cyclic load applications, provided sufficient salt surrounds the openings. Cyclic loads applied via insoluble fluids to previously fractured salt reservoirs apparently cause progressive deterioration of their pressure retaining capacity, even for load magnitudes significantly smaller than initial fracture values. The presence of brine in a reservoir may alter this effect however.

Tests performed in the laboratory and in situ employ only small amounts of material from a rock salt formation. Thus they cannot represent effects of megascopic features such as "anomalous zones", described by Kupfer (1980), which usually include large scale trends of gas and brine occurrence in salt domes. The effects of megascopic features on geostorage applications in rock salt formations appear worthy of further study.

5. ACKNOWLEDGEMENTS

The assistance and mine access provided by Domtar Chemical, Ltd., and Diamond Crystal, Inc., are gratefully acknowledged.

This work was supported by the U. S. Department of Energy (DOE) under Subcontract No. B-67966-A-0, Laboratory Tests of Rock Salt Subjected to Compressed Air Energy Storage (CAES) Load Environments, through Pacific Northwest Laboratory, operated for the DOE by Battelle Memorial Institute.

6. REFERENCES

Aufricht, W. R. & K. C. Howard 1961, Salt characteristics as they affect storage of hydrocarbons, J. of Pet. Tech., Aug: 733-738.

Gehle, R. M. 1980, Finite element analysis of slow, time-dependent, rock salt deformations, thesis for Master of Science in Engineering Science, Louisiana State University, Baton Rouge.

Gehle, R. M. & R. L. Thoms 1981, Monitoring cyclic load effects on rock salt in situ, Proc. third conf. on acoustic emissions in geol. struc. and matls, The Penn. St. U., Hardy, R., and F. Leighton (eds), in press.

Gipson, G. S. & R. L. Thoms 1981, On the transport of gaseous matter through permeable media between cylindrical cavities, Int. J. Engr. Sci., V 19, N8, 1095-1100.

Herbst, H. C. 1981, The CAES power plant, a tool at the load dispatcher's hands in an electric utility system, Proc. Int. Conf. on Energy Storage, Seattle, in press.

Jaeger, J. C. & N. G. W. Cook 1979, Fundamentals of rock mechanics, 3rd ed., 169, 389, London, Chapman and Hall.

Kupfer, D. 1980, Problems associated with anomalous zones in Louisiana salt stocks, USA, Proc. Fifth Symp. on Salt, Hamburg, N. Ohio Geol. Soc., Coogan, A. H. & L. Hauber (eds), 119-134.

Mine Safety and Health Administration 1981, The Jefferson Island Mine Inundation, Nov. 20, 1980, U.S. Department of Labor, Aug. 13.

Obert, L. 1963, An inexpensive triaxial apparatus for testing mine rock, BOM report 6332, U.S. Bureau of Mines.

Quast, P. 1981, The Huntorf plant: over three years operating experience with compressed air caverns, Proc. Int. Conf. on Energy Storage, Seattle, in press.

Scheidegger, A. E. 1960, The Physics of flow through porous media, University of Toronto Press, 93, 105.

Sutherland, H. J. & S. P. Cave 1980, Argon gas permeability of New Mexico rock salt under hydrostatic compression, Int. J. of Rock Mechs. and Mining Sci., V 17, N5, 281-288.

Thoms, R. L. & R. M. Gehle 1981a, Experimental study of rock salt for compressed air energy storage, Proc. Int. Conf. on Energy Storage, Seattle, in press.

_____ 1981b, In situ response of rock salt to cyclic loads, Proc. first conf. mech. behavior of salt, The Penn. St. U., Hardy, R., and M. Langer (eds.), in press.

Thoms, R. L., M. Nathany & R. Gehle 1980, Low-frequency cyclic loading effects on rock salt, Rockstore 80, Stockholm, V 2, 755.

Warne, L. K., R. R. Beasley, P. J. Langdon, A. K. Jacobson 1979, Direct measurement of change in width of horizontal fracture in oil shale, SAND-78-2008, Sandia Laboratories Energy Report, Albuquerque.

THERMOMECHANICAL CALCULATIONS CONCERNING THE DESIGN OF A RADIOACTIVE WASTE REPOSITORY IN ROCK SALT

Thermomechanische Berechnungen zum Entwurf eines Endlagerbergwerks für nukleare Abfälle im Steinsalzgebirge

Calculs thermomécaniques relatifs au dimensionnement des installations souterraines d'un dépôt de déchets radioactifs dans le sel gemme

M.WALLNER
Bundesanstalt für Geowissenschaften und Rohstoffe, Hannover, Bundesrepublik Deutschland
A.WULF
Control Data GmbH, Hamburg, Bundesrepublik Deutschland

SUMMARY:
Computer calculations concerning a nuclear waste repository will require a high accuracy in the predictions of the deformations and the stability of the repository over very long times and therefore a hight level of sophistication in geomechanical modeling. For the Waste Isolation Pilot Plant (WIPP) project near Carlsbad, New Mexico a benchmark II problem was stated in order to compare various computer codes with respect to their capability for calculating the thermal mechanical response of a hypothetical drift configuration for nuclear waste experiments and storage demonstration. Structural computations were made with ANSALT, a new FEM-code, especially developed for the analysis of thermomechanical processes related to the storage of heat producing radioactive wastes in rock salt. The computed results are illustrated and discussed.

ZUSAMMENFASSUNG:
Stabilitätsberechungen für ein Endlagerbergwerk für nukleare Abfälle erfordern geomechanische Modelle und Rechenverfahren, die es erlauben, zuverlässige Vorhersagen über thermomechanische Auswirkungen der Einlagerung auch über sehr lange Zeiträume zu machen. Für das "Waste Isaolation Pilot Plant (WIPP)" Projekt in New Mexico, U.S.A., wurden Vergleichsberechnungen mit verschiedenen Rechenprogrammen durchgeführt, um die Möglichkeiten, die Genauigkeit und Leistungsfähigkeit der verschiedenen Rechenprogramme zu untersuchen. Im Rahmen dieser Studie wurden Berechnungen auch mit dem von der BGR in Zusammenarbeit mit CD nach neuesten Erkenntnissen der Salzmechanik und der Rechentechnik entwickelten FEM-Programm ANSALT durchgeführt. Die Berechnungsergebnisse für eine hypothetische Lagerstrecke für wärmeentwickelnden radioaktiven Abfall unter Zugrundelegung einer differenzierten geologischen Situation werden dargestellt und erläutert.

RESUME:
Les calculs de stabilité pour des installations souterraines d'enfouissement requièrent des modèles géomécaniques aussi que des procédés de calculs permettant de faire, même sur de très lonques périodes, des pronostics sûrs en ce qui concerne les conséquences thermomèchaniques d'enfouissement. Pour le "Waste Isolation Pilot Plant (WIPP)", Projet à New Mexico, U.S.A., ont été effectués des calculs de comparaison, avec différents programmes de calcul afin d'étudier les possibilités, l'exactitude et le rentement des différents programmes de calcul. C'est dans le cadre de cette étude que les calculs ont été réalisés avec également le FEM-Programm ANSALT, mis au point par le BGR en collaboration avec le CD, d'aprés les théoris les plus récentes de la mécanique du sel et de la technique de calcul. On y décrit et y expliquer les résultats de calculs concernant une galerie pour des déchets radioactifs thermogènes, et ce, en prenant pour base une situation géologique differenciée.

1 INTRODUCTION

The design of a nuclear waste repository is based on a multiple barrier storage concept taking into account a system of sequential or interconnected natural and technical barriers (Albrecht et al 1980). The natural barrier provided by a rock salt formation could act as an encapsulated system due to the very low permeability and the high ductility of rock salt contrary to other host rock types. However, the assessment of the integrity of the rock salt mass over very long times among other things requires a thorough understanding of the long-term thermomechanical process taking place due to the decay heat of high level waste.

In the framework of the US/FRG bilateral agreement on cooperation in research and development for nuclear waste management the BGR, Hannover, in cooperation with CD, Hamburg, had the chance to participate in the second benchmark problem for the Waste Isolation Pilot Plant(WIPP) initiated by Sandia National Laboratories, Albuquerque NM in order to compare different thermal-structural computational codes.

The purpose of the WIPP project is to investigate the feasibility of storing defence transuranic waste in the bedded salt formation of Southeastern New Mexico and to perform experiments with defence high level waste (Hunter 1979). Structural calculations are used for reliable and detailed predictions for the WIPP experiments and storage demonstration as well as for extrapolating the long-term behavior of the repository to hundreds or thousands of years needed for nuclear waste isolation.

2 GEOMECHANICAL MODELING

2.1 Model and code requirements

It is obvious that geomechanical modeling of an underground structure can only reach a certain level of accuracy because the rock mass itself will always remain unknown up to a certain extend. Beyond that all input data for a computer calculation like the material properties, the loading and the boundary conditions may vary within the investigated system, whereby the exact variability of those values will not be known.

The engineer's approach to overcome this general difficulties is a continuous improvement to the model appropriate to the improved knowledge of the input data within an integrated cycle. The features of this cycle are the establishment of a constitutive model for the material behavior, the quantification of site relevant input data, the prediction and monitoring of the structural response and from that the necessary feedback to check the validity of the constitutive law, input data and modeling process in an iterative manner. Applying this method a final structural design will be based on a balanced combination of experiences, calculations and measurements.

For many geotechnical problems this approach allows to use a geomechanical model which is as simple as possible and as correct as necessary. Quite different from most geotechnical problems computer calculations concerning a nuclear waste repository will require a high accuracy in the predictions over very long times in advance. Since the design and construction of a nuclear waste repository in any case will be a prototype regarding the long-term behavior it is therefore extremely important to establish a highly sophisticated geomechanical model and to verify such a model in a comprehensive feasibility study.

In this context it is clear that the computer code used for thermal-mechanical calculations first must be verified, that means it must be demonstrated that the code is mathematically correct and internally consistent. Besides that it must be proved that the model in the code and particular the mathematical formulation of the constitutive model is qualified to solve thermal-mechanical problems with sufficient accuracy. Model qualification will be achieved through field confirmation tests and related to laboraory investigations.

2.2 Constitutive modeling of rock salt

The mechanical parameters of rock salt are highly nonlinear dependent on time, temperature, stress, etc. (Langer 1979, Wawersik & Hannum 1978). Deriving an accurate constitutive model for rock salt it is important to understand the physical mechanisms which control the nonlinearities in the mechanical behavior. On this basis it seems to be possible to identify dominant mechanisms for different environmental conditions and to derive constitutive relations from test data which can be extrapolated beyond the temporal and spatial region the tests were conducted for.

From this point of view the mechanical properties of rock salt have been clearly understood and correctly studied only for the last one or two decades.

Table 1: Constitutive model for rock salt

$$\underset{\sim}{\varepsilon}_{ges} = \underset{\sim}{\varepsilon}^{el} + \underset{\sim}{\varepsilon}^{cr} \mid \underset{\sim}{\varepsilon}^{f} \tag{1}$$

$$\underset{\sim}{\varepsilon}_{ij}^{el} = -\frac{\nu}{E}\underset{\sim}{\sigma}_{kk}\delta_{ij} + \frac{1+\nu}{E}\underset{\sim}{\sigma}_{ij} + \alpha_t \Delta\vartheta\delta_{ij} \tag{2}$$

$$\dot{\underset{\sim}{\varepsilon}}_{ij}^{cr} = \frac{3}{2}\frac{\varepsilon_{eff}^{cr}}{\sigma_{eff}^{cr}}\underset{\sim}{s}_{ij} \tag{3}$$

$$\dot{\varepsilon}_{eff}^{cr} = \sqrt{\frac{2}{3}\dot{\underset{\sim}{\varepsilon}}_{ij}\dot{\underset{\sim}{\varepsilon}}_{ij}} \tag{4}$$

$$\sigma_{eff} = \sqrt{\frac{3}{2}\underset{\approx}{s}_{ij}\underset{\approx}{s}_{ij}} \tag{5}$$

$$\dot{\varepsilon}_{eff}^{cr} = \sum_{i=1}^{3}\dot{\varepsilon}_{eff}^{cr}\,i(S,\sigma_{eff},\vartheta) \tag{6}$$

$$\dot{\varepsilon}_{eff}^{cr}1 = A_1 e^{\frac{-Q_1}{R\vartheta}}\left(\frac{\sigma_{eff}}{G}\right)^{n_1} \tag{7}$$

$$\dot{\varepsilon}_{eff}^{cr}2 = A_2 e^{\frac{-Q_2}{R\vartheta}}\left(\frac{\sigma_{eff}}{G}\right)^{n_2} \tag{8}$$

$$\dot{\varepsilon}_{eff}^{cr}3 = 2\left(B_1 e^{\frac{-Q_1}{R\vartheta}} + B_2 e^{\frac{-Q_2}{R\vartheta}}\right)\sinh\left(D\left\langle\frac{\sigma_{eff} - \sigma_{eff}^{o}}{G}\right\rangle\right) \tag{9}$$

$$\dot{\underset{\sim}{\varepsilon}}_{ij}^{f} = \dot{\lambda}\frac{\delta_f}{\delta\sigma_{ij}} \tag{10}$$

$$f = II_s - fkt(I_\sigma, II_{\dot{e}}, \vartheta, m, S) = 0 \tag{11}$$

$$f = \tau_o - C_1\sigma_o^{\alpha}\cdot e^{-C_2\sigma_o(\vartheta-\vartheta_o)^2}\left(1 + C_3\ln\frac{II_{\dot{e}}}{II_{\dot{e}}^{o}}\right) \tag{12}$$

In the meantime a lot of test results under well-defined test conditions are available (Herrmann et al 1980, Langer et al 1979, Hunsche 1981, Parrish & Gangi 1981) which led to a reliable constitutive model for rock salt. The mathematical formulation of this model is summarized in table 1. In the present version this model is mainly focused on the elastic properties (eq. 2) and the steady state creep behavior (eq. 3-9).

From the present data also a preliminary first approximation for a more general failure criterion which includes creep fracture was derived (eq. 10-12) (Wallner 1981a).

Up to now a constitutive equation for transient creep is not included in the model. The concept of three stages of creep deformation derived from the retardation test and described as primary creep, secondary creep, and tertiary creep is not suitable in many practical cases, e.g. continuously varying deviatoric stresses or temperatures. Therefore an appropriate laboratory test program is just performed at the BGR to give a data base for a more general law for transient creep.

3 ANSALT - DESCRIPTION

ANSALT (Special Purpose Code for Analysis of Nonlinear Thermomechanical Response of Rock Salt) is a finite element code cooperatively developed by BGR and Control Data, Hamburg, in order to offer an optimized and efficient computer code to calculate nonlinear thermomechanical response of rock salt within a nuclear waste repository (Wallner 1981b).

The base code for ANSALT is ANSR II (1979) developed by D.P. Mondkar at the Earthquake Engineering Research Center, University of California. This base code satisfies the following requirements:

a) Modularity: ANSR II is modular so that new code capabilities, such as new finite elements, new constitutive laws, etc., can be added by developing a few subroutines, without changes to the existing code. This has been achieved by structuring the code as a base code to which a number of auxiliary codes can be added.

Table 2: ANSALT, code capabilities

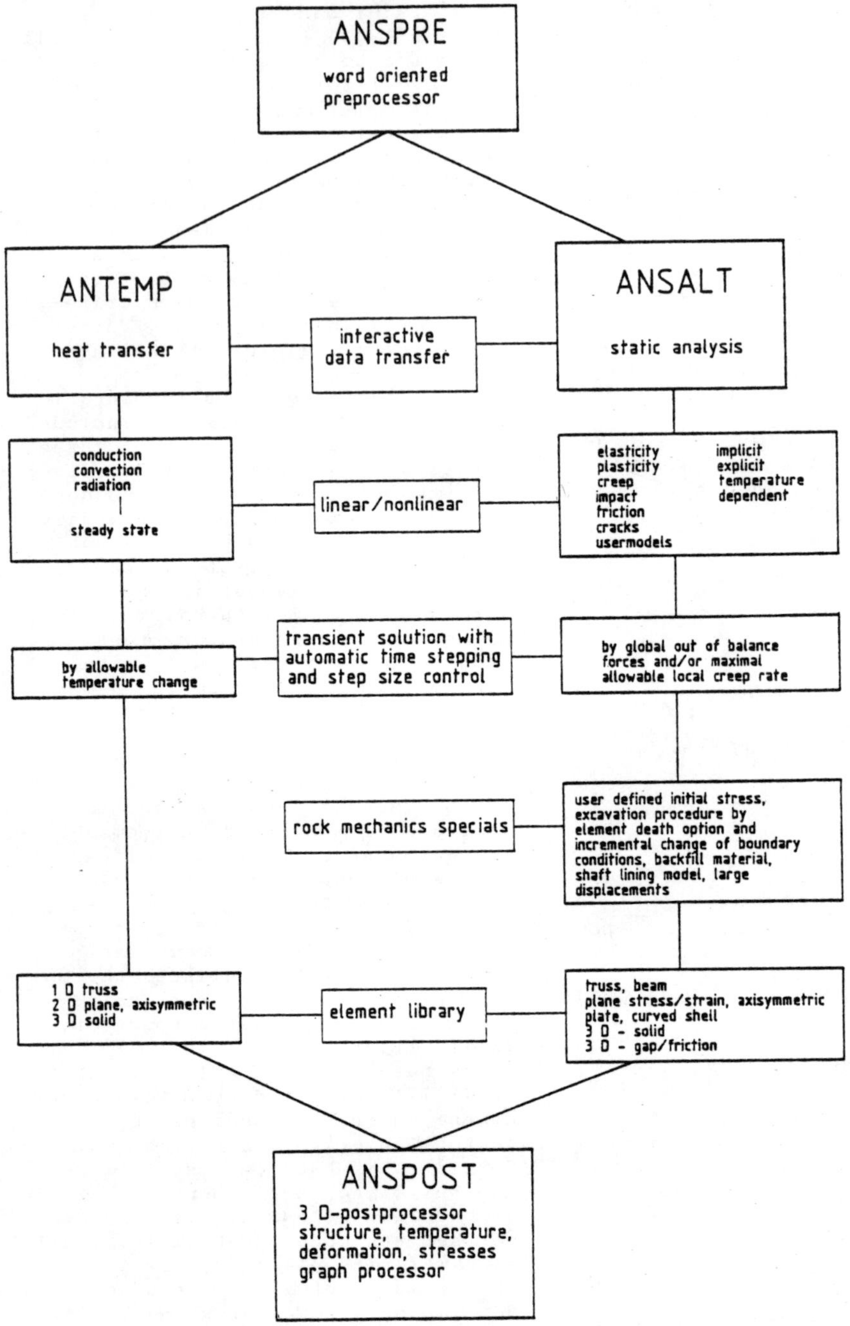
ANSPRE
word oriented preprocessor
ANTEMP
heat transfer
interactive data transfer
ANSALT
static analysis
conduction
convection
radiation
steady state
linear/nonlinear
elasticity
plasticity
creep
impact
friction
cracks
usermodels
implicit
explicit
temperature dependent
by allowable temperature change
transient solution with automatic time stepping and step size control
by global out of balance forces and/or maximal allowable local creep rate
rock mechanics specials
user defined initial stress, excavation procedure by element death option and incremental change of boundary conditions, backfill material, shaft lining model, large displacements
1 D truss
2 D plane, axisymmetric
3 D solid
element library
truss, beam
plane stress/strain, axisymmetric
plate, curved shell
3 D - solid
3 D - gap/friction
ANSPOST
3 D-postprocessor
structure, temperature,
deformation, stresses
graph processor

Storage allocation and computations common to all finite elements are performed within the base code, whereas computations associated with specific elements are carried out within the auxiliary code.

b) Computational efficiency: The code includes efficient symmetric and nonsymmetric out of core equation solvers optimized due to dynamic allocation of core storage and buffering of data into blocks for direct transfer to disc storage. For further improvement the code will be vectorized.

c) Solution strategy: The wide variety of solution schemes like step by step, iterative, mixed schemes and automatic step size control permits the user considerable flexibility in selecting an optimal scheme for his particular nonlinear problem. During the solution stresses and geometrical and temperature boundary conditions can be changed linear or stepwise as defined by the user in each increment.

Besides these advantages of the base code a library of elements and material models corresponding to the current knowledge of constitutive modeling of rock salt has been established in ANSALT. A brief description of the code capabilities is summarized in table 2.

4 BENCHMARK II PROBLEM FOR WIPP STRUCTURAL COMPUTATIONS

4.1 Objectives and philosophy

Although agreement with field data within a field confirmation test is ultimately necessary for final code qualification, this agreement alone does not provide sufficient confidence that all aspects can be properly modeled. In general only displacements can be measured accurately in the field which then can be compared against code results. Moreover experimental results can be strongly dependent on local inhomogenities near the instrumentation. The calculations could easily be erroneous and still compare well with measured data because one error compensated for another. As a result, in a code-experiment comparison the influence of a particular material property or nonlinearity cannot be studied independently to determine its effects on the problem.

A useful and important first step to field confirmation tests is a controlled comparison of codes with each other. The overall objective of the benchmark II study therefore was to assess the capabilities of various thermal-structural codes to solve complex boundary value problems which represent idealisations of drifts located in the WIPP stratigraphy (Matalucci et al. 1981, Morgan et al 1981).

Each participant in the benchmark activity had to analyse the benchmark II problem as completely as possible and no changes in geometry, boundary conditions, material properties, or creep law were allowed. Direct comparisons of the calculated results were used to identify disparaties in the results.

A benificial aspect of the code-comparison study was the exchange of information on code capabilities, modeling techniques, and approaches used in solving a common problem. A comprehensive comparative analysis of the 9 codes used in the WIPP Benchmark II problem was done by Morgan et al (1981). In this report only the own calculated results using the ANSALT code will be presented.

4.2 Problem formulation

A detailed specification of the problem, i.e. the geometry, boundary conditions, mechanical and thermal loads as well as the material description was given by Krieg et al (1980).

The hypothetical heated drift configuration considered for the second benchmark problem is shown in fig. 1 together with the finite element mesh used for the analysis. The single drift, which is a part of regular arrays of long drifts, is simulated with a plane strain assumption and with symmetry planes through the drift and pillar centerlines.

The stratigraphy modeled in the problem consisted of horizontally bedded layers of halite, anhydrite, polyhalite, a mixture of these three, argillaceous halite, and clay seams. 4 clay seams located

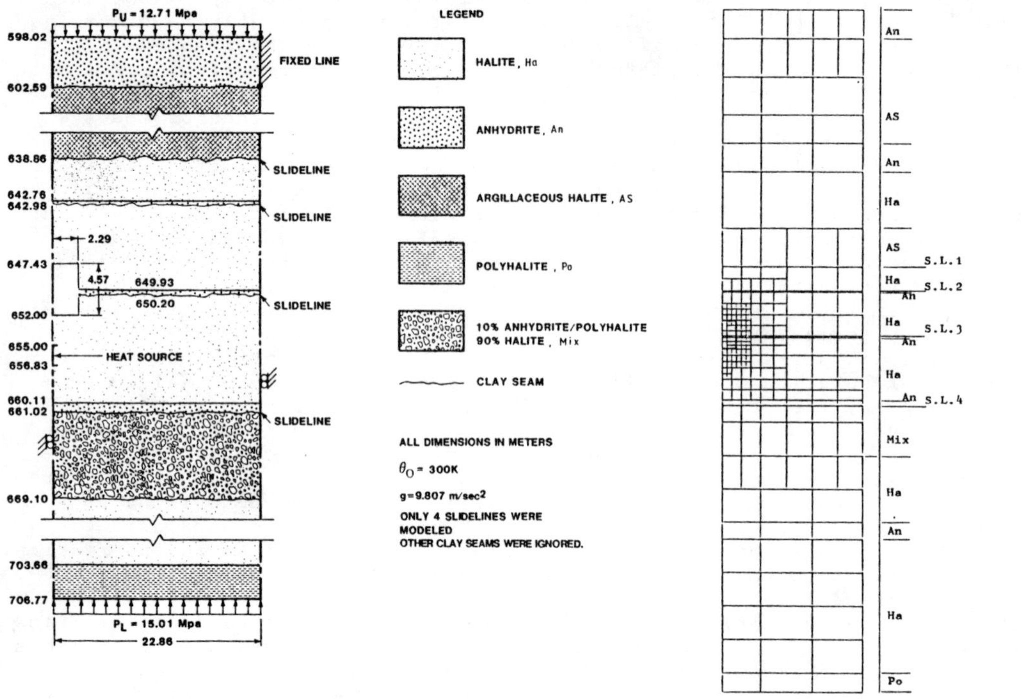

Fig. 1: Repository room configuration for the second benchmark problem, finite element mesh used in analysis

at specified levels were moduled as slide lines with a zero coefficient of friction.

The initial lithostatic state of stress was taken to the isotropic, i.e. $\sigma_x = \sigma_y = \sigma_z$; the initial temperature throughout the configuration was 300 K. Single canisters with radioactive waste are placed in boreholes at regular intervals beneath the floor. This heat source is to be modeled as a source that is continuously distributed along the drift length and has a height of 1.83 m. The heat output of this idealized plane source is approximately equal to a thermal power loading of 30 KW/acre (7.5 W/m²)

In the drift a nonstructural "thermal material" was used to simulate radiation heat transfer in a closed cavity.

The mechanical properties of all layers are summarized in table 3.

The parameter A, n and Q in table 3 are constants in the steady state creep law and correspond to A_2/G, n_2 and Q_2 respectively of table 1. The thermal properties of the various layers are presented in table 4.

Table 3: Mechanical properties for the second benchmark problem

Material	Elastic Constants v (-)	Elastic Constants E (Pa)	Creep Constants A ($Pa^{-4.9}s^{-1}$)	Creep Constants n (-)	Creep Constants Q (kcal/mole)
Halite	0.25	2.48E+10	5.79E-36	4.9	12.0
Arillaceous Salt	0.25	2.48E+10	1.74E-35	4.9	12.0
10% A-P, 90% H	0.25	2.65E+10	5.21E-36	4.9	12.0
Anhydrite	0.33	7.24E+10	0.0	---	---
Polyhalite	0.33	7.24E+10	0.0	---	---
Clay Seam	Friction Slip Line: μ static = μ dynamic = 0.0				

Table 4: Thermal properties for the second benchmark problem

Material	Density ρ (kg/m)	Specific Heat c_p (J/kgK)	Thermal Expansion α (K)	Thermal Conductivity $k=\lambda_o(300/\vartheta)^\gamma$ λ_o (W/mK)	γ
Halite	2167.0	860.0	4.50E-05	5.0	1.14
Argillaceous Salt	2167.0	860.0	4.00E-05	4.0	1.14
10% A-P, 90% H	2167.0	860.0	4.27E-05	5.0	1.14
Anhydrite	2167.0	860.0	2.00E-05	4.5	1.14
Polyhalite	2167.0	860.0	2.40E-05	2.0	1.00
"Equivalent Thermal Material"	1	1000.0	---	50.0	0.00

4.3 Results calculated with ANSALT

Some of the essential results computed by ANSALT for the benchmark II problem are illustrated in fig. 2-7.

Fig. 2 shows the temperature history for three selected locations. After 10 years, a temperature of 314.2 K in the center of the pillar is computed. A maximum temperature of 342.9 K at the heat source and 322.7 K at the midpoint of the floor are reached after 10 years.

Fig. 2: Temperature history
1 midheight of heat source
2 floor midpoint
3 center of the pillar

A deformed mesh showing the distribution of drift convergence at 10 years is presented in fig. 3. Remarkable displacements only occur in the immediate vicinity of the drift. The horizontal deformation below the anhydrite layer intersecting the drift is much greater than the deformation above due to the higher stiffness of the anhydrite layer which restricts the deformation.

Fig. 4 shows the vertical room closure and the midpillar horizontal displacement history. After 10 years the floor-to-ceiling convergence reaches a total value of 0.40 m. The midpillar horizontal displacement amounts to a value of only 0.04 m at the top of the stiff anhydrite layer.

The relative horizontal displacement profiles at 1,2 and 10 years for the slide line 3 which intersects the drift are plotted in fig. 5. At the drift wall a total relative horizontal displacement of 0.26 m is computed after 10 years. Only slide line 2 above the drift has a likewise remarkable slip which amounts to about 0.10 m after 10 years. Slip across the two other slide lines far away the drift is very small.

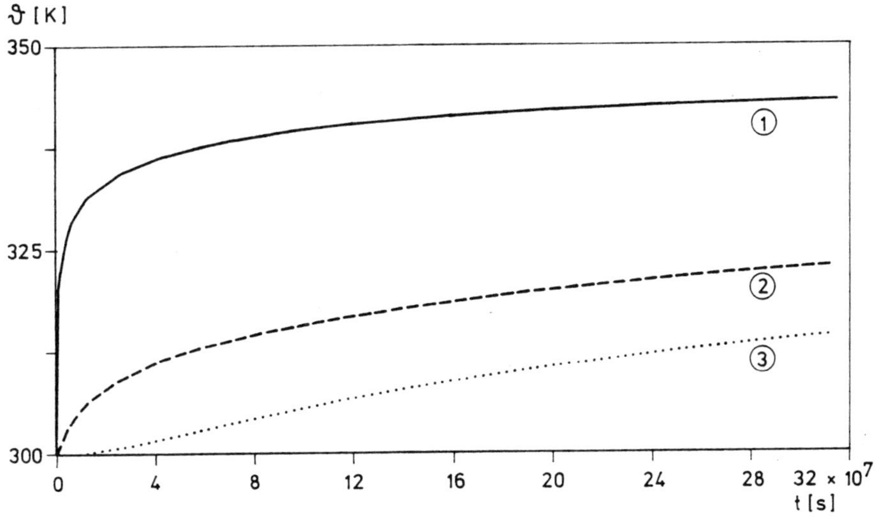

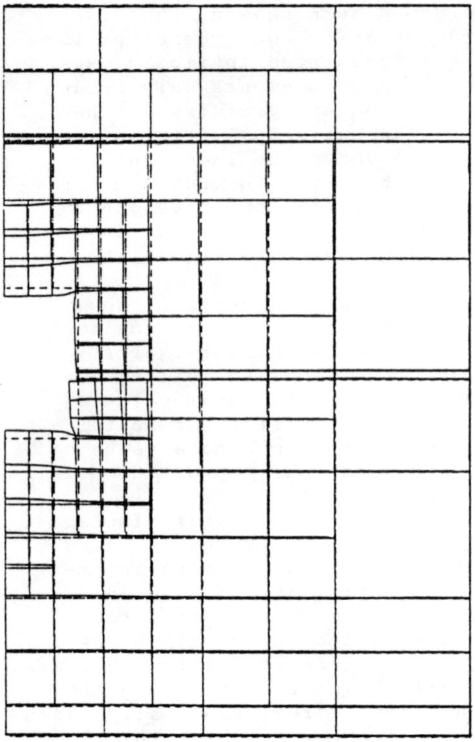

Fig. 3: Room closure, deformed mesh at 10 years (correct scale)

The horizontal stress profiles in the vertical centerline are shown in fig. 6. It is important to note, that the stress in the salt layers vary only little with time. In the stiff anhydrite layers however high stresses accumulate due to the creep deformations in the adjacent halite layers and dominate the entire stress distribution. After 10 years the horizontal stress in the anhydrite layer above the drift amount to 92.8 MPa and to 84.6 MPa for the anhydrite layer beneath the drift respectively.

5 CONCLUSION AND ASSESSMENT

Summarizing the results of the benchmark II problem it can be stated that the stratigraphy is very important for the entire system behavior. The thin but stiff anhydrite layers mainly control the stress field and the room closure. Besides that, the clay seams allow for slippage and dependent on their position will therefore strongly influence the deformation field. On the other hand only the closest slidelines to the drift significiantly effect the drift closure.

Furthermore, it should be mentioned that failure was not to be considered in the benchmark problem although it surely would affect the results. From a practical point of view

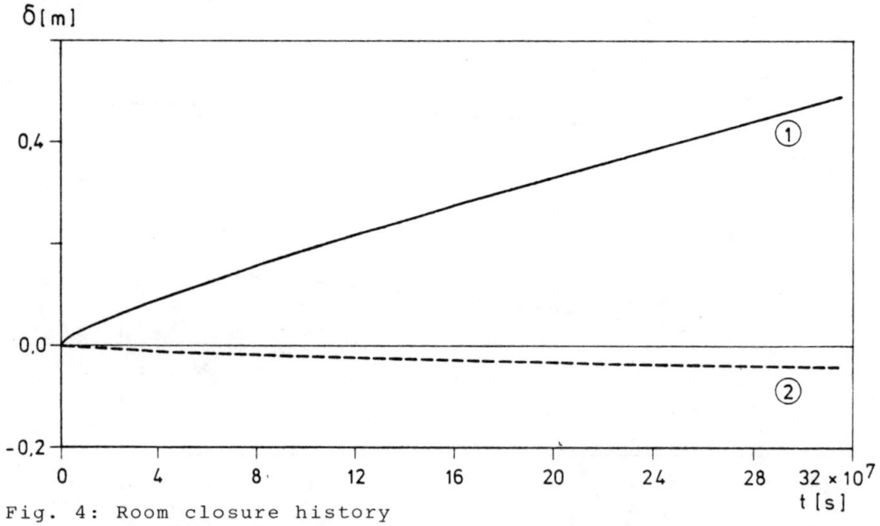

Fig. 4: Room closure history
1 vertical closure
2 midpillar horizontal displacement

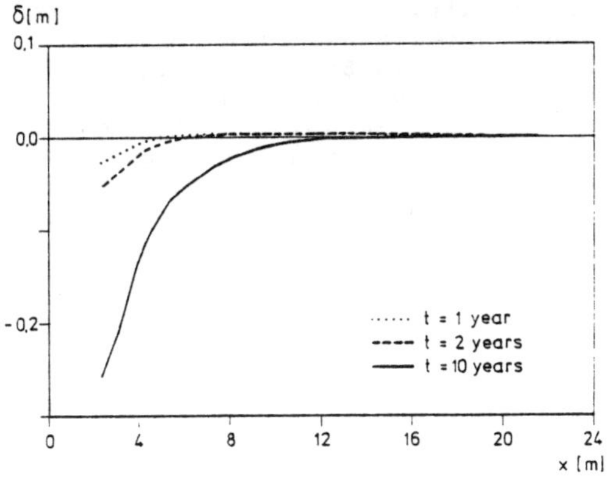

Fig. 5: Relative horizontal displacement along slide line 3

it would be expected that after a certain time especially the stress accumulation within the thin anhydite layers would cause failure and consequently change the reinforceing effect of those layers.

Comparison with other computer codes within the benchmark comparative study has shown that the new developed special purpose code ANSALT is very well qualified to solve even complex thermomechanical problems related to the storage of heat producing radioactive waste. On account of special features to simulate characteristic rock response to excavation ANSALT represents an efficient numerical tool to solve thermomechanical stability problems.

6 ACKNOWLEDGEMENT

The development of ANSALT as well as the participation in the benchmark II code comparison study was done within a research work for the Federal Ministry for Research and Technology, BMFT, by the Federal Institute for Geoscience and Natural Resources, BGR, under contract KWA 2070/8 in cooperation with Control Data GmbH under contract KWA 2070/8.

The authors would like to thank Sandia National Laboratories, Albuquerque NM for the permission to publish these results.

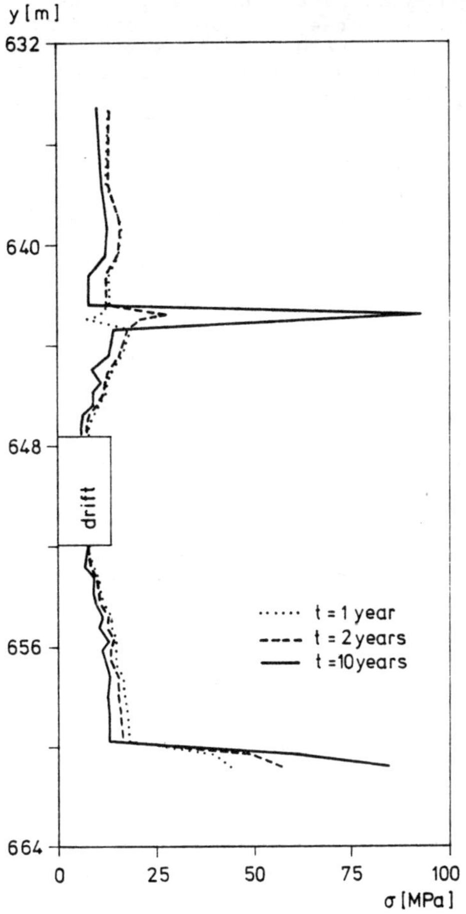

Fig. 6: Horizontal stresses along the vertical center line, stress peaks within the stiff anhydrite layers

7 REFERENCES

Albrecht, H., Langer, M. & M. Wallner 1980, Thermomechanical effects and stability problems due to nuclear waste disposal in salt rock, Proc. Rockstore 80, Stockholm, Vol.2, p. 801-809

BGR-Bericht 1980, Berechnung thermomechanischer Vorgänge bei der Endlagerung hochradioaktiver Abfälle im Salzgestein unter Verwendung eines optimierten Finite Element Programmes (ANSALT), BMFT-Forschungsvorhaben KWA 2070/8, Zwischenbericht 1980 (unpublished)

Herrmann, W., Wawersik, W. & H.S. Lauson 1980, Analysis of steady state creep of Southeastern New Mexico bedded salt, SAND 80-0558, Sandia National Laboratories, Albuquerque NM.
Hunsche, U. 1981, Results and interpretation of creep experiments on rock salt, Proc. 1st Conference on the Mechanical Behavior of Salt, The Pennsylvania State University
Hunter, T.D. 1979, Summary of results and plans of the experimental program for the Waste Isolation Pilot Plant, SAND 79-1950C, Sandia National Laboratories, Albuquerque NM.
Krieg, R.D., Morgan, H.S. & T.O. Hunter 1980, Second benchmark problem for WIPP structural computations, SAND 80 - 1331, Sandia National Laboratories, Albuquerque NM.
Langer, M. 1979, Rheological behavior of rock masses, Proc. 4. Int. Congr. on Rock Mechanics, Montreux, Vol. 3, 29-96.
Langer, M., Delisle, G. & M. Wallner 1979, Thermal mechanical modeling. Proc. U.S./FRG Bilateral Workshop Berlin, 248-318.
Matalucci, R.V., Morgan, H.S. & R.D. Krieg 1981, The role of benchmarking in assessing the capability to predict room response in bedded salt repositories SAND 81-1293C, Sandia National Laboratories, Albuquerque NM
Mondkar, D.P. & G.H. Powell 1979, ANSR II, Analysis of nonlinear structural response, user's manual UCB/EERC Report, S. 9-17, Earthquake Engineering Research Center, University of California, Berkeley
Parrish, D.K. & A.F. Gangi 1981, A nonlinear least squares technique for determining multiple-mechanism, high-temperature creep flow laws, Geophysical Monograph 24, Mechanical Behavior of Crustal Rocks, 287-298
Wallner, M. 1981a, Critical examination of conditions for ductile fracture in rock salt, Proc. OECD/NEA Workshop on Near Field Phenomena in Geologic Repositories for Radioactive Waste, Seattle
Wallner, M. 1981b, Analysis of thermomechanical problems related to the storage of heat producing radioactive waste in rock salt, Proc. 1. Conf. on the Mechanical Behavior of Salt, The Pennsylvania State University
Wawersik, W.R. & D.W. Hannum 1978, Mechanical Behavior of New Mexico rock salt in triaxial compression up to 200° C, Proc. V. Int. Symp. on Salt, Hamburg.

THERMAL STRESS INDUCED FRACTURING/STRESS-RELAXATION IN ROCK ADJACENT TO AN UNDERGROUND STORAGE VAULT

Durch thermische Spannung erzeugtes Bruch- und Fliessverhalten in Gestein, welches an ein unterirdisches Gewölbe angrenzt

Fissuration/fluage résultant des contraintes thermiques dans la roche voisine d'une enceinte d'évacuation souterraine

B.J.S.WILKINS, G.L.RIGBY & J.R.DRYDEN
Atomic Energy of Canada Research Co., Pinawa, Manitoba

SUMMARY:
Atomic Energy of Canada Limited is studying the underground storage of nuclear waste in a vault in hard rock in the Canadian Shield. As part of this work, models are being developed to assess the possible rates of escape of various waste components through the rock to the biosphere. At the temperatures expected (<150°C) in the vicinity of the vault, the response to stress perturbation will be creep, via macro- and microfracturing. As rock permeability and the overall stability of the vault will be affected by the extent of fracturing, it is important to establish the possible extent and kinetics of fracture processes. This paper describes some aspects of this work. It presents a two-dimensional finite element model that relates stress relaxation to microfracturing using linear elastic fracture mechanics. The kinetics of the process are derived from slow crack extension data for a local granite.

ZUSAMMENFASSUNG:
Atomic Energy of Canada Limited untersucht gegenwärtig die Möglichkeit radioaktiven Abfall in einem unterirdischen Gewölbe, das in das harte Gestein des kanadischen Schildes gehauen werden soll, zu lagern. Als Teil dieser Arbeit werden Modelle entwickelt, die es erlauben das mögliche Ausmass des Entweichens der verschiedenen Abfallkomponenten durch das Gestein in die Biosphare zu bestimmen. In diesem Vortrag werden einige Aspekte dieser Arbeit beschrieben. Es wird ein zweidimensionales Finite Element Modell vorgefuhrt, welches mit Hilfe der linear elastichen Bruchmechanik eine Relation zwischen Spannungsrelaxation und Microbruch-sowie Reissverhalten aufstellt. Die Kinetik dieses Prozesses wurde aus experimentell ermittelten Daten abgeleitet, die der Untersuchung des langsamen Bruchvergrösserungsmechanismus galten. Fur diese Untersuchungen wurde lokal vorkommender Granit im trockenen Zustand bei 20°C und im mit Wasser gesattigten Zustand bei 80°C untersucht.

RESUME:
L'Energie Atomique du Canada Limitée étudie l'évacuation souterraine des déchets nucléaires dans une enceinte pratiquée dans la roch dure du bouclier canadien. Dans le cadre de ces travaux, on met au point des modèles pour évaluer les taux possibles d'échappement de divers composants de déchets à travers la roche et vers la biosphere. Ce rapport décrit certains aspects de ces travaux. Il présente un modèle à deux dimensions, par éléments finis, reliant la relaxation des contraintes à la microfissuration. La cinétique des processus est dérivée des données de propagation lente des fissures, exprimées sous l'angle de la mécanique des fissures linéaires élastiques. Le résultat de l'analyse est une évaluation de la façon cont, pour la roche intacte, les contraintes, la densité des fissures et le facteur de sécurité varieront en fonction de l'espace et du temps.

1. INTRODUCTION

AECL is studying the possible disposal of solid nuclear waste in a vault in hard rock (Boulton 1978). Part of this work is to develop models that assess the rate of escape of various waste components to the biosphere. As active material can reach the biosphere through the rock mass, via water transport, a knowledge of rock permeability is essential. Hence, information is needed on rock fracture populations and on factors (stress state, etc.) that affect the flow of water through these fractures. Excavation of the vault and heat generated by active waste will disturb the original stress and temperature distributions in the rock mass. The major response to these disturbances in hard rock at the anticipated temperatures (<150°C) will be microfracturing that occurs both immediately and over a long time period. As the general stability of openings and rock permeability depend on the degree of fracturing, we must establish the kinetics and extent of the process. Also, because nuclear waste is involved, it is important to develop a sound theoretical basis for extrapolation to long times.

Rock is a complex solid. It consists of an aggregate of different constituents each with different, and usually anisotropic, mechanical and physical properties. Heating produces fracturing due to elastic strains generated by differential expansion and the inherent brittleness of the material (Davidge 1981). It occurs with or without the presence of thermal gradients. Deviatoric stress and confining pressure also cause microfracturing, which in hard rock results in stress relaxation, modified displacement and a reduction in effective elastic modulus (decrease in stiffness). This paper presents a two-dimensional analysis that relies on linear elastic fracture mechanics (LEFM) to relate stress relaxation to microfracturing. The kinetics of the process are obtained from experimental data for slow crack growth in hard rock (Wilkins 1980).

2. FRACTURE MECHANICS AND STRESS CORROSION CRACKING

In LEFM the important parameter is the stress intensity factor (K). It represents the magnitude of the stress occuring at a crack tip in an elastic solid (Rooke and Cartwright 1976). There are three modes of cracking, each characterised by a different stress intensity factor, i.e. tensile-opening (K_I), in-plane shear (K_{II}) and anti-plane shear (K_{III}). Above a critical value of the factor, for example K_{IC}, a crack is unstable and will propagate rapidly. In hard rock, crack shapes and orientations are widely distributed; hence, all cracking modes are possible. However, there is extensive evidence that the mechanism of compressive-shear failure of hard rock, in the brittle regime, derives from cumulative tensile microcracking (Brace, Paulding and Scholz 1966. Scholz 1968). Presumably, this follows because K_{IC} <

K_{IIC} and K_{IIIC}. In all modes of cracking, K is a function of applied stress and crack size. Also, it is a function of crack shape and the geometry of the solid containing the crack. K_I is given by an expression of the form

$$K_I = Y \sigma L^{1/2} \qquad (1)$$

where σ is the applied stress, normal to the crack, Y is a geometry factor and L is the crack length.

At values of $K_I < K_{IC}$, slow crack growth gives rise to the phenomenon known as static fatigue or delayed failure. In glasses, various silicates, and other materials the mechanism often depends on stress-dependent corrosion (Anderson and Green 1977). For a given material, temperature, and environment

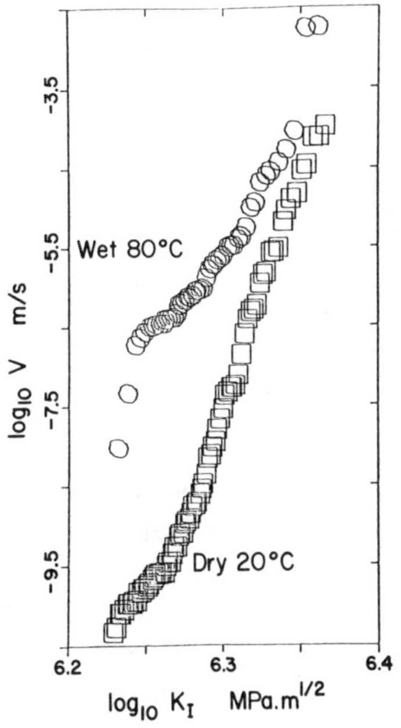

Fig.1 Crack growth velocity versus the stress intensity factor for Lac du Bonnet granite.

there is a unique relationship between the crack growth velocity (V) and K_I at the crack tip. Typical log log plots of V versus K_I for a hard rock (Wilkins 1980) at room temperature in air (approximately 50% relative humidity) and at 80°C in distilled water are shown in Figure 1.

For the purposes of this analysis, the kinetics of crack growth may be represented by a relationship of the form,

$$V = dL/dt = AK_I^{\,n} \qquad (2)$$

where t is time and A and n are material constants for a given environment. A best fit line, using the method of least squares, was drawn through each data set, in Figure 1, to allow evaluation of A and n. Integrating (2) and substituting from (1) allows crack growth time to be estimated e.g.,

$$\int_{L_o}^{L_1} Y^{-n} \; L^{-n/2} \, dL = A\sigma^{n} \int_0^t dt \qquad (3)$$

where L_o and L_1 are initial and final crack lengths.

3. STRESS RELAXATION AND FINITE ELEMENT METHODS

For simplicity this analysis considers the behaviour of a thick slab of rock, containing a single crack. Further, the rock slab is constrained to consist of one isotropic phase, under the conditions of plane strain and fixed grips. Details of the manner

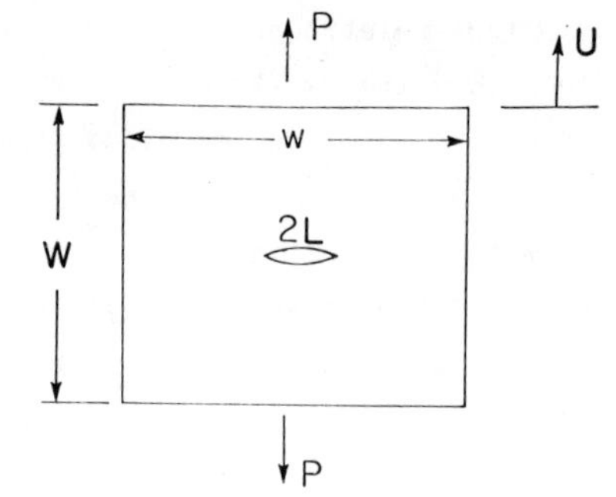

Fig.2 Dimensions and manner of loading of a thick rock slab containing a crack.

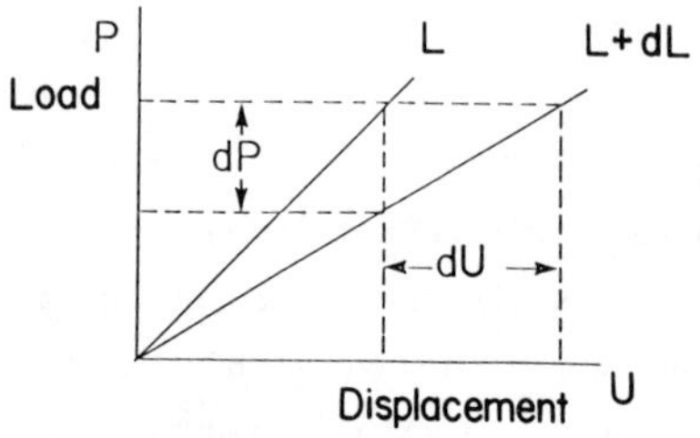

Fig.3 Load-displacement diagram.

of loading and dimensions of the slab are shown in Figure 2.

Consider the load-displacement diagram shown in Figure 3. Compliance (C) as a function of crack length is given by,

$$U = C(L)P \tag{4}$$

where P and U are load and displacement, respectively. Hence, with constant U (fixed grips)

$$CdP + PdC = 0 \tag{5}$$

Since the extrinsic stress (σ) is proportional to the load,

$$d\sigma/\sigma = -\, dC/C \tag{6}$$

Using the subscript o to indicate initial values, integration gives,

$$\int_{\sigma_o}^{\sigma} d\sigma/\sigma = -\int_{C_o}^{C} dC/C \tag{7}$$

hence,

$$\sigma/\sigma_o = C_o/C \tag{8}$$

Compliance is found from the constant load case using the finite element model shown in Figure 4.

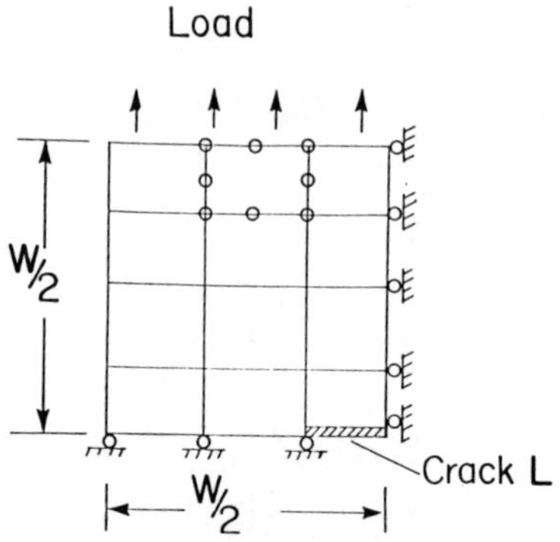

Fig.4 Finite element mesh for a quarter of the rock slab.

The standard, eight-noded, isoparametric finite element is used and from symmetry the mesh needs only to cover a quarter of the slab. Compliance is obtained as a function of crack length, normalised by the width (W) of the slab, see Figure 5.
A value of 0.2 was taken for Poisson's ratio.

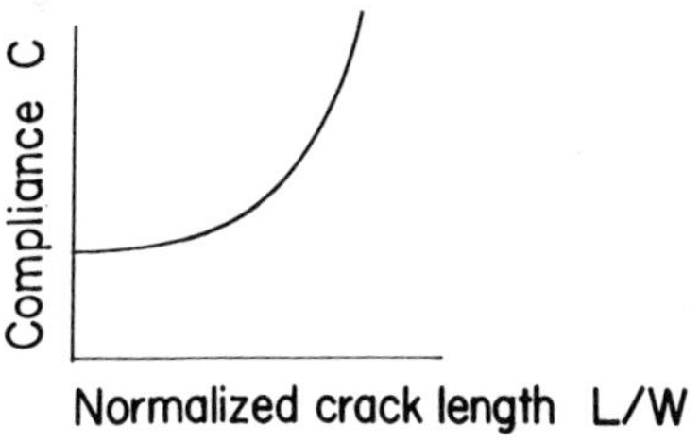

Fig.5 Compliance versus normalized crack length.

Stress and crack length as a function of time are found as follows. From equations (1) and (2),

$$dL/dt = AY^n \sigma^n L^{n/2} \quad (9)$$

Integrating and using equation (8)

$$t = (1/A\sigma_o^n)\int_{L_o}^{L_1} [(C/C_o)^n / Y^n L^{n/2}]dL \quad (10)$$

where t is the time taken for a crack to grow from length L_o to L_1. Also, note that for a different original stress, $\sigma_o{}^*$ say, the time t*, taken for the same crack growth is given by,

$$\log t^* = \log t + n\log(\sigma_o/\sigma_o{}^*) \quad (11)$$

4. RESULTS AND DISCUSSION

In this model, σ/σ_o decreases to zero and $(L/W)^{1/2}$ increases to 0.71 as 2L approaches W. Therefore, as $K_I \propto \sigma L^{1/2}$, it (and V) must pass through a maximum value as L/W increases from a small value. The maximum occurs at a value of L/W that depends only on the C versus L/W relationship. Hence, the K_I maximum is not present if L_o/W exceeds a large enough value. For small values of L_o/W an initial increase in L/W produces a small increase in C (Figure 5) and, therefore, a small decrease in σ (equation (8)). When L/W becomes larger, changes in C and σ are more significant. Therefore, both σ/σ_o and L/W as a function of time appear as complementary S-shaped curves. Figure 6 shows how σ/σ_o, L/W and K_I/K_{Io} vary with time.

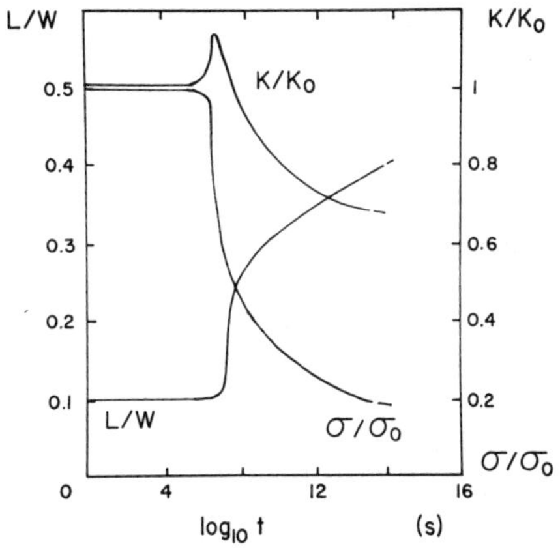

Fig.6 Variation of K,L and σ values with each other and with time.

The results for six cases, chosen to illustrate the range of behaviour, are presented in Figures 7 and 8. For that purpose equation (9) was integrated using Simpson's rule, with the geometry factor (Y) given by,

$$Y = (\pi L)^{1/2} \cdot f(L/W) \quad (12)$$

Details of each case are set out in Table 1.

TABLE 1 Test Case Details

No.	L_o/W	σ_o	n	$\log_{10}A$
1*	0.02	4.2	50	-321
2*	0.025	6.3	50	-321
3*	0.1	2.1	50	-321
4*	0.1	3.2	50	-321
5*	0.1	4.2	50	-321
6**	0.1	2.1	26	-169

Stress in MPa
* dry granite at 20°C
** wet granite at 80°C

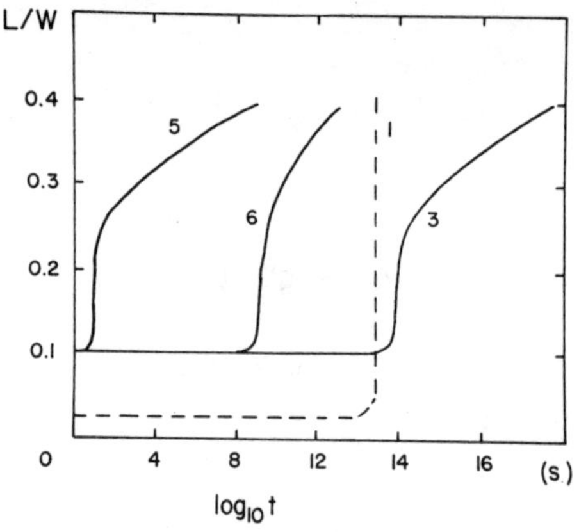

Fig.8 Normalized crack extension rate using data for granite, dry at 20°C(1,3 and 5), and wet at 80°C(6).

Figure 7 shows σ/σ_o versus log t for cases 1 to 5, all of which used A and n values for dry granite at room temperature. Figure 8 shows L/W versus log t for cases 1, 3, 5 and 6. Case 6 was calculated using A and n values for wet granite at 80°C.

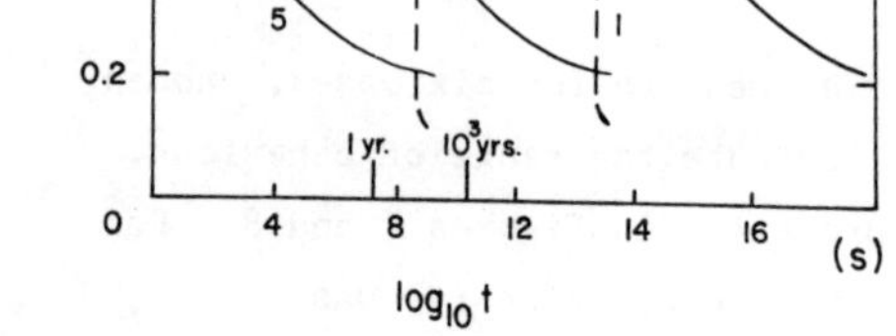

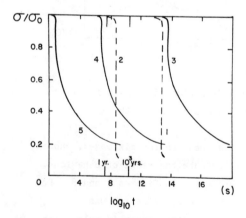

Fig.7 Stress relaxation curves using data for dry Lac du Bonnet granite at 20°C. (1,2)L_o/W=0.025; (3,4 and 5)L_o/W=0.1

The main observations are:

(i) Microfracturing and consequently stress relaxation are more rapid as σ_o is increased

(ii) All plots of σ/σ_o versus log t have the same shape regardless of σ_o values, (see equation (11)). The shape is a function of all the other parameters. This is illustrated in Figure 7, where cases 3 to 5 have the same shape and cases 1 and 2 have a different shape. Practically, this means that the time required, for the bulk of stress relaxation (microfracturing) to occur, is proportional to an incubation time (the time required for σ/σ_o to relax to 0.95, say). For cases 3, 4 and 5 the constant of proportionality for the ratio of relaxation times at (σ/σ_o) = 0.95 and 0.3 is approximately 10^3. Hence, an incubation time of one month would correspond to a bulk relaxation (70%) time of approximately 100 years. Extending the incubation time to one year would give a relaxation (70%) time of 10^4 years.

(iii) The incubation time varies inversely with L_o/W. However, the time required for the bulk of stress relaxation is independent of L_o/W. These effects are illustrated by cases 1 and 5 in Figure 7. Where a solid contains a variety of crack sizes there will be a range of L_o/W values. It is anticipated that the growth of cracks with large L_o/W values will be responsible for most of the stress relaxation. Hence, in a polycrystalline solid such as granite, type 3, 4 and 5 behaviour is expected, rather than type 1 and 2.

(iv) The influence of water and elevated temperature on granite is found by comparing cases 3 and 6 in Figure 8. The main effect is a much reduced incubation time for a given σ_o. Also, the bulk of stress relaxation occurs more quickly.

5. CONCLUSIONS

The model provides some insight into the possible stress relaxation (microfracturing) behaviour of hard rock. It suggests that estimating long term behaviour of heated rock may not be an intractable problem.

There appear to be two possible extremes of behaviour. Microfracturing either starts early and terminates rapidly or is slow to begin and takes a very long time to finish. Both situations lend themselves to the prediction of long-term microfracture population changes due to stress relaxation, and could assist in predicting the evolution of related phenomena, such as bulk hydraulic conductivity and mechanical properties in hard rock.

6. REFERENCES

Anderson, O.L. & Green, P.C., "Stress-Corrosion Theory of Crack Propagation With Applications to Geophysics", Rev. Geophys. Space Phys. Vol.15, pp. 77-104,(1977).

Boulton, J. (Editor), "Management of Radioactive Fuel Wastes: The Canadian Disposal Program", Atomic Energy of Canada Limited Report, AECL-6314, (1978).

Brace, W.F., Paulding, B. & Scholz, C.H., "Dilatancy in the Fracture of Crystalline Rocks", Pure Appl. Geophys. 116, pp. 807-839, (1966).

Davidge, R.W., "Cracking at Grain Boundaries in Polycrystalline Brittle Materials," Acta Met. Vol. 29, pp. 1695 to 1702, (1981).

Rooke, D.P. & Cartwright, D.J., "Compendium of Stress Intensity Factors", Her Majesty's Stationery Office, London, (1976).

Scholz, C.H., "Mechanism of Creep in Brittle Rock", J. Geophys. Res. Vol. 73, pp. 3295-3302, 1968.

Wilkins, B.J.S., "Slow Crack Growth and Delayed Fracture of Granite", Int. J. Rock Mech. Min. Sci. & Geomech. Abstr. Vol.17, pp. 365-369, (1980).

SOME CONSIDERATIONS OF RESEARCH ON STABILITY OF UNDERGROUND STORAGE CAVERNS

Über die Stabilität der unterirdischen Speicherkavernen

Quelques considérations de recherche sur la stabilité des cavernes souterraines de stockage

ZHU WEISHEN, FENG DINGXIANG & BAI SHIWEI
Institute of Rock & Soil Mechanics Academia Sinica, Wuhan, China

SUMMARY:
This paper presents some considerations of research on the stability of underground storage caverns in rock. At the beginning the author introduces a conception of transformations and distribution of energy in rocks confining the cavern and proposes an approximate equation of conservation of energy which is a fundamental criterion to be followed for studying and controlling the stability of a cavern.
Then, relating to a research work of a 40-meter-span cavern in China, this paper discusses some problems concerning the measurements of earth stress in the field, the non-linear finite element analysis and finally, the analytical method used for evaluating the fracture zone of rock mass and so on. At the end of this paper a great deal of numerical analogic computation with finite element method for studying the stability analysis of a cavern with various joint systems in various stress field is listed. Some significant conclusions for selecting the site and location of a large span cavern as well as for design and construction of the support are given.

ZUSAMMENFASSUNG:
In der vorliegenden Arbeit handelt es sich um einige Probleme über die Stabilität der unterirdischen Lagerfelshöhle im Felsen. Zuerst führt der Verfasser einen Gedanken der Energieübertragung und Energieverteilung um die Felshöhle ein und dann stellt eine Näherungsgleichung der Energieerhaltung vor, welche als grundliegendes Kriterium für die Untersuchung und Kontrollierung von der Stabilität der Felshöhle gilt.
In Verbindung mit einer Untersuchungsarbeit von einer weit gespannten Felshöhle mit 40 Meter Spannweite in China der Verfasser untersucht einige Probleme, welche die Gebirgedruckmessung auf dem Feld, nicht-lineare endliche Elementenanalyse und die analytische Methode des Kriteriums für die Bruchfläche und den Störungsbereich der Felsenmasse und des Gebirgskörpers.
Am Ende dieses Beitrags ist eine große Anzahl von numerischen Berechnungen mit der Finite Elementmethode als Parameterstudie zur Standsicherheitsberechnung einer Kaverne mit verschiedenen Trennflächengefügen und Spannungsfeldern aufgeführt. Einige wesentliche Schlüsse für die Standortwahl großer Kavernen aber auch für den Entwurf und die Konstruktion der Sicherungen werden gezogen.

RESUME:
On présente certaines considérations de recherche sur la stabilité des cavernes souterraines de stockage. D'abord, les conceptions de transformation et de répartition de l'énergie dans le massif rocheux

entourant une caverne souterraine sont controduites, l'auteur avance une équation approximative de la conservation de l'énergie qui est considérée comme un critérium fondamental suivi pour analyser et contrôler la stabilité d'une caverne souterraine de grande portée de 40 m en Chine, on discute certaines considérations, y compris la mesure in situ de contrainte, l'analyse non-linéaire d'éléments finis, la méthode analytique utilisée pour juger la zone de fracture des massifs rocheux, etc.. Enfin, au moyen de calcul analogique de beaucoup de numéros avec la méthode d'éléments finis de stabilité des massifs rocheux entourant une caverne souterraine avec les systèmes de joints variés dans les champs de contraintes variées, certaines conclusions significatives pour le choix de site et de ligne de caverne souterraine de grande portée ainsi que pour le projet et le construction du support sont données.

1 INTRODUCTION

The problem of stability of underground cavern is one of the practical subjects of rock mechanics. That course,as the whole of rock mechanics,is lack of ripe theory and methods for study. There are various factors to effect the stability of an underground cavern, the essential components can be summarized as follows: effect of geology (especially geological structure), effect of geo-stress state, effect of the mechanical properties of rock mass, engineering effect involving the shape of cavern and the technique of underground excavation and effect of underground water etc. For the rock mass is a complex body, it is almost impossible to establish a complete theory that is suitable for every conditions to get a quantitative solution. Therefore, at the present stage, the more reasonable way is that to classify the problems with different characters into different categories, to simplify them and to resolve them in approximately way separately.

This paper will present the main points briefly of our research for several problems.

2 CONCEPTION OF TRANSFORMATION AND DISTRIBUTION OF ENERGY IN ROCKS CONFINING THE CAVERN

It is well known that most rock formations unexcavated possess distinct elastic properties and therefore comprise of elastic potential energy. Mechanical effects such as deformation, fracture etc. in the confining rock after excavation may be regarded as the results of the work done by the release of potential energy. The rock mass has been analysed as homogeneous, linear elastic body by N.G.W.Cook and M.D.G.Salamon. The latter formulated the energy conservation equation, $W_c+U_m=U_c+W_r$, in which W_c is the work done by the internal stress, built up within the total volume of the confining rock during excavation, U_m is the strain energy released from the excavated portion of the rock mass, U_c is the strain energy newly accumulated in the immediately adjacent confining rock due to excavation, and W_r is the loss of elastic energy in the process of excavation.

Besides, when the stress redistribution around the opening takes place to a certain extent some forms of motion such as viscous or plastic deformation and brittle fractures etc. will dissipate energy. This non-elastic strain energy is W_n. If a mam-made structure (such as certain type of supports or refilling of mines) is built at a certain time after excavation, a portion of energy, W_f, will also be absorbed by it. Therefore, under normal condition the above-stated energy equation may be rewritten as below

$$W_c + U_m = U_c' + W_r + W_n + W_f \qquad (1)$$

In most cases, nonelastic deformations and fractures mainly develop in the immediate vicinity of the cavern opening. Many stress analysis data also prove that even if there exists a plastic or fractural region,

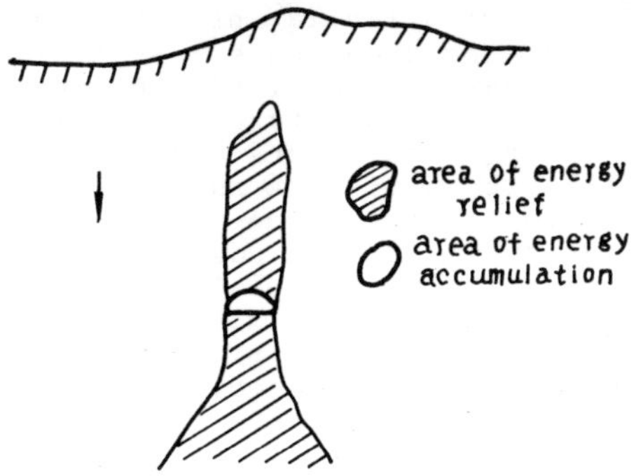

Fig.1 Re-distribution of the elastic energy after excavation under the gravitational field only

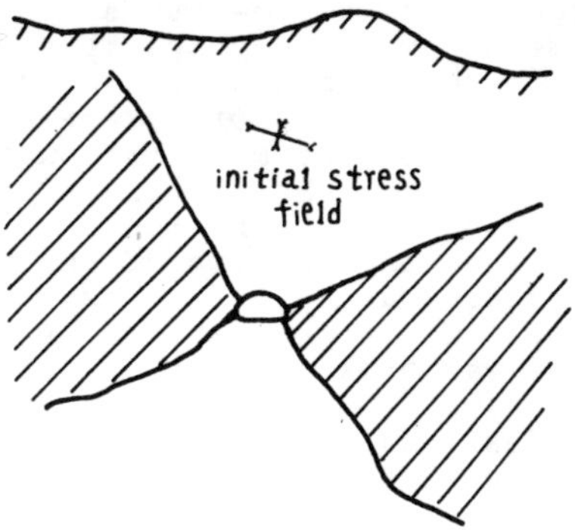

Fig.2 Re-distribution of the elastic energy after excavation under the approximate horizontal initial stress field

the stress redistribution mainly develops within the range of 1—1.5 times the major axis of the rock opening(for single opening). W_c ,in a given condition, may be assumed approximately to be constant and U_m and W_r may be more so. Therefore we may approximately have

$$U_c' + W_n + W_f \doteq \text{const.} \qquad (2)$$

This energy equation is a fundamental criterion to be followed for studing and controlling stability of a cavern. Generally, in order to reduce the cost of the structures, we should utilize, tothe utmost, the self-supporting capacity of the elasto-plastic property of the surrounding rock. So, W_f should be kept as small as possible. But the excessive plastic deformation of the confining rock would also affect its own stability and the use of the cavern. Hence, we should let $W_n < [W_n]$. The newly accumulated elastic strain energy should also be kept within a certain limit $U_c' < [U_c]$, otherwise, in some cases, rock burst would happen. Therefore, under various conditions, partition of each energy components should be well controlled, based on equ.(2), to ensure both safety and economy of the confining rock-structure system.

Besides, partition of the accumulated elastic energy U_c (or U_c') in the confining rock is also affected by the factors including rock media, in-situ stress and engineering features. For example, when initial stress field is non-homogeneous, the redistribution of the elastic potential energy after excavation is related to the orientation of this stress field. Fig.1and Fig.2 show respectively the distribution forms of energy after excavation, in the case of the gravitational direction and the near horizontal direction of stress field as the major component. These two figures are obtained from elastic analyses by means of finite element method which compares the first invariant of stress tensor J_1 ,and the second invariant of the stress deviator J_2' at each point before and after excavation.

3 IN-SITU STRESS MEASUREMENT

The stability of the underground cavern is discussed usually in the controlling of the strength and controlling of the deformation around the cavern, and these factors are related to the stress state of rock mass in excavation as before and after. So that the initial state of stress is a fundamental background for analysing the stability of underground cavern. Of course, rock stress was created by previous tectonical movements in history, and its stress field has been disturbed by multiple tectogenesis each other, thus it is so complex as to describe difficultly by a quantitative judgement, such as the investigation of region and in-situ geology. Everybody, who wants to know exactly the practical distribution of stress field, must conduct in-situ measurement.

We conducted the in-situ stress measurements over ten years at various projects and compared the measuring technique by means of several methods. At first, we measured on the surface of rock masses and afterwards in borehole. The experiences have shown that the results of surface method are unstable than that in borehole while the surface of rock masses was broken due to blasting.

The type of 36-2 Borehole Stress Gage designed and manufactured by ourselves has been put into use to measure a lot of in-situ stresses at several construction sites. The measuring results show that there existed horizontal stress with significant magnitude even if the overburden is more shallow or the properties of rock mass is much soft. The existed horizontal stress is a residual stress induced by tectonic movements but not by the weight of rock masses themselves.

Figure 3 is an arrangement for measuring with the stress relief method in deep borehole, that is used to analyse the stability of a large span cavern. One of the testing holes is up to 79m in depth. The result of the test shows that the direction of maximum principal stress intersects with the horizontal level forming an angle about 30°, the magnitude is up to 150—180 kg/cm^2.

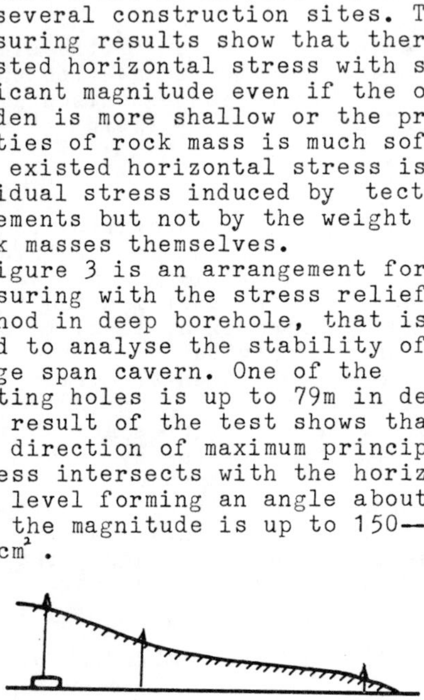

Fig.3 Arrangement of deep borehole of stress-relief on hillside

4 CALCULATION BY FINITE ELEMENT METHOD

The finite element method has been used as a powerful instrument to analyse the stability of underground cavern. Because of the complication of rock mechanics problems, all of the finite element analysis are used merely under a certain condition. Even though it has been considered the testing informations, the parameters choices could not be avoided the artificial effects. For instance, the assumption of the initial stress distribution, the simplification of the distribution law of joints and clefts, the adoption of physical and mechanical model of such meduim etc. The problems for any stability of underground cavern have individually characters. A successful calculation must require to make a serious analysis and judgement during formulating of calculation scheme. It must reflect the controlling factors and all of the simplifications and assumptions without any major excessive error. There are many key problems to effect the stability of a cavern. If we treat a certain problem wrongly, the calculating results will be far away from the practical condition. Therefore, we must pay attention to this calculation very carefully.

The finite element method is valid as a effective method for researching the variety factors effecting the stability of rock engineering. We shall present briefly a practical engineering as follows and analyse its stability by means of finite element method in calculation as a plane problem.

Non-linear analysis of the finite element method is applied in the calculation. A typical section is chosen and some "joint" elements are distributed on this section.The distribution law is established from the field investigation and from the law of average statistics in this region. Those "joint" elements represent both small faults and large joints.

For the rock elements, considering the hysteresis loop bounded by loading and unloading curves of the rock mass in situ, different stress-strain matrixes are chosen accordingly Fig.4. Criterion for defining loading and unloading is based on increase or decrease of the first invariant of the stress tensor J_1 and the second invariant of the stress deviator J_2'. The curve of complete stress-strain relationship is simplified to the form as shown in Fig.5. Before point A, the stress state belongs to elastic problems. Then shear failure is reached at point A and thereafter, the material enters into plastic state. If the tensile stress exceeds σ_T, the rock element is assumed in the state of tensile failure. These two types of failure will both undergo "stress transfer" process. After shear failure from point A to point B (Fig.5),

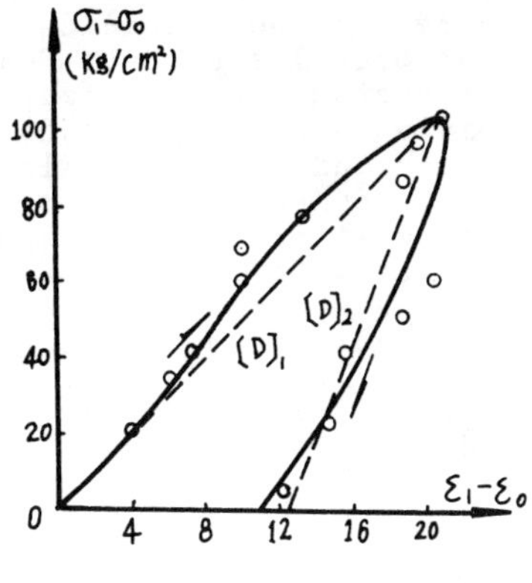

Fig.4 Relationship between principal stress deviator and strain deviator in triaxial test

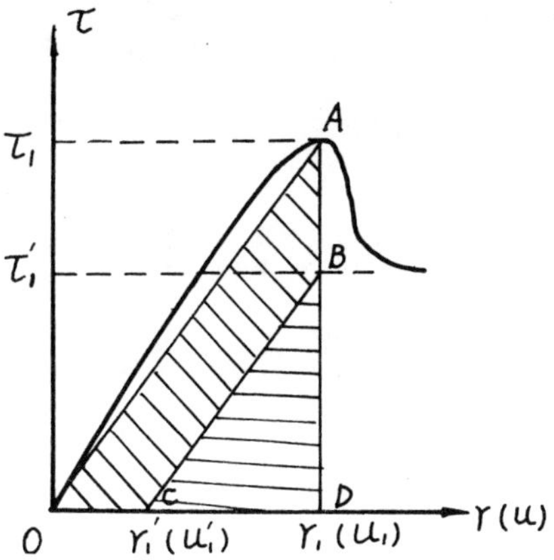

Fig.5 Shear stress-strain relationship of rock element

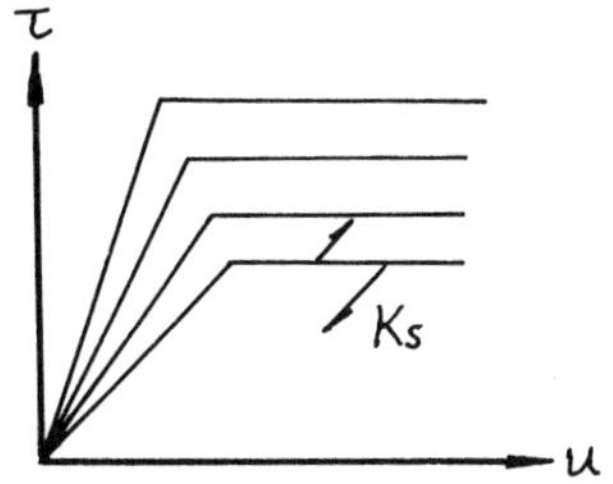

Fig.7 Shear displacement model for joint element

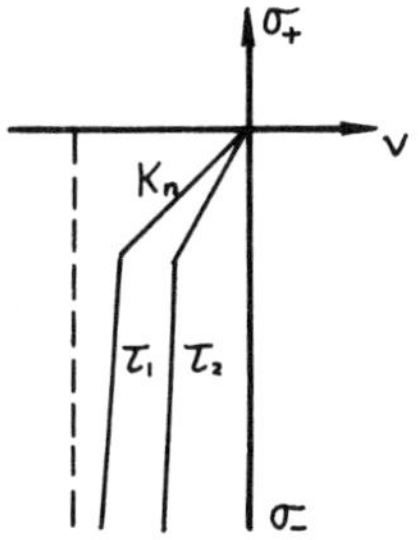

Fig.8 Normal deformation model for joint element

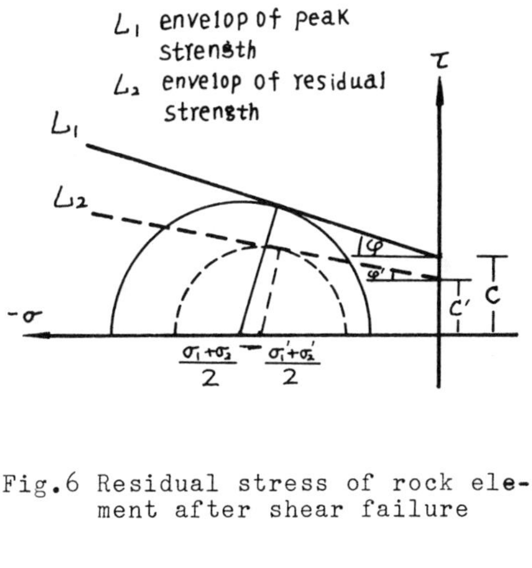

Fig.6 Residual stress of rock element after shear failure

position of the new Mohr stress circle and its center can be determined by "residual energy method" (Fig.6).

The selection of model for joint element is based on R.E.Goodman model. The relationship between stress and displacement is shown in Fig.7 and Fig.8. If Couloumbs criterion is chosen as the yield function and the joint elements are assumed to possess non-hardening characteristics in the plastic state, by using associated flow rule, the stress-strain matrix of the elastoplastic material may be expressed as below

$$[C_{ep}] = \begin{bmatrix} K_{ss} & K_{sn} \\ K_{ns} & K_{nn} \end{bmatrix} \qquad (3)$$

in which

$$K_{ss} = \frac{K_s K_n - f_1^2}{K_s f_2^2 + K_n f_1^2} \qquad K_{nn} = \frac{K_s K_n f_2^2}{K_s f_2^2 + K_n f_1^2}$$

$$K_{sn} = K_{ns} = \frac{K_s K_n f_1 f_2}{K_s f_2^2 + K_n f_1^2}$$

$$f_1 = -2\sin\varphi + \frac{2[2\sin^2\varphi\sigma_y + C\sin 2\varphi]\sin^2\varphi}{\{[2\sin^2\varphi\sigma_y + C\sin 2\varphi]^2 + 4\cos^4\varphi\tau^2\}^{1/2}}$$

$$f_2 = \frac{4\tau\cos^4\varphi}{\{[2\sin^2\varphi\sigma_y + C\sin 2\varphi]^2 + 4\tau^2\cos^4\varphi\}^{1/2}}$$

C cohesion of joint,

φ angle of friction of joint,

K_s unit shear stiffness,

K_n unit normal stiffness.

Then considering the actually measuring data of in-situ stress field and various mechanical parameters, it is possible to solve non-linear problems by means of the incremental stress tyansfer method. The cross section of the cavern is calculated, and the failure of the surrounding rock may be seen in Fig.9.

In order to investigate effect of some main factors on the stability of the cavern, a comprehensive analytical work and comparison for various cases of the jointed surrounding rock were made by using non-linear finite element method in 1977. Among them, efforts were concentrated on the study of the effect of geological structure features,

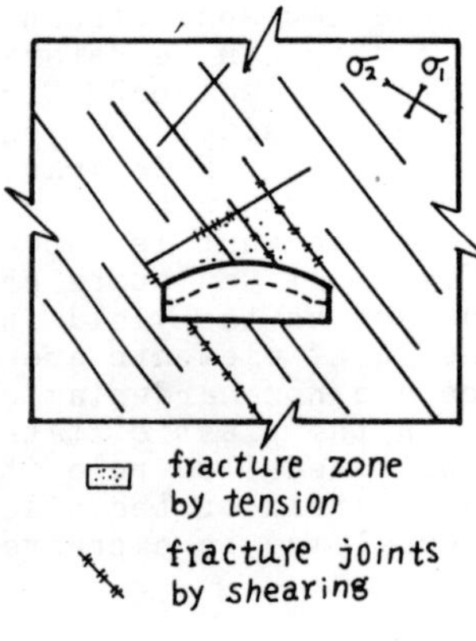

Fig.9 Fracture zone on a calculated section

in-situ stress field and the mechanical properties of the confining rock. For geological structrue features, three systems are adapted. Types of joints include horizontal, vertical, steep and moderately inclined ones. Some are thoroughgoing and some are non-thoroughgoing types. For initial stress field, the hill more than 100 meters high is taken as the background. Two basic cases, one of which gravity stress field dominates (gravitational stress is greater) and the other of which horizontal in-situ stress is supplemented (the horizontal stress is greater than vertical), are especially studies and respectively called "A" and "B" type stress field. The mechanical parameters and strength of the surrounding rock are classified into upper, middle and lower grade based on their magnitudes. About 30 cases are analysed. From these numerical simulation some fracture characters of surrounding rock can be found:

1. When the direction of joint group in the surrounding rock at the arch roof makes an acute angle with the principal direction of the initial stress field, this group is easiest to be sheared off, whereas the angle approaches to 90°, they are not sensitive to the changes of the in-situ stress.

2. Where the joint group is inclined and the initial stress field belongs to type "A", shear fracture of joints group grows in the direction of two oblique angles at the arch roof (Fig.10). For type "B" initial stress field, the shear fracture first occurs at the middle of the roof and then, continues laterally in both directions as the horizontal in-situ stress increases (Fig.11).

3. Where the two joint groups are both inclined at the arch roof, the shear fracture over the roof almost always takes place in "λ" shape. This is because the normal stresses to the fissured plane in that particular direction decrease as a result of unloading due to excavation.

4. Where there is a larger shear displacement along the joints due to shear failure, the adjacent rock elements may be liable to develop many induced tensile-shear fractures.

5. Where other conditions are the same, any changes in strength (increase or decrease)at the joint

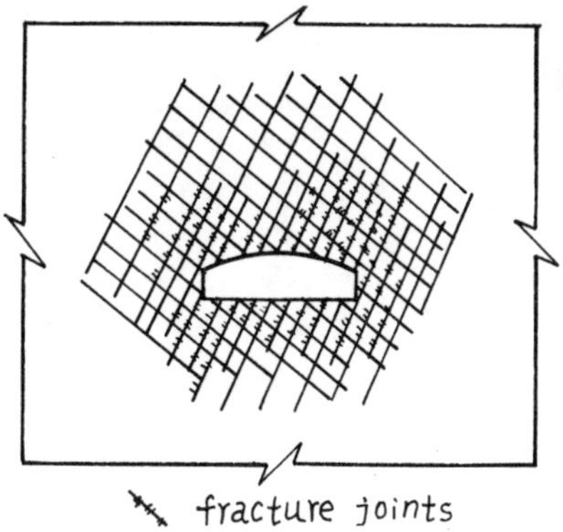

Fig.10 The sketch map showing the fracture zone of joints in the type "A" initial stress field

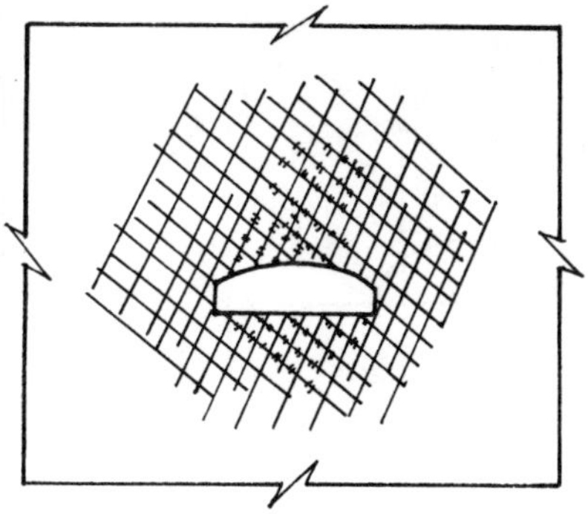

Fig.11 The sketch map showing the fracture zone of joints in the type "B" initial stress field

or rock elements in the surrounding rock will not change the distribution characteristics of the fracture region, but only affect the number of fractures.

From the above, some significent conclusions may be drawn for selecting the site and line of the large span cavern as well as for design and construction of the support.

1. In case the initial stress field belongs to type "A", it should try to avoid the site selection in the area with the joint systems having lower strength and steep dip (especially for two groups of joints).

2. In case the initial stress field belongs to type "B", the site selection should be avoided as much as possible in the region with gentle dip at the arch roof and with good thoroughgoing characteristics and low strength of the joint systems.

3. Where the joints are in horizontal orientation and have lower strength and in thinner beds, the joints and rock at the arch roof are easy to be fractured. If the horizontal in-situ stress is large, it is helpful to improve the rock strength, but not to lessen the joint fractures. So, the roof is always very difficult to be maintained.

4. If the joint groups at the cavern top are cut into triangular prisms and the strength of these joints is low, it is extremely difficult to prevent falls of these triangular prisms, no matter what type of in-situ stress field it may be.

5. Anchor support is one of the most effective supporting pattern for the jointed rock mass. But the direction of the initial stress field should be noticed during anchor supporting. When the direction of initial stress field makes a small angle with that of the joints to be anchor-supported, the anchoring effect is the best (the bolts should be normal to the joint plane to be supported). If they make an angle near 90° with each other, the effect is the worst.

6. Since most joint fractures in the roof are of "λ" type, anchor-bolt strengening should be made separately according to the directions of the different joint systems on either side of the arch crown.

5 AN ANALYSIS METHOD TO JUDGE THE FRACTURE REGIONS OF SURROUNDING ROCK

Because of the complex of the structure of rock masses, it is limited that some theoretical analysis methods to be applied in rock mechanics. But at a certain condition, however, these methods are more useful practically to predict the engineering problems conveniently and quickly, so that it could be provided a good reference for further discussion and study of our questions.

In our investigation, we have used

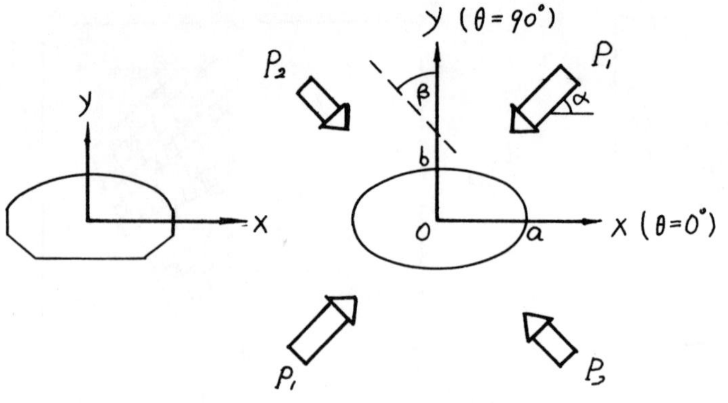

Fig.12 The sketch map showing the analysis method to judge the fracture regions of surrounding rock

the analysis method for researching underground cavern in a certain large span in order to judge the fracture region surrounding rock masses. The shape of the cavern is as shown in figure 12. Let us treat approximately this shape tyansformed into an ellipse as a plane strain problem. The long semi-axis is a, and short semi-axis is b. For the cavern is located deep, its stress field is also simplified as two external loads P_1 and P_2, the direction of which are so far from infinity. The maximum angle between P_1 and X-axis is defined α. The stress field arround the ellipse region may be found by applying the functions of a complex variable. Then we could establish the curvilinear coordinate "ρ, θ", the relation between the stress field of that ellipse rigion and the rectangular coordinate "X,Y" is that (when we coincide the long semi-axis with X-axis)

$$X = \frac{R}{\rho}(1+m\rho^2)\cos\theta$$
$$Y = \frac{R}{\rho}(1-m\rho^2)\sin\theta \qquad (4)$$

here

$$R = \frac{a+b}{2} \qquad m = \frac{a-b}{a+b}$$

In the curvilinear coordinate, the stress component may be expressed in the function of stress in complex number

$$\sigma_\theta + \sigma_\rho = 2\{\phi(\zeta) + \overline{\phi(\zeta)}\}$$
$$\sigma_\theta - \sigma_\rho + 2i\tau_{\rho\theta} = \qquad (5)$$
$$= \frac{2\zeta^2}{\rho^2\overline{\omega'(\zeta)}}\left[\overline{\omega(\zeta)}\phi'(\zeta) + \omega'(\zeta)\psi(\zeta)\right]$$

here

$$\phi(\zeta) = \frac{\varphi'(\zeta)}{\omega'(\zeta)} \qquad \psi = \frac{\psi'(\zeta)}{\omega'(\zeta)}$$

While we map the conformal mapping of ellipse-hole at external region to inside of a unit circle, the mapping function is

$$Z = \omega(\zeta) = R\left(\frac{1}{\zeta} + m\zeta\right) \qquad (6)$$

here $\zeta = \rho e^{i\theta}$

The expression of stress component for having external load $P=P_1$ in one direction would be obtained by deriving the final expression of stress function and differential to separate the real and imaginary parts. Furthermore, by adding another uniform external stress P_2 to this stress field again (the intersected angle of P_2 and P_1 is $\alpha/2$). Then we can obtain the stress expression which we desired as follows:

$$\sigma_\rho = \frac{1}{2}\{4A_4 - A(A_1A_2 - B_1B_2 + A_3) + B(A_1B_2 + A_2B_1 + B_3)\}$$

$$\sigma_\theta = \frac{1}{2}[4A_4 + A(A_1A_2 - B_1B_2 + A_3) - B(A_1B_2 + A_2B_1 + B_3)]$$

$$\tau_{\theta\rho} = \frac{1}{2}[A(A_1B_2 + A_2B_1 + B_3) + B(A_1A_2 - B_1B_2 + A_3)] \quad (7)$$

here, all of $A, B, A_1, A_2, A_3, A_4, B_1, B_2, B_3$ may be expressed by the apparent equations including ρ, θ, R, m, P_1, P_2 and α.

When the rock itself is only slight anisotropy it would be considered the direction of main joints β only (which is corresponding to θ plane), and then we can check approximately the joint strength of that point (Fig.13).

The normal stress σ and shear stress τ on the surface of any joint through a given point respectively are

$$\sigma = \frac{1}{2}(\sigma_\theta + \sigma_\rho) + \frac{1}{2}(\sigma_\theta - \sigma_\rho)\cos 2\beta - \tau_{\theta\rho}\sin 2\beta$$
$$\tau = -[\frac{1}{2}(\sigma_\theta - \sigma_\rho)\sin 2\beta + \tau_{\theta\rho}\cos 2\beta] \quad (8)$$

To substitute the above equations into Coulumb's formula

$$\tau = \sigma \, tg\varphi + c \quad (9)$$

and put it in order we get

$$(\sigma_\theta + \sigma_\rho)tg\varphi - a(\sigma_\theta - \sigma_\rho) = 2b\tau_{\theta\rho} - 2c \quad (10)$$

here a and b may be expressed by β, φ.

The region of the fracture arround the cavern can be defined according to equation (7) and (10).

It has been made to compare the dimension of the fracture regions obtained by above mentioned method with results by nonlinear finite element method which represents that the produced fracture radius ρ obtained by analytical method and a correct coefficient K will be very closed to the fracture radius obtained by FEM (Fig.14). In the cases which have been discussed K were coefficients little greater than unite. At the parts of cavern wall K=1.1—1.2 and at the arch crown parts K=1.2—1.4. Analytical method does not consider the effect of joints upon stress distribution and the effect of stress regulation which occurs after joint or rock fracture, so its solution is rather rough. However in case the joints with enough density rock mass are distributed uniformly and stress state is of compression character dominantly, the accuracy of this solution can still achiev the requirement desired by engineering practice.

6 CONCLUSIONS

1. A energy equation is advanced as a basical principle to research and to control the stability of underground cavern, which is that sum of the strain energy anew accumulated in the adjacent confining rock due to excavation the non-elastic strain energy dissipated

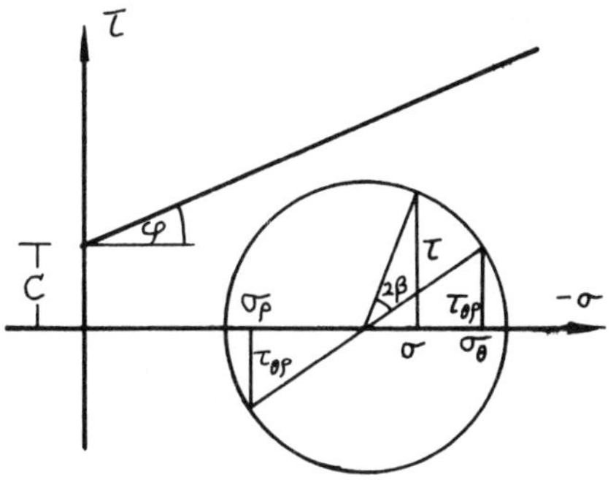

Fig.13 The check of the joint strength

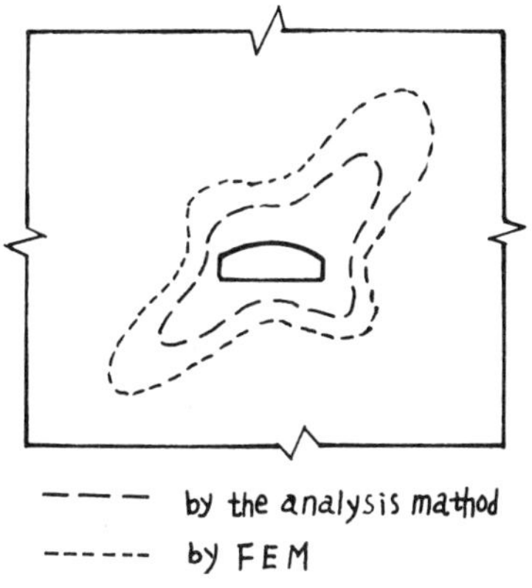

Fig.14 The sketch map showing contrast of results between the analysis method and FEM

after ex-cavation and the energy absorbed by artificial structure would be approximately constant.

2. In order to study the stability of underground cavern, rock stress measurement in-situ is very important. In many regions of China the horizontal components of rock stresses are often much greater than expected, even in the shallow depth of mountain area.

3. To study the stability of underground cavern in jointed rock mass great attention must be paid to the relation among the direction of maximum principle stress, the direction of main joint group and the direction of main free surface of cavern. With the relation changed the fracture characters of surrounding rock as well as the conditions of stability can be quite defferent.

4. Even for jointed rock mass in the case of great compression stress state the deep part of surrounding rock can still be approximately treated as continuous media. The evaluation of fracture regions by analytical method can be used with good approximation.

7 REFERENCES

Cook, N.G.W. 1966, The design of underground excavations, Proc. 8th Symp. on Rock Mech. , Univ. Minnesota, pp. 167-193.

Salamon, M.D.G. 1974, Rock mechanics of underground excavations, Proc. of the 3rd Congr. of the Intern. Soc. for Rock Mech.

Zhu Weishen. 1978, Stability of underground storage with large-span (internal research report).

Zienkiewicz, O.C. ,Valliappan, S. & King, I.P. 1968, Stress analysis of rock as a "no-tension" material, Geotechnique, 18,56-66.

Goodman, R.E. ,Taylor, R.L. & Brekke, T.H. 1968, A model for the mechanics of jointed rock, J. Soil Mech. and Found. Div. , V. 94, SM 3.

Zhu Weishen. 1979, Stability of underground rock chambers, chapter XX " theories and practices in rock mechanics" 1981.

Zhu Weishen. 1979, Stability of large-span in jointed rock mass, Proc. of 4th Intern. Congress on Rock Mechanics. Vol. 3.